A Sanskrit Dictionary

A concise sanskrit dictionary of words from principal traditional scriptures, major philosophical works,
Dhātu Pāṭhaḥ and various grammar texts.
Transliterated in English script and alphabetical order and including many Monier-Williams references.

compiled by John M. Denton

v 2.9 December 2013 ISBN 978-0-473-18314-1

A Sanskrit Dictionary

A concise sanskrit dictionary of words from principal traditional scriptures, major philosophical works, *Dhātu Pāṭhaḥ* and various grammar texts.
Transliterated in English script and alphabetical order and including many references to the traditional Monier-Williams Dictionary.

ISBN 978-0-473-18314-1

The Alphabet

ॐ

अ *a*	इ *i*	ऋ *ṛ*	ऌ *ḷ*	उ *u*
ए *e*	ओ *o*	ऐ *ai*	औ *au*	
क *ka*	च *ca*	ट *ṭa*	त *ta*	प *pa*
ख *kha*	छ *cha*	ठ *ṭha*	थ *tha*	फ *pha*
ग *ga*	ज *ja*	ड *ḍa*	द *da*	ब *ba*
घ *gha*	झ *jha*	ढ *ḍha*	ध *dha*	भ *bha*
ङ *ṅa*	ञ *ña*	ण *ṇa*	न *na*	म *ma*
	य *ya*	र *ra*	ल *la*	व *va*
	श *śa*	ष *ṣa*	स *sa*	
		ह *ḥ*		

Pronunciation

a	as u in but
ā	a in master
ai	y in my
au	ou in loud
b	b in bear
bh	bh in abhor
c	ch in check
ch	chh in catch him
d	d in dice
ḍ	d in drum
dh	dh in adhere
ḍh	dh in red-haired
e	a in evade
g	g in good
gh	gh in loghouse
h	h in hard
ḥ	h in oh
i	i in fix
ī	ee in feel
j	j in jam
jh	dgeh in hedgehog
k	k in kite
kh	kh in blockhead
l	l in love
ḷ	lry in jewelry
m	m in mother
ṁ	m in hum
n	n in not
ṇ	2nd n in none
ṅ	ng in sing
ñ	n in lunch
o	o in oh
p	p in put
ph	ph in uphill
r	r in red
ṛ	ri in river
ṝ	ri in reed
ś	sh in sure
ṣ	sh in show
s	s in sit
t	t in water
ṭ	t in true
th	th in fat-head
ṭh	th in anthill
u	u in suit
ū	oo in pool
v	w in water
y	y in you

a 1a/1 1. the first letter of the alphabet, 2. a vocative particle, e.g. *a ananta* O Viṣṇu 3. a prefix having a negative or contrary sense, *a-sat* not good , 4. the base of some pronouns and pronom. forms -*asya, astra*, etc. 5. an augment prefixed to the root for some tenses,

ā as a prefix to verbs, especially of motion and their derivatives – near, near to, towards, (may be separable from the verb in older language), to, unto, at, with roots like *gam, yā, i,* 1. *dā*, it reverses the action of the verb e.g. go becomes come, *ādatte* takes, 126/1 a particle of reminiscence, also of compassion or pain and of assent, 'sometimes used in the sense of comparison - as it were, like', as an adverb after words expressing a number or degree –fully, really, indeed; may indicate up to, until, as far as, from, thereto, besides, quite, entirely, all the way to, until, e.g. *ā-maraṇam* till death *ā-samudram* as far as the ocean, *ā-kumāram* from a child, or from childhood, or to a child, from or up to (with 5th),

abaddha 59/3 mfn unbound, unrestrained, at liberty, not yet visible,

abādhita mfn unreputed, a proposition remaining uncontradicted, not forbidden, unrefuted

abāhya 60/1 mfn not exterior, internal, without an exterior,

abbā f. a mother,

abbindu m. a drop of water, a tear

abda m. 'water-giving', a year, a cloud, the grass,

ābdika mfn annual, yearly, - *ābdika* ..-ennial, lasting .. years

ābhā P. *ābhāti,* to shine or blaze towards, to irradiate, outshine, illumine, to appear, become visible or apparent, to look like, f. light, appearance, splendour, a flash, colour, appearance, a reflected image,

abhāgya 61/1mfn unfortunate, wretched, unfortunately,

ā√bhaj P. to cause to share or partake, let anyone have anything, favour anyone, to revere, respect,

abhakṣya mfn not to be eaten by, (3rd or 6th), n. that which ought not to be eaten,

abhakta mfn one who is not a devotee, detached, unconnected with, not eaten, not received as a share,

ābhaṇḍana 145/1 n. defining, determining

ābharaṇa n. decorating, ornament, or collectively ornaments, jewels etc.,

ā√bhāṣ Cl 1 -*bhāṣate,* to call on, call upon, invite, to address, converse with, to talk, speak, name, promise,

ābhāṣa speech, talking, a saying, proverb, introduction, preface,

ābhāsa 45/2 splendour, light, appearance, reflection, semblance, intention, purpose, phantom, mere appearance, fallacious appearance, looking like, understood, as a reflection of *Brahman* , including personal aspects. reflection (of the Self), (in logic) fallacy, semblance of a reason, ifc. looking like, having the mere appearance of a thing,

ābhāsamātra m. mere appearance, in name only,

ābhāsavāda a theory in Advaita Vedānta that the *jiva* (individual) is an illusory appearance of the Brahman, a doctrine holding that all creation is a reflection of the Absolute, 2. a *śaiva* and *śakta* theory that all appearances are real as aspects of ultimate reality,

ābhāti f. shade, splendour, light, 1/s/pres *ā√bhā* becomes visible, shines, looks like, blazes towards, illumines, appears,

abhāva 60/3 m. non-existence, nullity, absence, non-entity, negation,

proof from non-existence, 'since there are no mice, there must be cats here',
annihilation, death, privation,

abhāvamātra mere absence, of a merely negative character,

abhāvanā f.n. absence of judgement or right perception,

abhāvarūpa having the nature of non-existence, an unreal cause,

abhāvarūpa dharma (W) a negative attribute

abhavat became, 1/s/impf. √*bhū*

abhāvātmaka (W) a type of motion (*dharma*) in Jainism, which indicates the distinction of one thing from another ,

abhāvayat mfn non-perceiving, non-concentrating, un-meditative, unwise, unconscious,

abhāvin mfn not about to be, not destined to be,

abhautika mfn not relating to or produced by the gross elements, not material, subtle,

abhavāya for deliverance from material existence, for liberation,

abhāvya mfn what is not to be or will not be, not destined to be, a person not capable of release from the bondage of transmigration, (Jain)

abhaya mfn absence of fear, fearless
n. f. (*ā)* fearlessness

abhaya mudrā a hand gesture often used pictorially or in sculpture (one hand raised with the palm outward) indicating fearlessness or 'do not fear',

abheda 75/1 m. non-fracture, compactness, closeness of array, absence of difference or distinction, identity,
mfn not different, identical,
G. non-difference, non-duality,

abhedabhakti highest devotion that has culminated in merging of the identities of the worshipper and the worshipped, devotion without the sense of duality, (U)

abhedabhāva sense of non-separateness,

abhedabuddhi the *buddhi* that beholds unity,

abhedacaitanya n. undivided consciousness, constant thought of the identity of the *jīva* with Brahman,

abhedadarśana self-realization, non-perception of duality,

abhedāhaṁkāra m. the pure ego that identifies with Absolute/Brahman,

abhedajñāna knowledge of the identity of the individual with Brahman,

abhedaka mfn not dividing, not causing any distinction,

abhedin mfn not different,

abhedya mfn not to be divided or broken, indivisible, not to be betrayed (secret formula), (*am*) n. a diamond,

abhedyatā f. or *–tva* n. indivisibility, impenetrability,

abhi prefix, to, towards, into, over, upon, moving towards, approaching
as a prefix to nouns not derived from verbs expresses superiority, intensity
as an adverb or prep. (with 2nd.) to, towards, in the direction of, against, into, for, for the sake of, on account of, before, in front of

abhī mfn fearless,

abhī 2. (√*i) abhy-eti,* to come near, approach, go up to or towards, to go along or after, to enter, join, go over to, to begin to, to reach, obtain, to come to, fall to one's share,

abhi√*bādh –bādhate* to check, stop, to attack (in battle), to cause pain,

abhi√*bhā* to glitter (around), be bright, appear,

abhibhā 2. f. apparition, phenomenon, inauspicious omen, (Buddhist) act of overpowering, superiority,

abhi√*bhaj* to turn or flee towards

abhibhaṅga mfn breaking down, destroying,

abhi√ *bhañj* to break down, destroy

abhibhartṛ ind. towards the husband, before (in the presence of) the husband,

abhi√*bharts* to scold, threaten so as to terrify, to deride, ridicule,

abhi√*bhāṣ* Cl 1 *-bhāṣate* to reply to, answer,

to address, speak to, converse with, to utter,

abhibhāṣaṇa n. the act of addressing or speaking to,

abhibhāṣin mfn addressing, speaking to,

abhibhāṣita mfn spoken to, addressed, accosted,

abhibhāṣya mfn to be addressed,

abhibhava 66/3mfn overpowering, powerful m. prevailing, overpowering, predominance, defeat, subjugation, disregard, disrespect, humiliation

abhibhāvaka mfn overpowering, surpassing,

abhibhavana n. causing to overcome making victorious,

abhi√bhṛ to lay or throw blame or fault upon

abhibhu or 2. *abhibhū* one who surpasses, a superior,

abhi√bhū 'be against', to overcome, overpower, predominate, conquer, surpass, overspread, to attack, defeat, humiliate, to approach, come near to, to be victorious or prospering in,

abhibhū mfn one who surpasses, a superior, m. name of a month, name of a die,

abhi√3.bhuj P. to be useful to,

abhibhūta mfn surpassed, defeated, humbled, overcome, injured,

abhibhūti f. superior power, overpowering, disrespect, humiliation, mfn overpowering, superior,

abhibhūty-ojas mfn having superior might,

abhibhūya n. superiority, ind. overpowering, subduing,

abhibuddhi f. name of a function of the intellect in Sāṁkhya phil.(comprising *adhyavasāya, abhimāna, icchā, kartavyatā, kriyā),*

abhi√cakṣ -caṣte to look at, view, perceive, to cast a kind look upon, to address, looks on,

abhicakṣaṇa n. conjuring, incantation, observation of the sky (in augury),

abhicakṣya mfn manifest

abhi√car to act wrongly towards anyone, to be faithless as a wife, to charm, enchant, bewitch,

abhicara m. a servant

abhicāra m. employment of spells for a malevolent purpose, exorcising, incantation, magic,

abhicāraka m. a magician, mfn conjuring,

abhicārita mfn enchanted, charmed,

abhicchāyam ind. in darkness,

abhi√cint cl 10, to reflect on

abhi√cud caus. *codayati* to impel, drive on, inflame, animate, to invite, fix, settle, to announce, inquire for,

abhi√1. dā -dadāti to give, bestow for a purpose,

abhi√dah to singe, burn

abhidakṣiṇam ind. to or towards the right,

abhidarśana n.becoming visible, appearance,

abhi√dās –dāsati, to consider and treat as an enemy

abhidaṣṭa mfn bitten

abhīddha mfn inflamed, 74/3

abhi√dhā –dadhāti to surrender anyone to, A.P. to put on or round, to bring upon (4th), put on or round (esp. the furniture of a horse), to cover a country with an army, to cover, protect, to set forth, explain, tell, speak to, pass. *–dhīyate* to be named or called, caus. *–dhāpayate* to cause to name,

abhidhā f. name, appellation, the literal power or sense of a word, a word, sound, m.f. surrounding,

abhi√dham to blow towards or against,

abhi√2. dī to radiate, beam forth or towards

abhidigdha polished, glazed (in the fire *tapāsa*), i.e. sharp,

abhi√dhā –dadhāti to surrender anyone to, to bring upon, to put on or round, to cover, protect, to set forth, explain, L. Cl 1, designate, mention,

abhidhā 2. f. name, appellation, the literal power or sense of a word, a word, sound, primary meaning,

abhidhāna n. telling, naming, speaking, speech, manifesting, a name, title, expression, word, a vocabulary,

dictionary putting together, bringing in close connection,
abhidhānakam n. a sound, noise,
abhidhānamālā f. a dictionary
abhidharma m. the dogmas of Buddhist philosophy or metaphysics, (in Pāli *abhidhamma),*
abhidharṣaṇam n. possession by demonic spirits
abhidhāsyati he shall set forth, shall explain, 1/s/fut/act *abhi √dhā*
abhidhātavya to be told or named, to be manifested,
abhidhātṛ mfn saying, telling,
abhi√dhāv –dhāvati to run up towards or against, to rush upon, attack,
abhidhāvana n. running up, attack,
abhidheya mfn to be named mentioned or expressed, being spoken of or expressed,
a nameable or denoteable thing, spiritual practices, activities in devotional service,
abhi√3.dhi to satisfy,
abhi√dhī to reflect upon, consider,
abhidhīyate 63/2 it is called or explained 1/s/pres/indic/pass *abhi √dhā*
abhi√dhṛ caus.*dhārayati* to uphold, maintain
abhi√dhṛṣ to overpower,
abhi√dhū to shake,
abhi√dhvan to resound, whiz (as arrows),
abhidhyā f. wish, longing for
abhi√dhyai –dhyāyati, to direct one's intention to, set one's heart upon, intend, desire, to meditate,
abhidhyāna n. desiring, meditation, 'intense meditation' (Gam.),
abhidhyāyin mfn giving one's attention to
abhi√dih to wrap up, envelope, 63/1
abhi√dīkṣ to consecrate one's self (for a purpose),
abhiḍīnam n. the act of flying towards, 62/3
abhi√dīp to blaze towards, caus. *–dīpayati* to cause to shine, make brilliant, to blaze or shine all round, 63/1
abhidipsu mfn wishing to deceive, cunning
abhi√diś to point out,
abhi√2. drā to overtake, 63/1
abhidroha m. offense, injuring,
abhi√dṛś to look at, caus. *–darśayati* to show, to point out, denounce anyone, pass. to be in view, appear,
abhi√2.dru to run up to or near, to attack, overrun, infest
abhidrugdha mfn injured, oppressed,
abhi√druh –druhyati to hate, seek to injure, do violence to,
abhidruh mfn seeking to injure, inimical,
abhidruta mfn run towards, attacked,
abhi√2. du to burn or pain by burning
abhi√duṣ -duṣayati to contaminate, wound
abhidūṣita mfn wounded, 63/1
abhiduṣṭa mfn contaminated,
abhidyu mfn directed to heaven, tending or going to heaven, heavenly, bright,
abhi√gā -jigāti, to go near to, to approach, arrive at, get, gain, 61/3
abhigacchat mfn approaching,
abhi√gai to call or sing to, to enchant, to sing, to fill with song, to celebrate in song, 61/3
abhi√gāh A. to penetrate into,
abhi√gam –gacchati to go near to, go unto, approach, to follow, to meet with, find, to cohabit, to get, gain, obtain, caus. *–gamayati* to study,
abhigama m. approaching, visiting, sexual intercourse,
abhigamana 61/3 the act of cleansing the way to the image of the deity, morning devotions,
abhigamya 1. to be visited, accessible,
2. ind. having approached,
abhigantṛ m. one who understands, insidious
abhigarjana n. ferocious roaring, uproar,
abhigara m calling out with approval, the priest who does so, 61/3
abhigata approached,
abhighāra m. sprinkling over, scattering over, mingling with, clarified butter or ghee,
abhighāta m. (*√han*) striking, striking back,
abhighātaka mfn counteracting, removing,
abhi√ghrā –jighrati to snuffle, smell at, to

smell, scent, to bring the nose close to another's forehead in caressing or as a token of affection,
abhighrāṇa n. smelling at, caressing,
abhigīta mfn addressed or praised in song, n. a song, 61/3
abhi√gī to call to or address with approbation, to join, to welcome, praise, to approve of, accept propitiously, allow,
abhi√grah –gṛihṇāti to take hold of, take up (from the soil), to accept, receive, to set (as a blossom), to lay together, to fold (the hands), caus. *–grāhayati* to catch, surprise, 62/1
abhigraha m. seizing, taking hold of, attack, onset, defiance, challenge, robbing, plundering, resolution, a vow,
abhigumphita mfn strung together, interwoven
abhigupta mfn guarded, protected, 61/3
abhi√gur to assent, agree, approve of,
abhigūrta mfn approved of,
abhi√2.hā to rush upon, seize hastily, 74/1
abhi√han to strike, kill, beat, beat (drum),
abhihara mfn carrying off, removing,
abhihāra m. bringing near, robbing, seizing,
abhi√hary 74/1 *–haryanti* to wish anything to be near, call it near, to like, love,
abhihāsa m. jest, joke,
abhihasya mfn ridiculous,
abhihata struck, killed,
abhihati f. striking (as an arrow), multiplication, the product of multiplied numbers,
abhihava 74/2 m. pouring the oblation upon, 2. m. calling near
abhihita mfn harnessed or put to (as a horse),named, called, said, declared, spoken, spoken to, n. a name, expression, word,
abhihitā 74/1f. or *–tva* n. the having been said, stated or named, called, spoken, a holding forth, declaration,
abhihiti f. telling, manifesting, title,
abhi√hṛ to bring, offer, to pull off, tear off, to attack, put on (a cuirass), to be angry with,
abhi√hṛṣ caus. to gladden,
abhihruti f. fall, damage, injury,
abhi√hu to make oblation upon or for the sake of, shed or pour over,
abhihūti f. calling near (gods at a sacrifice),
abhihvāra m. a crooked or damaging way or place,
abhi√hve to call near,
abhija mfn 62/2 produced all around,
abhijājvaliti rises up, blazes up (as anger), desid. *√jval*
abhi√jalp 62/2 to address, , to accompany with remarks, to advocate, to settle by conversation,
abhi√jan cl 4 A. *– jāyate* to be born for or to, to claim as one's birthright, to be born or produced, to be born again, to become,
abhijana m. family, race, descendants, ancestors, noble descent, the head or ornament of a family, native country, fame, notoriety,
abhijānāti 62/2 recognizes, perceives, knows, be or become aware of comes to know or realize, to acknowledge, agree to, own, to remember, 1/s/pres/indic/act *abhi√jñā*
abhi√jap to mutter over or whisper to,
abhijāta mfn born in consequence of, born, produced, noble, well-born, obtained by birth, in-bred, fit, proper, wise, learned, handsome, n. nativity, high birth, nobility,
abhijāti f. descent, birth,
abhijaya m. conquest, complete victory,
abhijāyate is born, is produced, is reborn, is born again *abhi√jan* 1/s/pres/indic/pass
abhi√ji -jayati to conquer completely, acquire by conquest
abhijighrat mfn caressing,
abhijit mfn victorious,
abhijña mfn knowing, skilful, clever, understanding, conversant with, remembrance, recollection, supernatural faculty of a buddha – said to be-

taking any form at will,
hearing to any distance,
seeing to any distance,
penetrating men's thoughts,
knowing their state and antecedents,

abhi√jñā 62/2 *–jānāti, jānīte* to recognize, perceive, know, be or become aware of, to acknowledge, agree to, own, to remember,

abhijñā 62/2 mfn knowing, skilful, clever, understanding, f. remembrance, recollection,

abhijñānam n. remembrance, recollection, knowledge, ascertainment, a sign or token of remembrance, any sign or token serving as a proof, recognition

abhijñānāti recognizes, knows, perceives, is or becomes aware of

abhijñāti P. becomes wise

abhijñāpaka mfn making known

abhi√juṣ to be pleased with, like, 62/2

abhi√jval to blaze forth, caus. *–jvālayati* to enlighten, illuminate,

abhijuṣta mfn visited, frequented, surrounded by, possessed of,

abhīka mfn fearless, 2. longing after, lustful, 3. meeting together, collision , near, towards,

abhikalpanā formation of a conception in respect of a non-physical thing in order to express it in words for common use,

abhi√kam to desire, love,

abhikāma m. affection, desire, mfn affectionate, loving, desirous, (*am*) ind. with desire,

abhi√kāṅkṣ -kāṅkṣati (te), to long for, desire, strive, 61/1

abhikāṅkṣā 61/1 longing for, desire

abhikāṅkṣita mfn longed for, desired

abhi√kāś to illuminate, irradiate, to look on, to perceive,

abhi√khan to dig up, turn the soil, 61/2

abhi√khyā to see, view, perceive, to cast a kind or gracious look on anyone, to be gracious, caus. *–khyāpayati* to make known

abhikhyā f. a gracious look, splendour, beauty, fame, glory, telling, calling,

abhikhyāna n. fame, glory,

abhikhyāta mfn become known, manifested,

abhikhyātṛ m. a supervisor,

abhi√klṛp A. to be adequate to, be in accordance with, caus. *kalpayati* to put in order,

abhiklṛpta mfn being adequate to, in accordance with,

abhi√1.kṛ to do with reference to or in behalf of , to procure, effect,

abhi√1. kī –kirati to pour over, throw over,

abhi√kram to step or go near to, approach, to attack, overpower, to step upon, undertake, begin, caus. *–kramayati* to bring near, 61/2

abhikrama m. stepping near, approaching, effort, approaching, assault, attack, M. attempt, effort,

abhi√krand to shout at, roar at,

abhikrānta mfn approached,attacked, begun,

abhikratu mfn insolent, haughty,

abhi√krī to buy for a special purpose,

abhikrośaka m. a reviler

abhi√kṛṣ -karṣati to overpower,

abhi√krudh to be angry with,

abhi√kruś to cry out at, call out to, lament, call to (in a scolding manner)

abhīkṣ (√īkṣ) A. to look towards, 74/3

abhikṣadā mfn giving without being asked,

abhi√kṣam to be gracious, propitious to, to pardon,

abhi√kṣar to flow near or round,

abhikṣattṛ one who carves and distributes (food), a host,

abhi√kṣip to fling at (as the lash of a whip at a horse), to excel,

abhikṣita mfn not asked for alms,

abhīkṣṇa 74/3 mfn. constant, perpetual, (*am*) ind. repeatedly, again and again, perpetually, constantly, presently, at once, very, exceedingly, *-śas* ind. constantly,

ābhīkṣṇya 145/3 continued repetition

abhi√kūj to twitter, warble,

abhi√kuṣ -kuṣṇāti to tear, pull at, pinch

abhi√kuts to revile, inveigh against,

abhikrama 61/2 m. stepping near, effort,

approaching, assault, attack, ascending, undertaking, attempt
abhilabh A. to take or lay hold of, to reach, obtain,
abhi√lakṣ to appear 68/2
abhilakṣaṇa n. the act of marking with signs,
abhilakṣita mfn fixed or indicated by, determined for, selected as, indicated, pointed out, appearing, visible,
abhilaṅgh caus. to jump across or over, to transgress, violate,
abhilaṅghana n. jumping over, violating, acting contrary to,
abhi√lap to talk or speak about, 68/3
abhilāpa m. expression, word,
abhi√laṣ -laṣati to desire or wish for,
abhilāṣa m. desire, wish, covetousness, affection, craving, passion for,
abhilaṣaṇa n. craving after, desiring,
abhilaṣin mfn desirous, anxious,
abhilāva m. cutting, reaping, mowing,
abhilekhana n. writing upon, inscribing,
abhilekhita n. a written document 68/3
abhi√lī -līyate to adhere to, cling to,
abhi√likh to engrave, write upon, draw, paint, caus. to cause to paint, have anything painted, to cause to write down,
abhilīna mfn adhering to, clinging to,
abhi√lip to smear with,
abhilipsā f. desire of obtaining,
abhi√lok caus. to view, look at (from a height),
abhi√lubh caus. *–lobhayati* to entice, allure,
abhilulita mfn touched or grazed by anything, shaken about, agitated,
abhi√lup to rob, plunder,
abhilupta mfn disturbed, injured,
abhīma mfn not terrifying, causing no fear
abhi√3.mā to measure upon 2. f. measure (breadth),
abhi√mad to be inebriated,
abhimāda m. intoxication
abhi√man –manyate to think of, long for, desire, to intend to injure, threaten, be insidious, to allow, agree, to think of self, be proud of, to think, suppose, imagine, take for,
abhimāna 67/1 pride, egoistic feeling self-conceit, arrogance, arrogating to one-self, obsession,
abhimanas having the mind directed towards, desirous of
abhi√mand P. to gladden, A. to be pleased with, enjoy,
abhimānī " the claimant of the experience" HH " unless there is an *abhimānī*, pleasure and pain, even if registered by the witness, will have no effect."
abhimānin 67/2 thinking of oneself, imagining oneself to be, laying claim to,
abhimānita n. sexual intercourse
abhimantavya mfn to be considered/desired
abhi√manth to churn or rub (to produce fire)
abhi√mantr A. to address or consecrate with a Mantra, to address with any formula (as when inviting a guest),
abhimantṛ m. one who refers all objects to self
abhimantraṇa n. consecrating, addressing,
abhimara m. killing, slaughter, combat, treachery, mutiny, fettering,
abhimarda m. devastation (of a country etc. by an enemy), battle,
abhimarśana n. touching, contact, mfn touching, coming in contact with,
abhimārutam ind. against the wind
abhimata mfn longed for, desired, loved, dear, allowed, imagined, supposed, respected, honoured,
abhimati f. self-reference, referring all objects to self (as the act of *ahaṁkāra* or personality), 67/1
abhimāti mfn insidious, f. striving to injure, an enemy,
abhimāya mfn perplexed, confused,
abhimethana n. insulting, injurious speech,
abhi√mih to wet by urinating upon
abhi√mṛ A. to touch or defile while dying,
abhi√mṛḍ to protect graciously from
abhi√mṛd to oppress, to devastate,
abhi√mṛj to wipe, cleanse

abhi√mṛkṣ to smear, anoint,
abhi√mṛś P. to touch, come in contact with,
abhimṛṣṭa mfn touched, struck (weapon),
abhimṛta mfn afflicted or rendered impure by the death of (3rd), defiled,
abhi√muc P. *–muñcati* to let go, to let loose, A. to throw or shoot (arrows),
abhi√muh to lose consciousness, to faint away,
abhimukha mfn face towards, ind. towards, (with 6th) against, f.(*ī*)
abhimukhaya Nom P °*yati* to face
abhimukti turned towards liberation, (W), the stage of *arhat,*
abhimūrchita mfn augmented, intensified, excited, stirred up (as by passions),
abhinabhas ind. towards the sky,
abhinabhyam ind. near the clouds or the sky,
abhi√nad to sound towards, to sound, raise a noise,
abhinaddha tied round, blindfold,
abhinahana a bandage over the eyes,
abhi√nakṣ -nakṣati, to approach, come to, arrive at,
abhi√nam to bow or bend or turn towards,
abhināmadheya n. a surname,
abhi√nand to please, rejoice at, salute, welcome, greet, to praise, applaud,
abhinanda 63/3 m. the delight, pleasure (of sensuality), wish, desire for,
abhinandita mfn delighted, made happy, saluted, applauded,
abhi√nard P.A. to roar towards, to roar,
abhi√naś to attain, reach,
abhinata bent, inclined,
abhinava mfn quite new or young, very young, fresh, modern,
abhinaya m. (indication of a passion or purpose by look, gesture, etc.), acting, dramatic action (expressive of sentiment), stream forth, mfn controlling, training, discipline,
abhīndh (*√indh*) to surround with flames, inflame, 74/3
abhinetṛ m. one who brings near,
abhi√nī to conduct towards, bring near, to represent dramatically, act, to quote
abhini√dhā to place upon or into, A. to place upon oneself as a burden, to touch slightly with(3rd), be in close contact
abhiniḥdhāna placing upon
abhini√dhyai to give attention to,
abhini√gad to speak to
abhini√han to beat, strike,
abhinihata mfn put on (as on a spit),
abhinihita mfn touched with, m. close contact, 64/1
abhini√kram to tread down,
abhiniḥsṛta mfn issued or issuing from,
abhinīla mfn very dark or black,
abhini√mantr to summon, invite
abhini√mruc –mrocati (said of the sun) to set upon anyone who is sleeping or has not finished his work,
abhinimrukta or *abhinimukta* mfn upon whom while not doing any work or while sleeping the sun has set,
abhininartam ind. so as to accomplish step by step, i.e. repeating separately,
abhini√nī to pour out or upon, 64/1
abhini√pat caus. *–pātayati* to throw down,
abhini√pīḍ to press, squeeze, trouble,
abhinipīḍita mfn pained, tormented,
abhi-niḥ-√sṛ to stream forth, issue, 63/3
abhiniḥ√sṛp to move towards, 64/1
abhinir√2. as to throw towards,
abhinir√bharts to scold thoroughly,
abhinir√diś to point out, indicate, to appoint, characterize,
abhinir√gam to go out or away from,
abhinirjita mfn conquered
abhinirmita mfn made, created,
abhinir√nud to drive out, frighten away
abhinir√vad to declare with regard to
abhinir√2.vap to share out or add anything to another,
abhinir√vṛt to result from, proceed, caus. –*vartayati* to produce, accomplish,
abhinirvṛtta mfn resulting from,
abhinirvṛtti f. resulting, proceeding, accomplishment,
abhinir√yā to march out, go out towards,
abhiniṣad to sit down or settle round,
abhini√śam to perceive, notice,
abhiniścita mfn quite convinced of, settled or fixed with regard to,

abhiniṣkārin intending evil against, injuring,
abhiniṣ√kram to go out towards, to leave the house in order to become an anchorite, to lead towards (as a door),
abhiniṣkramaṇa n. going forth (as above),
abhiniṣ√pad to come to, to enter into, become, to appear, caus. *–pādayati* to bring to
abhiniṣ√pat to fly out towards, to spring forth, shoot forth,
abhiniṣpatti f. appearance,
abhini√śri to pass from one thing to another,
abhiniṣṭāna m. a sound which dies away – the *visarga,* sounding heavily (as a drum,
abhini√ṣṭhiv to spit upon, 64/2
abhini√syand or *ṣyand* to trickle upon,
abhniṣyanda m. trickling,
abhinīta mfn brought near, performed, highly finished or ornamented, fit, proper,
abhinīti f. gesture, expressive gesticulation, friendship, civility,
abhinivartam ind. so as to turn back towards,
abhiniveśa 64/2 m. attachment, application, intentness, study, affection, devotion, determination, tenacity, persistent fondness, a clinging to life and dread of death, will to live,
abhiniveśin mfn intent upon, devoted to,
abhiniveśita mfn made to enter into, plunged into,
abhini√viś –viśate to enter, to devote one's self entirely to, caus. *–veśayati* to cause to enter, lead into, cause anyone to devote himself entirely to, to devote one's attention to, to cause one to devote himself entirely to,
abhiniviṣṭa mfn entered or plunged into, intent on, endowed with, concentrated, determined, persevering,
abhiniyukta mfn occupied in
abhinna uncut, unbroken, uninterrupted, (in arith.) undivided, integer, whole (as numbers), unchanged, unaltered, not different from (5th or in comp.),
abhinnataraka mfn not at all different,
abhinṛmṇa exceedingly propitious,
abhi√nṛt –nṛtyati to dance towards or in imitation of,
abhi√3.nu to turn oneself towards,
abhi√4.nu to shout towards,
abhi√nud to push, press, caus. *–nodayati* to excite, spur or urge on,
abhiny √2.as -asyati to depress (as fire),
abhiny√ubj to press down, hold down,
abhi√1.pā to drink of
abhi√2.pā –pāti, to guard, to behold with attention, caus.P. *–pālayati* to protect, assist,
abhi√pac to boil up (as milk),
abhi√pad to come near or approach, to seize, catch, take possession of,
abhīpada m.whose foot or step is without fear,
abhipāla m. protector,
abhipālana n. protecting,
abhipale to follow after anyone running away,
abhipanna mfn approaching for imploring the help of, assisted, seized, overpowered, taking in hand, one who has acted wrongly toward,
abhiparā√vad to speak to, address
abhipare to go away towards, (√*i*)
abhipariglāna mfn tired, exhausted,
abhipari√han to overpower entirely,
abhparihāra m. moving round,
abhipari√hṛ to move round in a circle,
abhipari√grah to clasp, embrace,
abhipariplutа overflowed with, attacked,
abhipariṣvañj to embrace
abhiparīta mfn filled or taken with,
abhiparivṛta mfn filled or taken with, (3rd, as with anger),
abhiparyā√dhā to surround (as a pan with fire),
abhiparyā√sic to pour out round,
abhiparyā√vṛt to turn oneself towards, to turn oneself round,

abhiparye (said of time) to pass away or elapse,
abhiparyv1.ūh abhparyūhate to carry or bring towards,
abhi√paś –paśyati to look upon or at, to perceive, notice, to know,
abhi√1.pat -patyate to be lord over,
abhi√2.pat to fly near, hasten near, rush towards, fall down upon,
abhipāta m. hastening near,
abhipatana n. flying towards,
abhipaṭhita mfn denominated, named
abhipatti f. seizing, possession,
abhi√pīḍ cl 10 *–pīḍayati* to press upon, oppress, torment,
abhipīta mfn watered, (as the earth by rain)
abhipitva n. approaching, visiting, evening
abhi√plu to swim or navigate towards, approach, to overflow, to jump near to, caus. to wash (said of the sea),
abhipluta mfn overflowed, overrun, overwhelmed, affected by,
abhi√pī -pūryate to become full or abundant, caus. *–pūrayati* to make full, fill, to load with, to present with, to fill the heart of anyone (sorrows), overwhelm, accomplish,
abhipṝ to fill up, *-pūryate* to become full or abundant, caus. *–pūrayati* to make full, fill, to load with, cover with, to present with (3rd), to fill the heart of anyone (sorrows), to overwhelm, accomplish,
abhiprabhaṅgin mfn breaking completely
abhipra√bhū to assist, 66/1
abhipra√bhṛ to offer to, to throw, dart,
abhipra√cakṣ to see
abhi√prach to ask or inquire after,
abhipra√cud caus. *–codayati* to impel, induce, persuade,
abhipra√cyu to move towards, arrive at,
abhipradarśana n. pointing out, indicating,
abhipra√diś caus. –deśayati to urge on,
abhipra√gāh –gāhate, to dip or plunge into, penetrate,
abhipra√gai to begin to praise,
abhipra√2.hā -jihīte to jump or fly upwards in the direction of .. (2nd),
abhipra√han to overpower,
abhiprahata mfn struck at, hurt,
abhiprahita mfn sent hither, 66/2
abhipra√jan to bring forth, bear, generate for the sake of,
abhipra√jval to flare up,
abhipra√kamp caus. *–kampayati* to stir, allure
abhipra√kāś -kāśate to become visible,
abhipra√kram P. *–krāmati* to go up to
abhiprakramya to be stepped upon or walked on,
abhipra√kṣal -kṣālayati to clean thoroughly, polish up (as a jewel),
abhipra√kṣar to stream towards,
abhiprakṣarita mfn poured out,
abhipra√man A. to take anyone for, look on anyone as,
abhipra√1.mand to gladden, to confuse, infatuate, 66/1
abhipra√math caus. *–manthayati* to churn thoroughly
abhipra√mṛś to seize, grasp,
abhipramur mfn bruising, crushing
abhiprāṇ (√an) –prāṇiti to exhale, breathe forth, 66/2
abhipraṇana n. exhaling,
abhipra√ṇad to begin to roar or sound,
abhipra√ṇakṣ to overpower,
abhipraṇam to bow before,
abhipraṇata bent, bowing before,
abhipraṇaya m. affection,
abhipra√nī to bring towards,
abhipraṇīta mfn brought to (as fire to the altar),
abhipraṇu to shout towards, praise highly,
abhi√prāp to reach, obtain,
abhiprāpta mfn obtained,
abhprāpti f. arrival,
abhipra√pac pass. –pacyate to get ripe, develop itself,
abhipra√pad to come towards, reach at, enter into, to resort to, to undertake,
abhiprapanna mfn approached, attained,
abhipra√paś to look out after,
abhipra√pīḍ caus. –pīḍayati to cause pain, torture,

abhiprapī –pūryate to be filled, fill oneself completely,
abhiprārc (√arc) to celebrate in song
abhiprārth (√arth) to long for, wish
abhipra√ruh to put forth or produce shoots,
abhpra√sad to sit down or settle along, caus. *–sādayati* to cause to be well-disposed or gracious, pray for grace or favour,
abhipra√sah to be able to,
abhipra√śaṁs to praise highly,
abhiprasāraṇa n. stretching out the feet towards,
abhipra√skand to jump into,
abhipraśnin mfn inclined to ask, inquisitive,
abhipra√sṛ caus. to stretch oneself out towards, stretch a foot towards,
abhipra√sṛp to creep near,
abhiprasṛta mfn devoted to,
abhipra√sthā to start or advance towards, reach, to surpass, have the precedence of, caus. to drive (as cattle to pasture), 66/2
abhiprasthita mfn one who has set out, started,
abhipra√stṛ to scatter,
abhipra√stu to praise with a *stoma* (hymn?)
abhipra√śudh caus. *–śodhayati* to clean thoroughly
abhipra√sū to drive towards,
abhiprasupta mfn fallen asleep,
abhiprasūta mfn engaged, induced, ordered, 2. generated, born,
abhipra√tan to spread over 65/3
abhipratapta mfn intensely heated, dried up, exhausted with pain or fever,
abhiprtar ind. towards morning, early,
abhi√prath to spread, extend itself towards, caus. *–prathayati* to spread or scatter over, to spread (as one's fame),
abhiprati√pad to begin with or at, 65/3
abhiprati√piṣ to dash or crush out
abhipratyava√ruh to step down upon
abhipratyave to move down towards,
abhipratye to come back towards,
abhipra√vah to carry or bring towards,
abhpravartana n. coming or flowing forth,
abhipra√vip to move against, threaten,
abhipra√viś to flow out (as a river into the sea, or into another river),
abhpraveśa m. entering into,
abhipraviṣṭa mfn fallen or come into
abhipra√vraj to step or advance towards,
abhipravṛdh caus. –vardhayati to enlarge, render prosperous, 66/1
abhipra√vṛṣ to pour down rain,
abhipra√vṛt A. to advance up to, go forth, advance, disembogue into, caus. –*vartayati* to cause to advance against, throw against,
abhipravṛtta 66/1 mfn. being performed, advancing, proceeding
abhipra√yā to come towards, approach, to set out, go to battle,
abhiprāya m. aim, purpose, intention, wish, opinion, inclination,
abhiprayāyam ind. so as to approach,
abhiprayāyin approaching,
abhipra√yuj -yuṅkte to seize grasp, bring in one's possession,
abhipre –praiti, to go near to, approach, to approach with one's mind, to think of, to aim at, intend, 66/2
abhipreks (√ikṣ) to look at, see, view,
abhiprepsu desirous of gaining,
abhiprer (√īr) caus. *–prerayati* to drive forwards, push on
abhipreraṇa n. pushing, setting in motion
abhipreṣ (√1.iṣ) to summon, command,
abhipreṣita mfn that which has been commanded or ordered,
abhipreta mfn meant, intended,
abhipretya ind. intending, meaning by
abhiprī mfn gladdening,
verb caus. *abhiprīṇāyati* to gladden, refresh,
abhiprīta mfn pleased,
abhiprīti 66/2 f pleasing, pleasure
abhiprokṣaṇa sprinkling upon, pouring on
abhipṛṣṭa mfn inquired after,
abhipṛṣṭhe ind. at the back of, behind,
abhi√pru to hasten near or towards, jump into,
abhīpsat mf longing for, desiring,
abhīpsita mfn desired, (*-am*) ind. thing desired, desire,

abhīpsu mfn desirous of obtaining, 77/2
abhi√pū -pavate to flow purified towards or for, to blow towards, to make bright, glorify, 65/2
abhi√pūj to honour, reverence greatly, approve of,
abhipūjita mfn honoured, approved,
abhipūraṇa n. filling,
abhipūrṇa mfn full of,
abhipūrta n. that which has been fulfilled,
abhipūrva following in regular order,
abhipuṣpa mfn covered with flowers, n. an excellent flower,
abhi√pyai to swell, abound with,
abhīr (√īr) caus. to bring near
ābhīra m. cowherd, (sometimes incorrectly *abhira*), name of a people, 145/3
abhi√rabh A. to embrace,
abhirāddha mfn rendered propitious, propitiated, conciliated, 68/2
abhi√rādh caus. *–rādhayati* to propitiate, conciliate, caus.pass. *–rādhyate* to be rendered propitious,
abhi√rai to back towards,
abhi√rāj -rājate to shine, be brilliant, 2. mfn reigning everywhere
abhi√rakṣ P.A. *-rakṣati (te),* to guard, protect, preserve, to govern or command,
abhirakṣā f. protection,
abhirakṣaṇa n. guarding, protecting,
abhirakṣantu 3/pl/impv protect!
abhirakṣita (*abhi √rakṣ*) guarded, protected
abhirakṣya to be protected,
abhirakta mfn devoted to,
abhi√ram –ramate to dwell, to repose, to delight in, be delighted, caus. –*rāmayati* to gladden, to delight in,
abhirāma mfn pleasing, delightful, agreeable, beautiful,
abhirāmam ind. 1. so as to be agreeable to, 2. referring to Rāma
abhiramaṇa n. delighting in, delighting,
abhiramaṇīya mfn delightful,
abhirambhita mfn embraced, seized by,
abhi√rañj –rajyate to be pleased with, caus. P. to colour,
abhirañjita mfn tinted, coloured,
abhi√1. ras to neigh towards,
abhirāṣṭra mfn overpowering or conquering dominions,
abhirata 68/1 mfn reposing, pleased or contented with, satisfied, engaged in attentive to, performing
abhirati f. pleasure, delighting in
abhi√riṣ to fail, miscarry,
abhiroruda mfn causing tears (indicative of strong passion),
abhiroddhṛ mfn one who wards off,
abhi√ruc A. to be bright, shine, to please anyone, caus. P. to delight, amuse, P.A. to be pleased with, approve of, be inclined to, like,
abhiruci f. delighting in, being pleased with,
abhirucira mfn very bright,
abhirucita mfn pleasing, agreeable to, pleased with,
abhi√rudh to keep off,
abhirudita mfn cried, lamented,
abhi √ruh cl 1 *–rohati,* to ascend, mount, climb up,
abhiruhya having ascended,
abhirūpa mfn corresponding with, conformable to, pleasing, handsome, beautiful, wise, learned, m. the moon, *-tā* f. the state of being learned or well-educated,
abhiruṣita mfn very angry,
abhīṣ (√3.*iṣ*) to seek for long for,
abhiśabdaya Nom P. to name, call,
abhiśabdita mfn announced, mentioned,
abhi√ṣac 1. A. *–sacate*, to turn to, be favourable to, P. *-siṣakti* to approach for revering, 2. m. following, accompanying, devoted to, 71/1
abhiṣad (√*sad*), *-sīdati* to beseige,
abhīṣah (√sah) mfn overpowering,
abhīṣahā ind. (3rd) by force,
abhiṣakta mfn possessed by evil spirits, humiliated, defeated, reviled, cursed
abhi√sāntv to conciliate, pacify, comfort,
abhisāntva m. consolation, conciliation,
abhi√śam -śāmyati to be calmed, cease,
abhisam√2.as to put together, group, collect, 73/1

abhisamā√gam to approach together, to come to,

abhisamāhita mfn fastened to, connected with

abhisamā√hṛ to scrape up or together,

abhisamā√pad A. to enter upon,

abhisamā√sic to pour together,

abhisamavāya m. union, association,

abhisamā√vṛt to return home,

abhisamaya m. agreement, clear understanding,

abhisamā√yā to approach together,

abhisamā√yam –yacchati to fasten to

abhisamāyukta mfn connected or endowed with (3rd),

abhisam√bandh –badhnāti to refer to, mean by,

abhisambādha mfn pressed together, crowded,

abhisambandha m. connection with, relation to, being connected with, belonging to, sexual connection,

abhisambhṛta mfn endowed with, (in comp.)

abhisam√bhū to reach, come to, arrive at, be changed into, caus. to salute,

abhisambodhana attaining the *Bodhi*

abhisambuddha mfn deeply versed in, having attained the *Bodhi (Buddh*).

abhisaṁ√car to go up to, seek for,

abhisaṁcārin 'moving in every direction', inconstant, changeable,

abhisaṁ√1.ci A. *–cinute* to pile up the sacrificial fire for the benefit of oneself

abhisaṁ√cint to remember

abhisaṁdaṣṭa mfn compressed or tightened together

abhisaṁdeha n. organ of generation,

abhisaṁ √1.dhā 72/3 to take aim at, to aim at, have in view, to acknowledge unanimously, to overcome, master, to snap at for devouring, to ally, associate with, 2. f. speech, declaration,

abhisaṁ√dham to blow at

abhisaṁdhāna n. being allied or connected, connection between (in comp.), 'speech, deliberate declaration' (ifc.), attachment or interest in any object, special agreement, overcoming, deceiving, making peace or alliance,

abhisaṁdhāya ind. aiming at, having in view, coming to an agreement regarding, overcoming, bringing in contact with (as a bow with an arrow), place upon (3rd),

abhisaṁdhi m. speaking or declaring deliberately, purpose, intention, object, meaning, special agreement, cheating, deceiving, making peace or alliance, joint, junction,

abhisam √e (-ā-√i) to join in coming near, approach together,

abhisameta mfn assembled,

abhisaṁ√gam to approach together, to join in welcoming, to meet with,

abhisaṁgata mfn together with,

abhisaṁ√1.gī to promise,

abhisaṁ√grah to grab at once with several fingers,

abhisaṁgupta mfn guarded, protected,

abhisaṁ√han to combine, confederate,

abhisaṁhata mfn attacked

abhisaṁdhāya having in view, having in mind, aiming at,

abhisaṁhita mfn aimed at, agreed upon, acknowledged by(in comp.), overcome, (ifc.) connected with attached to ,

abhisam √i –eti, to approach together, come together, meet at (2nd)

abhisamīkṣya ind. seeing, viewing, noticing, perceiving, learning from, considering, with reference to,

abhisam √indh to set on fire, kindle,

abhisam √īr caus. to put in motion,

abhisaṁjāta mfn produced (√*jan*) (as joy)

abhisaṁ√jñā to agree, allow, concede anything,

abhisaṁ√jvar to envy, regard with spite,

abhisaṁ√khyā to enumerate

abhisaṁkhya mfn inferable, clearly ascertainable f.(*ā)* number

abhisaṁkhyeya to be enumerated,

abhisaṁ√krudh to be angry with,
abhisaṁkruddha mfn angry with,
abhisaṁ√kruś to call out to,
abhisaṁ√kṣip to compress, render quite small (the body by magical power),
abhisaṁkṣipta mfn one who has shrunk his body
abhisammata mfn honoured, esteemed,
abhisammūḍha mfn entirely confused,
abhisammukha mfn looking respectfully towards
abhisam√mūrch to assume a solid form with regard to,
abhisaṁnaddha mfn armed
abhisaṁ√nah to bind or string together,
abhisaṁ√nam to alter, modify,
abhisaṁ√nī to lead to or upon,
abhisaṁniviṣṭa mfn being united or combined in
abhisaṁ√4.nu A. to rejoice or cheer together at or towards,
abhisam √pad –padyate, to become, become similar to, be changed to, to come to, arrive at, obtain, caus – *pādayati* to make equal to, change into,
abhisam √pat to fly to, hasten to,
abhisampāta m. concourse, war, battle
abhisampatti f. becoming anything, becoming similar or equal to,
abhisampluta mfn poured upon, overflowed with, deeply engaged in,
abhisamprāp to reach, come to, arrive at, obtain
abhisampra√pad -padyate, to be changed to, assume or obtain the shape of,
abhisampravṛtta mfn having begun,
abhisampra√yā to go towards,
abhisamprekṣ to look at, perceive,
abhisam √pūj to honour, revere greatly,
abhisam √ṛ A. to reach, seize,
abhisaṁrabdha mfn excited, furious,
abhisaṁ√rabh A. to take hold of for support
abhisaṁrādhana n. pacifying, conciliating
abhisaṁrakta mfn intensely attached to
abhisaṁrambha m. fury, rage, 72/1
abhi√śaṁs to accuse, blame, to praise, 70/2
abhiśaṁsaka mfn accusing, insulting,
abhiśaṁsana n. accusation, insult (w 6th),
abhisaṁśīna or *°śyāna* mfn coagulated, congealed, 72/1
abhisaṁskāra m. 'the being formed' development (as of seeds), preparation, conception, idea,
abhisaṁs√1.kṛ –s-karoti, to shape, form, to render or make oneself anything
abhisaṁskṛta mfn consecrated,
abhisaṁśraya m. refuge, connection,
abhisaṁ√śliṣ to cling to each other,
abhisaṁ√smṛ to recollect (with 2nd),
abhisaṁ√spṛś to wash one's self
abhisaṁ√sṛ to run against or assail each other,
abhisaṁ√śri P. to resort to for refuge, have recourse to, to give way to, devote oneself to, to attain
abhisaṁśrita mfn who has resorted to anyone (for refuge), (for a visit)
abhisaṁsṛta mfn one who has come near
abhisaṁ√śru to hear, learn
abhisaṁ√sru to unite in flowing into,
abhisaṁ√stambh to support, render firm,
abhisaṁstava m. praise,
abhisaṁ√sthā -tiṣṭhate to stop at, finish at,
abhisaṁstham ind. in regular order,
abhisaṁsthita mfn stopping or standing or watching at some place, reflecting upon (7th),
abhisaṁstuta mfn. highly praised
abhisaṁstīrṇa mfn entirely covered with
abhisaṁ√stu to praise highly,
abhisaṁ√svṛ to praise or call or invite unanimously
abhisaṁ√tan to use for bridging over or stretching across,
abhisaṁ√tap to press hard on all sides,
abhisaṁtapta mfn tormented,
abhisaṁtata mfn spread over, covered with (in comp.),
abhisaṁ√tī to cross over towards,
abhisaṁtrasta mfn terrified, much alarmed,
abhisaṁ√tyaj to abandon, give up, stop
abhisam √ubj to spread a covering upon
abhisam √1.ūh -ūhati to heap up, heap up and cover with (as with ashes)
abhisaṁ √vāñch to long for, pray to

abhisaṁ√4.vas A. to wrap oneself into,
abhisaṁ√5.vas A. to settle round together
abhisaṁ√1.vid to know thoroughly
abhisaṁ√3.vid to meet each other, to relate, explain,
abhisaṁ√vīkṣ to look at in astonishment, gaze at,
abhisaṁ√viś P.A. to meet round or near, surround, to enter into, dissolve in, merge with,
abhisaṁ√1.vṛ to cover, conceal,
abhisaṁvṛddha mfn having grown a very long time, very old, (said of a tree)
abhisaṁ√vṛt A. to turn oneself towards,
abhisaṁvṛta mfn covered, concealed, surrounded or accompanied by, filled with, furnished with,
abhisaṁvṛtta mfn undertaking, beginning,
abhisaṁ√yā -yāti to visit, approach to, to approach in hostile manner,
abhisaṁyatta mfn being taken care of or governed by,
abhisaṁyoga close contact or relation to,
abhisaṁ√yuj caus. to bring in close contact with (3rd),
abhisaṁyukta mfn furnished/endowed with
abhisandhaka mfn deceiving,
abhiṣaṅga m. propensity or inclination to, the state of being possessed by evil spirits or disturbed in mind, humiliation, defeat, curse or imprecation, false accusation, oath, embracing,
abhiṣañj (√sañj) to be in close contact with, have a claim to or lay claim to, put a slur upon, revile, curse,
abhi√śaṅk A. to doubt, suspect, have doubts about,
abhiśaṅkā f. suspicion, apprehension, fear,
abhiśaṅkita mfn having doubts, suspecting, being alarmed, (*am*) ind. without fear or shyness,
abhiśaṅkya mfn suspicious,
abhiṣaṇṇa mfn besieged, oppressed,
abhi√śap to curse, caus. to conjure, to implore with solemnity,
abhi√sap to carry on, manage
abhiśāpa m. curse, charge, accusation, false accusation,
abhiśapana n. false accusation, slander,,
abhiśapta mfn cursed, accursed, reviled, defamed,
abhisara m. a companion,
abhisāra m. attack, assault, meeting, rendezvous (of lovers),
abhisaraṇa n. meeting, rendezvous,
abhisarga m. creation,
abhisārin mfn going to meet,
abhisarpaṇa n. approaching, the ascent of sap in trees,
abhi√śās -śāsati to assign, allot, to rule, govern,
abhiśas f. accusation, imprecation,
abhiśastaka mfn accused, defamed,
abhiśāstṛ mfn one who assigns, allots,
abhiśasti f. curse, imprecation, damnation, misfortune, evil, one who curses or injures, blame, defamation, asking, begging,
abhiṣāta mfn gained,
abhisatkṛ (√1.kṛ) to honour, receive a guest with reverence,
abhisatkṛta mfn honoured, received with reverence
abhisatvan m. surrounded by heroes,
abhiṣava 71/2 pressing out (*soma*), distillation, ablution, religious bathing, sacrifice, n. sour gruel, consecration,
abhisāyam ind. about evening, at sunset,
abhiṣeka m. anointing, inaugurating, consecration, ritual bathing, sprinkling,
abhiṣic (√sic) to sprinkle, water, wet, to consecrate, anoint, appoint by consecration,
abhiṣicyatām let (him) be anointed, impv.
abhi√3.sidh –sidhyati to be accomplished, to obtain, win,
abhisiddhi f. the state of being effected or realized,
abhiṣikta mfn sprinkled, anointed, installed, enthroned,
abhi√ścut caus. P. to sprinkle with, A. to scatter over oneself with (3rd),

abhiṣeka m. anointing, coronation,sprinkling
abhiṣeṇa m. directing arrows against,
abhiṣeṇana marching against with an army,
abhisevana n. practising, cultivating,
abhi√śī 1. to lie upon,
2. to fall down upon,
abhi√ṣic Cl 6 *–siñcati* to pour upon, consecrate,
abhiṣiddha mfn driven hither,
abhiśīna or abhiśyāna mfn coagulated, congealed,
abhiśīta or *abhiśyāta* mfn cold, chilly,
abhi√śikṣ caus. to teach,
abhiṣikta mfn anointed, installed, enthroned, sprinkled, 71/1
abhiṣiv to sew round,
abhi√skand to ascend, 74/1
abhiskandam ind. running near,
abhi√smi to smile upon,
abhi√śnath to pierce through,
abhisneha m. affection, desire,
abhiṣo to fetter, chain, to put an end to,
abhiśobhita mfn adorned, looking bright or smart,
abhiśoca mfn shining, glowing with heat,
abhiśocana n. a tormenting spirit or demon
abhiśoka m. ardour,
abhisphurita fully expanded (as a blossom),
abhi√sphūrj to sound towards,
abhi-spṛś to touch, to influence, affect
abhi√śri 1. to spread, extend (as brightness),
2. to mix, mingle *–śrīṇāti* to prepare or dress, produce, cause,
3. mfn attached to each other, arranging, putting in order,
abhiśrāva m. hearing a prayer, granting an answer,
abhiśravaṇa n. repeating Vedic texts while sitting down to a *śrāddha* ceremony,
abhi√sṛ to flow towards, to approach, go towards, advance in order to meet, attack, lead to battle, invite to a rendezvous, to approach, visit,
abhi√sṛj to pour into or upon, pour out for a purpose or for the sake of, to let loose in a special direction, to surrender, give, grant,
abhi-sṛp to approach silently or softly,
abhiśriṣ f. a ligature
abhisṛta mfn gone near, directed towards,
abhi√śru to hear, learn,
abhi√sru to cause to flow near,
abhiśruta mfn renowned,
abhiśrutya ind. hearing of, learning,
abhīṣṭa mfn wished, desired, m. a lover, *(ā)* f. a mistress, *(am)* n. wish, m. betel, *-tama* dearest, m. a dearest lover, *-tā* state of being desired,
abhiṣṭan to thunder, roar,
abhiṣṭava m. praise, eulogy,
abhiṣṭhā -tiṣṭhati to tread or step upon, to overpower, defeat, to extend or rise over, to step or advance towards, to stay, live, to stop,
abhīṣṭi f. wish
abhisthiram ind. very firmly, intensely,
abhiṣṭhita mfn trampled upon, defeated, stepped upon, serving as basis
abhiṣṭhiv to spit upon,
abhiṣṭi m. an assistant, protector, f. assistance, protection, help,
abhi√stṛ to scatter over, cover,
abhiṣṭuta praised, consecrated, addressed
abhiṣṭu -ṣṭauti to praise, extol,
abhiṣṭubh -ṣṭobhati to sing or recite in addition to,
abhiṣṭuvat mfn praising,
abhiṣu to press out the Soma juice,
abhīṣu m. rein, bridle, ray of light, *-mat* mfn having rays of light, radiant, bright,
abhiṣū -ṣuvati to endow with, to consecrate for a purpose,
abhi√śubh A. to adorn oneself with, be bright,
abhi√śuc 1. to mourn, 2. to flame towards, burn, consume,
abhisūcita mfn pointed out,
abhiśuna mfn successful, having an advantage over (as in wrestling)
abhiṣvaṅga m. intense attachment to or affection towards,
abhiṣvaṅgin mfn intensely attached to or mad for
abhiṣvañj to embrace,
abhisvar f. invocation,
abhisvare ind. (4th) for calling into one's

presence, just behind (with 6th),
abhisvartṛ (tā) m. an invoker
abhi√śvas to blow towards or hither, to whistle, to groan
abhi√svṛ to join in praising or invoking, to hold a note in singing,
abhiṣyand to run towards or along (said of liquids or creepers), flow,
abhiṣyanda oozing or flowing, running at the eyes, great increase or enlargement,
abhīta mfn fearless,
abhi√taḍ to thump, hit, beat, wound,
abhitaḥ ind. near to towards, near, all around, around, on both sides, before and after (all with 2nd),
abhitāḍita mfn knocked, struck
abhi√taṁs to shake out of, rob,
abhi√tan to stretch or spread across, or over, be prominent,
abhi√tap to radiate heat, to heat, to pain, distress, caus. *–tāpayati* to distress,
abhitāpa m. extreme heat, agitation, affliction, great pain, emotion,
abhitapta mfn scorched, burnt,
abhitaptābhyaḥ 5/pl from those (matters) deliberated over, (see *abhyatapat)*
abhitaram ind. nearer,
abhīruka mfn m. fearless
abhīruṇa not terrific,
abhitas ind. near to towards, near, around on both sides, before and after (all with 2nd), 61/1
abhi√tarj –tarjayati to scold, abuse,
abhītavat ind. fearlessly,
abhīti f. fearlessness, assault,
abhitrāsa m.putting in fear, intimidating,
abhi√tṛd –tṛṇatti to burst open, open, obtain water by bursting the clouds or digging a well, to procure
abhi√tṛp caus. *–tarpayati* to satiate, refresh
abhitṛtti f. the act of procuring or gaining
abhi√tsar to catch, entrap,
abhitsāra m. catching, entrapping,
abhitti f. not bursting, mfn having no walls i.e. no solid foundation,
abhi√tuṣ -tuṣyati to be glad or pleased,
abhi√tvar to be in haste,
abhi√tyaj to abandon,
abhi√2.vā to blow upon or towards,
abhi√vac to declare or utter a verse with reference to,
abhi √vad address or salute with reference, declare with reference to, express by, say, speak, to present oneself to (4th case.), caus. to greet someone,
abhivāda m. reverential salutation, unfriendly speech, abuse
abhivadana n. salutation, addressing,
abhivādana 69/1 respectful salutation
abhivadet may talk to, 1/s/opt/act see above
abhi√vadh to strike
abhvādin mfn telling, enunciating, signifying, describing, m. an explainer, interpreter,
abhivādya ind. to be respectfully saluted,
abhi√vah to convey or carry near to or towards, caus. *vāhayati* to pass time
abhivahana n. carrying near to,
abhivāhatas in consequence of the flowing towards,
abhivāhya n. n. conveyance, transmission,
abhi√valg to jump towards, to bubble up, (said of boiling water),
abhi√vam to spit upon
abhi√van to long for, desire
abhi√vand A. to salute respectfully
abhi√vāñc to long for, desire, 69/1
abhivañcita mfn cheated, deceived, 68/3
abhivāñcita n. wish, desire
abhi√vand cl 1 *–vandate,* to greet, salute,
abhi√2.vap to scatter over, cover with,
abhivardhana 1315/2 strengthening, increasing
abhī-varga circuit, compass,
abhivarṇana n. description,
abhivarṇita mfn described
abhivarṣa m. rain
abhivarṣaṇa n raining, raining upon,
abhīvarta mfn rendering victorious, m. victorious attack, victory,
abhivartin mfn coming towards, approaching, going towards (in comp.),
abhi√vaś -vaṣṭi P. to rule or be master over, P.A. to long for, desire

abhi√4.vas -vaste, to wrap oneself up in, to clothe, cover,
abhivāsa m. covering,
abhivāsas ind. over the garment,
abhivat containing the word *abhi*
abhivāta mfn ill, sick,
abhivātam ind. windwards,
abhivayas mfn very youthful, fresh
abhivedhin mfn (in geom.) cutting (as one line cuts another)
abhivī to come towards from different parts, to urge, impel,
abhivi√car A. to go near to, caus.*–cārayati* to consider, reflect upon
abhivi√cakṣ -caṣṭe to look towards
abhi√1.vid caus. *–vedayati* to report, relate,
abhi√3.vid to find, obtain, to know,
abhivi√bhā –bhāti to illuminate,
abhivi√bhaj A. to distribute,
abhivi√budh –budhyate to notice, learn from
abhividdha mfn wounded, 70/1
abhivi√dhā to bring near to or in contact with,
abhivi√dhāv to run near to,
abhividhi m. complete comprehension or inclusion, (*au*) 7th ind. inclusively,
abhividīpita mfn entirely inflamed,
abhivi√dṛś caus. *darśayati* to show to,
abhividruta mfn run towards, run away, fled,
abhivi√dyut to break open, open by force,
abhivihita mfn covered entirely,
abhivi√hṛ to divide,
abhi√vij to tip over a vessel,
abhi√vīj caus. to fan
abhivi√jaṁh to struggle, convulse,
abhivi√jñā to be aware of, perceive, 69/2
abhivijñāpta mfn notified, made known,
abhivijñāya ind. being aware of, perceiving
abhivi√jval to flame or blaze against or opposite to,
abhivi√khyā to look at view,
abhivikhyāta mfn universally known, renowned, known as, called,
abhivikrama mfn endowed with great courage,
abhivīkṣ A. -*vikṣate* to look at view, perceive, to examine, look upon as, behave as, regard as, with regard to, to be affected towards,
abhivikṣepa m. flapping one's wings over
abhivi√kṣip to flap one's wings over
abhivīkṣita mfn seen, perceived,
abhivīkṣya ind. having seen or perceived,
abhivi√lī caus. to cause to melt
abhivimīna endowed with *abhimāna* (self-reference),
abhivi√manth to grind, grind to powder,
abhivi√mṛj to rub in, rub with,
abhivinīta mfn well-disciplined, well-educated, versed in,
abhivi√nud caus. *–nodayati,* to gladden, cause to rejoice
abhivipaṇyu mfn absolutely indifferent,
abhivi√paś -paśyati to look at, view, to look hither,
abhivīra mfn surrounded by heroes,
abhivi√rāj to govern, to shine, be radiant,
abhivi√ruc A. to shine or be brilliant over,
abhivi√ṣañj to be entirely devoted to, have one's heart set upon,
abhiviśaṅkin mfn afraid of,
abhiviśruta mfn widely celebrated,
abhiviṣṭa mfn entered by, seized by, being in the power of,
abhivi√ṣṭhā A. to extend one's self towards or over,
abhivi√śvas caus. –śvāsayati to render confident
abhivīta mfn desired, driven, impelled by,
abhivi√tan to stretch the bowstring over or across the bow
abhivi√2.vas to shine forth during or at the time of
abhivivṛddhi f. increased prosperity,
abhivi√yā -yāti, to approach, visit
abhivlaṅga m. turning off, shaking off,
abhi√vlī to sink down, fall down,
abhivoḍhṛ m. one who conveys towards,
abhi√vṛ caus. *–vārayati* to keep off, fend off 2. *–vṛṇīte* to choose, prefer,
abhi√vraj to go up to, to pass through, to go to,
abhi√vṛdh to grow higher than, surpass, to grow up, increase more, prosper,

abhivṛddha mfn increased, augmented,
abhivṛddhi f. increase, growth, prosperity
abhi√veṣṭ caus. to cover with (3rd),
abhi√vṛh caus. to strengthen, encourage,
abhi√vṛṣ P. cl 1 *-varṣati,* to rain upon, to bedew, cover with, a shower (arrows or blossoms), to cause to rain (said of gods),
abhi√vṛt to go towards, approach, to attack, to make for, be victorious, to turn up, arise, to take place, happen, exist,
abhivṛta or abhīvṛta mfn surrounded by, bordered by, 2. chosen, selected,
abhivṛtti f. coming towards, approaching,
abhi√vyadh P. to wound
abhivyaikhyat he manifested or he gazed around,
abhivyakta mfn manifest, evident, visible, distinct, manifested, (*am*) ind. manifestly,
abhivyakti f. manifestation, distinction,
abhi√vyañj to be manifested, become manifest, pass. *–vyajjate*
abhivyañjaka mfn revealing, manifesting, indicative, showing,
abhivyañjana n. making manifest,
abhi-vy-√āp (ind. p. °*vyāpya*), (said of a rule) to extend to, have value unto,
abhi-vy-ā-√hṛ to utter, pronounce, to speak or converse about, 70/2
abhivyāhāra m. pronunciation, utterance, an articulate significant word or phrase,
abhivyāhṛta mfn pronounced, spoken, addressed, (*am*) n. what has been said, speaking carried out, '*vācā yadi abhivyāhṛta*' – if speaking be done by speech,
abhivyāhṛtya mfn to be said,
abhivyaikhyat manifested
abhivyakta mfn evident, distinct, manifest, (*-am)* ind. manifestly,
abhivyāpaka mfn (in Gram.) extending to, including, comprehending,
abhivyāpti f. inclusion, comprehension,
abhivyāpya ind.1. up to a certain point, inclusive, 2. mfn to be included,
abhi√yā to go up to in a hostile manner, attack, approach, obtain, to devote one's self to, 2. mfn going up to, approaching, assailing
abhi√yāc to ask for, solicit, request,
abhiyācana n. asking for, entreaty, request,
abhiyācita asked for, requested,
abhi√yaj to honour with sacrifices, to offer a sacrifice, to honour,
abhiyaṣṭavya mfn to be honoured with sacrifices
abhiyāta mfn approached, attacked,
abhiyāti -tin, m. an assailant, enemy
abhiyoga 68/1 m application, energetic effort, exertion, perseverance in, constant practice, attack, assault,
abhiyoktṛ mfn assailing, attacking, m. an enemy, (in law) a plaintiff, claimant, pretender, accuser,
abhi√yuj A. –yuṅkte to put to (as horses to a carriage) for a special purpose, to summon, invite to, to order, charge with, to encounter, attack, to accuse of, to undertake, to apply to, make one's self ready to, caus. to furnish with, make anybody share in,
abhiyukta 68/1 applied, intent on, the steadfast, diligent, versed in, united to yoga, blamed, rebuked, (in law) charged, prosecuted, a defendant,
ābhoga m. satiety, enjoyment, fulness, completion, expanse, curving, curve, the hood of the Cobra, circuit, circumference, variety, (G) immediate experience, engrossed attachment of the mind to one thing,
abhokta m. non-enjoyer,
a-bhokṭri mfn not enjoying, not using, abstemious
√*abhr* 79/3 cl 1 P *abhrati* to err, wander about, DP in the sense of *gati*, going, moving
abhra 79/3 n. water-bearer, cloud, thunder-cloud, rainy weather, sky, gold, camphor, the *ratan*
abhragaṅgā the celestial *Gaṅga*
abhraghana mfn thickly covered with

clouds,
abhraka n. talcum, mica
a-bhrama mfn not blundering,
abhramliha mfn cloud-licking, touching the clouds, high, lofty, m. the wind,
abhrampatha m. sky, atmosphere
abhramu f. female elephant of the east, mate of *airāvata* (Indra's elephant), *-priya* or *–vallabha* the male elephant of the east or *airāvata,*
a-bhrānta mfn un-perplexed, not in error, clear, composed, not mistaken, (G) non-illusory, real, true,
a-bhrānti f. absence of perplexity or error
abhrapruṣ f. sprinkling of the clouds, rain
a-bhrātṛ mfn brotherless
abhravakāśika mfn affording an opportunity for the rain, exposing one's self to the rain,
abhravakāśin having the clouds or sky as shelter – an ascetic
abhravarṣa dripping or raining from clouds
abhri f. a wooden scraper or shovel, spatula,
a-bhuj mfn one who has not experienced or enjoyed,
a-bhuñjat mfn not being useful to, stingy
abhūta 75/1 mfn whatever has not been or happened,
abhūt 1/s/aor. √*bhū* he became,
abhūtābhiniveśa (N) false attachment
abhūtapūrva mfn unprecedented,
abhūtārtha m. anything unheard of or impossible,
abhūtatva n. or *–tā* f. not having existed or happened at any time, impossibility,
a-bhukta mfn uneaten, unenjoyed, unused, unexpended, one who has not eaten, enjoyed or expended,
a-bhuñjāna mfn not eating, fasting,
abhyā√*bhū* to happen to, occur to,
abhyā√*cakṣ* to look at, speak,
abhyā√*car* to approach, to undertake, practise, 77/2
abhyācāre in the reach or compass,
abhyā√*1.dā* A. P. to seize, snatch away, A. to put on as a wreath, (with *vākyam)* to commence to speak,
abhyādāna n. beginning,
abhyā√*dhā* to lay on fuel etc.
abhyādhāna n. laying on (fuel),
abhyadhika mfn additional, more, superior, surpassing, superior to, 75/3
abhyadhvam ind. upon the way,
abhyā√*gam* to come near to, approach,
abhyāgama m. approaching, arrival, visit, arriving at or enjoying a result, neighbourhood, rising to receive a guest, 77/1
abhyāgare 7th ind. in the house
abhyāgārika diligent in supporting a family
abhyāgata mfn come, arrived,
abhyāghāta m. interruption, attack,
abhyagra quick, constant, perpetual, having the point directed towards,
abhyāhanana n. impeding, interruption,
abhyahanyanta 1/pl/impf/pass √*han* they sounded
abhy-aj to combine, unite,
abhyājñāya m. order, command,
abhyākāṅkṣita n. a groundless complaint or false accusation,
abhyā√*khyā* to accuse falsely
abhyākhyāta one charged with some doubtful guilt,
abhy-akta mfn oiled, anointed,
abhyalaṁkāra m. decoration,
abhyalpa very small,
abhyamitra mfn ind. against the enemy
abhyānana mfn having the face turned towards,
abhy-aṅga n. rubbing with unguent,
abhy√*añj* P. to smear, anoint, A. to anoint oneself, to decorate, decorate oneself,
abhyantara 75/3 being inside of, interior, interval, space, next, nearly, related, intimate, (*am*) n. inner part, interior, inside, middle, (*am*) ind. ifc. into,
abhy√*āp* *-āpnoti* to reach to, get, obtain
abhyantaraka m. an intimate friend
abhy-anu-√*jñā* 1. to assent to, approve, allow, permit, concede, to authorize, direct, to allow one to depart, dismiss, 2. f. assent, approval, permission, granting leave of

absence, dismissing, (G) a logical concession,
abhy-anujñāna n. assenting to approval,
abhyanūkta mfn stated or uttered with reference to,
abhy-anu-√mud caus.to assent to, approve of
abhy-anu-√prach to inquire after, ask for,
abhy-anu-√śās to indicate, denote,
abhy-anu-√sṛ to learn by investigating,
abhy-anu-√vac to declare or state or utter with reference to,
abhy-anu-√vad to utter with reference to
abhy-anu-√yuj to apply to, ask,
abhy-apa-√śri to retire towards,
abhyā√pad to enter into, come to,
abhyāpādam ind. so as to enter into or pass through,
abhyā√pat to jump on, hasten near to,
abhyāpāta m. calamity, misfortune,
abhyā√rabh A. to lay hold of, to commence,
abhyāram ind. near, at hand
abhyārambha m. beginning, re-beginning, repetition,
abhy√arc to praise, celebrate in song, 76/1
abhyarcana n. worship, reverence,
abhyarcya mfn to be reverenced,
abhy√ard to oppress, afflict
abhyardha m. opposite to, in the face of,
abhyardita mfn distressed, oppressed,
abhyarhaṇa n. reverencing,
abhyarhanīya mfn to be greatly honoured, venerable, *-tā* f. honourableness
abhyarhita mfn greatly honoured, venerable, more honoured, more important than, fit, proper, becoming,
abhyarṇa near, proximate,
abhyāroha m. ascending
abhy√arth A.P. to request, ask for
abhyarthana n. asking, requesting, generally
abhyārūḍha mfn ascended,
abhyā√ruh *abhyārohati* to ascend, mount, step upon,
abhy√1. aś *-aśnoti*, to pervade, reach, gain
abhy√1.as *-asti,* to be over, reign over, excel, surpass, overpower,
abhy√2.as to throw towards or upon,
abhyāśa m. reaching to, pervading, an expected result, proximity, near, *(am)* ind. near, at hand,
abhyāsa repetition, reduplication, practice, military practice, repetition, exercise, use, act of adding anything, inculcation of a sacred truth by repetition,
abhyasta mfn accumulated by recent practice (as food), practised, exercised, learnt by heart, repeated, studied, multiplied, familiar, (in Gram.) reduplicated, n. the reduplicated base of a root,
abhyā√yā to come up to, approach,
abhyā√yam to lengthen (as a syllable in speaking, A. to assume,
abhyā√sad to sit down into, to attain, obtain
abhyāsa m. reaching to, pervading, any expected result or consequence, proximity (with 5th or 6th), *(am)* ind. near, near at hand, 2. the act of adding anything, (in Gram.) 'what is pre-fixed', the first syllable of a re-duplicated radical, *(am)* n. the reduplicated base of a root, in poetry – repetition of the last verse of a stanza or of the last word of a chapter, (in arithmetic) multiplication, repeated or permanent exercise, discipline, use, habit, custom, repeated reading, study, military practice, (in later Vedānta phil.) inculcation of a truth conveyed in scripture by persistent repetition of the word or passage, (in Yoga phil.) the effort of the mind to remain in its unmodified condition of purity (*sattva*), "practice, knowledge into action by repetition" HH
abhyāsakta mfn closely linked together,
abhyaśana n. reaching, gaining
abhyasana n. practice, exercise,
abhyāsaṅgya mfn to be closely linked together (as days)
abhyāsaparivartin mfn wandering about or near,
abhyāsatā f. constant practice, use, habit,

abhyāsavat m. (in Yoga phil.) 'being in the condition called *abhyāsa'* i.e. a Yogin of the first degree,
abhyāsayoga m. the practice of frequent and repeated meditation on any deity or abstract spirit, repeated recollection,
abhyāsin mfn practising, repeating,
abhyasta mfn accumulated by repeated practice, practised, exercised, learnt by heart, repeated, studied, multiplied, (in gram. re-duplicated (as roots),
abhyastam said of the sun setting upon anybody not working, or with action incomplete, n. the reduplicated base of a root,
abhyasūya 77/1 to show indignation, be indignant at, P.A. *–asūyati* speaks evil of, sneers at
abhyasūyā f. indignation, anger, envy, jealousy
abhyasūyaka having envy, the envious, or indignant
abhyā√tan to take aim at, shoot, 77/2
abhyā√tap to torment, pain
abhyatapat he undertook *tapas,* austerities, he deliberated over, resolved, 1/s/impf *abhi √tap*
abhy-atī√i to pass over, to get through towards,
abhy-ati√kram to step over, walk through, to transgress,
abhy-ati√kṣar to flow over to,
abhy-ati√nī to bring or place upon,
abhy-ati-√ric to remain for the sake of
abhy-ati√sṛj to let pass,
abhy-atita one who has walked towards, one who visits,
abhy-atīta mfn passed away (as time),
abhy-ati-√vad to speak louder or better, surpass in disputing,
abhy-ati√vṛt –vartate, to drive past,
abhyātma mfn directed towards one's self,
abhyātmam ind. towards one's self,
abhyā√tī to come up to,
abhyātta mfn encompassing,
abhy√av to refresh
abhyava√1.dā to place into, 76/2
abhyava√3.dā to cut off in addition to,
abhyavadānya mfn depriving of
abhyava√dhā to allay, lay, (as dust),
abhyā√vah to convey, bring towards,
abhyavahāra 76/3 m taking food
abhyava√hṛ to throw down into water, to bring near, to take food, eat,
abhyava√jval to enlighten, illuminate, caus. *-jvālayate*
abhyavakarṣaṇa n. extraction, drawing out
abhyavakāśa m. an open space,
abhyavakīrṇa mfn covered,
abhyava√kṝ to throw or cast on, pour on, cover,
abhyava√man –manyate to despise, reject,
abhyava√nam caus. to bow, incline
abhyava√nī to lead down (into water), to pour into or upon,
abhyava√nij P. *–nenekti* to wipe or wash clean, clean,
abhyava√pat to fly near,
abhyāvartam ind. so as to repeat, repeatedly,
abhyāvartin mfn coming near, coming repeatedly, returning (as days),
abhyava√ruh to step down upon
abhyavaskanda m. impetuous assault,
abhyava√sṛ to retire from(5th), towards (2nd),
abhyavasthita mfn resisting,
abhyava√syand to drive towards
abhyava√tan -tanoti, to send out or spread (as rays ,3rd,) towards, or to be sent out etc.
abhyava√vṛt to turn oneself away from,
abhyavāyana n. going down,
abhy-ave (√i) –avaiti to go down, descend into water, to condescend
abhy-avekṣ, -avekṣate to look at or upon,
abhyā√viś to rush into, to enter into, penetrate
abhyā√vṛt -vartate to roll (as a cart) towards, come up to or towards,
abhyāvṛtta mfn come near, approached,
abhyāvṛtti f. repetition,
abhyāvṛtya ind. turning oneself towards,
abhyaya m.approach of darkness, setting of the sun,
abhyā√2.yu to strive towards, 77/3
abhyāyin mfn going towards, approaching

abhyetya having approached,
abhyūḍhi f. conveying towards,
abhyāyuka mfn coming up to,
abhy√ṛ -ṛṇoti to run towards, reach,
abhy√ṛch –archati, to come to, visit or afflict with, strive to overpower,
abhy√ṛñj A. *–ṛijyate* to stretch out the hand for, hasten towards,
abhy√uc -ucyati to like, take pleasure in visiting,
abhyucchrita mfn raised aloft, elevated, prominent, excellent through (3rd)
abhyuccaya m. increase,
abhyuc√car to rise over,
abhyuc√1.ci to bring together in one place,
abhyudaya 78/2 m. sunrise or rise of luminaries, beginning, commencing, increase, prosperity, good result
abhyudayin mfn rising,
abhyude ind.to go out in order to meet anyone,
abhi√yudh to fight against, to acquire by fighting, to fight,
abhyud√dhā to rise together with,
abhyuddhṛ to take out (fire), to take or draw out, draw(water), to take up, lift up, to elevate, render prosperous, to re-obtain
abhyuddhṛta mfn taken up, drawn (as water), collected (for a purpose),
abhyuddṛṣṭa having become visible (as the moon) during anything,
abhyudgama m. rising from a seat to honour anyone, 78/3
abhyudgata mfn risen (as the moon), one who has gone out in order to meet anyone, extended (as fame),
abhy-ud-√i to rise over (the sun), rise, to engage in combat with,
abhy-ud-√īkṣ to look towards,
abhy-ud-√īr caus. to raise one's voice, to be stirred up, intensified,
abhyudita 78/2 mfn. 1. risen, arisen, rising (said of the sun or moon), 'one over whom, while sleeping, the sun has risen', engaged in combat, happened, arisen, elevated, prosperous,
2. expressed (in words)
abhy-ud-√1.ūh to move or push further out,
abhyūḍha mfn concluded, inferred,
abhyūha m. reasoning, deduction, inference, conjecture,
abhyūhati infers, guesses,
abhy-uj-√ji to obtain by conquering,
abhy-uj-√jīv -jīvati to preserve life,
abhyukta mfn declared or uttered (as a verse) with reference to, uttered with reference to, is revealed,
abhyullasat mfn gleaming, flashing,
abhyupā√1.dā to pick up as fruit from the ground,
abhyupa√dhā to place upon (the fire) together with, cover with,
abhyupagama agreeing with someone elses argument,
abhyupagantṛ mfn one who assents or admits,
abhyupagata mfn gone near to, approached
abhyupāgata mfn come near, approached,
abhyupā√hṛ to bring near, offer,
abhyupā√kṛ to prepare, make preparations
abhyupā√kṛṣ to draw toward oneself,
abhyupa√lakṣ to perceive, notice,
abhyupa√mantr to address with a formula,
abhyupapanna mfn protected, rescued, asking for protection or help, agreed to, admitted, agreeing to,
abhyupapatti f. approaching in order to assist, for protection or defence, favour, the conferring of a benefit or kindness, impregnation of a woman (especially of a brother's widow, as an act of duty),
abhyupa√sad to reach (a town),
abhyupaśānta mfn allayed, calmed,
abhyupa√sev -sevate to observe religiously
abhyupa√sṛ to come near,
abhyupa√sthā to honour
abhyupasthita come, arrived, attended or accompanied by
abhyupāva√hṛ to bring or set down upon,
abhyupa√viś to sit down upon, to sit down,
abhyupā√vṛt to turn oneself or go towards,
abhyupa√yā to approach, go towards, (with *śamam*) to enter the state of rest,
abhyupāya m. an agreement, promise, enagagement, a means an expedient,
abhyupā√yā to come up to, approach
abhyupāyana n. a complimentary gift, an inducement,
abhyupayukta mfn employed, used,
abhyupe 1. to go near, approach, arrive at, enter, to bathe, to enter a state or condition, obtain, share, to admit as

an argument or a position, to agree with, approve of,

abhyupekṣ to overlook, allow,

abhy√uṣ to burn, consume by fire,

abhyuṣita having dwelt, having passed the night with

abhy-ut-√kram to go up to, ascend,

abhy-ut-√kruś to raise loud acclamation towards,

abhy-ut-√pat to fly or jump or rush up to,

abhyut√sah to be able to resist, feel competent, venture

abhyut√smi to smile on, smile,

abhyut√thā to rise for going towards, rise to do someone honour, rise in rebellion, desist from,

abhyutthāna n. rising from a seat through politeness, rising, setting out, rebellion, elevation, gaining a high position, gaining authority, respectability, power; rise, origin, birth

abhyut√tī to cross over towards, penetrate to

abhyukta 78/1 mfn declared or uttered (as a verse), with reference to (2nd), spoken of,

abja mfn born in water, a conch, the moon, (*am*) n. a lotus,

abodha m. non-perception, ignorance, stupidity, mfn ignorant, stupid, puzzled, perplexed, 60/2

abodhagamya mfn incomprehensible,

abodhanīya mfn unintelligible, not to be awakened or aroused,

ābrahma 145/1 ind. up to or including brahman,
stamba 1257/3 a clump or tuft of grass, *paryanta* 607/1 bounded by
ābrahmastambaparyanta from *Brahmā* to a tuft of grass

abravīt he said, spoke, 1/s/impf/act √*brū*

abuddha 60/1 mfn unwise, foolish, not seen or noticed,

abuddhi f. want of understanding, ignorance, stupidity, mfn ignorant, stupid, unintelligent,

abuddhimat mfn unwise, foolish,

abuddhyā f. want of understanding, ignorance, stupidity, mfn ignorant, stupid, ind. unintentionally,

abudh or *abudha* mfn stupid, foolish, m. a fool,

abudhna mfn bottomless,

abudhya mfn not to be awakened,

abudhyamāna mfn not being awake,

√ac 8/3 cl1 P *acati, añcati* , Ā *acate* to go, move, tend, honour, make round or curved, request, ask
DP in *gati*, going, moving,
or *yācana* 850/2 asking, entreaty, begging, soliciting,

ā√cakṣ A. -*caṣṭe* to look at, inspect, to tell, relate, announce, declare, make known, confess, to acquaint, introduce to, to address anyone, to call, name, to signify,

ācakṣus mfn learned,

ācakṣva (V) kindly inform, kindly calculate, please describe, please tell,

acala mfn. not moving, immovable
m. a mountain, not changing,

acalā f. the earth

ācamana n. sipping water from the palm of the hand for purification, the water used, rinsing of the mouth,

ācamanīya m. a vessel used for *ācamana,* (*am*) n. the water used for *ācamana,* an offering of water,

acāpalam freedom from restlessness, steadiness, determination,

ā√car Cl1 to conduct oneself, act, do,

acara mfn not moving, (substantive) a plant (as distinguished from an animal), immovable, impassable,

ācara 484/3 to be practised or performed,

ācāra 131/3 m. conduct, manner of action, good conduct, good behaviour, acting lawfully, usage,
walk and conversation, agreeing with what is taught by the teacher (Buddhist),

acaraṇa n. improper conduct,

ācaraṇa n. behaviour, conduct, behaving, following, undertaking, character, observing, cart, performing, carriage, approaching, practising, manners, processing (theme), activity,

ācarata undertaking, moving towards
acarat walked
ācarati he does, he behaves, he practices 1/s/pres/indic/act *ā√car*
ācāravarjita mfn out of rule, irregular, outcast,
ācāravat mfn well-conducted, virtuous,
ācāraviruddha mfn contrary to custom,
ācārika n. habit of life, diet, regimen,
ācārin mfn following established practice,
ācarita mfn passed or wandered through, frequented by, observed, exercised, practised, (in Gram. enjoined or fixed by rule), (*am*) n. approaching, arrival, conduct, behaviour, -*tva* n. custom, usage,
ācaritavya gve. to be practised, should be practised, to be acted in a customary way,
ācārya 131/3 m. 'knowing or teaching the *ācāra* or rules', a spiritual guide or teacher, (especially one who invests the student with the sacrificial thread), and instructs him in the Vedas, in the law of sacrifice and religious mysteries, the title affixed to the names of learned men is like the use of Dr.
ācāryopāsanam n. sitting with a teacher, attendance on a teacher
accha mfn not shaded, not dark, transparent, clear, m. a crystal, a bear, a separable verbal prefix or preposition –to, unto, hither sometimes *acchā*
ā√chad Cl10 *āchādayati* to hide, conceal,
ācchādana 132/1 covering, concealing, hiding, cloth, clothes, mantle, cloak,
acchāya 9/1 mfn without shadow, casting no shadow
acchedya mfn not to be pierced or cut not able to be cut, indivisible,
acetana inanimate, inert, not conscious, insensible, unconscious,
acetas 9/1 mfn. imprudent, unconscious, insensible, the non-discriminating
acintayat he or she thought
acintya 9/1 mfn inconceivable, surpassing thought, unthinkable, unimaginable, incomprehensible,
acira mfn not of long duration, brief, instantaneous, recent, ind. not long, not for long, not long ago, soon, speedily,
acirāt mfn not of long duration, brief, instantaneous, recent, soon, ind. soon, not long, not for long, after a little while,
acireṇa ind. soon, within a short while,
acīrṇavrata m. one who has not fulfilled the vow,
acit 8/3 mfn without understanding, not knowing, irreligious, bad, f. matter, not spirit,
acit śakti great darkness, *tamas,* the root of matter,
acit vastu non-sentient matter,
ācit f. attention,
acitti f. not wisdom, folly, want of sense, infatuation,
acitvā ind. without piling, (L)
acyuta 9/2 imperishable, unshaken, not fallen, permanent, unchanging one, name of *Viṣṇu*, *Kṛṣṇa*
√aḍ 11/3 cl 1 P *aḍati* to endeavour DP in *udyamana* trying, exerting
√ad 17/3 cl 2 P *atti* to eat, consume, devour, caus. *ādayati*, DP in *bhakṣaṇa* eating,
2. mfn ifc. 'eating' as in *matsyād* eating fish,
ād id then indeed,
ada or *adaka* eating
ā√dā Cl 3 *–datte,* to receive, take, accept, to seize, take away, rob, to take back, reclaim, bring,
adadāt gave
adagdha mfn unburnt
adaḥ pron. n. (mediate, in between, neither near nor far), that, that one,
ādahana n. burning place, place of cremation
adahat he, she or it burned
adāhayat set alight 1/s/past/imperf/act
adāhyas not to be burned,

not able to be burned, *a√dah*

adakṣiṇam 17/3 not dexterous, not handy, not right, left, inexperienced, simple-minded,
not offering a present to the priest

adambha mfn. free from deceit,
m. straightforwardness

adambhitva 18/1 n. sincerity, unpretentiousness,

adana 17/3 the act of eating, food

ādāna 136/3 taking, receiving, taking for oneself, drawing near to oneself, taking away or off, a cause of disease, binding on or to, fettering

adanīya to be eaten

adantajāta mfn not having teethed,

adaṁṣṭrin n. without tusks or large teeth,

ādara 138/1 m. respect, regard, notice, care, trouble,

ādaraṁ√kṛ take care (to)

ādarśa 18/1 *adarśa* for *ādarśa* m. a mirror, ideal, model, act of perceiving by the eyes, sample, commentary, template, ideal perfection, pattern, day of new moon,
Apte 79/3 1.showing, displaying, 2. a mirror.

ādarśamadhyasthe 470/3 *darśa* looking at, viewing. root *dṛś* 491/1 to see, -*madhya* in the middle, standing between, belonging to neither or both parties 7/s (ref. A and C) existing in a mirror,

adarśam I saw, I have seen, 1/s/aorist

adarśana 18/1 n. not seeing, a latent condition, beyond the range of vision, lack of discernment, non-vision, disregard, neglect, non-appearance, latent condition, disappearance, mfn latent, invisible,

ādarśapuruṣa m. an exemplary person,

adas, adaḥ pron. (mediate i.e. neither near nor far), this, that, then,
yon, yonder, that there,
a designation of some-one not named e.g. *asāv (asau) aham*
I am so and so, a certain,

adasta mfn unexhausted, imperishable,

ādau in the beginning, at first, 7/s of *ādi*

adatta mfn not given, given unjustly, not given in marriage, one who has given nothing, f. (*ā*) an unmarried girl,

ādatte 136/2 gives to one self, takes, accepts, receives from, seizes, takes back *√dā*

ādāya 136/3 1.mfn ifc. taking, seizing,
2. ind. having taken, with, along with

adbhuta 19/1 wonderful, marvellous

adbhutarūpa mfn having wonderful beauty,

ādbika mfn additional, subsequent, later, annual, surpassing, superior,

aḍḍ 11/3 cl 1 *aḍḍati* to join, to infer, argue, meditate, discern, attack, DP in *abhiyoga*

aḍḍana n a shield

adeha 'bodiless', the god of love,

ādeśa 137/3 m. advice, instruction, account, information, declaration, injunction, precept, rule, command, order, foretelling, soothsaying, 'instruction through analogy', a divine command from within the being,

adeśakāle in the wrong place and time

adeva m. non-god, who is no god,

ādevana n. gambling place, place for playing,

adha 19/3 ind. used mainly as an inceptive particle, now, (or expressing a sequence) then, so then, therefore, moreover, and
adha yad just then when,

ā√dhā Cl 3 *–dadhāti, -dhatte,* to place or put on (with loc.), entrust to, take on, assume, to impregnate, impress, apply, appoint, give, supply, lend, accept, receive,

adhaḥpatana downward distillation, deterioration, downfall,

adhaḥśākha (whose) branches are below

adhaḥśayin mfn lying low, sleeping on the ground

adhama 19/3 mfn lowest, vilest, worst, (often ifc. e.g. *narādhama* the lowest of men, degraded,

adhamādhama the lowest of the low,
adhama uddharaka uplifter of the down-trodden,
adhanya mfn not rich, poor, unhappy,
adhara mfn inferior, lower, West,
m. the lower lip, the lip,
n. the lower part, a reply, the vulva
ādhāra 139/1 m support, prop, stay, substratum, the power of sustaining or the support given, a vessel, a reservoir, pond, dam, receptacle, (in phil. and gram.) comprehension, location, the sense of the locative case, ifc. belonging or relating to, the subject in a sentence, 'the system composed of the 5 principles constituting the physical, vital, mental, intellectual and bliss sheaths,'
ādhāra-ādheya-saṁbandha relation of the support and the thing supported; relation of location and the thing located; relation of abode and abiding,
adharedhyus ind. the day before yesterday,
adharma injustice, wrong, against the law, cheating, sin, unrighteousness, f. (*ā*) unrighteousness, demerit,
Jain – the principle of rest which pervades the universe,
adharmacarin mfn practising wickedness,
adharmāstikāya Jain- the medium of rest,
adharmatas ind. unrighteously, unjustly,
adharottara mfn lower and higher, worse and better, topsy-turvy, nearer and further, upside-down,
adharastāt 19/3 ind. below
adhārṣṭa mfn absence of - boldness, audacity, violence, arrogance, not proceeding,
adhas 20/1 ind. below, down, in the lower region, beneath, under,
adhastāt 20/2 ind. below, the lower region, under, the nadir,
ādhatsva keep! place!
2/s/impv/mid *ā√dhā*
adhāvat ran
ādhāya having placed or put, placed, put gerund *ā√dhā* 138/2
ādheya n. a placing esp. of the sacred fire, being based, contained, the 'superstratum as opposed to substratum' as 'pot is to clay'
to be deposited or placed,
to be pledged or mortgaged,
to be assigned or attributed,
to be effected, to be fixed,
being, contained, comprehended, included,
(G) a type of power (*śakti*) that is occasioned in a thing by some new operation (as in an idol when it is consecrated),
adhi (*upasarga* – indeclinable prefix to nouns and verbs) 20/2, expresses above, over, besides,
a separable adverb or preposition,
(with 5th) – over, from above, from, from the presence of, after, for, instead of,
(with 7th) – over, on, at, in comparison with,
(with 2nd) over upon concerning,
also 'different'
as a figure of speech
adhī-(√i) adhyeti to turn the mind towards, observe, understand, to mind, remember, care for, long for, to know, know by heart, to go over, study, to learn from (a teacher's mouth), to declare, teach, A. *adhīte*, *adhīyate*, to study, learn by heart, read, recite, caus. *adhyāpayati* to teach,
ādhi m. a receptacle, place, situation, a pledge, deposit, hire, rent, an attribute, title, epithet, 2. anxiety, pain, mental anguish, mental disease, 138/2
adhi√bādh to vex, annoy, 21/2
ādhibhautika 138/3 belonging or related to created beings, elementary, derived or produced from the primitive elements, material, physical, to do with inanimate objects, elemental,
adhibhojana an additional gift, 21/2

adhi-bhū m. a master, a superior,
adhi√3.bhuj to enjoy,
adhibhūta Supreme Being, aggregate of physical elements, the spiritual or fine substratum of material or gross objects, the all-penetrating influence of the Supreme Spirit, 'the transitoriness of the elements-', nature, (*am*) ind. on material objects, 'with regard to natural things',
adhibhūtavidyā f. science of the physical or material world,
adhi√brū to speak in favour of or favourably to, intercede for, 21/2
adhi√car to walk or move on or over, to be superior to,
adhicaraṇa n. the act of walking or moving on or over,
adhi√ci to pile upon,
adhidaiva or *-daivata* 21/1 Supreme God, the divine agent operating in material objects 'beyond Indra and other gods', a presiding or tutelary deity, (*am*) ind. on the subject of the deity or the divine agent,
adhidaivavidyā f. science of the heavens,
adhidaivika mfn spiritual, divine, relating to deities,
ādhidaivika 138/3 relating to or proceeding from gods or from spirits, proceeding from divine or supernatural agencies
adhi-daṇḍa-netṛ, tā m. presiding over punishment,
adhidārva mfn wooden,
adhideva m. or *–devatā* f. a presiding or tutelary deity
adhidevam or *–devatam* ind. concerning the gods or the deity,
adhidevana n. a gaming table or board,
adhi√dhā to place upon, give, share between, A. to acquire additionally
adhidīdhiti mfn having excessive lustre,
adhi√dhṛ caus. to carry over or across
adhi√diś to bestow,
adhi√2.dru to cover (said of a bull),
adhi√gā P. to obtain, to remember, notice, P or generally A. to go over, read, learn, study, to attempt, resolve,
adhi√gam *-gacchati* 20/3 to go up to, approach, arrive at, go to, go unto, approach for sexual intercourse, to fall in with, to meet, find, discover, to accomplish, to study, read, obtain, attain, realise, perceive,
adhi√gaṇ to enumerate, to value highly,
adhijigamiṣati seeks,
adhijigāṁsate to be desirous of study or reading,
adhigantṛ (tā), one who attains or acquires,
adhigartya mfn being on the driver's seat
adhigata mfn found, obtained, acquired, gone over, studied, learnt
adhigṛham ind. in the house or houses
adhiguṇa mfn possessing superior qualities
adhigupta mfn protected,
adhihari concerning Hari
adhihasti ind. on an elephant,
adhi√hṛ to procure, furnish,
adhi√hu to make an oblation on or over,
adhija mfn born, superior by birth,
adhi√jan to be born,
adhijanana n. birth,
adhijānu ind. on the knees,
adhi√ji to win in addition,
adhijya with bowstring mounted/stretched,
adhijyotiṣam ind. on the luminaries, (treated of in the Upanishads),

adhika 20/2 mfn. additional, subsequent, later, superior, going beyond
adhikāra m. jurisdiction, authority, prerogative, claim, privilege, royalty, title, office, right, ownership, property, reference, relation, a topic, subject, a governing rule (the influence of which over any succeeding rules is called *anuvṛtti*
adhikaraṇa n. subject, location, receptacle, substratum, sense of the locative or 7th case, category, supremacy, relationship of words in a sentence, relation, paragraph, minor section,
adhika mfn, additional, surpassing the usual

measure, superior, extraordinary, n. surplus,
adhikānurāga m. superior affection or most affection,
adhikāra m. authority, government, administration, rule, jurisdiction, prerogative, right, privilege, ownership, property, a subject, topic, (in gram.) a governing rule, (the influence of which over any number of succeeding rules is called *anu-vṛtti*),
adhīkāra m. superintendence over, interest, business, affair, authorization, capability, authority, duty, right,
adhīkāramukta readiness to receive spiritual knowledge,
ādhikāra sutrāṇi these are statements that govern particular following groups of *sutrāṇi* in *Pāṇini'*s work
adhikaraṇa 20/3 n. the act of placing at the head, supremacy, (in phil.) the substratum; a subject (e.g. *ātman* is the *adhikaraṇa* of knowledge), (in gram.) location, the sense of the locative case, relationship of words in sentence (which agree together), a set of arguments or text-book chapter,
adhikaraṇasiddhānta an agreed conclusion from which further reasoning may follow,
adhikaraṇika m. a government official, a magistrate, judge,
adhikaraṇya n. authority, power
adhikārin mfn possessing authority, entitled to, fit for, m. a superintendent, governor, official, a rightful claimant, a man, a qualified aspirant for liberation (G), the qualifications including – truthfulness, humility, a fitness to be taught, and a capability to learn,
adhikārivāda the doctrine of a distinct course of discipline for each aspirant according to his capacity,
adhikarman n. superintendence, *-karmakṛt* an overseer,
adhikarūpavant mfn surpassingly beautiful,
adhikārtha mfn exaggerated,
adhikatā addition, excess, redundancy, preponderance,
adhikatara greater, surpassing, (comparative)
adhi√kṛ to place at the head, appoint, to aim at, regard, to refer or allude to, to superintend, be at the head of, A. – *kurute* to be or become entitled to, to be or become superior to, overcome,
adhi√kram to ascend, mount up to,
adhikrama m. an invasion, attack,
adhi√krīḍ to play or dance over,
adhikṛta mfn placed at the head of, appointed, ruled, administered, m. a superintendent, especially a controller of public accounts, *-tva* the being engaged in or occupied with,
adhikṛti f. a right, privilege, position,
adhīkṣ to expect *√īkṣ*
adhikṣepa m. abuse, insult, dismissal,
adhi√kṣi to be settled in or over, be extended over or along, to rest upon
adhi√kṣip to throw upon, insult, scold,
adhikṣipadabjanetra mfn having eyes which eclipse the lotus,
adhikṣipta mfn insulted, scolded, placed,
adhikṣit m. a lord, ruler,
adhilokam ind. on the universe,
adhi√man to esteem highly
adhimanthana n. friction for producing fire,
adhimātra mfn above measure, excessive, (*am*) ind. on the subject of rhythm, stress and intonation of speech,
adhimukta mfn inclined, inclined towards, confident,
adhimukti f. propensity, confidence,
adhīna mfn resting on or in, situated, depending on, subject to, subservient to, 22/3
adhi√nam to incline over,
adhinātha m. a supreme lord, chieftain,
adhi√nī to lead away from, to raise above the ordinary measure, enhance,
adhi-ni√dhā to place upon, impart, grant
adhinir√han to destroy, root out from
adhinir√muc to escape from,
adhinirṇij covered over, veiled,

adhini√ṣad to settle in a place,
adhini√5.vas to dwell in,
adhini√vyadh to pierce through,
adhipa m. a ruler, commander, overlord,
adhipāṁśula mfn being dusty above, dusty,
adhipatham ind. over or across a road,
adhipati m. a particular part of the head (where a wound is instantly fatal), lord, king, master, overlord,
adhipatipratyāya the defining cause,
adhipatnī f. a female sovereign or ruler,
ādhipatya 138/3 n. supremacy, sovereignty, power,
adhi-pra-√1.dhāv to approach hastily from
adhiprajam ind. on procreation as a means of preserving the world (Taittirīya Upanishad)
adhi-pra-√1. sū to send away from
adhipuruṣa or *-pūruṣa* m. the Supreme Spirit
adhīra mfn imprudent, excitable,
adhirāj m. a supreme king,
adhirāja or –rājan m. an emperor,
adhirajju mfn carrying a rope, fastening, fettering,
adhirājya n. supremacy, imperial dignity, an empire,
adhiratha mfn being on or over a car, m. a charioteer,
adhirathyam ind. on the high road
adhiroha m. ascent, mounting, overtopping, mfn riding, mounted,
adhirohin mfn rising above, ascending, f. a ladder, flight of stairs,
adhiropita mfn raised, placed above,
adhirūdha mfn ascended, mounted,
adhirūdhasamādhiyoga mfn engaged in profound meditation,
adhi√ruh cl 1 P.A. to rise above, ascend, mount,
adhirukma mfn wearing gold,
adhīśa m. a lord or master over others,
adhi-saṁ-√dhā to put or join together,
adhi-saṁ-√5.vas to dwell or reside together,
adhi-saṁ-√vṛt to originate from,
adhiśasta mfn notorious, 22/2
adhiśaya m. addition, anything added or given extra
adhiśayana mfn lying on, sleeping on,
adhiśayita mfn recumbent on, used for lying or sleeping on,
adhi√śī to lie down upon, lie upon, sleep on
adhi√spardh to compete for an aim, strive at
adhi√spṛś to touch lightly or slightly,
adhiśraya m. a receptacle,
adhi√śri to put in the fire, spread over,
adhiśrita mfn put on the fire (as a pot), resided in, dwelt in, occupied by, (in phil.) are superimposed,
adhi√sṛp to glide along
adhi√sru to trickle or drop off,
adhīṣṭa mfn solicited, asked for instruction, (as a teacher), m.n. instruction from a teacher solicited for it,
adhi√ṣṭhā (√sthā) - *tiṣṭhati* to stand upon, depend upon, to inhabit, abide, to stand over, to superintend, govern, to step over or across, to overcome, to ascend, mount, to attain, arrive at,
adhiṣṭhāna n. standing by, being at hand, approach, standing or resting upon, a basis, base, the standing place for the warrior on a car, a position, site, residence, abode, seat, a settlement, town, the Absolute as the only real , a dwelling place or manifestation of the soul (L), standing over, government, authority, power, a precedent, rule, a benediction, background, support, basis, substratum, repository (Brahman), underlying truth or essence,
adhiṣṭhātṛ mfn superintending, presiding, governing, tutelary, *(ā)* m. a ruler, the Supreme Ruler (or Providence personified or identified with one or other of the Hindu gods, a chief, a protector, - *devatā* presiding divinity,
adhiṣṭāya controlling, governing, standing over, gerund *adhi √sthā,* experiences
adhiṣṭhita mfn settled, inhabited, controlled, superintended, regulated, appointed, superintending,
adhistri concerning a woman or a wife,
adhi√ṣvan to roar along or over,

adhīśvara m. a supreme lord or king,
adhīta mfn attained, , studied, read, well read, learned, *adhī√i*
adhīti f. perusal, study, desire, recollection,
adhītin mfn well read, proficient, occupied with the study of the Vedas
adhitiṣṭhati see *adhi√ṣṭhā*
adhītya ind. having studied, gone over
adhi√vac to speak in favour of, advocate,
adhivacana n. an appellation, epithet,
adhi√vad to speak, pronounce over or at,
adhivāda m. offensive words,
adhivāka m. advocacy, protection,
adhivaktṛ tā m. an advocate, protector, comforter,
adhi√2.vap A. *–vaste* to put on or over (clothes etc.)
adhi√4.vas A. *–vaste* to put on or over (clothes etc.)
adhi√5.vas to inhabit, to settle or perch on
adhi√vās to scent, perfume,
adhivāsa m. an upper garment, mantle,
2. m. an inhabitant, a neighbour, one who dwells above, a habitation, abode, settlement, site, dwells, presides,
3. m. perfume, fragrance, application of..,
adhivāsana n. causing a divinity to dwell in an image, 2. application of perfumes etc. preliminary purification of an image,
adhīvāsas over the garment,
adhivāsin mfn inhabiting, settled in,
adhivāsita mfn scented, perfumed,
adhivastra mfn clothed,
adhivijñāna n. the highest knowledge,
adhivedam concerning the Veda
adhivedana n. marrying an additional wife,
adhivelam ind. on the shore
adhi√3.vid -vindati to obtain, to marry in addition to,
adhi-vi-√dhā to distribute or scatter over
adhividyam ind. on the subject of science, (treated of in the Upanishads)
adhi-vi-kartana n. the act of cutting off
adhi-vi√kram A. to come forth on behalf of
adhi-vi√rāj to surpass in brightness
adhi√viś caus. *–veśayati*, to cause to sit down, to place upon,
adhivīta mfn wrapped up, enveloped in,
adhi√vṛdh to refresh, gladden, A. *–vardhate* to prosper through or by
adhi√vṛj cl 7 P. *–vṛṇakti* to place near or over (the fire),
adhi√vṛt to move or pass along or over
adhi-vi√yat caus. to subjoin, annex
adhi√vye to envelope
adhi√yā to escape
adhiyajña m.the chief or principal sacrifice, mfn relating to a sacrifice, lord of sacrifice, 'he who is to be propitiated by sacrifice'(*am*) ind. on the subject of sacrifice,
adhi√yat to fasten, caus. *–yātayate* to reach, join
adhi√yuj to put on, load,
ādhmāta mfn puffed up, blown up, inflated, sounding, heated, burnt
adho'dhaḥ below (with 2nd),
adholoka the lower world, hell,
adhomukha mfn down-faced, with face bent down, headlong, upside down,
adhonivīta mfn sacred cord (worn) low,
ādhoraṇa m. rider or driver of an elephant,
ādhṛṣya mfn to be ventured against,
adhruva 23/3 mfn. not fixed, uncertain, doubtful, impermanent
adhunā 22/3 ind. now, immediately
ādhunika mfn present, current, new, recent, of the present moment,
adhvan m.f. *ā* a road, way, orbit, a journey, course, distance, time, means, method, resource, the zodiac, sky, air, a place, a recension of the Vedas and the school upholding it,
adhvara m. religious/liturgical service, sacrifice, mfn not injuring, n. sky or air,
adhvaryati P. performs sacrifice,
ādhvaryava n. service of sacrificing priest,
adhvaryu m. priest, who did the actual work of the sacrifice, and appears in the oldest period as companion of the *hotṛ*,
āḍhya mfn wealthy, rich, abounding in,
adhyadhi ind. on high, just above,

adhyakṣa 23/1 mfn. perceptible, observable, exercising supervision,
m. an eyewitness, superintendent,
*adhyakṣaram*23/1 ind. on the subject of syllables, above all syllables (as *om*) observable, exercising supervision.
adhyāpaka mfn a teacher(sacred knowledge)
adhyāpana n. instruction, lecturing
adhyāpayitṛ, *tā*, m. a teacher,
adhyāpita mfn instructed
adhi√yam to erect or stretch out over
ādhyāna 139/2 n meditating upon, reflecting on, remembering with regret,
adhyāropa 23/1 m. (in Vedanta phil.) wrong attribution, erroneous transferring of a statement from one thing to another, erroneous knowledge, incorrect attribution, (N) super-imposition, from Buddhism – the mistake of believing something to exist which does not exist,
adhyāropakalpanā (N) imagination based upon superimposition,
adhyaropita mfn erroneously transferred from one thing to another, fictitiously ascribed,
ādhyāsa (G) 13, super-imposition; illusion; false-attribution... e.g. a rope seen as a snake and with all the qualities of snake. super-imposing ignorance and the empirical world upon the Absolute- hence not being aware of the Absolute, m. case of mistaken identity,
adhyasta mfn placed over, disguised, supposed, n. upper part of a bone,
adhyasta astitva reflected existence,
adhyātma 23/2 n.the Supreme Spirit, own, belonging to self, ind. concerning self or individual personality,
'in the context of the soul, with regard to the indwelling Self', (Gam.),
pertaining to the self,
adhyātmacetas 23/2 m. one who meditates on the Supreme Spirit
adhyātmajñāna 23/2 knowledge of the Supreme Spirit or of the Self
adhyātmavid knower of the Self,
adhyātmavidyā 23/2 f. knowledge of the Supreme Spirit or of *ātman*,
adhyātmayoga 'the yoga of the unity of the Self' HH 'to clarify the world and to put everything in perspective from multiplicity to singularity' HH
ādhyātmika 139/3 relating to Self or to the soul, relating to the Supreme Spirit, spiritual, holy,
adhyavasāna n. attempt, effort, exertion, energy, perseverance, determining, (in rhetoric) concise and forcible language,
adhyavasāya m. (in phil.) mental effort, apprehension, resolution, the determining function of the *buddhi* (intellect),
adhyavasita mfn resolved, completed, accomplished,
adhyava√so Cl4 *adhyavasyati* to resolve, decide, accomplish,
adhyāya m. study, reading, a lesson, lecture, chapter, study, proper time for reading or a lesson, ifc. a reader,
adhyāyaka m. one who has studied the Vedas, a teacher,
adhyayana 22/3 n. reading, studying, study especially the Vedas, 'the knowledge that arises from studying the scriptures' (Gam.), recitation
adhyāyin engaged in reading, a student reading, proper time for reading etc.
adhyeṣyate will study, will recite 1/s/fut/mid *adhi √i*
adhyeti (√i)to turn the mind towards, observe, understand, to mind, remember, care for, long for, to know, know by heart, to go over, study, to learn from (a teacher's mouth), to declare, teach, A. *adhīte*, *adhīyate*, to study, learn by heart, read, recite,
adhyetṛ, *tā*, m. a student, reader,
adhyuṣita mfn inhabited,
ādi 136/3 m. beginning with, etc, and so on

e.g. *ādi śaṅkara* the original or first *śaṅkara,* pl. *ādīni,* precedence, foremost, inception, beginning, *-ādi* ifc. having ... as the beginning, and so forth, beginning with *ā,*

ādideva primal god, existing from the beginning

ādiḥ the first (of a series)

ādika as for *–ādi* ifc. above,

ādima first, prior, primitive, original

ādimat first, mfn having a beginning, *-tva* n. the state of having a beginning,

ādin mfn eating, devouring,

adīna mfn not depressed, noble-minded,

adīnātman mfn with cheerful spirit, undaunted, 18/2

ā√diś Cl 1 *–diśati,* to point out, direct, to aim at, have in view, to report, to order, direct, profess as one's aim or duty, announce, teach, determine, specify,

ādi-tattva the first principle –Brahman,

aditi mfn not tied, free, boundless, unbroken, entire, unimpaired, happy, f. having nothing to give, destitute, a goddess ('infinity' or 'the Eternal and Infinte Expanse', mother of the *āditya* s and of the gods), boundlessness, immensity, inexhaustible abundance, unimpaired, condition, perfection, creative power, a cow, milk, the earth, m. devourer, death,

āditya (s) m. months of the year, 12 divine powers, the sun, 12 as representing the sun in the months of the year, name of the sun god, belonging to or coming from the *āditya,* son of Aditi,
mfn belonging to or coming from,

ādityavāra 137/1 Sunday *āditya* the name for seven deities of the heavenly sphere, the chief of whom is *Varuna* to whom the name *āditya* is particularly applicable, the name of a god in general, particularly *Sūrya* the sun.

ādivāsī original inhabitants, indigenous people

adīyata was given 1/s/impf/pass

admasad m. a fly, a companion at table,

adoṣa mfn faultless, guiltless,

ā√dṛ Cl4 *ādriyate* to regard with attention, attend to, be careful about, respect, honour, reverence, defer to, refer to,

adravya n. a nothing, a worthless thing, non-substance - attributes such as purity, activity, inertia, sound, sight, form, mfn having no possessions,

adṛḍha 18/3 mfn not firm, not decided, fragile, impermanent,

adri m. a mountain, a stone, a rock, a stone for pounding soma, a slingstone, a thunderbolt, a mountainous cloud, a tree, the sun,

adroha m. freedom from malice or hatred,

adṛś mfn blind,

adṛṣṭa mfn not seen, unseen ,
sometimes used to express that 'the Absolute may not be seen or experienced', 'the unseen principle', destiny, influence, fate,
the power of latent *saṁskāra,*
unforeseen danger or calamity,
not visible, not perceptible, latent, unseen, unforeseen, not experienced, unperceived, beyond the reach of observation or consciousness, (*am*) ind. unperceived,

adṛṣṭakāraṇa of unknown cause,

adṛṣṭapurva previously unseen,

adṛśya changeless – 'for *dṛśya* is anything meant to be seen, i.e. any modification, for a modification is meant to be seen. What is not *dṛśya* is *adṛśya* – changeless', (Gam.) mfn invisible, latent, not fit to be seen, unassailable, proud, that which cannot be seen by the physical eye (Brahman),

adṛśyat 18/3 mfn invisible,

adravya n. non-thing, unworthy object,

adri m. rock, stone, Soma-stone, missile stone, a cloud, a tree, the sun, the number seven,

adrivant mfn having or armed with a throwing stone,

adṛṣṭakāma m. love for one not yet seen,
adurmaṅgala mfn bringing no bad luck, not inauspicious,
advaita 19/3 mfn destitute of duality, sole, unique, non-duality, identity of spirit and matter, the ultimate truth, the philosophy by that name,
advaita niṣṭha establishment in non-duality,
advaitavāda monism, the doctrine of *advaita*
advaya 19/2 mfn not 2, without a second, only, unique, as One, the ultimate Truth, One without a second, *(am)* n. non-duality, unity, identity (esp. the identity of Brahma with the human soul or with the universe, or of spirit and matter, the ultimate truth (Gam.), a non-dualist (Gam.),
advayatā non-duality, oneness
adveṣa mfn not malevolent,
adveṣṭṛ non-hater, not an enemy, a friend
advitīya mfn without a second, sole, unique, matchless,
advitīyata mfn state of being without a second,
adya 19/1 today, nowadays, now, to this day, *-tas* from today, initial, first, earliest,
adya niśi in this night (just past),
adyayāvat until now,
adya ārabhya from now on,
adya prabhṛti from today onward,
ādya 1. 137/1 being at the beginning, first primordial, original, primitive, primal, ifc. *(bahuvṛhi)* having ... as first, beginning with ....
adyāpi this very day, even now, until today
ādya-śakti primordial power,
√*ag* 4/2 cl1 *agati* to move tortuously, DP in *kuṭilā gati*
kuṭilā 288/2 bent, crooked, curved, round, dishonest,
gati 347/3 going, moving
aga mfn unable to move, m. sun, water jar, mountain, tree, snake, #7,
āgacchā come!
āgacchat came
agacchat went
āgacchati comes, arrives
agada mfn not having disease, well, healthy, whole, wholesome, m. medicine,
agādha – 4/3 deep, unfathomable, a hole,
agadita mfn untold, unasked,
√*agadya* Nom P.4/2 to have good health, to heal, DP in *nīrogatva* 565/2 freedom from disease, health, being without disease
agālita mfn unfiltered,
ā√*gam* Cl 1 *–gacchati,* to come, arrive at, attain, reach, have recourse to, ascertain, learn from, caus. *āgamayati* acquire,
agama mfn impassable, not going, unable to go, m. a mountain,
āgama m. 'a coming', approaching, arrival, a grammatical augment, (N) an authoritative statement, (G) scripture, what has come down from tradition, revealed scripture, recognized scriptures in particular fields, traditionally 28 in number but hundreds are spoken of,
āgamana n. a coming, coming hither,
āgamāpāyin mfn 'coming and going', transitory,
āgama pramāṇa the Veda as proof,
āgāmika mfn relating to the future,
āgāmikarma m. result of actions performed during the present life,
āgamiñyati will come
āgamya having come
agamyarūpa mfn of unsurpassed form,
agandhā f. without smell,
agandhi mfn without smell, scentless,
āgantu m. a stranger, guest, mfn anything added or adhering, incidental, adventitious, accidental,
agāra 4/3 a house, apartment,
āgas n. sin, (orig. a slip),
agastya name of a *ṛṣi*
āgata 129/2 come, arrived, having come to or into, entered, ppp. Reached,
agati mfn halting, without resource,

helpless, not going, f. unsuccessfulness, stoppage, want of resource

āgati f. origin, rise, arrival, origination, coming, return,

āgatya having come

agatyā ind. unavoidably, indispensably,

agāyat sang

agha name of a demon, 6/3 mfn. bad, dangerous, sinful, impure, sin, impurity, pain, suffering,

aghamarṣaṇa mfn sin-effacing, purifying,

aghāta no injury, no damage

aghātin mfn not fatal, not injurious, harmless,

āghāta 130/3 m. striking, a blow, killing, misfortune, pain, a striker, beater, place of execution, slaughter-house,

√*aghāya* *aghāyati* to intend to injure, to plan mischief,

aghnya m. a bull

aghnyā f. a cow,

aghora not terrifying, a benevolent power,

aghoracakṣus mfn not evil-eyed,

aghoṣa unvoiced, an unvoiced sound is one in which the vocal chords do not vibrate e.g. zzzzzz can be felt vibrating when a finger is placed against the throat but the sound sssssssss can not.

āghrāpayati caus .√*ghrā* to cause to smell,

āghrāṇa 131/1 smelling, satiety, satisfaction

āghṛṇi mfn glowing with heat, beaming,

agīta mfn unsung,

agni 5/1 fire, sacrificial fire, the god of fire (mediator between men and gods, messenger who carries the sacrifice to them, protector from the terrors of darkness, keeper of house and hearth,), the element fire , has the property *rūpa* – form, shape, beauty, a symbol of consciousness

agni astra a fire missile,

agnihotra fire sacrifice, a burnt offering of fresh milk made twice daily,

agnihotrahavaṇī f. fire sacrifice ladle,

agnikuṇḍa a round hole in the ground for the sacred fire,

agnipurogama mfn 'having Agni as leader' led by Agni,

agnisaṁyoga joined, united with fire, (referring to utterance?)

agniṣṭut laudatory of god of fire, he who sings the praises of Agni (in Vedic sacrifice),

agni-tattva the fire-principle,

agnivelā f. fire-hour, time for kindling the sacred fire, afternoon,

agnyādheya n. placing or setting up of the sacred fire,

agotram unconnected, solitary, alone,

agra mfn top, tip, first, chief, best, the nearest end, the beginning, n. foremost point, tip, front, top, summit, surface, point, the nearest end, the climax or best part, goal, aim, multitude, a weight, a measure of food given as alms, remainder, sharpness (fig.),

agraha mfn = *mukhya*, m. non-acceptance, 'free from all illusion of perceptions' (Gam.), non-perception, non-cognition,

āgraha m. insisting on, strong or obstinate inclination for, obstinacy, whim, seizing, taking, favour, affection, (*āt, eṇa)* ind. obstinately,

agrahaṇa n. non-comprehension or non-perception, not knowing the truth, lack of right perception, not meaning, mfn not afflicted by disease,

agrahāyaṇa m. commencement of the year (about November 12th), name of a month,

agrāhya 6/3 mfn not to be conceived or perceived or obtained or admitted or trusted, ' beyond one's grasp, i.e beyond the range of the organs of action', inconceivable, inadmissable, (N) not to be grasped,

agram mfn, n. top, foremost point, tip, first, chief, point, beginning, best, the nearest end, the beginning

agratas ind. in front, before (one's self), in the beginning, (with 6th) in the presence of, (with *kṛ*) place in front, cause to lead,

agrayāna 6/2 n. stepping in front to defy the enemy, the first vehicle,

agre (7th *agra*) in front, before, in presence of (with 6th), beginning, in the beginning, in the first place, first, tip, end, in the presence of,

ā√ghrā Cl1 *ājighrati* smells,

agṛhya mfn impercepible, independent,

agrya mfn foremost, best, proficient, intent, closely attentive,

aguṇa without *guṇa* or quality,

aguṇin mfn devoid of merit, not requiring *guṇa* change,

√ah 1. a verb limited to only a few parts, to say, speak, express, signify, to call (by name), hold, consider, regard as, state or declare with reference to, to acknowledge, accept, state,
cl 5 P.to pervade or occupy DP cl 1, in *vyāpti* pervading
2. to pervade or occupy

āḥ a particle expressing joy or indignation

aha particle, certainly, of course, namely, for *ahan* in compounds,

āha he said, says, 1/s/perf/act, *√ah* say, speak,
a particle implying reproof,
ind. an interjection,

ahaḥ in comp. for *ahar* n. a day,

ahaḥ ahaḥ daily, every day,

ahaha exclamation of joy or sorrow,

ahaituka 125/3 mfn. causeless, unexpected, having no motive, disinterested

aham 124/2 pron. 1/s I, the ego,

ahamahamikā f. rivalry, assertion or conceit of superiority,

ahamika egoism, pride,

ahaṃkāra 124/2 conception of one's individuality, ego, pride, 'the individual or ego which asserts and distinguishes itself from others' (U),

ahaṃkāriṇī conceited, proud, thinking of "me" and "mine"

ahaṁkartavyam mfn 'the object of egoism' (Gam.),

ahaṁkṛta 124/2 egotistic, conscious of one's individuality

aham pratyaya 'I' feeling, self-consciousness,

ahaṁtā f. self-consciousness, 'I-ness',

aham vṛtti a self-arrogating thought,

ahan see *ahar*

āhanas mfn swelling, fermenting, foaming, to be beaten or pressed out, unchaste, lascivious, profligate,

ahar (also *ahan* or *ahas*)124/3 n. a day, a sacrificial or festival day, also *–ahaḥ, -ahnaḥ,*

āhāra mfn ifc. bringing near, procuring, being about to fetch, going to fetch, m. eating, what one takes, food, bringing near, taking food, taking, employing, use, object of the senses, anything taken in by the senses,

- āhāra ifc. bringer, carrier,

āhāradāna n. giving of food,

āhāradi n. food and so forth,

āhāraparityāga m. relinquishment of food,

aharāgama m. the approach of the day,

āhāraḥ 162/3 food, taking food, fodder,

aharahaḥ karman n. daily work,

aharahar ind. day by day, daily,

āharaṇa n. bringing, fetching,

āhārārthin n. seeking food,

ahardala n. midday,

ahardiva mfn daily,

ahardivi ind. day by day,

ahardṛś mfn beholding the day, living,

ahargaṇa m. a series of days, any calculated term, a month,

aharjaram ind. 'so that the days become old', by and by,

aharniśa n. day and night, a whole day, (*am*) ind. day and night, continually,

ahārya mfn not liable to be stolen,

āhārya mfn to be taken or seized, to be fetched or brought near, to be extracted or removed, adventitious, accessory, accidental, m. a kind of bandage, n. any disease to be treated

by extraction,
āhāryāśobhā f. adventitious beauty, (achieved with paint, ornaments etc.)
ahas see *ahar*
ahasat laughed
ahasta mfn handless
ahata mfn 1. not beaten, 2. unwashed (of a garment), new,
āhati f. a blow, hitting, striking,
āhava 162/2 1.m. sacrificing, sacrifice, 163/1 2. m. n. challenge, war, battle
āhāva m. a trough, pail, vessel, a trough for watering cattle,
āhavana n. offering an oblation, offering sacrifice, a sacrifice,
āhavanīya mfn of or for the oblation, one of 3 consecrated fires to which householder oblations are offered,
ahi m. 125/1 a snake, serpent, esp. the dragon of the sky, a cloud, water, the sun, a traveller,
ahigopā mfn having the dragon as their keeper, guarded by a serpent,
ahihatya n. the slaying of the dragon, victorious fight with the dragon,
ahimsā 125/2 f. harmlessness of thought speech and action, non-violence
ahipati m. lord of the snakes (*Vāsuki*),
ahita 125/2 mfn. unfit, improper, noxious, hostile, not propitious, m. an enemy
āhitāgni mfn having a set or established fire, m. one who is keeping a sacred fire alive,
āhituṇḍika m. snake-charmer,
ahivat ind. as a dragon,
āhlādana 163/1 the act of gladdening, refreshing
āhnika mfn daily, a day's work etc,
aho ind. exclamation of astonishment, pleasant or unpleasant, Oh!, alas,
aho aho ind. expression of surprise or alarm, like "Oh My",
aho bata oh alas!
ahorātra m. = *aharniśa* a day and night,
ā√hṛ Cl1 *āharati* to fetch, bring, take away, to conceive (a woman), to bring home (a bride),
ahrīka shamelessness, mfn 'shameless beggar', a buddhist mendicant,
ahṛṇāna mfn not being angry,
āhṛtya 163/1 ind. p. having fetched or brought, having offered, to be fetched or offered,
ā√hu sacrifice, offer oblation, sprinkle *ājuhoti, ājuhote*
ā√hū Cl 1 *–hvayati* to call to, summon, invite, f. calling, invoking,
āhuḥ they say, they assert, 1/pl/perf *√ah*
āhuta mfn offered as an oblation, sacrificed, laid in the fire as a corpse, offering made to men, hospitality, nourishment of all created beings,
āhuti 162/3 f. offering oblations with fire to the deities, any solemn rite with oblations, oblation, offering,
āhvāna 165/2 calling, inviting, a call or summons, invocation of a deity, a challenge, legal summons, an invitation,
ā√hve Cl1 *āhvayati* to summon, call,
āhūya ind. having invited,
āhūyatām let (him) be called (impv)
aikadeśika present only in one place (*Jīva*),
aikamatya n. unanimity, conformity,
aikṣata mfn seen, thought, desired, saw, looked at,
aikṣvāka descended from King Ikṣvaku
aikya n. oneness, unity, harmony, sameness, identity, identity of the soul or of the universe with the deity, an aggregate, sum,
aikyāropa m. equalization,
aindrābārhaspatya mfn belonging to *Indra* and *Bṛhaspati*
airāvata 'produced from the ocean' the name of Indra's elephant 234/2
aiśvara 234/3 mfn. relating to a mighty lord or king, powerful, majestic (*am*) n. supremacy, might
aiśvarya n. glory, glory of wealth, 234/3 the state of being a mighty lord, sovereignty, supremacy, dominion, superhuman power (eight listed), power, lordliness,

aitadātmya n. state of having the nature or property of this,
aitihāsika m. teller of legends, mfn traditional, legendary, historical,
aitihya n. traditional instruction, tradition,
√*aj* 9/2 cl1 P *ajati* drives, throws, propels, casts, DP in *gati*, or *kṣepaṇa*
aja 1. m. a drove, a driver, mover, instigator, leader, a ram, vehicle of Agni, beam of the sun, troop,
aja 9/3 2. not born, existing from all eternity, name of *prakṛti, māyā* or illusion, birthless,
ajā f. she-goat,
ajaḍa mfn not inanimate, not stupid, (W) immaterial, non-material,
ajāgara mfn not awake, not wakeful,
ajānanta not knowing, ignorant of
ajānat knew, 1/s/impf/pass
ajānata not cognising, not knowing, unaware,
ajara mfn not aging, ageless, undecaying,
ajarāmaravat ind. as if ageless and immortal,
ājarasam ind. till old age,
ājarasāya ind. till old age,
ajasra 10/1 not to be obstructed, perpetual (said of fire), not dying out,
ajasram ind. perpetually, for ever, ever,
ajāta mfn unborn, not yet born, not yet developed,
ajātivāda the view that no creation has occurred ever and that Brahman alone exists, nothing is real from this standpoint,
ajayat conquered
ajāyata evolved, not born,
ājāyate *(ā√jan)* is born, begets,
āji m. race, contest, battle,
ājighrati he smells (as in he smells an odour), to smell at, to kiss, kiss on, √*ghrā* caus. *āghrāpayati*
ajighṛkṣat wished to catch, tried to take up, wanted to take up, √*grah* desid. 1/s/impf.
ājighṛkṣat willing to catch, (E)
ajina 10/2 the hairy skin of a (black) antelope or of a tiger, goat-skin, pelt
ajira mfn agile, swift,
ajirāya A. *ajirāyate* to be swift, press swiftly onward, to be agile,
ajīva mfn life-less, insentient,
ājīva 133/1 livelihood, subsisting through, living by, *ājīvam* ind. for life, throughout life
ajjū f. a mother,
ajña 10/3 mfn. not knowing, ignorant, inexperienced, unconscious, unwise
ā√jñā Cl 9 *–jānāti,* to mind, perceive, notice, understand, caus. *ājñāpayati -te,* orders, commands, directs,
ājñā f. an order, command, authority, unlimited power, permission,
ājñāpayati commands,
ajñāna n. non-cognizance, ignorance, (in phil.) spiritual ignorance, the power of the *guṇā* to cause identification with personality thus preventing identification with Brahman, mfn ignorant, unwise, (- *āt*) ind. ignorantly
ājñāna *(am),* n. noticing, perceiving, rulership, the state of lordliness,
ajñānajam born of ignorance
ajñānāt or °*atas* out of ignorance,
ājñānavāda non-belief, agnosticism,
ajñāta mfn unknown, unexpected, unaware, (*am*) ind. without the knowledge of,
ajñātajñāpana what is not known becoming known, what has been unreal becoming real,
ajñātakulaśīla mfn whose character and family are unknown,
ajñātvā ind. without knowing, not having known or ascertained,
ājuhoti, ājuhote see *ā√hu*
ājya 133/2 n. melted or clarified butter
ājyabhāga m. a portion of clarified butter, mfn partaking of the clarified butter,
ājyabhāgau the 2 portions of clarified butter belonging to Agni and Soma
ājyāhuti f. oblation of clarified butter,

ājyaśeṣa remainder of the clarified butter,
√*ak* 1a/3 cl1 P *akati*, moves tortuously (like a snake), DP in *kuṭilā gati*
kuṭilā 288/2 bent, crooked, curved, round, dishonest,
gati 347/3 going, moving
akala mfn not in parts, entire, not skilled in the arts,
akalka mfn free from impurity, f. moonlight,
akalkala as *akalkana*
akalkana mfn not deceitful, honourable,
akalpa 2/1 mfn not subject to rules, uncontrolled,
akalpaka devoid of imagination, non-conceptual, (Gam.)
akalpita mfn not manufactured, not artificial, not pretended, natural, genuine,
akāma 2/1 mfn. desireless,
akāṇḍa mfn accidental, causeless, unexpected, without a trunk, ind. (*e*) causelessly, unexpectedly
ākāṅkṣ 126/3 to desire, longing for, to expect , *ākāṅkṣet* 1/s/pres/opt/act. he should desire, he might desire,
ākāṅkṣa mfn (in gram.) requiring a word or words to complete the sense, (*ā*) f. desire, wish, (also as for mfn),
ākāṅkṣin mfn ifc. wishing, desirous, hoping, expecting,
akāra 1/1 the letter or sound *a*
ākara m. one who scatters, i.e. distributes abundantly, accumulation, abundance, 2. a mine, a rich source of anything, *-ja* produced in a mine, a mineral,
ākāra m. make, shape, appearance, form, category, expression of the face (furnishing a clue to the disposition of the mind),
akāraṇa 2/ mfn. causeless, (*am*) n. absence of a cause, ind. causelessly
ākāravant mfn shapely, having a shape, embodied,
ākāravat mfn shapely, well-formed, having a shape, embodied,
akārin 2/1 mfn. inactive, not performing, an evil-doer, neglecting duty,
akarman n. 'non-action', inaction, not working, not performing good works, wicked,
ākarṇayati P. gives ear to, listens,
ākarṇya 126/2 ind. to give ear to, listen to. part. hearing, having heard,
akarot 1/s/past imperf./act. he/she made or did, built
a kārpaṇya free from misery, limitlessness, liberality,
ākarṣa m. attraction, drawing towards oneself (as a rope), fascination or an object used for it, dragging (as a stone), bending (of a bow), spasm, playing with dice, a die, a playing-board, an organ of sense, a magnet,
ākarṣaka mfn attractive, m. a magnet, a town,
akartavya mfn that which should not be done,
akartṛ 1/3 not an agent, (of the Absolute), not active,
-tva n. a state of non-agency,
akārya not to be done, improper,
ākaṣa m. a touchstone,
ākāśa m. 'not visible' 126/3 the ether, sky, or atmosphere, the element space, the first great element (having the property Sound).
ākāśaga mfn going/moving in the sky',
ākāśaja m. born of *ākāśa*
akāśakalpa 'slightly different from space i.e. resembling space' (Gam.),
ākāśa tattva the ether principle,
ākāśavāṇī ethereal voice, heavenly voice,
akasmād-āgantu m. an accidental arrival, a chance comer,
akasmāt ind. without apparent cause, unexpectedly, accidentally,
ākasmika 126/3 causeless, unforeseen, unexpected, sudden, accidental
akathayat told
akathya 1a/3 mfn unspeakable, unutterable, unmentionable, indescribable,
akāya 2/1 mfn. bodiless, incorporeal
ākha m. a spade, a pitfall,

akhādat ate

akhaṇḍa 4/1 not fragmentary, whole, complete, "the unlimited is pervading everywhere and there is no end to it, and this is what does exist in reality. This is the substratum. It always remains the same and always remains one. It has no division. Therefore it is called *akhaṇḍa.*" HH. indivisible,

akhila 4/2 without a gap, complete, all, entire,

ākhu m. a mouse, 'burrower', a mole, a rat, a hog, a thief,

ā√khyā Cl 2 –*khyāti,* to behold, to tell, mention, to call

ākhyā f. name, at end of compounds – 'having ... as name'

ākhyāhi tell! speak! 2/s/impv. *ā√khyā*

ākhyāna 129/2 n. telling, communication, a tale, report, story,

ākhyānabhāga the narrative part of a sacred text (G),

ākhyāta ppp. told, explained, has been spoken of, made known, called,

akhyāti f. infamy, bad repute, disgrace,

ākhyāti f. telling, communication, publication of a report, name,

akiñcana 2/2 without anything, utterly destitute, disinterested,

ākīrṇa mfn scattered, strewn,

akīrti 2/2 f. mfn ill-fame, disgrace

akīrtikara mfn causing disgrace, disgraceful

akledya not to be wetted, not able to be wetted or moistened, *a√klid*

akleṣa m. freedom from trouble,

akliṣṭa mfn untroubled, unmoved, undisturbed, unwearied,

akra 1. mfn inactive,
2. m. a banner, a wall, fence

ā√kram Cl 1 –*krāmati,* to come upon, attack, to step or go near to, come towards,

akrama mfn not happening successively, happening at once, m. want of order, confusion,

ākrama m. approaching, attaining, obtaining, overcoming,

ā√krand shouts out, invokes, calls for help,

ākrānta mfn come to, approached, attacked, overcome, seized, filled with (3rd),

akratu 2/3 mfn destitute of energy, foolish,

akriya 3/1 inactive, abstaining from religious rites, impious, inactive

akriyamāna mfn not being accomplished,

akrodha mfn absence of anger, '*krodha* is anger or rage. Anger or rage is instrumental to violence. Therefore not to be agitated, not to fall into rage is to avoid violence. ...to be enraged and to be violent is against the law.'

ākrośa 128/2 assailing with harsh language, scolding, reviling,

akrośat cried out

ākrośati scolds, cries out in anger

ā√kṛṣ Cl 1 -*karṣati ,* Cl 6 –*kṛṣati,* to draw toward, attract,

akṛta 2/2 mfn undone, not committed, not made, uncreated, unprepared, incomplete, one who has done no works, (*ā*) f. a daughter who has nor been made a sharer in the privileges of a son, (*am*) n. an act never before committed, spontaneous,

akṛtārtha whose aim is unachieved, unsuccessful,

ākṛti f. make, shape, appearance,

ākṛtī 127/3 f. form, shape

akṛtrima 2/3 1/s/m inartificial, unmade, not created,

akṛtsna 2/3 mfn incomplete

akrūra mfn not harsh,

√akṣ 3/1 cl1,5 *akṣati, akṣnoti*, to reach, pass through, penetrate, pervade, DP in *vyāpti* 1037/3 accomplishment, pervasion, inherence, inherent and inseparable presence of any one thing in another, e.g. oil in sesame seed, universal pervasion, a universal rule without an exception, omnipresence,

akṣa 1. ifc. for *akùan,* 2. a die or dice,

akṣa an axle or wheel,

akṣa 3. 3/2 an organ of sense, sensual perception, eye, son of *Rāvaṇa*

akṣama mfn unfit, unable to endure,

impatient, incompetent, envious,
akṣamālā a garland of seeds of the eleocarpus serratus tree, a rosary,
akṣan n. eye,
akṣānta mfn impatient,
akṣapriya mfn beloved of the dice, i.e. lucky at gaming,
akṣara 3/2 mfn. imperishable, undying, unalterable, m. a sword, n. (am) a syllable (*om*), , a sound, a word
akṣāra mfn not pungent,
akṣārālavaṇa n. that which is not pungent and not salt,
akṣārālavaṇāśin mfn eating that which is not pungent and not salt, abstaining from seasoned and salted food,
akṣaranyāsa m. establishment of the alphabet, writing,
akṣaraśaḥ ind. by syllables, syllable by syllable,
akṣaravinyāsa 3/3 array of letters or syllables, the alphabet
akṣaya mfn imperishable,
akṣaya 3/2 mfn exempt from decay, imperishable, everlasting,
akṣayatva n. imperishability,
akṣauhiṇī f. a complete army,
akṣauhiṇīpati m. master of an army, a general,
ākṣepa 128/3 drawing together, convulsion, applying, laying, throwing away, giving up, removing, reviling, abuse, harsh speech, objection,
akṣi n. eye, the number two,
ā√kṣip Cl 6 -*kṣipati,* throw at, cast at, deride, put to shame,
akṣipat threw
akṣita 4/1 mfn undecayed, uninjured, undecaying, *(am)* n. water,
akṣiti f. imperishableness,
akṣobha mfn unagitated, unmoved, m. post to which an elephant is tied, freedom from agitation, tranquillity,
akṣobhya 4/1 unagitated, emotionless, unmoved, imperturbable,
akṣubdha 331/3 m. unperturbed
akta 1. mfn driven, 2. mfn smeared over, bedaubed, tinged, characterised, (often ifc.), *(am)* n. oil, ointment,
aktu m. 1. ointment, 2. light, a beam of light, 3. night,
akuha m. no deceiver,
akula mfn not of good family, low, a name of *Śiva,*
-tā f. lowness of family,
ākula 127/2 mfn. confounded, confused, agitated, distressed, overburdened, bestrewn, covered, filled
ākulayati Nom.P . confuses,
ākulī√bhū becomes confused
ākulībhūta being in confusion,
ākulita mfn at one's wits end, bewildered, confused, made muddy (as water),
akuñcana n. bending, contraction,
akūpāra mfn unbounded, m. the sea, tortoise, the mythical tortoise that holds up the world,
akūrca m. 'the guileless one', a Buddha
akurvan 1/pl/past imperf/act. they (many) made or did (dual – *akurutām*)
akurvata they did √*kṛ* 1/imperf/mid
akuśala 2/2/ inauspicious, evil, demerit, *(am)* n. evil, an evil word
akusuma mfn flowerless,
ākūta n. intention, idea,
√*al* 93/3 cl 1 P *alati to* adorn, be competent or able, to prevent, DP in *bhūṣaṇa* adorning, *paryāpti* being competent or able, and *vāraṇa* preventing
alābha 95/1 m non-acquirement, want, deficiency, loss
alabhamāna mfn not catching, not gaining,
alabhata found, obtained,
alaka m. a curl or lock of hair,
alakṣana 94/1 n. a bad, inauspicious sign, mfn having no signs or marks, without characteristic, having no good marks, inauspicious, 'without any logical ground for inference i.e. uninferrable' (Gam.), (N) translated in some Chinese Buddhist texts as 'without form',

alakṣita mfn unnoticed, unseen,
alakṣya 94/1 invisible, unobserved, not indicated
alakta m. red lac, a resin from insects,
alam 94/2 ind. with 3rd, enough of, sufficient, adequate, (with 4th), Apte 56/1 -no need of, needless, with infinitive – capable of,
ālamarthya n. the condition of having the sense of *alam*
ālamba 153/2 m. that on which one rests, support, prop, depending on, a perpendicular, mfn hanging down,
ālambanam n. depending upon or resting on, supporting, sustaining, a yogic exercise, a silent repetition of a prayer, the 5 qualities distinguishable by the senses, form, sound, smell, taste and touch
ālambana pratyaya primal idea, base cause,
alam √kṛ adorn, embellish,
alaṁkṛta mfn made ready, adorned,
alaṅkāra 94/2 the act of decorating, (in rhetoric) embellishment of sense or sound, literary figure, embellishment
alaṁkaraṇa n. making ready, preparation, decoration, ornament,
ālāpa m. talk, conversation,
alasa 94/3 inactive, idle, lazy, dull,
ālasya 153/3 n. idleness, sloth, want of energy, laziness,
alāta n. a fire-brand, coal,
alāta-spandita movement of a fire-brand,
alāta cakra a burning stick whirled round and appearing as a circle of fire,
alaukika mfn not current in the world, uncommon, unusual (esp. said of words), not relating to this world, supernatural, transcendental,
alavaṇa mfn not salt,
alaya m. non-dissolution, permanence, mfn restless,
ālaya vijñāna 'the continually changing stream of consciousness or the Absolute itself' (W), 'internal cognition, (U)
ālaya vijñāna pravāha train of self-cognition' (U),
ālaya m.n. a house, dwelling,
ālaya vijñāna repository of everything, the store-house of consciousness, may be either 'the continually changing stream of consciousness or the Absolute Being itself (G)',
ali m. a black bee, a scorpion, a crow, a cuckoo, liquor,
alīka 95/1 , not pleasing, disagreeable
ā√likh Cl6 ālikhati draws (a picture)
ā√liṅg Cl1 *āliṅgati* embraces,
aliṅga 95/1 n. absence of marks, mfn having no marks, (in gram. having no gender), liṅga ... 'that sign through which anything is comprehended i.e. intellect etc. (Gam.)', 'he who is without that *liṅga* is *aliṅga*'
āliṅgana 153/3 n clasping, embracing, an embrace
alobha m. non-greed, absence of desire, steadiness, moderation,
ā√loc *-locayati,* to consider, reflect, to make visible, show,
alocana mfn without eyes, without windows,
ālocana n seeing, perceiving, considering, reflecting, attention,
ālocya mfn to be considered or reflected on, ind. having considered or reflected on,
alohita mfn bloodless, free from qualities associated with redness, reddish,
ā√lok Cl10 *ālokayati* gazes, looks at, proves, beholds, perceives,
āloka m. looking, seeing, beholding, sight, aspect, vision, light, lustre, splendour, glimmer, flattery, praise, panegyric,
ālokaka m. a spectator,
ālokana n. the beholding, seeing, looking, sight, mfn looking at, contemplating,
ālokya 154/2 mfn beholding, ind. having seen,
aloluptva 95/2 n. free from desire
alpa mfn small, tiny, mean,

alpadhī mfn small-minded,
of small intelligence,
alpajña mfn knowing little, ignorant,
alpamedha 95/3 of little understanding,
ignorant, silly
alpaprāṇaḥ 'small breath' unaspirated – referring to the pronunciation of sounds,
alpaśaktimān impotent, weak, feeble,
alpaśas ind. to a small degree, a little,
alpībhāva 96/1 becoming smaller,
being small
√*am* cl1 P *amati* to go, to go to or towards, to serve or honour, to sound, DP in *gati* going, *śabda* sounding, or *saṁbhakti* honouring,
am ind. quickly, a little,
ām ind. yes
ama pron. this he,
ama m. impetuosity, violence, strength, power, depriving of sensation, fright, terror, disease,
āma ind. yes, mfn raw,
amā ind. at home, *amā* √*kṛ* keep by one
amahātman mfn not high-minded,
amala 81/1 1/s/m spotless, stainless, clean, shining, pure, crystal,
amalā f. umbilical cord,
āmalaka m.n. indian gooseberry,
amanaḥstha one who has reached mindlessness
amanas 80/2 n. non-perception, want of perception, mfn without perception or intellect, mindless,
amanaska mindless
amanaskata state of mindlessness,
amanāva not human, superhuman,
amānī without false ego, without desire for prestige, (V)
amanībhāva 80/2 m. the state of not having perception or intellect,
amānitva 81/2 modesty, humility, absence of pride or arrogance,
ā√*mantr* Cl10 *āmantrayate*, salute, takes leave of,
āmantraṇa 146/2 addressing, speaking to, calling, summoning, inviting, deliberation, interrogation, greeting, welcome, taking leave, the vocative case
amantu mfn silly, ignorant,
amanyata he thought 1/s/impf/mid √*man*
amara mfn deathless, immortal, m. an immortal, a god, author of the *amarakośa*
amaravat ind. like a god,
āmarda(na) 147/2 the act of crushing, pressing , squeezing, handling roughly
amāri non-violence to extreme extent, prohibition of animal sacrifice, mfn immortal
amaropama mfn like a god,
amarottama mfn chief of gods,
amarṣa 81/1 impatience, anger, passion, anger and jealousy combined,
āmarśana 147/2 touching, wiping off
āmarṣaṇa *ā*√*mṛṣ* bearing patiently?
amartya mfn immortal, imperishable,
amātra mfn without measure, boundless, not metrical or prosodical,
amātrā (G) modeless, the fourth (*turīya)* state,
amātrayā ind. in a boundless manner,
amātya m. a King's minister, an inmate of the same house, a relative,
amāvāsa m. a dwelling (of the moon) at home (with the sun),
amāvāsya mfn the night of *amāvāsa* i.e. the night of the new moon,
āmaya 146/2 sickness, disease
amāyā f. without guile, sincerity,
āmayitnu mfn sickening,
√*amb* 83/2 cl 1 P *ambati* to go
DP in *gati* going, moving
cl 1 A *ambate* to sound,
DP in *śabda*, sounding
amba/ambā a mother, good woman, as title of respect, a name for several goddesses,
ambara 83/2 n. circumference, compass, neighbourhood, apparel, garment sky, atmosphere, ether
√*ambarya* 83/2 P Nom. *ambaryati* to bring together, collect,

DP in *sambharaṇa* bringing together

ambayā mother

√*ambh* 84/1 *ambhate* to sound, DP in *śabda* sounding, going, honouring

ambhaḥ (in comp. for *ambhas),*

ambhaḥpati m. the lord of the waters, *Varuṅa,*

ambhaḥsāra m. a pearl,

ambhaḥstha mfn standing in water,

ambhaḥsū m. smoke,

ambhas n. water, the celestial waters, power, fruitfulness, a world, n.pl. a collective name for gods, men, Manes and Asuras,

ambho in comp. for *ambhas*,

ambhoda m. a cloud,

ambhodhara m. a cloud,

ambhodhi 84/1 the ocean,

ambhogarbha mfn containing water (as a cloud)

ambhoja 'water-born' n. the day lotus,

ambhojanman n. the lotus,

ambikā f. mother, good woman (as a term of respect),

ambu 83/3 n. water

ambuja mfn water-born, n. lotus,

ambuvega m. water currents, esp.swift currents,

amedhya 83/1mfn impure, foul, n. excrement,

aṁh 1. 01/2 cl1 *aṁhate* to go, set out, commence, DP in *gati* 347/3 going, approaching, setting out 2. 01/2 to press together, to strangle, DP in *tatkriyā* 'doing that', any particular action

amī pronoun 1/pl those, all those these, all these,

amilat (+3rd) met

amīmāṁsya 82/1 mfn not to be called in question, not to be discussed,

āmis 147/1 n. raw flesh, meat, a dead body ,

āmiṣa n. flesh, food, meat, prey,

āmiṣāśin mfn flesh-eating, carnivorous,

amiśraṇa 81/3 not causing to mix or unite

amita mfn immeasurable, boundless, infinite, unmeasured, *(am)* ind. immensely

amitābha of unmeasured splendour, m.pl.

amithuna mfn not forming pairs, not both sexes promiscuously,

amīva f.(*ā*), plague, distress, disease, n. tormenting spirit, pain, grief,

amīva-cātana f.(ī) driving away distress,

amīva-han mfn slaying the tormenting spirits, destroying pains,

amla 841/1 mfn sour, acid, m acidity, vinegar, m.n. sour curds,

āmnāya m. sacred tradition, sacred texts handed down by tradition, that which is to be remembered or studied or learnt by heart, received dosctrine, traditional usage, family or national customs, advice, instruction in past and present usage, a family, series of families,

amloṭa m. ebony,

āmoda mfn gladdening, m. fragrance, fragrancy, smell, strong smell, asparagus,

amogha mfn unfailing, unerring, hitting the mark, m. the not erring or not failing, 83/1

āmra n. mango, fruit of the mango tree,

amṛdaya mfn pitiless,

amṛkta mfn unhurt,

amṛta 82/2 mfn.not dead, immortal, imperishable, beautiful, beloved, m. (as) an immortal, a god, f. (*ā*) a goddess, a plant, liquor, n. (*am*) world of immortality, immortality, the nectar conferring immortality, ambrosia, nectar-like food, infinity, indestructible by nature,

amṛtattva (or °tatā) 82/2 n. immortality

amṛtatvāya 4/s/n for immortality

amṛtavarṣin mfn giving a shower of nectar, 82/3

amṛtyu m. non-death, immortality, mfn immortal,

√*aṁś* 01/2 cl10 to divide, distribute DP in *samāghāta* 1163/3 m. striking together, collision, conflict, war,

aṁśa 1a/1 m. a share, portion, the portion of a sacrifice that goes to the gods,
aṁsa m. shoulder,
aṁśu m. a shoot of the soma plant, a shooting ray of light,
aṁśuka n. a fine upper garment (*śāṭī*)
aṁśuman radiant, shining, grandson of King Sagara
aṁśumat mfn radiant, shining, luminous, m. moon, sun,
aṁśumant mfn rich in beams, radiant
aṁsumat mfn possessing beams or rays, radiant, m. the sun, name of a grandson of King Sagara
amu the base of a pronoun (*adas*) that 2nd *amum, amūm*, 3rd *amunā, amuyā*, 4th *amuṣmai, amuṣyai* etc.
amuc *-k* f. not setting at liberty,
amūḍha 82/1m. not perplexed , the intelligent man, not infatuated,
amūdṛkṣa or *–dṛś* or *–dṛśa* mfn like such a one,
amūla mfn rootless, baseless, without authority, not resting on authority,
amūlya mfn priceless, invaluable,
amuka mfn such and such a person or thing, a thing or person referred to without name, so and so,
amukhya mfn not chief, inferior,
amukhya karaṇa subordinate cause, secondary cause,
amukta mfn not loosed, not let go, not liberated from birth and death,
amuktavat as if not free,
amukti f. non-liberation,
amum pron. 2/s/f that
amūra mfn not ignorant, wise, intelligent, sharp-sighted,
amūrchayat (he) shaped or gave form to it, see √*murch*
amurhi ind. at that time, then,
amūrta mfn formless, shapeless, subtle unembodied, not forming one body, consisting of different parts,
amūrti f. shapelessness, absence of shape or form, mfn formless,
āmuṣmika 147/1 mfn of that state, being there, belonging to the other world,
amuṣmin ind. in the other world, in Reality, in the next world,
amuṣya 6/s/m *adas,* of such a one, of him
amuṣyāḥ (6th /s of *adas)* of such a one, of her, 5/s from her,
amutas ind. from there, there, from above, from the other world, from heaven, hereupon, upon this,
amuthā ind. thus, in that manner, like that,
amutra 82/1 there, in the other world, in the life to come,
amuvat ind. like such person or thing, a thing or person referred to without name,
amuyā ind. (3rd f.) in that manner, thus or thus, so,
an- occasionally (before a vowel) substituting for *a* as a negative
an 24/1 cl 2 P *aniti* to breathe, respire, gasp, to live, to move go, DP in *prāṇava*, breathing
aṇ 11/3 cl 1 P to sound, *aṇati*, DP in sense of *śabda,* sounding cl 4 A *aṇyate* to breathe, DP in *prāṇava* living, breathing
ana a pronoun stem related to *idam* (this)
ana m. breath, respiration,
anābhāsa 'free from appearance', (Gam.), i.e. without manifestation, 'does not appear in the form of any object, imagined outside' (Gam.), imagelessness,
anabhibhūta mfn not overcome, not beset, unsurpassed, unobstructed,
anabhidya non-covetousness, not thinking vain thoughts, not brooding over perceived injuries,
anabhisaṁdhāya without interest in, not aiming at, without regard for
anabhisneha mfn. 26/1 without affection, cold, non desirous, unimpassioned,
anabhiṣvaṅgas absence of clinging, non-attachment, without self-identification such as 'I am this, or I am that', 26/1
anabhivyakta mfn indistinct, unmanifest, potential,
anabhyudita not expressed, not uttered,

(Gam.)
anādara 28/1mfn. indifferent, calm
m. disrespect,contemptuous neglect,
anādayaḥ eternal (Gam.),
anadhigata mfn unstudied,
not acquired or obtained,
original,
anadhyavasāya m. irresolution, hesitation,
anadhyayana n. intermission of study, not reading or studying, freedom from study, academic holiday,
anādhṛṣya mfn unapproachable, invincible, not to be meddled with,
anādi mfn not having a beginning, eternal, existing from eternity,
ind. perpetually, incessantly,
anāditva n. beginninglessness
anādimat 28/1 mfn. having no beginning,
anādṛtya ind. part. having not heeded, without reference to, without respecting (regardless),
ānaḍuha mfn of or from a bull, taurine,
anaḍvah m. bull, a bull kept for breeding,
anadyatanaù 'not of today' a tense not referring to the current day, e.g. periphrastic future, past imperfect or perfect tense
anāgāmin mfn not coming, not arriving, not future, not subject to returning, third among the four Buddhist orders,
anāgas mfn without sin,
anāgata mfn not arrived, not yet come, impending, future,
anāgatavant mfn to do with the future,
anāgatavidhātṛ m. arranger for the future, forethought, name of a fish,
anagha 24/2 mfn. sinless, faultless (*Kṛṣṇa)*
anahaṁkṛta mfn free from self-conceit,
anahamvādin 27/2 free from self-conceit, not given to asserting his ego
anāhata mfn unbeaten, unwounded, intact, new and unbleached (as cloth),
the fourth *cakra,* (the lotus of the heart),
anaikāntika mfn unsteady, variable, having many objects or purposes, n. (in *Vaiśeṣika* phil.) a particular fallacy of inconsistency in reasoning, 42/3
anaikāntikatva n. unsteadiness, uncertainty, inconclusiveness,
aṇaka 11/3 mfn insignificant, small, contemptible
anaka mfn inferior,
anala 26/2 m. fire, god of fire, wind, digestive power, gastric juice,
anāmaka mfn without name, infamous,
anamat bowed, 1/s/ past, √*nam*
anāmaya 28/2 mfn. free from disease, healthy, salubrious, not pernicious
n. health
anāmayitnu mfn not sickening, healing,
anamīva mfn without sickness or trouble,
n. good health, happy state,
ānana n. mouth, face, entrance, door,
anānātva non-duality (Gam.), non-difference, undifferentiated, (Q)
ānanda 139/3 pure happiness, bliss,
ānandabhuk full of joy, enjoying bliss, 'enjoyer of bliss',
ānandamaya 140/1 consisting of bliss or happiness, made of bliss,
ānandamayakoṣa the 'bliss sheath',
ānandavigraha embodied bliss, embodiment of bliss,
ānandayāti gladdens, enlivens,
ānandena blissfully, very happily
ananta mfn 25/1 limitless, boundless, eternal, infinite, endless
anantamahāmbhodhi *ananta* 25/1 boundless, limitless, *mahā* 794/2,3 great, *ambhodhi* 84/1 receptacle of waters, the ocean, the great limitless ocean,
anantara mfn having no interior, having no interstice or interval or pause, uninterrupted, unbroken, continuous, immediately adjoining, contiguous, next of kin, compact, close, (*as*) m. a neighbouring rival, a rival neighbour, (*am*) n. contiguousness, Brahma or the supreme soul (as being of one entire essence), *(am)* ind. straight away, after (time), immediately after, after, afterwards,
anantaraya m. non-interruption, 25/1

anantaśeṣa name of the great serpent –the couch of Viṣṇu during dissolution,
ananuṣṭhāna n. non-observance, neglect, impropriety,
ananya 25/2 mfn not another, not different, identical, self, identical, without a second, undeviating,
ananyata mfn non-difference,
ananyatā f. or *–tva* n. identity, exclusive dedication, single-mindedness,
ananyayoga m. not suitable to any others, (am) ind. not in consequence of any other (word),
ananyayogena with single-minded concentration, with undivided concentration
anapara 25/3 mfn without another, having no follower, single, sole, without effect,
anaparāddha mfn unoffending, innocent,
anapatya mfn childless, without offspring,
anapekṣa 25/3 mfn. indifferent, impartial, careless,
anāpnuvan pres.part. not getting, not accepting,
anārabhya mfn. improper or impractical, to be commenced or undertaken,
anārambha 28/2 m. absence of beginning, non-commencement, not attempting or undertaking, having no commencement
anarghya mfn not to be priced, priceless,
anarghyatva n. pricelessness,
anartha 26/2 nonsense, having no meaning, non-value, worthless, evil, bad, (L) non-advantage, disadvantage,
anārya 28/3 mfn not honourable or respectable, inferior, (not Aryan)
anāruhya ind. without going into (danger), not having gone into, not having surmounted,
anas n. a cart for heavy burdens, a mother, birth, offspring,
anāśa 1. 29/1 mfn hopeless, despairing, 2. mfn √*naś* undestroyed, living,
anāsakti yoga 'the yoga of detachment, which comes through understanding the unity of object and subject of observation. This makes everything and every action blissful and then all else does not exist. ' HH76
'Objects of the material world need no change and the actions of the subtle world of mind need no change. The change takes place in the *bhāva*, the emotional level. Once understanding is achieved, once knowledge is gained fully, then alone change will follow'.
'Only if one could change one's centre of understanding that all observed things and the observer are the same, then one could have achieved all changes; for the view of the world, of the beauty and the action will all change diametrically'.
anaśanam n. abstinence from food, fasting
anāśayat destroyed
anāśin mfn imperishable, 2. not eating,
anaśnan fasting
anāśrita 29/1 mfn. not supported, detached, independent, not depending on,
anāśraya m. non-support, absence of anything or person to depend upon, defencelessness, self-dependence, isolation, mfn defenceless, unprotected, isolated,
anaśru mfn without tears,
anaṣṭa mfn not lost, undestroyed, unimpaired,
anaṣṭapaśu mfn who loses none from his herd,
anasūya 27/2 not spiteful, not envious, absence of ill-will or envy, not sneering or scoffing
anasūyanta not sneering, not spiteful, not speaking ill of, pres. part.
anātha mfn having no master or protector, widowed, fatherless, helpless, poor, (*am*) n. want of a protector, helplessness,
anatidbhuta mfn 'transcending what has existed', unsurpassed,
anātman 27/3 m. not-self, another,

something different from spirit or soul, mfn not spiritual, corporeal, destitute of spirit or mind, unembodied,

anaupādhika unconditional (relationship), uncontaminated,

āṇava mfn fine, minute, the sense of individuality causing ignorance of one's true nature, (*am*) n. exceeding smallness,

ānava mfn kind to men, humane, a foreign man,

anavacchinna 26/3 not intersected, not interrupted, unbounded,

anavadhāna 26/3 inattention, inadvertence, inattentive, careless

anavadya mfn blameless, faultless,

anavadyāṅga mfn having a faultless body,

anavakāśa having no opportunity or occasion, whose potential remains unfulfilled, uncalled for, inapplicable,

anavasāna mfn having no termination, free from death, endless,

anavalokayan not looking toward, not looking, 1/s/m pres/caus/act part. *an ava* √*lok*

anavāpta unattained, not attained, not reached, mfn *an ava* √*āp*

anavastha mfn unsettled, unstable, (*ā)* f. unsettled condition or character, instability, loose conduct, (in phil.) non-finality (of a proposition), endless series of statements, infinite regress,

anavasthāna 27/1 mfn unstable, fickle, m. wind, n (*am*) instability, unsteadiness,

anavasthita mfn unsettled, unsteady, loose in conduct,

anavekṣa mfn regardless, without any looking around, (*am*) ind. without looking around, without regard to, irrespectively,

anavekṣamāna mfn not looking around,

anaviprayukta 'not applied divergently to different objects', (Gam.),

ānaya bring! , m. leading to, leading to a teacher, √*nī*

anāyāsa (in which there is no exertion), mfn not troublesome, not tiring, m. ease, idleness, neglect,

ānayat brought

ānayati brings,

anayat led

anayoḥ of these two 6/du/m

anāyudha mfn weaponless, defenceless,

√*añc* 10/3 cl1 P *añcati* A *añcate*, to bend, curve, incline, curl, to reverence (with inclined body), to honour, to tend, move, go, wander about, to request, in *gati* or *yācana,* or *pūjana* cl 10 or caus. *añcayati* to unfold, make clear, produce DP in *viśeṣaṇa* particularising

añc ifc. turned to, going or directed towards,

√*āñc* 133/2 see √*añc* above, DP in *āyāma* -extending

añcala m. border (of a dress)

√*and* cl 1 P *andati* to bind, DP in *bandhana,* binding

aṇḍa n. an egg, a testicle, the scrotum,

aṇḍaja mfn. egg-born, -*as* m. a bird, a fish, a snake,

aṇḍaka m. the scrotum, (*am*) n. an egg,

aṇḍakāra mfn egg-shaped, oval, elliptical, m. an ellipsis,

√*andh* cl 10 *andhayati* make blind DP in *dṛṣṭi-upaghāt* growing blind or in *upasaṁhāra* withdrawing

andha 44/3 mfn blind, blinding, dark, (*am*) n. darkness, dark water, water

andhaka mfn blind,

andhakāra m.n. darkness,

andhatāmisra utter darkness, complete darkness of the soul, doctrine of annihilation after death,

anedya mfn not to be blamed, blameless,

anenas mfn free from guilt,

anejat 42/2 mfn. not moving, immovable √*ej*

aneka mfn not one, more than one, many, several,

anekadhā ind. in many ways, many times, in various ways,

anekarūpa mfn. multiform, of various kinds or sorts
anekaśas 42/2 mfn not one, many, much, ind. not one, in great numbers
aneke, anekāni many
anena pron. 3/s/m. n. by this, by him from this, with this
√ *aṅg* 7/2 cl1 P *aṅgati* to go, cl10 P *aṅgayati* to mark, DP in *gati,* in the sense of going, moving, motion in general, passage, procedure, progress, path,
aṅga n. a limb, member, body, person, form, division,
aṅga a particle used to assert emphatically, *yad aṅga* just when, *te aṅga* they only
āṅga 131/1 mfn (in gram.) relating to the base (*aṅga*) of a word, n. a soft delicate form or body,
aṅgadam 7/3 an armlet worn on the upper arm,
aṅgaṇa as below,
aṅgana 8/1 the act of walking, place to walk in, a court, *(ā)* f. any woman or female, a woman with well-rounded limbs, the female elephant of the north,
aṅgāra m. coal, a heap of charcoal,
aṅgī√kṛ to make a part, subordinate, adopt, accept, promise,
aṅgīkṛta mfn promised, agreed to, undertaken,
aṅgiras a sage, a race or tribe among the forefathers (regarded as half divine),
aṅgirasa mfn descended from *aṅgiras*
√*aṅgh* 8/2 cl1, Ā *aṅghate* to go, set out, commence, DP in *gati* (see *aṅg* above), or in *ākṣepa* 128/3 drawing together, convulsion, applying, laying, throwing away, giving up, removing, reviling, abuse, harsh speech
āṅgika mfn 131/1 expressed by bodily action or attitude or gesture etc. (as dramatic sentiment, passion, etc). a player on a tabor or drum
aṅgiras a sage
aṅguli f. a finger, a toe, the thumb, the big toe, the finger-like tip of an elephant's trunk,
aṅgulīyaka or *aṅgurīyaka* n. a finger ring,
aṅgulīyam a ring
aṅguṣṭha 8/2 m. the thumb, the great toe, a thumb's breadth,
aṅguṣṭha-mātraḥ having the size of a thumb,
aṇi 11/3 m. the point of a needle or of a fine stake,
ā√nī Cl 1 *–nayati,* to bring, bring to,
aniccha 29/2 mfn. undesirous, unwilling
anicchā f. absence of wish or desire,- indifference
aṇīci m.f. bamboo, cane,
anīḍa mfn having no nest, having no settled abode, incorporeal, bodiless,
anidra 29/2 mfn sleepless, awake, (ā)f. sleeplessness,
aniha mfn one who has or knows no 'here',
anīha mfn listless, indifferent, (*ā*) f. indifference, apathy,
anihita mfn not set down, not ending with a consonant,
anīhita- 31/1disagreeable displeasing unwished,
anīka n. 1. face, 2. fig. appearance, 3. of a hatchet (face), sharp edge, 4. front, troop,
anīkam army, fighting force, appearance, face, edge, 2/s/m or n
anila 30/1 m. air or wind, the god of wind, one of the demi-god *Vasus*
anilayana a non-sustaining thing , n. no home or refuge, see *nilayana*
aṇimā f. subtle essence, spirit, (see *aṇiman)*`
aṇiman 11/3 m minuteness, fineness, thinness, atomic nature, n. the smallest particle,
animitta 29/3 mfn having no adequate occasion, causeless, groundless, (am) n. absence of an adequate cause or occasion, groundlessness,
animittatas ind. groundlessly,

aniṅga 29/2 mfn not divisible (said of words,

anirdeśya 30/1 undefinable, inexplicable, incomparable, indescribable,

aniruddha mfn unobstructed, ungovernable, self-willed, m. a spy, secret emissary,

anirukta 29/3 mfn unuttered, not articulated, not explained, inexpressible, unspeakable,

anirvacanīya mfn unutterable, indescribable,' neither identical with nor different from', 'neither real nor unreal', relating to the ontological existence of the world, not determinable as either real or unreal,

anirvācya 30/1 unutterable, indescribable

aniśa 30/2 mfn 'nightless', sleepless, uninterrupted, continually, n. ceaselessly,

anīśa 30/3 mfn one who has no Lord or superior, paramount, powerless, unable, not independent, *(ā)* f. a feeling of powerlessness, helplessness

anisarga mfn unnatural, unnaturally affected,

aniścita 30/2 unascertained, uncertain, not well ascertained,

aniṣṭa mfn undesired, disagreeable, unapproved, unlawful, 2. not honoured with a sacrifice, not offered as a sacrifice,

aniṣṭacintana n. thinking about something unlawful,

aniṣṭvā ind. without sacrificing,

anīśvara mfn without a superior, unchecked, paramount, powerless, unable, godless, atheistic, *tā* f. or *tva* n. absence of a supreme ruler,

anītijña mfn not knowing discreet conduct, clever in immoral conduct, not discreet or politic,

anitya 29/2 impermanent, transient, occasional, incidental, irregular, unusual, unstable, uncertain, destructible, (*am*) ind. occasionally,

anityatā f. or *tva* n. transient or limited existence, transitoriness,

aniveśana mfn having no resting place, unsettled,

aniviśamāna mfn not going to rest, restless

aniyama 29/3 absence of rule or fixed order, uncertainty, doubt

aṇīyaṁsa more minute, smaller, subtler, m comparative

a-niyata 29/3 mfn. not regulated , not well-defined, uncontrolled, uncertain, unrestricted

√*añj* 11/1 cl 7 P A *anakti, aṅkte* ... .*kte* to apply an ointment or pigment, smear with, anoint, decorate, prepare, honour, celebrate, cause to appear, make clear, be beautiful, DP in *vyakti, mrakṣaṇa, kānti* and *gati*

āñjana n. ointment, collyrium for the eyes or a box filled with that,

añjas n. an ointment, a mixture ind. quickly, suddenly,

añjasā ind. instantly, suddenly, soon, right, truly, justly, quickly,

añjali 11/1 m. a reverent or respectful gesture made with the hands, joined hands,

√*aṅk* 7/1 cl1 Ā *aṅkate* to move in a curve, DP in *lakṣaṇa* 892/1 marking, stepping, cl10 P *aṅkayati* to move in a curve, to stamp, brand, *DP in gati going*

aṅk brand, stamp,

aṅka m. 1. the lap body-fold, the lap, 2. the hip bend that carried babies may be rested on, 3. a hook, 4. a mark or sign like a pot-hook, a bend in the arm, wall, shore,

aṅkana the act of marking, branding, stamping, writing

√*aṅkhaya* p. *aṅkhayati,* to hook on, grapple, *pari+* clasp, embrace,

aṅkita mfn marked,

aṅkura 7/2 a sprout, a shoot, a blade

aṅkuśa a goad, esp. an elephant goad,

anna 45/1 mfn. eaten, n. food (esp. rice), food in a mystical sense, water

annamayakoṣa 45/1 m. the food sheath, the gross material body,
annaprāśana n. rice-feeding, the first-feeding of an infant with rice,
annarasa n. food and drink, m. taste in distinguishing food, chyle,
annavant mfn provided with food,
annāyu 45/2 m. living by food, desirous of food, dependent on food,
anirviṁṇa 30/1 mfn. not downcast
ano ind. no, not,
anoṁkṛta mfn not having *om* uttered, unaccompanied by *om*,
anṛta 42/2 not true, untruth, false and with all the qualities of snake. super-imposing ignorance and the empirical world upon the Absolute-hence not being aware of the Absolute
anṛtabhāṣaṇa lying, falsehood, speaking untruth
anṛtika mfn untruthful,
√*ant* 42/3 cl1 *antati* to bind, DP in *bandhana* binding
anta 42/3 m. end, limit, termination, border, inner part, inside, internal, certainty, (L) 1. vicinity, proximity, *ante* in the end, *antena* finally,
antagata mfn end-gone, come to an end, being at the end of,
antaḥ end, boundary, final word syllable ,
antaḥkaraṇa 43/1 the internal organ, the seat of feeling and thought, the mind, the thinking faculty comprising *buddhi, citta, manas*, and *ahaṅkara*
antaḥkaraṇa-pratibimba-caitanya reflection of the intelligence in the mind,
antaḥkaraṇa-vyāpāra thought-construction, working of the mind,
antaḥprajña mfn internally wise, knowing one's self, inner subjective consciousness,
antaḥpura
antaḥstha 'in-between' semi-vowel
antaḥsukhas he who has happiness within
antaka m. border, boundary mfn making an end, causing death, m. ender (death),
antakāla 42/3 time of death, death
antakara mfn end-making, destroyer, causing death, 42/3
antakarman death, destruction, the end or cessation of action
antama mfn next, nearest, the last, intimate (as a friend), 43/1
antaḥprajña mfn internally wise, aware of internal objects i.e. in the mind, knowing one's self, internal consciousness, inwardly cognitive, (G) the dream state where consciousness still functions but is not externally manifested (*taijasa)*,
antaḥpura n. inner stronghold, citadel, inner apartment of the citadel, gymnasium, harem, female apartments,
antar ind. 43/2 within, between, amongst, inside, interior, within, along with,
antara 43/3 mfn being in the interior, interior, near, related, different from, n. the interior, a hole, opening, the interior part of a thing, the contents, soul, heart, supreme soul, interval, intermediate space or time, period, term, distance (between two things), the difference, representation, different, other, another, occasion, juncture, ifc. in the interior, within, a different, another,
antarā 44/1 ind. in the middle, inside, within, between, amidst, among, on the way, by the way, near, nearly, almost, in the meantime, now and then, for some time, between, during, without, except, without, assoc with case 2.
antarā or *–ram* or *-re* or *–reṇa* between,
antarābhavadeha or *antarābhavasattva* n. the soul in its middle existence between death and regeneration,
antaraṅga mfn interior, being essential to, internal organ, mind,
antarātman m. the in-dwelling soul, heart,

the internal feelings, the heart or mind,
antarāya m. intervention, obstacle,
antarbhava mfn being within, inward, internal, generated internally
antarbhauma mfn subterranean,
antardhāna n. hiding, disappearance, invisibility,
antardhauti inner cleansing,
antardhi 44/2 m. concealment, covering, disappearance, interim, meantime,
antardṛṣṭi inner vision,
antareṇa between, without, regarding, except, with reference to (with 2nd), on account of,
antareṣu in between
antargata mfn gone within, hidden, immanent,
antarikṣa 44/1 n. the intermediate space between heaven and earth, the atmosphere or sky, the air,
antarikṣaga passing through the atmosphere, a bird,
antarikṣaloka m. atmosphere world, the atmosphere as a world,
antarita mfn hidden, concealed, separated, departed, gone within, withdrawn, perished, disappeared,
antarjyotis mfn he who has light within, inner light,
antarlajjā f. inner shame,
antarmukha mfn inner gaze, turned inwards,
antarmukha-vṛtti a state in which the mind is turned inwards and is withdrawn from objects,
antarvedi ind. within the sacrificial spot,
antaryāga inner sacrifice,
antaryāmin 43/3 m. checking or regulating the inner feelings, the soul, 'he alone entering into all, directs everything from within', (*Māṇ* 6, trans. *Nikhilānanda*), 'the inner controller' (Gam.) , the inner guide, the witness who dwells within,
antataù ind. finally, ultimately, in the end,
antavat 43/1 mfn. having an end or term, limited, perishable, containing a word which has the meaning of anta, ind. like the end, like the final of a word
antaya to make an end of, *antayati* P
ante in the end 7/s
antevāsin 43/1 mfn dwelling near the boundaries, dwelling close by, m. a pupil who dwells near or in the house of his teacher, a disciple,
√*aṇṭh* or *aṭh* 11/3 cl1 A *aṇṭhate* to go, move,
tend, DP in *gati*, going, moving
anti ind. before, in the presence of, near, opposite, in front,
antika 44/2 mfn.near, proximate, n. vicinity, proximity, near, (*am*) ind. until, near to, into the presence of, etc.
2. reaching to, reaching to the end of, lasting till, until
antima mfn last, final, ultimate, ifc. immediately following, very near,
antya mfn last in place, in time, or in order, immediately following, lowest in place or condition, the inferior, of the lowest caste,
antyajāti mfn having the lowest birth, of the lowest caste, 44/3
antyastrī f. a woman of the lowest caste,
antyeṣṭi f. funeral sacrifice, last rites,
aṇu 11/3 mfn fine, minute, atomic, an atom of matter or of time, subtle ind. minutely
anu 31/1 mfn = *aṇu*
m. a non-Aryan man, of a non-Aryan tribe,
ind. prefix after, along, alongside, lengthwise, near to, subordinate to, with, When pre-fixed to nouns, especially in adverbial compounds, - according to, severally, each by each, methodically, one after an other, repeatedly,
As a separable adverb – after, afterwards, thereupon, again, further, then, next
anubaddha mfn bound to, obliged to, connected with, related to, belonging to, followed by,

anu√bādh pass. to be oppressed/tormented
anubadhnat mfn following, seeking,
anubala a rearguard, an auxiliary army following another,
anu√bandh Cl 9 *anubadhnāti* to attach, tie, to bind (by an obligation), to stick, adhere, follow, endure, to be followed by, to pursue, importune,
anubandha 36/2 m. binding, connection, consequence, inevitable result, consequence accruing, sequence, an indicatory letter or syllable attached to roots etc., (marking some peculiarity in their inflection).
anubandhaka mfn connected, related, allied,
anubandhin 36/3 connected with, attached, resulting, permanent, having in its train or as a consequence
anubandhya mfn principal, primary, liable to receive an adjunct (as a root, a disease),
anubha mfn neither, no one of two,
anu√bhā to shine after another, shine in accordance
anubhāga intensity,
anu√bhaj to worship
anubhartṛ mfn supporting, strengthening, penetrating,
anu√bhāṣ to speak to, address,
anubhāṣitṛ mfn speaking to, saying,
anubhava m. perception, apprehension, fruition, understanding, impression on the mind not derived from memory, experience, knowledge from personal observation or experiment, result, consequence, cognition, consciousness, custom, usage, intuitive consciousness (self-realisation), (*am*) ind. at every birth, (N) perception by intuition, -*siddha* mfn established by experience or perception,
anubhāva m. sign or indication of a feeling *(bhāva)* by look or gesture, dignity, authority, consequence, firm opinion, ascertainment, good resolution, belief, dignity,
anubhava-advaita actual living experience of oneness,
anubhava-gamyam obtainable by direct perception (through *samādhi)*
anubhāvaka causing to apprehend, making understand,
anubhāvana n. the act of indicating feelings by sign or gesture,
anubhavati he/she feels, experiences, encloses, embraces, attains, equals, perceives, understands, √*bhū*
anubhavi guru teacher with spiritual realisation,
anubhāvin mfn perceiving, knowing, being an eye-witness, showing signs of feeling,
anu√bhṛ to support, to insert, enter,
anu√bhrāj to illuminate,
anubhrātṛ m. a younger brother
anu√bhū Cl1 *anubhavati* to enclose, embrace, to be after, attain, equal, to be useful, to help, to turn to, to notice, perceive, understand, to experience, enjoy, to bear, to attempt
anubhū 36/3 mfn perceiving, understanding, *anubhūyate* 1/s/pres/indic/passive is experienced
anu√bhuj to suffer the consequences of one's actions, to enjoy successively, to enjoy, participate,
anubhūta experienced, perceived understood, apprehended, resulted, followed as a consequence; that has experienced, tasted, tried or enjoyed,
anubhūti 36/3 f. perception, knowledge from any source but memory, (in phil.) knowledge gained by perception by the senses, inference, comparison and verbal authority. G40 direct apprehensions, experience which reveals new knowledge, experience
anubhūya ind. having experienced, having enjoyed,
anubhūyate is experienced,
anubodha m. recollection, an after-thought, perception,

anubodhana n. recollecting, reminding,

anubodhita mfn reminded, convinced by recollection,

anubrāhmaṇa n. a work resembling a Brāhmaṇa, (*am*) ind. according to the Brāhmaṇa

anu√brū cl2 P. *–brāviti* to pronounce, recite, to utter, address, invite, to repeat another's words, learn by heart,

anu√budh to awake, to recollect, to learn (by information), caus. – *bodhayati* to communicate, to remind, 36/2

anubuddha mfn unawakened,

anu √cakṣ to look at or up to, 32/2

anūcāna one competent to repeat the Vedas and Vedāṅgas, one who repeats his lesson after his master, devoted to learning, well-behaved, 41/3

anu √car to walk or move after or along, to follow, pursue, seek after, adhere to, attend, behave

anucara mfn following, attending, m. companion, follower, servant,

anucarci mfn reciting or repeating in a chorus,

anucca mfn not high, low, humble,

anucchid to cut lengthwise

anucchinna not cut off, not uprooted

anucchitti non-destruction, indestructibility

anuccho to cut open, or cut up,

anu √2.ci to remember,

anūcīna mfn coming after, successive,

anūcīnāham ind. on successive days,

anu √cint 32/2 to meditate, consider, recall to mind,

anucintana n. thinking of, meditating upon, recalling, recollecting, anxiety, f. *anucintā*

anucintayan meditating, thinking of pres/act/caus/part 1/s/m

anucintita mfn recollected, recalled, thought of

anucita 1. mfn set in rows, 2. mfn improper, wrong, unusual, strange,

anucitārtha m. an unusual meaning,

anūcya 1. n. elbow piece of a seat, 2. mfn to be repeated or learnt, mfn having instructed (Gam.)

anudagra mfn not lofty, low, not projecting

anu√1.dā to permit, restore, to give way, yield, to remit,

anu√dah to burn up, to take fire,

anudaka mfn waterless, (*am)* ind. without touching water, without adding water,

anūdaka n. want of water, aridity

anudara mfn thin

anudāra 1. niggardly, mean, 2. mfn adhered to or followed by a wife,

anudarśanam 33/2 keeping in view or in mind, consideration, 1/s/n

anudatta mfn granted, remitted, given back

anudātta mfn not raised, not elevated, not pronounced with the *udātta* (raised) accent, having the neutral general tone neither high nor low, m. one of the 3 accents to be observed in reading the Vedas,

anudaya m. not rising, not rising of a luminary

anudbhaṭa mfn not exalted, unassuming,

anūddeśa m. describing, mentioning according to or conformably with,

anuddhata mfn not lifted up, humble, unsurpassed, unopposed,

anudeham ind. behind the body,

anudeśa m. a rule or injunction pointing back to a previous rule, reference to something prior,

anūḍha mfn not borne, not carried, an unmarried woman,

anu √dhā to add in placing upon, to stimulate to, to concede, allow,

anu √dhāv –dhāvati, to run after, pursue,

anu √2.dhāv to cleanse

anudhāvana 1. chasing, pursuing, 2. cleansing, purification,

anudhāvati runs after, pursues,

anu √dhī to think of

anudhūpita mfn puffed up with pride

anu dhyā f. sorrow

anudhyāna n. meditation, religious contemplation, solicitude

anu √dhyai to consider attentively, think of, muse,

anūd √*i* to go up or out after (another)
anudigdha mfn covered,
anudinam ind. every day,
anu√*diś* to point out for, assign,
anudiśam ind. in every quarter,
anudita mfn not risen, not appeared,
2. mfn unsaid, unuttered, unutterable, blamable
anudivasam ind. every day
anu√*dī* to break through after another, to be scattered or confused due to the confusion of others
anudra mfn waterless,
anu√*2.dru* to run after, pursue, to run over in reciting,
anu√*dṛś* to survey, behold, to keep in view or in mind, to foresee,
anu√*duṣ* to become demoralized as a result of
anudvegakara 33/3 not causing apprehension not overawing
anudvigna 33/3 mfn. free from apprehension or anxiety, easy in mind
anudya mfn unutterable,
anūdya mfn to be spoken to afterwards, 2. having said afterwards or in reply,
anudyamāna not being spoken,
anūdyamāna mfn spoken in reply to or according to,
anudyata mfn inactive, idle, nil perseverance
anudyoga m. inactivity, laziness
anu √*1.gā* to go after, follow, to act in conformity to, or according to the wishes of
anuga mfn going after, following, adapted to, corresponding with, a companion, a follower, a servant,
anugacchati 1/s/pres/ind/act he/she follows
anugāḍha mfn plunged or immersed in,
anugādin repeating another's words
anu √*gāh* to plunge after, be immersed in,
anu √*gai* to sing after or to, to celebrate in song
anu √*gam* cl 1 P. *-gacchati* to go after, follow, seek , approach, visit, arrive, to practise, observe, obey, imitate, to enter into, to die out, be extinguished,
anu √*gaṇ* to count over,
anugaṇita mfn counted over,
anugaṅgam ind. along the Ganges
anugata mfn followed by, following, a follower, acquired, extinguished, tallying with, practising,
anugati f. following, imitation, dying out, a going after,
anugatika m. a follower, an imitator,
anu √*ghrā* to smell at, to kiss,
anu √*ghuṣ* to name aloud,
anugiram ind. on the mountain,
anugra mfn not harsh or violent, mild, gentle
anu√*grah* Cl 9 *anugṛhṇāti* to favour,
anugraha m. conferring benefits, obligation, loving kindness, obligation, assistance, showing favour, kindness,
anu √*gī* *-gṛṇāti* to join in praising, to rejoin, answer, repeat,
anu √*grah* to follow in taking or plundering, to support, uphold, to receive, welcome, treat with kindness, favour, oblige, to foster
anugraha 32/1 favour, kindness, showing favour, conferring benefits, grace,
anugrāhaka mfn favouring, furthering, facilitating, favourable, kind,
anugrahita mfn occupied, engaged,
anugrāmam ind. village after village,
anugṛhīta mfn favoured, obliged,
anugu ind. behind the cows
anuguṇayati he,she favours
anuguṇa mfn having similar qualities, congenial to, according or suitable to, m. natural peculiarity, *(am)* ind. according to one's merits,
anugupta mfn protected, sheltered,
aṇuḥ subtle, 11/3 mfn. fine, minute, atomic, m. an atom of matter or time, *aṇu* n. ind. minutely
anūha mfn thoughtless, careless,
anuharaṇa n. or *–hāra* m. imitation, resemblance
anuhava m. inviting, stirring up, calling after, calling back,
anu√*hve* to call again, call after,

anu√i cl 2 -*eti,* go along or after, accompany,
anu√iṣ -*icchati,* look for, search after, seek after,
anuja mfn born after, later, younger, m. younger brother
anu √jalp to follow in talking, A. –*jalpate* entertain by conversation,
anu √jan to follow in being born or produced, to take after one's parents,
anujanam according to people, popularly
anujanman m. younger brother, younger,
anu √jap to follow or imitate in muttering,
anujāta mfn later, younger, born again, regenerated by the sacred cord,
anu √ji to subdue,
anujihīte A. runs after √2.*hā*
anu √jīv to follow or imitate in living, to live for anyone, to live by or upon something, be dependent on,
anujīvin mfn living upon, dependent, m. a dependent,
anujjhat mfn not quitting,
anujjhita mfn undiminished, unimpaired, not left or lost,
anu √jñā to permit, grant, allow, consent, to excuse, forgive, to authorize, dismiss, farewell, to entreat, to behave kindly, assent,
anujñā f. approval, permission, assent,
anujñāpaka m. one who commands or enjoins,
anujñāpti f. authorization, permission,
anujñāta mfn assented to, allowed,
anu √juṣ to seek, to devote oneself to, to indulge in,
anuka mfn subordinate, dependent, 31/1
anūka m.n. the backbone, spine, the back part of the altar, a former state of existence, n. race, family,
anukāla mfn opportune, occasional,
anukalpa m. permission to use an alternative or substitute,
anukalpita mfn followed by,
anu√kam to desire,
anukāma m. desire, according to one's desire, agreeable, (*am*) ind. as desired at pleasure,
anukāmīna mfn one who acts as he pleases
anu√kamp to sympathize with, be compassionate, pity,
anukampā f. compassion, with compassion, causeless mercy, (V),
anukampaka m. sympathizer, mfn ifc.
anukampana n. sympathy, compassion, sympathizing, being compassionate,
anukampayā out of compassion, with compassion, mercifully, (V)
anukampya mfn worthy of sympathy, pitiable, m. an ascetic
anukāṅkṣā f. desire after, 31/1
anukara mfn imitating, m. an assistant,
anukaraṇa n. the act of imitation or of following an example, resemblance, similarity,
anukārin mfn imitating, acting, m. imitator,
anukarṣa m. attraction, drawing, invoking, grammatical attraction (including a subsequent in a preceding rule), delayed performance of a duty,
anukāśa m. reflection (of light), clearness, regard, reference,
anu√kath to repeat what has been heard, to relate after some other,
anukathana n. orderly narration, discourse, conversation,
anukathita related after (other), repeated,
anu √khyā to descry, 31/3
anukhyāti f. act of descrying, revealing,
anukīrṇa mfn crowded, crammed full,
anu√kīrt to narrate,
anukīrtana n. narrating, publishing,
anu √kḷp to follow in order,
anukḷpti f. agreement
anu √kṛ to do after, to follow in doing, to imitate, copy, to equal, to requite, to adopt,
anu√1.kṝ to scatter along, to strew, fill with,
anu √kram to go on, go after, follow, to go through in order, enumerate, supply with an index or abstract,
anukrama m. succession, arrangement, order, method, an index,
anukramaṇa proceeding methodically or in order, following,

anukrameṇa in succession,
anu √krand to shout or cry after one,
anukrānta mfn gone over, read, done in due order, enumerated,
anukrī mfn bought subsequently,
anu √krīḍ to play
anukrośa m. tenderness, compassion,
anu √kṛp –kṛpate to mourn for, long for,
anukṛṣṭa mfn drawn after, attracted, included or implied in a subsequent rule,
anukṛta mfn imitated, made like
anu √kruś to shout at, to join in lamenting
anukṣaṇam ind. momentarily, perpetually, every instant,
anukṣapam ind. night after night,
anu √kṣar to flow into or upon,
anu √2.kṣi to settle along,
anukta mfn unuttered, unheard of, unsaid, extraordinary
anūkta mfn spoken after, recited after, occurring in the (sacred) text, studied, n. study,
anukti f. not speaking, improper speech,
anūkti f. mentioning after, repeated mention, repetition by way of explanation, study of the Veda *-tva* n. state of requiring repetition or explanation, 41/3
anukūla mfn following the bank or slope, according to the current, favourable, agreeable, conformable, friendly, kind, well-disposed, a good husband
anukuñcita mfn bent, made crooked,
anu √kuṣ to drag along
anu√labh to grasp or take hold of (from behind) 37/3
anulagna mfn attached to, intent on, followed, pursuing after,
anulāpa repetition of what has been said, (tautology)
anulbaṇa mfn not excessive, not prominent, keeping the regular measure,
anulepana n. 38/1 anointing the body, unguent so used, ointment,
anu √lī to disappear after
anu√lip to anoint, besmear, A. to anoint oneself after bathing
anulipta mfn smeared, anointed,
anuloma mfn 'with the hair or grain', in a natural direction, in order, regular, successive, of mixed castes, (*am)* ind. in regular order,
anulomana n. due regulation, sending or putting in the right direction,
anu √lubh to long for, desire
anu√2. mā to roar or bleat towards,
anu√3. mā to be behind in measure, to be unable to equal, to infer, conclude, guess, conjecture
anumā f. inference, conclusion from given premises,
anu√mad to rejoice over, gladden, to praise
anumādya to be praised in succession,
anu√man to approve, assent to, permit, grant, caus. P. *–mānayati* to ask for permission, ask for, to honour,
anumāna n. the act of inferring, inference, reflection, consideration, guess, conjecture, one of the means of obtaining true knowledge, the forming of a conception,
ānumānika mfn relating to a conclusion, derived from inference, subject to inference, inferrable, inferred,
anumantā f. permitter, consenter, the giver of sanction to the movements of nature,
anu√mantr to accompany with or consecrate by magic formulas, to dismiss with a blessing, 36/3
anumantraṇa n. consecration by hymns and prayers
anumaraṇa n. following in death, the burning of a widow with her husband's corpse
anumārga m. following, seeking,
anumarśam ind. so as to seize/take hold of
anumata mfn approved, agreed to, permitted, allowed, agreeable, pleasant, loved, beloved, concurred with, being of one opinion, (*am*) n. consent, permission
anumati f. approbation, favour (of gods to the pious), grace (personified),

M. approval, consent, permission
aṇumātra mfn having the size of an atom,
aṇumātrika mfn having the size of an atom, containing the atomic elements (*mātrā*) of the body,
anumeya mfn to be measured, inferable, to be inferred, proved or conjectured,
anumimāna mfn concluding, inferring
anumiti f. conclusion from given premises, inference,
anumoda m. a subsequent pleasure, the feeling of pleasure from sympathy,
anumodaka mfn assenting, showing sympathetic joy,
anumodana n. pleasing, causing pleasure,
anumodita mfn pleased, delighted, applauded, agreeable, acceptable,
anu√mṛ to follow in death,
anu√mud to join in rejoicing, to sympathize with, express approval, applaud,
anu√muh to feel distressed at, troubled about
anūna or *anūnaka* mfn not less, not inferior to, whole, entire, having full power, -*guru* having full weight, very heavy -*varcas* mfn having full splendour,
anunāda m. sound, vibration,
anunadi ind. along the river,
anu√nand to enjoy
anunāsika a sound pronounced through the nose and mouth
anunaya m. conciliation, salutation, courtesy civility, showing respect or adoration to a guest or a deity, humble entreaty or supplication, reverential deportment, regulation of conduct, discipline, tuition, mfn conciliatory, kind, (*am*) ind. fitly, becomingly, 34/1
anunāyaka mfn submissive, humble
anunayin mfn courteous, supplicating,
anu√nī to bring near, lead to, to induce, win over, conciliate, pacify, supplicate
anu-ni-√kram,-kramati to follow in the steps
anu-ni-√pad –padyate, to lie down by the side of
anu-nir-√dah to burn down in succession
anu-nir-jihāna mfn proceeding out of
anu-nir-√2.vā, -vāti to become extinct, go out after
anu-ni-√śam to hear, perceive, to consider, 2. *anuniśam* ind. every night
anuniśītham at midnight,
anunīta mfn disciplined, taught, obtained, respected, pleased, pacified, humbly entreated,
anunīti f. conciliation, courtesy, supplication
anu-ni-√vṛj to plunge into
anu-ni-√vṛt caus. *–vartayati* to bring back,
anu-ni√yuj to attach to, place under the authority of
an-unmāda m. not being mad, soberness,
an-unmatta mfn not mad, sane, sober, not wild
an-unnata mfn not elevated, not lifted up,
anunaya m. conciliation, salutation, courtesy, civility, showing respect or adoration to a guest or deity, humble entreaty or supplication, reverential deportment, regulation of conduct, discipline, tuition, mfn conciliatory, kind, (am) ind. fitly, becomingly,
anu√4.nu to follow with acclamations of praise
anu√1.pā to drink after or thereupon, follow in drinking, drink at, 2. caus. P.A. *-pālayati (te),* to preserve, keep, cherish, to wait for, expect,
anūpa mfn situated near the water, watery, m. a watery country, pond, bank of a river, a buffalo,
anupabādha mfn unobstructed,
anupabhukta mfn, unenjoyed, unpossessed,
anu√pac to make ripe by degrees, to become ripe by degrees,
anu√pad to follow, attend, be fond of, to enter upon, to notice, understand,
anupad 2. mfn coming to pass,
anupada mfn following closely, a chorus, refrain, (am) ind. step by step, word by word, on the heels of,
anūpa√das to fail, become extinct,
anūpa√dhā to place upon, pile up after or in addition to,
an-upadhi-śeṣa mfn in whom there is no

longer a condition of individuality, Buddh. 34/2
anupadin m. a searcher, inquirer, one who follows or seeks for,
anupadiṣṭa mfn untaught, uninstructed,
anupaghnat mfn not detrimental,
anupahata mfn unimpaired, uninitiated, not rendered impure,
anupahūta mfn not called upon or invited,
anupajīvanīya mfn yielding no livelihood, having no livelihood,
anupakārin 34/2 mfn. not assisting, disobliging, ungrateful, not making a return for benefits received
anupākhya mfn not clearly discernible,
anupakṛta unassisted,
anupakṣita mfn uninjured, undecaying,
anupalabdha mfn unobtained, unperceived, unascertained
anupalabdhi f. non-perception, non-recognition, non-apprehension,
anupalakṣita mfn untraced, unperceived, unmarked, not discriminated
anupalakṣyavartman mfn having ways that cannot be traced,
anupalambha m. non-perception, non-apprehension,
anupalambhana n. want of apprehension or knowledge
anupālana n. preserving, maintaining,
anupama mfn incomparable, matchless excellent, best,
anupamita mfn uncompared, matchless,
anupāna n. a fluid vehicle in medicine, drink taken with or after medicine, drink after eating, drink to be had near at hand,
anupapatti f. non-accomplishment, failure of proof, inconclusive argument, irrelevancy,
anupaplava mfn free from disaster,
anupapluta mfn not overwhelmed,
anuparata mfn uninterrupted, not stopped
anuparihāram ind. surrounding,
anupari (√i) –pary-eti to follow in going round, make the round of,
anupari√kram to walk round in order, make the circuit of,
anuparimāna atomic, of the size of an atom,
anuparśva mfn along or by the side, lateral
anu-pary-ā-√dhā to place round in order,
anu-pary-ā-√1.gā to revolve, return to
anu-pary-ā-√vṛt to follow in going off, to follow
anu√paś P.A. *–paśyati (te),* to look at, see, perceive, discern, notice, discover, to consider, reflect upon, to look upon as, take as,
anupasamhārin (G) nonconclusive reason, a type of fallacious reasoning...
anupāsana n. want of attention to
anupāsita mfn not attended to, neglected,
anupasarga m. a word without an *upasarga*, a word that is not an *upasarga*, that which needs no additions (as a divine being)
anupaśaya m. any aggravating circumstance,
anupaskṛta mfn unfinished, unpolished, not cooked, genuine, blameless,
anūpa√sthā to approach in order,
anupasthāna n. not coming near, not being at hand, absence,
anupaśya mfn. keeping in view, perceiving, seeing, following with looks,
anupaśyāmi I foresee, I anticipate, consider, notice, look at, keep in view, 3/s/pres/indic/act *anu √paś*
anupaśyati 35/1 he/she realizes, looks at, notices, discovers, reflects upon, takes as, look upon as, sees, realizes directly
anu√pat to pass by flying, to fly after, run after, go after, follow,
anu√paṭh to say after, repeat,read through
anupatha mfn following the road
anupaṭhita mfn read through aloud, recited
anupatita mfn fallen, descended, followed,
anūpa√viś to sit down in order, lie down (said of an animal about to birth),
anupāya without means, the path without any means, '*anupāya* denotes liberation itself and not a path to it' 'liberation through grace'
anupāyin mfn not using means or expedients,
anupayogin mfn unsuitable, useless,

anupayukta mfn unsuitable, improper,
useless, unserviceable
anuplava m. a companion or follower,
anu√plu to float after (as clouds),
anu√pè to fill,
anupra√āp *-āpnoti,* cl 5, to go up to,
reach, to arrive, get, get back,
to get by imitating,
anupra√bhā to shine upon, 35/3
anupra√bhūṣ to serve, attend, offer,
anuprabhūta mfn passing through,
penetrating,
anu√prach to ask, to inquire after,
anupra√1.dā to surrender, make over,
anupra√hi Cl 5 *anuprahiṇoti* to send
someone for something, despatch,
anuprahita mfn sent after, shot off, 36/1
anupra√jan to be born after, to propagate
again and again,
anupra√jñā to track, trace, discover,
anupramāṇa mfn having a suitable size or
length, sources of valid knowledge,
perception, inference and valid
testimony,
anupra√muc to let loose or go successively
anupra√mud caus. *–modayati* to consent,
anu-prāp to come or go up to, to reach,
attain, arrive, get, get back,
anuprapādam ind. going in succession,
anupra√1.pā P. to drink one after
the other,
anuprapanna mfn following after,
conformed to, conforming to,
anuprapātam ind. going in succession,
anuprāpta mfn arrived, returned, having
reached, having got,
anuprāsa m. alliteration, repetition of
similar letters, syllables and words,
anupra√sad to be content or satisfied with
anuprasakta mfn strongly attached,
anuprasakti f. close connection with,
anupra√sañj to adhere to, fasten,
anupraśna m. a subsequent question,
(referring to the teacher's reply)
anupra√sṛ to extend over,
anupra√sṛp to creep towards or after,
anupra√sthā to start after another,
anupra√śuc *-śocate* to regret/mourn deeply
anuprasūta mfn created afterwards,
anupravacana Veda study with a teacher
anupra√vad to repeat the words of another,
to speak of, cause to resound,
to play an instrument,
anupra√viś to follow in entering, enter,
anupraviśya having entered into,
anupra√vraj to follow into exile, to
become an ascetic after,
anupra√vṛt to proceed along or after
anupravṛtta mfn following after,
anupra√yā to follow after,
anupra√yam to offer,
anuprayoga m. additional use
anupra√yuj to employ after, add after,
to join, follow,
anupre (√i) –praiti to follow, follow in
death, to seek after,
anupṛkta mfn mixed with,
anuprapanna 35/3 following after,
conformed to, conforming to
anu-prekṣ (√ikṣ) to follow with the eyes,
anu-prekṣā concentration of thought,
contemplation, reflection,
anu-preṣ (√iṣ) caus. P. *-preṣayati*
to send forth after,
anu-proh (√1.ūh) to insert,
anupṛṣṭhya held lengthwise 35/2
anupta mfn unsown (seed), *-sasya* mfn
fallow, meadow,
anupuruṣa m. the before-mentioned man,
a follower,
anupūrva mfn regular, orderly, in
successive order from the beginning,
anupūrveṇa ind. regularly,
anūpya mfn being in bogs or ponds
anu√rādh to carry to an end, to finish with
anurāddha mfn effected, accomplished,
anūrādha mfn causing welfare, happiness
anurāga m. attachment, affection, love,
passion, red colour, intense love
toward God,
anurāgin mfn impassioned, attached,
causing love, f. personification of a
musical note,
anuragitā f. the state of being in love with,
anurahasam ind. in secret, apart,
anu√raj *-rajyati*, cl 4 'have a strong feeling

for', feel an affection for, be enamoured of,
anu√rāj to be brilliant or shine in accordance with,
anurajyate is fond of (with 6th)
anurakṣaṇa n. the act of guarding
anurakta mfn fond of, attached, pleased,
anurakti f. affection, love, devotion
anu√ram P. *–ramati* to stop, A. to be fond of,
anu√rañj to be attached or devoted, to become red in imitation of,
anurañjyate becomes attracted
anurasa m. (in poetry) a subordinate feeling or passion, a secondary flavour,
anurata mfn fond of, attached to,
anurathyā a path by a road, a side-road,
anurātram ind. in the night,
anūrdhva mfn not high, low,
anūrjita mfn not strong, weak, not proud,
anūrmi mfn not fluctuating, inviolable,
anurodha m. obliging or fulfilling the wishes of anyone, means for winning the affection of, compliance, considerance, respect, reference or bearing of a rule, conformity, ifc. with regard to, according to,
anurodhin mfn complying with, compliant, obliging, having respect/regard to,
anuroha m. mounting or growing up to,
anuru mfn not great
anūru m. the charioteer of the sun, the dawn,
anu√rudh to bar (as a way), to surround, confine, overcome, cl4 A. *-rudhyate* or P. *–rudhyati* to adhere to, be fond of, love, to coax, soothe, entreat, comply, 2. mfn adhering to, loving,
anuruddha mfn checked, opposed, soothed, pacified,
anu√ruh P. to ascend, mount, A. to grow
anurūpa mfn following the form, conformable, corresponding, like, fit, suitable, according to, n. (am) conformity, suitability, appropriate,
anuruta mfn resounding with,
anuśabdita mfn verbally communicated, spoken of,
anusajjate he or she is attached or clings onto, 1/s/pres/indic/mid *anu √sañj*
anu√śak to be able to imitate, come up with, to teach, instruct,
anuṣak or *anuṣaṭ* ind. in continuous order, one after the other, 39/3
anuṣakta mfn closely connected with, supplied from something preceding,
anuṣakti f. clinging to, adherence,
anu√śam to become calm after or in consequence of
anusamā√car to carry out, accomplish 40/3
anusamā√dhā to Clm, compose,
anusaṁ√āp caus.P. to complete, or accomplish further or subsequently,
anusamā√rabh A. tp place oneself in order after
anusamā√ruh to rise after,
anusamā√hṛ to join or bring in order again
anusambaddha mfn connected with, accompanied by
anusam√bhid to bring into contact, combine,
anusam√bhū to be produced after, proceed after,
anusaṁ√car to walk alongside, to follow, join, to visit, seek after, penetrate, traverse, cross, to become assimilated
anusaṁcara mfn following or accompanying,
anusaṁ√cint to meditate,
anusaṁ√dah to burn along a whole length
anusaṁ √diś to assign, to make over,
anusaṁ√dṛś to consider successively
anusaṁ√dhā to explore, ascertain, inspect, plan, arrange, to calm, compose, set in order, to aim at
anusaṁdhāna n. investigation, inquiry, setting in order, arranging, planning,
anusaṁ√grah to oblige, favour, to salute by laying hold of the feet,
anusaṁ√hṛ to compress, reduce a subject, to drag the foot,
anusaṁ√man to approve,
anusamprāp to arrive, reach, get
anusamprāpta mfn arrived, come

anusampra√yā to go towards,
anusaṁ√rabh to catch hold of (mutually),
anusaṁrakta mfn attached or devoted to,
anu√śam to become calm after or in consequence of,
anu√śaṁs to recite or praise after another
anusaṁ√smṛ to remember, to long for the dead or absent,
anusaṁ√sthṛ P. to follow a road, A. to become finished after,
anusaṁ√tan to overspread, diffuse, extend everywhere, to join on, continue,
anusaṁtati f. continuation,
anusaṁ√tī to carry to the end, go on (in spinning),
anusamudram ind. along the sea,
anusaṁvatsaram ind. year after year,
anusaṁ√1.vid to know together with or in consequence of (something else),,
anusaṁ√viś to retire for sleep after,
anusaṁ√yā to go up and down (as guards), to go to or towards,
anusandhyam ind. evening after evening, every twilight,
anuṣaṅga m. close adherence, connection, conjunction, coalition, connection of word with word or effect with cause, necessary consequence, tenderness, compassion,
anu√ṣañj to cling or adhere to,be attached to
anusānu ind. from ridge to ridge, along a table-land or summit,
anu√śap to curse,
anūṣara mfn not salted, not saline,
anusara mfn following, a companion
anusāra m. going after, following, custom, usage, nature, natural state or condition, prevalence, currency, received or established authority (esp. codes of law), accordance, conformity to usage, consequence, result,
anusāraka mfn following, attendant on,
anusaraṇa n. following, going after, searching,
anusarati follows – an instruction
anu √śās 39/2 to rule, govern, to order, to teach, direct, advise, address, to punish, correct, to impart after,
anuśāsaka mfn one who governs, directs etc.
anuśāsana n. instruction, direction, precept
anuśāsanapara mfn obedient,
anuśāsita mfn defined by rule, directed
anusātam ind. according to delight,
anusavanam ind. at every sacrifice, constantly
anuśaya m. close connection as with a consequence, close attachment to any object, (in phil.) the consequence or result of an act which clings to it and causes the soul after enjoying the temporary freedom from transmigration to enter other bodies, repentance, regret,
anusāyam ind. evening after evening, every evening,
anuśayin mfn having the consequence of an act, connected as with a consequence, devotedly attached to, faithful, repentant, regretful, hating deeply, penitent, (also) indifferent to everything,
anuśāyin mfn lying or extending along,
anu√sev to practise, observe,
anusevin mfn practising, observing, habitually addicted to,
anu√1.śī cl 2 A. *–śete,* to sleep with, lie along or close, adhere closely to,
anusiddha mfn gradually effected or realized
anu√śikṣin mfn exercising oneself in, practising , 39/2
anuśīlana n. constant practice or study (of a science etc.), repeated and devoted service, exercise,
anuśīlita mfn studied carefully, attended to
anuśiṣṭa mfn. 39/3 taught, revealed, done according to law, instructed
anuśiṣṭi f. instruction, teaching, ordering
anuśiṣyāt it/he/she should be taught, 1/s/opt/act
anūṣita mfn living near another, 42/1
anuskandam ind. having gone into in succession,
anūṣmapara mfn not followed by a sibilant,

anusmara remember! think of 2/s impv/act *anu √smṛ*
anusmaran meditating on, thinking about pres/act/part
anusmaraṇa n. remembering, repeated recollection, constant memory of Brahman
anusmarati he remembers
anusmaret he should meditate on or call to mind 1/s/opt/act
anu√smṛ to remember, recollect,
anusmṛta mfn remembered,
anusmṛti f. cherished recollection, recalling some idea to the exclusion of all others
anusmṛtya ind. having remembered, remembering
anuṣṇa mfn not hot, cold, apathetic, lazy, (*am*) n. the blue lotus
anuṣṇaka mfn chilly
anuṣṇāśīta mfn neither hot not cold,
anuśocita mfn regretted, repented of,
anuśoka m. or-*śocana* n. sorrow, repentance, regret,
anuspaṣṭa mfn noticed,
anu√sphur to whizz toward,
anusphura whizzing as an arrow,
anu√spṛś to touch, extend to,
anu√sṛ to go after, pursue,
anuśrava Vedic tradition (acquired by repeated hearing)
anu√sṛj to dismiss, let go, to create successively,
anu√sṛp to glide after or towards, approach
anusṛta mfn followed, conformed to,
anusṛti f. going after, following,conforming,
anusṛtya ind. following, imitating, searching out

anu√śru cl 5 P –*śṛṇoti* to hear repeatedly,
anuśruta mfn handed down by Vedic tradition,
anustaraṇa m. a suitable animal to be chosen as a secondary victim, f. the cow sacrificed at the funeral ceremony,
anuṣṭhā stand near or by, to follow out, to carry out, attend to, to perform, do, practise, to govern, rule, superintend, to appoint,
anuṣṭhāna n. carrying out (duties), undertaking,doing, performance, f.(*ī*) performance, action, devotion to, observance, systematic perfomance of religious duties over a long and stipulated period of time,
anuṣṭhati practises, follows, carries out
anuṣṭheya mfn to be effected or done, to be observed, to be proved or established,
anuṣṭhi f. being near, present, at hand,
anuṣṭhita 40/1 mfn. done, practised,
anuṣṭhu or -ṣṭhuyā presently, immediately
anu-ṣṭubh (√stubh) to praise after, to follow in praising, 2. f. following in praise or invocation, a metre of 4 quarter-verses of 8 syllables each, speech, *Sarasvatī*
anu√1. śuc 39/3 to mourn over, regret, wail, be sorry for,
anusūcaka mfn indicative of, pointing out,
anusūcana n. pointing out, indication,
anu√śuṣ to dry up gradually, to become emaciated by gradual practice of religious austerity, to languish after another,
anuśuśruma we have heard, we have heard repeatedly, 3/pl/perf/act *anu√śru*
anuṣvadham ind. according to one's will, voluntary, 40/2
anusvāna sounding conformably
anuṣvāpam ind. continuing to sleep,
anusvāra m. after-sound, the nasal sound marked by a dot above the line and which belongs to a preceding vowel, *-vat* mfn having the *anusvāra*
anusyūta mfn sewed consecutively, strung together, or connected regularly and uninterruptedly,
anu √takṣ to procure or create for the help of, 31/1
anutamām ind. (superl.) ind. most
anu√tan to extend along, to carry on, continue, develop,
anutaṭam ind. along the shore,

anu √tap to heat, to vex, annoy,
anutāpa m. repentance, heat, remorse,
anutāpana mfn occasioning remorse, repentance or sorrow,
anutapta mfn heated, filled with regret,
anu √tark to follow in thought, to regard as or take for,
anutarṣa m. thirst, wish, desire, a drinking vessel for liquor
anūti f. no help,
anutiṣṭhanti practises, follows, carries out
anutilam ind. grain by grain, minutely,
anutka mfn free from regret, self-complacent,
anutkarṣa m. non-elevation, inferiority,
anūt√kram to go up or out after,
anūt√1. pā –pibati to drink up or empty by drinking after another,
anūt√5.pā to rise along,
anutpāda m. non-production, not coming into existence, not taking effect, not being born again,
anutpādya mfn not to be created, eternal,
anūt√pat to fly up after another, raise oneself into the air, jump up afterwards,
anutpatti f. failure, non-production, birthlessness,
mfn not (yet) produced,
anutpatti-dharma-kṣānti f. acquiescence in the state which is still future, preparation for a future state, (Buddhist)
anutsāha m. non-exertion, want of effort, listlessness,
anutsanna mfn not lost,
anutsuka mfn not eager, calm, moderate,
anutseka m. absence of arrogance or high-mindedness, modesty,
anutsūtra mfn not anomalous
anu √tī to follow across or to the end,
anu √tṛd to split open,
anu √tṛp to take one's fill or refreshment after or later than another,
anutta mfn not cast down, un-moved, i.e. invincible,
anuttama mfn unsurpassed, excellent, the best or chief, excessive,
anuttara mfn chief, principal, best, excellent, low, inferior, base, south, southern , (am) n. a reply which is incoherent or evasive and therefore held to be no answer, without a reply, unable to answer, silent, fixed, firm,
anūtthā (√sthā) anūttiṣṭhati to rise after,
anutthita mfn not risen, not grown up (grain)
anutunna mfn muffled (sound)
anutva n. minuteness, atomic nature,
anu √vā cl2 P *–vāti* to blow upon, blow along or after, 2. f. blowing after, 38/2
anu √vac to recite the formulas inviting to the sacrificial ceremony, to repeat, recite, communicate, study
anuvacana n. speaking after, repetition, reciting, reading, lecture, a chapter, recitation of texts as responses,
anu √vad to repeat the words of, to imitate (in speaking),to resound, insist upon
anuvāda m. saying after or again, repeating by way of explanation, translation, explanatory repetition with corroboration or illustration, explanatory reference to anything already said, a passage of the Brāhmaṇas which explains or illustrates a rule (*vidhi),*
anuvāda reassertive corroborative statement e.g. "Fire is the remedy for cold", in which a known fact is restated. (Gam.), see *arthavāda*
anuvādaka or *anuvādin* mfn repeating with comment and explanation, corroborative, conformable, in harmony with, translator,
anuvādita mfn translated
anu √vah to convey or carry along, take after
anuvāka m. reciting, repeating, reading
anuvakra mfn somewhat crooked or oblique
anuvāram ind. time after time,
anu √varṇ to mention, describe, praise
anuvartana 39/1 n. obliging, serving or gratifying another, compliance, obedience, following, result, concurring, continuance,

anuvartate he, she, it follows
1/s/pres/indic/mid *anu √vṛt*
anuvartin mfn following, compliant, obedient, resembling,
anuvartman mfn following, attending,
anuvartmana n. a path previously walked by another,
anu √4.vas to clothe, cover
anu √5.vas to dwell near to, to inhabit along with, to settle after another,
anu √vās to perfume,
anuvaśa m. obedience to the will of, mfn obedient to the will of
anuvāsin mfn residing, resident,
anuvāte ind with the wind blowing in the same direction, to windward,
anuvedha m. piercing, obstructing, blending, intermixture,
anuvelam ind. now and then,
anu√ven to allure, entice,
anuveśa m. entering after, following,
anu√veṣṭ to be fixed to, cling to
anuvi√bhū to equal, to correspond to,
anu-vi-√car to walk or pass through
anviccati searches after,
anu-vi-√cint to recall to mind, meditate upon
anuviddha mfn pierced, intermixed, full of
anu-vi-√dhā to assign to in order, to regulate, to lay down a rule, pass. yields or conforms to,
anuvidhāna n. obedience, obedient to instruction,
anuvidhīyate it is guided, ordered, regulated,
1/s/pres/pass *anu vi √ dhā*
anuvidvas mfn having found,
anuvi√han to interrupt, derange,
anu-vī (√i) cl 2 P. *–vyeti* to follow or join in going off or separating, to extend along
anu√vīj to fan
anu-vi-√kas to blow, expand, as a flower,
anu-vi-√kāś to penetrate with one's vision
anu-vi-√1.kṛ to shape after
anu-vi-√1.kṝ to bestrew
anu-vi-√kram to step or walk after
anuvīkṣ to survey, examine,
anuvi√lī to dissolve
anuvi√mṛś to consider
anuvi√nad to make resonant or musical
anuvi√naś to disappear, perish, disappear one after another
anuviniḥ√sṛ to go or come out in order
anuvi√paś to look at, view
anuvi√rāj to be bright after or along
anuvi√sraṁs to separate, loose,
anuvi√sṛj to shoot at or towards
anu-vi-√tan to extend all along or all over
anuvitta mfn found, obtained, at hand
anuvitti f. finding
anuvi√vā to blow while passing through
anu√1.vid cl 2 P.-*vetti* to know thoroughly,
anu√3.vid cl 6 P.A. *–vindati (te*), to find, obtain, discover, to marry, to deem,
anuvidya mfn having known,
anu√viś to enter after, enter, follow,
anuvi√viś to settle along separately,
anu√vraj to go along, to follow a departing guest as a sign of respect, to obey, do homage, to visit one after another,
anuvrata mfn devoted to, faithful to, ardently attached to, acting according to the will or command of another, obedient, the first five vows in Jainism abstinence from gross violence, gross falsehood and gross stealing, contentment with one's own wife, limitation of one's possessions,
anu√vṛdh to grow, increase,
anu√vṛṣ to rain upon or along
anuvi√vṛt to run along, go after, attend upon,
anu√vṛt A. to go after, to follow, pursue, to follow from a previous rule, be supplied from a previous sentence, to attend, to obey, respect, imitate, resemble, assent, expect,
anuvṛtta mfn following, obeying, complying, rounded off, *(am)* n. obedience, conformity, compliance,
anuvṛtti f. sequence, continuance, following, acting suitably to, having regard or respect to, turning round and round, complying with, the act of

continuance, (gram.) continued course or influence of a preceding rule on what follows, reverting to, imitating, doing or acting in like manner, 39/1

anuvyāhāra m. cursing, execration, 39/2

anuvyāhāraṇa n. repeated utterance

anuvyā√hṛ to utter in order or repeatedly, to curse,

anu-vy-ā√khyā to explain further,

anuvyākhyāna n. that portion of a Brāhmaṇa which explains or illustrates difficult Sūtras, texts or obscure statements occurring in another portion

anuvyā√sthā caus. *–sthāpayati* to send away in different directions

anuvyam ind. behind, after, inferior to,

anuvyavasāya a in Yoga philosophy -'the function of the mind in its intelligent (*sāttvika*) aspect by which sensations ...are associated, differentiated, integrated and assimilatedinto percepts and concepts', (Ananta Sukla, Art and Representation'), perception of a sentiment or judgment, introspective cognition, knowledge of perception, 'the object is known by me' as opposed to 'this is an object' (an activity of *cidābhāsa),*

anu-vy-ava-√so to perceive

anu√yā to go towards or after, follow, to imitate, equal, 2. mfn following,

anu√yam to direct, guide, give direction to

anu√yat A. *–yatate* to strive to attain or reach,

anuyata mfn followed (in hostile manner),

anuyātṛ m. a follower, companion,

anuyātra n.f. retinue, attendance, that required for a journey

anuyāyin mfn a dependant, follower, following, going after, m. follower, dependant, attendant, companion,

ānuyātrika mfn belonging to a servant, belonging to a retinue, a servant, m. an escort,

anuyoga m. a question, examination, censure, reproof, exposition, religious meditation, spiritual union, a group of texts in Jainism, in Buddhism 'the teachings of the Perfection Process' emphasizing insight and removal of mental conditioning,

anuyogin mfn combining, uniting, connected with, questioning,

anuyojana n. question, questioning,

anuyojya mfn to be questioned or examined, to be enjoined or ordered, censurable, a servant, agent, delegate,

anuyū mfn depending, dependent,

anuyugam according to the Yugas (ages)

anu√yuj to join again, to question, examine, to order, to enjoin,

anuyukta mfn ordered, enjoined,

anuyuktin m. one who has enjoined, examined,

anvaicchat he/she searched after

anvaicchatām (they two) searched

anvajāryat suffused, endowed

anvañc mfn directed after, following after, being behind, ind. in the rear, behind

anvaśocas you have mourned
anu a śocas 2/s/impf/act *anu √śuc*

anvaya 46/1 m. following, succession, connection, association, logical connection of cause and effect, syntax, natural order of words, proposition and conclusion, race, family, positive knowledge as opposed to *vyatireka* – (knowledge gleaned through negation and process of elimination).
succession, lineage, family,

anvaya-vyatireka positive and negative assertions; proof by assertion and negation, a traditional method of separating that which exists in name and form alone from the eternal existence-consciousness-bliss,

ānvayika mfn of a good family, well-born, (W) directly connected,

anveṣaṇa or *anveṣa* 47/2 seeking for, searching, investigating,

anveṣin mfn searching for, inquiring,
anveṣṭavya mfn to be investigated,
anviccha seek!, wish for, desire
2/impv/act *anu* √*iṣ*
anvicchā f. 1313/3 seeking after
ānvīkṣikī (W) 'the science of logic' one of the branches of study to be studied by a prince under reputable guidance,142/1 logic, logical philosophy, metaphysics, an argumentative mind (with buddhi),
anviṣ *(anu + iṣ)* Cl1 *anveṣate* to look for, desire, seek after, search for, enquire,
anvita 47/2 gone along with, accompanied by, reached by the mind, full of, understood, joined, endowed with
anvitāḥ 47/2 endowed with
anvicchati searches after
anya pron. other, another, else, different,
*anya (*or *eka)... anya*
the one.... the other,
another person, one of a number,
anyabhāva 1313/2 m. change of state,
anyac ca and another thing, i.e. again, moreover,
anyadā at another time, sometimes, one day, once, in another case,
anyad api also another, something more
anyaśarīravat anya 45/2 other, different, *śarīra* body, suffix *vat* - like, like another's body
anyatas ind. from anywhere, from another direction, otherwise, elsewhere, to another place,
anyatama mfn one of several, someone, any one of many, either, any,
anyatara mfn either, one of two, 45/3
anyatarasyām optionally (in gram.),
anyatarathā in one of two ways,
anyathā 45/3 ind. otherwise, in a different manner, otherwise, in another way, in different ways, separateness; the state of being otherwise, in other circumstances,
anyathābhāna (W), becoming otherwise, one thing appears as another without really changing, e.g. a straight stick appears bent when poked in water,
anyathābhāva m. alteration, difference, 'birth, transmutation' (Gam.), (W) existing otherwise, 'when gold is made into a bangle it no longer appears as a lump of gold'
anyathāgrahana 'grasping the truth otherwise', (W) misapprehension,
anyathājñāna 'the misapprehension of one attribute for another',
anyathākhyāti 'appearance of a real thing in a wrong way' (Gam.), (W) cognition of a thing other than what it is, 'the object of error exists but not where it is perceived', the assertion that something is not really what it appears to be,
anyathāsiddha (W) an accidental circumstance, not the true cause of an effect, e.g. a bird lands on the coconut tree and a coconut falls off, 45/3 wrongly defined, wrongly proved or established, effected otherwise, non-essential,
anyatobhuvaḥ adventitious, i.e. added from without, accidental, casual, supervening,
anyatra ind. aside from, otherwise, elsewhere, apart from, anywhere else, another,
anyāyena by unjust or foul means
anye 1/pl/m others, other
anye-dyus ind. on the next day,
anyonya 46/1 pron. one another, mutual, (W) reciprocity, a figure of speech in which two things perform the same act towards each other,
anyonyābhāva mutual non-existence,
anyonyādhyāsa 'When two things of different nature come together, they influence each other. The interchange of their qualities is known as *anyonyādhyāsa,* i.e. inter-superimposition.'
anyonyasakta 'joined one to another' (Gam.), combined,

anyonyāśraya (N) interdependent, 46/1 m. mutual or reciprocal support or connection or dependence, mutually depending, mutual support, a type of fallacious reasoning 'A depends on B and B depends on A'

ap 1. n. work, 47/3
2. f. water, air, the intermediate region, the Waters considered as divinities, *āpaḥ* f.pl.

√āp 142/1 cl 5 P *āpnoti,* to reach, overtake, meet with, fall upon, obtain, gain, take possession of, undergo, suffer, to fall, come to anyone, enter, pervade, occupy, to equal, to arrive at one's aim or end, become filled, DP in *vyāpti* pervading, in *lambhana* obtaining
2. to arrive, come towards,

apa ind. prefix away, off, back, down when prefixed to nouns it may sometimes = the negative prefix *a*-, or may express deterioration, inferiority,
As a separable particle or adverb (with 5th), away from, on the outside of, without, with the exception of,

āpa 142/2 1. mfn obtaining, ifc. to be obtained, 2. name of a Vasu (demi-god), 3. n. water, the waters

apa√bhaj to cede or transfer a share to, satisfy the claims of, divide in parts

apabhaya mfn fearless, undaunted,

apabhraṁśa (N) corrupted language, ungrammatical language,

apabhrāṣṭa mfn fallen off, deviating (from good grammar), provincial, dialect,

apa√bhū to be absent, be deficient,

apaca mfn not able to cook,

apa√car to depart,

apacāra m. want, absence, defect, fault, improper conduct, offence,
(W) beginningless impurity, disobedience to Śiva's will,

apacārin mfn departing from, disbelieving in, infidel, doing wrong, wicked

apacarita mfn gone away, departed, dead,

apacaritam n. fault, offence,

apacāy to fear, to respect, honour,

apacaya m. diminution, decay, decrease,

apacāyin mfn not rendering due respect,

apacāyita mfn honoured, respected,

apa-cchad (√chad) caus. *–cchādayati,* to take off a cover,

apa-ccheda m.n. cutting off/away, separation

apa-cchid (√chid) to cut off/away,
2. f. a cutting, shred, chip

ā√pad Cl4 *āpadyate* attains, comes to, happens, occurs,

āpaddharma (W) the law of calamity, during times of distress there is a certain laxity in the rules and regulations of the law. This is based upon the idea that before a good life may be secured, life itself must be preserved, e.g. a Brahmin may adopt the profession of a Kṣatriya or Vaiśya but after the emergency is over he should follow his own profession,

apacetas mfn not favourable to,

apacetṛ, m. a spendthrift,

apa√1.ci *-cinoti* to gather, collect, to grow less, to wane,

apa√2.ci to pay attention to, respect,

apa√cit caus.A. to abandon, turn off from,
2. f. a noxious flying insect,

apacita mfn honoured, respected,
n. honouring, esteeming,
2. mfn expended, wasted, diminished, emaciated, thin

apaciti f. honouring, reverence,
2. f. loss, expense,
3. f. compensation, either recompense or retaliation, revenge, punishing

apacyava m. pushing away

apa√cyu to fall off, go off, desert

apad mfn footless, m.f. *apād* footless,

ā√pad to come, walk near, approach, to enter, get in, arrive at, go into, to fall in or into, to be changed into, to get into trouble, fall into misfortune, to get, take possession, to happen, occur,

āpad 142/3 f. misfortune, calamity, distress, hardship, *āpadā* (3rd) through mistake or error, unintentionally,

apa√dah to burn up, to burn to drive out,

apadakṣiṇam ind. away from the right, to the left side,

apadama mfn without self-restraint, of wavering fortune,

apadāna n. a great or noble work,

apādāna, am, n. taking away, removal, ablation, a thing from which another thing is removed, 'The eternal unmoving from which all movement comes'

apadārtha m. nonentity,

apa√das to fail i.e. to become dry,

apadeśa m. assigning, pointing out, pretence, feint, pretext, disguise,

apadevatā f. an evil demon

apa√dhṛṣ to overcome, subdue,

apa√dhvaṁs -dhvaṁsati to scold, revile,

apadhvaṁsa m. concealment, degradation,

apa√dhyai to have a bad opinion of, curse mentally

apadhyāna n. envy, jealousy, meditation upon things not to be thought of, (W) cessation fron inflicting bodily injuries, killing, etc.

apa√diś to assign, to point out, indicate, to betray, pretend, use as a pretext,

apadiśam ind. in an intermediate region of the compass (half a point),

apadiṣṭa mfn assigned as a reason or pretext,

apadoṣa mfn faultless,

apadravya n. a bad thing, m

apadrāva n. a side-entrance

apa√dru -dravati, cl 1 run off or away,

apa√gā to go away, vanish, retire,

apaga mfn going away, turning away from

apa√gam to go away, depart, vanish,

apagama m. going away, giving way, departure, death,

apagata departed, remote, dead, diseased

apaghana 1. m. a limb or member (hand or foot), 2. mfn cloudless,

apagoha m. hiding place, secret,

apagopura mfn without gates (a town),,

apagoram ind. disapproving, threatening,

apagūḍha mfn hidden, concealed,

apa√guh to conceal, hide,

apa√gur to to reject, disapprove, threaten,

apahāni f. diminishing, vanishing,

apahara mfn carrying off

apahāra m. taking away, stealing, spending another's property, concealment,

apaharaṇa 53/3 n taking away, carrying off, stealing

apaharati carries away

apa√has to deride, ridicule,

apahāsa m. a mocking laugh

apahata mfn destroyed, warded off, killed

apahatapāpman (W) sinless, free from evil,

apahatapāpmatva (W) n. purity, free from all sins, the Supreme Soul,

apahāya ind. p. quitting, leaving, avoiding, leaving out of view, excepting

apahnava m. concealment, denial of or turning of of the truth, dissimulation, appeasing,

apa√hnu Cl2 *apahnute* conceals, disguises, excuses one's self, gives satisfaction to,

apa√hṛ cl 1 *–harati* take off or away, steal

apahṛta 53/3 mfn. taken away, stolen

apahṛtya having taken away or carried off

apaiśuna 56/3 n. absence of slander, absence of vilification

apa-jāta m. a bad son who has turned out ill,

apajaya m. defeat, discomfiture, 48/3

apajñāna n. denying, concealing,

apa√jñā –jānīte to dissemble, conceal,

apa√jī to ward off, keep out or off,

apāka 1. coming from a distant place, distant, 2. mfn immature, unripe, m. immaturity, indigestion, 53/3

apākā ind. far

apakalaṅka m. a deep stain of disgrace

apakalmaṣa mfn stainless, sinless, 47/3

apakāma m. aversion, abhorrence, abominableness, (*am*) ind. against one's liking, unwillingly,

apakāra m. injury, offence, hurt, despise, disdain, 48/1

apakāraka or *apakārin* mfn acting wrongly,

offending, injuring,
apakaraṇa n. acting improperly, doing wrong, ill-treating, offending
apākaraṇa n. driving away, removal, payment, liquidation, 53/3
apakārin mfn injuring, acting wrongly,
apakarman n. discharge of a debt, evil doing, violence, any impure or degrading act,
apakarṣa m. drawing or dragging off or down, detraction, diminution, decay, decline, inferiority,
apakarṣaka mfn drawing down, detracting,
apakarṣaṇa mfn taking away, forcing away, diminishing, n. taking away, depriving, abolishing, denying,
apakartṛ mfn injurious, offensive,
apakaruṇa mfn cruel,
apa√kaṣ to scrape off,
apakaṣāya mfn sinless
apakīrti f. infamy, disgrace,
apa√1.kṛ to carry away, remove, drag away, to hurt, wrong, injure, 48/1
apa√kṝ to scrape with the feet, to spout out, spurt, scatter,
apa√kram to go away, retreat, retire from, to glide away, measure off by steps,
apakrama m. going away, flight, retreat, not being in proper order (poetry),
apakrośa m. reviling, abusing,
apakṛṣṭa mfn taken away, removed, lost, brought down, depressed, low, vile, m. a crow
-*tva* n. inferiority, vileness
apa√2.kṛt cl 6 P –*krintati* to cut off,
apakṛta done wrongly or maliciously, committed offensively or wickedly, practised as a degrading or impure act e.g. menial work, n. injury, offence,
apakṛti f. oppression, wrong, injury,
apakṛtya n. damage, hurt,
apa√kruś to revile
apakṣa mfn without wings, without followers or partisans, not on the same side or party, adverse, opposed to,
apakṣaya m. decline, decay, wane,
apa√kṣi to decline, wane (as the moon),
apakṣīṇa mfn declined, decayed,
apakṣita mfn waned,
apakti f. immaturity, indigestion,
apakva mfn unripe, immature, undigested,
-*tā* f. immaturity, incompleteness,
apakvabuddhi mfn of immature understanding,
apala n. a pin or bolt, 2. mfn fleshless, 51/3
apa√lap to explain away, to deny, conceal,
apalapana n. denial or concealment,
apalapita mfn concealed, denied, suppressed, embezzled,
apalāṣin mfn free from desire
apalāya not retreating or fleeing
apa√likh to scrape off,
apamada mfn free from pride/arrogance,
apamala mfn spotless, clean,
apamāna 50/2 dishonour, disrespect, disgrace
apamārin mfn dying or pining away,
apāmārjana n. cleansing, keeping back, removing of diseases &other evils
apāmitya n. equivalent, 54/2
apāṁ-nātha m. the ocean, 47/3
apāṁ-nidhi m. the ocean,
apām-pati or *ap-pati* m. the ocean, M. 'lord of the waters', Varuṇa,
apām-pitta or *ap-pitta* n, fire, a plant,
apamud mfn joyless, pitiable,
apāṇa 54/2 m. that of the 5 vital airs (*prāṇas)* which goes downwards and out at the anus, the anus, G48 'carrying downwards breath', inspired breath, outbreath, inhalation, digestive energy. The life breath which removes all waste from the human system. excreting, etc.
āpaṇa m. market, shop, waves, commerce, trade, 142/3
apanābhi without a navel, without a focal point,
apa√nah to bind back, to loosen,
apa√nam bend away from, give way to, to bow down before,

āpāna mfn one who has reached, n. a tavern, the act of drinking, a drinking party, banquet, 142/2
apanāma m. curve, flexion, 49/3
apanāman n. a bad name, mfn having a bad name
apa√2.naś to disappear,
apanata mfn bent outwards, bulging out,
apanaya m. leading or taking away, bad policy, bad or wicked conduct,
apanayana 49/3 n taking away, withdrawing, destroying, healing, acqittance of a debt
apañcikaraṇa the unquintuplicated form of matter, subtle form of matter before mixing to form the 5 elements,
apaṇḍita mfn unlearned, illiterate,
apa√nī to lead away or off, to steal, remove, drag away, to put off or away, to extract, take from, deny, except, exclude from a rule,
apani√dhā to place aside, hide, conceal, to take off,
apanidra 1. mfn sleepless,
2. mfn opening (as a flower), bristling, erect (as hair on the body),
āpanika m. shopkeeper, merchant,
apanīta mfn taken away, removed, paid, badly executed, spoiled,
n. imprudent or bad behaviour,
apani√hnu to deny, conceal,
apani√lī to hide oneself, disappear,
apāṇipāda without hands and feet,
apanirvāṇa mfn not yet extinct
āpanna 143/1 entered, got in, gained, obtained, acquired, afflicted, unfortunate
apannadat mfn (whose) teeth have not fallen out,
āpannasattva mfn pregnant,
apanodana mfn, n. removing, driving away
apānṛta mfn free of falsehood,
apa√3.nu to put aside,
apa√nud cl 6 –nudati, to push or drive away, to remove, dispel,
apanudyāt it should remove, it should take away/dispel 1/s/opt/act
apāpa 54/2 mfn. sinless, virtuous, pure
-viddha not afflicted with evil
apa√pad to escape, run away 50/1
apapādatra mfn having no protection for the feet, shoeless,
apāpakāśin mfn not ill-looking, revealing virtue,
apapāṭha m. a mistake in reading, a wrong reading in a text, 50/1
apapra√1.gā to go away from, yield to,
apapradāna n. a bribe,
apara 50/2 mfn. 1. having nothing beyond or after, having no rival or superior,
2.posterior, later, latter, following, inferior, lower, other, another, distant, opposite *aparā* the west, lower, inferior (used in the Upanishads to describe knowledge relating to the phenomenal world) , (*am*) n. the future, ind. in future, for the future, again, moreover, in the west of (5th), (*eṇa* with 2nd) ind. behind, west, to the west of,
apāra mfn not having an opposite shore, unbounded, boundless, (*am*) n. a bad shore 'the reverse of *pāra',* a kind of mental indifference or acquiescence, the reverse of mental acquiescence, the boundless, sea,
-pāra mfn carrying over the boundless sea of life, (*am*) n. non-acquiescence,
aparabhāva m. after-existence, succession, continuation,
aparābhāva m.the state of not succumbing, not breaking down,
aparabrahman (W) the Supreme Brahman as conditioned by attributes, it is immanent, limited and with name and form, master of the universe, ... omnipresent, omnipotent, creator, sustainer, destroyer, (in Advaita Vedānta), *saguṇa-brahman* or *īśvara*
apara brahman " a synonym for *saguṇa brahman*" HH
apa√rādh to miss (one's aim), to wrong, offend against, to offend, sin,
aparāddha mfn having missed, offended or sinned, criminal, guilty, erring
aparāddhi f. wrong, mistake,

aparāddhṛ mfn offending, an offender,
aparādha m. offence, transgression, crime, sin, fault, mistake, mfn guilty,
aparādhin mfn offending, criminal, guilty, m.one guilty of offence
aparāga m. aversion, antipathy,
aparaja mfn born later
aparājiṣṇu mfn unconquerable, invincible,
aparājita mfn unconquered, unsurpassed,
aparakāla m. a later period
aparakta mfn changed colour, grown pale, disaffected, disloyal, unfavourable,
aparaloka m. another world, paradise,
aparam mfn posterior, later, latter, following, western, inferior, lower, m. the hind foot of n elephant, f. the west, the hind quarter of an elephant, the womb, the future, n. the future, ind. in future, for the future, again, moreover, west,
aparamārtha (W) not real, relative,
aparaṁ ca and another thing, and further, moreover,
aparāmṛṣṭa mfn untouched, 51/1
aparāṅmukha mfn not having an averted face, i.e. not turning the back,
aparamukta (W) souls failing to understand, unliberated beings,
aparapakṣa m. latter half of the month, other or opposing side, defendant,
aparapara one and the other, various
aparapuruṣa m. a descendant,
aparasad mfn being seated behind,
aparaspara one after the other
aparaśvas ind. the day after tomorrow
aparata mfn turned off from, unfavourable to,
aparatā f. *tva* n. distance, posteriority (place or time), opposition, contrariety, relativeness, nearness,
aparatra ind. in another place,
apararātra m. the latter half of the night, the last watch, end of the night,
aparava m. contest, dispute, discord
aparavarṣā f. pl. the latter half of the rains
apara- vidyā knowledge of the material world, worldly knowledge,
aparavojjhita mfn free from dispute, undisturbed, undisputed,
apare some, others, 1/pl/m
apariccheda m. want of distinction or division, want of discrimination or judgment, continuance,
aparicchinna mfn connected, unlimited, without interval or division, uninterrupted, infinite, never-ending
aparicita mfn unacquainted with, unknown,
aparigata mfn unobtained, unknown,
aparigraha m. non-acceptance, renouncing, deprivation, destitution, mfn destitute, without possessions, the concept of non-possessiveness-limiting possessions to what is necessary or important, absence of avarice, non-clinging,
aparigrāhya mfn unfit or improper to be accepted, not to be taken,
aparihāṇa or *aparhāṇa* n. the state of not being deprived of anything,
a-pariharaṇīya mfn. not to be avoided, inevitable, not to be abandoned or lost, not to be degraded,
aparihārya gve. unavoidable, unable to be got around,
aparihvṛta mfn unafflicted, not endangered, approved,
aparijāta mfn not completely grown (an embryo) i.e. prematurely born, stillborn,
aparijñānam 'want of knowledge of reality' (Gam.)
aparikhedita mfn not afflicted, exhausted, depressed or destroyed, indefatigability,
aparikleśa mfn lack of annoyance,
aparikṣita mfn untried, unproved, not considered, inconsiderate,
aparīkṣita mfn untried, unproved,
aparimāna mfn without measure, immeasurable, immense, n. immeasureableness,
aparimeya 51/2 immeasurable, illimitable,
aparimita mfn unmeasured, indefinite , unlimited,
aparimita dṛṣṭi the view transcending the limitation of space, time and causation,
aparimlāna m. not withering, not decaying,
aparimoṣa m. not stealing,
aparimsya mfn immeasureable, illimitable,
apariṇāma m. unchangeableness,
apariṇāmin mfn unchanging,
apariṇīya ind. without any leading around,
aparipakva mfn not quite ripe, mature,
aparisamāptika mfn not ending, endless,
aparisara mfn non-contiguous, distant,
apariśeṣa mfn not leaving a remainder, all-surrounding, all enclosing

apariṣkāra m. want of polish or finish, coarseness, rudeness,
aparīta mfn unobstructed, irresistible
aparitoṣa mfn unsatisfied, discontented
apariveṣaṇa absence of - *pariveṣaṇa* 601/1attendance, waiting, distributing food, n circumference, the rim of a wheel
apariviṣṭa mfn not enclosed, unbounded,
aparṇa mfn leafless,
aparodha m. exclusion, prohibition,
aparokṣa 51/3 not invisible, perceptible, in the sight of, directly knowable, direct and actual experience, immediate and direct perception of one's own self, (Vimuktananda)
aparokṣajṇāna direct knowledge of Brahman
aparokṣānubhāva-svarūpa the essence of direct intuitive perception; of the nature or form of direct realisation, (U),
aparokṣānubhūti direct experience of the truth, self-realization,
aparokṣatva feeling of directness or immediateness, (U)
apartu mfn untimely, unseasonable, not the right time, not the season,
apa√2.rudh to expel, drive out,
aparūpa n. monstrosity, deformity, mfn ill-looking, odd-shaped,
aparyanta mfn unbounded, unlimited,
aparyāpta mfn *(a pari √āp)* mfn unable, incompetent, not enough, inadequate incomplete, insufficient, unlimited
aparyāya m. want of order or method,
apas 1. n. work, action, esp. sacred act, sacrificial act,
2. mfn active, skilful in any art, f. name of the hands and fingers (pl.) while engaged in certain religious tasks ,
3. mfn watery,
āpas n. a religious ceremony, water,
āpas-tattva water principle, (U)
apaśabda bad or vulgar speech, ungrammatical language
apa√sac to escape, evade,
apaśakuna n. a bad omen
apaśama m. cessation,
apaśaṅka mfn fearless, having no fear or hesitation, (*am*) ind. fearlessly,
apasara m. (in geom.) distance,
apasaraṇa n. going away, retreating,
apasāraṇa n. removing to a distance, dismissing, banishment,
apasarjana n. abandonment, gift or donation, final emancipation of the soul,
apasarpa m. a secret emissary or agent,
apasarpaṇa n. going back, retreating, moving away, escape,
apasiddhānta m. an assertion or statement contrary to orthodox teaching
apa√śiṣ to leave out,
apasmāra the desire to ignore the Truth HH epilepsy, want of memory, confusion of mind,
apasmṛti mfn forgetful, absent in mind, confused,
apasphur mfn bounding or bursting forth,
apaśoka mfn sorrowless,
apaśṝ mfn deprived of beauty
apāśraya 1. mfn helpless, destitute,
2. refuge, recourse, the person or thing to which recourse is had for refuge, the portion of a bed or couch on which the head rests, a yard or court awning
apā√śri P.A. *–śrayati (te)* to resort to, to use, practise,
apaśrita mfn retired, retreated, absconded
apāśrita mfn resting on, resorting to,
apa√sṛp Cl1 *apasarpati* gets away, escapes,
apaṣṭhu mfn contrary, opposite, left, perversely, badly,
apaśuc m. without sorrow, the soul,
2. driving off by flames
apasvara m. an unmusical sound or note,
apaśya mfn not seeing,
apasya Nom P to be active,
2. mfn watery, melting, dispersing,
apasyā f. activity, mfn watery, melting, dispersing,
apaśyanā f. not seeing, Buddh.
apaśyat mfn not being in view of, not

noticing, not considering,
1/s/imperf./act he saw,
apaśyat 1/s/imperf./act he/she saw
ā√pat Cl1 *āpatati* to occur, befall, appear suddenly, hasten towards, fall out, happen,
āpatana n. reaching, coming, happening,
apataram ind. farther off
āpātaramaṇīya mfn good for the time being, 'beautiful at first sight; looking beautiful to the non-discriminative; superficially attractive and beautiful, (U)'
apatarpaṇa fasting (in sickness),
apatat he fell
apaṭha m. unable to read,
apatha n. not a way, absence of a road, pathless state, wrong way, deviation, heresy, heterodoxy, mfn pathless, roadless,
-*gāmin* mfn going by a wrong road, pursuing bad practices, heretical,
-*prapanna* mfn out of place, in the wrong place, 49/1
apathin m. absence of road,
apathya mfn unfit, unsuitable, inconsistent,
apathya-kārin traitor,
apati m. not a husband or master,
f. without a husband or master,
apatighnī mfn , f. not husband-slaying,
āpatkāla m. emergency, hard times, season or time of distress,
apatnīka mfn not having a wife,
where the wife is not present,
apātra 54/1 n. unworthy, undeserving
apa√trap to be ashamed or bashful
apatrapaṇa n. bashfulness
apa√tṛp caus. –*tarpayati* to starve, cause to fast
āpatti f. happening, occurring, fault, transgression, entering into relationship with, misfortune,
apattra mfn leafless,
apaṭu mfn not clever, awkward, uncouth, ineloquent, -*tva* n. awkwardness
apatya n. offspring, child, descendant,
-*tā* f. state of childhood,
apauruṣa n. unmanliness, superhuman power, mfn unmanly, superhuman,
apauruṣeya not coming from men, e.g. the Vedas, impersonal, 57/1
apa√vad to revile, abuse, distract, divert, console by tales,
apavāda m. evil-speaking, denial, refutation, negation, sublation, contradiction, exception, command, withdrawal of the *adhyāropa* or superimposed attribute,
in Buddhism – the mistake of regarding as non-existent something which does exist,
apavādaka mfn blaming, defaming,
apavāda-yukti 'the employment of the logical method of *apavāda*
apavādin mfn blaming, decrying,
apavāhita mfn carry off, carried off,
apavana 1. mfn without air, sheltered,
2. n. a grove
apavāraṇa 52/2 n covering, concealment
apavarga m.completion, end, the emancipation of the soul from bodily existence, exemption from further transmigration, final beatitude, gift, donation, -*da* mfn conferring final beatitude,
apavārita mfn covered, concealed,
(-*am)* ind. in theatrical language as an aside, secretly, apart, aside,
apavarjana n. completion, discharging a debt or obligation, final emancipation or beatitude,
apavarjanīya mfn to be avoided,
apavarjita mfn abandoned, quitted, got rid of, given or cast away, made good (as a promise), discharged (as a debt), M. fulfilled,
apavarjya ind. p. excepting, except
apavarṇa mfn faulty/incorrect sound,
apa√2.vas to drive off by excessive brightness, to become extinct,
apavarta m. reduction to a common measure (in arithm. or alg.), the divisor,
apavartaka m. a common measure,
apavat mfn watery
apa√ve to unweave what has been woven
apa√ven to turn away from,

apa√veṣṭ to strip off
apa√vī *-veti* to turn away from, be unfavourable to,
apa√vic cl 7 –vinakti to single out from, select
apaviddha mfn pierced, rejected, dismissed, *-leka* mfn 'who has given up the world'
apavighna mfn unobstructed, unimpeded,
apa√viś to send away,
apavitra mfn impure,
apa√1.vṛ to open, uncover, exhibit,
apa√vṛj *-vṛṇakti,* cl 7 turn away, caus. *–varjayati* gets rid of, fulfils,
apa√vraj to go away,
apavrata mfn disobedient, unfaithful, perverse, stubborn,
apavṛkta mfn finished, completed,
apavṛkti f. fulfilment, completion
apāvṛnoti 54/3 opens, uncovers, reveals √*vṛ*
apāvṛnu open! reveal! 1/s/pres/impv
apavṛta mfn uncovered, opened up,
apāvṛta 54/3 mfn. open, unconcealed, unrestrained, self-willed,
apavṛtta mfn reversed, inverted, overturned, finished, carried to the end, 52/2
apa-vy-ā-√1.dā to open (the lips)
apa-vy-ā-√hṛ to speak wrongly or unsuitably
apavyaya m. prodigality
apa√vye to extricate oneself, deny
apa√yā Cl2 *apayāti* to go away, depart, retire from,
apāya m. going away, departure, what takes one from the mark, danger, destruction, death, annihilation, injury, loss, misfortune, evil, calamity,
apāyin mfn going away, departing, vanishing, perishable, 56/2
apcara m. an aquatic animal, 47/3
apekṣā f. regard, expectation, need,
apekṣābuddhi f. (in Vaiśeṣika phil.) a mental process, the faculty of arranging and methodizing, clearness of understanding,
āpekṣika mfn having relation or reference to, relative,
āpekṣita mfn required, considered, expected, referred to, looked for, wished, (*ā*) f. expectation,
apeta mfn departed, free from, gone, lacking,
api 55/1 or sometimes *pi* expresses placing near or over, uniting to, annexing, reaching to, proximity etc. in later sanskrit *abhi* is frequently used instead,
as a separable adv. and, also, moreover, assuredly, besides, surely, very, even, even now, though, also,
apiapi or *apica* as well as, *na vāpi* or *na apivā* or *nacāpi* neither nor,
cāpi and (at the beginning of a sentence) *apica* moreover,
api nāma (with opt.) could it be that? if only,
api used to express emphasis in the sense of even, also, very, e.g. *anyad api* also another, something more,
api may be fixed to an interrogative to make it indefinite, e.g.
ko'pi anyone,
kutrāpi anywhere,
āpi m. friend, 'who stands near another'
apī (√i) *apy-eti* to go in or near, enter into or upon, to come near, approach, to partake, have a share in, to join
apibaddha mfn fastened,
api√bandh A. to fasten upon, put on a wreath
apibat drank
apibhāga mfn having part in, sharing in,
api√bhū to be in, to have part in,
api ca moreover
apicchila mfn clear, free from sediment,
apīcya mfn secret, hidden, very handsome,
āpīḍa m. compressing, giving pain, chaplet tied on the crown of the head,
apīḍā f. ind. not unwillingly
api√dah *-dahati* to touch with fire, singe,
apīḍana n. not giving pain, gentleness, kindness, 56/1
apīḍayant mfn non-oppressing,
api√dhā to place upon or into, put to, give to shut, close, cover, conceal,

apidhāna n. placing upon, covering, a lid, a cover, a cloth for covering,
api√dham to blow upon,
api√dhāv to run into,
api√gā to enter, get into, mingle with,
api√gam to go into, enter, approach, join,
apigīrṇa mfn praised,
api√grah to close the mouth or nose etc.
apiguṇa mfn excellent
apihita mfn. placed into, concealed, covered
api√hnu to refuse,
api√hve to call in addition to or besides
apija m. born after or in addition to,
apījū mfn impelling,
api√1.kṛ to bring into order, prepare, arrange
api√2.kṛt to cut off,
apimantra mfn giving an explanation or an account of,
api√mṛṣ A. to forget, neglect,
apinaddha mfn closed, concealed,
api√nah to tie on, tie up, close, stop up
apināma (at the start of a phrase) perhaps, in all probability, I wish that,
apīnasa m. dryness of the nose, loss of smell, cold,
api√nī to lead towards or to, bring to a state or condition,
api√pad to go in enter,
apipakṣa m. the region or direction to the side,
apipāsa mfn free from thirst or desire,
api√path caus. *–pāthayati* to lead upon a path,
apiprāṇa mfn uttered or produced with every breath,
api√pṛc to mix with,
apiripta mfn grown blind
api√ruh, apirohati, to grow together, grow whole again,
apisaṁgṛbhāya Nom P. to assume,
apisarvara mfn being at the beginning or end of the night
api√sic to sprinkle with,
api√sṛ to flow upon,
api√śī P. to break off,
api√sṛj to place to or upon, to add to, mingle to
apiśīrṇa mfn broken,
api√ṣṭhā to stand too near, stand in anyone's way
apiṣṭhita mfn approached,
apiśuna unmalicious, upright, honest,
apit 1. mfn not swelling, dry,
apīta mfn gone into, entered, f. entering into, dissolving, dissolution, 2. mfn not drunk, not having drunk,
api tu but, but yet,
apitva n. having part, share,
api√vap to scatter upon,
api√vat to understand, comprehend,
apivatī f. intelligible,
api√vṛ to conceal,
apivrata mfn sharing in the same religious acts, blood-related,
api√vṛt to throw into, 55/3
apivṛta mfn concealed, covered,
api√vye to cover,
api√yāc caus. *–yācayate* to despise
apiyat mfn entering the other world, dying, dissolving, disappearing,
apiyanti they merge,
ap-kṛtsna n. deep meditation performed by means of water,
a-pañcī-kṛta n. 'not made of the five gross elements', the five subtle elements,
āplāvya 144/3 ind. having washed, wetted or sprinkled, mfn serving for bathing bathing (anyone) to be washed, to be used as a bath, n. washing, bathing
*āpnoti*142/1 reaches, 1/s/pres/indic/act he/she/ it reaches, attains
āpnuvan pres.act.part. overtaking, meeting with, reaching, obtaining, experienced
āpnuyām I should attain, I should reach, may have, 3/s/opt/act √*āp*
apoha m. pushing away, removing, (in disputation) reasoning, arguing, denying, negating,
apohana 56/3 reasoning, arguing, denying
ā√pṝ Cl 9 *–pṛṇāti,* to fill up,
ā√prach Cl6 *āpṛcchati* takes leave of, says goodbye

apracyuta 57/2 mfn unmoved, not fallen or deviating from (with 5th), observing, following, unwavering,
āpradāna receive? (Manu 3.31 – some translators, others express doubt)
apradāya not offered, not offering
apradhāna mfn not principal, subordinate, secondary, *-tā* f., *tva* n. inferiority,
apraiṣyat he sent
apraja mfn having no offspring, childless, unprolific,
aprajñāta mfn undistinguished, not known, not known clearly, (*ā*) f. ignorance,
aprakāśa 57/2 not shining, unenlightened, dark, not visible,
aprakaṭa mfn unmanifested, unapparent, not published, concealed, hidden, (*am)* ind. without having been perceived,
aprākṛta 59/1 mfn. not principal, not original, G. 50 non-material, 'is eternal' HH,
apramā f. incorrect knowledge, a rule without authority,
apramāda m. care, vigilance, mfn careful, cautious, mindfully guarding,
apramādam ind. carefully, with attention
apramādin mfn careful, vigilant,
apramā nika mfn unauthentic, unauthoritative,
apramatta 58/2 mfn careful, attentive, vigilant, unerring, m. one who is careful,
apramattā sane, attentive to her husband, without inebriation,
aprameya 58/3 mfn. immeasurable, unlimited, unfathomable,
aprāṇa 59/2 1. m. no breath, 2. mfn inanimate, lifeless, without the vital force, Brahman,
aprāpya ind. not attaining or reaching, unobtainable, gerund *a pra√āp*
aprasiddha mfn not brought about, accomplished or established, not settled, unestablished, unusual, uncommon, of no real existence, not current, not generally known,
apratarkya mfn unimaginable, not to be discussed, undefinable, unthinkable, incomprehensible by reason,
apratibhā mfn modest, bashful, f. shyness, timidity,
apratīkāra 57/3 mfn unopposing, unresisting, without remedy, defenceless,
apratima mfn without match or equal,
apratipanna mfn unaccomplished, unascertained,
apratiṣṭha 58/1 mfn. having no solid ground, fluctuating, unsafe
apratisaṅkhyā-nirodha 'natural annihilation (G), 'cessation not dependent on a sublative act of mind' (U),
apratīta mfn not gone against, not withstood, invincible, not understood, uncommon (expression)
apratta mfn not given (in marriage), not given back,
apratyakṣa mfn not present to the sight, invisible, imperceptible, *-tā* imperceptibility, *śiṣṭa* mfn not distinctly taught,
āpravaṇa 144/2 mfn a little precipitous
apravartin mfn immovable
apravṛtti f. not proceeding, no further effect or applicability of a precept, abstaining from action, non-excitement, stagnation, ceasing to function as, want of news about,
aprayucchant mfn not heedless, watchful,
apṛcchat asked
aprīti 59/2 f dislike, aversion, enmity, m. a foe, an enemy,
apriya uncherished, unloved, disliked,
apṛthak (°g) 56/2 ind. not separately, with, together with, collectively,
apsaras f. a beautiful heavenly nymph, semi-divine wives of Gandharvas
āpta mfn trusted, respected, intimate, a trustworthy person, a sage or adept, competent person, reached, overtaken, met, received, gained, obtained, filled up, taken, come to, reaching to, abundant, full, complete, fit, true, clever,
āpta-dakṣiṇa mfn having or accompanied

by suitable presents,

āpta-dharma duty laid down by the great ones or sages (U)

āptakāma m. free from desires for everything, self-fulfilled, desiring the Self alone, a realised sage,

āptavāc f. a credible assertion or the assertion of a credible person, trustworthy testimony, the Veda, a Muni,

āptavacana (N) intuition of the Brahman, words of reliable authority,

āptavākya n. = *āptavacana* a correct sentence, the evidence of the wise, *veda* or *śruti*

āpti f. 142/2 reaching, meeting with, obtaining, attaining, abundance, fortune, fitness, aptitude, 'pervasiveness' (Gam.),

āptopadeṣa historical truth, reliable assertion, knowledge,

āptum 142/1 to reach, obtain, gain infin. √*āp*

āptvā having attained

aptya mfn watery

apuccha mfn tailless

apūjā f. irreverence, disrespect,

apuṁs m. not a man, a eunuch

apunar ind. not again, only once,

apunaranvaya mfn not returning, dead

apunarāvṛtti f. final exemption from life or transmigration,

*apunarbhava (*or *–bhāva)*not occuring again, exemption from further transmigration, final beatitude,

apunarukta (ti) mf no superfluous repetition

apuṇya mfn impure, wicked,
-*kṛt* acting wickedly, wicked,

apūpa m. a cake of flour or meal, a kind of fine bread, honeycomb, wheat,

apurāṇa mfn not old, modern, new,

apuruṣa mfn unmanly, a cruel man or servant,

apūrṇa mfn incomplete, not full, imperfect, deficient, n. incomplete number, fraction,

apūrva 56/2 mfn unprecedented, without prior cause), unrecorded, not having existed before, quite new, strange, unparalleled, incomparable, extraordinary, not first, n. the remote or unforeseen consequence of an act, a consequence not immediately preceded by its cause, without any cause preceding it, *(eṇa)* ind. never before,

apūrvatā f. incomparableness, strangeness, unprecedented, not having existed before, uncommon nature of proof,

apūrva vidhi (W) an injunction which enjoins something not previously known, an unknown or unseen injunction, 'enjoins an individual to a specific act for a particular result',

āpūrya having filled, filling, (gerund)

āpūryamāṇa mfn becoming filled or full pres/mid/part *ā*√*pṝ*

apuṣkala mfn not eminent, mean, low, empty of meaning, shallow,

apuṣṭa mfn unnourished, lean, soft, invalid, unimportant,

apūta mfn impure, not purified (by rites),

aputra m. not a son, mfn sonless,

apya mfn being in water, coming from water, connected with water,

āpya 1. mfn to be reached, obtainable, acceptable, (am) n. confederation, alliance, relationship, friendship, a friend, 2. mfn belonging or relating to water, watery, liquid, consisting of water, living in water,

apyaya m. joint, juncture, pouring out (of a river), entering into, vanishing,

apyayana n. union, copulating,

āpyāyana 144/1 mfn causing fullness or stoutness, increasing welfare, gladdening, n. satiating, satisfying, refreshing, pleasing, increasing, causing to thrive, satiety, satisfaction,

ara 86/2 mfn swift, speedy, little, m. the spoke or radius of a wheel, a Jaina division of time, name of an ocean, n. the spoke of a wheel,

āra m. brass, iron, a sting, an angle, a

corner, 2. a spoke,

ā√rabh Cl 1 *–rabhate,* grasp, take hold of, undertake, make an effort to achieve,

ārabdha ppp. having started, begun, commenced, undertaken,

ā-rabhate begins, commences, engages, lays or takes hold of, enters, reaches, attains,

ārabhya having begun, beginning with, having performed,

ā√rādh caus. *–rādhayati,* Cl 1 *–rādhate,* to propitiate, honour, strive to obtain the favour of or gain a boon from,,

ārādha m. gratification, paying homage,

ārādhana 150/2 mfn. propitiating, rendering favourable to one self, (*am*) n. homage, worship, adoration (*ā*) f. worship, homage, propitiation of the deities,

ārādhita ppp. propitiated, honoured, pleased

ārāga m. dispassion, through the sky,

arāla mfn curved, crooked,

aram ind. so as to fit or suit, ready, at hand, enough, with *kṛ* make ready, serve, with *gam* attend upon,

ārāma 150/1 m. delight, pleasure

aramat rejoiced

ā-rambha 150/1 m. undertaking, beginning, a thing begun, origin, mental initiation of an action, *saṅkalpa,*

ā-rambhakopadhāna 'material cause which gives birth to an effect as an essentially different entity, e.g. atoms of the Vaiśeṣika School' (U),

ā-rambha upādāna 'material cause which is distinguishable from its effect as cloth is different from threads in some respects,' (U)

ā-rambha-vāda 'The theory of causation that states the effect is a new production from the cause. The cause is one thing and the effect another.' Nyāya Vaiśeṣika theory (G)

araṇa mfn distant, strange, foreign, a refuge, without fighting (as death),

araṇi f. piece of (*sami* tree) wood for kindling fire by friction,

araṇya n. wilderness, forest, 'strange land'

*āraṇyaka*149/3 mfn. forest, wild, forest-born, name of a class of religious and philosophical writings closely connected with the Brāhmanas, the name indicating written or studied in forests, the *upaniṣad*s are considered to be attached to them, forest discussion of *vedā–*

araṇya 86/3 n. a foreign or distant land, a wilderness, desert, forest

araṇyānī f. wilderness, large forest,

araṇyarājya n. forest sovereignty,

araṇyavāsin mfn living in the forest,

arapas mfn without infirmity, whole,

√ararya P *araryati* to work with an awl

ārāt ind. from a distant place, distant, to a distant place, far from, near, directly, immediately,

arati 86/3 f. dissatisfaction, discontent, anxiety, regret, distress

arāti f. non-liberality, malignity (personified), pl. malign hags, m. (is) an enemy

āratī a lamp waving ceremony as an act of worship, crying out desparately for help,

ārati a ritual to ward off jealousy

aravinda n. a lotus, the Indian Crane, copper,

arāya m. an evil spirit

√arb 93/1 cl 1 P *arbati* to go, to hurt, DP in *gati* going

arbha mfn little, small, unimportant m. child, boy

arbhaka mfn small, minute, young, childish

arbhaga mfn youthful

arbuda m. a serpent-like demon, a swelling, tumour, n. ten millions,

√arc 89/3 cl 1 P *arcati,* shine, be brilliant, praise, sing, honour, *arcitum* infin. to shine, DP in *pūjā* worshipping

arc 2. m. shining, brilliant

arcā f. worship, adoration, an image or idol to be worshipped,

arcaka mfn honouring, worshipping, m. a worshipper

arcas n. worship, praise,
arcana 90/1 mfn. honouring, praising,
n. f. homage paid to deities and to superiors, worshipping an image of the divine, 'offering of flowers and sacred leaves etc. at the time of worship, uttering the names of the object of worship' (U),
arcat mfn (pres.part.) shining, praising,
arcāvatāra a consecrated image,
arci 90/1 m. ray, flame,
arcimat or *–vat* mfn shining, blazing, bright,
arcis n. flame,
arciṣmat mfn brilliant, resplendent, m. fire, the god of fire, a stage through which a *bodhisattva* must pass,
arcitvā gerund from *ṛc* having worshipped, worshipping, worshipping in this way, after worshipping,
√*ard* 91/3 cl 1 P *ardati* to go, move, be moved, be scattered (as dust), dissolve, torment, hurt, kill, ask, beg for, DP in *gati* going, moving or *yācana* begging, asking, cl10 in *hiṁsā* injuring
ardana 91/3 moving restlessly, disturbing, distressing, annihilating,
n. pain, trouble,
ardha 1. m. side, part, place, region
2.mfn half (portion), m. the half, forming a half,
ardhāṅginī partner in life (wife), better half,
ardharātra m. midnight,
ardhaspṛṣṭa 'half–contacted' sibilant sounds,
ardhika mfn amounting to half,
ārdra mfn wet, fresh, moist, tender,
ārdrabhāva 152/1m wetness
dampness, tenderness of heart
ārdravāsas mfn having wet garments,
ārdrendhana wet or green firewood/fuel,
are a word of address, Ah! (voc. of *ari)*
argha m. worth, price,
arghya mfn of price (or) that may be priced, deserving a respectful, reception,
n. an offering of water or a garland,
√*arh* 93/3 cl 1 P *arhati*, (rarely A *arhate*), to deserve, merit, be worthy of, have a claim to, to be worth, should, ought, counterbalance, be able,
DP in *pūjā* honouring, worshipping
arha 93/3 mfn meriting, deserving, obliged, proper, fit, worthy of, proper,
n. worship,
arhaka mfn comp. entitled to,
arhanta mfn worthy, m. a Buddha, a buddhist mendicant, 'destroyer of the enemies' i.e. passions, in Jainism enlightened or holy one, the fourth stage in an aspirant's spiritual evolution – perfection of non-violence,
arhat a buddhist stage of enlightenment,
mfn deserving, entitled to, worthy, respectable, venerable, m. a superior divinity with the Jainas, an intensely spiritual being radiating purity to all,
arhati is worthy, is able, is capable
√*arh* 93/3 to be worthy of
be allowed to do anything
be obliged or required to do ..
he ought, should (with infinitive)
ari 87/3 1. mfn faithful, attached to, pious, 2. greedy, 3. mfn. envious, hostile, m. an enemy
ariṣṭa mfn unharmed,
ariṣṭanemi name of a king, the felly of whose wheel is unharmed,
ariṣṭatāti f. without harm, health,
mfn making auspicious/fortunate,
arisūdana slayer of the enemy, name for *Kṛṣṇa*
√*arj* 90/1 cl1 P *arjati* to procure, acquire,
DP in *arjana*, gaining, earning,
A cl 10? *arjate* to go, stand firm, procure, be of good health,
DP in *pratiyatna* care bestowed on anything, endeavour, preparation
arjana 90/1 procuring, acquiring, gaining, earning
ārjava 151/3 straightness, honesty, sincerity, rectitude, virtue, renouncing deception and wrongdoing,
arjayitvā 90/1 *arjayati* he acquires, part. having acquired

arjuṇa a prince and a principal in the *bhagavad gītā,* mfn silver-white
√*ark* 89/1,2 *arkayati* to heat, to praise, DP in *stavana* praising, *tapana*, heating, warming
arka 89/1 m. a ray, flash of lightning, the sun, copper, praise, hymn
alakṣya mfn insignificant in appearance, unmarked, invisible, unobserved, not indicated, having no particular marks,
ālakṣya mfn scarcely visible, visible, apparent, ind. having observed or beheld
arṇas 90/2 m.n. a wave, flood, stream, the ocean, m. a letter, syllable, the teak tree, *(ā)* f. a river,
arṇava 90/2 mfn. agitated, foaming, restless, m. a wave, flood, the foaming sea, the ocean of air, m.n. the sea, *-ja* m. sea-born, cuttlefish, the earth, *-pati* m. lord of the seas (the ocean), *-potam.* a boat or ship,
arpaṇa n. the sending, consignment, entrusting, procuring, inserting, fixing, piercing, placing in or upon,
arpayati causes to partake of, inflicts, injures, settles, 1/s/pres/caus. √*ṛ*
arodat cried, wailed
aroga mfn not having disease, healthy,
ārogya 151/2 n. freedom from disease, health, mfn healthy, giving health,
āroha m. one who mounts or ascends, one who is seated in a carriage, ascent, rising, mounting, haughtiness, pride, the swelling hips or buttocks of a woman, increase, the hip-seat on which an infant is carried, a particular measure, a chief elephant driver,
ārohaka mfn ascending, rising, raising up, m. a rider, a tree,
ārohaṇa mfn. 151/2 arising, ascending, n. the act of rising, a carriage, a ladder, staircase,
ārohati climbs
āropa 151/1 m. imposing (as a burden), burdening with, placing in or on, super-imposition, arousing consciousness,
āropita mfn raised, elevated, fixed, placed, made, strung (as a bow), interposed, imposed, accidental, adventitious,
arpaṇa 92/3 mfn. procuring, consigning, entrusting, n. inserting, fixing, offering, entrusting, giving back, placing in or upon,
arpiṣa n. fresh meat,
arpita 92/3 mfn fixed upon (eyes or mind) placed, entrusted, thrown, delivered,
arṣa relating to or derived from the *ṛṣi*, 'that which comes from a *ṛṣi'*
arṣat he ran (*īṣā Up.*)
arṣati √ *ṛṣ* to flow, flow quickly, moves with a quick motion, to spear, perforate, pierce,
ārta mfn. pained, distressed, L. mfn visited esp. by trouble, afflicted,
√*arth* 90/2 cl 10 A, *arthayate*, to strive to obtain, desire, wish, request, ask for, to point out the sense of , comment upon, DP in *upa-yācñā* requesting, begging, supplicating
artha n.m. 1. aim, object, purpose, errand, sake, intent, meaning,
2. object, thing, object of the senses, matter, cause, motive, reason, business, substance,
3. advantage, profit (with 3rd), wealth, property,
artham and *arthe* for the purpose of, for the sake of, on account of, for, (frequently ifc.),
arthābhāsa (N) false appearance as objects, (related to self-manifestation in the appearance of an object), appearance of an object,
artham *artham* and *arthe* for the purpose of, for the sake of, on account of, for, (frequently ifc.),
arthāntaranyāsa m. substantiation, introduction of some other matter, antithesis,
arthāpatti assumption, inference from circumstances, one of the proofs of

knowledge,
arthārjana 91/2 acquisition of property
arthāpatti f. inference from circumstances,
arthārtha mfn effective for accomplishment of the aim in view, ind. on account of money, longing for wealth,
arthārthatattvajña mfn knowing the essence of the very aim of anything, knowing thoroughly,
arthatattva n. true state of the matter, the real object or nature or cause of anything, the true state of a case, fact of the matter,
arthārthin mfn selfish, desirous of gaining wealth or making a profit, (*ā*) f. desire of wealth,
arthavāda m. explanation of the meaning (of any precept), speaking for gain, praise, eulogium, persuasive expression,
'corroborative statements (3 kinds)-
(a) *guṇavāda* – attributive corroborative statement, e.g. "the sun becomes the sacrificial stake", where the statement contradicts experience and is taken to mean "a stake shining like the sun"
(b) *anuvāda* reassertive corroborative statement e.g. "Fire is the remedy for cold", in which a known fact is restated.
(c) *bhūtārthavāda* factual corroborative statement e.g. "Indra raised his thunderbolt against Vṛtra" a fact known from the Vedas alone.' (Gam.),
arthāya for the purpose of, 4/s/m
arthayate (ti) A. P. seeks for an object
arthin mfn having an object, desiring, seeking, needy, wishing for, begging, 91/3 active, industrious, one who wants or desires anything, longing for, m. a beggar, petitioner, wooer, a plaintiff, prosecutor, one who supplicates with prayers,
arthotsarga m. expenditure of money,
arthya mfn wealthy, proper, fit, rich, intelligent, wise, n. red chalk,
arti 90/2 pain, L. f. a visitation (of evil), i.e. trouble, misfortune,
ārti 149/2 pain, injury distress, the end of a bow,
ārūdha 151/1 mfn. mounted, ascended, undertaken, reached,
ā√ruh -Cl 1 *–rohati,* rise up to, mount, ascend,
āruhya 151/1 ind. having mounted or ascended, riding
arūkṣa mfn not of cruel or crooked disposition, soft,
arula n. water, a small, boat,
aruṇa mfn the colour red, ruddy, reddish,
arundhatī f. name of the morning star, wife of *Vasiṣṭha,*
arundhati-nyaya The star Arundhati is rarely visible to the naked eye; to point it out, therefore, some very big star near it is shown at first as Arundhati; then it is rejected and a smaller star is pointed out as Arundhati and so on till the actual Arundhati is located. This method of leading from the gross to the more subtle is called Arundhati-nyaya. This method is followed specially in Indian philosophy where in the beginning men are goaded to have faith in the lower form of worship with the help of Agamas and Tantras; then guided to the Bhakti method or the dualistic religion of the Puranas; then, again, to the rigour of the Smritis, and finally, to the non-dual (Advaita) Vedanta of the Upanishads and Ajati- vada. (Compare this with the Bhramara-kita-nyaya which is a direct meditation on the Absolute at one stretch without any such preliminary stages of religion as in the case of the former.) (U)
arūpa emancipation, formless,
arūpaloka the world of the formless,
arūpaka mfn formless,
āruruksu 151/1 mfn. desirous to rise, ascend

or advance, 'one who is attempting to rise to the state of yoga' (U),

aruṣ mfn not angry, good tempered,

aruṣa mfn or *aruṣī* f. ruddy,

√*arv* 93/2 cl 1 P *arvati* to hurt, kill DP in *hiṁsā* hurting, injuring,

arvācīna mfn turned towards, favouring, turned towards (in a hostile manner),

arvāk 93/2 ind. before (time), from a certain point (with 3rd), on this side, before, after, (with 7th) within, near,

arvākkālikatā f. the belonging to a proximate time, the state of being more modern (than anything else),

arvāṇc mfn directed towards this place,

arvaśa mfn running, quick

arya mfn faithful, attached, kindly, favourable, devoted, dear,

ārya L. mfn belonging to the faithful, (as) m. man of one's own tribe, an Aryan, mfn Aryan, noble one, reverend, (used in respectful address),

aryaman m. bosom-friend, esp. a bride-groom's friend, the sun,

Aryaman 93/1 chief of the departed spirits

āryaputraḥ son of a noble one

āryasatya n. noble or sublime truth

√*aś* 112/2 cl 5 A *aśnute* (Vedic *aśnoti),* to reach, come to, arrive at, get, gain, obtain, to visit, to master, become master of, to offer, enjoy, pervade, penetrate, fill, accumulate DP in *vyāpti* pervading and *saṁdhāta* accumulating

2. *aśnāti* cl 9 to enjoy, to cause to eat, feed, DP in *bhojana* eating

√*aṣ* 116/1 cl 1 P *aṣati,* A *aṣate,* to go, move, shine, take or receive, DP in *gati* going, *dīpti* shining, *ādāna* taking or seizing

√*as* 117/1 cl 2 P *asti,* to be, live, exist, be present, to take place, happen, to abide, dwell, stay, to belong to, to fall to the share of, happen to anyone, to be equal to, turn out, tend towards any result, prove (w 4th), to become, to be, DP in *bhū* being,

2. cl 4 P *asyati* to throw, cast, shoot at, to drive or frighten away, DP in *gati* going, *dīpti* shining, *ādāna* taking or seizing,

3. *asati, asate,* see √*aṣ* DP in *gati* going, *dīpti* shining, *ādāna* taking or seizing,

ās 1. ind. interjection implying – joy, anger, menace, pain, recollection

√*ās* 2. 159/3 cl 2 A *āste* and *āsate*, to be present, exist, to sit, sit down, rest, dwell in, abide, remain, make one's abode in, continue, continue doing anything, to cease, have an end, solemnize, celebrate, do anything without interruption, continue in any situation, to last, DP in *upaveśana* sitting down

3. P. *asyati* to throw upon, lay or put upon,

4. n. mouth, face, by word of mouth, before one's eyes, personally, present, in one's own person, immediately

āśa m. food, reaching, obtaining,

āsa there was, m. the posterior of the body, ashes, dust, n. a bow,

āśā 157/1 f. wish, desire, hope, expectation, prospect, region, quarter of the sky,

aśabda mfn soundless, (*am*) ind. soundless (refers to Brahman) (U),

ā√*sad* caus. *āsādayati* to reach, overtake, find, acquire,

asadāvaraṇa 'a power of *āvaraṇa śakti* which screens the existence of Brahman and which makes us think there is no Brahman; it is removed through *aparokṣa jñāna* (direct knowledge),' (U)

asadbhāva m. non-existence, absence, an evil temperament or disposition,

āṣāḍhaḥ name of a month (corresponding to parts of June and July),

asādhāraṇa mfn not common, special,

asādhāraṇa kāraṇa uncommon cause

asādhāraṇa nimitta primary or chief cause,

asaddhetukam having an unreal thing for a cause, the product of an unreality

(Gam.),

asādhu mfn not good, wicked, evil, disgrace, m. a wicked man, n. anything bad or evil, ind. interjection – bad! shame!

asādhya mfn not proper or able to be accomplished, not to be effected or completed, incurable, not to be overpowered, not susceptible of proof,

asadrūpa imperceptible to the senses,

āsādya attaining, approaching, having attained/approached, confronting,

asaha 120/1 mfn not able to , intolerant of, impatient, incapable of bearing or producing young, n. the middle of the breast,

āsakta mfn fastened, fixed, attached to, accompanied or furnished with, following directly, immediately proceeding from (2nd), intent on, zealously following or pursuing,

āsakti f. adherence, intentness (on),

aśana n. food, eating, mfn reaching (across), reaching,

asaṅga 118/1 mfn free from ties, independent, unattached, m. non-attachment, non-inclination, ind. non-impediment (3rd), unobstructedly or at pleasure (5th),

aśaṅka mfn without hesitation, fearless, secure, certain, to be relied on, ind. fearless,

aśaknuvant mfn not being able, being unable to bear,

asakta 118/1 mfn not stopped or intercepted by or at, unattached, detached from worldly feelings, not hanging on to, not clinging, ind. without obstacle or resistance, uninterruptedly, immediately, at once, eternal, continual,

āsakta 160/1 mfn. fixed or fastened to, attached to, intent on, wound round, encircled, accompanied or furnished with, following directly, immediately proceeding from, n. darkness,

aśakta 112/3 mfn. unable, incompetent,

aśakti mfn inability, disability, without power or energy, incapability,

āsaktamanas 160/1 mfn. having the mind deeply engaged in or fixed upon (any object), intent on, devoted to, absorbed in

asakti 118/1 f. being detached from worldly feelings or passions

aśakya mfn impossible, impracticable, not to be overcome, invincible,

āsam I was

aśama 113/1 disquietude, uneasiness, 'not resting',

asamañja a son of Sagara by Keśini, 'unbecoming, good for nothing'

asamāpya not having attained or obtained, not completing,

asamartha 119/1 mfn. unable to, not having the intended meaning, n. incapability of

asamavāyi 'not intimately related; a cause forming part of an effect; not being the substance', (U)

asamavāyi kāraṇa n. accidental cause, 'non-concomitant cause; the wheel and stick of the potter that help in the manufacture of the pot,' (U)

asambaddha mfn unconnected, incoherent, without meaning or absurd (words),

asaṁbandha 119/2 mfn unconnected, separate, not closely associated, distant, not related, want of relationship, incoherent, not meaningful, absurd,

asaṁbhava m. 'non-existence', destruction, non-happening, cessation, interruption, absence of, want, impropriety, inconsistence, impossibility,

asaṁbhāvanā f. not regarding as possible, impossibility of comprehending, want of respect, spiritual doubt having the nature of improbability or impossibility,

asambhāvya mfn not supposable, impossible, inconceivable,

incredible,

asambhūti f. non-existence (unborn), destruction, *prakṛti* as primal material cause,

asaṁbodha m. non-knowledge, ignorance, mfn unconfined, spacious, wide, large, unobstructed, unimpeded, scarcely, frequented, *(am)* n. non-confinement, open space,

asaṁdigdha mfn not indistinct, undoubted, unsuspected, certain, *(am)* ind. without any doubt, certainly,

asaṁhita mfn unconnected, unsteady,

asaṁhrādayant mfn not causing to rattle,

asaṁjñin unreasonable, not having reason, without rationality,

āśaṁkā f. fear, apprehension, doubt, uncertainty,

asaṁkhya mfn countless,

asaṁkhyāta innumerable, number without end,

asaṁkrāntam 'unassociated with any other object' (Gam.),

asaṁmūḍha mfn free from delusion, deliberate,

asampatti f. non-success, failure, not being sufficient,

asaṁprajñāta samādhi - the consciousness of the object of meditation is transcended,

asaṁsakta 117/3 unconnected, incoherent, not joining (eyebrows), separate, indifferent,

asaṁsakti the fifth stage of realisation, "attachments very close to the individual begin to drop"

asaṁśaya 117/3 m. absence of doubt, certainty, surely, without doubt

asaṁśayam adv. without doubt, surely

asaṁskrita mfn not consecrated, not originated or constructed, not prepared, unadorned, unpolished

asaṁtoṣa m. displeasure, dissatisfaction,

asaṁvedana n. 'non-receptivity of the mind; imperishable state of quiescent *jñāna* ; *nirvikalpa samādhi ;* thoughtless state,' (U)

asamyagdarśana n. consciousness of the objective universe; imperfect vision,

asamyagdarśin 'a person who has not risen to perfect knowledge; one who has no proper vision and has the consciousness of the world',

asamyak ind. wrongly, incorrectly,

asaṁyama m. non-restraint (as of one's senses),

asaṁyata 117/2 mfn not kept together, not shut (as a door), unbridled,

asan in comp. for *asat,*

āsan they were

aśana n. food, eating, mfn reaching, reaching across,

asana 117/2 n throwing, sending a shot, mfn one who throws or discharges f *(ā)* a missile, an arrow

āsana 159/3 2. *ās* to sit, be present, exist, *āsana* n. sitting, sitting down, sitting in particular posture, the manner of sitting forming part of the eightfold observances of ascetics, a seat, couch, place, stool, abiding, dwelling, maintaining a post against an enemy, f. stay, abiding,

aśanāya Nom P. *°yati* to desire food, be hungry,

aśanāyā f. desire of eating or consuming, hunger, 112/3

aśanāya °ti, (or -nāyā) to desire food, be hungry

aśanāyita mfn hungry,

aśanāyāpipāṣe f. du. hunger and thirst

asaṅga 118/1 mfn free from ties, independent, moving without obstacle, having no attachment or inclination for or interest in, m. non-attachment, non-inclination, non-impediment, generally without obstacle,

asaṅga-bhāvanā 'feeling or attitude of the mind, of non-attachment',

asaṅgatā f. non-attachment,

asaṅgena ind. without obstacle,

asaṅgin mfn not attached to the world, free from worldly desire,

asaṅgo-ayam-puruṣaḥ 'this Self is unattached (referring to Brahman)

aśani f. a bolt of lightning, the tip

of a missile, a hailstone,

ā√śaṅk Cl1 *āśaṅkate* fears, doubts, suspects, is afraid,

āśaṅkā f. fear, apprehension, uncertainty,

āsanna 160/2 mfn. seated down, set down, near, proximate, *(am)* n. nearness, end, death

asanskāra 117/3 non consecration, want of embellishment or care, natural state

asant mfn non-existing, n. non-existence,

aśānta 113/1 restless, violent, wild, unconsecrated, not sacred,

aśānti f. restlessness, distraction, absence of peace of mind,

āśāpāśa trap of hope, shackles in the form of hope

asapatna n. unrivalled, without a rival, undisturbed condition,

āśāpratīkṣe hope and expectation

asāra 120/2 mfn spoiled, unfit, sapless, without strength or value, worthless, faithless, m. worthlessness, dry, barren, without essence,

āsāra m. pouring rain, surrounding an enemy, incursion, attack,

aśaraṇa mfn helpless, without help, defenceless, without refuge, m. helpless person, n. not proceeding, not going,

aśaraṇya mfn without refuge, wanting refuge, not yielding refuge,

aśarīraka mfn bodiless

asarvopayoga
asarva not whole, incomplete
upayoga employment, use, application, consuming, taking, any act leading to a desired end engagement, contract, use, fitness

aśas 113/1 mfn cursing, hating, aversion

āśas f. wish, hope, desire, praise,

aśastra n. unarmed, without weapon, having no invocation,

aśāśvata mfn impermanent, inconstant

asat 118/2 not being, not existing, unreal, non-being, untruth, unrighteous,

asat sat false existence

asatas of the non-existent, of the unreal, pres.part. *a√as* 6/s/n

asatkṛta 118/2 badly treated, not treated respectfully or properly

āsatti f. vicinity, proximity, intimate union, uninterrupted sequence (of words),

asatya (N) lack of reality, 118/2 mfn untrue, false, lying, n. untruth, falsehood,

asatyasaṁdha mfn unfaithful, treacherous,

asau 18/1 (see *adas*) pron. that, a certain 1/s/m or f he, she, that

aśauca n. impurity, contamination, defilement, uncleanness,

āsava ' signifies attachments arising in the mind from the impact of outside influences, and the ideas born of outside influences that intoxicate the mind' 160/3 m. distilling, distillation, decoction, rum, the nectar or juice of a flower,

āśāvant mfn hopeful,

āśaya 157/3 resting place, abode, the mind, heart, soul , the seat of feelings and thoughts, thought, meaning, intention, disposition of mind, mode of thinking, the will, pleasure, virtue, vice, fate, fortune, property, a miser,

āśaya bīja potent seed, a seed containing a seed of potential diverse growth,

āścarya 158/1 n. a wonder, appearing rarely, curious, miracle, a prodigy, mfn marvellous,

āścaryavat adv. like a marvel, wondrously

āsecana 160/3 pouring into, wetting, sprinkling, cavity (into which one pours),

āsecanavant mfn having a cavity, hollow,

aśeṣa 113/3 without remainder, entire, perfect, all, wholly,
-tas ind. entirely, without exception,

aśeva mfn not dear, hostile, not causing pleasure, hostile

asi 120/2 m. a sword or knife, a shark, alligator,

asi 2/pres/indic/act of *as* to be thou art, you are

āsi you are

asiddha 120/3 mfn. imperfect, incomplete, unaccomplished, unproved, not existing or not having taken effect (e.g. a rule in grammar),

asiddhi f. non-attainment, failure, want of proof, conclusion not warranted by the premises,

āsīḥ you (s) were

āśi f. eating, P. to sharpen, make zealous,

āśin mfn eating (in compounds),

āsīn n. the act of sitting, sitting, posture, a posture in Yoga, a seat,

āśina 157/1 aged, eating 2. √*aś*

āśīrvāda m. expression of a (good) wish, i.e. a benediction, benison,

āśirvādābhidhānavant mfn containing a designation of a benediction,

aśīrya

āśīs 157/2 f. asking for, prayer, wish, blessing, benediction,

āsīt √*as* 1/s/impf/act was

āsīta he might sit, he should sit, 1/s/opt/mid √*ās*

Asitaḥ Devala a legendary sage

aśīti eighty,

aśiva mfn unkind, unfriendly, inauspicious,

āśīvarda m. a blessing, benediction,

ā√*skand* Cl1 *āskandati* to leap upon, attack,

āskandana 161/1 going towards, assailing attack, battle, reproach, abuse,

aślīla mfn ugly, vulgar, coarse, low abuse,

aśliṣṭa mfn incoherent,

aśma 114/1 a stone

asma pron. stem we, us

āsma pron. we (pl) were

asmābhiḥ pron. by us pl.

asmabhyam pron. for us pl.

asmad pron. personal pronoun base, I we, us, at beginning of a compound

asmadīyaiḥ our

asmadīya our

asmākam pron. of us, ours, our 6/pl.

aśman m. 1. stone, 2. thunderbolt, 3. vault of heaven,

asmān pron. us 2nd pl.

aśmanvant mfn stony,

asmaraṇa n. not remembering,

asmāsu pron. in us pl.

asmat pron. from us (pl.

asmi verb to be 1/s/pres/act I am

asmin pron. 7/s in this

asmitā f. egoism, 'by which a person appropriates undeserved attributes to himself' (U), 'erroneous identification of the Self with the mind-body complex' (G),

asmitā-nāśa destruction of egoism

asmṛti forgetfulness, state of unconsciousness

aśnan eating pres/act/part √*aś*

aśnat 114/1 part. eating

asnāvira 123/1 mfn. without sinews

asnihyat fell in love

aśnute attains, reaches, 1/s/pres/indic/mid √*aś*

aśobhana mfn disagreeable, vicious, bad, inauspicious, not beautiful,

a-śocya 114/1 mfn. not to be lamented

aśoka m. name of a tree, 'sorrowless', 'saraca asoca',

aśokavṛkṣaḥ a kind of tree with magnificent red flowers

aśoṣya ind. not to be dried, not able to be dried, withered, *a*√*śuṣ*

aspandamāna mfn free from vibration,

asparśa 123/1 mfn not having the faculty of perception by touch, intangible, m. non-contact with, touchless, name of Brahman,

asparśayoga the 'yoga of no contact' through control of *manas,* relates to exercises in the 3rd and 4th chapters of the *Māṇḍūkya-Kārikā,*

asphuṭa mfn not quite correct, indistinct, n. indistinct speech,

aspṛha 123/2 mfn desireless

aspṛśant mfn not touching,

aspṛśat mfn not touching,

aśraddha mfn (*ā*) f. want of trust, unbelief,

aśraddadhāna 114/2 mfn not trusting in, unbelieving, incredulous,

aśrama mfn indefatigable,

āśrama m.n.a halting place, stage of

life,158/2 one of 4 stages in the life of a *brāhman, (brahmacārin-* student of the *veda*, *gṛhastha-* household life, *vānaprastha-* forest life, - *saṁnyāsin-* abandoner of worldly concerns)
āśramin belonging to..one of the 4 stages
m. hermitage, abode of ascetics, the cell of a hermit or retired sages, a hut built on festive occasions, a college, school, a wood or thicket,

āśrama-dharma duties pertaining to the four orders or stages of life (U)

āśrama- karaṇī duties of the four stages of life,

āśramapada n. a hermitage, site of a hermitage, a period in the life of a Brahman,

aśrauṣam I have heard 3/s/aorist/act √*śru*

aśrauta non-scriptural, not *śruti,*

āśrava mfn listening to, obedient, compliant, m. promise, engagement,

āśraya 158/2 that to which anything is closely connected or on which anything depends or rests, resting place, place of refuge, shelter, depending on, having recourse to, help, assistance, protection, authority, sanction, warrant,

āśrayabhūta mfn having become a protector, i.e. a protector, one who is the refuge or support of another ,

āśrayet should cling to or lean on, 1/s/opt/act *ā√śri*

ā√śri Cl1 *āśrayati/te* to resort to, take shelter with, to affix, to apply anything, to adhere, rest on, depend on, to choose, prefer, to be subject to, keep in mind,

āśritya having resorted to, at, in, by,

asṛj or *asṛk* n. blood, saffron, m. Mars, a kind of religious abstraction,

asṛjata mfn created,

aśṛta mfn uncooked,

āśṛta mfn slightly cooked,

ā√śri Cl 1 *–śrayati,* to lean or rest on, happen to, befall, come to,

āśrita 158/3 atttaching ones-self to, joining, having recourse to, seeking refuge or shelter from, subject to, depending on, concerning, practising, observing, using

āśritya 158/3 part. employing, practising, having recourse to, taking refuge in, depending on ,

asṛj n. blood,

asṛjata created

aśṛṇot listened

asṛṣṭānna 121/3 mfn who does not distribute food, not offered, (as in sacrificial food not offered to Brāhmaṇas)

aśru 114/3 n. a tear (as in crying)

aśrumukha mfn tearful-faced,

aśru-pāta falling of tears

aśruvimocana releasing tears, crying

asta mfn thrown, cast, n. home, esp. of the sun, m. setting (the sun or other luminaries, end, death,

āsta pron. you (pl) were

aṣṭa eight

aṣṭādaśan eighteen,

aśṭadhā eightfold

āstam pron. you two were

āstām pron. they two were

aṣṭama mfn eighth,

astamauna mfn having thrown aside or abandoned silence,

aṣṭan eight,

aṣṭaṅgamana n. 'going home', setting of the sun or other celestial object,

aṣṭāṅga yoga of *pataṇjali* the eightfold *yoga* of p... consisting of *yama, niyama, āsana, prāṇāyāma, pratyāhāra, dhyāna, dhāraṇā, samādhi*

aṣṭāṅgapāta m a profound obeisance on hands, knees, feet, breast and face,

aṣṭāvakra a wise counsellor of king *Janaka*

aṣṭavidha mfn of eight sorts, eight-fold,

āste √*ās* to sit, be present, 159/3 sits, to be present, to exist, 1/s/pres/indic/mid sits

asteya n. not stealing, '.. to be fair, equitable, is the human law, to steal is against the law'
ā√sthā Cl 1 -*tiṣṭhati,* to stand on, mount, ascend, resort to, act according to, to undertake, perform, do, practise, be of the opinion of, to maintain, affirm, to acknowledge, to cause to stay or stop, to arrest, stop, have regard for, to fix into, put into, to strengthen, to introduce,
asthā ind. at once,
asthan n. bone,
asthāna n. non-permanency, inconstancy (as of a sound), not a fit place for (6th), without abode, not established, (in comp.) in a wrong place, wrong time, unseasonably, unsuitably,
asthāne ind. in a wrong place,
asthāpayat placed, put
asthāvara mfn not standing, not fixed, moving, movable,
āsthāya having recourse to, following, practicing, gerund
asthi n. a bone, the kernel of a fruit,
asthira 123/1 mfn. unsteady, trembling transient, doubtful, changeable,
āsthita 161/2 mfn abiding being, existing, attained, obtained, established, seated in, mounted, staying or sitting on, stayed, dwelt, inhabited, ascended, undertaken, performed,
asthūla not gross or bulky, delicate,g
aṣṭi f. attainment, reaching, #16,
asti 1/s/pres/act/indic √*as* to be, he, she or it is
asti f. being, exists, is, Brahman,
āsthita 161/2 mfn. staying or sitting on, abiding, one who has undertaken or performed, being, existing
asthūla mfn delicate, not bulky or gross, Brahman,
āstikya faith, respect for the teaching of the scriptures
astināsti ind. partly true and partly not, doubtful, either is or is not,
astitā 122/2 f. existence, reality,
astra n. arrow, weapon, missile,
astu let there be, let it be 1/s/impv/act √*as,* existence, reality,
asu 121/1 m. breath, life, 'any function calculated to sustain life's activity, such as breathing etc.'(Gam.)
āśu 157/3 mfn. fast, quick, going quickly, ind. quickly, immediately,
asu m. life of the spiritual world or departed spirits, respiration, vital breath, vital breaths or airs of the body, animal life, life, n. grief, spirit,
aśubhaś 113/3 mfn bad, vicious (as thought or speech) sin, evil, inauspicious,
aśubha mfn disagreeable,
aśuci mfn unclean, impure
aśuddha mfn impure, incorrect, wrong, unknown, unascertained,
aśuddha-māyā impure *māyā*
aśuddhi f. impurity,
āśu-drāvaṇa n. melting quickly, softening quickly
āśugamana 157/3*āśuga* mfn going or moving swiftly, swift, fleet
āśugrahaṇa comprehending swiftly, quickly taking to oneself
asukhi unhappy, miserable,
aśukla mfn not white, black,
asunīti f. the leading or continuing of life (in the other world), spirit-life
asunva mfn not pressing (Soma), i.e. indifferent to the gods, godless,
aśūnya 113/3 mfn not empty, not vain or useless, -*tā* f. non-emptiness, completion (as of the seasons),
asura 121/1 mfn. spiritual, incorporeal, divine, (*as*) m. a spirit, good spirit, supreme spririt, the chief of the evil spirits, an evil spirit, demon, ghost, opponent of the gods, demons of the first order in perpetual hostility with the gods, (*ī*) f. a female demon, (L) 1. mfn spiritual (used of the gods and designating esp. the difference between celestial and mundane existence), 2. m. a spirit of life, a god, 3. (later) demon, enemy of the gods, an Asura, a not-god,

evil tendency in man,
asūra n. absence of sunlight, (*e*) ind. in the night, 121/3
āsura 160/3 mf(*i*)n. spiritual or divine, belonging or devoted to evil spirits, demonic, m. an *Asura* or demon,
asurabhi disagreeable smell,
asurī f. a female demon, wife of an *asura*,
āsurī 160/3 female demon, surgery,
asurya 121/2 mfn. incorporeal, spiritual, divine, demoniacal, L. mfn godlike, (*as*) n. pl. godhead,
n. spirituality, divine nature, the collective body of spiritual beings
asūrya mfn. sunless, demoniacal, inaccessible, unknown,
(am) ind. at night
aśuśrūṣā 113/3 non-desire of hearing, disobedience (from desid. √*śru*)
aśuśrūṣāve 4/s/m of above to one who does not wish to listen
aśutośa 'who is easily pleased', who is easily satisfied (name of a person), attribute of *Śiva*
asuṭrp mfn enjoying or profiting by another's life, bringing it into one's possession, enjoying one's life, devoted to worldly pleasures, insatiable, life-robbing,
asūya 121/3 *asūyayati* Nom. P to murmur at, be displeased or discontented with, f. displeasure, indignation, envy, jealousy, DP in *upatāpa* envying, being jealous, grumbling, detracting from
asūyā f. impatience, envy,jealousy,
āsva pron. we two were
aśva a horse, salt, *aśvā* f. mare, steed,
ā√*svad* to eat, consume, *svadati*, caus. *svādayati*, eat with relish,
āsvādana 162/1 n. the act of eating, tasting, enjoying
asvādu mfn tasteless, sour
aśvakovida mfn well-skilled with horses,
aśvamedha m. horse sacrifice,
aśvanāya m. horse-herder,
asvapant mfn not sleeping,
asvapna dreamless, 124/1 m. sleeplessness, mfn not sleeping, watchful,
not dreaming, m. 'sleepless', a god
asvargya 124/1 mfn. not leading to heaven
ā√*śvas* 159/2 Cl 2 –*śvasiti,* to breathe, breathe again or freely, get one's breath, become quiet,
take heart or courage, revive,
caus. *śvāsayati* to cause to take breath, to encourage, comfort, to calm, console, cheer up,
āśvāsa m. breathing again or freely, feeling of comfort, optimism,
āśvāsana n. causing to revive, refreshing, reviving, consoling, encouraging, cheering up, refreshment, recreation, consolation, comfort,
āśvāsayām he caused to take heart caus/peri/perf *ā*√*śvas*
asvastha mfn not well, ill, not self-contained, not master of one's self,
asvāsthya n. illness, sickness, discomfort, indisposition,
aśvatara m. mule, f. (*ī*), a better horse, a male calf,
aśvattha 115/3 'under which horses stand', the holy fig tree, ficus religiosa,
'the tree of life whose roots are in heaven', the sun, peepul tree,
Aśvatthāmān a *Kaurava* warrior 'having the strength of a horse'
asveda mfn free from sweat, not perspiring,
aśvin 116/1 mfn. possessed of horses, consisting of horses, mounted on horseback, a cavalier, name of two divinities (horsemen of the sun)– they bring treasures to men and avert misfortune and sickness,
āśvina mfn like riders or horsemen,
m. name of a month,
n. a day's journey for a horseman,
aśvya mfn belonging to or coming from horses, consisting of horses, n. a number of horses, possession of horses, son of *aśva*,
asya pronoun of this, his
asya fut/pass/part of √ *as* is likely to be
asyām in it, in this, 7/s/f

āsyam mouth, face,

at ind. a prefix said to imply surprise

√*aṭ* 11/2 *aṭati, aṭate*, to roam, wander about, frequently used of religious mendicants, DP in *gati*

√*at* 12/1 cl1 P A *atati* to go constantly, walk, run, to obtain, DP in *sātatya-gaman*, uninterrupted going, wandering, pervading

āt ind. afterwards, then, further, also, therupon, *ād id* then indeed, (may be strengthened by *-aha,-id, -īm, -u,*), may be used after an interrogative pronoun to give emphasis to the pronoun,

atad not that

atadam ind. undeservedly, unjustly,

atadvyavṛtti the process of knowing the truth through a thing opposed to it; e.g. the Self is distinct from the three bodies, (U), exclusion of cow from non-cows,

atadarha mfn not deserving that,

ata eva that is why,

ataḥ ind. hence, from here, from this, then, from that time, therefore, for this reason,

ataḥ param from then on, henceforth, hereafter, in the future,

atajjñā mfn not knowing That, i.e. Brahma and the soul's identity

aṭaka mfn roaming,

atala n. mfn bottomless, name of a hell,

atana m. a passer on, n. act of passing on

atandra 12/1 mfn. free from lassitude, alert, unwearied

atandrita as above

aṭanī f. the notched end of a bow,

atanu not thin, not small

atanū f. bodiless, Brahman,

ātaṅka 134/2 disease, sickness, apprehension, fear

ātapa 134/2 mfn causing pain or affliction, m. heat (esp. from the sun), sunshine,

atapaska 12/1 mfn one who neglects austerities,

ātapavāraṇa n. umbrella, parasol,

ātapya mfn being in the sunshine

atarat crossed,

atarkya mfn incomprehensible, surpassing thought or reason, that which cannot be reasoned out, Brahman,

atas 12/1 ind. hence, so, from this, hence, from here, from that time, therefore,

atasmintadbuddhiḥ (G) 'cognition of something as something else' *śaṅkara's* definition of super-imposition (*adhyāsa),*

ātatāyin 134/2 having one's bow drawn, endeavouring to kill someone, a murderer, M. 'having a drawn bow', a warrior,

atathya mfn untrue, unreal, not really so

atattvārthavat 12/1 mfn not conformable with the nature of truth, without true purpose, not concerned with truth

ata-ūrdhvam 12/1 ind. henceforth, afterwards

aṭavī f. forest, 'roaming place',

atavyas not stronger, not very strong,

atejas n. absence of brightness or vigour, dimness, shade, shadow, feebleness, dullness, insignificance, mfn not bright, dim, not vigorous, 16/3

√*aṭh* 11/2 cl 1 P *aṭhati* A *aṭhate* to go, DP in *gati*, going, moving

atha 17/3 ind. an auspicious and inceptive particle, then, now, and, after this, next,

atha ca ind. moreover, and likewise,

atha kadācit then one day,

atha kim how else? what else? certainly, assuredly, sure enough,

atha kim u ind. how much more, so much the more,

athāpi thus

atharva 4th division of the Veda, in comp. for *Atharvan* (Brahmā's eldest son)– to whom was revealed the *brahma-vidyā,*

atharvan m. a priest who has to do with fire and *soma*, name of the first priest to institute fire worship and offerings, offerings of *soma* and prayers,

author of the Atharva Veda,
atha tu ind. but, on the contrary,
athavā 17/3 ind. or rather, but no, however, ind. is it not so, what? or, rather, however, or else, but, otherwise, when repeated, either or, or rather, or perhaps, is it not so? however
atho 17/3 ind. now, likewise, next, or, and,
ati 12/2 ind. passing, going, beyond, across, past, overmuch, too, very,
as a verbal prefix - beyond, over
as a nominal prefix – beyond, surpassing , passing, going, excessive,
as a separable adv. or prep. beyond, over, at the top of
as a prefix to nouns, adj. & verbs- intense, extraordinary, excessive, excessively, exceedingly, very, too e.g. too hard,
atī (√i) cl 2 P. *atyeti* to pass by elapse, pass over, overflow, to pass on, get over, to pass through, to defer, to enter, to overcome, overtake, outdo, to pass by, neglect, to overstep, violate, to be redundant, to die,
atibahu mfn very much, too much,
atibālaka m. an infant, mfn infantile,
ati√bhā -bhāti to blaze or be very bright
atibhāra m. excessive burden, excessive obscurity (of a sentence),
atibhāva m. superiority, overcoming,
atibhojana n. eating too much,
ati√bhū to originate or arise in an excessive way, P. to excel, surpass,
atibhūmi f. extensive land, culmination, eminence, superiority, excess,
atibodha *ati* 12/2 prefix expressing excessive, intensity, *bodha* 734/2 knowing, understanding. 1/s/m increase in knowledge
ati√brū to insult, abuse,
aticaṇḍa mfn very violent,
ati√car to pass by, overtake, surpass, to transgress, offend, be unfaithful to,
aticara mfn transient, changeable,
aticāra m. passing by, overtaking, surpassing, transgression, incorrect behavior, infraction by accident,
aticaraṇa n. excessive practice,
aticchandas mfn past worldly desires, freedom from all desires,
ati√ceṣt to make extraordinary efforts,
aticira mfn very long, (*am*) ind. a very long time, (*asya*) ind. for a very long time, very long, (*āt)* ind. at last,
ati√cṛt to stick on fasten,
ati√1.dā to surpass in giving, to pass over in giving,
ati√dagh to go beyond, to pass,
atidagdha mfn badly burnt,
ati√dah to burn or blaze across, to burn or distress greatly,
atidāha m. great heat, violent inflammation
atidāna n. munificence, excessive munificence,
atidarpa m. excessive conceit,
atidarśin mfn very far-sighted,
atidāruṇa mfn very terrible,
ati√dāś to favour with a gift, present,
atidātṛ m. a very or too liberal man,
atideśa m. transfer, extended application, inference, analogy, overruling, influence, assimilation, substitution, mfn over-ruling, previously stated,
ati√dhyai to meditate deeply,
atidīpta mfn exceptionally brilliant,
atidīrgha mfn very long, too long,
ati√diś to make over, transfer, assign,
atidiṣṭa mfn overruled, attracted, influenced, inferred, substituted, (in gram. to be over-ruled or attracted or assimilated,
atidoṣa m. a great fault,
atidrutam ind. extremely quickly,
atiduḥkhasaṁvega extremely sharp feelings of pain,
atiduḥkhita , greatly afflicted, very sad,
atiduḥsaha mfn hard to bear, unbearable,
atidūra mfn very distant, (am) n. a great distance
atidurgata mfn very badly off,
atidurlambha mfn very hard to attain
atidurvṛtta mfn excessively wicked,
atiduṣkara mfn very difficult,

atiga mfn exceeding, overcoming, surpassing, transgressing, violating
ati√1. gā or ati√gam to pass by or over, to surpass, overcome, to escape, neglect, to pass away, die,
atigāḍha mfn very important, very intensive, (*am*) ind. exceedingly, intensively,
ati√gāh to emerge over, to rise upon,
atigahana mfn very deep,
ati√gam see *ati√gā*
atigambhīra 'profound, unfathomable like an ocean' (Gam.),
atigarvita mfn very conceited,
atigata mfn having passed, being past,
atigha m. a weapon, bludgeon, wrath,
atighnī f. utter oblivion or profound sleep, (obliterating all that is disagreeable in the past and regarded as the highest condition of bliss)
atighnya mfn one who is in *atighnī,*
atigo mfn an excellent cow,
ati√grah to take beyond or over usual measure, to surpass,
atigraha m. act of taking over or beyond, surpassing, one who takes or seizes to an extraordinary extent,
atigrāha the object of a *graha* or organ of apprehension,
apāna fragrant substance,
nāman name, *rasa* flavour,
rūpa form, *śabda* sound,
kāma desire, *karman* action,
sparśa touch,
atiguṇa mfn having extraordinary qualities,
atigupta mfn closely concealed, very mysterious
ati√gur tocry out, give a shriek,
atiguru mfn very heavy
ati√2.hā to jump over, jump past,
atihāsa m. excessive laughter,
atihastaya Nom. to stretch out the hands, to overtake on an elephant,
atihata mfn firmly fixed, utterly destroyed
atihimam ind. after the frost, past the cold,
ati√hṛ to hold over, reach over, cause to jut over, to add,
ati√hve to call over to one's side,
ati√i cl 2 *eti*, to go beyond,
atijāgara mfn very wakeful,
atijala mfn well watered,
atijana mfn beyond men, uninhabited,
atijara mfn very aged,
atijava m. extraordinary speed
ati√ji to conquer,
atijīrṇa mfn very aged
atijīrṇatā f. extreme old age,
ati√jīv to survive, to surpass in the mode of living,
atijīva mfn quite alive, very lively,
atikalyam ind. very early, too early,
atikānta mfn excessively beloved,
atikarṣaṇa excessive exertion,
atikatha mfn exaggerated
atikaṭhora mfn very hard, too hard
atikāya mfn of gigantic body or size,
ati√khyā to survey, overlook, to neglect, pass over, abandon,
ati√kram to step or go beyond or over or across, to pass, cross, pass time, to surpass, excel, overcome, to pass by, neglect, to overstep, transgress, violate, to pass on or away, to step out, to part from, lose,
atikrama m. act of overstepping or overcoming, transgression, violation, neglect, determined onset,
atikrāmaka mfn exceeding, transgressing,
atikramaṇa 13/2 n. the act of passing over, surpassing, overstepping, passing (spending) time, excess,
atikramin, mfn exceeding, violating,
atikramya having passed beyond or over,
atikrānta mfn having passed or transgressed, exceeded, surpassed, overcome, past, bygone,
atikrānti f. transgression,
atikṛṣa mfn very thin, emaciated,
atikṛṣṇa mfn very or too dark (or blue),
atikṛta mfn overdone, exaggerated,
atikruddha mfn excessively angry
ati√kṣip to throw beyond,
atikutsita mfn greatly despised,
atilāghava exceeding lightness, smallness, brevity or thoughtlessness,
atilakṣmī mfn very prosperous,
atilamba mfn very extensive,

atilaulya n. excessive eagerness or desire,
atilulita mfn closely attached or adhering,
atimahat mfn very great, too long,
atimām (3rd of *aty-aham)* surpassing me,
atimaṅgalya mfn very auspicious,
ati√man -manyate to disdain, despise, value less than oneself, to pride oneself
atimānita mfn honoured highly
atimānitā f. excessive pride, arrogance, great haughtiness,
atimānuṣa mfn superhuman, divine,
atimanuṣyabuddhi mfn having a superhuman intellect,
atimarśa m. close contact
atimartya mfn superhuman,
atimāruta mfn very windy, m. a hurricane
atimaryāda mfn exceeding the proper limits, (*am*) ind. beyond bounds,
atimati f. haughtiness, mfn exceedingly wise,
atimātra mfn exceeding the proper measure, *(am)* ind. or *–śas* ind. beyond measure,
atimāya mfn free from illusion, liberated,
atimirmira mfn twinkling exceedingly,
atimita mfn beyond measure, exceeding, 2. mfn not moistened,
atimodā f. extraordinary fragrance,
atimokṣa m. final liberation,
atimokṣin mfn escaping,
atimṛtyu mfn overcoming death,
ati √muc to avoid, escape, giving up
atimucya ind. having dismissed or given up,
atimukta mfn entirely liberated, seedless, m. 'surpassing pearls in whiteness'
atimukti f. final liberation (from death),
ati√nam to bend aside, keep on one side,
atināṣṭra mfn beyond danger, out of danger,
atīndriya mfn transcending the senses, beyond the realm of the senses, n. soul, spirit, the mind, 16/2
atīndriya sukha happiness beyond the reach of the senses, the bliss of Brahman,
ati√ned to stream or flow over, 14/2
ati√nī to lead over or beyond, to help a person over anything,
atinidra mfn given to excessive sleep,
atinipuṇa mfn very skilful,
ati√3.nu caus. to turn away,
ati√nud to drive by,
ati√pad to go beyond, jump over,
atipanna mfn gone beyond, transgressed, missed, past,
atipāpa mfn extremely evil, very evil,
atipara mfn one who has overcome his enemies, m. a great enemy
atiparī to pass round, *(pari√i)*
ati√paś to look beyond, look through,
ati√2.pat to fall or fly by or past, beyond, over, to neglect, miss,
atipāta m. lapse, neglect,
atipatana mfn act of falling or flying beyond, passing, missing, transgressing,
ati√paṭh to be greatly celebrated, proclaimed
atipatita mfn passed beyond, transgressed, n. complete fracture of a bone,
atipātaka m. a very heinous sin,
atiparokṣa mfn far out of sight, no longer discernible,
atiparokṣavṛtti (in gram.) having a nature no longer discernible, i.e. obsolete
atipeśala mfn very dexterous,
ati√1.pṛ to convey across, to help over, to cross, pass over,
ati√pṝ cl 4 P. *–pūryati* to become full or overflowing,
atiprabandha m. complete continuity,
ati√prach to go on asking,
atipra√cit –cekite to be clearly, distinct or distinguishable,
atipra√cyu to pass by
atipra√jval to flame or blaze exceedingly,
atipramāṇa mfn beyond measure, immense,
atiprāṇam ind. exceeding life,
atiprāṇapriya mfn dearer, than life,
*atipraṇaś (√2. naś)*to be entirely deprived of
atipra√ṇī (nī) to lead by or beyond
atipraṇud (√nud) to press or incite very strongly
atipra√sad P. *–sīdati* to become completely cheerful
ati –prasaṅga m. excessive attachment, stretch of a rule too far,
atiprasakti f. or *–prasaṅga* m. excessive attachment, stretch of a rule too far
atipra√śaṁs to praise highly,
atipraśna a transcendental question,

questioning to the extreme, too much questioning,
atipra√sthā to have an advantage over,
atipra√2.vā cl 4 P. *–vāyati* to blow violently,
atipra√vah to extend or carry beyond,
atipra√yam to give or hand over,
atipra√yuj to separate from,
ati√pū P. to clarify or purify through,
atipuruṣa m. a first-rate man, a hero
atipūta mfn quite purified, over purified,
atirabhasa m. extraordinary speed,
atirai exceeding one's income, extravagant,
ati√rāj to shine over,
atirājan m an extraordinary king, one who surpasses a king,
atirakta mfn very red,
atiraṁhas mfn extremely rapid,
atiratha m. a great warrior, fighting from a car
atirātra mfn prepared/performed overnight, an optional part of a partic. sacrifice,
atireka or *atīreka* m. surplus, excess, redundancy, difference,
ati√ric to be left with a surplus, to surpass, be more than, (with negative connotation) be less than, inferior to,
atiricyate it exceeds, it surpasses, ati √ric 1/s/pres/indic/mid
atirikta 15/2 mfn left with or as a surplus, left apart, redundant, unequalled,
ati√ruc to shine over or along, surpass in shining,
ati√ruh to climb or ascend over, grow higher
atirucira mfn very lovely
atirūpa mfn very beautiful,
atiruṣ mfn very angry,
atiśakta (ti) mfn very powerful,
atisakti f. excessive attachment,
atisamartha mfn very competent,
atisaṁcaya m. excessive accumulation,
atisaṁdheya mfn easy to be settled,
atisamīpa mfn very near,
atisaṁnidhāna n. excessive nearness,
atisaṁtuṣṭa mfn extremely pleased,
atiśānta m. completely at rest, completely peaceful,
atisarga m. the act of parting with, giving away, granting permission
atisarjana 16/1 n. the act of giving away, granting, liberality, a gift, sending out of this world, killing
atisarva mfn too complete, superior to all,
atiśarvara n. the dead of night,
atiśasta mfn very excellent
atiśaya mfn pre-eminent, superior, m. pre-eminence, eminence, one of the superhuman qualities attributed to *jaina arhat,* ind. superiority, eminently, very,
atisiddhi f. great perfection,
atisparśana contact between tongue and palate too marked in pronunciation,
ati √sṛj to glide over or along, to send away, dismiss, abandon, to remit, forgive, give away, present, to create in a higher degree,
atisṛjya 16/1 to be dismissed, or given up
ātiṣṭha undertake, perform, carry out 2/s/impv/act *ā√sthā* n. superiority,
atiṣṭhat stood
atisujana mfn very moral, very friendly,
atiśukra mfn too bright,
atisūkṣma mfn extremely subtle,
atisvapna too much sleeping, oversleeping, (*am*) n. excessive dreaming tendency
atīta mfn gone by, past, passed away, dead, one who has gone through or got over or beyond, transcendent, one who has passed by or neglected, negligent, passed, left behind, excessive, *(am)* n. the past, 16/2
atītakāla m. the past time or tense,
ati√tap to be very hot, to heat, to affect greatly, 13/3
atitapasvin mfn very ascetic,
atitarām 13/3 ind. (compar. of *ati)* above in rank, better, higher, more, very much, exceedingly, excessively,
atitārin mfn crossing,
atitārya to be crossed or passed over or overcome
atitata mfn stretching far, conceited,
atithi m. 14/1 a guest, a person entitled to hospitality, name of *Agni*
atithikriyā f. hospitality

atithin mfn travelling,
atithi-satkāra m. honouring of guests, hospitality,
ātithya n. hospitality, proper for a guest,
ati√tī to pass through or by, or over, cross, overcome, escape,
atitrasnu mfn over timid,
ati√tṛd to split, pierce through, penetrate
ati√tṛp to be satiated,
atitṛpti f. too great satiety,
atitṛṣṇa mfn excessively thirsty, rapacious,
atiṣakta or *atisakta* mfn connected with,
atisaṁ√dhā to overreach, deceive, to wrong or injure,
atisaṁdhāna mfn overreaching, cheating
atisaṁdheya mfn easy to be conciliated, easy to be settled,
atisandhita mfn overreached, cheated,
atisara m. effort, exertion,
atisāra m. purging, dysentery,
atisarga m. act of parting with, dismissal, giving away, granting permission,
atisarjana n. act of giving away, granting, liberality, a gift, sending out of the world, killing,
atisarva mfn superior to all, m. the Supreme
atiśaya m. pre-eminence, eminence, superiority in quality, quantity or numbers, advantageous result, mfn pre-eminent, superior, abundant, surpassing, (*am, ena*) ind. eminently, very,
atiśayana mfn eminent, abundant, (*am*) ind. excessively,
atiśayita mfn surpassing, superior,
atiśayokti f. exaggeration, verbosity,
atiśeṣa m. remainder, remnant,
ati√sev to use or enjoy immoderately, to practise excessively,
ati√śī Cl.2 *atiśete* to surpass, triumph over,
ati√2.śiṣ to leave remaining,
atiśiṣṭa mfn remaining,
atiśreṣṭha mfn superior to the best, the best of all,
ati√sṛ caus. to cause to pass through,
ati√sṛj *atisṛjati* to glide over or along, to send away, dismiss, abandon, to remit,forgive, to give away, present, bestow, lavish, leave as a remnant,
atisṛjya 16/1 to be dismissed, or given up
atisṛṣṭi f. a higher creation, an excellent creation,
ati√sru to flow over or excessively,
atiṣṭhā (√sthā) to be at the head of, govern, to jut over or out,
2. f. precedence, superiority,
m.f. superior in standing,
atiṣṭhant mfn not standing, restless,
atiṣṭhat mfn not standing, unstable,
ati√śubh to be brilliant, to please,
atiśva mfn superior to or worse than a dog, name of a tribe,
atīta 16/2 gone by, passed away, dead, transcended, gone beyond,
atitārin 14/1 crossing,
atitārya to be crossed or passed over or overcome
atitīvra mfn extremely severe, very sharp, pungent or acid, doob grass,
atitvam surpassing thee
ati√tvar to hasten overmuch,
atītya going beyond, transcending, gerund *ati√ī*
ati-tyad surpassing that,
ati√2.vā cl 2 P –*vāti* to blow beyond, cl 4 P. –*vāyati* to blow violently
atīva very, very much, excessively, intensively,
ati√vac to blame, or speak too loudly in blaming or praising
ati√vad to speak louder or better, to ask for too much,
ativādī a tall talker, one who is apt to go beyond in his talk,
ati√vah to carry over or across, to pass by, to pass time,
ativāhana n. excessive toiling or enduring,
ativāhya n. the passing of time,
ativakra mfn very crooked or curved,
ativaktṛ mfn very loquacious,
ativartana n. a pardonable offence,
ativartanti they transcend 1/pl/pres *ati√vṛt*
ativartate he goes beyond, he transcends, 1/s/pres/indic/mid *ati √vṛt*
ativartula mfn very round, a kind of grain

or pot-herb,
ativāta m. high wind, a storm,
ativela mfn passing the proper boundary, excessive, (*am*) ind. excessively,
ativi√dhā –dhatte to distribute too much
ativi√rāj to shine or be exceedingly brilliant,
ativiśrabdha mfn entirely trusting, or confiding in
ativikaṭa mfn very fierce, m. a vicious elephant,
ativodhṛ m. one who carries over or across,
atīvra mfn not sharp, blunt, not pungent,
ati√vraj to pass by, to fly over, to pass or wander through
ativṛddha mfn very large, very old,
ativṛddhi f. extraordinary growth,
ati√vṛṣ to rain violently
ativṛṣṭi f. excessive rain,
ativyādhya mfn vulnerable,
ativyāpti redundancy – one of 3 tests of understanding an object, there is redundancy when the characteristics in question are found to be common to other objects, e.g. cows are four-legged, other animals are also found to have 4 legs, hence redundancy,
ativyāpti doṣa f. an unwarrantable stretch of an argument,
atiyāja m. great sacrificer, very pious,
atiyaśa mfn very illustrious,
atiyoga m. excessive union, excess,
atiyuvan mfn very youthful,
atka m. a traveller, a limb or member, armour, mail, garment,
ātma (in comp. for *ātman*), rarely ifc. see *ātman*
ātmā 135/1 m. the Self (in all)
ātmā-anātmā-viveka discrimination between the Self and the not-self
ātmabhava m. becoming or existing of one's self, 'mind-born', mfn produced in or caused by one's self, coming into existence of one's self, the existence of himself,
ātmabhāva m. existence of the soul, the self, proper or peculiar nature, feeling that everything is the Self,
ātmabhāvasthaḥ situated in one's own being, dwelling in one's own being
ātmābhimānitā f. self-respect,
ātmabhū m. self-born
ātmabhūta mfn 'become another's self', attached to, faithful,
ātmabhūya n. peculiarity, own nature
ātmabodha m. having knowledge of the soul or supreme spirit, knowledge of the Self,
ātmabuddhi f. self-knowledge,
ātmadā mfn granting breath or life,
ātmadāna n. gift of self, self-sacrifice,
ātmadarśana n. seeing the soul of or in, (in comp).
ātmādhīna mfn depending on one's own will, sentient,
ātmādhika mfn dearer than one's self,
ātmadrohin mfn self-tormenting, fretful,
ātmadūṣi mfn corrupting the soul,
ātmagata mfn being on its self, (*am*) ind. 'gone to one's self', in drama –an aside to the audience,
ātmagati f. one's own way, 'course of the soul's existence', life of the spirit,
ātmaghāta m. suicide,
ātmagrāhin mfn taking for one's self,selfish
ātmahita mfn beneficial to one's self, n. one's own welfare,
ātmaja mfn self-originated,
ātmajaḥ m. a son
ātmajā f. a daughter,
ātmajanman n. the birth or re-birth of one's self, i.e. the birth of a son, m. a son,
ātmajña mfn knowing one's self, knowing the Supreme Spirit, knower of the Self,
ātmajñāna n. self-knowledge, knowledge of the soul or supreme spirit, "the experience of the Self, not as this and that, but as Itself". HH
ātmajyotis n. the light of the soul or Supreme Spirit, mfn receiving light from one's self,
ātmaka Apte 78/2 made up or composed of, (*am*) n. of the nature of, consisting of, L. ifc. nature, character, peculiarity, e.g. *māra-ātmaka* murderous-natured, murderous,
ātmakāma mfn loving one's self,

self-conceited,

ātmakarman n. one's own act,

ātmakārya n. one's own business, private affairs,

ātmakīya mfn one's own,

ātmakrīḍa mfn playing with the Supreme Spirit, rejoicing in the Self alone,

ātmakṛpā the grace of the Self

ātmakṛta mfn done or committed against oneself, done of one's self, self-executed,

ātmalābha m. one's own profit, acquisition (of the knowledge) of the supreme spirit, coming into existence, attaining realisation of the Self,

ātmalakṣya mfn having the Self as the goal, Self as the object of meditation,

ātmamāna n. regarding one's self as (e.g. learned etc.),

ātmamāṁsa n. one's own flesh,

ātmamaya mfn issued from one's own self,

ātmamūlī f. striking root in self, self-existent,

ātmamūrti mfn one whose body is the self,

ātman 1/s/m *ātmā* 135/1 the soul, principle of life and sensation, the individual soul, self, abstract individual e.g. *ātman karoti* 'makes his own' *ātmanā akarot* 'he did it himself', *ātman* in the singular is used as a reflexive pronoun for all three persons and genders,
[a reflexive pronoun (myself, himself, herself, yourself etc.) is used e.g. when the person being seen is the same as the person seeing, "I see myself", "she sees herself"],
essence, nature, character, peculiarity, the Self, the highest personal principle of life, the breath, the individual soul, Brahma, effort, the sun, fire, a son, the body, ifc. the understanding, intellect, mind. 'In Advaita Vedanta – the substratum of all is apparently individualised and yet identical with the Brahman or Absolute, all-pervasive, "That moves, That does not move; That is far off, That is very near; That is inside all, and That is outside all"', (from the *Īśopaniṣad.*)
Buddhism – '*Ātman* is an essence of things that does not depend on others; it is an intrinsic nature. The non-existence of that is selflessness', (*Candrakīrti*)
Advaita postulates the existence of a monistic metaphysical 'being in itself' i.e. *Brahman/Ātman* while Buddhism does not.

ātmanaḥ his

ātmānapekṣa mfn not selfish, not regarding one's self,

ātmānanda mfn rejoicing in the soul or supreme spirit

ātmanepada n. word to oneself, word for oneself, i.e. that form of the verb which implies an action belonging or reverting to self, the terminations of the middle voice,

ātmanindā f. self reproach,

ātmaniṣṭhā f. established in the Self,

ātmanitya mfn constantly in the heart, greatly endeared to one's self,

ātmanivedana 135/2 n. offering oneself to a deity, self-surrender,

ātmanvat mfn animated, having a soul,

ātmanya mfn being connected with one's self,

ātmapa mfn guarding one's self,

ātmapañcama mfn being one's self the fifth with four others,

ātmāpahāra m. concealing of self, dissimulation, 'taking away self'

ātmāpahārin mfn self-deceiving, dissembling, self-concealing,

ātmapakṣa m. one's own party,

ātmāparādha m. one's own offence, personal transgression,

ātmaparājita mfn one who has lost himself (at play),

ātmapāta m. descent of the soul, rebirth,

ātmaprabha mfn shining by one's own light, self-illuminated,

ātmaprakāśa mfn self-shining, self-luminous, the light of the Self,

ātmapratikṛti f. one's own reflection or

image,
ātmaprātyakṣa direct perception of the Self,
ātmapratyaya belief in the self, trust or faith in the Self, firm conviction in the self,
ātmaprayojana mfn selfish,
ātmapūjā f. self-praise,
ātmārāma 136/1 one who rejoices in his own Self or in the supreme spirit,
ātmarati mfn rejoicing in one's self, centred in the Self,
ātmārtham indef. for the sake of one's self,
ātmaruha mfn growing on itself,
ātmasācin m. one's own companion,
ātmasad mfn dwelling in (my)self,
ātmaśakti f. one's own power or effort,
ātmasama m. equal to one's self,
ātmasamarpaṇa n. offering oneself to a deity,
ātmasaṁyama m. self-restraint,
ātmasaṁdeha m. personal risk,
ātmasani mfn granting the breath of life,
ātmasantuṣṭi contentment or satisfaction in one's own Self,
ātmasāt √*kṛ* to appropriate,
ātmasatya mfn the Truth that is the Self,
ātmaśoṇita n. one's own blood,
ātmāśraya m. dependence on self or on the supreme spirit, self-reliance, a type of logical fallacy (G),
ātmastham ' tam ātmastham - "Him as residing in the space of the heart within the body"', 'pervading the individual self', residing in the Self, the Self within, seated in the intellect, pure consciousness,
ātmaśuddhi f. self-purification,
ātmatā f. essence, nature,
ātmatantra n. the basis of self, mfn depending only on one's self, independent,
ātmatattva n. the true nature of the soul or of the Supreme Spirit, the reality of the Self,
ātmatattvajña mfn knowing or versed in the Vedānta doctrines,
ātmatṛpta mfn self-satisfied, one who rests contented in the Self,
ātmatṛpti f. satisfaction in one's own Self,
ātmatva n. essence, nature,
ātmatyāga m. self-forgetfulness, absence of mind, suicide,
ātmaupamya n. likeness to one's self i.e. putting one's self in another's place,
ātmavadha m. suicide,
ātmavaśa 135/3 mfn. dependent on one's own will, self-controlled, self-restrained
ātmavat 135/3 mfn. having a soul, self-possessed, composed, prudent,
ātmavattā f. self-possession, self-regard, prudence, self-resemblance, proportion, analogy,
ātmavān possessed of the Self, full of the Self 1/s/m
ātmavañcanā f. self-delusion,
ātmavat 135/3 mfn. having a soul, prudent, composed, self-possessed, L. ind. as one's self,
ātmavanta as above
ātmavibhūti f. spiritual wealth after self-realisation, (U)
*ātmavibhūtaya*s self powers or manifestations
ātmavid mfn knowing the nature of the soul or supreme spirit,
ātmavidhitsā f. selfishness,
ātmavidyā f. knowledge of soul or the supreme spirit,
ātmavinigrahas control of the aggregate of body and organs, self-control,
ātmavīra m. a mighty man, a living being, a son, a wife's brother,
ātmavṛtti f. one's own circumstances,
ātmayoga m. union with the supreme spirit
ātmeśvara m. master of one's self,
ātmībhāva m. becoming part of the supreme spirit,
ātmikā having the nature of Self, ifc. having ..... as its nature,
ātmī√*1.kṛ* to make one's own, take possession of,
ātmīya mfn one's own,
ātmodaya m. self-advantage or elevation,
ātmopajīvin mfn living by one's own labour,
ātmopama mfn like one's self,

atna, atnas, atnu, atnus, m. the sun,
ato'nya other than it, differing from this,
āṭopa m. swelling, pride, flatulence, a multitude, redundancy, haste,
atra 1. ind. here, with regard to (this), in this place, in this respect, at this time, there, then, in it, in this case, in that case, in this or that place, here, there, in that world, in that time, on this matter, about this,
2. not enjoying or affording protection,
3. a devourer, demon
4. n. food,
atra antare in the interim, meantime, on this occasion, at this juncture,
atrabhavat or atrabhavant mfn his Honour here, your Honour etc.
atrabhavatī f. her Honour here, this lady,
atradaghna mfn reaching so far up, having such and such a stature,
atra tatra sarvatra here, there, everywhere
atraiva ind. on this very spot,
atrasad mfn sitting here,
atratya mfn connected with this place, produced or found here,
ātreyī f. proper name,
atri m. a devourer, name of a *ṛṣi*
atṛpa mfn not satisfied,
atṛpnuvat mfn insatiable,
atsaruka (without handle), a vessel,
√*aṭṭ* 11/2 cl1 A *aṭṭate* to exceed, to kill, cl 10 P *aṭṭayati* to view with contempt, despise, lessen, diminish, DP in *atikramaṇa* and *hiṁsana*, cl 10 in *anādara* despising, viewing with contempt,
aṭṭa ind. high, lofty, loud, a watchtower, over-measure, market-place,
ātta mfn taken, obtained, taken away or off, withdrawn from, seized, grasped, perceived, felt, undertaken, begun,
aṭṭaka m an apartment on the roof
aṭṭālaka m. a watch-tower,
aṭṭaṭṭa ind very high, very, loud
atti m. an eater, an elder sister, a mother,
atudat (he or she) was hit

atuhina mfn not cold,
atula mfn unequalled, destitute of weight- the sesame seed and plant,
atulya mfn unequalled,
atunda mfn not stout, thin
atuṅga mfn not tall, short,
atura mfn not liberal, not rich,
ātura 135/1 suffering, sick, afflicted with sorrow, affected by, desirous of,
atūrta mfn not outrun, not outdone, not obstructed,
atuṣṭi f. displeasure, discontent,
atūtuji mfn not quick, slow,
atvara mfn not hasty, deliberate,
atya mfn rapid, swift, m. a steed,
atyājya mfn not to be abandoned,
ātyantika mfn continual, uninterrupted, infinite, endless, entire, universal (as the world's destruction), 136/1
atyācāra m. performance of works beyond duty, mfn negligent of custom
atyadbhūta extremely marvellous, very surprising,
atyādhāna n. act of imposing or placing upon, imposition, deception,
atyāditya mfn surpassing the sun,
atyā√*dṛ* take great care of, be anxious about
atyāgī who do not resort to renunciation
atyagni mfn surpassing fire, m. too rapid digestion,
atyāhita mfn disagreeable, great calamity, great danger,
atyajighāṁsat desired to run away, ?
atyakṣara mfn inarticulate,
atyaṁhas mfn beyond the reach of distress,
atyaṅkuśa unmanageable, beyond the elephant-driver's hook,
atyanta 16/3 beyond the proper end or limit, excessively, endless, thoroughly
atyantābhāva m. absolute non-existence,
atyantaga mfn going very fast,
atyantaganin mfn having extraordinary qualities
atyantagata mfn completely pertinent, always applicable,
atyantakopana mfn very passionate
atyantasaṁyoga mfn immediate proximity

atyanta-asat extremely non-existent,
atyantika mfn too close, final, ultimate,
ātyantika 136/1 continual, uninterrupted, infinite, endless, entire, universal
ātyantika pralaya immediate liberation with complete annihilation of all phenomena subjectively,
atyantīna mfn going far
atyartha 17/1 excessively, beyond, exceedingly, beyond proper worth,
atyaśnata mfn eaten too much,
atyāśramin m. an ascetic of the highest degree
atyaya m. passing, lapse, passage, passing away, perishing, death, danger, risk, evil, suffering, transgression, guilt, vice, attacking, overcoming, mastering mentally,
atyāya m. the act of going beyond, excess, transgression,
atyā√yā to pass by
atyā√yat A.to make extraordinary efforts for
atyayin mfn passing,
atyāyus mfn very old,
aty√eṣ to glide over,
atyeti see *atī*
aty√ṛj to convey across towards.., to admit to,
atyucchrita raised too high, *aty-ud -√śri*
atyuddhā to surpass,
atyugra mfn 'excessively strong', very fierce, very pungent,
atyugrapuṇyapāpa mfn extraordinarily good and bad (e.g. pl deeds),
aty√1.ūh or *atyuh* to convey across
2. *√2.ūh* to scorn, disdain,
atyūha m. excessive deliberation, a peacock
aty√2.ukṣ to surpass,
atyupadha mfn superior to any test, tried, trustworthy,
atyuśṇa mfn very hot
atyut√kram to surpass, excel
audārya n. generosity, nobility, liberality, magnanimity, noble style,
-*tā* f. liberality,
aucitya n. fitness, suitableness, decorum,
audāsīnya 237/3 indifference, apathy, disregard, 'indifference to all sense-experience and pairs of opposites; a high state of *jñāna*' (U),
audayika mfn to be reckoned from sunrise, relating to or happening in an auspicious time, prosperous,
aupadhika mfn deceitful, deceptive, m. an imposter, cheat,
aupādhika mfn depending on or relating to special qualities, limited by particular conditions, valid only under particular assumptions, (G) due to limiting adjuncts, '(enjoyment) through the medium of the senses'(U),
aupamya 238/3 n. the state or condition of resemblance or equality, likeness, comparison, analogy
aupaniṣada 238/2 mfn. contained or taught in an *upaniṣad*, a follower of the *U*°, a *vedāntin*
aupapādika mfn self-produced,
aupaveśi m. patronymic of Aruna,
aurasa mfn produced from the breast, innate, own, produced by one's self, coming from or belonging to,
auṣadha 240/2 n. consisting of herbs, a herb, medicine, medicine in general,
autsukya n. anxiety, eagerness, longing,
√av 96/1 cl 1 P *avati,* to drive, impel, animate, (as a horse or car), promote, favour, satisy, refresh, to offer (as a hymn to the gods), to lead or bring to, (said of the gods) to be pleased with, like, accept favourably, (said of kings or princes), to guard, defend, protect, DP in *rakṣaṇa* protecting, *gati* going, *kānti* being beautiful, brilliant, desiring, *prīti* loving, pleasing, *tṛpti* being satisfied, *avagam* understanding, *praveśa* being satisfied, *śravaṇa* hearing, *svāmin* ruling, *yācana* begging, *kriyā* acting, *icchā* wishing, *dīpti* shining, *avāpti* reaching, obtaining, *āliṅgana* embracing, *hiṁsā* hurting, injuring, *ādāna* accepting, *bhāga* dividing, *vṛddhi* prospering,

ava 1. m. favour
2. ind. as a prefix to verbs and verbal nouns expresses- off, away, down, (with prep and 5th) down from,
avabaddha mfn put on (as a helmet), fastened on, fixed, sticking (as an arrow or nail), captivated, attached to
ava√bādh A. to keep off,
avabāḍha mfn dug out, discovered, (√*bāṁh)*
ava√bandh A. to tie or fix on, put on,
avabandha m. palsy
ava√bhā, -bhāti, to shine downwards, to shine, be brilliant, to appear, become manifest,
avabhagna mfn broken off, broken, injured (as honour),
avabhaṅga m. breaking off,
avabharjana n. 'frying', destroying as seeds,
avabharjita mfn 'fried' destroyed (as seeds),
ava√bharts to deter by threatening/scolding
ava√bhās, -bhāsate to shine forth, be brilliant, to become manifest, appear as, caus.P. *–bhāsayat* to illuminate, to make manifest,
avabhāsa m. splendour, lustre, light, appearance (esp. ifc. with words expressing colour), (in *Vedānta* phil.) manifestation; reach, compass,
avabhāsaka (in Vedānta phil.) mfn illuminating, making manifest,
avabhāṣaṇa 101/2 n. speaking against, speaking
avabhāsana m. shining, becoming manifest, (in Ved. phil.) illuminating,
avabhāsin mfn shining, bright, making manifest,
avabhāṣita mfn spoken against, reviled,
avabhāsita mfn shining, bright, illumined, lighted,
avabodha m. waking, being awake, perception, knowledge, faculty of being resolute in action or knowledge,
avabodhaka mfn awakening (as faculties),
avabodhana 101/2 n informing, teaching, instructing
avabodhanīya mfn to be reminded, admonished, censured,
avabodhavya mfn to be kept in mind,
avabodhita, mfn awakened,
avabuddha mfn learnt (as skilfulness),
ava√budh, -budhyate, -budhyati, to become sensible or aware of, perceive, know, caus. to make one aware of, remind of, to cause to know, inform, explain,
avācaka mfn not expressive of,
ava√cakṣ A. *-caṣṭe* to look down upon, to perceive,
avacana n. absence of a special assertion, mfn not expressing anything, not speaking, silent,
avacanakara mfn not doing what one is bid or advised,
avacanīya mfn not to be spoken, improper,
avacanīyatā or *tva* n. impropriety of speech,
ava√car to come down from,
avacara m. the dominion or sphere or department of,
avacāraṇa (in med.) application,
avacaskara mfn silent, not speaking,
avacaya m. gathering (flowers, fruits etc.)
avacchada m. a cover,
avaccheda m. anything cut off, part, portion, separation, discrimination, (in logic) distinction, particularising, discrimination, a predicate,
avacchedaka mfn distinguishing, m. that which distinguishes, a predicate, characteristic, property,
avacchedāvaccheda m. removing distinctions,generalising,
avacchid to refuse anyone
avacchinna mfn separated, detached, distinguished, particularised,
avaccho (√cho), to cut off, skin,
ava√1.ci *-cinoti* to gather, collect, (fruit from a tree),
avā√1.ci *-cinoti* to dissipate what is accumulated, use up,
2. ci to examine,
ava√chid Cl 7 *–chinotti,* to cut down or off,
avacita mfn gathered,
ava√cṛt to let loose,
avacūri or *–cūrikā* f. a gloss, a short commentary
avācya 106/3 what should not be spoken, not to be spoken to,

2. mfn southern, southerly,
avadagdha mfn burnt down
ava√dah expel from with heat or fire, to burn down, consume,
ava√dal –dalati to burst, crack asunder,
avadalita mfn burst, cracked open,
avadaṁśa m. any pungent food which excites thirst, stimulant,
avadāna n. a great or glorious act, achievement, 2.n. cutting off,
avaḍaṅga m. a market, mart,
avadānya mfn niggardly,
avadāraṇa 99/2 n breaking, shattering in pieces, breaking/bursting open
avadat said
a-vadat mfn not speaking,
avadāta mfn cleansed, clean, clear, pure, blameless, excellent, of white splendour, dazzling white, clear, intelligible, m. white colour,
avadāvada mfn undisputed, uncontested,
avadha mfn not hurting, beneficent,
*ava√dhā*P. to place down, plunge into, deposit, to place or turn aside, to be applied or directed (mind),
avadhāna n. attention, attentiveness, intentness,
avadhānin mfn attentive,
avadhāra m. accurate determination, limitation,
avadhāraka mfn determining, bearing upon, meaning, restricting,
avadhāraṇa n. ascertainment, affirmation, emphasis, stating or holding with positiveness, accurate determination, restriction to a certain instance or instances, limitation of the sense of words, mfn restrictive,
avadhārita mfn ascertained, known, certain, heard, learnt,
avadhārya 100/1 mfn to be ascertained or known, aware that
avadhi m. attention, a term, limit, conclusion, termination, environs, (G) supernatural cognition, transcendental knowledge, clairvoyance, limit,
ava√dhī to watch or lie in wait for
avadhijñāna n. the faculty of perceiving even what is not within the reach of the senses, name of the 3rd degree of knowledge (Jain),
avadhijñānin mfn having the above knowledge
avadhīrayati P. despises, rejects,
ava√dhṛ to consider, ascertain, determine accurately, limit, restrict, to conceive, understand, resolve, caus. *avadhārayati* determines, resolves,
avadhṛta mfn ascertained, determined, certain, heard, learnt,
avadhūta mfn 'shaken off' (as evil spirits), removed, discarded, spiritual adept, one who has shaken off from himself worldly feeling and obligation, the highest (6th) state of ascetism,
avadhvansana 100/2 sprinkling, abandoning, despising, disrespect,
avadhya mfn inviolable, not to be harmed, unable to be killed,
avadhyabhāva m. inviolability,
avadhyāna n. disregard
avādin mfn not speaking, not disputing, peacable,
ava√diś to show or practise kindness etc.
avadoha m. milk
avadya mfn censurable, blamable, low, inferior, disagreeable, n. anything blamable, want, imperfection, vice, blame, shame, disgrace,
avadyotaka mfn illustrating, making clear,
avadyotana n. illustrating,
ava√dyut caus. *–dyotayati* to illustrate, show
ava√1.gā to pass away, be wanting, to go to, join with,
avagacchati he goes down, understands,
avagaccha understand! 2/s/impv. *ava√gam*
avagāḍha mfn immersed, bathed, that in which one bathes, deepened, low, having disappeared, vanished,
avagadita mfn unsaid,
ava√gāh *-gāhate* to plunge into, bathe in, to go deep into, be absorbed in,
avagāhana 97/2 n immersion, bathing,

also as immersion in study, mastering, learning,
ava√gal to fall down, slip down,
ava√galbh to be brave, valiant,
avagalita mfn fallen down, slipped down,
ava√gam *-gacchati,* to go down, descend to, ‘ to come to, visit, approach, to reach, obtain, get power or influence, to go near, undertake, to hit upon, think of, conceive, know, understand, anticipate, be convinced, confident of, to recognize, consider, believe anyone to be,
avā√gam to undertake, begin, learn, know, suppose, consider,
caus. *avagamayati* procure
avagama m. understanding, comprehension, intelligence,
avagamaka mfn making known, conveying a sense, expressive of
avagamana 97/2 n making known, proclamation,
avagamin mfn ifc. conceiving understanding
avagamya mfn intelligible,
ava√gaṇ to disregard, disrespect,
avagaṇa mfn separated from one's companions, isolated,
avagaṇana n. disregard, disrespect,
avagaṇita mfn disregarded, despised,
avagata mfn conceived, known, learnt, understood, comprehended, assented to, promised,
avagatha mfn bathed early in the morning,
avagati f. conceiving, guessing, anticipating,
avaghāta m. a blow, threshing corn with a pestle/ mortar, a hole in the ground,
ava√ghaṭṭ to push away, push open,
avaghaṭṭa m. a cave, cavern,
ava√ghrā to smell at, kiss,
avaghra mfn kissing, m. smelling at, being in immediate contact with,
ava√ghuṣ to proclaim aloud,
avaghuṣita mfn approved of,
avaghuṣṭa mfn proclaimed aloud, offered publicly as food, sent for, summoned, addressed aloud to attract attention,
avagoraṇa n. menacing,
ava√grah to let loose, let go, to impede, stop, to divide, (in gram.) to separate as words or parts of a word,
avagraha m. separation of the component parts of a compound, or of the stem and certain suffixes and terminations, the mark or the interval of such a separation, mark of the elision of an initial ‘*a*’, obstacle, impediment, restraint, drought, nature, original, temperament, perception with the senses, a form of knowledge, an imprecation, an elephants forehead, a herd of elephants, an iron hook for driving elephants,
avagrāha m. obstacle, impediment, a bucket, the forehead of an elephant,
avagrāham ind. so as to separate the words, the forehead of an elephant,
avagrahana n. act of impeding, restraining
ava√guh *-gūhati,* to cover, hide, conceal, put into or inside, embrace,
avagūhana n. hiding, concealing,
avaguṇa mfn deficient in good qualities
avaguṇḍita mfn pounded, ground,
ava√guṇṭh *-guṇṭhayati* to cover with, conceal
avaguṇṭhana n. hiding, veiling,
ā√vah P.A. to *āvahati* to drive or lead near or towards, to bring, fetch, procure,
ava√3.hā to leave, quit, pass. to be left remaining, left behind, to be excelled, be abandoned, caus. to cause to remain behind on or to deviate from a path (5th),
āvaha 155/1mfn. bringing, bringing to pass, producing, what bears or conveys, m. inviting, invitation, one of 7 winds or bands of air, or fires
avahālikā f.a wall, hedge, fence,
ava√han to throw down, strike, hit, to drive away, expel, keep off,
āvāhana n. appeal, invitation, invocation, bringing near,
avahanana mfn threshing, winnowing,
avahant mfn not flowing, standing,
āvahantī a bringer,

avahāra m. truce, suspension of arms, cessation of playing, summoning, inviting, a thief, apostasy,
avahāraka mfn one who stops fighting, etc
avaharaṇa n. putting aside, throwing away,
ava√has to laugh at, deride,
avahāsa 106/2 jest, joke, laughing
avahasana n. deriding,
avahāsya mfn to be derided, ridiculous,
avahata mfn threshed, winnowed,
avahela n.f. disrespect, disregard, (*ayā* 3rd) ind. without any trouble, quite easily,
avahita plunged into, fallen into, placed into, confined within, attentive,
avahittha n. dissimulation, f. (*ā*)
ava√īkṣ Cl 1 *-īkṣate,* to look after, look upon, see, regard,
avaikalya n. perfection, non-distraction,
avaiklavya absence of frailness, distress or despair
avajānanti they despise or treat with contempt 1/s/pres/indic/act *ava √jñā*
avajaya m. overcoming, winning by conquest,
ava√ji to spoil (deprive of by conquest), win, conquer, ward off,
avājin m. a bad horse,
avajita mfn won by conquest,
avajiti f. conquest, victory,
ava√jñā –jānāti to have a low opinion of, treat with contempt, despise, 2. f. contempt, disesteem, disrespect, disdain, mfn treated with contempt, humiliated,
avajñāta 98/2 mfn. despised, disrespected
ava√jval caus. *–jvalayati* to set on fire,
avajvalana n. illumining,
avajyotana n. causing a light to shine upon, illumining,
ava√jyut caus. *–jyotayati* to light up or cause a light to shine upon, illumine,
avāk ind. downwards, headlong, being or situated below, turned downwards,
avakā f. a grassy swamp plant,
avakalkana n. mingling, mixing together,
avakāśa m. 1. an open place, 2. opportunity, occasion, scope,
avakhaṅḍana 97/1 breaking into pieces, destroying
ava√kāṅkṣ to desire, long for,
avakara m. dust or sweepings,
avakarṣaṇa n. taking off, etc.
ava√kāś to be visible, be manifest,
avakāśa m. place, space, room, occasion, opportunity,
avakāśada mfn giving opportunity, granting the use of,
avakāśavat mfn spacious,
ava√khyā to look down, to see, perceive,
avākin mfn not speaking,
avākka mfn speechless,
avakleda m. *–kledana* n. trickling, descent of moisture,
ava√klṛp -kalpate, to correspond to, answer, be right, to be fit for, serve to, caus.*-kalpayati* to put in order, prepare, make ready, to consider as possible, to emply becomingly,
avaklṛpta mfn corresponding with, right, fit,
avaklṛpti f. considering as possible,
ava√1.kṛ to direct downwards (as the face),
avā√1.kṛ to ward off, remove,
avakra mfn not crooked, straight, upright, honest,
ava√kram to step down upon, to tread down, overcome,
avakrāmin mfn running away,
ava√krīḍ A. to play,
ava√kṛṣ to draw off or away, take off, take off (a garment or wreath) to turn off, remove, drag down,
ava√kṛt Cl 6 *–kṛntati* cut down, cut off, to destroy,
avākṣaka 106/3 having shoots turned down, (as the Ficus Indica),
avākśruti mfn deaf and dumb,
avakṛṣṭa mfn dragged down, being underneath anything, 'removed' being at some distance,
avakṣāma mfn meagre, lean,
avakṣaya m. destruction, waste, loss,
avakṣepaṇa 97/1 n throwing down, overcoming, reviling, blame, (G) downward motion,

avakṣipta mfn thrown down, said sarcastically, imputed, insinuated,
ava√kṣṇu to rub off, efface,
avaktavya mfn not to be said, indescribable,
ava√kūj to make a sound, utter,
ava√kūl to singe, burn,
avakuñcana n. curving, flexure, contraction,
avakuṇṭhana n. investing, surrounding, covering,
avakvaṇa m. a discordant or false note,
ava√lag to fasten to,
ava√lamb, -lambate, to hang down, glide or slip down, descend, to set (the sun), to catch hold, hold on, rest upon, depend upon, to hold up anything, adopt (a position),
avalamba mfn hanging down from, m. depending, resting upon, support, a prop, a stay,
avalambana mfn hanging on, clinging to, (am) n. hanging down, depending upon, dependance, support, basis, making a halt, stopping at,
avalambate 103/2 rests on, 1/s/pres/indic/mid depends upon,
avalambin mfn hanging down to rest upon,
avalambitavya to be held onto, caught hold of, to be clung to,
ava√laṅgh to pass or spend time,
avalaṅghita mfn passed (as time)
avaleha m. licking, lapping,
avalekha m. anything scraped off, (*ā*)f. drawing, painting,
avalekhana n. brushing, combing,
avalepa m. pride, insult, arrogance, ointment, ornament,
avalepana n. ointment, proud behaviour, arrogance,
ava√lī A. to stick to, to bow, stoop,
āvali m. (ī) f. a continuous line, series, dynasty, a row, range,
ava√lih to lick, lap,
ava√likh to scratch, graze,
avalīlā f. play, sport, ind. quite easily,
ava√lip P. to smear, A. to smear oneself,
ava√lok cl 1 A. *-lokate*, to look, cl 10 P. –*lokayati* to look upon or at, view, behold, see, notice,
avalokana 103/3 n. seeing, viewing, view, observing, looking at, gazing on, a look, glance, appearance of, the aspect, observation,
avalokin mfn looking at, beholding,
avalokita mfn seen, viewed, observed, having been seen,
avalokya having seen, to be looked at,
avalopa m. interruption,
ava√lup P.A. to cut or take off, to take away by force, wrest,
avalupti f. falling off,
āvām *pron.* we/us two
ava√3.mā to measure off,
avama n. undermost, inferior, lowest, base, next, intimate, last, youngest,
ava√majj to immerse,
ava√man to despise, treat, contemptuously to repudiate, refuse,
avamāna 101/3 disrespect, contempt, dishonour
avamarda m. appresion, giving pain,
avamarśa m. touch, contact, reflecting upon
avamarśam m. touch, contact, reflecting upon, ind. so as to touch,
avamarśita mfn touched,disturbed (sacrifice)
avamata mfn despised, disregarded,
avamati f. aversion, dislike, disregard
avamocana n. loosening, setting at liberty, 'where horses are unharnessed', a place for resting, settling,
ava√mṛś to touch, to reflect upon,
avaṁśa m. a low or despised family, n. that which has no pillars or support
ava√muc P. to loosen, let go, to unharness, take off a garment, A. to liberate oneself from, strip off
ava√mūrch to be appeased or allayed,
ava√muṣ to take away,
avana n. favour, preservation, protection, satisfaction, joy, pleasure, mfn preserving, a preserver,
avanaddha mfn bound on, tied, covered with, n. a drum,
ava√nah to cover with

avanāha m. binding or putting on,
ava√nam to bow, make a bow to,
to bow down
avanāma m. bending, bowing,
avanamra mfn bowed, bent,
ava√2.naś to disappear, perish,
avanata mfn bent down
avanatakāya mfn with bent down body,
avanāya m. placing down,
avanayana n. pouring down,
avāñc,āṅ, ācī āk, (fr.2. *añc)*, turned downwards, being or situated below, lower than, *avāñcam* ind. downwards,
avāñca mfn turned or bent down,
avanejana mfn washing the feet, n. ablution of hands or feet,
avaneya mfn to be led away,
avaṅgmanogocara beyond the reach of speech and mind; Brahman or the Self, (U)
avani f. course, bed of a river, stream, earth,
avani√nī to put or bring into water,
ava√nij to wash esp. the feet, wash oneself,
avanikta mfn washed,
avanipāla m. ruler of the earth, a king,
avaniścaya m. inference, deduction, ascertainment,
avāntara mfn intermediate, respectively different, respective, (*am*) ind. differently from (5th), ind. between,
avantiḥ name of a city (now Ujjain)
ava√3.nu A. to move towards,
ava √āp Cl 5 *–āpnoti* to reach, obtain, attain, incur,
to get by division (quotient),
-*vat* mfn reaching, obtaining,
ava√pad –padyate to fall down,
glide down into,
avapāda m. falling down,
avapāna n. drinking, a pond or pool for watering,
avapanna mfn fallen down, that on which anything has fallen down,
ava√paś P. *–paśyati* to look down upon,
A. *–paśyate* to look upon
avāpa-sthāna the place where the oblations are poured,
ava√pat to fly down, jump down, fall down,
avapatana n. falling down,
ava√pīḍ to press down, compress,
ava√piṣ to crush or grind to pieces, to crush
ava√plu to jump down as from a cart,
avapluta mfn jumped down from, plunged into, gone away from, departed,
avaplutya ind. jumping down,
avāpnoti 107/1 to reach, obtain, get, gain, 1/s/pres/act. to cause to obtain anything, he attains
avāpnu 107/1 *avāpnuhi* to reach, obtain, attain. -*nuyāt* opt.act. 1/s should attain
avapothita mfn thrown or knocked down,
avapothikā f. anything used for knocking down, e.g. stones on besiegers,
avapūrṇa mfn filled with,
avāpya ind. having attained/obtained, mfn to be obtained,
avāpsyasi you will attain, you will incur
avāpsyatha you shall attain, you shall achieve, 2/pl/fut/mid *ava √āp*
avāptavya to be attained or reached gerundive
avāpti 107/1 f. obtaining, getting
avāptum infin. to attain, reach *ava √āp*
avāpyate it is attained or reached, 1/s/pres/indic/pass *ava √āp*
avara 102/2 mfn below,later, inferior, low, mean, posterior, West,
n. the lowest, the meanest
avāra this side, the near bank (river),
ava√rādh to commit a fault
avaraja n. of low birth, inferior, younger,
ava√ramb to hang down,
āvaraṇa 'the limiting of the limitless or superimposing one limit on another' such as 'the presumption of snake over rope. N. covering, the act of covering, This superimposition causes agitation (*vikṣepa*).
156/1 mfn. covering, hiding, concealing, (*am*) n. the act of covering, concealing, cloth (in phil. mental blindness), an outer fence, wall, shield, the 'veil of ignorance',
āvaraṇa- abhava absence of the covering

veil,
āvaraṇa- bhaṅga destruction of the veil of ignorance,
āvaraṇacyutiḥ 'destruction of covering' (Gam.),
āvaraṇaśakti f. the power of illusion (that which veils the real nature of things),
avāraṇīya not to be stopped or kept back, unrestrainable (as water), belonging to *āvaraṇa* or mental blindness,
avarapara ind. one upon the other, n. preceding and following
avarārdha m. ifc. the least part, the minimum 102/2
avarārdhya mfn being on the lower or near side, beginning from below,
avaratara mfn farther down,
avaratas ind. at least, below,
avarati f. stopping, ceasing,
avaravarṇa m. a low or despised caste,
avaravarṇaja born in a low caste,
avaravrata m. the sun,
avarcas mfn having no vigour or energy,
avardhata grew
avardhamāna mfn not growing,
avārita mfn unimpeded, unobstructed,
avarjanīya mfn inevitable,
avarṇa 1. mfn having no outward appearance, colourless, featureless m. blame, speaking ill of, 2. the vowel *a* or *ā*
avarṇya mfn indescribable,
avaroha m. descent, mounting, a shoot or root sent down from a branch, a creeping plant climbing to the top of a tree, descending from a higher tone to a lower one, heaven,
avarṣa n. want of rain, a drought,
avasarpiṇī f. 'going or gliding down gradually',
avarṣin mfn not raining,
āvarta m. an eddy, turning, winding, turning round, deliberating,
avartamāna mfn not of the present time,
avarti f. poverty, distress, bad fortune,
avartra mfn unimpeded, unrestrained,
avarocaka m. want of appetite,
avarodha 1. mfn hindrance, obstruction, injury, harm, seclusion, imprisonment, an enclosure, confinement, a covering, a lid, fence, pen, the inner apartments, the queen's or women's apartments, 2. m. moving down, a shoot or root sent down by a branch,
avarodhaka mfn hindering, being about to besiege, m. a guard, f. a female of the inner apartments, a barrier, fence,
avarodhana mfn procuring, n. siege, blockade, a closed or private place, the innermost part of anything, secluding, imprisonment, 2. n. descending motion,
avaroha m. descent, also musically by tone
avarokin mfn shining, brilliant,
avaropana n. planting, causing to descend, depriving, diminishing,
avaropita, mfn caused to descend, taken down from, deprived of, lowered, lessened, curtailed, lost, silenced,
avaropya ind. having made or making to descend,
āvarta 156/1 m. turning, winding, turning round, deliberating
ava√ruc, -rocate to shine down,
avaruddha mfn hindered, checked, stopped, kept back, shut in, enclosed, imprisoned, secluded,
ava√2.rudh to check, keep back, restrain, to expel, put aside, seclude, remove, to shut in, keep anything (as grief) locked up (in one's bosom),
avarudita mfn that upon which tears have fallen
ava√ruh to descend, alight, dismount, caus. *avaropayati* cause to descend, dismiss from office,
avā√ruh to bring down from (5th),
avarūpa mfn misshapen, deformed,
avas 1. n. favour, furtherance, protection, assistance, refreshing, enjoyment, pleasure, wish, desire, (as of men for the gods or of waters for the sea), 2. ind. downwards, (as a prep) down from,

avās (√2. as) to put down,
avaśa 104/1mfn unsubmissive to another's will, without will, against will, unrestrained, independent, free, powerless, helpless,
āvāsa m. dwelling, house, abode,
avaśā f. not a cow, a bad cow,
avasa n. refreshment, food, provisions,
avasā f. liberation, deliverance,
avasāna n. ending, cessation, end, completion, building site,
avāsana n. abatement,
āvasāna mfn dwelling on the boundaries of a village,
avāsas mfn unclothed,
ava√sad P. *–sīdati,* to sink (as in water), to sink down, faint, grow lean, become exhausted or disheartened, slacken, come to an end, come to naught, perish, caus. *avasādayati* causes to sink down weakens (ignorance etc), renders down-hearted, ruins, frustrates,
avasāda m. sinking (as of a chair), growing faint (as of a sound), failing, exhaustion, fatigue, lassitude, defeat, want of energy or spirit, (in law) poorness of a cause, end, termination,
avasādaka mfn causing to sink, frustrating, exhausting, tiresome, wearisome, ending, finishing,
avasādana 105/1 oppressing, disheartening
avasādayet one should degrade, cause to sink, render downhearted, dispirit, 1/s/caus/act/opt *ava √ sad* 104/3
avasādita mfn made to sink, exhausted,
avasakta mfn suspended from, attached to, bound round, being in contact with, belonging to, hung with (wreaths),
avasaṁcakṣya mfn to be shunned, avoided,
ava√sañj to suspend, attach to, append, A. *–sajjate,* to adhere or cleave to, not leave undisturbed,
avasāna mfn not dressed, 2. n. where the horses are unharnessed, stopping or resting place, residence, a chosen building site, conclusion, termination, cessation, death, boundary, limit, end of a word, last part of a compound, end of a phrase, end of a line of verse or the line itself, conclusion,
avasānabhūmi f. the highest limit,
avasañjana n. the Brāhmanic thread hanging over the shoulder,
avasanna mfn sunk down, pressed down,
avasara 105/1 m. rain, occasion, moment, favourable opportunity, seasonableness, appropriate place for anything (6th) , anyone's turn (6th), leisure,advantageous situation, a year, ind. (7th *–e*) at the right moment, *avasarakāle* or *–velāyām* 7th ind. on a favourable opportunity,
avasāraṇa n. moving away
avasarga m. letting loose, letting go, relaxation, laxity, following one's own inclinations, independence,
avasare ind. at the right moment, opportune,
avasarjana n. liberation,
avasarjita mfn who has abandoned,
avasarpa m. one who creeps up, a spy,
avasarpaṇa n. descent, going down to,
avaśas 104/1 unsubmissive to another's will, without will, against will, unrestrained, independent, free, 104/2 f. wrong desire,
avasat dwelt
avaśātana n. withering, drying up,
avasatha m. habitation, a village, a college, school, n. a house, dwelling,
āvasatha 155/1 m. dwelling place, abode, habitation, night's lodging, a dwelling for pupils and ascetics, a village,
avasathin mfn having a habitation,
avasathya mfn belonging to a house, domestic, m. a college, school,
avasātṛ, tā m. a liberator,
avasavi ind. to the left,
avasavya mfn not left, right,
avasāya .2.m. taking up one's abode,
avasāyaka mfn (said of an arrow *sāyaka*), 'bringing to a close' destructive,
ava√ścut to trickle down,
avasecana n. sprinkling, water for irrigating

(trees), bathing, bleeding,
avaseka m. sprinkling, irrigating, syringing, bleeding,
avaśeṣa n. leavings, remainder, (*am*) ind. so as to leave as a remnant,
avaśeṣita mfn left as a remnant, remaining,
avaśeṣya mfn to be left or kept remaining,
avaseya mfn to be ascertained, understood, be made out, be learnt from,
ava√3.śī A. to fall or drop off,
ava√sic to sprinkle, pour upon, pour out,
ava√2.sidh to keep back or off from,
avasikta mfn sprinkled,
avaśīna or *–śyāna* mfn coagulated,
avaśīrṇa mfn broken, shattered,
ava√śiṣ pass. -śiṣyate, to be left as a remnant, remain,
avaśiṣṭa mfn left, remaining,
avaśiṣṭaka n. remainder,
avaśiṣyate 104/2 to be left as a remnant, remain, 1/s/pres/indic/pass remains
avaśīta or *–śyāta* mfn cooled, cool,
avasita mfn terminated, over, fulfilled, one who dwells, rests, resides ended, finished, completed, determined, ascertained, known, understood, one who is determined to (7th), stored (as grain), gone, being at the end of a line of verse,
avaskanda m. assault, attack, storm,
avaskandana n. descending, bathing, (in law) accusation,
ava√so, -syati to loosen, deliver from, to unharness, put up at anyone's house, settle, rest, to finish, terminate, to be finished, be at an end, , be exhausted, to decide, to obtain, caus.pass. *–sāyayati* to ascertain, clearly distinguish,
avaspandana having a sense of movement, quivering, a movement away
avaspartṛ m. a preserver, saviour
ava√sphūrj to thunder, make a noise like a thunderclap,
avasphūrja m. the rolling of thunder,
ava√smi A. to flash down, (lightning),
ava√spṛ to defend, preserve from,
ava√śṝ to break (as anyone's anger), to be dispersed, fly in every direction,
ava√sṛ caus. to move anything aside/away
avasraṁsana 1317/1 n falling down
avasrasta mfn fallen down,
ava√śrath caus. to loosen
avaśrayaṇa n. taking (anything) off the fire,
ava√sṛj to fling, throw, (arrows, thunderbolt) to throw or put into, to let off, let loose, let go, send, dismiss, abandon, surrender, to give up (one's anger or one's life), to pardon, to deliver (a woman), to be delivered, bring forth, to produce, form, shape, to relax, lose energy and power, to attach to,
ava√sṛp, -sarpati to set (the sun), to flow back (as in low tide), to creep to or approach unawares, to flow over gradually,
avasṛṣṭa mfn let loose, thrown (as arrows, thunderbolt), mfn made over, dismissed, sent, brought forth (from the womb),
ava√sru caus. to cause to flow down
avasruta mfn run or dropped down,
avaṣṭabdha mfn standing firm, supported by, resting on, seized, arrested, standing near, being near, approaching,
avastabdha mfn stiff, (with cold etc.),
avaṣṭabhya 104/2 ind. having rested upon, leaned upon, barricaded, mfn to be seized or stopped, supported by, ind. to be seized or stopped,
avaṣṭambh (√stambh), -ṣṭabhnoti to lean or rest upon, to bar, barricade,
avaṣṭambha m. leaning or resting on, having recourse to anything, applying, self-confidence, resoluteness, beginning, obstruction, impediment, a post or pillar, gold,
avaṣṭambhana n. having recourse to,
avastāra m. a litter, bed,
avastaraṇa n. strewing, a cover for a bed,
avāstava mfn unsubstantial, unreal, fictitious, unfounded, irrational
ava√sthā 105/3 P. *-tiṣṭathi* to go down

into(2nd), reach down to (2nd), to go away from (5th), to be separated from or deprived of (5th), A. to take one's stand, remain standing, stay, abide, stop at any place, to abide in a state or condition (3rd), to remain or continue doing anything, to be found, exist, be present, to enter, be absorbed in, to come to rest, (7th), to penetrate as sound or fame, caus. to cause to stand or stop, to place upon, fix, set, to cause to enter or be absorbed in (7th), to render solid or firm, to establish (by arguments), (G) state of experience, state of consciousness, condition,

avastha m. penis, *(ā)* f. appearance (in a court of justice), stability, consistence, state, condition, situation, circumstance of age or position, stage, degree, f.pl. the female organs of generation,

avasthābheda (G) difference in condition, any individual state of experience of ignorance,

avasthā-catuṣṭaya the 4 periods of human life – childhood, youth, manhood, old age,

avasthādvaya n. the two states of life – happiness and misery,

avasthāna 106/1 standing, taking up one's place, situation, condition, residing, abiding, dwelling,

avasthānāntaragataprāpti 'the state of the effect being resolved or involved into the cause' (U),

avasthāsthiti permanent abiding, changelessness,

avasthātraya n. the 3 states, waking, dreaming, sound sleep,

avasthātum 105/3 to stand, to remain standing, infinitive of *ava √sthā*

avasthāvan mfn possessed of stability,

avasthāyin mfn staying, residing in, abiding in a particular condition

avasthita 106/*1* mfn. standing near, arrayed, having its place or abode, abiding, resident, continuing to do anything, stationed, placed

avasthiti f. residence, abiding, stability,

avastra mfn without clothes, naked,

avastu n. a worthless thing, the unreality of matter, insubstantiality, unreality

avastutvāt because of being ultimately unreal,

avāstu mfn having no home,

avastuka mfn unsubstantial, not an existent thing

avasupta mfn asleep,

ava√śuṣ, -śuṣyati to become dry,

avasvadvat mfn united with the desirous one,

avaṣvan (√svan) -ṣvaṇati to smack one's lips, eat noisily

avasvat mfn desirous,

avasya Nom P. to seek favour or assistance,

avaśya mfn necessary, ind. necessarily, inevitably, certainly, at all events, by all means, (also) disobedient,

avaśyā f. hoar frost, dew,

āvaśyaka mfn necessary, inevitable, (*am*) n. necessity, inevitable act or conclusion,

avaśyam ind. necessarily, surely, of course, indeed,

avaśyāya m. hoar frost, dew,

avasyu mfn desiring favour or assistance, desirous of helping or assisting,

avaṭa m. a hole, vacuity in the ground, a hole in a tooth, any depressed part of the body, a sinus, a juggler,

avata m. a well, cistern,

avāta mfn not dried up, fresh,
2. mfn windless, windless atmosphere
3. mfn unattacked, untroubled,

ava√taḍ caus.–*tāḍayati* to strike downwards,

avatakṣaṇa n. anything cut in pieces,

avataṁsa m. ear-ring,

avatamasa n. slight darkness, obscurity,

avataṁsana n. a garland,

ava√tan -tanoti to stretch or extend downwards, to overspread, cover, to loosen, undo,

avatansana 98/3n a garland, pushing on a

carriage
ava√tap to radiate heat or light downwards, to heat or light from above,
avatapta mfn heated,
avatara m. descent, entrance, opportunity,
avatāra m. descent (esp. of a deity from heaven),appearance of any deity on earth, an incarnation of *Viṣṇu,* any new and unexpected appearance, (any distinguished person in the language of respect is called an Avatāra or incarnation of a deity), opportunity of catching anyone, translation,
avataram ind. more favourably or with greater pleasure
avataraṇa n. descending, alighting, 'rushing away', translating,
avatarati comes down, descends
avatāra-vāda the doctrine that holds that God takes human form,
avatarda m. splitting, perforation,
avatārita mfn caused to descend, fetched down from, taken down, laid down, set aside, set going, rendered current, accomplished,
avatata mfn extended downwards, covered
avatati f. stretching, extending,
avatīrya gerund, having descended, incarnating,
avatiṣṭhati 105/3 remains standing, stays, abides, takes his stand, remains firm
avātita mfn gone down,
ava√tṝ cl 1 P *–tarati* to descend into, alight from, alight, descend (as a deity) in becoming incarnate, make one's appearance, arrive, arrive at, to be in the right place, to fit, undertake, Ved. cl 6P. to overcome, sink, caus. *avatārayati* to remove,
avatrasta mfn terrified,
avatṛṇṇa mfn split, having holes
ava√tsar to fly away,
avatta mfn cut off, divided,
avatu √*av* cl 1 P *avati,* to drive, impel, animate, to promote, favour, satisfy, refresh, to offer, to lead or bring to, to be pleased with or accept (gods), to guard, defend, protect, 1/s/pres/impv/act may he protect, let him protect,-
ava√tviṣ to glitter, shine, give, dwell,
ava√vā *-vāti,* to blow down, to snort towards (a bull), to crackle towards (a fire),
ava√vad to speak ill of or against,
avavāda m. speaking ill of, evil report,
avavadana n. speaking ill of,
avavadita mfn instructed, taught,
avavaditṛ m. one who speaks finally, gives the definitive opinion,
avāvan mfn one who carries off, a thief,
avāya m. going down(into water),
ava√yaj *1.* to offer a sacrifice a for result, to get rid of by sacrifice,
2. f. share of the sacrificial oblation,
avayava 102/2 a limb, member, part, portion, particle,
avayavin mfn having portions or subdivisions, a whole,
āvayoḥ pron. of/in us two
ava√1.yu to separate from, to keep off,
avāyu mfn without wind,
avayuna mfn indistinguishable, indistinct, dark,
avayuti f. separation, ind. separately (3rd),
āvābhyām pron. by/for/from us two
āvega m. hurry or haste produced by excitement, flurry, agitation,
avekṣ *ava√īkṣ* Cl1 *avekṣate* watches, watches over,
avekṣā f. a looking around, observation, care, attention to (7th),
avekṣe I see, I behold, 111/1 *ava √īkṣ* 1/s/pres/indic/mid
avekṣya looking at, perceiving, beholding, mfn to be attended to,
āveśa 155/3 m. joining one's self, taking possession of, absorption of the faculties in one wish or idea, an attack of emotion, intentness, devotedness to an object, possession, anger, wrath, pride,

arrogance, indistinctness of idea, 'agitative charge or aggressiveness'
aveśita entering, abiding in,
āveśya having caused to enter, fixing, concentrating
caus.gerund *ā√viś*
avi m. sheep, a protector, lord, the sun, f. ewe, mfn favourable, kindly disposed,
āvi, āvis, āvī f. pain, suffering, (*yas*) f.pl. pangs of childbirth,
avibhāga m. non separation, non distinction between, inseparability,
avibhakta 109/2 mfn. undivided, not shared, joint, (*am*) n.
avicchindant mfn not severing,
avicchinna mfn not severed, continuous, undivided, not cut off,
avīci mfn waveless, m. a partic. hell,
avicikitsat mfn not having doubts,
ā√vid Cl1 to know well or thoroughly
caus. *āvedayati*, to make known, report, declare, to offer, present,
Cl3 to reach, obtain, to get into, to exist,
avidāsin mfn not drying up, perennial,
avidhānatas ind. not according to regulation, irregularly,
avidhavā f. not a widow,
avidhi mfn abnormal, anomalous, perverted, f. anomaly, aberration, partic. rites not done in accord with rules,
avidhipūrvakam 109/1 ind. not according to Vedic rule, in the absence of fixed rules,
avidita 108/3 mfn. unknown
without the knowledge of (6th),
(am) ind. so that nobody knows
avidūrataḥ mfn not very far away, near,
avidvāṁa the unwise perf.act.part *a √vid*
avidvān mfn ignorant,
avidvas mfn ignorant, not knowing,
*avidyā*108/3 mfn. unlearned, unwise,
1/s/f ignorance, spiritual ignorance, illusion; 'a *śakti* or illusive power in Brahman which is sometimes regarded as one with *māyā* and sometimes as different from it. It forms the condition of the individual soul and is otherwise called *ajñāna* or *aśuddha-māya.* It forms the *kāraṇa śarīra* (causal body) of *jīva.* It is *malina* or impure *sattva.'* (U), it is beginningless and removed by right knowledge, (G)
avidyāgranthim the knot of ignorance,
avidyā-nāśa m. destruction of ignorance, liberation from bondage of embodiment,
avidyā-nivṛtti removal of ignorance, *mokśa,*
avidyā-saṁskāra the impression of basic ignorance
avidyopādhikasattva (N) existence which has *avidyā* as its limiting adjunct
avidyopādhi-paricchinna the nature of the *jīva* – '*paricchinna* is divided, finite. *Jīva* is finite with the limiting adjunct of ignorance', (U)
avighāta m. without hindrance or obstacle, mfn unimpeded,
avighna mfn unimpeded, uninterrupted, n. want of obstacle, undisturbedness
āviḥ self-effulgent, before the eyes, openly, manifestly, evidently,
avihvala 110/3 not disquieted, unperturbed mind undisturbed, not hesitating, having courage,
avijñeya mfn unknowable, not distinguishable, not discernible,
avijñāna 108/2 mfn not having any information, (*am*) n. no knowledge, (*āt* 5th) ind. without knowing, unawares, devoid of sentience, insentient stone etc.
avijñāta mfn unknown, indistinct, doubtful, not noticed, passed unawares, Brahman,
avijñāya ind. without discerning, not having discriminated,
avijñeya not to be known or understood gerundive 1/s/n
āvika mfn relating to or coming from sheep, woollen, f.n. a sheepskin,
avikalpita mfn undoubted,
avikampa unwavering

avikāra m. non-change of form or nature, non-alteration, mfn unchangeable, immutable,

avikārin mfn unchangeable, unchangeable in character, faithful, not exhibiting any alteration, Brahman,

avikārya mfn. invariable, not able to be changed,

avikriya 107/3 unchangeable, invariable,

avikṛta 107/3 unchanged, not prepared being in its natural condition

āvila mfn turbid, foul, not clear, confused,

avilambam ind. without delay, m. non-delay, following immediately, mfn prompt, expeditious,

avimukta mfn not loosened, the un-liberated soul,

avinābhāva m. necessary connection of one thing with another, inherent and essential character, 109/1

avinābhāvin mfn necessarily connected with, inherent, inseparable relationship,

avināśa 109/1 m. non-destruction

avināśin imperishable, not decaying or putrefying,

avinaśyanta mfn indestructible,

avinaya mfn misbehaving, m. bad behaviour, disrespect, rudeness, pride, want of good manners, arrogance, immodesty,

avipaścit 109/1 mfn. unwise, ignorant, non-discriminating,

avipluta mfn not dishonoured, unsullied, unviolated, undeviating,

aviprayukta 109/2 mfn not separated, 'diversely used' (Gam.),

avirata mfn uninterrupted, continuous, not desisting from, (*am*) ind. continuously,

avirati f. lack of control, incontinence, intemperance, non-restraint, sensual indulgence,

āvirbhāva m. manifestation, becoming visible, presence,

āvir√bhū cl 1 *–bhavati,* to be or become visible, to manifest, be present before the eyes,

āvirbhūta mfn become apparent, visible, manifest,

avirodha m. non-opposition to, living or being in agreement with, non-conflict, without contradiction,

aviruddha 109/3 mfn. unobstructed, unimpeded, not incompatible with, consistent with, not opposed to, not encountering resistance from, not contradictory,

ā√viś to go or drive in or towards, approach, enter into or upon, settle, reach, obtain
with *kṛ* make visible,

āvis ind. before the eyes, in view, openly, manifestly, evidently,

aviśabdana 107/2 means *pratijñāna* - the disclosure of one's intentions by means of words, favourable or kindly disposed speech

aviśaṅka 110/1 having no doubts, not hesitating, (*ā*) f. 'no hesitation', (*ayā)* ind. 3rd without hesitation, undoubtingly,

aviśaṅkita mfn unapprehensive, not having doubts, not hesitating,

āviśati he, she enters, 1/s/pres/act √*viś*

aviṣaya m. a non-province, something out of one's line or that one has no business to do, unlawful thing, anything impossible or improper, matter beyond the scope of,

aviśeña 110/1 m. non-distinction, non-difference, uniformity, ind. without a special distinction or difference, not differently, equally, (in *sāṁkhyā* phil.) name of the five elementary substances (pl.),

aviśiṣṭa " a synonym for *nirguṇa*" HH uniformity,

āviṣkāra 155/3 making visible, manifestation,

aviṣṭa *m.* taken possession of, fallen into, overcome by, ppp. *a* √*viś*

āviṣṭa 155/1 *ā*√*viś,* mfn. entered, being on or in, intent on, subject to, possessed, engrossed, filled (by sentiment)

aviśvāsa m. distrust, suspicion, mistrusted, mfn not inspiring with confidence,
āviśya entering, approaching, having entered or approached, gerund *ā√viś*
āviśyā f. desire, ardour,
avīta mfn not enjoyed (as a sacrificial oblation), 110/3
avittvā not having found,
avivāda m. non-disputed, agreement,
aviveka mfn without discrimination, absence of judgment or discrimination, non-separation, non-distinction,
avivekatā f. lack of judgment, inconsiderateness,
avināśin 109/1 imperishable
avratī (A) p60 desireless (E) p132 passionless
avitatha 108/2 mfn not untrue, true, not vain or futile, *(am)* ind. not falsely, according to truth,
avivāda 110/1 m. non-dispute, agreement, mfn not disputed, agreed upon, (N) 'not making dispute',
ā √vṛ 156/1 to cover, hide, conceal, encompass, surround,
avṛaṇa not wounded, unscarred, entire,
āvriyate he is covered, he is enveloped 1/s/pres/indic/pass *ā √vṛ* 156/1
avṛka mfn not harmful, (*am*) ind. harmlessly, lovingly,
āvṛta covered, enveloped, covered, obscured, surrounded,
ā √ vṛt 1.turn or draw round or back or near
āvṛt 2. f. a turning towards or home, entering, turn of path or way, course, process, direction,
āvṛta 156/1 mfn. enveloped, covered, concealed
āvṛtta turned round, stirred, whirled, reverted, averted, retreated, fled, (*am*) n. addressing a prayer or songs to a god,
āvṛtti f. turning towards, entering, turning back or from, reversion, retreat, flight, recurrence to the same point, repetition, turn of a way, occurrence, revolving, going round, worldly existence, return, rebirth, use, employment, application, repetition,
āvṛtti-cakṣu whose gaze is turned inwards,
āvṛtya ind. enveloping, covering, obscuring, having enveloped, spread or pervaded, 2. having turned, turning towards etc.
avyabhicāra 111/3 m. non-deviation, not going astray or wandering, non-transgression, unwavering, conjugal fidelity,
-cārin mfn. as above, permanent
avyākṛta mfn undeveloped, unexpounded, undifferentiated, undefined, (Buddhism) unanswerable questions, questions Buddha declined to answer, inconceivable, *(am)* n. elementary substance from which all things were created, considered as one with the substance of Brahma,
avyakta 111/2 mfn undeveloped, not manifest, invisible, imperceptible, "..the unmanifest nature of the Absolute, .. it is here that the divine regulations are held and may be known" LM,
unmanifest (in seed or causal form), m. the Universal Spirit,
avyakta-dṛṣṭi the view from the standpoint of Absolute
avyakta-nāda unmanifested sound,
avyakta śabda - *avyakta* as above
śabda sound, word, speech, language
avyaktāyām vāci in unmanifest speech
avyapadeśya 111/3 mfn not to be defined, indescribable (by words) (Gam.),
avyāpti non-comprehensiveness, inadequate pervasion, failure of an argument because a definition is too narrow or incomplete, e.g. 'a pot is blue',
avyāpyavṛtti mfn being of limited application, of partial inherence,
avyasana mfn free from evil practices, (G) absence of attachment,
avyavahāra m. improper conduct or

practice, free from worldly activities or concerns,

avyavahārya 112/1 mfn not to be practised, not to be discussed in law, unactionable, beyond empirical dealings (Gam.), non-usable, (G) unrelatable, (N) Xuan Zang translates (as principle of the Void [Buddh.]) 'not to be argued about',

avyavahita mfn uninterrupted, not separated, adjoining, contiguous, separated by the letter *a,*

avyavasāya m. irresolute, wavering,

avyavasāyin mfn inactive, negligent, remiss, mfn not possessing resolution, irresolute,

avyaya 111/3 1.mfn made of sheepskin, belonging to or consisting of sheep, 2. an indeclinable word, particle, imperishable, undecaying, words or particles which do not change their grammatical form whatever the position in a sentence, not liable to change, undiminishing, undecaying, imperishable

aya 84/2 m. ifc. going, a move towards the right at chess, a die, the number 4, good luck, favourable fortune,

ā√yā Cl 2 *–yāti,* to come near or towards, to arrive, approach, reach, attain, get or fall into any state or condition, to be reduced to, become anything,

ayam m. pron. 1/s this, this one, he, here (is), see, hereby,

ayāma m. not a night-watch, anytime during daylight, not a path,

āyāma 148/2 m. stretching, extending, restraining, stopping, expansion, length (in space or time), breadth (in mensuration), extent, extension,

āyamya 1. mfn to be stretched, to be restrained, 2. ind. having extended, drawn out, e.g. a bowstring, *ā√yam*

ayana mfn going, (*am*) n. walking a road, a path, the sun's road north and south of the equator, the half year, way, progress, manner, place of refuge,

ayaneśu 7/pl/n in positions, progress, movements

ayas n. metal, iron, an iron weapon (axe etc.), gold, steel,

ayaśas 85/1 n. infamy, disrepute, bad reputation, mfn devoid of fame, disgraced,

āyasa 148/2 mfn of iron, made of iron or metal, iron-coloured, armed with an iron weapon, f. (*ī*) body armour, a breastplate, coat of mail, n. (*am*) anything made of iron, iron, a wind-instrument,

āyāsa 148/2 effort, exertion, (bodily or mental), trouble,

āyāsadam suffix *dam* indicates an adverb of time, (W 1103b) persistent effort,

ayasmaya mfn iron,

a-yat 84/3 mfn. not making efforts

ā√yat 148/1 P. A. to arrive, enter, to adhere, abide, to attain to, to rest on, depend on, to be at the disposition of, to make efforts,

āyat mfn coming near to,

a-yata mfn unrestrained, uncontrolled

āyata mfn stretched, lengthened, wordy, put on (as an arrow), stretching, extending, extended, spread over, directed towards, aiming at, long, future, m. an oblong figure in geometry, f. *ā* a musical interval, ind. (*am* and *ayā)* without delay, on the spot, quickly,

āyatalocana mfn having long eyes,

āyatana 148/1 n. resting place, home, house, abode, an altar, a plot of ground, the place of the sacred fire, field of operation, basis, support, (Buddhist) the five senses and Manas (considered as the inner seats or *āyatana*s and the qualities perceived by the above i.e. the outer *āyatana*s),

ayathā 84/3 ind. not as it should be, unfitly,

ayathārtha mfn incorrect, incongruous, erroneous, false,

ayathāvat incorrectly, wrongly

a-yati no ascetic

āyāti 148/3 coming near, arrival, coming from, coming back, comes, to reach, attain,
āyatta dependent on, resting on, being ready or prepared, cautious, circumspect,
āyātu 1/s/pres/impv/act may cease
ayaugapadya non-simultaneity, non-contemporaneous existence,
aye ind. an interjection showing surprise
ayi ind. a voc. particle , introducing encouragement or a kind enquiry,
ayoddhṛ m. non-fighter, a coward,
ayodhyā a capital city, home of *Rāmaḥ*
āyodhyaka mfn inhabiting Ayodhyā
ayogata mfn disconnected,
ayomaya mfn made of iron,
ayonija not of human birth, origin unknown,
ā√2.yu to draw or pull towards oneself, to seize, take possession of, to procure, provide, produce, to stir up, agitate, meddle with,
āyu 2. 148/3 mfn living, moving, active, m. a living being, man, mankind, son, descendant, offspring, family, lineage,
n. life, duration of life,
ayuddha mfn unconquered, irressistible,
n. not war, absence of war, peace,
āyudha 149/1 n. a weapon, implement, gold used for ornaments,
āyuhana accumulated, conglomeration,
ayuj mfn not paired, in odd numbers,
ayuja mfn not paired, uneven, 'without a companion, without an equal,
ayukta 85/3 mfn. not right (wrong), not yoked, not harnessed, not connected, not united, not joined, inattentive, without concentration, not dextrous, (*am*) ind. not being yoked,
āyur-veda 'the complete knowledge for long life', a system of traditional medicine,
āyus n. activity, liveliness, life, period or duration of life, long life, vigour, living creatures, m. name of the first son of Urvaśi and Purūravas, age,
āyuṣmant mfn having life or vitality, long-lived, old, blessed with a long life,
ayuta unimpeded, detached, separate, uninterrupted, undisturbed,
ayuta-siddha proved to be inseparable and inherent,
ayuta-siddhi the proof of inseparability of certain things/notions (*Vaiśeṣika* Phil.),
āyuta mfn melted, mixed, mingled, ifc. combined with,
ayutasiddha mfn (in phil.) proved to be not separated (by the intervention of space), proved to be essentially united (as organic bodies etc.),
-siddhi f. establishing by proof that certain objects or ideas are essentially united and logically inseparable,
babhāra exhibited, he maintained,
babhūva he/she/it was or became 1/s/perf/act *√bhū*
√bad 719/3 or *band* cl 1 P *badati* or *bandati* to be firm or steady DP in *sthairya* being firm,
√bāḍ cl 1 A *bāḍate* to bathe, dive,
baddha 720/2 mfn bound, tied, fixed, fastened, tied, bound by the fetters of existence, m.n. that which binds or fetters the embodied spirit, mfn bound, clenched (fist), built or constructed (as a bridge), embanked (as a river), congealed, clotted (as blood), taken up (an abode), contracted (friendship or enmity), alloyed (as quicksilver),
baddhavā having bound
√badh *badhya* see *vadh, vadhya* to strike, slay, murder, kill, defeat, DP in *saṁyamana* restraining,
√bādh 728/1 cl1A *bādhate* to press, force, drive away, repel, remove, harass, pain, trouble, grieve, resist, oppose, check, stop, prevent, to set aside (as a rule), annul, invalidate, suffer annoyance or oppression, to be acted upon, suffer, DP *viloḍana* pressing, harassing,

bādha mfn distressing, m. distress, a molestation, affliction, *(ā)* f. injury, detriment, hurt, damage, suspension, annulment (of a rule), obstruction, a contradiction,objection, absurdity, molestation, damage,

bādhaka mfn oppressing, harassing, opposing, hindering,

bāḍha mfn strong, loudly, strongly, mightily,

bāḍham ind. certainly, yes, so be it, (generally used as a particle of consent, affirmation or confirmation),

bādhana 728/1 mfn oppressing, harassing, opposing, refuting, f uneasiness, trouble, pain, n opposition, resistance, molestation, affliction,

bādhate troubles, attacks

badhira mfn deaf,

bādhita mfn pressed, oppressed, (in gram.) set aside, annulled, (in logic) contradictory, absurd, false, incompatible, cancelled, refuted, contradicted,

bādhitavya mfn to be pressed hard, harassed, to be suspended or annulled ,

badhnāti binds

badhura mfn handsome,

badrīnāṭh a village in the Himalayas established as a pilgrimage site by *ādi śaṅkara*

√*bāh* to bear down, endeavour, make effort, try, DP in *prayatna* endeavouring,

bahala mfn thick, abundant, firm, solid, wide, extensive, bushy or shaggy (tail), deep or intense (colour), harsh (tone), manifold, copious, abundant, m. a kind of sugar-cane, f. large cardamoms,

bahavaḥ 1/pl/m. many

bahiḥparidhi ind. outside the enclosure,

bahirdhā ind. Outward, outside of, away from (5th), external,

bahis ind. outside, as prep. outside of (house, village, country), out, forth, outwards, (the final s is changed before *k* and *p* to *ṣ*

bahiḥ-prajñā objective consciousness as in the waking state,

bahiraṅga-lakṣya concentration upon an external object or point in space,

bahir-dhaiti external washing & cleansing,

bahirmukha-vṛtti 'the outgoing mode or tendency of the mind' (U),

bahiṣkārya to be put outside, to be banished

bahiṣkṛta mfn put out, expelled, a yogic inner cleansing practice,

bahiṣprajña 727/1 mfn one whose knowledge is directed towards external objects, conscious of the outside world,

bahu 724/2 much, many

bāhu m. arm esp. fore-arm, of beasts –the fore-leg esp. the upper part,

bahūdaka 2nd level Sannyasin who wears a tuft of hair,

bahudakṣiṇa mfn marked by many fees or donations, bountiful, lavish, liberal, *aśvamedha* sacrifice,

bahudhā 726/2 many times, in many ways, variously, repeatedly, 'diverse through the differences in the impure conditions of name and form', diversely,

bāhu m. arm, fore-arm,

bahukālam ind. for a long time,

bahula mfn thick, abundant, much, much, many, copious, dense,

bahulauṣadhika mfn having abundant herbs, overgrown with herbs,

bāhulya n. abundance, commonness, state of being usual, usual order of things, *-āt* in accordance with the usual order of things, *-ena* mostly,

bahu√man esteem highly, think highly of,

bahuman mfn consider as much, think much of, esteem, a long-armed god

bahumāna m. esteem, respect,

bahumānapuraḥsaram ind. with respect,

bahumata mfn highly regarded,

bahunā 724/2 much, many, '*kim bahuna'* = 'in short'

bahūni many 1/pl/n

bahuśas ind. repeatedly, often, much,
bahutva plurality,
bahuvacana case-endings and personal terminations in number, plural,
bahuvāram ind. many times, often,
bahuvidha of many kinds or sorts, manifold, various, ind. diversely, in several directions, up and down,
bahuvīrya mfn very powerful or efficacious,
bāhuvīrya mfn strength of arm, strong armed
bahuvrīhi 'much rice' a compound the principal of which is outside the word e.g. he who has much rice i.e. is wealthy,
bāhuyuddha n. arm-fight, wrestling,
bahvya many
bāhya 730/3 mfn being outside, outer, external, expelled from caste or community, not belonging to the family or country, strange, foreign, diverging from, conflicting with, opposed to, having nothing to do with, m. a corpse, the outer part, exterior, ibc. outside, without, out, ind. outside, without, out,
bāhya kāraṇa outer instrument, eye, ear etc.
bāhyatas ind. outside, externally,
bāhya-viṣaya-pratyakṣa external object perception, direct cognition of sense-objects,
baijika mfn relating to seed, seminal, paternal, pertaining to semen, sexual, belonging to any primary cause or source or principle, original, m. a young shoot, sprout, cause, source, the spiritual cause of existence, soul, spirit,
baka m. heron, crane, fig. a hypocrite, cheat, rogue, the crane being regarded as a bird of great cunning and deceit as well as circumspection,
baka-mūrkha m. fool of a heron,
bakula m. name of a tree, (said to put forth flowers when sprinkled with nectar from the mouths of lovely women), (X)
√*bal* 722/2 1. intensive only *balbalīti* to whirl round in a circle, 2. cl 1 P *balati* to breathe, live, to hoard grain or prevent wealth, to be distressed(?) A. *balate* (*bhalate*) to mention, to hurt, to give,
cl 10 P *balayati* to live, *bālayati* to nourish, rear, A. *bālayate* to explain, describe,
DP in *prāṇana* breathing, living, *dhānyā-varodha* hoarding grain, preventing wealth, cl 1, in *prāṇana* living cl 10
bala 722/3 n. power, strength, might, force, vigour, validity, force personified, power of, (5th) forcibly, expertise, stoutness, bulkiness, emphasis in pronunciation, pl. troops,
m. a crow,
bāla 728/3 young, a child, childish, foolish, a boy under 5, 'unenlightened, the non-discriminating', (Gam.),
- *vat* like a child,
balā f. military force, troops, an army, shape, body, semen, gum, blood, a young shoot, bone,
bālā f. a girl
baladā m strength-giving, an ox, bullock, mfn conferring or imparting power,
balādhika mfn superior in strength/power,
bālaka little boy (-*ka* diminutive)
balāka m. a kind of crane,
balānvita mfn connected with power, suggestive of power, leading an army,
bālātpatya n. young offspring, of men and animals,
balāt ind. forcibly
balātkāra 723/2 m employment of force, violence, oppression, injustice,
balavat mfn possessing strength, mighty, strongly, extremely,
balavant mfn powerful,
balavṛtrahana mfn slaying Bala and Vṛtra, m. slayer of Bala and Vṛtra, a name of Indra,
balavṛtraniṣūdana m. slayer of Bala and Vṛtra,
bali 723/3 m. tribute, offering, gift,

portion of meal or sacrifice offered as tribute, tax, fragments of food at a meal,

bālikā girl, young woman,

balin mfn mighty, strong, m. a soldier, hog, buffalo, camel,

bāliśa 729/3 mfn childish, ignorant, m. a fool

baliṣṭha mfn most mighty, very strong, stronger than

balivarda or *balīvarda* m. bull, ox,

ballava m. cowherd, cook, f.(*ī*)

balonmatta mfn frenzied/crazed with power

bālya 729/3 n. boyhood, childhood, immaturity of understanding, crescent state of the moon,

√*baṇ* see *vaṇ* to sound, DP in *śabda* sounding,

bāṇa 727/2 (or *vāṇa*) m. a reed-shaft, an arrow, a cow's udder, (*ā*) f. the feathered end of an arrow, n. the body, 'aggregate of body and senses' (Gam.),

baṇḍa mfn maimed, defective, crippled, emasculated, f. an unchaste woman,

√*bandh* 720/2/1 cl 9 P A *bandhāti, badhnīte,* cl 1 P A *bandhati (te)*, cl 4 P b*adhyati* to bind, tie, fix, fasten, chain, fetter, bind round, put on, 'on oneself', to catch, take or hold captive, met. to attach to world or sin, to fix, direct, fasten, rivet, (eyes ,ears or mind), to arrest, hold back, restrain, suppress, stop, shut, close, bind a sacrificial victim, offer, sacrifice, to punish, chastise, to join, unite, put together or produce anything in this way, fold the hands, clench the fist, knit the brows, assume a posture, set up a limit, construct a dam or bridge, conceive or contract friendship or enmity, compose, construct a poem or verse, to form or produce in any way, cause, effect, do, make, bear fruit, strike roots, take up one's abode, to entertain, cherish, show, exhibit, be bound by the fetters of existence or evil, be affected by experience, suffer, caus. *bandhayati* to cause to bind or catch or capture, imprison, cause to be built or dammed, to bind together, DP in *bandhana* binding

bandha 720/3 mfn binding esp. a binding to the sacrificial post, , tying, bondage, imprisonment, custody, sacrifice, m. a binding, (in phil.) mundane bondage, attachment to this world, knot, 2. band, string,

bandha-mokṣa bondage and liberation,

bandhana 721/1 mfn binding, tying, fettering, captivating, holding fast, stopping, dependent on, n. the act of binding, tying, a bond, tie, rope, cord, tether, binding on or around, binding up, bandaging, a bandage, capturing, confining, detention, custody, building, construction, m. (having connection or relationship), a relative, friend

bandhu 721/1 m. connection, relation, association, friend, companion,

bāndhava m. kinsman, relation, brother, friend,

bandhu 721/1 m. connection, relation, association, kinship, a relative, kindred, a friend, a husband, a brother, *bandhūn* 2/pl/m relatives, kinsmen,

bandin m. prisoner, a praiser, bard, captive,

√*barb* 722/1 cl 1 P *barbati* to go, move, DP in *gati* going

barbara mfn stammering, m. foreigners (applied to non-Aryans by Aryans), a man of lowest origin, a wretch,

√*barh* 722/1 or *varh* cl 1 A *barhate* to speak, to hurt, to give or cover, cl 10 P to speak, to shine, DP in *hiṁsā* (cl 10) hurting, *bhāṣā* (cl 10) speaking, shining, *prādhānya* (cl 1) being pre-eminent or excellent, in *paribhāśā* (cl 1) speaking, *hiṁsā* (cl 1) hurting, *chādana* (cl 1) covering

barha m.n. tail feather (partic. peacock),

barhin m. having tail-feathers, the peacock,

barhiṇa m. peacock, adorned with peacock feathers,

barhis n.grass or straw spread for seating and oblations, sacrifice, water, ether,

bāṣpa m. a tear (as in crying), tears, steam, vapour, iron,

bāṣpākala mfn agitated by tears, inarticulate through tears,

bata 719/3 1. ind. an interjection expressing astonishment or regret, alas! oh! (later – *vata*)
2. m. a weakling,

baṭu m. boy, lad, stripling, youth, a class of priests, a young Brahmin (student), a fellow (contemptuously)

bauddha mfn being in the mind, mental (not uttered), relating to intellect or understanding, relating or belonging to Buddha, Buddhist,

bhā 750/3 1. cl 2 P *bhāti* to shine, be bright or luminous, shine forth, appear, show oneself, be splendid or beautiful or eminent, to appear as, seem, look like, to be, exist, to show, exhibit, manifest,
DP in *dīpti* shining,

bhā 2 f. light, brightness, splendour, m. the sun, m. the planet Venus, the sun, n. a star, planet, asterism, sign of the zodiac,

bhadra mfn praiseworthy, pleasing, blessed, fortunate, auspicious, good, gracious, friendly, kind, excellent, fair, beautiful, lovely, n. happiness, good fortune, good, happy, name of the elephant guarding the western quarter, ind. happily, fortunately, joyfully, voc. my good man, dear lady, with √*kṛ* or *ā*- or √*car* to do well, m. a sanctimonious hypocrite, a kind of elephant, a bullock, a water wagtail, name of *Śiva*, f. a cow,

bhādra m. name of a rainy month from mid-August to mid-September,

bhadraṁ vaḥ if you please, (parenthetical),

bhadrakṛt mfn causing welfare, blessing,

bhadram ind. with *kṛ* or *ā-car* do well, see *bhadra* above,
3. favourable, auspicious,

bhadre voc. dear lady, madam,

bhaga 743/2 m. 'dispenser', gracious lord, patron (applied to gods esp. *Savitri)*, the sun, the moon, fortune, happiness, welfare, prosperity, (ifc.f.*ā*) dignity, majesty, distinction, excellence, beauty, loveliness, n. the sun, moon, good fortune, happiness, welfare, prosperity,love, affection, sexual passion, amorous pleasure, dalliance, (ifc. f.*ā* and *ī*) the vulva, dignity, majesty, distinction, excellence, beauty, loveliness,

bhāga 751/2 a part or portion, share, inheritance, fortune, luck, destiny, place, spot, region, the numerator of a fraction, a quotient, a degree or 360th of the circumference of a circle, part of anything given as interest,

bhāgadheya n. (bestowal or allotment of a part), portion, esp. bestowal of a goodly lot, blessing, m. one to whom a share is due (heir, co-heir), mfn the share of a king, tax, impost,

bhāgaśas ind. part by part, gradually, one part after another, by turns,

bhagatyaga-lakṣaṇa 'defining by division and separation' (U), see Grimes 81, and 144,

bhagavan 743/3 (voc. form of *bhagavat* mfn*),* in comp. for *bhagavat,* holy, glorious, illustrious, used as a form of address to gods, demigods, and saints, O Blessed One,

bhagavān the Lord, the greatly fortunate, your lordship, 1/s/m *bhagavat*

bhagavant mfn fortunate, possessing a happy lot, blessed, 2. heavenly, august, lordly, applied to Indra, Brahma etc. esp. in voc. (above) as a form of address,

bhagavat mfn ' possessing good fortune', fortunate, prosperous, glorious, blessed, heavenly, venerable, holy, lordly, m. the divine or adorable one,
bhāgavata m an adorer of Bhagavān or Viṣnu as God, mfn divine, holy,
bhāgavata dharma the law of Vaiṣnava dispensation of adoration and love,
bhagin mfn fortunate, happy, splendid, prosperous, perfect, glorious,
bhāgin mfn 751/3 entitled to or receiving or possessing a share, partaking of, m. a partner, owner, possessor, fortunate man, the 'whole' as consisting of parts, a co-heir or co-heiress,
bhāgineya m. sister's son, f. (*ī*) a sister's daughter,
bhaginī sister,
bhagīratha m. an ancient king who brought the Ganges down from heaven, son of Dilipa and grandson of Sagara
bhāgīratha mfn of *bhagīratha* , f. (*ī*) the stream of B°, the Ganges,
bhagna mfn broken, split, torn, defeated,
bhagnabhāṇda mfn having broken pots or who broke the pots
bhagnāśa mfn having broken hopes, disappointed in expectation, ,
bhāgya n. lot, fate, esp. happy lot, luck, *bhāgyena* luckily,
bhaikṣa 766/3 n. living on alms, begging,
bhaima descended from Bhīma, Bhīma's daughter Damayantī,
bhaimī f. descended from Bhīma, Damayantī
bhairava mfn fearful i.e. awful, m. Terrible -name of a hunter, a jackal,
√*bhaj* 743/1 cl1 P *bhajati* A *bhajate* to serve, honour, revere, love, adore, P. to divide, distribute, allot or apportion to, share with, A. to grant, bestow, obtain as one's share, partake of, enjoy, possess, have, to turn or resort to, engage in, assume (as a form), put on (garments), experience, incur, undergo, feel, go or fall into, to pursue, practise, cultivate, to fall to the lot or share of, to declare for, prefer, choose caus. *bhājayate* to divide, deal out, distribute, cause anyone to partake of, pursue, chase, to cook, dress (food), DP in *sevā* (cl 1) serving, *viśrāṇana* (cl 10) giving,
bhaja 2/s/pres/impv/act (you) cultivate
bhajāmi I share with, I love, I reward 3/s/pres/indic/act √*bhaj*
bhajana n. the act of sharing, possession, ifc. reverence, worship, adoration, devotional singing,
bhājana n. a vessel. pot, receptacle, a fit object, sharing, division, a recipient, the act of representing, representation, a partic. measure,
bhajante they get or obtain 1/pl/pres/mid
bhajati 743/1 he honors, loves or worships
bhāk from root *bhāj* 752/1 enjoying, devoted to, to serve, honour, love, adore, enjoy
√*bhakṣ* 742/3 cl 10 P A *bhakṣayati (te)* cl 1 P A *bhakskati (te)* to eat or drink, partake of, to sting, bite, consume, use up, waste, destroy, drain the rsources of, impoverish, DP in *adana* eating,
bhakṣa m. the enjoying, eating or drinking, food, at the end of adjectival compounds – having ... as food, living on... ,
bhakṣaka m. eater,
bhakṣakāra m. 'food-maker', a cook, baker,
bhakṣaṇa 742/3 mfn eating, one who eats, n. the act of eating, drinking
bhakṣin mfn eating, devouring,
bhakṣita mfn eaten
bhakṣitavya to be eaten,
bhakṣya to be eaten, edible, n. proper food,
bhakta m. a lover of God, a devotee, a worshipper, a votary, a follower of Bhaktiyoga, mfn ifc. forming part of, belonging to, ifc. loved, liked, served, worshipped, attached or devoted to,

faithful, honouring, worshipping, serving, dressed, cooked,
n. food or a meal, cooked rice, any edible grain boiled with water, a vessel, a share, portion,

bhakti 743/1 f. distribution, partition, share, belonging to, attachment, devotion, fondness for, devotion to, homage, worship, piety, faith or love,

bhaktila mfn attached, faithful, trusty, (said of horses),

bhaktimān full of devotion

bhakti-marga the path of devotion

bhaktiyoga m. the yoga of devoted attachment, loving devotion,

√*bhal* 748/2 /3 (or bal) cl 1 A *bhalate* to describe or expound or hurt or give, cl 10 A *bhālayate* to describe or behold, to throw up(?) DP in *paribhāṣaṇa* (cl 1) describing, *hiṁsā* hurting, *dāna* giving, in *ābhaṇḍana* (cl 10) seeing,
beholding, expounding, explaining,

√*bhall* 748/3 cl 1 A *bhallate* = *bhal, bhalate*

bhalla mfn auspicious, favourable, a bear

bhallaka m. a bear

√*bhām* cl 1 A *bhāmate* cl 1 P *bhāmayati* to be angry or impatient, DP in *krodha* being angry

bhāma m 1. light, brightness, splendour, 2. rage, fury, (*ā)* f. a passionate woman,

bhāmin mfn radiant, splendid, 2. passionate, angry, (*ī*) f. a passionate or angry woman, vixen (often used as a term of endearment)

bhāminī mfn shining, radiant, beautiful, splendid,f. a passionate woman,

bhāmita mfn enraged, angry,

√*bhaṇ* 745/2 cl 1 P *bhaṇati* to speak, say to, call, name, caus. *bhāṇayati* DP in *śabda* sounding,

bhāṇa m. recitation,

bhāna perception, appearance, evidence, light, lustre, manifestation,

√*bhaṇḍ* 745/3 cl 1 A *bhaṇḍate* to reprove, deride, jest, speak, cl 1 .10. P *bhaṇḍati, bhaṇḍayati* to be or render fortunate, to do an auspicious act, DP in *paribhāṣaṇa* (cl 1) speaking, conversing, in *kalyāṇa* (cl 10) making fortunate,

√*bhand* 745/3 cl 1 A *bhandate* to be greeted with praise, receive applause, to be or make fortunate, to be or make glad, to shine, to honour or worship, caus. *bhandayati* to cause to prosper, DP in *kalyāṇa* making fortunate, or *sukha* being glad,

bhāṇḍa n. 1. vessel, pot, vat, dish, box,
2. generalised as – utensil, wares, ware,

bhāṇḍāra m. a storehouse, store,

bhandiṣṭha mfn most loudly/best praising,

bhaṅga 744/3 mfn breaking, bursting,
m.the act of breaking, splitting, dividing, a break or breach, disturbance, interruption, frustration, downfall, decay, bending,
a wave, a water-course, a bend,
a round-about way of speaking, plucking (of buds), dispersal of crowds (X),

bhaṅgara mfn fragile,

bhaṅgi f. breaking, a bend, curve, circumlocution, mode, manner,

√*bhañj* 744/2 cl 7 P A *bhanakti* to break, shatter, split, break into, make a breach in, rout, put to flight, defeat, dissolve (an assembly), break up, divide, bend, to check, arrest, suspend, disappoint, DP in *āmardana* breaking, tearing down, shattering,

bhañjana mfn breaking, a breaker, destroyer, m. tooth decay, n. breaking, shattering, violent pain, disturbing, interrupting, smoothing (of hair),

bhānu m. appearance, brightness, light or a ray of light, lustre, splendour, the sun, a king, prince, master,

bhara 1. mfn bearing, carrying,
2. m. burden, weight,
3. mass, quantity,

4. a partic. quantity or measure,
bhāra m. burden, load,
bharaṇa 747/2 mfn bearing, maintaining, n. the act of bearing, carrying, bringing, procuring, wearing, putting on, maintaining,
bharaṭa 747/2 m. a potter or servant, a priest, actor, dancer, tumbler,
bharata mfn to be supported or maintained, esp. to be kept alive by the care of men, m. name of a patriarchal hero,
bhārata mfn descended from Bharata, m. descendant of *Bharataḥ,* a name for *Yudhiṣṭhira,*
Bharatarśabha Bull of the *Bharatas (Arjuna)*
bhāratī goddess of speech (Sarasvatī), speech, voice, word, eloquence, literary composition, dramatic art, a quail, one of the 10 orders of religious mendicants who trace back to pupils of *Śaṅkarācārya*
bhargas n. radiant light, glory, lustre, splendour, mfn clear, shrill (voice),
bhārika m. carrier, porter, forming a load, heavy, burdensome,
bharjana 748/2 mfn roasting, burning, n. the act of roasting or frying
bhartā supporter, bearer, sustainer, *Īśvara*
bhartṛ 748/1 m. one who bears or carries or maintains, a bearer, protector, maintainer, lord, a husband, f. *(trī)*
bhartṛhari m. a seventh century a.d. grammarian and philosopher of language,
a n 11th century king who renounced his kingdom to become a sage,
√*bharts* 748/2 cl 10 A *bhartsayate (ti)* cl 1 *bhartsati,* to menace, threaten, abuse, revile, deride, DP in *tarjana* threatening, menacing,
bhartsana n threatening, a threat, menace, curse
√*bharv* 748/2 cl 1 P *bharvati* to chew, eat, hurt, injure, DP in *hiṁsā* hurting

bhārya gve. to be borne or supported or maintained or cherished, m. one supported by or dependent on another, a servant, mercenary, soldier,
bhāryaka ifc. a wife,
bhāryā f. a wife or the female of an animal,
bhāryātva n. condition of being wife or (among animals) mate,
√*bhaṣ* 750/1 cl 1 P A *bhaṣati (te*), to bark, growl, rail against, reproach, revile, DP in *bhartsana* abusing, reproaching, growling, barking,
√*bhāṣ* cl 1 A P *bhāṣate (ti)* to speak, talk, say, tell, speak of or about, announce, declare, to call, name, describe as, to use or employ in speaking, 755/2 , DP in *vyaktāvāc* speaking articulately
√*bhas* cl 3 P *babhasti* or *bapsati* to chew, masticate, consume, to blame, abuse, to shine, DP in *bhartsana* blaming, abusing, *dīpti* shining,
√*bhās* 756/1 cl 1 A *bhāsate* to shine, be bright, to appear or occur to the mind, be conceived or imagined, become clear or evident, DP in *dīpti* shining
bhās n. light, brilliance, effulgence, m. the sun, an image, reflection, shadow, glory, splendour,
bhāsa 756/1 m. light, lustre, brightness, impression made on the mind, fancy, a bird of prey, vulture,
bhāṣā f. speech, conversation, language, definition,
bhāsaka mfn causing to appear, enlightening, ifc. making evident or intelligible,
bhaṣaṇa 750/1 barking, barking (like a dog)
bhāṣaṇa 755/3 n. the act of speaking, talking, speech, talk, f. resembling
bhāsana 756/1 shining, glittering, brilliance, splendour, illuminating
bhāsate 755/3 he/she/it shines, appears, or is appearing,
bhāṣase you speak, say 2/s/pres/act √*bhāṣ*

bhāṣate (or *–ti*) speaks, says, tells
bhāsayate causes to shine or illuminate,
bhāṣita mfn spoken, n. what is spoken, the words,
bhasita mfn reduced to ashes, n. ashes,
bhāṣitum inf. to speak,
bhāskara mfn 'making light' mfn shining, glittering, bright, m. the sun, a hero, n. gold,
bhasman 750/3 devouring, consuming, pulverizing, (what is pulverized by fire) ashes,
bhasmāntam reduced to ashes, (the body)
bhasmasāt ind. with √*kṛ* to reduce to ashes
bhasmībhūta mfn become/ turned to ashes,
bhasmīkaraṇa 750/3 reducing to ashes, burning
bhastrā f. a leather bag, bellows,
bhastrikā f. a yogic breathing exercise, a little bag,
bhāsvara mfn shining, brilliant, bright, resplendent, m. the sun, a day, mfn light-coloured, having the colour of light,
bhāṣya commentary to a major work
bhāsya mfn to be made visible, to be brought to light,
bhāṣyakāra m. a commentator,
√*bhaṭ* 745/1 cl 1 P *bhaṭati* to hire, nourish, maintain, cl 10 P *bhaṭayati* to speak, converse, caus. *bhāṭayati* to hire, DP in *bhṛti* (cl 1) in nourishing, hiring, receiving wages, in *paribhāṣaṇa* speaking, conversing,
bhaṭa m. soldier, mercenary, combatant, warrior,
bhāti 750/3 √*bhā* to shine, be bright or luminous, shine forth, to appear as, be, exist, exists or shines,appear, show one's self, shine forth, appear as, seem, look like, to be, exist,
bhāti 2. f. light, splendour,
'that which exists proclaims itself through its brilliance and is known to be there; this is called *bhāti'* HH .
'The word *bhāti* is the act of knowing, known, so it is directly related to knowledge. The knowledge is again only one and it arises from that which is in existence. ... includes knowledge of existence and knowledge of ignorance, ... knowledge of the Brahman and knowledge of the world'.
bhatsanā f. threat
bhaṭṭa m. lord, my lord, mfn venerable,
bhaṭṭāra m. lord,
bhaṭṭāraka m. lord, applied to gods and learned men,
bhaṭṭārakavāra m. lord's day, Sunday,
bhauma mfn relating or dedicated to the earth, produced or coming from the earth, earthly, terrestrial, n. dust of the earth (pl.), corn, grain, ifc. floor, story,
bhaumavāra Tuesday *bhauma* 768/3 name of the planet Mars whose day is Tuesday, also to do with the earth -and production from the earth, earthy, corn, grain,
bhutika mfn physical, worldly, n. a sort of monk, anything elemental or material, pearl, qualities of the elements,
bhava 748/3 m. coming into existence, birth, life,
2/pres/impv. √*bhū* you be, be! exist! become! let be,
bhāva 754/1 becoming, being, existing, turning or transition into, occurring, appearance, state of being anything, true state, manner of being, that which is or exists, way of thinking or feeling, being or living creature, states of existence
'the emotional realm' HH
bhavadāhārārtham ind. for your food, 'having your food as object'
bhavadīya mfn your honour's, your,
bhavaduttaram having *bhavant* as last word in the begging formula,
bhāvagrāhin mfn understanding the sense, appreciating the sentiment,
bhāvagrāhya mfn to be conceived with the heart, 'who is realised through the

pure heart' (T),

bhāvaka 755/1 mfn causing to be, effecting, promoting anyone's (6th) welfare, imagining, fancying (6th or comp.), having a taste for the beautiful or poetical, singing with expression, m. sentiment, affection, the external expression of amatory sentiments,

bhāvaṁgama mfn touching the heart, charming, lovely,

bhavān a form of *bhavat* 749/2 a respectful form of address – your honour, your worship, (lit. the gentleman or lady present) 1/s/m you

bhavana n. dwelling, abode, house, palace,

bhāvana mfn causing to be, effecting, producing, displaying, manifesting, promoting or effecting anyone's welfare, imagining, fancying, teaching, m. a creator, producer, efficient, f.n. the act of producing or effecting, forming in the mind, conception, apprehension, imagination, supposition, fancy, thought, meditation,

bhāvanā 755/1 causing to be or become, manifesting, imagining, thought, the act of producing or effecting, feeling of devotion, faith in, reflection, contemplation, right conception or notion, emotional intent, "sometimes used as emotion and being" HH "the individual is free in *bhāvanā*. This should be taken as dedication. An individual can dedicate any *bhāvanā* to anyone. He can deliberately create a *bhāvanā* within himself and work accordingly. even in miserable conditions, people become happy or in happy conditions become miserable because they choose it like that." HH "the emotion with which the work is being done, the real motive with which the first move into the activity was made". HH "The *bhāvanā* is the most basic factor of all activity. That must be pure. It should be a dedication, an offering to the Absolute, or a service to *samaṣṭi*. That will bestow on it the pleasure of the Lord and give it the most glorious meaning." HH

bhavan-madhya mfn having *bhavant* as middle word (of one's begging formula),

bhavanam n. palace, abode

bhavant mfn lordly, 'used in respectful address as a substitute for the 2nd person pronoun and translatable as' your honour, thou, ye, 'used in the pl. of a single person to express greater courtesy, used in the voc/s/m (*bhavas* [contracted] *bhos*, f. *bhavati*, as word of address' (lord, master,mister,) sir, lady, (prob. a contraction of *bhagavant*),

bhavantas 1/pl/ honorific, your lordships

bhavaroga 'the disease of existence' HH

bhāvarūpa mfn really existing, real, actual,

bhāvasaṁśuddhis purity of being, purity of heart, absence of manipulation

bhavat mfn being, present, *bhavat* m.f. respectful address, you sir, your honour,

bhavata be! become! pl.

bhavati verb to be 1/s/pres/indic/act he/she becomes

bhavat-pūrva mfn having *bhavant* at the beginning of one's begging formula, *-am* ind.

bhāvarūpa mfn actual, real, really existing,

bhavatu let it be! 1/s/act/ impv.

bhāvayantas cherishing, fostering, pres. part. 1/pl/m *bhū*

bhāvayanti root *bhū* to think about, consider, 760/2 1/pl/causative *bhū* they consider,

bhāvayantu may they cherish or foster, may they cause to be, may they increase the well-being of 1/pl/caus/impv/act *bhū*

bhāvayata may you cherish, or foster, may you cause to be, may you increase the well-being of, 2/pl/caus/opt/act *bhū bhāvayati* protects, cherishes, fosters, causes to be or become, call into existence or life, originate, produce, create, 1/s/caus.

bhāvayitavyā to be nourished or protected, fut.pass.part.

bhāvayitrī the nourisher,

bhāve in meaning or in intention 7/s

bhavet verb to be 1/pres/opt he might be/ should be/become , it would be

bhāvin mfn becoming, coming into existence, about to be, destined to be

bhāvinī f. a beautiful woman,

bhaviṣyāmaḥ we shall be, we shall exist, 1/pl/fut/act √*bhū*

bhaviṣyasi 2/s/fut you will be

bhaviṣyat 750/1 mfn about to become or be, future, n. the future

bhāviṣyati 760/1 1/s/fut/act. of *bhṛ,* will come into being, he will be, it will arise

bhaviṣyatkāla future tense

bhavitā he, she, it will become, will be, 1/s/periphrastic future

bhāvitaḥ transformed into, caused to become, caus. part.

bhavitavya deserving to become, destined to be, about to be,

bhavitum infinitive of verb to be *bhū,* 760/1 to become

bhavya mfn being, existing, present, to be about to be or become, future, (in Jainism –one who is capable of attaining liberation,

bhāvya 755/2 about to be or be effected or performed, future or what ought to be, what is to be accomplished,

bhaya 747/1 n. fear, alarm, dread, danger, apprehension

bhayaṁkara mfn causing or inspiring fear, fearsome,

bhayana n. fear, alarm,

bhayānaka 747/2 fearful, terrible, dreadful, m. the sentiment of terror, a tiger

bhayārta mfn stricken with fear,

bheḍa m. a ram, a raft, float,

bheda 766/1 m. breaking, splitting, cleaving, opening, expanding, a cleft, separation, disclosing, divulging, betrayal(of a secret), separation, division, partition, part, portion, distinction, difference, kind, sort, species, variety, interruption, violation, dissolution, disunion, dissension, change, modification, contraction, (in phil.) dualism, duality,

bhedābhāva (G) absence of duality or difference,

bhedābheda (N) the theory that Brahman and the individual self are neither one nor different, (interpretations of this differ according to the scholar), 766/2 m. union and disunion, dualism and non-dualism, *-vādin* a maintainer of the doctrine both of the d ifference and the identity of God and the Universe,

bheda-ahaṁkāra the differentiating ego, sense of separateness,

bheda-buddhi ' the intellect that creates differences, the *vyāvahārika buddhi* that diversifies everything as opposed to *pāramārthika buddhi* that unifies everything', (U)

bheda-jñāna consciousness of difference, worldly consciousness,

bhedana 766/2 mfn breaking, splitting, piercing, dividing, separating, causing to flow, n.disunion, discord,

bhedanimna mfn having an inclination towards duality, worldly,

bhedita mfn broken, split, cleft, ifc. divided into,

bheka m. a frog, a cloud, a timid man,

bheryas 1/pl/f large drums

√*bheṣ* 766/3 cl 1 P A *bheṣati (te*) to fear, dread, DP in *bhaya* fearing

bheṣaja 766/3 curing, healing, medicine, remedy,

bhetavya gve. to be feared,

Bhīma a powerful warrior, brother of *Arjuna*, tremendous, awful

√*bhī* 1.758/1 cl3 P *bibheti* A *bibhyati*

cl 1 A *bhayate*, pass. *bhidyate* cl 10 P *bhāyayati* to fear, be afraid of, fear for, be anxious about, DP in *bhaya* fearing

bhī 2. 758/1 f. fear, apprehension, fright, alarm, dread of,

√*bhid* 756/3 cl 7 P A *bhinatti, bhintte* , cl 1 P *bhedati* split, cleave, break, cut or rend asunder, pierce, destroy, to disperse (darkness), transgress, violate (a compact or alliance), to open, expand, loosen, disentangle, dissolve, to disturb, interrupt, stop, disclose, betray, disunite, set at variance, distinguish, discriminate, to be opened (as a hand, eyes,), to overflow (as water), to be loosened, become loose, be distinguished, pass. *bhidyate* is untied etc.
2. mfn. ifc. breaking, splitting, piercing, destroying, f. a wall, separation, distinction, a sort, kind, species, DP in *vidāraṇa* breaking, cleaving, splitting,

bhidura mfn fragile, breaking, splitting, piercing, easily split or broken, brittle,

bhīkara mfn causing fear,

√*bhikṣ* 756/2 cl 1 A P *bhikṣate (ti)* to wish for, desire, to beg anything, be weary or distressed, DP in *bhikṣā* begging, *alābha* not finding, *lābha* finding,

bhikṣā 756/2 f. the act of begging or asking, hire, wages, service, alms, food etc received from begging, n. asking alms etc, mendicancy,

bhikṣāka m. a beggar, mendicant,

bhikṣita mfn begged, solicited or obtained as alms,

bhikṣu 756/3 one who subsists entirely on alms, a mendicant, beggar,

bhikṣuka m. a beggar, mendicant, a Brāhman of the mendicant order,

bhīma mfn fearful, terrible, m. name of a king of *Vidarbha*, father of *Damayantī*, 2nd son of *Pāṇḍu*,

bhīmakarman mfn formidable in action, dreadful,

bhīmaparākrama m. terrible strength or courage, mfn possessing awesome strength or courage,

bhīmaśāsana n. command/summons of *bhīma*

bhīmat mfn fearful,

√*bhind* 757/3 = *bind*

bhinna 757/1 changed, altered, different from, broken, distinct from, other than, cut off,

bhīru mfn timid, fearful,

bhiṣaj mfn healing, m. healer, physician,

√*bhiṣajya* 757/3 Nom P *(°ti)* to heal, cure, possess healing power, to be physician to anyone, to be a physician or remedy for i.e. to gain mastery over anything,
2. mfn sanative, healing, healthful, f. healing, cure, remedy,
DP in *cikitsā* doctoring

bhīṣaṇa mfn terrible,

bhīṣma m. name of a son of *Śāṁtanu* and *Gaṅgā,* who fought for the *Kaurava*s against the *Pāṇḍavas* famous warrior, 'awesome', 'terrible' great uncle of *Arjuna* but fighting for the opposing *Kuru* army,

bhiṣṇajya 757/3 Nom P (°*ti)* to heal, refresh, DP in *upasevā* serving, practising,

bhiṣuj m. a physician,

bhīta mfn afraid, fearful, (*am*) ind. timidly, n. fear, danger,

bhīti f. fear, alarm, dread, danger,

bhitti f. breaking, splitting, a mat (of split reeds), a wall (of earth or masonry), panel, a wall-like surface, a fragment, bit, portion, a place, a rent, fissure, a flaw, deficiency, an opportunity, occasion,

bhittika mfn breaking, splitting, a wall, (ā) f. a partition, wall, a small house-lizard,

bhittikhātana m. 'wall-digger' a rat,

bhiyas 758/1 m. fear, apprehension

√*bhlakṣ* 771/1 cl 1 P A *bhlakṣati (te)* to eat, DP in *adana* eating,

√*bhlāś* 771/1 cl 1.4 A *bhlāśate, bhlāśyate* to shine, beam, glitter,
DP in *dīpti* shining,

√*bhleṣ* 771/1 see *bhreṣ* in *gati* going,

bho *(bhos)* 768/2 m. used in addressing another, Oh Your Honour, Sir,
voc. of *bhavat,*

bho-bhāva m. the becoming *bhos*, (with *nāmnām)* the becoming *bhos* of names, i.e. the use of *bhos* instead of a person's real name, see *bhavant*

bhoga 767/2 1. any winding or curve, coil (of a serpent), the expanded hood of a snake, a snake,
2 m. experiencing, feeling, sense of enjoyment, eating,

bhogabhūta involuntary action arising from the latency of previous actions,

bhogārtha for the sake of enjoyment,

bhogatva n. the state of being curved or winding, curvedness,

bhogavat mfn ringed, coiled, curved (as a snake), furnished with a hood,

bhogavatī the underworld city of the *Nāgas*,

bhogin 1. curved, ringed, coiled (as a serpent), m. a serpent,
2. mfn enjoying, esp. enjoying food, well-fed,

bhogya mfn to be enjoyed, to be used (in the sense 'to be eaten'), what may be used or enjoyed, useful, profitable, n. an object of enjoyment, an object of experience,

bhojana 768/1 mfn feeding, giving to eat, voracious, n. the act of enjoying, using, the act of eating,
a meal, food,

bhojya 768/2 to be enjoyed or eaten, a festive dinner, object of enjoyment,

bhokṣyase you shall enjoy, you shall eat, 2/s/fut/mid √*bhuj*

bhoktā 759/2 [under *bhuj* to enjoy, use, possess], f. the enjoyer

bhoktāra m. enjoyer, eater

bhoktṛ 760/1 m. one who enjoys or eats, enjoyer, eater, experiencer

bhoktṛ-bhāva the sense of being the enjoyer,

bhoktṛtva having the nature of an enjoyer,

bhos Oh!

√*bhṛ* 764/3 cl 1 P A *bharati (te)*, cl 3 P A *bibharti bibhṛte,* cl 2 P *bharti* to bear, carry, convey, hold on or in, to wear i.e. let grow, (hair, beard, nails), to balance, hold in equipoise (as a pair of scales), possess, have, keep, support, maintain, cherish, to hire, pay, carry off or along, to bring, offer, procure, grant, endure, experience, suffer, undergo, to lift up, raise (the voice or a sound), to fill (the stomach), to become pregnant, take care of, rule, submit to, obey, DP in *bharaṇa* bearing, supporting, or *poṣaṇa* nourishing,

√*bhrāj* 770/1 cl 1 A P *bhrājate (ti),* to shine, beam, sparkle, glitter,
DP in *dīpti* shining,
2. f. light, lustre, splendour,

√*bhrakṣ* see *bhṛkṣ* P.A. *bhṛkṣati, bhrakṣati, te,* to eat,

√*bhram* 769/2 cl 1 P *bhramati* , cl 4 P *bhrāmyati (te)*, to wander or roam about, rove, ramble, fly about, roll about, to move to and fro or unsteadily, to move round, circulate, revolve, to spread, waver, be perplexed, doubt, err, DP in *clana* moving, walking, in *anavasthāna* roaming, wandering about,

bhrama 769/3 confusion, mistake, error, mistaking anything for, illusion, wandering or roaming about, turning round, revolving,

bhrāmaja-adhyāsa m. 'the misconception consequent upon false identification of the Self with *cidābhāsa* (reflection of consciousness),' (U),

bhrāmaka mfn false, causing error, deceitful, m. turning round, m.n. causing to turn round,

bhramaṇa 769/3 n. wandering or roaming about, moving about, rolling, turning round, a whirlpool, eddy, spring, dizziness, perplexity, a circle, auger, gimlet,

bhramara m. a bee, bumble-bee, a young man, lad, a potter's wheel,

bhramati he/she/it wanders or roams about 1/s/pres/indic/act √*bhrams* 769/2

bhramabhūta 769/3 being an error, erroneous, unreal

bhramara m. a large black bee, any bee, a young man, lad, libertine, a potter's wheel, a position of the hand,

bhramati 769/2 wanders or roams about,

brahmavid mfn m. knower of Brahman,

bhrāmayan causing to move, causing to wander, revolving, caus/pres/part

√*bhraṁś* (or *bhraś*) 769/1 sometimes written *bhraṁs*, cl 1 A *bhraṁśate* , cl 4 P *bhraśyati* (*te*), to fall, drop, fall down or out or in pieces, to strike against, rebound from, to fall (fig) decline, decay, fail, disappear, vanish , be ruined or lost, be separated from or deprived of, lose, to slip or escape from, swerve or deviate from, abandon, DP in *avasraṁsana* falling or dropping down, slipping off or down,

bhraṁśa m. fall, ruin, loss, falling or slipping down or off, straying or deviating from, abandonment of,

√*bhraṇ* 769/2 cl 1 P *bhraṇati* to sound, utter a sound, DP in *śabda* sounding,

bhraṅśa m. fall, ruin, loss,

bhrānta 770/1 moving about unsteadily, being in doubt or error, confused, perplexed, m. an elephant in rut,

*bhrānti*770/1 f. confusion, error, mistaking something for, false impression of, supposing anything to be or exist, wandering or roaming about, moving to and fro, driving (of clouds), staggering, reeling, turning round, rolling (of wheels), moving round, circumambulating,

bhrānti-darśana mistaken notion,

bhrānti-ja born of delusion / misconception

bhrānti-mātra mere illusion or delusion,

bhrāntvā ind. having roamed,

√*bhraś* see *bhraṁś*

√*bhrāś* 770/3 = *bhrās,* cl 1.4. A *bhrāśate, bhrāśyate*, (or °*śyati*), to shine, glitter, DP in *dīpti* shining,

bhraṣṭa mfn fallen, dropped, broken down, decayed, lost, gone, fled or escaped from, strayed or separated from, depraved, vicious, a backslider, f. a fallen or unchaste woman, 769/1

bhrātra m. a brother,

bhrātṛ m. brother or an intimate friend, 770/2

bhrātṛhatyā f. fratricide,

bhrātṛmat mfn having a brother or brothers,

bhrātṝn brothers, 2/pl/m

bhrātṛ-sthāna mfn taking the brother's place, m. representative of a brother,

bhrātṛvya m. a father's brother's son, a cousin, a hostile cousin, rival, adversary, enemy,

bhrātrīya m. a nephew, mfn fraternal, belonging or relating to a brother,

√*bhṛḍ* 765/3 cl 6 P *bhṛḍati* to dive, plunge, DP in *nimajjana* sinking, diving,

√*bhrej* 771/1 cl 1 A *bhrejate* to shine, glitter, DP in *dīpti* shining,

√*bhreṣ* 771/1 cl 1 P A *bhreṣati* to totter, waver, slip, make a false step, be angry, to fear, to go, DP in *gati* going,

bhṛgu 765/1 name of a mythical race of men associated with bringing fire to men, name of a *ṛṣi* (supposed author of the *ṛk veda*)

√*bhrī* 770/3 cl 9 P *bhrīṇāti,* or *bhriṇāti*, to injure, hurt, to be angry, DP in *bhaya* fearing,

√*bhṛj* 765/3 cl 1 A *bharjate* to fry, parch DP in *bharjana* parching

√*bhṛṁṣ* 765/1 cl 1.10 *briṁśati, briṁśayati* to speak or to shine, DP in *bhāṣā* speaking, shining,

√*bhṝ* 766/1 cl 9 P *bhṛṇāti* to bear, to

blame, to fry, to be crooked, DP in *bhartsana* blaming, censuring, or *bharaṇa* supporting,

bhṛṅga m. a a species of large black bee, a bee, wasp, shrike, libertine, golden vase or pitcher,

√*bhṛś* 765/3 cl 4 P *bhṛśyati* to fall, fall down, cl 6 P *bhṛśati* to be strong or vehement, DP in *adhaḥ-patana* falling down,

bhṛśa 765/3 mfn mighty, strong, often (*am*) ind. frequently , greatly, strongly, violently, excessively, very much, harshly, without hesitation, often, frequently, eminently, in a superior manner,

bhṛśaduḥkhita mfn exceedingly pained or unhappy,

bhṛt 764/3 mfn. bearing, carrying, bringing, maintaining, supporting

-bhṛt a bearer

bhṛta 764/3 mfn borne, carried, gained, acquired, ifc. filled, full of, hired, paid, m. a dependant, a servant, a hireling, mercenary, labourer,

bhṛti 764/3 f. bearing, carrying, bringing, fetching, support, maintenance

bhṛtya m. (one who is to be maintained), a servant,

bhrūḥ 770/3 f. an eyebrow, the brow

bhrūkuṭī f. contraction of the brows, the space between the eyebrows,

√*bhrūṇ* 771/1 cl 10 A *bhrūṇayate* to hope or wish or fear, DP in *āśā* hoping, or *viśaṅka* fearing,

bhruva ifc. for *bhrū*

bhruvos 6/du/f of the 2 eyebrows

√*bhū* 1. 760/1/2 cl 1 P A *bhavati*, (*te*) to become, be, arise, come into being, exist, be found, live, stay, abide, happen, occur, to fall to the share of, belong to, be on the side of, assist, serve for, tend to, be occupied with, devote oneself to, thrive or prosper in, be of consequence or useful, A. fall or get into, attain to, obtain, to obtain it, be successful or fortunate, caus. *bhāvayati (te),* to cause to be or become, call into existence or life, originate, produce, cause, create, to cherish, foster, animate, enliven, refresh, encourage, promote, further, to addict or devote one's self to, to subdue, control, to manifest, exhibit, show, betray, purify, present to the mind, think about, consider, know, recognize as or take for, to mingle, mix, saturate, soak, perfume, DP in *sattā* (cl 1) being, becoming, in *prāpti* (cl 10) obtaining, gaining, in *avakalakana* reflecting, or *miśrīkaraṇa* (cl 10) mixing,

2. mfn. becoming, being, existing, springing, arising, f. the place of being, space, world, universe, the act of becoming or arising, the earth as one of the 3 worlds and therefore a symbolical name for the number one, earth as a substance, ground, soil, land, floor, pavement, a place, spot, piece of ground, the base of a geometrical figure, object, matter, a sacrificial fire,

bhūbhāga m. spot of the earth, place,

√*bhuj* 1. 759/1 cl 6 P *bhujati* to bend, curve, to sweep, DP in *kauṭilya* bending, curving,

2. see *tri-bhuj*

3. 759/2 cl 7 P A *bhunakti, bhuṅkte* cl 6 P A *bhuñjati (te*) , to enjoy, use, possess, enjoy a meal, eat, eat and drink, consume, enjoy (carnally), make use of, exploit, take possession of, rule, govern, suffer, experience, undergo, P. be of use or service to, DP in *pālana* protecting, or *abhyavahāra* eating,

4. f. enjoyment, profit, advantage, possession or use of, m. an enjoyer, eater, mfn. enjoying (also carnally), eating, consuming, partaking of, possessing, ruling, m. enjoying the reward of, suffering for, passing, through, fulfilling

bhuja m. an arm (of the body), trunk, a branch, bough, a bending, curve, coil (of a snake), the base of a triangle, side of a geometrical figure, the base of a shadow,

bhūja f. a winding, coil (of a snake), the arm or hand, the side of any geometrical figure,

bhujaga m. snake,

bhujaṁ-gama m. serpent, snake,

bhukti f. enjoyment, eating, consuming, fruition, possession,

bhūmā the almighty Lord,

bhūman n. earth, world,

bhūmi 763/1 f. ground, earth, element, land, place (esp. fit place), proper vessel, soil, foundation, floor,

bhūmibhāga m. spot of ground,

bhūmikā f. earth, floor, soil, spot, ground, step, decoration, introduction, story

bhūmipa m. king

bhūmipāla m. king, ruler,

bhūmipati m. lord of the land, king, prince,

bhūmṛt m. mountain, king,

bhūmi-ṣṭha mfn standing on the ground,

bhuṅkṣva enjoy! 2/s/impv √*bhuj*

bhuṅkte root *bhuj*, 759/2 1/s/pres/indic/mid eats

bhūmyām on the ground, 7/s/f *bhūmya*

bhunaktu √3.*bhuj* 759/2 cl7 P.A. *bhunakti,* to enjoy, use, possess, enjoy a meal, eat, consume, 1/s/pres/act/impv may he enjoy, protect, possess,

bhuñjāna mfn enjoying

bhuñjīthāḥ you should enjoy or experience yourself, or make use of , (*īṣā up* protect or enjoy yourself), 2/s/opt/mid

bhuñjiya I should enjoy, I should eat, 3/s/opt/mid √*bhuj*

bhuṅkte he enjoys, he eats, he possesses 1/s/pres/indic/mid √ *bhuj*

bhūpa m. protector of the earth or land, king, prince,

bhūpati m. lord of the land, king, prince,

bhuraṇa mfn 1. moving quickly, 2. active, busy

bhuranya 760/1 Nom P *bhuranyati* to be active or restless, stir, DP in *dhāraṇa* holding, supporting, or *poṣaṇa* nourishing,

bhūri mfn abundant, much, frequent,

bhūri-kāla m. long time,

bhūriśas 764/1 manifoldly, variously, in diverse ways

bhūristhātra mfn having many stations, being in many places,

bhūrloka m. this earth

bhūrṇi mfn stirring, vigilant, excited, jealous (of a god),

bhūs it should be, it should arise 1/s/aor/subj √*bhū*

√*bhūṣ* 764/2 cl 1 P *bhūṣati* to strive after, use efforts for, be intent upon, to seek to procure, to adorn, caus. *bhūṣayati* to adorn, embellish, attire, DP in *alaṅkāra* adorning, decorating,

bhūṣā 764/2 ornament, decoration

bhūṣaṇa mfn decorating, adorning, n. ornament, jewel,

bhūṣanā f. adorned or decorated with,

bhūṣita mfn adorned,

bhūta 761/3 mfn become, been gone, past, (n. the past), actually happened, true, real, (n. matter of fact, a reality), existing, present, ifc. being or being like anything, consisting of, mixed or joined with,
m. a son, child, n. that which is or exists or has come into being, any living being (divine, human, animal or vegetable), the world, a spirit (good or evil), a ghost, demon, goblin, an element, one of the 5 elements, or a *tanmātra (subtle-element),* well-being, welfare, prosperity,

bhūtabhāṣā f. language of the goblins or *piśācas*

bhūtabhāva m. state of being, mfn existing in all beings,

bhūtabhāvanaḥ 1/s/m causing beings to be, causing beings to come into

existence, mfn causing welfare in living beings,
bhūtabhṛt mfn sustaining the elements or creatures, supporting beings,
bhūtadayā f. compassion towards all creatures, universal benevolence,
bhūtadhara mfn retaining (in the mind) or remembering the past,
bhūtadharā f. supporting beings, the earth,
bhūtādi 762/2 original or originator of beings, the origin of beings, the beginning of beings,
bhūtagaṇa 761/3 the host of living beings, a multitude of spirits or ghosts,
bhūtagrāma 761/3 any aggregate or elementary matter, the body, see also *bhūta,* 761/3 any living being and *grāma* 373/1 people 7/s in all beings,
bhūtajanya born of the elements,
bhūtakāla m. past time,
bhūtakoti f. 'the highest culminating point for all human beings',absolute non-entity, (= *śūnya-tā* Buddhist),
bhūtala n. earth-surface, ground, earth,

bhūtārtha m. anything that has really happened or really exists, real fact,
bhūtaśakti energy in matter subtle material elements,
bhūtasiddhi perfect control over the elements and the body,
bhūtastha abiding in beings, existing in beings, 761/3 mfn living on the earth, m. a man,
bhūtaśuddhi purification of the elements of the body,
bhūtāni beings, creatures 1/pl/n, 2/pl/n
bhūtapati the Lord of beings, a name of Śiva
bhūtaprādurbhāva the manifestation of beings
bhūtārthavāda factual corroborative statement e.g. "Indra raised his thunderbolt against Vṛtra" a fact known from the Vedas alone, (Gam.)
bhūtatā 762/1 f. reality, truth,
bhūtatanmātra the root elements of matter,
bhūtātma he lower self,
bhūtatva n. the state of being an element,
bhūtavat 1. ind. as if it were past, 2. mfn having been, 'as if real' (Gam.),
bhūtayajña an offering to the sub-human creatures,
bhūtayoni the source of all creation,
bhūti 762/3 f. existence, being, well-being, thriving, prosperity, might, power, wealth, fortune, riches,
bhūtikāla m. time of prosperity, a happy moment,
bhūtikāma mfn desirous of wealth or property, m. a king's counsellor,
bhūtvā having become, having been
bhuvas ind. the air, atmosphere, the world of becoming,
bhuvana –760/3 being, existence, man, the world, earth, *bhuvi* on earth, with *viśva* (singular) all beings,
bhuvana-traya n. world triad, heaven, atmosphere and earth,
bhuvaneṣa m. lord of the world,
bhūya m.763/3 more, very much, becoming more, more numerous, greater, larger, most, moreover, still more, once more, again, generally, usually, repeatedly,
n. becoming, being
bhūyāṇs mfn more, greater, (becoming in a higher degree, increasing),
bhūyas comparative adj. more, greater, moreover, furthermore,
bhūyāya 4/s/n to oneness with, for becoming Brahman
bhūyiṣṭha 763/3 mfn. most numerous or abundant or great or important, chief, principal (*am*) ind. mostly, chiefly
√*bhyas* 769/1 cl 1 A *bhyasate* to fear, be afraid, tremble, DP in *bhaya* fearing,
bibharti 764/3 bears, carries, upholds, maintains, √*bhṛ*
bībhatsa mfn loathsome, disgusting, horrible, n. repulsiveness,
bibheti he fears, is anxious about, 1/s/pres

√*bhī* 758/1 cl3

√*bid* (or *bind*) cl 1 P *bindati* to cleave, split, DP in *avayava* cleaving, splitting,

biḍāla m. a cat, the eyeball,

bīja 732/2 n. seed (of plants), semen, seed-corn, grain, primary cause or principle, source, analysis, truth (as the seed or cause of being) ,
seed sounds – the seeds of all sounds,

bījajanman life from seed? growth?

bījakṣara the seed letter of a *mantra*

bījāṅkura 732/3 m. a seed-shoot, seedling, du. seed and sprout, -*nyaya* the rule of seed and sprout (where two things stand to each other in the relation of cause and effect),

bījaprada 732/3 m. yielding or sowing seed, a generator, who deposits the seed

bījasantāna sowing ..scattering seed, generation of seed,

bījātma the subtle inner self,

√*bil* 732/1 (or *vil,* connected with *bid*) cl 6.10. P *bilati, belayati* to split, cleave, break, DP in *bhedana* splitting, breaking,

bila n. cleft, hollow, cave, hole,

bimba m.n. the sun disk or moon disc, a disk made of gold or silver, a mirror, an image, shadow, m. a lizard, chameleon,

bimba-pratibimba-vāda 'the doctrine that the *jīva* ia a reflection of Brahman; *jīva* who is the reflection of Brahman is not, therefore, a distinct thing from but is absolutely one with It.' (U)

√*bind* see *bid*

bindu m. a detached particle, drop, dot, spot, a pearl, a drop of water taken as a measure, a spot or mark of coloured paint on an elephant, the dot over a letter representing an *anusvāra,* a zero, a coloured mark made on the forehead between the eyebrows, f. *bindi*

bindu-jagrat the first state of ignorance,

bisa the lotus plant, stalk, fibre or root,

√*biṭ* 731/1 (or viṭ) cl 1 P to swear, shout, address harshly, DP in *ākroṣa* sounding, swearing,

boddhavya mfn to be attended to or noticed, to be known or perceived or observed or recognized, perceptible, intelligible, to be enlightened or admonished, or instructed or informed, one who is informed, to be awakened or aroused, n. (impers.) it is to be watched or awakened,

boddhavya-lakṣaṇa that which is to be known,

boddhṛ m. one who perceives or comprehends, one who knows or is versed in in comp. or 7th),

boddhum 733/2 infin. √*budh* to wake up, wake, be awake, to know, to understand, to perceive,

boddhyavyam to be known or enlightened, to be learned, gerundive √*budh*

bodha 734/2 knowing understanding, becoming or being awake or conscious, consciousness, awakening, the opening of blossom, bloom, thought, knowledge, understanding, intelligence, arousing, making known, informing, instructing,

bodhā f. the ascertainer,

bodhadhiṣaṇa m. one whose intellect is knowledge,

bodhagamya mfn attainable by the intellect, intelligible,

bodhaikaṭa oneness of consciousness (U)

bodhakara mfn one who wakens, rouses, teaches or informs, m. awakener,

bodhamātra m. the full and simple measure of anything, pure consciousness,

bodhamaya mfn consisting of pure knowledge,

bodhana 734/2 mfn causing to awake or expand, arousing, exciting, enlightening, teaching, instructing
f. intellect, knowledge,
m. the planet Mercury,

bodhāna mfn prudent, clever, wise, m. a wise man,

bodhanīya mfn to be admonished, to be known or understood, to be made known or explained, 734/3

bodhatas ind. through wisdom or understanding,

bodhātman m. the intelligent and sentient soul (Jainas),

bodhavyam what is to be ascertained (Gam.)

bodhayanta enlightening, causing to enlighten, awakening, pres/act/caus/part. √*budh*

bodhayitṛ m. an awakener, teacher, preceptor,

bodhi m.f. (with Buddhists or Jainas) perfect knowledge or wisdom, (by which a man becomes a Buddha or a Jina), the illuminated or enlightened intellect of the above, m. the tree of wisdom under which perfect wisdom is attained or under which a man becomes a Buddha, the sacred fig tree, enlightenment,

bodhicitta includes the following aspects, awakening mind, the wish to attain complete enlightenment in order to be of benefit to all beings, the aim to bring happiness to all beings and relieve them of all suffering, loss of attachment to the illusion of a personal self, limitless compassion and wisdom,

bodhida m. an Arhat (Jaina),

bodhin mfn intent upon, careful of, knowing, familiar with, causing to know or perceive, awakening, enlightening,

bodhinmanas mfn one whose mind is awake, watchful, attentive,

bodhisattva m. an aspirant for enlightenment whose essence is perfect knowledge, one who is on the way to perfect knowledge and has only one birth to go, a Buddhist saint,

bodhita mfn made known, apprised, explained, informed, instructed,

bodhya mfn to be known or understood, to be regarded or recognized as, to be made known, to be enlightened or instructed, 735/1

brahma 738/1 in a compound for *brahman*, m. a priest, n. the one self-existent Spirit, the Absolute, note nom. n. is used for the impersonal spirit and nom. m. (*brahmā*) for the personal god,

brahmā m. 'one who is all-surpassing, great, i.e. excels all others in virtue, knowledge, detachment, and splendour' (Gam.), 'the name for cosmic *buddhi* is *brahmā'* HH 'The primal manifestation of the *nirguṇa brahman* into *saguṇa brahman* in the imagery of the creative deity is known as *brahmā*. It is a figurative term used for the point of departure from the *nirguṇa*. This is the state of the universal *buddhi*' HH. "... when one thinks and reasons with one's *buddhi*, one is acting as *brahmā* on the individual level" 738/1 the one impersonal universal spirit manifested as personal Creator and as the first of the triad of personal gods,

brāhma 741/1 relating to *brahmā*, holy, sacred, divine, relating to sacred knowledge, prescribed by the veda, scriptural,

brahmabhāvanā feeling of identity with Brahman as well as of everything as Brahman,

brahmabhūta 739/2 absorbed in *Brahman*, identification with *Brahman*, one who has become *Brahman*

brahmabhūyā 739/2 n. identification with or absorption into Brahman

brahmābhyāsa m. study and repetition of the Veda, practice of the presence of Brahman (thinking of Brahman alone, talking of Brahman alone, ... in whole-souled surrender and dedication of one's being to the Universal Reality, meditation on

Brahman, *nididhyāsana* etc. for the realisation of Brahman), (U)

brahmacārin 738/2 practising sacred study as an unmarried student, observing chastity and obedience, m. a young Brāhman who is a student of the Veda (under a preceptor) or who practises chastity, a young Brāhman before marriage,

brahmacarya n. study of the Veda, the state of an unmarried religious student, a state of continence and chastity,

brahma-cintana constant meditation on Brahman,

brahmadāya m. sacred word heritage, heritage consisting of the sacred word, imparting or teaching sacred knowledge,

brahmadāyahāra mfn receiving the sacred word as a heritage,

brahmadhāman n. abode that is Brahman, Brahmā's place or abode,

brahmadvara n. entrance into Brahman, door to Brahman,

brahmadviṣ mfn devotion hating, godless, hostile to sacred knowledge or religion, impious,

brahma-granthi the knot of ignorance at the *mūlādhāra chakra*

brahmahan mfn brāhman-slaying, m. murderer of a brāhman,

brahmajajña mfn one that is born from *Brahmā* and illumined, born from and knowing Brahma, knowing what is Brahma-born i.e. knowing all things,

brahmajijñāsā f. the desire to know Brahman, enquiry into reality,

brahmajña mfn holy, knowing the sacred text, possessing sacred knowledge, spiritually wise,

brahmajñāna m. self-realization, spiritual wisdom, direct knowledge of Brahman

brahmakāra vṛtti 'in *samādhi* or absorption there is the transformation of all *vṛtti*s into the *brahmakāra vṛtti* which destroys ignorance, desires and actions, and settles down, extinguishing itself like burnt camphor' (U),

brahmaloka 739/3 the world or heaven of *brahmā* (a division of the universe and one of the supposed residences of pious spirits) "where there are beings who have acquired great merits .."

brahma-muhūrta period of an hour and a half before sunrise,

brahman 737/3 n. lit. 'growth, expansion', a sacred word, the sacred syllable Om, religious or spiritual knowledge, the one self-existent impersonal Spirit, the one universal Soul (or one divine essence and source from which all created things emanate or with which they are identified and to which they return, the Self-existent, the Absolute, the Eternal, (not generally an object of worship but rather of meditation and knowledge,) religious or spiritual knowledge, n. the class of men who are the repositories and communicators of sacred knowledge, the Brahmanical caste as a body, food, wealth, final emancipation,

G.96 the Absolute Reality, or all-pervasive principle of the universe, it has nothing similar to it and nothing different from it, the nature of *Brahman –sat* existence absolute, *cid* consciousness absolute, *ānanda* bliss absolute

brāhmaṇa mfn. relating to or given by a *brāhman*, befitting or becoming a *brāhman*,

m. one who has divine knowledge, a *brāhman*, a man belonging to the first of the classes or castes, generally a priest but often in present day a layman engaged in non-priestly occupations although the name is strictly only applicable to one who knows and repeats the *Veda,*

n. that which is divine, the divine, sacred or divine power, Brahmanical explanation, explanations of sacred knowledge or doctrines (esp. for use in sacrifices etc.), a soma vessel, the *brāhmaṇas* the explanatory part of the *veda*- rules for recitation, legends, detailed explanations of origins, meanings and legends, each Veda has its *brāhmaṇa*
part 1 – *viddhi* rules or directions for rites,
part 2 – explanatory remarks,

brahmānanda bliss of the Absolute

brāhmaṇavāda m. a statement of the *brāhmaṇas*

brahmāṇḍa 740/2 brahmā's egg, the universe

brahmaniṣṭha mfn absorbed in contemplating the Absolute, one who is established in Brahman,

brahmānubhāva self realisation,

brahmānusaṁdhāna exploration into the nature of Brahman; receiving of the *upadeśa* (instruction) about Brahman and reflection upon it.

brāhmaṇya (N) 'the state of one who knows Brahman', m. the planet Saturn, n. the state or rank of a Brahman,

brahmanirvāṇa n. 'blown out", ceasing to exist, in Brahman, extinction in Brahma, absorption into the one self-existent Spirit,

brahmaniṣṭha 'who is absorbed in Brahman', mfn absorbed in contemplating Brahmā or the one Supreme Spirit, 'devoted to the inferior Brahman, seeker of the knowledge of the Supreme Brahman (Gam.)',

brahmaṇya mfn pertaining or attached to the holy life and study, i.e. pious, attached or friendly to Brahmans, the planet Saturn, the mulberry tree,

brahmapara 'devoted to the inferior Brahman, mistaking that for the superior Brahman', (Gam.),

brahma-pārāyaṇa 'one whose faith and sole refuge is in Brahman' (U)

brahmaprāpti f. obtainment of or absorption into Brahman, liberation,

brahmāpyayam absorption in the Brahman, merger in Brahman,

brahmarandhra n. a suture/aperture in the crown of the head (through which the soul is said to pass on death),

brahmarṣi m. priest-sage, priestly sage,

brahma-sakṣātkāra realisation of Brahman,direct experience of the Supreme Being,' (U)

brahmaśakti the power of Brahman,

brahma-śrotriya he who has knowledge of the Vedas and the Upanishads,

brahma-saṁsthā grounded in Brahman, Sannyasin,

brahma-sthīti establishment or dwelling in Brahman,

brahmāstra n. name of a terrible weapon,

brahmasūtra n. the sacred thread worn over the shoulder, name of a work,

brahmāsūtrāṇi a harmony of *sūtra*s. teaching the single truth. "I am Brahman"

brahmatattva the reality of Brahman,

brahma-tejas the effulgent splendour of Brahman

brahmavādin mfn discoursing on sacred texts, a defender or expounder of the Veda, one who asserts that all things are to be identified with Brahman,

brahmavākya divine revelation e.g. the upanishads

brahmavarcas or *-varcasa* n. divine glory or splendour, pre-eminence in holiness or sacred knowledge, sanctity or superhuman power,

brahmavarcasvin mfn eminent in divine knowledge,

brahmavedin mfn knowing divine knowledge,

brahmavicāra enquiry into the nature of Brahman

brahmavid 740/1 mfn knowing the one *Brahmā*, a Vedic philosopher,

brahmavidvara one who has reached the fifth *jñāna bhūmika* or *asaṁsakti, brahmavidvariṣṭha* a full *jñāni,* a *jīvanmukta* who has attained to the seventh *jñāna-bhūmika* or *turīya,*

brahmavidvariya one who functions in the sixth *jñāna-bhūmika* or *padārthābhāvanā*

brahmavidvas mfn one who knows *Brahmā* or the one Universal Spirit,

brahmavidyā 740/1 f. knowledge of the 'the one self-existent Being', sacred knowledge,

brahmavihāra m. pious conduct, perfect state,

brahmavit knower of Brahman, one who is in the fourth *jñāna-bhūmika* or *sattvāpatti,*

brahmayoga the Yogi finds himself and the whole universe as Brahman,

brahmayoni 'the Brahman that is the source' or 'the source of the inferior Brahman ' (Gam.),

brāhmī 742/1 the *śakti* or personified energy of Brahmā

brāhmīsthitiḥ the state of Brahman, Brahmanic position, standing in the Brahman, existence in Brahman,

brahmopāsanā worship of Brahman

bravīmi 1/s/pres/indic/act I tell, I speak, I am speaking,

bravīsi 2/s you tell, say

√*bṛh* 1. 735/3 (or *vṛh),* cl 6 P *brihati (vṛhati*), to tear, pluck, root up, DP in *udyamana* growing, increasing, in *vṛddhi* growing, or *śabda* sounding,
√**2.** *bṛḥ* or *bṛṁh* see *bṛṁh* below, DP in growing, increasing, expanding, sounding
3. f. prayer =*bṛhaspati* , L. conceived as a swelling and filling of the heart in devotion,
4. or *bṛṁh* (also written *vṛh* or *vṛṁh*), cl 1 P to roar, bellow, trumpet, (said of an elephant), also cl 10 P to speak, to shine, DP in *bhāṣā* speaking, shining,

bṛhadaśva mfn possessing great or powerful horses, name of the sage who relates the story of Nala,

bṛhanta mfn great, mighty, lofty,

bṛhaspati 737/1 'lord of prayer or devotion', head priest of the gods with whom he intercedes for men, the mediator between gods and men, later – god of wisdom and eloquence

bṛhat 735/3(or *vṛhat* in later language) mfn lofty, high, tall, great, extended or bright, name of a man, name of a *marut,* name of various *sāman*s, (a metrical hymn or song of praise) composed in *bṛhatī* form, name of *Brahman*, big, strong,

bṛhat-brahmāṇḍa the great macrocosm,

bṛhatkathā f. Great Story – name of a story collection,

bṛhatsāma 736/1 having the *bṛhat-sāman* for a *sāman* (see above)

bṛhattva vastness, largeness, absoluteness,

√*bṛṁh* 735/3 or *bṛh* cl 1 P *bṛṁhati* to be thick, grow great or strong, DP in *vṛddhi* growing, increasing, or *śabda* sounding, in *vibhāga* dividing, or *utsarga* discharging, emitting,

√*brū* 742/2 cl 2 P A *bravīti (te*), present stem only (other forms provided by √*vac),* to speak, say, tell, to speak about any person or thing, to proclaim, predict, to answer, to call or profess oneself to be.., A. to designate for oneself, choose, to be told by itself, tell itself, DP in *vyaktā-vāc* speaking, declaring,

brūhi 742/1 *brū* 2/s/mid/*lot* (impv) speak, say, tell !

brūte 742/1 he says, tells, speaks, 1/s/pres/indic/mid

brūvan √ *brū* 742/1 to speak say, part. speaking

bubhukṣā 735/1 f. desire to enjoy anything appetite, hunger, will to enjoy,

bubhukṣu mfn wishing to be or become anything, wishing to become powerful or prevail, desiring power or personal change,
735/1 mfn wishing to eat, hungry, desirous of worldly enjoyment,

bubhutsā 734/2 desire to know, curiosity

about,

budbuda 733/1 a bubble m/1/plu often used as a symbol of something transitory

buddha 733/2 awake, awakened, expanded, conscious, intelligent, wise, learnt, known, understood, m. a wise or learned man, sage, (with Buddhists) a fully enlightened man who has achieved perfect knowledge of the truth and thereby is liberated from all existence and before his own attainment of Nirvāṇa reveals the method of obtaining it, n. knowledge, L. enlightened, (N, S,)'one who has understood truth' full of knowledge,

buddhacakṣus one of the 5 sorts of vision, 'Buddha's eye',

buddhacarita n. 'the acts of Buddha',

buddhāgama m. Buddha's doctrine (personified),

buddhaguru m. a Buddhist spiritual teacher,

buddhajñāna n. Buddha's knowledge, knowledge of Buddha,

buddhakalpa m. name of the present Buddha era,

buddhamarga m. the way of Buddha,

buddhānta m. waking condition, the being awake,

buddhānusmṛti f. continual meditation on Buddha,

buddhatva n. the condition or rank of a Buddha,

buddhavacana n. 'Buddha's word', the Buddhist Sūtras,

buddhayā . through judging it to be, 3/s

buddhayas insights, enlightenments, 1/pl/f

buddhi 733/3 reason, the organ of discrimination, reflects the light of the *ātman*, intellect, the power of forming and retaining concepts and general notions, intelligence, reason, discernment, judgment, mind, perception, the name for cosmic *buddhi* is *brahmā,*
'*buddhi* is used in two main ways: reason or common-sense, intelligence to help deal with worldly affairs; and discrimination between conscious and inanimate, which is known as *viveka*, to exorcise the ghost of *ahaṅkāra* or *prakṛti*.' L. insight, understanding, intellect, mind, wit, wits, reflects the light of the *ātman,* functions as intellect with the character of determination and will (U).

buddhijīvin mfn living by one's mind, employing one's intelligence, intelligent, (L)

buddhim √*kṛ* make up one's mind, (L)

buddhim pra√*kṛ* (mid) put a plan before one's self, decide,

buddhimān m. full of wisdom, wise, enlightened, intelligent,

buddhimant mfn possessing understanding, intelligent,

buddhi-śakti intellectual power,

buddhi-śuddhi purity of intellect,

buddhi-tattva the principle of intelligence,

buddhitva understanding, having the nature of Buddhi,

buddhi-vyāpāra functioning of the intellect,

buddhiyoga 734/1 devotion of the intellect, intellectual union with the Supreme Spirit, yoga of discrimination

buddhiyukta mfn endowed with understanding, intelligent,

buddhiyuktas he who is disciplined in determination through buddhi. 734/1 mfn endowed with understanding, intelligent,

buddhvā 733/2 ind. understanding, having learned, having realised, having awakened, gerund, √ *budh*

√*budh* 733/2/1 cl 1 P A *bodhati (te*), cl 4 A P *budhyate (ti),* to wake, wake up, be awake, to recover consciousness (after a swoon), to observe, heed, attend to, perceive, notice, learn, understand, realize, become or be aware of or acquainted with, to know to be, recognize as, to deem, consider or regard as, to be awakened or restored to

consciousness, caus. *bodhayati (te)* to wake up, arouse, restore to life or consciousness, revive the scent of a perfume, cause a flower to expand, cause to observe or attend, admonish, advise, to make a person acquainted with, remind or inform of, impart or communicate anything to, DP in *avagamana* waking, understanding, knowing, understanding, perceiving, in *bodhana* waking up, knowing, understanding,
2. mfn awaking, intelligent, wise,

budha 734/1 mfn awaking, intelligent, wise, m. a wise or learned man, name of the planet Mercury, father of Purūravas,

budhna n. the bottom, lowest point, the sky, the body,

√*bukk* 733/1 cl 1. 10. P *bukkati, bukkayati* to bark, yelp, sound, talk, to give pain, DP in *bhaṣaṇa* barking

√*bund* 735/1 cl 1 P A (also *cund* and *bundh),* to perceive, learn, understand, DP in *niśāmana* perceiving, knowing,

√*buṅg* 733/1 (or *vuṅg*) cl 1 P *buṅgati* to forsake, abandon, DP in *varjana* forsaking, abandoning,

√*bus* 735/2 cl 4 P *busyati* to discharge, pour forth, emit, to divide, distribute, DP in *vibhāga* dividing, or *utsarga* discharging, emitting, pouring out,

√*bust* 735/2 cl 10 P *bustayati* to honour, respect, DP in *ādara* respecting, regarding, or *anādara* disrespecting, condemning,

√*byus* 737/3 = √*vyuṣ* cl 4 P to burn, divide, distribute, cl 10 P to reject, discharge, emit,
DP in *vibhāga* dividing,
2. dawn, daybreak,

ca and, also, when more than two words are connected it is used with the last only

√*cad* 386/2 cl 1 *cadati, cadate* to ask or beg, DP in *yācana* begging, requesting

√*cah* 391/3 cl 1.10 P *cahati cahayati* to cheat, DP in *parikalkana* cheating, deceiving,

caila 402/3 made of cloth, bred in clothes (insects),

caitanya 402/2 consciousness, intelligence, sensation, spirit, Universal Soul or Spirit, pure consciousness,

caitanyamayi full of consciousness; an attribute of *māyā*

caitra m. name of the 2nd spring month, a buddhist or Jain mendicant,

caitya m. the individual soul, a funeral mound, monument or *stūpa,* pyramidal column containing personal ashes, sacred tree growing on a mound, hall or temple or place of worship,

√*cak* 380/2 cl 1 P A *cakati (te)* to be satiated or contented or satisfied, to repel, resist, to shine, DP in *tṛpti* being satiated, and *pratighāta* repelling,

√*cakās* 380/2 cl 2 P *cakāsti* to shine, be bright, DP in *dīpti* shining
2. mfn shining,

cakās n. bad rice

cakita mfn trembling, timid, frightened, n. trembling, timidity,

√*cakk* 380/3 cl 10 P *cakkayati* to suffer, to give or inflict pain, DP in *vyathana* suffering, inflicting pain,

cakra 380/3 n. a wheel, a discus, a circle, G100. Centres (6) of energy in the subtle body where the *(nādi)* channels converge. These junctions, *cakras* or centres of consciousness regulate the body mechanism.

cakraka n. a circular argument, mfn resembling a wheel or a circle,

cakravartin mfn rolling everywhere without obstruction, supreme, holding the highest rank, m. an emperor, sovereign, supreme, holding the highest rank,

cakravāta m. the whirlwind demon, a whirlwind,

cakrin 381/3 mfn bearing a discus, having wheels, driving in a carriage, m. a potter, an oil-grinder, a king,

√*cakṣ* 382/1 cl 2 A *caṣṭe* to appear, become visible, to see, look at, observe, notice, to tell, inform, DP in *vyaktāvāc* distinct speech?

cakṣas n. radiance, clearness, look, eye, sight, m. a teacher, spiritual instructor,

cakṣu 382/1 m. the eye, the subtle organ of sight, sense of seeing,

cakṣuḥpīḍā f. eye-ache, eye pain,

cakṣus *m.* seeing, n. light, clearness, the act of seeing, faculty of seeing, sight, a look, the eye,

cakṣuṣā by the eye

cakṣuṣmant mfn having eyes,

√*cal* 391/1 cl 1 P A *calati (te)* to be moved, stir, tremble, be agitated, to move on or forward, proceed, go away, start off, depart, to set (said of the day), to be moved from one's usual course, be disturbed, become confused or disordered, go astray, to turn away from, swerve, deviate from, sport about, frolic, play, to cherish, foster, DP in *kampana* shaking, trembling, *vilasana* sporting, playing, *bhṛti* cherishing

cala 391/1 mfn. moving, trembling, changing,

calābhāsa 'appears as though moving', 'appears to admit movement',

calana 391/2 moving, movable, shaking motion, walking about, wandering

calati 391/1 moves, is agitated, moved from one's usual course, is disturbed

√*cam* 388/2 cl 1 *camati* to sip, drink, to eat, DP in *adana* eating, *bhakṣaṇa* eating

cāmara mfn coming from the yak (*cam*), m. a chowrie (a fly-whisk made from the bushy tail of a yak,)

camasa m. beaker, a cup made of wood, square and with a handle,

camat ind. (only in comp.) an interjection of surprise,

caṁcala mfn moving to and fro, unsteady, inconstant, flickering, inconsiderate, m. the wind, a lover, libertine,

caṁcalatva fickleness, tossing of the mind,

caṁcalavṛtti natural wavering tendency of the mind,

caṁcu f. beak,

camatkaraṇa n. also *camatkāra* m. astonishment, causing surprise or wonder, spectacle, festival, esteemed poetry,

√*camp* 388/3 cl 10 *campayati* see √*champ* DP in *gati* going

campaka m. a tree, a kind of perfume,

campakavant mfn abounding in *campaka*s

camūḥ f. army or division of an army, heaven and earth, six times,

√*caṇ* 383/1 cl 1 P *caṇati* to give, to go, to injure, to sound, DP in *gati* going and *dāna* giving

√*can* 386/2 cl 1 P *canati* to sound, utter a sound, to hurt, injure, DP in *hiṁsā* injuring, *śraddhā* trusting, *upakanana* killing,

cana 386/2 ind. and not, also not, even not, not even, (this particle is placed after the word to which it gives force), a preceding verb is accentuated, in Classical Sanskrit it is only used after interrogatives beginning with '*k*' making them indefinite,

caṇa mfn impetuous, wrathful, n. heat, passion, wrath, circumcised, (*am*) ind. violently, in anger,

caṅaka m. chick-pea, f. linseed,

canas n. delight, satisfaction, with √*dhā* 'to delight in, be satisfied with',

√*cañc* 382/2 cl 1 P *cañcati* to leap, jump, move, dangle, be unsteady, DP in *gati* going

cañcala 382/2 mfn. moving to and fro, shaking, flickering, movable, unsteady, inconstant, inconsiderate, m. the wind, a lover, intensive from √*cal* Cl 1 391/1

cañcu f. beak, bill, m. a deer, the castor-oil plant,
√*cand* 386/2 cl 1 *candati* cl 1 to shine, be bright, to gladden, DP in *āhlādana* being glad, rejoicing, and *dīpti* shining
√*caṇḍ* 383/1 cl 1. 10 A *caṇḍate, caṇḍayate* to be angry or wrathful, DP in *kopa* growing angry
cāṇḍala m. a *Chāṇḍāla*, (a person of the lowest caste), an outcast,
candana m. sandalwood, sandalwood tree,
caṇḍila m. a barber,
candra *m.* the moon, glittering, shining, having the hue of light
cāndra mfn. shining, shimmering, lunar, m. a lunar month, the moon, the moon god,
ī f. moonlight
candramas m. the moon, the moon god,
cāndramasa n lunar
candramasi 7/s in the moon
candramus m. the moon,
candranādi lunar psychic current that flows through the left nostril,
candravarṇa mfn of shining hue, of brilliant colour,
cāndrāyaṇa an observance or lunar penance, a fast,
candrikā f. moonlight,
cāpa m. n. a bow, (as in bow and arrow), Sagittarius, arc, rainbow,
capala mfn fickle, shaking, unsteady, thoughtless, ill-mannered,
capalā f. lightning,
capalatā mfn rudeness, fickleness, f. inconstancy
cāṇūraḥ name of a demon
√*cap* 388/1 cl 1 *capati* to caress, soothe, console, cl 10 *capayati* to pound, knead, to cheat, DP in *sāntvana* consoling, soothing, in *parikalkana* being proud or haughty,
cāpa 393/1 m. n. a bow, arc, rainbow
capeṭa m. a slap with the open hand,
√*car* 389/1 cl 1 P A *carati (te)* to move oneself, go, move, walk, stir, roam about, wander, to spread, be diffused (as fire), to move or travel through, pervade, go along, follow, to behave, conduct oneself, act, live, treat, be engaged in, occupied or busy with, have to do with, have intercourse with, to continue performing or being, to undertake, set about, undergo, observe, practise, do or act in general, to consume, eat, make or render, caus. *cārayati* to cause to move or walk about, to pasture, send, direct, turn, move, cause anyone to walk through, to drive away from, cause anyone to practise or perform, DP in *gati* going, *bhakṣaṇa* eating, *saṁśaya* doubting,
cara 389/2 mfn moving, movable, walking, wandering, living, practising, m. spy
carācara mfn moving and not moving, n. the moving and not moving, i.e. all living things, animal & vegetable,
carama mfn last, ultimate, final,
caraṇa 1. m.n. foot, ifc. pl. 'the feet of the venerable', a pillar, support, a line of a stanza, the root (of a tree), a school or branch of the Veda, n. going round or about, motion, course, conduct of life, good conduct, practising, 2. n. a wandering,
cāraṇa mfn depending on a Vedic school, belonging to the same Vedic school, m. wanderer, esp. wandering singer or player, celestial singer,
caraṇāmṛta water in which the feet of a Brahman or spiritual guide have been washed,
√*caraṇya* 389/3 Nom P *caraṇyati* to move DP in *gati* going,
caraṇya mfn foot-like
carata pass.part. living, wandering
carati 389/1√ *car* – to move, walk, go 1/s/pres/indic/act walks, moves, grazes,
√*carb* 390/2 cl 1 *carbati* to go DP in *gati* going, *adana* eating
√*carc* 390/2 cl 1 *carcati* to abuse, censure,

menace, cl 10 *carcayati* to repeat a word (in reciting the Veda), also A. to study, DP in *paribhāṣaṇa* saying, *hiṁsā* injuring, *tarjana* threatening,

carcā f. a going over, repetition (Veda recitation), troubling one's self about, trouble, concern,

cārin 393/3mfn moving, ifc. living, being, moving, walking or wandering about, acting, doing, proceeding, m. a soldier, a spy,

carita 389/3 gone to, attained, done, 2. conduct, behaviour, proceedings, deeds,

caritārtha mfn having accomplished what one set out to do, successful in any undertaking,

caritra n. m. a foot, leg, n. going, acting, behaving, behavior, habit, practice, acts, an adventure, nature, disposition, custom, law as based on custom, f. the tamarind tree,

cāritra m. proceeding, manner of acting, conduct, good conduct, good character, reputation, peculiarity of customs, a ceremony, tamarind tree,

carita-vrata 389/3 mfn one who has observed a vow,

√*carkarīta* 390/2 n. a term for any intensive formed without the syllable *ya* e.g. *carkarīti*

carman n. skin, pelt, leather, bark, parchment,

carṣaṇi mfn active, busy, f. pl. busy mortals, men, folk,

caru grains to be offered in a fire sacrifice with milk, sugar and ghee

cāru mfn lovely, pretty, pleasant, fair,

cāruhāsin mfn sweetly laughing, smiling sweetly,

√*carv* 391/1 cl 10 *carvayati* cl 1 *carvati* to grind with the teeth, masticate, chew, to taste, DP in *adana* eating

Cārvāka founder of a materialist philosophical school

carya gve. to be accomplished, practised or performed, n. ifc. driving (in a carriage), *(ā)* f. . going about, wandering, n. behaviour, conduct, due observance of all rites and customs, a religious mendicant's life, practising, performing,

caryā mfn to be practised or performed, f. going about, wandering, walking or roaming about, visiting, driving (in a carriage), n. proceeding, behaviour, conduct, due observance of all rites and customs, a religious mendicant's life, occupation with or concern for a thing,

√*caṣ* 391/2 cl 1 *caṣati* to hurt, P A to eat, DP in *bhakṣaṇa* eating,

√*caṭ* 382/3 cl 1 P *caṭati* to fall in (as the flood), to reach (with loc.) fall to the share of or into, to hang down from, to rain, to cover, DP in *varṣa* raining, and *āvaraṇa* screening, covering, in *bhedana* piercing, breaking,

√*cat* 383/3 cl 1 *catati* to hide oneself, P A to go, ask, beg, DP in *yācana* asking, begging, requesting,

cāṭa 391/3 a cheat, rogue. Apte – one who wins the confidence of the person he wishes to deceive, *-vaḥas*, like , in a cheating way, in an ingratiating way

cātaka m. a bird said to subsist on raindrops,

cātana mfn driving away,

catasṛ f. pl. of *catur*

cāṭu flattery, pleasing or graceful words or discourse,

catur 384/1 four,

catura mfn clever, swift, quick, dexterous,

caturbhuja mfn having 4 arms, four-armed, a quadrangular figure,

caturdaśa fourteen

caturmāsya n. 'four months', the monsoon season, a four-monthly sacrifice, beginning a four-month season,

caturtha fourth, f. (*ī*)

caturvarga fourfold aims – *dharma, artha, kama, mokṣa*

caturvidhā the 4 divisions - those born

from the womb, those born from eggs, those born from vapour or sweat, those born from seeds or sprouting, four kinds of foods,

caturyuga the four ages – *kṛta, tretā, dvāpara, kali*

catuṣpad mfn a quadruped, collectively the four-footed beasts,
having taken 4 steps,

catuṣpada possessed of 4 quarters, quadruped, having 4 divisions,

catuṣpāt mfn having (taken) four steps, consisting of four parts,

catuṣṭaya consisting of four, four-fold, collection of four,

catvār strong form of *catur*, four

catvara n. or m. a quadrangular place, place in which many ways meet,

catvāra four

cauḍa n. ceremony of tonsure,

caura m. thief,

caurya 403/1 trickery, theft, fraud

√cay 389/1 cl 1 *cayate* to go DP in *gati* going

√cāy 393/2 cl 1 *cāyati* to observe, perceive, notice, to fear, be afraid of, A. to behave respectfully, DP in *pūjā* worshipping, *niśāmana* observing

cayana 394/2 n. piling up, collecting, stacked wood,

ced 401/3 ind. (*ca* + *id*) if (never begins a sentence or half-line), *na ced* if not, *no ced* and if not,

cel 402/1 cl 1 = √*cal*, DP in *calana* moving, shaking,

cela n. cloth, clothes, garment,
m. a slave or servant, a disciple,

√ceṣṭ 402/1 cl 1 *ceṣṭati (te)* to move the limbs, move, stir, make effort, struggle, strive, be busy or occupied with, act, do, perform, DP in *ceṣṭā* trying,

ceṣṭa 402/1 n. action, bodily activity, gesture, behaviour, manner of life, effort, conveying meaning by body movement,

ceṣṭā 402/1 f. behaviour or manner of life, action, effort, activity, doing, endeavour, exertion, performance

ceṣṭita mfn performed, set in motion, done with effort, exerted,
n. deeds, moving any limb, gesture,

cet Nom. P. *–tati,* to recover consciousness,

cet if

ceṭa m. a servant, slave, kind of fish,

ceta m. the mind (V)

cetā f. consciousness

cetana 397/3 mfn.distiguished, visible, intelligence, conscious, sentient, m. an intelligent being, man, soul, mind, m. an intelligent being, man, soul, mind, n. conspicuousness, consciousness f. (*ā)* intelligence, consciousness, understanding, sense

cetas 398/1 n. splendour, consciousness, intelligence, thinking soul, heart, mind, subconscious mind,

cetasāḥ thoughts, 1/pl/m

cetaso'rpaṇa recollection of the mind,

cetaya mfn sentient, enlivening,

cetavitavyam 'the object to be conscious of' (Gam.),

ceto in comp. for *cetas*

cetomukha 398/1 mfn one whose mouth is intelligence, 'he is the doorway to the consciousness of the experiences in the dream and waking states'(Gam.), 'or he is called *cetomukha* because consciousness, appearing as empirical experience, is his doorway to the states of dream and waking'(Gam.)

cetoṁśūn 'rays of consciousness' (Gam.),

cettṛ mfn attentive, guardian,

cetu m. heedfulness,

cetya mfn perceivable

√chad 404/1 cl 1 *chadati* to cover, caus. (or cl 10) *chādayati* to cover, cover over, clothe, veil, to spread as a cover, to cover oneself, to hide, conceal, keep secret, to protect, DP in *saṁvaraṇa* covering
2. mfn covering

3. or 2. √*chand* cl 10 *chadayati (te)* *chandayati,* cl 1 *chandati* [=*arcati]* to seem, appear, be considered as, to seem good, please, A. to be pleased with, delight in, *chandayati* to gratify anyone, try to seduce anyone. DP in *apavāraṇa* n. covering, concealment,
4. mfn appearing as, pleased with,
5. cl 1 to nourish DP in *ūrjana* strengthening, animating

chadmagati 404/2 approaching clandestinely

chadman n. external covering, deceptive dress, disguise, pretext, pretence, deceit, fraud

chāga m. goat, mfn coming from a goat,

chala 405/2 n. fraud, deceit, pretense, delusion

√*cham* 405/2 cl 1 *chamati* to eat, DP in *adana* eating,

√*champ* 405/2 cl 10 *champayati* to go

√*chand* 405/2 see √1 & 3 *chad* also = *chṛd,* DP in *saṁvaraṇa* covering

chanda mfn pleasing, inviting, alluring, praising,
m. appearance, look, shape, will, pleasure, delight, appetite, desire, according to the wish of, involuntarily,
n. pleasure, ind. (3rd) according to one's own wish

chandāṁsī the Vedic hymns pl.,

chandas 1. roof, deceit

chandas 2. 405/1 desire, longing for, incantation, hymn, metre, the science of metre, singing of verses

chandatas 404/3 ind. at will, at pleasure, according to choice

channa mfn covered, covered over, obscured (the moon), hidden, secret, ind. secretly, (with √*gau* to sing) privately, in a low voice,

√*chaṣ* 405/3 cl 1 P A to hurt, DP in *hiṁsā* hurting, injuring

chātra m. pupil, disciple,

chatra n. umbrella,

chaviḥ f. beauty, colour, aura,

chāyā 406/1 shade, shadow, a shady place, shelter, protection, a reflected image, reflection, shading or blending of colours, lustre, light, colour, gracefulness, beauty,

chāyādvitīya mfn having one's shadow as second, accompanied by one's shadow,

√*ched* in *dvaidhīpana* bisecting, dividing in two,

cheda m. cut, cutting off, failure, dearth, want, lack, cutting out, removing,

chedana 407/1 cutting asunder, splitting, destroying, removing, cessation,

√*chid* 406/2 cl 7 *cinatti, cintte*, cut off, amputate, cut through, hew, chop, split, pierce, divide, separate from, destroy, annihilate, efface, blot out, pass. *chidyate* is dispelled etc.DP in *dvaidhīkaraṇa* cutting, taking away, removing
2. mfn ifc. cutting, cutting off, cutting through, splitting, piercing, destroying, annihilating, removing, m. the divisor, denominator
f. the cutting off, annihilation of

chidra n. hole, defect, weak spot, chink,

√*chidraya* 406/3 Nom *chidrayati* to perforate, DP in *karṇabhredana* piercing the ear,

chindanti they cut, they pierce √*chid*

chinna 406/3 past part. of *chid,* cut, cut off, taken away, nibbled,

chittvā cutting away, having cut away, having split,

√*cho* 407/2 cl 4 *chayati* to cut off, cut, DP in *chedana* cutting,

choṭī a lock of hair left on top of the head, f. petticoat,

√*chṛd* 407/2 cl 7 to vomit, to utter, leave, P A *chṛntte* to shine, to play, cl 1 *chardati* or charpati to kindle, caus. *chardayati* to cause to flow over, to vomit, eject, to cause to spit or vomit, DP in *dīpti* shining, *devana* playing, *sandīpana* kindling,

√*chṛp* 407/2 cl 1. 10 for √*chṛd,* DP in *sandīpana* kindling, *chucchundara* m. musk-rat,

√*chuḍ* 407/1 cl 6 = √*thuḍ,* to cover,DP in *samvaraṇa* covering, screening,

√*chup* 407/1 cl 6 *chupati* to touch DP in *sparśa* touching

√*chur* 407/2 cl 6 *churati* to cut off, cut, incise, etch, caus. *churayati* to strew or sprinkle with, *chorayati* to abandon, throw away, DP in *chedana*, cutting,

churikā f. knife,

churita mfn studded with, inlaid with, n. flashing of lightning,

√*chuṭ* 407/1 cl 6 *chuṭati* to bind, cl 10 *choṭayati* to cut, split, DP in *chedana* cutting, dividing,

√*ci* `1. 394/2 cl 5 *cinoti cinute* to arrange in order, heap up, pile up, construct (an altar), to collect, gather together, accumulate, acquire for oneself, to search through (for collecting), to cover, inlay, set with, DP in *cayana* collecting

2. Ved. cl 3 *ciketi* to observe, perceive, to fix the gaze upon, be intent upon, cl 5 *cinoti* to seek for, investigate, search through, make inquiries,

3. cl 1 *cayate* to detest, hate, to revenge, punish, take vengeance on,

√*cīb* 399/3 = √*cīv* to take,DP in *katthana* boasting,

cibuka n. chin, tongs,

cid 397/3 in compounds for *cit* 395/2 /3 thought, intellect, spirit, consciousness

cid pure uninfluenced consciousness, "is experienced as consciousness" HH, (see *cit*) "unlimited consciousness" HH "Cid is *akhaṇda* and it is also known as *ātmajñāna*, the experience of the Self, not as this and that, but as Itself". HH

cid 2. 398/1 even, indeed, (often merely laying stress on a previous word), requiring a previous simple verb to be accentuated, in Class. used after interrogative pronouns and adverbs to render them indefinite, as well as, both, and,

cidābhāsa reflected consciousness, the reflection of intelligence *(jīva),* "consciousness of knowledge or appearance of knowledge on the consciousness" "That consciousness which shines or seems to reflect in the *antaḥkaraṇa*". HH 'all experiences are called *cidābhāsa,* that is the illusion of being conscious' HH, 'the *ātman* reflected in the *sattvika buddhi* is called *cidābhāsa'* (U) , 'fallacious presentation of consciousness located in the *buddhi*', (*Nikhilānanda*), 'performs various actions and enjoys their results therefore it is called *jīva',*

cidābhāsa - caitanya reflection of consciousness from Brahman

cidacit thought and non-thought, sentient and insentient, mind and matter,

cidākāśa 'the space of consciousness', 'the infinite dimension of undivided consciousness', 'Brahman in its aspect as limitless knowledge (the pure consciousness is like *ākāśa* [ether, space], an all-pervading continuum)',

cidānanda consciousness-bliss,

cidātman m. 397/3 pure thought or intelligence, *cid/cit* 395/3 pure thought or intelligence + *ātman* 135/1 essence, nature, character, 6/s whose nature is consciousness,

cidrūpa 397/3 mfn = *cinmaya* wise, n. the Universal Spirit as identified with pure thought, consciousness,

cihnam n. a sign, mark, symbol, characteristic, symptom,

√*cīk* 399/2 =√*sīk* cl 1.10. to endure, DP in *āmarṣaṇa* enduring, bearing,

cikīrṣamāna pres.mid.part. desiring to make ,

cikīrṣita n. purpose, design, intention, designed, intended to be done,

cikīrṣu desiring or intending to do or make 1/s/desiderative √ *kṛ*
cikitsā 395/2 medical attendance, practice or science of medicine, medical treatment,
cikitsaka m. a physician
cikitu mfn shining, f. understanding,
cikitvit ind. with understanding, with deliberation,
√*cil* 399/1 cl 6 *cilati* to put on clothes, DP in *vasana* putting on clothes,
√*cill* 399/2 cl 1 to become loose, to exhibit a *bhāva* or *hāva* DP in *śaithilya* becoming loose, and *bhāvakaraṇa* intimating one's desire, exhibiting emotion,
cīna m. chinese, a kind of deer, a thread, a banner, lead,
cīnāṁśuka n. silk,
cinmātra adj. 397/3 consisting of pure thought, pure consciousness
cinmātra 397/3 consisting of pure thought, *cin* in comp. for *cit, cit* 5. 395/3 pure thought, *mātra* –(suffix) in full measure, entirely, only , pure consciousness, consiousness alone,
cinmaya 397/3 consisting of pure thought, pure consciousness,
chinna mfn cut, cut off, taken away, nibbled,
√*cint* 398/1 cl 10 *cintayati*, cl 1 *cintati,* to think, have a thought or idea, reflect, consider, to think about, reflect upon, direct the thoughts towards, care for, to find out, to take in to consideration, treat of, to consider as or that, DP in *smṛti* remembering, pondering over,
cintā f. thought, care, anxiety, consideration, anxious thought about, (in comp.) worry anxiety,
cintaka 398/1 mfn ifc. one who thinks or reflects upon, an overseer,
cintāmaṇi m. a wish-fulfilling jewel, philosopher's stone,
cintana n. thinking, thinking of, reflecting upon, anxious thought,
cintāpara mfn depressed, attached to sadness or sorrow, lost in thought,
cintayet 1/s/pres/opt/act he should reflect
cintāmaṇi m. a wish-fulfilling jewel, philosopher's stone,
cintana 398/1 thinking, reflecting upon, anxious thought, consideration,
cintānurodhī *cinta* 398/1 thought, care, anxiety, *anurodhin* 37/3 complying with, compliant, thought compliant,
cintāviṣa-ghna mfn destroying the poison of sorrow,
cintayanta directing thought to, meditating on, concentrating on
cintayati 398/1 √*cint* 1/s/pres/indic/act he or she thinks
cintayet he should think of, he should reflect on, 1/s/caus/opt/act √*cint*
cintitopasthita mfn thought of and (immediately) at hand, at hand as soon as thought of,
cintya mfn to be thought about or imagined, to be considered or reflected or meditated upon, gve.
cira 398/2 long, lasting a long time, at all times, ever, for a long time, mfn long, existing from ancient times, (*am*) or *cireṇa* ind. for a long time, after a long time, at last, finally, too late,
cīra n. strip of bark or cloth worn by an ascetic, crest, a stripe, stroke, line,
ciragata mfn gone for a long time,
cirajīvikā f. a long life
cirakālīna mfn of a long time, long-standing, old, chronic,
cirakāra mfn slow, working slowly,
cirakārin m. slow, mfn slow, making slow progress,
cira-mitra n. an old friend,
ciraṁjīva m. long-lived,
ciraṁjīvin one who has attained deathlessness,
cirantana mfn existing from ancient times, f. (*ī*) old, ancient, m.pl. the ancients,
cirasya ind. for a long time, after a long time, at last, late,
cirāt after a long time,
cireṇa after a while

√ciri 399/1 cl 5 *ciṛnoti* to hurt, kill, DP in *hiṁsā* hurting, killing

cīrṇa 399/3 mfn practised, observed (a vow, austerity), n. conduct,

√ciṭ 395/2 (derived from *ceṭ)* cl 1 P *ceṭati* to send out, DP in *parapreṣya* -sending forth, serving another,

cit 1. 394/2 mfn piling up, forming a layer or stratum, piled up,
2. 394/3 mfn ifc. knowing giving heed to or revenging
3. mfn as 2 above
1.2.3. *cit* relate to √*ci* 1.2.3.

√cit (4.) cl 1 *cetati,* cl 2 A pass. *cite*, cl 3 irreg. *ciketati* A. and pass. *cikete*, A. pass. *cicite*, A. pass. *aceti* and *ceti*, to perceive, fix the mind upon, attend to, be attentive, observe, take notice of, to aim at, intend, design, be anxious about, care for, to resolve, to understand, comprehend, know, (perfect often in the sense of present), P A to become perceptible, appear, be regarded as, be known, caus. *cetayati (te*) to cause to attend, make attentive, remind of, to cause to comprehend, instruct, teach, to observe, perceive, be intent upon, A. to form an idea in the mind, be conscious of, understand, comprehend, think, reflect upon, P to have a right notion of, know, to recover consciousness, awake, A to remember, have consciousness of, to appear, be conspicuous, shine, DP in *sañjñāna* perceiving, seeing, noticing, observing, knowing, understanding, remembering, thinking, in *sañcetana* perceiving, understanding
5. mfn thinking
f. thought, intellect, spirit, soul,
f. pure thought,
ind. only in compound
5. *cit* 395/3 mfn ifc. thinking,
f. thought, intellect, spirit, soul, consciousness, *cin* =*cit*
influenced consciousness in *antaḥkaraṇa,* " in *cit* are involved all concepts from *adhyātma* and *vyavahāra* (spiritual knowledge and practical knowledge) with which the individual relates himself to the universal", HH "limited consciousness" HH (see *cid*) "*cit* is closely associated with the *antaḥkaraṇaḥ* and it is changeable, destructible. *cid* on the other hand is unchangeable, indestructible. *Cit* is powered by *cid* and the light of *cid* shines in the *cit* and goes through its modifications." HH

citā f. funeral pyre,

citghana mass or substantiality of awareness or consciousness,

citi 1. f. pile, stack, funeral pile, collecting, gathering, a heap, multitude, an oblong, understanding,
2. f . 395/3 understanding, thought, intellect, spirit, m. the thinking mind,

cit-dharma the essential quality or nature of the mind, spiritual nature or the characteristic function of a conscious being,

cīt-kāra m. the sound *cīt* the braying of an ass, noise,

citra 396/1 mfn conspicuous, excellent, distinguished, bright, clear, bright-coloured, clear (a sound), variegated, spotted, agitated, various, different, manifold, (execution) having different varieties (of tortures), strange, wonderful, m. variety of colour, ind. so as to be bright, f. a kind of snake, a metre of 4x 16 syllabic instants, a stringed instrument, illusion, unreality, n. anything bright or coloured which strikes the eye, a bright or extraordinary appearance, a brilliant ornament, the ether, sky, a picture, sketch, punning in question and answer, facetious conversation, riddle

citrāṅga m. dapple-coat, name of a deer, n. vermilion, yellow pigment,
citraratha 397/1 mfn having a bright chariot, m. the sun, the polar star, the king of the Gandharvas
citraśravas mfn whose praise is loud, or whose fame is excellent,
citrastha mfn being in a picture, painted, represented in a picture,
citrīkaraṇa making variegated, decorating, painting
citrita decorated, made variegated,
citśakti the power of consciousness, conscious energy, power of intelligence,
citsāmānya mfn universal consciousness,
citsvarūpa having the nature of pure intelligence or consciousness,
citta 395/3 n. the heart, mind, memory, storehouse of *saṇskāra,*
thinking, imagining, reflecting, thought, intention, aim, wish, intelligence, reason,
mfn noticed, aimed at, longed for, appeared, visible, the seat of memory,
cittadṛśya 'things perceived by consciousness' (Gam.),
cittahārin mfn mind or heart captivating,
cittaikāgrya (N) concentration of the spirit,
cittakāla time according to mental fancy, 'objects in the mind are *cittakāla* – lasting as long as the mind imagines them'
cittapramāthin mfn disturbing the mind, confusing the mind,
cittaprasādana n. gladdening of mind, peace or tranquillity of mind,
cittaspanditam 'a vibration of consciousness' (Gam.),
cittaśuddhi purification of the mind,
cittavidyā science of the mind,
cittavimukta detached from the mind,
cittavṛttaya m. movements of the mind,
cittavṛtti 396/1 continuous course of thoughts, (as opposed to concentration), thinking, imagination, 397/1 f. any astonishing act or practice,
citti f. understanding, wisdom, thinking, thought, intention, a wise person, pl. thoughts, devotion,
cittīkṛta mfn made an object of thought,
cittin mfn intelligent,
√cīv 399/3 or *cīb* cl 1 *civati (te)* to take, to cover, cl 10 *cīvayati* DP in *ādāna* taking, receiving or *samvaraṇa* covering, in *bhāṣā* (cl 10) speaking, shining
cīyate 1.√ci pass. arranges in order, becomes covered with, is piled up, is constructed,
codana 400/2 impelling, *(ā)* f. n. direction, rule, precept, injunction, invitation, command, *(ā)* f. reproof,
codita mfn caused to move quickly, driven, impelled, incited, carried on (a business), invited, directed, ordered, informed, apprised, inquired after, enjoined, fixed, appointed,
cora m. thief,
corayati steals
corita mfn stolen,
corya n. theft,
√cṛp 401/2 cl 1. 10. variation for *√chṛd* to vomit, to utter, to leave, DP in *sandīpana* inflaming, exciting
√cṛt 401/2 cl 6 *cṛtati to* tie, to hurt, kill, cl 1 *cartati* to shine, to light, fasten together, DP in *hiṁsā* hurting, killing, or in *granthana* binding
√cucy 400/1 for *√śucy* to distil, to perform ablution, DP in *abhiṣava* squeezing, expressing (as juice), distilling
√cuḍ 400/1 cl 6 *cuḍati* to conceal, DP in *samvaraṇa* covering
√cud 400/1 cl 1 *codati (te)* to impel, incite, animate, to bring or offer quickly, A. to hasten, caus. *codayati* to sharpen, whet, to impel, incite, cause to move quickly, accelerate, to request, petition, ask, urge on, help on, assist in the attainment of, to

bring or offer quickly, to ask for, to inquire after, to enjoin, fix, settle, to object, criticise, to be quick DP in *sañcodana* sending, directing, asking,

cūḍa m. a tonsure, crest of a cock or peacock, plume, diadem,

cūḍā f. tuft of hair left on the crown of a child's head after the tonsure ceremony,

cūḍākarman n. tonsure ceremony,

cūḍāmaṇi m. a crest-jewel,

√cuḍḍ 400/1 cl 1 *cuḍḍati* =*√cull*, to exhibit coquettish gestures, dally blandish, DP in *bhāvakaraṇa* sporting, dallying, hinting one's meaning,

√cukk 399/3 cl 10 to suffer pain DP in *vyathana* suffering, inflicting pain

√cul 400/3 cl 10 *colayati* to raise, (for √bul) to dive into, DP in *samucchrāya* raising, elevating,

√cull 400/3 = *√cuḍḍ* to exhibit any *bhāva* or *hāva,* DP in *bhāvakaraṇa* – exhibiting any *bhāva*, intimating one's desire,

√cumb 400/2 cl 10 to hurt, cl 1 *cumbati (te)* to kiss, to touch with the mouth, to touch closely or softly, caus. *cumbayati* to cause to kiss, to kiss, DP (cl 10)in *hiṁsā* injuring, hurting, DP (cl 1) in *vaktrasañyoga* kissing

cumbakamaṇi m. magnet,

cumbana 400/2 kissing, a kiss

√cup 400/2 cl 1 *copati* to move, 2. cl 6 for *√chup*, DP in *mandāgati* moving slowly, creeping, stealing along

√cuṇḍ 400/1 = √ *cuṭ* to split, cut off, DP in *alpībhāva* becoming small, decreasing,

√cuṇṭ = *√cuṭ* DP in *chedana* cutting off, dividing

√cur 400/2 cl 10 *corayati (te)* to steal, to rob anyone, to cause to disappear, DP in *steya* stealing

√cūr 401/1 cl 4 *curyate* to burn, for cl 10 *cūrayati* see*√cur*, DP in *dāha* burning

curā f. theft,

√curaṇya Nom. *curaṇyati* to steal DP in *caurya* stealing

√cūrṇ 401/1 cl 10 (or Nom) *cūrṇayati* to reduce to powder or flour, pulverise, grind, pound, crush, bruise, DP in *preraṇa* setting in motion, urging, inciting, activity, action, in *saṅkocana* the act of contracting or closing

cūrṇa m.n. meal, powder, chalk, lime, flour , pounded sandal,

cūrṇita 401/2 mfn crushed, powdered,

cūṣ 401/2 *cuṣati* to suck, suck out, DP in *pāna* drinking, smoking

√cuṭ 400/1 also *cuṇṭ* and *cuṇḍ,* cl 6.10. *cuṭati, coṭayati* to split, cut off, cl 1 *coṭati* to become small, DP in *chedana* cutting off, dividing

cūṭa m. a mango tree,

√cuṭṭ 400/1 cl 10 *cuṭṭayati* to become small DP in *alpībhāva* becoming small, decreasing,

cyavante they get deprived etc. *√cyu*

cyavati moves from one's place, deviates

√cyu 403/2 (and *cyus),* cl 10 *cyāvayati* = *√sah* or *√has,* cl 1 *cyavate* or *cyavati* to move to and fro, shake about, to stir, move from one's place, go away, retire from, to deviate from, abandon (duty etc.), come forth from, come out of, drop from, trickle, fall down, slide, slide from, to fall from any divine existence (so as to be re-born as a man), to die, be deprived of, lose, fade away, disappear, to fail, to sink down, sink, to decrease, to bring about, create, to cause to go away, make forget, caus. *cyāvayati* P to cause to move, shake, to loosen, remove from a place, drive away from, to cause (rain), A to be moved or shaken, DP in *hasana* laughing, or *sahana* suffering pain, cl 10 in *gati* going

√cyus 404/1 see √1 *cyu*, cl 10 *cyosayati* to leave, = *√sah* or *√has* DP in *hasana* laughing, or *sahana* suffering, pain,

√*cyut* 403/3 cl 1 *cyotati* to flow, trickle, ooze, to fall down, to cause to stream forth, DP in *āsecana* sprinkling, wetting

-da ifc. giver, giving, administering,

da 464/3 2. mfn. √*dā* 1. ifc. giving (in compounds),granting, offering, effecting, producing, (in compounds),
2. *da* m.n. a gift, f. *dā* a gift
3. *da* mf(*ā)*n the act of cutting off

√*dā* 1. cl 3 P *dadāti* A *dadatte* to give, bestow, grant, yield, impart, present, offer to, to hand over, to give back, to pay (a fine or debt), to give up, cede, to sell, to sacrifice (oneself), to offer (an oblation), to communicate, teach, utter (blessings), to permit, allow, to place, put, apply, to add, permit sexual intercourse, grant a boon, to direct a gaze,
A. to carry, hold, keep, preserve, to show,
2. m. a giver, mfn giving, granting,
3. for √*do* to cut,
4. cl 4 P *dyati* to bind,
5. for √*de*,
6. f. √*de* protection, defence,
7. for √*dai,*
8. for √das cleansing, purifying, DP in *dāna* (1&3)giving, bestowing, *lavana* (cl 2) cutting,

√*dabh* 469/2 or *dambh* cl 1 to hurt, injure,destroy, deceive, abandon, impel,*dambhayate* to accumulate, DP (*dambh*) in *dambhana* deceiving, cheating, injuring or hurting

dabha m. deception,

√*dad* 467/3 cl 1 *dadati* = √*dā*
DP in *dāna* giving

dadat giving pres/act/part

dadāmi I give, 3/s/pres/indic/act

dadāti 473/2 1/s/pres/indic/act gives

dadau he gave 1/s/perf/act √*dā*

√*dadh* 468/1 cl 1 *dadhate* to hold, to give, DP in *dhāraṇa* holding

dadhan n. sour milk, curds,

dadhāti puts, places, allots

dadhi n. curds,

dadhikarṇa name of a cat (ears as white as curds), milk-ear,

dadhmau 1/s/perf. √*dhmā* he blows, sounded, blew,

dadhṛk ind. firmly, strongly, boldly,

dadṛh mfn firm,

dadṛśe 1st or 3rd /s /perf √*dṛś* indistinctly seen as in haze (?) (Gam.)

dadṛśivān having seen

dagdha mfn. burnt, scorched, consumed by fire, tormented, pained,

dagdhendhana burning fuel,

dagdhodhara n. one's cursed belly, the hungry stomach,

dagdhvā ind. having set alight

√*dagh* 466/2 cl 5 to fall short of, with *adhas* reaching below regular height, to strike, protect,
cl 4 to go, to flow, DP in *ghātana* killing, hurting, *pālana* protecting

√*dah* 473/2 cl 1 *dahati (te*) to burn, consume by fire, scorch, roast, to cauterise, destroy completely, torment, torture, pain, distress, disturb, grieve, pass. *dahayate* to be burnt, burn, be in flames, to be consumed by fire or destroyed, to be inflamed (a wound), to be consumed by internal heat or grief, suffer pain, be distressed or vexed, caus.
dāhayati to burn or be burned, to cause to be cooked, A. to be burnt completely, DP in *bhasmīkaraṇa* burning (making ashes),
2. mfn burning

-daḥ giver

dāha 477/2 m burning, combustion, conflagration, heat, place of cremation, glowing, redness, cauterizing, cautery (of a wound) internal heat, fever

dahati burns *Dh° dah*

dāhayati sets light to

√*dai* 497/1 cl 1 P *dāyati* to purify, cleanse, DP in *śodana* purifying, cleansing,

dailya m. demon,
dainya 497/2 n. wretchedness, affliction, depression, meanness, poverty,
Daitya 497/1 a son of *Diti*, a demon, slave,
daiva 497/2 mfn of the gods, divine, (*as*), chance, or fate , destiny, deity, n. divine power or will, fortune, destiny, chance,
daivavāṇī f. voice from heaven,
daivapara m. fatalist, fated, predestined, trusting to fate,
daivata mfn pertaining to a divinity, (*as*) n. a divinity, the divinities, an idol,
daivatya mfn having as one's deity, sacred to a deity, ifc. ... as divinity, ...addressed to,
daivī peculiar or relating to the gods, coming from gods, divine,
daivī saṁpatti divine properties
daivika mfn of the gods, divine,
daivya mfn of the gods, divine, n. divine power or effect, fate, fortune,
√*dakṣ* 465/1 cl 1 P to act to the satisfaction of, A. to be able or strong, to grow, increase, to act quickly, to go, to hurt, DP in *vṛddhi* growing or *śīghra* doing, going, acting quickly,
dakṣa mfn able, dexterous, strong, m. ability, faculty, strength, power, industrious, intelligent, esp. spiritual power, will,
dakṣiṇa mfn. South, right (as relative position), able, clever, benign, straightforward, candid, sincere, m. the right (hand or arm), (*am*) ind. to the right, 465/2
dakṣiṇā f. donation to a priest for services, a gift, donation, a prolific cow,
dakṣīṇābhimukha mfn facing south,
dakṣīṇāhi in the South, far to the right,
dakṣīṇāmūrti personification of an aspect of *śiva* as supreme awareness, understanding and knowledge, a teacher of yoga, music and wisdom, expounding on the scriptures,
dakṣīṇāpara mfn south-westerly,
dakṣīṇapaścima mfn south-westerly,
dakṣiṇāpathika mfn belonging to the Deccan
dakṣīṇapravaṇa mfn sloping to the south-east,
dakṣīṇapūrva mfn south-easterly,
dakṣīṇāraṇya n. the southern forest,
dakṣiṇataḥ ind. from the right or south on the right side or southward
dakṣīṇāvant mfn abounding in gifts to the priests, pious,
dakṣīṇāyana n. southern sun phase, the summer solstice a sacred and auspicious day, southern way,
dakṣiṇī + kṛ to place on the right,
dākṣiṇya mfn belonging to or worthy of a sacrificial fee, n. politeness, dexterity, skill, gallantry, kindness, consideration, piety, energetic, capable, strong, heightening or strengthening of the intellectual faculties,
dākṣya 475/1 n. cleverness, skill, fitness
√*dal* 471/2 =√*dṝ*, cl 1 *dalati* to crack, fly open, split, open (as a bud), DP in *viśaraṇa* bursting open, splitting, cracking, *vidāraṇa* splitting, tearing
dala n. a leaf, petal, a fragment, a part or degree, cinnamon leaf, unclean gold, a clump, heap, a detachment,
√*dam* 469/2 cl 4 *dāmyati* to be tamed or tranquillised, to tame, subdue, conquer, cl 9 irreg. caus. *damayati* A to subdue, overpower, DP in *upaśama* (cl 4) making calm, tranquil or tame
dam 2. m. a house
dama m.n. house, home,
dama mfn taming, subduing, m. control of mind, speech, senses, body, self-restraint, 'is self-control, the control of the organs of action' '... not to have self-control is against the law', the name of a son of King Bhīma, *(śamaḥ* = control of the inner organs of mind)
dama ifc. mfn conquering,
dāma in comp. for *dāman*
dāman n. m. a giver, donor, a liberal man, giving, a gift, m.f. allotment, share, a girdle, chaplet, wreath, garland for the forehead, 2. n. bond,
damana mfn conquering, name of a sage,

name of a son of King Bhīma
damanya 469/3 Nom. to subdue
ḍamara m. a tumult, riot, an evil omen,
ḍāmara mfn causing tumult, extraordinary, surprising, m. surprise, a lord,
damayantī name of *bhīma*'s daughter,
damayantyartham adverbial phrase – for the sake of Damayantī
damayatām of rulers pres/part. 6/pl/m
√*dambh* 469/3 = √*dabh*
dambha 469/3 deceit, fraud, hypocrisy, ostentation, pride, Indra's thunderbolt,
dambhana damaging, n. deceiving
dāmbhika mfn deceitful, deceiver, m. a cheat, hypocrite,
dambhin mfn deceiver, acting deceitfully, m. hypocrite,
dampati m. master of the house, as dual – master and mistress, husband and wife,
√*daṁś* 464/3 or *daṁs* cl 1.10 P *daṁśati daṁśayati* or *daṁsati* to speak or to shine,
cl 1 P and cl 10 A to show, cl 1 *dāśati* to bite,
DP in *daśana* biting, *daṁśana* biting, *darśana* seeing
daṁśa m. gadfly, sting,
daṁśati he bites
daṁṣṭā f. a large tooth or tusk, fang,
daṁṣṭra 464/3 m. tusk, fang
daṁṣṭrin mfn having tusks or large teeth,
√*dān* 475/3 cl 1 PA *dānati (te)* to cut off, desid . *dīdāṁsati (te)* to be or make straight, DP in *khaṇḍana* cutting, dividing,
dāna 474/1 n. the act of giving, giving up, giving in marriage, communicating, imparting, teaching, generosity, paying back, charity, restoring, adding, addition, donation, gift, oblation, liberality,
self-sacrifice, giving without thought of reward,
2. n. cutting off, splitting, dividing, pasture, meadow, rut-fluid (which flows fro an elephant's temples), m. distribution of food, imparting, communication, liberality, part, share, possession, distributor, dispenser,
3. n. purification
dānadharma m. the virtuous practice of alms-giving, duty of liberality,
dānakriya act of giving, charity
dāna-pāramitā benevolence, giving with pure motivation, 'perfection of giving',
dānasamiti careful giving and receiving (to avoid transgressing),
dānava 474/3 a class of demons
daṇḍa m. a staff (stick), 466/2 a stick, staff, staff given at investiture, power over (symbol of dominion and punishment), , the vertical stroke used in forming letters, the vertical line at the end of a sentence.
daṇḍabhaya m. fear of the rod,
daṅḍanipātana application of the rod, punishing
daṇḍanīti f. administration of justice, application of the rod, the system of law courts that administer justice,
daṇḍāpūpa n. stick and cake,
dandaśūka malignant, a snake, biting, venomous
√*daṇḍaya (ti)* 467/2 Nom to chastise, punish, DP in *daṇḍanipātana* beating with a stick
daṇḍaya punish! impv.
daṇḍayati punishes
daṇḍin mfn bearing a staff, m. *(as)* warder,
danta m. tooth, ivory, a tusk,
dānta mfn tamed, mild, subdued (one's passions), name of one of Bhīma's sons', patient,
dantadhauti cleaning of the teeth,
dantin 469/1mfn tusked, m. an elephant
dantura mfn uneven, jagged, having projecting teeth,
dānu m. name of a demon,
2. dripping fluid,
f.n. drop, dew, dewdrop,
√*dap* [illegible] cl 10 A *dāpayate* to

accumulate, DP in *saṁghāta* collecting, accumulating,

dara m. cleft, hole, the navel,

dāra m. hole, rent,wife, cleft,

dāraka m. boy, son,

darbha m. grass-tuft, grass used at ceremonies esp. *kuśa* grass,

daridra mfn poor, without riches, wandering about, mendicant, a poor man, m. a beggar, *Dh° drā* in making haste, being in need

dāridrya n. poverty, neediness,

darpa m. pride, arrogance, insolence, conceit, wildness, impudence,

darpaṇa m. a mirror,

darśa 470/3 *darśa* mfn looking at, viewing, m. sight, 'appearance' the new moon when just become visible, day of new moon, half-monthly sacrifice performed on that day,

darśaka mfn 1. seeing, 2. (from caus.) showing, making clear,

darśana 470/3 mfn showing, insight, way of seeing, vision, making visible, ifc. seeing, looking at, 'knowing', exhibiting, teaching, n. seeing observing, looking, noticing, observation, perception, inspection, examination, visiting, audience, meeting, experiencing, contemplating, observation, discernment, understanding, intellect, opinion, intention, view, doctrine, philosophical system, the eye, the becoming visible or known, presence, appearance (before a judge), a vision, dream, semblance, aspect, a mirror, a sacrifice, experience, foreseeing, doctrine, appearance

darśanagocara m. range of vision,

darśanamohanīya 'deludes the understanding and is responsible for the wrong assessment of the ultimate values'resulting in mental bias,

darśanāvaraṇīya apprehension or perception obscuring *karma* that restricts realization of the truth,

darśanīya mfn visible, worthy of being seen, good-looking, beautiful,

darśapūrṇamāsa m. du. new and full moon, the days and the festivals of the new and full moons,

darśata mfn to be seen, visible, beautiful, striking the eye, conspicuous,

darśaya cause to be seen, allow me to see, show! 2/s/caus/impv/act √*dṛṣ*

darśayati causes to see, 1/s/pres/caus/act

darśibhiḥ by the seers, by the perceivers, by the discerners, by the knowers, 3/pl/m *dṛś*

darśin mfn seeing, looking, experiencing, observing, knowing, understanding, teaching, receiving, examining,

darśita *mfn* manifested, shown,

dāru mfn liberal, breaking, splitting, n. wood, log or billet of wood, ore,

dāruṇa mfn harsh m. cruel, severe, m. plumbago, n. harshness, severity,

√*das* 473/1 cl 1.4 to suffer want, become exhausted, DP in *upakṣaya* fading away, becoming exhausted,

√*dās* cl 1 P A *dāsati (te)* to give, cl 5 P *dāsnoti,* to hurt, injure, DP in *dāna* giving

√*dāś* 476/3 cl 1 P A *dāśati, (te)* to serve or honour a god, offer or present, grant, give, bestow, DP in *dāna* giving, in *hiṁsā* hurting 2. f. worship, veneration, m. worshipper

daśa numeral ten

daśā f. the threads projecting at the end of a weft, fringe, lamp-wick, fig. wick of life, course of life, time of life,

dāsa m. 1. foe esp. supernatural foe, evil demon, 2. foe of the gods, infidel, 3. servant, slave, *dāsī* female slave, servant of God,

daśadhā in ten ways, in 10 parts, ten-fold,

daśāha m. space of ten days,

daśama mfn tenth,

dāsamārga the path of the servant,

daśan ten
daśana 472/3 m. a tooth, a bite, peak,
dāsapatnī mfn f. having the demon for their master, being in the power of demons,
daśarathaḥ father of *rāmaḥ* a king
daśaśākha mfn having 1000 fingers
daśaśata n. a thousand,
dāsī f. a female slave or servant,
dāsya 477/2 n. servitude, slavery, service, surrendering to the will of god,
dāsyante they will give 1/pl/fut/mid √*dā*
dāsyati he will give
dasyu 473/1 m. robber, thief, demon, foe of gods and men, slave,
dātavya to be given (gerundive *dā*), it should be given, to be communicated,
dātṛ m. giver, donor mfn generous,
datta 467/2 part. 1. protected, 2. mfn given, granted, m. a son given for adoption,
dattvā having given
dauhitra 499/3 m.daughter's son, rhinoceros
daur 499/1 bad-heartedness, wickedness, depravity, *daur-bala*, weakness, impotence,
daurbalya weakness, impotence feebleness
daurmanasya n. dejectedness, melancholy, evil disposition, despair,
dautya n. message, mission, the state or function of a messenger,
dava m. forest-fire, burning, heat, fever,
davāgni m. a forest-fire, conflagration,
daviṣṭha mfn (superlative) remotest, ind. very far away,
√*day* 469/3 cl 1 A *dayate* to divide, impart, allot, partake, possess, to divide asunder, destroy, consume, to take part in sympathize with, have pity on, to repent, to go DP in *dāna* giving, granting, *gati* going, *rakṣaṇa* protecting, *hiṁsā* hurting, *ādāna* accepting
dāya 474/2 a gift, a present, mfn giving, 2. portion, inheritance,
dayā 469/3 sympathy, compassion, mercy empathy, grace, conquering callous, cruel and insensitive feelings towards all beings,
dāyāda m. heir, a son or distant kinsman,
dāyaka mfn giving, m. heir
dayālu mfn compassionate, kind, merciful,
dayāvant mfn compassionate,
dayayāḥ please, by showing mercy,
dāyin mfn giving, permitting, granting, yielding, ceding, owing, having to pay, producing,
dayita mfn beloved, dear,
√*de* 492/2 cl 1 A *dayate* to protect, defend, DP in *rakṣaṇa* protecting,
dedīpyamāna pres/mid/part √*dīp*, radiant, shining intensely, glowing,
deha 496/3 m.n. the body, manifestation
deha-bheda the fall of the body,
dehābhimāna m. egoistic attachment to the body
dehādhyāsa m. false identification with the body,
dehaśuddhi f. purification of the body,
dehātmabhava considering the body to be the Self,
dehātmabuddhi the intellect that chooses to identify with the body,
dehātmavāda m. 'assertion that the body is the soul, materialism,
dehabhṛt 497/1 mfn. embodied, corporeal, the embodied one, the *ātman*
dehavidyā f. physiology of the body
dehatyāga m. death, giving up the body,
dehi give! (s.),
dehī the embodied one, (T),the Self identifying itself with the intellect, the conscious embodied self, *jīva,*
dehin 497/1 mfn. having a body, corporeal, a living creature, man, m. (*dehī*) the spirit, soul (enveloped in the body), the Self
dehi dayayā please give, please pass deliberation, examination, (discursive thought), + *nir* – without
deśa 496/2 m. place, part, country, kingdom, locality
deśabhāṣā f. dialect of the country,
deśakāla m. space-time, place and time for,
deśakāla m. space-time relation, having

connection with space and time,
deśapabandha limitation of place, (G)
deśavakāśika restriction of movement, a Jaina ethical code of conduct, (G)
dese in or at the proper place 7/s
deśika mfn familiar with a place, a guide, m. a guru or spiritual teacher,
deśita mfn shown, directed, instructed,
deśīya mfn belonging to the country, bordering on, resembling, almost, nearly,
deṣṭṛ m. pointer, guide, instructor,
deṣṭṝ f. instructress as a deity,
√*dev* 492/2 see √1.2. *div*
DP in *devana* playing,
deva 492/2 mf(*ī*)n. heavenly, divine, m. a deity, god, goddess, shining one, one who shines, universal power or deity, lord, (rarely) evil demons,
-*deva* at the end of Brahman names, having ...as god e.g. *manuṣyadeva* god among men,
king or queen,
devadaivatya mfn having the gods as divinity
Devadatta god-given (Arjuna's conch-horn)
devadāsī servant of god, a temple-dancer,
devadeva God of Gods
devadūta m. messenger of the gods,
devahūti f. invocation of the gods,
devakāma mfn having love for the gods
devakula n. temple,
devaliṅga n. god-characteristic, mark by which a god may be distinguished from a man,
devaloka the world of the gods or heaven,
devamandira n. 'dwelling house of a god or gods', a temple,
devana 1. 492/2 n wailing, grief, sorrow
2. m dice for gambling
f sport, pastime, service
f service
n shining, splendour, play, sport, pleasure ground, garden, a lotus, praise, desire, business
devanāgarī the Indian script most commonly used by Sanskrit scholars, 'city of the gods' urban script, script of the cultured establishment,
devapāna mfn serving the gods for drinking
devapati m. lord of the gods, Indra,
devapūjā 493/3 worship of the gods
devara m. husband's brother,
devarāja m. king of the gods i.e. Indra,
devarṣis divine seer
devaśabda divine sound e.g. thunder
devasaṁnidhi m. presence of the gods,
devasva 495/1 divine property
deva-svabhāva m. divine nature,
devatā 495/3 godhead, divinity, image of a deity, name of the organs of sense,
ind. with divinity, with a god or gods, among the gods,
the world of the gods,
devatā-gṛham house of the god, temple,
devātman 495/1 m. the divine soul,
mfn being of divine nature, containing a deity,
devātmaśakti f. the power of the soul,
devatva n. divinity, godhead,
devavāṇī f. divine voice, oracle
devavat ind. like a god /gods
devayājas m. worshippers of gods,
devayajña sacrifice or worship for the divine
devayāna m. the path of the gods ,
devī a feminine deity, goddess, lady, queen, resplendent, see *deva*
devīkoṭṭa m. goddess-fort, name of a town,
devīkṛta mfn made by Durgā
devīvat like a queen, goddess
devīvinirmita mfn laid out by Durgā
devṛ m. husband's brother,
deya 492/2 to be given or presented,
dha mfn bestowing, granting, placing, putting, holding, possessing, having, m. virtue, merit, n. wealth, property,
√*dhā* 1. cl 3 P A *dadhāti*, cl 1 P A *dadhāti (te)* , cl 2 P *dhāti* to put, place, set, lay in or on, to take or bring or help to, A to direct or fix the mind or attention upon, think of, fix or resolve upon, to destine for, bestow, on, present ot impart to, appoint, establish, constitute, to render, to make, produce, generate, create,

cause, effect, perform, seize, take hold of, hold, bear, support, wear, put on (clothes), A. to accept, obtain, conceive (esp. in womb), get, take, take pleasure or delight in, DP in *dhāraṇa* holding, *poṣaṇa* maintaining (giving),

dhā 2. 508/1 mfn ifc. placing, putting, holding, possessing, having, bestowing, granting, causing, m. virtue, merit, n. wealth, property, placer, bestower, holder, supporter,

dhā (in compounds)bestowing, granting, drink

dhairya 520/2 n. intelligence, forethought, calmness, patience, gravity, fortitude, 2. n. constancy, 'patience as an aspect of constancy, as Absolute is constant' n. firmness, earnest or resolute bearing,

√*dhakk* 508/1 cl 10 P *dhakkayati* to destroy, annihilate, DP in *nāśana* destroying,

dhakṣyati will burn, will consume by fire

ḍhāla n. a shield

ḍhālin mfn armed with a shield,

√*dham* to blow, or to blow a conch shell, *dhamati* blows

dhama 509/3 mfn blowing, melting, m. the moon,

dhāma in comp. for *dhāman*

dhamaka m. 'a blower', blacksmith,

dhamākāra m. a blacksmith,

dhāman 514/3 n. dwelling place, house, abode, domain, site of the sacred fire and Soma, with *priyam* favourite thing or person, the inmates of a house or members of a family, class, troop, band, law, rule, established order, state, condition, manner, mode, tone, form, appearance, effect, power, strength, majesty, glory, splendour, light,

√*dhaṇ* 508/1 cl 1 P *dhaṇati* to sound, DP in *śabda* sounding,

√*dhan* 508/1 cl 1 P *dhanati* to sound, cl 3 P *dadhanti* to cause to run or move quickly, to bear fruit, *(te)* to cause to move or run, to move or run, DP in *dhānya* bearing fruit,

dhana 508/2 n. wealth, riches, the prize,

dhāna mfn holding, containing, n. receptacle, case, seat, the site of a habitation, coriander,

dhānā f. pl. corns, grain, coriander, bud, shoot,

dhanadhānyabāla power of estate and wealth,

Dhanaṁjaya conqueror of wealth (*Arjuna*)

dhanika mfn rich,

dhanin mfn wealthy, virtuous, 'possessing wealth', m. a rich man, owner, a husband, coriander, f. a virtuous or excellent woman,

dhanu 509/1 m a bow (as in bow & arrow)

dhanudharas m. an archer or bowman

dhanus m. n. a bow, a measure (4 hands), Saggitarius, f. sandy shore or bank,

dhānuṣka mfn armed with a bow, m. bowman, archer,

dhanuṣkāṇḍa n. bow and arrow,

dhanuveda m. the science of archery

√*dhanv* 509/2 cl 1 P A *dhanvati (te)* to run or flow, cause to run or flow, DP in *gati* going, moving

dhanvan n. bow, rainbow, Saggitarius, m. dry soil, shore, a desert, a waste,

dhanvantari name of the gods' physician

dhanvin mfn having a bow, bowman, cunning, shrewd,

dhanya 509/1 mfn bringing or bestowing wealth, opulent, rich, fortunate, happy, auspicious, good, virtuous, blessed, wholesome, healthy, m. infidel, atheist, a spell for weapons,

dhānya mfn consisting or made of grain,cereal, n. cereal, grain, corn, a measure (4 sesame seeds), coriander, a kind of house, being rich, richness,

dhānyāvarodha storing grain or hoarding riches

dhara 510/1 mfn.holder, holding, bearing, sustaining, preserving, observing, m. a mountain, flock of cotton, a frivolous or dissolute man, a sword, the womb, a vein or tubular vessel of the body, a marrow, a mass of gold or heap of valuables,

dharā the earth, also = *dhara*

dhārā f. stream of water, jet, shower, edge, blade, a leak or hole in a pitcher, the pace of a horse (5 specified), uniformity, sameness, custom, usage, continuous line or series, line of a family,

dhāraka mfn keeping in the memory (with 6th), m. a receptacle or vessel, a water-pot, the highest point, f. prop, pillar, a division of time, the vulva,

dhāraṇa 515/1 mfn holding, bearing, keeping (in remembrance), concentration of mind, retention, preserving, protecting, maintaining, possessing, having, enduring, m. the two female breasts,
n. the act of holding, bearing, wearing, suffering, enduring, keeping in remembrance, memory, immovable concentration of the mind upon (7th), restraining, established ordinance, rule,

dhāraṇā 515/2 f. the act of holding, supporting, maintaining, concentration of the mind (joined with the retention of breath), understanding, intellect, steadfastness, righteousness,

dhāraṇaśakti power of grasping and retaining ideas,

dhāraṇayoga the yoga of concentration, before the stage of *dhyāna* and *samādhi*

dharaṇī f. the earth, any tubular vessel of the body, a verse or charm to relieve pain, a row or line,

dhārāsāra m.pl. stream pouring, violent pouring, m. rain-shower,

dhāraya 515/2 mfn holding, bearing, owing a sum

dhārayan resolving, maintaining, believing, being convinced pres/caus/act/part.

dhārayati wears, puts on, carry, maintain, preserve, employ, practise, restrain, suppress, remains,1/s/pres/caus/act √*dhṛ* 519/3

dhārin mfn holding, possessing, keeping in memory, maintaining, observing,

dharma 510/3 m that which is established or firm, steadfast decree, statute, ordinance, law, virtue, morality, correct conduct, duty, right, justice [√*dhṛ* 519/1 in holding, supporting] the law, that which upholds, system of duties, rewards, punishments, etc., righteous way of living,Will of the absolute (fine laws of the universe), Universal justice ensuring happiness, freedom and virtue. (an aspect of *puruṣārtha*),
'the aspirant' (Gam.), (N) 'in Buddhism – thing, what exists, fact, object',

dharmacakra n. the wheel or range of the law, a partic. mythical weapon,

dharmacakṣus n. the eye of the law,
mfn having an eye for the law or for what is right,

dharmacārin mfn virtuous, observing the law, fulfilling one's duties, dutiful, moral, (*iṇī)* f. a female helpmate in the fulfilment of duties, an honest wife, a virtuous woman,

dharmacchala m. fraudulent transgression of the law or duty

dharmacintā f. consideration of the law or duty, virtuous reflection,

dharmadāsa m. slave of duty, lawful slave,

dharmadhātu the essence or realm of *dharma,* the *dharma* realm of Buddhism, (N) 'that which is not produced', 511/2 the element of law or of existence,

dharmaghna mfn 'destroying law or right', unlawful, immoral,

dharmaja mfn produced by a sense of duty,

dharmajīvana mfn living by fulfilment of duties, m. a Brahman who lives according to rule,

dharmajña mfn knowing the law or one's duty or what is right,

dharmajñāna n. knowledge of the law,
dharmakāya m. 'law-body' having the law for body, a Buddha, 'It constitutes the unmanifested, "inconceivable" (Sanskrit: *acintya*) aspect of a Buddha, out of which Buddhas (and all phenomena) arise' (K),
dharmakśetra n. law-field
dharmamūla n. the root or foundation of the law,
dharmamegha 'cloud of righteousness' name of a partic. *Samādhi,*
dharman n. established ordinance, steadfast decree,
dharmaṇā according to the established order of things, in a way that accords with nature,
dharmapariṣāt assembly of the wise,
dharmapatnī f. lawful wife,
dharmārthakāmamokṣa a traditional expression for "the 4 objectives of life" *dharma* 510/3 justice, virtue, doing one's duty, right action *artha* 90/2 wealth, prosperity. *kāma* 271/3 pleasure, sensual pleasures, *mokṣa* 835/1 freedom, liberation *dharmārthakāmamokṣeṣu*7/pl /m in the matter of meritorious behaviour, prosperity, pleasure, and freedom,
dharmaśāstra the Laws of *Manu* according to *dharma,* lawbook,
dharmastha m. judge, 'abiding in the law'
dharmasthānam n. tribunal, being in a lawful state, the seat of *dharma,*
dharmatā f. essence, inherent nature, the being law or right,
dharmatantra n. s.pl. the beginning and end of the law, 'summum jus',
dharmatas ind. in a way which starts from *dharma* i.e. in accordance with good usage, rightly, justly,
dharmatattva n. the real essence of the law,
dharmātman mfn having virtue or right as one's nature,
dharmātmika mfn virtuous by nature,
dharmavid mfn knowing the law or one's duty, acquainted with good usage,
dharmika mfn righteous, just, virtuous,
dhārmika mfn righteous, virtuous, just, resting on right, conforming with justice, m. judge, a bigot, a juggler, a Bodhisattva
dharmin mfn knowing or obeying the law, faithful to duty, virtuous, pious, just, ifc. following the laws or duties of, m. the bearer of any mark or attribute, object, thing,
dharmya 513/1 mfn. legal, legitimate, usual, customary, just, virtuous, endowed with properties, suitable to righteous, proper,
dharṣita mfn overpowered, (having been) overcome, insolence, copulation,
dhārṣṭya 516/1 boldness, audacity, violence
dhārtarāṣṭra m. a son of *dhṛtarāṣṭra,* a kind of goose,
dhāryate it is sustained or supported 1/s/pres/indic/caus/pass √*dhṛ*
dhātā the establisher, arranger, ordainer, creator, supporter,
dhātāra the supporter, one who places or puts,
dhātṛ m. creator, establisher, founder, supporter, arranger,
dhātrī nurse, foster-mother,
dhātrikā f. wet-nurse,
dhatte 513/2 to be given, put,place, intend, middle voice to accept, obtain, 1/s/pres/mid accepts
dhātu 513/3 element of words, grammatical or verbal root or stem, realm, minerals,
√*ḍhauk* 431/2 cl 1 A *ḍhaukate* to approach, caus. *òhaukayate* to bring near, , cause to come near, offer to anyone, DP in *gati* moving, going,
dhaurtya 520/3 fraud, dishonesty
dhauti f. kind of penance, washing, rivulet, creek, spring, well,
√*dhāv* 516/1 cl 1 P A *dhāvati (te)* to run, flow, stream, move, glide, swim, run after, run towards, run a race, run as fast as possible, run to and fro, run away, flee, to advance or rush

against, caus. *dhāvayati* to make run, impel, drive in a chariot, jump, dance,
2. cl 1 P A to rinse, cleanse, wash, purify, polish, make bright, DP in *gati* moving, going, *śuddhi* purifying,

dhāvaka m. washerman, forerunner, mfn running,

dhavala mfn dazzlingly white, m. an old or excellent bull, white, a kind of dove, one of the elephants of the quarters, f. a white cow,

dhāvasi 516/1 *dhāvati* to run, run to and fro, 2/s/pres/indic/act. you run

dhāvata m. a runner

dhāvati 516/1 runs, runs after, seeks for, 1/s/pres/indic/act seeks

√*dhe* 520/1 cl 1 P *dhayati* to suck, drink, take to oneself, absorb, appropriate, caus. *dhāpayati* to give suck, nourish, DP in *pāna* sucking, drinking,

dhenu 520/1 mfn. yielding or giving milk, f. a cow, milch cow, the earth (metaphorically),

dhetu see *hetu,* m. impulse, motive, cause, cause of, reason for, a logical reason or deduction or argument, the reason for an inference, primary cause (Buddhist),

dheya mfn to be held or taken, to be created or what is created, to be applied or put in practice,n. the giving, imparting,

√*dhi* 516/2 1. cl 6 P *dhiyati,* to hold,
2. m. receptacle,
3. cl 5 P *dhinoti* to nourish, satiate, satisfy, delight, please, DP in *dhāraṇa* holding, having,

dhi (in cpds.) containing, granting,

√*dhī* 516/3 cl 3 A *dīdhīte* to perceive, think, reflect, wish, desire,
2. f. thought, (esp.) religious thought, reflection, meditation, devotion, prayer, understanding, intelligence, wisdom, knowledge, science, art, mind, disposition, intention, design, notion, opinion, mental attitude, intelligence,
'the intellect in the employment of obedient service, listening to discourses, reception of good ideas, accepting these ideas, analysis, science of meaning or semantics and philosophical or spiritual principles is the human law, To misuse the intellect is against the law.'
3. cl 4 A *dhīyate* to contain, hold, to slight, disregard, propitiate, DP in *ādhāra* holding, containing, disregarding, disrespecting,
4. f. for *dī* splendour,

dhik ind. used as a prefix or expletive expressing annoyance, menace or reproach, 'shame on', 'what a pity', (with 2nd case)

dhikkṛta 516/2 *dhik* a prefix expressing reproach, + root *kś* to do or make. - reproach, deride, part.expressing contempt

√*dhikṣ* 516/2 cl 1 A (desid. of √*dah?),* to kindle, to live, to be weary or harassed, DP in *sandīpana* kindling, *kleśana* harassing, *jīvana* living,

dhīmān *dhī* 516/3 intelligent, wise, learned *dhīmān* 1/s/m the wise man

dhīmat mfn wise, intelligent, learned, sensible,

dhīmant mfn gifted with understanding, wise,

√*dhinv* 516/2 see √3. *dhi* DP in *prīṇanā* gladdening, being glad

dhīra 517/1 mfn steady, constant,composed, intelligent, wise, one of steady mind, the discriminating one, the wise one, firm, resolute,

dhīrya n. prudence, intelligence,

√*dhiṣ* 516/2 cl 3 P *didheṣṭi* to sound, DP in *śabda* sounding,

dhīradhī 517/1 *dhīra* steady, steady-minded, *dhṛ* 516/3 2. understanding, wisdom, one of steady wisdom

dhīti f. thought, devotion, skill, reflection, intention, wisdom, *dhīvara* m. 'a very clever or skilful man', a fisherman,

dhiyā by, with or through intelligence,

dhīyādhīyā with each thought, every time it occurs to one,

dhmā 520/3 1. see *dham* DP in *śabda* blowing an instrument, *agni-saṁyoga* blowing a fire 2. m. blowing,

dhobī the washerman

√*dhor* 520/2 cl 1 P to run, trot, be quick or alert, DP in *gari-cātur* going quickly, being skilful, trotting,

√*dhṛ* 519/2/1 cl 1 P A *dharati (te*), to hold, bear, carry, maintain, preserve, keep, possess, have, use, employ, practise, undergo, to preserve body or soul, continue living, survive, to hold back, keep down, stop, restrain, suppress, resist, to place or fix in, bestow or confer on, to destine for, to present to, to direct or turn (attention, mind etc.), towards, fix or resolve upon, A. to be ready or prepared for, P. A to owe anything to, to prolong (in pronunciation), to quote, cite, so be firm, keep steady, continue living, exist, remain, to begin, resolve upon, undertake, DP in *avadhvaṁsana* (cl1) holding, suffering, destroying, *avasthāna* (cl 6)being, existing, living, *dhāraṇa (*cl 1)holding, supporting,

√*dhrāḍ* 521/2 *dhrāḍate* =√*drāḍ* DP in *viśaraṇa* cutting, dividing, cl 1

√*dhrāgh* 521/2 *dhrāghate* = *drāgh* DP in *sāmarthya* being able, sufficing

√*dhrai* 522/1 cl 1 P *dhrāyati* to be pleased or satisfied, cl 2 *dhrāti,* DP in *tṛpti* being pleased,

√*dhraj* 521/2 cl 1 P or, *dhrañj or dhrāj* , *dhrañjati or dhṛñjati,* to move, go, glide, fly, sweep on, DP in *gati* going

√*dhrākh* 521/2 *dhrākhati* = *drākh* DP in *śoṣaṇa* becoming dry, *alam* being sufficient, warding off, cl 1

√*dhraṇ* 521/2 cl 1 P *dhraṇati* to sound, DP in *śabda* sounding

√*dhrāṅkṣ* 521/2 *dhrāṅkṣati* = *dhvāṅkṣ* DP in *ghoravāsita* making a discordant sound, desiring,

√*dhras* 521/2 cl 9. 10 P *dhrasnāti*, *dhrāsayati* to glean or to cast upwards, DP in *uccha* throwing or tossing up, gleaning,

√*dhrek* 522/1 cl 1 A *dhrekate* to sound, DP in *śabda* sounding, or *utsāha* growing, showing joy, increasing

√*dhṛj* 519/3 or *dhṛñj* cl 1 P *dharjati* *dhṛñjati* to go, move, DP in *gati* going,

√*dhṝ* 520/1 cl 9 P *dhṛṇāti* to be or grow old, DP in *vidāraṇa* growing old, withering,

√*dhṛṣ* 519/3 cl 5 P *dhṛṣnoti,* cl 1 P *dharṣati* to be bold or courageous or confident or proud, to dare or venture, to dare to attack, treat with indignity, to surpass? caus. *dharṣayati* to venture on attacking, to offend, violate a woman, overpower, overcome, DP in *prāgalabhya* being proud, overbearing, in *prasahana* assailing, attacking, outraging,

dhṛṣṇu mfn daring, courageous, doughty,

dhṛta 519/2 mfn borne, maintained, measured, continuing existing, being, kept back, supported , held firmly, drawn tight (reins), turned towards or fixed upon, continuing, existing, being, proplonged (in pronunciation), quoted, cited by,

Dhṛtarāṣtra 519/2 a powerful king

dhṛti 519/2 f. holding, seizing, keeping, firmness, constancy, satisfaction, content, joy, resolution, patience '*dhṛtiḥ* means *dhairya* or patience as an aspect of constancy, as Absolute is constant', fortitude, steadfastness, 'overcoming non-perseverance, fear and indecision',

dhṛtvā having put on, having held or borne,

√*dhru* 521/2 cl 6 P *dhruvati* to go,

to be firm or fixed, cl 1 P *dhravati* DP in *sthairya* (cl 1) being firm or fixed, in *gati* going or *sthairya* cl 6,

dhruti f. a deceiving, infatuation, seduction

√*dhruv* 521/2 *dhruvati* = √*dhru*

dhruva 521/2 mfn. fixed, firm, immovable, constant, permanent, sure, eternal *(am)* n. the fixed point (from which a departure takes place), the pole star, air, atmosphere, *(am)* ind. firmly, constantly, certainly, surely, (*āya*) ind. for ever,

dhruvā f. sacrificial ladle, lit. holder,

√*dhu* 517/1 1. = 1. *dhū,* 2. f. shaking, trembling, DP in *kampana* trembling,

√*dhū* 517/3 cl 5 P A *dhūnoti, dhunote, dhunoti, dhunute,* cl 6 P *dhuvati*, cl 9 P A , cl 1 P *dhavati,* cl 2 A *dhuvate*, to shake, agitate, cause to tremble, to shake off, remove, liberate oneself from, to fan, kindle (a fire), to treat roughly, hurt, injure, strive against, resist, DP in *kampana* (cl5, 9, 10) trembling, *vidhūnana* (cl 6) shaking, agitating,
2. f. shaking, agitating,

√*dhukṣ* 517/2 cl 1 A *dhukṣate* to kindle, to be weary, to live, DP in *sandīpana* kindling, *kleśana* being weary, *jīvana* living,

dhūli f. dust,

dhūma 518/1 m. smoke, vapour, mist ,

dhūmaka ifc. smoke, also f. *–ikā*

dhūmamarga m. chimney, the path of smoke as distinguished from the way of light- referring to the *jīva* on its journey after death, the path of the *manes,*

dhūmra mfn purple, gray, m. a camel, incense, smoke-coloured,

dhuni mfn shaking, stormily moved, boisterous, wild,

dhūpa m. incense, perfume, aromatic vapour or smoke,

√*dhūpaya* or *–pāya* Nom P (*ti)* to fumigate, perfume, *dhūpaya* to obscure with mist, to speak or to shine, DP for *dhūp* in *santāpa* great heat, sorrow, anguish, *bhāṣā* speaking, shining, with incense,

dhur f. a yoke, burden, load, top, summit, place of honour (at the head, in front, in presence of,),

√*dhūr* 518/3 cl 4 A *dhūryate*, to hurt or kill, to move or approach, 2. in comp for *dhur*, DP in *hiṁsā* hurting, killing, in *gati* going,

dhurā f. load, burden, shaft, yoke, pole,

dhūrdhara m. chief, leader, mfn bearing a burden, managing affairs,

dhurīna 517/2 m. leader, chief, mfn fit to be harnessed, charged with, bearing,

dhūrta mfn shrewd, sly, cunning, m. a rogue, cheat, deceiver, gambler,

dhūrtatraya n. trio of rogues, swindlers,

√*dhurv* 517/3 = *dhūrv* DP in *hiṁsā* hurting

√*dhūrv* 518/3 or *dhurv* cl 1 P *dhūrvati* to bend, cause to fall, hurt, injure

√*dhūś* 519/1 or *dhūṣ* or *dhūs* cl 10 P *dhūśayati* to embellish, DP in *kānti-karaṇa* adorning, decorating

dhūsara mfn dusted over, dusty, grey,

dhūta mfn agitated, shaken, fanned, kindled, n. morality,

dhūtapāpa mfn 'having one's sins shaken (off)' whose sins are removed, destroying sin,

√*dhvaj* 522/1 or *dhvañj* cl 1 P *dhvajati, dhvañjati*, to go, move, DP in *gati* going

dhvaja m. a banner or standard, flag, sign of any trade, a distiller or vendor of spirits (liquor), the organ of generation,

√*dhvaṁs* 522/1 cl 1 P A *dhvaṁsati* to go *(te)* to fall to pieces or to dust, decay, be ruined, perish, to be gone, vanish, scatter, cover, *(ti)* to be destroyed, perish, caus. *dhvaṁsayati* to scatter, destroy, disperse, to violate (a woman), *dhvasayati* to scintillate, sparkle, DP in *ava-sraṁsana-gati* falling down,

dhvaṁsa m. the perishing, destruction, (*ī*) f. a mote in a sunbeam,

√*dhvaṇ* 522/2 cl 1 P *dhvaṇati* to sound, DP in *śabda* sounding,
√*dhvan* 522/2 1. to become covered or extinguished (as anger), caus. to envelope, wrap up, darken, to cover wrap up, extinguish, vanish,
2. cl 1 P *dhvanati* to sound, roar, make a noise, echo, reverberate, to mean, imply, caus. *dhvānayati* to cause to sound, make resound, *dhvanayati* to allude to, hint at, DP in *śabda* sounding,
dhvaṇḥ m. sound, echo, noise, voice,
dhvani m. sound, echo, noise, audible part, suggested meaning, allusion,
√*dhvāṅkṣ* 522/3 cl 1 P *dhvāṅkṣati* to utter the cry of birds, to caw, croak, to desire, DP in *ghoravāsit* crowing, cawing, desiring,
dhvasira mfn covered, dusty, sprinkled,
√*dhvṛ* 523/1 cl 1 P *dhvarati,* to bend, cause to fall, hurt, injure, DP in *hūrchana* bending, killing,
√*dhyai* 521/1 cl 1 P A *dhyāyati (te)*, cl 2 *dhyāti,* to think of imagine, contemplate, meditate on, call to mind, recollect, brood mischief against, be thoughtful or meditative, to let the head hang down (said of an animal), DP in *cintā* thinking of meditating upon,
dhyāna n. 521/1 meditation, reflection
dhyānagamya attainable through meditation,
dhyānika pertaining to meditation,
dhyānanimagna mfn immersed or deep in meditation,
dhyānapara mfn having meditation as highest object, absorbed in contemplation, thoughtful,
dhyātṛ m. the meditator, one who reflects upon,
dhyayamāna 521/2 mfn being reflected or meditated on,
dhyāyamīna m. while engaged in meditation,
dhyāyanta meditating on, thinking of, 1/pl/pres/act/part √*dhyā*
dhyāyat 521/2 mfn. thinking, meditating, contemplating
dhyeya the object or aim of meditation, purpose behind action,
dhyeyatyāga renunciation of objects in meditation,
√*ḍī* 1. 480/2 cl 4. P A *dīyati, ḍīyate*, to soar, fly, DP in *vihāyasā-gati* flying, passing through the air,
2. cl 3 P to shine, be bright, shine forth, excel, please, be admired, bestow upon by shining,
3. cl 4 A *dīyate to* decay, perish, DP in *kṣaya* wasting, decaying,
4. f. decay, ruin
√*dīdhī* 481/1 cl 2 A *didhte* to shine, be bright, P. to appear as resemble,
2. cl 2 A *didhīte* to perceive, think, be intent upon, to wish, desire, DP in *dīpti* shining, in *devana* gaming, playing,
didhiṣu mfn desirous to win, m. suitor, husband esp. second husband,
dīdivi mfn shining, bright, risen (as a star), m. the planet Jupiter, heaven, final emancipation,
didṛkṣu mfn desirous to see, wishing to examine or try,
didyu m. missile,
digambara mfn naked (sky clothed), m. darkness, naked mendicant (Jain)
diganta m. end of the horizon, a remote distance,
digvijaya conquest of the quarters (of the world), either military or cultural, mfn being in remote distance,
√*dih* 480/2 cl 2 P A *degdhi, digdhe* to anoint, smear, plaster, increase, accumulate, caus. *dehayati,* DP in *upacaya* thriving,
dilīpa the son of Aṁśumat & father of Bhagīratha, ancestors of Rāmaḥ
dik direction,
√*dīkṣ* 480/3 cl 1 A *dīkṣate* to consecrate or dedicate oneself to a monastic order, caus. *dīkṣayati* to consecrate, initiate, to make ready, prepare, DP in *mauṇḍya* shaving one's head, *ijya*

sacrificing, *upanayana* investing sacred thread, *niyama* practising self-restraint, *vrata* dedicating oneself to or vowing, *ādeśa* consecrating, initiating,

dīkṣā f. preparation or consecration for a religious ceremony, dedication, initiation, any serious preparation, complete resignation or restriction to, consecration,

ḍimba m. an egg, a chrysalis, new-born child, a child, a young animal,

dina 478/1 n. a day *dināni* 1/pl days mfn cut, divided, mowed, clear,

dīna 480/3 mfn scarce, scanty, sad, miserable, wretched, disturbed, humble, helpless,
n. distress, wretchedness,
f. female mouse or shrew,

dīnabandhu friend of the poor and the helpless, God,

dinacaryā f. daily work, daily activity,

dīnadayālu mfn merciful towards the helpless,

dinakara mfn making day or light,
m. the sun

dinakaratanaya m. the planet Saturn,

dinakarātmaja m. daughter of the sun,

dinanātha m. the sun, day-lord,

dinapati the sun, day-lord,

dīnāra m. denarius, name of a gold coin,

dinatraya n. space of 3 days,

dīnatā 480/3 scarcity, weakness, timid, (A. humility), timid

ḍiṇḍama m. drum, clamour, great noise, loud assertion,

ḍiṇḍima a dainty meal,

√*ḍip* 430/3 *ḍimp, ḍimbh,* cl 10 A to heap together, *ḍepayate, ḍimpayate, ḍimbhayate,*
cl 4.6.10 P *ḍipyati, ḍipati, depayati* A. *ḍimbayate* to throw,
DP in *kṣepa* (cl 4) throwing, *kṣepa* (cl 6.10) throwing, sending, *saṁghāta* (cl 1) collecting, accumulating,

√*dīp* 481/1 cl 4 A *dīpyate, dipyati,* to blaze, flare, shine, be luminous or illustrious, glow, burn(also with anger), to kindle, set on fire, inflame, illumniate, make illustrious, excite, rouse, DP in *dīpti* shining, blazing

dīpa 481/1 m. a light, lamp, lantern,

dīpikā f. a light, torch, lantern, lamp,

dīpita 481/2 mfn. set on fire, inflamed, excited, illuminated, manifested
m. an illuminator, enlightener

dīpta mfn ablaze, flaming, shining,

dīptamat m. possessing brilliance or radiance, brilliant, radiant

dīpti f. brightness, light, splendour, beauty

dīptimat 481/3 mfn. bright, splendid, brilliant

dīrgha mfn long in space, time and sound, lofty, high, tall, deep,

dīrghadarśin far-seeing, m. a bear, vulture,

dīrghakālam ind. for a long time,

dīrghakarṇa m. Long-ear – name of a cat

dīrgharāva m. Long-yell – name of a jackal,

dīrghasvapna long dream, used to indicate the unreal nature of the world,

dīrghasūtratā “such characters would take ten hours to do a job which could easily be done in two hours..” HH 482/3 n. procrastination, dilatoriness,

dīrghasūtrī 482/3 dilatory, procrastinating

dīrghavarṇa m. a long vowel,

dīrghavarṇānta mfn having a long vowel as final,

dīrghāyus mfn long-lived,

√*diś* 479/3 cl 3 P *dideṣti* to point out, show, exhibit, to produce, bring forward (as a witness in a court of justice, to promote, effect, accomplish, to assign, grant, bestow upon, to pay (tribute), to order, command, bid, to order, command, DP in *atisarjana* giving, granting, bestowing,
2. f quarter or region pointed at, direction, cardinal point (NESW), quarter, region, direction, place,

point of the compass, country, foreign country, abroad, the numeral 10, a hint, reference, instance, example, precept, order, manner,

diś f. direction, point, cardinal point, quarter of the heavens,

diśā 480/2 f. compass direction, region, cardinal point, quarter,

diśas 480/2 direction, region, quarter,

diṣṭa mfn assigned, settled, shown, fixed, appointed, directed, pointed out, bidden, time, direction, decree, goal, fate, allotment, description according to time and space, instruction, order, assignment, directive,

diṣṭyā ind. fortunately,

dīti f. glance, flame,

√div 1. cl 1 P *devati* cl 10 P *deyavati* to cause to lament, to pain, vex, ask, beg, to go, A. to suffer pain, DP in *pari-kūjana* suffering pain, lamenting, moaning, in *mardana* vexing, tormenting,
2. cl 4 *divyati (te)* to cast, throw, (esp. dice), play, gamble, lay a wager, bet with, play, sport, joke, trifle with, have free scope, spread, increase, shine, be bright, praise, rejoice, be drunk or mad, to sleep, to wish for, to go, DP in *krīḍā* playing, *vijigīṣā* desiring to conquer, *vyavahāra* activity, *dyuti* shining, *stuti* praise, *moda* joy, *mada* intoxication, *svapna* sleep, *kānti* beauty, desire, *gati* going,

div m. sky, heaven, heaven, day, daily, day by day,
personified as father (of the dawn),

diva n. heaven, sky, day, *divedive* day by day, daily,

divā ind. by day, during the day,

divānaktam day and night,

divārātram day and night,

divasa m. a day, heaven

divātana mfn daily, diurnal, m. a crow,

divaukas m. god, an inhabitant of heaven, a deity, 'having heaven as a dwelling',

a deer, a bee, an elephant,

divi on the day, in the day, 7/s/ *dyu*
m. the blue jay,

divya 479/2 1. Nom.P. *–yati* to long for heaven,
2. mfn divine, heavenly, celestial, wonderful, magical,
n. the divine world or anything divine, pl. the celestial regions, the sky, heaven, sacred, luminous, supernatural, an ordeal, oath, solemn promise, cloves,
m. barley,
f. a kind of perfume,

dīyate it is given, bestowed,
1/s/pres/indic/pass *√dā*

√do *498/1* cl 2.4. P *dāti* to cut, divide,
reap, mow, pass. *dīyate* to be cast down or dejected?
DP in *avakhaṇḍana* cutting, dividing, reaping, mowing,

dogdhṛ mfn yielding milk or profit of any
kind, m. calf, cowherd, milker, poet who writes for reward, exploiter,

doha mfn. milking, yielding, granting, m. milking, milk, a milk-pail,

dohada m. any morbid desire or wish for, longing of a pregnant woman for objects, pregnant,

dohana mfn giving milk, a milker, yielding
profit, f. milk-pail, n. milking, milk, milk-pail,

dolā litter, hammock, swing,

dolāya (*dolāyate)* to swing like a swing, move to and fro, waver, be doubtful or uncertain,

dolāyamānamati mfn having a wavering mind

ḍoma m. a man of low caste living by singing and music,

dos n. arm, fore-arm, side of a

triangle or square,

doṣa 498/2 m. evening, darkness,
2. m. fault, vice, deficiency, badness, wickedness, offence, wrong, weakness, sin, crime, guilt, harm, bad consequence, imperfection, blemish,

doṣā f. darkness, night, night persomified, the arm, ind. in the evening, at dusk, at night,

doṣadṛṣṭi vision that perceives defects,

doṣarahita mfn devoid of faults,

doṣāvastṛ m. illuminator of the darkness, mfn lighting up in the dark,

doṣmat mfn strong-armed, having arms,

√*dṛ* cl 6 A *driyate* to respect, honour, DP in *hiṁsā* hurting, *ādara* respecting, honouring,

√*dṝ* 492/2 cl 9 P *dṛnoti,* cl 2 P. A. *darṣate* to burst, break asunder, split open, to cause to burst, tear, rend, divide, DP in *vidāraṇa* tearing or rending asunder, splitting, *bhāya* fearing,

drā 501/2 /3 1. = *drai*
2. cl 2 P *drāti* to run, make haste, DP in *kutsā* being ashamed or *gati* going

√*drāḍ* 501/3 cl 1 A *drāḍate* to split, divide, go to pieces, DP in *viśaraṇa* cutting, dividing,

√*drāgh* 501/3 cl 1 A *drāghate* to be able, to stretch or lengthen, to exert oneself, to be tired, tire, torment, to roam, stroll, to be long or slow, tarry, delay, DP in *sāmarthya* being able, sufficing, in *āyāma* exerting, stretching,

drāghiman m. length, a degree of longitude,

drāghimavat mfn long, lengthy,

drāghiṣṭha superlative of *dīrgha* , longest, m. a bear,

drāghīyaṁs comparative of *dīrgha,* longer,

drāghīyas mfn longer

√*drāh* 502/1 cl A *drāhate* to wake, to deposit, put down, DP in *nidrā-kṣaya* waking, in *nikṣepa* throwing,

√*drai* 502/3 or *drā* cl 1 P A *drāyati (te)* cl 2 P *drāti* to sleep, DP in *svapna* sleeping,

drāk ind. instantly, quickly, shortly, soon,

√*drākh* 501/3 cl 1 P *drākhati* to become dry or arid, to be able or competent, to adorn, to prohibit or prevent, DP in *śoṣaṇa* being dry, *alam* being sufficient,

drākśā f. vine, grape, mfn made of grapes,

drakñyati he will see

√*dram* 500/3 cl 1 P *dramati* to run about, roam, wander, DP in *gati* going about,

√*drāṅkṣ* 501/3 cl 1 P *drāṅkṣati* to utter a discordant sound, croak or caw, to desire, long for, DP in *ghora-vāsita* making a discordant sound, desiring,

draṣṭā f. the seer, the pure consciousness comprehending all objects (G),

draṣṭavya gve. to be seen, to be regarded or considered as,

draṣṭṛ m. spectator, observer, witness,

draṣṭum to see, to behold (infin. *dṛṣ*)

draupadeyās sons of *Draupadī,*

draupadī wife of the Pandava brothers,

dravatā f. wetness, fluidity, liquidity,

dravati 502/1 runs, hastens, dissolves, melts

dravatva n. fluidity, wetness,

draviḍa m. Dravidian,

dravīkaraṇa 501/1 liquefaction, melting

draviṇa 501/1 n. movable property, substance, wealth,

dravya 501/1 n. a substance, thing, object, the ingredients of anything, property, worthy object, (N) the Brahman (Bhartṛhari)

dravyatas ind. in substance, according to substance,

dravyatva n. substantiality, substance,

dravyatvābhāva (N347) substancelessness,

dravyavinimaya exchange of substances? intersuperimposition, superimposition, ?

√*dṛbh* 491/1 cl 1.10 *darbhati, darbhayati* to fear, be afraid,
DP in *bhaya* fearing,
2. cl 6 P *dṛbhati*

1.10. P *darbhati* and *darbhayati* to string or tie together, tie in a bunch, DP in *grantha* tying, fastening, stringing together, in *sandarbha* tying, fastening stringing together,

dṛḍha 490/2 mfn fixed, firm, hard, solid steady, resolute, persevering, shut fast, strong, massive, whole, complete, n. anything fixed or firm or solid, stronghold, fortress, iron, (*am*) ind. firmly, fast, steadily, thoroughly, much, very well,

dṛḍhatā f. hardness,

√*drek* 502/3 cl 1 A *drekate* to sound, to be in high spirits, to grow or increase, DP in *śabda* sounding, or *utsāha* growing, increasing, showing joy, being exhilarated,

√*dṛh* 492/2 see √*dṛṁh*, √*dhṛk* DP in *vṛddhi*, growing, increasing,

dṛk seer, perceiver,

√*dṛṁh* 490/1 or *dṛh* cl 1 P *dṛhati* to make firm, fix, strengthen,

A. (*te*) to be firm or strong,

B. cl 4 P A be strong, cl 1 *darhati* to grow, DP in *vṛddhi* growth, increase, welfare, √*dṛmph* see 1. √*dṛp* DP in *utkleśa* paining, torturing,

droha 502/3 m. injury, mischief, harm, wrong, perfidy, treachery

Droṇa a *Kaurava* warrior and martial arts master, the preceptor of the Pāṇḍavas and Kauravas,
n. a wooden vessel, bucket, trough,
m.n. a measure of capacity,
a measure for fields,
a lake or large area of water,
m. a cloud from which water streams as water from a bucket, a raven or crow, a scorpion,

√*dṛp* 491/1 or *dṛph* cl 6 P *dṛpati* or *dṛmpati* to pain, torture,
cl 4 P *dṛpyati* to be mad or foolish, to rave, to be extravagant or wild, to be arrogant or proud, to be wildly delighted, to light, kindle, inflame, DP in *utkleśa* paining, torturing, in *harṣa* being delighted, *mohana* being mad or foolish,

√*dṛś* 491/2 1. (present tense forms supplied by √*paś)* to see, behold, look at regard, consider, to wait on, visit, to see with the mind, learn,
to understand, to notice care for, look into, try, examine, to see by divine intuition, think or find out, compose, contrive, (hymns, rites), become visible, appear, to be shown or manifested, appear as, caus. *darśayati (te), adadarśat* to cause to see or be seen, to show a thing, to show = prove, demonstrate, reveal, DP in *prekṣaṇa* seeing,

dṛś 2. m. seeing, viewing, looking at, knowing, discerning, f. sight, view, look, appearance, the eye, theory, doctrine, (in compounds) look, appearance,

dṛśa m. the seeing, (in compounds) look appearance, f. the eye,

dṛṣad f. stone, esp. the lower mill-stone,

dṛṣadupala n. grindstone for condiments, dual f. both millstones,

dṛśaye for beholding,

dṛśi f. seeing, the power of seeing,

dṛṣṭa mfn seen, perceived, discerned, realised, noticed, visible, apparent, considered, regarded, appeared, manifested, existing, found, real, experienced, learnt, known, understood, seen in the mind, imagined, settled, decided, n. perception, observation, the visible, that which is perceived,

dṛṣṭānta 491/3 m. example, paragon, standard, allegory, type, illustration, instance, exemplification, a *śāstra*, death,

dṛṣṭāntabhāsa an erroneous example,

dṛṣṭaphala a visible result, tangible fruits,

dṛṣṭapūrva mfn seen previously, seen,

dṛṣṭārtha mfn having the aim or object apparent, obvious, practical, a perceptible result, knowing the matter or the real nature of anything,

dṛṣṭavān having seen, seeing, perf/part
dṛṣṭāye so as to be seen, for the purpose of finding out,
dṛṣṭe is seen (passive)
dṛṣṭī 492/1 f. seeing, viewing, beholding, (also with the mental eye), view, opinion, the sense of sight, glance, look, the mind's eye, wisdom, intelligence, regard, consideration, view, notion, theory, doctrine, system, eye, look, glance, gaze, a wrong view (Buddhist),
dṛṣṭin 492/1 mfn.having an insight into, or familiar with anything, having the looks or thoughts directed upon anything,
dṛṣṭipāta m. glance,
dṛṣṭisṛṣṛtivāda the theory that creation is just a perception, that the creation is a projection of intellect,
dṛṣṭiṣu *dṛṣṭi* 492/1 seeing, sight, hence any sense experience
7/pl (in the matter of) sensory experiences
dṛṣṭvā gerund, having seen
dṛṣṭyupaghāta blindness, ignorance
dṛśya 491/3 mfn. visible, conspicuous, to be looked at, any visible object, worth seeing, beautiful, pleasing, m. a given quantity or number, n. any visible object, the visible world, 2. having seen,
dṛśyamānā pres.part. being perceived, perceiving,
dṛśyaprapañca the phenomenal world visible to the eye
dṛśyate 1/s/pres/indic/pass is seen
dṛśyatva n. objectivity, visibility, vision, sight,
dṛti m. bag of leather, bellows, hide,
√*dru* 502/1 cl 5 P *druṇoti* to hurt, injure, to repent, to go,
2. cl 1 P *dravati* to run, hasten, flee, run up to, attack, assault, to become fluid, dissolve, melt, caus. *drāvayati* cause to run, make flow, make fluid, melt, to drive away, put to flight,
DP in *gati* going,
3. mfn running, going, f. going, motion,
4. m.n. wood or a wooden implement (e.g. cup, oar), m. a tree or branch
√*drū* 502/3 cl 9 P *drūṇāti* to hurl, throw, cl 5 P *drūṇoti* to kill or to go,
2. mfn taking any shape at will, f. gold DP in *hiṁsā* hurting, injuring
drugdha mfn one who has tried to harm, hurtful, malicious, n. offence, misdeed, impers. harm has been done,
√*druh* 502/3 cl 4 P A *druhayati* *(te)* to hurt, seek to harm, be hostile to, to be a foe or rival, DP in *jighāṁsā* bearing malice or hatred, seeking to hurt,
2. mfn. injuring, hurtful, hostile to, mf. injurer, foe, fiend, demon, f. injury, harm, offence,
druma m. a tree,
drumāyati passes for or is regarded as a tree, 1/s/pres/act/
√*druṇ* cl 6 P *druṇati* to make crooked, bend, to go, move, to hurt, kill, DP in *hiṁsā*hurting, *gati* going, *kauṭilya* bending, malking crooked
druta mfn quick, speedy, swift, quickly or indistinctly spoken, flown, run away, dissolved, melted, fluid, *(am)* ind. hastily, rapidly, without delay, m. a scorpion, a tree,
√*du* 1. cl 1 P *davati* to go DP in *gati* going,
2. cl 5 P *dunoti* cl 4 A *dūyate (ti)*, to be burnt, to be consumed with internal heat or sorrow, *dunoti* only – to burn, consume with fire, cause internal heat, pain, or sorrow, afflict, distress,
DP in *upatāpa* burning,
√*dū* see 2. √*du* above,
dū 1. in comp. for *dus,*
2. f. pain distress from 2. √*du*
ducchunā f. calamity, harm, mischief,
ducchunāyate 1/s/pres/mid, seeks to harm,

dūda mfn afflicting, harassing,
dūdabha mfn difficult to be deceived
dūdāś mfn not worshipping, irreligious
dūdhī mfn malevolent,
dūḍhya mfn malevolent,
dugdha 483/3 mfn. milked, milked out
sucked out, impoverished,
n. milk, 2.√*duh*
√*duh* 1. cl 1 P *dohati* to pain DP in *ardana*
distressing, paining,
2. cl 2 P A *dogdhi, dugdhe* or *duhe*
cl 6 P A *duhati (te)*
cl 4 *duhyati (te)* to milk (a cow or udder), take advantage of, enjoy, to milk or squeeze out, extract (milk, soma, any good thing), draw anything out of another thing, (mostly A *dugdhe*) – to give milk, yield any desired object, DP in *prapuraṇa* milking
3. mfn milking, yielding, granting,
duḥ 483/1 in comp for *upasarga*
(prefix) *dus,*
duhitṛ f. daughter,
duḥkha 483/2 mfn uneasy, uncomfortable, unpleasant, difficult, n. pain, sorrow, trouble, difficulty, (*am*) ind. with difficulty, scarcely, hardly, 2. Nom P. *–khati* to pain,
duḥkhabodha mfn difficult to understand
duḥkhabhāgin mfn having pain as one's portion, unhappy,
duḥkhadagdha mfn burnt by affliction, pained, distressed,
duḥkhaduḥkha n. (3rd) with great difficulty,
duḥkhaduḥkhin mfn having sorrow upon sorrow
duḥkhagata n. adversity, calamity
duḥkhahā sorrow destroying, pain destroying, *duḥkha* √*han* 1/s/m
duḥkhahan mfn removing pain,
duḥkhajāta mfn suffering pain, distressed,
duḥkhajihāsā desire to avoid pain and sorrow,
duḥkhajīvin mfn living in pain or distress,
duḥkhakara mfn causing pain to, afflicting,
duḥkhākara m. a multitude of sorrows,
duḥkhakṣaya m. the removal of misery,
duḥkhāya Nom A. (te) to feel pain,
be distressed,
duḥkhā√*kṛ* to cause pain, afflict, distress
duḥkhākula mfn filled with sorrow,
duḥkhaloka m. the world of pain,
duḥkham misery
duḥkhamaraṇa mfn having a painful death,
duḥkhamaya mfn consisting in suffering,
duḥkhamokṣa m. deliverance from pain,
duḥkhanirodha cessation of suffering,
duḥkhaparītāṅga mfn whose limbs are filled with pain,
duḥkhasāgara m. ocean of pain, great sorrow, the world,
duḥkhasaṁcāra mfn passing unhappily (time),
duḥkhaśīla mfn bad-tempered, irritable,
-tva n. irritability,
duḥkhaśokavat mfn feeling pain and sorrow,
duḥkhatara greater hardship, greater pain, greater misery , discomfort, (comparative)
duḥkhātmaka mfn whose essence is sorrow,
duḥkhānarha mfn deserving no pain,
duḥkhānta m. the end of pain or trouble,
duḥkhavega m. a violent grief,
duḥkhavyābhaṣita mfn pronounced with difficulty,
√*duḥkhaya* Nom P *duḥkhayati*
DP in *tatkriyā* causing pain,
duḥkhayantra n. torture,
duḥkhayoga m. infliction of pain,
duḥkhena unhappily
duḥkhin mfn pained, afflicted, grieved,
duḥkhita mfn sad, pained, distressed,
duḥkhitacitta mfn grieved in mind,
duḥsādhya mfn difficult to perform, manage or accomplish, difficult to cure, difficult to conquer,
duḥsaha mfn unbearable, irresistible,
n. an evil demon
duḥsahāya mfn having bad companions, forsaken by all,
duḥśaka mfn impractical, impossible,
duḥśakta, °ti, mfn powerless,
duḥsākṣin m. a false witness,
duḥṣama 1. a partic. weight, 2. n.
a bad year, (*am*) ind. unevenly,

improperly, at a wrong time,

duḥsama mfn unequal, uneven, unfit, perverse, bad,

duḥsamartha mfn difficult to be conceived,

duḥsaṁcāra mfn difficult to walk, pass

duḥsaṁcintya difficult to conceive, imagine

duḥsamīkṣya mfn difficult to perceive

duḥśaṁsa mfn wishing or threatening evil,malicious, wicked,

duḥsaṁskāra m. a bad custom or practice,

duḥsaṅga m. bad inclination,

duḥsarpa m. a vicious serpent

duḥśāsa mfn difficult to control

duḥśasta mfn badly recited,

duḥśāsus mfn malevolent,

duḥsattva n. evil being, noxious animal

duḥśeva mfn envious, malignant,

duḥsevya mfn intractable, difficult to manage

duḥśikṣita mfn ill-bred, impertinent,

duḥśiṣya m. a bad scholar,

duḥśīla mfn badly disposed, ill-behaved

duḥsmara mfn unpleasant to remember,

duḥsparśa difficult or unpleasant to touch,

duḥspṛṣṭa slight contact, the action of the tongue producing the sounds, *y,r,l,v,*
m. a sound thus produced,

duḥśodha mfn difficult to be cleaned,

duḥśoṣa mfn difficult to be dried,

duḥśrava mfn unpleasant to be heard,

duḥśṛṅgī f. a disloyal wife,

duḥśṛta mfn not well cooked, underdone

duḥṣṭhu mfn badly behaved, ind. badly

duḥśruta mfn badly or wrongly heard,

duḥstha mfn unsteady, 'standing badly' uneasy, unhappy, unwise, a fool, covetous, (*am*) ind. badly, ill,

duḥsthiti f. ill condition,

duḥstrī f. a bad woman

duḥṣupta mfn sleeping badly, having bad dreams

duḥsvapna m. a bad dream,

dukhin mfn pained, afflicted, unhappy,

√*dul* cl 10 P *dolayati* to swing, throw up, shake to and fro,
DP in *utkṣepa* swinging,

dūlabha mfn difficult to be deceived

dūṇaśa mfn unattainable, inaccessible,

dūṇāsa mfn as above + imperishable, incessant, perpetual,

dundubhi m.f. drum, a poison,

dur the form taken by *dus* before voiced letters, in comp. denoting 'bad' or 'difficult' etc.
n. great crime or wickedness,

dūra mfn. distant, far, remote,
n. distance, remoteness, a long way, far from, a long way back or from a remote period, come from afar (with a past participle),
ind. (*am*) far, far from, in a high degree, far above or below,

durācāra m. bad conduct, wicked,

dūrada mfn difficult to scratch, hard,

dūrādha mfn difficult to accomplish

dūradṛṣṭi f. discernment, foresight, long-sightedness, prudence,

durāgama a poor or bad text or scripture,
m. bad income, improper gain,

dūrakṣya mfn difficult to be guarded or preserved,

dūrakta mfn badly coloured or dyed

dūram 489/2 ind. distant, far, remote, far from, a long way off or a long period back, far above or below,

durāsada 485/1 mfn. dangerous to approach, unheard of, unparalleled,

durāśaya mfn evil-minded, malicious,
m. the subtle body which is not destroyed by death,

dūrastha 489/3 mfn. being in the distance, remote,

dūrāt ind. from a distance, from afar,

durātman mfn evil-minded, bad, villain

duratikrama mfn hard to overcome,

duratyaya 484/2 mfn. inaccessible, unfathomable, (*ā*) f. difficult to penetrate, difficult to master,

dūri -√*kṛ* P. *–karoti*, put far away, send off, remove, repel,

durbala 486/1 of little strength, weak, feeble,

durbhaga mfn ill-portioned, ill-favoured,
f. (*ā*) an ugly woman, a bad or ill-tempered woman, a shrew,
old age (personified),

durbhāgya mfn unfortunate, unlucky, n. ill-luck,
durbhikṣa mfn (time) in which alms-getting is hard, n. famine, want, distress,
durbodha mfn unfathomable, difficult to understand,
dur-buddhi 486/1 f. weak-mindedness, foolish, ignorant, malignant, evil-minded,
durdānta mfn overcome with difficulty, m. hard to tame (name of a lion), a calf, strife, quarrel,
durdivasa m. bad or rainy day,
dūre 489/2 ind. far away, away from, in a distant place, far,
dūreṇa (3rd) by far,
durga 487/2 m. difficult of access or approach, impassable, unattainable, n. a difficult or narrow passage, a citadel, rough ground, roughness, difficulty, danger,
Durgā f. (Pārvatī) a goddess, mfn difficult of access or approach, impassable, unattainable,
durgandha 485/2 mfn ill smelling, stinking m. the mango tree, an onion,
durgata mfn ill-conditioned, unfortunate,
durgati 485/2 misfortune, distress, poverty
durgraha 485/2 m seizing badly, cramp, illness, obstinacy, mfn difficult to seize, catch or attain,
duriṣṭha very bad or difficult or wicked,
durjana m. bad person, scoundrel, mfn malicious, wicked,
durjñeya mfn 'dificult to be known' difficult,
durlabha 486/3 scarce, rare, hard to find, difficult to attain or obtain,
durlabhatara more difficult to attain, harder to attain, comparative
durmada mfn badly intoxicated, drunken,
durmanas mfn in low spirits, sad, melancholy, n. perversity of mind, bad disposition,
durmanāyate to be miserable,
durmaṅgala mfn bringing bad luck,
durmati 486/2 f. bad disposition of mind, envy, hatred, m. fool, blockhead, ill-will,
durmitra 486/2 mfn unfriendly
durnigraha 486/1 mfn. difficult to restrain or conquer
durnimitta mfn ill-measure, irregular,
durnirīkṣya difficult to see or look upon, gerundive *dus nis* √*īkṣ*
durnivāra mfn whose warding off is hard, hard to get rid of, irrepressible,
dūrūḍha mfn badly grown or cicatrized
√*durv* cl 1 P to hurt, injure, kill, DP in *hiṁsā* hurting
dūrvā f. millet-grass, bent grass,
durvāra mfn hard to restrain, irrepressible, irresistible,
durvāsas m. an irascible sage, famous for his tendency to curse people for minor offences, mfn barely clad, naked,
durvijñeya mfn hard to distinguish, hardly conceivable, unintelligible,
durvipā evil consequences (destiny),
durvipāka mfn having evil consequences, m. evil result or consequence,
durvṛtta mfn of evil life, wicked, badly-behaved, n. bad conduct, meanness,
Duryodhana dirty fighter, chief of the *Kuru* army, son of *Dhṛtarāṣṭra*,
duś 487/3 in comp. for *dus.*
√*duṣ* 1. in comp. for *dus,*
2. cl 4 P *duṣyati* (te) to become bad or corrupted, to be defiled or impure, to be ruined, perish, to sin, commit a fault, be wrong, caus. *doṣayati* to spoil or corrupt (the mind) DP in *vaikṛtya* becoming bad or corrupted,
dus 488/1 ind. a prefix to nouns and adverbs implying evil, ill, bad, difficult, hard, slight, inferior, opp. to s*u* , the final consonant changes according to the letter following
dūṣa mfn defiling, corrupting,
dūṣaka n. corrupting, spoiling, disgracing, seducing, offending, transgressing, m. offende, seducer, disparager,

a kind of rice, pencil or paint-brush,
dūṣaṇa mfn corrupting, spoiling, violating, n. the act of corrupting, dishonouring, detracting, disparaging, objection, adverse argument, refutation,
dūṣaya Nom P. °yati to corrupt, spoil, contaminate, to dishonour or violate (a woman), to adulterate, falsify, to object, refute, disprove, blame, find fault with, accuse, to offend, hurt, fault, offence, guilt, sin,
duścakṣas mfn evil-eyed,
duś√car to act wrongly or badly towards, to behave badly,
duścarita n. misbehaviour, wickedness, (pl. Buddhist the 10 chief sins) – murder, theft, adultery, lying, slander, lewdness, evil speech, covetousness, envy, heresy,
duścaritra having false or bad character, see *duścarita*
duścarmaka n. leprosy
duśceṣṭā f. misconduct, error,
duśceṣṭita mfn doing evil, misbehaving,
duścikitsa mfn difficult to be cured, (*ā*)f. a wrong treatment,
duścintin mfn 'thinking evil thoughts',
duścintita n. a bad or foolish thought,
duścintya mfn difficult to be understood,
duścit mfn thinking evil,
duścitta mfn melancholy, sad,
dūṣi 489/1 mfn corrupting, defiling, (the mind), f. a poisonous substance,
dūṣin mfn corrupting, polluting, violating
dūṣita mfn spoiled, corrupted, blamed, contaminated, defiled, blemished, compromised, falsely accused of, f. a girl who has been violated or deflowered,
duṣkāla m. an evil time,
duṣkara mfn hard to be borne, difficult to do, arduous,
duṣkaraṇa n. a difficult or miserable work,
duṣkīrti f. dishonour, mfn infamous,
duṣkrama mfn ill-arranged, not methodical,
duṣkrīta mfn badly or dearly bought, demerit, sin, evil action,
duṣkriyā f. evil act a misdemeanour
duṣkṛt mfn acting wickedly, criminal, evil-doer
duṣkṛta mfn wrongly or wickedly done, badly arranged or organized or applied, n. evil action, sin, guilt,
duṣkṛta 487/3 mfn wrongly or wickedly done, evil action, bad action
duṣkṛti mfn acting wickedly, an evil-doer,
duṣkuhaka mfn incredulous,
duṣkula n. a low family or race, mfn of a low family, low-born,
duṣpada mfn unfathomable or inaccessible,
duṣpāna difficult to drink,
duṣpāra mfn diff. to be crossed or overcome
duṣparājaya 'difficult to be conquered'
duṣparigraha mfn difficult to seize or keep
duṣparihantu mfn diff. to remove/destroy
duṣparīkṣya mfn diff. to investigate, examine
duṣparimṛṣṭa mfn badly considered,
duṣparināma mfn of undefined extent,
duṣpatana n. falling badly,
duṣpoṣa mfn difficult to nourish
duṣprabhañjana m. hurricane,
duṣprabodha mfn awaking with difficulty
duṣprada mfn causing pain or sorrow,
duṣpradharṣa mfn not to be assailed or touched, intangible,
duṣprajñāna n. want of understanding, weak intellect,
duṣprakāśa mfn obscure, dark,
duṣpralambha difficult to deceive,
duṣpramaya mfn difficult to measure
duṣpraṇīta mfn badly led or managed, n. ill-conduct or behaviour,
duṣprāpa difficult to attain, hard to reach *duṣ pra √āp*
duṣprapadana mfn difficult to attain or enter,
duṣprasāda mfn to be propitiated,
duṣprasādhana diff. to be managed
duṣprasaha mfn diff. to be supported, suffered, irresisitible, terrible,
duṣpratyabhijña diff. to recognise
duṣpravāda m. ill speech, slander,
duṣpraveśa mfn difficult to enter,
duṣpravṛtti f. bad news,
duṣprayukta mfn falsely used,

duṣpūra mfn difficult to fill/satisfy
duṣpuruṣa m. a bad man,
duṣputra m. a bad son,
duṣṣanta m. an ancient king, the husband of *śakuntalā,*
duśṭa mfn evil, spoilt, corrupted, defective, bad, offensive, guilty, culpable, m. a villain, rogue, (*ā*) f. a bad or unchaste woman, n. sin, offence, crime, guilt,
duṣṭabhāva mfn evil-natured, malignant,
duṣṭabuddhi mfn illl-disposed against,
duṣṭacaritra mfn ill-conducted, evil-doer,
duṣṭacetas mfn evil-minded, malevolent
duṣṭadamana n. 'taming of the bad'
duṣṭadurjana m. villain, reprobate,
duṣṭagaja m. a vicious elephant,
duṣṭahetu defective reason, (G)
duṣṭahṛdaya mfn bad-hearted,
duṣṭanigraha destruction of the wicked,
duṣṭānvita mfn defiled, rendered impure,
dustapa mfn difficult to endure (penance),
duṣṭara mfn difficult to pass or overcome or endure, unconquerable, irresistible, incomparable, excellent,
dustara difficult to pass or overcome, unconquerable, invincible,
dustarka m. false reasoning, faulty argument
dustarkya mfn difficult to reason about,
duṣṭātman mfn evil-minded, malevolent,
duṣṭavāc mfn uttering bad language,
duṣṭi f. corruption, defilement, depravity, growing worse (a wound),
dustoṣa mfn difficult to satisfy,
dustyajya mfn difficult to relinquish or quit
dūṣya mfn corruptible, liable to be soiled, defiled, violated, hurt, reprehensible, culpable, vile, bad, m. wicked man, a villain, n. matter, pus, poison,
dūta m. messenger, ambassador, envoy,
duvas 1. mfn stirring, restless, 2. n. gift, oblation, honour, worship, reverence
duvasya Nom P *–yati* to honour, worship, celebrate, reward, give as a reward, DP in *paritāpa* glowing, scorching, *paricaraṇa* serving attending
duvasyu mfn worshipping, reverential,
dva numeral two,
dvādaśa twelve, f.(*ī*) twelfth
dvaidha 507/2 mfn twofold, double n. a state of duality, duplicity
dvaidhīkaraṇa 507/3 making into two, separating
dvaita 507/2 duality
dvaitabhāva sense or feeling of duality,
dvaitavāda dualism, the doctrine of duality,
dvaṁdva see *dvaṁdva* 503/2 n. pair, couple, male and female, a pair of opposites, argument, a copulative compound or any compound in which the members if uncompounded would be in the same case and connected by the conjunction "and"
dvaṁdvata state of duality,
dvaṁdvātita mfn gone beyond or freed from opposites,
dvandva see *dvaṁdva*
dvāpara yuga 503/3 the bronze age, (864,000 years) 3rd of the 4 traditional ages, the age of heroes, qualities no longer pure,
dvār door, gate, entrance or issue, fig. expedient, means, opportunity,
dvāra n. door, gate, passage, entrance, opening, aperture (esp. human body),
dvārakāraṇa intermediate cause,
dvārapakṣa m. side of the door,
dvaya 503/2 mfn (from and in comp. *dvi*) twofold, double, of 2 kinds or sorts, m. a pair, n. a couple, pair, two things, falsehood, both, (*am*) ind. between,
dvayābhāsa appears to have two aspects (Gam.)
dvayābhāva 'non-existence of duality' (Gam.), the appearance of duality,
dvayam laukikam dualist world view, external objects exist, awareness exists,
dve, dvau two
dvedhā ind. in two, in two kinds or ways,
dveṣa 507/1 aversion, dislike, hostility
dveṣas n. hatred, hater, foe,

dveṣṭa 506/3 *root 2.* adj. *dviṣ* hates, *dveṣṭi* dislikes.

dvi two, (a form of *dva)*

dvidhā ind. in two parts, 'in two ways',

dvigu 'worth 2 cows' the name of a class of *karmadhāraya* compound that begins with a number,

dvija mfn twice-born twice-born, a member of one of the 3 highest castes, re-born by virtue of the ceremony known as the investiture with the sacred thread, any animal born of an egg is also called twice-born,

dvijanman mfn having double-birth, (same as *dvija*)

dvijāti mfn (*as*)m. a man of the three upper castes, an Aryan esp. a Brahman, a bird or snake,
ind. for or to Brahmans,

dvijottama highest of the twice-born, a brahman

dvipa m. elephant,

dvīpa m. island

dvipad mfn having two feet, (*as*) m. the two-footed one, man, n/ s that which is two-footed (collectively) men (bipeds),

dvipada f. (*ī)* mfn having (taken) two steps, two-footed, consisting of 2, containing 2 words, binomial,
m. a biped, a man (with contempt),

dviparārdhika mfn equal to 50 of Brahmā's years,

dvīpicarman n. tiger-skin,

dvīpin 507/1m tiger, panther, leopard, having islands or island like spots

dvipravrājin mfn going after two (men), unchaste,

dvirepha m. bee

dviṣ 1.(in compounds for *dvis*) twice

√*dviṣ* 2. cl 2 P A *daveṣṭi daviṣṭe* also *daviṣati (te),* to hate, show hatred against, be hostile or unfriendly, to be a rival or a match for, DP in *aprīti* hating,
3. f. hostility, hatred, dislike, mf. foe, enemy, mfn hostile, hating, disliking,

dviṣata envious,

dvita mfn second,

dvitā ind. just so, so also, equally, doubly so, certainly,
f. doubleness, the number 2, duality,

dvitaya n. a pair or couple,
, mfn consisting of two, twofold, double, both,

dvitīya mfn 506/2 second, a second, another, a further,

dvitva n. twoness, duality, dual, reduplication,

dvivacana (in gram.)the dual and its endings

dvividha 505/3 mfn. twofold, of 2 kinds,

dvyaṇuka n. combination of 2 atoms, diatom,

√*dyai* 500/3 cl 1 P *dayāyati* to despise, ill-treat, DP in *nyakkaraṇa* treating with contempt, ind. fie! for shame!

dyāvāpṛthivī dual f. heaven and earth,

dyotana 500/2 mfn. shining, illuminating enlightening, a lamp, n. shining, being bright, illumination

√*dyu* 1. cl 2 P *dayauti* to go against, attack, assail, DP in *abhigamana* advancing towards, assailing, ?
2. *dyu* 1/s *dyaus* 478/3/2 m. heaven, the sky, (rarely n.) day, by day, daily, every day, day by day, by day or in the course of days, a long time, brightness, sheen, glow, fire,

dyumant mfn heavenly, bright, splendid,

√*dyut* cl 1 A *dayotate (ti),* to shine, be bright or brilliant,
caus. *dayotayati* to make bright, illuminate, irradiate, cause to appear, make clear or manifest, express, mean, DP in *dīpti* shining, 2. f. shining, splendour, ray of light,

dyut 499/3 mfn. advancing against

dyūta n. gambling, play, gaming, fig. battle or contest for, booty won in battle,

dyūtakāra m. gambler,

dyuti 500/1 f. splendour (as a goddess)

, lustre, brightness, majesty, dignity

e 227/2 a particle of recollection, addressing, censure, contempt, compassion,

e ā-√i P. *eti* to come near or towards, go near, approach, reach, attain

ebhyaḥ pron. this (indefinite) 4/pl or 5/pl from these,

√edh 231/3 cl1 *edhate, -ti,* to prosper, increase, become happy, grow strong, grow big with self-importance, become insolent, become intense, extend, spread, to swell, rise (as waters),
caus. *edhayati* to cause to prosper or increase, wish for the welfare or happiness (of any one), bless,
DP in *vṛddhi* prospering

edha 231/3 m. fuel, mfn. ifc. kindling

ehi come! impv

√ej cl 1 P *ejati* stir, move, shake, tremble cl 1 A *ejate* to shine,
DP cl 1 in *kampana* trembling,
cl 1 in *dīpti* shining

ejat 231/1 pres.p. anything moving or living

ejati he/she/it moves

eka 227/3 mfn one, alone, solitary
a certain, happening only once,
the same, one and the same, identical,
one of two or many *eka....eka*the one...the other, , *eka...dvitīya,*
esp. pl. *eke* some, *eke—apare,* some—others),
(*eka* repeated twice either as a compound [*ekaika*] or uncompounded, may have the sense of 'one and one', 'one by one'),
single of its kind, unique, singular, chief, pre-eminent, excellent, sincere, truthful, little, small, sometimes used as an indefinite article 'a', 'an', *(am)* n. unity, a unit,

ekabhakṣa m. sole food, ifc. eating ... alone,

ekabhavika of the same source or nature,

ekabindu one drop

ekacaryā 'observing one rule of conduct, moving alone without company,' 'one-conduct' concentration

ekadā once (upon a time), at one time, simultaneously, at a certain time,

ekadaṇḍin bearing one staff (Sannyasin),

ekādaśa num. eleven, mfn eleventh,

ekādaśī eleventh day of lunar fortnight,

ekadeśa m. a certain place, a place or spot or part, being in the same place,

ekadeśika mfn one-sided, localised,

ekadhā ind. in one way, together, at once, simply, singly,

ekāgra 230/1 one-pointed, closely attentive, intent, undisturbed, close and undisturbed attention, intentness in the pursuit of an object

ekāgratā 230/1 f. intentness in the pursuit of one object, close and undisturbed attention, 'one-pointed attention'

ekāgratas ind. with undivided attention,

ekāgrya 230/1 mfn closely attentive,
n. close attention, concentrating

ekāha m. the period of one day,

ekaika mfn one by itself, one singly, each one singly, every single one,
one by one, each

ekaikaśas ind. one by one, severally,

akaikaśya n. single state, severalty,

ekaikasya each one has, single state,

ekākin 231/1 mfn alone, single, solitary

ekākśara n. having one syllable, the sole imperishable thing,

ekam n. unity, a unit

ekamati mfn having one mind, unanimous, concentration of mind,

ekamevādvitīyam one, alone, without a second, Brahman,

ekāṁśa m. one part, single part,

ekanakṣatra n. an astral mansion (star),

ekāñjali m. one handful,

ekānta m. an end, a retired/ secret spot,
a single part, part, portion,
the only end or aim, exclusiveness, absoluteness, necessity, devotion to one object, worship of one being, monotheistic doctrine, ind. solely, only, exclusively, absolutely,

necessarily, by all means, in every respect, invariably
ekāntabhāva m. devotion to one object alone, feeling of isolation or solitariness,
ekāntavāda monism,
ekāntika 230/2 mfn. devoted to one aim or object or person or theory, final or ultimate, the Absolute,
ekāntam 230/2 ind. solely, only, exclusively absolutely, necessarily, invariably, a lonely place,
ekapada f. *(ī)* having (i.e. taking) one step, n. one and the same place or spot, a single word, a simple word, a simple nominal formation, one and the same word, *ekapade* ind. on the spot, in one moment, at once,
ekapatnī f. wife of only one man, faithful wife, pl. women who have the same husband,
ekāpāya m. diminution by one,
ekapṛthaktva n. unity and distinctness, (G) distinct separateness,
ekarasa 229/1 m. the only pleasure, mfn. having only one pleasure or object of affection, unchangeable, 'on an even keel' homogenous, uniform, one essence, Brahman,
ekarṣi or ekariṣi the only or chief *ṛṣi*
ekārṇava m. general inundation, only one ocean, nothing but ocean,
ekārtha m. one purpose, i.e. one and the same purpose, one and the same meaning, mfn having the same purpose or aim, having the same meaning, synonymous, expressing one thing,
ekārthasamaveta mfn come for one (and the same) purpose,
ekastha standing together, standing as one resting or abiding in one, conjoined, combined, assembled, remaining in the same place,
ekatā f. union, unity, oneness, coincidence, identity,
ekatara one of two, either, other,
ekatatpara mfn solely intent on,
ekatra ind. at one place together, in one place,
ekatva 228/1oneness, unity, union, singularity, coincidence, soleness,
ekavacana singular (in grammar)
ekavarṇa mfn having one colour,
ekayā through that one, by one, with one,
ekāyana mfn passable for one only, fixing one's thoughts on one object, closely attentive, absorbed in, n. worldly wisdom, unity, meeting-place, centre of union, absorption in one, absolute devotedness to one,
eke some
ekendriya mfn having but one organ of sense,
ekī in comp. for *eka*
ekībhāva m. the becoming one, coalition,
ekī√bhū 231/1 to become one, be blended or combined,
ekībhūtaḥ m. undifferentiated, (Gam.)
ekīkaraṇa n. the act of making one, uniting, combination,
ekoddiṣṭa n. a funeral ceremony,
ekona mfn lacking one, less by one, minus one,
elāya 232/2 Nom. P *elāyati* to be wanton or playful, be merry, DP in *vilāsa* being merry or frolicsome,
ema *(m), eman* n. a course or way
ena a pronoun base
ena enclitic 3rd case of *idam,* him, her, it, them, also this, that
enā ind. here, there, thus, then, in this way, *para enā* beyond here, beyond (with 3rd) there, *yatra...enā* whither ... thither,
enam (pron.) -is substituted for *imam* or *etam* when something is referred to which has already been mentioned in a previous part of the sentence,
enas n. mischief, crime, sin, evil, unhappiness, misfortune
enasvant mfn sinful,
enasvin mfn wicked, sinful,
enat pron. this Supreme Lord (*īṣā up*)
eraṇḍa m. castor-oil plant, long pepper,
eṣ 232/3 cl 1 P A *eṣati* to go, move,

creep, glide, to glide or hasten towards, attain, obtain, 2. *-īṣati (te)* to hasten near or towards, fly at, to endeavour to reach or obtain, to desire, request, DP in *gati* going

eṣā mfn seeking, m. the act of seeking or going after, wish, option,

eṣaḥ pron. 1/s/m of *etad* this, "*eṣaḥ* denotes *aham* and not *idam* which is used for all that is not *aham*" HH "This, the *prājña*, the mere consciousness undifferentiated, is the lord of all, the omniscient and resides in each *antaḥkaraṇa*, the cause of everything and the beginning and end of all existence." HH

eṣām pron.6/pl of these

eso a *prakrit* form for *eṣas*

eṣyasi you shall come or attain 2/s/fut/act √*i*

eta 1. come near, approached, 2. mfn rushing, darting, of a variegated colour, varying the colour, shining, brilliant, m. a kind of deer or antelope, the hide of the same,

etad 231/2 mfn this, this here, referring to what precedes, ind. in this manner, thus, so, here, at this time,

etadartham ind. for this purpose, therefore,

etādṛś mfn such, such like, so formed, of this kind, similar to this,*etādṛk* 2/s/n such as I have

etādṛśa such, *...yat* such ... that

etān 2/pl/m these

etarhi ind. at this time, nowadays, then, n. a measure of time,

etasya pron. 6/s of this

etat-kahaṇe ind. in this moment, now

etat-para mfn intent on or absorbed in this

etatsama mfn equal to this,

etatsamīpa n. presence of this one,

etat *1/s/n* pron. *eṣaḥ* this

etat-tulya 231/3 mfn similar to this, equal to this

etāvan 231/3 of this measure/quantity, so great, *etāvantam* suffix *tam* pres.part.

etāvant mfn thus much, *etāvan... yena* so great... that

etāvat 231/3 of such extent, so great, so far, so much (and no more)

ete 1/pl/m these

eteṣām pron. 6/pl/m of these, to them

eti he goes, he attains 1/s/pres/act *ā*√*i*

√*eṭh* 231/1 cl 1 A *eṭhate* to be a rogue or rasCl, to cheat, DP in *vibādhā* causing pain

eva 232/2 ind. only, even, so, indeed, truly, indeed, only, alone, just(emphasizes previous word)

evam 232/2 ind. thus, in this way, in such a manner, likewise, so, *yathā... evam* as... so, with *ukta or śrutvā* – upon saying or hearing this, *evam ukta* thus addressed, *evam astu* so be it *mā evam* not so! *yady evam* if that's the case, *evam* in that case, *evam* likewise,

evambhūta mfn such, of such a quality or nature,

evaṁrupa mfn having such a form, provided with such a form,

evaṁvidha mfn of such sort, such,

evaṁvit (D) a knower of this kind, well instructed, familiar with what is right,

√*gā* 352/1 cl 3 P *jigāti* to go after, pursue, to fall to one's share, be one's due, to come into any state or condition, undergo, obtain, to go away, to come to an end, to walk, to be born, A. *gāte* to go, go towards, come, approach, DP in *stūti* praising, singing, in *gati* going

-ga goer, (in compounds) going, ifc. mfn singing,

gabhīra mfn deep, profound, sagacious, grave, serious, solemn, secret, dense, impervious, not to be penetrated or investigated or explored,

gaccha go! (singular)

gacchan mfn going

gacchata go! (pl)

gacchati he/she/it goes

√*gaḍ* 342/3 cl 1 P *gaḍati* to distil or drop, run as a liquid, cl 10 P *gaḍayati* to cover, hide, DP in *secana* distilling, drawing out,

√*gad* 344/2 cl 1 P *gadati* to speak articulately, speak, say, relate, tell anything to anyone, cl 10P *gadayati* to thunder, DP in *vyaktāvāc* speaking articulately, in *devaśabda* thundering, sounding of the gods

gada m. disease, sickness, a sentence,

gadā f. a series of sentences, mace, club,

√*gadgadya* 344/3 Nom P *gadgadyati* to stammer, DP in *vāk-skhalana* stammering

gadgada mfn stuttering,

√*gādh* 353/2 cl 1 A *gādhate* to stand firmly, stay, remain, to set out for, to desire, to compile, string together, DP in *pratiṣṭhā* standing, *lipsā* seeking or coveting, and *grantha* compiling

gādha mfn shallow, fordable, m. desire, cupidity,

gadin 344/3 armed with a club

gaḍu m. any superfluous addition, a spear, hunch, earthworm, water-pot, goitre, hump hump on the back, humpbacked man, javelin,

gagaṇa n. the sky , heaven, atmosphere,

gagaṇakusuma n. 'flower in the sky' an expression of impossibility, a fanciful thing,

gagaṇacara m. 'moving in the air', a bird,

gagaṇaga m. 'moving in the sky', a planet,

gagaṇakusuma n. 'flower in the sky' an impossible or fanciful thing,

gagaṇaravinda n. sky-lotus, an impossibility indicating a non-existent thing,

gagaṇatala n. the vault of the sky, firmament,

√*gāh* 354/3 cl 1 A P *gāhate (ti)* to dive into, bathe in, plunge into, penetrate, enter deeply into, to roam, range, rove, to be absorbed in, DP in *viloḍana* shaking, turning, agitating,

gahana 352/1 mfn deep, dense, impenetrable, thicket, hard to be understood, depth, hiding place,

gahvara 352/1m. a cave, cavern, arbour, bower, mfn M. thick, impenetrable, n. a hiding place, thicket, wood,

√*gai* 363/2 cl 1 P A *gāyati (te)* , cl 2 *gāti,* cl 3 P *jigāti* to sing, speak or recite in a singing manner, sing to, praise in song, relate in metrical language, to sing before, to be called, to be sung or praised in song, to be asserted obstinately, DP in *śabda* singing, speaking

√*gaj* 342/1 cl 1P *gajati* to sound, roar, to be drunk or confused, cl 10 P *gajayati* to sound, roar, DP in *śabda* sounding, in *mada* being drunk or confused,

gaja m. elephant

gajayūtha m. herd of elephants,

gajendra 342/2 a princely elephant

√*gal* 1. 350/3 cl 1 P *galati* to drip, ooze, drop. trickle, distil, to vanish, perish, pass away, to fuse, liquefy, dissolve, melt, A. (*te*) to flow, DP in *sravaṇa* flowing
2. cl 1 P *galati* to eat, swallow, DP in *adana* swallowing, *āsvādana* tasting

gala m. throat, neck, a reed, a rope,

galana mfn dropping, flowing, trickling,

galanīya mfn fusible, soluble,

√*galbh* 351/1 cl 1 A *galbhate* to be bold or confident, DP in *dhārṣṭya* being bold, confident, arrogant,

√*galh* 351/1 =√*garh* to blame, DP in *kutsā* contempt, reproach,

gāli f. verbal abuse,

galita 350/3 lost, perished, melted, dissolved, 2. swallowed,

√*gam* 347/1 Ved. cl 1 P *gamati*, cl 2 P *gamanti*, cl 3 P *jaganti*, Ved. and Class. cl 1 P A *gacchanti*, to go to or towards, approach, to go or pass (as time e.g. *kāle gacchati* time going on, in the course of time), to fall to the share of, to go against with hostile intentions, to decease, die, to approach carnally, have sexual intercourse with, to go to any state or condition, undergo, partake of, participate in, receive, obtain, (*manasā* √*gam* to go with the mind, observe, perceive,) to observe, understand, caus. *gamayati* spend, pass (time), DP in *gati* going

gām the earth, the planets, cow,

gama ifc. mfn going, riding on (comp.), m. course, going, march, decampment, going away from, intercourse with a woman (in comp.), removal (in math. as of fractions), a road, superficiality, a similar reading in two texts, hasty perusal, a game played with dice and men, 348/1

gamaka mfn causing to understand, making clear or intelligible, explanatory, leading to clearness or conviction, -*tā* f. convincingness,

gamana 348/1 n. going, moving, going to or approaching, undergoing, attaining, manner of going, going away, departure, setting out (for war or an attack), a going (journey),

gamanakriyā f. action of going,

gamas you should undergo, partake of

gambhīra mfn deep (voice, character, navel), dignified, grave, m. the lemon tree, a lotus, a hiccup,

gāmbhīrya 354/1 mfn being in the depths, n. deepness, depth, depth or profundity of character, depth of meaning, generosity, calmness, (N) 'the contents of the instruction are profound', i.e. not easily understood, gravity of demeanour,

gāmin 353/3 mfn. going anywhere, going or moving on or in or towards or in any particular manner

gamiṣyati will go 1/s/fut/*gam*

gamya mfn to be gone, to be gone to, approachable, accessible, passable, attainable, -*tā* f. accessibility, perceptibility, intelligibleness, clearness, being intended or meant,

gamyate it is attained, reached, gone to 1/s/pres/pass √*gam*

√*gaṇ* 343/1 cl 10 P A *gaṇayati (te)* to count, number, enumerate, sum up, add up, reckon, take into account, to think worth, value, to consider, regard as, to enumerate among, ascribe, attribute to, to attend to, take notice of, to imagine, to count one's number (said of a flock or troop), DP in *saṅkhyāna* counting, numbering, enumerating

gaṇa m. a group, troop (of Maruts), crowd (of friends), host (of stars), flock (of birds), tribe list, the verb root classifications

gāna n. song, singing, a sound,

gaṇācāra (G)working for the uplift of all,

gaṇācārya m. teacher of the people, (Buddhist),

gaṇadhara a primary disciple of a Tirthankara (Jaina),

gānadhārī wife of *Dhṛtarāṣṭra*

gaṇanā f. a numbering, calculation, counting, considering, supposing, regarding,

gāṇapatya m. a worshipper of *gaṇeśa*

√*gaṇḍ* 344/1 cl 1 P *gaṇḍati* to affect the cheek, DP in *vadana-ekedeśa* affecting the cheek,

gaṇḍa m. the cheek, whole side of the face (including the temple), the side, a bubble, boil, pimple, a joint, bone, the bladder, a mark, spot, part of a horses trappings (stud or button fixed on the harness), a rhinoceros,

gaṇḍaka m. rhinoceros,

√*gandh* cl 10 A *gandhayate* to injure, hurt, to move or go, DP in *arddana* tormenting

gandha 345/1 m. smell, odour, fragrance, scent, a fragrant substance, pounded sandal-wood, a sectarial mark on the forehead, myrrh, connection, relationship, perfume,

gandharva m. celestial musician

gāndharva mfn pertaining to a *gandharva* or *gandharva(s),* (with *vivāha*) a marriage by mutual consent,

gandharvanagara n. clouds seen as a castle or city in the sky, any fanciful conception, the world,

gandhatanmātra n. the subtle element of smell,

Gāṇḍīva the name of *Arjunas* bow

gaṅgā f. the Ganges, a goddess, 'one who goes swiftly',

gaṅgādhāra a name of *Śiva* as upholder of *gaṅgā*

gaṇikā f. harlot, whore, coutesan,

gaṇita mfn calculated, n. calculation, arithmetic,

√*gañj* cl 1 P *gañjati* to sound, give out a particular sound, DP in *śabda* sounding,

gañja m. disrespect,
m.n. a treasury, jewel room,
m.f. a mine
f. a tavern, drinking vessel, hemp, a hut, hovel, abode of low people,

gantā going to, goes, will go, he will go,

gantāsi thou shalt go 2/s/peri/fut/act

gantavya to be attained, to be gone, to be approached, be accomplished gerundive √*gam*

garala m. n. poison, the venom of a snake, a bundle of grass or hay, a measure (in general),

√*garb* 349/2 cl 1 P *garbati* to go or move, DP in *gati* going,

garbha 349/2 m. the womb, the inside, middle, sleeping chamber, foetus, seed, conception? ifc. f. (*ā*) containing, filled with,

gārbha mfn relating to the embryo or gestation, born from a womb, ifc. containing,

garbhagṛha the central shrine of a temple, inner apartment, sleeping room,

garbhastha mfn being in the womb, unborn

garbhavant adj.(f. only) pregnant,

gārbhika mfn relating to the womb, pre-natal,

garbhin i

garbhodaka the primeval waters,

√*gard* 349/2 cl 1 P *gardati* to shout, give shouts of joy, to emit any sound, cl 10 *gardayati* DP in *śabda* sounding,

gardabha m. donkey, ass, *(ī)* f. she-ass,

gārddhya 354/2 desire, greediness

Gārgī a woman philospher (Bṛhad. Up.)

√*garh* 350/2 cl 1.10. P A *garhati, garhate, garhayati, garhayate*, to lodge a complaint before someone, to accuse, charge with, reproach, blame, censure, anyone or anything, DP in *kutsā* reproach, in *vinindana* blaming, reproaching,

gārhapatya mfn pertaining to the householder, n. being head of the house, the housekeeping, the householder's ancestral fire,

gārhasthya n. being a householder,

garimā f. heaviness, weight, importance, dignity, venerableness, a venerable person, the power to make oneself heavier,

gariman m. weight, heaviness, dignity,

garīyas 348/3 mfn. (comparative), heavier, extremely heavy, greater than, more precious or valuable, very honourable, dearer than

garīyān m. glorious, worshipable, more great, more glorious, more heavy,

√*garj* 349/1 cl 1 P *garjati* to emit a full or deep sound, sound as distant thunder, roar, thunder, growl, DP in *śabda* sounding, roaring, making noise

garjana n. roar, rumbling of clouds, passion, battle, excessive indignation, reproach,

garta m. a high seat, throne, the seat of a war-chariot, a chariot, a table for dice, 'earth-cut' ditch, hole, cave, the hollow of the loins,

garuḍa m. a mythical bird, 'devourer', the vehicle of Viṣṇu,
garut n. the wing of a bird, ,
garutmant or *garutmat* mfn winged, m. a bird, *garuḍa,*
√*garv* 350/2 cl 1 P, *garvati* cl 10 A, *garvayate* to be or become proud or haughty, DP in *darpa* being proud, boasting, in *māna* being proud,
garva 350/2 m. pride, arrogance
garvita mfn proud
gata 347/1 mfn gone, gone to any state or condition, departed, departed from the world, deceased, dead, past (time), gone by, disappeared (often in comp.) come, come forth from,arrived at, being in, attained, restored, n. going, motion, manner of going, having disappeared, the place where anyone has gone, anything past or done, event, diffusion, extension, celebration, manner, concerning,
gatāgatam going and coming, what comes and goes, going to and fro, growth and decline, to enter into a negotiation or treaty (with *kṛ*),
gatāgati f, dying and being born again, going and coming,
gatakalmaṣa mfn whose sins are gone,
gatakleśa *gata* 347/1 gone, gone away. *kleśa* 324/1 pain, affliction, free from pain
gatānugati f. going after he who has gone before, following in the old ruts,
gatānugatika addicted to following old ways or ruts, (L)
gataprāṇa mfn whose breath is gone, dead,
gatarasa 347/2 mfn having lost its flavour or sap, withered, tasteless,
gatasaṁkalpa mfn whose purpose or resolution is for the moment gone, purposeless,
gatasandeha 347/2 2/s free from doubt
gatāsu mfn whose life is gone,
gatavyatha free from concern, 'whose anxiety is gone'
gāthā f. a pot, a verse,
gati 347/3 f. going, arriving at, gait, obtaining, passage, progress, way, path, road , destination, condition, state, motion in general, manner or power of going, means, resource, the way or course esp. of the soul during transmigration, (in gram.) a term for prepositions and some other adverbial prefixes e.g. *alam* when immediately connected with the tenses of a verb or with verbal derivatives
gati-cāturya dextrous movement, an amiable condition,
gati-kauṭilya crooked movement, a false or dishonest state
gati-nivṛtti return to rest or stillness, cessation of movement, end of activity
gatipratighāta prevention of movement, resistance to movement
gati-vaikalya defective movement, weak movement
gātra 352/1 n. instrument of moving, a limb or member of the body
gātraprakṣaraṇa oozing from a member of the body,
gātravicūrṇana wounding,
gātravigharṣaṇa rubbing the limbs
gātravikṣepa dancing
gātravināma deformity
gātu m. motion, movement, course, progress, refuge, abiding-place,
gatvā ind. having gone
gatyākṣepa - *gati* + *ākṣepa* 128/3 drawing together, convulsion, applying, laying, giving up, removing, charming, reviling, abuse
gatyartha for the purpose of movement, object of movement, meaning to go,
gauḥ cow,
gauṇa mfn indirect, indirect meaning, secondary, relating to a quality, having qualities, attributive, subordinate, unessential, the less immediate object of an action, metaphorical, figurative,

gauṇabhakti devotion through rituals as a preliminary step on the path of love,
gauṇatva n. the state of being subordinate or secondary,
gauṇavṛtti a figurative or secondary way of expression as in 'he is a lion' – he is not a lion but may be as brave as a lion,
gauṇika mfn standing in relation to the three guṇa's
gauṇya m. merit, n. subordination, being secondary,
gaura mfn white, pale, shining, brilliant, clean, beautiful,
gaurakṣya n. cattle-tending
gaurava n. admiration, dignity, m. saffron, pride, respectability, importance, gravity, weight, heaviness, significance,
gaurī a name of *Pārvati,*
gautama patronymic from Gotama, name of Buddha,
gava bull, cow, cattle, (equiv. of *go* in compounds),
gavala m. the wild buffalo, n. buffalo horn,
gavaya m. the Gayal, a species of ox,
gavyūti f. pasture-land, territory, abiding-place,
gāyati sings
gāyatrī a sacred text,
gāyatrīvidyā meditation on *gāyatrī* as Brahman,
gaurakṣya cattle-tending
√*gaveṣ* 351/2 cl 1 A *gaveṣate* to seek, search or inquire for,
cl 10 *gaveṣayati* , DP in *mārgaṇa* seeking, searching
geha 363/2 n. a house, dwelling, habitation, n.du. 'the 2 habitations' (house and body), a kind of ant, family life,
√*gep* 363/2 = √*kep* cl 1 A *gepate* to go, move, DP in *kampana* trembling, moving, in *sevana* serving,
√*geṣ* 363/2 cl 1 A *geṣate* to seek, search, DP in *anvicchā* seeking, searching, investigating,
gha ind. (used to lay stress on a word), at least, surely, verily, indeed, especially, the vowel is often lengthened and it is usually preceded by other particles, or by a pronoun or preposition,
mfn striking, killing,
f. a stroke,
m. a rattling, gurgling or tinkling sound, a bell, a tinkling ornament worn by women round the waist,
√*ghaggh* 375/1 cl 1 P *ghagghati* and *ghaghati* to laugh,
√*ghagh* see *ghaggh* DP in *hasana* laughing
ghana 376/1 mfn a striker, killer, destroyer, compact, solid, material firm, hard, dark, deep (sound or colour), complete, all, auspicious, fortunate,
m. cloud, an iron club, mace
any compact mass or substance,
a collection, multitude, mass, quantity, talc, vulgar people, slaying,phlegm, the body, cymbal, bell, gong, iron, tin,
ifc. mere, nothing but, closely,
ghanaprajña undifferentiated consciousness,
ghanatva n. compactness, firmness, thickness, solidity
√*ghaṇṭ* 375/3 cl 1 .10. P *ghaṇṭati, ghaṇṭayati* to speak or to shine, DP in *bhāṣā* speech, language,
ghaṇṭā f. a bell or gong,
gharma m. warmth, heat, sunshine
√*ghas* not used in present cl1 *ghasati* to consume or devour, eat, DP in *adana* eating
ghāsa m. food, meadow or pasture grass, gradually,
√*ghaṭ* 375/1 cl 1 A P *ghaṭate (ti)* to be intently occupied about, be busy with, strive or endeavour after, exert oneself for, to reach, come to, to fall to the share of, to take effect, answer, to happen, take place, be possible, suit, to be in connection or united with,
caus. P A *ghaṭayati (te)* to join together, connect, bring together, unite, to shut, put or place or lay on,

to bring near, procure, to effect, accomplish, produce, make, form, fashion, to do a service, to impel, to exert oneself, (for √*ghaṭṭ* caus.) to rub, graze, touch, move, agitate, DP in *ceṣṭā* (cl 1) being busy with, stirring after, in *saṅghāta* (cl 10) collecting together, or in *hanti* injuring, killing, in *bhāṣā* speech, language

ghaṭa 375/1 mfn intently occupied or busy with, m. a jar, pitcher, jug, the sign Aquarius, a measure, the head, a part of a column, a border, f. effort, endeavour, an assembly, a number, collection, assemblage, a troop of elephants (for martial purposes), justification, a kind of drum, a sweet citron, a water jar,

ghāta mfn killing, m. a blow, bruise, slaying, killing, injuring, the product (as in multiplication),

ghatābhāva non-existence of a pot

ghātaka mfn deadly, murderer, killer destroying, executioner,

ghātana 377/2 mfn killing, n slaying, killing, slaughter, immolating

ghātayati he causes to slay, 1/s/caus/act √*han*

ghaṭākāśa *ghaṭa* + *ākāśa* space in a jar or jug

√*ghaṭṭ* 375/3 cl 1 A *ghaṭṭate* cl 10 P *ghaṭṭayati* to rub the hands over, touch, shake, cause to move, stir round, have a bad effect or influence on, to hurt with words, speak of malignantly, DP in *calana* shaking, moving,

√*ghiṇṇ* 377/2 cl 1 A *ghiṇṇate* to take, grasp, DP in *grahaṇa* taking, receiving

ghna 379/3 mfn killing, killer, murderer, striking, removing, removing, multiplied by, ifc. striking with, n. killing, they are striking

ghnata kill, those who are killing, those who are about to kill, pr.part √*han*

ghnya mfn to be slain,

ghora mfn dreadful, horrible, terrible

ghoracakṣus mfn having an evil eye,

ghorākṛti mfn having an awful form,

ghoravāśita a terrible roaring noise

ghoṣa 378/1 voiced, m a voiced sound is one in which the vocal chords vibrate e.g. zzzzzz can be felt vibrating when a finger is placed against the throat but the sound ssssssss can not. voiced consonants g,gh,j,jh,ḍ,ḍh,d,dh,b,bh,ṅ,ñ,n,m,y,r,l, v,h, (all vowels are voiced), the vowels and *anusvara*

ghoṣaṇā f. slogan, proclamation, declaring,

√*ghṛ* 378/2 cl 3 *P jigharti* , cl 1 *gharati* to besprinkle, wet, moisten, DP in *secana* sprinkling, 2. cl 3 P *jigharti* to shine, burn DP in *kṣaraṇa* sprinkling or *dīpti* shining, in *prasravaṇa* sprinkling over, wetting, moistening (cl 10)

√*ghrā* 379/3 irregular. Cl 1 P Aor cl 3 P *jighrati* (*te*) cl 2 P *ghrāti* to smell, perceive odour, to perceive, to smell at, snuffle at, to kill, DP in *gandha-upādāna* smelling, taking scent, kissing

ghrāṇa 379/3 mfn smelled, smelling, sense of smell, m.n. smelling, smell, sense of smell, odour, n. the nose, nose of a bull,

ghrātā f. one who smells something, having scented, smelled at,

√*ghṛṇ* see 2. *ghṛ* DP in *dīpti* shining, burning

ghṛṇā f. a warm feeling towards others, compassion, tenderness, aversion, contempt,

√*ghṛṇṇ* 379/1 cl 1 A *ghṛṇṇate* = √*ghiṇṇ* to take, grasp, DP in *grahaṇa* taking, receiving,

√*ghṛṣ* 379/2 cl 1 P *gharṣati* to rub, brush, polish, grind, crush, pound, A. to rub oneself, DP in *saṅgharṣa* rubbing

ghṛta mfn sprinkled, n. butter – clarified and then hardened, (anglo-indian *ghee*)

ghṛtapaśu m. sacrificial beast made of *ghee*
ghṛtaścut mfn dripping with *ghee*
√*ghu* 377/2 cl 1 A *ghavate* to utter or produce a peculiar sound, DP in *śabda* sounding, making an indistinct sound,
m. a kind of sound
√*ghuṁṣ* to diffuse lustre, DP in *kānti-karaṇa* causing beauty, beautifying
√*ghuṇ* 377/3 cl 6 P *ghuṇati* to go or move about, cl 1 A *ghoṇate*, DP in *bhramaṇa* wandering or roaming about, unsteadiness, turning round, falling into error
√*ghuṇṇ* 377/3 cl 1 A *ghuṇṇate* = √*ghiṇṇ* DP in *grahaṇa* taking, receiving
√*ghur* 377/3 cl 6 P *ghurati* to cry frightfully, frighten with cries, DP in *bhīma* being frightful or terrible, or *śabda* sounding, crying in distress,
√*ghūr* 378/2 cl 4 A *ghūryate* to hurt, injure, kill, to become old, decay, DP in *hiṁsā* hurting, killing, in *vyohā* growing old,
√*ghūrṇ* 378/2 cl 1 P A *ghūrṇati (te*) to move to and fro, shake, be agitated, roll about, DP in *bhramaṇa* rolling, staggering
√*ghuṣ* 378/1 cl 1 P A *ghoṣati (te),* P to cry or proclaim aloud, call out, announce publicly, declare, A. to sound DP in *viśabdana* = *prat-jñāna* admission, assertion, assent, in *aviśabdana* non-assent, non-assertion
2. cl 1 P to kill
√*ghuṭ* 377/3 cl 6 P *ghuṭati* to strike again, resist, oppose, to protect, cl 1 A *ghoṭate* to turn, to barter, exchange
ghuṇī mfn worm-eaten,
gir mfn addressing, invoking, praising, f. invocation, addressing with praise, praise, verse, song, speech, speaking, language, voice, words,
gira 355/1 ifc. speech, speaking, voice, also mfn
giri 355/2 m. a mountain, hill, rock
girijā f. 'daughter of the mountain' (*Himavat)*, another name for *Pārvatī* or *Dūrga,* the wife of *Ṣiva*
gīta 356/1 mfn. sung, chanted, praised in songs, n. singing, song, (*ā*) f. a song, sacred song or poem
√*glah* 374/2 cl 1 A *glahate* to gamble, play with anyone (at dice), win by gambling, to take, receive, DP in *grahaṇa* taking
√*glai* 374/3 cl 1 P A *glāyati (te)* cl 2 P *glāti* to feel aversion or dislike, be averse or reluctant or unwilling or disinclined to do anything, to be languid or weary, feel tired or be exhausted, fade away, faint, to be hard upon anyone, caus. *glāpayati* A (*te)* to exhaust, tire, be hard upon, injure, cause to faint or perish, (with *manas*) to make desponding, DP in *harṣa-kṣaya* being despondent, being dejected in spirit
glāna feeling aversion or dislike, wearied, exhausted, sick, exhausted,
n. exhaustion, sickness,
glāni 374/3 f. exhaustion, languor, lassitude, depression, sickness,
√*glas* 374/2 cl 1 A *glasate* to eat, DP in *adana* swallowing, eating up, consuming
glau m. a round lump, wen-like, lump, the moon, camphor, the earth,
f. a ball or globe,
√*glep* cl 1 A *glepate* to be poor or miserable, t o shake, tremble, to move, DP in *gainya* being poor, in *kampana* shaking
glepana shaking, trembling, moving, poor
√*gleṣ* 374/3 cl 1 A *gleṣate* to seek, investigate, DP in *anvicchā* seeking, stealing, investigating
√*glev* 374/3 cl 1 A *glevate* to serve, worship, DP in *sevana* serving, worshipping
√*gluc* 374/3 cl 1 P *glocati* to steal, rob, go, move, DP in *steya-karaṇa* stealing

√*gluñc* 374/3 cl 1 P *gluñcati* to go, move, DP in *gati,* going

go f. *gau* m. a bull or cow, the sun, moon, a singer, praiser, a 'goer' horse, an organ of sense, water, the eye, a billion, the sky, the thunderbolt, 2. flesh, 3. the earth,

gocara 364/1 m. pasture ground for cattle, range, field for action, offering range or field or scope for action, domain, place,
mfn being within the range of, attainable for, perceptible, having (or used in) the meaning of, a place where birds are fed,

goghna mfn cattle killing, m. cowslayer, one for whom a cow is killed (a guest),

gokarṇa mfn cow-eared,
m. a cow's ear, a deer, mule, the span from thumb-tip to that of the ring-finger, a place of pilgrimage sacred to Śiva, (Malabar coast)

gokula n. a herd of cows,

gola m. a globe or ball, myrrh, a widow's bastard, conjunction of all the planets in one sign,

√*gomaya* 366/1 Nom P *gomayati* to smear with cow dung, DP in *upalepana* smearing with cow dung

gomaya mfn bovine, consisting of cattle, n. cowdung, dung in general,

gomukha m. a trumpet, a crocodile,

gonaya m. cowherd,

gopa cow-herd, keeper in general,

gopā m. cow-keeper, keeper in general, protector, (*ās*) a female guardian,

gopālaḥ cowherd, master of the cows,

gopana 368/2 guarding, protecting, preserving, hiding, concealment, abuse, hurry, alarm, light, lustre

gopati lord of cattle, lord in general,

gopī f. milk-maid,

goptā m.defender, protector

goptṛ m. a protector, guardian,

gopura n. a monumental tower, town-gate,

gorakṣaka m. cattle-keeper, cow-herd,

goṣakhi mfn having cattle as companions, rich in cattle,

√*goṣṭha* 367/2 Nom P *goṣṭhate* to assemble, collect, DP in *saṅghāta* close union or combination, collection

goṣṭha m. cow-stall, byre, meeting-place, water vessel, refuge of men (Śiva), (*ī*) f. an assembly, meeting, society, family connections, partnership, fellowship, conversation, dialogue,

gotama m. a vedic seer,

gotra n. 1. cow-stall, cattle-pen, 2. poss. pen of cattle, 3. group esp. family, 4. family name, lineage,

gotraja 364/3 mfn born in the family, m. a relative,

gotva having a cow-like nature,

govindaḥ Govinda, the Lord, grace, love, attachment, cow-finder, cow-master,

goyukta mfn yoked with cattle, (with *cakra)* wagon drawn by cattle,

√*gṛ* 361/2 cl 1 P *garati* to sprinkle, moisten, DP in *secana* sprinkling

√*gṝ* 363/1 cl 9 P A *gṛṇāti gṛṇīte* to call, call out to, invoke, to announce, proclaim, mention with praise, praise, extol, pronounce, recite, to relate, teach in verses, DP in *śabda* sounding, calling out, proclaiming
cl 6 P A *girati (te)* to swallow, devour, emit or eject from the mouth, DP in *nigaraṇa* swallowing,
cl 10 A *gārayate* to know, make known, teach, DP in *vijñāna* making known, reading, relating

grābha mfn grasping, grasper, taking possession of,

√*grah* 371/2/3 372/1 or *grabh* cl 9 P *gṛbhṇāti* or *gṛhṇāti* A *gṛhṇīte* to seize, take by the hand, grasp, lay hold of, take by the hand in marriage ceremony, marry, to arrest, stop, take captive, capture, imprison, take possession of, gain over, captivate, seize, overpower, eclipse, abstract, take away (by robbery), lay the hand on, claim, gain, win, obtain, receive, accept, keep, acquire by purchase, choose, choose anyone (as a wife), draw water, pluck, pick, collect a store of anything, use, put on (clothes), assume (a shape), place upon, include, undertake, undergo, receive hospitably, take back (a divorced wife), take into the mouth, mention, name, perceive, observe, recognise, cognise, receive into the mind, apprehend, understand, learn, admit, approve, obey, follow, to take for, consider as, DP in *upādāna* seizing, perceiving, learning, acquiring, accepting allowing,

graha 372/1 mfn seizing, taking, grip, grasp, perceiving, recognising, accepting, m. seizure (with a claw), bite, a planet (as affecting men's destinies), a crocodile, anything seized, 'booty', spoil, imprisoning, imprisonment, seizure, eclipse, stealing, robbing, effort,

grāha 372/3 mfn seizing, receiving, holding, catching, m. any large marine animal, conception, notion of, a prisoner, the handle of a sword, seizure, grasping, morbid affection, disease,

grāhaka 372/3 (in phil.) mfn the subject (grasper), that which seizes or perceives, one who seizes, one who receives or accepts, a puchaser, containing, including, perceiving, perceiver, captivating, persuading; that which seizes or perceives (sense organ), m. a hawk, falcon,

grahaṇa 372/2 mfn seizing, holding, taking, gaining, obtaining, n. the hand, an organ of sense, a prisoner, a word mentioned or employed, seizing, holding, taking by the hand, marrying, taking captive, seizure, demoniacal possession, gaining, obtaining, acceptance, reception, eclipse, purchasing, taking or drawing up (fluid), attraction, putting on clothes,

grahītā f. a receiver, recipient, one who comprehends,

grahītavya mfn to be taken or received, to be taken (a fluid), to be perceived, to be learned, obligation to take or receive,

grāhya G.130 the object of knowledge (graspable),
373/1 mfn to be received or accepted or gained, fit to be received, to be overpowered, to be picked or gathered, to be seized or taken or held, to be captured or imprisoned, to be taken in marriage, to be received in a friendly or hospitable way, to be perceived or recognized or understood, to be understood in a particular sense, meant, to be accepted as a rule or law, to be acknowledged or assented to, to be attended to or obeyed, to be admitted in evidence, to be undertaken or followed (a vow),
n. poison, the objects of sensual perception, perceivable,
(ā) f. archery exercise,

grāhyabhāve in the absence of things to be perceived (Gam.),

grāma 373/1 n. a village, m. an inhabited place, a village, hamlet, the collective inhabitants of a place, community, race, multitude, troop, the old women of a family, a number of tones,

grāmakāma mfn having desire for the village, fond of living in the village,

grāmaṇī m. head-man of a village,

√*grāmaya* 373/3 Nom P *grāmayati* to invite, DP in *āmantraṇa* inviting

√*granth* see √*grath*

grantha 371/1 m. tying, binding, stringing together, a knot, a literary work, a verse or couplet, a book,

granthana tying or connecting together, arranging, composing

granthi 371/1 a knot, tie, knot of a cord, unreal and illusory complexity and ignorance,
granthin mfn having books, bookish, well read, strung together,
√*gras* cl 1 P A *grasati (te)* to seize with the mouth, take into the mouth, swallow, devour, eat, consume, to swallow up, cause to disappear, to eclipse, to swallow or slur over words, pronounce indistinctly, to suppress, stop or neglect (a lawsuit), DP in *adana* swallowing, devouring, eating up, consuming, in *grahaṇa* eating, devouring,
2. mfn swallowing
grāsa mfn swallowing, m. mouthful, food, nourishment, an eclipse,
grasamāna swallowing, devouring pres/part/mid √*gras*
grasiṣṇu 371/2 mfn accustomed to swallow or absorb
√*grath* = *granth*, 370/3 cl 9 P *grathnāti* to fasten, tie or string together, arrange, connect in a regular series, to string words together, compose (a literary work), P *granthati* A. *granthate* to be strung together or composed (a literary work), or cl 1 A *granthate* to be crooked, DP in *sandarbha* writing, composing, in *kautilya* being crooked, being wicked, bending, in *bandhana* fastening, tying
grāvan m. stone, esp. stone for pressing the Soma, a stone or rock, a mountain, a cloud, mfn hard, solid,
√*gṛbh* 361/3 *gṛbhāyati* to grasp, seize, related to √*grah* grasping seizing, *gṛbhayat*, seizing, DP in *grahaṇa* taking
√*gṛdh* cl4 P 361/2 *gṛdhyati* endeavour to gain, covet, desire, A *gṛdhyate* to deceive, cheat, DP in *abhikāṅkṣā* coveting, desiring, being greedy,
gṛdha m.. or *gṛddha* ppp.. coveting, desirous of,
gṛdhra mfn desiring greedily or fervently, m. a vulture
gṛh = *gṛbh* f. grasping, seizing, mfn grasping,
gṛha 361/3m. n. a house, a home, a servant, a family,
gṛha-jana m. family, member of the family,
gṛhamedhin mfn one who performs the domestic sacrifices,householder,
gṛhāṇa just accept, please take now,
gṛhapati m. master of the house,
gṛhapatnī f. mistress of the house,
gṛhāśrama m. house-stage, second stage in a Brahman's life,
gṛhastha mfn abiding in a house, m. householder or Brahman in the second stage of his religious life, f. a housewife, mfn ifc. living or staying in anyone's house,
gṛhiṇī f. mistress of the house, housewife,
gṛhīta mfn grabbed, grasped, taken, held received, accepted, received hospitably, obtained, gained, perceived, understood, 'received completely into one's mind',
gṛhītārtha mfn comprehending the sense or meaning, acquainted,
gṛhītvā ind. having grabbed, taken, grasping, taking up,
gṛhṇāti 371/2 root *grah*, takes, seizes, receives, he accepts
gṛhṇan accepting, pres/act/part √grah 371/3
grīva m. the neck, a corridor, the nape, the neck of a bottle,
√*gṝ* 363/1 to call, invoke, praise, extol, recite
gṛdhra mfn greedy, m. vulture,
gṛdhrakūṭa m. vulture-peak, a mountain in Magadha,
grīṣma m. summer,
grīva 374/1 m. the neck, nape of the neck, f. (*ā*)
√*gṛj* 361/2 = √*gurj* cl 1 *garjati* or *gṛñjati* to sound, roar, DP in *śabda* roaring, sounding,
gṛṇanti they extol 1/pl/pres/act
√*gṛñj* see √*gṛj* above,
gṛtsa mfn clever, wise, dextrous
√*gruc* 374/2 cl 1 P *grocati* to steal, to go, DP in *steya-karaṇa* stealing
√*gu* 356/1 cl 1 A *gavate* to go, 356/2 cl 1 A *gavate* to sound,

cl 6 P *guvati* to void by stool, DP in *śabda* sounding, in *avyaktaśabda* speaking indistinctly, in *purīṣotsarga* evacuating, defecating,
f. cow, n. water, the hair on the body

guccha m. bundle, bunch, a bush, shrub, bunch of flowers, a pearl necklace, a section in a tale,

√*gud* 358/3 cl 1 A *godate* to play, sport, DP in *krīḍā* playing

√*guò* 356/3 cl 6 P *guḍati* to guard, preserve, DP in *rakṣā* defending, preserving,

guda n. anus,

guḍa 356/3 m. globe or ball, lumpy sugar, treacle, molasses, an elephant's trappings or armour, a ball to play with

guḍaka m. a ball, molasses,

guḍākeśa O Thick-Haired One *(Arjuna)*

√*gudh* 358/3 cl 4 P *gudhyati* to wrap up, envelope, cover, clothe, cl 9P *gudhnāti* to be angry, cl 1 A *godhate* to play, sport, DP (cl 4) in *pariveṣṭana* wrapping up, covering, enveloping, in (cl 9) *roṣa* being angry,

gūḍha n. deep mystery,

gūḍhapraśna m. enigma

gūḍhavāsanā f. hidden subtle desire,

√*guh* 360/2 cl 1 P A *gūhati (te)* to cover, conceal, hide, keep secret, DP in *samvaraṇa* covering,

guh f. hiding place,

guhā cave, hidden place, ind. in secret, the heart,

guhācara moving in secret i.e.in the heart,

guhya 360/3 mfn to be covered or concealed, or kept secret, secret, genital, m. hypocrisy, a tortoise, (am) ind. secretly, privately, n. a secret, mystery,

guhyaka m. one of a class of demi-gods,

guhyatama most secret (superlative)

√*guj* 356/2 cl 1. 6. P *gojati, gujati* to buzz, hum, DP in *avyaktaśabda* making an indistinct noise, in *śabda* sounding, humming, buzzing,

gulma m. a clump of trees, thicket, a troop or guard of soldiers, a fort, entrenchment, disciplining an army, the spleen,

gulpha m. ankle,

√*gumph* 359/1 cl 6 P *gumphati* to string together, tie or string as a garland, DP in *grantha* tying, binding, stringing together,

guṇa 357/1 m. the attributes of nature (*sattva, rajas* and *tamas*) ,
In Vedānta philosophy, there are three major guṇas that serve as the fundamental operating principles or 'tendencies' of *prakṛti* (universal nature) which are called: *sattva*, *rajas*, and *tamas*. The three primary gunas are generally accepted to be associated with creation (*rajas*), preservation (*sattva*), and destruction (*tamas*). They are the three basic qualities of nature which determine the inherent characteristics of all created things, " the whole creation is in the grip of the *guṇāḥ* and they never stay the same, so they keep on changing all beings and all situations. Everyone, wherever he is placed, whether at level one or even at level nine, is tossed by them. Some are totally affected while others are only outwardly affected. This means that one of the *guṇāḥ* may be predominant now and after a few moments, another, and yet after a few more moments, you may be caught by another *guṇa*. Thus the fluctuation of *guṇāḥ* will keep on forcing changes in all beings and in all situations." HH
a single thread or strand of a cord, string or thread, rope, a garland, a bowstring, chord, a multiplier, coefficient, subdivision, species, kind, a quality, peculiarity, attribute or property or virtue,

an attribute of the 5 elements (each of which has its own peculiar quality or qualities as well as organ of sense; thus 1. ether has *śabda* or sound for its *guṇa* and the ear for its organ; 2. the air has touch and sound for its *guṇāḥ* and the skin for its organ; 3. fire or light has form, touch and sound for its *guṇāḥ,* and the eyes for its organs; 4. water has taste, form, touch and sound for its *guṇāḥ* and the tongue for its organ; 5. earth has smell, taste, form, touch and sound for its *guṇāḥ* and the nose for its organ,

the first gradation in the strengthening of a vowel (by adding one measure of '*a*' ; the second (adding a second measure of '*a*') is called *vṛddhi,*

m. a single thread or strand of a cord or twine, string or thread, rope,

guṇabhedata 357/2 ind. according to the difference of quality, i.e. according to the *guṇā* relationships at the time

guṇāḍhya 'rich in virtues or excellences',

guṇāḥ the 3 constituents of the universe,

guṇamaya mfn 3 constituent properties of *prkṛti,* full of qualities or attributes,

guṇamayī f. made or produced by the *guṇa,* a product of the *guṇāḥ,*

guṇānvita mfn endowed with excellence,

guṇaśālin mfn possessing virtues, excellent,

guṇasamya where the *guṇāḥ* are in equilibrium – the Absolute,

guṇāśraya m. one endowed with virtues, very virtuous man, abode of qualities, matter,

guṇātīta mfn freed from or beyond all properties,

guṇavāda – attributive corroborative statement, e.g. "the sun becomes the sacrificial stake", where the statement contradicts experience and is taken to mean "a stake shining like the sun" (Gam.)

guṇavat mfn endowed with excellent qualities, virtuous, excellent,

guṇavant mfn virtuous, excellent,

guṇānvita 358/1 endowed with virtues, excellent, associated with the *guṇā*

guṇātītas g + ppp. *ati* √*ī* going beyond the *guṇāḥ* , transcending the *guṇāḥ*

√*guṇaya* 358/2 Nom P *guṇayati* to multiply, to advise, invite, DP in *āmantraṇa* inviting,

√*guṇḍ* 358/2 cl 10 *guṇḍayati* to cover, conceal, protect, to pound, comminute, DP in *rakṣaṇa* guarding, protecting, or *veṣṭana* covering or *ketana* summons, invitation

guṇī mfn good-natured, posessor of a quality or qualities,

guṇin mfn virtuous, excellent, endowed with good qualities, auspicious (a day), endowed with the good qualities of or contained in... (ifc.), requiring the first gradation (a vowel), possessing qualities- an object or thing or noun or substantive, m. 'furnished with a string', a bow,

√*guñj* 356/2 cl 1 P *guñjati* to buzz, hum, DP in *avyaktaśabda* sounding, humming, buzzing,

√*guṇṭh* 358/2 cl 10 P *guṇṭhayati* to enclose or envelope, surround, cover, DP in *veṣṭana* surrounding, enveloping, covering,

√*gup* 358/3 cl 4 P *gupyati* to become perplexed or confused, to guard, defend, protect, preserve, to hide, conceal, to seek to defend oneself from, be on one's guard, to beware of, shun, avoid, detest, to feel offended or hurt DP (cl4) in *vyākulatva* being confused or disturbed,

in (cl1) *gopana* hiding, in *rakṣaṇa* guarding, protecting,

√*guph* 359/1 cl 6 *guphati* to string together, tie or string as a garland, DP in *grantha* tying, binding, stringing together,

guptaparibhāṣaṇa speaking secretly

gupti f. preserving, protection, guarding, restraint of body, mind and speech, concealing, hiding, keeping secret (ifc.), a means of protection, fortification, rampart, a prison, a place of concealment, a hole in the ground, cellar, a leak in a ship,

√*gur* 359/2 cl 6 *gurate* to raise, lift up, to hurt, to go, to eat, DP in *udyamana* making an effort or exertion

√*gūr* 361/1 see *gur* above DP in *hiṁsā* hurting, *gati* going, DP in *udyamana* making an effort or exertion

√*gurd* 360/1 cl 1 *gurdate* or *gūrdate* to play, sport, jump, cl 10 *gurdayati* or *gūrdayati* to dwell, inhabit, DP (cl 1) in *krīḍā* playing, in (cl 10) *pūrva-niketana* former dwelling place,

guru 359/2 mfn heavy, important,
m. a spiritual parent, teacher, or guide, G133 6. "The root *gu* stands for darkness; *ru* for its removal. The removal of the darkness in the heart is indicated by the word *guru.*" , 'one who is firmly convinced that he is the supreme consciousness, one whose mind is rooted in the highest reality, one who has a pure and tranquil mind, one who has realized identity with Brahman"

gurukṛpā the grace of the teacher

gurūkti words from a *guru*

gurukula n. the house of a guru, a teaching place for guru and students

gurukulavāsa m. living with the guru,

gurūpassati devotion to the guru,

gurutva n. weight, heaviness, greatness, magnitude, respectability, dignity, venerableness, length of a vowel,

√*gurv* 360/1 cl 1 P *gūrvati* to raise, lift up or to make an effort, DP in *udyamana* endeavouring,

ha m. water, a cipher (representing zero), meditation, auspiciousness, sky, heaven, paradise, blood, dying, fear, knowledge, the moon, battle, a horse, pride, a physician, cause, motive, m.f. laughter, n. the supreme spirit, pleasure, delight, a weapon, the sparkling of a gem, calling, mfn mad, drunk,
a particle emphasizing a previous word or simply used as an expletive in poetry, i.e may be meaningless in the verse but used as a metrical filler,
mfn killing, destroying,

ha vai once upon a time, may indicate recalling to mind some well-known fact,

hā 1. expresses astonishment or satisfaction, pain,
2. m. water, the arithmetical figure which expresses zero, meditation, auspiciousness, sky, heaven, paradise, blood, sex, dying, fear, knowledge, the moon, *viṣṇu*, war, battle, a horse, pride, a physician, cause, motive, m.f. laughter, f. coition, , a lute, n. the supreme spirit, pleasure, delight, a weapon, the sparkling of a gem, calling, ind. = *aham*, mfn mad, drunk, cl 3 A *jihīte* to start or spring forward, bound away, give way to, to go or depart, to fall or come into any state, DP in *gati* going
3. cl 3 P *jahāti* cl 1 *jahati* to leave, abandon, desert, quit, forsake, relinquish, to discharge, emit, to put away, take off, remove, lay aside, give up, resign, avoid, shun, abstain or refrain from, disregard, neglect, to lose, be deprived of, to get rid of, escape from, to cause to emit, fart, to be left behind, fall short of, be excluded from, be overtaken by, be deficient, suffer loss or wanting, decrease, wane, decline, come to an end, to weigh less, to be given up or avoided, to be subtracted, to become detached from, fall out (as hair), caus. *hāpayati (te)*, to cause to leave or abandon, to omit, neglect, fall short of, be wanting in, to give up (life), to lose (time), DP in *tyāga* abandoning,
5. mfn. abandoning, deserting, f. abandonment, desertion

hā hā alas! alas!

√*had* 1287/1 cl 1 P A *hadati (te)*, to

evacuate, excrete, DP in *purīṣotsaga* excreting,

haima mfn wintry, caused/produced by snow or ice, covered with snow, golden, consisting of or made from gold, f. yellow jasmine,

haituka 1304/1 mfn having a cause or reason, ifc. caused by or dependent on, founded on some motive, caused, motivated,
m. a reasoner, rationalist, skeptic, heretic, a follower of the *mīmāṁsa* doctrines,

√*hal* 1293/1 1. cl 1 P *halati* to plough, make furrows, DP in *vilekhana* ploughing,

hala m. a plow, the earth, water,

halāhala m.n. a certain deadly poison, a kind of lizard, kind of snake,

√*hamm* 1288/2 cl 1 P *hammati* to go, DP in *gati* going,

haṁsa the one caste in the golden age,
haṁsa 1286/1 a swan or goose, used to represent 'the Universal Soul or supreme Spirit', the soul or spirit, 'I am he', the individual soul,

√*han* 1287/2 cl 2 P *hanti,* A. *hate* cl 1 *hanati, jighnate (ti),* to strike, beat (also a drum), pound, hammer, strike upon, smite, slay, hit, kill, mar, destroy, to put to death, cause to be executed, to strike off, ward off, to hurt, wound (the heart), to obstruct, hinder, repress, give up, abandon (anger, sorrow etc.,), to go, move, caus. *ghātayati* cause to be slain or killed, put to death, punish, to notify a person's death, to mar, destroy, DP in *hiṁsā* killing, or *gati* going,
2. mfn killing, a killer, slayer,

hāna 1296/2 gone or departed, the act of abandoning, relinquishing, giving up

hanana mf a killing, a killer, n. the act of striking or hitting, killing, destroying, removing, dispelling, multiplication,

hāni 1296/2 f. abandonment, relinquishment, decrease, diminution, damage, loss, failure, ruin, deficit, cessation, non-existence,

hānopāya 'means of avoidance', means of avoiding association thus leading to liberation, means of liberation,

hanta 1288/2 ind. an exclamation here, look, see, oh,

hantāra slayer, killer

hantavya gdv to be slain, to be violated, to be refuted,

hanti he slays, he kills, 1/s/pres/indic/act.

hantṛ mfn slayer, destroyer,
m. a measure of food,

hantum to kill, to slay, infin. of √*han* slay

hanu f. jaw, a weapon, death, disease, a prostitute,

hanumān or *hanumat* wisest and most capable of monkeys

hanyamāne in being slain or killed pres/mid/part. 7/s/m

hanyate he is slain, killed 1/s/pres/indic/pass

hanyus they should kill, they may kill, 1/pl/opt/act √*han*

hara mfn (only ifc.) bearing, carrying, bringing, conveying, taking, removing, charming, √*hṛ*

hara 1289/1 m. a name of *śiva,* seizer, destroyer, a stallion, an ass,

hāra mfn bearing carrying, carrying away, stealing, levying, raising (e.g. taxes), ravishing, charming, delightful, m. a garland of pearls, a necklace, taking away, removal, confiscation, forfeiture, waste, loss, war, battle, a carrier, porter, a girl unfit for marriage,f. a pearl, Nom. P. to be like a string of pearls,

haraṇa 1289/1 mfn carrying, holding, containing, taking away, removing, m. 'taker' a hand, an arm,
n. the act of carrying or bringing or fetching, offering, carrying off, robbing, removing, destroying, dividing, division,

haras n. a grasp, grip, esp. the seizing or

devouring, power of fire, flame, fire,
harati seizes, carries away 1/s/pres/act
hari 1.mfn bearing, carrying,
2.mfn brown, tawny, yellow, (esp. horses), m. yellow, reddish-brown, 1289/3 a lion, a horse, steed, the sign of the zodiac Leo, the sun, a ray of light, the moon, a monkey, jackal, parrot, peacock, the wind, a name used for many gods, the Lord, 'who destroys the evil deeds of those who take refuge in him', a name of *Nārāyaṇa* or *Kṛṣṇa*
hari 1289/3 1/s/m the Lord, a name of – *Vāyu, Indra, Viṣnu- Kṛṣṇa*
hārin taking, carrying, carrying away, stealing, robbing, taking to one's self, surpassing, exceeding, ravishing, captivating, having or wearing a garland of pearls,
hariṇa mfn yellowish, greenish, a deer, antelope, the sun, 'full of rays' (Gam.),
harita mfn green, pale yellow, pale
haritabhāva in becoming pale
harivant mfn having fallow steeds, lord of the coursers, i.e. Indra,
harmya n. a strong building, dwelling, stronghold, prison, a fiery pit, place of torment, region of darkness, mfn living in houses,
harṣa 1292/2 m. bristling, erection, joy, pleasure, excitement, happiness, sexual excitement, lust, desire,
harṣa kṣaya loss of enjoyment, weariness
hartṛ m. 'one who takes away' a robber, thief,
√*hary* 1292/2 cl 1 P *haryati (te),* to like, delight in, be fond of, or pleased with, yearn after, long for. to go, to threaten, DP in *gati* going or *kānti* delighting,
hārya to be taken away or stolen,
√*has* 1294/2 cl 1 P *hasati (te*), to laugh, smile, laugh at, to deride, mock, ridicule, to surpass, excel, to expand, open (as a blossom), caus. *hāsayati* to cause to laugh, DP in *hasana* laughing,
2. ind. an exclamation of laughter or loud merriment,
hāsa m. laughter, laughing, mirth, a jest, joke, fun, dazzling whiteness, pride, arrogance,
hasana 1294/2 mfn laughing, jesting or sporting with, f. a jest, encouraging shout, next, n. a laugh,
hasati laughs
hāsin mfn laughing, dazzlingly white, brilliant or adorned with,
hasta m. hand, an elephant's trunk, the fore-arm, position of the arm, hand-writing,
hastagrābha mfn grasping the hand,
hastagṛhya taking by the hand, having taken by the hand,
hastin 'possessing a hand', *hastinaḥ* m. elephant, *hastāt* 5/s/m from the hand, from the elephant,
hastināpura a town on the Ganges, home of the Kurus, Elephant City,
hastirāja m. elephant- king, leader of a herd,
hastisnāna n. ablution of an elephant,
hāsya to be laughed at, (as) m. laughter, ridicule, fun, amusement,
√*haṭ* 1287/1 cl 1 P *haṭati* to shine, be bright, DP in *śabda saṅghāta dīpti* sounding, heaping or collecting together, shining, being bright,
hata slain, killed ppp. √*han* 1/s *hatam* n. *hatā* f. killed
hataka ifc. cursed, mfn struck, hit, wretched
hāṭaka n. gold,
√*haṭh* 1287/1 cl 1 P *haṭhati* to leap, jump, be wicked, to treat with violence, oppress, to bind to a post, DP in *pluti* leaping, *śaṭhatva* being wicked, *balātkāra* treating with violence, oppressing,
haṭhayoga 1287/1 a kind of forced yoga, 'in which the physical activity of control of body and breath predominates'

hātum 1296/2 infin.to relinquish, give up, to renounce,

hatvā having killed

hatya n. slaying,

hava m. an oblation, burnt offering, sacrifice, call, invocation, direction, order, command, mfn calling,

havanī f. sacrificial ladle,

havis n. an oblation or burnt offering, sacrificial gift or food, water, fire,

haviṣmant mfn having an oblation, m. offerer,

havya 1294/1 1. n, anything to be offered as an oblation, sacrificial gift or food, gdv. to be invoked,

havyavah m. bearing the oblation

havyavaha fire,

havyavāhana mfn fire

√*hay* 1288/2 cl 1 P *hayati* to go, move, to be weary, to worship, or to sound, DP in *gati* going,

haya 1288/2 m. a horse, a yak, *hayaiḥ*, 3/pl/m by/with horses

he ind. O used as in O King

√*heḍ* (or *heḷ*), 1303/3 cl 1 A *heḍate, heḷate, helate,* to be or make angry or hostile, to act or treat, carelessly or frivolously, cl 1 P *heḍati* to surround, clothe, attire, caus. *heḍayati*, DP in *veṣṭana* (cl 1) surrounding, in *anādara* disregarding,

helā 1305/2 f. sport, play, disrespect, contempt, L. carelessness, levity, moonlight,

hema or *heman* n. gold,

hemanta m. winter, the cold season,

√*hep* DP in *gati* going

√*heṣ* 1305/ 2 cl 1 A *heṣate (ti),* to neigh, whinny, DP in *avyakta śabda* neighing

hetavaḥ causes, 1/pl/m

√*heṭh* 1303/3 also written *heṭ, heḍh*, cl 1 P A *heṭhati (te)* to be wicked, vex, harass, hurt, injure, cl 9P *heṭhṇāti* see *heḍh*, caus. heṭhayati see vi √*heṭh,* DP in *vibādhā* (cl1) causing pain to, in *bhūta-prādurbhāva* (cl9) being born,

heto m. for, for the sake of,

hetu 1303/3 m. impulse, reason for, motive, the cause, by reason of, (6th) *hetoḥ* for, for the sake of, a logical reason or argument or deduction, the reason for an inference,

hetunā by/with reason, from reason 3/s/m

hetupaṇāyā f. application of reason,

hetuphalayoḥ of cause and effect,

hetuśāstra n. reason-book, rationalist work, dialectics,

hetvābhāsa m. fallacious semblance of an argument, fallacious inference or reason,

heya 1297/1mfn to be left or abandoned, rejected, 1296/1 to be gone, rejectable,

√*hi* 1297/2 cl 5 P *hinoti, hinute, hinvati, (te),* to send forth, set in motion, impel, urge on, hasten on, to stimulate or incite to, assist or help to, discharge, hurl, cast, convey, bring, procure, forsake, abandon, get rid of, *hinvati* to gladden, delight, caus. *hayuyati*, DP in *gati* going, or *vṛddhi* promoting,

hi 1297/3 ind. for, because, on account of, of course, truly, indeed, since, (enclitic),

√*hikk* cl 1 P A *hikkati (te),* to hiccup, sob, caus. P. *hikkayati* to cause to hiccup, A. *hikkayate* to injure, kill, DP in *avyakta śabda* hiccuping,

√*hil* 1300/3 cl 6 P *hilati*, to sport amorously, dally, be wanton, express amorous inclination, DP in *bhāva- karaṇa* sporting amorously,

hima m. snow, the cold, winter, the sandal tree, the moon, camphor, n. frost, hoar-frost, snow, tin, a pearl, fresh butter, a lotus, mfn cold, cool, f. cold season, winter,

himādri m. Himalaya mountain,

himāga m. Himalaya, snow-mountain,

himāla m. Himalaya mountain,

himālaya 1299/2 abode of snow,

possessing snow, snowy,
himapāta m. snowfall,
himavat M. the *himālaya* personified as father of *Pārvatī* (*Śiva*'s wife also called *Girijā* 'daughter of the mountain') and *Gaṅgā*, the Ganges river,
√*hiṁs* 1297/3 cl 1.7.P *hiṁsati hinasti,* also A. *hiṁsate, hiṁste* to injure, harm, wound, kill, destroy, caus. or cl 10 P *hiṁsayati* to injure, harm, kill, slay, DP in *hiṁsā* injuring, killing, 2. mfn injuring, striking,
hiṁsā see 1297/3 mfn injuring, injurious, mischievous, hostile, f injury, harm, hurt, wrong (3kinds – mentally bearing malice, verbal abusive language, personal acts of violence), desire to hurt,
hiṁsana 1297/3 m. an enemy, n. the act of hurting, injuring, killing, slaying
hiṁsātmaka mfn cruel by nature, violent natured, intent on doing harm,
hiṁsra mfn harmful, harming, m. a savage or cruel man, a savage animal, beast of prey,
hīna 1296/2 mfn abandoned, left forsaken, devoid of, free from, left behind, excluded or shut out from, lower or weaker than, inferior to, left out, omitted, deficient, defective, incomplete, low, vile, bad, deprived of, poor, little, m. a faulty or defective witness, subtraction, (*am*) n. deficiency, want, absence
hīnā f. a female mouse, ,
hinasti 1297/3 he/she injures, wounds, kills, destroys 1/s/pres/indic/act.
hīnayāna the 'small or lesser vehicle' referring perhaps condescendingly to *theravāda* (classical) buddhist schools as opposed to *mahāyāna* buddhism, *theravāda* is said to be aimed at personal salvation rather than the more universal approach of transformation of all, *theravāda* is earlier than *mahāyāna* which arose in early christian times,
√*hiṇḍ* 1298/2 cl 1 A *hiṇḍate* to go, move, wander or roam about, to disregard, slight, DP in *gati* going, or *anādara* disregarding, slighting,
√*hinv* 1298/3 see √1. *hi,* DP in *prīṇanā* being glad, gladdening,
hiraṇmaya 1299/3 mfn. golden, gold-coloured, effulgent,
hiraṇyagarbha '...the seed-form of the creation as the golden egg or womb' HH. 1299/3 a golden egg, in which the Self-existent *Brahma* was born as *Brahmā* the Creator, who is therefore regarded as a manifestation of the Self-existent, possessed of the twofold power of knowledge and action, called Sūtra when conceived of as the principle of action, 'the highest created being through whom the Supreme Being projects the physical universe; cosmic mind,
hiraṇya n. gold, a vessel or ornament made of gold, coined gold or money, a gold piece or coin, a cowry, semen, substance, imperishable matter, a partic. measure, the thorn apple,
√*hiṣk* 1300/3 see *hikk* and *kiṣk,*
√*hiṭ* 1298/2 see *biṭ* , DP in *ākrośa* swearing, shouting, exclaiming,
hita 1298/2 mfn sent, impelled, urged on, going, running, speeding,
2. mfn set, put, placed, planned, arranged, prepared, made ready, beneficial, wholesome, favourable, good (as in diet),
m. a friend, benefactor, pl. veins or arteries,
n. anything useful or suitable or proper, benefit, advantage, profit, service, good, welfare,
the means to the end,
hitā f. a causeway, a pl. noun. of particular veins or arteries. 'a *hitā* nerve constitutes part of the subtle body'. HH . f. a causeway, dike,

hitakāma mfn wishing well to, desirous of benefitting,
hitakāmyā 1298/2 desire for another's welfare
hitecchā f. desire for the welfare of another,
hitopadeśa m. salutary instruction, name of a collection of fables, good advice,
hitvā 1296/2 having left or abandoned, letting alone, slighting, disregarding, excepting, with the exception of,
√*hlād* 1307/3 cl 1 A *hlādate* to be glad or refreshed, rejoice, to sound, shout (for joy), caus. *hlādayati* to refresh, gladden, exhilirate, delight, DP in *avyakta śabda* sounding, shouting, or *sukha* being glad or delighted, rejoicing,
hlādaka mfn cooling, refreshing, gladdening
hlādikāvant mfn rich in cooling, (L)
hlādinī f. name of a mythical river' refreshment, gladness, delight, potential for giving pleasure,
√*hlag* 1307/3 cl 1 A *hlagate* to cover, hide, DP in *saṃvaraṇa* hiding, covering,
√*hlap* 1307/3 cl 10 P *hlāpayati* to speak, DP in *vyaktā-vāc* speaking distinctly
√*hlas* 1307/3 cl 1 P *hlasati* to sound, DP in *śabda* sounding,
√*hmal* 1306/3 cl 1 P *hmalati* to shake, move, DP in *sañcalana* walking, moving about,
√*hnu* 1306/3 cl 2 A *hnute, hnauti, hnavati, (te),* to hide from, to drive or take away, DP in *apanayana* taking away, robbing,
√*hoḍ* 1305/3 cl 1 A *hoḍate* to disregard, disrespect, DP in *gati* going, in *anādara* disrespecting,
ho ho alas ! alas! (stronger than *aho*)
homa m. pouring into the fire, oblation, sacrifice, (older word is *āhuti*),
homi m. fire, clarified butter, water,
homin mfn offering, presenting an oblation of, only ifc.
homīya mfn relating/belonging to or fit or destined for an oblation or sacrifice,
hotādhvaryū m.du. the *hotṛ* and *adhvaryu* priests,
hotṛ m. an offerer of an oblation or burnt offering (with fire), sacrificer, priest esp. a priest who at a sacrifice invokes the gods or recites the Rig-Veda
hotra n. sacrificing, a burnt offering, both the action and the thing offered,
√*hṛ* 1302/1 cl 1 P A *harati (te),* to take, bear, carry in or on, carry, convey, fetch, bring, to offer, present, to take away, carry off, seize, deprive of, steal, rob, to shoot, cut or hew off, sever (the head or a limb), remove, destroy, dispel, frustrate, annihilate, to turn away, avert the face, A. take to oneself, appropriate (legitimately), come into possession of, receive (as an heir), raise (tribute), marry (a girl), to master, overpower, subdue, conquer, win, win over (also by bribing), to outdo, eclipse, surpass, enrapture, charm, fascinate, withhold, withdraw, keep back, retain, to protract, delay, to divide (arithmetically), caus. *hārayati* (te), DP in *haraṇa* (cl1) taking, conveying, in *prasahya-karaṇa* (cl 3) taking by force, cl 9 A *hṛṇīte* to be angry or wroth,
√*hrād* 1307/2 cl 1 A *hrādate* to sound, roar, make a noise, caus. *hrādayati* to cause to sound, to refresh, delight, DP in *avyatkta śabda* sounding, roaring,
hrada m. pool, lake, a ray of light, a ram,
hrāduni f. hailstones, hail, 'rattling',
√*hrag* 1306/3 cl 1 P *hragati* to cover, conceal, DP in *saṃvaraṇa* hiding, covering,
√*hras* 1307/1 cl 1 P A *hrasati (te)* to become short or small, be diminished or lessened, to descend from, P. to sound, caus. *hrāsayati* to make small or less, shorten, curtail, diminish, DP in *śabda* sounding,
hrāsa m. loss, diminution,

hrasva mfn short , weak, small, dwarfish, unimportant, insignificant, less by, m. a dwarf, a short vowel,

hṛcchaya mfn lying or abiding in the heart, the eternal monitor in the heart, the conscience, m. love 1302/2

hṛcchayapīḍita mfn love-pained, lovesick,

hṛcchayavardhana mfn increasing or arousing love,

hṛcchayāviṣṭa mfn entered by or filled with love,

hṛcchayāviṣṭacetana mfn possessing a love-filled mind,

hṛd 1302/2 n. the heart (as seat of feelings and emotions)
hṛdi 7/s/n in the heart

hṛdaya 1302/3 n. the heart as seat of feelings and sensations, mind as centre of mental operations

hṛdaye + √*kṛ* to take to heart, take seriously,

hṛddeśe in the region of the heart

hṛdistha mfn being in the heart, beloved, dear, existing in the heart, in the space within the heart,

hṛdya mfn being in the heart, internal, inward, inmost, innermost, pleasing or dear to the heart, beloved, cherished, proceeding from or produced in the heart, agreeable, pleasant, pleasant to the stomach, savoury, dainty (as food),

√*hreṣ* 1307/2 cl 1 A P *hreṣate (ti*), to neigh, whinny, to go, move, DP in *avyakta śabda* neighing,

√*hrī* 1307/2 cl 3 P *jihreti* to feel shame, blush, be bashful or modest, be ashamed of anyone or anything, caus. *hrepayati* to make ashamed, cause to blush, confound, put to shame, DP in *lajjā* being ashamed,

hrī 1307/2 2. f. shame, modesty, shyness, timidity,

√*hrīcch* DP in *lajjā* being ashamed,

√*hṛṇīya* 1302/2 Nom A *hṛṇīyate* to be angry, DP in *roṣaṇa* being angry, *lajjā* feeling ashamed,

√*hṛṣ* 1303/2 cl 1 P A *harṣati (te),* to be excited or impatient, rejoice in the prospect of, be anxious or impatient for, to speak or affirm falsely, lie, cl 4 P *hṛṣyati (te),* to thrill with rapture, rejoice, exult, be glad or pleased, become sexually excited, become erect or stiff or rigid, bristle, become on edge, caus. *harṣayati (te),* to excite, make impatient or eager for (victory etc.), to rejoice, be glad, to cause to bristle, be impatient or excited, DP in *alīka* (cl1) telling a lie, becoming erect, bristling, being delighted, in *tuṣṭi* (cl 4) being delighted,

hṛśīkeśa m. bristling haired, erect haired, M. a reference to *Kṛṣṇa* as lord of the senses,

hṛṣīta mfn 'bristling' the hair erect, through fear,
M. unwithered, fresh (flowers),

hṛṣitasragrajohīna mfn having unwithered garlands and free from dust,

hṛṣṭa mfn delighted, joyful,

hṛṣṭaroman 1303/2 hair standing on end

hṛṣyati 1303/2 rejoices, exults, rejoices, is glad or pleased 1/s/pres/act/rejoices

hṛta 1302/1 taken, taken away

hṛtstha 1302/3 mfn. standing or abiding in the heart

hriyate he is carried on, he is conveyed 1/s/pres/indic/pass. √*hṛ*

√*hu* 1301/1 1. cl 3 P *juhoti* A *juhute* to sacrifice, offer or present an oblation, sacrifice to, worship or honour, to sprinkle on, to eat, caus. *hāvayati* to cause to sacrifice or to be sacrificed or to be honoured with sacrifice, DP in *dāna* giving, *ādana* eating, *ādāna* receiving,
2. ind. an exclamation

√*huḍ* 1301/2 cl 6 P *huḍati* to collect, accumulate, to dive, sink, be submerged, cl 1P *hoḍati* to go, DP in *gati* going,

√*hūḍ* 1301/3 cl 1 P *hūḍati* to go, DP in *gati* going,

√hul 1301/3 cl 1 P *holati* to go, to cover, conceal, to kill, DP in *gati* going,
√huṇḍ 1301/2 cl 1 A *huṇḍate* to collect, accumulate, to select, choose, take, DP in *saṅghāta* collecting, in *varaṇa* choosing,
√hurch 1301/3 cl 1 P *hūrchati* to go crookedly, creep stealthily, totter, fall, to fall off from, caus. *hūrchayati* to cause to fall from, DP in *kauṭilya* acting crookedly,
hūrchana 1301/1 n. cunning, crookedness, going crookedly
huta 1301/1 mfn. offered in fire, poured out, burnt, sacrified, the oblation, the pouring out
hutabhuj m. fire, the south-east, plumbago,
hutahoma mfn having offered oblation,
hutāśa 1301/1 m. oblation-eater, fire
hutāśana m. 'having the oblation as food', a name for Agni, hence fire,
hūti f. invocation,
√hval 1307/3 cl 1 P *hvalati (te),* to go crookedly or astray, or wrong or deviously, stumble, fall, fail, caus. *hvalayati, hvālayati* to cause to tremble, shake, DP in *sañcalana* moving about, agitation, trembling
√hve cl 1 P A *hvayati (te), havate, huvati (te),* to call, call upon, summon, challenge, invoke, to emulate, vie with, caus. *hvāyayati* to cause anyone to be challenged by
√hvṛ 1308/1 or *hvī* cl 1 P *hvarati, hvarate, hvṛṇāti* to deviate or diverge from the right line, be crooked or curved, bend, go crookedly or wrongly or deviously, stumble, fall down, caus. *hvārayati* to cause to go crookedly, lead wrong or astray, A. to go wrong or astray, DP in *kauṭilya* being crooked,
hyaḥ yesterday, = *hyas*
hyas ind. yesterday,
i ind. an interjection of anger, sorrow, distress, compassion,
√i 163/2 cl. 2 P *eti,* cl 1 P &A *ayati, ayate* to go, flow, walk, advance, blow, advance, spread, get about, to go to or towards, to go away, escape, pass, retire, arise from, come from, return, succeed, arrive at, reach, obtain, fall into, come to, approach with prayers, gain by asking, to undertake anything, be employed in, go on with, continue in any condition or relation, appear, make one's appearance, approach anyone with requests, DP in *gati* going cl 1&2, *adhyayana* studying cl 2, *smaraṇa* remembering cl 2,
ī ind. an interjection of pain or anger, a particle impling consciousness or perception, consideration, compassion,
√ī DP in *gati, vyāpti, prajana, kānti, asan, khādana, gati*
ibha 167/3 m. an elephant, fearless, servants, domestics, dependants, household, family,
icchā f.. desire, inclination, wish , in math.- a question or problem, in gram.-the desiderative form, ind. according to wish or desire,
icchāmātra mere desire, mere will,
icchāmi I would like, I desire *√iṣ* 3/s/pres/indic/act
icchānicchāvivarjane *icchā* (above) + *an for a* not *anicchā* 29/2 undesirous, averse, *vivarjana* 988/3 the act of avoiding, shunning, leaving, 7/s in the matter of abandoning desire and aversion
icchanta mfn thinking, as though thinking, imagining, (Gam.)
icchasi 169/1 *√iḥ* 2/s/pres/act. you wish, seek for, desire,
icchati he/she desires, wants
icchu mfn desirous, wishing, desiring,
id ind. a particle of affirmation, even, just, only, indeed, assuredly,
√īḍ 170/2 cl 2 A *īṭṭe* to implore, request, ask for, to praise, DP in *stuti* praising,
iḍā 164/2 f. refreshing draught, vital

spirit, stream or flow of praise and worship, a partic. artery on the left side of the body, a tubular vessel (one of the principal channels of the vital spirit, that which is on the right side of the body)

idā later, 165/3 now, at this moment

idam pron. 1/s/n this, 'this world diversified through names and forms, and the object of direct perception', ind. now, here,

idamtā f. being this, identity, thisness,

idānīm now, at this moment, in this case, just, even, now-a-days,

iḍenya 170/2 praiseworthy, to be invoked or implored, adorable

idhma m. fuel, fuel for the sacred fire,

idhmaciti f. fuel-pile,

īdṛś or *īdṛk* mfn endowed with such qualities, such

īdṛśa 170/2 mfn. such, endowed with such qualities. of such a kind, of this kind

īḍya 170/2 praiseworthy, to be invoked or implored, adorable, gve. ind.

√*īh* 171/2 cl 1 A *īhate*, to endeavour to obtain, to aim at, attempt, to long for, desire, to take care of, to have in mind, think of

iha, 169/3 ind. here, in this place, now, at this time, in this world, in this case

īha m. attempt, (*ā)* f. effort, exertion, activity, request, desire wish,

ihaloka m. this world, this life,

ihāmutra 170/1 in the other world, in the life to come, in this world and the next, now and hereafter

īhate 171/2 endeavours to attain, seeks for, wishes for

īhita 171/3 mfn sought, wished, desire, effort, n. desire, request, wish, attempted, desired,

√*īj* 170/2 cl 1 P *ījati* to go, blame or censure, DP in *gati* going or *kutsana* censuring, blaming,

īje M. (having been) sacrificed, 1/s/mid/perf/ √*yaj*

ijya 164/2 mfn. to be revered/honoured, m. a teacher, deity, the planet Jupiter, a gift, donation, worship, reverence, meeting, union, f. a sacrifice,

ijyā sacrifice, making offerings, gift, donation, worship, reverence

ijyate it is performed, offered or sacrificed 1/s/pres/pass √*yaj*

√*ikh* 164/1 cl 1 P *ekhati*, to go, move, DP in the sense of *gati*, moving

√*īkṣ* 170/1 cl 1 A *īkṣiṣyate* to see, look, view, behold, look at, gaze at, to watch over, to see in one's mind, think, have a thought, regard, consider, observe (the stars etc.), to foretell for
īkṣate 1/s/pres/indic/mid sees

īkṣa mfn ifc. seeing, looking, visiting, f. (*ā*) sight, viewing, considering, (*am)* n. anything seen,

īkṣaka m. a spectator, beholder,

īkṣaṇa n. 170/1 look, view, sight, glance, the eye, regarding, looking after, caring for,

īkṣata mfn thought, saw, perceived, considered, regarded, deliberated,

īkṣate he/she sees, observes

ikṣurasa 164/1 7m sugarcane juice

ikṣvākave to or for (king) *Ikṣvāku*

Ikṣvāku the founder of the line of kings who ruled Ayodhyā. use of the plural indicates' descendants of' (including Sagara),

√*il* 168/2 cl 6 P *ilati*, to come, send, cast, sleep, cl 10 P *ilayati,* to keep still, not to move, to become quiet, DP cl 6 in *svapna* sleeping, *kṣepaṇa* throwing, cl 10 in *preraṇa* impelling, driving out, setting in motion

√*īl* 170/3 Caus. P *īlayati* to move DP in *preṣaṇa* sending, impelling,

ilā f. the mother of *Purūravas,* flow, speech, the earth,

iḷenya 170/2 praiseworthy, to be invoked or implored, adorable

imāḥ pron. 1/pl/f these (indefinite),

imam 2/s/m this

imāni pron. (indefinite) these 1/pl/n

ime 1/pl/m these
√*ind* 165/3 cl 1 P *indati*, to be powerful, to see,
DP in *paramaiśvarya* supreme lordly power
√*indh* 167/3 cl 7 P *inddhe,* to kindle, light, set on fire, to blaze, flame, DP in *dīpti* kindling, blazing,
indhana m. fuel, n. kindling, lighting, fuel, wood, grass etc. for this purpose,
-*vat* mfn possessed of fuel,
indra m. *Indra*, Lord of the minor gods, universal *manas*, thunder, the mind or the soul; the lord of the senses; a Hindu deity; chief of the celestials; the ruler of heaven; the rain-god.
indrābṛhaspati m. Indra and Bṛhaspati,
indrāgni m. Indra and Agni
indragopa m. the cochineal insect, a fire-fly, mfn having Indra as one's protector,
indrajāla 166/2 magic, illusion,
indrajit eldest son of *Rāvaṇa*
indraloka m. Indra's world, Indra's heaven,
indrapurogama mfn having Indra as leader, preceded by Indra
indraśatru mfn conquered by Indra,
indrasenā f. Indra's missile- weapon, personified as his bride,
name of a woman,
indrāyudha n. Indra's weapon, the rainbow, diamond,
indriya 167/2 n. power, force, power of the senses, fit for or belonging to Indra,
indriyāṇi the senses, -five of knowledge (*jñānendriya*) and five of action (*karmendriya*)
indryagocara mfn field of action of the senses, field perceptible to the senses, object of the senses,
indryāgocara mfn imperceptible to the senses,
indriyagrāma all the senses
indriyajñāna sense-knowledge, perception,
indriyanigraha control of the senses, 'mastery over sensory organs of knowledge and perceptions. Mastery over senses requires choice of perceptions conducive to righteous life.' 'Not to master the senses of knowledge or to pervert the senses of knowledge is against the law.'
indriyārtha sense-objects, objects of the senses, anything exciting the senses,
indriyārthasaṁnikarṣa contact with or attraction of the objects to the appropriate sense organs,
indu m. moon, a bright drop, a spark, time of moonlight, night, camphor, the point on a die, a symbolic expression for the number 1, a coin,
indura m. mouse, rat,
√*iṅg* 164/1 cl 1 P, A *iṅgati* (*-te*), to go, go to or towards, move or agitate, (in gram.) to divide or separate the members of a compound word, use a word or bring it into such a grammatical relation that it is considered *iṅgya,* DP in gati, going, moving,
iṅgate 164/1 it moves or agitates, goes to or towards, flickers or stirs,
1/s/pres/indic/mid √*iṅg*
iṅgita n. movement, gesture, sign, hint, indication, palpitation, aim, intention, real but covert purpose,
√*iṅkh* 164/1 *iṅkhati* to go, move,
DP in *gati* going, moving
√*īṅkh* 170/1 cl 1 P *iṅkhati* to go, move,
in *gati*, going
√*inv* 167/3 cl 6 P *invati* or cl 8 P *inoti,* to advance upon, press upon, drive, to infuse strength, invigorate, gladden, to use force, force, drive away, keep back, remove, to have in one's power, take possession of pervade, to be lord or master of anything, have the disposal of,
DP in *vyāpti* pervading
īpsā 170/2 f. asking, desire, wish to obtain,
īpsita mfn desired, sought after,
n. desire, wish,
īpsu 170/2 mfn striving to contain/obtain, wishing to get or obtain,
irasya 168/1Nom. P. *–ti,* to be envious,

to be angry

√*ir* 168/1 cl 6 P *iriti* to go, DP in *svapna* sleeping and *kṣepaṇa* throwing

√*īr* 170/3 cl 2 A *īrte* to go, move, rise, arise from, to go away, retire, to agitate, elevate, raise one's voice, DP in *gati* going, *kampana* agitating, in kṣepa throwing,

iras n. ill-will, anger, hostility

√*irasya* Nom. P *irasyati* to show enmity to, be angry or envious, DP in *īrṣyā* envying 170/3

irasyā f. ill-will, wrath,

iriṇa n. a water-course, rivulet, gulch, well, desert, inhospitable region, a bare plain, barren or salt soil, desert land, any excavation in the ground, a hollow, hole,

īrṣā f. impatience, envy of another's success

īrṣy or *īrkṣy* 170/3 cl 1 P *īrṣyati* to envy, feel impatient at another's prosperity, DP in *īrṣya* envy

īrṣya f. ill-will, envy, jealousy,

īrṣyā f. envying, impatience at another's success, spite, malice, jealousy

īryā walking with care, i.e. without harming any creature,

√*iṣ* 1. cl 1.P to seek, search, *eṣati*, A *eṣate*, cl 4 P *iṣyati*, cl 9 P A *iṣṇāti*, to cause to move quickly, throw, let fly, cast, swing, to send out or off, stream out, pour out, discharge, deliver a speech, proclaim, impel, animate, promote, DP cl 9 in *ābhīkṣṇya*

2. mfn sacrificed, worshipped with sacrifices, m. sacrifice,

iṣ 168/3 mfn ifc. moving quickly, speedy

√*iṣ* 3. 169/1 cl 6 P *icchati*, A *iccate*, to endeavour to obtain, strive, seek for, endeavour to make favourable, to desire, wish, long for, request, to wish or be about to do anything, to strive to obtain anything, from anyone, to assent, be favourable, concede, to choose, to acknowledge, maintain, regard, think, pass. *iṣyate* to be wished or liked, to be wanted, be asked or requested, be prescribed or ordered, be approved or acknowledged, be accepted or regarded as, to be worth, to be wanted as a desideratum, DP cl 4. in *gati*, cl 6 in *icchā* desiring

iṣ 169/2 mfn ifc. seeking for

iṣ f. wish

iṣ f. anything drunk, refreshment, enjoyment, libation, the refreshing waters of the sky, sap, strength, freshness, comfort, increase, good condition, affluence,

√*īś* 171/1 1. cl2. A *īṣte* (*Ved*) *īṣe* to own, possess, to belong to, to dispose of, be powerful, be master of , to command, rule, reign, behave like a master, allow,

īś 2. m. master, lord, the Supreme Spirit, name of *śiva*
f. (*ā*) power, dominion, faculty

īś, ṭ, m. master, lord, the Supreme Spirit, mfn. power, dominion one who lords it over is *īṭ*

īṣ cl 1 A (with prep. also P), *īṣate* (*ti),* to go, to fly away, escape, to attack, hurt, to glean, collect a few grains, to look, DP in *gati*, moving, *hiṁsā* attacking, hurting, *darśana* looking, seeing, *uñcha* gleaning

iṣa 1. = *iṣ,* 2. (*as*) mfn vigorous, fruitful, seeking, possessing sap and strength, well-fed, strong,

īśa mfn. owning, possessing, one who is completely master of anything, powerful, supreme, a ruler, master, lord, m. a husband, name of *śiva*

īśā by the Lord 3/s/m

īṣaddhasana slightly laughing, smiling,

īśana n. commanding, reigning,

īśāna mfn owning, possessing, wealthy, reigning, m. ruler, master, controller, an older name of *śiva-rudra,* one of the Rudras, the sun as a form of *śiva*, (*am*) n. light, splendour,

īśānakṛt mfn acting like a competent person, making use of one's possessions or faculties, rendering one a master or able,

īśasamsthaḥ fully established as the Lord (T),

īṣat mfn attacking, hurting, ind. a little, slightly, a few,

īṣatspṛṣṭa mfn uttered with slight contact of the organs of speech, (said of the semi-vowels),

īśāvāsya n. to be clothed or pervaded by the Supreme

iṣīkā 168/3 f. a reed, rush, stalk or stem of grass used as an arrow, a sort of sugarcane, the eyeball of an elephant,

iṣita mfn. moved, driven, willed, directed, caused, quick, speedy

iṣṭa 169/2/3 mfn sought, wished, desired, liked, beloved, desirable, reverenced, respected, approved, m. a lover, a husband, object of desire n. wish, desire, 2. mfn. sacrificed, worshipped with sacrifices, m. sacrifice, n. sacrificing, sacrifice, sacred rite, sacrament,

iṣṭadevatā f. favourite god, chosen tutelary deity, one particularly worshipped,

iṣṭalābha m. acquisition of a desirable object,

iṣṭajana m. beloved person, loved one,

iṣṭakā f. brick used in the sacred fireplace,

iṣṭakāmaduh 169/2 f. granting desires, the name of the cow of plenty

iṣṭāpūrta the merit of sacred rites, the fruit of sacrifice, work for the benefit of others, the public good,

iṣṭasiddhi attainment of the desired goal,

iṣṭi 1. impulse, acceleration, hurry, invitation, order,
2. f. seeking, going after, any desired object,
3. f. sacrifice (simple offering of butter, fruit etc.),

iṣṭikā f. brick used in the sacred fireplace,

iṣṭvā worshipping, offering, having worshipped, (gerund)

iṣu 168/3 m. an arrow

√*iṣudhya* 169/1 Nom. P A *iṣudhyati* to be a quiver, contain arrows, DP in *śaradhāraṇa* cl.11 containing arrows, imploring, requesting, desiring oblations, 169/2 Nom. P *iṣudhyāti* to implore, request, crave for, DP cl 6 in *icchā* desiring, wishing for

īśvara 171/1 m. able to do, master, Lord capable of , a husband, the Supreme Being, 'the cosmic reflection of Brahman in the *sattva* aspect of *prakṛti*..., the creator, preserver and destroyer of the universe,' (U)

īśvarabhāva 171/1 royal or imperial state, lordliness, exercising rulership

īśvarapraṇidhāna n. devotion to *īśvara*, self-surrender,

īśvaraprayatna the will of *īśvara*,

īśvarapujana (K) the cultivation of devotion through daily worship and meditation, the return to the source,

īśvarasṛṣṭi 'that which has been created by *īśvara* such as the elements etc.' 'things as they are in themselves' (U),

iṣyate is wanted 1/s/pres/pass √*iṣ*

√*iṭ* 164/2 cl 1 P *eṭati*, to go, to go to or towards, to make haste, to err, DP in *gati*, going,

itaḥ in comp. for *itas*, adv. from here, from hence, from this world, in this world, from this time, now, therefore,

itara 164/3 another, the other one, different from, other, may signal a contrary idea to the preceding word e.g. *sukhetareṣu* in happiness and distress, in a *tatpuruṣa* compound may express an idea implied in the contrary of that idea e.g. *dakṣiṇetara* - the left hand,

itarajana m. an ordinary man, (*ās*) m.pl. other men (spirits of darkness),

itarajātīya mfn ordinary, commonplace,

itaramātra mfn of such extent or quality,
itarapāṇini ind. thus according to Pāṇini
itaratas ind. otherwise than, different from, from or to another direction,
itarathā in the other way, anyone else than, else, otherwise,
itara itara the one- the other, this – that,
itaravṛtta n. occurrence, event,
itaretara mfn one another, one with another, mutual, respective, several, *(am)* n. mutually,
itas adv. from here, from hence, from this world, in this world, from this time, now,
itas itas here, there
itastataḥ 165/1 adv. hither and thither
iti 165/1 ind. signifying the end of thought or speech, thus, in this manner,
itiha ind. thus, indeed, according to tradition,
itihāsa 165/2 'so indeed it was', tradition, history, traditional accounts, an epic story,
itthā ind. thus, often used to lay stress on a following word, truly, really,
ittham ind. thus, in this way,
itthaṁbhūta mfn become thus, being thus or in such manner,
ityādi mfn having such (thing or things) at the beginning, thus beginning, and so forth, et cetera, used at the end of compounds to signify 'that which has ... as its beginning',
ityanta mfn ending thus,
ityartha mfn having such a sense or meaning, *(am)* ind. for this purpose,
ityukta n. 'so said', information, report,
iva 168/3 ind. like, as it were, as if, seems
iyacchiram ind. so long, such a time, 168/1
iyam pron. 1/s/f this (indefinitely),
iyant mfn so great, so much
iyat mfn so much, only so much, so large, only so large,
ja mfn(in cpds. ifc.) born, born from, growing in, living at, 'belonging to, connected with', m. a son of, a father, birth,
jā f. a race, tribe, ifc. a daughter,
√*jabh* 412/1 or *jambh* cl 1 *jabhate* or *jambhate* to snap at, caus. *jambhayati* or *jabhayati* to crush, destroy, or cl 1 *jabhati* or *jambhati* A *jabhate* = √*yabh* to know carnally, DP in *gātravinām* copulating,
jaḍa 409/3 mfn cold, frigid,motionless, inert, void of life, apathetic, senseless, inanimate, unintelligent,
jaḍadhī dull-witted
jaḍa- jaḍa- bheda difference between various classes of matter,
jāḍya 417/2 n. coldness, chilliness, insensibility, dullness, absence of soul or intellect, inactivity
jagadguru m. guru of the world,
jagadiśvara 408/2 Indra, world-lord
jagadvyāpāra m. creation and support of the world, world-business,
jagannātha m. world-lord, Viṣṇu
jāgaritasthāna ' the sphere of activity as the waking state',
jāgara 417/1 mfn. awake or watchful, m. waking, wakefulness
jāgarita 417/1 mfn. n. waking, waking state,
jāgarayati Cl 2 awakens, √*jāgṛ* caus.
jagarti 417/1 to be awake or watchful 1/s/pres/indic/act. awakes
jāgarti 417/1 awaken, be attentive to 1/s/pres/indic/act awakens f. waking, vigilance,
jagat 408/1 mfn moving, movable, living, m. pl. people, mankind, n. that which moves or is alive, the world , the universe
jagatpati 408/1 Lord of the Universe,
jagatprapañca world appearance,
jagatyām 7/s/f on the earth
jagdha 407/3 mfn. eaten, exhausted by, n. a place where anyone has eaten
jaghana m.n. the hinder parts, the buttocks, hip, rear-guard, ind. behind, following, once, so as to turn the back towards,
jaghanya 408/3 mfn. hindmost last, latest lowest, worst, vilest, least, least

important, of low origin or rank

√*jāgṛ* 417/1 cl 2 *jāgrti*, cl 1 *jāgarati* to be awake or watchful, to awake, to watch over, be attentive to or on, care for, provide, superintend, to go on burning (said of fire), to be evident, to look on, DP in *nadrā-kṣaya* awakening,

jāgradavasthā f. the waking state,

jāgrat 417/1 m. waking, the waking state,

jahadajahallakṣaṇā 'defining by rejecting and taking in' (U), 'part of the primary meaning of a word is given up and part of it is retained' (see Grimes 144), used to understand the *mahāvākyas,*

jahāti 1296/2 see 3. √ *hā*, to give up, renounce, resign, 1/s/pres/ind/act. gives up, leaves, casts off

jahi kill! destroy! 2/s/impv/act √ *han*

jāhnava 420/2 m. the Ganges, (the daughter of *Jahnu*)

jāhnavī f. name of the Ganges as daughter of *Jahnu*

Jahnu m. name of a sage who swallowed the Ganges then discharged it through his ears, the Ganges is said to be his daughter

jahuḥ they give up,

√*jai* 425/1 Cl 1 *jāyati* to wane, perish, DP in *kṣaya* declining, decaying,

jaina M. mfn pertaining/relating to the Jinas, viz. a teacher of the Jaina religion, m. a Jaina or follower of the Jaina religion, an Indian religion that prescribes a path of non-violence towards all living beings. Its philosophy and practice emphasize the necessity of self-effort to move the soul towards divine consciousness and liberation. Any soul that has conquered its own inner enemies and achieved the state of supreme being is called *Jina* (Conqueror or Victor). Jainism is also referred to as *Shraman (self-reliant) Dharma* or the religion of *Nirgantha* (who does not have attachments and aversions) by ancient texts. Jainism is commonly referred to as *Jain Dharma* in Hindi and *Samanam* in Tamil.
Jain doctrine teaches that Jainism has always existed and will always exist, but for academic purposes, historians date the foundation of organized Jainism to sometime between the 9th and the 6th centuries BCE. Some have speculated that the religion may have its roots in much earlier times, reflecting native spirituality prior to the Indo-Aryan migration into India. In the modern world, it is a small but influential religious minority with as many as 4.2 million followers in India, and successful growing immigrant communities in North America, Western Europe, the Far East, Australia and elsewhere. Jains have successfully sustained this longstanding religion to the present day and have significantly influenced and contributed to ethical, political and economic spheres in India. (K)

√*jaj* 409/1 Cl 1 P to fight, DP in *yuddha* fighting,

jaja m. a warrior

√*jakṣ* 407/3 Cl 2 *jakṣiti* to wish to eat, to eat, consume, (redup. √*has* to laugh), DP in *bhakṣa* eating and *hasana* laughing,
2. laughing,

√*jal* 414/2 Cl 1 *jalati* to be rich, or to cover, to be sharp, to be stiff or dull, Cl 10 *jālayati* to cover, DP in *ghātana* sharpening, in *apavāraṇa* covering,

jala 414/2 n. water, any fluid, the element water with the property of taste, mfn stupid, m. a stupid man,

jāla mfn watery, n. a net (for fish or birds), a hairnet, a snare, a cob-web, mail-coat, lattice window, the webbing of web-feet, lion's mane, a

cluster (buds etc.), collection, multitude, kind, species, not real, illusion, m. a small cucumber,
jalacara mfn any aquatic creature,
jalada m. cloud,
jaladhara m. raincloud, a mountain,
jaladhi m. ocean, a lake, the number 4,
jālakāra m. spider,
jalākāśa Ether which is reflected together with clouds, stars, etc., in the water contained in the jar; ether belonging to the water of the jar. (U)
jalakriyā f. a water ceremony of offering to the dead,
jālapāda a web-footed bird, a goose,
jalāśaya m. water-abode, lake, pond, mfn lying in water, stupid,
jālavān 'possessor of the net' ruler of *Māyā*
jālma mfn despicable, contemptible cruel, inconsiderate, (*ī*) f. m.f. a wretch,
√*jalp* 416/2 Cl 1 *jalpati (te)* to speak inarticulately, murmur, to chatter, prattle, to say, speak, converse with, speak about, = √*arj* to praise, DP in *vyaktā-vāc* murmuring, speaking,
jalpa m. talk, speech, discourse, pl. chatter, gossip, a kind of dispute (overbearing reply and disputed rejoiner),
√*jam* 412/2 Cl 1 *jamati* to go, to eat, DP in *adana* eating,
jāmātṛ m. son-in-law, brother in law, husband, 'maker of (new) offspring',
√*jambh* 412/3 see *jabh*
Jambūdvīpa m. one of the seven continents, India,
jambūka m. a jackal, a low man,
jāmbūnada mfn coming from the river Jambū, n. golden ornament, gold, thorn-apple,
√*jaṁs* 407/3 Cl 1. 10 *jaṁsati, jaṁsayati* to protect, DP in *rakṣaṇa* protecting, liberating,
√*jan* 410/1 Cl 1. 10 *janati (te)* to generate, beget, produce, create, cause, to produce (a song of praise), Cl 10 or caus. to cause to be born, to assign, procure, Cl 4 *jāyate (ti)* to be born or produced, come into existence, to grow (as plants, teeth) to be born as, be by birth or nature, to be born or destined for, to be born again, to become, to be changed into, to take place, happen, to be possible or applicable or suitable, to generate, produce, DP in *janana* begetting, in *prādurbhāva* (Cl 4) being born, arising, being produced,
janādhipa m. ruler of men
jana 410/1 m. a man , living being, person, creature, pl. people,
jāna 418/3 n. birth, origin, birthplace,
janaka m. father, *Janaka,* father of *Sītā,* king of *Videha*
jānan knowing pres/act/part
janana 410/3 mfn generating, begetting, m a progenitor, creator n birth, coming into existence, life, production, causation
jānāna 426/1 in comp for *jñāna* pres.mid. part. knowing
jananī f. mother
janapada m. district, community, nation, people, an empire, inhabited country, mankind,
janarava m. gossip, rumour, slander, popular saying or belief,
janārdana agitator of men, mover of men (*Kṛṣṇa)*
janasaṁsad 410/3 an assembly of men, an assembly of common people
janasamūha jana 410/1 living being , people, *samūha* 1170/3 assemblage, multitude, *janasamūhe* 7/s in a multitude of human beings
janati √*jan* generates, begets, produces, creates,
jānāti root *jñā* 425/2 to know 1/s/pres/indic/act knows
janavāda m. gossip, rumour,
janayet should cause to give birth to or arise, or produce, 1/s/opt/act/caus
janayitṛ m. one who generates, begets or produces, progenitor, father,

jāne I know 3/s/pres/indic/mid √*jñā*
jaṅgama 408/2 mfn moving, living, 'moving on feet'- (Gam.), f. a living being,
jaṅgha f. (*ā*) the shank (ankle to knee),
jaṅghākara mfn running quickly, m. a runner,
jaṅghāla m. 'running swiftly, runner', a class of animals (antelopes etc.),
jani or *janī* f. woman, wife,
janiman n. production, creation, birth, offspring, a creature, being, genus, kind, race,
janitra n. origin, birthplace, home, pl. parents, relatives,
janitva n. wifehood, m. father, m.du. parents, f. mother,
√*jañj* Cl 1 P see √*jaj*
jañjatī f. glittering, flashing,
janma in comp. for *janman*
janmamṛtyū birth and death
janman 411/3 birth, re-birth , existence, life, birthplace, origin, home, father, natal star, a creature, being, coming into being,
jantu 411/2 a child, offspring, a creature, living being. pl. *jantavas*
jānu 418/3 n. knee,
janus n. origin, nature, creation, innate character,
januṣā ind. by birth, from birth, by nature, originally, essentially, necessarily,
janya mfn born, produced, occasioned by, produced from,
belonging or relating to the people, national, belonging to a race or family or the same country,
m. a father, the friend or companion of a bride-groom, a son-in-law, a common man,
n. the body, a portent occurring at birth, people, community, nation,
m.n. rumour, report, a war, a market,
(*ā*) f. a bridesmaid, a newly married wife, pleasure, affection,
√*jap* 412/1 cl1 *japati* to utter in a low voice, whisper, mutter, (esp. prayers or incantations), to pray to any one in a low voice, DP in *vyaktāvāc mānasa* muttering, low voice or repeating internally
japa 412/1 muttering, whispering, muttering prayers, repetition, chanting mantras daily,
japamālā f. a rosary for *japa*,
japayajña muttering prayers as a sacrifice,
jāpya mfn relating to a muttered prayer, to be muttered, n. prayer to be muttered, muttering of prayers, muttered prayer,
jara mfn becoming old, m. the act of wearing out, wasting,
jarā the act of becoming old, old age
jāra mfn becoming old, m. a lover, sweetheart,
jaradaṣṭi mfn long-lived, very old,
jaraddāsa m. old slave or servant,
jaradgava m. old bull (name of a vulture),
jarant mfn aging, old,
jaras f. the growing old, old age, decay,
jaraṭha mfn old, bent, drooping, decrepit,
jarayanti they are wasting, wearing out, becoming old √*jṝ*
jarayu mfn becoming old,
jarāyu mfn withering, dying away, n. the cast off skin of a snake, a perishable covering,
jarāyuja 414/1 viviparous, born of wombs, born in a living state,
jaritṛ m. invoker, singer, praiser,
√*jarj* 414/2 Cl 1 see √*jarc* to speak, abuse, threaten,
jarjara mfn decayed, broken, divided (a realm), dull, hollow (sound), m. an old man, f. an old woman,
jāruja 419/3 mfn. = *jarāyuja* 414/1 viviparous, born of wombs, born in a living state,
√*jaṣ* 416/2 Cl 1 P A to hurt, DP in *hiṁsā* hurting, injuring
√*jas* 416/3 Cl 1 A to be exhausted or starved, P *jasati* to go,
Cl 4 P to liberate, caus. *jāsayati* to exhaust, weaken, cause to expire, to hurt, strike, contemn,

DP in *mokṣaṇa* (Cl 4) setting free, liberating, in *hiṁsā* (Cl 10) injuring, killing, in *tāḍana* (Cl 10) striking,

jāspati m. head of a family,

jasra mfn dying out,

√jaṭ 409/1 Cl 1 P = *√jhaṭ* to become entangled or intermixed,

jaṭā mfn wearing twisted locks of hair, f. matted hair, tangled locks,

jāta 417/2 mfn. born, grown, produced, '*saḥ jātaḥ* he, being born, having entered into the body', happened, become, present, apparent, manifest, ready at hand, belonging to (6th), possessed of (3rd), m. a son, a living being, n. a living being, creature, birth, origin, race, kind, sort, class, species,

jātakarman n. birth-ceremony,

jātāmarṣa mfn having anger aroused, vexed, enraged,

jātāni born, brought into existence, 1/pl/n

jātarūpa mfn having native beauty, splendid, beautiful, brilliant, golden, n. gold, the thorn- apple,

jātasaṁkalpa mfn feeling a passion for another, a purpose or desire having arisen,

jātasya of the born 6/s/m

jātāvamāna mfn contempt having arisen, filled with contempt,

jātavedas mfn 'all-possessor', 'knowing or known by all creatures', m. fire

jātavedasa mfn belonging or relating to *jātavedas,* 'endowed with enlightenment' (Gam.), name of *Agni*

jātaviśvāsa mfn inspired with confidence,

jaṭāyu m. king of the vultures

jaterṣya mfn jealous, jealousy aroused, (L)

jaṭhara n. belly, womb, mfn hard, old

jaṭharāgni m. digestive stomach-fire, gastric juice,

jāti 418/1 f. birth, production, re-birth, the form of existence (man, animal etc.), fixed by birth, position assigned by birth – rank, caste, race, (N) class, classification,

jātimātra n. mere rank, position in life obtained merely by mirth,

jātismara mfn remembrance of incidents of previous births,

jātu 418/2 ind. at all, ever, some day, once, once upon a time,

jātyābhāsa (N) appears to have an origin,

java 416/2 mfn. swift, m. speed, velocity, swiftness

javayukta mfn having fleetness

javana mfn quick, swift, fleet, m. a fleet horse, kind of deer, n. speed, velocity,

javasā forcefully

javavat mfn having fleetness

javīyas mfn. quicker, faster

jaya 412/3 m. victory, conquering, winning, conquest, triumph, mfn ifc. conquering, winning, mastery,

jāyā f. wife, 'bringing forth',

jayājayau victory and defeat (1/2/dual/ m *dvandva* comp.)

jāyamāna becoming, generating, producing, creating, causing pres.p. *√jan* as if born, seeming to be born or created, born

jayanta mfn victorious, m. the moon,

jāyante they are born, originated 1/pl/pres/pass

jayanthi the day of birth, birthday,

jāyate 410/1 is born (root *jan*) Cl.4 to be born or produced, be, become 1/s/pres/indic/pass

jayati root *ji* 420/2 conquers, excels, surpasses, wins, to conquer (the passions),

jayema we should conquer, we should prevail, 3/pl/opt/act

jayeyus they should conquer, 1/pl/opt/act

jayya part. to be conquered or gained,

√jeh 425/1 Cl 1 A to open the mouth, breathe heavily, be excessively thirsty, to gape, to move, DP in *prayatna* endeavouring, in *gati* going,

√jeṣ 424/3 Cl 1 A to move, DP in *gati* going,

jetāsi you will conquer 2/s/peri/fut *√ji*

jhalla m. a cudgel fighting athlete,
√*jham* 428/3 Cl 1 P =√*cham, jam,* to eat, DP in *adana* eating,
jhaṁjhā mfn roaring,
jharā f. waterfall,
√*jharjh* 428/3 Cl 1 *jharjhati* to blame, DP in *paribhāṣaṇa* saying, *bhartsana* blaming, *hiṁsā* injuring, *tarjana* threatening,
jharjharita mfn bruised, worn, wasted, withered,
√*jhaṣ* 429/1 Cl 1 *jhaṣati* to hurt, (also A. to take, to cover, DP in *hiṁsā* hurting, in *ādānasamvaraṇa* putting on or wearing,
jhaṣa 429/1 m. a large fish, the sign Pisces, sun-heat, a desert,
√*jhaṭ* 428/3 Cl 1 *jhaṭati* to become entangled or intermixed, DP in *saṅghāta* clotting, becoming twisted or matted together (as hair)
jhaṭiti 428/3 ind. at once, instantly immediately, suddenly,
jhillī f. a cricket, the wick of a lamp,
jhillika m. a cricket,
jhī 429/2 = √*jī* Cl 4.9. *jhiryati, jhriṇāti* to become old, DP in *vayohāni* growing old withering,
√*ji* 420/2 Cl 1 *jayati (te*), Cl 9 *jināti* (=√*jyā),* to win or acquire (by conquest or in gambling, conquer (in battle), vanquish (in a game or lawsuit), defeat, excel, surpass, to conquer (the passions), overcome or remove (any desire or difficulties or diseases), to expel from, win anything, vanquish anyone in a game, be victorious, gain the upper hand, often pres. in sense of impv. "long live", "glory to", Caus. *jāpayati* to cause to win, to conquer, Desid. *jigīṣati (te)*DP in *jaya* surpassing, excelling, in *abhibhava* conquering, overcoming, 2. mfn. conquering
*jighānsā*421/1 wish or intention to slay or strike, malice, revenge
jighran 421/1 mfn smelling
jighrati 379/3 he smells, perceives odour, √*ghrā* to smell,
jighṛkṣā f. wish or intention to take or seize, √*grah*
jighṛkṣu 421/1 mfn intending to take/seize,
jigīṣatām of those who desire victory desid/pres/part/act 6/pl/m √*ji*
jihāsā 421/3 desire to abandon or give up
jihma 421/3 mfn oblique, transverse, athwart, squinting, crooked, morally crooked, deceitful, false, dishonest, slow, lazy, n. falsehood, dishonesty,
jihva 422/1 m. the tongue or the organ of taste and speech,
jihvā f. various forms of flame,
jihvāgra n. tip of the tongue,
jihvāmūlīyaḥ formed at the base of the tongue, *kh* or *ḥ* before *k,*
jijñāsa m. one who desires to know, a spiritual aspirant,
jijñāsā f. desire to know, wish to determine,
jijñāsana n. investigation, desire for knowing,
jijñāsu mfn 421/1 desirous of knowing
jijīviṣāmas we desire to live 3/pl/desid/act √*jīv*
√*jim* 421/3 Cl 1 *jemati* to eat, DP in *adana* eating
jīmūta m. thundercloud, a cloud, mountain, sun, Indra, a sustainer, nourisher,
jina mfn victorious, m. victor, a Buddha, an Arhat (Jaina),
√*jinv* 421/2 Cl 1 P A *jinvati (te)* to move one's self, be active or lively, to urge on, cause to move quickly, impel, incite, refresh, animate, promote, help, to help anyone to anything, to receive favourably (prayers or acts of devotion), DP in *prīṇana* pleasing, delight, gladdening,
jīra mfn quick, speedy, active, m. quick movement, a sword,
jīradānu swift dripping, well-watered,
√*jiri* 421/3 Cl 5 P *jirinoti* to hurt, DP in *hiṁsā* hurting, killing
jīrṇa 422/2 mfn. old, worn out,

ancient tradition, digested, m. an old man, n. old age

√*jiṣ* 421/3 Cl 1 *jeṣati* to sprinkle, DP in *secana* sprinkling

jita mfn won, acquired, defeated, conquered, subdued, overcome or enslaved by, given up, discontinued,

jitakāśin arrogant, full of victory,

jitāpsaras surpassing the Apsaras, having conquered the Apsaras

jitendriya mfn having the senses tamed or subdued, one who controls the senses,

jītitavyam should be lived,

jitvā having conquered

√*jīv* 422/2 Cl 1 *jīvati* to live, be or remain alive, to revive, to live by (instr.), caus. *jīvayati* to make alive, restore to life, vivify, to support life, keep alive, nourish, bring up, to shout *jīva* (long live!), DP in *prāṇadhāraṇa* living, breathing (in supporting life),

jīva 422/2 mfn living, existing, alive, ifc. living by, causing to live, vivifying, m.n. alive, any living being, existence, life, m. the principle of life, vital breath, the living or personal soul (as distinguished from the universal soul), G.148 -consciousness inseperably qualified by the internal organs. G 147, the phenomenal self subject to experience and empirical changes- a blend of *puruṣa* and mind, G. a blend of the Self and not-Self with a wrong identification each of the other, consciousness qualified by the internal organs. In truth the Self is ever free, this is about what we think ourselves to be –erroneously, 'the transmigrating individual soul', 'the *jīva* with his mind devoted to the worldly existence does not know that he is the self-evident *ātman'* (P), *pāramārthika jīva* 'the real *jīva'* – not different from the *brahman.*

jīvabhūta consisting of the *jīva*s, or souls, or spiritual beings, 422/3 become alive, endowed with life,

jīvacaitanya individual consciousness,

jīvaghana 422/3 m. receptacle of everything living, a mass of creatures,

jīvagrāmā living things, multitude of *jīvas* or individual souls, (U)

jīva-jīva-bheda difference between one individual and another, (U)

jīvakoṭi belonging to the category or class of the individual soul (U)

jīvaloka m. the world of the living,

jīvana mfn giving life, enlivening, (said of the wind, sun, etc.), m. a living being, wind, a son, manner of living, living by, making alive, (*am*) life, manner of living, livelihood, means of living, enlivening, making alive,

jīvanmukta 423/2 emancipated while still alive, liberated while living,

jīvanmukti (G) liberation while living,

jīvapati or *–patni* mfn f. having one's husband yet alive, m. a living husband,

jīvapraja mfn having one's children alive,

jīvasṛṣṭi that which has been created by the *jīva,* e.g. egoism, mine-ness, individual imagination,

jīvati 422/2to live, be or remain alive 1/s/pres/indic/act. lives √*jīv*

jīvātman 423/1 m. the living or personal or individual soul, the vital principle,

jīvavīcayaḥ waves of individual existence

jīvavīci waves of individual existence

jīveśvarabheda difference between the individual soul and God ; the fundamental tenet of the dualistic school of thought.

jīvikā f. livelihood,

jīvin mfn living, m. a living being,

jīvita 423/2 mfn living, alive, lived through (a period of time), returned to life, enlivened, animated, n. a living being, life, duration of life, livelihood, lifetime,

jīvitās 1/pl/m lives, as in their lives
jīvitāśā f. the wish for life, hope to save one's life, hope for life,
jīvitavya n. impers. to be lived, possibility of living, the life to be expected, duration or enjoyments of life, possible return to life,
jīvite from root *jīv* 422/2 to live, being alive, 1/s/pres/mid/indic being alive,
jivri mfn old, worn out, decrepit, m. time,
-jña knower of (at end of a compound)
√*jñā* 425/2/3 Cl 9 PA *jānāti jānite* to know, have knowledge, become acquainted with, perceive, apprehend, understand, experience, recognise, ascertain, investigate, to know as, know or perceive that, regard or consider as, to acknowledge, approve, allow, to recognise as one's own, take possession of, visit as a friend, to remember (with 6th),A. to engage in, caus. *jñapayati* to teach anyone *jñāpayati* to make known, announce, teach anything, A. to request, ask, *jña* 2. mf(*ā*)n knowing, familiar with, intelligent, having a soul, wise, m. a wise and learned man, the thinking soul, the planet Mercury or Mars, *brahmā*, DP in *avabodhana* (Cl 9) knowing, in (Cl 10) *māraṇa* killing, *toṣaṇa* satisfying, *niśāmana* observing, *niyoga* ordering, directing
jñāna 426/1 n. knowing, knowledge, (esp, Spiritual Knowledge), the higher knowledge, 'wisdom', true knowledge.
'The primary knowledge is Pure Consciousness or *svarūpajñāna* (knowledge in itself);i.e. not other than the Self'
'The secondary sense, and the one most commonly used, is the expression or reflection of the Pure Consciousness in *antaḥkaraṇa*. As such it could be lofty or otherwise, and it may be valid (*pramā*) or invalid (*apramā*), unlike the word "knowledge" in the West, which usually refers to valid knowledge only. In the scriptures of course the secondary sense refers to spiritual knowledge such as in the Upanishads or conversation with a fully realized man.' see *vijñāna* and *prajñāna*
jñānābhāsa "The limited manifests in the *antaḥkaraṇaḥ*. That consciousness which shines or seems to reflect in the *antaḥkaraṇaḥ*. is called *cidabhāsa*. in this reflected light of knowledge is the knowledge one acquires from the creation, communication, operative skills, etcetera. All this is known as *jñānābhāsa"*.
jñānābhyāsa the way of *vedānta sādhanā*
jñānacakṣu the eye of wisdom or eye of intuition,
jñānadīpa 426/1 the lamp of knowledge
jñānagamya 426/2 mfn. attainable by the understanding (*am*) n. goal of knowledge
jñānāgni fire of spiritual knowledge or wisdom,
jñānakāṇḍa n. that portion of the Veda which relates to knowledge of the one Spirit,
jñānākara m. knowledge-mine,
jñānakarmaṇoḥ samuccayaḥ (N) 'the conjunction of thought and action'
jñānāloka the light of knowledge,
jñānamarga m. the way of knowledge,
jñānamaya mfn consisting of knowledge, made of knowledge,
jñānaniṣṭha mfn engaged in cultivating true knowledge,
jñānaśakti f. intellectual faculty,
jñānasphūrti flash of knowledge,
jñānasvarūpa embodiment of wisdom or knowledge,
jñānavān wise man, man of wisdom,
jñānavat 426/2 endowed with knowledge,

having spiritual knowledge, intelligent, wise,

jñānayajña m. sacrifice of knowledge, dissemination of knowledge,

jñānayoga m. yoga based on the acquisition of true knowledge, the path of knowledge,

jñānayogin one practising the path of knowledge,

jñānendriyāṇi five senses of knowledge, seeing, hearing, touch, taste, smell,

jñānin 426/2 mfn. knowing, wise, endowed with knowledge or intelligence, knowing the higher knowledge or knowledge of spirit, m. a fortune-teller, astrologer, a sage,

jñānodaya m. the dawn of knowledge,

√jñapaya Nom. DP in *jñāna* knowing, informing, *jñāpana* informing others,

jñapti f. understanding, ascertainment of, the exercise of intelligence, intelligence,

jñaptimātra (N 264) 'the actual existence of "higher truth" is *jñaptimātra'*, (N301) 'pure consciousness'

jñāsyasi you will know, thou shalt know 2/s/fut/act *√jñā*

jñāta 425/3 mfn known, ascertained, understood, comprehended,

jñatā f. being known or understood, the knower,

jñātajñeya ind. having understood what is to be known,

jñatatā f. being known or understood,

jñātatattva knowing the truth,

jñāti m. kinsman, close relative,

jñatṛ mfn the knower, one who knows or understands, a witness,

jñatṛtva n. knowledge,

jñātvā ind. having known or understood,

jñātavya to be known or understood or investigated,

jñāyān m. elder, elder brother,

jñeya 426/2 mfn. to be known, knowable, to be learnt or understood or inquired about, (the object of knowledge) –gerundive

jñeyābhinna 'non-different from the knowable' identified with Brahman, (Gam.),

jñīpsā 426/2 asking for information, desire for knowledge

jogū mfn loudly singing, praising,

joṣam ind. arbitrarily, according to one's wish or liking,

joṣam √ās āste to remain silent (X),

joṣas n. pleasure,

joṣayet should cause to enjoy or delight 1/s/opt/caus/act

jrayas n. space, flat surface, stretch, expanse,

√jri 428/1 Cl 1 P *jrayati* to go, overpower,
Cl 1.9.10. *jrayati, jriṇāti, jrāyayati* to grow old, DP in *abhibhava* (Cl 1) conquering, in *vayohāni* (Cl 10) growing old,

√jṛmbh 424/2 Cl 1 *jrimbhate (ti),* to open the mouth, yawn, to gape open, open (as a flower), to fly back or recoil (as a bow when unstrung), to unstring a bow, to unfold, spread, expand, to feel at ease, DP in *gātra-vināma* copulating, gaping, yawning,

√jṝ 424/3 Cl 1 P to make old or decrepit,to cause to grow old, to humiliate, Cl 4 P A *jīryati (te)* Cl 9 *jṛnoti*, Cl 10 *jārayati* to grow old, become decrepit, decay, wear out, wither, be consumed, break up, perish, to be dissolved or digested, caus. *jarayati* to make old, wear out, consume, cause to be digested,
2. Cl 1 A *jarate* to crackle (as fire), to call out to, address, invoke, praise DP in *vayohāni* (Cl 9 and 10), growing old, withering,

√ju 423/3 =√1. *jū*

√jū 424/2 Cl 1 A Cl 9 P *javate, junāti,* Cl 1 P *javati* to press forwards, hurry on, be quick, to impel quickly, urge or drive on, incite, to scare, to excite, promote, animate, inspire, DP in *gati* going

2. mfn quick, speedy, inciting, driving, m. couser, f. speed, the atmosphere, a female goblin

√juḍ 423/3 Cl 6 *juḍati* to bind, to go, Cl 10 *joḍayati* to send, DP in *bandhana* binding, *gati* going, *preraṇa* sending

jugupsā 423/3 dislike, abhorrence, disgust,

juhosi you offer (in sacrifice) 2/s *√hu*

juhū sacrificial ladle for melted butter, a tongue (flame),

juhurāṇa mfn. crooked, deceitful, (*√hvṛ* to deviate or diverge from the right line, go crookedly or wrongly or deviously)
m. the moon

juhvati they offer, they sacrifice, 1/pl/pres/indic/act *√hu*

√jun 423/3 Cl 6 *junati* for *√juḍ* DP in *gati* going

√juṅg 423/3 Cl 1 *juṅgati* to exclude, DP in *varjana* leaving,

√jūr 424/2 cf *√jur,* Cl 4 A *jūryate* to hurt, to be angry with, DP in *hiṁsā* hurting, or *vyohāni* growing old,

√juṣ 424/1 Cl 6 *juṣote (ti*), Cl 3 P *jujoṣati* , Cl 1 P *joṣati*, to be pleased or satisfied or favourable, to like, be fond of delight in, enjoy, to have pleasure in, to give pleasure to, to choose for, to devote oneself to, practise, undergo, suffer, delight in visiting, frequent, visit, inhabit, enter, to afflict,
caus. A to like, love, behave kindly towards, cherish, delight in, approve of, DP in *prīti* pleasing, enjoying, *sevana* devoting aor attaching oneself to, in *paritarkaṇa*, reasoning, *paritarpaṇa* injuring, hurting, satisfying,
2. mfn liking, fond of, devoted to, dwelling in, visiting, approaching, having, showing, similar,

√jūṣ Cl 1 P = *√yūṣ*, to hurt, kill, DP in *hiṁsā* injuring,

juṣṭa 424/1 mfn. pleased, propitious, liked, agreeable, usual, acceptable, loved, adored, welcome, agreeable,

juṣṭi f. love, service, favour, satisfaction,

√jut 423/3 Cl 1 *jotate* to shine, DP in *bhāsana* shining

jūti 424/2 f. going or driving on, quickness, velocity, speed, flowing without interruption, impulse, incitement, instigation, inclination, energy, 'mental suffering, owing to disease etc. –Gam.'

√jval 428/2 Cl 1 P A *jvalati* to burn brightly, blaze, glow, shine, to burn (as a wound), to set on fire, light, kindle, make radiant, illuminate, DP in *dīpti* shining,

jvāla mfn burning, blazing,
m. flame, torch,
f. illumination, causing a flame to blaze, burnt rice,

jvalati 428/2 burns brightly, blazes, glows

jvalana mfn combustible, flaming, shining, m. a fire, n. blazing,

√jvar 428/1 Cl 1 *jvarati* to be feverish, DP in *roga* being diseased or feverish

jvara 428/1 m. fever, fever of the soul, mental pain, affliction, grief

jyā 426/3 Cl 9 P *jināti* to overpower, oppress, deprive anyone of property, to become old, Cl 4 A *jīyate* to be oppressed or badly treated, be deprived of property, DP in *vayohāni* growing old, decaying,

jyā f. superior power, force, bowstring, the chord of an arc, the earth,

jyaiṣṭha oldest, m. name of a month (May-June), the full moon in *jyeṣṭhā*

jyāyāṁs mfn stronger or superior, older,

jyāyas 426/3 mfn. superior, greater, larger, stronger, most excellent,
M. older, elder,

jyāyasī better, superior, 1/s/f comparative

jyeṣṭha 426/3 mfn most excellent, pre-eminent, first, chief, best, greatest, m. the chief, greatest eldest, eldest brother, n. what is most excellent, f. the eldest wife, the middle finger, misfortune, a small house lizard, (*am*) ind. most, extremely,

jyeṣṭhaprathama mfn having the oldest as the first,

jyotiḥśāstra n. astronomy,

jyotirmaya mfn starry, full of light, brilliant, consisting of light,

jyotis light (of sun, dawn etc.), as pl. the heavenly bodies, stars, illumination, luminosity, effulgence,

jyotiṣa m. the sun, the illuminator, n. science of astronomy and planetary influence, 427/2 mfn. luminous, brilliant, shining, belonging to the world of light, celestial, spiritual, pure 'the brilliance of light' LM

jyotiṣkṛt mfn light-making, creating light,

jyotiṣmant mfn full of light, light,

jyotiṣmat mfn luminous, pure, belonging to the world of light, shining, brilliant, spiritual, celestial, sun,

jyotiṣām of the lights, of stars 6/pl/n

jyotiṣmatī mfn spiritual, pure, effulgent, the m. the sun, f. 'star-illumined' night,

jyotiṣṭoma a soma ritual (not well understood),

jyotsnā f. a moonlit night, moonlight, pl. light, splendour,

√*jyu* 427/1 Cl 1 A to go, =√*cyu* DP in *gati*, going near, approaching

ka 240/2 interrogative pronoun, who? what ? which,
2. m. the soul, a comet, the sun, fire, splendour, light, air, a peacock, the body, time, wealth, sound, a king,
3. n. happiness, joy, pleasure, water, the head, hair, a head of hair,
4. a *taddhita* affix often used to form adjectives and may be added to nouns to express diminution, deterioration or similarity, e.g. *putraka* a little son, *aśvaka* a bad horse or like a horse

kā who? what? etc.1/s/f

√*kab* 251/3 Cl 1 A *kabate* to colour, tinge with various hues, to praise, DP in *varṇa* colouring

kabandha a heavenly being cursed to live in a *rākṣasa* body

√*kac* Cl 1 P *kacati* to sound, cry, A *kacate* to bind, fetter, to shine, DP in *bandhana* binding, 242/3

kāca m. glass, 268/2

kācamaṇi m. rock-crystal jewel, quartz,

kaccha m. border, shore, marsh-land, bank, watery soil, marshy ground, morass, m.f. the hem or end of a lower garment (tucked into the waistband), f. (*ā*) a cricket,

kaccha-pa m. tortoise, turtle,

kaccit(d) ind. 'a particle of interrogation', is it that? has it? has this? I hope that, sometimes, now and then, used in questions expecting the answer 'yes',
ibc. marks the uselessness, badness or defectiveness of anything e.g. -*akṣara* n. a bad letter, bad writing, with *na* in no way or manner,

√*kaḍ* 244/3 Cl 1 P *kaḍati* to be confused or distressed by pleasure or pain, to be elated or intoxicated, Cl 6 P *kaḍati* to eat, consume, caus. *kāḍayati* to break off a part, separate, divide, to remove the chaff or husk of grain, to preserve, DP in *mada* being disturbed or confused, being proud, being intoxicated

√*kad* cl 1 A. *kadate,*to be confused, suffer mentally, to grieve, confound, kill, hurt, to call, to cry or shed tears,
2. a particle of interrogation, anything wrong or bad,
used like *kim,* with the particles *cana* and *cid,* sometimes, now and then,

kadā 248/1 ind. when? at what time?
na kadā cana not at any time so-ever, never,
kadā cid once on a time, one day,
kadā cid api na never,

kadācana at any time, at any time whatsoever

kadāpi ever (after *na*) never

kadācid (t) 248/1 at some time,

or other, at any time, at any time whatever, one day, sometimes, perhaps,

kadala m. or *kadalī* (f.) banana tree

kādambinī f. a bank of clouds, row of clouds,

kadāpi ind. anytime, ever, at any time,

√*kaḍḍ* 245/1 Cl 1 P *kaḍḍati* to be hard or rough, to be harsh or severe, DP in *kārkaśya* being harsh or severe, being hard or rough,

kadru mfn brown, m. tawny,

√*kag* 242/1 cl1 P *kagati* to act, perform, DP in *saṅga* 1132/3 m. relation to, association with.

kaḥ interrogative pronoun, who? which? what?

kaḥ api or *kaḥ cit* anyone, anything, someone, something, a certain, a few

√*kai* 311/1 Cl 1 P *kāyati* to sound, DP in *śabda* sounding,

kaiḥ by whom? with whom? 3/pl/m interrog.

kaikeyī mother of *Bharata*

kailāsa m. a Himalayan peak, 'crystalline', 'abode of bliss',

kailāsastha mfn standing/being on Kailasa,

kaiṅkārya n.service to god as a personal servant, servitude, servant's work place,

kais by what, 3/pl/n

kaitava 311/2 mfn deceitful, n gambling, fraud, deceit, cheating, roguishness

kaivalya 311/3 mfn leading to eternal happiness or emancipation, n. isolation, absolute unity, detachment from all other connections, beatitude, established in unity, detachment of the soul from matter or further transmigration

kaivarta m. fisherman, f. the wife of a fisherman, the grass,

kajjala n. collyrium (an eye-salve), a cloud, lampblack (applied near the eyes medicinally or as decoration,

√*kal* 311/1 Cl 1 A *kalate* to be unsteady, to be proud, DP in *kaulya* being unsteady

kāka m. a crow, an impudent or insolent fellow, a lame man, a cripple, washing the head, a sectarial mark, a partic. measure,

√*kakh* 242/1 Cl 1 P *kakhati* to laugh, laugh at, deride, *kakhayati* cause to laugh, DP in *hasana* laughing

kakṣa m. lurking place, hiding place, a wood, forest of dead trees, large wood, underbrush, an inner recess, the interior of a forest, grass, dry grass, sin, a gate, a buffalo, (*as,ā* m.f.) the armpit, the region of the girth, a girdle, zone, belt, girth, hem, border, the scale of a balance, a surrounding wall, a wall, any place surrounded by walls, the orbit of a planet, the periphery, circumference, balance, equality, similarity, resemblance, emulation, rivalry,

kakṣyā f. a wall, enclosure or inner apartment, girth of an animal, girdle, zone, the orbit of a planet, the scale of a balance, an upper garment, similarity, equality, effort, exertion, f. pl. the fingers,
mfn being or abiding in shrubs or dry grass, filling out the girth, well-fed,

kāku f. emphasis, cry of sorrow, tongue, complaint, muttering, lamentation, murmuring, stress, peculiar tone or change of the voice from fear etc. tone of voice,

kakubh f. a region, space, quarter of the heavens, a peak, summit, unornamented hair or a ponytail hairstyle, a wreath of *campaka* flowers, splendour, beauty, a science,

kakud f. a peak, summit or hump, a chief or head, any projecting corner, the hump over the shoulders of indian cattle,

kakum or *kakubh* f. a peak, summit, space

region, pony tail hair, a wreath of *campaka* flowers, splendour, beauty,

√*kal* 260/1 1. Cl 1 A *kalate* to sound, to count,
2. Cl 10 P *kālayati (te)*, to push on, drive forward, drive before oneself or away, carry off, go after, persecute, count, tell over,
3. P *kalayati (te),* to impel, incite, urge on, bear, carry, betake oneself to, do, make, accomplish, utter a sound, murmur, DP (cl1)in *śabda* sounding, or *saṅkhyāna* counting, *kṣepa* (cl10) impelling, *gati* going, 3. in *āsvādana* tasting

√*kāl* 277/1 from 3. *kal*? DP in *kāla-upadeśa* counting the time

kala mfn dumb, indistinct, (am) ind. emitting a soft or gentle tone, humming, melodious, a faulty pronunciation of vowels, weak, crude, undigested, m. humming, buzzing (a low or soft and inarticulate sound),

kāla 278/1 mfn black, of a dark colour, blue-black, 1. m. a black or dark-blue colour, the pupil of the eye, the Indian Cuckoo, a poisonous snake, the planet Saturn, 2. the right or proper or appointed time, 3. a period of time, time (in general), time (as leading to events i.e. fate, destiny), time (as destroying all things – death, time of death), indistinct, inarticulate, (*am*) ind. for a certain time, (*ena*) ind. in the course of time,

kalā mfn indistinct, dumb, ifc. indistinct or inarticulate on account of tears, emitting a soft tone, melodious, a kind of faulty vowel pronunciation, m. a low or soft tone (humming, buzzing),
f. a small part of anything, any single part or portion of a whole, esp. a sixteenth part, a measure of time, a syllabic instant, an atom, the elements of the gross or material world, an embryo shortly after conception, skill, ingenuity, ignorance, any practical art, any mechanical or fine art, pl. constituents,

kāladharma m. the law or rule or operation of time, death, dying, influence of time, seasonableness, suited to the time or season, with √*gam* die, (go to the law of time),

kalaha m. strife, contention, quarrel, a scabbard, a road, way, deceit, abuse, beating, kicking,

kalahakāra mfn quarrelsome, contentious,

kālaharaṇa n. waste time, lost time, losing time, wasting time,

kalakala m. noise, racket, uproar,

kālakṣepa m. wasting time, delay

kālam 278/1 for a certain time, death, time of death

kalaṅka m. spot, stain, mark,

kālapāśa m. snare of Death,

kalaśa m. pot, jar, pitcher, butter churn,

kālaśakti f. all-destroying time,

kalatra n. hip and loins, vagina, wife, royal citadel, consort, stronghold, female of an animal,

kālātīta mfn elapsed, passed away, become unseasonable,

kalatra 260/3 n. a wife, consort, the female of an animal, the hip and loins, a royal citadel,

kalayatām of the calculators or regulators or subduers,of all masters, pres/part/act √*kal* 6/pl/m

kāle in time, at the proper time 7/s

kāle kāle ind. from time to time, sometimes,

kālena in course of time

kalevara 262/2 the body

kālī 'the black one' , a goddess associated with eternal energy, consort of *śiva,* also means 'the time' or 'death' (as in time has come), hence Kali is considered the goddess of time and change, sometimes presented as dark and violent, also seen as Bhavatarini 'redeemer of the universe' and as a benevolent mother goddess, (K)

kālika mfn fit for any partic. season, seasonable, relating to time, lasting a long time, m. species of heron,

kalikā f. bud, blackness or black colour, division of time, unblown flower,

kalila mfn mixed with, full of, covered with, impenetrable, impervious, inscrutable, (*am*) n. a large heap, thicket, confusion,

kāliyaḥ *Kāliyaḥ* a serpent demon

kaliyuga the iron age, the fourth of four ages in the cycle, 432,000 years long, selfishness, ignorance and conceit prevail,

kalkana 262/2 n. meanness, wickedness

√*kall* 263/3 Cl 1 A *kallate* to utter an indistinct sound, to be mute, DP in *avyaktaśabda* sounding indistinctly,

kallola 263/3 m. a wave, billow

kalmaṣa 263/1 n. stain, dirt, darkness, moral stain, mfn. impure, sinful

kalmaṣa-dhvaṁsa-kārin mfn sin-destruction-causing, preventing a crime,

kālopadeśa referencing to time, telling the time, measuring time

kalpa 1. mfn practicable, feasible, possible, proper, fit, able, competent, m. a sacred precept, ordinance, manner, way, manner of acting, proceeding, practice, one side of an argument, an alternative, investigation, research, resolve, determination, treatment of the sick, manner of curing, the art of preparing medicines, the doctrine of poisons and antidotes,
first duty, a rule to be observed before any other rule, one of two cases, one side of an argument, an alternative, investigation, research, investigation, resolve, determination, treatment of the sick, manner of curing, the art of preparing medicine, pharmacy,
ifc. having the form or manner of anything, similar to, resembling, like but with a degree of inferiority, almost,
a fabulous period of time, a day of Brahmā or one thousand yugas, a period of 4,320,000,000 years of mortals measuring the duration of the world, a month of Brahmā is supposed to contain thirty such *kalpa*s, 12 months of Brahmā constitute his year, and one hundred such years his lifetime, at the end of a kalpa the world is annihilated, fourteen *manwantaras,* one day in the life of *brahmā,* one *manvantara* = 71 cycles of the 4 *yugas*

kalpādau at the beginning of a kalpa

kalpakṣaya 262/3 the end of a kalpa, destruction of the world

kalpana 263/1 creating in the mind, assuming anything to be real. (*ā)* f. making, manufacturing, preparing, fixing, settling, arranging, imagining, creating in the mind, assuming anything to be real, fiction, hypothesis, form, shape, image,

kalpāṇa mfn noble, good, blessed, n. good fortune,

kalpanamātra mere imagination, resting only in imagination,

kālpanika mfn imaginary, fictitious, artificial, fabricated, invented

kalpānta 262/3 the end of a *kalpa,* (cycle, a day of *brahmā,* 4320 million years) the end of a cycle

kalpate √*kḷrp* 308/2 is ordered or regulated, is or becomes fit, is adapted well managed, succeeds, prepares, arranges, happens, becomes, occurs, creates, makes, executes, brings about, contrives, invents 1/s/pres/indic/mid

kalpita mfn made, fabricated, imagined,

kalpitasaṁvṛti (N) 'covering due to false construction', G 157 'imaginary relative point of view',

kalya mfn well, healthy,

kalyāṇa 263/2 mfn. beautiful, agreeable,

illustrious, noble, virtuous, good, beneficial, auspicious, good conduct, good fortune, fortunate, auspicious

kalyāṇakaṭaka Fairdale, name of a place,

kalyāṇakṛt 263/2 mn doing good, virtuous,

√*kam* 252/1 Cl 1 A caus. *kāmayate* to wish, desire, long for, to love, be in love with, have intercourse with, DP in *kānti* desiring,

kam 1. particle emphasizing the previous word in an affirmative sense,
2. interrog.whom? which?

kāma 271/3 m. longing, desire, 'sex energy' pleasure, enjoyment, love, esp. sexual love or sensuality, 'desire for a remote object, hankering, - Gam.'

kāmabhāj mfn partaking of sensual enjoyment, enjoying all desires,

kāmabhāja partaker in enjoyment, fit for enjoyment,

kāmabhoga m. gratification of desires, sensual gratification,

kāmacāra 272/1 moving freely, following one's own pleasure, unrestrained, independent, following one's own desires 1/s/m spontaneous action,

kāmadhena = *kāmadhuk* = *kāmadhenu* the cow of plenty, the wish-giving cow,

kāma 271/3 m. wish, desire, longing, desire for, longing after, love, affection, pleasure, sensual pleasures, sexual love,

kāmadeva m. god of love,

kāmaduh (*-dhuk, -duham, -dhugbhis*, etc.) mfn granting every wish,
2. =*Dhenu* the wonder-cow,

kāmāgni m. fire of love, passion, lust,

kāmajata mfn born of desire or passion,

kāmakāmī m. desirer of the objects of desire

kāmakāra 272/1 mfn. fulfilling the desires of anyone, m. the act of following one's inclinations, spontaneous deed, free will

kāmakāmin mfn one who desires desires, following the dictates of passion,

kāmakāñcana lust and wealth – enemies of self-realisation,

kamala 252/1 m.n.a name of *Brahmā,* a lotus, a rose-coloured lotus-flower, mfn pale-red, rose-coloured,- *ja* 407/3 born or descended from, *Brahmā*, born of the lotus

kamalapattrākṣa mfn lotus petal-eyed, *Kṛṣṇa*

kāmam ind. at will, gladly, indeed, according to wish or desire, certainly, if you please, no doubt,

kāmamaya full of desire and lust,

kāmanā f. desire, longing, pleasure-seeking,

kamaṇḍalu m. water-jar, pitcher,

kāmarūpam desire-form, having the form of desire

kāmāśakti f. addiction to love, force of love or desire,

kāmasaṁkalpa mfn having all kinds of wishes,

kāmātman 272/3 mfn whose very essence is desire, whose selves are desirous, given to lust, sensual

kāmavaśa 272/3 m. subjection to love (lust), subject to the power of lust,

kāmāya ind. out of love for, according to desire for, agreeable to the wishes of,

kambala m. blanket, woollen cloth,

kambu m. shell, a conch.

kambu-grīva m. Shell-neck name of a tortoise,

kāmika mfn desired, wished for, satisfying desires, ifc. relating to or connected with a desire or wish, m. a wild duck,

kāmin mfn affectionate (spouse), desirous, longing after, loving, fond, in love with, m. (ī) a lover, anxious husband, pigeon, sparrow,

kāminīsakha mfn in the company of his wives, (L)

√*kamp* 252/2 Cl 1 A *kampate* to tremble, shake, DP in *calana* moving, trembling

kampa m. a trembling, shaking,

kampana 252/3 trembling, shaking,

unsteady, causing to tremble, quivering, vibration m. an earthquake

kampate he trembles, shakes

√*kaṁs* 241/1 Cl 2 A *kaṁste* to go, to command, to destroy, DP in *gati* going or *śāsan* destroying,

kaṁsa m. *Kaṁsa* name of a person, metallic vessel, metallic implements,

kāṁsya mfn brazen, n. brass, a drinking vessel of brass,

kāmyā 273/3 mfn desirable, beautiful, amiable, lovely, agreeable, to one's liking, agreeable to one's wish, f. wish, desire, longing for or striving after, will, purpose, intention,

kāmya-karman n. any act or ceremony done from interested or selfish motives,

√*kaṇ* Cl 1 P *kaṇati* to become small, to sound, cry, to go, approach, Cl 10 P *kāṇayati* to wink, close the eye with the lids or lashes, to sigh, sound, DP in *śabda* sounding, *gati* going, Cl 10, *nimīlana* closing the eye, winking,

√*kan* 248/2 Cl 1 P *kanati* to be satisfied or pleased, to agree to, accept with satisfaction, to shine, to go, DP in *dīpti* shining, *kānti* loving, wishing, or *gati* going

kaṇa m. a small grain, (as of dust or rice). particle of dust, a flake of snow, drop of water, spark of fire, any minute particle, atom, f.(ā) a minute particle, atom, drop, long pepper, cummin seed, kind of fly,

kāṇa mfn one-eyed, blind, pierced, perforated, m. a crow,

kāṇabhūti name of a demon,

kanaka 248/2 n. gold, a thorn-apple, mfn of gold, golden,

kanaka-stambha-rucira mfn shining with gold columns,

kanaka-sūtra n.a golden cord or chain,

kānana n. forest, grove, a house,

kāṇayati Nom. P. makes blind, destroys the sight,

√*kāñc* 268/2 Cl 1 A *kāñcate* to shine, Cl 10 to bind, DP in *dīpti* shining, and *bandhana* binding,

kāṇcana 268/2 n. gold, money, wealth, property, the filament of the lotus, mfn golden, made of gold, m. a covenant binding for life, a form of temple,

kāñcanāra m. mountain ebony,

√*kand* 249/2 Cl 1 P *kandati* to cry, utter lamentations, A *kandate* to be confounded, confound, DP in *āhvāna* crying, weeping, shedding tears, or *rodana* calling out to, exclaiming, in *vaiklavya* being confounded, perplexed,

√*kañc* 243/1 Cl 1 A *kañcate* to bind, to shine, DP in *dīpti* shining, and *bandhana* binding

kañcuka mfn armour, mail, m. the skin of a snake, husk, shell, cover, envelope,

kañcukin m. a chamberlain, an overseer of the women's apartments, a libidinous man, a debauchee, a snake, mfn furnished with armour or mail,

√*kaṇḍ* 246/1 Cl 1 P A *kaṇḍati (te),* to be glad or wanton, Cl 10 P *kaṇḍayati* to separate (the chaff from the grain) DP Cl 1 in *mada* being proud, Cl 10 in *bhedana* cutting, dividing

kāṇḍa m.n. section, joint of a stalk from one knot to another, arrow, chapter, mfn part of the trunk of a tree from where the branches come out, the source of all *nāḍī s*

kandamūla n. a radish,

kandara n. a natural cave, ginger, f. a lute, m. a hook for driving an elephant,

kandarpa m. 249/3 the god of love, love, lust,

kanduka m. a ball, a boiler, saucepan, a pillow, a betel-nut,

√*kaṇḍuya* 246/1 Nom P *kaṇḍūyati* to scratch, scrape, rub, DP in *gātravigharṣaṇa* rubbing limbs together, scratching,

kaniṣṭha mfn smallest, youngest, leat,

m. a younger brother, youngest, least, smallest, lowest, decending bucket of a well, (*ā*) f. inferior wife, one married later, little finger, younger wife,

kaniṣṭhaka mfn smallest, f. *–ikā* little finger

kaniṣṭhaprathama mfn having the youngest as the first,

kanīyāsa mfn smaller, younger, less,

kanīyas comparative mfn -younger, a younger brother or sister, younger son or daughter, smaller, less, inferior, very small or insignificant,

√*kaṅk* 242/1 Cl 1 A *kaṅkate* to go, DP in *gati* going, moving,

kaṅka m. a heron, kind of mango,

kaṅkāla m.n. a skeleton,

kaṅkana n. ring shaped ornament, a bracelet an ornament or trinket, a crest,

√ *kāṅkṣ* 268/1 Cl 1 P A *kāṅkṣati (te),*to wish, desire, long for, hope for, expect, wait for, strive to obtain, look for anything, DP in *kāṅkṣā* desiring, wishing for,

kāṅkṣā 268/1 f. wish, desire, inclination,

kāṅkṣe I will wish for, desire, 3/s/fut/mid/ √*kāṅkṣ* 268/1

kāṅkṣin mfn desiring, wishing, waiting for,

kānta mfn beloved, liked, loved, desired, lovely, beautiful, dear,

kaṇṭaka m. thorn, prickle, sting, a fishbone, a fingernail, unevenness/roughness,

kaṇṭaki-kṣīrin m. pl. thorn plants & milk plants,

kaṇṭakin mfn thorny, m. thorn plant,

kāntāra 271/1 a large forest, a difficult road through a forest, living in the world compared to a difficult road through a forest

√*kaṇṭh* 245/3 Cl 1 P A *kaṇṭhati (te*), Cl 10 P to mourn, long for, desire, DP in *śoka* being anxious, regretting,

kaṇṭha m. throat, using the *kaṇṭha* mouth, throat, and tongue position, for pronunciation of *kaṇṭha* letters *k,kh, g, gh, ṅ,* neck

kaṇṭhamūla n. the base of the neck, throat,

kānti f. desire, wish, loveliness, beauty, splendour, female beauty, personal embellishment, brightness

kaṇva m. a sage, foster father of *śakuntalā*

kanyā f. daughter, maiden, young girl,

kanyakā f. girl, maiden, unmarried girl,

kanyārala n. a gem of a girl, excellent girl,

kanyāratna n. girl-jewel, excellent maiden, lovely girl,

kapāla n. 1. cup or dish, alms-bowl,
2. cover or lid,
4. cranium, skull, the shell of an egg or tortoise,

kāpālarandhra hollow or cavity of the skull

kāpālika mfn relating to or belonging to a skull, m. a kind of śaiva ascetic who carries a human skull and uses it as a food bowl,

kaparda m. small shell used as a coin,

kapardaka m. small shell used as a coin, the cowrie shell,

kapaṭa m.n. fraud, trickery, cheating, also *kāpaṭa*

kapaṭaprabandha m. series of frauds,

kapha m. phlegm

kapi m. monkey, ape

kapi-dhvajas banner of the monkey , monkey-bannered, (*Arjuna)*

Kapila a sage and founder of the *Sāṁkhya* philosophical system

kapila n. brown, (monkey colour)

kapola m. cheek,

kapota m. dove, pigeon,

kāpuruṣa m. miserable man, coward,

kara 253/1 1. mfn a doer, maker, causer, doing, making, causing, producing, the act of doing, making etc. the 'doer', the hand, the trunk of an elephant, a measure (24 thumbs),
2. a ray of light, sunbeam, moonbeam

-kara ifc. causing or making,

kāra 274/2 n. making, doing, working, a maker, doer, an author, m. ifc. an act, action, a term used in denoting a letter or sound or indeclinable word, effort

kārā f. prison, gaol,
kārāgṛham n. prison, gaol,
kāraka 1. mfn. making or causing, doing, acting, who or what does or produces or creates,
*(am)*n. instrumental in bringing about the action denoted by a verb, (*karman, karaṇa, kartṛi, sampradāna, apādāna, adhikaraṇa*)
karāla 255/2 mfn. cleaving asunder, formidable, dreadful, terrible, a kind of deer,
karālī f. the terrific one, one of the seven togues of flame or fire,
karaṇa 254/1 mfn doing, making, effecting, causing, clever, skilful, a writer, instrumentality, (in Gram.) a sound or word as an independent part of speech (or as separated from context; in this sense usually n.), the act of making, doing, producing, instrument, means of action, method, cause, means, m. a helper, companion, a scribe, writer,
kāraṇa 274/2 1. n. cause, reason, the cause of anything, instrument, means, motive, origin, agency, instrumentality,
kāraṇabrahman saguṇa brahman, the Absolute qualified by māyā,
karaṇabhedana the act of splitting,
karaṇādhipa the god presiding over each sense,
kāraṇajagat the causal world,
kāraṇaśarīra the causal body
kāraṇavastha period of cosmic dissolution,
karatala m. palm, palm of the hand,
karavāri n. water from the hand,
karavāvahai √*kṛ* to do, make, perform, accomplish, cause, effect, undertake, 3/du/mid/impv. may we accomplish
kārayan causing to act, causing action, 1/s/pres/caus/act part.
√*karb* 258/2 Cl 1 P *karbati* to go, move, approach, DP in *gati* going,
√*kard* 258/1 Cl 1 P *kardati* to rumble (as the bowels), caw (as a crow), to make any unpleasant noise, DP in *kusitaśabda* rumbling (as the bowels),
kardama m. mud, slime, mire, clay, filth
karhi ind. when? at what time?
(with *svid, cid or api*) at any time,
(with *cid* and a particle of negation) never or at no time,
karhicit 260/1 at any time
kārikā f. 274/3 concise statement of doctrines, commentary, treatise,
karin mfn ‘possessing a hand’, an elephant,
kārin mfn causing, doing, making, effecting, producing, m. a mechanic, a tradesman, mfn rejoicing, praising,
kariṣyati will do or make
kariṣyasi you will do or make
kārita ppp caused to be made,
√*karj* 256/2 Cl 1 P *karjati* to pain, torment, DP in *vyathana* teasing, giving pain,
karkaśa mfn harsh, hard, firm, rough, m. a sword, scimitar, species of sugar-cane,
kārkaśya 275/2 n. roughness, hardness, rough labour, firmness, sternness, firmness, sternness, rough labour,
karkaṭa m. crab,
karma 258/2,3 for *karman* in cpds.
act, action, work, any religious act or rite (as sacrifice, oblation etc., esp. as originating in the hope of future recompense and as opposed to speculative religion or knowledge of spirit),
the accumulated effect of deeds in past, present or future, ‘as one sows so shall one reap’,
karma-bandha bondage of karma TP compound
karma-bandha m. the bonds of action (i.e. transmigration or repeated existence as a result of actions),
karmaceṣṭā f. active exertion, activity, deed, performance, action,
karmacodanā 258/3 the motive impelling

to ritual acts, inducement to action, inducer of all actions ,

karmadhāraya a class of *tatpuruṣa* compounds the members of which refer to the same object and would be in the same case if the compound were dissolved,

karmādhyakṣa m. over-seer of actions

karmadoṣa m. a sinful deed, vice, error,

karmaja deed-born, resulting from the actions of a life, originating in action, resulting or produced from any act (good or bad),

karmaja-adhyāsa identification of the ego with the body,

karmajña mfn skilled in any work, acquainted with religious rites,

karmakāṇḍa 258/3 that part of *śruti* which relates to ceremonial acts and sacrificial rites,

karmakṛt 258/3 mfn. performing any work, skilful in work, one who has done any work, m. a servant, workman, labourer,

karmamārga 'the way of action', 259/1m. the course of acts, activity

karman 258/2 n. act, action, performance, business, office, special duty, occupation, obligation (ifc. the first member of the compound being the person who performs the action or the person or thing for whom the action is performed or a specification of the action, any religious act or rite, work, labour, activity, action consisting in motion (Nyāya phil.), product, result, effect, organ of sense or of action, (in gram.) the object (of a sentence or an action), action with implied reference to the effect of deeds in past, present or future,

karmaṇaḥ 5/6/s/n from action, than action, from deeds, than deeds, of work, of actions, activities, whose activities,

karmaṇi 7/s/n in action, to action

karmaṇi prayoga a term for 'passive' sentence construction in which the *kartṛ* (agent) is in the 3rd (instrumental) case and the *karman* (object) is in the 1st (nominative) case,

karmāṇi actions, works 1/pl/n

karmānugāni in accordance with the actions,

karmānuṣṭhānam 259/2 act of practising one's duties, acting appropriately

karmaphala n. fruit of action

karmasākṣin m. witness of actions, sun,

karmasamāpti completion or perfection of action, concluding ceremony,

karmāśaya m. accumulation of the effects of good and evil acts to be played out later,

karmayoga m. agriculture and commerce, practical application, active exertion, the 'discipline of action', 'the process of achieving perfection in action', 'union through action',

karmayogin one on the path of *karmayoga*

karmendriyāṇi five senses of action, speaking, grasping, moving, evacuating, generating

kārmuka mfn efficacious, m. a tree, bamboo, a bow, rainbow, an arc, Saggitarius,

Karṇa a *Kaurava* warrior, half-brother of *Arjuna*

karṇa m. ear

karṇabhedana piercing the ear

kārpaṇya 275/3 n. pitiful circumstances, poorness of spirit, weakness, meekness,

karomi I do, I make, 3/s/pres/indic/mid √*kṛ*

karoṣi you do 2/s/

karoti 301/2 1/s/pres/act/indic. √*kṛ* he or she makes or does, puts on

karotu √ *kṛ* 1/s/impv/act let him do, he or she may do

karpūra m.n. camphor, made of camphor,

karpūrapaṭa 'camphor-cloth' name of a washerman or dyer,

karpūravilāsa 'camphor-joy' name of a washerman

karṣa 259/3 m. the act of drawing, dragging, ploughing, agriculture, a weight of gold or silver,
karta m. (earth)-cut, ditch, hole, cavity, separation, distinction,
kartā f. from *kṛ* 300/3 the agent of the action, the doer, worker, the creator,
kartakāma mfn desiring to do or perform,

kartana n. the act of cutting off, excision, act of extinguishing, extinction, 2. the act of spinning cotton/thread,
kartanī f. scissors,
kartāra m. creator, maker,
kartari prayogaḥ agent construction (the normal method of sentence construction), the *kartṛ* (subject or 1st case) is the agent of the action and the *karman* (object) is in the second case,
kartavya 257/3 to be done or made or accomplished, that which ought to be done, duty, obligation, having to be done, needing to be done, n. what has to be done, ind.'the will of the Absolute as the laws of nature reflecting through the framework of the individual' The little Absolute has to respond to the big Absolute. The interaction is the *kartavya.*' fut/pass/part √*kṛ*
kartavyatā f. or *–tva* n. the to-be-doneness, necessity, obligation, task,
kartavyam to be done, to be accomplished gerundive 1/s/n √*kṛ*
kārtika m. name of a month (October-November),
kārtikeya god of war,
√*kartr* 258/1 Cl 10 P *kartrayati* to unloosen, remove, DP in *śaitilya* relaxing
kartṛ 257/3 mfn. one who makes or does or acts, a doer, maker, agent, author, (in grammar) the agent of an action (who acts of his own accord [*sva-tantra*]), the active noun, the subject of a sentence,
kartṛtva 258/1 n. agency, means of action, state of performing action, the state of being the performer or author of anything,
kartṛvāda the claim of being an independent 'doer', (U)
kārtsna n. totality, whole,
kārtsnyena ind. entirely, fully,
kārttikeya m. name for *Skanda* god of war,
kartṛtā 258/1 the state of being the agent of the action,
kāru mf a maker, doer, artisan, mechanic, m. praiser, poet, singer, an art, science,
kartum 257/3 *kartu* , *kartum* infinitive of *kṛ* to do, (needing) to be done,
karuṇa 255/2 mournful, miserable, compassionate, (*ā*) f. pity, compassion, m. pity
karuṇāpara mfn compassionate,
karuṇaviṣṭa full of compassion,
kāruṇya 275/1 n. compassion, kindness,
√*karv* 259/3 Cl 1 P *karvati* to be proud, boast, DP in *darpa* being proud, boasting,
kārya 276/1 mfn going to be done, having to be done, to be made or done, n. business, task, work, duty, matter, M. an effect as opposed to cause (in philosophic texts), 'derived in the sense of anything produced, means the state of being the effect' 'evolves into the effect' (Gam.), fut.pass. part. (gerundive) 'the physical body as contrasted to the causal body *kāraṇa,'* (U)
kāryabrahma effected Brahman, *hiranyagarbha*
kāryahantṛ m. business-destroyer, one who obstructs an affair,
kāryakāla m. time for action, appointed time, season, opportunity,
kāryakāraṇasaṁbandha he relation between the cause and the effect,
kāryākṣama mfn unequal to or unfit for work,
kāryatattvārthavit (U) 'one who knows the meaning of the essence of actions'
kāryavimukti liberation from activity,

final emancipation,
kāryate is caused or forced to perform, 1/s/pres/pass/caus √ *kṛ*
kāryavastha period of cosmic manifestation,
√*kaś* 265/1 Cl 1 P *kaśati* to go, move, sound, strike, punish, hurt, DP in in *gati* going or *śāsana* destroying,
√*kāś* 280/2 Cl 1 A *kāśate* to be visible, appear, to shine, be brilliant, have an agreeable appearance,
Cl 4 *kāśyate* DP in *dīpti* shining
√*kaṣ* 265/2 Cl 1 P A *kaṣati (te)*, to rub, scratch, scrape, to rub or scratch oneself, test, try, hurt, destroy, DP in *hiṁsā* injuring, killing,
√*kas* 266/1 Cl 1 P *kasati* to go, move, approach, to beam, shine, DP in *gati* going, Cl 2 *kaste* in *śāmana* destroying and *gati* going
√*kās* Cl 1 A *kāsate* to cough, DP in *śabdakutsā* coughing or making a sound indicative of any disease,
kāśa m. visibility, 'the becoming visible, appearance', a kind of grass used for mats, roofs etc.
kaśā f. a whip, a rein, bridle, whipping, flogging, a string, rope, thong,
kāsāra m. a pond, pool,
kaṣāya mfn astringent, fragrant, red, dull red, yellowish red (as the garment of a Buddhist Bhikṣu), m.n. an astringent flavour or taste, a yellowish red colour, an astringent juice, an extract of juice, a decoction or infusion, any healing potion, juice, gum, resin, ointment, smearing, anointing, colouring or perfuming,
265/3 attachment to worldly objects, a translucent screen which fogs the subtle body and puts the person into a chamber of misty darkness made of ignorance, known by some as *āvaraṇa* covering or veiling,
kaścana 240/3 any, anyone at all, in any way
kaścid(t) 240/3 anyone, someone,
kāśī the city of Benares, Varanasi,
kaśmala 265/2 mfn foul, dirty, impure, timid, m.n. consternation, stupefaction, dejection, despair
kasmāt ind. why? wherefore? whence?
kasmin pron. 7/s in whom
kaṣṭa n. hardship, mfn ill, evil, wrong, bad, painful, severe, miserable, pernicious, noxious, injurious,
kāṣṭha n. stick of wood, log, firewood, an instrument for measuring lengths, a kind of measure, wood or timber in general,
ind. with a verb expresses excellence or superiority,
kāṣṭhā f. race-course, course, track of the winds and clouds in the sky, a measure of time, the mark, goal, limit, the highest limit, top, summit,
kāṣṭha-bhārika m. a wood-carrier,
kāṣṭha-ccheda m. dearth of wood,
kāṣṭhika m. woodman,
kasya pron. whose
kasyacid of anyone, of anyone whatever
√*kaṭ* 243/2 Cl 1 P to go, Cl 1 P *kaṭati* to rain, to surround, encompass, cover, screen, divide, DP in *varṣa* raining, and *āvaraṇa* screening, covering,
ind. a particle of exclamation,
kaṭa m. a mat, the hip, the hip and loins, the temples of an elephant, a glance or side look, a corpse, a hearse, a burning ground, a time or season, excess, superabundance, grass,
kaṭaka 243/3 m. a twist of straw, a straw mat, a bracelet of gold or shell, m.n. a valley, dale, an army, circle, wheel, dale, a royal camp, troop, caravan, a multitude, an army,
katama mfn who or which of many, best, excessively good-looking, often a strengthened substitute for *ka,* the superlative affix imparting emphasis, occasionally 'who or which of two', when 'followed by *ca* and preceded by *yatama* an

indefinite expression is formed equal to "any whosoever" or "any whatsoever"', e.g. *yatamad eva katamac ca vidyāt,*
"he may know anything whatsoever",

kaṭāra libidinous man, lecher,

katara who or which of two, (comparative) sometimes used to express which or who of many,

kātara mfn timid, nervous, embarrassed, cowardly, disheartened, afraid of, faint-hearted, m. kind of large fish, n. timidity, despair, agitation,

√*kaṭh* 244/2 Cl 1 P *kaṭhati* to live in distress, DP in *kṛcchrajīvana* living in distress

√*kath* 247/1 Cl 10 P *kathayati* to converse with anyone, tell, relate, narrate, report, inform, speak about, declare, explain, describe, announce, show, exhibit, order, command, suppose, state, DP in *vākyaprabandha* telling, narrating

kathā f. story, tale, fable, discussion, conversation, speech, talk, mention, ind. how? whence? why? sometimes merely a particle of interrogation,

kathāchala n. guise of a fable,

katham or *kathā* 247/2 ind. how? in what way? *katham etat* how's that, *kathaṁ nu* how indeed, *kathaṁ cana* in any wise whatsoever (emphasizing a preceding negation), *katham api* somehow, *katham cit* somehow, only just,

katham-cana ind. in some way

kathā-pīṭha n. pedestal of *kathā,* name of the first book of the -

kathā-sarit-sāgara m. story-stream-ocean , title of *Somadeva's* collection,

kathāvatāra m. incarnation of *kathā,*

kathayanta speaking of, explaining, describing, pres/act/part 1/pl/m

kathayata please speak, please tell,

kathayati tells

kathayiṣyanti they will relate, they will tell, 1/pl/fut/act

kaṭhina mfn hard, cruel, firm, inflexible,

kathita° told, things spoken, conversation,

kaṭhora mfn cruel, hard, stiff, offering resistance, sharp, piercing, full-grown,

kaṭhora-garbha late pregnancy, having a full-grown foetus,

kathyate 247/1 from *kath* to converse, to be called, be regarded or considered as, 1/s/pres/indic/pass it can be described

kati 246/3 how many? some, several,

katipaya mfn indef. several, some, a few, a certain number, so many,

√*katr* 247/1 Cl 10 P *katrayati* to loosen, slacken, remove, DP in *śaithilya* relaxing,

√*katth* 246/3 Cl 1 A *katthate* to boast, praise, celebrate, DP in *ślāghā* boasting

katthana 246/3mfn. boasting, praising, m. the act of boasting

kaṭu 244/1 mfn pungent, acrid, sharp, m. pungency, acerbity,

kaulāla n. pottery, m. a potter,

kaumāra mfn juvenile, youthful, belonging to a youth or young girl, maiden, maidenly, n. childhood, youth,

kaumudī f. moonlight, day of full moon,

Kaunteya m. son of *Kuntī,* (*ā*) f. – mother of Yudhiṣṭhira, Bhīmasena & Arjuna,

kaupīna 316/2 a loin cloth, a small piece of cloth worn over the genitals by poor persons, the genitals, *kaupīnatve – tva* 7/s in having a loin cloth, having nothing but a loin cloth i.e. very poor,

kaurāvya m. descendant of the Kuru

kauśala 317/3 n. skilfulness, welfare, good fortune, prosperity, cleverness, experience, well-being, health, prosperity

kausalyā f. *Kausalyā*

kaustubha n. the name of a jewel worn on the chest of Viṣṇu,

kauṭilya 315/2 n crookedness, curvature, falsehood, dishonesty, curliness of the hair,

kautūhala m. curiosity, interest in anything,
kautuka 316/1 n. curiosity, interest in anything, eagerness, impatience,
kautukāt ind. eagerly, out of curiosity or interest,
kavaca m. armour, a coat of mail, any covering, n. an amulet, an amulet or charm inscribed with mystic words or a syllable,
kavaya m. the intelligent, enlightened one, the advancement of scholars or philosophers in spiritual life (V),
kavi 264/2 mfn. gifted with insight, intelligent, knowing, enlightened, wise, m. (*ḥ*) a wise man, sage, seer, prophet, poet
seer of the *krānta* (past)
seer of all, 'there is no other seer but this'
kavikratu mfn having the power or insight of a wise one, intelligent,
kavya mfn a sacrificer , sacrificial priest, n. *(am)* an oblation of food to ancestors,
kāvya mfn endowed with the qualities of a sage or poet,descended or coming from a sage, prophetic, inspired, n. poetry, poem, m. happiness, welfare, pl. poems, f. intelligence, 280/1
kāvyaśāstra-vinoda m. entertainment with poetry and science,
kayā 253/1 ind. 3/s/ *ka* in what manner? by what?
kāya 274/1 2. m.the body, trunk of a tree, body of a lute, mfn relating or devoted to the god *Ka*,
kāyakleśa m. bodily suffering, toil, mortification and torment of the body,
kāyasampat (d), f. perfection of the body
kāyasiddhi f. perfection of the body through yoga,
kāyastha m letter-writer, writer -caste, dwelling in the body, Supreme Spirit,
kāyavyuha m. supernatural power of assuming several bodies simultaneously,
kāyika mfn corporeal, performed by the body,
ke pron.which two, which many,
kecid some, whoever,
√kel 309/3 Cl 1 P *kelati* to shake, tremble, to go or move, to be frolicsome, sport, DP in *calana* moving, trembling, shaking, playing, sporting,
keli 309/3 sport, amorous sport, pastime, amusement,
keliśikṣayā śikù 1070/1 to wish to be able, to learn, study, practice, to practise oneself in, verbal noun – practises 3/s by amorous practise
kena pron. by or with whom, what or which
kenacid with anything
kendra n. centre, m. the centre of a circle, the equation of the centre, the argument of a circle, the argument of an equation, the heart,
√kep 309/2 Cl 1 A *kepate* to shake or tremble DP in *kampana* trembling
keśa m. hair of the head, the mane of a horse or lion, a kind of perfume, name of a mineral,
keśānta m. hair-end, long hair hanging down, locks,
keśapakṣa m.du. the 2 sides of the hair of the head, the temples,
kesara m. hair, mane, filament,
kesarāgra n. ends of a mane,
keśava mfn having long or much or handsome hair, 'o handsome haired one' voc/s/m a name for *Kṛṣṇa*
keśa-śmaśru-loma-nakha n.pl. hair of the head, beard, the body, plus the nails,
Keśi a demon in the form of a horse slain by *Kṛṣṇa*
keśin mfn maned, with flowing mane,
keśiṇī M. 'she who has fine hair', the wife of King Sagara of Ayodhyā, daughter of the king of Vidarbha and mother of the wicked Asamañja
keta m. intention, desire, will, intention, a house, abode, mark, sign,

ketaya 308/3 nom. P *ketayati* to summon, call or invite, to fix or appoint a time, counsel or advise, to hear

ketu m. brightness, clearness, bright appearance, flag, banner, a chief, leader, eminent person, intellect, judgment,discernment, unusual phenonema – comet, meteor, pl. rays of light, beams,

√*kev* 309/3 Cl 1 P *kevate* to serve, attend to, DP in *sevana* serving,

kevala 309/3 mfn exclusively one's own (not common to others), alone, only, mere, sole, one, the Absolute, excluding others, not connected with anything else, isolated, abstract, absolute, simple, pure, uncompounded, unmingled, entire, whole, all, selfish, envious, n. alone, absolute, entire, whole, all, the Absolute, mere, the doctrine of the absolute unity of spirit, the highest possible knowledge,
m. certainly, decidedly, a dancer,
f. 'the whole of a philosophical system',
(*am*) ind. only, merely, solely, entirely, only, absolutely,

kevala asti mere existence,

kevala astitva absolute being,

kevala caitanya pure consciousness or intelligence, without thought,

kevalajñāna n. the highest possible knowledge (Jaina),

kevalakumbhaka sudden restraint of breath,

kevalānandasvarūpa Brahman, having the nature of mere bliss,

keyūra m. an armlet worn on the upper arm,

kha n. 1. hole, hollow, 2. opening, aperture of the human body,
3. hole in the hub of a wheel,
4. void space, the sky, air, ether,
m. the sun,

√*khac* 335/1 Cl 1 P *khacati* to come forth, project (as teeth), Cl 9 P *khacñāti* to be born again, to cause prosperity, to purify, Cl 10 P *khacayati* to fasten, bind, DP in *bhūta-prādurbhāva* being born again appearing of beings,

√*khaḍ* 335/2 Cl 10 P *khāḍayati* to divide, break, DP in *bhedana* cutting, dividing

√*khad* 336/2 Cl 6 P *khadati* to be steady or firm or solid, to strike, hurt, kill, (for √*khād*) to eat, DP in *sthairya* being steady or firm, or *hiṁsā* striking, hurting

√*khād* 339/1 Cl 1 P A *khādati (te)* to chew, bite, eat, devour, feed, prey upon, to hurt, ruin, DP in *bhakṣaṇa* eating,

khāda eat! (sing.)

khadana mfn striking, hurting, killing, n. juice, firmness, solidity,

khādana 339/2 n. chewing, eating, food, victuals, m. a tooth,

khādata eat! (pl)

khādati eats

khaḍga m. a sword, scimitar, large sacrificial knife, a rhinoceros,

khādiṣyati will eat

khādita mfn eaten

khāditavya to be eaten,

khāditvā ind. having chewed, having eaten,

khadyota m. sun,

khadyotā f. left eye,

khaga also *khagama* (sky-goer),
1.mfn moving in the sky, flying,
2. m. bird,

√*khai* 340/3 Cl 1 P *khāyati* to make firm, be firm or steady, to strike, injure, kill, to mourn, sorrow, DP in *khadana* being steady and firm, striking, hurting, killing

√*khaj* 335/1 Cl 1 P *khajati* to churn or agitate, DP in *mantha* churning, stirring,

√*khal* 338/1 Cl 1 P *khalati* to move or shake, to gather, DP in *sañcalana* shaking, and *sañcaya* gathering, collecting,

khala m. 1. threshing floor, granary, earth, mould, soil, 2. a mean low-living fellow, a rogue, (*ā*) f. a mischievous woman, 3. contest, battle, sediment, dregs of oil, the sun,

khalu 338/2 ind. indeed, verily, certainly, may emphasize the previous word, please, pray (in entreaty)
L. 1. now (continuative),
atha khalu now
2. indeed – emphasizing the previous word,
na khalu certainly not,

√*khan* 336/3 Cl 1 P *khanati* to dig, dig up, delve, turn up the soil, excavate, root up, to pierce (said of an arrow), DP in *avadāraṇa* digging

√*khaṇḍ* 336/1 Cl 1 A *khaṇḍate* to break, divide, destroy, Cl 10 P *khaṇḍayati* to break, tear, break into pieces, crush, cut, divide, to destroy, remove, annihilate, defeat, conquer, refute, interrupt, disturb, to disregard (an order), DP in *mantha* churning, in *bhedana* cutting, dividing,

khaṇḍa mfn broken, deficient, defective, crippled, m. a break, section, piece, a continent, part,

khaṇḍaka m. lump-sugar, treacle, molasses, a fragment, part, piece, mfn breaking to pieces,

khaṇḍana breaking, dividing, reducing to pieces, hurting, injuring, removing, frustrating, cheating, deceiving, rebellion, opposition,

khaṁḍaśas ind. in pieces, by pieces, bit by bit, piece by piece,

khaṅga 335/1 see *khaḍga* 335/3 a sword, scimitar, sacrificial knife,

khani mfn digging or rooting up, f. a mine,

khanitavya gve. to be dug, dug up,

khanitra n. a digging tool, spade, shovel,

√*khañj* 335/1 Cl 1 P *khañjati* to limp, walk lamely, mfn limping, DP in *gati-vaikalya*, limping

khañja mfn lame,

khara mfn harsh, rough, pungent, acid, m. ass, donkey, mule, an osprey, heron, crow,

√*kharb* 338/1 337/3 Cl 1 P *kharbati* to go or move, DP in *gati* going

√*khard* 337/3 Cl 1 P *khardati* to bite, sting, sting venomously, DP in *dandaśūka* biting, stinging,

√*kharj* 337/3 Cl 1 P *kharjati* to creak (like a wagon-wheel), to worship, treat with respect or courtesy, to pain, make uneasy, to cleanse, DP in *vyathana* causing pain, or *pujana* worshipping

√*kharv* 338/1(= √*garv*), Cl 1 P *kharvati* to be proud or haughty, DP in *darpa* being proud, boasting,

√*khaṣ* Cl 1 P *khaṣati* to hurt, injure, kill, DP in *hiṁsā* hurting, killing

√*khaṭ* 335/1 Cl 1 P *khaṭati* to desire, DP in *kāṅkṣā* desiring, wishing, ind. a particle of exclamation,

khāta mfn dug up, m. a ditch, n. a ditch, moat, pond, well, digging a hole,

√*khaṭṭ* 335/2 Cl 10 P *khaṭṭati* to cover, screen, DP in *saṁvaraṇa* covering, screening,

√*khav* 338/3 Cl 9 P *khaunāti* or *khunāti* to be born again, to cause prosperity, to purify, DP in *bhūta-prādurbhāva* being born again, manifestation of beings,

khecara mfn moving in the sky, flying, what moves in the sky, a celestial being, a bird

khecaratva n. power of flying (by magic),

√*kheḍ* 340/3 variation of √*kheṭ* DP in *bhakṣaṇa* eating

kheda 340/1 m. lassitude, depression, fatigue, pain, affliction

khedavaśa mfn having depression as one's controlling influence, under the dominion of sorrow,

√*khel* 340/3 Cl 1 P *khelati* to shake, move to and fro, swing, tremble, DP in *gati* going, in *calana* moving, shaking, playing, sporting,

khela 340/3 moving, trembling, sport, play, pastime, (*ā*) f. sport, play

√*khelāya* 340/3 Nom P *khelayati* to play, sport, DP in *vilāsa* sporting

√*kheṭ* 340/2 Cl 10 *kheṭayati* to eat, consume, DP in *bhakṣaṇa* eating

√*khev* 340/3 = √*seva* to serve, wait upon, DP in *sevana* serving,

√*khid* 340/1 Cl 6 *khindati* to strike, press, press down, be depressed or weary, Cl 7 A *khintte* to be pressed down, suffer pain, Cl 4 A P *khidayate (ti)* to be pressed down or depressed, be distressed or weary, feel tired or exhausted, caus. P *khedayati* to press down, molest, disturb, make tired or exhausted, DP in *parighātana* (Cl 6) striking, pressing down, afflicting, in *dainya* (Cl 4 & 7) suffering pain or misery

khidyate 339/3 is wearied , suffers pain, 1/s/pres/indic/pass. is wearied or sad

khila m. 1. a piece of waste-land between cultivated fields, 2. a gap

khinna 340/1 mfn depressed, distressed, afflicted, exhausted,

√*khiṭ* 339/3 Cl 1 P *khedati* to be terrified or frightened, to terrify, alarm, DP in *trasa* fearing, frightening, causing fear,

√*khol* 341/1 = √*khor* DP same

√*khor* 341/1 Cl 1 P *khorati* to limp, be lame, DP in *gati-pratighāta* limping, being lame

√*khoṭ* 340/3 Cl 1 P *khoṭati* = √*khor*, DP in *bhakṣaṇa* eating

√*khru* DP in *śabda* sounding

khu a Prakrit form for *khalu*

√*khuḍ* 340/1variation of √*khuṇḍ*, DP in *saṃvaraṇa* covering

√*khuj* 340/1 Cl 1 *khojati* to steal, DP in *steya-karaṇa* stealing,

√*khuṇḍ* 340/2 Cl 1 A *khuṇḍate* to break in pieces, to limp, Cl 10 P *khuṇḍayati* to break in pieces, DP in *bhedana* breaking, dividing,

√*khur* 340/2 340/2 Cl 6 P *khurati* to cut, cut up, break in pieces, DP in *bhedana* cutting, scratching,

khura m. hoof, razor,

√*khurd* 340/2 Cl 1 A *khūrdate* to play, sport, DP in *krīḍā* playing

√*khyā* 341/1 Cl 2 P *khyāti* also A in some tenses, to be named, be known, caus. *khyāpayati* to make known, promulgate, proclaim, to relate, tell, say, betray, denounce, DP in *prakathana* telling,

khyāta mfn named, called, denominated, known, well-known, celebrated,

khyāti f. assertion, view, idea, perception, knowledge, being well-known, fame,

khyātim gam become famous,

√*ki* 282/1 Cl 3 P *ciketi* see √*ci* DP in *jñāna* knowing

kīdṛc mfn of what sort?

kīdṛg–vyāpāra m. what business

kīdṛg–vyāpāravant mfn having what business

kīdṛś(a) *(ī)* what kind of..?

√*kil* 284/1 Cl 6 P *kilati* to be or become white, to freeze, to play, Cl 10 P *kelayati* to send, throw, DP in *śvaitya* being or becoming white, or *krīḍana* playing, sporting,

kila or *kilā* ind. indeed, certainly, as they say, (follows the word it emphasizes), m. play, trifling,

kilbiṣa 284/2 n. fault, offence, sin, guilt

kim 282/2 ind. interrogative, what, why, expecting the answer 'no', sometimes used as a question marker without meaning,

kimapi somewhat, much more, still further

kimartha mfn having what as object

kimartham ind. why?

kim bahunā 724/2 "what occasion is there for much talk?" i.e. "in short"

kim bhṛtya m. a bad servant,

kiṁ ca moreover

kiṁcit something, somewhat, slightly,

kimiti wherefore? why? with what in mind?

kimiva wherefore?

kimprabhu m. a bad master,

kim punas tu but what besides, how much more?

kim nu to say the least of,

kim nu khalu can it be that?

kiṁsuhṛd m. a bad friend,

kiṁśuka m. name of a tree,
kiṁtu but, however, (may be used first in a sentence)
kimuta
kiṁ vā perchance?
kim + vadantī 282/3 1/s/f "what do they say", (it is) a common saying, rumour,
kimicchasi what would you like? (at meals), what do you desire?
kiñcana 283/1 something, anything, (with negation), in no way, nothing, anything,
kiñciccalana subtle movement
kiñcid 283/1 whatever , anything, something
kiñcijjña partial knowledge,
kinnara m. a heavenly musician, (associated with the Gandharvas),
kintu but
kiraṇa m. dust, very minute dust, a ray or beam of light, a sun or moon-beam,
kīri m. praiser, poet,
kirīṭa 284/1 any ornament used as a crown
kirīṭin mfn having a crown/diadem,
kirīṭina crowned
√*kīrt* 285/1 Cl 10 P. *kīrtayati* to mention, make mention of, tell, name, call, recite, repeat, relate, declare, celebrate, praise, glorify
kīrtaya 285/1 *kīrtayati* mentions, celebrates, praises, glorifies pres/caus/
kīrti f. mention, esp. good report, fame,
kirītita 285/2 mfn said, mentioned, asserted, declared, celebrated, known, notorious,
kīrtana 285/1 n. mentioning, repeating, saying, singing the praises of the Lord, chanting, √*kīrt* recite, repeat, celebrate, praise, glorify (with gen.), 'praise-singing' HH
kīrti 285/1f. good report, fame, renown, glory, lustre
kiśalaya or *kisalaya* m. n. sprout, shoot, Nom. P. to cause to shoot or spring forth,
kiṣkindhā the capital city from which *sugrīva* was exiled
kiśora m. a colt, the young of any animal, (*ī*) f. young, a female colt,
√*kiṭ* 282/2 Cl 1 P *keṭati* to go or approach, to alarm or terrify, to fear, DP in *gati* going, *trāsa* fearing, frightening
√*kit* 282/2 Cl 3 *ciketti*, see 2. *cit* and *ketaya*, DP in *nivāsa* living, roga-*apanayana* healing, curing
kīṭa m. worm, caterpillar, the scorpion in the zodiac, n. faeces, ifc. an expression of contempt,
kitava m. gambler, rogue f. *vī* addicted to gaming,
kiyat mfn how great, how large, how far, how much, of what extent, of what qualities, little, small, unimportant, of small value, ind. how far, how much, how,
kiyad-dūra n. small distance, (-*re*) ind. a little way,
kiyāmbu n. waterlily,
kiyān what is this, what, of what extent, how much, (V)
kiyant 1. how great? how much? what sort of a?
2. (how great in a derogatory sense) not great, small,
kiyat how great,
√*klad* 323/2 see √*kland* DP in *vaiklavya* being perplexed, and *vaikalya* confounding,
klaibya n. 324/1 impotence, unmanliness, weakness, timidity, cowardice
√*klam* 323/3 Cl 1.4. *klāmati*, *klāmyati* to be or become fatigued, be weary or exhausted, DP in *glāni* being fatigued or tired
√*kland* 323/2 Cl 1 P *klandati* to call, to lament, weep, A. *klandate* to be confounded or troubled, to sound, DP in *āhvāna* crying, weeping, and *godana* calling out to exclaiming DP (A) in *vaiklavya* being perplexed, and *vaikalya* confounding,
√*klap* see √*hlap* to speak, DP in *vyaktavāc* speaking, sounding, creaking

√*klath* 323/2 Cl 1 P to be formed into clots or lumps, to hurt, kill, DP in *hiṁsā* injuring

kleda 323/3 m. wetness, dampness

kledana making wet, moistening, oozing

kledayanti they cause to become wet, 1/pl/pres/caus/act √*klid*

√*kleś* 324/2 Cl 1 A *kleśate* to speak articulately, to speak inarticulately, to strike, kill, DP in *avyaktāvāc* speaking inarticulately, *bādhana* impeding, hindering,

kleśa 324/1 m. pain, affliction, distress, wrath, anger, worldly occupation, care, trouble,

kleśana n. disgust

√*klīb* 324/1 Cl 1 A *klibate* to be impotent, behave like a eunuch, to be timorous or modest or unassuming, Cl 10 A. *klībayate* to be unmanly or timorous, DP in *adhārṣṭya* being impotent,

√*klid* 323/3 Cl 4 *klidayati* (rarely A) to be or become wet or damp, to rot, putrefy,
DP in *ārdrībhāva* becoming wet, being damp, being moist

√*klind* 323/3 Cl 1 P A *klindati (te)* to lament, DP in *paridevana* lamenting,

klinna mfn moistened, wet, running (as an eye), rotted, putrefied,
soft or moved (the heart),

√*kliś* 324/1 Cl 9 P *kliśnāti* to torment, trouble, molest, cause pain, afflict, to suffer, feel pain, Cl 4 P *kliśjati* to torment, cause pain, A. *kliśyate* to be tormented or molested, be afflicted, feel pain, P. to be sinful, DP in *upatāpa* suffering pain, in *vibādhana* tormenting, afflicting

kliṣṭa mfn molested, tormented, afflicted,

√*kḷp* cl 1 A *kalpate,* to be well ordered or regulated, be well managed, succeed, to bear suitable relation to anything, correspond, be adapted to, in accordance with, to accomodate oneself to, be favourable to, to partake of, to fall to the share, be shared, to become, to happen, occur, to prepare, arrange, to produce, cause, create, to bring into suitable connection with, caus. *kalpayati* to arrange, prepare, DP in *nikṣepa* scattering, *hiṁsā* injuring, hurting, killing, *saṁśabdana* mentioning, uttering, naming, calling,

kḷpta 308/3 mfn arranged, prepared, ready, in order, complete, right, perfect, at hand, made, done, formed, caused, produced, effected, invented, created, fixed, settled, prescribed, ascertained, determined, cut, clipped, pared, shorn,

kḷpta-keśanakhaśmaśru mfn having hair, nails and beard in order
i.e. trimmed,

kḷptānta having its end prescribed, limited,

klṛpta mfn arranged, made, ready, in order, created

kḷpti f. preparation, making or becoming conformable, accomplishment, invention, contrivance, obtainment, description,

√*klu* 324/2 Cl 1 A *klavate* to move, DP in *gati* going

√*kmar* 318/3 Cl 1 P *kmarati* to be crooked in mind or body, be fraudulent, DP in *hūrchana* being crooked, acting dishonestly,

√*knas* 318/3 Cl 4 P *knasyati* to be crooked in mind or body, to shine, caus. *knasayati* to shine DP in *hvaraṇa* being crooked or *dīpti* shining

√*knu* or *knū* 318/3 Cl 9 P A *knunāti* or *knunīte* or *knūnāti* to sound, DP in *śabda* sounding,

√*knūy* Cl 1 A *knūyate* to be wet, to make a creaking sound, to stink, caus. P *knopayati* to make wet, DP in *śabda* sounding or *und* being wet,

kodaṇḍa m. bow (of an archer), an eyebrow shaped like a bow,

kodaṇḍāṭanī f. the notched end of a bow,

kokila m. an Indian cuckoo, a kind of mouse, a kind of snake,

kola m. a hog, a raft, the breast, haunch,

hip or flank, an embrace, embracing, a kind of weapon, the planet Saturn, a barbarian, a man of mixed caste, (*am*) n. the jujube tree or its fruit,

kolāhala m.n. uproar, confused cry, din,

komala mfn tender, soft, sweet, charming,

koṇa m. a corner, angle, the number 4, the sharp edge of a sword, a club,

kopa 313/1 m. √*kup*, anger, fury, passion, rage, disorder or imbalance in the body, being in contradiction with, reversal, incompatibleness,

kopākula mfn full of anger,

kopāt angrily

ko'pi ind. indefinite. anyone,

kośa 314/1 m.a cask, cover, sheath, subtle body, treasure, wealth, treasury, encasement, coccoon, vocabulary,

koṣa m.n. pocket, bud, store-room, treasury, vessel, store, box,

koṭara n. hollow of a tree, hollow,

koṭi f. a crore, =10,000,000 or 100 *lakh,* the curved end of a bow, end or top of anything, horns or cusps, the highest point, eminence, the complement of an arc to 90°, perpendicular side of a right angle triangle,

koṭṭa m. a fort, stronghold,

kovida mfn knowing well, skilled, learned,

√*kṛ* 301/1 Cl 8 P *karoti* A *kurute* to do, make, perform, accomplish, cause, effect, prepare, undertake, to do anything for the advantage or injury of another, to execute, carry out (as an order or command), to manufacture, prepare, work at, elaborate, build, to form or construct one thing out of another, to employ, use, make use of, to compose, describe, to cultivate, bring to completion, spend (time), place, put, lay, bring, lead, take hold of, to direct the thoughts/ mind towards any object, turn the attention to, resolve upon, determine on, to think of, to make, render, procure for another, bestow, grant, A to procure for oneself, appropriate, assume, give aid, help anyone to get anything, make liable to, injure, violate, appoint, institute, give an order, commission, cause to get rid of, proceed, act, worship, sacrifice, make a sound, utter, pronounce,
Also exists in
class 1 P *karati* A *karate*,
class 2 P *karti* A *kṛte* (meanings as above) and
304/1 class 3 P *cikarti* A *cikṛte*, to make mention of, praise, speak highly of, injure,
Cl 5 P *kṛṇoti* A *kṛṇute*,
DP in *karaṇa* (Cl 8) doing, and *hiṁsā* hurting, injuring, (Cl 3).

√*kṝ* 308/2 Cl 6 P *kirati* to pour out, scatter, throw, cast, disperse, to throw up in a heap, heap up, A. to throw off from oneself, P. to strew, pour over, fill with, cover with, DP in *nikṣepa* scattering,

√2.*kṝ* Cl 5,9, P A *kṛṇoti* to hurt, injure, kill, DP in *hiṁsā* hurting, killing

√3*kṝ* Cl 10 A *kārayate* to know, to inform,

√*krad* 319/2 see *krand* DP in *vaiklavya* being perplexed and *vaikalya* confounding,

krakaca m.n. a saw,

√*kram* 319/3 Cl 1 P A *krāmati*, or *kramati* or *kramate,* also Cl 4 P *krāmyati* or *kramyati,* to step, walk, go, go towards, approach, to approach in order to ask for assistance, to go across, go over, to climb (as on a branch), cover (as in copulation), stretch over, project over, tower above, take possession of, A. to proceed well, advance, make progress, succeed, to read according to the *krama* arrangement of a Vedic text, P. to be liable to the peculiar arrangement of a Vedic text called *krama* (i.e. to be doubled as a letter or word), DP in *pāda* walking, or *vikṣepa* stepping,

krama m. a step, going, proceeding, course, regular progress, process, sequence, order, series, regular arrangement, succession, hereditary descent, method, manner, order, rules regarding rituals,

kramamukti progressive emancipation of devotees from this world to the world of Brahman and from there attain *kaivalya*

kramaśaḥ ind. step by step, gradually, in order, consecutively,

krameṇa ind. step by step, gradually,

√*krand* 319/2 Cl 1 P A *krandati (te)* to neigh (as a horse), roar, (metaphorically applied to clouds, wind and water), to creak (as a wheel), to sound, make a noise, to cry piteously weep, grieve, be confused with sorrow, to roar, rave, DP in *āhvana* crying, weeping, or *rodana* calling out to, exclaiming, in *vaiklavya* being perplexed and *vaikalya* confounding,

√*krap* 319/2 Cl 1 A *krapate* to be compassionate, DP in *kṛpā* pitying or *gati* going,

kratava mfn relating to Indra,

√*krath* 319/2 Cl 1 P *krathati* to hurt, kill, caus. *krāthayati* to hurt, injure, destroy, to rejoice, revel, DP in *hiṁsā* hurting, injuring

kratu 319/1 m. plan, intention, desire, will, intelligence personified, conviction, determination, a firm belief, inspiration, enlightenment, a sacrificial rite or ceremony, sacrifice, offering, worship, 'resolution – Gam.' '*bhadra kratu*'- right judgment, good understanding,

kratumaya mfn. endowed with intelligence, identified with a conviction

kraurya n. hard-heartedness, fierceness, terribleness, cruelty,

kravya n. raw flesh, corpse, carrion,

kravyād mfn consuming corpses,

kravyāda mfn consuming corpses (as Agni),

kravya-vāhana mfn carrying off the corpses (said of Agni),

kṛcchra mfn distressful, troublesome, causing trouble or pain, bad, evil, m.n.. trouble, difficulty, hardship, ind. (am) miserably, painfully,

kṛcchrajīvana a life of hardship, badness, trouble or confusion,

kṛcchrakarman n. hard work, drudgery,

√*kṛḍ* see √*kūḍ* (cl 6 P *kūḍati,* to graze, eat, become firm or solid, cl. 10 P *kūḍayati* to burn, scorch,

√*krī* 321/2 Cl P A *krīṇāti, krīṇīte* to buy, purchase, DP in *dravya-viniyama* buying or exchanging goods,

√*krīḍ* 321/3 Cl 1 P *krīḍati* or *krīḷati* to play, sport, amuse one's self frolic, gambol, dally(used of men, animals, the wind and waves, etc.), to jest, joke with, DP in *vihāra* playing, amusing oneself,

krīḍā mfn playing, sporting (said of the winds),m. sport, play, pastime, amusement, amorous sport

krīḍana 321/2 playing, play, sport

kṛdanta –(*pāṇini s* name for) participles, m. a word ending with a *kṛt* affix,

krīḍārtha for the sake of amusement,

krīḍati plays, 1/s/pres/

kriṣṇa see *kṛṣṇa*

krītotpanna mfn bought or on hand (food)

krītvā ind. having done, made, performed, having bought,

kriya m. sign Aries,

kriyā means activity. 'There is only one activity in truth. The entire creation is this activity, manifesting the glory and substance of the Absolute. At different times this activity may be called –speaking, writing, resting, going or living, but at all times it is manifesting the substance of the absolute. Name and form change but the Absolute does not. The ocean and its waves are of the same substance; the waves are in motion and ever changing, but the substance, water, remains the same.' L..M. verbs in general, action (as the general idea expressed by any verb). The activity in a sentence, the verb. the form of the *kriyā* can express a range of aspects of the activity such as its time or mood.

kriyā f. doing, rites, offerings, action, performance, business, act, action, undertaking, activity, work, labour, bodily action, exercise of the limbs, (in gram.) action as the general idea expressed by any verb, verb, sacrificial act, sacrifice,

kriyā'dvaita 321/1 n. efficient cause (as resigning all to God), oneness in action or practical living of Oneness

kriyājñāna the intellectual processes which are the means taken to acquire *svarūpajāna*

kriyamāṇa ..that "which would gather in the future through the activities performed by the person." pass.part. √*kṛ* being performed, performed, being made, the *saṁskāra* of the future produced by present action

kriyānivṛtti relief from action, emancipation,

kriyāśakti f. capability to act, supernatural power as appearing in actions,

kriyate it is performed, done, made 1/s/pres/pass √*kṛ*

kriyāvān 'one who is possessed of i.e. devoted to, (spiritual) practices like knowledge, meditation, detachment and so on' (Gam.)

kriyāviśeṣaṇa a word which "expands the remainder" from a verb, bringing out a previously unmanifested character, (an adverb)

kriyāyoga yoga of action, yoga of self-purification through external service or worship,

kṛmi m. a worm, spider, silk-worm, ant,

krodha 322/1 m. anger, wrath, passion

kroḍa 323/1 m. the interior of anything, cavity, a cave, breast, bosom, f.*(ā)* a woman with a well-formed breast,

krośa m. a call, cry, yell, calling distance,

krośamātrāvasthita mfn stationed at the distance of a *kos*

krośati cries out

kroṣṭu m. a jackal,

kṛp 1. f. (only instr.*kṛpā*) beautiful appearance, beauty, splendour,

√2.*kṛp* 305/1 Cl 6 A *kṛpate* to mourn, long for, lament, implore, Cl 10 P mourn, grieve, to pity, to be weak, DP in *daurbalya* being weak

Kṛpa a *Kaurava* warrior and instructor in arms

kṛpā 305/1 f. pity, tenderness, grace, compassion (with gen. or loc.),

kṛpālu mfn merciful, compassionate,

kṛpaṇa 305/1 mfn miserable, poor, wretched, inclined to grieve, miserable, feeble, resulting from tears, low, vile, miserly, stingy, m. a poor man,

kṛpāṇa m. dagger, sword,

kṛpāya to mourn, grieve, lament

√*kṛś* 305/3 Cl 4 P *kṛśyati* to become lean or thin, become emaciated or feeble, to cause the moon to wane, caus. *karśaysati* to make thin or lean, attenuate, emaciate, keep short of food, lessen, diminish, DP in *tanukaraṇa* becoming lean or emaciated, waning,

√*kṛṣ* 306/1 Cl 1 P rarely A *karṣati* to draw, draw to oneself, drag, pull, drag away, to lead or conduct (as an army), to bend (a bow), to draw into one's power, become master of, overpower, to obtain, to take away anything from anyone, to draw or make furrows, plough, Cl 6 P A *kṛṣati* to draw or make furrows, A – to obtain by ploughing, travel over, draw, drag, draw or tear out, cause pain, torture, DP in *vilekhana* ploughing, killing

kṛśa mfn lean, haggard, emaciated, weak, feeble, small, insignificant,
kṛśā mfn lean,
kṛṣaka m. a ploughman, farmer, an ox, a plough, f. (*ā*) cultivation of the soil,
kṛṣi 306/1 f. ploughing, cultivation, the harvest, the earth
kṛṣivala m. a cultivator, peasant, farmer,
kṛṣṇa Great lord, reincarnation of *Viṣṇu*
kṛṣṇa mfn black, the dark lunar fortnight, m. the black antelope,
kṛṣṇājina n. skin of the black antelope,
kṛṣṇapakṣa the dark fortnight,
kṛṣṇaśakuni 'blackbird' a crow,
kṛṣṇasarpa m. poisonous black cobra
kṛṣṇavat as if it were all, as if it were the whole, like or as Kṛṣṇa,
kṛṣṇāyate blackens
kṛṣṭi f.pl. people, folk, ploughing, cultivating, attracting, drawing, harvest, consequences, m. a teacher, learned man,
kṛt 1. 301/1 mfn. making, doing, performing, accomplishing, effecting, manufacturing, acting, one who accomplishes or performs anything, author, m. an affix used to form nouns from roots, a noun formed from that root,
√2. *kṛt* 304/2 Cl 6 P A *kṛntati* (*te*) to cut, cut in pieces, cut off, divide, tear asunder, destroy, DP in *chedana* cutting,
√3.*kṛt* 304/3 Cl 7 P *kṛṇatti* to twist threads, spin, to wind (as a snake), to surround, encompass, attire, DP in *veṣṭana* surrounding, encompassing,
-*kṛt* m. an affix used to form nouns from roots, a noun formed with that affix, -maker, doing, performing,
kṛta 1. made, done, 2. prepared, 3. attained, 4. well done (good), 5.n. deed, 6. the side of the die marked with 4 spots, 7. a period of time, the golden age, name of the first *yuga* or age in the cycle, also called the Satya Yuga,
kṛtabuddhi mfn mind made up, of resolute character, of formed mind, learned, wise, discriminative, rational,
kṛtajña grateful, knowing what is right, correct in conduct,
kṛtajñatā f. gratefulness, gratitude,
kṛtakṛtya his duties fulfilled becoming freed from duties, 302/1 mfn one who has attained any object or purpose, contented, satisfied with , n. what has been done and what is to be done,
kṛtakṛtyatā f. condition of having performed one's duty, the full discharge of any duty or realization of any object, accomplishment, success,
kṛtamauna mfn having kept a silence, silent
kṛtāñjali mfn having made a gesture of reverence, with reverent gesture, by whom the gesture has been made,
kṛtānna n. prepared or cooked food,
kṛtānta 303/1 mfn. causing an end, bringing to an end, whose end is action, destiny, fate, doctrine, dogma
kṛtapuṇya mfn happy, one who has accomplished meritorious acts in a previous life, one who has accomplished, fortunate, lucky,
kṛtārtha 303/1 one who has attained an end or object or has accomplished a purpose or desire, successful, satisfied, contented, clever, f. success,
kṛtasaṁketa mfn having made an agreement, agreed upon as a rendezvous,
kṛtātman 303/1 mfn one whose spirit is disciplined, whose Self is established in its own superior aspect through knowledge, established in identity with the Supreme Self,
kṛtāvajña mfn disdained, having contempt shown to one,
kṛtavedin mfn grateful, observant of propriety, thankful,
kṛta yuga or satya yuga golden age, 1,728,000 years , people realised the

Self and remembered without difficulty

kṛtaniścaya mfn confident, determined, decided to act, one who has ascertained anything, resolute, sure,

kṛttama the best (person) to act,

kṛtānta 303/1 mfn. causing an end, bringing to an end, whose end is action, destiny, fate, doctrine, dogma

kṛtartha 303/1 one who has attained, successful, satisfied, contented, self-fulfilled,

-kṛte for the sake of , on account of, for, (with 6th) e.g. *mama kṛte* or *mat kṛte* on my account, for me,

kṛtena 3rd, as previous entry,

kṛti 303/2 f. the act of doing, making, performing, manufacturing, composing, action, activity, literary work, a production, a literary work,

kṛtī in comp. for *kṛti,* one who has attained an object or accomplished a purpose,

kṛtin mfn one who acts, active, expert, clever, skilful, knowing, learned, good, virtuous, pure, pious, obeying, doing what is enjoined, one who has attained an object or accomplished a purpose, satisfied,

kṛtnu mfn working well, able to work, skilfull, clever, a mechanic, artist

kṛtrima mfn artificial, not natural, adopted, fostered,

kṛtsna 304/3 mfn. all, whole, entire n. water, the flank, hip or belly, f. (*ā*) totality, completeness

kṛtti f. pelt, hide, a garment of skin, the skin on which a religious student sits or sleeps, the bark of a birch tree (used for writing on and hooka pipes),

kṛttikā f. pl. the Pleiades, white spots, a cart

kṛtu a doing, a time, see *kṛtvas*

kṛtvā 304/1 past part. having done, gained,

kṛtvas ind. times, (as in 10 times 2),

kṛtvā having done, having put on, made

kṛtya 303/3 to be done or performed, duty

√*kru* 322/1 to be rough or raw, 'embraces many cries from the harshest to the softest' Muller, see *mitra-kru* DP in *śabda* sounding,

√*kruḍ* 322/1 Cl 6 P *kruḍati* to sink, dive, to be or become thick, DP in *nimajjana* sinking, diving

kruddha mfn irritated, provoked, angry with

kruddhvā ind. having been angry,

√*krudh* 322/1 Cl 4 P *krudhyati* to become angry, be wrathful or angry with, caus. *krodhayati* to make angry, provoke, irritate, DP in *krodha* being angry

krudh f. anger, wrath,

krudhā f. anger,

krudhmi mfn irritable,

krudhyat or *krudhmin* mfn being angry, feeling provoked, wrathful,

krudhyate becomes angry,

√*kruñc* 322/1 Cl 1 P *kruñcati* to curve or make crooked, or be crooked, move crookedly, to become small, shrink, or to make small, lessen, to go towards, approach DP in *gati-kauṭilya* making crooked or *alpībhāva* making small

krūra 322/3 mfn wounded, hurt, sore, cruel, fierce, pitiless, harsh, bloody, raw, hot, sharp, disagreeable, ind. in a formidable manner,

krūramati one with a cruel mind or intention,

krūrata mfn cruelty, pitilessness,

√*kruś* 322/2 Cl 1 P *krośati* to cry out, shriek, yell, call out, to exclaim, to lament, weep, to make a singing noise (as the ear) DP in *āhvāna* crying out or *godana* weeping,

kṣa 324/3 1. m. a field, the protector or cultivator of a field, peasant, 2. m. destruction, loss, destruction of the world, lightning, a demon, the 4th incarnation of *Viṣṇu* as *nara-siṁha*

√*kṣai* 333/1 Cl 1 P *kṣāyati* to burn, catch

or take fire, DP in *kṣaya* , wasting or wearing away, declining

√*kṣaj* or √*kṣañj* 324/3 Cl 1 A *kṣajate* to go, approach, to give, Cl 10 P *kṣañjayati* to live in pain or want, DP in *gati* going, *dāna* giving, in *kṛcchrajīvana* (Cl 10) living in distress or pain

√*kṣal* 327/2 Cl 10 P *kṣālayati* to wash, wash off, purify, cleanse, DP in *śauc-karmana* washing, purifying, cleansing,

kṣālayati washes, wipes

√*kṣam* Cl 1 A P *kṣamate (ti)* Vedic Cl 2 P *kṣamati*, Cl 4P *kṣāmyati*, to be patient or composed, suppress anger, keep quiet, to submit to, to bear patiently, endure, put up with, suffer, to pardon, forgive anything, to allow, permit, DP in *sahana* suffering, enduring,

kṣam 326/2 f. the ground, earth,

kṣama mfn patient, , bearing or enduring, suffering, submissive, resisting, adequate, able, competent, fit for, favourable to, bearable, tolerable, equal to a thing, able, m. 'the patient' (Śiva), n. propriety, fitness,

kṣamā 326/2,3 f. patience, forbearance, indulgence, tameness, resistance, the earth, the number 1,
forgiveness, 'to forgive is the *dharma* , the human law , and not to forgive is against the law.'

kṣamī forgiving, remaining unperturbed even when abused or assaulted

kṣāmaye I beg pardon, request indulgence 1/s/caus/mid √*kṣām*

kṣamp 327/1 Cl 1.10. P *kṣampati*, *kṣampayati* to suffer, bear, to love, like, DP in *kṣānti* patience, enduring,

kṣāmya part. to be borne patiently, or pardoned

√*kṣaṇ* see √*kṣan* DP in *hiṁsā* hurting, killing,

√*kṣan* cl 8 P *kṣaṇoti,* to hurt, injure, wound, to break (a bow), to hurt oneself, be injured or wounded, DP in *hiṁsā* hurting, injuring, killing,

kṣaṇa 1. 324/3 m. any instantaneous point of time, instant, twinkling of an eye, moment, measure of time (4 min.), leisure, opportunity, dependence, the centre, middle, n. an instant, moment, in a moment,
ind. (3rd) in a moment, (5th) after an instant or immediately,
kṣaṇe kṣaṇe n. every instant, every moment,

kṣaṇam ind. an instant, moment, for a moment,

kṣaṇika mfn momentary, transient, transitory, temporary,

kṣaṇikatva n. momentariness,

kṣaṇika vijñāna momentary consciousness,

√*kṣañj* see √*kṣaj*

kṣānta 326/3 mfn. borne, endured, enduring, patient,

kṣānta

kṣantavya to be put up with or pardoned,

kṣānti 326/3 f. patiently waiting for anything, patience, forbearance, endurance, the state of saintly abstraction,

√*kṣap* 326/1 Cl 1 P A *kṣapati (te)* to be abstinent, fast, do penance, Cl 10 P *kṣapayati* to throw, cast, DP in *preraṇa* driving out,

kṣapā f. night, ind (3rd) at night,

kṣapāha n. a night and day,

kṣapaṇaka m. a mendicant, a Jaina mendicant who wears no clothes,

kṣapita 326/1 mfn. destroyed, ruined

√*kṣar* 327/1 Cl 1 P A *kṣarati (te)* Vedic Cl 2 P *kṣariti* to flow, stream, glide, distill, trickle, melt away, perish, fall or slip from, be deprived of, to cause to flow, pour out, to give forth a stream, give forth anything richly, to overflow or soil with acrid substances, DP in *sañcalana* oozing, flowing,

kṣara mfn perishable, melting away,

kṣāra mfn pungent, saline, caustic, biting, m. any caustic, corrosive, acrid or saline substance, juice, essence, treacle, molasses,

kṣaraṇa 327/1 n. flowing, trickling, distilling, dropping, pouring forth, splashing

kṣata 325/3 mfn wounded, hurt, injured, broken, rent, torn, destroyed, impaired, diminished, (*ā*) f. a violated girl, (*am*) n. a hurt, wound, sore, contusion,

kṣati 326/1 f. injury, hurt, loss, want, Apte 170/2 *kṣati* decline, decay, diminution

kṣatra n. 1. rule, dominion, power, 2. (later) the temporal power (as distinguished from the spiritual),

kṣātra 325/3 belonging or relating to the warrior class, n. the dignity of a ruler or governor,

kṣātrabandhu m. one who belongs to the second caste,

kṣātradharma m. bravery, duty and conduct of a *kṣatriya,* military conduct,

kṣātravidyā f. knowledge or science possessed by the *kṣatriya* or military order,

kśatriya m. 1. ruler, 2. one who belongs to the second class or caste – warriors, kings, statesmen, n. the power or rank of the sovereign,

kṣatriyadharma m. the duty or occupation of the warrior-tribe, war, government, etc.

kṣatriyadharman mfn having the duties of a soldier or of the second caste,

kṣātriyavidyā

kṣaya 327/3 1.m. dominion, dwelling, residing, abode, seat, house, 328/1 loss, waste, diminution, destruction, decay, wasting or wearing away, end, termination mfn. dwelling, residing

kṣema 332/3 mfn giving rest or ease or security, at ease, habitable, m. basis, foundation, residing, resting, abiding at ease, m.n. safety, tranquillity, peace, security, happiness,

kṣematara n. greater ease, greater tranquillity, (comparative)

kṣepa 329/1 m. a throw, cast, throwing, tossing, stretching, moving to & fro, sending, dismissing, transgressing, delay, procrastination, disrespect, contempt, pride, haughtiness,

kṣepaṇa the act of throwing, casting, letting fly, throwing away, sending, directing, passing away, spending time, sling, f. an oar, sling, net,

kṣetra 332/1 n. the field, land, any geometrical figure, place of origin, place where anything is found, the body (considered as the field of the indwelling soul), , a holy place,

kṣetrajñā 332/2 m. the soul, the conscious principle in the corporeal frame, the knower of the field, mfn knowing localities, familiar with cultivation of the soil, clever, dextrous, skilful,

kṣetrapati m. farmer, master of a field, landowner, landlord,

kṣetre in/on the field 7/s/n

√*kṣev* see √*kṣiv,* DP in *nirasana* spitting

√*kṣi* 1. 327/3 Cl 1 P *kṣayati* to possess, have power over, to rule or govern, be master of, DP in *kṣaya* wasting, decaying,

2. Cl 2.6. P *kṣeti, kṣiyati* , to abide, stay, dwell, to remain, be quiet, to inhabit, to go, move, DP in *nivāsa* abiding, dwelling, staying, or *gati* going, moving,

3. f. abode,

4. Cl 1 P *kṣayati* to destroy, corrupt, ruin, make an end, kill, injure, be diminished, decrease, to pass (said of the night), DP in *hiṁsā* hurting, killing,

5. f. destruction, waste, loss,

√*kṣīb* 329/2 Cl 1 P *kṣībati* or *kṣīvati* to eject from the mouth, spit, to be drunk or intoxicated, caus. *kṣībayati* to excite, DP in *mada* being drunk or intoxicated

√*kṣīj* 329/2 Cl 1 P *kṣījati* to sound inarticulately, sigh or groan (as in distress), DP in *avyaktaśabda* making indistinctive noise,

√*kṣiṇ* 328/3 Cl 8 P A *kṣiṇoti, kṣiṇute* see 4. √*kṣi* above, DP in *hiṁsā* hurting, killing,

kṣīṇa 328/2 diminished, wasted, lost, worn away, eradicated, attenuated, powerless, weak,

kṣīṇadoṣa 'whose mental defects or impurities e.g. anger, have been attenuated',

√*kṣip* 328/3 Cl 6 P A *kṣipati (te)* Cl 4 P *kṣipyati* to throw, cast, send, despatch, to move hastily (the arms or legs), to throw a glance (the eye), to strike or hit (with a weapon), to put or place anything in or on, pour on, scatter, to direct (the thoughts) upon, get rid of, lay the blame on, to utter abusive words, insult, to disdain, excel, beat, strike down, ruin, A. to destroy one another, go to ruin, to pass or while away the time or night, to lose time, to skip or pass over a day, to add (in math), DP in *preraṇa* n. driving out, setting in motion, direction, command, activity,

kṣipati throws or shoots

kṣipra 329/1 quick, speedy, swift, elastic (as a bow), (*am*) ind. quickly, immediately, directly, (*am*) n. a measure of time,

kṣiprakārin mfn skilful, inconsiderate, precipitate, unmindful, rash, acting quickly,

kṣipratā f. quickness

kṣipta n. 'scattered' distraction or absence of mind, f. night, mfn thrown, cast, sent, dispatched

kṣipta -laguḍa mfn having thrown the cudgel,

kṣīra n. milk, milky sap,

kṣīravṛkṣa Indian fig tree or *nyagrodha*,

kṣīrābdhi ocean of milk

kṣīrin mfn milky, m. milk-plant,

kṣīrodaka n. milk and water,

kṣit mfn ruling, dwelling, inhabitant of, ifc. inhabitant, ruler,

kṣiti f. dwelling, abode, piece of ground or land, the earth, the ground, destruction, the period of destruction of the universe,

kṣitipati m. 'lord of the earth', king,

√*kṣiv* 329/2 Cl 1.4. P *kṣevati, kṣīvyati* to eject from the mouth, spit, vomit, DP in *nirasana* spitting, ejecting from the mouth,

√*kṣmāy* 334/1 Cl 1 A *kṣmāyate* to shake, tremble, DP in *vidhūnana* shaking,

√*kṣmīl* 334/1 Cl 1 P *kṣmīlati* to twinkle, close the eyelids, DP in *nimeṣaṇa* closing or contracting the eyelids,

√*kṣṇu* 333/3 Cl 2 P *kṣṇoti* to whet, sharpen,
DP in *tejana* whetting, sharpening

kṣobha 331/1 m. agitation or disturbance, emotion, a strong current of water,

kṣoda m. stamping, shattering, crushing, the stone or slab on which anything is ground or pounded, mortar,
any pounded or pulverised substance – flour, meal, powder, dust,
a drop, a lump, piece,

√*kṣot* 333/2 *kṣoṭayati* Cl 10 P to throw, cast, DP in *kṣepa* throwing

√*kṣu* 330/2 Cl 2 P *kṣauti* to sneeze, cough,
DP in *śabda* sneezing, coughing

√*kṣubh* 331/3 Cl 1 A *kṣobhate*, Cl 4 P A *kṣubhyati (te)* to shake, tremble, be agitated, or disturbed, be unsteady, stumble, f. a shake, a push, DP in *sañcalana* shaking, being agitated,

√*kṣud* 330/2 Cl 1 P *kṣodati* to strike against, shake, A. to move, be agitated or shaken, to stamp or trample upon, to crush, pound, pulverise, to reduce, diminish, DP in *sampeṣaṇa* bruising, pounding down,

√*kṣudh* 331/2 Cl 4 P *kṣudhyati* to feel

hungry, be hungry, DP in *bubhukṣā* being hungry
f. hunger,

kṣudhā f. hunger,

kṣudhārta mfn distressed with hunger,

kṣudhita mfn hungry

kṣudra 330/2 very small, little, base, low, niggardly, avaricious, mean, vile, poor, indigent, m. a small particle of rice,

kṣudrabrahmāṇḍa n. universe, world, cosmos, brahmā's egg, cosmic, cosmic ray,

kṣudrabuddhi m. Smallwit, name of a jackal, of little understanding, of a low character,

kṣud-vyādhi m. hunger and disease,

√*kṣur* 331/3 Cl 6 P *kṣurati* to cut, dig, scratch, to make lines or furrows, DP in *sañcaya* collecting, *vilekhana* making lines or furrows

kṣura a razor, arrow barb, cow's hoof, foot of a bed,

kṣuradhāna m. a razor case

kṣurin m. a barber,

√*kṣvel* 334/1 Cl 1 P *kṣvelati* to leap, jump, play, to shake, tremble DP in *calana* playing, sporting, shaking, moving,

√*kṣvid* see √*kṣviḍ* DP in *snehana* being greasy or unctuous, loving, and *mocana* releasing,

√*kṣviḍ* 334/1 Cl 1 P *kṣveḍati* to utter an inarticulate sound, hum, murmur, growl, roar, Cl 1 A *kṣveòate* to be wet or unctuous, exude, emit sap, CL 4 P *kṣviòayati* DP not given

ktvānta a gerund with a *tvā* ending, meaning carried out the action e.g. *bhūtvā* having become

ku 1. a pronominal base seen in *kutas, kutra* etc., a prefix implying deterioration, depreciation, deficiency, want, littleness, hindrance, reproach, contempt, guilt,
3. f. the earth, the base of a triangle or other plane figure, the number 1,

√*kū* 299/1 Cl 2 P *kauti* or Cl 1 A *kavate* or Cl 6 *kuvate* or Cl 9P A *kūnoti (te)*, to sound, make any noise, cry out, moan, cry, coo (as a bird), hum like a bee, move, cry aloud, DP in *śabda* cooing, humming like a bee
2. ind. where?
3. f. a female goblin,

kubera *Kubera*, the god of wealth

kubuddhaya mfn unintelligent,

kubuddhi 286/2 having vile sentiments, stupid, f. wrong opinion, part. *kubuddhayaḥ* the unintelligent,

√*kuc* 287/3 Cl 1 P *kocati* to sound high, utter a shrill cry, to polish, go, connect, mix, bend, make curved, to be curved or crooked, to oppose, impede, to mark with lines, to contract, to be or make small, DP in *śabdatāra* uttering a shrill cry like a bird, in *samparcana-kauṭilya-pratiṣṭambha-vilekhana* connecting, making, crooked or curve, stopping or delineating, in *saṅkocana* contracting,

kuca m. the female breast, , teat,

√*kuḍ* 289/1 Cl 6 P *kuḍati* to play or act as a child, trifle, to eat, to heap, to plunge, dive, DP in *bālya* playing or acting like a child,

kudṛṣṭi f. a bad or false view, unorthodox philosophy,

√*kuh* 298/3 Cl 10 A *kuhayate* to surprise or astonish or cheat by trickery or jugglery, DP in *vismāpana* cheating, deceiving,

kuha ind. where? m. a rogue, cheat,

√*kuj* 287/3 Cl 1 P *kojati* to steal, Cl 6 P *kujati* to be crooked, DP in *steyakaraṇa* stealing

√*kūj* 299/2 Cl 1 P *kūjati* to make any inarticulate or monotonous sound, utter a cry (as a bird), coo (as a pigeon), caw (as a crow), utter any indistinct sound, to blow or breathe the flute, DP in *avyakta śabda* uttering inarticulate sound,

kūjana n. the uttering of any inarticulate

sound,warbling, cooing, moaning, rumbling of the bowels,

√*kuk* 287/1 Cl 1 A *kokate* to take, accept, seize, DP in *ādāna* taking, accepting, seizing,

kukkura m. dog

kukkuṭa m. a cock, spark of fire, small house-lizard, hypocrisy,

√*kul* 294/2 Cl 1 *kolati* to accumulate, collect, to be of kin, behave as a kinsman, to proceed continuously, to count, DP in *saṁstyāna* accumulating, collecting, or *bandhu* behaving as a kinsman

√*kūl* 300/3 Cl 1 P *kūlati* to cover, hide, or to keep off, obstruct, DP in *āvaraṇa* covering,

kula 294/2 n. herd, troop, family, community, flock, number, a house, abode, a noble or eminent family or race, high station, the body, the front, forepart, a blue stone, swarm of bees,

kūla n. a shore, bank, declivity, slope, a heap, mound, pool, army rear,

kuladharma family or caste duty,

kulaghna mfn slaying/destroying a family,

kulāla m. potter, wild cock, owl,

kulaśīla n. character or conduct honourable to a family,

kulavidyā f. knowledge handed down in a family,

kulin mfn well-born,

kulīna mfn of good family,

kulīra m. crab, zodiac sign (cancer),

kuliśa m. an axe, hatchet, a diamond, the thunderbolt of Indra,

kumanas mfn displeased, angry,

kumāra m. 'easily dying' a child, boy, youth, son, a prince,
(-ī) a young girl 10-12, daughter,

kumāradatta name of a man,
(-ī) a young girl 10-12, daughter

kumāraka m. young man, son,

kumāraya 292/2 Nom. P *kumārayati* to play (as a child). DP in *krīòā* playing

kumārga m. a bad way (lit. and fig.),

kumārī f. name of a goddess, virgin, daughter, princess,

kumati f. vile sentiment, weak intellect, folly, wrongheadedness,

√*kumb* 292/3 Cl 6, 10 P *kumbati, kumbayati* to cover, DP in *ācchādana* covering, screening, concealing,

√*kumbh* as *kumb* above

kumbha 293/1 m. a water jar, pitcher, jug pot, zodiac sign Aquarius, a measure of grain, a yogic breathing exercise

kumbhaka m.n. temporarily closing the nostrils with the fingers of the right hand and closing the mouth to suspend breathing – a yogic exercise, m. a pot, a measure of grain, the base of a column, f. a small pot or pitcher,

kumbhakāra m. pot-maker, potter,

kumbhamela (K) a mass Hindu pilgrimage. The normal Kumbh Mela is celebrated every 3 years, the *Ardh* (half) Kumbh Mela is celebrated every six years at Haridwar and Prayag, the *Purna* (complete) Kumbh takes place every twelve years, at four places (Prayag (Allahabad), Haridwar, Ujjain, and Nashik). The *Maha* (great) Kumbh Mela which comes after 12 'Purna Kumbh Melas', or 144 years, is held at Allahabad.
The last Ardh Kumbh Mela was held over a period of 45 days beginning in January 2007, more than 70 million Hindu pilgrims took part in the Ardh Kumbh Mela at Prayag, and on January 15, the most auspicious day of the festival of Makar Sankranti, more than 5 million participated.
The previous *Maha Kumbh Mela*, held in 2001, was attended by around 60 million people, making it at the time the largest gathering anywhere in the world in recorded history,

kumbhikā f. pitcher,

kumbhīra m. a shark, Gangetic crocodile,
√*kuṁś* or *kuṁs* 287/1 Cl 1 or 10 P *kuṁśati* or *kuṁśayati* or *kuṁsati* or *kuṁsayati* to speak or to shine, DP in *bhāṣā* speaking or shining,
kumuda m.a white lotus, red lotus, camphor,
√*kuṇ* 289/2 Cl 6 P *kuṇati* to sound, to support or aid (with gifts), to be in pain? Cl 10 P *kuṇayati* to converse with, address, invite, DP in *śabda* sounding, or *upakaraṇa* supporting, giving aid,
√*kūṇ* 299/3 Cl 1 *kūṇati* to contract, shrink, shorten, caus. P A *kūṇayati (te)* to draw together, contract, close, DP in *saṅkocana* contracting, closing,
√*kuṇḍ* 289/3 Cl 1 P *kuṇḍati* to mutilate, Cl 1 A to burn, *kuṇdate*, Cl 10 *kuṇḍayati* to protect, DP in *vaikalya* agitating, mutilating, *dāha* burning, Cl 10 *rakṣaṇa* protecting
kuṇḍa n. a round vessel, round hole in the ground for fire or water, a bowl shaped vessel,
kuṇḍala n. ring, esp. ear-ring, a bracelet, fetter, tie, the coil of a rope,
kuṇḍalinī (K) literally means coiled. In yoga, a "corporeal energy"- an unconscious, instinctive or libidinal force or Shakti, lies coiled at the base of the spine. It is envisioned either as a goddess or else as a sleeping serpent, hence a number of English renderings of the term such as 'serpent power'. The kundalini resides in the sacrum bone in three and a half coils and has been described as a residual power of pure desire.
√*kundr* Cl 10 P *kundrayati* to tell a lie, DP in *anṛtabhāṣaṇa* lying
√*kuñj* 288/1 Cl 1 P *kuñjati* to murmur, DP in *gati,* going, *kautilya* making crooked and *alpibhāva* making small
kuñja m. bower, a place overgrown with creepers, arbour, the lower jaw, an elephant's tusk or jaw,
kuñjara m. elephant, anything pre-eminent of its kind, the number 8,
√*kuṇṭ* 289/3 see √*kuṇḍ* DP in *pratighāta* warding off, keeping back, in *veṣṭana* surrounding, enveloping, covering,
√*kunth* 291/2 Cl 1 *kunthati* to hurt, injure, suffer pain, want, to cling to, twine round, embrace, to injure, DP in *hiṁsā* injuring, hurting, suffering , or *saṁkleśana* causing pain, or *saṁśleśaṇa* clinging to
Kuntī f. one of the two wives of Pāndu
Kuntīputra son of K*unti*
√*kup* Cl 4 P A *kupyati (te)* to be moved or agitated or excited, heave or boil with rage or emotion, be angry, be angry with, P A *kopayati (te)* to cause to swell with anger, provoke, make angry, Cl 10 P *kopayati* to speak or to shine, DP in *krodha* being angry
kūpa m. a well, cave, hollow, a mast, mooring post, navel,
kupita mfn angry, incensed, offended,
kupyati 291/2 *kup* to be excited, agitated, angry, *kupyati* is angry
√*kur* 293/3 Cl 6 P *kurati* to utter a sound, DP in *śabda* sounding,
kuraṅga m. deer, species of antelope,
√*kurd* see √*kūrd*
√*kūrd* 300/2 Cl 1 P A *kūrdati (te)* to leap, jump, A *kūrdate* to play, DP in *krīḍā* playing
kūrma m. tortoise, turtle, the earth considered as a tortoise,
kuru 301/1 2/s/impv/act of *kṛ* to do do/ make! perform! let do/make etc.
Kuru 294/1m. name of a people of India and of their country, a person of that tribe, collectively also called by a patronymic Kaurava, boiled rice,
Kurukśetra an extensive plain north of *Delhi* where the great battle described in the *Mahābhārata* took place,
kurunandana voc. O descendant of Kuru,

m. scion or offspring of the Kurus
kuruśravaṇa m. name of a prince, 'glory of the Kurus',
kuruṣva do! make! 2/s/mid/impv √*kṛ*
kurute √ *kṛ* 300/3 acting, doing, mid voiceor *ātmanepada* – implies an action belonging or reverting to oneself), he does, makes, acts
kurvan pres. act. part. of *kṛ* 300/3 performing, doing, acting, 1/s/m
kurvāṇa mfn doing, making, acting as an agent or servant,
kurvanti they do, perform, make 1/pl/pres/indic/act √*kṛ*
kurvat 294/2 n. cause, pres. pass. part. doing, acting as an agent, or servant, present, actual,
kurvat 294/2 doing, acting as an agent, or servant, present, actual,
kurvīta he should do, 1/s/mid/opt √*kṛ*
kuryām I should perform or do 3/s/opt/act √*kṛ*
kuryāt he should act, perform, make, do 1/s/opt/act
√*kuś* 296/3 Cl 4 P *kuśyati* to embrace, enfold, DP in *saṁśleṣaṇa* embracing, surrounding
√*kuṣ* 297/3 Cl 9P *kuṣṇāti* to tear asunder, to pinch, to force or draw out, extract, to knead, test, examine, to shine, Cl 6 *kuṣati* to gnaw, nibble, pass. to weigh, balance, DP in *niṣkarṣa* tearing, extracting, drawing out,
kuśa 296/3 a grass with long pointed stalks, sacred grass,
kuśāgra mfn the tip of a blade of *kuśa* grass,
kuśahasta mfn having *kuśa* in the hand,
kuśala 297/2mfn right, proper, good , auspicious, well, healthy, in good condition, prosperous, fit for, competent, conversant with, (*am*) n. welfare, well-being, happiness, benevolence, virtue, cleverness, competence, (*am*) ind. well, in a proper manner, properly, welfare, (in comp.) happily, cheerfully,
kuśalabuddhi mfn wise, able, intelligent,
kuśalapraśna m. friendly enquiry after a person's health or welfare, salutation, 'how do you do',
kuśalaṁ te greetings, hail to thee,
kuśalavāc mfn eloquent,
kuśalavat mfn well, healthy,
kuśalin mfn well, prosperous,
kuśapiñjūla n. tuft or bunch of *kuśa* grass,
kuśruta mfn indistinctly heard,
kuṣṭha m.n. leprosy, n. a sort of poison, f. the prominent part of anything,
√*kuṣubhya* Nom. P *kuṣubhyati* to throw or to despise, DP in *kṣaya* throwing, abusing,
kusuma n. a flower, blossom,
kusumākara m. Spring , (abounding with flowers)
kusumāyudha m. (flower-weaponed) the God of Love,
√*kuṭ* 288/1 Cl 6 P *kuṭiti* to become crooked or curved, bend, curve, to be dishonest, cheat, Cl 4 P *kuṭyati* Cl 10 A *koṭayate* to break into pieces, tear asunder, divide, to speak indistinctly, be warm, burn, DP in *kautilya* being crooked or curved, in *chedana* cutting, dividing,
√*kūṭ* 299/2 Cl 10 P *kūṭayati* to burn, to give pain, be distressed, to counsel, advise, A *kūṭayate* to avoid or decline giving, to render indistinct, or unintelligible, render confused or foul, be distressed, despair, DP in *āpradāna* abstaining from giving, *avasādana* censuring Cl 10, *paritāpa* being distressed, or *paridāha* burning
kūṭa 1.n. the bone of the forehead, horn, m.n. a summit or peak, the highest, most excellent, first, a heap, multitude, part of a plough, an iron mallet, a deer trap, a concealed weapon, illusion, fraud, trick, untruth, falsehood, enigma, elemental uniform ethereal substance,
kutas 290/2 ind. from whom, from where, whence, wherefore, why,

how? in what manner, (indefinite with particles *api, cid, cana*)

kutaścid 290/2 from or through any or some, *kutas* from whom + indefinite modifier *cid* through some cause

kūṭastha 299/3 mfn immovable, uniform, unchangeable, 'standing on the summit' keeping the highest position, standing in a multitude, a name for Brahman, m.n. a kind of perfume, n. the soul,

kūṭastha-caitanya immutable consciousness, individual consciousness destitute of egoism,

kūṭasthanitya eternally unchanging,

√*kuth* 290/3 Cl 4 *kuthyati* to stink, become putrid, DP in *pūtībhāva* becoming putrid, stinking,

kuṭhāra m. axe,

kuṭila mfn crooked or bent,

kuṭilā gati

kuṭilā 288/2 bent, crooked, curved, round, dishonest,

gati 347/3 going, moving

kuṭīra m. a hut, cottage, hovel, n. sexual intercourse,

kutra ind. where? in what or which place, to what or which place, whither? 290/2 –where, + *api* anywhere, + *na,* not, nowhere

kutracidapi anywhere (or with preceding *na* not anywhere, nowhere

kutracit 290/2 somewhere, wheresoever, anywhere

kutrāpi anywhere,

√*kuts* 290/3 Cl 10 P A *kutsayati (te*) to depise, abuse, revile, slander, DP in *avakṣepaṇa* abusing, reviling,

kutsā reproach, contempt

kutsana 290/3 abuse, reviling, reproach

kutsita śabda reproachful speech

√*kuṭṭ* Cl 10 *kuṭṭayati* to crush, bruise, to grind or pound, paw (the ground), to strike slightly, to multiply, to censure, abuse, to fill, DP in *chedana* cutting, dividing, *bhartsana* blaming, censuring, or *pūraṇa* filling, *pratāpana* burning,

kuṭṭana 288/3 mfn breaking, bruising, grinding, cutting, pounding

kuṭṭanī n. cutting, pounding, grinding, abusing, f. a kind of spear, a bawd,

kutūhala n. 1. interest felt in something extraordinary, eagerness, *(āt)* ind. eagerly, 2. interest caused by something remarkable,curiosity,

kutuka n. curiosity, eagerness, desire for,

kuṭumba n. household, family, members of a household, m.n. name, race, a relation, offspring,

kuṭumbhadhāraṇa protecting, preserving, maintaining the family

kuṭumbin m. householder, family man,

kva interrogative, where? in whom, in what place,
if repeated with another question expresses great incongruity or incompatibility
na kva ca nowhere
yatra kvāpi wherever, in whatsoever place

kvacana anywhere,

kvacid anywhere, somewhere, to any place, in a certain place,
na kvacid nowhere, never, by no means, also = *kvacid api na,*

kvacid ... *kvacid* here...there, here and there, in various places, now...then, now and then,

kvacit 324/2 kva where, + indefinite article, anywhere, any whatever, at some time

kva kva or *kutra kva* (implies excessive incongruity), where is this?, where is that? how distant is this from that, how little does this agree with that,

kvāpi anywhere, somewhere, to some place, in a certain place, sometimes,

√*kvaṇ* 324/2 Cl 1 P *kvaṇati*, to sound, make any sound, tinkle, to hum (as a bee), caus. *kvaṇayati* to cause to sound, make sound (as a musical instrument) , blow (the flute), DP in *śabda* sounding, jingling, humming, tinkling, singing

√*kvath* 324/3 Cl 1 A *kvathate* to boil, prepare by heat, to digest, to be hot (as the heart), DP in *niṣ-pāka* boiling, decocting, digesting

la m.n. cutting,

√*lā* 899/2 Cl 2 P *lāti* to take, receive, obtain, to undertake, begin, to give, DP in *ādāna* taking, receiving, obtaining,

labdha 896/2 mfn taken, seized, arrived at, got at, found, gained

labdhi f. obtaining, gaining, acquisition, gain, profit,
in arithmetic the quotient,

labdhṛ mfn one who obtains or receives, a receiver, gainer, recipient,

√*labh* 896/2 Cl 1 A *labhate* also *ti* and *lambhate,* to take, seize, catch, catch sight of, meet with, find, find an opportunity, make an impression, be effective, gain possession of, obtain, receive, succeed in, be permitted to, possess, have, perceive, know, understand, learn, find out, caus. *lambhayati* cause to take or receive or obtain, give, bestow, to get, procure, DP in *prāpti* getting, obtaining,

√*lābh* 900/3 Cl 10 P *lābhayati*, to throw, direct, DP in *preraṇa* sending,

lābha 897/1m. acquisition, gain, profit, meeting with, finding, perception, knowledge,

lābhālabhau gain and loss, (dual *dvandva* compound)

labhate finds

labhante they (pl) find or attain 1/pl/pres/indic/mid √*labh*

labhasva attain! find! 2/s/impv

labhet he should obtain, find or get 1/s/opt/act

labhya able to be reached or attained, attainable, to be found or met with, capable of being reached/attained, to be understood or known, suitable, proper, fit, to be allowed to (inf. with pass. sense),to be furnished or provided with (3rd),

√*lach* 895/2 Cl 1 P *lacchati* to mark, DP in *lakṣaṇa* marking,

√*laḍ* 895/3 Cl 1 P *laḍati* to play, sport, dally, Cl 10 P *laḍayati* to loll the tongue, lick, put out the tongue, *lāḍayati* to throw, toss, to cherish, foster, *lāḍayate* to wish, desire, DP (Cl 1) in *vilāsa* dallying, playing,
(Cl 10) *upasevā* fondling, caressing,

√*lag* 893/2 Cl 1 P *lagati* to adhere, stick, cling or attach oneself to, DP in *saṅga* sticking, adhering to,

√*lāgh* 899/3 Cl 1 A *lāghate* = *rāgh* DP in *sāmarthya* being able, sufficing,

lāghava 899/3 n. swiftness, rapidity, speed, alacrity, versatility, skill, lightness, M. n. 'lightness', making light or little of,lightness of heart, disdain,

laghiman m. lightness, levity, absence of weight, faculty of levitation, lowness, meanness of spirit, thoughtlessness, frivolity,

laghu 893/3 mfn light, easily digested, short, swift, low, insignificant, causing easiness or relief, well, in good health, unimpeded, small, light, young, clean, pure, soft, gentle, m. a light carriage, a slender or delicate woman, a measure of time, ind. lightly, quickly, easily,

laghu-cetas mfn small-minded, low-minded,

laghuka mfn light, unimportant, insignificant,

laghu-krama mfn having a quick step, (*am)* ind. quickly, hastily

lagna ppp. adhered or stuck to, attached to, an auspicious time for action, one who has entered on a course of action, one who has begun to (inf.), meeting, intersecting, cutting, immediately ensuing, passed (as days), consumed by or spent in (3rd), auspicious, m. a bard or minstrel, mn. the point of contact or intersection (of two lines), m. the decisive moment or time for action, decisive measure, a scheme or figure of the 12 zodiacal signs or houses,

laguḍa m. cudgel, stick, staff,

laharī f. a large wave, billow,

√*laj* 895/2 1. Cl 6 A *lajate* to be ashamed, DP in *vrīḍā* being ashamed, blushing, in *apavāraṇa* covering, screening,

√*laj* 2. 895/2 Cl 1 P *lajati* to fry or to blame, DP in *bharjana* frying

√*laj* 3. Cl 10 P *lajayati* to appear, DP in *prakāśana* making clear,

√*lāj* 900/1 Cl 1 P *lājati* to fry or to blame DP in *bharsana* blaming, parching,

lāja m.pl. parched or roasted grain,

√*lajj* Cl6 *lajjate* to be ashamed, blush, caus. *lajjayati* (or *lajjapayati?*) to embarrass, inspire with shame,

lajjā 895/2 f. shame, modesty, shyness, embarrassment n. causing shame,

lajjākara mfn shameful, causing shame, disgraceful, embarrasing,

lajjāvant mfn having shame, embarrassed,

lajjāvat mfn having shame, embarrassed,

lakāra the ten tenses/moods

laṭ	present indicative,
liṭ	perfect – remote past action not witnessed by speaker,
luṭ	periphrastic future – not of today,
lṛṭ	simple future,
leṭ	subjunctive (only in Vedic Sanskrit)
loṭ	imperative –command, demand,
laṅ	imperfect – past, not of today,
liṅ	optative, potential, what should, ought, could, might, be done,
luṅ	past, of today,
lṛṅ,	aorist conditional, would have

√*lakh* 893/2 Cl 1 P *lakhati* to go, move, DP in *gati* going

√*lākh* 899/3 Cl 1 P *lākhati* = √*rākh* DP in *śoṣaṇa* being dry, or *alam* being sufficient, refusing, warding off,

√*lakṣ* 891/3 Cl 1 A *lakṣate* to perceive, observe, (P. *ti*) to recognize, Cl 10 P A *lakṣayati (te*), to mark, sign, characterize, define, to indicate, designate indirectly, to aim at, direct towards, have in view, mean, to consider or regard anyone as, to know, understand, notice, perceive, observe, see, view, DP (Cl 10) in *darśana* noticing, observing, seeing, or *aṅkana* marking, denoting, in *ālocana* seeing, looking at

lakṣa n. 1. mark, token, 2. a hundred-thousand, 3. a mark for aiming at,

lākṣā f. a kind of red dye from the cochineal beetle, lac,

lakṣaṇa 892/1 mfn. indicating, expressing indirectly, (*ā*) f. a line or symbol, token, characteristic, accurate description, definition, characteristic (auspicious) mark,

lakṣaṇā vṛtti implied meaning, 'the inherent power in a sound that gives rise to a thought of certain qualities like name, for, etc., directly associated with it.' (U),

lakṣasaṁkhya mfn numbered by hundreds of thousands,

lakṣita 892/2 mfn marked, indicated, distinguished or characterized by, vaguely indicated or expressed, equivocal, ambiguous, aimed at, called, named, considered or regarded as, taken for, enquired into, examined, perceived, observed, beheld, seen, evident, known, understood, proved, excellent,

lakṣman n. a good or lucky mark or sign,

lakṣmaṇa brother of Rāma

lakṣmī f. 1. mark, sign, 2. bad sign or omen, something ominous, bad luck, 3. (oftenest) a good sign, good luck, prosperity, wealth (royal) splendour, consort of *Viṣṇu,* the power of increase and prosperity

lakṣya 893/1 mfn to be marked, target, characterized, defined, to be indicated or expressed, to be kept in view or observed, to be regarded as, taken for, to be recognised, known, recognisable by (3rd or comp.),observable, perceptible, visible, n. an object aimed at, a target, prize, an aim, mark, goal,

lakṣaṇa n. indication, sympton, relating to or acquainted with, f.(*ā*) indication, characteristic, sign, aim, labelling, object, mark, attribute, hint, view, quality,

lakṣyārtha m. indirectly expressed meaning, underlying indicative meaning, e.g. the *lakṣyārtha* of *tat* is Brahman,

√lal 897/3 Cl 1 P *lalati* to play, sport, dally, frolic, behave loosely or freely, to loll or wag the tongue, caus. *lālayati* cause to dally, caress, fondle, foster, cherish, to wave, flourish, to favour, A. to desire, DP in *vilāsa* (Cl 1) dallying, sporting, in *īpsā* (Cl 10) desiring,

lālā f. saliva, spittle, n. a secret matter, persuasion, the wife of another,

lālasa 900/3 eagerly longing for, desirous of, totally given up to

lalāṭa n. forehead, brow,

lalita mfn artless, naive, lovely, wanton, amorous, innocent, soft, gentle, m. a position of the hands in dancing,

√lamb 897/1 Cl 1 A *lambate (ti),* to hang down, depend, dangle, hang from or on, to sink, go down, decline, fall, set (as the sun), to be fastened or attached to, cling to, fall or stay behind, be retarded, lag, loiter, delay, tarry, caus. *lambayati* cause to hang down, to hang up, suspend, cause to be attached or joined, to stretch out, extend the hand, DP in *śabda* sounding, *avasraṁsana* hanging down

lambhana 896/3 the act of obtaining or attaining, receiving, recovery, causing to get, procuring

lampaṭa mfn greedy, covetous, lustful, m. a libertine, lecher, dissolute person,

√lāñch 900/1 Cl 1 P *lāñchati* to mark, distinguish, characterize, caus. *lāñchayati,* DP in *lakṣaṇa* marking,

√laṇḍ 895/3 Cl 10 P *laṇḍayati* to throw or toss up, to speak, DP in *utkṣepaṇa* tossing up, in *bhāṣā* speaking, in *āpyāyana* increasing,

√laṅg 895/1 Cl 1 P *laṅgati* to go, to limp, DP in *gati* going,

laṅga mfn lame, limping, m. lameness, union, association, a lover,

lāṅgala n. a plough, a palm tree, kind of flower, penis,

√laṅgh 895/1 Cl 1 P A *laṅghati (te)*, to leap over, go beyond, to ascend, mount upon, abstain from food, fast, to dry, dry up, waste, consume, caus. or Cl 10 *laṅghayati (te)* to leap over, cross, traverse, mount, ascend, tread upon, enter, overstep, transgress, violate, neglect, to get over, shun, escape from, to frustrate, prevent, avert, offend, insult, injure, to excel, surpass, outshine, obscure, eclipse, to remove, transport, fast, DP (Cl 1) in *gati* going, and *bhojana-nivṛtti* fasting, *śoṣana* drying, (Cl 10) *āpyāyana* increasing, *bhāṣā* shining, speaking,

lāṅgūla n. tail,

√lañj 1. 895/2 Cl 1 P *lañjati* to fry or to blame, DP in *bharjana* frying, 2. Cl 10 P *lañjayati* to be strong, to strike, to dwell, to give, to speak, to shine, DP in *hiṁsā* hurting, *balā* being strong, powerful, *dāna* giving, taking, *niketana* living, dwelling, in *bhāṣā* speaking, shining, *āpyāyana* increasing, *prakāśana* making clear

√lāñj 900/2 Cl 1 P *lāñjati* = *√lāj* DP in *bhartsana* blaming, parching,

√laṅkh 895/1 to go, DP in *gati* going

laṅkà the island where *rāvaṇa* lived,

√lap 896/1 Cl 1 P *lapati (te), lapyati,* to

prattle, chatter, talk (also of birds), to whisper, to wail, lament, weep, DP in *vyaktā-vāc* speaking distinctly,

lapsyate will find

√*larb* 897/3 Cl 1 P *larbati* to go, DP in *gati* going,

√*laś* 899/1 Cl 10 P *lāśayati* to exercise an art , DP see *las*

√*laṣ* 899/1 Cl 1.4 *laṣati (te), laṣyatī (te),* to wish, desire, long for, to strive after, approach, caus. *lāṣayati* to exercise an art, DP in *kānti* wishing, desiring,

√*las* 899/1 Cl 1 P *lasati* to shine, flash, glitter, to appear, come to light, arise, to sound, resound, to play, sport, frolic, embrace,
Cl 10. *lāsayati* to dance, to exercise an art, to cause to teach to dance, DP (Cl 1) in *śleṣaṇa* embracing, or *krīḍana* playing, (cl10) in *śilpa-yoga* exercising or practising any art,
2. mfn shining, glittering,

lasa mfn moving quickly hither and thither, lively, shining, playing,
f. saffron, turmeric,
n. red sandalwood,

√*laṭ* 895/2 Cl 1 P *laṭati* to be a child, to cry, DP in *bālya* acting like a child, prattling

latā f. a creeper, a slender woman, a whip, a string of pearls, a streak, line,

√*lāṭyāya* 900/2 Nom P *lāṭyāyati* to live, DP in *jīvana* living

lauhāyasa mfn metallic, made of metal or copper, n. metallic ware,

laukika 909/2 mfn worldly, common, usual, not sacred, m. common or ordinary men, men of the world, men in general, people, mankind, n. a person's ordinary occupation, (*am*) ind. worldliness,

laukika vākya everyday language

laulya 909/3 n. restlessness, unsteadiness, inconstancy, lustfulness, eagerness, greediness, passion, ardent longing for,

lava m. little piece, bit, fragment, moment, particle,

lāva mfn cutting off, plucking, destroying, killing, reaping, gathering, cutting,

lavaṇa mfn saline, salt, briny, tasteful, graceful, handsome, beautiful,
n. salt, esp. sea-salt, saltiness,
f. (*ī*) lustre, grace, beauty, charm,

lavana 898/3 mfn a cutter, reaper,
n. the act of cutting, reaping, sickle, knife,

lāvaṇya n. the taste or property of salt, beauty, loveliness, charm,

lavaśas ind. in small pieces, bit by bit, in minute divisions or instants, after some moments,

lavaśo lavaśa piece by piece,

laya 903/2 m. the act of sticking or clinging to (7th),melting, dissolution, disappearance, or absorption in, Apte 477/3 mind absorbed, 903/2 spiritual indifference, rest, repose, place of rest, extinction, destruction, mental inactivity, spiritual indifference, making the mind inactive or indifferent, sport, diversion, merriness, delight in anything, an embrace, (G p.175) dissolution, absorption, to merge, said to be a precursor to *samādhi*, dissolution

layacintana concentration of the mind with a view to dissolving it, meditation where the mind progresses to ever more subtle activity until it becomes non-apparent in unity or *yoga*,

layana n. the act of clinging, adhering, lying, rest, repose, a place of rest, house, cell, etc.

lekha m. a writing, letter, line, stroke, manuscript, written document,

lekhā m. a line, stroke, a writing, letter, manuscript, any written document,
f. a scratch, streak, line, furrow, the act of drawing, painting,

writing, a drawing, likeness, figure, impression,

lekhaka m. a writer, copyist, scribe, one who delineates or paints, f. a little stroke, n. a writing, written message,

lekhāya 901/2 Nom P *lekhāyati* to be wanton or to waver, DP in *vilāsa* sporting or dallying wantonly, or *skhalana* tottering, wavering,

lekhana m. pencil

lekhin mfn scratching, grazing, touching, f. (*ī*) a spoon, ladle,

lekhinī pencil

√*lekhya* 901/3 1. Nom P *lekhyati* = *lekhāya*

√*lelāya* P A (*te*), *lelāyati* to move to and fro, quiver, tremble, shake, shoot up (flame), DP in *dīpti* shining

leliha 903/1 m.constantly licking, a serpent

lelihyase you lick 2/s/intens/*lih*

lelihyate licks constantly,

√*lep* 905/3 Cl 1 A *lepate* to go, to serve, DP in *gati* going

lepa 902/3 m. the act of smearing, daubing, anointing, spot, stain, impurity, anything smeared on, food, victuals, (A) attachment

leśa m. a little, particle, little bit, smallness, littleness, a small portion a short space of time,

leśataḥ ind. very slightly,

leśa-avidyā a trace of ignorance,

leśya mfn light, colouration (Jaina),

√*lī* 903/2 Cl 9 P *lināti* to adhere, obtain, Cl 1 P *layati,* to melt, liquefy, dissolve, Cl 4 A *līyate,* *lāyate,* to cling, stick, adhere, to remain sticking, to lie, recline, alight or settle on, hide or cower down in, disappear, vanish, caus. *lāpayati* or *lāyayati* to cause to cling etc. A. *lāpayate* to deceive, to obtain honour, to humble, DP in *śleṣaṇa* (Cl 9) adhering, melting, (Cl 4) sticking, adhering, clinging to, (Cl 10) in *dravīkaraṇa* melting,

lī 2. f. clinging to, adhering,

√*lih* 903/1 Cl 2 P A *leḍhi līḍhe* also *lihati* to lick, lap, lick at, taste, sip, DP in *āsvādana* licking,

√*likh* 901/1 Cl 6 P *likhati (te)* to scratch, scrape, furrow, tear up (the ground), to pick, peck, (said of birds), to scarify, lance, draw a line, write, copy, trace, sketch, paint, make smooth, polish, DP in *akṣaravinyāsa* writing

likhanaphalaka m. writing table

likhati he writes

likhitvā ind. having written,

līlā 903/2 f. play, sport, game, diversion, grace, elegance, comeliness,

līlāmaya mfn consisting of or relating to play or enjoyment,

limpati 902/2 smears, anoints with, stains

līna mfn clung or pressed closely together, attached or devoted to, merged in (7th or comp.), sticking, lying or resting on, staying in, lurking, hiding, dissolved, absorbed in (7th or comp), disappeared, vanished, n. the clinging to, being absorbed or dissolved in, disappearance, -*tā* f. (ifc.) concealment in, complete retirement or seclusion, -*tva* n. sticking or concealment in,

līnayati disssolves, melts,

√*liṅg* 901/3 Cl 1 P *liṅgati* to go, Cl 10 P *liṅgayati* to paint, variegate, to change or inflect a noun according to its gender, DP in *gati* going, in *citrīkaraṇa* painting,
disguise, proof, evidence,
a sign of gender or sex, male organ (in gram.) gender, 'that sign through which anything is comprehended i.e. intellect etc. (Gam.)',

liṅga 901/3 a mark, spot, sign, token, a sign of gender or sex, male organ (in gram.) gender, an indicatory mark in the sense that smoke indicates fire,

liṅgadeha m.n. the subtle body,

liṅgadhāraṇa n. the wearing of one's characteristic marks, *liṅga-śarīra* the subtle body – the marks or signs of one's individuality,

liṅgin 902/2 mfn having a mark or sign, characterized by, bearing false signs, a hypocrite, one whose external appearance coincides with inner character, having a subtle body

√*lip* 902/2 Cl 6.1. P A *limpati (te)* to smear, anoint with, stain, soil, pollute, defile, to inflame, kindle, burn, pass. *lipyate (ti)* to be smeared, to be attached to, stick, adhere, etc. caus. *lepayati,* DP in *upadeha* besmearing, in anointing, covering,

lipi f. rubbing over, writing, painting, drawing, anything written, letter, manuscript,

lipsā 897/1 the desire to gain, wish to acquire, longing for

lipta mfn smeared,

lipyate is smeared, defiled, contaminated, affected, 1/s/pres/indic/pass

√*liś* 903/1 Cl 4 A *liśyate* to be or become small, lessen, Cl 6 P *liśati,* to go, move, caus. *leśayati,* DP in *alpī-bhāva* (cl6) becoming small, decreasing, (cl4) in *gati* going

√*liṭya* 902/2 Nom P *liṭyati* to be little or to think little of, DP in *alpa* being small, *kutsana* abusing, reviling

lobha 905/1 m. perplexity, confusion, eager desire or longing for , greed, avarice, 'greed' HH

lobha-viraha m. freedom from avarice,

√*loc* 907/3 Cl 1 A *locate* to see, behold, perceive, caus/Cl 10 *locayati* to speak, to shine, DP in *darśana* seeing, viewing, perceiving, in *bhāṣā* speaking, shining,

locana 1. mfn enlightening, 2. (*as*) n. eye,

√*loḍ* see *loṭ* DP in *unmāda* being foolish or mad

loga m. clod of earth,

loha 908/3 mfn red, reddish, copper-coloured, iron, steel, gold or any metal, a weapon, a fish-hook, blood, m. the red goat, a kind of bird, (*ī*) f. a pot, n. any object or vessel made of iron,

lohakāra m. blacksmith,

lohāyasa n. coppery metal, any metal alloyed with copper,

lohita mfn red, red-coloured, reddish, made of copper, metal, m. red, redness, n. any red substance, f. (*ā*) blood,

√*lok* 906/1 Cl 1 A *lokate* to see, behold, perceive, caus./cl10 *lokayati* to know, recognize, DP in *darśana* seeing, viewing, perceiving, in *bhāṣā* speaking, shining,

loka 906/1 m. space, room, place, a region, the world, people, heaven, ordinary life, common practice or usage, the world of names and forms,

lokāḥ pl. inhabitants, people, humanity

lokādi m. the beginning of the world, the creator of the world

lokakṛt mfn world-making, world-creating,

lokampṛṇa mfn world-filling, penetrating everywhere,

lokapāla m.pl. the protectors of the worlds, a king, prince,

lokapravāda m. world saying, common saying,

lokasaṅgraha 907/1 the propitiation or conciliation of men, the whole of the universe, aggregate of worlds, the welfare of the world, uplift of the world,

lokavat 907/1 mfn. containing the worlds, ind. as in the ordinary life

lokāyata mfn materialistic, m. a materialist,

lokottara 907/3 mfn excelling or surpassing the world, beyond what is common or general, unusual, extraordinary, super-normal, (N) beyond the world-view, here external objects do not exist, nor does awareness, realizing the non-existence of external objects and not being bound in relation to them, the state of success,

lola mfn 1. moving hither and thither,

uneasy, 2. anxious for, desirous of, greedy, fickle, longing,

lolupa 908/2 very destructive,very desirous, eager longing for, longing,

lomaharṣa m. thrill or shudder, thrilling, causing the hair to bristle,

loman n. the body-hair of men and animals, a tail,

lopa m. omission, want deficiency, breaking, hurting, neglect, violation, robbing, plundering, absence, (in gram.) dropping, elision,

loptum inf. to cut off,

√*loṣṭ* Cl 1 A *loṣṭati* to heap up, gather into a heap or lump, DP in *saṅghāta* assembling, collecting,

loṣṭa 908/2 a lump of earth or clay, a clod

√*loṭ* 907/3 Cl 1 P *loṭati* or *loḍati* to be mad or foolish, (in gram.) name of the imperative tense and of its terminations, DP in *dhaurtya* deceiving, *pūrvabhāva* being first, or *svapna* sleeping,

√*lū* 905/2 Cl 9 P A *lunāti, lunīte, lunoti,* to cut, sever, divide, pluck, reap, gather, cut off, destroy, annihilate, caus. *lāvayati,* DP in *chedana* cutting, 2. mfn cutting, dividing,

√*lubh* 904/3 Cl 6 P *lubhati* Cl 4 P *lubhyati* to be perplexed or disturbed, become disordered, go astray, to desire greatly or eagerly, long for, be interested in, to entice, allure, caus. *lobhayati* to confound, bewilder, cause to desire or long for, excite lust, allure, entice, attract, to efface, DP in *vimohana* (Cl 6) bewildering, confounding, perplexing, in *gārdhya* (Cl 4) coveting, longing for,

lubdha 904/3 mfn bewildered, confused, greedy, covetous, avaricious, n. a hunter, a lustful man,

lubdhaka m. a hunter, a covetous or greedy man, the star Sirius, the hinder parts,

√*lumb* 905/1 Cl 1 P *lumbati* to torment, harass, Cl 10 P *lumbayati* to be invisible, DP in *ardana* (Cl 1) tormenting, in *adarśana* (Cl 10) becoming invisible, or *ardana* tormenting,

√*luñc* Cl 1 P *luñcati* to pluck, pull out, tear off, to peel, husk, DP in *apanayana* removing,

√*luṇḍ* 904/2 see *luṇṭ,* DP in *ālasya* being lazy, *pratighāta* striking,

√*luñj* 904/1 see *lañj*

√*luṇṭ* cl 1 P *luṇòati,* to rob, plunder, DP in *upaghāta* striking against, resisting, in *viloḍana* suffering pain, in the sense of *bhāṣā* speaking,

√*luṇṭh* to stir, agitate, to go, to be idle, to be lame, to resist, to rob, plunder, DP in *steya* robbing, stealing, *gati* going,

√*lunth* 904/2 Cl 1 P *lunthati* to strike, hurt, cause or suffer pain, DP in *hiṁsā* hurting, or *saṁkleṣaṇa* suffering pain,

√*lup* 904/2 Cl 6 P A *lumpati (te*), to break, violate, hurt, injure, spoil, to seize, fall or pounce upon, to rob, plunder, steal, to cheat, to take away, suppress, waste, cause to disappear, elide, erase, omit (a letter, word, etc.),
Cl 4 P *lupyati* to disturb, bewilder, perplex, confound, caus. *lopayati* to cause to break or violate, to break, violate, infringe, neglect, (in gram.) to be suppressed or lost or elided, A. cause to disappear, efface, to be greedy,
DP (Cl 6) in *chedana* cutting off, breaking, in *vimohana* (Cl 4) troubling, effacing, making smooth, 2. (in gram.) falling out, suppression, elision, mfn fallen out, dropped, elided,

lupta mfn deprived, robbed, plundered, (in gram.) dropped, elided, n. stolen property, plunder, booty,

luptvā ind. having attacked, having plundered,

√*lūṣ* 905/3 Cl 1 P *lūṣati* to adorn, decorate, Cl 10 P *lūṣayati,* to hurt, injure, kill, to steal, DP in *bhūṣā* (Cl 1) adorning, in *hiṁsā* (Cl 10) hurting, injuring,

√*luṭ* 904/1 1. Cl 1 A *loṭate* to resist, to suffer pain, to shine, Cl 10 P *loṭayati* to speak, to shine,

2. Cl 1.4. P *loṭati, luṭyati* to roll, roll about, wallow, Cl 1 A *loṭate* to go, Cl 10 *loṭayati,* DP in *viloḍana* rolling or wallowing on the ground,

√*luṭh* 1. 904/1 Cl 1 P *loṭhati* to strike, knock down, roll, wallow, Cl 1 A *loṭhate* to resist, suffer pain, to go, Cl 10 P *loṭhayati* to rob, pillage, sack, DP in *upaghāta* striking,
2. Cl 6 P *luṭhati* to roll, move about or to and fro, wallow, welter, flutter, dangle, to touch, to agitate, move, stir, DP in *viloḍana* rolling or wallowing on the ground,

ma 771/1 m. time, poison
a magic formula,
the moon, name for various gods,

mā 804/1 ind. a particle of prohibition or negation not, that not, do not, f. a mother, measure, authority (*-tva* n.) , light, knowledge, binding, fettering, death, a woman's waist, n. happiness, welfare, water,

√*mā* 2. Cl 3 P *mimāti* A *mimīte, mimeti,*
to sound, bellow, roar, bleat, (calves, cows, goats etc.), DP in *māna* measuring, or *śabda* sounding,

√*mā* 3. Cl 2 P *māti,* Cl 3 A *mimīte*, Cl 4 A *māyate,* to measure, mete out, mark off, traverse, measure (by any standard, compare with, measure out, apportion, grant, to prepare, arrange, fashion, form, to show, display, exhibit, DP in *māna* measuring,

√*mabhr* 789/1 Cl 1 P *mabhrati* to go, move, DP in *gati* going,

√*mac* 773/2 Cl 1 A *macate* to cheat, be wicked or arrogant, to pound, grind, DP in *kalkana* cheating, being vain,

macchisya m. pupil of me, my pupil,

mac-citta 777/2 mfn. having the mind fixed on me, thinking of me

māciram ind. shortly, straightaway,

mad 1. base of the first person pronoun

√*mad* 777/3 Cl 4 P *mādyati, (te)* also *madati (te*), to rejoice, be glad, exult, delight or revel in, be drunk, enjoy heavenly bliss, to boil, bubble (as water), to gladden, exhilarate, intoxicate, animate, inspire, A. to gladden, delight, satisfy, DP in *harṣa* (Cl 4) revelling, delighting, rejoicing, (Cl 1) in *harṣa* or *glepana* being poor, (Cl 10 in *tṛpti-yoga* pleasing, gratifying,

mada 777/3 m. hilarity, rapture, lust, wine, excitement, inspiration, intoxication, 'pride of possession' HH

māda m. revelry, drunkenness, passion,

madana m. passion, love or the god of love, a kind of embrace, a bee, beeswax, *(ā*) f. any kind of intoxicating drink, musk, n. the act of intoxicating or exhilirating,

madarthe 7/s/m for my sake, 'of me in purpose'

madāśraya m. dependent on me , taking refuge in me,

madbhakta worshipping me, devoted to me

madbhāva my state of being, originating from me, my essence,

madgataprāṇāḥ those who have concentrated the vital breath on me 1/pl/m, whose goal of their life's breath is..

madgatena by going to me

madgu 'diver' m. a water-fowl, kind of snake, galley or vessel of war,

mādhava mfn relating to spring, vernal, m. descendant of *Madhu* (*Kṛṣṇa*)

madhu m. honey, mfn sweet,

madhujñāna that from which is known

madhu – nectar i.e. the cause of immortality (Gam.),
madhukāra (or *–kara*) 'honey-maker' a bee,
madhulih 'honey-licker', a bee,
madhura mfn sweet, (of speeches) honeyed, charming, delightful, melodious,
mādhurya 809/1 n. loveliness, beauty, charm, sweetness or tenderness, sweetly speaking
Madhusūdana a name of *Kṛṣṇa*, slayer of *Madhu* (not the ancestor above)
madhya mfn central, moderate, n. middle, middle-most, intermediate, central, impartial, neutral, of a middling size, quality or quantity,
madhya-cārin mfn moving in the middle of,
madhya-ga mfn situated in the middle of, tarrying amongst, going or being in the middle or among,
madhyama mfn. middle, middlemost, central, m.n. middle of the body, waist, m. In Sanskrit grammar the *madhyama puruṣaḥ* (middle or second person of the verb) is expressed as 'you' e.g. *gacchasi* - you (2/s) go. f. (*ā*) An aspect of speech or sound manifestation, "when the move is made to one of the possibilities and the sound related to the knowledge to be expressed has risen only in the mental realm of the being, then it is called *madhyamā*" HH
madhyastha m. standing in the middle, neutral
madhye (+ 6th case) in the middle of
madirā f. liquor,
madīya mfn mine, my own,
madvyapāśrayas trusting in me, taking refuge in me, one to whom I am the refuge, 1/s/m *mat vi apa ā* √*śri*
madya n. wine
madyājinas those who are devoted to me (those sacrificing to me)
Magadha an ancient country (now part of south Bihar and west Bengal) - *āḥ* m.pl. Magadhans, name of the people of Magadha,
magadhadeśa the land of Magadha,
√*magadhya* 772/1 Nom P °*ti* to surround, to serve, be a slave, DP in *pariveṣṭana* surrounding (serving),
magha 772/2 m. a gift, reward, bounty, wealth, power, liberal gift,
māgha m. a month corresponding to January/February,
maghavan mfn abounding in liberal gifts, generous, esp. as m. a rich patron or lord who institutes a sacrifice and pays the priests, Indra – 'rewarder of priests and singers', the generous one',
maghavan(t) 772/2 mfn possessing or distributing gifts, bountiful, liberal, munificent, a name for Indra,
magna mfn sunk, submerged, immersed in,
√*mah* 794/1 cl1.10. P *mahati, mahayati,* A *mahate, mahayate,* elate, exalt, arouse, magnify, esteem highly, honour, revere, worship,
A. *mahate*, *mahayate*, rejoice, delight in, give, bestow, DP in *pūjā* (Cl 1) worshipping, in *pūjā* (Cl 10) honouring, *stambha* being proud,
2. mfn great, strong, powerful, mighty, abundant,
√*māh* 815/1 Cl 1 P A *māhati (te)* to measure, mete, DP in *māna* measuring,
mah f. *mahī* mfn great, mighty,
maha mfn great, mighty, strong, abundant, a feast, festival, a sacrifice, a buffalo, light, lustre, brilliance, n. pl. great deeds, f. (*ā*) a cow,
mahā 794/3 used in compounds for *mahat* or *mahant,* used for *mahat* as an independent word in 2nd s. *mahām* = *mahāntam*
mahā 794/3/2 great, mighty,
mahābaho O mighty armed one
mahābāhu mfn great-armed, stout-armed
mahābhāga m. fortunate, illustrious, venerable,
mahābhārata an epic story,
mahābhiḥ pl. greatly, mightily, right heartily,

mahābhāmi a great country, a vast region
mahābhūta 798/2 mfn being great, great, m. a great creature or being, n. a great element, gross element, see next
mahābhūtāni 1/pl/n. five gross elements, earth, water, fire, air, space, 'that are the materials of all the bodies and that constitute the foods and the eaters, -Gam.' (properties*), śabda, sparśa, rūpa, rasa, gandha*
mahādeva m. great god, Śiva, Viṣṇu,
mahādevī f. the principal wife of a king
mahādhana mfn having great wealth,
mahādhī mfn having a great understanding, a man of great intellect,
mahāguru mfn exceedingly revered, m. person worthy of unusual honour,
mahaḥ (G) heaven, the world of vastness,
mahāhrada 802/1 m. a great tank or pool
mahā kāla m. a form of *śiva* in his character of destroyer,
mahākalpa m. great cycle of time,
mahākāśa 'the limitless space held in consciousness' HH
mahākathā f. great tale,
mahākavi m. great poet,
mahākula n. great (noble) family,
mahāmanas mfn great-minded,
mahāmati mfn 'having great understanding' wise,
mahāmāyā f. great deceit or illusion, the divine power of illusion, the illusory nature of worldly objects..
mahāmuni m. great sage,
mahān n. greatness, might, power, abundance,
mahant f. *mahatī* (actually a hindi word from the sanskrit *mahat*)1. mfn great in space, time, quantity or quality, large, long, mighty, important, significant, m. great or noble man, 2. m. the intellect,
mahānubhāva 797/1 of great might, mighty, high-minded, noble-mighty, generous,
mahāpadma the elephant supporting the southern quarter of the earth,
mahāpaṇḍita mfn exceedingly learned,
mahāpaṅka m.n. deep mire,
mahāparādha m. great crime,
mahāprājña mfn very wise,
mahāpralaya m. cosmic dissolution at the end of a *kalpa*, ,
mahāprāña 'great breath' aspirated, - referring to pronunciation of sounds,
mahāprasthāna n. setting out on the great journey, departing this life, dying,
mahāpuruṣa 797/2 m. a great or eminent man, a great sage or saint, the great soul, the Supreme Spirit, a realised being,
mahāpuruṣa m. supreme spririt, great Soul, great or eminent man, a sage,
mahārāja 799/3 a great king, supreme sovereign,
māhārajana dyed with Indian saffron (turmeric),
mahāraṅga m. a great amphitheatre, a large stage,
mahārathās 'those whose chariots are great' –great warriors 1/pl/m
mahārgha mfn high-priced, very precious or valuable, costly, expensive,
mahrāva m. great howl,
mahāsāmanya n. the widest universality, generality in the broadest sense,
maharṣayāḥ the great seers, great sages,
maharṣi 794/2 any great sage or saint
mahas n. greatness, might, glory, gladness,
mahāsamādhi 'great union', (the great and final samādhi) is the act of consciously and intentionally leaving one's body at the time of death. A realized yogi (male) or yogini (female) who has attained the state of *Nirvikalpa Samadhi* (enlightenment), will, at an appropriate time, consciously exit from their body and cease to live. This is known as *mahāsamādhi* . This is not the same as the physical death that occurs for an unenlightened person. (K)
mahāsaṁghika m. pl. name of a Buddhist school which eventually led to the *Mahāyāna* School,

mahāśaya 801/1 "great receptacle", the ocean, having a noble disposition, gentleman, high-minded, magnanimous, open, sometimes a term of respectful address, sir or master, the master,

mahāsiṁha m. great lion,

mahāstra 802/1 a great or powerful missile, powerful bow,

mahāśūnya n. great vacuity or vacancy, the great void (Buddhist),

mahat 794/2 mfn great, mighty, strong,
n. (G) the Great Intellect, The first evolute of primordial nature (*prakṛti*). It is the cosmic aspect of the intellect and, along with the intellect, ego, and mind, it is the cause of the entire creation. It is also called *buddhi* which is the psychological aspect of the intellect in individuals. It is both eternal and non-eternal. Its special function is determination. From it evolves egoity 'self-consciousness' and manas 'the mind'.

mahatā mfn long, great, extended,
f. greatness, mightiness,

mahātapas mfn practising great austerity, Great Penance m. name of a sage

mahatattva 794/2 n. 'the great principle (name of universal *buddhi*)', the intellectual principle as source, 'the great That Thou', "here are universal feeling of existence and individual feeling of existence," the subtle world, 'the principle of intelligence' (Gam.),

mahātejas mfn of great splendour, full of fire, of great majesty (said of gods and men),

mahati 7/s/m in the great, in the mighty

mahātmā 'great souled', an honorific title,

mahātman 796/1 mfn. high-souled, great souled one, magnanimous, having a great or noble nature, exceedingly wise, eminent, distinguished,
the Supreme Spirit, *mahātmanaḥ* of the exceedingly wise,

māhātmya n. magnanimity, high-mindedness, exalted state or position, majesty, dignity,

mahattara mfn greater,

mahattva 794/3 great size or extent, magnitude, violence, intensity, moral greatness,

mahaujas mfn having great strength,
n. great might or power,
m. a hero, a champion,

mahāvākya 800/2 n. a principal sentence, the name of 4 sacred utterances of the *upaniṣads*,

mahāvana n. a great forest or jungle,

mahāvikrama mfn having great might or courage, Great-might –name of a lion,

mahāvīra m. great hero,

mahāvrata n. great vow, the first five vows in Jainism - abstinence from gross violence, gross falsehood and gross stealing, contentment with one's own wife, limitation of one's possessions,
mfn having undertaken a great vow,

mahāvratin mfn practising the five fundamental duties of Jainas, a devotee, ascetic,

mahāyaśas mfn having great glory,

mahāyajña m. great sacrifice,

mahāyāna n. 'great vehicle', name of the later (esoteric) system of Buddhism, The Mahāyāna tradition is the larger of the two major traditions of Buddhism existing today, the other being that of the Theravāda school. According to the teachings of Mahāyāna traditions, "Mahāyāna" also refers to the path of seeking complete enlightenment for the benefit of all sentient beings, also called "Bodhisattvayāna", or the "Bodhisattva Vehicle.
In the course of its history, Mahāyāna Buddhism spread from India to various other Asian countries. (K)

mahāyuga one cycle of the four yugas 4,320,000 years

mahendra m. Great Indra, great chief,

mahendratva n. the name or dignity of

Great Indra,

maheśa 802/2 great lord or god, a name of *Śiva*

maheṣu m. a great arrow, mfn armed with a great arrow,

maheśvara 802/2 Great Lord, sovereign, chief, name of *Śiva*

maheśvāsā mighty archers (*mahā iṣu āsās* mighty arrow hurlers) 1/pl/m

mahi mfn great,

mahī 803/2 f. the great world, the earth, earth as substance, the base of a triangle or other plane figure,

mahīdhara mfn 'earth-bearing' supporting the earth, m. a mountain,

mahī-kṛte for the sake of the earth

mahīkṣit m. earth-ruler, king,

mahilā f. woman,

mahimā = *mahiman*

mahiman 803/1 greatness, power, majesty, the power of assuming great size,

mahimāna mfn greatness,

māhina mfn glad, blithe,

mahīpāla m. earth-protector, king,

mahī-pate voc. O Lord of the Earth

mahīpati m. earth-lord, king,

mahiṣa mfn mighty, f. *mahiṣī* the powerful one, - a woman of high rank, first wife of a king, m. buffalo, f. (*ī*),

mahiṣī f. the mighty or powerful one, the first wife of a king,

mahītala n. the surface of the earth,

mahitva n. greatness, might,

√*mahīya* 803/3 Nom A *mahīyate* to be joyous or happy, to prosper, to be exalted, rise high, be highly esteemed or honoured, becomes glorified, DP in *pūjā* being honoured,

mahodadhi 802/2 m. the great ocean

mahodaya m. great fortune or prosperity,

mahotpāta (in comp.) a great portent or prodigy,

mahotsava m. a great festival, any great rejoicing, the god of love,

mahyam pron. for me

maithuna 834/2 mfn paired, coupled, connected by marriage, n. union, connection, copulation

maitra 834/1 mfn. friendly, amicable, benevolent, kind, belonging or relating to Mitra, m. 'friend of all creatures', friendship

maitrī f. friendship, friendliness, benevolence, goodwill, (one of the four perfect states for Buddhists, benevolence personified (daughter of Dakṣa and wife of Dharma), close contact or union, ifc. equality, similarity,

mājāra-s cat

√*majj* 773/2 Cl 6 P *majjati* to sink, go down, go to hell, perish, become ruined, to sink (in water), dive, plunge, caus. *majjayati* cause to sink, submerge, drown, overwhelm, destroy, to inundate, DP in *śuddhi* cleansing, purification,

majja mfn diving, sinking,

majjā f. bone marrow,

majjao Prakrit for *mājāra-s* (cat) and for *majjāra-s* (my lover)

makara 771/2 m. a kind of sea-monster, crocodile, f.(*ī*)

makāra 771/1 the letter or sound *ma*

makh 772/1 Cl 1 P *makhati* to go, move, DP in *gati,* going,

makha mfn jocund, cheerful, m. a feast, a festival, a sacrifice,

makṣika m. (*ā*) f. a fly, bee,

-*mala* n. excretion of bees, beeswax,

mākṣīkaḥ m. spider,

√*mal* 792/1 Cl 1 A 10 P. *malate, malayati,* to hold, possess, DP in *dhāraṇa* holding, possessing,

mala 792/1 m.n. dirt, filth, dust, impurity (physical and moral), "*mala* is due to the *saṁskārāḥ* which form a thick layer of dirt in the subtle body" (Jaiswal)

mālā f. crown, wreath, garland, string of beads, rosary,

mālākāra m. gardener,

mālava m. Malva –name of a country in west-central India,

mālavadeśa m. the land of Malva,
mālavaviṣaya m. the land of Malva,
malaya m. name of a mountain,
malīmasa mfn dirty, foul,
mālin mfn crowned, wreathed, garlanded,
m. a gardener, a florist,
malina mfn dirty, filthy, impure, soiled, tarnished, of a dark colour, grey, dark grey, black, tainted,
m. a religious mendicant wearing dirty clothes,
n. a vile or bad action, buttermilk, water, borax,
-*tā* f. dirtiness, impurity, moral impurity, blackness,
-*tva* n. blackness,
malinasattva impure *sattva,* nescience, *avidyā* in the individual,
mālinya 814/2 n. foulness, dirtiness, impurity, obscurity,
√*mall* 792/3 Cl 1 A *mallate* to hold, have, DP in *dhāraṇa* holding, possessing,
malla 1. Mallas – a people, 2. professional boxer/wrestler,
mālya 814/1 n. wreath, garland, flower,
mām pron. me (2nd)
mama pron. 6/s my, of me
māma mfn of mine,
voc/s/m as word of address of a dog to an ass – uncle, dear friend, uncle,
māmaka mfn mine, my, selfish, greedy, a miser, a maternal uncle,
mamakāra m. feeling of mineness in relation to the body and things connected with it, e.g. wife, children, friends, home, wealth,
māmakīna mfn my, mine,
mamatā 789/1 f. sense of "mine", "egotism" ownership
mamatva 789/1 n. the state of mineness,
√*maṁh* 771/2 Cl 1 A *maṁhate* to give, grant, bestow, to increase, to speak or shine, DP in *vṛddhi* increasing, in *bhāṣā* speaking, shining
maṁhiṣṭha mfn granting most abundantly, most generous, quite ready for (4th),
māmikā my, mine, my own 1/s/f

māṁs or *māṁsa* n. meat, flesh,
māṁsala mfn fleshy
māṁsa-lubdha mfn desirous of meat,
māṁsa-ruci mfn having pleasure in meat, greedy for meat,
mamukṣu one who hankers after liberation (Gam.),
√*maṇ* 774/3 Cl 1 P *maṇati* to sound, murmur, DP in *śabda* sounding,
√*man* 783/1 cl8 *manute, manyate* to think, believe, imagine, suppose,
to regard or consider anyone or anything, to think oneself or be thought to be, appear as, pass for, to be of opinion or think fit, to set the heart or mind on, to perceive, observe, learn, know, understand, comprehend, consider, to remember, meditate on, caus. *mānayati* to honour, esteem, value highly, DP in *avabodhana* considering, in *jñāna* knowing, thinking,
√*mān* 809/1 Cl 1.10 P *mānati, mānayati,* to honour, respect, DP in (cl1) *pūjā* honouring, (Cl 10) *pūjā* honouring, respecting, *stambha* being proud,
māna 809/1 m.n. regard, respect, opinion, honour, arrogance, pride,
notion, conception, idea, purpose, wish, design, consideration,
a wounded sense of honour, anger or indignation excited by jealousy,
m. structure, castle,
manā f. devotion, attachment, zeal, eagerness, envy, jealousy
manā masc. form of *manas* in a *bahuvṛhi* comp.
māna-da mfn showing honour (to others),
m. honour-giver (address of a woman to her lover),
manaḥkalpitajagat the world created by the mind or imagination, (U)
manaḥśuddhi purification of the mind,
manāk 784/2 ind. a little, in a small degree, even slightly, shortly, immediately, at once, only, merely,
manana 783/3 mfn. thoughtful, careful,

n. thinking, reflection, meditation, intelligence, understanding, (esp. intrinsic knowledge or science, as one of the faculties connected with the senses, homage, reverence, 2nd stage of reflection, (*śravanam, mananam, nididhyāsanam) q.v.* (G) … removes the doubt of an aspirant regarding the nature of the object (*prameya*) to be contemplated. reflection is to be employed so as to get an intellectual conviction of the truth. It is the constant thinking of the Absolute (Brahman).

mananaśakti the power of reflection and concentration,

mana(s) 783/3 the mind (in its widest sense) in phil. the internal organ of perception and cognition, the faculty or instrument through which thoughts enter, considered perishable, the information gatherer, an instrument of knowing, the lower level of mind which thinks, deliberates, has the function of general indeterminate thinking,

manasaḥ than the mind, more than the mind, of the mind, from the mind

mānasa 810/1 mfn belonging to the mind or spirit, mental, spiritual (opp to corporeal), expressed only in the mind, conceived or present in the mind, the mental powers, mind, spirit, heart, performed in thought , mentally, deriving from mind, name of a lake in the Himālaya,

manasā name of a goddess, 3rd case of *manas* (in comp.)

manasapūja a kind of ritualistic worship,

manasaspati 784/1 m. the lord or presiding genius of the mental powers and life of men,

mānasika mfn existing in the mind alone (imaginary), committed (only) in the mind(a sin), mental, spiritual, imaginary,

mānasikajapa m. mental repetition,

mānasikakriyā f. mental action

māṇava m. boy, youngster, young Brahman

mānava 809/3, a human being, man, f. (*ī*) Manu(s)- ancestors of man,

mānavadharma the essential nature of man, the duties of man, (U)

mānava dharmaśāstra n. law book of the *mānava* school

mānava ka m. manikin, dwarf, a young Brahman

manavāṇīkriyā mind, word and deed

manave to Manu 4/s/m

mānayitavya mfn requiring to be honoured

mānayitvā ind. having honoured,

√*mañc* 773/3 = √ Cl 1 A *mañcate* to cheat etc., to hold, to grow high, to adore, to shine, DP in *dhāraṇa* wearing, *ucchrāya* exalting, *pujana* worshipping

√*maṇḍ*775/2 Cl 1 P *maṇḍati* to deck, adorn, A. *maṇḍate* to distribute or to clothe, caus. *maṇḍayati* to adorn, decorate A. oneself, to glorify, extol, to rejoice, exhilarate, DP in *bhūṣā* (Cl 1) adorning, decorating, Cl 10 in *bhūṣā* adorning or *harṣa* rejoicing,

√*mand* 787/3 1. Cl 1 A P *mandate (ti),* to rejoice, be glad or delighted, be drunk or intoxicated, to gladden, exhilarate, intoxicate, inflame, to shine, be splendid or beautiful, DP in *stuti* praising, *moda* being glad, *mada* being drunk, *svapna* sleeping, *kānti* being beautiful, shining, *gati* going,

manda 787/3 mfn slow, dull-witted, tardy, weak, dull, feeble, ill, sick, m. the planet Saturn, a stupid or slow elephant, the end of the world, f. a pot, vessel, inkstand,

*mandā*787/1 f. a pot, vessel, inkstand

mandabhāgya mfn having little luck, unlucky, n. misfortune

mandādara mfn having little regard for, careless about, indifferent to,

mandākinī Ganges name, (going slowly)

maṇḍala 775/3 circular, round, globe, ring,

circumference, orbit of a heavenly body, a disk, territory, province, M. a bunch or quantity of anything,
mandaṁ mandam slowly slowly, very slowly
maṇḍana 775/3 mfn adorning, being an ornament to, n. ornament, decoration
mandana mfn 787/3 gay, cheerful
maṇḍapa m.n. open hall or pavilion (erected on festive occasions), tent, temple, arbour, bower,
maṇḍapikā f. small shed or shop,
mandara mfn slow, tardy, sluggish m. Mandara , a sacred mountain, heaven, a mirror,
mandāra m.n. coral tree, name of a man,
māndārya mfn descended from Mandāra, m. descendant of M°,
mandira n. house, palace, temple, a horse-stable, the body, m. the sea, back of the knee
maṇḍūka m. frog f. (*ī*)
√*maṅg* 772/3 Cl 1 A √*maṅgate* to go, move, DP in *gati* going
maṅgala n. welfare, luck, 2. anything lucky, auspicious or of good omen, m. the planet Mars,
māṅgalya 806/1 mfn conferring or indicating happiness, auspicious, m. welfare, propitiousness, luck, n. an auspicious prayer, any auspicious thing, sour curds, sandal wood, gold, red lead,
√*maṅgh* 773/2 Cl 1 P √*maṅghati* to adorn, decorate, A √*maṅghate* to go, start, begin, to blame, to cheat, DP in *maṇḍana* decorating, adorning,
maṇi m. pearl, jewel, 2. water-jar,
maṇigaṇa 774/3 pearls
maṇipūra m. navel, sort of bodice,
maṇipūra cakra the third *cakra,* situated in the vicinity of the navel,
mānin mfn thinking, being of opinion, thinking to be or have, high-minded, haughty, highly honoured or esteemed,
manīṣā 784/2 f. thought, reflection, wisdom, intelligence, concept, idea, prayer, hymn, desire, wish, 'independent thinking, genius, intellect –Gam.'
manīṣī m. ruler of the mind, a saintly person, intelligent man, philosopher
manīṣikā 784/2 f. wisdom, intelligence
manīṣin thoughtful, intelligent, wise, sage, prudent, devout, offering prayers or praises, m. a learned Brahman, teacher, Paṇḍit
mañjara n. a cluster of blossom, panicle,
mañjarī f. a cluster of blossoms, bud, flower, foliage, a parallel line, a pearl,
mañju mfn beautiful, lovely, charming,
mañjula mfn beautiful, pleasing, lovely,
mañjuṣā f. basket, chest, case, box,
√*maṅk* 772/2 Cl 1 A *maṅkate* to move or to adorn, DP in *maṇḍana* decorating, adorning,
√*maṅkh* 772/2 Cl 1 P *maṅkhati* to go, move, DP in *gati* going,
√*māṅkṣ* 806/1 Cl 1 P *māṅkṣati* to wish, long for, desire, DP in *kāṅkṣā* desiring, wishing for,
manmāṁsa my flesh,
manman n. thought, esp. devotion, prayer or praise,
manmanā mind fixed on me
manmatha m. love, the god of love, mfn relating to or concerning love,
manmaya 777/2 mfn. consisting of or proceeding from me, full of me, like me
manobuddhi mind and intelligence f.
manodharma m. natural attributes or properties of the mind,
manodṛśya perceived by the mind,
manogata 785/1mfn. mind-gone, existing or concealed in the heart or mind, n. thought, opinion, notion
manogati f. 'heart's course', wish, desire, mfn going where one will,
manogrāhin mfn captivating the mind, fascinating,
manogupta mfn cherished or concealed in the mind, thought or meditated on secretly, f. red arsenic, a species

of sugar-cane,
manohara mfn 'heart-taking', captivating, fascinating, attractive,
manokṛtena through the action of the mind, 3/s/m
manolaya m. loss of awareness, loss of consciousness, used to indicate an intense spiritual experience, dissolution of the mind in its cause,
manomātrajagat mind alone is world, the world is made from mind alone,
manomaya 785/2 consisting of spirit or mind, mental, consisting of that knowledge, associated with the mind,
manomayakośa the mental sheath, one of the five coverings of the Self,
manonāśa m. loss of mind, destruction of mind,
manonirodha m. restraint of the mind,
mano'nukūla mfn pleasant to the mind,
manorājya n. castles in the mind, the realm of fancy,
manoratha 785/2 "heart's joy", fancy, illusion, a wish, desire,
manoviśuddhi f. purity of mind,
manovṛtti f. activity or disposition of the mind,volition, fancy, imagination,
maṁsyante they will think, they will believe 1/pl/fut/mid √*man*
-mant possessive suffix,
mantā f. the thinker,
mantavya mfn to be thought, to be thought of, to be regarded or considered as, what should be reflected on,
mantavyam 'the object of the mind' (Gam.),
√*maṇṭh* 775/2 Cl 1 A *maṇṭhate* to long for, desire eagerly, DP in *śoka* being anxious,
√*manth* 777/1 see 1. √*math*
mantha 787/1 m. stirring round, churning, agitating, a stirred drink, a churning stick
manthān m. a churning (fire-lighting) stick,
manthara mfn slow, dull, low or hollow or deep (sound), bent curved, crooked, m. fruit, spy, antelope, anger, treasure, hair,
√*mantr* 787/1 Cl 10 A *mantrayate, (ti)* to speak, talk, say, deliberate, take counsel, resolve upon, to propose any measure, give anyone advice, to consecrate, enchant, DP in *gupta-paribhāṣaṇa* consulting, giving advice, speaking,
mantṛ m. the thinker,
mantra 785/3 m. 'instrument of thought,' speech, sacred text or speech, a prayer or song of praise, a sacred formula addressed to any individual deity, G187 a sacred word or phrase of spiritual significance and power.
mantracaitanya the dormant potency of mantra (U),
mantra-da mfn giving i.e. imparting the sacred texts,
mantradīkṣā initiation of an aspirant through giving/accepting of *mantra*, *dī* – what is given or the person capable of bestowing divine grace, *kṣa* – one who is capable of assimilating,
When the *Guru* initiates His disciple with the *mantra*, He also bestows His sensitive power of intuition and empowers the disciple with His '*sankalpa*' (benign resolve) as well. *Mantra* = *mananam* (reflection) + *antar* (interior, inner,); that which is to be reflected upon in the heart.
mantravant mfn accompanied by sacred texts,
mantra-varṇa m. the wording of a sacred text,
mantrayate A . speaks with solemn or formal utterance,
mantrin 786/3 mfn wise or eloquent, a king's counsellor, minister, a conjurer, in chess – the queen,
mantu m. counsel, deliberation, (then) result of deliberation, plan, intent, an adviser, manager, disposer, lord of men, a king
f. thought, understanding, intellect,
mantūya 785/3 Nom P A *(°ti, °te)* to

become angry, to transgress against, to be offended or be jealous, DP in *aparādhe* offending, becoming angry,

manu 1. m. man, mankind, Manu a lawgiver, father of mankind, mfn thinking, intelligent, wise,

manuja m. man, sprung from Manu,

manujendra m. 'prince of men', king,

manus m. man or *manu* the father of men

mānuṣa m. pertaining to man, human, man,

mānuṣadaivika mfn of men and gods,

manusmṛti the laws of *Manu* according to *dharma*

manuṣya mfn human, manly, useful or friendly to man, m. man

manuṣyadeva m. human god, or man-god, or god among men, Brahman,

manuṣyaloka m. world of men,

manuṣyāṇām of men, of mankind

manuṣyajajña sacrifice for mankind

manuṣyatva n. condition of being man,

manuṣyeṣu 7/pl among men,

manvantara 7 cycles of the 4 *yugas*, supervised by one *Manu* (Lawgiver), an age of Manu,

manya 786/3 thinking oneself to be, passing for, appearing as, ifc

mānya mfn descended from a poet or from *Māna,* m. the poet's son or *Māna*'s son,

manyamāna pres/mid/part. thinking oneself to be, while brooding,

manyatā f. one thinks to know, belief, recognition,

manyate he thinks, he imagines 1/s/pres/indic/mid √*man*

manye I think or believe, 1/s/pres/indic/mid √*man,* (may be added to a sentence without affecting the construction).

manyu m. 1. mood (temper of mind), 2. anger, rage, heat of temper,

mara m. dying, death, the world of death, the earth, mfn killing, m.pl. the inhabitants of hell,

māra n. killing, murder,

maraka 789/3 m. an epidemic, plague, mortality ,

marakata n. emerald,

mārakata mfn having the properties of an emerald, m. emerald,

*maraṇa*789/3 n. death, the act of dying

māraṇa 811/3 n. killing, slaying, a killing, slaughter, death

mārātmaka mfn having murder in one's nature, murderous,

√*marb* 791/2 Cl 1 P *marbati* to go, move, DP in *gati* going,

√*marc* 791/1 Cl 10 P *marcayati* to sound, to seize, take DP in *śabda* sounding

mardana 791/2 mfn crushing, grinding, bruising, tormenting, destroying, m. crusher, subduer, n. friction,

mārdava 813/2 softness, gentleness, kindness, leniency towards all beings, mildness,

mārdavena gently

mārīca m. uncle of *rāvaṇaḥ*

marīci chief of the storm gods, 790/1 a particle or ray of light

√*mārg* 812/2 Cl 1.10. P *mārgati, mārgayati,* to seek, look for, to seek after, strive to attain, to request, ask, beg, DP in *anveṣaṇa* seeking,

marga see

mārga 812/2 m. seeking, search, hunting, the track of a wild animal, any track, way, a way, road or path, usage, custom

mārgamāna seeking after, looking for,

mārgaṇa 812/3 mfn desiring, requiring, asking, seeking, n. investigation, inquiry

mārgaśīrṣa a month (approx November/December)

mārja mfn (in cpds.) cleaning, a cleaner, m. a washerman, cleansing, purification, smoothness, unctuousness,

mārjāra m. a cat, (the cleaner),

marīci 790/1 m.f. a particle of light, shining mote or speck in the air, a ray of light (of the sun or moon), the sky (a world),

marīcikā f. a mirage

marīcimālā f. garland of rays,
marīcimālin mfn having a garland of rays,
√*mārj* 812/3 Cl 10 P *mārjayati,* to wipe, cleanse, purify, sound? DP in *śabda* sounding,
mārjana 813/1 mfn wiping away, cleaning, a cleaner, f. wiping off, washing, purifying, the sound of a drum, a broom, a brush
markaṭa m. ape, monkey, kind of bird, spider,
marma-jña mfn knowing the weak spots,
marman n. mortal part, vulnerable or weak spot,
marmāra m. murmur,
marṣa m. patience, endurance,
marṣaṇa 792/1 enduring, forgiving
marta 791/1 m. mortal, a man, the world of mortals, the earth,
mārtāṇḍa m. sprung from a lifeless egg, bird, bird in the sky, the sun, sun or the god of the sun *āditya*s
martavya mfn liable to die, n. death being inevitable,
martya 791/1 mfn who or what must die, mortal, subject to death, m. man, person, the world of mortals, the earth, *(ā)* f. dying, death, n. that which is mortal, the body,
martyaloka mortal world, world of mortals
martyatā f. or *–tva* n. mortality, human condition,
maru m. a waste, desert, abstinence from drinking,
marubhūmi f. wilderness, desert,
marusthalī f. desert-land, desert,
marut pl/m the storm gods, 790/2 the flashing or shining ones
maruta 790/3 m. wind, a god
māruta relating or belonging to the Maruts
√*marv* 792/1 Cl 1 P *marvati* to fill, to go, move, caus. *marvayati* to utter a particular sound, DP in *pūraṇa* filling,
marya m. a mortal, man, esp. young man, lover, suitor, a stallion, a camel,
maryādā f. limit, a frontier, boundary,
√*maś* 793/2 Cl 1 P *maśati* to hum, buzz, make a noise, to be angry, DP in *śabda,* sounding, or *roṣakṛta* being angry,
√*maṣ* 793/3 Cl 1 P *maṣati* to hurt, injure, DP in *hiṁsā* hurting, injuring,
√*mas* 793/3 Cl 4 P *masyati,* to measure, mete, DP in *pariṇāma* weighing, measuring, changing form,
mās m. 1. moon, a month, n. flesh, meat,
māsa 814/3 m. the moon, a month
māsāhāra mfn eating only once a month,
maśaka m. gnat, biting/stinging insect, mosquito,
māsala 815/1 m.a year
māsaṣaṭka n. six months,
māsatraya n. three months,
maṣī or *maṣi* f. bone-black, 2. ink,
√*mask* 794/1 Cl 1 A *maskate* to go, move, DP in *gati* going
masṛṇa mfn smooth, tender, mild, bland,
mastaka n. m. the head, skull, top, summit, tuft of leaves on a palm,
māstu *(mā astu)* let there not,
maṣyabhāva m. lack of ink,
mat may indicate any singular form of *aham* i.e. my, me etc.
mat pron. from me
mata 783/1 ppp. *mata* thought, believed, thought to be, regarded as, imagined, f. opinion, notion,
māta 804/2 mfn. formed, made, composed
mātaṅga m. elephant,
mātaṅgavadana mfn elephant-faced,
mātariśvā air, lord of the atmosphere, L. mystic name of Agni,
mātariśvan m. breeze, wind, air,
mate thought, thought to be 1/du/f
√*maṭh* 774/2 Cl 1 P *maṭhati* to dwell or to be intoxicated, DP in *mada* being intoxicated, or *nivāsa* dwelling,
√*math* or *manth* 777/1 Cl 1.9. P *mathati, manthati, mathnāti* also A *mathate, manthate, mathnīte,* to stir or whirl round, to produce fire by rotating one dry stick in another, to churn milk, shake, stir, agitate, afflict, hurt, destroy, DP for *manth-* in

hiṁsā hurting, injuring, *saṁkleśana* being afflicted, crushing, grinding, *viloḍana* churning, shaking, stirring, DP for *math* in *viloḍana* churning, shaking, stirring

maṭha m.n. a hut, cottage, monastery, esp. the hut/cell of an ascetic or student, a cloister, college (esp. for young Brāhmans), temple, m. a cart or carriage drawn by oxen,

maṭhākāśa the space bounded by a temple, house or room,

maṭhara mfn persistent, hardness, harshness, m. name of a man,

māṭhara m. name of a man, superintendent of a monastic school,

mathitvā ind. having agitated, stirred by discerning

mathurā f. a city in the north Indian state of Uttar Pradesh, an ancient city,

mati 783/2 f. thought, design, intention, devotion, prayer, determination, inclination, wish, desire, thinking, 'cognition, developing a spiritual will and intellect with the guru's guidance', (K),

matimat mfn clever, intelligent, wise,

matiprakarṣa m. wit-superiority, i.e. a fine dodge, cleverness, talent,

matkarmakṛt performing my action

mat-paras 777/2 mfn. me intent on, with me as highest

matparāyaṇaḥ with me as supreme aim or object, devoted to me,

matprasādāt from or through my grace

mātṛ 2. 807/1mother, air, space, L. applied also to the earth, the Dawn,

-mātra merely,or (in cpd.) merely, the one thing and no more, nothing but, only, *mātra* 804/2 elementary matter, measure,

mātrā 1. f. material, measure, quantity ifc. having ... as its measure, so and so long, high, large etc.
2. the full measure i.e. limit, at end of adjectival cpds. 'having ... as its limit', 'not more than ...', '....merely', '...only', 'mere...', (such a compound may be the first member of another compound),
3. measure i.e. height, depth, length, breadth, distance,

mātrāsparśa M. m. material contact, contact with material objects,

mātratā f. being as much as, no more nor less than,

mātrata(s) 804/3 ind. from the first moment of

mātṛkā "the basic forces which initiate all formal and informal creation of causal, subtle, and physical bodies. They have in them all those qualities which are seen to be manifest in this creation." HH, the *śakti* or powers in 16 particular sound syllables,

matṛtas ind. from the mother, on the mother's side,

mat-ṛte me without, without me

matṛvat ind. as one's mother,

matsama-(tva) 777/2 resemblance of me,

mat 777/2 for *mad* me,
-sama 1152/1 same, like, like me

matsamsthā 777/2 f. union with me

matsara 776/2 exhilarating, intoxicating, selfish, greedy, envious, 'envy' HH

mātsarya n. envy, jealousy, displeasure, dissatisfaction,

matsthāni n.pl.in me abiding, living, resting,

matsya m. fish

matta mfn mad, in rut, furious, drunken,

mattaḥ 5/s pron. *mat* from me +*taḥ* adv. abl. term. from me

mātula m. maternal uncle

matvā ind. having considered or meditated on, having thought,

matyā ind. knowingly, purposely, wittingly, thinking to be,

mauli m. head, diadem, top of anything, a 'topknot',

mauna 836/3 m. silence, taciturnity,

mauṇḍya 836/3 shaving the head, baldness

mauñja mfn made of Munja –grass,

mauṅjīnibandhana n. tying of the Munja girdle,

√*mavy* 793/2 Cl 1 P *mavyati* to bind, DP in *bandhana* fastening, binding,
√*may* 789/1 Cl 1 A to go, move, DP in *gati* going,
-maya ifc. mfn made of, consisting of, containing, 2. maker, former,
mayā by me, with me, 3/s/m
māyā 811/1 illusion, unreality, deception, trick, magic G. 189 the principle of appearance. The force which shows the unreal as real and presents that which is temporary and short-lived as eternal and ever-lasting. The force that conceals our divinity.
māyā-kapota m. illusion-pigeon,
māyā-kapota-vapus mfn having the form of a phantom-pigeon,
māyāmātra nothing but *māyā*
māyāmohajala the jugglery or deception set up by infatuation with *māyā*
mayas n. invigoration, refreshment, cheer, gladness, joy,
māyāvāda m. the doctrine affirming the world to be illusion,
mayi pron. 7/s in me
māyī 'the ruler of Māyā' (T)
māyin mfn wily, cunning, deceptive, m. conjurer, magician,
māyobhavya n. gladness, happiness,
mayobhū mfn refreshing, gladdening, m. Agni,
māyopadhi the *upādhi* or apparently limiting conditions produced by *māyā* or appearance,
mayūkha m. ray of light, flame, brightness,
mayūra m. peacock,
√*me* 831/2 1. Cl 1 A P *mayate (ti)* to exchange, barter, DP in *pra-ṇi-dāna* exchanging, bartering,
me pron. 6/s of me, my
√*med* 832/3 strong form of √*mid*
medas n. fat, marrow, lymph, corpulence,
√*medh* 832/3 strong form of √*midh*
medha m. broth, sap, pith, essence, L. 2. sap and strength, essential part, 3. sacrificial victim, animal sacrifice,
medhā 833/1 f. mental vigour or power, intelligence, wisdom, prudence, 'ability to understand and retain the purport of books', worldly intelligence,
medhākāra mfn causing or generating intelligence,
medhas n. sacrifice, intelligence, knowledge, understanding,
medhas wisdom in *su-medhas*
medhāvat mfn possessing wisdom, wise,
medhāvin mfn = *-vat,* m. a learned man, teacher, a parrot, an intoxicating beverage,
medhya mfn full of sap, vigorous, fresh, mighty, strong, fit for a sacrifice or oblation, free from blemish, clean, pure, not defiling (by contact or being eaten), wise, intelligent, m. a goat
medura mfn fat, dense, unctuous, bland,
megha m. cloud,
meka 1. m. a goat, 2. a setting up, *su-meka* establishing,
mekhalā f. girdle, (of Munja –grass),
melaka m. assembly, with *kṛ* assemble,
melana n. meeting, union, association,
menakā f. an Apsara, mother of Śakuntalā by Viśvāmitra
meṇaṭha m. elephant-keeper,
√*mep* 833/2 Cl 1 P *mepati* to go DP in *gati* going,
meṣa m. ram, (*ī*) ewe, zodiac sign Aries,
meru a famous sacred legendary mountain (not possible to identify geographically),
merudaṇḍa m. the spine, spinal column,
√*meth* 832/2 strong form of √*mith*
meṭha m. elephant –keeper,
√*mev* 833/3 Cl 1 A *mevate* to worship, serve, DP in *sevana* serving,
√*mi* 815/3 1. Cl 5 P A *minoti, minute*, to set up, found, build, construct, mete out, measure, judge, observe perceive, know, cast, throw, scatter, to fix or fasten in the ground,DP in *prakṣepaṇa* throwing, casting,
√*mī* 818/2 Cl 9 P A *mīnāti, mīnīte,*

mināti, minoti, mīyate, to lessen, diminish, destroy, A. to perish, disappear, die, to lose one's way, go astray, to transgress, violate, frustrate, change, alter, DP *hiṁsā* hurting, killing,
3. Cl 1. 10. P *mayati* or *māyayati* to go, move, DP in *gati* going

√*mich* 815/3 Cl 6 P *micchati* to hurt, pain, annoy, DP in *utkleṣa* hindering, annoying,

√*mid* or *med* 817/2 1. Cl 1 P A =√*mith*, to understand or to kill, DP in *medhā* being wise or *hiṁsana* killing,
2. Cl 1 A or 4 P *medate medyati*, to grow fat, Cl 10 *mindayati* or *medayati*, to make fat, DP in *snehana* being unctuous, greasy,

√*mid* or *mind* 817/2 2. Cl 1 A or 4 P *medate,medyati*, Cl 10 p *mindayati* or *medayati* to grow fat, DP in *snehane* loving, being unctuous, greasy,

mīdhvāṁs mfn bestowing richly, bountiful, (L)

√*midh* 817/2 or *medh*, Cl 1 P A *medhati* (*te*) see √*mith*, DP in *medhā* being fat, *hiṁsana* injuring, *saṅgam* meeting

√*mih* 818/2 Cl 1 P *mehati*, to void or pass urine, make water upon or towards, DP in *secana* wetting, moistening,

mih f. mist, fog, downpour of water,

√*mil* 817/3 Cl 6 P A *milati (te*) to meet, encounter, join, fall in with, come together, assemble, concur, DP in *śleṣaṇa* joining or *saṅgama* meeting,

√*mīl* 819/1 Cl 1 P A *mīlati (te*) to close the eyes, wink, twinkle, to assemble, be collected, DP in *nimeṣaṇa* 551/2 closing or contracting the eyelids

milati meets (with 3rd),

mīlati 819/1 closes the eyes

√*mīm* Cl 1 P *mīmati* to move, to sound, DP in *gati* going or *śabda* sounding,

mīmāṁsā 818/3 f. profound thought or reflection, consideration, investigation, examination, discussion, evaluation, an enquiry into the nature of a thing, examination of the Vedic text, the *Pūrva-mīmāṁsā* usually called the *mīmāṁsā,* concerning itself chiefly with the correct interpretation of Vedic ritual and text, 'calls for understanding of the will of the Absolute and expects one to put it into practice exactly as prescribed, Only then the result follows. In *Uttaramīmāṁsā* (also known as *Vedānta*) it has been presented differently, The real understanding of the unity of the Absolute and the individual brings all these two parts together and one becomes the Absolute oneself.

mīmāṁsaka a follower of the *pūrva mīmāṁsa* teaching

mīmāṁsya gve. to be called in question,

mīna m. a fish, Pisces zodiac sign,

√*miñj* 815/3 Cl 10 P *miñjayati* to speak or to shine, DP in *bhāṣā* speaking, shining,

√*minv* = *pinv*, Cl 1 P *meśati,* DP in *sevana* sprinkling, or *secana* honouring,

√*miś* 817/3 Cl 1 P *meśati* to sound or to be angry, DP in *śabda* sounding, or *rośa-kṛta* being angry,

√*miṣ* 818/1 Cl 6 P *miṣati* to open the eyes, wink, blink, DP in *sparddhā?*
2. Cl 1 P *meṣati* to sprinkle, moisten, wet, DP in *secana* sprinkling,

miṣat winking, blinking, living

miśla see *miśra*

√*miśr* 817/3 Cl 10 P *miśrayati* or *miśrāpayati* to mix, mingle, blend, combine, DP in *samparka* mixing

miśra 817/3 mfn. mixed, mingled, blended

miśraṇa 818/1 n. mixing, mixture, addition

miśrībhāva m. becoming mixed, mingling,

miśrībhāva-karman n. mingling-action, process of becoming mixed,

miśrībhū to become mixed, mix, intertwine, meet together,

miśrīkaraṇa 818/1 n. the act of mixing,

seasoning, an ingredient

miśrita mfn mixed, blended with (comp.)

mit f. post, pillar, prop,

mita 815/3 mfn fixed, set up, founded, established, cast, scattered, the sea,

mitāhāra mfn m. moderate food, scanty diet,

√*mith* 816/3 Cl 1 P A *methati (te)*, to unite, pair, couple, meet, alternate, engage in altercation A. to dash together, DP in *medhā* being wise, or *hiṁsana* injuring,

mithas ind. together, mutually, among each other, in turns, reciprocally,

mithilā a city, capital of *Videha* the kingdom of *Janaka* (father of *Sītā*)

mithu mfn wrong, false, ind. wrongly, falsely, alternately,

mithuna 816/3 mfn paired, forming a pair, m. a pair (male and female but also any couple or pair), ifc. f. (*ā*), n. pairing, copulation, a pair or couple, the other part, complement or companion of anything, honey and ghee, a root compounded with a preposition, *-tva* the state of forming a pair,

mithuyā f. wrongly, falsely, ind. falsely,

mithyā false, unreal, illusory, illusion, 817/1 ind. contrarily, wrongly, vainly, in vain, improperly, incorrectly, ibc. false, untrue, sham,

mithyābhimāna free from ego or selfishness, error-prone ego,

mithyācāra 817/1 improper conduct, acting hypocritically, m.a hypocrite

mithyādṛṣṭi f. false doctrine, heresy, atheism, wrong view, vision that the world is unreal,

mithyāhamkāra m. free from ego or selfishness, error-prone ego,

mithyājñāna n. a false conception, error, mistake, wrong knowledge,

mithyājñānanimitta n. based on wrong knowledge,

mithyāsaṁbandha m. false relationship,

mithyātva n. falsity, unreality, perversion or illusion,

mithyāvāda m. phenomenal doctrine, doctrine of unreality, falsehood, false view,

mithyopacāra m. false service or simulated kindness, wrong treatment (med.),

miti 1. 815/3 fixing, erecting, √*mi* establishing,
2. 816/1 f. measuring, measure, weight, accurate knowledge, evidence,

mitokti f. moderate speech,

mitra n. 816/1 friend, m. friendship, friend, comrade, an *āditya*

mitrabandhu-hīna mfn destitute of friends and relatives,

mitra-kru m. name of an evil person,

mitralābha m. 'friend acquisition', name of the 1st book of the *Hitopadeśa,*

mitrātithi name of a man 'having Mitra as his guest',

mitrāvaruṇā Mitra and Varuna 1/du/m

√*mīv* 819/1 1. Cl 1 P *mīvati* to move, 2. to grow fat or corpulent, DP in *sthaulya* growing fat,

√*mlai* 838/1 Cl 1 P *mlāyati (te), mlāti*, to fade, wither, decay, vanish, be languid, or exhausted or dejected, have a worn appearance, caus. *mlapayati* DP in *harṣa-kṣaya* being sad or dejected,

mlāna mfn faded, withered, exhausted, languid, weak, feeble, dejected, sad, melancholy, vanished, gone, black, dark-coloured, foul, dirty m. a house frog, n. faded or withered condition, absence of brightness or lustre,

mlānakśīṇa mfn withering and languishing,

mlānamanas mfn depressed, dispirited,

mlāna-sraj mfn having a withered garden, having a withered or faded garland,

mlānasragrajaḥsvedasamanvita mfn provided with withered garlands, dust and perspiration,

mlāni f. decay, dejection, withering, fading, depression, disappearance, foulness, blackness, vileness,

√*mlech* 837/3 Cl 1 P = *mlich* Cl 1 P *mlecchati* to speak indistinctly, (like a foreigner or barbarian who does not speak sanskrit), DP in *avyaktāśabda* speaking indistinctly, incorrectly, in *avyaktāvāc* speaking confusedly, *chedana* cutting, smearing, anointing,

mleccha m. barbarian, foreigner, non-Aryan, man of an outcast race, (ī) f. a wicked or bad man, sinner, one who lives by agriculture or making weapons,

mlecchana 838/1 n. the act of speaking confusedly or barbarously

√*mleṭ* 838/1 Cl 1 P *mleṭati* to be mad, DP in *unmāda* being mad,

√*mlev* 838/1 Cl 1 A *mlevate* to serve, worship, DP in *sevana* serving,

√*mluc* 837/3 Cl 1 P *mlocati* to go, move, to go down, set, DP in *gati* going,

√*mluñc* 837/3 = √*mluc* Cl 1 P *mluñcati* DP in *gati* going

mna minded, (?)

√*mnā* 837/2 Cl 1 P *manati* cf. √*man* with which *mnā* was originally identiCl, DP in *abhyāsa* learning diligently, repeating in mind,

mocana 835/2 n. release, liberation, mfn freeing or delivering from,

moda 835/3 joy, delight, gladness, pleasure, fragrance, perfume

modaka gladdening, delighting, m. sweetmeat, (in medicine) a kind of pill,

modate rejoices √2. *mud*

modinī f. the earth, musk, an intoxicating drink, mfn rejoicing, glad,

modiṣya I shall rejoice √*mud*

mogha 835/2 mfn. vain, fruitless, useless, (*am*) in vain, uselessly, without cause

moha 836/1 loss of consciousness, perplexity, ignorance, delusion, error "attachment or infatuation" HH

mohana 836/1 mfn depriving of consciousness, bewildering, confusing, perplexing, leading astray, infatuating,

mohanīya mfn 'to be deluded', resulting from illusion, error or infatuation,

mohanīya karma 'deluding karma',

mohayati 825/1 cause to err or fail, stupefy, bewilder, caus. √ *muh*

mohita 836/2 mfn. stupefied, bewildered, deluded

mokṣa 835/1 freedom, liberation from the bondage of *saṁsāra* emancipation, liberation, release from worldly existence or transmigration,

mokṣakāma 835/1 emancipation, liberation, freedom, *kāma* 271/3 wish, desire, - one who longs for liberation

mokṣaṇa 835/1 mfn liberating, emancipating n. liberation, releasing, rescuing, giving up, abandoning,

mokṣārthe intent on liberation

mokṣyase you shall be released or liberated 2/s/fut/pass √*muc*

mora *(mātra)* (N 322) the unit that may be considered when the individual syllables have been dissected, m. a peacock, f. name of a family cat,

√*mrad* 837/3 Cl 1 A *mradate* to smooth, DP in *mardana* smoothing

mradas n. softness,

√*mrakṣ* 837/2 Cl 1 P *mrakṣati,* or *mṛkṣati*, to rub, stroke, curry, to smear, to accumulate, collect, caus./Cl 10 *mrakṣayati, mṛkṣayati*, to rub, smear, anoint, to accumulate, to speak indistinctly or incorrectly, DP (Cl 1)in *saṅghāta* accumulating, (Cl 10) in *chedana* cutting, smearing, anointing, accumulating,

mrakṣaṇa 837/2 n. rubbing in, annointing, ointment, oil,

√*mṛ* 827/2 Cl 6 A *mriyate* Cl 1 P A *marati, marate*, to die, decease, caus. *mārayati* cause to die, kill, slay, DP in *prāṇa-tyāga* dying, giving up breath,

√*mṝ* 831/2 Cl 9 P *mṛṇāti* to crush, smash, break, kill, destroy, DP in *hiṁsā* hurting, killing,

√*mṛḍ* 829/3 Cl 6 P *mṛḍati , (mṛḷati)* Cl 9 P *mṛḍnāti* Cl 10 *mṛḍayati (mṛḷayati) (te*), to be gracious or favourable, pardon, spare, to treat kindly, make happy, rejoice, DP (CL 6) in *sukhana* being delighted or happy, (Cl 9) in *kṣoda* squeexing, pressing, rubbing, or *sukha* being delighted or happy,

√*mṛd* 830/1 1. Cl 9 P *mṛdnāti*, Cl 1 P A *mardati (te),* to press, squeeze, crush, trample, destroy, ravage, kill, to rub, stroke, rub into, mingle with, rub against, touch, overcome, surpass, DP in *kṣoda* squeezing, pressing, rubbing,

mṛd 830/2 earth, clay, soil, loam, a piece of earth, lump of clay,

mṛdā f. clay, loam, earth,

mṛdaṅga m. drum,

√*mṛdh* 830/3 1. Cl 1 P A *mardhati (te*), Cl 6 P A *mṛdhati (te*), to neglect, forsake, abandon, to be moist or moisten, DP in *undana* moistening, 2. f. fight, battle, adversary, foe,

mṛdu mfn soft, weak, slight, moderate,

mṛdutā f. tenderness, gentleness, softness, weakness, mildness,

mṛdya mfn pressed, mild form of dispassion or detachment,

√*mreḍ* 838/1 Cl 1 P *mreḍati* to be mad, DP in *unmāda* being mad

√*mreṭ* 837/3 see *mleṭ*

√*mṛg* 828/2 Cl 4 P 10 A *mṛgyati, mṛgayate* to chase, hunt, pursue, seek, search for, or through, investigate, examine, to visit, frequent, seek or strive after, DP in *anveṣaṇa* seeking,

mṛga 828/2 m. a forest animal or wild beast, deer, gazelle,

mṛgatṛṣṇi f. a water mirage in the desert,

mṛgayā f. hunting, the chase,

mṛgendra 829/1 m. king of beasts, a lion, zodiac sign Leo,

mriyate dies

√*mṛj* 829/2 Cl 2 P *mārṣti* A. *mṛṣte,* Cl 6 P A *mṛjati (te),* to wipe, rub, cleanse, polish, clean, purify, embellish, adorn, to make smooth, curry e.g. a horse, to stroke, wipe off or out, destroy, to carry away, win, DP in *śauca* washing off, cleansing,

√*mṛkṣ* 828/1 weak form of √*mrakṣ*

mṛīka n. grace, mercy,

√*mṛṇ* 829/3 Cl 6 P *mṛṇati* to crush, slay, kill, to thread, winnow, DP in *hiṁsā* hurting, killing,

mṛṇāla n. f.(*ī*) 'liable to be crushed'edible fibrous lotus root or lotus stalk fibre,

mṛnmaya mfn made of earth, with *gṛha* house of clay, the grave, (L)

√*mṛś* 831/1 Cl 6 P A *mṛśati (te*) to touch, stroke, handle, to touch mentally, consider, reflect, deliberate, DP in *āmarśana* rubbing, stroking, touching, handling

√*mṛṣ* 831/1 1. Cl 4 P A *mṛṣyati (te*), Cl 1 P A *marṣati (te*), to forget, neglect, disregard, not heed or mind, bear patiently, put up with, to pardon, forgive, excuse, DP in *titikṣā* suffering, enduring, putting up with, *sahana* suffering, enduring, caus. *marṣayati* to overlook, excuse, 2. ifc. one who bears or endures, bearing, one who strokes or touches, 3. Cl 1 P A *marṣati (te)* to sprinkle, pour out, DP in *secana* sprinkling,

mṛṣā 831/1 in vain, wrongly, false, unreal,

mṛṣṭa (having been) rubbed, polished,

mṛta mfn 827/2 dead, deceased, departed

mṛtavat ind. as if dead,

mṛttikā f. clay

mṛtvā ind. having died,

mṛtyu 827/3 death, dying

mṛtyumatya 'encompassed by death, within the grasp of death',

mṛtyumukhāt from the jaws of death

mṛtyuṁjaya mfn overcoming disease, conqueror of death, *Śiva*

mṛtyupāśān 'the fetters of death', (T)

mṛtyuproktam told by death,

√*mruc* 837/3 Cl 1 P *mrocati* to go, move, DP in *gati* going,

√*mruñc* 837/3 = √*mruc*

mṛyate he dies, he is dead, 1/s/pres/pass.

√*mū* 825/2 1. Cl 1 A *mavate* to bind, tie, fix, DP in *bandhana* binding, tying, 2. mfn. binding, tying,

√*muc* 820/3 Cl 6 P A *muñcati (te),* to loose, let loose, free, let go, slacken, release, liberate, to spare, let live, set free, allow to depart, dismiss, despatch, to relinquish, abandon, leave, quit, give up, set aside, to die, yield, grant, bestow, to send forth, emit, shed, utter, discharge, throw, cast, caus. *mocayati (te*), to set free, liberate, absolve from, to cause to loose or let go, to gladden, delight, Cl 1 A *mocate,* to cheat, DP (Cl 10) in *pramocana* liberating, or *modana* gladdening, delighting, (Cl 6) in *mocana* liberating, loosening,

√1. *mud* cl10 822/2 P *modayati* to mix, mingle, blend DP in *saṁsarga* mixing, uniting,

√2. *mud* cl1 A *modate* (*ti)* to be glad, happy, rejoice, delight in, caus. *modayati* (*te)* to gladden, give pleasure, exhilirate, DP in *harṣa* rejoicing

3. *mud* f. joy, delight, gladness, intoxication, frenzy

mudā f. joy, pleasure, gladness,

mūḍhavastha a state of the mind, state of ignorance, forgetfulness of one's real nature,

mūḍha 825/2 mfn bewildered, confused, deluded, foolish, simple

mūḍhavat like a fool

mūḍhadhī 825/2 silly-minded, simple, foolish

mudita mfn glad, joyful, rejoicing in,

muditā f. complacency, gladness, joy,

mudrā f. name of partic. finger/hand signs or signals, a seal, signet-ring, any ring, any stamp, print, mark or impression, a stamped coin, rupee, cash, medal, an image, sign, badge, a pass, passport, a lock, stopper,

mudrayati stamps, seals,

mugdha mfn ignorant, foolish, artless, young, gone astray, attractive or charming, simple, innocent, lovely, naive, perplexed, foolish,

mugdhata mfn a state of deluded forgetfulness of the true divine nature through infatuation,

√*muh* 824/3 Cl 4 P A *muhyati (te*), to become stupefied or unconscious, be bewildered or perplexed, err, be mistaken, go astray, become confused, fail, caus. *mohayati* to stupefy, bewilder, confound, perplex, cause to err or fail, DP in *vaicitya* mental confusion, absence of mind,

muhur ind. occurring repeatedly, suddenly, at once, in a moment, constantly, recurring, at every moment

muhur muhur or *muhurmuhuḥ* 825/1 again and again, suddenly, at once, in a moment, at every moment, constantly,

muhūrta m.n. 1. a moment, 2. an hour (30th of a day, 48 minutes, an auspicious moment,

muhus in comp. for *muhur*

muhyamāna mfn being deluded, becoming deluded or bewildered,

muhyati he is deluded, confused, 1/s/pres/indic/act

√*muj* 821/3 (or *muñj)* Cl 1 P *mojati* or *muñjati* to give out a particular sound, Cl 10 P *mojayati* or *muñjayati* to sound or to cleanse, DP in *śabda* sounding

mūka mfn mute, speechless, tongue-tied, m. a fish, the offspring of a mule and a mare, f.(*ū*) a crucible,

√*mūl* 826/2 Cl 1 P *mūlati* to be rooted or firm, caus. *mūlayati* or *molayati* to plant or to grow, DP in *pratiṣṭhā* (Cl 1)being firm, standing fast, taking root, (Cl 10) in *rohaṇa* planting, growing,

mūla mfn original, own, first, n. source,

base, origin, root, original text, firmly fixed, square root, beginning, thicket, native inhabitant,
mūlya mfn being at the root, to be torn up by the root, purchasable, n. price, original value, value, worth, wages, salary, payment for service rendered,
mūka 825/2 mfn silent, speechless, mute, m. a fish, offspring of a mule and a mare,
mukha n. 1. mouth, jaws, 2. visage, countenance, face, snout or face of an animal,
mukhara mfn loquacious, garrulous,
mukhocchvāsa m. breath, mouth-breath,
mukhya 820/2 mfn being in or coming from or belonging to the face or mouth, being at the head or at the beginning, primary, first, principal, chief, eminent, ifc. the first or best among.., m. a leader, guide, n. an essential rite, reading or teaching the *veda,* a month from new moon to new moon, a moustache,
mukhyaprāṇa chief vital air
mukhyārtha m. the primary meaning of a word, mfn employed in (or having) the original sense, mfn employed in or having the original sense,
mukhyavṛtti direct interpretation, direct meaning,
mukta 820/3 liberated (one who is….), free from bondage, let go, free, loose, liberated, with 5th – freed, √ *muc*, 1/s/m free
muktā f. pearl,
muktaśāpa mfn having a laid aside curse, leaving his curse behind him,
mukti 821/2 f. liberation, setting or becoming free, giving up, final beatitude, [√ *muc* in liberating, or gladdening, delighting]
muktvā having been liberated
mukula n. a bud, the body, the soul,
mukuṭa m. diadem, tiara, crown,
mūla 826/2 n. firmly fixed, rooted, a root, basis, foundation, cause, origin, commencement, beginning, capital (city), an original text,
mūlaccheda 826/2 cut up by the roots
mūlādhāra n. G 195 the *cakra* or spiritual centre at the base of the spine where the Kuṇḍalinī (latent spiritual power) lies dormant,
mūladhauti cleaning of the anus,
mūlājñāna primal ignorance containing all potentialities (U),
mūlamantra m. a principal, primary or fundamental text, a spell,
mūlaprakṛti f. primary cause or originant, original root or germ out of which matter or all apparent forms are evolved (U),
mūlāvidyā primal ignorance containing all potentialities (U),
mūlya n. price, capital,
mumukṣu 821/2 mfn desirous of freeing, eager to be free, striving after emancipation , m. one who strives after liberation,
mumukṣubhiḥ by the seekers of liberation,
mumukṣutva intense longing for liberation,
mumurṣā f. death wish, impatience with life
mumūrṣu mfn wishing to die, about to die, moribund,
√*muṇ* 822/1 Cl 6 P *muṇati* to promise, DP in *pratjñāna* promising,
√*muñc* 821/3 Cl 1 P *muñcati* to go, move, Cl 1 A. *muñcate* to cheat, be wicked, DP in *kalkana* cheating, being vain,
muñcati root *muc* 820/3 to loose, liberate, relinquish, quit, to free oneself, get rid of, 1/s/pres/act liberates,
√*muṇḍ* 822/1 Cl 1 P to cut, crush, grind, Cl 1 A. to cleanse, to sink, to shave, DP in *mārjana* cleansing, sinking, *khaṇḍana* shaving, crushing,
muṇḍa mfn bald, head shaved. hornless (a cow or goat), stripped of top leaves or branches, hornless, m. a shaven-head man, a bald man, the trunk of a lopped tree, a barber,
muni 823/1 m. a sage, saint, seer, sage,

ascetic, silent one, an austere person, L. 1. pressure, impetus, pressing on, impulse,
2. a man driven on by inward pressure or impulse, person in a (religious) ecstasy, 3. any distinguished sage or seer or ascetic, esp. one who has taken a vow of silence,

munijanaḥ a monk

√*muñj* 821/3 see *muj* DP in *śabda* sounding

muñja m. sedge,

√*muṇṭh* 822/1 Cl 1 A *muṇṭhate* to run away or to protect, DP in *pālana* protecting,

√*mur* 823/2 1. see *murch*, 2. see *murv*, 3. Cl 6 P *murati* to encompass, entwine, bind together, DP in *sañceṣṭana* encircling, surrounding,

√*murch* 823/3 (or *mūrch*) Cl 1 P *mūrchati* to become solid, thicken, congeal, assume shape or substance or consistency, expand, increase, grow, become or be vehement, or intense or strong, to fill, to shape, pervade, penetrate, spread over, to have power or take effect upon, to grow stiff or rigid, faint, swoon, become senseless or stupid or unconscious, to deafen, to cause to sound aloud, DP in *moha* loss of consciousness, or *samucchrāya* growing,

mūrchā f. hallucination, infatuation, stupor, melody, swoon, delusion, fainting,

mūrdha(n) 826/1m. the forehead, head in general, skull, the foremost or topmost part of anything roof (of the mouth), a mouth position for pronunciation,

mūrkha mfn foolish, stupid, m. fool,

mūrta 824/1 mfn formed, substantial, material, embodied, incarnate,

mūrtāmūrta personal and impersonal (U),

mūrti 824/1 f, any solid body or material form, material elements, solid particles, embodiment, the gross, manifestation, incarnation, personification, anything which has definite shape or limits, (in phil. as mind, earth, water, fire and air), a person, form, figure, appearance, image, idol, statue, beauty,

mūrtikāra m. a sculptor

mūrtimant mfn having bodily form, incarnate,

mūrtivat mfn possessing bodily form,

√*murv* 824/1 Cl 1 P *mūrvati* to bind, tie, DP in *bandhana* binding tying,

√*muṣ* 824/1 1. Cl 1 P *moṣati* to steal, rob, plunder, to ravish, captivate, enrapture (the eyes or the heart),see *maṣ*, DP in *steya* stealing,

√*mus* 824/3 Cl 4 P *musyati* to break or cut in pieces, destroy, DP in *khaṇḍana* cleaving, dividing,

mūṣ cl 1 P to steal, rob, plunder, 2. m.f. mouse, 'the thief',

mūṣaka m. thief, mouse, rat, Mousey as name of a man,

mūṣakākhyā f. the name 'Mousey',

musala m.n. pestle,

mūṣika m. mouse, rat,

mūṣikanirviśeṣa mfn undistinguished from a mouse,

muṣita mfn stolen, robbed, carried off,

muṣka m. 1. testicle, 2. region of the female genitalia,

muṣkadeśa m. region of the testes, groin,

√*must* 824/3 Cl 10 P *mustayati* to gather, collect, DP in *saṅghāta* heaping up gathering,

muṣṭi m.f. fist, clenched hand, stealing,

√*muṭ* 821/3 Cl 1.6.10. P *moṭati, muṭati, moṭayati* to crush, grind, break, DP (Cl 1) in *mardana* crushing, grinding, (Cl 6) in *ākṣepa* blaming, rebuking, or *pramardana* crushing, (cl10) in *sañcūrṇana* crushing, grinding, powdering,

mūtra n. urine,

-na used to form adjectives or participles

na ind. not, no, nor, neither, with indef. pron. no if repeated *(na na)* or with an (*a*)generally forms a strong affirmation, with 3rd or 5th case indicates deficiency, often joined with other particles, it may also like (*a*) form compounds meaning – that not, lest, for fear lest, like, as, as it were,

na... vā neither... nor

na anyat kiṁcana nothing else whatsoever,

na kaścit, na ko'pi not anyone, no one,

na bahiṣprajña not conscious of the outside world,

√*nabh* 527/2 Cl 1 A *nabhate* to burst, be torn or rent asunder,
Cl 4.9. P *nabhyati, nabhnāti* to hurt, injure, caus. *nabhayati* to cause to burst, tear open,
DP in *hiṁsā* injuring,
2. f. or m. injury or injurer,

nabhas n 527/3 sky or atmosphere, ether (as an element), period of life, age, mist, clouds, vapour,
m. period of life, age, clouds, rainy season, the nose or smell, a rope,

nabhas-tala n. sky-surface, the sky,

nābhiḥ or *nābhī* 535/3 f. the navel, a navel-like cavity, centre, central point, point of junction or of departure, home, origin, the nave of a wheel, m. a chief, sovereign,

nābhicakra the third *cakra* at the navel,

nābhivardhana n. the cutting of the umbilical cord,

nabhīta mfn not afraid, fearless,

Naciketā a name in the *Kaṭha Upaniṣad* meaning – that which is unperceived i.e. spirit

nacira 523/1 mfn. not long (in time),
(*am*) ind. shortly, soon,

nacirāt ind. soon,

naciréṇa ind. shortly, soon

√*nad* 526/1 Cl 1 P *nadati* to sound, thunder, roar, cry, howl, caus. *nadayati (te)* to make resound or vibrate, Cl 10 *nādayati (te*), to make resonant, fill with noises or cries, DP in *avyakta-śabda* (Cl 1) inarticulate sound, in *bhāṣā* speaking, (Cl 10)

naḍa m. a species of reed, a reed,

nada n. 'the bellower' a bull, a reed, river

nāda m.a loud sound, roaring, bellowing, crying, any sound or tone, a praiser, *anahata nāda* 'the unstruck sound' said to be an unheard sound of primordial energy, endless and unlimited,

√*nādh* 535/1 Cl 1 A *nādhate* seeking help, asking, begging, DP in *yācñā* asking, *upatāpa* heating, *aiśvarya* having power, *āśīḥ* blessing

nādhīta mfn not learned, unread,

nadī f. roaring stream, river,

nāḍi 2. f. any tube or pipe, esp. a tubular organ of the body e.g. a vein, artery, nervous system,

nāḍī f. the tubular stalk of any plant or any tubular organ (as a vein, artery or nervous system), any pipe or tube, a flute, the pulse, any hole or crevice, a sort of bent grass, a leather strap or thong, a measure of time, a juggling trick, deception,

nadīna mfn not small or insignificant,
m. 'lord of the river', the ocean,

nadṛśya mfn invisible,

nadūṣita mfn uncorrupted,

nāga m. serpent, snake, also a class of demons, ordinary men (Buddhist), name of a tribal group, a cruel man, an elephant,

nagara n. and *–rī* f. town, city,

nāgarika mfn born or living in a town, civic, polite, courtly, clever, cunning,
m. a citizen of a city or town,
a policeman, police superintendent,
n. the toll raised from a town,

nagaropānta n. neighbourhood of the town, outskirts of a town,

nagna mfn naked, bare, desolate, desert,
m. a naked mendicant,

√*nah* 532/2 Cl 4 P *nahayati (te*) to bind, tie, fasten, bind on or round or together, A. to put on (as armour etc), arm oneself, DP in *bandhana* binding, 2. a bond, tie,

nahi ind. not, to be sure, *nahi me asti* to

be sure, I have no.... , by no means, not at all, surely not,

nahus m. neighbour, fellow-creature, man, pl. neighbourhood, mankind,

nahuṣa m. name of an ancient king who took Indra's throne but was later dethroned and turned into a serpent. Father of his successor Yayāti,

nāhuṣa mfn neighbouring, kindred, m. descendant of *nahuṣa* neighbour, kinsman,

naiḥ for *nis* in comp.

naiḥsaṅgya n. absence of attachment, indifference,

naiḥśreyasa mfn leading to happiness or future beatitude,

naikṛtika mfn dishonest, vile, wicked, given to destroying the livelihood of others

naimittika 570/3 mfn occasional, special, accidental, work not usually known in advance – arising out of a situation or need

naimittika-karma obligatory rites for special occasions,

naipuṇa mfn or *naipuṇya* n. dexterity, experience in, skill, requiring skill, completeness, totality,

nairātmya 'without soul' (Buddhist) indicating *nirvāṇa,* having no separate soul or no individual existence,

nair for *nis* in comp.

nairantarya n. uninterruptedness, close succession, compactness, immediate consequence,

nairaśya 570/2 n. hopelessness, non-expectancy, despair at

nairguṇya n. absence of qualities or properties, want of good qualities or excellencies,

nairukta mfn pertaining to the Nirukta, based on etymology, explained etymologically, m. an etymologist,

naiṣadha mfn pertaining to Niṣadha, m. prince of the Niṣadhans, i.e Nala

naiṣkarmya n. actionless, inactive

naiṣṭhika Apte 304/2 1. final, last, concluding, 2. decided, definitive, 3. fixed, firm

naiṣkarmya 570/2 n. freedom from action, inactivity, state beyond *karma,* abstinence or exemption from acts and their consequences

naitya mfn continually done or to be done, regularly repeated, n. eternity, perpetuity,

naityaka mfn to be always or regularly done (not occasionally), constantly repeated, obligatory, food regularly offered to a deity,

naivedya food offered to a deity or image,

naiyāyika knowing the *nyāya* philosophy, a follower of such,

nāka 532/3 m. 'where there is no pain', vault of heaven, firmament, sky, the sun, mfn painless,

na kadāpi never (not ever)

√*nakh* 524/3 or *naṅkh* Cl 4. 1. P *nakhyati, nakhati, naṅkhati,* to go, move, DP in *gati* going

nakha m.n. nail (on fingers or toes), claw, talon, spur of a cock, m. part, portion,

nakhin mfn having claws, thorny, m. beast with claws,

nakīm ind. not, not at all, never,

nakiṁcana mfn having nothing, very poor,

nakiṁcid n. nothing,

nakiṁcidapisaṁkalpa m. no desire for anything,

nakis 1. no one, 2. nothing, 3. never,

√*nakk* 524/1 Cl 10 P *nakkayati* to destroy, kill, DP in *nāśana* destroying completely,

nakra m. a crocodile, n. the nose, f. a swarm of bees or wasps,

√*nakṣ* 524/2 Cl 1 P A *nakṣati (te*) to come near, approach, arrive at, get, attain, DP in *gati* going,

nakṣatra n. heavenly body, sun, stars, constellation, 524/2 any heavenly body, collectively the stars,

nakta n. night, eating only at night,

ind. (*am*) by night,
nakula m. a mongoose,
Nakula a *Pāṇḍava* prince, (colour of the mongoose)
nakutaścid ind. from nowhere,
na kutracidapi nowhere at all
na kutracit nowhere
√*nal* 530/2 /1 Cl 1 P to smell or to bind, Cl 10 P to speak or shine, to bind or confine, DP in *gandha* (Cl 1) smelling, *bandhana* binding, in *bhāśā* (Cl 10) speaking, shining,
nala (or *naḷa*) m. reed, stalk, name of a prince of Niṣadha, chosen by Damayantī to become her husband in preference to the gods,
nala m. a monkey architect, reed species,
nalinī f. 'the reedy one' name of a mythical river, day lotus,
nalopākhyāna n. Nāla episode,
√*nam* 528/1 Cl 1 P *namati (te)* to bend or bow, (transitive or intransitive), to bow to, subject or submit oneself, to turn towards, to aim at, to yield or give way, keep quiet or be silent, (in gram. –to change a dental letter into a cerebral), DP in *prahvatva* bowing, or *śabda* sounding,
nāman n. a name, personal name, a characteristic mark or sign, form, nature, kind, manner, a noun (as opposed to a verb), a great name, renown, fame, water,
nāma 536/1 ind.by name, named, called,
nāmadhātu verbs derived from nouns or nouns derived from verbs.
nāmadheya n. a name, title, appellation, 'an indirect name –Gam.' naming, name-giving,
nāma graha mentioning a name, personal name, (family name *gotra),*
nāman name in general including proper names and nouns, a characteristic mark or sign, form, nature, kind, name, substance, essence, renown
-nāman named
nāmarūpa n. du. name and form,
nāmarūpajagat the world of name and form,
nāmarūpakāraṇa the creation or evolution of names and forms,
namas a bow, obeisance, adoration (by gesture or word), reverence, salutation to (with 4th),
namaskāra m. making of *namas,* adoration, greeting (in a form of worship),
namas-kṛ do homage,
namaskuru be reverent, make obeisance, 2/s/impv. *namas* √*kṛ*
nāmasmaraṇa remembrance of the Lord through memory or repetition of his name,
namasya 528/2 1. Nom. P. *namasyati,* to pay homage to or worship, be humble or deferential,
2. mfn. deserving or paying homage, venerable, humble,
namati bows, pays homage,
nameran they should bow, 1/pl/opt/mid
nāmnā 536/2 n. a characteristic name or sign, form, nature, kind, manner, name, personal name, merely the name, a noun, substance, essence, a good or great name, ind. by name, called,
namra mfn bent, humble,
namratā f. modesty, humility,
namṛta mfn not dead, alive,
namuci m. name of a demon, the god of love,
nānā 535/1 ind. variously, separately, differently, various, distinct from, without, f. coin,
nānābhāva mfn manifold, various, the feeling of plurality or multiplicity,
nanāndṛ f. husband's sister,
nānātva n. difference, variety, manifoldness, plurality,
nānāvidha 535/2 of various sorts or kinds, multiform, manifold, diversity,
√*nand* 526/2 Cl 1 P *nandati (te*) to rejoice, delight, be pleased or satisfied with, be glad of, DP in *samṛddhi* being glad, pleased, delighted, rejoicing at,
nanda m. joy, delight, happiness, a flute, a drum, (*ā*)f. delight, felicity, prosperity, happiness, = *nānda*
nanda or *nandana* m. son,

nandana mfn. rejoicing, gladdening, m. a son, a frog, causer of joy, f. (*ā*) a daughter, n. gladdening or gladness,
nāndana = *nandana*
nandi m. 'the happy one' name of *Viṣṇu*, of *śiva* and others, *śiva's* vehicle, f. joy, happiness, welfare,
nandideva m. name of a Brahman,
nandita mfn overjoyed,
nanu surely, certainly, indeed, no, not at all, never, a particle implying kindness or reproach, or perplexity,
napāt, *naptṛ* m. 1. in the Veda – a descendant in general - son, grandson, 2. grandson,
nāpita m. barber, shaver,
naptī f. daughter, grand-daughter, great grandchild,
naptṛ m. grandson,
napuṁsaka m. a eunuch, neuter,
napuṁsakaliṅga neuter gender, " not pertaining to generation"
nārada m. an immortal sage,
narādhama m. vile man, wretch, hostile,
narādhipa lord of men
nara 528/3 m. a man, a male, a person, the primal man or spirit,
nāra 536/3 m. relating to or proceeding from men, human, mortal,
nārada name of an ancient *devarṣi* who relays news between men and gods,
narādhipa m. lord of men, i.e. king, prince
naraka 529/3 m.n. place of torment, hell
naranārī f. man and woman,
nāraṅga m. orange, orange tree,
narapati m. lord of men, king,
narapuṅgavas man bull, bull of a man
naraśārdūla m. man-tiger, i.e. best among men,
nārasiṁha mfn relating or belonging to the man-lion, m. man-lion, Viṣṇu as man-lion, great warrior (man-lion),
naraśreṣṭha mfn best of men,
narasūnu f. daughter of the primal man or spirit,
naravāhana mfn 'having men as his team', drawn by men, a name of Kubera (god of wealth) and of a king,
naravāhanadatta m. name of a son of King *Udayana*
naravyāghra m. man-tiger, i.e. brave and noble man,
narayāna n. palanquin, a carriage drawn by men,
nārāyaṇa m. son of the primal man, synonym of *Viṣṇu,* meaning- a Being that supports all things, that is reached by them and that helps them to do so, one who pervades all things, one who sleeps on waters,
√*nard* 530/1 Cl 1 P *nardati (te)* to bellow, roar, shriek, sound, to go, move, DP in *śabda* sounding
nareśvara m. lord of men, i.e. king, prince,
nārī 537/1f. a woman, a female, wife, any object regarded as feminine,
nārikela m. a coconut, a fermented drink made from the coconut,
narīṇa (*ā*?)feminine, womanly,
nārī ratna n. 'a gem of a woman or wife' an excellent woman or wife,
narmada mfn granting or causing fun, making gladness,
narman n. fun, jest, sport, pastime,
naroga mfn not ill, well,
narottama mfn best of men,
nas pron. us, of us, to us, for us
√*naś* (or *noś*) 531/3 Cl 1 P A *naśati (te)* to reach, attain, meet with, find,
2. Cl 4 P *naśyati* to be lost, perish, disappear, be gone, run away, to come to nothing, be frustrated or unsuccessful, caus. *nāśayati* (*te*), to cause to be lost or disappear, drive away, expel, remove, destroy, to lose(also from memory), to violate, deflower, extinguish, DP in *adarśana* being lost, perishing, disappearing,
3. mfn perishing,
√*nas* 532/2 Cl 1 A *nasate* to approach, resort to, join, copulate, to be crooked or fraudulent, DP in *kauṭilya* being crooked,
√*nās* 538/1 Cl 1 A *nāsate* to sound,

DP in *śabda* sounding,

nas f. nose,

nas pron. we two,

nasa in cpds. for *nas* the nose,

nāśa 538/1 m. attainment, being lost, destruction, disappearance, annihilation, flight, desertion, elimination (arithmetic),

nāsā 538/1 f. the nose, the two nostrils,

naśakti f. inability,

nasaṁvid f. unconsciousness, forgetfulness,

nāśana mfn 538/1 destroying
m. destruction, removal,
causing to be lost or to perish,
forgetting

nāśayati destroys

naśeṣa mfn without remainder, all, entire

nāsikā f. nose, nostril,

nasikāgra m. point of the nose,

nāsikāgra n. point of the nose,

nāsikāgradṛṣṭi gazing at the tip of the nose,

nāśita lost, destroyed, ppp.

naṣṭa 532/1mfn. lost, disappeared, perished, spoiled, in vain

nastātmanas who have lost their selves

nāstika m. an atheist or non-believer,
mfn atheistic,

naśubha mfn unpleasant, inauspicious,

nasukara mfn not easy to be done, difficult,

naśvara mfn perishable, transitory,

√*naṭ* 525/2 Cl 1 P *naṭati* to dance, to hurt or injure, caus. *nāṭayati* to represent anything dramatically, act, perform, imitate, to fall, to shine, DP in *nṛti* (Cl 1) acting on the stage, *avaspandana* (Cl 10) dancing, acting, in *āpyāyana* becoming full, increasing,

naṭa m. dancer, mime, actor, (these form a despised caste),

natadvid mfn not knowing that,

nāṭaka n. play, drama. m. pond, actor,
mfn dancing, acting,

naṭarāja the Lord of Dance, *Śiva*

natarām ind. not at all, never,

√*nāth* 534/3 Cl 1 A *nāthate* to seek aid, approach with prayers or requests, to ask, solicit, beg for, to have power, be master, to harass, DP in *yācñā* asking, *upatāpa* heating, *aiśvarya* having power, *āśīḥ* blessing,

nātha n. a refuge, help, m. a protector, lord, husband, rope through the nose of a draft ox,

nāti not very or much, not too,

nātidūra mfn not very far,

natvā ind. having bowed,

nāṭya n. dance, dancing, the costume of an actor,

nau 571/2 alternative enclitic pronoun 2nd,4th, 6th, du. of 1st person pronoun we two, both, to us both,

nau f. boat, ship, vessel,

naukā f. boat, ship

nava or *navan* nine

nava mfn new, 530/3 fresh, recent, young, modern, a new oven dish (unburned)

nāva 538/1 1. m. a shout of joy or triumph
2. a boat, a ship, f. *(ā)*

navadvārapurī f. the nine-gated city, the body,

navakṛtva nine times,

navam ninth

navanīta n. fresh butter

navati ninety

navavidha mfn nine-fold, consisting of nine parts,

navavidhabhakti nine ways of devotion, hearing his names and glories, singing them, remembering the Lord, worship of his feet, adoration with flowers, prostrations, regarding oneself as his servant, as his friend, total self-surrender,

naveda mfn knowing well, cognizant of,

navidya, navidvas mfn ignorant,

nāvika m. boatman,

navīn mfn new

√*nay* 528/2 Cl 1 A *nayate* to go DP in *gati* going, *rakṣaṇa* protecting,

naya 528/2 m leading (of an army), conduct, behaviour, prudent conduct or behaviour, good management, polity, wisdom, prudence, reason, principle, system, method, an opinion or viewpoint (Jaina), mfn fit, proper

nāyaka m leader, chief, master, hero,

nayana n. eye (organ of sense that leads), the pupil of the eye, n. leading, directing, managing, conducting,carrying, bringing, fixing, pl. prudent, conduct, the eye,
nayati leads fut. *neṣyati,* past *anayat* √*nī*
nayet he should lead or direct 1/s/caus/opt/act √*nī*
nāyikā f. heroine in a drama, a noble lady, mistress, courtezan,
nayuta m.pl. a myriad,
√*ned* 569/1 Cl 1 P *nedati*, to go, flow, to censure, blame, to be near, DP in *kutsā* blaming, or *sannikarṣa* being near,
ned ind. not, not indeed, in order that not, lest, (*na* +*id*)
nediṣṭha mfn the nearest, next, very near, (*am)* ind. next, in the first place, (*āt*) ind. from the neighbourhood,
nedīyas mfn nearer, very near, ind. near, hither, *-yastā* f. nearness, neighbourhood,
nedya gve. to be blamed, blameless,
nejaka m. washerman,
nema mfn half, several, one, one...other m. portion, dancing,
nemi f. felly (the exterior rim of a wheel), foundation of a wall,
nepathya n. (in drama) the part of a theatre behind the scenes (where costumes were changed etc.),
√*neṣ* 569/3 Cl 1 A *neṣate* to go, move, DP in *gati* going,
neṣyati will lead
netavya gve. to be carried, to be led or guided, to be led away, to be led towards or to or into, to be applied or examined,
neti a method of cleaning the nostrils with a thread,
neti neti not this, not this, (*na iti na iti),* a process of negating all names and forms in order to arrive at the eternal underlying truth, (U)
netṛ mfn leading, guiding, one who leads or will lead, m. leader, guide, conductor, bringer, offeror, a master, owner, hero of a drama,
netra n. the eye (as guiding organ), a leader, guide, n. leading, guiding, conducting, m. a leader, guide,
ni- 538/3 prep. prefix to verbs or nouns, down, back, into, within, (with nouns has a sense of negation or privation e.g. down-hearted). often may be translated as without
ni, niḥ, nir, nis, niś, niṣ have the same meaning and are used in appropriate sandhi situations,
2. (for *nī*), mfn
3. (in music) the 7th note
nī *for nis* (before *r*)
√*nī* Cl 1 P A *niyati (te*) to lead, guide, conduct, direct, govern, to lead towards or to, to lead or keep away, exclude from, A. to carry off for oneself, to lead home, marry, to draw (a line), to pass or spend time, conduct a ceremony, trace, track, find out, ascertain, settle, decide, A. be foremost or chief, DP in *prāpaṇa* leading,
nī mfn leading, guiding, a leader or guide,
ni√*as* Cl 4 *–asyati,* to cast or throw down,
nibaddha mfn securely bound, tied to, fastened onto, *ni* √*bandh*
ni√*bādh* A. *–bādhate* to press down or together, confine, obstruct,
nibadhnāti 550/1 see *ni*√*bandh* he binds fetters
nibadhyate he is bound 1/s/pres/indic/pass *ni* √*badh*
ni √*bandh* P. *–badhnāti* to bind on, tie, fasten to, join, enchain, fetter, to contract, unite, to compose, draw up, write down, to catch, win, acquire, to hold fast, restrain, to fix, place, locate,
nibandha m. binding on, fastening, tying
nibandhana mfn binding, fastening, fettering, n, binding, that on which a thing is fastened, rests or depends,

condition, means, cause, origing, basis, seat, receptacle, band, fetter, tie, composition, arrangement, commentary, (in gram.) syntax, f. (*ī*) band, bond, fetter,

nibha mfn ifc. resembling, like, similar,

ni√bhal P.A. *–bhālayati (te),* to perceive, see

nibhalana n. seeing, perception, 550/3

nibhatā f. similarity, likeness,

ni√bhid to be opened, open,

nibhṛta mfn borne or placed down, hidden, secret, nearly set (moon), firm, immovable, shut, closed (as door), fixed, settled, decided, fixed or intent upon (comp.), filled with, full of, attached, faithful, still, silent, quiet, humble, modest, mild, gentle, free from passions, undisturbed, lonely, solitary,

ni√1.bhuj to bend (head and knees),

nibhūta mfn past, gone, quite frightened

nibiḍa or *niviḍa* mfn without spaces, close, compact, thick, dense, firm, full of, abounding in,

nibiḍaya Nom P. °*yati* to make tight, embrace firmly,

nibiḍita 550/2 made tight, pressed close to, become heavy or thick,

nibodha know! understand! 2/s/impv/act

nibodhata understand

ni√budh P. Cl1 *nibodhati* to learn or hear anything, to attend or listen to, to know, understand, consider as, caus. *-bodhayati* to cause to know or learn, to inform, tell,

nīca mfn low, not high, dwarfish, depressed (navel), short (hair, nails), deep, lowered (voice), low, vile, base, mean,

nīcā ind. below, down, downwards, mfn going or directed downwards, lying with the face downwards, bent down, depressed, deep, low (voice), humble, vile, slow, lazy, whole, entire,

nīcāvayas mfn whose strength is diminished,

nīcaiḥ ind. low, below, underneath, humbly, modestly,

nīcakarman mfn having a low occupation (as a servant),

nīcakula n. a low family,

nīcatā f. lowness, baseness, inferiority,

ni √cāy to regard with reverence, honour, worship, observe, perceive

nicāyya looking on (meditating on) something as one's own Self, realising, realising directly,

niceru mfn gliding, creeping,

nicetṛ m. observing, observer, minder,

ni√1.ci to pile up, heap up, collect,

ni√2.ci P.*-ciketi* to perceive, notice, observe

nīcīna mfn below, being low, flowing down, cast down,

nicira mfn attentive, vigilant,

nicita 1. mfn piled up, heaped up, erected, covered, full of, constipated, 2. mfn observed, beheld, appearing

nicula m. an upper garment, overcoat,

niculaka m. outer garment, case, box

niculita mfn being in a case, cased,

nīcya °*cyati* to be in a low situation, be a slave,

√nid 547/3 see *√nind* and *√ned,* DP in *kutsā* blaming, or *sannikarṣa* approaching, 2. f. mocking, ridiculing, mocker, scoffer,

nida m.n. poison

nīḍa m.n. resting place, esp. bird's nest,

nīḍagarbha m. nest-interior,

ni√4.dā P. *–dyati* to bind on, fasten, f. blame, contempt,

nidāgha m. heat, warmth, the hot season, internal heat, sweat,

ni√dah P. *–dahati* to burn down, consume by fire

nidāna mfn reproached, ridiculed, n. a band, rope, halter, a first or primary cause, original form or essence, a cause of existence (12 in number), any cause or motive, the cause of a disease and enquiry into it, cessation, end, purification,

nidaṇḍa mfn one who has laid down the stick, (given up the use of force),

nidarśaka mfn seeing into, perceiving,

proclaiming, announcing,

nidarśana mfn pointing to, showing, indicating, announcing, teaching, pleasing, n. seeing, viewing, sight, appearance, vision, showing, proof, evidence, example, refutation of an argument, a sign, mark, omen, a system, scheme, injunction, precept, ordinance, authority, text,

nideśa m. order, command, direction, talk, conversation, vicinity,

nideśin mfn showing, directing, pointing out f. region, point of the compass, *nideśinī* mfn showing, directing, pointing out f. region, quarter, compass-point

nideṣṭṛ m. who points out or orders, explaining, advising, commanding,

ni√dhā P.A. Cl 3–*dadhāti, -dhatte,* to put or lay down, deposit, lay up, preserve, (A. for oneself), to entrust, commit, present to, put into, fix in, 2. f. a net or snare,

nidhana 548/3 2. mfn having no property, poor, n. domicile, settling down, conclusion, end, death, destruction

nidhāna 548/3 mfn containing anything, n. putting or laying down, depositing, a hoard or treasure,

nidhātṛ m. one who lays down, or leaves a footmark,

nidhāya ind. having put down, having fixed or placed, (with *manasi*) fixing or laying up in the mind, reflecting,

nidhi m. a place for deposits, a receptacle, treasure, *apāṁ nidhi* the ocean, sea, setting down or setting up food,

nidhruvi mfn constant, persevering, faithful

ni√dhyai P. –*dhyāyati* to observe, perceive, meditate, think of, remember,

nidhyāna n. intuition, seeing, sight,

nidhyapti f. reflection, philosophical meditation,

ni√2.dī to shine down upon,

nididhyāsana 549/1 n. profound and repeated meditation, contemplation, the third stage of reflection. (see *śravanam mananam,)* (G).. removes the contrariwise tendencies of the mind, ..a continuous stream of ideas of the same kind as those of Brahman, one of the principal aids to liberation, assimilating the teaching by inquiry within until the teaching becomes one with the seeker, 'when the mind is totally free from all doubts and does not stand in need of even the reasoning process and gets fixed firmly on the object of contemplation, and there is only a single *vṛtti* or mental modification, i.e. *vṛtti* of meditation, it is said to be in the state of *nididhyāsana.'* (U)

nididhyāsitavya to be meditated on, or contemplated, to be realized,

nidigdha mfn smeared, plastered, clinging,

ni√diś P. –*diśati* to direct, order, point out,

nidrā f. sleep, slumber, sleepiness, sloth, non-perception, the budding state of a flower, 'a negative condition of the *vṛtti*s where the activities of the mind are adjourned for a future time, and all the psychological processes are wound up temporarily' (U), 'however the state is still a modification, for, upon waking, one has the consciousness that one has slept well, ' (G),

nidrāṇa 548/2 mfn. asleep, sleeping, shut up, closed,

nidrā kṣaya destruction of sleep, awakening

nidrāti falls asleep 548/2 1/s/pres/indic/act sleeps

nidrālu mfn sleepy,

ni√dṛś caus. –*darśayati* to cause to see, show, point out, introduce, to impart knowledge, teach, instruct,

nidrita 548/2 mfn asleep, sleeping

ni√1.gā to enter, come or get into, attach oneself to,

nigacchati 545/3 settles down upon or near, enters, resorts to, undergoes, attains

ni√gad P. –*gadati* to recite, proclaim, announce, declare, tell, speak,

nigaḍa m. the heel chains for an elephant, mfn bound, fettered,
nigada m. reciting, audible recitation, speech, discourse,
nigadana n. reciting from memory,
nigaḍayati to bind, put in fetters,
nigāḍayati cause to recite,
ni√gai P. *–gāyati* to accompany with song, sing, chant,
ni√gam P. *–gacchati,* to settle down upon or near, to enter, resort to, undergo, incur, become, to acquire knowledge, to be inserted,
nigama m. the place where a word occurs or the word quoted from such a passage, a sacred precept, the words of a holy man, doctrine, instruction in, certainty, assurance, trade, traffic, a town,
nigamana n. insertion, quotation of words and the word quoted, the summing up of an argument, deduction, going in or into, conclusion,
nigaraṇa 546/1 the throat, the smoke of a burnt offering, absorbing, taking up
nigha mfn as high as broad, equally distant, m. with height and width equal,
nighaṇṭa m. a vocabulary, glossary,
nighna mfn dependent, subservient, obedient, ifc. dependent on, ruled by, devoted to, full of, (after a numeral) multiplied with,
nighnat mfn killing, slaying,
nighnatā f. subjection,
nighuṣṭa n. sound, noise,
nigīta mfn sung, proclaimed,
nigrābha 546/2 m. pressing down, letting sink, suppressing (the voice),
ni√grah P.A. *–gṛhṇāti, (ṇīte*), to hold down, lower, depress, to keep or hold back, draw near, attract, to seize, catch,
nigraha m. keeping down or back, binding, restraining, coercion, suppression,
nigrāha m. punishment, chastisement,
nigrahasthāna n. position of being unfit to carry on an argument from impossibility of agreeing about first principles,
nigṛhīta 546/1 mfn held down or back, seized, caught, checked, under control, withdrawn,*√grah*
nigṛhīti f. restraint, check, overpowering
nigu mfn pleasing, charming, m. the mind, dirt, a root, a painting,
nigūḍha mfn concealed, secret, obscure,
ni√guh to cover, conceal, hide,
ni√2.gup to conceal,
nigut m. an enemy
niḥ- 538/3 for *nis* before a sibilant and rarely before *k, kh, p, ph.* (with nouns has a sense of negation or privation e.g. destitute of and may be translated as 'without'
ni√2.hā A. *–jihīte,* to descend, stoop, yield,
nihākā f. a storm, whirlwind, an iguana, the alligator of the Ganges,
ni√han P.Cl 2 *–hanti,* to strike down, strike or fix in, hurl in or upon, to make an attempt upon, attack, kill, overwhelm,
nihan m. a killer, destroyer,
nihanana n. killing, slaughter,
nihantṛ m. a killer, destroyer,
nīhāra m. mist, fog, hoar-frost, heavy dew,
nihata mfn hurled, thrown, hit, touched, struck down, killed, lost, gone,
nihatya ind. striking down, killing, having killed, gerund *ni√han*
nihīna mfn low, vile, mean
nihita 564/3 mfn. laid, placed, deposited, fixed or kept in (7th), delivered, given, bestowed, laid (as dust by rain), encamped, seated e.g. seated in the body, uttered in a deep tone,
nihitārtha of hidden aim, inscrutable design,
niḥkṣepa m. throwing, sending away, removing, 544/1
niḥ√1.kṣi P. *-kṣiṇoti* to destroy, remove an illness,
niḥkṣipta mfn thrown away, spent (time),
nihnava m. begging pardon, making amends or reparation, atonement, expiation, denial, secrecy, mistrust,
ni√hnu A. *–hnavate*, to make reparation or amends to, to disown, deny, conceal, evade, dissimulate, negates, refutes,

nihnuta mfn denied, disowned, concealed, given out for something else,
nihnuti f. denial, reserve, secrecy,
ni√hṛ P. *–harati,* to offer (as gift or reward),
ni√hṛṣ P. *–hṛṣyati* to sink down (as a flame),
niḥśabda mfn noiseless, silent, still, m.n. silence, *(am)* ind. noiselessly,
niḥśabdaniścala mfn (night) noiseless and motionless
niḥsādhāra mfn supportless, (*am*) ind.
niḥsādhvasa mfn fearless, bold, n. fearlessness, boldness, (*am*) ind. fearlessly, boldly,
niḥsaha mfn not able to support or resist, powerless, weak, intolerable, irresistible,
niḥsahāya mfn without helpers, unassisted,
niḥsākha mfn branchless,
niḥśalāka mfn free from grass, lonely, solitary
niḥsalila mfn waterless,
niḥśalya mfn freed from an arrow, thorns, pain, (am) ind. without pain, easily, willingly,
niḥśama m. uneasiness, anxiety,
niḥśāmam ind. at the wrong time, unseasonably
niḥśāmānya mfn extraordinary, uncommon,
niḥśāmarthya mfn unfit, unsuitable,
niḥsambādha mfn not crowded, lonely, solitary,
niḥsambandha mfn without relatives,
niḥsambhrama mfn unembarrassed, not perplexed,
niḥsaṁdhi mfn having no joints perceptible, well-knit, compact, close, firm,
niḥsaṁdigdha mfn not doubtful, certain
niḥsaṁjña mfn senseless, unconscious,
niḥsaṁkakṣa mfn not perplexed or confused
niḥsaṁkalpa mfn having no determination or will
niḥsaṁkhya mfn innumerable, numberless
niḥsaṁkṣobha mfn unshaken,
niḥsampāta mfn affording no passage, m. thick darkness, midnight,
niḥsaṁśaya mfn undoubted, certain,
niḥsaṁskāra mfn uneducated, ill-mannered
niḥsaṁtati mfn childless,
niḥśāṇa m.n. march, procession,
niḥsaṅga m. absence of attachment, entire concentration, mfn unobstructed, moving freely, unconnected, separated, detached, indifferent to, free from worldly attachment, unselfish, disinterested, (*am or ena*) ind. without interest, without reflection, at random,
niḥśaṅka mfn free from fear or risk, not afraid of (comp.), careless, secure, (*am*) ind. fearlessly, securely, easily, m. (in music) a measure, dance (*ā* f. absence of fear/ hesitation *-supta* mfn sleeping calmly,
niḥsapatna mfn having no rival, not sharing, unrivalled, unparalleled,
niḥsāra mfn sapless, pithless, worthless, vain, unsubstantial,
niḥsara mfn issuing out,
niḥsaraṇa n. going forth or out, issue, egress gate, means, expedient, means to get rid of (comp.), departure, death, final beatitude,
niḥśaraṇa mfn defenceless, unprotected,
niḥsaraṇi mfn pathless, impractical,
niḥśas f. refusing
niḥ√śās to drive away, expel,
niḥśastra mfn weaponless, unarmed,
niḥśatru mfn free from enemies,
niḥsattva mfn without existence, weak unsubstantial, wretched, mean, low, insignificant, n. want of power or energy, insignificance, non-existence
niḥsatya mfn untrue, false, *-tā* f. falsehood, insincerity,
niḥśeṣa mfn without remainder, whole, finished, passed away,
niḥsīman mfn unbounded, grand, immeasurable, infinite,
niḥśmaśru mfn beardless,
niḥsneha mfn not greasy, not wet, dry, insensible, unfeeling, indifferent, not loved, uncared for, hated,
niḥśodhya mfn not to be cleansed or purified, clean, pure,

niḥśoka mfn free from sorrow or care
niḥspanda mfn motionless
niḥ√sphur P. *–sphurati,* to jerk or hurl away
niḥsphura mfn (heart) not throbbing,
niḥspṛha free from desire or longing, abstaining from (5th), desirelessness,
niḥ√śī to break, crush,
niḥ√sṛ P. *–sarati,* to go out, come forth, depart, withdraw, caus. *–sārayati* to cause to go out, turn out, expel, to conclude, finish
niḥśreyas the Highest Good, supreme bliss, *mokṣa*
niḥśreyasa 538/3 mfn. having no better, best, most excellent, n. the best, ultimate bliss, final beatitude or knowledge that brings it,
niḥśrīka mfn deprived of beauty, ugly, unfortunate, inglorious,
niḥ√sṛj P.A. *–sṛjati (te),* to pour out, to let loose, set free, to separate (words), to remove, destroy (as sorrow),
niḥsṛta gone out or forth, departed, prominent (eyes), having emerged,
niḥ√sru P. *–sravati,* to flow out or off, rise from, to disappear, be lost to/from,
niḥsruta mfn flowed out or off, passed away (time)
niḥ√ṣṭhā P.*nistiṣṭhati* to grow forth, rise, bring to an end, finish, make ready, prepare, caus. to drive out into,
niḥṣṭhita mfn grown forth, finished, accomplished, ready,
niḥ√śuc to shine forth,
niḥśūka mfn beardless (corn), merciless
niḥsukha mfn joyless, unhappy, sad, disagreeable, distressing,
niḥśukra mfn without fire or energy,
niḥśūnya mfn quite empty,
niḥsva mfn deprived of one's own, poor, indigent,
niḥsvabhāva m. poverty, without property, mfn without peculiarities
niḥsvādu mfn insipid, tasteless,
niḥsvana mfn soundless
niḥ√śvas P. *–śvasiti* to hiss (serpent), snort (elephant), to breathe, to sigh,
niḥśvāsa m. sigh, exhalation, breathing out,
niḥśvasana n. breathing out or sighing,
niḥśvasaparama mfn much addicted to sighing,
ni√hve to call down or near, invoke,
√nij 546/1 Cl 2. A. *niṅkte*, Cl 3 P.A. *nenekti,* to wash, cleanse, purify (A oneself), to nourish, DP in *śauca* cleansing, or *poṣaṇa* nourishing,
nija 547/1 innate, native, of one's own party or country, m.pl. one's own people, constant, continual, in later language used as a reflex pron. like *sva* – my own, his own, our own,
nijabodharūpa n. state of self-awareness, having the nature of inherent consciousness,
nijakarman one's own work,
nijamukta mfn liberated for ever,
nija-lābha-pūrṇa self-satisfied, engrossed in self-interest,
nijārtham ind. for one' own sake, for one's self
nijasva n. one's own property
ni√kam to long or wish for, lust after,
nikāma m. desire, wish, pleasure, ibc =(*am*) according to wish or desire, to one's heart's content, abundantly, at will, excessively, mfn desirous, covetous,
nikāmajala mfn (a river) yielding abundant water
nikāmatapta mfn excessively burnt,
nikāmavarṣa mfn having plenty of rain,
nikānamakṣi ind. having closed the eyes,
nikara m. a heap, pile, a multitude, a bundle, mass, collection, pith, sap, essence, suitable gift, a treasure, the best of anything, an honorarium.
nikāra 1. 544/2 piling up or winnowing corn, tossing or lifting up, 2. 545/1 bringing down, humiliation, wrong, offence, injury, wickedness, malice, opposition
nīkāra m. disrespect, contempt, degradation
nikāraṇa n. killing, slaughter,
nikarṣa m. lowering, decreasing, reducing

nikarṣaṇa n. an open place in or near a town, an entrance court, a neighbourhood,
nikartana mfn cutting away, robbing, impoverishing *(ni√1.kṛt)*
nikartṛ mfn m. one who acts badly, basely,
ni√kaṣ to scratch, rub,
nikaṣa m. rubbing in, smearing, f. a roller, harrow, m.f. the touchstone,
nikaṣā 544/2 ind. near to (with acc.), proximate, in the middle, between
nikāśa m. horizon, range of sight, proximity ifc. having the appearance of, similar, like,
nikāṣa m. scratching, rubbing, grinding,
nīkāśa m. appearance, look, mien, certainty, ascertainment, mfn like, similar,
nikaṭa mfn being at the side, near, m.n. nearness, proximity, *(-ṭam)* ind. near to, towards, *-te* near, at hand
nikaṭībhūya ind. having become near *-bhūta* mfn become near, approached,
nikāya a heap, an assemblage, a group, class, association, congregation, school, the Supreme Being
niketa m.n. a mark, sign, a house, habitation, a stage in the life of a Brāhman, state of being, one's support e.g. the reality of the Self, one's place of abode, the body or external objects,
niketana 545/1 n. a house, mansion, habitation, temple, m. an onion,
ni√khan P. *–khanati* to dig into the ground, bury, fix, implant, erect (post etc), to dig or root up,
nikhanana n. digging in, burying,
nikharva mfn dwarfish, a dwarf, n. a billion,
ni√khid P. *–khidati* to press down,
nikhila 545/2 mfn complete, all, whole, entire, *(ena)* ind. completely,
nikoca m. closing
ni√1.kṛ P.A. to bring down, humiliate, subdue, overcome,
ni√kram P. *–krāmati,* to put down the feet, tread down, to enter,
nikramaṇa n. footstep, footfall,
ni√1.kṛṣ P. *-karṣati* to draw or drag down, *-kṛṣati* to plough in
nikṛṣṭa mfn debased, despised, outcast, n. nearness,
ni√kṛt *-kṛntati (te)* to cut or hew down, cut away, chop off, cut through or to pieces, massacre, Ā to cut one's self, (or one's nails etc.),
nikṛta mfn brought down, humiliated, injured, tricked, deceived, low, base, wicked, removed, set aside, dismissed, n. lowering, humbling, humiliation,
nikṛtta mfn cut off, m. cut up,
nikṛti mfn deceitful, dishonest, f. low conduct, baseness,
nikṛtya 545/1 f. wickedness, dishonesty,
√nikṣ 545/2 Cl 1 P *nikṣati* to pierce, to kiss, DP in *cumbana* kissing,
nikṣa mfn kissing, f. a nit,
nikṣepa 545/2 m. putting down, throwing or casting on, a deposit, pledge, trust, sending away, wiping,
ni√kṣip P. Cl 6 *-kṣipati* to entrust, to install, appoint to, to lay aside, to throw or cast or put or lay down, throw etc in or upon, to pour in, to deliver anything, to give or hand over, deposit, give up, leave, abandon, cast off, repel, to put down figures, count,
nikṣipta mfn thrown down or upon, deposited, pawned, pledged, rejected, abandoned, given away, sent off, appointed, installed,
nikṣipya ind. having thrown
nikta mfn washed, cleansed, purified,
nikubja mfn curved, bent
ni√kūd P. to burn, set on fire,
nikūla mfn going downhill,
ni√kūṅ P. to close, contract,
ni√kuñc to draw in, contract,
nikuñca m. a key
nikuñcana n. shrinking together, contraction,
nikuñja m. an arbour, a thicket,
nikuramba m.n. a flock, mass, multitude,
nikvaṇa or nikvāṇa m. sound,

√*nil* 558/3 Cl 6 P *nilati* to understand with difficulty, to be impassable, or impenetrable, DP in *gahana* understanding with difficulty, being impenetrable,

√*nīl* 566/1 Cl 1 P *nīlati* to be dark, dye dark,DP in *varna* being dark colour,

nīla mfn of a dark colour esp. blue, green or black, dyed with indigo, m. the sapphire, a monkey architect, (*ā*)f. the indigo plant, a black and blue mark on the skin, n. dark, darkness, any dark substance, poison,

nīlabha 'of bluish or dim appearance', the moon, a cloud, a bee,

nīlābha mfn bluish, m. a cloud,

nīlābhra m. a dark cloud,

nīlakamala n. a blue water-lily

nīlalohita mfn dark blue and red, purple, dark red

nīlamaṇi m. a sapphire,

nīlapadma n. the blue water-lily

nīlapata m. dark garment,

nīlaphalā f. the egg-plant,

nīlarāji f. a dark line or mass, darkness,

nīlaruna m. the dark red or first dawn of day

nīlasaṁdhāna-bhāṇḍa n. a vat for the mixing (preparing) of indigo,

nīlatā f. blueness, a dark colour,

nīlataru m. the coconut tree

nīlatoyada m. a dark cloud,

nīlavarṇa mfn blue coloured, blue

nīlavat mfn blackish, dark,

nilaya m. rest, resting place, hiding or dwelling place, often ifc. (*ā*) f. living in, inhabiting, inhabited by

nilayana 558/3 2. n. settling down, alighting on, a nest, a sustaining thing,

nilāyana n. hiding oneself

ni√*lī* A.-*līyate*, to settle down, alight, descend, to become settled, to hide one's self, disappear, perish,

nīlībhāṇḍa-svāmin m. indigo-vat proprietor,

nilīna mfn clinging to, sitting on, hidden in, intent upon, devoted to, resorted to, sought for shelter, involved, encompassed, wrapt up, changed

ni√*lip* -*limpati (te)* to besmear, anoint, P. cause to disappear, A. to disappear,

nīlotpala n. a blue lotus,

nima m. a pin, stake,

ni√*mā* A. –*mimīte* to measure, adjust,

ni√*mad* to pronounce slowly &distinctly

nimagna mfn sunk, fallen into (water etc.), submerged, plunged or immersed in, penetrated or fixed into, gone down, set (as the sun), sunk in, depressed, not prominent,

ni√*majj* P.A. Cl 1–*majjati (te),* to sink down, dive, sink or plunge or penetrate into, bathe in, to disappear, perish, to immerse or submerge in water,

nimajjana 550/3 bathing, diving sinking, immersion

ni√*man* to regard or consider as

nimāna n. measure,

ni√*mantr* to invite, summon, call to, to offer anything to

nimanyu mfn unresentful, appeased,

ni√*math* to strike down, kill,

nimba 551/3 the *nimb* or neemb tree, (it has bitter fruit and it's leaves are chewed at funerals)

nimeṣa m. closing or winking of the eyes,

nimeṣaṇa 551/2 shutting the eyes, winking

ni√*1.mi* –*minoti* to fix or dig in, raise, erect, to perceive, notice, m. the closing or winking of the eyes,

nimīlana 551/2 shutting the eyes, closing (a flower), complete obscuration, a total eclipse,

ni√*miṣ* 551/2 *nimiṣati,* to shut the eyelids, wink, fall asleep to be shut (eyelids),, *nimeṣa* shutting the eye, *nimiṣa* close the eyes, 6/du. *miṣ*818/1 to open the eyes, wink, blink, *meṣita* etc

nimiṣa 551/2 m winking, shutting the eye, n. the interval of a moment, in a moment,

nimiṣati closes the eyes

nimiṣan closing the eyes pres/act/part *ni* √*miṣ* 551/2

nimiśla mfn devoted or attached to,

nimita mfn fixed, raised, erected, measured, caused,
nimittārtha m. (in gram.) infinitive mood,
nimitta 551/1 a mark, target, sign, omen, cause, reason
nimitta -tā f. *–tva* n. (in phil.) the state of being a cause, causality, instrumentality,
nimittahetu m. the efficient cause,
nimittakāraṇa n. instrumental or efficient cause, e.g. the potter who makes the pot,
nimittamātra n. the mere efficient cause or instrument,
nimittanaimittika n. du. cause and effect
nimittanimittin mfn operating &operated upon,
nimittasaptamī f. a 7th case indicating the cause or motive,
nimittavedin mfn hitting a mark,
nimloca m. setting of the sun,
nimlukti f. disappearance in,
ni√mruc P. to set, diappear (as the sun), mfn slack, loose,
nimrukti f. sunset, evening,
√niṁs 538/3 Cl 2 A *niṁste, niṁsate*, to touch closely, kiss, salute, DP in *cumbana* kissing,
nimna n. depth, low ground, cavity, depression, (*ais*) ind. downwards, mfn deep, low, depressed, sunk, ifc. inclined towards,
nimnadeśa m. a low or deep place,
nimnagā f. 'going downwards, descending', a river, mountain stream,
nimnagata mfn going in deep or low places,
nimna -tā f., *-tva,*n. depth, lowness, profundity
nimnita mfn deep, depressed, sunk
ni√nad P °*nadati*, to sound, cry out, resound
ninada m. a sound, noise,
nināda m. a sound, noise, crying, humming
ninādita mfn filled with noise, resonant with
ni√nard P. *–nardati* to prolong a note in chanting, slur or trill, to sound
ninarda m. a slur or trill,
√nind 549/2 or *nid,* Cl 1 P *nindati (te)* to blame, censure, revile, despise, ridicule, DP in *kutsā* blaming,
nindā 549/2 f. blame, censure, reproach
nindaka mfn blaming, abusive, scoffer,
nindāyām 7/s/f in blame
nindati 549/2 1/s/pres/ind/act he blames, censures, despises
nindita 549/2 blamed, censured, despicable, condemned
ninditṛ m. scorner, scoffer,
ni√nī P.A. *–nayati (te*), to lead to carry or bring forwards, bring or cause to, to incline, bend, to pour down, pour out or in,
niṇik ind. secretly, mysteriously,
√niñj 547/1 Cl 2 A *niṅkate* see *√nij* DP in *śuddhi* cleansing, purification,
ni√nṛt P. *–nṛtyati* to repeat a portion of a verse or syllable, 'dance again',
ninṛtta mfn repeated (as above),
√ninv 549/2 Cl 1 *ninvati* to wet or to attend, DP in *sevana* serving or *secana* wetting,
niṇya mfn interior, hidden, concealed, n. a secret, mystery, (*am*) ind. secretly, mysteriously
nīpa mfn situated low, deep, m. the foot of a mountain,
ni√1.pā P. *–pibati* to drink or suck in, kiss, to absorb, dry up,
ni√2.pā P. *–pāti* to guard or protect from, to observe, watch over, caus. *pālayati* to protect, guard, govern
ni√pad A. *–padyate* to lie down, rest, lie down with
nipāda m. low ground, a valley,
nipaka mfn intelligent, wise, m. chief,
nipāka cooking, maturing, ripening
nipalāśam ind. (as softly or quietly as) the falling of leaves,
nipāna 1. drinking, imbibing, a place or trough for watering cattle, a well, pool, tank, a milk-pail, 2. n. a place of refuge
ni√pat P. Cl 1 *–patati* to fly down, settle down, descend on, alight, to rush upon, attack, fall down, fall upon or into, to fall into ruin or decay, to

befall, happen, take place, miscarry, to enter, be inserted, get a place,

nipāta 549/2 m. falling down, descending, alighting, falling from, into or upon,rushing upon, decay, destruction, ruin, death, accidental occurrence or mention,(in gram.) ready-made form, irregular forms, exceptions, particles. words without case,gender or number i.e. without endings so that they appear in a sentence already complete, an indeclinable particle

nipātaka a bad deed, a sin

nipaṭha m. recitation, study,

nipatana n. falling down, falling, descending, flying,

nipatita mfn flown or fallen down, descended, fallen upon or into,

niphālana n. seeing, sight,

niphena n.opium

ni√pīḍ caus. to press close to or against, press together, impress, to oppress, afflict, trouble,

nipīdita mfn squeezed, pressed, embraced,

nipīlana n. pressing out,

ni√prath to spread or increase,

nipuṇa mfn clever, adroit, skilful, sharp, acute, skilled in, conversant with, capable of, kind or friendly towards, perfect, complete, absolute (as purity, devotion etc.), (*am*) ind. in a clever or delicate manner, completely, perfectly, absolutely, exactly, precisely,

nipur f. the subtle body, (*sūkṣma deha*)

nipūta mfn strained, purified, filtered,

nīpya mfn being low or on the ground,

nir- 539/2 for *nis* before vowels and soft consonants, , see *nis* 543/2
543/2 ind. out, forth, away. also used as a prefix to verbs and nouns in which case it takes the meanings- out of, away from, without, destitute of, free from, also may be used as a strengthening particle – entirely, very liable to be changed to *niḥ, nir, niś, niṣ,* or *nī*

ni√ī P.A *–riṇati, ṇīte,* to dissolve, scatter, tear, to unveil, discover

nīra n. water, juice, liquor,

nirābādha mfn undisturbed, unmolested,

nirābhāsa mfn without fallacious appearance,

nirabhibhava mfn not subject to disgrace, or humiliation, not to be surpassed

nirabhilapya mfn unutterable, inexpressible

nirabhilāṣa mfn not desiring, indifferent to,

nirabhimāna mfn free from pride,

nirabhīmāna mfn unconscious,

nirabhimānata mfn state of mine-lessness, egolessness,

nirabhimānī without honour, without conceit,

nirabhiprāya mfn purposeless,

nirabhisaṁdhāna n. absence of design, *-dhin* mfn free from egoistic designs,

nirabhra mfn cloudless,

nirā√cakṣ to refute, reject

nīracara m. moving in water, a fish or other acquatic creature,

nirācāra mfn without approved usages, customs, lawless, barbarian, 540/1

nīrada mfn toothless, 2. m. water-giver, a cloud

nirādāna mfn taking or receiving nothing,

nirādara mfn showing no respect

nirā√dhā –dadhāti to take out of or away

nirādhāra mfn without a receptacle or support,

nirādhi mfn free from anxiety, secure,

nīradhi or *nīranidhi* m. 'water-receptacle' the ocean

niradhiṣṭhāna mfn having no resting place or basis, supportless, untenable, independent,

niradhva mfn one who has lost his way,

nīradin mfn cloudy,

nirāga mfn passionless, dispassionate,

nīraga mfn colourless, free from passion,

nirāgama not founded on revelation

nirāgas mfn sinless, innocent,

niragha mfn sinless, free from faults,

niragra or –agraka divisible without remainder, 539/2

nirāgraha mfn not insisting on, not obstinate,
nīragraha m. taking up water in a ladle,
nirāha m. call, exclamation,
niraham mfn without self-conceit,selfishness
nir ahaṃkāraḥ nir without, *ahaṃkāra* 124/2 conception of one's individuality, ego, 1/s/m egoless
nirahaṁstambha mfn free from egotism, *nirāhāra* mfn abstaining from food, having no food, not having eaten, fasting, m. want of food, f. fasting, having no food,
nirāhavat mfn accompanied by exclamation
nir√aj P. *–ajati* to drive out or away,
nī√rāj caus. *–rājayati,* to cause to shine upon, illuminate, irradiate,
nirāja m. marching off,
nīraja mfn free from dust, free from passion, 2. m.n. a water-lily, lotus, m. an otter, a species of grass, a pearl,
nīrajākṣī f. a lotus-eyed or beautiful woman
nīrājana n. offering or waving of light or lighted camphor before a deity during a ceremony,
nīrajāta mfn water-born, produced from water, acquatic,
nīrājita mfn shone upon, illuminated, consecrated,
nīrājya mfn clear, pure, limpid,
nirākāṅkṣa mfn desireless, hopeless, complete
nirākāra 540/1 mfn formless, shapeless, incorporeal (brahman), making no appearance or show, insignificant, unimportant, having no object, m. heaven, the Universal Spirit, god,
nirākaraṇa n. separating, driving away, repudiating, opposing, contradicting, denying, forgetting, neglecting the chief religious duties,
nirākāśa mfn having no free space, completely filled,
nīrākhu m.'water-rat' an otter,
nirā√kṛ P.to separate or divide off, to drive away, keep off,
nirā√kram to come forth, go out of,
nīrakta mfn colourless, faded,
nirākula mfn clear, steady, serene, unconfused, calm, n. clearness, calmness ,
nirālamba mfn independent, friendless, alone, self-supported,
nirālambana mfn supportless or self-supported, not resting on another, free
nirālāpa mfn not talking,
nirālasya mfn not slothful,
nirāloka mfn not looking about, dark or blind, ifc. looking at, investigating,
ni√ram A. *-ramate* to rest, come to rest, cease, caus. cause to rest, stop, -*ramayati* to gladden, give pleasure (sexual),
nīra n. water, juice, liquor,
niramaṇa n. resting, ceasing, 2. mfn worn out, exhausted,
niramārṣa mfn not impatient, patient, apathetic,
nirāmaya 540/1 m. freedom from illness, health, welfare, mfn free from illness, healthy, well, complete, entire, pure,
nirambara mfn undressed, naked,
nirambu mfn abstaining from water, not having any water,
nirāmiṣāśin mfn not meat-eating,
niramitra mfn free from enemies,
nirānanda mfn joyless, sorrowful, sad,
nirandhas mfn foodless, hungry
nīrandhra mfn having no holes or openings, close, thick, dense, uninterrupted,
niraṅga mfn incomplete, having no resources or expedients,
nirañjana mfn unpainted, spotless, pure, simple, void of passion or emotion, free from taint, free from suffering, n. the Supreme Being,
nirañjano'ham I am spotlessly pure,
niraṅkuśa uncontrolled, independent, free unruly, extravagant
niranna mfn wanting food, starving, giving or yielding no food,
nirantara 539/2 having no interval,

uninterrupted, continuous perpetual, constant, faithful, true, abounding in, full of, not other or different, identical, not hidden from view, (*am*) ind. closely, tightly, firmly, constantly, continually, immediately, at once,

nirantarābhyāsa m. constant repetition or study, diligent exercise or practice,

nirantarāla mfn without intervening space, close, narrow,

niranubandha mfn having no indicatory letter,

niranuga mfn without followers, unattended

niranugraha mfn ungracious, unkind,

niranukrośa mfn pitiless, hard-hearted, m. cruelty,

niranumāna mfn not bound to conclusions or consequences,

niranunāsika mfn not nasal

niranurodha mfn unfavourable, unfriendly,

niranuśaya mfn without consequences

niranuyojya mfn faultless, unblamable,

niranvaya mfn childless, unconnected, unrelated, illogical, unmethodical, unaccompanied,

nirapa mfn waterless, secure, fortunate, prosperous, f. security, prosperity,

nirāpad f. no misfortune, security, prosperity

nīrapatatrin m. water-bird

nirapakrama mfn not to be escaped from,

niraparādha mfn guiltless, blameless,

nirapavarta mfn not returning

nirapāya mfn imperishable, infallible, free from harm or evil,

nirapekṣa 539/3mfn regardless of, indifferent to, independent of, disinterested, unaffected by prior, consideration, without expectation, absolute (not relative), f. independence, indifference, (*am*) ind. regardlessly, accidentally, -*tā* f. –*tva* n. disregard, indifference,

nirārambha mfn abstaining from all work,

nīrarāśī m. 'water-mass' the ocean,

nir√ard P. –*ardati* to stream forth,

nirargala mfn unbarred, unimpeded, free,

nirartha mfn without wealth, poor, useless, vain, meaningless, m. loss, detriment, m.pl. nonsense,

nirarti mfn painless,

nīraruha n. 'water-grown' the water-lily, lotus,

nir√2.as to cast out, expel, remove, banish, to ward off, keep away, to strip off, stretch out, to reject, refuse, destroy,

nīrasa mfn without juice, sapless, dried up, withered, flavourless, insipid, without charm, dull, m. the pomegranate,

nirāśa 540/2 mfn. without any hope or wish or desire, f. hopelessness, despair,

nirāśaya mfn not deep, without resting-place or retreat,

nirasana 553/1 casting out, driving away, expelling, removing, rejecting, denying, refusal, contradiction, n. vomiting, spitting, denying, refusal, banishment from, scattering, dispersing, destruction, extermination,

nirāśis 540/2 mfn. hopeless, despairing without desire or wish

nirāśraya mfn shelterless, supportless, not dependent or resorting to, destitute, alone,

nirasta 553/1mfn rejected, removed, destroyed, shot off (arrow), spit out, vomited, pronounced hurriedly or dropped in pronouncing, n. dropping or leaving out (considered a fault in pronunciation),

nirasti f. removal, destruction,

nirata mfn pleased, satisfied, delighting in, attached or devoted to, intent upon, deeply engaged in,

nirātaṅka 540/1 free from fear or pain, not feeling or causing it,

nirātapa mfn shady, not reached by the sun, f. the night,

nīrataraṁga m. a water-wave

niratisaya mfn unsurpassed, perfect,

niratisayānanda infinite bliss, supreme bliss,

nirātithya mfn inhospitable, lonely,

nirātmaka mfn having no individual existence or separate soul, *niravadhi* mfn unlimited, endless, infinite,

nirā√vah P. *–vahati* to carry off, to fetch,

nirāvaraṇa 540/2 unveiled, manifest, evident,

niravayava mfn having no limbs or members, indivisible, not consisting of parts,

nirā√viś to retire, keep away from,

niraya m. egression from earthly life, or Hell (without happiness),

nirā√yam to bring or get out,

nirāyāsa mfn not causing trouble or fatigue, easy,

nirāyata mfn stretched out, extended, contracted, compact,

nirāśa 540/2 without any hope or wish free from expectation

nīrasa mfn without juice, sapless, dried up, withered, tasteless,

niraśana mfn abstaining from food, n. going without food, fasting,

nirāśaṅka mfn fearless, (*am*) ind. without fear or hesitation,

nirāśis free from desires, indifferent, hopeless,

nirāsrava mfn sinless,

nirāśrayā 540/2 destitute, alone, without support, shelterless,

niraṣṭa *(√akṣ)* emasculated, deprived of vigour,

nirāstha mfn not interested in anything, not intent upon (comp).

niraśva mfn without horses,

nīrata mfn not delighting in, indifferent,

nirātaṅka 134/2 mfn free from fear or pain, comfortable, not feeling/causing it,

niratīcāra mfn inviolable,

niratiśaya mfn unsurpassed, perfect,

niratyaya mfn free from danger, secure, infallible, faultless,

nirava mfn unprotected,

nīrava mfn soundless, noiseless, (*am*) ind. silently,

nirava√day to satisfy anyone in respect to-

nirava√dhe P. *–dhayate* to suck out,

niravadhi mfn unlimited, endless, infinite,

nirava√do P. *–dāti* or *–dyati* to distribute or divide completely, give anyone his share, appease,

niravadya mfn not liable, unobjectionable, n. blamelessness, excellence,

niravagraha mfn unrestrained, independent,

niravaha m. a kind of sword,

niravalamba mfn supportless,

nirāvaraṇa mfn unveiled, manifest, evident

niravarodha mfn unrestrained, unopposed,

niravasāda mfn not cast down, cheerful,

niravaśeṣa mfn without residue, complete,

niravaskṛta mfn clean, pure,

nirava√so caus, *-sāyayati* to establish, settle,

niravatta mfn distributed, completely divided or allotted

niravayava mfn not consisting of parts, indivisible,

niraveks (√īkṣ) to observe, perceive,

niravyaya mfn undecaying, eternal,

nirāya mfn yielding no income, profitless

nirāyāsa mfn not causing trouble or fatigue,

nirāyata mfn unextended, compact, contracted,

nirāyati mfn one with no future, whose demise is at hand,

nirbaddha mfn fixed or fastened upon, clung to, pressed hard, urged,

nirbādha mfn free from vexation/annoyance

nirbala mfn powerless, weak,

nir√bandh P. *–badhnāti* to fix or fasten upon, attach oneself to, insist upon, persist in, urge,

nirbandha m. 555/3 perseverance, insisting upon, objection, obstinacy, attributing anything to, accusing of (comp.),

nirbandhu mfn without relations or friends,

nir√bhā P. *–bhāti* to shine forth, appear, arise, to look like, seem to be,

nirbhāga mfn not consisting of parts,

nirbhāgya mfn unfortunate,

nir√bhaj P.A. *–bhajati (te),* to exclude from participation, to satisfy with (3rd),

nirbhara 541/2 without weight or measure, measureless, excessive, vehement, violent, ardent, full of, abounding in,

nirbhara mfn 'without weight or measure'

excessive, vehement, violent, deep (as sleep), ardent (embrace), full of, abounding in,
nirbharam ind. in full measure, completely,
nirbharata m. unsupported, not maintained,
nir√bhās caus. *–bhāsayati* to illuminate,
nirbhāsa m. appearance, similar, like,
nirbhāsana n. illuminating, illustrating, making manifest,
nirbhāsita mfn illuminated, illumined,
nirbhaṭa mfn hard, firm,
nirbhāṭa mfn shone or shining forth, appeared, arisen,
nirbhaya n. fearlessness, security, mfn fearless, free from danger, tranquil, beyond fear,
nirbheda m. breaking asunder, splitting, bursting, split, rent, channel (of a river), betraying, revealing,
nirbhinna mfn broken asunder, budded, blossomed, divided, separated, penetrated, found out, betrayed,
nirbhūti f. disappearing, vanishing,
nirbīja mfn seedless, impotent, attributeless,
nirbījasamādhi in which the seeds of *saṁskāra* are fried and therefore unable to germinate,
nirbodha 541/2 see *nirbuddhi* 541/2 m. dull, stupid, senseless
nir√brū P. *–bravīti* to speak out, pronounce, interpret, explain,
nirbuddhi unintelligent, senseless, ignorant,
nirdagdha 2.mfn burnt, burnt up,
nirdahana mfn not burning, n. burning up, consuming, *nirdāha* n. burning
nirdainya mfn free from misery, comfortable, at ease
nirdākṣiṇya mfn not courteous, rude
nirdara m. a cave, cavern
nirdaravāsin mfn inhabiting a cave
nirdāridriya mfn free from poverty, wealthy,
nirdātṛ m. a weeder, reaper,
nirdaya mfn pitiless, unkind, cruel,
nirdeśa 555/2 m. pointing out, indicating, directing, command, instruction, description, designation, specification, details or particulars,
nirdeva mfn abandoned by the gods, without gods or idols,
nir√dhā P. *–dadhāti* to take or find out,
nirdhana mfn without money or property, m. an old bull,
nirdhanin mfn without wealth, poor,
nirdharma mfn unrighteous, lawless, impious, m. unrighteousness,
nirdhauta washed off, cleansed, purified,
nir√dhṛ to settle, ascertain, caus. *–dhārayati* to hold back (the breath), to take or pick out,
nirdhūma mfn smokeless,
nirdhūta shaken, agitated, harassed, shaken off, deprived or bereft of (comp.), a man abandoned by his relatives or friends,
nir-dhyai 555/3to think of, reflect upon,
nirdhyāta mfn thought of, meditated,
nirdigdha mfn anointed, well-fed, stout,
nir√diś P. *–diśati* to point to, show, to assign anything to, destine for, to indicate, state, name, to take for, regard as, to proclaim, prophesy, recommend, advise,
nirdiṣṭa mfn pointed out, shown, announced, foretold, enjoined, meant or determined for, appointed to, learned, wise,
nirdoṣa without evil, guiltless, see 2. *doṣa* 498/2
nirdravya mfn immaterial, without property,
nirdroha mfn friendly, not hostile/malicious
nirdruma mfn treeless,
nirduḥkha mfn painless, not feeling or causing pain,
nirdurdina mfn 'free from bad weather', serene, bright,
nirdvaṃdva 541/2 indifferent to the pairs of opposites, e.g. pain and pleasure, independent, not double, not contested, not acknowledging two principles,
nirebha mfn soundless, noiseless,
nireka *1.* mfn excluding one, 2. prominence, superiority, above all, in a high degree
nirenas mfn free from guilt,
nirga m. a country, region, district,
nir√gā to go out, come forth,

nirgacchati comes out,
nirgalita mfn flowed out, dissolved, melted
nirgama m. going forth, setting out, escaping from, vanishing, cessation, end, exit, issue, outlet, a door,
nirgata mfn departed, gone out, come forth, appeared, become visible, disappeared, extinct, freed from, f. the state of being entirely freed from sin, freed from fear, fearless,
nir√gam P. *-gacchati* to go out, leave, comes forth, depart from, set out, to start, come out, or appear, to go away, disappear, to enter into any state, to undergo,
nirgahana mfn knowing no difficulties, intrepid, 541/1
nirgamya ind. having gone out, 554/2
nirgarha mfn blameless,
nirgarva mfn free from pride, humble,
nirgata mfn gone out, come forth, appeared, become visible, extinct, disappeared, freed from,
nirgaurava mfn without dignity
nirghaṇṭa, °ṇṭu, °ṇṭuka = nighaṇṭa etc. collection of words, vocabulary,
nirghaṭa n. a great fair, crowded market,
nirghāta m. removal, destruction, whirlwind, hurricane, thunderstorm, earthquake,
nirghoṣa mfn soundless, noiseless, 2. sound, noise, rattling, tramping,
nirgrāhya mfn perceivable, to be traced or found out,
nirgrantha mfn free from all ties or hindrances, without possessions, a saint who has withdrawn from the world and lives either as a hermit or a religious mendicant wandering about naked, a fool, idiot, a gambler, murder, manslaughter, m. a naked Jaina or Buddhist mendicant, n. Jainism or Buddhism, free from knots, knotless, without blemish, perfect, poor, a religious mendicant, a fool,
nirguṇa 541/1 devoid of all qualities or properties, having no epithet, (said of the Supreme Being), "synonym for *para brahman* and *aviśiṣṭa*" HH
nirguṇatva having the nature of being without *guṇā*
nir√han to strike off, expel, remove, strike or knock out, kill, destroy,
nirhāra m. a hoard, a private store,
nirharaṇa n. taking out, extracting, expelling, carrying out (esp. a dead body),
nirhārin mfn diffusively fragrant, taking forth or out, having wealth,
nirhata mfn struck down,
nirhetu mfn causeless, reasonless, *-tā* f. *tva* n. want of a cause or reason,
nirhlāda mfn joyless, uncomfortable, uneasy,
nir√hrād to cause to sound, beat a drum,
nirhrāda m. sound, noise, humming, roaring, murmuring, etc.
nirhrāsa m. shortening, abbreviation,
nirhrasita mfn shortened (as a vowel),
nirhrasta mfn abridged, diminished,
nirhṛta mfn taken forth or out, removed,
nir√hve P.*–hvayati* to call off,
nir√i P. *–eti* to go out, come forth, go off, depart,
nī-rī *(nis +√rī)* P.A. *–riṇāti, riṇīte*, to loosen, separate from, allure, seduce
niriccha mfn without wish or desire, indifferent,
nirīha mfn motionless, inactive, desireless, indifferent, not anxious,
nir√īkṣ A. *-īkṣate (ti),* to look at or towards, behold, regard, observe,
nirīkṣe I see, I behold, *3/s/mid, nir √īkṣ*
nirīkṣya ind. having contemplated, having looked at or viewed
nirindhana mfn without fuel,
nirindriya mfn impotent, without manly vigour or strength, a barren cow, having no organs of sense,
niriṅga mfn immovable, not flickering,
nirjala mfn waterless, dry, m. or n. a dry country, desert, waste
nirjana mfn unpeopled, lonely, desolate,
nirjara mfn not becoming old, young, fresh,

imperishable, immortal, m. a god 2. mfn completely wearing down or destroying, m. the gradual destruction of all actions (Jain)

nirjarjalpa mfn tattered,

nirjāta come forth, appeared, visible,

nirjaya m. conquest, subduing, mastering,

nirjhara m. a waterfall, cataract, cascade, a mountain torrent, burning chaff, an elephant, (ī) f. a river,

nirjharin m. a mountain,

nir√ji P. –jayati to conquer, win, acquire,

nirjijñāsa mfn not desiring to know or understand,

nirjita mfn conquered, subdued, won,

nirjīva mfn lifeless, dead,

nirjñāna mfn ignorant, silly, stupid,

nir√jī caus. *–jarayati* to wear down, crush,

nirjuṣṭa mfn frequented, inhabited,

nirjyotis mfn lightless, dark,

nirlakṣmīka mfn devoid of lustre or splendour,

nirlakṣya mfn not observable, invisible,

nirlekhana n. a scraper,

nir√likh P. *–likhati* to scratch, scarify,

nirlina mfn cut through or off,

nirlipta m. unsmeared, undefiled,

nirlobha mfn free from desire, not avaricious

nir√lup P. *–lumpati* to draw out, extract,

nir√luṭh 1. caus. *loṭhayati* to roll down 2. *-loṭhayati* to rob, steal,

nir√mā A. *–mimīte, -māti,* to mete out, measure, to build, make out of, form, fabricate, produce, create, compose or write,

nirmā f. value, measure, equivalent,

nirmada mfn sober, quiet, humble, modest

nirmādhyastha n. absence of impartiality, interest, sympathy

nirmagna mfn to sink under, sunk into i.e. firmly fixed upon,

nirmala mfn spotless, unsullied, clean, pure, shining, resplendent, bright, sinless, virtuous, having a pure mind, n. cleansing, purification stainlessness, cleanness, without stain or impurity,

nirmalīmasa mfn spotless, clean, pure,

nirmama mfn unselfish, disinterested, esp. free from all worldly connections, regardless of, indifferent to, 541/3

nirmāṁsa mfn emaciated, fleshless,

nirmāṇa n. measuring, measure, reach, extent, forming, making, transformation, pith, the best of anything, , manufacture, building, producing, creation,

nirmāna free from pride, without self-confidence,

nirmāṇacitta manufactured mind, manufacturing mind,

nirmāṇakāya m. body of transformations, manufactured body,

nirmanaska mindless, having no *manas,*

nirmantra a ceremony without holy texts,

nirmantu mfn faultless, innocent,

nirmanuja mfn not peopled, uninhabited,

nirmānuṣa mfn not peopled, desolate,

nirmanyu mfn free from anger, or resentment

nirmārga mfn roadless, pathless

nirmaryāda mfn boundless, immeasurable, innumerable, unlimited, unrestrained unruly, wicked, criminal, *(am)* ind. confusedly, topsy-turvy,

nir√math or *manth* P.A. *–manthati (te)*, to produce fire by rubbing wood together, to stir rub or churn, 556/1

nirmatha mfn rubbing,

nirmathana mfn rubbing, churning, making butter, lighting a fire,

nirmātṛ m. maker, builder, creator, author,

nirmatsara mfn without envy or jealousy,

nirmāya mfn powerless, weak,

nirmedha mfn without understanding, stupid

nirmita mfn constructed, built, formed, created, performed (ceremony),

nirmithya mfn not false, true,

nirmiti f. formation, creation, making, adding, addition(of a word),

nirmocana n. deliverance,

nirmoha mfn free from illusion, without attachment, without delusion,

nirmoka m. setting loose or free,

nirmokṣa m. liberation, deliverance from,

nirmoktṛ m. a looser, resolver of doubts,
nir√muc P. *–muñcati* to loosen, free from, liberate, pass. *–mucyate* to be freed, or free oneself from, get rid of, to be abandoned or given up,
nir√muh caus. *–mohayati* to confuse, bewilder,
nirmukta 556/2 loosed, separated, liberated, given up, lost, disappeared, vanished, free from every attachment,
nirmukti f. liberation, deliverance from,
nirmuṭa m. a tree, a free market, the sun
nirmūla mfn rootless (as a tree),
nirṇāma m. bending, twisting, turning,
nirṇamana n. bending,
nirnamaskāra mfn offering no homage, not respecting, unrespected,
nirnara mfn deserted, abandoned by men
nirnaṭa m. bent outward, prominent,
nirṇaya m. taking off, removing, complete ascertainment, decision, settlement, determination, (in logic) deduction, inference, conclusion, (in law) sentence, verdict, (in rhet.) narration, discussion, consideration,
nirṇāyana n. rendering certain, the outer angle of the elephant's eye,
nirṇāyaka mfn settling, conclusive,
nirṇejaka m. a washerman, washer,
nirṇejana n. washing cleaning, atonement for an offence, expiation, water for washing or rinsing,
nirṇeka m. washing, ablution, expiation,
nirṇenekti P. washes off, cleans,
nir√ṇī (√nī) P.A. *–nayati (te)*, to lead or take away, carry off, to find out, investigate, decide, fix on, settle,
nirnidra mfn sleepless,
nirṇikta mfn washed, cleaned, polished, purified, pure,
nirṇiktamanas mfn pure-hearted,
nirnimeṣa mfn not twinkling, not closing the eye,
nirnimitta mfn without reason or motive, causeless, having no ego motive, free from cause,
nirnirodha mfn unobstructed,
nirṇīta mfn (having been) decided,
nirṇoda m. removal, banishment,
nirodha 554/1 m. confinement, imprisonment, restraint, check, suppression, suppression of pain, covering up, hurting, injuring, aversion, disfavour, dislike, a state of intense concentration in which the distinction between subject and object is destroyed, control (of the mind), in buddhism the cessation or removal of suffering, a stage of meditation – cessation of activity, see *nivṛtti,* 'unrealisable' (Gam.),
nirodha pariṇāma cessation of mental activity
nīroga mfn free from sickness, healthy,
nirogatva n. health, being without disease
nī-roha m. shooting out, growing,
nir√ṛ to go out or off, fall away from, be deprived of, to separate, disjoin,
nir√ṛch P. *–ṛchati* to go asunder or pass away, to be deprived of,
nir√ṛj P. *–arjati* to let out, deliver,
nirṛta mfn dissolved, decayed, debilitated
nirṛti f. dissolution, destruction, calamity, evil, adversity, m. death
nirṛtha m. destruction, personified as the destroyer
nir√ubj P. *–ubjati* to cause to flow down, let loose,
nī-ruc *(nis +√ruc)* to drive away by shining
nirudaka mfn waterless,
niruddeśam ind. without any statement,
niruddrāva mfn immovable, undecaying,
ni √rudh 553/3 to hold back, stop,
niruddha mfn. held back, withheld, stopped, controlled,
nirūḍha mfn unmarried, 2. mfn grown up, conventional, accepted, m. (in rhetoric) the force or application of words according to their natural or received meanings, (in logic) the inherence of any property in the term implying it (as of redness in the word 'red' etc. 3. drawn out, put aside, separate, purged, eviscerated
nirūḍhi f. fame, celebrity,

nirudhya gerund confining, suppressing
nirudvigna mfn unexcited, calm, sedate,
nirudyama mfn effortless, inactive, lazy,
nirudyoga mfn disheartened, causeless, without effort, indolent,
ni√ruh caus. *–ropayati* to transplant, transfer from,
nir√1.ūh P.A. *–ūhati* to push or draw out, put aside or apart, remove,
nirūha 1. m. a complete sentence, 2. m. logic, disputation, certainty, ascertainment, mfn = *niścita*
nirūhaṇa n. ascertainment,
nīruj mfn healthy, wholesome,
nirukta 553/3 mfn uttered, pronounced, expressed, explained, defined, explicitly mentioned or enjoined, distinct, loud, interpreted i.e. become manifest, fulfilled, accomplished (as a word), n. explanation or etymological interpretation of a word, that which is definable.. , the science of etymology (one of the limbs of the Veda),
nirukti f. etymological explanation of a word, word derivation, communication of an event that has taken place,
niruktu mfn uttered, pronounced, expressed, explained, defined, explicitly mentioned, distinct, loud, interpreted,
niruṇaddhi, confines, restrains, holds back,
nirunmāda mfn free from pride or arrogance
ni√rūp P. *–rūpayati* to perform, represent on stage, act, gesticulate, indicate by gesture, to perceive, notice, find out, ascertain, to investigate, examine, consider, reflect upon,
nīrūpa mfn shapeless, m. air, wind, heaven, ether,
nirūpādhika mfn unconditional (logic), absolute, categorical, without attributes or qualities, without any limiting adjunct,
nirūpaka mfn observing, observer,
nirūpaṇa mfn stating, determining, defining, f. the act of stating, examination, sight, appearance, form, shape,
nirupabhoga mfn not enjoying,
nirupādāna mfn free from desire or clinging to life,
nirupadhi mfn guileless, blameless, honest,
nirupādhi (and *–dhika*) mfn without attributes or qualities, absolute, unconditioned,
nirupadrava mfn free from affliction or danger, neither inflicting nor incurring adversity, harmless, peaceful, secure, happy,
nirupahita mfn (in phil) without *upādhi* or *upadhi*
nirupākhya mfn without qualification, immaterial, unreal, false, non-existent, indescribable, inexpressible,
nirupakrama mfn incurable,
nirupakriya mfn not useful or profitable,
nirupama mfn peerless, incomparable,
nirupapatti mfn unfit, unsuitable,
nirupaplava mfn untroubled, unmolested,
nirupasarga mfn free from portents, auspicious
nirupaskṛta mfn unimpaired by, simple, pure
nirupasṛṣṭa mfn undamaged,
nirupasthāyaka mfn unattended,
nirupāya mfn without expedients, helpless, unsuccessful,
nirūpayati he sees, describes
nirupayoga mfn useless, unserviceable,
nirupekṣa mfn not neglectful,
nirūpita mfn seen, observed, considered, discovered, defined, appointed, elected, chosen, n. the state of having been discussed or ascertained,
nirūpiti f. statement, definition,
nirupti f. scattering, pouring out, offering,
nirūpya ind. performing, acting, gesturing, having seen, considered, 2. mfn to be seen, defined, ascertained, not yet certain, questionable,
nirutkaṇṭha mfn free from longing/desire
nirutsāha m. absence of exertion, indolence, mfn without energy or courage,

nirutsuka mfn careless, indifferent, tranquil, without eagerness,
niruttara mfn having no superior, answerless silenced,
niruttha mfn irrecoverable,
nir√vā P. *–vāti* to blow (wind), to cease to blow, to be blown out or extinguished, to be allayed, refreshed, exhilarated,
nir√vac mostly used in pass. *–ucyate*, to speak out, express clearly or distinctly, declare, interpret, explain, to derive from,
nirvacana mfn not speaking, silent, unobjectionable, blameless, *(am)* ind. silently, 2. n. speaking out, pronouncing, a saying or proverb, interpretation, explanation, etymology,
nir√vad P.A. *–vadati (te*), to order off, warn off, expel or drive away, to speak out, utter, to abuse, revile, to deny
nirvāda m. absence of dispute or railing, 2. m. obloquy, censure, rumour,
nir√vadh to split off or asunder, sever,
nir√vah P. *–vahati* to lead out of, save from, to bring about, accomplish, to be brought about succeed, be successful, overcome obstacles,
nirvāha m. carrying on, accomplishing, describing, narrating, perseverance, steadfastness,
nirvahaṇa n. end, issue, completion,
nirvāhaṇa n. carrying off, removing, destroying,
nirvāhin mfn leading or carrying out,
nirvaira without enmity, peaceable,
nirvākya, nirvāc, mfn speechless,
nirvaṁśa mfn having no family, alone
nirvāṇa 557/3 mfn. blown or put out, extinguished (as a lamp or fire), set (as the sun), calmed, quieted, dead, deceased (having the fire of life extinguished), lost, disappeared, immersed, plunged, immovable, n. blowing out, extinction, cessation, vanishing, disappearance
nir√vañc A. *–vañcate,* to deceive,
nirvāñc mfn outward, exterior,

nir√vap P.A. *–vapati,* to pour out, sprinkle, offer, present (esp. sacrificial items), to choose or select for, distribute, perform a sacrifice or funeral oblation,

nirvara mfn excellent,
nirvartaka mfn bringing about, finishing, accomplishing, performing,
nirvartana n. completion, execution,
nir√varṇ *–varṇayati* to look at, contemplate
nir√5.vas P. *–vasati* to dwell, finish dwelling, dwell abroad, to dismiss, banish, 557/2
nirvāsa m. leaving one's home, banishment
nirvaśa mfn having no free will dependent on another, 542/1
nirvāsana mfn without fancy or imagination, n. expelling from home, banishment, leading out to some other place,
nirvāsita mfn exiled, banished, dismissed
nirvasu without property, poor,
nirvāta mfn free from wind, sheltered, still
nirveda 542/2 mfn not having the Vedas, infidel,
2. 557/3 m. complete indifference, disregard of worldly objects, loathing, disgust for (6th,7th in comp.), -*duḥ-saham* ind. in a despairingly unsupportable manner, -*vat* mfn despondent, resigned, indifferent,
nirvedha m. penetration, insight,
nirvedya ind. unknowable, without having known
nirvega mfn without violent motion, quiet, calm
nirveśa m. payment, returning, offering, wages, reward, atonement, expiation, entering, attaining, fainting, swooning, 558/1
nirvi√bhās caus. *–bhāsayati* to illumine, enlighten
nirvicāra mfn not needing consideration, not reflecting or considering, *(am)* ind. without reflection, inconsiderately, without inquiry,
nirviceṣṭa mfn motionless, insensible,
nir√3.vid P. *–vindati* to find out,
A. *–vide,* to get rid of, do away with, pass. *–vidyate* to be despondent or depressed, be

disgusted with, caus. *–vedayati,* to cause despair,
f. despondency, despair,

nirviddha mfn wounded, killed, separated from each other, isolated,

nirvidya mfn unlearned, uneducated

nirvighna mfn uninterrupted, unhindered,

nirvikalpa mfn without attributes, not admitting an alternative,
free from change or differences,
2. *nirvikalpa* G209 nonconceptual, the highest state of *samādhi,* 'free of judgement', 'free from ideation' (Gam.), 542/1 mfn not admitting an alternative, free from change or differences, admitting no doubt, not wavering,
'devoid of all imaginations' (Gam.),

nirvikalpa samādhi unqualified unity HH

nirvikalpaka n. knowledge not depending upon or derived from the senses,

nirvikāra mfn unchanged, unchangeable, uniform, normal,

nirvikāsa mfn not opening or expanded,

nirvi√kram –krāmati to step out,

nirvimarśa Apte 293/1 void of reflection, unthinking, 542/2 unreflecting, inconsiderate,

nirviṇṇa mfn despondent, depressed, sorrowful, afraid, loathing, disgusted with, abused, degraded, humble,

nirvirodha mfn not being opposed to

nirvīrya mfn powerless, unmanly, m. a weakling, *-tā* f. unmanliness, powerlessness, impotence,

nir√viś P. *–viśati* to enter into, to settle in a home, become a householder, to marry, to pay, render, offer, to enjoy, delight in, to go out or forth, to embellish,

nirviṣaya mfn having no dwelling place or expelled from it, supportless, hanging in the air, having no object or sphere of action, not attached to sensual objects,

nirviṣaṅga indifferent, not attached,

nirviśaṅka mfn fearless, confident,

nirviśeṣa mfn showing or making no difference, undiscriminating, without distinction, not different from, same, like, n. absence of difference, likeness, without special characteristics,

nirviśeṣacinmātra undifferentiated consciousness alone,

nirviśeṣākṛti mfn having like appearance, looking alike, whose forms are precisely alike,

nirviśeṣatva absence of distinctive attributes,

nirvi√śī to peel or drop off, fall asunder,

nirviṣṭa mfn entered, sticking in, sitting, married, paid off, rendered, enjoyed, earned, gained,

nirvitarka mfn unreflecting, inconsiderate,

nirvi√vah P. *–vahati* to carry out, export, expel,

nir√vai P. *–vāyati* to be extinguished, go out,

nirviveka mfn undiscriminating,

nirveṣṭana n. a weavers shuttle

nirveṣṭita mfn denuded,

nirvitarka mfn unreflecting, inconsiderate,

nirvoḍhṛ mfn accomplishing, performing,

nir√2.vṛ A. *vṛṇīte* to choose, select,

nirvraṇita mfn whose wounds are healed

nirvraska mfn uprooted, extirpated,

nirvrata mfn neglecting religious duties,

nirvṛṣṭi f. cessation of rain,

nir√vṛt A. *–vartate,* to come forth, originate, become, to be accomplished or affected, or finished, come off, take place, caus. *vartayati* to cause to come forth, bring out, turn out, remove, bring about, complete, to gladden, satisfy,

nirvṛta mfn satisfied, happy, tranquil, at ease, contented,

nirvṛti 558/1 f. complete satisfaction, bliss, emancipation, final beatitude, attainment of rest, extinction (of a lamp), destruction, death,

nirvṛtta mfn sprung forth, originated, developed, accomplished, finished, ready, grown out (fruit)

nirvṛtti mfn having no occupation, destitute, 2.f. originating, development, growth, completion, termination,

nirvyādhi mfn free from sickness, healthy

nirvyagra mfn unconfused, calm, prudent

nirvyāja mfn free from deceit or ambiguity, exact, honest, sincere, pure,
nirvyākula mfn not troubled or excited, calm, -*tā* f. calmness, tranquillity,
nirvyañjaka mfn indicating, betraying
nirvyañjaṇa mfn without condiment, *(e)* ind. in a plain manner, explicitly,
nirvyāpāra mfn not busy, at leisure, passive
nirvyasana mfn free from bad inclinations,
nirvyatha mfn free from pain, quiet, calm,
nirvyāvṛtti mfn (emancipation), not involving any return (to worldly existence),
nirvyūḍha mfn pushed out, expelled from, arrayed in order of battle, carried out, finished, completed, succeeded, successful, lucky, left, abandoned, n. bringing about, accomplishing,
nirvyūḍhi f. end, highest point or degree
nirvyūha n.m. a turret, a helmet or its ornament, a crest, a door, gate, A peg to hang things on,
nir√yā P. *–yāti,* to go out, come forth, set out for, to go hunting, to die, to weed a field, to drive away, expel
niryā f. getting out of order, disturbance, defect (esp. of a rite),
nir√yāc P.A. *–yācati (te),* to beg or solicit from, to ask, entreat,
niryāma m. a sailor, pilot,
niryāmaka m. an assistant,
niryāṇa n. going forth or out, exit, issue,
niryāṇika mfn conducive to emancipation,
niryantraṇa mfn unrestrained, self-willed, independent, (*am*) ind. without restraint
niryāsa m. an exudation, juice, resin, milk, any thick liquid, extract,
niryāta mfn gone out or forth, issued,
niryāti f. departure, dying, final emancipation
niryatna mfn inactive, immovable, lazy
niryoga m. a decoration, a tie-rope for cows
niryūha n. prominence, projection, a kind of pinnacle or turret, a helmet, crest, a peg or bracket, a door, gate, m. extract, juice,
niryukta mfn constructed, built, erected
niryukti f. want of union or connection, unfitness, impropriety, mfn unfounded, illogical, wrong, 2. f. explanation of a sacred text (Jain)
niryūṣa m. extract, juice, etc.
nis- 543/2 ind. out, forth, away. also used as a prefix to verbs and nouns (with nouns has a sense of negation or privation - often may be translated as without), in which case it takes the meanings- out of, away from, without, destitute of, free from, also may be used as a strengthening particle – entirely, thoroughly, very, very liable to be changed to *niḥ, nir, niś, niṣ,* or *nī* usually according to the following letter,
niś 542/3 for *nis* in comp.
√niś 560/2 Cl 1 P *neśati* to meditate upon, be absorbed in meditation, DP in *samādhi* meditating upon, 2. f. night, every night,
niś- with nouns has a sense of negation or privation e.g. destitute of and may be translated as 'without', for *nis* before *c* or *ch* for *nis* in compounds,
niṣ- for *nis* before *k, kh, p, ph,* *see nis- / niś-* above, 2. Cl 1 P. *neṣati,* to moisten, sprinkle,
niśā f. night, a vision, dream, turmeric,
niśabda mfn speechless, silent,
ni-ṣac *√sac* to be closely connected or associated
niśācara m. night-wanderer, a kind of demon, a fiend, a jackal, an owl, a snake, mfn night-walking, moving about by night,
ni√sad Cl 1 *–sīdati,* to sit down, be seated,
niṣād mfn sitting inactive,
niśāda m. a man of low caste, an out-caste, a man of any degraded tribe,
niṣadha name of a people, *Niṣadha* - name of a country,
niṣadhādhipa m. ruler or king of *Niṣadha*
nīṣāh mfn overpowering
niṣakta mfn hung or hanging on, fixed in,

fastened to,
ni√śam P. *–śamyati* to be extinguished, caus. *śamayati* to appease, make quiet, to cool down, *śāmayati* to observe, perceive, hear, learn,
niśāma m. observing, perceiving,
niśamana n. perceiving, hearing,
niśāmana 560/3 observing, perceiving, repeated observation
niśamaya mfn perceiving, coming into contact with, reaching to (comp.)
niśāmita mfn perceived, heard, learnt,
niśamya ind. having perceived or heard,
niśāna sharpening, whetting, observing, perceiving
niṣaṅga m. clinging to, attachment, quiver,
niṣaṅgathi mfn embracing, m. an embrace, a bowman, a charioteer, a car, the shoulder, grass,
niṣaṅgin mfn having a quiver or sword, cleaving, clinging, sticking, attached to, m. a bowman, warrior,
niṣaṇṇa mfn sitting, seated, resting or leaning on, sunk down, distressed,
niṣanna mfn dejected
niṣaṇṇaka mfn sitting, seated, n. a seat
niśānta m.n. daybreak, 2. 560/3 mfn allayed, tranquil, calm, customary, traditional, n. a house, dwelling, habitation, a harem,
nīśāra m. a warm cloth or outer garment, curtains esp. mosquito curtains,
nisarga m. voiding excrement, giving away, granting, bestowing, relinquishing, abandoning, natural state or condition,
nisargabhāva m. natural state or condition,
nisargabhinna mfn naturally distinct,
nisargaja mfn innate, inborn, produced at creation, natural,
nisarganipuṇa mfn naturally clever,
nisargapadva n. inclined, feeling attracted towards,
niśāna n. sharpening, whetting, observing, perceiving,
niśata 560/3 m. shining at night,
niśāta mfn sharpened, whetted, polished,
niśatayati mitigates,
niśaṭha mfn not false, honest,
niśāvana m. hemp,
niśāyin mfn lying down, sleeping,
nis√bhid Cl 7 *–bhinatti,* to split open,
niścakṣus mfn eyeless, blind,
niścakrika mfn without tricks/deceit, honest
niścala mfn motionless, immovable, fixed, steady, invariable, unchangeable, *ā)*f. the earth,
niś√car P. *–carati* to come forth, go out, proceed, appear, rise (as sounds)
niścarati moves away, wanders away
niścaya 561/2 m. inquiry, ascertainment, fixed opinion, conviction, certainty, '*iti niścayaḥ* this is a fixed opinion,' resolution, resolve, design, purpose, aim,
"to differentiate the two (see *cid* and *cit*) is called *niścaya* (resolution) ." HH
niścayabodha. (E. p.434) sure-knowledge,
niścayaka mfn who or what ascertains and determines, determining, decisive,
niścayavṛtti a resolute state of mind,
niścayin 561/2 of firm opinion or resolution, one who has come to know
niśceṣṭa mfn incapable of motion, motionless, powerless, helpless, *(am)* ind. without motion, *(ā)* f. motionless
niścetana mfn unconscious, unreasonable,
niścetas mfn out of one's senses,
niś√2.ci P. *–cinoti,* to ascertain, investigate, decide, settle, fix upon, determine, resolve,
nis√ci Cl 3 *–ciketi,* to decide, settle, determine as certain,
niścinta mfn not thinking, thoughtless,
niścita mfn one who has come to a conclusion or formed a certain opinion, determined to, resolute upon, determined, settled, decided, (*am*) ind. decidedly, positively, n. certainty, decision, resolution, design, careless, unconcerned,
niściti f. ascertainment, fixing, settling,
niśchandas mfn not studying Vedic texts,

niśchāya mfn shadeless, without shade,
niścheda mfn indivisible, reduced by the common divisor to the least term
niśchidra mfn having no rents or holes, without weak points or defects, unhurt, uninterrupted,
niścita 561/2 mfn one who has come to a conclusion, or formed a certain opinion, ascertained, determined, certainty, decision, knowing with certainty, n. certainty, decision, resolution, design, (*am*) ind. decidedly, positively,
niścitya 561/2 ind. having ascertained or decided, surely, without doubt,
niṣedha 562/1 hindering, prohibition, keeping off , prevention,
niṣeka m. sprinkling, infusion, an injecting esp. of semen, impregnation, the ceremony performed upon impregnation,
niṣeva mfn practising, exercising, observing, enjoying, (*ā*) f. exercising, practice, service, use, employment, devotion, adoration,
niṣevaka mfn visiting, frequenting, using, employing, observing, enjoying,
niṣevaṇa n. visiting, frequenting, living in, practice, performance, use, employment, adherence or devotion to, honour, worship,
niṣevin mfn practising, enjoying, observing,
nis√gam Cl 1 *–gacchati,* go out, issue forth,
ni√ṣidh to drive away, ward off, keep back, forbid, prohibit, suppress,
niṣiddhakarma action(s) forbidden by scripture
niṣiddhi f. prohibition, defence, warding off,
nis√īkṣ Cl 1 *-īkṣate,* look upon, survey,
ni√śi P. *–śiśāti* to sharpen, whet, to excite, strengthen,
niśita mfn sharpened, sharp, stimulated, n. iron, steel,
niśitā f. night,
niśītha m. midnight, night,
niśiti f. exciting, refreshing,
√niṣk 562/2 Cl 10 A *niṣkayate* to measure, weigh, DP in *parimāṇa* measuring, weighing,
niṣkaivalya mfn mere, pure, absolute,
niṣkala mfn without parts, undivided, waned, diminished, decayed, infirm, m. an old man, a receptacle, f. a woman past childbearing, *-tva* n. indivisibility, the state of the absolute Brahma,
niṣkalaṇka mfn stainless, immaculate,
niṣkālika mfn one who has no more time to live, whose term of life is elapsed
niṣkalmaṣa mfn stainless, sinless, pure,
niṣkāma mfn desireless, disinterested, unselfish, *-cārin* acting without interest or selfishness,
niṣkampa mfn motionless, immovable,
niṣkāmuka mfn free from worldly desires,
niṣkāṅkṣa mfn free from doubts
niṣkānta mfn not lovely, ugly,
niṣkaṇṭaka mfn free from thorns or enemies
niṣkapaṭa mfn guileless, free from deceit
niṣkāraṇa mfn causeless, unnecessary, disinterested (as a friend), groundless, not proceeding from any cause, (*am* and *āt*) ind. causelessly, without special motive
niṣkarman mfn inactive, exempt from or neglecting religious or worldly acts,
niṣkaruṇa mfn pitiless, cruel
niṣkāsa m. issue, egress, a portico, verandah
niṣkaṣāya mfn free from dirt or impure passions,
niṣkarṣa 562/3 drawing out, extracting, chief or main point, essence, measuring, ascertainment,
niṣkevala mfn belonging exclusively,
niṣkilbiṣa mfn free from sin,
niṣkiṁcana mfn having nothing, poor,
niṣkleśa mfn free from pain/moral faults,
niṣkoṣa m. tearing off or out, husking, shelling,
niṣ√1.kṛ to bring out, extract, drive away, expel, remove, to arrange, set in order, prepare, to break in pieces, to restore, cure,
niṣ√kram to go out, come forth, to leave

(worldly life), to make an exit (in drama),
niṣkrama m. going out, coming forth, an exit, departing from, degradation, loss of caste, intellectual faculty,
niṣkramaṇa n. going forth or out, departing, ceasing, disappearing, the first going out with a child,
niṣkraya m. redemption, ransom, reward compensation, hire, wages,
niṣkrayaṇa mfn redeeming, ransoming, n. redemption, buying off, ransom,
niṣkṛti f. complete development, cure, restoration, redeeming, redemption, expiation, atonement,
niṣkṛpa mfn pitiless, cruel,
niṣkriya 543/1 n. the actionless One the Supreme Spirit, *-tā* f. inactivity, neglect of (comp.)
niṣkriyarūpa of actionless nature (Brahman),
niṣkrodha mfn free from wrath, not angry with,
niṣ√kṛṣ Cl 1 *-karṣati,* to draw out, extract, pull out,
niṣkṛta mfn done away, removed, expelled, atoned, expiated, made ready, prepared, n. atonement, expiation, removal, doing away, escaping, avoiding, neglecting,
niṣkṛti f. complete development, restoration, cure, requital, atonement, expiation, removal, doing away, escaping, avoiding, neglecting,
niṣkūja mfn noiseless, still
niṣkula mfn having no family,
niṣkuṣita mfn torn off, stripped off,
niṣkūṭa mfn free from deceit,
niṣkutūhala mfn having no curiosity,
niśliṣ mfn clinging, sticking, caus. to fasten, paste on or up,
nis√mā Cl 3 *–mimīte,* to form, make, see *nir√mā*
niṣṇa mfn clever, skilful, versed or experienced in,
niṣṇāta mfn deeply versed in, skilful, clever, learned, agreed upon,
nis√nī Cl 1 *–nayati,* to decide, see *nir√nī*
niṣ√1.pā P. *–pibati* to drink out or up, drink from,
niṣ√3.pā P. *–pāti* to protect from,
niṣ√pad to fall out, to come forth, issue, arise, be brought about or effected, become ripe, ripen,
niṣpad mfn footless, f. excrement,
niṣpādaka mfn accomplishing, developing, effective,
niṣpādana n. effecting, causing, producing,
niṣpālaka mfn without guardian, unprotected
niṣpāka boiling, de-cocting, digesting
niṣpakva mfn well-cooked or ripened
niṣpāna mfn drinking out or up,
niṣpanda mfn motionless, immovable,
niṣpandahīna mfn motionless,
niṣpaṅka mfn free from mud, clear, pure
niṣpanna mfn gone forth or sprung up, arisen, descended from, (in gram.) derived from, brought about, effected, succeeded, completed, finished, ready,
niṣpāpa mfn sinless, guiltless,
niṣpāra mfn boundless, unbounded,
niṣparāmarśa mfn incapable of thinking, without advice, helpless,
niṣparicaya mfn not becoming familiar,
niṣparidāha mfn not combustible,
niṣparīhāra mfn not avoiding, not observing caution,
niṣparihārya mfn not to be omitted, to be applied,
niṣparikara mfn without preparations or provisions,
niṣparīkṣya not examining accurately,
niṣparyanta mfn boundless, unlimited,
niṣparyāya mfn out of order, 543/1
niṣ√pat to fly out of, rush out, jump out, depart, hasten away,
niṣpatana n. rushing out, issuing quickly,
niṣpatita mfn flown or fallen out,
niṣpathya mfn unwell, ill,
niṣpatti 563/2 going forth or out, being brought about or effected, completed, consummation, coming or being derived from, a partic. state of ecstasy,

niṣpattra mfn leafless, unfeathered,
niṣpauruṣa mfn unmanly,
niṣpavana n. winnowing, fanning, purifying,
niṣpayoda mfn cloudless,
niṣphala mfn fruitless, vain,
niṣpīḍana n. pressing, squeezing, wringing out (cloth),
niṣpīta mfn drunk out or up, emptied by drinking, dried or sucked up, exhausted,
niṣphāla or *niṣphala* mfn bearing no fruit, fruitless, barren, without result, without success, useless, vain, seedless, impotent
f. a woman past child-bearing,
n. unfruitfulness, uselessness,
niṣphena mfn foamless, frothless,
niṣpoṣa mfn not being nourished,
niṣ√1.pṛ P. *–piparti* to bring out, rescue or deliver from,
niṣprabha mfn deprived of light or radiance, gloomy, dark
niṣprabhāva mfn powerless,
niṣpracāra mfn not moving, staying in one place, fixed or concentrated (as mind),
niṣpradeśa mfn having no certain place,
niṣprajña mfn ignorant, stupid,
niṣprakampa mfn immovable,
niṣprakāraka mfn without distinction or specification,
niṣprakāśa mfn not transparent, lightless, dark,
niṣprakrama mfn unruly, rash,
niṣpramāda mfn not careless or negligent,
niṣpramāṇaka mfn without authority,
niṣprāṇa mfn breathless, lifeless, quite exhausted,
niṣprapañca 543/2 mfn subject to no expansion or manifoldness, pure, honest,
niṣpratāpa mfn without dignity, mean, base
niṣpratibandha mfn unimpeded, unopposed
niṣpratibha mfn devoid of splendour, stupid,
niṣ pratibhā appearance
niṣpratibhāna mfn not bold, cowardly,
niṣpratidvaṁdva mfn having no adversary, unopposed, unequalled,
niṣpratigha mfn unhindered, unimpeded,
niṣpratigraha mfn not accepting gifts,
niṣpratīkāra mfn unobstructed, uninterrupted, *(am)* ind. 543/2
niṣpratikriya mfn incurable, irremediable,
niṣpratīpa mfn unhindered, unconcerned,
niṣpratyāśa mfn hopeless, despondent of
niṣpratyūha mfn unimpeded, irremediable
niṣprayatna mfn abstaining from exertion,
niṣprayojana having no motive, impartial, indifferent, harmless, needless, groundless, unnecessary,
nispṛh mfn greedy for, desirous of,
*nispṛha*564/2 mfn free from desire, not longing for (7th, or comp.), abstaining from (5th),
ni√spṛś to touch softly, caress, fondle, 564/2
niṣprīti mfn not pleased with or delighting in
ni√śī 561/1 to break off,
niśrama m. labour bestowed upon anything, continued practice,
niśraya m. refuge, resource,
niśrayaṇī f. a ladder, staircase,
nisṛṣṭa mfn hurled, thrown, sent forth, set free, dismissed, allowed, authorized, kindled(as fire), intrusted, committed, transferred, granted,
nisṛta mfn gone away, disappeared, come forth, unsheathed (as a sword),
niṣṣah mfn overpowering, mighty, 563/3
niṣṣidh f. granting, bestowing, gift,
nistabdha mfn paralyzed, numbed, stopped, fixed,
nistala mfn not flat, round, globular, trembling, down, below,
nistamaska mfn free from darkness, not gloomy, light,
nistandra or nistantra mfn not lazy, fresh, healthy
nistantu mfn having no children, childless,
niṣ√ṭap to singe, scorch, heat thoroughly, melt, anneal, purify by heat,
niṣṭapana mfn burning,
niṣṭapta mfn burnt, scorched, heated thoroughly, melted, well cooked
nistaraṁga mfn motionless, still,
nistāra m. crossing, passing over, rescue, deliverance, acquittal, requital,

payment, discharge of a debt, means, expedient, final liberation,
nistāraka mfn (*ikā*)n. rescuing delivering, a saviour,
nistaraṇa n. passing over, going forth, coming out of danger, rescue,
nistāraṇa n. crossing, passing over, overcoming, rescuing, liberating,
nistarkya mfn unimaginable, inconceivable,
nistattva mfn not comprehended in the 24 *tattva* s or principles,
nistejas mfn destitute of fire or energy, impotent, spiritless, dull,
niṣṭha mfn resting upon,
niṣṭhā 563/1 to give forth, emit, yield
mfn. *niṣṭha* being in or on, situated on, grounded on or
resting on, depending on,
relating or referring to
f.(*ā*)state, condition, posi tion,
steadiness, devotion, firmness,
attachment, application, skill in
2. mfn excelling, eminent,
niṣṭhāna n. sauce, condiment,
niṣṭhita mfn being in or on, fallen from the hand, grown forth, complete, perfect, consummate, attached or devoted to, conversant with, skilled in, firm, fixed, certain, ascertained,
niṣṭhura mfn hard, rough, harsh, severe,
nistīrṇa mfn crossed, passed over, spent, gone through, fulfilled, accomplished, escaped, rescued,
nistodana n. piercing, pricking, stinging,
nistoya mfn waterless, without water, grass, trees,
nis√tṝ P. –*tarati,* to come forth from, get out of, escape from, to pass over or through, pass or spend time, to overcome or master an enemy, to fulfil, accomplish, perform, to suffer for, expiate,
nistraṁśa mfn fearless,
nistrapa mfn shameless, 543/3
nistṛṣ mfn desireless, satisfied,
nistṛṣṇa mfn free from desire,
nis√tud P. –*tudati*, to pierce, prick, sting,
nistula mfn matchless, incomparable,
nistuṣa mfn freed from chaff, (fig.) purified, cleansed, simplified,
ni√śuc -*śocati* to be burning hot,
ni√sūd Cl10 –*sūdayati,* to destroy, put an end to,
niṣūdana 562/1 m.removing, destroying,
n. killing, slaughter,
L. m. finisher, one who makes an end of, destroyer,
nis√vā Cl 2 –*vāti,* to blow out, go out be extinguished, see *nir√vā*
niṣvabhāvatā (G) devoid of nature, devoid of existence, (Buddhist),
ni√svap to fall asleep, to meet death, die,
nisvara mfn soundless, noiseless,
ni√śvas P. –*śvasiti* to draw in the breath, inspire, to hiss, snort,
nis√vas Cl 1 –*vasati,* to stay/dwell abroad, caus. *nivārsayati* expels, 'causes to stay abroad', see *nir√vas*
niśvāsa m. a sigh,
nis√vṛt Cl 1 –*vartate,* to evolve, develop, turn out, roll out, be effected, accomplished, completed, caus. *nirvartayati* finishes, completes, see *nir√vṛt*
niṣyūta mfn sewn in, embroidered,
nīta mfn led, guided, brought, gained, obtained, well-behaved, correct, modest, entered, gone or come to,
n. wealth, corn, grain,
ni√tam caus. –*tamayati* to choke, suffocate,
nitamba m. the buttocks, the ridge or side or swell of a mountain, the sloping bank or shore of a river,
ni√tan P.A. –*tanoti,-tanute*, to pervade, penetrate, pierce, cause to go or grow downwards,
nitānta mfn extraordinary, excessive, considerable, important, (*am*) ind. very much, in a high degree,
ni√tap P. –*tapati* to emit heat downwards, to consume by fire,
nitara mfn deeply fixed, standing firm,
nitarām ind. downwards, in a low tone, completely, entirely, wholly, by all means, at all events, especially, in a high degree, always,

nītha m. leading or a leader, f. trick, art, stratagem, a musical air, song,
nīti 565/1 f. leading or bringing, guidance, management, conduct esp. right or wise or moral conduct or behaviour, prudence, righteousness, political wisdom or science, moral philosophy or precept, relation to, dependence on, presenting, offering, L. conduct esp, right conduct, the knowledge of all that governs virtuous, discreet and statesmanlike behaviour, political and social ethics, morality, 2. leading,
nīti m. moral (of a story), statesmanship
nītijña mfn a statesman or politician, knowing how to conduct oneself discreetly,
nitikta mfn excited, roused up,
nitikti ind. quickly, speedily
nītimat mfn of moral or prudent behaviour,
nītiśāstra n. doctrine or science of political and social ethics,
nītivartani f. the path of prudence or wisdom,
nītividyā f. knowledge of *nīti* or political and social ethics,
nitoda m. piercing, a hole, ,
ni√tud to pierce, penetrate,
nitośana mfn sprinkling, distributing, granter of (6th),
ni√tṛd to pierce, cleave, split,
ni√1.tuś
nitya 547/2 mfn innate, native, one's own, continual, perpetual, eternal, ifc. constantly dwelling or engaged in, intent upon, devoted or used to, ordinary, usual, fixed, necessary, obligatory, always,
m. the sea, ocean, f. a ploughshare, (*am*) ind. always, constantly, regularly, by all means,
nityabhāva m. eternity,
nityabuddhi mfn considering anything as constant or eternal,
nityācāra m. constant good conduct,
nityadāna n. daily alms-giving,
nityadhṛta mfn constantly maintained
nityagati mfn moving continually, m. wind or the god of wind,
nityahoma perpetual sacrifice,
nityajāta mfn always born, constantly born,
nityakāla m. uninterrupted time, (*am*), ind. always, at all times,
nityakarman n. a constant act or duty, any daily and necessary rite,
nityakṛtya n. a regular or necessary act or ceremony
nityamaya mfn formed or consisting of anything eternal,
nityamukta mfn emancipated for ever,
nityānanda m. eternal happiness,
nityanarta mfn constantly dancing
nityānitya 547/3 mfn eternal and perishable, permanent and temporary, who discriminates the eternal from the transient
nityānityavastuviveka discrimination between the Real and the unreal,
nityaparīkṣaṇa n. constant investigation or inspection,
nityapralaya m. the constant dissolution of living beings, dissolution of everyday events during sound sleep,
nityapramudita mfn always delighted or satisfied,
nityapuṣṭa mfn always well supplied,
nityasarga daily creation, awakening of the individual in the morning (U),
nityaśas ind. always, constantly, eternally,
nityaśaya mfn always sleeping, reclining,
nityasevaka mfn always serving others
nityasiddha mfn ever perfect (the soul), -Jain
nityasnāyin mfn constantly making sacred oblations, constantly bathing,
nityaśrī mfn of lasting beauty,
nityastha mfn always abiding in,
nityastotra mfn receiving perpetual praise,
nityaśuddha eternally pure,
nityasukha ever happy,
nityasvādhyāyin mfn always engaged in the study of the Veda
nityatā f. perpetuity, continuance, continual repetition of, permanence, necessity,
nityatṛpti f. ever content, ever satisfied,
nityatva having the nature of the eternal,

steadfastness, constancy,
nityavrata n. a perpetual observance (lasting for life),
nityayauvana mfn always young,
nityayuj mfn having the mind always fixed on one object,
nityayukta mfn always busy or intent on
nityopalabdhṛ (N) one eternally aware
ni√vac to speak, say
nivacana expression, proverbial expression
ni√vad A. *–vādayate* make resound, (drum)
nivaha mfn bringing, causing, m. multitude, heap, quantity,
nivāha m. leading down,
nivanā ind. downwards, downhill,
nivāpa m. seed, or a sown field, an offering
nivāpaka m. a sower, 559/1
nivāpin mfn throwing, scattering,
nivara m. covering, protection, a protector,
nīvara m. a trader, an inhabitant, a beggar, mud, n. water,
nīvāra m. wild rice,
nivāra m. keeping off, hindering, impediment, warding off,
nivāraka mfn keeping off, defending,
nīvārakaṇa m. wild rice grain,
nivaraṇa n. hindrance, trouble, disturbance,
nivāraṇa n. keeping back, preventing,
nivārita mfn kept off, hindered, forbidden,
nivarta mfn causing to turn back, *ni√vṛt*
nivartaka mf(*ikā*)n turning back, flying, causing to cease, abolishing, removing, desisting from, ceasing,
nivartana mfn causing to turn back, n. turning back, returning, retreating, fleeing, desisting from, a means of returning, averting or keeping back from, reforming, repenting, a measure of land,
nivartanti they return, they turn back 1/pl/pres/indic/act *ni√vṛt* 560/1
nivartate it turns away 1/s/pres/indic/mid he returns, turns back, is born again
nivarteta 'you (pl) would cease to be' 2/pl /opt/act *√vṛt* or 'it would cease to be' 1/s/opt/act/
nivartita mfn turned or brought back, averted, prevented, given up, abandoned, suppressed, removed,
nivartitum 560/1 to turn back, return from, return into life, be born again, infin. *ni-√vṛt*
ni√vas P. *–vasati* to sojourn, pass or spend time, dwell or live or be in, to keep one's ground, withstand, to inhabit, to incur or undergo, to cohabit, approach sexually, caus. *-vāṣayati* to cause to stay, receive as a guest, to populate, to choose as a dwelling place, inhabit, to put or place upon,
nivāśa mfn roaring, thundering,
nivāsa 559/1 m. clothing, dress, living, dwelling, residing, abode, house, habitation,
nivasana n. dwelling, habitation,
nivāsana n. living, residing, sojourn, abode
nivāsin mfn dwelling, living, being in, m. an inhabitant,
nivasatha m. a village,
nivasati lives
nivāsin mfn dressed in, living or being in, wearing, m. inhabitant
nivasita mfn dwelt, lived,
nivat f. depth, any deep place or valley,
nivāta 559/2 1. mfn sheltered from the wind, calm, n. a place sheltered from the wind, absence of wind, calm, stillness, 2. mfn unhurt, safe, secure, (n. security), dense, compact, m. asylum, refuge, an impenetrable coat of mail,
nivedaka mfn communicating, relating,
nivedana mfn announcing, proclaiming, n. making known, publishing, announcement, information,
nivedayati cl2 causes to know, informs,
nivedin mfn knowing, aware of, reporting, offering,
nivedita mfn made known, announced, told, presented, given,
niveśa m. entering, settling in a place, encamping, halting, a dwelling place, habitation of any kind, founding a household, matrimony,

founding a town, putting in order, arrangement,

niveśana mfn entering, bringing to rest, providing with a resting place, n. entering, entrance into (comp.), going or bringing to rest, founding a household, marrying, camp, house, home,

niveśaya cause to enter or approach, direct,
2 unhurt, uninjured, safe, secure graft (a branch or shoot,

√nīv 567/1 Cl 1 P *nīvati* to become fat, DP in *sthaulya* becoming fat

ni√1.vid Cl 2 *–vetti,* to tell, communicate, proclaim, report, relate, to offer, present, give, deliver, caus. *nivedayati,* causes to know, informs,

nivid f. instruction, information,

nīvi or *nīvī* f. a piece of cloth wrapped round the waist, a kind of skirt or petticoat, a hostage, capital, principal stock,

ni√viś A. *–viśate* to enter or penetrate into, to alight, descend, to come to rest, settle down or in a home, to encamp, to sit down upon, to resort to, to settle, take a wife, to be fixed or intent on, to sink down, sink, disappear, caus. *–veśayati* to bring to rest, to cause to enter, introduce, to build, erect, populate,

niviṣṭa mfn settled down, come to rest, drawn up, encamped (army), placed, located (guardians), entered, penetrated into,
lying in, resting in,
seated upon or in, situated (town), turned to, intent upon,
occupied, settled (country),

niviṣṭi f. coming to rest,

nivīta mfn hung or adorned with, having the Brahmanical thread round the neck, n. the thread worn round the neck,

ni√1.vṛ to ward off, restrain, to surround, to prohibit, hinder, stop, suppress, to put off, remove, banish from,

ni√vṛt A. Cl 1-*vartate,* to turn back, stop, to return from, to return into life, revive, be born again, to turn away, retreat, flee, abstain or desist from, get rid of, to fall back, rebound, cease, end, disappear, to be withheld from, not belong to, to be omitted, not to occur, to be ineffective or useless, to be wanting, not to exist, to pass over to, to lead or bring back, return, to keep back from, to give up, abandon, suppress, withhold, refuse, to annul, remove, destroy, to bring to an end, to procure, bestow,

nivṛta 560/1 mfn held back, withheld, surrounded, enclosed, a veil, mantle, wrapper,

nivṛti f. covering, enclosing,

nivṛtta 560/1 mfn turned back, returned, retreated, fled, set (the sun), averted from indifferent to, having renounced or given up, abstracted from this world, quiet, rid or deprived of, passed away, gone, ceased, disappeared, with *karman* n. (an action) causing a cessation (of mundane existence), omitted, left out, finished, completed, desisting from or repenting of any improper action, n. return, m. a virtuous man, one uninfluenced by worldly desires,

nīvṛti f. an inhabited country, a realm,

nivṛttātman m. one whose spirit is abstracted, a sage,

nivṛtti 694/1f. in-active life, inactivity,
560/2 returning, return, disappearance, leaving off, desisting from, ceasing, cessation, ceasing from worldly acts, abstaining from action, inactivity, rest, repose, attainment of rest, emancipation, liberation "renunciation", non-participation,
HH (*pravṛtti* = participation)

nivṛttimarga the path of renunciation or *Saṁnyāsa,*

nivṛttirūpa having the nature of renunciation and detachment,
nivyūḍha n. perseverance, resolution,
ni√yā P. *–yāti* to pass over (with a carriage), to come down to, to fall into, incur,
ni√yam P. *–yacchati* to stop, hold back, A. to stop, stay, remain, to keep back, refuse, to fail, be wanting, to fasten, tie to, to hold over, extend, to bring near, procure, bestow, grant, to hold in, keep down, restrain, govern, regulate (as breath, the voice, organs of sense), to suppress or conceal one's nature, to destroy, fix upon, settle, determine, establish, (in gram.) to lower, pronounce low, caus. *niyamayati* to restrian, check, curb, suppress, restrict,
niyama 552/1 restraining, checking, holding back, preventing, controlling, any fixed rule or law, necessity, certainty, obligation, a rule or precept, limitation, restriction, obligation, agreement, vow (also *niyāma*), the ten traditional Niyamas

1. are:*hṛ*: remorse, being modest and showing shame for misdeeds
2. *santoṣa* contentment; being satisfied with the resources at hand - therefore not desiring more
3. *dāna* giving, without thought of reward,
4. *astikya* faith, believing firmly in the teacher, the teachings and the path to enlightenment,
5. *īṣvarapūjana* worship of the Lord, the cultivation of devotion through daily worship and meditation, the return to the source;
6. *siddhānta śravaṇa* scriptural listening, studying the teachings and listening to the wise of one's lineage;
7. *mati* cognition, developing a spiritual will and intellect with the guru's guidance,
8. *vrata* sacred vows, fulfilling religious vows, rules and observances faithfully
9. *japa* recitation, chanting mantras daily
10. *tapas* the endurance of the opposites; hunger and thirst, heat and cold, standing and sitting etc.*ahiṁsa* 'harmlessness' is sometimes included , another version is- modesty, contentment, giving without thought of reward, faith, worship –devotion and meditation, scriptural study, developing spiritual will and intellect, fulfilling rules, vows and duties, chanting of mantras, endurance of adversity, self-surrender,

niyamadharma m. law prescribing restraints
niyāmaka mfn governing, subduing, limiting, contolling, restraining, defining, restrictive, m. sailor or boatman, charioteer, guide or ruler,
niyamalaṅghana n. transgression of a fixed rule or obligation
niyamana mfn subduing,n. act of subduing
nīyamāna m.n. pres.pass.part. √*nī* to lead, guide, conduct, govern, lead towards, to, or away
niyamānāsu 7/pl in leading towards or away
niyamaniṣṭhā f. rigid observance of prescribed rites,
niyamapara mfn observing fixed rules
niyamasthiti f. ascetism, self restraint
niyamavidhi a restrictive injunction,
niyamita 552/2 regulated, prescribed, bound by, destined to be, governed, guided
niyamya 552/2 ind. having restrained or checked, or bound
mfn. to be restrained, limited, restricted or defined
controlling, subduing

niyāna n. a way, access,
niyantā f. controller, arranger,
niyantṛ m. who or what holds in, restrains, governs, a restrainer, governor, horse-trainer,
niyantrana n. restraining, checking, restricting to a certain sense, defining, definition,
niyantrita mfn restrained, checked, dammed up, embanked, restricted to a certain sense (a word), governed by, depending on, 551/3
ni√yat A. *–yatate* to arrive at, come to
niyata 552/1 mfn held back or in, fastened, tied to, put together (hands), restrained, suppressed, restricted, connected with, dependent on (7th), disciplined, self-governed, temperate, constant, steady, quite concentrated upon or devoted to (7th), fixed, established, settled, sure, regular, invariable, positive, definite, ind. always, constantly, decidedly, surely, inevitably, n.pl. the organs of sense,
niyatakāla mfn limited in time, temporary
niyata-mānasa 552/1 of subdued mind or spirit, whose mind is subdued,
niyatātman mfn self-controlled,
niyatavibhaktika mfn standing always in the same grammatical case
niyatavrata mfn constant in the observance of vows, regular in observances, pious, religious,
niyatendriya mfn passions subdued or restrained
niyati f. the fixed order of things, necessity, destiny, fate, restraint, restriction, self-restraint,
niyava m. compact order, continuous series
niyayin mfn going over, passing over
niyoga 552/3 tying or fastening, use, employment, application, injunction, entrusting, order, command, commission, charge, appointed duty, necessity, obligation
niyogakārya what is to be done,
niyogin mfn appointed, employed, a functionary, official, minister,
niyogya m. lord, master,
niyojana. mfn enjoining, urging, n. the act of tying, fastening,
niyojayasi you cause to yoke, you urge, 2/s/pres/indic/caus/act *ni √yuj*
niyojita 552/3 mfn. put, placed, laid,connected with, attached to, appointed, directed,
niyojya mfn to be endowed or furnished with, to be enjoined, to be committed or entrusted, m. functionary, official, servant,
niyokṣyati will impel, enjoin, command 1/s/fut/act *ni √yuj*
niyoktṛ m. one who joins or fastens, a ruler, lord, master,
ni√2.yu to bind on, fasten, to bring near, procure, bestow,
ni√yudh A. *–yudhyate* to fight,
niyuddha n. fighting (esp. with fists), close or personal struggle,
ni√yuj Cl 7 *–yunakti,* to fasten on, enjoin something on somebody, set to a task, caus. set (a trap/snare),
niyukta, mfn bound on, chained, fettered, appointed, directed, ordered, (*am*) ind. by all means, necessarily
niyuktaka mfn appointed, elected,
niyukti f. injunction, order, command
niyut team of horses, pl. series of verses, words, a poem, mfn drawn by a team of horses, forming a series, flowing continuously,
niyuta mfn fixed, fastened, m.n. a very high number, generally a million,
no 571/1 ind. and not, not,
no ced and if not
nodana mfn driving away, removing, n. impelling, impulse,
nṛ 567/3 m. a man, hero, person, mankind, people, in gram. a masculine word nom. *nā*
√nī 568/3 Cl 9 p P *nṛnāti* to lead, see *nṛ,* DP in *naya* leading, going
nṛcakṣas mfn beholding or watching men (said of gods), leading or guiding men a *ṛṣi*

nṛloka the world of men

nṛmṇa n. manliness, courage, strength,

nṛṇām 567/3 a man, hero, person, mankind, people *nām* 6/pl/m of men

nṛpa m. protector of men, king

nṛpati m. lord of men, prince, king

nṛśaṁsa mfn man-cursing, malicious, mischievous, cruel, m. monster,

√*nṛt* 568/3 Cl 4 P *nṛtyati (te),* to dance, act on the stage, represent, dance about, DP in *gātra vikṣepa* dancing, moving about,
2. f. dancing, gesticulation,

nṛti 568/3 f. dancing, gesticulation, dance, grand or solemn appearance, show,

nṛtya n. dance,

nṛtyati dances,

nṛyajña m. hospitality, service or offering to humans, feeding of guests or the poor etc. one of the 5 daily sacrifices

√*ṅu* 379/3 Cl 1 A *ṅavate* to sound, DP in *śabda* sounding,

nu 567/1 1. at the beginning of a verse, ind. now, still, just, at once, so now, now then, indeed, surely,
often = *nu* +*u,*
nahi nu by no means,
nakir nu no-one, nothing at all, etc.
nū cit for ever, evermore, at once, forthwith, or nevermore,
katham nu how indeed,
sometimes lays stress on a previous word, also employed in questions partic. where there are two or more clauses when it may be repeated or one repetition replaced by *yadi, vā,*
a particle used to express reflection,
2. m. a weapon, time,

√*nu* 3. Cl 1 A. *navate* to go, caus. *nāvayati* to move from the place, remove,
4. Cl 2.6. P *nauti, nuvati, navate, navati*, to sound, shout, exult, praise, commend, 5. m. praise, eulogium,

√*nū* 567/1/2 Cl 2.6. = √*nu*
DP in *sthauti* (Cl 2) praising,
ind. = *nu*
2. a weapon,
3. Cl 1 A *navate* to go,
4. *nu* or *nū* Cl 2.6. P. *nauti, nuvati,* to sound, shout, praise, recommend,
5. praise, eulogium,
7. = *nau,* a ship,

√*nud* 567/2 Cl 6 P A *nudati (te),* to push , thrust, impel, move, remove, caus. *nodayati,* to push on, urge, incite, DP in *preraṇa* pushing, impelling,

nuda mfn (in cpds.) dispelling,
2. mfn pushing, impelling, driving,

nūnam ind. in all probability, assuredly, now, at present, just, immediately, for the future, now then, therefore, certainly, indeed,

nūpura 567/3 m. an anklet, an ornament for the toes, ankles or feet,

nuta mfn praised, commended,

nūtana mfn of now, recent, young, modern, fresh, new

nuti f. praise, laudation, worship, reverence,

nyac low,

nyācam ind. bending down,

nyag-rodha m. 'downwards-growing' banyan tree, *śamī* tree

nyagrodhapādapa a banyan tree

nyakkaraṇa 571/3 lowering, degrading, treating with contempt,

nyañc mfn directed downwards,

nyāsa m. giving up, renunciation *ni* √ *2. as* depositing, putting down or in,
L. m. a putting down, commitment,

nyāsī kṛ to make deposit, entrust

nyāya 572/2 m. that into which a thing goes back, an original type, standard, rule, norm, a general or universal rule, in the right manner, a logical or syllogistic argument or inference, likeness, analogy, justice, law, rule, judicial sentence

nyāyya mfn regular, normal, right, (*am*) ind. rightly, properly,

nyeti √4.*nī* to go into, enter, come or fall into, incur, to undergo the nature of i.e. be changed into,

nyuna mfn less, inferior, defective,

nyupta mfn thrown down, cast (dice), scattered, sown, offered,

odana m.n. grain boiled with milk, porridge, rice, 235/3

ogha m. a flood, stream,a heap or quantity, flock, multitude, abundance, uninterrupted tradition, instruction,

ojas mfn. odd (as opposed to even) n. bodily strength, vigour, energy, vitality, light, splendour, lustre,

ojodā mfn strength-giving,

oka n.m. a house, home, refuge, a bird,

√*okh* 235/1 Cl 1 P *okhati,* to be dry or arid, to be able, suffice, to adorn, to refuse, ward off, DP in *śoṣaṇa* being dry or having the sense of *alam* being sufficient, refusing,

√*olaṇḍ* 236/1 Cl 1.8.10 P *olaṇḍati* to throw out, eject, DP in *utkṣepaṇa* tossing or throwing up,

om 235/3 ind. a word of solemn affirmation and respectful assent, the *praṇava* sound, the object of profound religious meditation, the highest spiritual efficacy being attributed not only to the whole word but also to the three sounds *a, u, m* of which it consists.

oma m. a friend, helper, protector,

oman m.*(ā)* help, protection, kindness, a friend, helper, protector,

omanvat mfn helping, useful, favourable, propitious,

omātrā f. protection, favour, readiness to help,

oṁkāra 236/1 m. the sacred and mystical syllable om, the exclamation om, pronouncing the syllable om, a beginning, a prosperous or auspicious beginning to any activity,

oṁkṛta mfn accompanied by *om*

om tat sat a designation of Brahman, a benediction, a solemn invocation for divine blessing,

omyāvat mfn helping, useful, favourable,

√*oṇ* 235/2 Cl 1 P *oṇati,* to remove, take away, drag along, DP in *apanayana* removing, taking or dragging along,

opaśa m. top-knot, plume, cushion, pillow

oṣa 236/1 m. burning, combustion, mfn burning, shining,

oṣam ind. with ardour or vehemence, eagerly, quickly, while burning

oṣadhaya the herbs and plants

ośadhi(ī) f. a herb, plant, medicinal herb, an annual plant,

ośadhiyoga yoga of using herbal preparations to cure illness,

oṣṭha 236/1 the lip

*pa*1. drinking, 2. (in cpds.) keeper, keeping, 3. m. wind, a leaf = *pūta*

ota *mfn* woven, interwoven, addressed, invoked, summoned

√*pā* 1. class 1 P *pibati* drink, quaff, suck, sip, swallow, (metaphorically) to imbibe, draw in, appropriate, enjoy, feast upon (with eyes, ears, ...), to drink up, exhaust, absorb, to drink intoxicating liquors, DP in *pāna* drinking,
2. mfn drinking, quaffing,
3. Cl 2 P *pāti* to watch, keep, preserve, protect from, defend against, protect a country i.e. rule, govern, to observe, notice, attend to, follow, DP in *rakṣaṇa* protecting, mfn guarding, protecting, ruling, f. guarding, protecting,
4. mfn. keeping, protecting, guarding,

√*pac* or *pañc,* Cl 1 P A *pacati (te), pañcati (te),* to spread out, make clear or evident,

√*pac* 2. Cl 1 P A *pacati,* Cl 4 A *pacyate* to cook, bake, roast, boil, to cook anything out of..., to bake or burn (bricks), to digest, ripen, mature, bring to perfection or completion, cure, heal, DP in *pāk* cooking, boiling,

pac mfn cooking, baking,

pacana n. the act of cooking, baking (firing a pot),

pacati 575/1 cooks, bakes, roasts, boils,

ripen, mature

√*pad* 1. 582/3 *padati* to stand fast or fixed,
2. Cl 4 A *padayate (ti)* to fall, fall down or out, perish, to go, resort or apply to, participate in, keep, observe, caus. *pādayati (te)* to cause to fall, DP in *gati* going, moving,
3. m. a foot, also on foot, a step, a fourth part, a quarter,

pad m. foot,

pada 583/1 n. a word, an inflected word, the stem of a word in some cases, a foot, a foot as a measure, a step, a footstep, a footing, position, standpoint, rank, cause matter, business, abode, home, receptacle,

pāda 617/1 m. the foot, column, pillar, a wheel, a foot as a measure, the foot of a tree, foothill, a quarter, a ray, a fourth part of a quadruped, quarter of a verse, foot (of a heavenly body) i.e. a ray, beam,

pādamūla n. foot of a mountain, sole or heel,

padāni words

padanīya mfn to be investigated, steps to be followed,

pādapa m. plant esp. tree, 'drinking with its feet', a footstool or foot-cushion

padapātha words without sandhi

pādarajas n. foot-dust, dust of the feet,

padārtha 583/3 the meaning of a word, that which corresponds to the meaning of a word, a thing, object, man, person, a category, objects of experience, substance, topic,

padārthābhāvanī the sixth stage of realisation, "the constituent elements of the creation begin to lose their lustre for the aspirant" " the glory of the form, the pleasures of the senses, the beauty, the rhetoric and everything to lure the mind, does not lure anymore." HH "Every *padārtha* is said to have existence and therefore to have some essence. So the word indicates its negation, not its existential negation but only the negation of its essential attraction." HH

pādaśas 617/3 ind. foot by foot, quarter by quarter,

pādasevana 617/3 n. 'foot-salutation', service, duty

padāti m. foot-soldier, pedestrian, peon,

padavī f. track, path, way, to go the way of..., tread the footsteps of.. station, situation, place, m. a leader, guide, forerunner, n. footsteps, track,

pādavikṣepa moving about, walking, dancing, horse's paces, pace,

paddhati f. path, row, footpath, track, a class of expositional writing, method, system,

pade pade 583/1 at every step, everywhere, whatever happens,

pādika mfn amounting to or lasting one fourth (of a time), goin on foot, one *pada* long, f. a sandal, shoe,

padma m. n. a lotus, a goddess,

padmagarbha mfn containing lotuses, Lotus-filled, name of a lake,

padmarāga mfn having the colour of a lotus, m. ruby,

padmāsana 'lotus posture'

pādodara a snake

pādukā f. shoe, slipper, sandals, the sandals of the guru,

padya n. a verse, water offered to wash the feet with,

padyartha for the purpose of a word, action or step

√*pai* 649/1 Cl 1 P *pāyati* to dry, wither, DP in *śoṣaṇa* drying, withering,

√*paiṇ* 649/2 Cl 1 P *paiṇati* to go, to send, DP in *gati* going, *preraṇa* approaching, *śleṣaṇa* sending, embracing,

paiśāca mfn relating or belonging to the *piśāca* (goblins or demons),

paiśunya 649/3 tale bearing, backbiting, slander, malignity, wickedness

pāka 613/3 m cooking, baking, roasting,

boiling, a capable or competent person, an adept in, master of, anyone worthy of or fit for or abounding in, propriety, fitness, an order, command, a measure of capacity (m or n), maturity, full development, completion, perfection, greyness (hair), old age, development of consequences, result, any act having consequences, the domestic fire, a cooking utensil, a king's counsellor or minister, L. mfn young, (a calf) 2. simple, ignorant, honest,

pākadūrva f. young millet-grass,

√*pakṣ* 573/2 Cl 1 .10. P *pakṣati, pakṣayati* to take, seize, to take a part or side, DP in *parigraha* taking, accepting, receiving,

pakṣa m. 1. wing, 2. side, (of a door, or of the hair of the head), 3. faction e.g. *aripakṣaḥ* enemy faction, 4. half esp. half of a lunar month,

pakṣabala n. strength of wing,

pakṣapāta m. partiality, a partisan, adherent, the moulting of birds,

pakṣapātin mfn prejudiced, favouring, siding with, flying,

pakṣimṛgatā f. condition of bird or beast,

pakṣin mfn winged, m. bird,

pakṣiśāvaka m. young of a bird, young bird,

pakṣman n. eyelash, the hair of a deer, filament of a flower, a thin thread, a petal, a wing, a whisker,

paktvā ind. having cooked,

pakva mfn cooked, roasted, baked, burnt, prpared on a fire, warmed, mature, digested, ripe, near to death, fully developed, perfect, perishing, decrepit,

pākya ind. in simplicity, in ignorance,

pākya 614/1 mfn fit to cook edible, obtained by cooking or evaporation, ripening, n. a kind of salt, saltpetre,

√*pal* 609/3 *palati* to go, DP in *gati,* going,

√*pāl* 622/3 Cl 10 P *pālayati (te)* to watch, guard, protect, defend, rule, govern, to keep, maintain, observe (a promise or vow), DP in *rakṣaṇa* protecting,

pāla m. protector, herdsman,

pālana 623/1 mfn guarding, nourishing, defending, maintaining, keeping, serving, n. the act of guarding etc. milk of a cow recently calved,

palāy 610/1 to flee, run away, escape, *palāyante* 1/pl/pres/indic/mid they run away, *palāyate* he flees

palāyana n. flight (escape),

palāyya ind. having departed, having run away

palita mfn gray, hoary, old, aged,

pālita mfn protected, cherished, gurded, nourished,

pallava m. shoot, twig,

pallavāda m. twig-eater, deer,

pallī f. hut, below, small village,

√*palpūlaya* 610/2 Nom P *palpūlayati* to wash with alkaline water, DP in *lavaṇa* salty, *pavana* purifying,

palvala n. a pond, puddle, pool,

√*pampasya* 585/3 Nom P *pampasyati* to feel pain, DP in *duḥkha* uncomfortable, unpleasant, difficult, pain, sorrow,

√*paṁs* or *paṁś* 573/2 Cl 1 .10. P *paṁśati* or *paṁsati, paṁśayati* or *paṁsayati* to destroy, DP in *nāśana* destroying,

pāṁsu m.pl. dust, sand, crumbling soil, dung, manure, pollen,

√*paṇ* 580/1 Cl 1 A *paṇate* to honour, praise, to barter, purchase, buy, negotiate, bargain, bet, stake, lay a wager, play for, win anything, DP in *vyavahāra* transacting business, buying or *stuti* praising

pan 1. 584/1 = 3. *pad* in comp. before nasals

pan 2. 585/2 Cl 1 A *panate* to be worthy of admiration or to admire, caus. *panyate, panayati (te),* to regard with surprise or wonder, to admire, praise, acknowledge, A. to rejoice at, be glad of, DP in *stuti* praising, *paṇa* m. 1. bargain, stipulation, 2. wage, gauge, prize, 3. a certain coin, 3. play, gaming, playing for a stake, a bet or wager,

pāna 613/1 1. n. drinking (esp. spirits), kissing, a drink, drinking-vessel, a canal, 2.observing, keeping, protecting, guarding,

pāṇa = *pāṇi* 615/2 m. the hand, a stake at play, trade, traffic,

paṇava m.a cymbal or drum

paṇāyitṛ m. seller, hawker,

√*pañc* see 1.√*pac* DP in *vyaktīkaraṇa* (Cl 1) making manifest or clear or distinct, in *vistāra-vacana* explaining fully, amplifying, (Cl 10)

pañca 1. spread out, a measure in music, five, in comp for *pañcan* (five),

pañcadhā ind. five-fold, in five parts, in five forms,

pañcāgnividyā f. doctrine of the 5 fires, (five processes of sacrifice),

pañcakośa five sheaths of ignorance,

pañcākṣara mfn having five syllables,

pañcakṛtva five times,

pañcama fifth,

pañcan five,

pañcapada having (taken) five steps,

pañcaśīla the five virtues to be maintained by a lay Buddhist not injuring, not stealing, restraint from sexual misconduct, restraint from harmful speech, not becoming intoxicated,

pañcaśīrṣa mfn five-headed,

pañcatantra n. name of a collection of fables,

pañcatapas mfn having five fires, name of an ascetic,

pañcatva n. fiveness, dissolution of the body into the five elements i.e. death, with *gam* – die,

pañcayāma mfn having five courses,

pañcamahāyajña five great sacrifices to the
deva – the divine
ṛṣi s – the sages
pitṛ s – the fathers or ancestors
manuṣya s – men
bhūta s – lower beings

pañcāyata a village council of five members

pañcikaraṇa n. causing anything to contain the five elements, making into 5, the interpenetration of the five causal elements,

pañcīkṛta mfn made into five, quintuplicated,

√*paṇḍ* 580/2 Cl 1 A *paṇḍate* to go, move, Cl 10 P *paṇḍayati* to heap together, pile up, Cl 1 or 10 P *paṇḍati, paṇḍayati* to destroy, annihilate, DP in *gati* (Cl 1) going, in *nāśana* (Cl 10) destroying,

pāṇḍava adj. pertaining to the Sons of *Pāṇḍu,* a son of...

pāṇḍava -anīkam army of the Sons of *Pāṇḍu* TP cpd. , 2/s/m or n

pāṇḍavāḥ 1/pl/m the sons of *Pāṇḍu*

pāṇḍavaḥ 1/s/m son of *Pāṇḍu* (*Arjuna*)

paṇḍita 580/3 mfn. learned, wise, most learned, m. a scholar,

paṇḍitasabhā f. assembly of *pandits*,

paṇḍitatam mfn most learned, m. most learned one, (*ā*) f. cleverness, knowledge, learning, skill, wisdom

pāṇḍitya 616/1 scholarship, erudition, learning, cleverness, skill

pāṇḍu mfn whitish, pale, m. name of a prince of the Lunar Race,

pāṇḍura mfn white, pale,

pāṇḍuravāsin mfn wearing a white (garment),

pāṇḍunandana m. son of *pāṇḍu*

pāṇḍuvarṇa mfn pale-coloured,

pāṇḍvāvika n. a sheepswool shawl,

paṅga mfn lame,

paṇi m. 1.a bargainer, who gives naught without return, haggler, 2. niggard, esp. one who is stingy towards the gods, an impious person, 3. a malicious demon,

pāṇi 615/2 m. the hand, market, shop,

pāṇigrāha m. hand-grasper, husband, hand-taking, marriage,

paṇitṛ m. a trader,

pānīya gve. to be drunk, for drinking,

drinkable, n. drink, water,
pānīyavarṣa m. rainwater, downpour of water,
pañjara m. cage, body, skeleton, ribs,
pañka n. mud, mire,
pañkaja mfn 'born in mud', n. a lotus,
pañkila mfn muddy, miry,
pāñkta mfn consisting of five parts, fivefold,
paṅkti f. set or series or row of five, row in general, queue, line,
paṅktikrama m. order of a row, order, succession, *eṇa* in a row,
pannaga m. a serpent or serpent demon, snake, mfn snaky,
√*panth* 585/3 Cl 1 .10. P *panthati* or *panthayati* to go, move, DP in *gati* going,
pāntha m. wayfarer, visitor, wanderer,
panthā f. see *panthan*,
panthan m. road, path, way,
paṇya gve. to be bargained for or bartered,
pāṇya mfn praiseworthy, excellent, belonging to the hand,
pāpa 618/2 mfn wicked, evil, bad , sin, essence of bad action , m. bad fellow, n. trouble, harm, evil (deed),
pāpā wicked woman
pāpakarman mfn 'wrong-doing', wicked, sinful, m. an ill-doer, criminal, sinner, villain, n. a wicked deed,
pāpapuruṣa m. evil personified,
pāpaśīla mfn having evil as one's nature,
pāpīya (s) mfn worse, worse off, lower, poorer, more or most wicked or miserable, *-tva* n. wickedness, depravity,
pāpman 619/1 m. evil, unhappiness mfn hurtful, injurious, evil,
pāpmāna pres.part.being a devil, being evil
paprachha he/she asked 1/s/perf √*prach*
para 1. 586/1 mf(*ā*)n. far, distant, remote (in space), opposite, ulterior, beyond, after, highest, supreme, far, remote, more than, other than, another, superior, supreme, later, subsequent, beyond, on the farther or other side of, previous (in time), former, ancient, past, later, future, next, following, succeeding, subsequent, final, last, exceeding (in number or degree), better or worse than, other than, different from, m. another (different from oneself), a foreigner, enemy, a following letter or sound e.g. *ta para* –the next sound will be *t*,
m. or n. the Supreme or Absolute Being, the Universal Soul, m. another (different from one's self), a following letter or sound (ifc.),
f. (*ā*) a foreign country, abroad, name of a sound in the first of its 4 stages, 'pure consciousness and knowledge in substance' HH ;
a partic. measure of time, having as the chief object, given up to, pre-occupied with, engrossed in, intent upon, resting on, consisting of, serving for, synonymous with etc., the wider meaning of a word, existence (regarded as the common property of all things),
(*am*) ind. afterwards, later, beyond, after e.g.
paramvijñānāt beyond human knowledge,
ataḥ param after this, farther on, hereafter,
itaḥ param henceforward, from now,
tataḥ param after that, thereupon,
nāsmāt param no more of this, enough,
n. highest point or degree, final beatitude, chief matter or paramount object, engrossed in, intent upon,
in a high degree, excessively greatly, completely, rather, most willingly, by all means, I will, so be it, no more than, nothing but, however, otherwise (*param tu* or *param kim tu),*
na param –api not only –but also
na param –yāvat not only – but even
parena ind. farther, beyond, past, thereupon, afterwards, later than,

pāra n. the further bank or bound,
parā 1. f. of *para* in comp.
2. ind. prefix to nouns and verbs, away, off, alongside, on,
parabhāga m. superior power or merit,
parabhakti supreme devotion,
parabhāva 1. mfn loving another,
2.m. being the subsequent or second member in a compound,
parābhava m. vanishing, disappearance, dissolution, separation, ruin
parābhāva m. defeat, overthrow,
parābhāvana n. suppression,
parābhāvuka mfn about to decline, going to pass away,
parābhṛta mfn borne or taken off, put aside, hidden, concealed,
parā√bhū to perish, disappear, be lost, succumb, yield, to overcome,
parabhūta mfn following or subsequent (said of words),
parābhūta mfn vanished, perished, forlorn
parābhūti f. defeat, humiliation, injury
parabrahman 587/1 n. the supreme spirit or *Brahman,* " a synonym for *nirguṇa Brahman*" HH
parāc mfn averted, turned away from,
parācais ind. away, aside, off,
parā√car to go away, depart,
parācīna turned away or downwards, or opposite, averted, being opposite or beyond or outside of, averse from, indifferent to, unfit, improper, (*am*) ind. away from, beyond, more than, after, before the time,
paracintā f. thinking of/caring for another,
paracittajñāna n. knowing the thoughts of another
parā√1.dā to give up or over, deliver, throw away, give in exchange for, barter against, to exclude from,
parādadi mfn giving up, delivering over
parādāna n. the act of giving up,
paradāra another's wife/wives, adultery,
paradevatā f. the highest deity,
paradhana n. another's wealth
paradharma 586/3 the duties of another or of another caste
parā√1.dhāv P. *–dhāvati* to run away
parādhīna mfn ifc. entirely engaged in, intent upon or devoted to,
parā√dhmā to blow away, 590/2
paradhyāna n. intent meditation,
paradravya n. another's property
paradroha m. injuring another,
parā√dru P. *–dravati* to run away, flee
para-adu(ū) rejects (slights)
parāg in comp. for *parāñc*
parā√1.gā to go away, fly, escape,
parāga m. pollen, dust, fragrant powder used after bathing, sandal, fame, celebrity, independence
parā√gam to go away, depart, die,
parāgama m. arrival, approach or invasion of an enemy, 587/2
paragata mfn being with/relating to another,
parāgata mfn gone, deceased, one who has reached the opposite shore of, passed over in safety, pure, holy, m. arhat or deified saint or teacher (Jain), ppp. returned,
pāragati f. studying, going through, reading
parāgdṛś mfn having the eye turned toward the outer world,
parāghātana n. place of execution, slaughter-house,
paraglāni f. the subjugation of a foe,
paragranthi m. an articulation, joint,
paraguṇa the virtues of another (ibc.), mfn beneficial to another or to a foe,
parāha m. the next day,
parā√han P. *–hanti* to strike down or away, to touch, feel, grope, mfn turned over, tilled (the earth)
parāhati f. contradiction,
parahita mfn friendly, benevolent,
parāhṇa m. the afternoon,
parāhṛta mfn carried off, removed,
parā√i Cl 2 *–eti,* to go off, go away,
parajana m. another person, a stranger,
parajanman n. a future birth,
parajāta m. a stranger or servant, 'born of another',
parājaya m. loss, defeat, conquest, desertion,
parā√ji A. *–jayate* to be deprived of, suffer

the loss of, be conquered, succumb, to submit to, be overcome by, 589/3
parājihīte gives way, lets slip, abandons,
parājiṣṇu mfn conquered, succumbing
parājita mfn conquered, defeated, overthrown, condemned by law,
parājitya ind. having overcome
parajñānamaya mfn consisting in knowledge of the Supreme Being,
parāk in comp. for *parāñc, -tva* n. not turning back, non-recurrence
parāke at a distance
parākāt from a distance
parākdṛṣṭi seeing outwards,
parakāla mfn relating to a later time,
parakaragata mfn being in another's hands
parākaraṇa n. setting aside, disdaining,
parakarman n. service for another,
parakārya n. another's business or affair,
parākāśa distant view, remote expectation,
parakathā f.pl. talk about another,
parakāyapraveśana n. entering another's body
parakīya mfn belonging to another, strange, hostile, dependent on others,
parā√kṛ P. *–karoti* to set aside, reject, disregard,
parā√kram P.A. *–kramati (te),* to march forward, advance, to show courage or zeal, excel, distinguish oneself,
parākrama m. bold advance, attack, valour, courage, strength, energy, power, going out or away, 589/3
parākrānta mfn advanced, strong, bold, energetic, eagerly intent upon, n. displaying power or energy,
parākṛṣṭa mfn disparaged, reviled,
parākṛta mfn set aside, rejected, disdained,
parakṛti f. the action or history of another, an example or precedent,
parakṣetra n. another's field or wife, the body in another life,
parākṣipta mfn upset, wrested away,
paraloka m. the other or future world,
param 586/2 ind. afterwards, later, beyond, after (with 5th), L. beyond
parama 588/1 mfn (superl. of *para)* most distant, remotest, extreme, last, chief, highest, primary, most prominent, best, most excellent, worst, n. highest point, extreme limit, chief part or matter or object, (ifc. f. (*ā*) consisting chiefly of, completely occupied with , devoted to, intent upon, (*am*) ind. yes, very well,
paramā 588/1 f. consisting chiefly of, completely occupied with or devoted to or intent upon,
paramabhāsvara mfn excessively radiant,
paramabrahman n. the Supreme Spirit,
paramacetas n. all the heart,
paramadāruṇa mfn very dreadful,
paramadhāma n. supreme abode, Brahman, *mokṣa,*
paramadharmātman mfn very dutiful or virtuous
paramaduḥkhita mfn deeply afflicted,
paramādvaita m. the highest being without a second, n. pure, non-duality,
paramadurmedhas mfn exceedingly stupid
paramagahana mfn very mysterious or profound
paramagati f. any chief resource or refuge (as a god or protector),
paramaguru the guru of one's guru,
paramahaṁsa m. an ascetic of the highest order, ..who has subdued all his senses by abstract meditation,
(N) 'best of the *haṁsa* birds' 'an honorific for those who spend a life of wandering with the mind exclusively devoted to Brahman - a metaphor for those who have no attachments', applies mainly to followers of Vedāntic thought, the bird (of the goose family), moves with the changes of the seasons to find dwellings appropriate to itself,
paramāha m. an excellent day,
paramaiśvarya 588/3 n supremacy
paramajyā holding supreme power (Indra)
paramaka mf (*ikā*)n the most excellent, highest, best, greatest, extreme,
paramakāṇḍa m.n. very auspicious moment,

paramakaraṇa the supreme cause,
paramākhya mfn called supreme, considered as the highest,
paramakruddha mfn extremely angry.
paramākṣara the sacred syllable Om or Brahmā
paramamahat mfn infinitely great
paramamokṣa m. final emancipation,
paramānanda m. supreme felicity, the Supreme Spirit, soul of the universe
paramānandaprāpti attainment of supreme bliss,
paramāṅganā f. an excellent or beautiful woman
paramaṇi m. excellent jewel
paramānu m. an infinitesimal particle or atom, *-tā* infinite minuteness, the state of an atom,
paramāpad f. the greatest misfortune,
paramapada n. the highest state or position, eminence, final beatitude,
paramaparama mfn highest or most excellent of all
paramaprīta mfn exceedingly rejoiced,
paramapuṁs the Supreme Spirit,
paramapuruṣa m. the Supreme Spirit,
paramarāja m. a supreme monarch,
paramardhhika m. excessively fortunate
parāmarśa m. seizing, pulling, bending (a bow), violation, remembrance, recollection, reflection, consideration, judgment, (in logic) inference, conclusion,
paramarṣi m. a great or divine sage
parāmarśin 590/3 calling or bringing to mind, referring to (memories, opinions)
paramārtha 588/3 m. the highest or whole truth, spiritual knowledge, the best sense, the best kind of wealth, °*ena, āt,* ibc. in reality, *-tas* ind. in reality, really, in the true sense of the word,
paramārthadarśin (N) name for the Buddha,
paramārthadṛṣṭi right vision, intuition,
paramārthata 588/3 the highest or whole truth, spiritual knowledge, any excellent or important object, the best sense, the best kind of wealth, reality, transcendence, consciousness, abstract noun transcendence, (ibc. °*ena, āt,* in reality), *-tas* ind. in reality, really, in the true sense of the word, *-tā* f. the highest truth, reality,
paramārthasattva (N) the existence in the highest truth
paramārthatasatya n. the real or entire truth
paramārthatavid m. one who knows the highest truth, a philosopher,
pāramārthika in an absolute sense as opposed to a relative sense,
pāramārthika jīva 'the real *jīva'* – not different from the *brahman.*
pāramārthika-satta the absolute reality, transcendental truth, *param brahman,*
pāramārthika-satya (N) the highest truth,
paramārya m. a Bodhisattva
paramasammata mfn highly esteemed, much revered
paramasaṁtuṣṭa mfn highly pleased or satisfied,
paramasamudaya mfn very auspicious or successful
paramasarvatra ind. everywhere,throughout
paramaśobhana mfn exceedingly beautiful or brilliant,
paramata n. a different opinion or doctrine
paramatā f. highest position or rank, highest end or aim,
paramatas ind. in the highest degree, excessively, worst of all,
paramatattva n. the highest truth,
paramātma 1. m. a partic. personification, 2. in comp. = °*tman*
588/2 mf(*ī*)n being entirely the soul of the universe, the Supreme Self
paramātmaka mf*(ikā)*n the highest, greatest
paramātman 588/2 m. all the heart, the Supreme Spirit, the Supreme Self, the Absolute,
paramattha (N) early Buddhist term – ultimate truth, highest truth,

paramāvadhi m. utmost term or limit,
paramavaśyatā supreme control over the mind and senses
paramavismita mfn greatly surprised
paramāyus mfn reaching a great age,
parambrahma(n) 88/2 the Supreme Spirit
parame 588/3 7th case of *parama* in comp.
parameśa m. the Supreme Lord, Supreme Being,
parameṣṭha mfn standing at the top, supreme, superior,
parameṣṭhin mfn standing in the highest place, supreme, principal,
parameśvara 588/3 the Supreme Lord, Supreme Being, God,
pārameśvara mfn relating or belonging to or coming from the supreme god *(śiva)* 620/2
pāramitā the perfection or culmination of certain virtues (Buddhism), these virtues are cultivated as a way of purification... (K) the virtues are *dāna* charity and love, *śīla* good behaviour, *kṣānti* patience, *vīrya* zeal, *dhyāna* meditation, *prajñā* wisdom,
paraṁjyoti supreme light, Brahman,
parampara mfn one following the other, proceeding from one to another, successive, repeated, *(am)* ind. successively, uninterruptedly, *-tas* ind. successively, continually, mutually,
paramparā succession, one to another, order, succession, continuation, mediation, tradition,
paramparita mfn forming an uninterrupted series, continuous,
parā√mriś P. *–mṛśati* to seize or lay hold of, touch, feel, stroke, handle, to handle roughly, violate (woman or temple), to point or refer to, to consider, deliberate,
parāmṛta 'the best nectar' rain, 2. mfn one who is beyond, no longer subject to death, ,
paraṁtapa mfn scorcher of the foe
paramukta supreme liberation, beyond *jivanmukta*
parāṅ in comp. for *parāñc*
paraṇa mfn crossing, n. reading
parānasā f. administering remedies, medical treatment,
parāṅāvṛtta mfn turned away, flying,
parāñc 589/3 mfn directed or going away or towards some place beyond, turned away, averted, distant, turning from, being beyond or outside of (5th), not returning, done away with, gone, departed, having anyone behind, standing or going behind one another, following (5th), directed outwards or towards the outer world (as the senses), n. the body, ind. away, off, outwards, towards the outer world,
parāñca mfn turned away, averted,
parāṅgava m. the ocean, 589/3
parā√nī to lead away or back,
paranirvāṇa n. the highest *nirvāṇa*
parāṅmanas mfn having the mind or thoughts directed backwards,
parāṅmukha face turned away or averted, flying from, averse from, hostile to, regardless of, shunning, avoiding, unfavourable, unkind, m. a spell, n. turning away, aversion,
parānta m. death, 'the last end', living at the remotest distance,
parāntaka m. a frontier,
parāntakāle 'at the time of final death' i.e. at the end of one's worldly state the supreme moment of departure,
parantu ind. but,
parā√nud to push or drive away, banish
parapada n. the highest position, final emancipation
parapakṣa m. party of the foe, enemy,
parāpara mfn remote and near, before and after, cause and effect, earlier and later, higher and lower, better and worse,
paraparibhāva m. humiliation or injury suffered from others,
paraparīṇa mfn hereditary, traditional,
parā√pat to fly away or past, escape,

depart, to fall out, fail, be missing,
parā√paś to look far off or to a distance, to see or perceive at a distance,
parāpātin mfn flying off, getting loose,
parapatṇī f. wife of another or a stranger,
parāpātuka mfn miscarrying, abortive,
parāpavana n. cleansing away, removing by purification,
parapraiśya service to/for another
parāprakṛti the higher cosmic energy through which the supreme Brahman appears as individual souls, (U)
parapreṣyatva n. service of another, slavery
parā√pū P. *–punati* to purify, cleanse away,
parārdhaka m.n. one half of anything,
parāri ind. in the year before last,
parārtha m. the highest advantage or interest, an important object, sexual intercourse, another's advantage or interest, mfn having another object, designed for another, dependent on something else,
parārtham ind. for the sake of others,
parāruka m. a stone or rock,
pararūpa n. the following sound
paras ind. beyond, further, off, away, in future, afterwards, on the other side of, beyond, higher or more than, without, exclusive of, except,
pārasa m. Persian
parā śabda the first unmanifest level of sound,
parasambandha m. relation or connection with another,
parasaṁjñāka m. called supreme, the soul,
parāsaṁvit supreme knowledge, supreme consciousness, (U)
parāsaṅga m. cleaving or adhering to,
parāsarati comes near, approaches,
pārāśarin m. mendicant of the *pārāśarya* order,
parāśas f. calumny, curse,
parasavarṇa mfn homogenous with a following letter,
parāsedha m. arrest, imprisonment,
parasmaibhāṣa mfn see *parasmaipada*
parasmaipada n. 'word for another'the transitive or active verb and its terminations,
parasmaipada 'word for another' the active form of verbal words
paraspa mfn protecting, n. =*-tva*
paraspā m. a protector, protecting,
paraspara mfn mutual, each other's, pl. like one another, (*-am, eṇa, āt, asya,)* ind. one another, each other, with or from one another, one another's, mutually, reciprocally,
parasparādhyāsa mutual superimposition, the body is considered as the Self and the Self is considered as the body (U)
parasparādin ind. devouring one another,
parasparahata killed by one another,
parasparahita n. one another's happiness
parasparajña m. knowing one another,
*parasparākrandin c*alling to one another,
parasparam ind. one another, mutually, mfn mutual, each other's, pl. like one another,
parasparanumati f. mutual concurrence,
parasparaprīti f. mutual delight/content
parasparasakhya n. mutual friendship,
parasparasamāgama m. meeting one another,
parasparāśraya m. mutual dependence mfn mutual, reciprocal,
parasparasthita mfn standing opposite one another
parasparasukhaiṣin wishing one another happiness
parasparaviruddha opposed to one another
parasparavivāda quarreling with one another
parasparavyāvṛtti f. mutual exclusion
parasparopakra m. mutual assistance, alliance,°*rin* m. an ally or associate
parā√sṛj P. *sṛjati* to give away, bestow,
parāśrita mfn a dependent, servant, slave,
parastaram or *–tāram* ind. further away, further,
parastāt 589/1 ind. beyond, further away or further on, towards, beyond, above, from afar off, from before or behind, afterwards, later, at the end,

parā√sthambh P.*-stabhnāti* to hold back, hinder
parasthāna n. another place, strange place,
parā√sū P. *–suvati* to frighten away,
parāsu one whose vital spirit is departed or departing, dying or dead,
paraśu m. a hatchet, axe, a woodcutter's axe, a thunderbolt, *-mat* mfn having an axe,
paraśvadha m. a hatchet, axe
paraśvadhāyudha mfn armed with an axe
parā√śvas to confide in,
paraśvas ind. the day after tomorrow,
parasvat m. the wild ass,
parasya of another
paratā f. highest degree, absoluteness, being devoted to or intent upon,
paratama superlative form
paratantra mfn dependent or subject to another, obedient, n. and *–tā* f. dependence on another's will, a rule or formula for another rite, 'dependent or relative nature' dependent reality,
paratantrābhisaṁvṛti (N) covering dependent on another (regarding relative knowledge), said to be the principle which establishes things in the phenomenal world, one of the 2 kinds of covering unreal from the standpoint of the highest truth,
paratantrasattabhava possibility of dependent existence, (U)
paratara higher, superior, (comparative)
parātaram ind. further away,
paratarkaka m. a beggar
paratas ind. farther, far off, afterwards, behind, *itas-paratas* here-there, high above in rank, after (in time), beyond, above (in rank), otherwise, differently,
paratastva n. being from elsewhere or without,
parātman m. the Supreme Spirit, mfn one who considers the body as the soul,
parātpara mfn superior to the best,
paratra ind. elsewhere, in another place, in a future state or world, hereafter
parātta mfn given up,
paratva n. distance, remoteness, difference, consequence, strangeness,
parā√2.vā to blow away, remove by blowing
parā√vac P. *–vakti* to contradict,
paravāda m. the talk of others, popular rumour or report, slander
paravairāgya highest type of detachment, the mind turns away from and cannot be brought back to worldly objects, (U)
parāvāka m. contradiction,
paravāṇi m. a judge, a year, name of a peacock,
parāvara mfn distant and near, earlier and later, prior and subsequent, highest and lowest, all-including, traditional, each successive, knowledge handed down from the higher (*para*) to the lower (*avara*), m.pl. ancestors and descendants, n. the distant and near, cause and effect, motive and consequence, the whole extent of an idea, totality, the universe,
paravaśa mfn obedient, subdued or ruled by, subject to another's will, subservient,
paravastu supreme substance, Brahman, (U)
parāvat mfn offering beatitude, f. distance
pārāvata mfn coming from a dstance, distant, foreign, remote, m. pigeon, kind of snake, turtle-dove, monkey,
parā vidyā the higher knowledge, direct knowledge of Brahman,
parā√vṛt A. *–vartate* to turn back or round, return, desist from, caus. *–vartayati* cause to return,
parā√yā to go away,
parāyaṇa 1. 587/3 n. final end or aim, last resort or refuge, principal object f. *(ā)* making anything one's chief object or final aim, wholly devoted or destined to, intent upon, wholly, mfn violent, strong (as pain), principal, being the chief object or

final aim, devoted to, universal medicine –panacea,
2. going away, final end, departure, last resort, 'the resort of all lives' (Gam.),

pārāyaṇa 619/3 n. going over, reading through, perusing, studying, (esp.) reading a Purāṇa or causing it to be read, the part of the Vedā that deals with the understanding of the world and its process of manifestation.

√*parb* 606/3 Cl 1 P *parbati* to go, move, DP in *gati* going

√*pard* 606/3 Cl 1 A to break wind downwards, DP in *kutsitaśabda* breaking wind

paredvayi ind. tomorrow,

paredyus ind. tomorrow,

pareṇa ind. (with 2nd) farther, beyond, after, past, thereupon, afterwards, later, than,

pareprāṇa mfn more precious than life

pareśa m. the highest lord

pareṣṭi m. having the highest worship,

pareta mfn departed, deceased, dead, m. a ghost, spirit,

paretabhūmi f. place of the dead, cemetery,

paretakalpa mfn almost dead,

paretara mfn not hostile, faithful, friendly

pareti f. departure,

pareyivas mfn one who has departed or died,

pari 591/2 ind. prefix round, around, about, round about, fully, abundantly (also *parī* to express fullness or high degree), richly,
as a preposition (with 2nd) –about (in space and time), against, opposite to, towards, to, in the direction of, ibc. beyond, more than, to the share of, successively, severally,
(with 5th) from, away from, out of, outside of, except,
ibc. or or at the end of ind. –after the lapse of, in consequence or on account of or for the sake of, in accordance with law or right,

parī 1. in comp. for *pari*
2. (*pari*√*i*) P. *pary-eti* to go about, move in a circle, go or flow around, circumambulate, surround, include, grasp, span, run against or into, reach, attain, perceive, ponder,

pari-ava-√*sthā* Cl 1 *-tiṣṭhati,* to stand or be firm, become steady,

paribaddha mfn bound, stopped, obstructed

paribandhana n. tying round,

paribarha m. 'surroundings', retinue, furniture, attire, property, wealth, the necessities of life,

paribhagna mfn broken, interrupted, disturbed, stopped,

paribhagnakrama stopped in one's course

pari√*bhaj* to divide,

paribhakṣaṇa n. eating up, consuming,

paribhāṇḍa n. furniture, utensils,

paribhartsana n. threatening, menacing,

pari√*bhās* A. *–bhāsate* to appear,

pari√*bhāṣ* A *-bhāṣate,* to speak to, address, admonish, to declare, teach, explain, define, to exhort, persuade, encourage,

paribhāṣā f. speech, discourse, words, blame, censure, any explanatory rule or general definition, (in gram.) a rule or maxim which teaches the proper interpretation or application of other rules, (in medicine) prognosis, a list of abbreviations

paribhāṣaka mfn abusive,

paribhāṣaṇa 598/1 speaking much, speaking, talking, discourse, admonition, reprimand, reproof, rule, precept, walking around the subject

paribhāṣā sutrāṇi these explain how to understand the *sutrāṇi* which define the laws of grammar in Pāṇini's exposition.

paribhāṣita mfn explained, said, taught, established as a rule, formed or used technically,

paribhava m. insult, injury, humiliation, contempt, disgrace,

paribhāva m. contempt, disregard,

paribhavana n. humiliation, degradation,

paribhāvana 598/2 n. cohesion, union, f. (*ā*)

thought, contemplation
paribhāvaya 2nd present impv.
Cinmayānanda – says that *paribhāvaya* indicates a state of utter balance within and total oblivion of outer happenings.
paribhāvita mfn enclosed, contained
paribhaya m.n. apprehension, fear,
pari√bhid to be broken or destroyed
- *bheda* m. hurt, injury,
-*bhedaka* mfn breaking through,
-*bhinna* mfn broken, split,
paribhoga m. enjoyment, esp. sexual intercourse, illegal use of another's goods, means of subsistence or enjoyment,
paribhoktṛ mfn eating, enjoying, living at another's cost,
pari√bhṛ P.A. –*bharati (te),*
to bring, to extend or pass beyond, to roam or travel about,
pari√bhrāj to shed brilliance all around,
pari√bhram to rove, ramble, wander about,
paribhrama m. wandering about, going about, circumlocution, wandering discourse, mfn flying round or about,
paribhrāmaṇa n. turning to and fro,
paribhrāmin mfn moving hither and thither (in comp.),
paribhraṁśa m. escape,
pari√bhram Cl 4 P –*bhramati, bhrāmyati,*
to wander about or through, roam about, rove, ramble,
paribhraṁśana n. falling from, loss of,
pari√bhū to be round anything, surround, enclose, contain, to go or fly round, accompany, attend to, take care of, guide, govern, to be superior, excel, surpass, subdue, to pass round or over, not heed, slight, despise, to disgrace, to disappear, be lost, caus. –*bhāvayati* to divulge, make known, surpass, exceed, to saturate, soak, sprinkle, to contain, include, to conceive, think, consider, know, recognise as,
paribhū mfn surrounding, enclosing, containing, pervading, guiding, exists above all,
paribhugna mfn bowed, bent,
paribhūḥ one who exists above all 'transcendent'
enclosing, containing, pervading
pari√1. bhuj P/ -*bhujati* to span, encompass, embrace,
pari√3.bhuj P.A. –*bhunakti, -bhuṅkte,*
to eat before another, to neglect to feed, to eat, consume, enjoy,
paribhukta mfn eaten, enjoyed, possessed, eaten before another,
pari√bhūṣ to run round, circumambulate, to wait upon, serve, honour, to be superior, surpass,
paribhūta overpowered, slighted, despised
paribhūti f. superiority, contempt, injury,
paribodha m. reason, n. exhortation, admonition, mfn to be admonished,
paribodhana n. exhortation, admonition,
paribodhavat mfn endowed with reason,
paribṛḍha mfn firm, strong, solid,
paribṛṁhaṇa 598/1 n prosperity, welfare, an additional work, supplement
paribṛṁhita mfn increased, augmented, strengthened by, connected or furnished with, n. the roar of an elephant,
paricakṣā f. rejection, disapproval
pari √cakṣ 593/3 to overlook, pass over, despise, condemn, mention, relate, to declare guilty, to mention, acknowledge, to call, name,
paricakṣante they regard as, see as, they declare 1/pl/mid
paricapala mfn always moving about, very volatile
pari√car P. –*carati* to move or walk about, go round, walk around, to attend upon or to, serve, honour,
paricara mfn moving, flowing, m. an attendant, servant, follower, patrol, body-guard, homage, service,
paricāra 593/3 mfn moving, flowing, m. a servant, follower, attendant, attendance, service, homage, a place for walking,

paricāraka m. an assistant or attendant, f. °*ikā*
paricaraṇa 593/3 going about, serving, attending to, waiting upon
paricāraṇa n. attendance,
paricāraya Nom.P. *–yati,* to attend on, wait on, to take a walk, roam about,
paricārayasva perform your own service, get your own service performed, e.g. washing of feet etc.
paricarmaṇya n. a strip of leather,
paricaryā attendance, service, worship, doing service, circumambulation, wandering about or through, 593/3
paricaya 1. heaping up, accumulation, 2. m. acquaintance, intimacy familiarity with, knowledge of, trial, practice, frequent repetition,
pari√1.ci to surround or enclose with, to heap up accumulate,
pari√2.ci to examine, investigate, search, to find out, know, learn, exercise, practise, become acquainted with
paricchada m. a cover, garment, dress, paraphernalia, goods and chattels, personal property, furniture, retinue, train, attendants, royal insignia, travelling necessities,
paricchanda m. train, retinue,
paricchanna mfn covered, veiled, clad
pariccheda m. cutting, separation, accurate definition, exact discrimination, resolution, determination, limit, boundary, obviating, remedying,
paricchedaka mfn ascertaining, defining, n. limitation, limit, measure,
paricchedana n. discriminating, dividing,
paricchinna mfn cut off, divided, detached, limited, circumscribed, limited *-tva* n. determined, ascertained,
paricchitti f. accurate definition, measure, limitation, limit, partition,
pari√cint to think about, meditate on, reflect, consider, to call to mind, remember, to devise, invent,
paricintaka mfn reflecting about, meditating on
paricintayan meditating on, reflecting on pres/act/caus/part *pari √cint*
paricintita mfn thought of, found out,
paricodita mfn set in motion, brandished, impelled, incited,
paricumbana n. the act of kissing heartily
paricumbita mfn kissed passionately, touched closely
paricyavana n. descending to be born a man
pari√1.dā P.A. *–dadāti, -datte*, to give, grant, bestow, surrender, intrust to, caus. *–dāpayati,* to cause to be delivered or given up,
paridā f. giving oneself up to the favour or protection of another, devotion,
pari√dah Cl 1 *–dahati* to burn thoroughly, pass. be on fire,
paridāha 595/3 m burning hot, mental anguish
paridāna n. as *paridā* , restitution of a deposit
paridagdha mfn burnt, scorched,
pari√dah to burn round or through or entirely, consume by fire, dry up, to be burnt through or wholly consumed,
paridāha m. burning hot, mental anguish, pain, sorrow,
parīdāha m. burning, cauterizing,
paridahana n. burning,
paridahyate it is burned, it burns 1/s/pres/indic/pass. *pari √dah*
paridaṣṭa mfn bitten to pieces, bitten,
parideva m. 595/3 lamentation
paridevana n. lamentation, complaint,
paridevita mfn lamented, bewailed, n. lamentation, wailing,
pari√1.dhā P.A. *–dadhāti, dhatte*, to lay or put or place or set round, to cast round, turn upon, to put on, wear, surround, envelop, enclose,
paridhāna n. putting or laying round, putting on, dressing, clothing, f. closing or concluding a recitation,
parīdhāna n. a mantle, garment,
paridhāpana mfn causing to put on clothes
paridhāraṇa n. bearing, supporting, enduring *(ā)* f. patience, perseverance

paridhāvana n. running away from, escaping,

paridhāya m. retinue, a water receptacle, the rear end,

paridhāyaka m. a fence, enclosure,

paridhi m. an enclosure, fence, wall, any circumference or circle,

paridhīra mfn very deep (tone or sound),

paridhṛta mfn borne (in the womb),

parī√dhyai to meditate, ponder,

paridīpaka a pointer (Gam.)

paridīpita flared up, highlighted,

paridīna mfn much dejected or afflicted

paridiṣṭa mfn made known, pointed out,

paridṛḍha mfn very firm or strong,

paridraṣṭṛ m. a spectator, perceiver, 'the seer on all sides',

pari√dṛś to look at, see, behold, regard, consider, find out, know, to see without clarity as when hazy,

paridṛṣṭa mfn seen, beheld, perceived, learnt, known

paridṛṣṭakarman mfn having much practical experience,

pari√dru P. *–dravati,* to run round,

pari√gā P. *–jigāti* to go round or through, enter, walk around, permeate, to come near, approach, reach, visit, to go out of the way, avoid,

pariga mfn going round, surrounding,

pari√gai P. *–gayati* to go about singing,s sing or celebrate everywhere,

parigalita mfn fallen down, sunk, fluid flowing, melted,

pari√gam to go round or about or through, walk around, , surround, enclose, to come to any state or condition,

parigaṇanā f. correct calculation/statement,

parigaṇita mfn calculated, enumerated

parigaṇitin one who has well considered everything,

parigata mfn gone round or through, surrounded, encompassed, filled, visited by, afflicted with, diffused, deceased, dead, known, experienced, learnt from,

parigha m. an iron bar or beam for closing or locking a gate, a bar, obstacle, hindrance, a gate, a house, pitcher,

parighātana 593/2 killing, destroying, removing, a club or iron bludgeon

parighopama mfn like iron bars,

pari√ghrā to kiss passionately, cover with kisses,

parigīta mfn sung, celebrated, declared,

pariglāna mfn languid, exhausted, wearied,

pari√grah P.A. *–gṛhṇāti °ṇīte,* to take hold of on both sides, embrace, surround, enfold, to fence round, hedge round, to seize, grasp, to put on, wear, to take or carry along, to master, overpower, take prisoner, conquer, take food, to receive (as guest), take by the hand, take a wife, accept, to adopt, conform to, assist, marry, to surpass, excel,

parigraha 593/1 m. laying hold on all sides, surrounding, enclosing, assuming a form, comprehending, summing up, taking, accepting, receiving, getting, attaining, property, gift, present, acquisition, possession, a house, abode, root, origin, foundation, hospitable reception, marrying, marriage, a wife, choice, selection, understanding, conception, undertaking, occupation with, homage, reverence, grace, favour, assistance, control, force, constraint, claim on, relation to, concern with, a curse, punishment,

parigrahaka mfn taking hold of undertaking,

parigrāhaka mfn favouring, befriending,

parigrahaṇa n. wrapping round, putting on,

parigredha m. excessive greediness

parigṛddha mfn very greedy,

parigṛhīta mfn taken hold of on both sides, surrounded, embraced, enclosed, seized, taken, accepted, adopted, admitted, followed, obeyed,

parigṛhīti f. grasping, comprehension,

parigṛhya 1. having taken or seized, in company or along with, considering, regarding, 2. to be taken or accepted or regarded, a married woman,

pariguṇḍita mfn covered with dust,
pariguṇṭhita mfn veiled in, hidden by
pariguṇita mfn reiterated, repeated, augmented by addition of,
pari√hā P. *–jahāti* to leave, abandon, quit, to omit, neglect, disregard, caus. *–hāpayati* to cause to relinquish or abandon, to interrupt, leave unfinished,
pari√han P. *–hanti,* to wind round, to extinguish (fire), pass. to be changed or altered,
parihāṇa 604/3 being deprived of anything suffering a loss
parihāṇi or *parihāni* f. decrease, loss, deficiency,
parihāpaṇīya mfn to be omitted,
parihāpita mfn robbed or deprived of,
parihāpya ind. excluding, excepting,
parihara m. reserve, concealment,
parihāra m. leading round, delivering or handing over, shunning, avoiding, excluding, abandoning, giving up, resigning, seizing, surrounding, concealment, reserve, leaving out, omission, taking away, removing, contempt, disrespect, objection
parihāra mfn repelling, refuting, m.n. an armlet,
parīhāra m. avoiding, shunning, caution, disrespect,
pariharaṇa n. moving or taking round, avoiding, shunning,
parihārasthāna bounty, largess, n. a space of common land round a village
parihāravat 1. avoidable, 2. ind. ifc. like the omission of
parihārin mfn avoiding, shunning,
pariharṣaṇa mfn greatly delighting,
pariharṣin mfn delightful,
pariharṣita mfn greatly delighted,
pari√has to laugh or joke with, laugh at, ridicule, deride,
parihāsa jesting, joking, ridiculing, deriding, a jest, joke, merriment, mirth,
parihāsakathā f. an amusing story,
parihāsapūrvam ind. jokingly, in jest
parihāsavastu n. an object of jest
parihāsavedin m. a witty person,
parihāsavijalpita mfn uttered in jest,
parihasita mfn laughed at, ridiculed,
parihāsya mfn laughable, ridiculous,
parihāṭaka mfn consisting or made of pure gold, a ring for arm or leg, an armlet, anklet
parihava m. crying or calling upon,
parihīṇa mfn omitted, lost, wanting, abstaining from, deficient in,
parihita mfn put round or on, clothed,
parihṇuta mfn denied, refused,
pari√hṛ P.A. *–harati, te,*to move or carry or take round, to put or wrap round, to put aside, save for, to leave, quit, to defend, to spare, to avoid,
pari√hṛṣ caus. *-harṣayati* to delight greatly, cause to rejoice,
parihṛṣita mfn delighted, very glad,
parihṛta mfn shunned, avoided, abandoned, taken, n. what has been put on or wrapped round,
parihrut mfn causing to fall,
parihṛti f. shunning, avoiding,
parihvālam ind. stammering, faltering,
parihvṛti f. deceiving, harming, injuring,
pari-jā f. place of origin, source,
parijagdha m. a proper name, *√jakṣ*
parijagrabha *√grah* perf. one may grasp, he may grasp,
parijahāti √3.*hā* leaves, abandons, quits,
parijana m. a surrounding company of people, servants, followers, a single servant, *-tā* the condition of a servant, service,
parijanman m. the moon, fire,
parijapita mfn muttered, prayed, whispered
parijāta mfn begotten by, descended from, L. completely grown,
pārijāta m. fragrance, jasmine,
parijman mfn running or walking or driving round, surrounding, being everywhere, omnipresent, 7th all around, everywhere, m. the moon, fire,
pari√jñā to notice, observe, perceive, learn,

understand, comprehend, ascertain, know or recognise as,
parijñā f. knowledge,
parijñāna 594/2 perception, thorough knowledge, discrimination, ascertainment, experience,
parijñāpti f. recognition or conversation,
parijñāta mfn thoroughly known, recognised, ascertained, learned,
parijñātā m. the knower, the experiencer
parijñātṛ mfn one who knows or perceives, an observer, knower, wise, intelligent,
pari√jval P. *–jvalati* to burn brightly, blaze,
parijvan m. the moon, fire, a servant, a sacrificer, Indra,
parījyā f. a secondary rite,
pari√2.kal P. *–kālayati* to chase, persecute, drive about,
pari√3.kal P. *–kalayati* to seize, take hold of, swallow, devour, to observe, consider as,
parikalayitṛ mfn surrounding, encircling
parikālita mfn persecuted, dogged,
parikalkana 591/2 deceit, cheating
parikalpa m. illusion, (Buddhist)
parikalpana n. fixing, settling, contriving, making, inventing, providing, distributing, *(ā)* f. making, forming, assuming, reckoning, calculation,
parikalpita mfn settled, decided, fixed upon, chosen, wished for, expected, made, invented, contrived, arranged, distributed, (Buddhist) imaginary, illusory,
parikandala mfn teeming with, full of,
parikāṅkṣita m. a devotee, religious ascetic
parikara mfn who or what helps or assists, m. (ifc.f. *ā*) attendants, followers, entourage, multitude, abundance, a girth, zone, waist-band,
parikaraśloka discrimination, judgment,
parikarita mfn accompanied by,
parikarkaśa mfn very harsh
parikarman m. a servant, assistant, n. attendance, worship, adoration, adorning the body esp. after bathing, cleansing, purification, preparation, arithmetical calculation,
parikarmayati Nom. P. anoints, adorns, decorates, makes ready,
parikarmita mfn arranged, prepared,
parikarṣana n. a circle,
parikarṣin mfn dragging away, carrying,
parikarṣita mfn dragged about, tortured
parikartana mfn cutting up or to pieces,
parikātara mfn very timid or cowardly,
pari√kath P. *–kathayati* to mention, call, name,
parikathā f. a religious tale or narrative
parikhā f. a moat, trench round a town or fort, the sea surrounding the earth,
parikhāta mfn dug round, m. a furrow, rut
parikheda m. (ifc. (*ā*) f.) lassitude, weariness
parikhinna mfn depressed, exhausted, sick
parikhyāta mfn regarded as, passing for, called, famous, celebrated,
parikhyāti P. to look round, look at, perceive, to overlook, disregard, f. fame, reputation,
parikiraṇa n. scattering, strewing about,
parikīrṇa mfn spread, diffused, scattered around, surrounded, crowded,
pari√kīrt P. to prclaim on all sides, announce, relate, praise, declare, call, name,
parikīrtana n. proclaiming, announcing, talking of, boasting, naming,
pariklānta mfn very tired, exhausted,
parikleda m. humidity, wetness,
parikledin mfn wetting or wet,
parikleśa m. hardship, trouble, pain,
parikliśa m. vexation, trouble,
parikliṣṭa mfn much vexed or troubled,
parikliṣṭam ind. reluctantly, grudgingly
parikopa m. violent anger, wrath,
parikopita mfn geatly excited, very angry
pari√1.kṛ P. to surround, to uphold,
pari√kram P. *–kramati* to step or walk round or about, go around, circumambulate, roam over, walk through, visit,
parikrama m. circumambulation, roaming about, walking around, walking through, pervading, transition,

succession, series, order, a remedy, a goat,
parikramana n. walking or roaming about,
parikrānta mfn walked round, stepped on,
n. the place stepped on, footsteps,
parikrānti f. moving round, revolution,
parikrayaṇa n. hiring, engaging,
parikṛśa mfn very thin, emaciate, wasted
-tva n. a slender shape,
parikṛtta mfn cut round, clipped, cut off
parikruṣṭa mfn lamented,
n. lamented by (3rd)
parikṣāma mfn excessively emaciated, dried up, fallen away,
parīkṣ (pari-ikṣ) A. *parīkṣate* to look round, inspect carefully, try, examine, find out, observe, perceive,
parīkṣā f. inspection, investigation, test, examination, trial by ordeal,
parīkṣaka mfn trying, examining,
m. a prover, examiner, judge,
parīkṣaṇa n. trying, testing, experiment, investigation,
parikṣāṇa mfn charred or burnt to a cinder,
parikṣaya m. disappearing, ceasing, dissolution, decay, loss, ruin,
parikṣepa m. throwing about, moving to and fro, surrounding, encircling, being surrounded, circumference, extent,
parikṣība mfn drunk, intoxicated,
parikṣīṇa mfn vanished, disappeared, wasted, exhausted, diminished, lost, (in law) insolvent,
pari√kṣip to throw over or beyond, to put or lay or wind round, to surround, encircle, embrace, to throw or put or fix in, to throw away, squander,
parikṣipta mfn thrown, thrown about, scattered, surrounded, overspread,
parikṣit mfn dwelling or spreading around, surrounding, extending,
parīkṣita mfn carefully inspected, tried,
parīkṣya ind. having inspected, inspecting,
parikūjana in rumbling all around
parikūla n. the land lying on a shore
parikupita mfn much excited, very angry,
parikvaṇana mfn loud-sounding, loud,
pari√labh to get, obtain,
parilaghu mfn very light or small,
easy to digest,
parilagna mfn stuck, held fast,
parilambana n. lagging, lingering,
parilaṅghana n. leaping to and fro,
parilekhana n. drawing lines round about,
parilikhana n. smoothing, polishing,
parilikhita mfn enclosed in a circle,
parilopa m. injury, neglect, omission,
parilupta mfn injured, lost,
pari√mā A. *–mimīte* to measure round or about, mete out, fulfil, embrace, to measure, estimate, determine,
parimā f. measure, periphery,
parimala m. fragrance, or a fragrant substance, perfume, copulation, connubial pleasure, a meeting of learned men, soil, stain, dirt,
parimalita, mfn soiled, deprived of freshness or beauty, perfumed,
parīman bounty, plenty, (°*maṇi*) ind. plentifully,
parimāṇa 599/1 n. measuring, meting out, measure of any kind, e.g. length, size, weight, number, value, duration, (ifc. 'amounting to'),
-tas ind. by measure, in weight,
parīmāṇa n. measure, circumference, size, weight, number, amount,
parimanda mfn very dull, weak, faint,
parimaṇḍala mfn round, circular, globular, of the measure of an atom, n. a globe, sphere, orbit, circumference, -*tā* f. whirling about, roundness, circularity, rotundity,
parimāṇin mfn having measured, measured, measurable,
parimanthara mfn extremely slow, tardy,
parimantrita mfn consecrated, enchanted,
parimanyu mfn wrathful, angry,
parimara mfn one round whom people have died, m. dying in numbers or round anyone,
parimarda m. wearing out, using up,
parimardana n. wearing out, rubbing in, a remedy for rubbing in,
parimārga m. searching about, 2. m. wiping, cleaning, friction, touch

parimārgaṇa n. tracing, searching,
parimārgitavya to be sought for or realized, gerundive *pari* √*mārg*
parimārjana n. wiping off, cleaning, washing
parimārjita mfn cleaned, polished,
parimarśa m. touching, contact, consideration, reflection,
parimarṣa m. envy, dislike, anger,
parimathita mfn produced by attrition
parimeya mfn measurable, limited, few,
parimeyatā f.measurableness,calculableness
parimilana n. touch, contact,
parimilita mfn mixed or filled with, met from all sides, pervaded by (3rd),
parimit f. a roof beam, rafter, joist,
parimita mfn measured, meted, limited, regulated, moderate, sparing,
parimitabhojana n. eating sparingly,
parimitakatha mf(*ā*)n of measured discourse, speaking little,
parimitatva moderation, limited condition
parimitāyus mfn short-lived,
parimiti f. measure, quantity, limitation,
parimlāna mfn faded, withered, exhausted, languid, emaciated, disappeared, gone, n change of countenance from fear or grief, soil, stain,
parimlāyin mfn stained, spotted,
parimocita mfn liberated, emancipated,
parimohana n. bewildering, fascination,
parimohin mfn perplexed, bewitching,
parimokṣa 599/2 m. setting free, liberation, deliverance, relieving, evacuation,
parimokṣaṇa n. unloosing, untying, liberation, deliverance from (6th),
parimoṣa m. theft, robbery,
parimoṣaka mfn stealing,
parimoṭana n. snapping, cracking,
parimṛṣṭa 1. mfn wiped off, rubbed, smoothed, polished, 2. touched, caught, found out, considered, spread, pervaded,
pariṁśa m. the best part of
pari√*muc* P. *–muñcati* to set free, liberate, deliver from, to let go, give up, part with, to discharge, emit, pass. *–muncyate,* to loosen or free one's self, get rid of, to be liberated or emancipated from the ties of the world,
parimūḍha mfn disturbed, perplexed,
parimugdha mfn bewitchingly lovely,
parimukham ind. round or about the face or any person,
parimukta mfn released, liberated from,
parimukti f. liberation,
parimūrṇa mfn worn out, decrepit, old (as a cow),
parinā f. taking in, deception,
pāriṇa mfn being or crossing to the other side, well acquainted or completely familiar with,
parinābhi ind. round the navel,
pariṇaddha mfn bound or wrapped round, broad, large,
parīṇah f. enclosure or anything enclosed, a box belonging to a carriage,
pariṇāha m. compass, circumference, extent, width, breadth, circumference of a circle, periphery,
parīṇāha m. circumference, width,
pariṇahana n. binding or girding or wrapping round, veiling, covering,
parinaiṣṭhika mf(ī)n highest, utmost, most perfect,
pari-ṇam (√*nam*) P.A. *–ṇ*
ṇamati to bend or turn aside, to bend down, stoop, to change or be transformed into, to develop, become ripe or mature, to become old, to be digested, be fulfilled,
pariṇāma 594/3 m. change, alteration, transformation into (instr.), development, evolution, ripeness, maturity, result, consequence, issue, end, a figure of speech by which the properties of any object are transferred to the object with which it is compared, change of characteristic
parīṇāma m. course or lapse of time,
pariṇāmadarśin looking forward to consequent issues, prudent, fore-sighted,

pariṇāmadṛṣṭi foresight, providence,
pariṇamana n. change, transformation, changing into,
pariṇāmana n. bringing to full development, the turning of things destined for the community to one's own use,
pariṇāmasṛṣṭi f. creation by evolution and actual change (*Saṁkhyā*)
pariṇāmapathya mfn suited to a future state or condition,
pariṇāma upādāna ' a kind of material cause in which the effect is of a different nature from the cause as milk becomes curd,
pariṇāmavāda the doctrine of transformation according to the qualified non-dualism system of Rāmānuja, i.e. 'the cause is continually transforming itself into its effects,' (G)
pariṇāmavat mfn having a natural development
pariṇāmin changeable, subject to transformation, developing, bearing fruits or consequences,
pariṇāmika mfn resulting from change, easily digestible,
pariṇāmin mfn changing, altering, subject to transformation, developing, ripening, bearing fruits or consequences,
pariṇāminitya mfn eternal but continually changing,
pariṇāmopādāna n. that material cause which evolves out of itself an effect which is essentially one with, e.g. the Pradhāna of the Saṁkhyās, (U)
parīṇas m. plenty, abundance, *-asā* ind. richly, abundantly,
pariṇata mfn bent down (as an elephant to strike), changed or transformed into, developed, ripened, mature, full-grown, perfect, full (as the moon), set (as the sun), digested, elapsed (as time), n. capital, wealth accumulated for profit,
pariṇataprajña of mature understanding,
pariṇatapratyaya mfn (an action) of which the results have matured
pariṇati f. bending, bowing, transformation, result, change, alteration, natural development, ripeness, maturity, mature or old age, result, consequence, issue, end, termination, fulfilment of a promise, digestion,
pariṇatiṁ √*yā* to attain one's final aim, fulfilment (of a promise),
pariṇaya m. leading round, esp. leading the bride round the fire, marriage,
pariṇāya mfn leading round, a chess move,
pariṇāyaka m. a leader, guide, a husband,
pariṇayana n. the act of leading round, marrying, marriage,
pariṇayati he marries
parīndana n. gratification, present, °*dita* mfn gratified, presented,
pariṇetṛ m. a husband, one who leads round
pariṇeya gdv. to be led around,
pari√*ṇī* Cl 1 *–nayati,* to lead around, esp. lead the bride round the sacred fire marry, carry away, discover,
pariṇi√*dhā* to place or lay round,
pariṇi√*han* to encompass (with stakes etc.)
parinimna mfn much depressed, deeply hollowed
pariṇiṁsaka mfn tasting, eating, an eater, kissing, °*ṇiṁsā* f. eating, kissing,
pariṇi√*viś* to sit down about,
parinindā f. strong censure,
parinirjita mfn vanquished, conquered,
parinirmita mfn formed, created, marked off, limited, settled, determined,
pari-nir-√*2.vā* P. *–vāti* to be completely extinguished or emancipated (from individual existence), attain absolute rest, caus. *–vāpayati* to emancipate completely by causing extinction of all re-births, 596/2
parinirvāṇa mfn completely extinguished or finished, n. complete extinction of individuality, entire cessation of re-births,
parinirvapaṇa n. distributing, giving
parinirvivapsā f. desire to give, liberality
parinirviṇṇa mfn extremely disgusted with

parinirviṇnacetas mfn faint-hearted, despondent,
parinirvṛta mfn (√1.vṛ) completely extinguished, finally liberated,
parinirvṛti f. final liberation, complete emancipation,
pariniścaya m. fixed opinion or resolution,
pari-niṣ-√pad A. *–padyate* to change or turn into,
pariniṣpādita mfn developed, manifested
pariniṣpanna mfn developed, perfect, real, existing, perfect knowledge (Buddhist),
pariniṣpatti f. perfection, 596/3
pari-ni-ṣṭhā (√sthā) caus. *-ṣṭhāpayati* to teach thoroughly,
pariniṣṭhā f. extreme limit, highest point,
pariniṣṭhāna n. the being completely fixed, mfn having a final end or object,
pariniṣṭhāpanīya mfn to be exactly fixed or defined,
pariniṣṭhita mfn quite perfect, accomplished,
parini√vṛt A. *–vartate* to pass away,
pari√nṛt P. *–nṛtyati* to dance about/around
pariṇuta mfn praised, celebrated,
pari√1.pā P. *–pibati* to drink before or after, to drink or suck out, take away, rob,
pari√3.pā P. *–pāti* to protect or defend on every side, to guard, maintain,
paripācana cooking, ripening, bringing to maturity,
paripad f. a trap or snare,
paripadin m. an enemy,
paripāka m. completely cooked, digestion, maturity, perfection, result, consequence, cleverness, shrewdness, experience,
parīpāka m. ripening, maturing, full development, the result or consequences of anything.
paripākin mfn ripening, digesting,
paripakva mfn completely cooked or dressed, completely burnt (as bricks), quite ripe, mature, accomplished, perfect, highly cultivated, very sharp or shrewd, near death, fully digested,
pari√pāl Cl10 to guard, protect, preserve,
paripālayati to be a protector,
paripālaka mf(*ikā)*n guarding, maintaining, taking care of one's property
paripālana n. the act of guarding etc.
paripāṇa n. protection, defence, covert,
paripāna n. a drink, beverage,
paripaṇana n. playing for, wagering,
paripaṇita mfn wagered, promised,
paripanna m. the change of *m* into *anusvara*
paripantham ind. by or in the way,
paripanthayati obstructs the way, opposes,
paripanthin mfn ambushing a path, m. waylayer, hinderer,
pariparin m. an antagonist, adversary,
paripārśva mfn being at or by one's side, near, at hand,
paripārśvacara mfn going at one's side,
pari√paś to look over, survey, to perceive, see, observe, to fix the mind or thoughts upon, to learn, know, recognise as, to see everywhere,
paripaśyati sees everywhere, 1/s/pres/act
paripaśyanti 'realise as existing in its fulness everywhere' (Gam.)
pari√pat Cl 1 *–patati,* fly around, rush to and fro, move hither and thither, to leap down from, to throw oneself upon, attack,
paripatana n. flying round or about,
paripāṭha m. complete enumeration, (*ena)* ind. in detail, completely
paripāṭhaka mfn detailing, enumerating completely
paripati m. the lord of all around,
paripāti f. succession, order, method, arrangement, arithmetic,
paripavana n. cleaning, winnowing corn, a winnowing basket,
paripelava mfn very fine, small, delicate,
pariphulla mfn widely opened (as eyes), covered with erected hairs,
paripīḍana n. squeezing or pressing out, injuring, prejudicing,
paripiñja mfn full of,
paripīvara mfn very fat or plump,
pariplava mfn swimming, running about,

unsteady, restless, m. inundation, trembling, bathing, restlessness, boat, tyrrany, ship, oppression,

pāriplava mfn wavering, irresolute, moving in a circle, moving to and fro, perturbed, swimming, agitated, m. boat,

pariplavā f. small spoon used at sacrifices,

pariploṣa m. burning, internal heat,

pari√plu Cl 1 *–plavati,* to swim around,

paripluṣṭa mfn burnt, scorched,

paripluta mfn bathed, flooded, immersed, visited by, n. a spring, jump,

paripoṣa m. full growth or development,

paripoṣaka mfn nourishing, confirming,

paripoṣana n. the act of cherishing, furthering, promoting,

pari√pī pass. *–pūryate,* to fill, become completely full, caus. *pūrayati* to fill, make full, cover or occupy completely, to fulfil, accomplish, go through,

pari√prach P.A. Cl 6 *–pṛcchati (te),* to interrogate or ask a person about anything, to inquire about,

pariprāpaṇa n. taking place, occurrence,

pariprāpti f. obtaining, acquisition,

pariprārdha n. proximity, nearness,

paripraśna 597/3 m. question, interrogation, inquiry about,

paripṛcchā f. question, inquiry,

paripṛcchaka m. an interrogator, inquirer,

paripṛcchanikā f. a subject for discussion

paripreraka mfn exciting, causing, effecting

paripṛī mfn very dear, valued highly,

paripṛīta mfn much gratified, delighted,

parīpsā f. desire of obtaining, preserving, haste, hurry,

pari√pūj P. *–pūjayati* to honour greatly, worship, adore, 597/2

paripūjana n. honouring, adoring,

paripūjita mfn honoured, adored, worshipped,

paripuṅkhita mfn feathered (as an arrow),

paripūraka mfn filling, fulfilling, causing fulness or prosperity,

paripūraṇa n.the act of filling, perfecting, rendering complete,

paripūraṇīya mfn to be filled or fulfilled

paripūrin mfn granting or bestowing richly

paripūrṇa mfn quite full, filled with, accomplished, finished, perfect, whole, complete, fully satisfied,

paripūrti f. fulness, completion,

paripūta mfn purified, winnowed, strained,

paripūti f. complete cleaning, purification

parirabdha mfn embraced, encircled, one who has embraced,

pari√rāj P.A. *–rājati (te)* to shine on all sides, spread radiance everywhere,

pari√rakṣ P. *–rakṣati* to guard well or completely,

rescue, save, defend, to keep, conceal, rule, govern, to avoid, shun, A. *–te* to get out of a person's (6th) way,

parirakṣā f. keeping, protecting, protection,

parirakṣaka m. a guardian, protector,

parirakṣaṇa mfn guarding, protecting, a protector,

parirakṣita mfn well-guarded, protected,

parirambhaṇa n. embracing, an embrace,

parirambhita mfn embraced, occupied with or engrossed by,

pariramita mfn delighted (by amorous sport)

parīraṇa n. a tortoise, a stick,

parirandhita mfn injured, destroyed,

parirāpin mfn whispering to, talking over, persuading,

parirāṭaka mfn crying aloud, screaming,

parirodha m. obstructing, keeping back,

pari√ruc A. *–rocate* to shine all around,

pari√2.rudh to enclose, obstruct

pariruddha mfn obstructed by, filled with,

pariśabdita mfn mentioned, communicated,

parisabhya m. a member of an assembly, an assessor,

pariṣad mfn surrounding, besetting, f. an assembly, group, meeting, circle, audience, council,

pari√sad P. *ṣadati, ṣīdati, sīdati* to sit round, besiege, beset, to suffer damage, be impaired,

parisādhana n. accomplishing, settling, arranging, determining, ascertaining,

pariṣadvala surrounded by a council

(a king), forming/containing assemblies, m. a member of an assembly, assessor, spectator,
pariṣadya mfn to be sought after, to be worshipped, a member of an assembly, spectator, guest,
pariṣadvan mfn surrounding, besetting,
pariṣahā f. forbearance, patience,
pariṣanna mfn lost or omitted,
parisakhya n. perfect or true friendship,
parisamanta m. circumference, circuit,
pari-sam-√āp to be fully completed, arrive at completion, to be contained in, to relate or belong to, 603/3
parisamāpana n. finishing completely
parisamāpta mfn finished, completed, centred, comprehended,
parisamāpti f.entire completion, end, conclusion, relating/belonging to,
parisamāpyate to be fully completed, arrive at completion, pass. *āpyate,* it is fully comprehended,attain consummation, culminate, get merged, it is finished,
parisam√bhū to arise, spring, be produced from
parisaṁcakṣya mfn to be avoided,
parisaṁcara mfn roving about, vagrant, m. 'a very difficult pass or defile', 'a critical period',
parisaṁcita mfn collected, accumulated,
parisame to go back to
parisaṁhṛṣṭa mfn geatly rejoiced, delighted
pariśamita, mfn allayed, quenched, destroyed,
parisaṁ√khyā to count, enumerate, to limit to a certain number, to calculate, add up, to make good, restore, f. enumeration, sum, total,
parisaṁkhyāta mfn reckoned up, enumerated, specified exclusively,
parisaṁ√krīd to play about, amuse oneself,
parisaṁ√kṣip to encompass, surround,
parisaṁ√spṛś to touch at different places, stroke,
parisaṁsṛṣṭa mfn got at from all sides, surrounded,
parisaṁ√stambh to strengthen, comfort,
parisaṁsthita mfn standing together on every side, standing i.e. stopping,
parisaṁśuddha mfn perfectly clean or pure,
parisaṁtāna m. a string, cord,
parisaṁ√tap to be tormented or afflicted,
parisaṁtapta mfn scorched, singed,
parisamūhana n. sweeping up or heaping together,
parisamutsuka mfn very anxious, agitated,
parisaṁvatsara m. a whole or full year, mfn a full year old or older, inveterate, chronic (disease), waiting a year,
pari√ṣañj P. -*ṣajati* A. –*sajjate*, to have one's mind fixed on, be attached or devoted to,
pariśaṅkā f. suspicion, distrust,
pariśaṅkanīya mfn to doubted or mistrusted or feared or apprehended,
pariśaṅkin mfn fearing, apprehending, afraid on account of (comp.)
pariśaṅkita mfn suspicious, distrustful, afraid of, suspected, questionable, believed, thought to be,
pariśanna mfn fallen away or by the side,
parisāntvana n. the act of consoling, pl. friendly words, flattering speech,
parisāntvita mfn consoled, conciliated
pariśapta n. cursing, reviling, anathema,
parisara mfn adjacent, adjoining, contiguous m. verge, border, proximity, neighbourhood, environs, a vein or artery, death, a rule, precept,
parīsara m. circumference, surroundings,
parisāra m. wandering about, perambulation
parisaraviṣaya m. an adjoining place,
parisarpa m. going about in search of, following, pursuing, roaming, surrounding, encircling,
parisarpaṇa n. crawling upon,running about
parīśāsa m. anything cut out, an excision, kettle tongs,
pariśāśvata mfn continuing for ever, perpetually the same,
pariśaṭha mfn thoroughly dishonest/wicked
parisatya n. the full or pure truth,
pariṣavaṇa n. grasping, bunching together,
pariśāyana n. causing to lie completely in, complete immersion

pariṣeṇaya °*yati* to surround with an army,
pariśeṣa mfn left over, remaining, m.n. remnant, remains, rest, supplement, sequel, termination, conclusion, (*eṇa*) ind. completely, in full, *(āt)* ind. consequently, therefore,
pari√ṣev to frequent, practise, pursue, enjoy, honour,
parisiddhikā f. a kind of rice gruel,
pari√sidh to drive about (cows),
pariṣikta mfn poured out, sprinkled, diffused, 603/1
pariśīlana n. touch, contact, intercourse with, application or attachment to, pursuit of (comp.), constant occupation, study,
pariśīlita mfn practised, used, employed, pursued, studied, inhabited,
parisīman m. a boundary, extreme term/limit
pari√śiṣ P. *ṣinaṣṭi* to leave over, leave as a remainder, A. to be left as a remainder, caus. *śeṣayati* to leave over, suffer to remain, spare, to quit or leave, to supply,
pariśiṣṭa mfn left, remaining, n. a supplement, appendix,
pariśithila mfn very loose or lax,
pari√ṣiv to sew round, wind round,
pariṣkanda m. a servant, a foster-child, 2. m. a temple
pariṣkaṇṇa spilled, scattered,
pariṣkara m. ornament, decoration,
pariṣkāra cooking, dressing, domestic utensils, furniture, purification, initiation, self-discipline,
pariṣkṛta mfn prepared, adorned, embellished, furnished with surrounded or accompanied by, cooked, purified, initiated,
pariṣkṛti f.finishing, polishing,
pariślatha mfn quite loose or relaxed,
pariśleṣa m. an embrace, 602/3
pariśliṣṭa mfn clasped, embraced,
parismāpana n. causing wonder, surprising,
parispanda m. vibration, throbbing, stirring, arising, maintaining a sacred fire,
parispandana n. vibration, motion,
parisphuraṇa glancing, shooting, budding
parisphurita mfn quivering, palpitating, dispersed, reflected on all sides,
parisphūrti f. shining forth, appearing, becoming clear or manifest,
parisphuṭa mfn very clear or manifest, *(am)* ind. very clearly/distinctly
parispṛdh f. a rival,
pari√spṛś Cl 6 *–spṛśati* to touch, stroke,
parispṛś mfn ifc. touching,
parispṛṣṭa mfn smeared or soiled with blood
pariśobhita mfn adorned or beautified by
pariśodhana n. cleaning, purification,
pariśoṣa m. complete dryness, dessication,
pariśoṣana mfn drying up, parching, n. drying, parching, emaciating,
pariśoṣita mfn dried up, parched,
parisraj f. a garland, 604/2
parisrajin mfn wearing a garland,
pari√śram Cl 4 *–śramyati,* to tire oneself, become exhausted,
pariśrama m. fatigue, exertion, trouble, pain,
pariśramaṇa mfn free from fatigue
pariśrānta mfn thoroughly fatigued, tired of, disgusted with,
parisrasā f. rubbish, lumber,
parisraṣṭṛ mfn being in contact or connected with,
parisrava m. flowing, a stream,
parisrāva m. flowing, efflux,
pariśraya m. an enclosure, fence, a refuge, an assembly, meeting,
pariśrayaṇa n. encompassing, fencing in,
pariśrit f. (encloser) one of the little stones surrounding the sacrificial altar,
pariśrita mfn standing round, surrounded by
parisṛṣṭa mfn surrounded, covered,
parirṣta m.n. ardent spirits, liquor
parisṛta mfn having roamed or wandered through, m.n. an enclosed place,
pariśruta mfn heard, learnt, known as, passing for (1st), famous, celebrated,
paristara m. strewing round, a cover,
pariṣṭavana n. praise,
pari√ṣṭhā to stand round, be in a person's way, obstruct, hinder, to crowd from all sides, A. to remain, survive, caus. to beset, surround, to place near, cause to stay close by,

pariṣṭhā mfn obstructing, hindering, f. obstruction, impediment,
pariṣṭhāna n. abode, residence, fixedness, firmness,
parīṣṭe is able to
pariṣṭhāla n. surrounding place or site,
pariṣṭhiti f. as *pariṣṭhāna*
pariṣṭi f. obstruction, impediment, distress, dilemma,
parīṣṭi f. investigation, research, inquiry, service, attendance, homage, freedom of will,
paristoma m. a coverlet, cushion,
pariṣṭubh mfn exulting on every side,
pariṣṭuta mfn praised, sung
pariṣṭuti f. praise, celebration,
pari√śudh to be washed off, become clean or purified, A. to purify or justify oneself, prove one's innocence, caus. to clear, clean, clear off, restore, to try, examine, to solve, explain, clear up,
pariśuddha mfn cleaned, purified, pure, cleared off, paid, acquitted, discharged, (ifc.) diminished by, that from which a part has been taken away,
pariśuddhi f. complete purification or justification, acquittal,
pariśūnya mfn empty, (ifc.) totally free from or devoid of,
pari√śuṣ Cl 4 *-śuṣyati,* to become completely dry or parched,
pariśuṣka mfn thoroughly dried or parched up, withered, shrivelled, shrunk (as a vein), hollow (as cheeks), n. meat fried in ghee, dried and spiced,
pariśuśrūṣā f. complete/ implicit obedience,
pariśuṣyati dries up, *pari √śuṣ* 1/s/pres/act
pariṣūta mfn urged, impelled to come forth,
pariṣūti f. urging from all sides, oppression, beleaguering, vexation,
pariṣvaṅga m. embracing, an embrace, touch, contact with, 603/2
pariṣvajana n. embracing, an embrace,
parisvajate he embraces
pariṣvajīyas mfn clasping more firmly,
pariṣvajya mfn to be embraced,
pariṣvakta mfn embraced, encircled,
pariṣvaṅgin mfn succumbing,
parisvaṣkita n. the act of leaping about,
pariṣyanda a river, stream (fig. of words), moisture, a sandbank, island, keeping a sacred fire, decoration of the hair, 603/2
pariṣyandana n. dropping, oozing,
pariṣyandin mfn flowing, streaming,
parīta mfn standing or moving around, surrounding, past, elapsed, expired, surrounded, encompassed, filled, seized, overcome, 605/2
paritādin mfn striking or hitting everywhere
paritakmya mfn wandering, unsteady, uncertain, dangerous, *(ā)* f. travelling, peregrination, night,
pari√tam P. *–tāmyati* to gasp for breath, be oppressed,
pari√tan to stretch round, surround, embrace
pari√tap to burn all round, set on fire, kindle, to feel or suffer pain, practice austerities
paritāpa 595/1 glow, scorching heat, pain, agony, grief, sorrow, repentance
paritapta surrounded with heat, heated, burnt, tormented,
paritapti f. great pain or torture, anguish,
pari√tark to think about, reflect, consider,
paritarkaṇa 595/1 consideration, reflection
paritarkita mfn thought about, expected, examined (judicially),
paritarpaṇa 595/2 mfn satisfying, n. the act of satisfying, a restorative,
paritas m 595/2 ind. all around, everywhere, as prep. with 2nd round-about, round, throughout,
paritatnu mfn embracing, surrounding,
paritikta mfn extremely bitter,
paritoṣa m. delight in, satisfaction,
paritoṣaka mfn satisfying, pleasing,
paritoṣaṇa mfn as above, n. satisfaction, gratification,
paritoṣita mfn satisfied, gratified, delighted,
pari√trai *-trāti,* or *-trāyate*, to rescue, save, protect, defend,
paritrāṇa 595/3 n. rescue, preservation,

protection or means of protection, refuge, retreat, deliverance (5th) from, self-defence, the hair of the body, moustaches,

paritrāta mfn protected, saved, preserved,

paritrāt mfn protecting, a protector,

paritrasta mfn frightened, much alarmed,

paritṛpta mfn completely satisfied/content,

paritṛpti f. complete satisfaction,

parītta 1. mfn given away, given up, 2. mfn cut round, circumscribed, limited,

parītti f. delivering,

pari√tud to trample down, crush,

pari√tuṣ P. *–tuṣyati* to be quite satisfied with (with 3rd, 6th, 7th), caus. *paritoṣayati* make satisfied, to appease, delight, flatter,

parituṣṭa mfn completely satisfied, delighted,

parituṣṭi f. complete satisfaction, contentment

parituṣya ind. being delighted or glad,

parityāga m. the act of leaving, forsaking, giving, renouncing

parityagin mfn leaving, quitting, renouncing

pari√tyaj to leave, quit, abandon, give, reject, disregard, not heed,

parityajati he completely abandons,

parityajya ind. at a distance from, excepting, having left or abandoned, with the exception of, leaving a space, having renounced,

parityajana n. causing to abandon, giving away, distributing, abandoning,

parityājana n. causing to abandon/give up,

parityaktṛ mfn one who leaves or abandons,

parityakta mfn left, quitted, let go, let fly (as an arrow), deprived of, wanting, n. anything to spare (*am*) ind. without (comp.)

pari-upa-√ās Cl 2 *–āste,* sit around, surround,

pari√vad to speak out, speak of or about, to speak ill of,

parivāda m. blame, reproach, accusation, detraction,

parivādaka m. a complainant, accuser,

parivādin mfn speaking ill of, abusing, blaming, m. an accuser, a plaintiff,

parivāhin mfn overflowing, ifc. streaming with,

parivakrā f. a circular pit,

pari√vañc P. *–vañcati,* to sneak about,

parivañcana n. taking in, deception,

parivañcita mfn deceived, taken in,

pari√vand P *–vandati* to praise, celebrate,

parivāpa m. fried grains of rice, standpoint, place, a reservoir, furniture, scattering, sowing,

parivāra m. a retinue, cover, covering, surroundings, followers, a sheath, scabbard, a hedge round a village, L. that which surrounds, a retinue,

parivāraṇa n. a cover, covering, keeping or warding off, retinue

parivardhaka m. a groom, rearer of horses,

parivardhana n. increasing, augmenting, multiplying, breeding, rearing (cattle),

parivardhita mfn cut, excavated, 2. mfn increased, augmented, grown, swollen (as the sea), reared, brought up,

parivarga m. avoiding, omitting, removing,

parivargya mfn to be avoided,

parivārita mfn surrounded by, covered with, veiled in,

parivarjaka mfn shunning, avoiding, giving up,

parivarjana n. the act of avoiding, giving up, escaping, abstaining from, killing,

parivarjita mfn shunned, avoided, abandoned or left by, deprived or devoid of, countless, innumerable, wound round, girt,

parivarman mfn wearing a coat of mail, armed

parivartman mfn going round about, describing a circle,

parivarta m. revolving, revolution, a period of time, a year, moving to and fro, turning back, flight, exchange, barter, requital, return, an abode, spot, place, a chapter, section, book

parīvarta m. exchange, barter,

parīvartam ind. in a circle, recurring, repeatedly,

parivartaka mfn causing to turn round or

flow back, bringing to an end, concluding, exchange, barter,

parivartana mfn causing to turn round, n. turning or whirling round, rolling about, moving to and fro, revolution, end of a period of time revolution, barter, exchange, cutting or clipping the hair, protecting, defending, inverting, taking or putting anything in a wrong direction, requital, return, change, reversal

parivartin mfn moving round, revolving, ever-recurring, ifc. changing, passing into, being or staying near, flying, retreating, exchanging, requiting, recompensing,

parivartita mfn turned round, revolved, exchanged, bartered, put aside, removed, destroyed, searched thoroughly, taken or put in a wrong direction, n. the action of turning or wallowing,

parivarttana 601/3 causing to turn around, turning or whirling around, moving to and fro, revolution, end of a period of time, barter, exchange, inverting,

parivartula mfn quite round or circular,

pari√4.vas A. to put on assume, surround, attend

pari√5.vas P. *–vasati,* to abide, stay, remain with,

pari√8.vas P. *–vāsayati,* to cut off all round, cut out,

parivāsa m. abode, stay, sojourn, the expulsion of a guilty member, 2. m. fragrance, odour,

parivāsana n. a shred, a chip,

parivasatha m. a village,

parivāsita mfn respectfully attentive to superiors

parivatsara m. a full year, a year,

pariveda m. complete/accurate knowledge,

parivedanā f. shrewdness, wit, prudence,

parivedin mfn knowing, shrewd,

parīveṣa m. a sun or moon halo

pariveṣaka a waiter, servant, one who serves up meals,

pariveśana 601/1 in attendance, waiting, distributing food, surrounding, n. circumference, the rim of a wheel,

pariveśas m. a neighbour

pariveṣṭita mfn surrounded, beset, covered,

pariveṣṭitāra all-encompassing entity (Gam.),

parivī mfn wound round,

pari√1.vid to know thoroughly, understand fully, caus. *–vedayate*

pari√3.vid P. *–vindati,* to find out, ascertain, to twine, twist round,

parivihvala mfn extremely agitated,

parivījita mfn fanned, cooled,

parivikāra m. walking about for pleasure,

pariviśrānta mfn quite rested or reposed,

pariviṣṭa mfn surrounded, beset, besieged, dressed, offered (as food),

pariviṣṭi f. service, attendance,

pariviśvasta mfn feeling secure, confident,

pariviṣyamāna mfn being waited on, being at table,

parivīta mfn veiled, covered, pervaded, overspread, surrounded, encompassed by, name of the bow of Brahmā

parivitarka m. thought, anything thought of

parivitta mfn twined or twisted round,

pari√1.vṛ P.A. *–varati (te),* to cover, hem in, surround, conceal, keep back, to encompass, embrace, A. *-vṛṇīte* to choose,

pari√vraj P. *–vrajati* to go or wander about, walk round, circumambulate, to wander about as a religious mendicant, to become a recluse (Jainas),

parivrāja m. a wandering mendicant, ascetic of the 4th and last order (who has renounced the world,

parivrājaka m. a wandering holy mendicant

parivrājya n. religious mendicancy,

parivrajyā f. strolling, wandering from place to place, leading the life of a religious mendicant, abandonment of the world, mfn to be gone about,

pari√vṛdh A. *–vardhate* to grow, grow up,

increase, caus. *–vardhayati, te,* to bring up, rear, increase, augment, to rejoice, delight (with 6th),

parivṛddha mfn grown, increased by (comp.), strong, powerful, *-tā* f. increase, extension, the swelling and becoming sour of food in the stomach,

parivṛddhi f. increase, growth,

pari√vṛj P. *-vṛṇakti,* to turn out of the way of, avoid, shun, spare, pass over, to cast out, expel, A. to surround, enclose, keep off, remove, avoid, shun, quit, disregard,
f. avoiding, removing, purification, expiation,

parivṛkta mfn avoided, despised, (*-ā* or *ī*) f. the disliked or despised one, a wife less esteemed than another,

pari√vṛt A. Cl 1 *–vartate,* to turn round, revolve, move in a circle or to and fro, roll or wheel or wander about, circumambulate, to return, go or come back to, to be reborn in, to change, turn out different, to abide, stay, remain, to act, proceed, behave, caus. *–vartayati* to vcause to turn or move round or back or to and fro, A. to roll or bring near, to renew, to overthrow, upset, invert, put in a reverse order, to change, barter, exchange, to understand or explain, wrongly,

parivṛta mfn surrounding, veiled in, filled by, full of (comp.)
n. a covered and walled place or shed used for sacrifices,

parivṛti f. surrounding, standing round,

parivṛtta mfn turned, turned round, revolved, rolling, lasting, remaining, passed, elapsed, ended, covered, surrounded, retreated, returned, n. rolling, wallowing, an embrace,

parivṛttabhāgya mfn whose fortune has changed or gone,

parivṛttanetra mfn rolling the eyes

parivṛttatejas mfn spreading brilliance all around,

parivṛtti f. turning, rolling, revolution, return (into this world), exchange,barter, staying in a place, end, termination,

parivyakta mfn very clear or distinct, (*am*) ind. very clearly or distinctly,

parivyākula mfn much confused/disordered

parivyatha mfn disquieted, afflicted, vexed,

parivyaya m. condiment, spices, expense, cost,

parivyayaṇa n. winding round, covering, the covered spot,

pari√yā P. *–yati* to go or travel about, go round or through, to run through, to surround, protect, guard, to ramble or wander about, to avoid, shun,

pari√yaj P. *–yajati* to obtain or procure by sacrificing, to sacrifice or worship before or after another, perform a secondary rite,

pariyajña m. a secondary rite,

pari√yam P. *–yacchati* to aim, hit,

pariyāṇa n. going about

pariyāṇika n. a travelling carriage,

pariyatta mfn surrounded, beset, hemmed in,

pariyuta mfn clasping, embracing,

parjanya 606/1 m. a raincloud, cloud, rain, rain personified or the god of rain

parkaṭa m. a heron, n. regret, anxiety, f. a fresh betel- nut,

parkaṭī f. wavy-leaved fig tree, a fresh betel- nut, m. a heron,
n. regret, anxiety,

√parṇ 606/2 cl 10 P *parṇayati,* to be green or verdant, DP in *harita-bhāva* making green,

parṇa 606/2 n. a pinion, feather (also of an arrow), wing, a leaf (regarded as the plumage of a tree),

parṇadhi m. feather-holder, the part of an arrow where the feathers are fixed

parṇagṛha n. leaf-house

parṇāla m. a boat, a spade or hoe, single combat,

parṇaśāda m. the falling of leaves,

parṇaśālā f. a leaf-hut,

parṇasi m. a house upon or by the water, a lotus, adorning, decoration

parṇavat mfn leafy,

parṇila mfn leafy,

parṇya mfn relating to leaves, leafy,

parṇin mfn winged, plumed, leafy, m. a tree

parobāhu mfn beyond the arm or reach,

parokṣa 589/1 mfn indirect, that which cannot be seen by eyes directly, unknown, unintelligible, past, completed, (ibc.) in an invisible or imperceptible manner, beyond the range of sight, invisible, absent, unknown,
(*am*) ind. out of sight, behind one's back, without the knowledge of, one's self not being present, indirectly,
(*eṇa*) ind. out of sight, secretly, mysteriously, indirectly,
(*āt)* ind. secretly, without the knowledge of,
(*e)* ind. behind the back of, one's self not being present, m. an ascetic,
(*ā*) f. a past or completed action, *-tā –tva* n. f. imperceptibility, invisibility,

parokṣārtha mfn having a secret or recondite meaning, n. an absent or invisible object,

parokṣajñāna indirect knowledge of Brahman through study of scripture etc.

parokta mfn contradicted,

parocya mfnto be contradicted,

paromātra mfn immense, huge, vast,

paropadeśa m. giving advice to others

paropaga mfn relating to something else,

paropakāra m. benevolence, charity, service to others,

paropasāpaṇa approaching others, begging

parorajas mfn beyond the dust or above the world, untouched by passion,

paroṣṇī f. a cockroach

paro'varam ind. from top to bottom, from hand to hand, in succession,

√*parp* 606/3 cl 1 P to go, DP in *gati* going

parpa n. a wheel-chair, young grass, a house

parparī f. a braid of hair,

parparīka m. the sun, fire, a tank of water

parparīṇa m. the vein of a leaf,

parśu m. rib, sickle,

pārśva mfn near, proximate,
n. side, immediate neighbourhood, a curved knife, a side of any square figure, the curve or circumference of a wheel, a crooked expedient,
m. the side horse of a chariot,
m.du. heaven and earth,

pārśvanātha 23rd *tīrthaṁkara* of the Jain religion,

pārtha son of *Pṛthā* - *Arjuna* referring to his mother *Kuntī* or *Pṛthā*

pārthiva mfn of or belonging to the earth,
m. king, prince,

pārthivasutā f. king's daughter,

pārthivendra m. most excellent of kings,

partṛ only 3rd pl. with aids, helpfully,

paru m. a limb, member, a mountain, the ocean, the sky, paradise,

parudvāra or *parula* m. a horse,

parus n. a joint or knot (esp. cane or reed), a limb or member of the body

paruṣa knotty (as reed), spotted, dirty-coloured, variegated, hard, stiff, rough, uneven, intertwined with creepers, harsh, sharp, unkind, m. a reed, an arrow, (*ā*) a kind of riddle,
n. harsh speech, abuse,

paruṣacarman n. a rough skin

paruṣaghana m. a dirty or dark cloud

paruṣākṣara mfn harsh-worded, harsh

paruśas ind. limb by limb, member by member,

paruṣatara mfn harsher, sterner,

paruṣatva n. roughness, harshness,

paruṣavacana mfn speaking harshly,
n. harsh speech

paruṣetara mfn gentle, mild,

paruṣiman m. rough or shaggy appearance

paruṣita mfn addressed/treated harshly,

pāruṣya 621/2 n. harshness esp. of speech, roughness, harshness, shagginess, dishevelled state, reproach, insult, violence (in word or deed), squalor

parut ind. last year,

parutka mfn having knots or joints (as grass)

√*parv* 609/1 cl 1 P *parvati* to fill,
DP in *pūraṇa* filling

parvan n. knot, joint, limb, a break, pause, division, step of a staircase, member of a compound, a period or fixed time, a half-month, a day, a festival, holiday, opportunity, occasion, a moment, instant,

parvata 1. mfn consisting of knots or ragged masses, of a mountain, 2. m. mountain, hill, 3. cloud-mountain, 4. rock or boulder, 5. name of a seer (companion of *Nārada*),

parvatakandara n. mountain cave,

parvataśikhara m.n. hill-top,

parvatastha mfn standing on or in the mountain, situated in the mountains,

parvatavāsina mfn dwelling in or on the mountain,

parvatī f. consort of *Śiva*, the power of law

parvatopatyakā f. mountain lowland,

paryā√bhṛ to carry near, fetch from (5th)

paryābhṛta fetched or extracted from,

paryā√bhū to turn upside down,

paryā√dā A. –*datte* to make one's own, take away from (5th), to seize, snatch, to appropriate, learn,

paryādāna n. end, exhaustion,

paryā√dhā P. –*dadhāti* to lay round, surround (with fire),

paryādravati runs to and fro,

paryā√car to come near, approach,

paryadhyayana averse from study

paryā√gā to pursue, be intent upon, to perform a revolution, elapse (time),

paryā√gal P. –*galati* to drop or trickle down on every side,

paryā√gam to go round, elapse, last, live,

paryagāt (V) cannot estimate, must know, (Gam.) is all pervasive –like space, (who) has attained or must know in fact,

paryāgata mfn revolved, elapsed, passed (as a year), finished, done, inveterate, (with *punar*) returned to life, encircled, being in a person's power,

paryagnikṛta mfn encircled with fire,

paryāhāra m. a yoke worn across the shoulders for carrying a load, conveying, a load, a pitcher, storing grain,

paryak ind. round about, in every direction

paryā√kṛ to turn round,

paryā√kṣip to wind round, bind with,

paryākula mfn full of, filled with (comp.), disordered, confused, excited,

paryāloca m. consideration, reflection,

paryālocana m.n. deliberation, consideration, reflection,(*ā*) f. plan,

paryālocita mfn considered, pondered,

paryā√muc to make loose, take off on all sides,

paryā√ṇah P. –*ṇahyati* to cover up, cover

paryāṇa n. a saddle, a circuit,

pary√añc to turn about or round, revolve,

paryā√ṇī to lead, lead round, bring forward

paryaṅgya mfn being about or at the side,

paryaṅka m. a bed, sofa, litter, palanquin, a partic. method of sitting (Buddh.) a cloth wound round the back, loins and knees while so seated,

paryaṅkabandhana n. the act of sitting, with the legs bent and binding a cloth round the back and loins and knees,

paryanta 607/1 ind. end, to the end of , as far as, end, extremity, bounded by, (*am*) ind. entirely, altogether, (ifc.) to the end of, as far as, (*e*) ind. at the end, mf(*ā*)n coming to an end with, being a match for, extending in all directions, m. circuit, circumference, edge, limit, border, side, flank, extremity, end,

paryāntam (for *paryanta*) as far as, up to (comp.)

paryantabhū f. ground contiguous to the skirts of a river or mountain,

paryantadeśa m. a neighbouring or adjacent district,

paryantaparvat m. an adjoining hill,

paryantasaṁsthita or –sthā or –sthita mfn limiting, confining, neighbouring,

paryantikā f. loss of all good qualities, depravity

paryantīkta mfn finished,

paryantīya mfn being at the end,
paryanubandha m. binding round,
paryanuyoga m. asking, inquiring, an inquiry in order to refute, censure, reproach,
paryanuyojya mfn to be blamed or censured,
paryanuyoktavya mfn to be questioned, to be urged to answer a question,
paryanuyukta mfn asked, questioned,
pary-anv-√3.iṣ P. *–icchati* to seek for, search after
paryanya for *parjanya*
pary√āp P. *–āpnoti* to reach, obtain, make an end of, be content,
paryā√pat to hasten forth, hurry or run away
paryāpta mfn obtained, gained, finished, completed, large, abundant, many, sufficient for, adequate, equal to, a match for, (*am*) ind. fully, completely, enough, one's fill, willingly, readily, abundant, sufficient, equal
paryāptā f. copiousness, abundance, satisfaction, gratification,
paryāptakāma mfn one whose desires are accomplished or allayed,
paryāptavat mfn able, capable,
paryāpti 608/3 end, conclusion, entireness, fulness, sufficiency, adequacy, competency, obtaining
paryārin mfn toiling long without success, success after a long effort,
paryasana n. throwing or tossing around, putting off or away,
paryaśnoti 1/s/pres arrives at, reaches
paryaśru mfn bathed in tears, tearful,
paryasta mfn thrown or cast about, spread, diffused, surrounded, encompassed, ensnared, strung, overturned, upset, inverted, changed, struck, killed, dismissed, laid aside,
paryastamayam ind. about sunset,
paryasti 1/s/pres is in the way of, passes or spends time,
paryasti f. sitting upon the heels or hams,
paryā√śvas P. *śvasiti* or *śvasati,* to breathe out, recover breath, take heart, be at ease, caus. to comfort, console,
pary√ās P *–āste* to sit or assemble round anyone, remain sitting or inactive,
paryāśvasta mfn comforted, consoled, tranquil, at ease,
paryasyati 1/s/pres throws or casts around, spreads around, diffuses, entraps, ensnares, turns round, overturns,
paryaṭ *pari√aṭ* P.A. *paryaṭati, te,* to roam or wander about, travel over,
paryā√tan to spread round, surround
paryaṭana n. wandering about,
paryaṭaka m. a tramp, vagabond,
paryaṭita mfn one who has roamed or wandered
pary-ava-dāta mfn perfectly clean or pure, very accomplished, well acquainted with, (*-tva*) well-known, very familiar, (*-śruta*) mfn perfectly skilled in art, (*tā*) f.
paryavadāpayitṛ m. a distributor
paryavadhāraṇa n. precise, determination careful consideration, refining,
paryavanaddha mfn overgrown,
paryavāp (ava+√āp) P. *–avāpnoti* to study
paryavapāda m. transformation,
paryavapādya mfn effecting transformation
paryavarodha m. obstruction, hindrance,
paryāvarta m. return, exchange,
paryāvartana n. coming back, returning,
paryāvartita mfn turned round, subverted, reversed
paryavasāna n. end, termination, conclusion, comprehending, including, amounting to(7th), *(āt*) ind. in consequence of
paryavasarpati 1/s/pres approaches in a creeping manner, creeps up to,(*√sṛp*)
*paryavasāya,*m. = *paryavasāna*
paryavasāyin mfn ending with, amounting to,
paryavaśeṣa m. end, termination,
paryavaśeṣita mfn left remaining, regarded as the end of all (i.e. God),
paryavasita living farther off, departed to, finished, concluded, resolved, settled, *-mati* mfn thoroughly acquainted or familiar with,

paryavaskanda m. jumping down from a carriage
paryavaṣṭabdha mfn surrounded, invested,
paryavaṣṭambhana n. surrounding, investing
paryava√sthā A. *-tiṣṭhate* to become firm or steady, to fill, pervade, caus. –*sthāpayati* to comfort, encourage,
paryavasthā f. °*sthāna* n. opposition, contradiction,
paryavasthita mfn standing, stationed, (with 7th) contained in, attached or devoted to, intent upon, occupied with, merry, content, comfortable, of good cheer,
paryavasyati 1/s/pres results or ends in, finishes, completes, includes, perishes, is lost, *(√so)*
paryavatiśṭhate he/she/it becomes steady, steadies, stands, 1/s/pres/indic/mid
pary-ave (ava+√i) P. *–avaiti* to turn round, turn in the right direction, to pass, elapse,
paryaveta mfn elapsed, expired,
paryāvila mfn very turbid, much soiled,
paryā√vṛt A. *–vartate*, to turn round, turn away from, return to
paryāvṛta mfn veiled, covered,
paryā√yā to approach from (5th), come near
paryaya m. revolution, lapse, expiration, waste or loss of time, change, alteration, inversion, irregularity, confusion with(comp.), contrariety, opposition, neglect of or deviation from duty,
paryāya m. going or turning or winding round, course, lapse or expiration of time, repetition, succession, (ibc. or-eṇa) ind. in turn, successively, alternately, *-tā* f. *–tva* n. way, manner, method of proceeding, probability, formation, creation, point of contact,
paryāyacyuta mfn one who has lost his turn, superceded, supplanted,
paryāyata mfn extremely long or extended
paryāyakrama m. order of succession, regular rotation or turn,
paryāyaśabda m. synonym
paryāyaśas ind. by phrases or sentences, periodically, in succession, by turns,
paryāyātman m. the finite nature, finiteness,
paryāyavācaka m. a synonym, mfn expressing a corresponding notion,
paryāyavacana n. a convertible term, synonym
paryāyavākya n. similar words,
paryāyin mfn embracing, including,
pary-e (ā √i) P. *–aiti*, to go round, circumambulate, to come back,
paryeṣaṇa n. search, inquiry, investigation, striving after,
paryeṣṭi searching for, inquiry, striving after worldly objects,
paryudañcana n. debt,
paryudāsa m. a prohibitive rule, exception,
paryudasana n. exclusion,
paryudasta mfn rejected, excluded,
paryudayam ind. about sunrise,
paryudbhṛta mfn brought out, extracted,
paryudita mfn spoken, uttered
paryūhana n. sweeping or heaping together,
paryukta mfn bewitched by words, conjured
paryupāsate 608/3 sits round, is present at, partakes of, practises, worships 1/pl/pres/indic/mid
paryupa√sthā P. *-tiṣṭhati* to be or stand round, to attend, serve, honour with, A. to join
paryupasthāna n. waiting upon, serving, rising, elevation,
paryupasthāpaka mfn leading to or upon,
paryupasthita mfn standing round, surrounding, drawing nigh, imminent, impending, slipped, escaped (a word), intent upon, devoted to,
paryupta mfn sown, set (as a gem in a ring),
paryupti f. scattering seed, sowing,
paryuṣaṇa n. spending the rainy season,
paryuṣita mfn having passed the night, having stood for a time or in some place, not fresh, stale, insipid,
paryuṣṭa mfn old, faded, withered,
paryuta mfn enclosed or set with,
paryutsuka mfn very restless, excited, eagerly desiring, longing for,

paryutthāna n. standing up, rising,
√*paś* 611/2 present tense only, P A *paśyati (te)* to see, behold, look at, observe, perceive, notice, to be a spectator, to see a person (either visit or receive as a visitor), to live to see, experience, partake of, undergo, to learn, find out, to regard or consider as, take for, to see with the spiritual eye, compose, invent (hymns, rites, etc.), to have insight or discernment, to consider, think over, examine,
2. f. sight or eye,
3. cl 10 P *pāśayati* to fasten, bend, DP in *bandhana* (cl 10) binding,
√*paṣ* 612/3 cl 1 P A *paṣati (te)* see *spaś*. cl 10 P *paṣayati* to bind, hinder, touch, to go, *pāṣayati* to bind, DP in *gati* going
pāśa 623/3 a snare, trap, noose, chain, fetter, the outer world, nature, edge, border, (ifc. expresses contempt or admiration), anything that binds the soul, i.e. the outer world, nature,
pāśāna m. a stone,
pāṣaṇḍa mfn heretical, impious,
paśava mfn derived from or belonging to cattle or animals,
m. beasts- both domestic and wild,
n. flock, herd,
paścā ind. behind, after, later, westward, in the west
paścāt ind. 612/2 beyond, from behind, in the rear, westwards, afterwards, hereafter, later, at last
paścāttāpa m. regret, sorrow, repentance,
pāścātya western, last,
paścima mfn later, last, final, west, westerly
paśu 1. ind. see, behold!
2. m. cattle, domestic animal,
paśubandha m. animal sacrifice,
paśughna mfn slaying cattle,
m. cattle-slayer,
paśumant or *-mat* mfn rich in cattle,
paśupati Lord of animals, Lord Śiva, Lord of individual souls,
paśuroman n. a hair of an animal,
paśutṛp mfn cattle-stealing,
paśuvadha m. slaughter of animals,
paśya 611/2 mfn. beholding, rightly understanding, seeing,
paśya see!, behold! 2/s/impv √*paś* 2/s/impv/act see!
paśyan pres/act/part. seeing
paśyanti they see 1/pl/pres/indic/act
paśyantī "the poised state of action" HH (2nd state of speech or sound)
paśyasi *paś* 611/2 to see, *paśyasi* 2/s/pres/indic/act. you see
paśyata 611/2 part. visible, conspicuous, seen, see!
paśyatas of the seeing, perceiving, pres.part. 6/s/m
paśyati m. 611/2 *paś* to see, *paśyati* he she or it sees or beholds
paśyatsu amongst those who have eyes i.e. among sentient beings(Gam.),
paśyema 3/pl/opt/act may we see
paśyet he should see or perceive 1/s/opt/act *paś*
√*paṭ* 579/1 cl 1 P *paṭati* to go, move, flow, split, open, burst asunder, cl 10 or caus. *paṭayati* to string together, wrap, *pāṭayati* to speak or shine, °*to* or °*te* to split, burst, cleave, tear, pierce, break, pluck out, remove, DP in *gati* (cl 1) going, *bhāṣā* (cl 10) speaking, shining, *grantha* (cl 10) stringing, weaving,
√*pat* 580/3 1. cl 4 A *patyate* to be master, reign, rule, govern, control, own, possess, dispose of, partake of, share in, to be fit or serve for,
2. cl 1 P *patati* to fly, soar, rush on, to fall down or off, alight, descend, fall or sink, fall (in a moral sense), lose caste or rank or position, to light or fall upon, fall to a person's share, to fall or get into or among, to occur, come to pass, happen, caus. *patayati* to fly or move rapidly along, to speed, to drop, °*te* to drive away or throw down, *pātayati (te)* to let fly or cause to fall, to fling, hurl, throw, to lay low, bring down, overthrow, ruin, destroy, to cut off

(a head), knock out (teeth), pour out or shed (water, tears), to kindle (fire), to cast (dice), to turn, direct, fix (eyes), to impose or inflict (punishment), set in motion, set on foot, to seduce to, betray into, subtract, A. to rush on, hasten, DP in *gati* going, falling
3. mfn. flying, falling,
4. in comp. for 3. pad.

paṭa 579/1 m. woven cloth, cloth, garment, painted cloth – a picture, monastic habit, f.(ī) a hem or edge of a garment, curtain of a stage,
n. a thatch or roof,

pata – flying, falling 1/s/pres. imperative it may descend,
mfn well fed, m. flying, falling,

pāta 613/2 mfn watched, protected, preserved,
616/3 m. fall, flying, mode of flying, flight, downfall,

paṭaha m. a drum, war-drum, beginning, hurting,

pātaka 616/3 mfn. causing to fall (from caste) , n. that which causes to fall, a sin, crime, loss of caste,

patākā f. 'flying'a banner or flag, a flag, banner, flagstaff, good fortune, auspiciousness,

patākin mfn having or bearing a flag, adorned with flags,
m. an ensign or standard bearer, a flag, a chariot,

patākinī f. an army,

paṭala n. veil, cover, a roof, thatch,
a chest, basket, box,
a film over the eyes, a cataract,
a chip, piece, portion, train, retinue,

pāṭala mfn pale red, pink,

pātāla n. hell, underworld,

pāṭali f. trumpet-flower,

pāṭaliputra n. capital of Magadha, now Patna,

patana n. the act of falling, a fall, downfall,

pataṅga 581/1 a flying insect, moth, bee etc. any flying thing,

paṭhati reads,

patati falls

patatra n. wing, pinion, feather,

patatrin 581/1 mfn winged, feathered, flying in the sky, m. a bird, a horse, an arrow, n.du. day and night,

patatu *pat* 580/3, 1/s/pres. imperative, fly! fall down!

pāṭava mfn clever, sharp, dextrous,
n. sharpness, cleverness, quickness,

pataya the guardians of the world , masters, (*lokapālas)* (T),

√*paṭh* 580/1 cl 1 P *paṭhati* to read or repeat aloud, to recite, rehearse, to repeat or pronounce the name of a god, to invoke, to read or repeat or recite to oneself, to peruse or study, to teach, cite, quote, mention, express, declare, learn from, caus. *pāṭhayati* to teach, instruct in, DP in *vyaktā-vāc* reading or repeating aloud, reciting, studying,

√*path* 582/2 cl 1 P *pathati* to go, move, to fly, caus. *pāthayati* to throw, send, DP in *gati* going, *prakṣepa* throwing, casting,

patha m. road, path way, see *panthan*,

pāṭha m. study, reading,

patha for *pathin* in cpds.

paṭhaka m. a reader,

pāṭhaka m. a reciter, reader,

paṭhana n. the act of reciting, recitation,

paṭhati reads, recites, studies, teaches,

pātheya n. provisions, food for a journey,

pathi on the way (7th of) *panthan,*
f. reciting, recitation,

pathika m. traveller,

pathirakṣi mfn guarding the paths,

paṭhitvā ind. having recited,

pathya mfn suitable, wholesome, (pertaining to the way, course or progress of a thing), *pathyā* f. pathway,

pati m. 1. master, possessor, lord, husband,

patighni mfn f. husband -slaying,

patiloka m. husband's place, abode of the husband in the future life,

pāṭin mfn splitting, cleaving, m.

a species of fish,
pātin mfn falling, flying, being in, causing to fall, sinking, emitting,
patisthāna n. husband's place,
patisthānīya mfn belonging to or in the husband's place, m. husband's representative,
patita 581/2 mfn fallen, descended, happened, occurred
patitva n. condition of spouse, wedlock,
patitvā ind. having fallen
pativrata n. loyalty or fidelity to a husband
pativratā f. girl, devoted and virtuous wife, virtuous woman,
pativratadharma the rules of life of a chaste woman devoted to her husband,
patnī f. 1. mistress, lady, 2. wife
patra n. a leaf, leaf of paper, page, wing
pātra 612/3 n. a drinking vessel, a cup, dish, bowl, utensil, a fit vessel or worthy person,
pātre to a/the (proper/worthy) person 7/s
pātrī f. a sacrificial vessel,
patsutaḥ-śī mfn lying at the feet,
patsutas ind. at the feet,
pattana n. a town
patti m. foot-soldier,
pattra n. 1. feather, wing, 2. leaf, 3. a leaf for writing on, a written leaf,
pattraśāka n. leaf-vegetable,
pattrin m. arrow, bird,
paṭu mfn 1. sharp, 2. fig. clever,
paudgalika mfn substantial, material, selfish,
pauṁsya n. manliness, manly deed,
paunarukta n. redundancy, repetition, tautology,
paura mfn urban, m. a townsman, citizen,
paurajana townspeople, citizens,
pauruṣa 651/2, mfn manly, human, n. manhood, virility, manliness, manly strength or courage, valour, heroism, force (as opposed to intellect),
pauruṣeya mfn made by man, man-made,
paurvadehika 651/3 mfn. belonging to or derived from a former body or existence, done in a former life
paurvāparyavivarjita (N) free from the relation of before and after, (Bhartṛhari regarding absolute truth),
pautra grandson
pautrī granddaughter,
√pav cl 1 A. *pavate,* to go, =√plav DP not given
pava m. purification, winnowing of corn, air, wind, a marsh, n. cow-dung,
pāvaka 623/2 mfn. pure, clear, bright, (said of Agni, Surya and other gods) m. fire, flame
pavana 610/3 m purifier, wind or the god of wind, breeze, air, breath, vital air, purification, blowing, winnowing fan,
pāvana mfn purifying, purificatory, pure, holy, living on wind, m. a partic. fire, incense,
pāvanī a mythical river, 'the purifier', a cow, the Ganges,
pavate purifies, sanctifies, 610/3 goes,
pavitra 611/1 m. a means of purification, filter, a means of purifying or clearing the mind, f.(ā) basil, saffron, mfn pure, holy, purifying, averting evil, sacred,
√pay 585/3 cl 1 A *payate* to go, move, DP in *gati* going,
payas n. milk, water, rain, semen, juice,
payasya mfn. made of milk, m. a cat, become, liquid, f. (*ā*) coagulated milk, curds, Nom P *payasyati* to flow, become liquid, DP in *prasṛti* flowing, becoming liquid,
payodhara m. a cloud or breast,
payomukha mfn having milk on the face or surface,
payovrata mfn subsisting on nothing but milk, n. vow to subsist on nothing but milk,
pāyu m. 'the organ of excretion' (Gam.), the anus, a guard, protector,
√pel 648/3 cl 1.10P *pelati, pelayati* to go,

DP in *gati,* going

pelava mfn soft, tender, delicate, fine, thin, slim, slender,

√*peṣ* 648/3 cl 1 A *peṣate* to exert oneself, strive diligently, DP in *prayatna* striving for

peṣala mfn lovely, clever, artificially formed, adorned, decorated, beautiful, charming, pleasant,

√*pes* 649/1 cl 1 P *pesati* to go, DP in *gati* going,

peṭa a box, basket, bag, a multitude, retinue, m. the open hand with the fingers extended,

√*pev* 648/3 cl 1 A *pevete = sev,* DP in *sevana* serving

peya mfn to be drunk or quaffed, drinkable, to be tasted, tastable, to be taken (as medicine), m. a drink offering, a libation, n. a drink, beverage, f. (*ā*) rice gruel,

√*phakk* 716/1 cl 1 P to swell, to creep, steal along, have a preconceived opinion, to act wrongly, behave ill, DP in *nācais-gati* moving slowly, going softly, gliding, creeping, acting wrongly

√*phal* 716/2 cl 1 P A *phalati (te*) to burst, cleave open, or asunder, split, to rebound, be reflected, to bear or produce fruit, ripen, be fruitful, have results or consequences, be fulfilled, result, succeed, to obtain (fruit or reward), to bring to maturity, fulfil, yield, grant, bestow, give out, emit (heat), DP in *niṣpatti* giving out, cleaving open, splitting, in *viśaraṇa* bursting, splitting,

phala n. fruit (esp. of trees), the kernel or seed of a fruit, a nutmeg, menstrual discharge, fruit –metaphysically – consequence, effect, result, retribution (good or bad), gain or loss, reward or punishment, advantage or disadvantage, benefit, enjoyment, compensation, the issue or end of an action, a gift, donation, the point of an arrow, a shield, a ploughshare, a spot on a die,

phalāhāra m. fruit only diet,

phalahetavas those who are motivated by the fruit of action

phalaka n. a plank, board, bench

phalākāṅkṣin mfn desiring fruit (results)

phalavant mfn fruitful, yielding good results,

phala-vyāpti 'by which knowledge or consciousness of the form of the object is given to the *jīva'* 'the illumination of the mental modification by consciousness' (U) see *vṛtti-vyāpti*

phālguṇa name of a month in Spring,

√*phaṇ* 716/1 Cl 1 P *phaṇati* to go, move, be accomplished (with *samāptim*), caus. *phāṇayati* to cause to bound, raw off the surface of a fluid, skim, bounding, leaping, DP in *gati* going,

phaṇā f. a snake's hood,

phaṇin 716/1 m. 'hooded' a serpent

phaṇī 1/s/m a snake

phaṭā f. a snake's hood,

√*phel* 719/1 Cl 1 P to go, move DP in *gati* going,

phena 718/3 m. foam, froth, saliva,

phenila mfn foamy, frothy,

√*phull* 717/3 (see *phulla*) Nom P *phullati* to open, expand, blow (as a flower), DP in *vikasana* opening, expanding, blowing (as a flower),

phulla mfn burst open, expanded, blooming abounding in flowers, flowery, dilated (eyes), puffed or inflated (cheeks) loose (a garment), n. a full-blown flower,

phullotpala n. having blooming lotuses, Blooming –lotus –name of a lake,

√*phurāphurāya* 718/3 Nom A °*yati* to tremble, flicker, DP in *saṁcalana* trembling, moving about,

phuṭa n. a snake's hood,

√*pi* 624/2 Cl 6 P *piyati* to go, move, DP in *gati* going,

√*pī* 629/1 connected with √1. *pā*

Cl 4 A *pīyate* to drink, Cl 1 A *payate* to swell, overflow, be exuberant, abound, increase, grow, (trans.) to fatten, cause to swell, or be exuberant, surfeit, DP in *pāna* drinking,

piba mfn drinking, who or what drinks, drink! s.

pibata drink! pl.

pibati drinks

√*picc* 624/2 Cl 10 P *piccayati* to press flat, squeeze, = √*pich,* DP in *kuṭṭane* cutting, ponding, grinding, beating, threshing

piccha n. tail-feather (bird or arrow), a tail, a wing, a crest, f.(ā) the scum of boiled rice, slimy saliva, venomous snake saliva, armour,

√*pīḍ* 629/2 Cl 10 P or caus. to press, squeeze, to hurt, harm, injure, oppress, vex, to beleaguer (a city), to break a vow, neglect (one's family), DP in *avagāhana* paining, tormenting,

pīḍā 629/2 f. pain, suffering, violation, damage, torture, a chaplet or garland for the head,

pīòita mfn squeezed, pressed,distressed, troubled, tormented,

pīdyate 629/2 root *pīd,*pass. to hurt or harm, to be pained or afflicted,

pihita mfn shut, hidden, concealed, covered or filled with, a figure of speech implying knowledge of personal secrets,

pihiti f. covering, stopping,

√*pīl* 630/2 Cl 1 *pīlati* to check or stop, to become stupid, DP in *pratiṣṭambha* checking, obstructing,

√*piṁs* 624/2 Cl 1 . 10 *piṁsati, piṁsayati* to speak, to shine, DP in *bhāṣā* speaking, shining,

pīna mfn thick, brawny, swollen, fat,

pināka m. staff or bow of Rudra/Śiva or trident of Śiva, falling dust, n. species of talc, staff or bow,

pinākin m. Śiva/Rudra

piṇḍ 625/2 Cl 1 A.10 P *piṇḍate, piṇḍayati*, to roll into a lump or ball, put together, join, unite, gather, assemble, DP in *saṁghāta* collecting, heaping, accumulating,

piṇḍa m. a ball of rice offered to ancestors, a ball, globe, lump, piece, body, has the sense of individuality as opposed to universality,

piṇḍapāta m. giving alms,

piṇḍi f. the nave of a wheel,

piṇḍī f. meal cake, a ball, lump of food,

piṅga mfn reddish-brown, tawny

piṅgalā 624/3 f. reddish-brown, tawny, a partic. vessel of the body, the right of 3 tubular vessels which according to yoga are the chief passages of breath and air

√*piñj* 624/3 Cl 2 A *piṅkte* to tinge, dye, paint, to join, to sound, to adore, Cl 10 P *piñjayati* to kill, be strong, give or take, to dwell, to shine or speak, to emit a sound,
DP in *varṇa samparcana* (Cl 2) tingeing, dyeing, colouring, in *hiṁsā* (Cl 10) hurting, killing, *bala* being strong or powerful, *ādāna* giving, taking, *niketana* living, dwelling, *bhāṣā* speaking, shining,

piñja mfn mfn confused, disturbed in mind, m. the moon, f. turmeric,

piñjara mfn reddish-yellow or tawny, m. a tawny-brown colour, n. a horse (bay or chestnut?), gold, yellow pigment,

piñjota f. the rustling of leaves,

piñjūla n. tuft of stalks, grass,

√*pinv* 627/3 Cl 1 P *pinvati,* to cause to swell, distend, cause to overflow or abound, A *pinvate* to swell, be distended, abound, overflow, DP ?

pipāsā 627/3 f. desire to drink, thirst,

pipasat 627/3 mfn wishing to drink, thirsty,

pipāsu mfn thirsty

pipīla m. ant,

pipīlikā f. ant,

pippala 627/3 the sacred fig tree, a kind of bird, a nipple, a jacket sleeve,

√piś 628/2 Cl 6 P *piṁśati (te),* to hew out, carve, prepare, (esp. meat), make ready, adorn, to form, fashion, mould, 2. f. ornament, decoration, DP in *avayava* shaping, forming, *nāśana* destroying,

√piṣ 628/3 Cl 7 P A *pinaṣṭi* to crush, bruise, grind, pound, hurt, injure, destroy, caus. *peṣayati* to crush, bruise, grind, to give, be strong, dwell, , DP in *sañcūrṇa* pounding, grinding,

√pis 629/1 Cl 4 P *pisyati* to stretch, expand, Cl 1 *pesati* to go, move, Cl 10 *pesayati* to hurt, be strong, give or take, to dwell, DP in *gati* (cl1, 10) going,

piśāca m. vampire, goblin, ghost

piśaṅga mfn reddish-brown,

piśita n. flesh, mfn made ready, prepared, dressed, adorned,

piṣṭa mfn milled, fashioned, prepared, n. meal, a cake, pastry, flour,

piṣṭapaśu m. sacrificial beast effigy of meal,

piśuna mfn back-biting, slanderous, wicked, base, m. cotton, a crow, a goblin, n. informing against, betraying, saffron,

√piṭ 625/2 Cl 1 P *peṭati* to sound, to assemble or heap together, DP in *śabda* sounding, or *manghāta* heaping or collecting together,

pīta mfn yellow, drunk, quaffed, ifc. having drunk, soaked, saturated, n. drinking, m. yellow colour, topaz, a yellow pigment,

pitāmahaḥ great father, grand- father, the Creator, the forefathers, the Manes,

pītāmbara mfn dressed in yellow clothes, m. religious mendicant wearing yellow garments, dancer or actor,

√piṭh 625/2 Cl 1 P *peṭhati* to inflict or feel pain, DP in *hiṁsā* hurting, or *saṁkleśana* feeling pain,

pīṭha n. 1. seat, chair, 2. image pedestal,

pīṭhacakra n. wagon with a seat,

pitṛ 626/2 a father, pl. forefathers, virtuous ancestors, the *manes,*

pitṛloka m. father's house, world of the *pitṛ*s

pitṛmitra n. father's friend,

pitṛtas ind. on the father's side,

pitṛvya m. father's brother,

pitrya mfn of one's father, of our fathers, of or belonging to or sacred to the *Mane*s

pitṛyajña m. sacrifice to the *Mane*s

pitṛyāna the path of ancestors,

pitta n. bile, one of the three humours,

pīvas n. fat,

pīyūṣa 630/1 nectar, cream, the drink of immortality produced at the churning of the ocean of milk
- *vat* like nectar

√plakṣ 714/3 Cl 1 P A *plakṣati (te*) to eat, consume, DP in *adana* eating

plava 715/2 mfn. swimming, floating, a float, boat, small ship, bird, frog etc. perishable,

plavaga m. frog, monkey,

plavagati 715/2 m moving by jumps, a frog, swimming, jumping, leaping,

plavana n.swimming, plunging into or bathing in, leaping, jumping over (comp) mfn inclined,stooping down towards, m. monkey,

plavate he jumps

plāvita ppp. submerged, inundated,

√plī 715/1 Cl 9 P *plināti* to go, move, DP in *gati* going

√plih 715/1 Cl 1 A *plehate* to go, move, DP in *gati* going

√plu 715/2 Cl 1A P *plavate (ti)* to float, swim, bathe, to go or cross in a boat, sail, navigate, to sway to and fro, hover, soar, fly, blow (as the wind), pass away, vanish by degrees, be lengthened (as a vowel), to hop, skip, jump, caus. *plāvayati* to cause to float or swim, bathe, wash, inundate, submerge, to wash away, remove (guilt, sin), to purify, prolate (lengthen) a vowel, cause to jump or stagger, DP in *gati* floating, swimming, jumping,

√pluṣ 715/3 Cl 1.4. P *ploṣati, pluṣyati* to

burn, scorch, singe, Cl 9 P *pluṣṇāti* to sprinkle, anoint, fill, DP in *dāha* (Cl 1.4.) burning, in *snehana* (Cl 9) anointing, or *secana* becoming wet or moist or *pūraṇa* pouring out, filling,

pluta mfn the protracted measure of a vowel (beyond *dirgha)*, bathed, overflowed, submerged, covered or filled with, leaped, leaping, n. a flood, deluge, leaping, moving by leaps, capering (one of a horse's paces),

pluti 715/3 f. overflowing, a flood, prolation (of a vowel), a leap, capering, curvet (one of a horse's paces),

plutvā having jumped

poṣa m. thriving, development, welfare,

poṣakā f. a nourisher, feeder, maintainer

poṣaṇa 650/2 mfn nourishing, cherishing, n. the act of nourishing, keeping, maintaining, supporting

poṭa m. the foundation of a house, putting together, uniting, mixing, (*ā*) f. a hermaphrodite or a woman with a beard, a female servant or slave, *(ī)* f. the rectum, a large alligator,

pota 650/1 m.n. a vessel, ship, foundation of a house, m. a young animal, a fetus without membrane, cloth, a garment,

poṭaka m. servant,

potaka m. site or foundation of a house, young animal or plant,

√*pṛ* 1. 645/2 Cl 3 P *piparti* Cl 9 P *pṛṇāti* to protect, to bring over or to, bring out of, deliver from, rescue, save, protect, escort, further, promote, to surpass, excel, to be able, preserve, keep alive, to get over, overcome, bring to an end, to resist, withstand, be capable of or able to,
DP in *pālana* nourishing or *pūraṇa* filling,
2. Cl 5 P Cl 6 A *pṛnoti*, or *priyate* to be busy or active,
DP in *prīti* (Cl 5) pleasing, delighting, in *vyāyāma* being busy or active

pra 652/1 ind. prefix – before, forward, in front, on, forth, (as a separate word) forth, away, (as prefix to an adjective) excessively, very much, (in nouns of relationship) great,
2. mfn filling, fulfilling, like, resembling, n. ifc. fulfilment,

√*prā* 701/3 1. Cl 2 P *prāti* to fill, 2. mfn filling, DP in *pūraṇa* filling
3.lengthened form of *pra* (prefix meaning before, forward, in front, on, forth) in compounds

pra√*āp* Cl 5 *prāpnoti,* to obtain, attain, get,

prārthayate (-ti) √*arth*, objectifies, wishes for, desires, asks for something,

prabaddha mfn bound, tied, fettered, dependent on (comp.), checked, stopped, suppressed,

prabala powerful, strong, mighty, important (as a word), dangerous, ifc. abounding in, (*am*) ind. greatly,
2. Nom.P. °*lati* to become strong or powerful,

prabalatara mfn stronger, very strong or mighty,

prabalatoya mfn abounding in water,

prabalatva n. strength, power, might,

prabalavat mfn strong, mighty,

prabalavirasā f. decay,

prābalya n. superiority of power, force, predominance, ascendancy, validity of a rule,

prabanddhṛ m. 'one who connects together', a composer, author, interpreter,

pra√*bandh* P. *–badhnāti,* to bind on, fasten, fetter, check, hinder,

prabandha m. a connection, band, tie, an uninterrupted connection, ininterruptedness, continuance, a composition, literary production, a commentary

prabandhakalpanā f. a work of fiction

prabandhana n. binding, fettering, bond, tie, connection,

prabandhavarṣa m. incessant rain,

prabarha m. the best, most excellent,

pra √bhā 683/3 shine forth, begin to become light, shine, gleam, seem, look like, reveal, to illuminate, enlighten,
pra √bhāṣ speak, tell, declare, manifest, explain, call, name, talk to,
prabhā 683/3 f. light, splendour, radiance
prabhadraka mfn exceedingly beautiful or handsome,
prabhākara m. 'light-maker' the sun, (du. the sun and moon), the moon, fire,
prabhākari f. illumination, enlightenment, 'shines light' (Buddhist),
prabhālepin mfn covered with splendour
prabhāmaṇḍala n. a circle or crown of rays
prabhāmaya mfn consisting of light, shining,
prabhāna n. light, radiance, shining,
prabhāpana n. causing to shine,
prabhāpanīya mfn to be caused to shine,
prabhāpraroha a ray or flash of light,
prabhaharati (te)√bhṛ P.A. brings forward, places before, offers, presents,
prabharman n. placing before, presenting, reciting, recitation,
pra√bhāṣ A.P. *-bhāṣate, (ti),* to speak, tell, declare, disclose, manifest, explain, call, name, to talk to, converse with
pra√bhās A.P. *–bhāsate, (ti),* to shine, glitter, be brilliant, caus. *–bhāsayati,* to irradiate, illuminate, enlighten,
prabhāṣa m. declaration, doctrine,
prabhāsa m. splendour, beauty,
prabhāṣana n. explanation,
prabhāsana n. irradiating, illumining,
prabhāṣita mfn spoken, uttered, declared,
prabhāṣin mfn saying, speaking,
prabhāsura, prabhāsvat, mfn shining forth, shining brightly, brilliant,
prabhāsvara mfn clear, shrill (as a voice), shining forth,
shining brightly, brilliant,
prabhāta mfn shone forth, begun to become clear or light,
n. daybreak, dawn, morning,
prabhātakāla m. time of daybreak,
prabhātakalpa mfn nearly become light, approaching dawn,
prabhātakaraṇīya n. a morning rite,
prabhātabhāva 684/1 shone forth, begun to become clear or light, dawn
prābhātika mfn relating to morning,
prabhava 684/2 mfn. prominent, excelling, distinguished. m. production, source, origin, cause of existence (as father or mother or the Creator), coming to be, f. (*ā*) springing or rising or derived from ,might, power,
prābhava n. superiority,
prabhāva m. (ifc f. *ā)* might, power, majesty, dignity, strength, efficacy,
prabhāvaka mfn prominent, having power or influence
prabhavana n. production, source, origin, ifc. springing from, ruling,
prabhāvana mfn creating, creative, explaining, disclosing, m. creator, (*ā*) f. disclosing, revealing, promulgation of a doctrine,
prabhavāpyayau
'the place of origin and dissolution' (Gam.),
prabhavat mfn coming forth, arising, mighty, powerful, potent, 684/2
prabhāvat mfn luminous, radiant, splendid,
prabhāvavin, mfn powerful, mighty,
prabhāvayitṛ mfn making powerful or mighty,
prabhaviṣṇu Lord of Creation, creator, lord over, *-tā* f. lordship, supremacy, dominion, tyranny,
prabhavitṛ mfn powerful, potent, m. a great lord or ruler,
prabhavya mfn being at the source, original,
prabheda m. difference, splitting, piercing, division, subdivision, variety, species, kind, sort,
prabhid P. *–bhinatti*, to cleave, split asunder, pierce, pass.- *bhidyate*, to be broken in pieces, crumble, to be dissolved, open, to split,
prabhinna, mfn split, cleft, pierced, flowing with juice (an elephant in rut), broken through, interrupted, disfigured, altered,
prabhīta mfn terrified, afraid, *(√bhī)*

pra√bhrāj A. *–bhrājate* to shine forth, gleam,

prabhrāj mfn shining forth,

pra√bhram P. *–bhramati* or *–bhrāmyati,* to roam about, wander through,

pra√bhraṁś A. *–bhraśyate* to fall away, drop down, disappear, vanish

prabhṛta 685/1 mfn. brought forward, introduced, ind. beginning with, from – forward or upward,

prābhṛta m. a present, gift, offering, m. a skilful physician,

-ka n. a present, gift,

resting upon authority, authenticity, authoritativeness, evidence, credibility,

prabhṛtha m. an offering, an oblation,

prabhṛti f. bringing forward, offering (sacrifice or praise), beginning, commencement, ifc commencing with or etcetera, from then onward (with 5th)

prabhu 684/2 mfn excelling, mighty, powerful, rich, abundant, more powerful than (5th), able, capable, having power to, constant, eternal, m. a sound, word, mercury, the Lord, a master, lord, king, *prabho* voc. O Lord, *-tā* f. lordship, dominion, supremacy, *-tva* n. lordship, sovereignty, high rank, might,

-tvabodhi knowledge joined with supreme power,

-bhakta mfn devoted to his master, m. a good horse,

-bhakti f. loyalty, faithfulness,

-bhū = *bhu*

pra√bhū P. A. *–bhavati, (te),* to dominate, prevail, to come forth, spring up, arise or originate from (5th), appear, become visible, happen, occur, to be before, surpass, to become or be numerous, increase, prevail, be powerful, to rule, control, have power over, be master of, to be equal to or capable of, to be a match for, to be able to (inf.), to profit, avail, be of use to, caus. *–bhāvayati* to increase, spread out, extend, augment, multiply, to provide more amply, endow more richly, cause to thrive or prosper, cherish, nurture,

pra√bhuj 1. to bend, incline,

3. to befriend, protect,

prabhukta mfn begun to be eaten (as rice),

prabhūṣati P.(he/she) offers, presents,

prabhūṣṇu mfn powerful, strong, able,

prabhūta 684/3 mfn come forth, risen, appeared, ifc. become, transformed into, abundant, much, numerous, considerable, high, great, abounding in, able to (infin.), governed, presided over, mature, perfect, (in phil.) a great or primary element, (=*mahābhūta*),

-tā f. *-tva* n. quantity, plenty, multitude, large number, sufficiency,

-rūpa n. great beauty,

-śas ind. many times, often,

°*totka* m. ardently longing for

-varṣa n pl. many years,

-vayas mfn advanced in years, old,

prabhūti f. source, origin, imperious demeanour, sufficiency, a ruler,

prabhūvarī f. reaching or extending beyond,

prabodha m. awaking (from sleep or ignorance), becoming conscious, consciousness, opening (of flowers), manifestation, appearance (of intelligence), waking, wakefulness, knowledge, understanding, intelligence, awakening, friendly admonition, good words,

prabodhacandra m. 'the moon of knowledge', knowledge personified and compared with the moon,

prabodhaka mfn awakening, causing to open or blossom, ifc = *-bodha,* understanding, intelligence, f. *(ikā)* easily intelligible,

prabodhana mfn awaking, arousing, n. waking, awaking, awakening, arousing, knowledge, understanding,

comprehension, enlightening, instructing,
prabodhita mfn awakened, aroused, etc.
prabodhin awaking, coming forth from(5th),
prabodhitā awaking, wakefulness,
prabodhya mfn to be awakened,
prābodhika m. dawn, daybreak,
prabravīmi I shall say 1/s/fut/act
pra√brū 683/3 *-bravīti, -brūte,* to exclaim proclaim, announce, declare, teach, praise, celebrate, speak kindly to, say, tell, relate
prabrūhi speak!
prabuddha mfn awakened, awake, roused, expanded, developed, opened, come forth, appeared, known, understood, enlightened, clear-sighted, clever, wise, *-tā* f. wisdom, intelligence,
pra√budh A. *–budhyate* to wake up, wake, awake, to expand, open, bloom, blossom, P.*-bodhati,* to become conscious or aware of, know, understand, recognize as, caus. *–bodhayati* to wake up, awaken, to cause to expand or bloom, to stimulate (with gentle friction), to make sensible, cause to know, inform, persuade, instruct, teach,
prabudha m. a great sage,
prabudh mfn watchful, attentive,
prāc eastern,
prācā ind. forwards, onwards, eastwards,
prācais ind. forwards,
pracakita mfn trembling, terrified
pracakra n. an army in motion,
pra√cakṣ A. *-caṣṭe* to tell, relate, declare, to suppose, regard or consider as, to name, call, caus. *-cakṣayati* to irradiate, illumine,
pracala mfn moving, shaking, what goes well, current, customary,
pracalāka m. shooting with arrows, a snake, a chameleon, peacock's tail or crest
pracalākin m. a peacock, a snake,
pracalana n. trembling, shaking, retiring, flight, going well, circulating, customary,
pracalat mfn moving, shaking, going, proceeding far or much, prevailing, being recognized (as authority or law),
pracalita mfn prevailing, set in motion, moved, received, in use, going away, departure, perplexed, confused,
pracaṇḍa mfn excessively violent, impetuous, fierce, passionate, great, large, hot, burning, sharp,
prācaṇḍya n. violence, passion,
pracapala, mfn very unsteady or restless,
pra√car P. *–carati* to proceed towards, go or come to, arrive at, to come forth, appear, to roam, wander, to circulate, be or become current (as a story), to set about, perform, discharge, to be active or busy, be engaged in, to proceed, behave, act in a peculiar manner, to come off, take place, caus. *–cārayati* to allow to roam, turn out to graze,
pracara m. a way, road, path, usage, custom, going well or widely,
pracāra m. roaming, coming forth, showing one's self, manifestation, appearance, occurrence, existence, application, employment, use, conduct, behaviour, prevalence, custom, usage, a playground, place of exercise, pasture, a driveway,
prācāra mfn contrary to or deviating from ordinary institutes and observances, m. a winged ant,
pracaraṇa n. going to graze, proceeding with, beginning, undertaking, circulating, being current, using,
pracāraṇa n. scattering, strewing,
pracaraṇīya mfn being in actual use,
pracārin mfn coming forth, appearing, following, sticking to, proceeding with, acting, behaving, going about,
pracarita mfn followed, practised, arrived at
pracaryā f. an action, process,
prācārya m. the teacher of a teacher or a former teacher,
prācas ind. from the front, facing, opposite, directed forwards or towards,

turned eastward, eastern, easterly, being to the east of, running from west to east, inclined, willing, lasting, long (as life),
previous or prior or former (esp. ibc.),
m.pl. the people of the east or grammarians,
f. (*ī*) a post for tying an elephant to,
pracaya m. collecting, gathering, heap, mass, accumulation, growth, ,
pracayana n. gathering, collecting,
pracchada m. a cover, coverlet, wrapper,
pracchādana mfn concealing, hiding, n. covering, concealment, concealing,
pracchādya ind. having covered, to be covered or hidden,
pracchana n.f. asking, inquiring, a question,
pracchanna mfn covered, enveloped, shut up, hidden, concealed, unobserved, private, secret, disguised, n. a private, door, lattice, loop-hole,
pracchāya n. a shadowy place, dense shade,
pra-cchid P.A. *–cchinatti, -cchinte* to cut off or through, pierce, split, cleave,
pracelaka m. a horse, 657/3
praceluka m. a cook
pracetana mfn illumining, illustrating,
pracetas mfn attentive, observant, mindful, clever, wise, happy, delighted,
pracetita mfn noticed, observed,
pracetṛ m. a charioteer,
pracetuna mfn affording a wide view or prospect,
√*prach* 658/2 Cl 6 P A *pṛcchati (te)*to ask, question, interrogate, to ask after, inquire about, to ask or interrogate anyone, A. asking oneself, to seek, wish, long for, to ask, demand, beg, entreat,
DP in *jñīpsā* asking, questioning,
pracchādana mfn hiding, concealing,
n. upper or outer garment, concealment, covering,
pracchanna mfn hidden, secret, stealthy,
n. lattice, loophole, private door,
(*am*) ind. stealthily,
pracchāya n. dense shade, shadowy place,

pra√*ci* to collect, gather, pluck, mow or cut down (enemies), to increase, augment, enhance,
prācī (see *prāñc* for associated forms)
f. (with *diś)* the east, the post to which an elephant is tied,
ind. before (in place, order, time), in the east, to the east of (5th), before the eyes, at first, formerly, previously, already, (with *eva*) a short while ago, recently, still more so, from now, henceforth, up to, as far as (with 5th esp. in gram.), between, early in the morning,
prācikā f. a mosquito, female falcon,
prācīna mfn turned towards the front or eastward, eastern, easterly, old, former, prior, preceding, ancient,
prācīnagāthā f. an ancient story, tradition,
prācīnakalpa m. a former kalpa or or period of the worlds duration,
prācīnamata n. an ancient belief, a belief sanctioned by antiquity,
prācīnāvītin or °*nopavīta* mfn wearing the sacred thread over the right shoulder,
pra√*cint* P. *–cintayati* to think upon, reflect, consider, find out, devise, contrive,
pracintya 1. ind. having reflected or considered, 2. mfn to be reflected or considered,
prācīra m.n. an enclosure, fence, hedge, wall
pra√*cit* P.A. *–ciketti, -cikitte*, to know or make known, to become visible or manifest, appear, caus. *–cetayati* to make known, cause to appear, A. to appear,
pracita mfn gathered, collected, heaped, covered or filled with (3rd or comp.)
praciti f. investigation, examination,
pracoda m. instigation,
pracodaka mf(*ikā*)n instigating, f. inflamer
pracodana n. instigating, exciting, direction, command, a rule or law, saying,
pracodin mfn driving forward, urging,
pracodita mfn driven on, urged, impelled, asked, requested, directed, decreed, determined, announced, sent,

pracṛtta-śikha mfn with loosened braids or flowing hair,
pra√cud P. Cl 1–*codati* to set in motion, drive on, urge, impel, caus. –*codayati* to excite, inspire, command, summon, request, A. to hasten, make haste,
pracudita mfn hurled, shot off,
pracura mfn much, many, abundant, ifc. abounding in, filled with, (opp. to *alpa*)
pracuracchala mfn hidden in many disguises,
pracurakaraṇa n. making abundant, augmenting, increasing,
pracura-tā f. –*tva* n. abundance, multitude,
prācurya n. multitude, abundance, plenty, amplitude, prolixity, prevalence, currency, (*eṇa*) ind. in a mass, fully, mostly,
prācya mfn being in front or in the east, eastern, easterly, prior, ancient, pl. the inhabitants of the east, the ancients
pracyava m. fall, ruin, withdrawal, 658/1
pracyavana mfn removing, destroying, n. falling down esp. from heaven i.e. being born again, departure, withdrawal, loss, deprivation,
pracyāvana n. means of removing or diminishing, a sedative, causing to give up,
pracyāvuka mfn transitory, fragile,
pracyuta mfn routed, put to flight, expelled,
pracyuti f. going away, withdrawing, loss, falling from, giving up, fall, ruin,
pra√1.dā P.A. –*dadāti, -datte,* to give away, give, offer, present, to give up, abolish, to sell, restore, pay, caus. –*dāpayati* to cause to give, to compel to give back or repay, to put or place in (7th),
prā√dā to give, bestow, offer, present, to give up, abolish, sell, restore, to pay, to put or place in, caus. -*dāpayati* to cause to give, to compel to give back or repay, to cause to put in or to,
prada mfn. giving, yielding, bestowing, causing, *pradā* f. a gift
pra√dah P. –*dahati* to burn, consume, destroy, to take fire, be burnt, burn,
pradāha m. burning, heating, consuming by fire, destruction, annihilation,
pradagdha mfn burnt, destroyed,
pradahati P. burns, consumes, destroys,
pradakṣiṇa mfn moving to the right, standing/placed on the right, auspicious, favourable, respectful, reverential, ind. from left to right, towards the south,
pradakṣiṇānuloma mfn respectful and obedient (said of a slave),
pradakṣiṇapaṭṭikā f. a yard, courtyard,
pradakṣiṇayati P. goes round left to right,
pradala m. an arrow,
pradāna n. giving, bestowal, presentation (esp. of an offering in the fire) a gift, donation, giving away in marriage, turning (the eyes), making (an attack), uttering (a curse), granting (a boon), teaching, imparting, declaring,
2. n. a goad
pradānaka n. an offering, donation,
pradānavat mfn giving, liberal,
pradaṇḍavat mfn inflicting severe punishment
pradarpa m. pride, arrogance,
pradarśa m. look, appearance,
pradarśaka mfn showing, indicating, proclaiming, foretelling, teaching, expounding, m. a teacher, n. a doctrine, principle,
pradarśana n. look, appearance, ifc. f. (*ā*) pointing out, showing, teaching, an example, prophesying, f. (*ā*) indication,
pradarśita mfn shown, pointed out, taught, mentioned, specified, prophesied,
pradarśin mfn ifc. seeing, viewing, pointing out, showing, indicating,
pradātṛ m. a giver, offerer, presenter,

an imparter (of knowledge),
a granter (of a wish),
pradatta mfn given away, offered, presented,
pradava mfn burning, inflaming, 680/1
pradaya mfn to be given or presented, or offered or communicated, to instructed or initiated in (7th), f.(ā) to be given in marriage, m. a present,
pradāya 679/3 m. a present
pradāyaka mfn giving, granting, presenting,
pradeha m. a plaster, a thick ointment, poultice, applying a poultice,
pradehana n. smearing, anointing,
pradeśa m. (ifc. *ā* f.) pointing out, showing, indication, direction, decision, determination, appeal to a precedent, an example (in gram. law etc.), a spot, place, region, country, a short while, a wall, the distance from tip to tip of thumb and forefinger, one of the obstacles to liberation (Jainas) 'atomic individuality',
prādeśa m. the span of the thumb and forefinger, place, country, mfn a span long,
pradeśabhāj mfn of short duration,
pradeśana n. a gift, present, offering, also *prādeśana*
pradeśaśāstra n. a book with examples
pradeśavat mfn having/occupying a place
prādeśika mfn having precedents, local, limited, a small land-owner, chief of a district, with *guṇa* m. the authorized function or meaning of a word,
prādeśin mfn a span long,
pradeśinī f. the forefinger
pradeśita mfn urged, directed,
pradeṣṭṛ m. one who pronounces, judgment, chief justice,
pradeya mfn to be given, presented, offered, communicated, imparted, taught, to be instructed or initiated in, (*ā*) f. to be given in marriage, marriageable, m. a present, gift,
pra√1.dhā A. *–dhatte,* to place or set before, offer, to send out (spies), to give up, deliver, to devote oneself to (2nd),
pradhana n. spoil taken in battle, the battle or contest, the best of one's goods, valuables,
pradhāna n. a chief thing or person, the most important or essential part of anything, ibc. the principal or first, chief, head of, primary or unevolved matter or nature, supreme or universal soul, intellect, understanding, (in gram.) the principal member of a compound, an elephant driver, the 1st attendant of a king, mfn chief, main, principal, most important, pre-eminent in (3rd), better than or superior to (5th), (in Sāṁkhya) the original germ of the material universe,
pradhānabhāj mfn 'receiving the chief share', most excellent/distinguished
pradhānabhūta mfn one who is chief person
pradhānādhyakṣa m. a chief superintendent
pradhānaka n. (in Sāṁkhya) the original germ of the material universe, *=pradhāna, avyakta,*
pradhānakarman n. chief or principal action, principal mode of treatment,
pradhānamantrin m. a prime minister,
pradhānāmātya m. a prime minister,
pradhānamitra n. a chief friend,
pradhānāṅga n. a chief member, the chief member, most eminent person in a state, principal branch of a science,
prādhanika n. an implement of war, weapon,
prādhānika mfn pre-eminent, distinguished,
prādhānya n. predominance, prevalence, ascendancy, supremacy,
-tas ind. in regard to the highest object or chief matter, chiefly, mainly, m. a chief or most distinguished person,
pradhānapuruṣa m. a chief person, a most distinguished person, an authority, the supreme soul,
pradhānasevā f. chief or principal service,
pradhānaśiṣṭa mfn taught or laid down as of primary importance,

pradhānatā f. pre-eminence, excellence, superiority, prevalence,
pradhānatama mfn most excellent or distinguished, most important,
pradhānatas ind. according to eminence or superiority,
pradhānātman m. supreme or universal soul,
pradhānatva n.pre-eminence, superiority, excellence, (in Sāṁkhya) the being *pradhāna*
pradhānavādin m. one who asserts the *sāṁkhya pradhāna* doctrine
pradhānavāsas n. the best clothes/full dress
pradhānavṛṣṭi f. copious or heaviest rain,
pradhanottama N. best of battles, a great battle or contest,
pradhānottama mfn best of the eminent, illustrious, warlike, brave,
pradhanya mfn forming the spoil or booty (as cattle),
pradhāraṇa mfn keeping, preserving, (*ā*) f. constantly fixing one's mind on a certain object,
pradhārṣa m. attacking, assaulting √*dhṛṣ*
pradhāvana m. a runner,
pradhāvita mfn run away, set out, started 2. m. air, wind, n. rubbing or washing off
pradhi m. the rim of a wheel, orb, disc (of the moon), a segment,
pra√*dhī* to long for, strive after,
pradhī 2. f. great intelligence, mfn of superior intelligence,
prādhī P.A. (pra-adhi-√i) *prādhyeti, °dhīte,* to continue to study, advance in studies,
pradhimaṇḍala n, a wheels circumference,
pradhmāpita mfn blown into, blown (conch shell),
prādhīta mfn one who has begun his studies, advanced in study, well-read, learned
pradhūmita mfn smothered with smoke, giving out smoke, smouldering,
pradhūpita mfn fumigated, perfumed, heated, burnt, inflamed, lit, afflicted,
pra√*dhṛ* to set the mind upon anything (4th), resolve, determine, to keep in remembrance, to reflect, consider,
prādhva mfn being on a journey, inclined, humble, distant, long, m. start, precedence, first place, a long way or journey, a bond, tie, a joke, sport, (*am*) ind. far away,
pradhvaṁsa m. utter destruction, √*dhvaṁs*
pradhvaṁsābhāva non-existence in the form of destruction, state of destruction,
pradhvaṁsin mfn passing away, transitory, perishable, ifc. destroying,
pradhvāna m. a loud sound,
pra√*dhyai* P.A. *–dhyāyati (te),* to meditate upon, think of, to reflect, consider,
pradhyāna n. meditating upon, reflection, thinking, deep thought, subtle speculation,
prādhyayana n. commencement of recitation or study, 707/1
prādhyeṣaṇa exhortation to study,
pra√*2.dī* to shine forth,
pradi m. a gift, present,
pradigdha 680/1 mfn. smeared over, stained, n.a dish prepared with meat, m. a kind ofgravy
pra√*dih* Cl 2 *–degdhi,* to smear, besmear,
praḍīna mfn flown up or forward, taking flight, n. the act of flying, flying forward,
pra √*dīp* A. *–dīpyate* to flame forth, blaze, burst into flames, caus. *–dipayati*, to set on fire, light, kindle,
pradīpa m. a lamp, light, lantern, also used as 'the (glory) of..' etc. used in titles as elucidation, explanation,
pradīpaḥ lamp, light
pradīpaka mfn a small lamp, a lamp, ifc. explanation, commentary,
pradīpana mfn inflaming, exciting, n. the act of kindling, inflaming,
pradīpta mfn kindled, inflamed, alight, lit, shining, excited, stimulated, blazing
pradīptabhās mfn shining bright,
pradīpti f. light, lustre, brilliancy
pradīptimat mfn bright, radiant, luminous,
pradīrgha mfn exceedingly long,
pra√*diś* 679/3 Cl 6 *–diśati* point out, show,

ordain, designate, declare, fix,
pradiś f. pointing to or out, indication, direction, order, command, dominion, a direction, quarter, region of the sky, the south, intermediate region (between the cardinal points),
2/pl in all directions, everywhere,
pradiṣṭa mfn pointed out, indicated, fixed, ordained,
praditsā f. desire to give,
praditsu mfn wishing to give,
pradiv f. existing from olden times, ancient, the 3rd or 5th heaven, ind. from of old, long since, always, ever, at all times,
pradivas ind. from of old, long since, always, ever, mfn existing from olden times, ancient,
pradoṣa mfn corrupt, bad, wicked, m. defect, fault, disordered condition, mutiny, rebellion,
2. mfn belonging or relating to the evening, evening, the first part of the night, *(am)* ind. in the evening, in the dark, 680/1
pradoṣāgama m. nightfall,
pradoṣaka m. evening,
pradoṣatimira n. the dusk of early night,
pradrāṇaka very needy or poor, distressed,
pradrava mfn fluid, liquid,
pradrāva m. running away, flight,
pradrāvin mfn fleeing, runaway, fugitive,
pradṛpta mfn proud haughty, conceited,
pradṛpti f. haughtiness, arrogance, madness
pra√dṛś pass. *–dṛśyate,* to become visible, appear, be seen caus. *darśayati,* to make visible, show, indicate, explain, teach,
pra√dru P.A. *–dravati, (te)*, to run forwards, run away, flee, to hasten towards, rush upon, to escape safely to,
prā√dru to run away, flee, escape,
pradruh mfn one who hurts or injures,
praduh mfn milking,
prādur ind. out of doors, forth, in sight, become manifest, be visible or audible, appear, arise, exist, (with *kṛ* to make visible or cause to appear), (with √as or √bhū to become manifest, be visible or audible, appear, rise, exist),
prādurbhāva 707/1 m becoming visible or audible, manifestation, appearance, appearance of a deity on earth
prādurbhūta mfn come to light,become manifest/evident, revealed,
pra√duṣ P. *-duṣyati* to become worse, deteriorate, to be defiled or polluted, fall (morally), to commit an offence against, to become faithless, fall off, caus. *-duṣayati* to spoil, deprave, corrupt, defile, to abuse, blame, be angry,
prāduṣ in comp. for *prādur*
prādus ind. forth to view, with *as* be visible, appear, reveal one's self, mfn apparently, seemingly,
pradūṣaka mfn polluting, defiling,
pradūṣaṇa mfn corrupting, defiling, impairing, n. pollution,
pradūṣita mfn corrupted, spoiled, made worse,
prāduṣkaraṇa n. bringing to light, manifestation, production,
prāduṣkṛta mfn made visible, brought to light, manifested, displayed, made to blaze (fire),
praduṣṭa mfn corrupt, wicked, sinful, bad,
praduṣyati 680/1 becomes worse, deteriorates, be polluted, fall (morally),
pradruta mfn run away, fled, departed,
pradvār f. a place before a door or gate,
pradveṣa m. dislike, repugnance, aversion, hatred, hostility to,
pradveṣaṇa n. hatred, dislike of,
pradveṣṭṛ mfn a disliker, hater,
pradviṣ 680/3 mfn disliking, hating
pra√dvṣ P.A. *-dveṣṭi, -dviṣṭe* to feel dislike or repugnance for, hate, show one's hatred against,
pradyota m. radiance, light, a ray of light,
pradyotana m. the sun, n. blazing, shining,
pradyotin mfn ifc. illustrating, explaining,
pradyu n. merit (of good works) leading

to or securing heaven,
pradyumna m. 'the pre-eminently mighty one', name of the god of love,
pradyutita mfn beginning to shine, illuminated, √1.*dyut*
prāg in comp. for *prāñc,*
praga mfn going before, preceding,
pra√gā P. *–jigati* to go forwards, proceed, advance, move, go
prāgabhāva m. the not yet existing, non-existence of anything which may yet be, previous non-existence, non-possession of property that may be possessed,
prāgabhihita mfn before mentioned,
pragacchati goes forward
pragāḍha mfn dipped or steeped in, mixed with, much, excessive, rich in, full of (ifc.), advanced, late (hour), hard, difficult, (*am*) ind. much, exceedingly, greatly, tightly, firmly, n. a crowd, pain, privation, penance,
pragadita mfn spoken, speaking, beginning to speak,
pra√gāh A. *–gāhate,* to dive into, penetrate, pervade,
pragāhana n. dipping or plunging into,
pra√gai P. A. *–gāyati (te),* to begin to sing, sing, celebrate, praise, extol, to sound, resound,
pragalbha mfn bold, confident, resolute, brave, strong, able, proud, arrogant, skilful, illustrious, eminent, mature (age), (*ā*) f. a bold and confident woman, (*am*) ind. courageously, resolutely, *-tā* f. *–tva* n. boldness, wilfulness, resolution, energy, strength, power,
prāgalbhī f. boldness, confidence resoluteness, determination,
pragalbhita mfn proud, arrogant, eminent, conspicuous, shining or resplendent with (3rd),
prāgalbhya 702/1 n importance, rank, manifestation, proficiency,
pragalita mfn dripped down,
pra√gam P. *–gacchati,* to go forwards, set out, advance, proceed, go to, reach, attain,
pragama m. the first manifestation of love, first advance in courtship,
pragāman n. walk, gait, step,
pragāmin mfn setting out, about to depart
pragamana n. a speech containing an excellent answer, progress, advance,
pragāṇa n. access, approach,
2. n. singing, song,
prāganurāga m. former affection,
prāgapam ind. from front to back, in a backward direction,
prāgāra m.n. a principal building,
pragardhin mfn pressing or hastening onwards, eager,
pragata mfn gone forward, started, separate, apart, gone with difficulty,
pragātṛ m. a singer, excellent singer,
prāgavasthā f. a former state, a former condition of life,
pragayaṇa n. an excellent answer,
pragāyin mfn beginning to sing, singing,
prāgbhāra m. the slope of a mountain,
prāgbhāva m. prior existence, superiority, excellence,
-tas from a prior state of existence
prāgdaihika mfn belonging to life in a former body,
prāgdakṣiṇa mfn south-eastern,
prāgdeśa m. the eastern country,
prāgdiś 1. f. the eastern quarter, the east,
2. mfn one who has been pointed to or mentioned before,
prage ind. early in the morning, at dawn, tomorrow morning,
pragenīśa one who sleeps in the early morning as if it were night
pragetana early, relating to the next day,
prāg-grīva mfn having the neck directed eastward,
praghaṇa m.n. a place or terrace before a house, an iron mace, crowbar, a copper pot,
praghāṇa m.n. the trunk of a tree,
pragharṣaṇa m. grinding, crushing, destroying, n. rubbing a remedy for rubbing in or anointing,

pra√ghaṭ A. -ghaṭate to exert oneself, devote oneself to, to commence, begin,
praghaṭā f. the rudiments or first elements of a science,
praghaṭaka ifc. a precept, rule, doctrine,
praghaṭṭaka m. a precept, rule, doctrine,
praghoṣa m. sound, noise,
praghṛṣṭa mfn rubbed in, embrocated, anointed
prāghuṇa m. a guest, visitor,
praghūrṇa mfn turning round, rolling violently, wandering, roaming, m. a guest, visitor
prāghūrṇika m. hospitable reception,
pragīta mfn recited in a singing tone, sung, resonant with singing, vocal, one who has begun to sing, n. song, a sing-song or drawling recitation (regarded as a fault),
prāgītya n, notoriety, celebrity, excellence,
prāgjanmaka mfn belonging to a former life,
prāgjanman n. a former birth, former life,
pragla mfn wearied, fatigued, exhausted,
pra√glai P. *–glāyati* to fade, wither away,
prāglagna n. horoscope,
prāglajja mfn being ashamed at first,
pragopana n. protection, preservation, salvation
pra√grah P.A. *gṛhṇāti, °ṇīte* to hold or stretch forth, hold, to seize, grasp, take hold of, take, to accept, receive, to draw up, tighten (reins), stop (horses), to befriend, favour, further, promote, to keep separated or isolated,
prāgra n. the highest point, summit,
prāgrahara mfn taking the best share, chief, principal among
pragraha m. holding in front, stretching forth, seizing, taking hold of, friendly reception, kindness, a favour, obstinacy, a rein, bridle, a ray of light, a rope, halter, cord, thong, a guide, leader, ruler, a companion, satellite, binding, taming, the arm, mfn receiving, kind, hospitable, *-vat* mfn one who has seized, holding, receiving kindly, obliging,
pragrāha m. seizing, taking, carrying, a rein, bridle, the string of a balance
pragrāham ind. taking the words separately, (without *saṁdhi* pronunciation*),*
pragrahaṇa m. a leader, guide, (ifc. (*ā*) f. 'led by'), stretching forth, offering, taking, seizing, holding, a means for taming or breaking in, being a leader or guide, authority, dignity, a rein or bridle, a check or restraint,
pragrahin mfn guiding the reins,
pra√gras P. *–grasati* to eat up, devour,
pra√grath P. *–grathnāti* or *–grathati,* to string together, join, connect,
pragrathana n. connecting or stringing together, intertwining,
pragṛhīta mfn held forth or out, taken, accepted, lofty, joined or united with (ibc.), kept separate, pronounced without observing *saṁdhi* rules,
pragṛhya 656/2 mfn to be taken or seized or accepted, (in gram.) to be taken or pronounced separately, not subject to the rules of *saṁdhi* ,2. ind. having taken or grasped, carrying away with
pragrīva m.n. a wooden fence round a building, a window, lattice, balcony
prāgrya mfn chief, principal, most excellent,
prāgudañc north-eastern,
prāgukti f. previous utterance,
praguṇa mfn straight, right, correct, honest, upright, being in a good state or condition, excellent,
praguṇana n. putting straight, arranging,
praguṇīkaraṇa n. putting straight arranging properly,
praguṇin mfn smooth or even, friendly towards,
praguṇita mfn made even or straight or smooth, put in order,
praguṇya mfn more exceeding, excellent,
prāguṇya n. right position or direction,
prāgutpatti f. first appearance, first manifestation (of a disease),
prāguttara mfn north-eastern,
prāgvacana n. a former decision, anything formerly decided or decreed,
prāgvaṁśa m. a former/previous generation,

prāgvat ind. as before, as previously, as in the preceding part (of a book),
prāgvāta m. east wind,
prāgvṛtta n. former behaviour,
prāgvṛttānta m. a former event, previous adventure,
prāgvṛtti f. conduct of life in a former existence,
prāh 709/3 (*pra√ah*) to announce, declare,
say, tell, to record, hand down by tradition, to call, name, regard or consider as,
prāha he told, he communicated 1/s/perf/act *pra √ ah*
prāha 709/3 m. dance instruction,
pra√hā Cl 3 *–jahāti,* to abandon, give up, leave, cast aside, get rid of,
prahā f. a good throw at dice, any gain or advantage,
pra√han P. *–hanti,* to strike, beat, kill, destroy,
prahāṇa n. relinquishing, abandoning, avoiding, abstraction, speculation, meditation, exertion,
prahaṇana n. striking etc. a kind of amorous sport
prahāṇi f. cessation, disappearance, want, deficiency,
prahara m. (ifc f.*ā*), a division of time (about 3 hours), the 8th part of a day, a watch, stroke on a gong marking the beginning or end of the watch,
prahāra m. striking, hitting, fighting, a blow or thump, a necklace,
prahārada mfn ifc. giving a blow to
praharaka m. striking the hours, a period of about 3 hours, a watch,
praharaṇa n. striking, beating, pecking, attack, combat, throwing of grass in the fire, removing, dispelling, a weapon, a carriage-box,
praharaṇās 1/pl/n striking, throwing
praharin m. one who announces the hours by beating a gong, a watchman,
prāhārika m. a police officer, watchman,
praharṣa m. erection of the male organ, erection of the hair, extreme joy, thrill of delight, rapture,
praharṣula m. the planet Mercury,
prahartavya gve. to be struck,
prahartṛ m. a sender, dispatcher, warrior,
pra√has Cl 1 *–hasati,* to burst into laughter, laugh aloud,
prahasana n. laughter, mirth, derision,
prahasat mf(*antī*)n n. laughing, smiling,
prahasati pra-√has bursts into laughter, laughs with or at, ridicules,
prahasant smiling, laughing, pres.part. 1/s/m above
prahasita mfn laughing, cheerful, n. bursting into laughter, displaying bright, gaudy colours,
prahasta mfn 'long-handed', the open hand with fingers extended,
prahāsyasi you shall leave or abandon, 2/s/fut/act *pra√hā*
prahata mfn struck, beaten, killed, hewn down, repelled, defeated, spread, expanded, contiguous, learned, accomplished, ifc. a blow or stroke with,
prahatamuraja mfn having drums beaten, resounding with the beating of drums
prahati f. a stroke, blow,
prahāvat mfn acquiring gain, gaining,
prahāyya m. one who is to be sent, a messenger
prahelā f. playfulness, free or unrestrained behaviour,
prahelayā ind. freely, without constraint,
praheli, prahelikā f. (6 kinds) an enigma, riddle, puzzling question,
praheti m. a missile, weapon,
prahetṛ m. one who sends forth or impels,
pra√hi P.A. to urge on, incite, direct, command, to convey or send to, to furnish, procure, bestow on (4th), to throw upon, discharge at, to turn the eyes towards, to drive away, dispatch messengers, send to, A. to rush on, to forsake,
prahi 2. m. a well,
prahima mfn having severe winters,
prahīṇa mfn left, remaining, having no relatives, cast off, worn out,

ceased, vanished, wanting, destitute of, m. removal, loss, waste, destruction,
prahīṇadoṣa mfn one whose sins have vanished, sinless,
prahīṇajīvita mfn one who has abandoned life, dead, slain,
prahita mfn urged on, incited, hurled, stretched forward (an arm), embedded (nails), directed/turned towards (eyes/mind) conveyed, sent, dispatched, *-vat* one who has sent out,
prahitaṁgama mfn going on a mission or errand to (6th),
prahitātman mfn resolute,
prahla mfn pleased, glad,
pra√hlād A. *–hlādate,* to be refreshed or comforted, to rejoice,
Prahlada a prince of the Daityas
prahlāda m. joyful excitement, delight, joy, happiness, sound, noise, a rice species
prahlanna mfn pleased, glad, happy,
prahlatti f. pleasure, delight,
prāhna m. before midday,
prahoṣin mfn offering oblations or sacrifices, accompanied by hymns of praise,
pra√hṛ P.A. *–harati (te),* to offer (esp. praise), to thrust or move forward, stretch out, to put into, fix in, to hurl, throw, strike, hit,
prahrāsa m. shortening, diminution, wane,
pra √hṛṣ 701/2 P.A. Cl 4 *–hṛṣyati (te*), to rejoice, be glad or cheerful, exult,
prahṛṣṭa mfn erect, bristling (as the hair of the body), thrilled with delight, exceedingly pleased,
prahṛṣṭacitta mfn delighted at heart,
prahṛṣṭamanas mfn having a delighted heart, happy,
prahṛṣṭamudita mfn exceedingly pleased and cheerful,
prahṛṣṭamukha mfn having a cheerful face,
prahṛṣṭarūpa mfn of pleasing form, erect in form,
prahṛṣyet one should rejoice, 1/s/opt/act
prahṛta mfn thrown (a stone), lifted up (a stick), struck, beaten, hurt,
prāhus they call, they say 1/pl/perf/act *pra √ah* with present meaning)
prahuta mfn offered up, m. sacrificial food offered to all created beings,
prahuti f. an oblation, sacrifice,
prahva mfn inclined forwards, sloping, bent, bowed, stooping, bowing before, humble, modest, intent upon, devoted to,
prahvala n. a beautiful body,
prahvatva 701/3 n bowed, stooping, bowed before, inclined towards
prahvāya m. call, invocation,
pra√hve A. *–havate*, to invoke
prahvībhūta mfn bowing, humble, modest
praiṣya n. servitude, mfn slave,
praiti (pra √i cl2) to come forth, appear, begin, go on, advance, go forwards, come to, arrive at, depart (die),
praja mfn bringing forth, bearing, m. a husband,
prajā f. procreation, propagation, birth, offspring, children, family, race, posterity, descendants, after-growth (of plants), a creature, animal, man, mankind, seed, semen, subject of a king,
prajahāti 700/3 deserts, gives up, abandons, 1/s/pres/indic/act √*hā*
prajahi kill!, destroy! 2/s/impv/act *pra √han* 700/2
prajādā f. 'granting offspring', shrub name,
prajādhara mfn supporting creatures,
prajāgara mfn one who wakes, waking, m. a watchman, guardian, waking, watching, attention, care, waking up,
prajāgaraṇa n. being awake,
prajāgarūka mfn wide awake,
prajāgupti f. protection of subjects,
prajahāti P. leaves, quits, abandons, renounces, breaks (a promise), sends off, throws, disappears, √3.*hā*
prajahita mfn quitted, abandoned (a fire),
prajāhita , mfn favourable or good for offspring or subjects, n. water,

prajāhan killing/destroying offspring
prajajñi mfn able to beget, 2. knowing, conversant with,
prājaka m. a driver, coachman,
prajākalpa m. the time of creation,
prajākāma mfn desirous of offspring,
prajākāra m. the author of creation,
prajalpa m. prattle, gossip, heedless or frivolous words,
prajalpana n. talking, speaking,
prajalpita mfn talked, spoken one who has begun to talk, n. spoken words, talk
pra√jan 658/2 A. *–jāyate (ti)* to be born or produced, spring up from, be begotten by from or with, to become an embryo, to be born again, to have offspring with or by, to bring forth, generate, bear, procreate, beget on, to provide, cause to be reproduced, caus. *–janayati*
prajana 658/2 m begetting, generation, bringing forth, one who begets, generator, progenitor, impregnation, n. one who begets, progenitor,
prājana m. a whip, goad, °*nin* one who bears a whip
prajānā f. the place of bringing forth,
prajānan being well aware of pres.part. *pra √jñā*
prajanana mfn begetting, generating, generative, vigorous, n. the act of begetting or bringing forth, generation, procreation, birth, production, generative energy, semen, the generative organ (male or female), offspring, children,
prajānāti distinguishes, discriminates 1/s/pres/indic/act *pra√ jñā*
prajanayitṛ m. a generator, begetter,
prajanikā f. a mother,
prajanu m.f. female organ of generation,
prajanuka m. the body,
pra√jap P. *–japati* to recite in a low tone, whisper, mutter,
prajāpa mfn muttering prayers, praying, protecting subjects, m. a prince, king,
prajāpāla m. protector of creatures, a prince, king,
prajāparipālana n. the protection of subjects
prajāpati sacrifice (a divine power), Lord of the Creatures, Virāt, 'the first embodied being – Gam.' m. 658/2 'protector of life', creator, a father, son-in-law, prince, king, the planet Mars, a partic. star,
prājāpatya son of *prajāpati*
prajārtham and °*rthe* ind. for the sake of offspring,
prajāsani mfn = °*vid,* bestowing or granting progeny,
prajsāṛj m. creator of beings, father, king
prajāta mfn born, produced, (*ā*) f. a woman who has borne a child,
prajātantu m. a line of descendants,
prajāti f. generating or generative power, generation, production, bringing forth, delivery, the raising of a grandson, initiation with the sacred thread,
prajātīrtha n. the auspicious moment of birth,
prajava m. haste, rapidity, *prajavam* ind. hastily, rapidly,
prajavana mfn running very quickly,
prajāvat having or granting offspring or children, prolific, fruitful, °*vatī* f. pregnant, bringing forth, mother of
prajavate hastens forward, (*pra√jū)*
prajāvid mfn bestowing or granting progeny,
prajavin mfn hastening, rapid, swift, m. a runner, courier, express,
prajavita mfn driven on, impelled, ifc. urged on, incited,
prajāvṛddhi f. increase/abundance of progeny
prajāvyāpāra m. care for/anxiety about the people
prajāvyṛddha-paśu-vyṛddha mfn one who has ill-luck with his children and cattle,
prajaya m. victory, conquest,
prajayati wins, conquers, (*pra√ji)*
prajāyinī f. about to bring forth, ifc, bearing, bringing forth, a mother of,

prajepsu mfn desiring offspring
prajeśa m. 'lord of creatures', name of the deity for procreation of offspring, 'lord of the people' a prince, king,
prajihīte P. drives off, springs up, √2.*hā*
prajijanayiṣitavya wishing to be born
prajijaniṣamāṇa wishing to be born
prājika m. a hawk,
prajina m. wind, air, also *prajīna*
prajinvati, prajiniti, refreshes, animate, promotes, furthers
prajīrṇa mfn digested,
prajit mfn conquering, defeating,
prajita mfn driven, impelled, urged,
prajīvana n. livelihood, subsistence, *(ā)* f. intelligence, understanding,
prajña *659/1* mfn. wise, prudent, intellectual, clever, m. a wise or learned man, intelligence dependent on individuality, a kind of parrot, ifc. knowing, conversant with
pra√*jñā* P. *–jānāti* to know, understand, (esp. a way or mode of action), discern, distinguish, know about, be acquainted with, to find out, discover, perceive, learn, caus. – *jñāpayati* to show or point out (the way), to summon, invite,
prajñā 659/2 f. wisdom, intelligence, knowledge, discrimination, enlightenment, judgment, device, design, a clever or sensible woman, wisdom personifed as the goddess of arts and eloquence, Sarasvatī,
prājña 702/1 mf(*ā* and *ī*)n intellectual, intelligent, wise, clever, m. a wise or learned man, intelligence dependent upon individuality, a kind of parrot, f.(*ā*) intelligence, understanding, awareness, '..is in the space within the heart' , (Gam.) conscious, (*ī*) the wife of a learned man, -*māna* m. respect for learned men -*tā* f.-*tva* n. wisdom, learning, intelligence,
prajñābhadra m. excelling in wisdom,
prajñācakṣus n. the eye of understanding, mfn 'mind-eyed' wise, intelligent, blind, name of a blind king,
prajñādeva m. god of wisdom
prajñāḍhya m. rich in wisdom,
prajñāditya m. sun of wisdom (applied to a very clever man),
prajñāghana m. nothing but intelligence
prajñāgupta mfn protected by understanding
prajñāhīna mfn destitute of wisdom, ignorant,
prajñāla mfn wise, prudent,
prājñamāna m. respect for learned men,
prajñāmātrā f. an element of cognition, organ of sense,
prajñāmaya mfn made of or consisting of wisdom,
prajñānaghanaḥ m. 'a mass of consciousness (since it is characterised by absence of discrimination)(Gam.)',
prajñānam n. wisdom, knowledge, intelligence, discrimination, sometimes translated as 'consciousness' (e.g. Māṇḍūkya Up.) , wisdom as the outcome of *vijñānam* and practical application, presence of mind,
prajñana mfn prudent, wise, easily known, n. knowledge, wisdom, intelligence, discrimination, a distinctive mark, token of recognition, any mark or sign, a monument, memorial,
prajñānetra variously quoted as – the window of awareness, the eye of awareness, the witness, all that is made to exist by consciousness,
prajñāntaka m. destroyer of wisdom
prajñāpāramitā f. perfection in wisdom
prajñāpeta mfn destitute of wisdom or knowledge
prajñāpratibhāsita m. illumined by wisdom, a partic. *samādhi*
prajñāpta mfn ordered, prescribed,
prājñapti 659/1 f. teaching, information, instruction, an appointment, agreement, experience, 'knowledge, perception of, sound etc.'(Gam.)
prajñāpti f. teaching, information, instruction, an appointment,

agreement, engagement,
prajñāsāgara m. sea of wisdom,
prajñāsahāya mfn having wisdom for a companion, wise, intelligent,
prajñāta mfn known, understood, found out, discerned, known as, well-known, public, common, notorious,
prajñāti f. knowing the way to (6th), or the right way,
prajñātman mfn whose nature is wisdom
prajñātṛ m. one who knows the way, guide, conductor,
prajñāvāda m. a word of wisdom,
prājñavādika mfn thinking oneself wise
prajñāvarman m. having wisdom for armour,
prajñāvat mfn wise, knowing, shrewd, intelligent,
prajñāvṛddha mfn old in wisdom or knowledge
prajñila mfn wise, prudent
prajñin mfn wise, prudent,
prajñu mfn bow-legged, bandy-legged,
prajotpādana f. the raising of progeny
prajotpatti n. the raising of progeny, 658/3
prajuhoti, –juhute, sacrifices continually, offers up, P.A. √*hu*
prajuṣṭa mfn strongly attached to/intent on,
pra√jval P. *–jvalati* to begin to burn or blaze, flame or flash up, shine, gleam,
prajvālā f. a flame, light,
prajvalana n. blazing up, flaming, burning
prajvālana n. kindling, setting on fire,
prajvāra m. the heat of fever (sometimes personified),
prājya mfn (having much ghee), copious, abundant, large, great, important,
prājyabhuja mfn long-armed,
prājyakāma mfn rich in enjoyments,
prājyavikrama mfn possessing great power,
prājyendhanatṛṇa mfn a place abounding in fuel and grass,
pra √kāś to become visible, appear, shine, become evident or manifest, caus. *–kāśayati* to make visible, cause to appear or shine, illumine, irradiate, show, display, manifest, reveal, impart, proclaim,
prāk 703/3 in comp. for *prāñc*
prāk ind. directed forwards, facing, in front, before, previous, prior in place or time, (see *prāñc* 703/3),
prakaca mfn having the hair erect,
pra√2.kal P.-*kālayati* to drive onwards, chase, pursue, to drive out cattle for grazing, to urge on, incite,
prakalā f. part of a part, a minute portion,
prakālana mfn driving on, pursuing,
prakālavid mfn knowing very little, ignorant
prakalpaka mf (*ikā)*n. being in the right place,
prakalpana n. placing in, raising to, (*ā*) f. fixing, settlement, allotment, n.f. supplying or mixing with,
prakalpate (ti), (pra√klṛp) to prosper, succeed, be fit or suitable,
prakalpayati caus. *(pra√klṛp)* to place in front, put at the head, honour, to put down on, to appoint or elect to, select for, to put in the place of, to contrive, invent, devise, prepare, provide, to fix, settle, determine, to prescribe, to ascertain, calculate, to make into,
prakalpita mfn made, done, prepared, arranged, appointed
prakalyāna mfn very excellent,
prakāma m. joy, delight, ibc. and *am* or *tas* ind. with delight, willingly, according to desire, sufficiently, very much, indeed,
prakāmabhūj eating till satisfied/enough
prakāmavikasat expanding or blooming abundantly
prakāmavinata mfn quite drooping
prakāmavistāra m. geat expansiveness,
prakāmālokanīyatā f. an object that may be viewed at pleasure,
prakāmāntastapta mfn internally consumed by heat,
prakāmodya n, talkativeness, talking to the hearts content,
prakampa mfn trembling, quaking,
prākāmya n. freedom of will, wilfullness,

irresistible will (one of 8 powers),

prakāṅkṣā f. desire of food, appetite,

prakāṇḍa m.n. a trunk from root to branches, a branch, shoot, anything excellent of its kind,

prakāṇḍara m. a tree,

prakaṇva m. freed from evil,

prakara mfn doing much or well, m. aid, friendship, usage, custom, respect, seduction, 2. m. a scattered heap, mulitude, quantity, plenty,

prakāra m. sort, kind, nature, class, species, way, mode, manner,

etena prakāreṇa in this way,

kena prakāreṇa in what way? how?

prakāraiḥ in one way or another,

prakāratā f. speciality,

triprakāra of three kinds,

prakāravat mfn belonging to a species

prākāra m. a wall, enclosure, fence, rampart,

prākārāgra n. the top of a wall,

prakaraṇa n. production, creation, treatment, discussion, explanation, book, chapter, a subject, topic, a kind of drama, treating with respect, doing much or well,

prakaraṇatas ind. occasionally

prakaraṇaśas ind. according to species/kind

prakarṣa m. pre-eminence, excellence, superiority, excess, intensity,

prakarṣaka m. harasser, disquieter,

prakarṣaṇa m. one who distracts or troubles, drawing away, pushing forth, advancing, ploughing, extension, length, duration, a bridle or whip, the act of harassing, superiority, excellence,

prākarṣika mfn deserving preference,

prakarṣin mfn drawing forth, causing to move, leading (an army), excellent, pre-eminent, distinguished,

prakartṛ mfn one who causes,

pra√kāś A. *–kāśate* to become visible, appear, shine, become evident or manifest, caus. *–kāśayati* to make visible, cause to appear or shine, illumine, irradiate, show, display

prakāśa 653/1 mfn shining out, clear, open, visible, shining, bright, manifest, open, public, expanded, universally noted, famous, ifc. having the appearance of, looking like, (*am*) ind. openly, publicly, before the eyes of all, aloud, m. clearness, brightness, splendour, lustre, light, (fig.) light, elucidation, explanation; appearance, display, expansion, diffusion, fame, renown, sunshine, open spot or air, n. bell metal, brass,

prākāśa m. a metallic mirror,

prakāśaka mf*(ikā)*n clear, bright, shining, brilliant, universally known, renowned, irradiating, illuminating, giving light, making clear, making apparent or manifest, m. light-giver, the sun, (N) that which illuminates,

prakāśakāma mfn wishing for renown,

prakāśakarman m. whose work is to give light N. of the sun,

prakāśakartṛ m. 'light-maker' N.of the sun

prakāśātmakatva n. the possession of a brilliant nature or character, brilliancy,

prakāśatva n. clearness, brightness, appearance, manifestation, renown,

prakāśavat mfn bright, brilliant, shining,

prakāśana 653/2 illuminating, giving light, causing to appear, displaying, bringing to light, a name of Viṣṇu

prakāśate 653/1 to become visible, appear, manifest, illumine

prakāśayati (*te*), 653/1 causes to appear or shine, illumine, display 1/s/pres/indic/caus/act *pra √kāś*

prakāśe publicly,

prakāśīkaraṇa n. giving light, illuminating,

prakāśin mfn visible, clear, bright, shining, making visible or manifest

prakāśita mfn become visible, brought to light, clear, manifest, apparent, evident, displayed, unfolded, discovered, illumined, enlightened, irradiated, published, promulgated,

prakāśya mfn to be brought to light or

made manifest, n. being evident, manifestness, celebrity, renown,
prakaṭa 1. mfn evident, clear, manifest (am) ind. evidently, visibly, openly, in public, 2. Nom P. °*ṭati* to appear, become manifest,
prakaṭana n. manifesting, bringing to light,
prakaṭaya Nom P. °*yati* to manifest, disclose, display, reveal,
pra√kath to announce, proclaim,
prakathana 653/2 announcing, proclaiming
prakaṭita mfn manifested, unfolded, proclaimed, public, evident, clear,
prākaṭya n. publicity, manifestation
prākciram ind. before it is too late, in good time,
praketa m. appearance, apparition, sight, perception, intelligence, knowledge
prakhāda mfn swallowing, devouring,
prakhala m. a great scoundrel or villain
prākharya n. sharpness (of an arrow), wickedness,
pra√khyā P. *–khyāti,* to see, to announce, proclaim, extol,
prakhya mfn visible, clear, bright, (*ā*) f. appearance, look, brightness, splendour (only ifc.),
prakhyāna 655/3 being perceived or known,
prakhyāta mfn known, recognised, celebrated, acknowledged, forestalled, pleased, happy, 655/3
prakhyātabalavīrya of celebrated strength and valour,
prakhyāti f. visibility, perceptibility, celebrity, praise, eulogium 655/3
prakīrṇa mfn scattered, thrown about, dispersed, squandered, disordered, dishevelled, waved, waving, mixed, containing various subjects, miscellaneous, standing alone, nowhere mentioned, confused, incoherent, expanded, open, spread abroad, published, m. a horse?, n. a miscellany, a chapter or section of a book, extent,
prakīrṇaka see above
prakīrṇakeśa having dishevelled hair,
prakīrtaṇa n. announcing, proclaiming,
prakīrti f. celebration, declaration,
prakīrtita mfn announced, proclaimed, revealed, stated, said, mentioned, named, called, approved, praised, celebrated,
prākkāla m. a former age or time
prākkālīna mfn belonging to former or ancient times, ancient, previous, former,
prākkalpa m. a former age or era,
prākkarman n. preparatory medical treatment, an action done in a former life,
prakkhara m. iron armour for horse or elephant
prākkṛta mfn done in a former life, done before,
prakleda m. moistness, wetness, humidity,
prakledana mfn moistening, wetting,
prakledin mfn as above, fusing, liquefying, resolving,
pra√klid A. *–klidyate* to be come moist or humid, to become wet
praklinna mfn moist, humid, wet, putrefied, moved with compassion/sympathy,
pra√klṛp *-kalpate,* to prosper, succeed, to be fit or suitable (with inf.), to place in front, put at the head, honour, to put down on (7th), to appoint or elect to, to put in the place of (6th), to contrive, invent, devise, prepare, provide, to fix, settle, determine, to prescribe, to make out, ascertain, to make into, to suppose, imagine,
praklṛpta mfn done, made, prepared, arranged, ready, being in the right place, being right, (*am*) ind. readily, easily,
prakopa m. effervescence, excitement, raging (of war, diseases etc,) tumult, insurrection, fury, rage, excess, superabundance,
prakoṣṭha m. inner courtyard, room, fore-arm,
prakotha m. putrefaction, putridity, mfn in *prakothedaka* filthy water,

prākpada n. the first member of a compound,
prākphalla m. the bread-fruit tree,
prākprahāna m. the first blow,
prākprastuta mfn mentioned before,
prākprātarāśika mfn to be studied before breakfast,
prākpuṇyaprabhava mfn caused by merit accumulated in former existences,
pra√1.kṛ P.A. *–karoti, -kurute, -kṛṇoti, kṛṇute*, to make, produce, accomplish, perform, achieve, effect, to make into, render, to marry, to appoint, charge with, to enable to, make fit for, to remove, destroy, kill, to violate, pollute (a girl), A. to induce, move, incline, to make a person perform anything, to set the heart upon, make up the mind to, resolve, determine, to gain, win, to lay out, expend, to put forward, to serve, honour, worship,
prā√kṛ P.A. to drive away,
pra√kram P.A. *–krāmati, -kramate,* to step or stride towards, set out, walk on, advance, proceed, resort to, march, pass, go, to cross, traverse, A. to undertake, commence, begin, to act or behave towards,
prakrama m.(ifc. f. *(ā)*,stepping, proceeding, a step, stride, pace (also as a measure of distance 2-3 ½ *padas*, commencement, beginning, procedure, course, leisure, opportunity, relation, proportion, degree, measure, method, order, regularity esp. in the order of words and gram. construction, discussing any point, the case in question,
prakramaṇa n. stepping forwards, proceeding, advancing towards (comp.)
prakrānta mfn proceeded, gone, commenced, begun, previously mentioned or stated, n. the setting out on a journey, the point in question, *-tva* commencement, beginning, what is meant or understood,
prakrantṛ m. one who proceeds or begins, conquering, surpassing,
prakrīḍa m. play, pastime, a place of sports
prakrīḍin mfn playing, sporting,
prakrīḍita mfn playing, sporting,
prakriyā f. producing, production, procedure, way, manner, a ceremony, formality, precedence, high position, elevation, privilege, characterisation, a chapter (esp. an introductory chapter), (in med.) a prescription, (in gram.) etymyological formation, rules for the formation and inflection of words, medical prescription,
prakṛnta m. one who cuts to pieces,
prakṛśita mfn attenuated, thin, emaciated
prakṛṣṭa mfn drawn forth, protracted, long (in space and time), superior, distinguished, eminent,
*prakṛṣṭatā,*f. *–tva* n.transcendent excellence, pre-eminence, superiority,
prakṛṣṭatama mfn violent, strong, harassed, eminent, superior, distinguished,
prakṛṣya mfn excessive, much
prakṛta mfn made, done, produced, accomplished, prepared, appointed, charged, commenced, begun or one who has begun, put forward, mentioned, genuine, real, *-tā* f. being begun or in process, *-tva* n. being the subject of discussion,
prākśta 703/1 original, normal, ordinary, unrefined, provincial, vernacular m. a low or vulgar man, With *laya* or *pralaya* –resolution or re-absorption into prakṛti, the dissolution of the universe, dialects akin to sanskrit,
prākśtajvara m. common fever,
prākśtamānuṣa m. a common/ordinary man
prākśtamitra n. a natural friend or ally,
prākṛta mfn original, natural, artless, normal, ordinary, usual, low, vulgar, unrefined, provincial, vernacular, m. a low or vulgar man,

n. any provincial or vernacular dialect cognate with sanskrit,

prakṛti 654/1 f. the original or natural form or condition of anything, original or primary substance, cause, original source, origin, extraction, nature, character, constitution, temper, disposition,
(ibc.and *–tyā* ind. by nature, naturally, unalterably, properly), fundamental form, pattern, standard, model, rule,
the original producer of (or rather passive power of creating) the material world, consisting of the 3 *guṇā (sattva, rajas* and *tamas*), Nature distinguished from Puruṣa – spirit as Māyā is distinguished from Brahman,
consisting of *avyakta, buddhi* or *mahat, ahaṁkāra,* and the 5 *tanmātras* or subtle elements,
the personified will of the Supreme in the creation,
the constituent elements or powers of the state,
(in gram.) the elementary form of a word, base, root, an uninflected word,
a co-efficient, a multiplier,
m. or f. organ of generation, a woman or womankind,
a mother, an animal,

prakṛtibhava mfn natural, usual, common,

prakṛtibhāva m. the natural or unaltered state of anything,

prakṛtibhojana n. usual food,

prakṛtibhūta mfn being in the original state or condition, original,

prakṛtibhūman n.pl. plurality of original form or nature,

prakśtija 654/1 mfn springing from nature, innate, inborn

prākśtika mfn relating to *prakṛti* or the original element, material, natural, common, vulgar,

praktikalyaṇa mfn beautiful by nature

prakṛtilaya m. absorption into *prakṛti,* the dissolution of the universe,

prakṛtimaṇḍala n. the whole kingdom,

prakṛtimat mfn having the original or natural form or shape, natural, usual,

prakṛtimaya mfn being in the natural state or condition,

prakṛtipāṭha m. a list of verbal roots,

prakṛtipuruṣa m. a minister, servant, a standard or model of a man,
(du.) nature and spirit,

prakṛtisampanna mfn endowed with a noble nature,

prakṛtisiddha mfn effected by nature, natural,

prakṛtistha existing in material nature, being in the original or natural state, genuine, unaltered, unimpaired, normal, healthy, inherent, innate, bare, stripped of everything,

prakṛtisubhaga naturally pleasant or agreeable,

prakśtitarala naturally changeful, volatile

prakśtitva n. the state or condition of being the original or natural or fundamental form of anything,

prakṛtivat ind. as in the original form,

prakṛtyā ind. by nature, naturally,

prakṣa m. to explain an etymology,

prakṣālaka mfn washing, one who washes,

prakṣālana mfn frequent ablution, one who washes frequently, n. washing, cleaning, purifying, bathing, a means of cleaning, anything used for purifying, water used for washing,

prakṣālanīya mfn to be washed away or purified,

prakṣālayitṛ one who washes the feet of his guest,

prakṣālita mfn washed, cleansed, expiated,

prāksaṁdhyā f. morning twilight,

prakṣapaṇa n. destroying,

prakṣara m. iron armour for horse/elephant

prakṣaraṇa n. flowing forth, oozing,

prākśas ind. eastwards, towards the east,

prakṣaya m. destruction, ruin, vanishing,

prakṣepa 655/2 m throwing, casting, putting, placing, adding to, increasing (e.g. a dose), an ingredient

prakṣepaṇa n pouring upon, throwing on or into, fixing (as a price)
prakṣībhita drunken, intoxicated,
prakṣīṇa mfn destroyed, vanished, perished, decayed, wasted, diminished, atoned, n. the spot where anyone has perished,
prakṣobhaṇa n. agitating, exciting,
prāktana mfn former, prior, previous, preceding, old, ancient,
prāktanajanman n. a former birth,
prāktanakarman n. any act formerly done or done in a former state of existence, fate, destiny,
prāktāt or *prāktas* ind. from the front, from the east,
prakula n. a handsome or excellent body
prakuñca m. a measure, (about a handful)
prakupita mfn moved, agitated, very angry,
prakupta mfn enraged, incensed,
prakuthita mfn putrid, putrescent,
prakvaṇa m. the sound of a *viṇa* or lute
prakvātha m. seething, boiling,
pralabdha mfn seized, cheated, deceived,
pralabdhavya mfn to be cheated/deceived,
pralabdhṛ mfn a cheat, deceiver,
pra√labh A. *–labhate* to lay hold of, seize, get, obtain, overreach, cheat, deceive, caus. *–lambhayati* to cheat, deceive,
pralaghu mfn very inconsiderable, very small (as an attendance),
pralamba mfn hanging down, depending, pendulous, prominent, slow, bending foward, a necklace of flowers or pearls, the female breast, *-bāhu* whose arms hang down, *-keṣa* one whose hair hangs down, *-nāsika* having a prominent nose,
prālamba mfn hanging down, female breast, a kind of gourd, pearl ornament,
pralambana n. hanging down, depending,
pra√lamb A. *–lambate* to hang down,
pralambha obtaining, gaining, overreaching, deceiving,
pralambhana 689/2 n. over-reaching, that by which anyone is deceived, deceiving
pra√lap P.*-lapati* to speak forth, prattle, talk idly or incoherently, trifle, lament,
pralāpa 689/2 m. prattling, chattering, raving, internal chattering,
pralāpaka m. speaking incoherently,
pralapan speaking pres/act/part *pra √lap*
pralapana n. prattling, talking,
pralāpana n. causing or teaching to speak
pralāpin mfn chattering, talking,
pralapita mfn spoken forth, spoken dolefully, invoked piteously, prattling
pralava m. a part cut off, a chip, fragment, a dead leaf, the sheath of a leaf,
pralavana n. the reaping of corn,
pralaya 689/3 m. dissolution, re-absorption, destruction, death, end, fainting, loss of sense or consciousness, sleepiness, the destruction of the world at the end of a kalpa presided over by Śiva the dissolver or destroyer,
pralayākala mfn an individual soul to which *mala* and *karman* still adhere,
pralayakāla m. the time of universal dissolution,
pralāyam ind. to hide one's self, be hidden
pralayana n. a place of repose, a bed
pralayānta mfn ending in death, extending to the end of life,
pralayatā f. °*tva* n. dissolution,
pralehana n. the act of licking,
pralepa m. cleaving to, an ointment, salve, plaster,
pralepaka mfn anointing, plastering, smearing, m. a plasterer, anointer, lime made of calcined shells, a fever
pralepana n. the act of anointing, smearing, an unguent, salve, plaster,
pralepya m. clean or well-trimmed hair,
prāleya mfn produced by melting, m. fever in goats or sheep, n. hail, snow, frost, dew,
prāleyavarṣa m. falling of snow,
pra√likh P.A. (P) to scratch or draw lines in, to draw lines, write, P.A. to scrape together, A. to comb one's head, to draw lines,
pralīna mfn dissolved, reabsorbed into (7th), disappeared, lost, died, dissolving,

dying, when one dies, tired, wearied, unconscious, insensible, flown away, *-tā* f. *–tva* n. dissolution, destruction, the end of the universe, unconsciousness, fainting,

pralīnendriya mfn one whose senses have slacked or languished,

pralipa mfn one who smears or plasters,

pralipta mfn cleaving or sticking to,

pralobha m. allurement, seduction,

pralobhana mfn causing to lust after, n. allurement, inducement,

pralola mfn in violent motion, agitated,

pralopa m. destruction, annihilation,

pralubdha mfn seduced,

pralūna mfn cut off,

pralupta mfn robbed,

pra√mā A. *–mimīte* to measure, mete out, estimate, to form, create, make ready, arrange, to form a correct notion of, understand, know, caus. *-māpayati* to cause correct knowledge, afford proof or authority,

pramā 685/3 f. basis, foundation,measure, scale, right measure, true knowledge, correct notion, *-tva* n. accuracy of perception,

pra√mad or *mand* P.A. *–madati, -mandati, -mādyati (te),* to enjoy one's self, be joyous, sport, play, to be careless or negligent, to be indifferent to or heedless about, caus. *-mādayati* to gladden, delight, A. *–mādayate* to enjoy, indulge in,

pramad f. lust, desire,

pramada m. joy, pleasure, delight, mfn wanton, dissolute, mad, intoxicated,

pramāda 685/2 m. intoxication, madness, insanity, an error, mistake, carelessness about through acting without prior consideration, through spontaneous action, inadvertence, negligence, non-performance of necessary duties, deviation,

pramādacārin mfn acting in a careless manner,

pramadā f. a young and wanton woman, *-jana* m. womankind, the female sex,

pramadana n. amorous desire, a pleasure-grove,

pramadavana n. pleasure-grove of a prince,

pramadāvana n. pleasure-grove of the wives of a prince,

pramādī idle people

prāmādika mfn arising from carelessness, erroneous, faulty, *-tva* n. erroneousness, incorrectness,

pramādita mfn trifled away, lost,

pramadvara mfn inattentive, careless,

prāmādya n. madness, fury, intoxication,

pramagna mfn immersed, dipped, drowned,

pramahas mfn of great might or splendour,

pra√man to think upon, find out by thinking,

pramāṇa 685/3 n. measure, scale, proof, standard, a measure of any kind, right measure, standard, authority, a means of acquiring *pramā* or certain knowledge, the process of the right perception of things through - (*pratyakṣa* sense perception, *anumāna* inference, *upamāna* analogy, *śabda* or *āptavacana* verbal authority or revelation, *anupalabdhi* or *abhāvapratyakṣa* negative proof, *arthāpatti* inference from circumstances), any proof or testimony or evidence, a correct notion, right perception, oneness, unity, accordance of movements in dance with music and song, measure of physical strength, principal, capital,

pramāṇābhāva m. absence of proof or authority

pramāṇabhūta m. authoritative,

pramāṇādhika mfn being beyond measure, excessive,

pramāṇadṛṣṭa mfn sanctioned by authority, demonstrable,

pramāṇaka ifc. measure, quantity, extent, argument, proof,

pramāṇakuśala mfn skilful in arguing,

pramāṇāntara n. another means of proof,

pramāṇānurūpa mfn corresponding to an

individual's physical strength,
pramāṇapuruṣa m. an arbitrator, judge,
pramaṇas mfn careful, attentive, kind, good-natured, cheerful,
pramanas mfn careful, tender, pleased, cheerful, willing,
pramāṇaśāstra n. any scriptural authority,
pramāṇastha of normal size, state, condition
pramāṇasūtra n. a measuring cord,
pramāṇatā f. (*-tva* n.) authority, warranty,
pramāṇatara having greater authority than,
pramāṇatas ind. according to weight or measure, according to proof or authority,
pramāṇatva, n. authority, warranty, correctness
pramāṇavākya n. authoritative statement,
pramāṇavat mfn established by proofs, well-founded,
pramāṇāyāmatas ind. according to size and length,
pramāṇayukta mfn having the right measure
prāmāṇika mfn forming or being a measure, founded on evidence or authority, authentic, credible, one who accepts proof or rests his arguments on authority, a president, the chief or head of a trade,
-tva n. authoritativeness, cogency,
pramāṇita mfn adjusted, proved, shown clearly, demonstrated,
pramantha m. a stick used for rubbing wood to produce fire,
prāmāṇya or *pramāṇya* being established by proof, truth,
pramanyu mfn incensed or enraged against, very sad,
pramāpaka mfn proving, m. an authority,
pramāpaṇa 1. form, shape, 2. a murderer
pramara m. death,
pramāra m. dying,
pramaraṇa n. dying, death,
pramārayati caus. P. to put to death √*mṛ*
pramardana mfn crushing, destroying,
pramārjaka mfn wiping off, causing to disappear,
pramata mfn thought out, wise,
pra√math or *manth* P. *–mathati* or *–mathnāti* to stir up violently, churn, tear or strike off, harass, distress, annoy,
pramatha m. a class of demons, pain, affliction,
pramātha 685/2 stirring about, tormenting, destruction (of enemies)
pramathabhāṣā A type of uttering. 'This is a state of abundance of energy either through ecstasy or some other intoxicating situation through emotional charge. In this state, when *rajas* would be predominant, then the uttering would be rather erratic and profuse. They may not respond to rules.'
pramāthin stirring about, tearing, rending
pramathita ppp. (having been) stirred up, agitated,
pramati f. care, providence, protection, provider, protector,
pramātṛ mfn one who has correct notion or idea, authority, m. an authority,
pramardana 687/2 crushing down, expelling, destroying,
pramatta mfn excited, wanton, lascivious, rutting, drunken, intoxicated, mad, insane, careless, inattentive, heedless, forgetful of, blundering, a blunderer,
-citta mfn careless-minded,
-tā f. inattentiveness, sleepiness, mental inactivity,
-vat mfn inattentive, 2. ind. as if drunk, like one intoxicated,
pramaya 1. m. measuring, measure, 2. m. ruin, downfall, death, killing, also °*mayā,*
pramayu liable to be lost, perishable,
prameya 686/1 n. the thing to be proved, the object of knowledge, the topic to be discussed, mfn to be measured, measurable, to be proved, provable,
prameyatva n. provableness, demonstrability
pra√1.mi P.A. *–minoti,-minute,* to erect, build, to judge, observe, perceive,
pra√mī to frustrate, annul, destroy, change
pra√mīl P. *–milati,* to close or shut the eyes,
pramīlā shutting the eyes, sleepiness,

lassitude, enervation,
pramīlaka m. *pramīlikā* f. shutting the eyes, sleepiness,
pramīlita mfn one who has the eyes closed, with closed eyes,
pramita mfn meted out, measured, ifc. measuring, of such and such measure, limited, moderate, little, few, known, understood, proved,
pramīta mfn deceased, dead, immolated,
pramiti f. a correct notion, right conception, knowledge gained or established by *pramāṇa* or proof, manifestation, inference or analogy, measuring,
pramlāna mfn faded, withered, soiled,
prāṁ-mukha mfn having the face directed eastward, facing east,
pramocana 686/3 mfn comp. liberating from, n. setting free, discharging, emitting
pramoda m. excessive joy, delight,
prāmodika mfn charming, enchanting,
pramodita mfn delighted, rejoiced,
pramoha m. bewilderment, infatuation,
pramohita mfn bewildered, infatuated,
pramohin mfn bewildering, infatuating,
pramoka m. liberation,
pramokṣa m. letting fall, dropping, losing, discharging, dismissing, liberation, liberation from (comp.), final deliverance,
pramoktavya mfn to be liberated,
pramoṣa m. stealing or taking away,
pramṛḍa mfn gracious, making glad/happy,
pramṛṇa mfn destroying, crushing,
pramṛśa mfn laying hold of, handling,
pramṛṣṭa mfn rubbed off, cleaned, polished, removed, given up, left,
pramṛṣṭa-maṇi m. polished or bright gem,
pramṛṣṭamaṇi-kuṇḍala mfn possessing bright gem ear-rings,
pramṛṣṭi f. rubbing over with (comp.),
pramṛta mfn deceased, dead, withdrawn or gone out of sight, covered, concealed, n. death, tillage, cultivation (as causing the death of many things),
pramṛtaka mfn dead,
prāṁśu mfn high, tall, long, strong, intense,
prāṁśuka mfn large, big (said of an animal),
pra√muc P.A. *–muñcati (te),* to set free, let go, liberate, release from (5th), to loosen, untie, undo, to give up, resign, renounce, to discharge, emit, caus. *–mocayati*
pramucyate (pass.) is liberated or released, becomes freed, one gets freed from, detached from, 1/s/pres/indic/pass *pra √muc*
pra√mud A. *–modate* to become joyful, rejoice greatly, exult, be delighted, caus. *–modayati* to make glad, delight,
pramud mfn pleased, happy, f. gladness, delight, pleasure (esp. sensual),
pramūḍha mfn bewildered, unconscious, infatuated, foolish,
pramudita mfn delighted, pleased, glad,
pramugdha mfn bewildered, unconscious, very charming,
pramuhyati P. faints, swoons, becomes bewildered or infatuated,
pra-mukha mfn. turning the face towards, first, foremost, honourable
-tas, before the face of, in front of
pramukhataḥ in front of, before (with 6th),
pramukhe ind. opposite, in front,
pramukta mfn. loosened, untied, released, forsaken, abandoned, given up, renounced,
pramukti f. liberation,
pramurchati P becomes thick/solid/congeals
pramūrṇa mfn crushed, destroyed,
pramuṣita mfn stolen, taken away,
pramuṣṇāti robs, takes away, steals away, distracted, beside one's self,
prāṅ in comp. for *prāñc*
prāṇ or *prān* P. *prāṇiti* or *prāniti* to breathe in, inhale, to breathe, to blow (as the wind), to live to smell, caus.
prāṇayati to cause to breathe, animate,
prāṇ mfn breathing,
praṇa mfn ancient, old,
prāṇa 701/3 1. mfn filled, full,
prāṇa 705/1 2. m. the breath of life, breath,

respiration, spirit, vitality, pl. life, a vital organ, vital air; the 5 vital airs are known as *prāṇa* – upwards, (expiration), *apāna*, downwards, (causes inspiration), *vyāna* – that by which these two are held, *samāna* – that which carries the grosser material of food to *apāna* and brings the subtler material to each limb, and *udāna* which brings up or carries down what has been drunk or eaten, *prāṇāḥ* pl. life,

prāṇabādha m. extreme peril, danger to life,

prāṇabhakṣa m. feeding only on breath/air,

prāṇabhāj mfn possessing life, m. a living being, creature, man

prāṇabhāsvat m. 'life-light', the ocean,

prāṇabhaya n. fear for life, peril of death,

prāṇabhṛt mfn supporting life,

prāṇabhūta mfn being the breath of life,

prāṇabuddhi f. life and intelligence,

prāṇacaya m. increase of vitality/strength,

prāṇaccheda m. destruction of life, murder,

prāṇaccid mfn cutting life short, deadly,

prāṇada mfn life-giving, preserving or saving life, n. water,

praṇāḍa m. a loud sound or noise, shout,

prāṇadā mfn giving breath,

prāṇāda mfn 'life-devouring', deadly, murderous,

prāṇadakṣiṇā f. the gift of life,

prāṇadāna n. gift of life (saving another's life), resigning life,

prāṇadaṇḍa m. the punishment of death,

prāṇadātṛ m. one who saves another's life,

prāṇadayita m. 'dear as life' a husband,

prāṇādhika mfn dearer than life, stronger, superior in vigour,

prāṇādhinātha 'life-lord', a husband,

prāṇādhipa m. the soul, master of the vital force, master of the senses,

praṇāḍikā or °*ḍī* f. a channel, watercourse, drain, ind. °*ḍikayā* or °*ḍyā* mediately indirectly,

prāṇadhāra mfn possessing life, living, animate, m. a living being, breath-awareness a meditation method, supporting life, that which supports lift,

prāṇadhāraṇa possessing life, living, animate, supporting life, that which supports life

prāṇadṛh mfn sustaining/prolonging the breath,

prāṇadroha m. attempt on another's life,

prāṇadurodara n. playing for life, staking life,

prāṇadyūta n. play or contest for life,

prāṇāghāta m. destruction of life, killing of a living being,

prāṇaghna mfn life-destroying, killing,

prāṇagraha m. the nose 'breath-grabber',

prāṇāha n. cement (used in building),

prāṇahāni f. loss of life, death,

prāṇahara mfn taking away or threatening life, destructive, fatal, dangerous to (comp.), capital punishment,

prāṇahāraka mfn taking away life, killing,

prāṇahīna mfn bereft of life, dead,

prāṇaka m. a living being, animal, worm,

prāṇakara mfn n. 'life-causing', refreshing, invigorating,

prāṇakarman n. vital function,

prāṇakṛcchra n. peril of life

praṇāla m. a channel from a pond, a water-course, a drain, a row, series, *(ī)* f. a channel, recension(of a text), intervention, interposition, °*nālikā* f. a channel. intervention, medium, (*ayā*) ind. indirectly,

prāṇalābha m. saving of life,

prāṇalipsu mfn desirous of saving life,

pranāma m. bow, reverent salutation,

prāṇamat mfn full of vital power, vigorous,

pra-ṇam (√nam) P.A *–ṇamati (te)*, to bend or bow down before, make obeisance to, caus. *–nāmayati* to cause a person to bow before, to bow, incline,

praṇāma m. respectful salutation, bow, bending, obeisance, n. bowing,

praṇamana n. bowing before, salutation, reverence

prāṇamaya 705/3 consisting of vital air or

breath, constituted of air, possessed predominantly of air,
praṇamayya ind. bowing
pranamya making obeisance, having bowed (gerund)
prāṇana 706/1 mfn enlivening, animating, m. the throat, n. breathing, respiration
prāṇanānta m. end of life, death,
prāṇanāśa m. loss of life,
prāṇanātha m. ifc. f.*ā* 'lord of life' a husband, lover,
prāṇanigraha m. restraint of breath,
prāṇanta m. air, wind, *(ī)* f. sneezing, sobbing,
prāṇānta m. 'life-end', death, mfn capital punishment,
prāṇāntika mfn dangerous to life, fatal, mortal, *(am)* ind. desperate, vehement,
prāṇāpāna m. du. air inhaled and exhaled
prāṇaparikṣīṇa mfn one whose life is drawing to a close,
praṇapāt m. a great grandson,
prāṇapata mfn °*pati* m.'life-lord', the soul,
prāṇapatnī f. 'breath-wife', the voice,
prāṇaprepsu mfn wishing to preserve his life, being in mortal fright,
prāṇapriya mfn dear as life,
pranaptṛ m. a great-grandson,
prāṇarakṣā f. preservation of life,
prāṇarodha m. suppression of breath,
prāṇārthavat mfn possessing life and riches
pra-ṇaś 659/3 √*1.naś* *naśati* reach, attain √2. *naś* *ṇaśati/ ṇaśyati* to be lost, disappear, vanish
praṇāśa m. vanishing, disappearance, loss, cessation, death
prāṇasadman n. 'abode of vital airs', the body,
prāṇasama mfn equal to or as dear as life, m. a husband or lover,
prāṇasaṁdeha m. danger to life,
prāṇasaṁdhāraṇa n. support of life,
prāṇasaṁśita mfn animated by the vital airs,
prāṇasaṁnyāsa m. giving up the spirit,
prāṇasaṁtyāga m. abandonment of life,
praṇāśana mf(ī)n causing to disappear, removing, destroying, n. destruction,
prāṇasāra n. vital energy, mfn full of strength, vigorous,
pra-ṇaṣṭa mfn destroyed, lost
praṇaṣṭādhigata mfn lost and found again
praṇaṣṭajñānika one whose knowledge or memory is destroyed,
praṇaṣṭavinaya mfn uncivil, rude,
prāṇasūtra n. the thread of life,
pranaṣyāmi I am lost or destroyed
praṇata mfn bent forwards, bowed, inclined bowed to, saluted reverentially, bent towards, offered respectfully, humble, submissive to, skilful, clever,
praṇatabahuphala mfn one to whom fruits or good things are offered
praṇatakāya mfn having the body bent down,
praṇataśiras mfn having the head bowed, inclined, stooping,
praṇatavat mfn bowing, bent, bowed,
prāṇatejas mfn whose splendour or glory is life or breath,
prāṇatha m. breathing, respiration, air, wind, the lord of all living beings, a sacred bathing place, mfn strong,
prāṇātilobha m. excessive attachment to life,
prāṇātipāta m. destruction of life, killing,
prāṇātman m. the spirit which connects the totality of subtle bodies like a thread,
prāṇatrāṇa n. saving of life,
prāṇatva n. the state of breath or life,
prāṇatyāga abandonment of life, breath, energy, - death, suicide
prāṇātyaya m. danger to life,
praṇava 'the first word is called the *praṇava* sound and is uttered as *om*, which is composed of *a,u* and *m.'*
prāṇāvarodha m. suppression of breath,
prāṇavat mfn vigorous, strong, powerful,
prāṇavidyā f. the science of breath or vital airs,
prāṇavināśa m. loss of life, death,
prāṇavṛtti f. vital activity or function, support of life,
prāṇavyaya m. renunciation or sacrifice of

life,

praṇaya m. M. 'bringing oneself forward', an expressing of one's feelings, a manifestation of one's affection, 659/3 m. a leader, guidance, conduct, manifestation, display, setting forth an argument, affection, confidence in (7th), love, attachment, friendship, favour, (ibc. *āt, ena, °yopetam* ind. confidentially, affectionately, openly, frankly), desire, longing for, an entreaty, request, reverence, obeisance, final beatitude, ind. *°yāt, °yena, °yopetam,* confidentially, affectionately, openly, frankly,

praṇayabhaṅga m. breach of confidence, faithlessness,

praṇāyaka m. a leader, army commander,

praṇayakalaha m. a quarrel of lovers, a trivial quarrel,

praṇayakupita mfn feigning anger, angry through love,

prāṇāyāma = prāṇayama 706/1 m. the name of specific breathing exercises *pūraka, recaka, kumbhaka*

praṇayamadhura mfn sweet through affection

praṇayamāna m. the jealousy of love

praṇayamaya mfn full of confidence

praṇayana n. bringing forwards, conducting, conveying, fetching, means or vessel for bringing or fetching, showing, betraying, inflicting punishment,

prāṇāyana n. an organ of sense, 2. the offspring of the vital airs,

praṇayapeśala mfn soft through affection,

praṇayaprakarṣa m. excess of affection, extraordinary attachment,

prāṇayātrā f. support of life, subsistence,

praṇayavacana n. a declaration of love

praṇayavat mfn possessing candour, frank,

praṇayavigāta averse to love/friendship,

praṇayavihati f. refusal of a request, non-compliance,

praṇayin mfn having affection for, attached to, beloved, dear, intimate, familiar, feeling attracted to, longing for, affectionate, loving, kind, ifc. clinging to, dwelling or being in, turned towards, aiming at, m. a friend, favourite, a husband, lover, *(inī)* f. a beloved female, wife, a worshipper, devotee, a supplicant, suitor,

prāṇayita mfn caused to breathe, kept alive, animated, longing to (inf.),

prāṇayoni f. the source or spring of life,

prāṇayuta mfn endowed with life, living,

praṇayya mfn dear, beloved, fit, worthy, blameless, desireless, rejected,

prāṇāyya mfn proper, fit suited,

prāñc 703/3 mfn (1st) *prāñ, prācī, prāk,* directed forward or towards, being in front, facing, opposite, with
√*kṛ* +2nd to bring, procure, offer, stretch forth the fingers, make straight, prepare/clear a path, with
pra-√*tir* or √*nī* to advance, promote, further, with √*klṛp* caus. to face, turn opposite to, turn eastward, eastern, easterly,

prāñcas m.pl. eastern people, grammarians,

praṇejana mfn washing or wiping away, n. the act of washing or bathing,

praṇenī mfn leading or guiding constantly or repeatedly,

prāṇeśvara 'lord of life', a husband, lover, pl. the vital spirits personified,

praṇetṛ m. a leader, guide, a maker, creator,

prāṅgaṇa n. a court, yard, courtyard, a kind of drum,

prāṇi in comp. for *prāṇin*

pra-ṇī (√*nī)* P.A. *–ṇayati (te),* to lead forwards, conduct, advance, promote, further, to bring or lead to, convey, to produce, perform, execute, finish, to do away with, remove, dispel, to manifest affection, love, desire, to show, to inflict (punishment), to establish, fix, institute, promulgate, teach, to

write, compose, A. to draw in (the breath),
praṇī m. a leader or guide, f. guidance, furtherance, devotion,
praṇidāna possibly as below, or, essential cause or motive
pra-ṇi-√dhā P.A. *–dadhāti, -dhatte*, to place in front, cause to precede, to put down, deposit, to place in, bring into, to put on, apply, to touch, to turn or direct (the eyes or thoughts) upon,
praṇidhāna 660/1 n laying on, fixing, applying, access, entrance, exertion, endeavour, respectful conduct, attention paid to, profound religious meditation, abstract contemplation of, applying the mind to, profound meditation on total surrender to.
praṇidhi m. prayer, spy, attention, request, spying, secret agent, emissary, watching, follower, sending out,
prāṇidyūta n. gambling on fighting animals
prāṇighātin mfn killing living beings,
prāṇin mfn breathing, living, alive, m. a living or sentient being, living creature, animal or man, etc.etc.
prāṇiṇiṣu mfn wishing to breathe or live,
prāṇipīḍā f. cruelty to animals,
prani√dhā Cl 3 *–dadhāti,* to put down,
praṇidhāyin mfn employing, sending out (spies),
praṅidhi m. watching, observing, spying, a spy, secret agent, emissary,
pra–ṇi-√dhyai to attend to,
prāṇigarbhavimocana giving birth, releasing from the womb
praṇi√han to slay, destroy, kill,
praṇihita mfn laid on, imposed, applied, put down, deposited, outstretched, stretched forth, directed towards, fixed upon (7th), delivered, committed, entrusted to (4th), contained in (comp.), sent out (as a spy), found out, discovered, ascertained or stated, one with thoughts concentrated on one point, intent upon (7th), obtained, acquired, prudent, cautious, resolved, determined, agreed to, admitted,
prāṅikṣaṇa n. looking eastward,
prāṇin 706/1 mfn breathing, living, alive m. a living being or creature
praṇināda m. a deep sound,
praṇindana or °*nindana* n. censuring upbraiding,
praṇinīṣeṇya mfn forming the entrance or beginning (as a day), 660/3
praṇi√pat P. *–patati* to throw one's self down before, bow respectfully to
praṇipāta 660/2 m. prostating oneself, bowing respectfully before
praṇīta mfn led forwards, advanced, brought, offered, conveyed, brought into, reduced to, directed towards, performed, executed, finished, inflicted, sentenced, awarded, established, instituted, taught, good (as food), entered, approached, f. a sort of cup (used at sacrifices), anything cooked or dressed, holy water,
praṇītā-praṇayana n. the vessel for fetching the holy water,
praṇīti f. conduct, leading, guidance, leading away, favour,
prāṇitva n. wished, desired, the state of a living being, life,
an author, promulgator of a doctrine, a performer, instrument player,
prāñjala mfn , straight, upright, honest, sincere, level (as a road), *-tā* f. straightness, plainness (of meaning),
prañjalayaḥ with palms joined (a reverent gesture)
prāñjali holding out joined and cupped hands in respect, humility or to receive alms,
prāñmukha facing east, inclined towards,
praṇoda m. driving, guiding, (horses etc.)
praṇodita mfn set in motion, agitated, driven, guided, directed,
prāṇopasparśana n. touching the organs of sense, 706/1
prāṇopeta mfn living, alive,

prāṇotkramana n. or °*otkrānti* f. death
prāṇotsarga m. 'giving up the ghost', dying,
pranṛtta mfn dancing, one who has begun to dance
prānta m.n. (ifc f.*ā*) edge, border, margin, verge, extremity, end, a point, tip (of a blade of grass), ibc. finally, eventually,
prāntabhūmi f. final place or term, (*au*) ind. finally, at last,
prāntadurga n. a collection of houses outside the wall of a town,
prāntaga mfn living close by,
prāntara n. a long desolate road, the country between villages, a forest, the hollow of a tree,
prāntaraśūnya n. a long dreary road,
prāntastha mfn inhabiting the borders,
prāntatas ind. along the edge or border,
prāntavṛti f. 'end-circle', the horizon,
praṇuda mfn driving or scaring away,
praṇuta mfn praised, celebrated, lauded
praṇutta mfn pushed away, repelled, set in motion,
praṇud P. to push on, propel, set in motion, drive or scare away, to move, excite, to press a person to do anything, mfn ifc. who enjoins, commands, *praṇyasta* mfn beat down, depressed in front
prāp (pra+√āp) P.A. *prāpnoti* to attain to, reach, arrive at, meet with, find, to attain, receive, to extend, reach to, to result (from a rule), caus. *prāpayati (te),* to cause to reach or attain, to advance, further, promote, A. to lead or bring to, to impart, communicate, announce,
pra√1. pā P *-pibati* to begin to drink, drink,
prapā f. a place for supplying water or watering cattle, a cistern or fountain for travellers, a supply of water,
pra√3. pā P. *–pāti,* to protect, defend from,
prāpa m. reaching, obtaining,
pra√2.pac to begin to cook, to be accustomed to cook,
pra√2.pad A. *–padyate*, to fall or drop down from, throw one's self down (at a person's feet), to go forwards, set out for, resort to, arrive at, attain, enter, take refuge with, reach, to fall upon, attack, come to a partic. state or condition, incur, undergo, to adopt or embrace (a doctrine), to undertake, commence, begin, do, to form (a judgment), to assume (a form), to enjoy (pleasure), caus. *-pādayati* to cause to enter, introduce into, A. *–pitsate* to be going to incur or undertake,
prapad 2. f. a way,
prapad 3. f. the forepart of the foot,
prapada n. the point of the foot, tip of the toes, (*ais,* ind. on tiptoe)
prapadana n. entering, entrance into, access,
prapadyante they take refuge in, they resort to, 1/pl/pres/indic/mid *pra√pad* 682/1
prapadye I take refuge or resort to 3/s/mid
prāpaka mfn causing to arrive at, leading or bringing to, procuring, establishing, making valid, m. a bringer, procurer,
prapakṣa m. the extremity of wing (of an army drawn up),
prapālaka m. a guardian, protector,
prapālana n. guarding, protecting,
prapālin m. protector
prapalāśa mfn whose leaves are fallen,
prapalāyana n. running away, flight, rout,
prapalāyita mfn run away, routed, defeated,
prapaṇa m. exchange, barter,
prāpaṇa 707/2 mfn leading or bringing to, n. occurrence, appearance, extension, attainment, acquisition, conveying, establishing, making valid, explanation
prapāṇa n. drinking, a drink or beverage,
prapañca 681/3 manifestation, expansion, development, manifoldness, diversity, amplification, prolixity, diffuseness, copiousness, (°*cena* and °*ca-tas* ind. diffusely, in detail), manifestation of or form of (6th), appearance, phenomenon, (in phil.) the expansion of the universe, the

visible world, (in gram.) the repetition of an obscure rule in a clearer form, deceit, trick, fraud, error, opposition, reversion, (N) in Buddhism – 'fruitless verbiage', falsehood, fiction, fallacy, word, various phenomena, discriminating, distinguishing variously what should not be distinguished, e.g. 'deciding whether to define *dharma* as eternal or not eternal is vain verbiage' , the original thing giving rise to discrimination,

prapañcabuddhi mfn cunning minded, artful

prapañcaka mf(*ikā*)n multiplying, amplifying, explaining in detail,

prapañcana n. development, diffusion, copiousness, prolixity,

prapañcanirmāṇa n. the creation of the visible world,

prapañcatva n.= *maraṇa* n. death

prapañcita mfn amplified, extended, treated at length, represented in a false light, mistaken, deceived,

prapañcopaśamam 'the one in whom all phenomena have ceased' (Gam.), (N) 'right annihilation of all vain talk', 'total extinction of vain talk',

prāpaṇika m. a trader, dealer,

prāpaṇiya gve. to be brought to, attainable

pra-panna 682/1 mfn. arrived at, fallen at a person's feet, suppliant, approached, appeared, happened, provided with (3rd), effecting, producing, poor, distressed,

praparṇa mfn whose leaves are fallen,

pra√paś P. A.*–paśyati, (te),* to see before one's eyes, look at, observe, behold, to know, understand, to regard as, take for,

prapaśya see! behold! 2/s/impv

prapaśyat 682/2 mfn. well-discerning, judicious, sensible, intelligent

prapaśyāmi I see, I perceive 3/s/pres/indic/act *pra √paś*

prapaśyati 682/2 sees before one's eyes, observes, beholds, 1/s/pres/indic/act sees

pra√pat P. *–patati* to fly away or along, hasten towards, fly or fall down upon, fall, caus. *–pātayati* to cause to fly away, to chase, pursue,

prapāta m. a partic. mode of flying, springing forth, an attack, starting off, setting out, departure, falling down, falling from, falling out, discharge, emission, letting fall, a cliff, precipice, a cascade, waterfall,

prapātana n. causing to fall, throwing down,

prapatha m. a way, journey (esp. to a distant place), ifc. f. (*ā*) a broad road or street, mfn 'about to go off, loose,

prapātha m. a road, way,

prapāṭha or °*pāṭhaka* m. a lecture (i.e. chapter or subdivision of a book),

prapāṭhita mfn taught, expounded,

prapathya mfn being on the road, wandering,

prapāṭika f. a young shoot/sprout,

prapatita mfn flown away or along, fallen, come down,

prapatti f. pious resignation or devotion,

prapautra m. a great grand-son,

prapavaṇa n. purifying, straining, (*soma*)

prapāvana n. fountain-grove, a cool grove,

prapharvī f. a wanton or lascivious girl,

praphulla mfn blooming forth, blooming, covered with blossoms or flowers, expanded, opened wide, smiling, shining, cheerful, pleased,

praphullanetra mfn having fully opened or sparkling eyes, having eyes expanded with joy,

praphullavadana mfn face expanded with joy, looking happy,

prapīta mfn swollen out, swollen up, distended,

prāpita mfn restored (to), led, conveyed or conducted to, possessed of, caused to attain to or arrive at,

prapitāmaha a paternal great grand-father

praplāvana n. flooding with water,

prāpnoti 707/2 attains to, obtains, receives 1/s/pres/indic/act he attains

prāpnuyāt he should attain or reach

1/s/opt/act *pra √āp*
pra√pṛ to carry across, bring over,
pra√pī P. *–pṛṇāti* to be filled, become full or satiated, be completed or fulfilled or accomplished, caus. *–pūrayati* to fill up, complete, to make rich, enrich,
prapra√jan to be born again and again,
prapra√pī to fill up, complete,
prapra√as P. (*praprās*) *–asti* to be in a high degree or prominently,
prapra√śaṁs to be praised
prapra√śru to be celebrated,
prapra√sthā to rise, advance,
prapra√vī to advance against, attack,
pra√prī caus. *–prīṇayati* to make pleasant,
prāpta 707/3 come to, arrived, present attained to, reached, meet with, find, to meet with, one who has attained to or reached, come to, arrived, accomplished, complete, mature, full-grown, (in gram.) following from a rule, valid,
prāptabhāra m. a beast of burden,
prāptabhāva mfn wise, handsome, one who has attained to any condition, of good disposition,
prāptabīja mfn sown,
prāptabuddhi mfn instructed, intelligent,
prāptajīvana mfn restored to life,
prāptakāla m. the time or moment arrived, a fit time, proper season,
prāptakārin mfn one who does what is right or proper,
prāptakarman n. that which results or follows from a preceding rule,
prāptakrama mfn fit, proper, suitable,
prāptapañcatva mfn (arrived at) dissolution into 5 elements, dead,
prāptaprakāśaka mfn advanced in intelligence
prāptaprāpya ind. having obtained what is to be obtained,
prāptatva the state of resulting (from a grammatical rule),
prāptavat mfn one who has attained to or gained, received,
prāptavya gve. to be obtained, about to be got,
prāptayauvana mfn having attained adolescence, reached a marriageable age,
prāpti 707/1 f advent, occurrence, reach, range, extent, reaching, arrival at (comp.) the power of the wind to enter or penetrate anywhere, the power of obtaining everything (one of 8 faculties), attaining to, obtaining, meeting with, finding, acquisition, gain, being met with or found, discovery, determination,
prāptis attainment, obtaining, reaching,
prāptum infin. to be attained,
prapūjita mfn honoured, respected,
prapūraka mf(*ikā*)n filling up, fulfilling, satisfying,
prapūraṇa 682/3 mfn filling up (oil), increasing (love), the act of filling up, filling, putting in, inserting, injecting, satiating, satisfying, adorning,embellishing
prapurāṇa mfn very old, kept a long time,
prapūrita mfn filled up, completed
prapuṣpita mfn flowering, in bloom,
praputra m. a grandson, descendant,
prāpya ind. obtaining, attaining, having encountered, having attained, having got,
prapyasa mfn swelling,
prāpyate it is attained, obtained or reached, 1/s/pres/pass *pra√āp*
prārabdha 708/2 begun, undertaken, (G p.241) accumulated past actions, the fruits of which are experienced now , events related to the past
prārabdha "This is what man gets in his present life and is the effects of his deeds which are ripe for use." HH "If one has performed good activities in the past, then good situations are presented in life, and if bad, then only bad situations confront him." HH "..presents itself as favourable or unfavourable situations for man's development"... HH 1967 S2 p3/4 "When some

event begins at the call of *prārabdha* the chain of events will follow its full course mechanically. Unless it is fully redeemed in the course of time, nothing will stop it" HH
the circumstances one encounters due to good and bad *saṁskāra*
'...has all that which the individual could use as his own capital in the present life'

prārabhate he undertakes, commences, begins, performs, 1/s/pres/indic/mid *pra ā √rabh*

prarakṣa mfn one from whom anyone is protected,

prarakṣaṇa n. protecting, protection,

prarakṣita mfn protected against, saved from (5th),

praramayati caus. P. delights or gladdens greatly, exhilarates,

prārambha m. beginning,

prarapati P. he/she talks, prattles,

*prarecana,*n. *prareka,*m. abundance, plenty

prarikvan mfn reaching beyond, surpassing,

prarocana mfn exciting or inciting to love (as a spell), seductive, *(ā)* f. highest praise, n. stimulating, exciting, seduction, praising, illustration, explanation,

prarocate A. *√ruc*, to shine forth, be liked, please, caus. *rocayati,* to enlighten, illuminate, to cause to shine, to make apparent or specious, make pleasing,

prarocita mfn commended, praised, liked

prarodhana n. rising, ascending,

praroha m. germinating, sprouting, a bud, shoot, an excrescence, a new leaf or branch, a shoot (fig.)= ray of light, *-vat* possessing or covered in vegetation,

prāroha m. a shoot, sprout,

prarohaka mfn causing to grow,

prarohaṇa n. germinating, sprouting, a bud, shoot, sprig,

prarohin mfn growing or shooting up, causing to grow, propagating,

praropita mfn sown, planted,

pra√arth 708/3 *prārthayate (*occ.*-ti)* to wish or long for, desire, to ask a person, to look for, search, have recourse to, attack,

prārthanā f. prayer, devotionals, request, entreaty, wish, desire,

prārthayante they seek, they ask for 1/pl/pres/indic/mid *pra √arth*

prārthayati asks for

prārthayitṛ mfn one who wishes for or asks, m. solicitor, suitor, aspirant, wooer, claimant,

prarūḍha mfn grown up, full grown, ifc. overgrown with, filled up, healed up, grown, widely spread, become great or strong, old, grown from a root, rooted, fastened, arisen or proceeded from (comp.),

prarūḍhakeśa mfn having long hair,

prarudita mfn one who has begun to weep, weeping,

pra√ruh P. –rohati to grow up, shoot forth, shoot up, to heal up (wound), to grow, increase,

praruh mfn shooting forth, growing up (like a plant), m. a mountain rising in the foreground,
f. a shoot, new branch

pra√rūp P. *–rūpayati* to expound, expose, explain,

prarūpaṇa n. exposing, teaching,

√pras 696/2 Cl 1 A *prasate* to extend, spread, diffuse, to bring forth young, DP in *vistāra* spreading,

prasabha 697/1 n. forcibly, violently, = *(am)* ind. forcibly, violently,

prāsaca m. congealing (water), freezing,

pra√sad P. A. *–sīdati, (te),* to settle down, grow clear and bright, become placid or tranquil, to become clear or distinct, to become satisfied/pleased, be gracious or kind, to fall into the power of (2nd), caus. *–sādayati* to make clear, purify, to make serene, gladden, to render calm, soothe, appease, propitiate, ask a person to (2nd), or for (infin. 4th) *prasāda* 696/3 m. clearness, brightness, calmness, tranquillity, kindness, absence of excitement, serenity of disposition, good humoured, grace, a propitiatory offering or gift (of food), gift, gratuity, well-being, welfare, graciousness, kindness, grace, a favour, aid, mediation, free gift, gratuity, the food presented to an idol, well-being, welfare, √*sad*

prāsāda m. lofty seat, building on high foundations, palace, top-story,

prasādabhāj mfn being in favour,

prasādabhūmi f. an object of favour, favourite,

prasādadāna n. a propitiatory gift, gift in token of a favour,

prasādaka mfn clearing, rendering, clear, gladdening, exhilirating,

prasādana mfn clearing, rendering, clear, calming, soothing, cheering, m. a royal tent, f. *(ā)* service, worship, n. clearing, rendering, clear, calming, soothing, cheering, rendering gracious, propitiating, boiled rice,

prasādanīya mfn cheering, pleasing, to be rendered gracious,

prasādastha mfn abiding in serenity, kind, propitious, happy,

prasādavat mfn pleased, delighted, gracious, favourable,

prasādavittaka mfn rich in favour, being in high favour with anyone, m. a favourite, darling,

prasādhaka mf(*ikā*)n ifc. adorning, beautifying, accomplishing, perfecting, cleansing, purifying, m. an attendant who dresses his master, *(ikā)*f. a ladies maid, wild rice,

prasādhana mfn accomplishing, effecting, m. a comb, n. arranging, preparing, bringing about, perfecting, embellishment, toilet and requisites

prasādin mfn clear, serene, bright, (as nectar, the eyes, face etc.), ifc. calming, soothing, gladdening, etc.

prasādita mfn cleared, rendered clear, pleased, conciliated, etc,

prasah, mfn = *prasāh* mfn overpowering, victorious

prāsah mfn mighty, strong, f. force, °*hā* ind. by force, violently,

prasaha mfn (ifc.) enduring, withstanding, M. endurance, resistance, a beast or bird of prey,

prāsaha m. force, power,

prasahana m. a beast of prey, n. resisting, overcoming, embracing,

prasahyakaraṇa 697/2 using force, forcibly, n. forcible abduction, robbing, plundering,

prasajya mfn to be attached to or connected with, applicable, *(pra√sañj)*

praśākha mfn having great branches, f. a branch or twig,

prasakala mfn very full (as a bosom),

prasakṣin mfn overpowering, victorious,

prasakta mfn attached, adhering or devoted to, fixed or intent upon, engaged in, occupied with (7th or comp.), clinging to the world, mundane, being in love, enamoured, ifc. supplied or provided with; resulting, following, applicable, continual, lasting, constant, eternal, used, got, obtained, expanded, contiguous, near, ibc. and (*am)* ind. continually, incessantly, eternally ever, *-dhi or –hṛdaya* mfn with heart or mind intent upon or occupied with,

prasaktavya mfn to be attached to (7th),

prasakti f. adherence, attachment, devotion or addiction to, indulgence or perseverance in, occupation with (7th or comp.), (in gram.) bearing upon, applicability (of a rule), connection, association, inference, conclusion, a topic of conversation, acquisition,

prasala m. the cold season, winter,

prasalavi ind. towards the right side,

pra√*śam* P. *–śāmyati* to become calm or tranquil, be pacified or soothed, settle down (as dust), to be allayed or extinguished, cease, disappear,

fade away, caus. *śamayati* to appease, calm, quench, extinguish, terminate, allay, subdue, 695/1
praśām mfn painless, unhurt,
praśama m. calmness, tranquillity, quiet, rest, cessation, abatement
praśāma m. tranquillity, pacification, suppression,
praśamaka mfn one who brings to rest, quenching, allaying,
praśamana mfn tranquillizing, pacifying, healing, n. the act of tranquillizing, securing, keeping safe,
praśamasthita mfn being in a state of quiescence,
prasaṁdhāna n. combination (e.g. words),
prasāmi ind. incompletely, partially, half,
prasamīkṣā f. deliberation, judgment,
prasamīkṣaṇa n. considering, discussing,
prasamīkṣita mfn looked at or upon, observed, considered, regarded,
praśamita mfn tranquillized, relieved, quenched, atoned for, expiated,
praśāmita mfn pacified, subdued, conquered, quelled, quenched,
prasaṁ√khyā P. *–khyāti* to count, enumerate
prasaṁkhyā f. total number, sum, reflection, consideration,
prasaṁkhyāna mfn collecting or gathering (for present needs only), payment, liquidation, a sum of money, n. counting, enumeration, reflection, meditation, reputation, renown, *-para* mfn absorbed in meditation, composed, indifferent
pra√śaṁs P.A. *-śaṁsati (te),* to proclaim, declare, praise highly, , laud, extol, urge on, approve, esteem, value, foretell, prophesy
praśaṁsā f. praise, fame, glory, a poem of praise, laudatory comparison,
praśaṁsaka mfn ifc. praising, commending,
praśaṁsana n. praising, commending
praśaṁsita mfn praised, commended,
praśaṁsya mfn to be praised, praiseworthy, preferable to, better than,
praśāmyati 695/1 to become calm or tranquil, cease,
prāśana n. 1. the eating, 2. the giving of food, feeding,
prasaṅga m. adherence, attachment, inclination or devotion to, indulgence in, fondness for, (*ena*) ind. zealously, eagerly, evil inclination or illicit pursuit, union, connection, occurrence of a possibility, contingency, an occasion, incident, time, opportunity,
prasaṅga 696/2 adherence, attachment, indulgence in, fondness for
prāsaṅgika mfn resulting from attachment or close connection, incidental, casual, occasional, inherent, innate
prasaṅgin mfn attached or devoted to (comp.), connected with, dependent on, belonging to, additional, occurring, appearing, occasional, incidental, secondary, subordinate, non-essential,
pra√sañj P. A. *–sajati, (te*), P. to hang on, attach to, cling to, engage with (quarrel), to be attached to the world, to be the consequence of anything, to cause to take place, A. to attach oneself to, Pass. *–sajyate* or *–sajjate,* to attach oneself to, cling to, be devoted to or intent upon or occupied with, to be in love –pres.p. *–sajjantī*, *-sajjate*, to be the consequence of something else, result, follow, be applicable, caus. P. *-sañjayati* to cause to take place, A. *–sajjayate* to attach to, stick in (7th), with *na* 'to fly through' said of an arrow,
prasañjana n. attaching, uniting, combining, connecting, applying, bringing into use, bringing to bear, giving scope or opportunity, introduction,
praśānta mfn. tranquillized, calm, quiet,
prasanna 696/3 clear, bright, pure, plain placid, tranquil, correct, just, gracious, kindly disposed to,
prasannajala mfn containing clear water,
prasannakalpa mfn almost quiet,

tolerably calm,
prasannatā f. brightness, clarity, purity, clearness of expression, good humour, complacence,
prasannatarka mfn conjecturing right,
prasannatva n. clearness, purity,
praśānta 695/1 mfn. calm, quiet, composed, indifferent, ceased, dead, extinguished, auspicious, indifferent, extinguished
praśāntaceṣṭa mfn one whose efforts have ceased, resting,
praśāntacitta mfn whose heart is calm, tranquil-minded, calm also = *praśāntadhī*
praśāntaka mfn tranquil, calm,
praśāntātman mfn composed in mind, peaceful, calm,
praśānti f. sinking to rest, rest, tranquillity, calm, quiet, pacification, abatement, extinction,
prasara m. (ifc. *ā)* going forwards, advance, progress, free course, coming forth, rising, appearing, spreading, extension, diffusion, range (of the eye), prevalence, influence, boldness, courage, a stream, torrent, flood, multitude, great quantity, a fight, war, an iron arrow, speed, affectionate solicitation,
prasāra spreading/stretching out, extension,
prasaraṇa n. going forth, running away, escaping, holding good, prevailing, amiability, spreading to forage,
prasāraṇa n. spreading/stretching out, extending, diffusing, displaying, developing, augmentation, increase, changing a semivowel into a vowel,
prasaraṇi f. surrounding an enemy,
praśardha bold, daring,
prasarga m. pouring or flowing forth,
prasārita mfn held forth, stretched out, expanded, spread, diffused, laid out, exhibited, published,
prasarjana mfn darting forth,
prasarpaṇa n. going forwards, entering, a place of refuge, shelter,
prasarpin, coming forth, issuing from (comp.), creeping along, crawling away,
prasarpita mfn crawling along,
praśas f. a hatchet, axe, knife,
pra√śās P. *–śāsti* to teach, instruct, direct, to give instructions to, order, command, to chastise, punish, to govern, rule, reign,
praśāsaka, praśāstṛ, m. 'director', name of a priest with a ritual function,
praśāsana n. guidance, government, rule,
praśasta 695/1 praised, commended, happy, auspicious, also *praśāsta*
praśasti f. praise, fame, glorification, to bestow praise upon, value highly, instruction, guidance, warning, excellence, eminence,
prāśastra government, rule, dominion,
praśastu let him rule, impv.
prāśastya n. celebrity, excellence, being praised,
praśasya mfn to be praised, praiseworthy, excellent, eminent, to be called happy, to be congratulated, ind. having praised or commended,
praśaṭha mfn very false or wicked,
prasatta mfn satisfied, pleased,
prasatti f. clearness, brightness, purity, graciousness, favour,
praśattvan m. the ocean, *(arī)* f. a river,
prasava 697/3 m pressing out (juice), n a Soma press
698/1 m. setting or being set in motion, impulse, course, stimulation, furtherance, aid, pursuit, acquisition, begetting, procreation, generation, conception, delivery, birth, origin, increase, augmentation, bithplace, offspring, posterity, a flower, fruit,
prasavabandhana n. the foot-stalk of a leaf or flower,
prasavadharmin mfn characterized by production, productive, prolific,
prasavagṛha n. a lying-in chamber,
prasavakāla m. the time of delivery or bringing forth,
prasavakarmakṛt m. one who begets,

prasavamāsa m. the last month of pregnancy
prasavana n. bringing forth, bearing children, fecundity,
prasavasthalī f. 'birthplace', a mother,
prasavasthāna n. a receptacle for young, nest
prasavavedanā f. the pangs of childbirth, throes of labour,
prasavat mf(*antī*)n bringing forth, bearing, a woman in labour,
prasaviṣyadhvam may you bring forth, bring forth, 2/pl/impv/fut/act *pra* √*su*
prasavitṛ m. a begetter, father, (*trī*) f. a mother,
prasavitra n. a soma press?
prasavya mfn *(am)* ind. turned towards the left, to the left side, contrary, reverse, favourable,
prasecana n. the bowl of a spoon or ladle, -*vat* mfn having a bowl or spout,
prasedivas mfn one who has become pleased or propitiated, favourable,
praseka m. flowing forth, effusion, discharge, vomiting, a running nose
prasena m.n. °*nā* f. a kind of jugglery,
praseva m. a sack or a leather bottle, √*siv*
prasevaka m. a sack, bag, a damper,
prasevana the producer of grains (Gam.),
prasīda be merciful, 2/s/impv/act *pra* √*sad*
prasīdati is pacified, calmed down, to fall into the power of, settle down, become placid, grow clear and bright, become clear or distinct, is pacified, calmed down, become fully satisfied, become reconciled, to become satisfied or pleased, be gracious or kind, (with 6th to favour), caus. *sādayati* to make clear, purify, to make serene, gladden, to render calm, soothe, appease, propitiate, *pra*√*sad* 696/3 1/s/pres/act
pra√*3.sidh* P. A. -*sidhyati (te),* to be accomplished or effected, succeed, to result from (5th), to be explained or made clear,
prasiddha mfn brought about, accomplished, well-known, notorious, celebrated,
prasiddhi f. accomplishment, success, attainment, proof, argument, general opinion, celebrity, fame,
prasiddhimat mfn universally known, famous,
prasiddhyet it should be accomplished, it might be accomplished, it should succeed or should be attained, 1/s/opt/act *pra* √ *sidh* 697/3
prasīdikā f. a small garden,
prasikta mfn poured out,
praśis f. order, direction, precept,
praśiṣṭa mfn ruled over, governed,
praśiṣṭi f. injunction, command, order,
praśiṣya m. the pupil of a pupil,
praśiṣyatva n. the condition of a pupil's pupil,
praśīta mfn congealed, frozen,
prasita mfn bound, fastened, diligent, attentive, attached or devoted to, engaged in, engrossed by, occupied with, lasting, continuous,
2. n. pus, matter,
praśithila mfn very loose, relaxed, very feeble, hardly perceptible,
prasiti f. continuation, extended path e.g. of life, a net for catching birds, a ligament, binding, fetter,
2. onward rush, attack, a throw, cast, shot, stretch, reach, extension, sphere, succession, duration, dominion, power, authority,
prāśitṛ m. eater,
prāśitra n. the portion of ghee to be eaten at a sacrifice by a Brahman, anything edible,
prāśitra-haraṇa the vessel holding the *prāśitra*
prasīvyati P. sews up √*siv*
praskandana mfn leaping foward, attacking, n. leaping over or across, one who has diahorrea, voiding excrement, a purgative,
praskandati P. leaps forth up or out, attacks, gushes forth, falls into, sheds, spills, pours out (an oblation),
praskanna mfn shed, spilt, lost, gone, having

attacked, m. a transgressor, sinner, one who has violated the rules of his caste or order,
praśleṣa n. close contact or pressure, coalescence (of vowels),
praśliṣṭa mfn twisted, entwined, coalescent (applicable to *saṁdhi* of some vowels)
prasmarati P. remembers, forgets, √*smṛ*
prasmartavya mfn to be forgotten,
prasmayate A. bursts into laughter, √*smi*
prasmṛta mfn forgotten,
prasmṛti f. forgetting, forgetfulness,
praśna m. basket-work, a plaited basket,
praśna 2. m. a question, demand, interrogation, query, a short section or paragraph (in books),
prasna m. a bath, vessel for bathing,
prasnapita mfn bathed,
prasnātṛ m. a bather,
prasnava m. a stream or flow (water, milk etc.), pl. tears, urine, √*snu*
prasnavana n. emitting fluid,
praśnaya Nom.P. to question, interrogate, inquire after,
praśnaya m. support, modesty,
prasnigdha mfn very oily or greasy, very soft or tender, √*snih*
praśnin m. a questioner, interrogator,
praśnottara n. question and answer, verse consisting of question and answer,
prasnuta mfn yielding milk,
praśocana mfn burning on, continuing to burn, √*śuc*
praśoṣa m. dryness, aridity,
praśoṣaṇa m. drying up,
praspardhin mfn ifc. rivalling, equalling,
prasphāra mfn swollen, puffed up, conceited,
prasphoṭana n. bursting, opening, striking, beating, winnowing, expanding, causing to bloom, making evident or manifest, winnowing corn, wiping away,
prasphuliṅga m.n. a glittering spark,
prasphuṭa cleft open, burst, expanded, published, open, evident,
praśrabdhi f. trust, confidence,
prasravaṇa 700/2 n streaming or gushing forth, trickling, oozing, a well or spring, a waterfall, perspiration, voiding urine, milk, milk flowing,
prāsravaṇa mfn coming from a spring (water),
prasravati P. flows forth, flows from (5th), lets flow, pours out, √*sru*
praśraya m. leaning or resting on, resting-place, inclining forward, respectful demeanour, modesty, humility, affection, respect, civility, -vat mfn deferential, respectful, civil, modest,
praśrayaṇa n. respectful demeanour, modesty, civility, courtesy,
praśrayin mfn courteous, modest, respectful
pra√*sṛ* P.A. *–sisarti , -sarati, (te)*, to move forwards, advance (for or against), proceed, spring up, come forth, issue from (5th), to break out (fire, disease), to be diffused (odour), to pass, elapse (as night), to commence, begin, to prevail, take place, to stretch out (hands), to agree, promise, caus. *–sārayati* to stretch out, extend, to spread out, to open wide (eyes, mouth), to diffuse, circulate, exhibit, to prosecute, transact, (in gram.) to change a semi-vowel into the corresponding vowel,
pra√*sṛj* P. *–sṛjati* to let loose, dismiss, send off to, to give free course, to (anger etc.), to stretch out (the arms), to scatter, sow, to argue with,
prasripta mfn spread, diffused,
prasṛṣṭa mfn let loose, dismissed, set free, undirected, uncontrolled, permitted
prasṛta 698/2 mfn. come forth, issued from, resounding, widespreading, extending over or to, intent upon, devoted to, prevailing, ordinary, intense, mighty, strong, set out, departed, fled, humble, modest, quiet, a handful (measure), (*ā*)f. the leg, grass, plants, vegetables, agriculture,
prasṛti 698/3 streaming, flowing, extension,

diffusion, swiftness, haste, a handful as measure,
prasṛtvara mfn breaking forth,
pra√sru Cl 1 *–sravati,* flow forth, flow from
prasruta mfn flowed forth, discharging fluid, humid, moist, wet,
prastabdha mfn stiff, rigid,
prastambha m. becoming stiff or rigid,
prastara m. ifc. (*ā*) f. anything strewed forth or about, a couch of leaves and flowers, a couch, a flat surface, flat top, level, a plain, a rock, stone, a gem, jewel, a leather bag, a paragraph, section,
prastāra m. (ifc. f. *ā*) strewing, spreading out, (fig. = abundance, high degree), a litter, bed of straw, a layer, steps to water, a flat surface, plain, a jungle, overgrown,
prastaraṇa m. *(ā*) f. a couch, seat,
prastārin mfn spreading out, extending to (comp.)
prastava m. a hymn of praise, chant, song, a favourable moment,
prastāva m. introductory eulogy, introducing a topic, preliminary mention, allusion, reference, topic, occasion, opportunity, season, turn, convenience, (*e* or *eṣu* on a suitable occasion, opportunity),
ena incidentally, occasionally, with *tava* at your convenience,
beginning, commencement,
prastāvakrameṇa m. introductory eulogy, intro. or prelude of a song, preliminary mention, allusion, by way of introduction,
prastāvanā f. sounding forth, blazing abroad, introduction, commencement, beginning, preface, the introductory part of a discourse,
prastāvatas ind. on the occasion of,
praṣṭavya mfn to be asked or questioned about, to be inquired into, n. (impers.) one should ask or inquire about,
pra√sthā P.A. *-tiṣṭhati* to stand or rise up (esp. before the gods, an altar etc.), to advance towards (2nd), to be awake, to set out, depart from, proceed or march to or with a view to or in order to, to move or abide in the open air , caus. *–sthāpayati* to put aside, to send out, send to (2nd) or for the purpose of, send away or send home, dispatch messengers, dismiss, banish, drive, urge on (horses),
praṣṭha mfn standing in front, foremost, principal, best, chief, m. a leader, conductor,
(*ī*) f. the wife of a leader or chief,
-tva n. being in front, pre-eminence
prastha mfn going on a march or journey, going to or abiding in, stable, firm, solid, expanding, spread, m.n. table-land on a mountain top, a level expanse, plain (esp. at the end of names of towns and villages, a partic. measure of capacity,
-vat m. a mountain,
prasthāna 699/3 n setting out, departure, procession, march, walking, moving, journey, sending away, dispatching, dying, religious mendicancy, a way to obtain any object, course, method, system, starting point,
prasthāyin mfn setting forth, departing, marching, going,
prasthita mfn set forth, prepared, ready (as sacrifice), rising, upright, standing forth, prominent, appointed, installed, set out, departed, gone to, n. setting out, going away,departure, ind. (impers.) a person (3rd) has set out,
prastira m. a bed or couch made of leaves and flowers,
prastīta or prastīma mfn crowded, together, swarming, making a noise, sounded,
prastobha m. allusion or reference to (6th),
praṣṭṛ m. one who asks or inquires
pra√stṛ P.A. to spread, extend, pour out, utter words, speak,
pra√stu P. *–stauti,* A. *–stavate,* to praise

before (anything else) or aloud, to sing, chant, introduce as a topic, commence, begin,
prastuta mfn praised, proposed, propounded, mentioned, introduced as a topic of conversation, in question, commenced, begun, ready, prepared, happened, made or consisting of, approached, proximate, done with effort or energy, n. beginning, undertaking,
prastutatāṅkura m. a figure of speech, allusion by the mention of any passing circumstance to something latent in the hearer's mind,
prastutayajña mfn having one's sacrifice begun, prepared for a sacrifice,
prastuti f. praise, eulogium,
prāstutya n. being propounded or discussed,
pra√1.sū P. *–suvati, -sauti,* to set in motion, rouse to activity, urge, incite, impel, bid, command, to allow, give up to,
pra√2.sū A. *–sūte, -sūyate, P. –savati, -sauti,* to procreate, beget, bring forth, obtain offspring or bear fruit, produce, A. to be born or produced, originate, arise,
prasū mfn bringing forth, bearing, fruitful, productive, ifc. giving birth to, f. a mother, a mare, a young shoot, tender grass,
pra√śubh to be bright, sparkle,
pra√śuc A. *–śocate* to glow, beam, radiate,
pra√sūc P. *–sūcayati* to indicate, manifest,
praśuci mfn perfectly pure,
praśuddhi f. purity, clearness,
prasūkā f. a mare
prasūmat, prasūmaya, prasūvara furnished with flowers,
praśūna mfn swollen,
prasūna mfn born, produced, n. (ifc.*ā)* a flower, blossom, fruit,
prasūnabāṇa m. 'having flowers for arrows' the god of love,
prasūnamālā f. a garland of flowers,
prasūnavarṣa m. a shower of flowers, (rained from heaven),
prasup mfn asleep,
prasupta mfn fallen into sleep, fast asleep, sleeping, having slept, asleep i.e insensible, quiet, inactive, latent,
prasupti f. sleepiness,
prasūta mfn procreated, begotten, born, produced, any productive source, the primordial essence or matter, *(ā)* f. a woman who has brought forth a child, recently delivered, n. a flower
prasūti f. procreation, generation, bringing forth, laying, parturition, birth,
prasūtitas coming forth, appearance, growth (fruit, flowers etc.), a production, product (of plants or animals), a procreator, father or mother,
prasūyat mf (*antī*) n being born
prasvādas mfn very pleasant or agreeable,
prasvana m. sound, noise,
prasvāna m. a loud noise,
pra√svap Cl 2 *–svapiti,* to go to sleep,
prasvāpa mfn causing sleep, soporific,
prasvāpaka mf(*ikā*)n causing to sleep, causing to die, slaying,
prasvāpana mfn causing sleep, n. sending to sleep,
prasvāra m. the extended syllable Om pronounced by a leader at the beginning of a lesson or discussion,
praśvāsa m. breathing in, inhaling,
praśvasitavya 696/1 n. recovery of breath, deep breathing,
prasveda m. great/excessive perspiration, sweat, m. an elephant,
prasvedate begins to sweat, becomes moist,
prasvinna mfn covered with perspiration, sweated, perspired, √*svid*
prasyanda m. flowing forth, trickling out,
prasyandin mfn oozing forth, shedding (tears), m. a shower of rain,
praṣyati sends
pratad-vasu mfn increasing wealth,
prātaḥ in comp. for *prātar*
prātaḥ at the dawn, early
prātaḥkāla m. morning time, early morning, daybreak,
prātaḥkalpa mfn night, almost morning, early dawn,
prātaḥsaṁdhyā f. morning twilight, dawn

prātaḥsnāna n. morning ablution,
pratakvan mfn rushing on, steep, precipitous,
pra√takṣ to build, make, produce,
pratala m. open hand with fingers extended, a division of the lower regions,
pra√tam P. *–tāmyati* to become exhausted or breathless, faint away, lose self-consciousness, perish,
pratamām ind. especially, particularly,
pra√tan P.A. *–tanoti, -tanute*, to spread or extend over, cover, fill, to spread, disperse, diffuse, continue, propagate, to show, display, to undertake, begin, perform, execute, cause, do,make,
-tanyute to be continued or extended or particularized,
pratana mfn ancient, old,
pratāna m. a shoot, tendril, a plant with tendrils, branching out, ramification, diffuseness, prolixity, tetanus, epilepsy
prataṅkam ind. gliding, creeping,
pratanu mfn very thin or fine, delicate, slender, minute, insignificant,
pra√tap P. *–tapati* to give forth heat, burn, glow, shine, to feel pain, suffer, to warm, heat, shine upon, to roast, bake, to kindle, light, illumine, to pain with heat, caus. *–tāpayati* to make warm, heat, to set on fire, irradiate, illuminate, torment, harass,
pratapa m. the heat of the sun,
pratāpa m. glowing heat, heat, warmth, splendour, brilliancy, glory, majesty, dignity, power, strength, energy,
pratāpana 661/2 mfn making hot, paining, distressing, tormenting, m. a partic. hell, n. warming, heating, turning, paining, distressing,
pratapat mf *(ānti)*n burning, glowing, shining, (lit. and fig.) feeling pain, doing penance,
m. the sun, an ascetic,
pratapatra n. a parasol,
pratapta mfn hot, glowing, shining, subjected to great heat, annealed, tortured, harassed, n. annealed gold,
prataptṛ m. one who burns or singes
prātar 706/2 in the early morning, at dawn, at daybreak, next morning, tomorrow
pratara m. passing over, crossing,
pratāra m. passing over, crossing (6th), deception, fraud,
prātarabhivāda m. morning salutation,
prātaradhyeya to be recited every morning
pratāraka mfn cheating, a deceiver,
prataram or *pratarām* ind. further, more particularly, in future,
prataraṇa mfn furthering, promoting, increasing, n. going to sea, passing over, crossing,
pratāraṇa n, ferrying over, carrying across, passing over, crossing, deceiving,
prātarāśa m. morning meal, breakfast
pratarati (te), √*tṝ* P.A. goes to sea, passes over, crosses, sets out, starts,
A. rises, thrives, prospers, raises, elevates, increases, furthers, extends, prolongs, caus. *–tārayati* to extend, widen, prolong (life), to mislead, take in, deceive, lead astray, seduce,
prātardina n. the early part of the day, forenoon,
pratareta should cross over
pratārita mfn misled, deceived, imposed upon, persuaded or seduced to,
pratarītṛ m. a furtherer, promoter
prātaritvan mfn going out early,
prātarjapa m. morning prayer,
pra√tark P. *–tarkayati* to form a clear view or notion of (2nd), to gather, conclude, to regard as, take for,
pratardana mfn piercing, destroying,
pratarka m. conclusion, supposition, conjecture,
pratarkaṇa n. judging, reasoning, discussion, logic,
prātarvikasvara mfn rising early,
prātaś in comp. for *prātar*
prātas in comp. for *prātar*
prātastarām ind. very early in the morning,
prātastana mfn relating to the morning, n.

early morning,
pratata n. a high bank
pratata mfn spread over, diffused, filled, covered (*am*) ind. continuously,
pratati f, spreading, extension, creeping plant,
pratavas mfn mighty, powerful, active
√*prath* 678/3 Cl 1 A P *prathate (ti),* to spread, extend, become larger or wider, increase, to spread abroad (as a name, rumour etc., become known or celebrated, to come to light, appear, arise, to occur (to the mind), to spread abroad, proclaim, celebrate, to unfold, disclose, reveal, show, to extend over, shine upon, give light to,
2. or *pṛth* Cl 10 P *prāthayati* or *parthayati* to throw, cast, to extend, DP in *prakhyāna* becoming known
prathā f. spreading out, extending, fame, celebrity, growing, becoming,
prathama 678/3 mfn (for *pra-tama* superlative of 1. *pra*), foremost, first, earliest, primary, original, prior, former, preceding, initial, chief, principal, most excellent, (*am*) ind. firstly, at first, for the first time, first of all, just, newly, at once, formerly, previously, In Sanskrit grammar (*ā*) f. the first or nominative case and its terminations, the first person (verbs) and its terminations,
the *prathamā puruṣaḥ* (first person of the verb) is he, she or it e.g. *gacchati* - he, she or it goes
prathamabhāvin mfn becoming or being like the first
prathamābhidheya n. original meaning,
prathamacchad mfn typical, figurative,
prathamāgāmin mfn occurring first, first mentioned,
prathamāham ind. on the first day
prathamāhāra m. the first application,
prathamamaṅgala mfn highly auspicious,
prathamaja or *–jā* mfn first-born, original, primary,
prathamajāta mfn first-born,
prathamakalpa m. a primary/principal rule
prathamam mfn foremost, first, earliest, primary, initial, chief, ind. firstly, at first, for the first time, just, newly, at once,
prathamadarśana n. first sight, (e) ind. at first sight,
prathamadivasa m. a first or principal day
prathamadugdha mfn just milked,
prathamaka mfn first, foremost,
prathamakalpika m. a beginnner Yogī
prāthamakalpika mfn being (anything) first of all or in the strictest sense of the word, m. a student who is a beginner, a Yogi just commencing his course,
prathamakalpita mfn placed first, first in rank or importance,
prathamakathita mfn afore-said,
prathamanirdiṣṭa mfn first-mentioned, first-named
prathamapuruṣa m. the first (our 3rd) person in the verb or its terminations
prathamapravada mfn uttering the first sound (a child),
prathamārdha m. the first half,
prathamāstamita n. having just set (the sun),
prathamataram ind. first of all,
prathamatas ind. first, at first, firstly, forthwith, immediately, before, in preference to (with 6th), ifc. before, sooner than,
prathamāvaratva n. the being the first and the last,
prathamayauvana n. early youth,
prathamarātra m. the beginning of night,
prathamaśravas mfn having a distinguished reputation,
prathamasukṛta n. a former service or kindness
prathamavaiyākaraṇa m. a beginner at grammar, a distinguished or first-rate grammarian,
prathamavayas n. earliest age, youth,
prathamavayasin mfn young,
prathamavittā f. a first wife,
prathamavṛttānta m. former circumstances,

earlier history,
prathametara mfn 'other than first', second,
prāthamika mfn belonging or relating to the first, occurring or happening for the first time, primary, initial, previous,
prathamodita mfn first uttered, previously uttered,
prathamotpanna mfn produced first, firstborn
prāthamya n. priority,
prathana n. spreading out, extending, the place for spreading, unfolding, showing, projecting, celebrating,
prathita mfn spread, extended, increased, displayed, published, intent upon, cast, thrown,
pratāpavat mfn. full of dignity, full of power, full of strength
pratareta should crossover,
prātharāśaḥ m. breakfast
prathas n. width, extension,
prathasvat mfn wide, spacious,
prathayat mfn spreading out, extending, seeing, beholding,
prāthayati cl 10 to throw, cast, extend
prathayitṛ mfn one who spreads, expands, or divulges, proclaims,
prathiman m. extension, width, greatness,
prathimin mfn having size or magnitude,
prathiṣṭha mfn broadest, widest, very large or great, steadfast, leading to, ending with, n. point of support, centre or base of anything,
f. (*ā*) stability, base security of position,
prathita 678/3 mfn spread, extended, divulged, published,
intent upon, engaged in,
known, known as, celebrated
prathiti f. extension of fame, celebrity,
prathivī for *pṛthivī* the earth,
prathu mfn wide, reaching farther than,
prathuka m. the young of any animal,
prati 1. ind. a prefix to roots, their derivative nouns and other nouns, sometimes *pratī*
towards, near to, against, in opposition to, down, upon, back again, in return, down upon, upon, on,
-before nouns it also expresses likeness or comparison, or
-forms indeclinable compounds of various kinds, e.g. *praty-agni*
- as a preposition with usually preceding 2nd case, in the sense of towards, against, to, upon, in the direction of e.g. *śabdam prati* in the direction of the sound, *agnim prati* or *praty-agni* (ind.) against the fire, also opposite, before, in the presence of, in comparison, on a par with, also with 5th or *–tas*
in the vicinity of, near, beside, at, on, at the time of, about, through, may be used distributively to express – at every, in or on every, severally, also – in favour of, for, on account of, in regard to, concerning,
pratī *prati√i* to go towards or against, go to meet (as friend or foe), to come back, return,
prāti √*prā* fills f. filling,
the span of the thumb and forefinger,
a lengthened form of *prati* in compounds,
pratibaddha mfn tied or bound to, fastened, fixed, twisted wreathed (garland), dependent on, subject to (comp.), attached to, connected or joined or provided with, harmonizing with (7th), hindered, excluded, cut off, kept at a distance, entangled, complicated, disappointed, thwarted, vexed, (in phil.) that which is always connected or implied (as fire in smoke), 668/1
pratibaddhacitta mfn one whose mind is turned to or fixed on (comp.)
pratibaddharāga mfn having passion in harmonious connection with,
pratibaddhatā f. the being connected with,
prati√bādh A. *–bādhate* to beat back, ward off, repel, to check, restrain, torment
pratibādhaka mf(*ikā*)n thrusting back,

repelling, preventing, obstructing,
pratibādhana n. beating back, repulsion,
pratibādhita mfn beaten back, repelled,
pratibādhin mfn obstructing, m. an opponent,
pratibadhya mfn to be obstructed/hindered,
pratibala 1. n. a hostile army, 2. mfn having equal strength or power, equally matched, a match for,
pratibanddhṛ m. a hinderer, obstructor,
prati√bandh P.A. *–badhnāti, -badhnīte*, to tie to, fasten, fix, moor, (A. anything of one's own), to set, to exclude, cut off, keep back or off, keep at a distance, to stop, interrupt,
pratibandha 668/2 connection, prop, support, siege, un-interruptedness, obstacle, impediment, opposition, resistance, inseparable connection, a logical impediment, obstructive argument, stoppage, cessation,
pratibandhaka ifc. = °*bandha,* impediment, obstacle, mf(*ikā*)n obstructing, preventing, resisting,
pratibandhakārin mfn creating obstacles, hindering,
pratibandhamukta mfn freed from obstacles,
pratibandhana n. binding, confinement,
pratibandhi m. contradiction, objection,
pratibandhin mfn meeting with an obstacle, being impeded or prevented, impeding, obstructing,
pratibandhavat beset with obstacles, difficult to attain,
pratibandhu m. an equal in rank or station
prati√bhā P. *–bhāti,* to shine upon, to come in sight, present or offer one's self to, to appear to the mind, flash upon the thoughts, become clear or manifest, occur to, to seem or appear to, to seem fit, appear good,
pratibha mfn wise, intelligent,
pratibhā f. an image, light, splendour, appearance, fitness, suitableness, intelligence, understanding, presence of mind, genius, wit, audacity, boldness, a founded supposition, fancy, imagination,
prātibha mfn intuitive, divinatory, n. intuitive knowledge, intuition, divination, (*ā*) f. presence of mind
pratibhābalāt ind. by force of reason or intelligence, wisely,
pratibhāga m. division, a share, portion, daily present (offered to a king),
pratibhāhāni f. dullness, darkness,
pratibhairava mfn dreadful,
pratibhākṣaya m. loss or absence of knowledge, want of sense,
pratibhāmukha mfn at once hitting the right, quick-witted, (confident, arrogant),
pratibhāna n. becoming clear or visible, obviousness, intelligence, eloquence, brilliancy, boldness, audacity,
pratibhānatva n. bright, brilliant, bold, audacious,
pratibhānavat mfn endowed with presence of mind, quick-witted, shrewd, intelligent,
pratibhaṇita mfn answered, replied,
pratibhānvita mfn intelligent, wise, confident, bold
prati√bhāṣ A. - *bhāṣate* to answer, tell,
prati√bhās A. - *bhāsate* 668/3 to manifest oneself, appear as, or look like, to shine, be brilliant, have a bright appearance,
prātibhāsika 706/3 mfn. having only the appearance of anything, existing only in appearance, the rope as a snake, in the dream state, m. the experiencer of the dream state,
prātibhāsika-satya the truth as false-appearance,
pratibhaṭa mfn a match for, vying with, m. an adversary, -*tā* f. emulation,
pratibhāta n. a symbolical offering,
pratibhātas ind. by fancy or imagination,
prātibhaṭya n. rivalry,
pratibhāva m. counterpart, corresponding character or disposition,
pratibhavam ind. for this & all future births,
pratibhāvat mfn endowed with presence of

mind, shrewd, intelligent, confident, bold, m. the sun, moon, fire,
prātibhāvya n. surety for, going bail for, certainty of or about (6th),
pratibhedana n. piercing, cutting, dividing, putting out (eyes)
prati√bhid P. *-bhinatti* to pierce, penetrate, disclose, betray, to reproach, be indignant with,
pratibhinna mfn pierced, divided, distinguished by (3rd or in comp.)
pratibhoga m. enjoyment,
pratibhojana n. prescribed diet,
pratibhojin mfn eating the prescribed diet,
prati√bhṛ P. *–bharati* to carry towards, offer, present, *-bibharti* to support a parent,
pratibhravīti replies, answers, *√bhrū*
pratibhṛta mfn offered, prevented,
prati√bhū P. *–bhavati,* to be equal to or on a par with (2nd), caus. *–bhāvayati* to observe, become acquainted with, pass. *–bhāvyate* to be considered as, pass for,
pratibhū m. a surety, security, bail,
pratibhūṣati *√bhūṣ* P. makes ready, fits out, serves, prepares, waits upon, agrees to, honours, worships, concedes,
pratibīja n. bad seed,
pratibījam ind. for every sort of grain,
pratibimba n. a reflection (as in a mirror), reflected image, the disc of the sun or moon reflected in water,
pratibimbana n. the being reflected, reflection, comparing together,
pratibimbayati reflects, mirrors,
pratibodha 668/2 m. awaking, waking, perception, knowledge, instruction, admonition,
pratībodha m. vigilance,
pratibodhaka mfn awakening (with 2nd), m. a teacher, instructor,
pratibodhana mfn awakening, enlivening, refreshing (ifc), (*ā*) f. awaking, recovering consciousness, n. awaking, expanding, spreading, awakening, instruction, explanation,
pratibodhanīya mfn to be awakened,
pratibodhavat mfn endowed with knowledge or reason,
pratibodhin mfn awaking, about to awake,
pratibodhita mfn awakened, instructed, taught,
prati√brū P.A. *–bravīti, -brūte* to speak in reply, answer, A. to answer (an attack), to refuse, deny,
prati√budh A. *–budhyate* P *–ti,* to awaken, awake, wake, perceive, observe, caus. *–bodhayati* to awaken, instruct, inform,
pratibuddha mfn awakened, awake, one who has attained to perfect knowledge, illuminated, enlightened, observed, recognized, known, celebrated, made prosperous or great,
pratibuddhaka mfn known, recognized
pratibuddhavastu mfn understanding the real nature of things
pratibuddhātman mfn having the mind roused or awakened,
pratibuddhi f. awakening, hostile disposition or purpose, mfn having hostile intentions,
prati√budh A. *–budhyate, (ti),* to awaken, awake, wake, to perceive, observe, learn, to expand, caus. *–bodhayati* to awaken, to instruct, inform, admonish, to commission, charge, order,
prati√cakṣ A. *-caṣṭe* to see, perceive, to expect, to cause to see, let appear, show
praticakṣaṇa n. looking at, viewing, appearance, look, aspect, showing,
praticakṣin mfn regarding, observing,
praticakṣya mfn visible, conspicuous,
praticāra m. personal adornment,
praticarati P. advances towards, approaches,
praticārin mfn exercising, practising,
pratcārita mfn circulated, proclaimed,
praticchadana n. a cover, covering,
pratīcchaka m. one who receives, a receiver,
praticchanda m. a reflected image, any image, likeness, substitute,
praticchanna mfn covered, enveloped, hidden, concealed, disguised,

endowed or furnished with,
praticchāyā f. reflection, likeness, image, shadow, phantom, °*yikā* f.
praticcheda m. cutting off, resistance,
praticikīrṣā f. wish to requite, desire to be revenged upon,
pratīcīna mfn turned towards, going or coming towards, turned away from, turning the back, being behind, coming from behind, turning westward, western, subsequent, future (with 5th), (*am*) ind. back to oneself, backwards, behind,
prati√cint P.A. to consider again, reflect upon, remember,
praticintana n. thinking repeatedly, considering,
praticintanīya mfn to be thought over again
praticodanā f. prevention, prohibition
praticoḍayati caus. drives/urges on, impels
praticodita mfn impelled or excited against,
pratīcya mfn being in the west, western country, n. designation of anything remote or concealed,
praticyavīyas mfn pressing closer against or towards,
prati√1.dā P.A. *–dadāti, -datte,* to give back, restore, return, to give,offer, present,
pratidahati P. burns towards, consumes,
prātidaivasika mfn happening or occurring daily
pratidaivatam ind, for each deity,
pratidāna n. restitution, restitution of deposit
pratidaṇḍa mfn disobedient, obstinate,
pratidāraṇa n. battle, fierce conflict,
pratidarśa m. looking at, viewing,
pratidarśana n. looking at, viewing, (*ā*) f. sight, look, appearance,
pratideham ind. in each body,
pratidevatā f. a corresponding deity,
prati√1.dhā P.A. *–dadhāti, -dhatte*, to put on or in or near or back, return, restore, to adjust an aim (arrow), to put to the lips (for drinking), to put down (the feet), to step out, to offer, present, to use, employ, to restrain, A. to commence, begin, approach,
pratidhā f. putting to the lips, a draught,
pratidhāna n. putting to or on, adopting precautions,
pratidhārayati (*te*),(√*dhṛ*) keeps back, stops, checks, keeps erect, supports,
pratidhārtṛ m. one who keeps back or stops,
pratidhāvati (te) P.A. runs back, rushes upon, attacks, (√*dhāv*)
pratidhāvana n. rushing upon, onset, attack
pratidhi m. cross-piece on a carriage-pole,
prati√dhī to expect, hope,
pratidhī mfn ifc. as intelligent as,
pratidhura m. a horse harnessed beside another
pratidhvani m. echo, reverberated sound,
pratidhvānin, °*nita* mfn sounding/resounding
pratidhvasta mfn sunk, hanging down,
pratidhyāta mfn thought upon, meditated,
pratidinam and *–divasam* ind. daily, day by day, every day,
pratidīpta mfn flaming against,
pratidiśam or °*deśam* ind. in every direction, all around,
pratidivan m. the sun, a day,
pratidīvan m. an adversary at play, the sun,
pratidivasam ind. every day, day by day
pratidoṣam ind. in the evening, in the dark,
prati√dṛś to look at, perceive, behold, notice, A. and pass. to become visible, appear, appear as, be, caus. to cause to see, show, teach,
pratidṛś mfn similar, like,
pratidṛśam ind. in or for every eye
pratidṛṣṭa mfn beheld, visible, conspicuous, famous, celebrated,
pratidṛṣṭānta m. a counter-example,
pratidṛṣṭāntasama m. an irrelevant objection by adducing a counter-example which ignores the opponents example,
pratidruh m. one seeking to injure in return
pratiduh n. fresh milk, milk still warm
pratidūṣita mfn defiled, rendered unclean,
pratidvaṁdva m. an adversary, rival, foe, n. opposition, hostility,
pratidvīpam ind. in every part of the world
prati√gā to go back, return,
pratigacchati he returns
pratigadati P.speaks in return, answers √*gad*

pratigāhate A. penetrates, enters, √*gāh*
pratigaja (R) m. hostile elephant,
prati√gam Cl 1 *-gacchati,to* go back, return,
pratigara m. an uttered response , encouraging words,
pratigarjana n. thundering or roaring against or in return, an answering roar,
pratigata gone towards or back, flying backwards and forwards, wheeling in flight, lost from the memory, f. °*gati,* n. *gamana* return
pratigātram ind. in every limb (ibc.),
pratigha m. hindrance, obstruction, struggling against (comp.), anger, enmity, wrath, combat, fighting, an enemy, contradiction,
pratighāta 665/2 m warding off, keeping back, repulse, prevention, resistance, struggling against, also *pratīghāta* as above
pratighātaka mfn disturbing, ifc. =°*ghāta*
pratighātakṛt mfn depriving anyone of,
pratighātana n. warding off, repulsing,
pratighātavid mfn knowing how to resist, apt to resist,
pratighna n. the body,
pratighoṣin mfn roaring or crying out against, (*iṇī*) f.a class of demons
pratigraha m. receiving, accepting, receiving of gifts (as a brāhman), friendly reception, favour, grace, marrying, hearing, a grasper, a spittoon, a gift, present,
pratigrāha m. accepting gifts, a spittoon,
pratigrāhaka or *pratigrāhin* one who receives or accepts
pratigrahaṇa mfn accepting, n. receipt, acceptance, marrying,
pratigrahin mfn one who receives a receiver,
pratigrahītṛ m. one who takes a wife, marries,
pratigrāhya mfn to be taken or accepted, acceptable, one from whom anything may be received,
pratigrāmam ind. in every village,
pratigṛbhāyati P. takes, receives, eats
pratigṛṇāti, -gṛṇīte, invokes, salutes, responds in recitation or chanting,
pratigṛdhyati P. is greedy or eager for,
pratigṛhīta mfn taken, received, accepted, married,
pratigṛhṇāti, -gṛhṇīte, takes hold of, grasps, seizes, appropriates, receives, accepts, gains, wins over, marries, receives a friend or guest, receives anything agreeable such as a good word or omen, assents to, approves, √*grah*
pratigṛhya mfn to be accepted, acceptable,
pratigṛham or *–geham* ind. in every house,
prati√3.gu to proclaim
pratigupta mfn guarded, protected, 665/1
prati√han P. *–hanti,* A. *–jaghne,* to beat against, attack, strike down, crush, strike back, repel, dispel, remove, check, prevent, frustrate, 673/1
pratihanana n. impeding, obstructing,
pratihantṛ m. one who wards off, preventer,
prātihantra n. vengeance,
pratihāra m. striking against, touch, contact, (esp. tongue with teeth for pronunciation of dentals), a door, gate, door-keeper, (*ī*) f. a female door-keeper, a juggler, juggling, trick, disguise,
prātihāra m. a juggler, doorkeeper
pratihāraka m. a juggler,
pratiharaṇa n. throwing back, repelling, avoiding, shunning,
pratiharṣa 673/2 expression of joy
pratiharṣaṇa mfn causing joy in return,
pratihartṛ m. one who draws back or absorbs, one who averts,
pratihāsa m. returning a laugh, laughing with or at, fragrant oleander,
pratihastaka m. proxy, 'person at one's hand',
pratiharyati (te) desires, loves, accepts gladly, longs for, √*hary*
pratihata mfn struck or striking against, repelled, impeded, dazzled (impeded eyes), dulled, blunted, hostile, disappointed, hated, disliked, tied, bound, sent, despatched,
pratihatadhī mfn having hostile intentions,

pratihatamati mfn hostile-minded,
pratihataraya mfn whose current is impeded
pratihati f. a stroke, blow, beating back, recoil, rebound, disappointment,
pratihatya ind. in inverse direction,
pratihiṁsā f. retaliation, revenge,
pratihita mfn put on or in, (*ā*) f. an arrow fitted to the bowstring,
pratihitāyin mfn one who adjusted an arrow
pratihiti f. adjusting an arrow,
pratihrāsa m. abridgement, abbreviation,
pratihṛdayam ind. in every heart,
pratihṛta mfn held back, fastened,
pratihvara m. a slope, the rising vault of the sky,
pratijāgara m. watchfulness, attention,
pratijāgaraṇa n. watching, attending to, guarding,
pratijāgarti P. watches beside (2nd),
pratijagdha mfn eaten, consumed,
pratijāgṛvi mfn watchful, attentive,
pratijahāti leaves unheeded, neglects, √*hā*
pratijalpa m. an answer, reply,
pratijalpaka m. a pilot but evasive answer,
pratijalpati P. answers, replies,
pratijana m. an adversary, mfn hostile,
pratijanam ind. in every one,
pratijāne I admit, acknowledge, approve, 3/s/pres/indic/mid *prati* √*jñā*
pratijānīhi 2/s/impv/act of above, be aware!, become aware!
pratijanman n. rebirth
prātijanīna mfn suitable for an adversary, suitable for everybody, popular,
pratijāpa . the act of muttering against
pratijapati P. mutters in response,
pratijāta mfn born again, renewed,
pratijayati P. conquers, defeats,
pratijihīrṣu wishing to return or requite
pratijīvana n. returning to life, resuscitation, also *pratijīvita*
pratijña mfn acknowledging,
prati√*jñā* 665/3 to admit, acknowledge, acquiesce in, consent to, approve, vow, promise, A. to confirm, assert, answer in the affirmative, to maintain, assert, to bring forward or introduce a topic, to perceive, notice, learn, become aware of,
prātijña n. the subject under discussion,
pratijñā f. admission, acknowledgement, assent, agreement, promise, vow, an assertion, declaration, affirmation, a proposition, the proposition to be proved, a complaint, indictment,
pratijñābhaṅga m. breach of a promise
pratijñāhāni f. giving up a proposition
pratijñāna 666/1 admission, assertion, assent, agreement, promise
pratijñāntara n. (in logic) a subsequent proposition on failure of the first,
pratijñāpāraga mfn one who keeps his word,
pratijñāpāraṇa fulfilment of a vow
pratijñāparipālana n. adherence to a promise,
pratijāpattra or °*traka* a promissory note, written contract, bond,
pratijāsaṁnyāsa breaking a promise, abandoning one's proposition,
pratijñāta mfn promised, admitted, acknowledged, agreed, declared, asserted, alleged, agreeable, desirable, °*tārtha* m. a statement, averment,
pratijñātavya mfn to be promised,
pratijñāvirodha m. contradiction between a logical proposition and an argument,acting contrary to a promise or agreement,
pratijñāvivāhita mfn promised in marriage, betrothed,
pratijuṣate A. is kind or tender towards, honours, serves, is gratified by, delights in,
pratijvalati P. flames, blazes, shines
pratīka mfn symbolic, turned or directed towards, looking at, going uphill, contrary, inverted, n. exterior, surface, outward form or shape, look, appearance, the face (esp. the mouth, an image, symbol, a copy, m. a part, portion, limb, member,
pratīkadarśana n. a symbolic conception,
pratikalam ind. at every moment,

constantly, perpetually,
pratikalpa m. counterpart,
pratikalpam ind in each cosmic period,
pratikalpya mfn to be arranged or prepared,
pratikāma mfn according to wish or desire, desired, beloved,
pratikāmin mfn contrary to desire, disagreeable,
prātikāmin mfn a servant or messenger,
pratikañcuka m. a critic, a critical work,
pratikāṅkṣin mfn wishing for, desirous of,
pratikāṅkṣitavya mfn to be expected
pratikaṇṭham ind. singly, severally one by one (so that each is reckoned),
prātikaṇṭhika mfn seizing by the throat,
pratikapālam ind. in every cup,
pratikāra mfn acting against, counter-acting, m. requital, compensation, retaliation, reward, retribution, revenge, opposition, prevention, remedy,
pratīkāra = *pratikāra* m. counteraction, remedy, revenge, etc.
pratikārajña knowing what remedy to use
pratikāravidhāna n. medical treatment,
pratikaraṇīya to be counteracted or prevented, remediable,
pratikarkaśa mfn equally hard,
pratikarman n. requital, retaliation, corresponding action, counteraction, cure, medical treatment, personal adornment, toilet,
pratikarṣa m. aggregation, combination, anticipating that which occurs afterwards,
pratīkāśa m. reflection, resemblance, appearance, ifc. similar, like
pratikaṣṭa mfn comparatively bad,
pratikartavya mfn to be requited or returned, to be repaid, to be counteracted or resisted, to be treated or cured,
pratikartṛ m. a requiter, recompenser, an opponent, adversary,
pratikāya m. an adversary, a target, mark, an effigy, likeness, picture, a bow,
pratikhyāti f. renown,
pratkīla m. an opposite peg or post,
pratikitava m. an adversary at play,
prati√klṛp A. – *kalpate* to be at the service of, receive hospitably, to regulate, arrange,
pratikopa m. anger against anyone, wrath,
pratīkopāsana n. image-worship, the service of idols,
prati√kṛ P.A. –*karoti, -kurute*, to do or make an opposition, to return, repay, requite (good or evil), to counteract, resist, to treat, attend to, cure, to repair, restore, to pay back a debt, caus. –*kārayate* to cause to be repeated,
prati√kī P. –*kirati* to scatter towards,
prati√kram P. –*kramāti* to come back, return, to descend, decrease, to confess,
pratikrama m. reversed or inverted order,
pratikramaṇa n. stepping to and fro, going to confession,
pratikriyā f. requital, retaliation, retribution, compensation, opposition, remedy, help, -*tva* n. venting of anger, embellishment, personal decoration
pratikṛta mfn returned, repaid, requited, n. recompense, requital, resistance
pratikṛti f. resistance, opposition, revenge, prevention, retaliation, return an image, likeness, model, substitute
pratikriyam ind. for every action,
pratikrodha m. anger in return,
pratikrośa mfn crying out to, halloing,
pratikṛṣṭa mfn ploughed back again, thrust back, rejected, despised
prati√krudh P. –*krudhyati* to be angry with (2nd) in return,
pratikrūra mfn cruel in return, returning harshness,
pratikruṣṭa mfn miserable, poor,
pratīkṣ *prati√ikṣ* to wait for, expect,
pratīkṣa mfn looking forward to, expectant of, f. (*ā*) expectation, consideration, attention, respect, veneration waiting for
pratīkṣaṇa n. looking to or at, considering, regard, attention,
pratikṣaṇam ind. at every moment, continually

pratikṣapam ind. every night,
pratīkṣate he watches for, anticipates, look at, beholds, perceives,
pratikṣaya m. a guard,
pratikṣepa m. contest, objection, contradiction, repudiation,
pratikṣepaṇa n. opposing, contesting, contradiction,
pratikṣetra n. place, stead, (*e*) ind. instead of
prati√kṣip P. *-kṣipati,* to throw into, push against, hurt, to reject, despise, oppose, contradict, ridicule,
pratikṣipta mfn thrown into, pushed against, hurt, rejected, despised, opposed, contradicted, ridiculed, sent, dispatched,
pratikṣita mfn contemplated, considered, respected, honoured, expected,
pratīkṣya ind. 'while expecting or waiting' gradually, slowly, to be observed or fulfilled or considered,
prātikūla mfn unfavourable, bad, against the bank, disagreeable, wrong, adverse, unpleasant, n. inverted order, opposition, f. adverseness,
prātikūlika mfn opposed to, contrary,
pratikūlam ind, contrarily, in the opposite direction,
prātikūlya n. contrariety, adverseness, opposition, disagreeableness, ifc. disagreement with,
pratikuñcita mfn bent, curved,
pratikuṇḍam ind. in every fire-pit, heat,
pratikuñjara m. a hostile elephant,
pratikūla mfn 'against the bank' contrary, adverse, opposite, inverted, wrong, refractory, inimical, unpleasant,
pratikūlabhāṣin mfn speaking against, contradicting,
pratikūlācarita n. an offensive action, injurious conduct,
pratikūladaiva mfn opposed by fate
pratikūladaivatā f. hostility of fate
pratikūladarśana mfn looking cross or awry, having an ungracious aspect,
pratikūlam ind. contrarily, against, in inverted order, n. inverted order, opposition,
pratikūlapravartin mfn a ship taking an adverse course or tongue causing unpleasantness,
pratikūlatā f. *–tva* n. adverseness, hostility, perverseness, contumacy,
pratikūlatas ind. in contradiction to,
pratikūlavacana n. contradiction, refractory speech
pratikūlavat mfn refractory, contumacious,
pratikūlavedanīya mfn causing an unpleasant effect,
pratikūlaśabda mfn sounding unpleasantly,
pratikūlavisarpin mfn a ship moving against wind or stream, a tongue moving unpleasantly,
pratikūlavṛtti mfn resisting, opposing,
pratikūlika mfn hostile, inimical,
pratikūlokta n. pl. contradiction,
pratikūpa m. a moat, ditch
prati√labh A. *–labhate*, to receive back, recover, to obtain, regain, partake of, to get back (be punished), to learn, understand, caus. *–lambhayati* to provide or present with,
pratilābha m. recovering, receiving,
pratilakṣaṇa n. a countermark, mark, sign
pratilambha m. receiving, getting, finding, recovering, regaining, conceiving, understanding, abuse,
prātilambhika mfn ready to receive, expecting,
pratilambhita n. obtaining, getting,
prati√laṅgh caus. to mount, sit down upon, to transgress, violate,
pratilaṅghayati mounts, sits down upon, transgresses, violates,
pratilati P. is desirous of sexual intercourse
pratiliṅgam ind. at every *liṅga*
pratilipi f. a copy, transcript, written reply
pratiloka m. every world,
pratiloma mfn against the grain, contrary to the natural course, reverse, inverted, adverse, hostile, unpleasant, vile, left (not right), contrary to caste, n. any disagreeable or injurious act, *(ena)* ind. in an unfriendly manner,
prātilomaka mfn against the hair or grain, adverse, disagreeable,

prātilomya n. contrary direction, inverse order, opposition,

pratimā m. a creator, maker, framer, (*ā)* f. an image, likeness, symbol, a picture, statue, figure, idol, measure, extent, an elephant's head between the tusks, having the measure of, as long or wide etc. as, ifc. like, similar, resembling,

pratimāgata mfn a deity present in an idol,

prati√man A. *–manute* to render back in return or in reply, contrast with, caus. *–mānayati* to honour, esteem, approve, consider, regard,

pratimāna n. a counterpart, well-matched opponent, adversary, a model, pattern, an image, picture, idol, comparison, likeness, similarity,

pratimāpūja f. worship of images

pratimatā f.-*tva* n. reflection, image, shadow

pratimātavya mfn comparable,

pratīmāna n. a weight (measure),

pratimānanā f. homage, reverence,

pratimaṇḍita mfn decorated, adorned,

pratimantraṇa n. an answer, reply,

pratimantrayati P. calls out, replys to, consecrates with sacred texts,

pratimantrita mfn consecrated with sacred texts,

pratimārga m. the way back, (*e*) ind. on the way,

pratimāsa ibc. or °*sam* ifc. monthly

pratimātṛ ind every mother

pratimātrā f. pl. every measure (of time),

pratimāyā f. counter-spell, counter-charm

pratimimīte A. √*mā* imitates, copies

pratimit f. a prop, stay, support,

pratimita mfn imitated, reflected, mirrored,

pratimiti f. reflected image,

pratimocana n. liberation, release from (comp.)

pratimocita mfn released, saved, delivered,

pratimodate A. rejoices at, glad to see, welcomes with joy, caus. *–modayate* gladdens, cheers,

pratimohayati bewilders, confounds,

pratimoka m. putting or hanging round

pratimokṣa m. liberation, deliverance, also *prātimokṣa*

pratimoṭayati caus. put an end to, kills, √*muṭ*

prati√*muc* P.A. *–muñcati (te*), to put (clothes, a garland etc) on, to fix or fasten on, append, to dress oneself, assume a shape or form, to attach or fasten to, to release, let go, send away, to give up, resign, to return, restore, pay back, caus. *–mocayati* to set free, rescue, save,

pratimuhūrta ibc. °*tam* ifc. every moment, constantly,

pratimuhus ind. again and again, repeatedly,

pratimukha n. the reflected image of the face, an answer, mfn facing, being near, present, towards, in front,

pratimukta mfn put on, applied, tied, bound, released, freed from (5th), liberated, given up, relinquished, flung, hurled

pratimūrti f. a corresponding form, an image

pratināda m. echo, reverberation,

pratinadi ind. at every river,

pratinādita mfn filled with sounds, resonant, echoing or echoed,

pratinagaram ind. in every town,

pratīnāha m. obstruction, constipation, a flag, banner,

prati√*nam* to bow or incline towards,

prati√*nand* P. to greet cheerfully, salute, bid welcome or farewell, favour, befriend, to receive thankfully, caus. to gladden, delight, gratify,

pratinaptṛ m. a great grandson,

pratinauti P. commends, approves,

pratinava mfn new, young, fresh,

prati√*nī* P. *–nayati,* to lead towards or back, to put into, mix,

pratini√*dhā* P. *–dadhāti,* to put in the place of another, substitute, to order, command, to slight, disregard,

pratinidhātavya mfn to be substituted,

pratinidhi m. substitution, a substitute, representative, proxy, surety, a resemblance of a real form, an image, likeness, statue, picture, similar, like,

prātinidhika m. a substitute,

pratinigrāhya mfn to be ladled out,

pratinihata mfn hit, slain, killed,
pratiniḥsarga m. giving back, abandonment,
pratiniḥsṛṣṭa mfn driven away,
pratininada m. echo, reverberation,
pratinindati P. abuses, blames, censures,
prati-ni-pāta m. falling down, alighting,
pratinirasyati P. throws back,
pratinirdeśa m. a reference back to (with 6th), renewed mention,
pratinirdeśaka mfn pointing or referring back,
pratinirdeśya mfn referred to or mentioned again,
pratinir√diś to point or refer back,
pratinirdiṣṭa mfn referred to again,
pratinirjita mfn appropriated, turned to one's own advantage,
pratinirvapati P. distributes in return,
pratinivāraṇa n. warding off,
pratiniryātana n. giving back, returning,
pratiniryāti P. comes forth again,
pratiniśam ind. every night,
pratiniścaya m. a contrary opinion,
pratiniṣkraya m. retaliation, retribution,
pratiniṣ√pū P. *–punāti* to cleanse or winnow again, purify, 666/3
pratiniṣpūta mfn cleansed, winnowed,
pratiniṣtarati P. accomplishes,
pratiniṣṭha mfn standing on an opposite side
pratinivartana n. returning, coming back,
pratinivartita mfn cursed to return, led back,
pratiniveśa m. obstinacy, obdurateness,
pratiniviṣṭa mfn quite prepossessed with, obstinate, obdurate,
-mūkha m. an obstinate fool,
prati-ni-√vṛt A. *–vartate*, to turn back or round, return, turn away from (5th), escape, run away, take flight, to cease be allayed or abated,
pratinivṛtta mfn turned back or from, come back, return,
pratinivṛtti f. coming back, return,
pratiniyama m. a strict rule applying a rule to particular persons or things only,
pratiniyata mfn particular or different for each case,
pratinoda m. thrusting back, repulse,
pratinṛtyati P. dances before (in contempt)
pratinudati, (te), thrusts back, repulses,
pratinyāgacchati P. comes back, returns,
pratinyāyam ind. in inverted order,
pratīpa mfn 'against the stream', going in an opposite direction, meeting, encountering, adverse, contrary, opposite, reverse, disagreeable, resisting, refractory, obstinate, impeding, hindering, backward, turned away, averted,
m. an adversary, opponent,
n. inverse comparison,
(*am*) ind. against the stream, backwards, against, in return, in inverted order
prati√pad A. *pratipadyate* to set foot upon, enter, step toward, attain, get, go or resort to, arrive at, reach, attain, to walk, wander, to come back to, return, to meet with, find, obtain, receive, take in or upon oneself, to receive back, recover, to restore to favour, to undertake, begin, practise, perform, accomplish, to give back, restore, to perceive, discover, understand, learn, discover, to consider, regard, to say yes, assent, agree, to begin to speak, commence, caus. *–pādayati* to convey or lead to, procure, give a present to, bestow on, to give in marriage, to spend, present with, to produce, cause, establish, explain,
pratipad f. access, ingress, entrance, the path to be walked, the right path, beginning, commencement, understanding, intelligence, taste for anything, rank, consequence, a kettle-drum
prātipada mfn forming the commencement,
pratipādaka causing to obtain, giving, explaining, teaching, effective, accomplishing, promoting,
pratipadam ind. at every step, on every occasion, at every place, everywhere, at every word, word by word, literally, expressly, each, singly,

pratipādana n. causing to attain, giving, granting, giving back, restoring, putting in, appointing to, causing, effecting, explaining, teaching, commencement, action, worldly conduct,

pratipadatva n. walking step by step,

pratipādayet one should offer, he should offer, 1/s/caus./opt/ *prati√pad* using strong case *pād* Cl 4

pratipādayitṛ m. a giver, bestower on, a teacher, propounder,

prātipadika n. the "stem" of a word, the crude form or base of a noun in its uninflected state,
mfn express, explicit, m. fire,

pratipādita mfn caused to attain, delivered, given (in marriage), stated, proved, explained, taught,

pratipadmam ind. at every lotus flower,

pratipāduka mfn recovering, determining, ascertaining, causing, effecting,

pratipādya mfn to be treated of or discussed, explained or propounded,

pratīpaga mfn going against, flowing backwards,

pratīpagamana or °*gati* a retrograde movement,

pratīpagāmin mfn going against, acting in contravention to,

pratīpaka mfn opposed to, hindering,

pratipakṣa m. the opposite side, hostile party, opposition, an obstacle, an opponent, foe, match for, equal, similar,

prātipakṣa mfn belonging to the enemy, hostile, adverse, contrary,

pratipakṣagraha m. the taking of the opposite side,

prati√pāl P. to protect, defend, guard, observe, maintain, wait, wait for, expect,

pratipalam ind. every moment,

pratipālayati P. protects, defends, guards, keeps, observes, maintains, waits, waits for, expects,

pratipālaka mf(*ikā*)n protecting, a protector,

pratipāla n. guarding, protecting, cherishing, maintaining, observing, expecting,

pratipālita mfn cherished, protected, practised, followed

pratipālin mfn guarding,

pratipaṇa 1. m. the stake of an adversary at play, 2.m. barter, exchange,

pratipāṇa 1. m. a counter-stake, revenge at play, 2.m. ready to exchange, bartering,

pratipāna n. drinking, water for drinking,

pratipanmaya mfn obedient, willing,

pratipanna mfn come or resorted to, got into (2nd), approached, arrived, met with, obtained, found, overcome, conquered, undertaken, begun, known, understood, familiar with (7th), sure of anything, one who has agreed to or promised, acknowledged (as a brother), admitted (as a debt), answered, replied, given, acting or behaving towards (7th),

pratipannaka m. arrived at an aim, name of the 4 orders of *ārya*s (Buddhist),

pratipaṇya n. merchandise in exchange

pratipāpa mfn wicked or evil in return

pratiparāharati P hands over

pratiparāṇayati (te) P.A. leads back,

pratipare returns again,

pratiparigamana n, walking round again or backwards,

pratiparyāharati turns round again

pratiparyāvartate turns round in an opposite direction

pratiparyāyam ind. at every turn,

pratiparyeti goes round in reverse direction

prati√paś to look at, perceive, see, to live, experience, to consider, A. (*te)* to see in one's own possession,

pratīpataraṇa n. sailing against the stream,

pratipatati P. hastens towards,

pratipatha m. way back, (*am*) ind. along the road, backwards,

prātipathika mfn going along a road or path, m. a wayfarer,

pratipatni f. a female rival, ind. for each wife,

pratipatti f. gaining, obtaining, acquiring, perception, observation, ascertainment, knowledge, intellect, supposition, assertion, admission, acknowledgement, giving, granting, causing, effecting, beginning, action, procedure in or with, welcome, homage, assurance, high rankor dignity, rule, reign,
pratipattibheda m. diversity of views,
pratipattidakṣa mfn knowing how to act or what is to be done,
pratipattidarśin mfn showing what ought to be done
pratipattikarman n. a concluding rite,
pratipattimat mfn knowing what to do, active, prompt, celebrated, high in rank, possessing appropriate knowledge,
pratipattiniṣṭhura mfn difficult to be understood,
pratipattiparāṅmukha obstinate, unyielding reluctant to comply, mfn
pratipattipradāna n. the giving of preferment or promotion,
pratipattṛ mfn one who perceives or hears, one who comprehends or understands, one who asserts,
prātipauruṣika mfn relating to manliness or valour,
pratīpavacana n. contradiction,
pratīpayati Nom P. being hostile to, causes to turn back,
pratīpayate Nom A. being hostile to,
pratipeṣam ind. rubbing/pressing against each other
pratiphala m. *pratiphalana* n. reflection, image, shadow, return, requital, retaliation,
pratiphalati P. bounds against, rebounds, is reflected, requites,
pratiphullaka mfn flowering, in blossom,
pratipīḍana n. oppressing, molesting,
pratipīḍayati presses, opresses, afflicts
prātīpika mfn contrary, adverse, hostile,
pratīpin mfn unfavourable, unkind,
pratipipādayiṣā f. desire of setting forth or discussing or treating of,
pratipipādayiṣu wishing to explain, about to treat of,
pratipitsā f. desire of obtaining, striving for,
pratipiṣṭa mfn rubbed/rubbing against each other (horses), crossed (swords), bruised, crushed,
pratipīyati P. abuses, reviles,
pratiplavana n. jumping or leaping back,
pratīpokti f. contradiction,
pratiprabhātam ind. every morning,
pratipra√dā P. *–dadāti* to give back again,
pratipradāna n. giving back, returning, giving in marriage,
pratiprahāra m. a counterblow, return blow,
pratiprahiṇoti P. drives or chases back,
pratiprajānāti seeks out or finds again,
pratiprajñāti f. discrimination, ascertainment, statement,
pratiprākāra m. an outer rampart,
pratipraṇāma m. abow or obeisance in return,
pratiprāni ind. in or for every living creature
pratprasarpati P. creeps near again,
pratiprasava m. counter-order, suspension of a general order in a particular case, an exception to an exception,
pratiprasavam ind. in each birth,
pratipraśna m. a question asked in return, an answer, (*am*) ind. with regard to the controversy, √*prach*
pratipraśrabdhi f. omission, removal,
pratiprasūta mfn re-enjoined after having been forbidden,
pratipra√1.sū A. *–suvate* to allow or enjoin again,
pratiprāsyati P. throws or casts upon,
pratipratta mfn given up, delivered,
pratiprati mfn counter-balancing, being a match for, equal to, ibc. at each initial word,
pratipra√vac reports, relates, tells,
pratipravartayati leads towards, caus. √*vṛt*
pratipravedayati proclaims, announces,
pratipraviśati goes back, returns,
pratiprayacchati P. gives back, returns,
pratiprayāṇa n. going back, return,
pratiprayāṇakam ind. with each day's journey

pratiprayāta mfn gone back, returned,
pratiprayāti P. goes back, returns,
pratiprāyāti P. comes near, approaches,
pratiprayoga m. counter-application or putting a parallel proposal,
pratiprayunakti, -yuṅkte, substitutes, adds instead of something else, √*yuj*
pratipṛcchati P. asks, questions, inquires of
pratipriya mfn agreeable to, n. kindness or service in return,
pratipīṇāti P. bestows in return, caus. *- pūrayati* fills up, makes full,
pratiprokta mfn returned, answered,
pratipūjā f. doing homage, honouring,
pratipūjaka mfn honouring, revering, a reverer,
pratipūjana n. doing homage, honouring, revering,
pratipūjita mfn honoured, revered, presented with (3rd), exchanged as civilities
pratipūraṇa n. filling up, filled, injecting a fluid, pouring a fluid over, being filled with, obstruction, congestion (of the head),
pratipūrita mfn filled with, full of, satisfied, content,
pratipūrṇa mfn, as above, full moon,
pratipūrti f. fulfilment, perfection,
pratipuruṣa m. a similar man, a companion, assistant, a deputy, substitute,
pratira 1. mfn furthering, granting success or victory, 2. carrying across, furthering, helping,
pratirāddha mfn counteracted
pratirādha m. obstacle, hindrance,
pratirāja or °*jan* m. a hostile king,
pratirājam ind. king by king, for every king
pratirajani ind. every night,
pratirājate A. shines like, equals in splendour,
pratirakṣā f. safety, preservation,
pratirakṣaṇa n. preserving, protecting,
pratiramati P. looks forward with joy, longs for, expects,
pratirambha m. passion, rage, violent abuse,
pratirapati P. whipers to, tells in a whisper,
pratirasati P. echoes, resounds,
pratirasita n. echo, resonance,
pratirata mfn delighting in, zealous for,
pratiratha m. an adversary, an adversary in a chariot,
pratirathyam ind. in every road,
pratirātram or °*tri* ind. each night, nightly,
pratiroddhṛ m. an opposer,
pratirodha m. opposition, impediment,
pratirohati P. sprouts or grows again, caus.*-ropayati* plants anything in its proper place, plants again, re-establishes, √*ruh*
pratiropita mfn planted again,
prati√*ruc* A *–rocate*, to please, caus. –*rocayati* to be pleased to, resolve, decide upon,
pratirūḍha mfn imitated,
pratiruddha mfn checked, prevented, rendered imperfect, impaired,
pratirūpa n. the counterpart of any real form, an image, likeness, representation, a pattern, model for imitation, a counterfeit, mfn like, similar, suitable, fit, agreeable, beautiful,
pratirūpacaryā f. suitable or exemplary conduct,
pratirūpaka n. an image, a picture, forgery, similar, having the appearance of .., m. a quack, charlatan,
pratirūpatā f. resemblance,
prātirūpika mfn counterfeit, spurious, using false weight or measure, °*pya* n. similarity of form,
pratiśabda m. echo, reverberation,
prati√*sac* A. *–sacate* to pursue with vengeance
prati√*sad* P. *–sīdati* to start back, abhor,
pratisadṛkṣa mfn similar,
prati√*śak* to hold one's ground against
prati√*śam* caus. *–śamayati* to re-establish, restore, put to rights,
pratiśama m. ifc. deliverance from, cessation of,
pratisama mfn equal to, a match for,
pratisamādhāna n. collecting oneself again, composure
pratisamādiṣṭa mfn bidden, directed, ordered , √*diś*

pratisamāhita mfn fitted to the bowstring, (an arrow),
pratisāmanta m. a hostile neighbour
pratisamantam ind. on every side, everywhere
pratisamāpana n. the going against, attacking
pratisamārthya n. relative suitableness,
pratisamāśrita mfn depending on,
pratisam√2.as P. *–asyati* to put back again in its place
pratisamayya ind. having arranged
pratisam√bhū P. to apply or give oneself to,
pratisambuddha mfn restored to consciousness, recovered,
pratisaṁ√car to meet, come together,
pratisaṁcara m. going or moving backwards, re-absorption or resolution (back into prakṛti), that into which anything is re-absorbed or resolved, a place of resort,
pratisaṁdeśa m. a message in return, an answer to a message,
pratisaṁ√1.dhā to put together again, re-arrange, A. to put on, adjust an arrow, to return, reply, P.A. to remember, recollect, A. to comprehend, understand,
pratisaṁdhāna n. putting together again, joining together, a juncture, the period of transition between 2 ages, memory, recollection, praise, panegyric, self-command, suppression of feeling for a time,
pratisaṁdhānika m. a bard, panegyrist,
pratisaṁdhātṛ m. one who recollects
pratisaṁdheya mfn to be opposed,
pratisaṁdhi m. reunion, re-entry into or into the womb, re-birth, the period of transition between two ages, resistance, adverseness (of fate),
pratisaṁdhita mfn fastened, strengthened, confirmed,
pratisaṁ√diś P. *–diśati* to send back a message to (6th), to order, command, to give a message or commission in return,
pratisaṁ√grah to receive, accept, to meet with, find,
pratisaṁhāra m. drawing in, withdrawing, giving up, resigning, keeping away, abstention from (5th), compression, diminution, comprehension,
pratisaṁhita mfn aimed at, directed against,
pratisaṁ√hṛ P.A. *–harati, (te),* to draw together, contract, to shrink, withdraw, to tke away, put off, to absorb, annihilate, to check, stop,
pratisaṁ√hṛṣ P. *-harṣati,* to rejoice again, be glad,
pratisaṁhṛṣṭa mfn glad, merry,
pratisamīkṣaṇa n. looking at again, returning a glance,
pratisaminddhe A. re-kindles,
pratisaṁjāta mfn born, sprung up, arisen
pratisaṁ√jñā A. *–jānīte* to be kindly disposed,
pratisaṁ√khyā to count or reckon up, number, f. consciousness,
pratisaṁkhyāna n. the tranquil consideration of a matter,
pratisaṁ√kram A. *–kramate* to go back again, come to an end,
pratisaṁkrama m. re-absorption, dissolution ifc. f. *(ā)* impression,
pratisaṁkruddha mfn angry with, wroth against,
pratisaṁlayana n. retirement into a lonely place, privacy, complete absorption,
pratisaṁlīna mfn retired, in privacy, complete retirement for the sake of meditation
pratisammodana n.f. greeting, salutation,
pratisammodanakathā f. friendly address as a salutation,
pratisaṁrabdha mfn holding hands, excited, furious,
pratisaṁruddha mfn contracted into itself, shrunk,
pratisaṁsaṁsṛṣṭa mfn mingled with, -*bhakta* mfn one temperate in eating,
pratiśaṁsati P. calls or shouts to, praises,
pratisaṁskāra (√*kṛ*) m. restoration
pratisaṁskṛta mfn joined or united with,
pratisaṁsmarati remembers,

pratisaṁśrayati seeks refuge or protection in reply,
pratisaṁ√śru to promise,
pratisaṁ√stambh to strengthen, encourage,
pratisaṁstāra n. friendly reception,
pratisaṁsthāna n. settling in, entering into (comp.),
pratisaṁvadate A. agrees with anyone,
pratisamvatsaram ind. every year, yearly,
pratisaṁvedaka mfn giving detailed information
pratisaṁvedana n. experiment, enjoyment,
pratisaṁvedin mfn feeling, experiencing, being conscious of anything,
pratisaṁveṣṭate shrivels, shrinks up,
pratisaṁ√1.vid caus. *–vedayati,* to recognize,
pratisaṁvid f. analytical science,
pratisaṁvidhāna a counteraction, stroke in return,
pratisaṁyāta mfn going against, assailing,
pratisaṁyatta mfn completely prepared or armed,
pratisaṁyoddhṛ m. an adversary in war,
pratisaṁyukta mfn bound or attached to something else
pratisaṅgin mfn (√*sañj)* clinging to, adhering, not meeting with any obstacle, irresistible,
prati√śaṅk A. *–śaṅkate* to be doubtful or anxious, hesitate, to trouble oneself about, care for,
pratiśaṅkā f. doubt, supposition, constant fear or doubt,
pratiśānta mfn extinguished, allayed,
pratiśāpa m. a curse in return,
pratisara m. a nuptial amulet of cord/ribbon n. a bracelet, circle, an attack, a wreath, garland, a follower, servant, the rear of an army, dressing a wound, day-break, m.n. a watch, guard, *(ā)* f. a female servant,
pratiśaraṇa n. confidence in, breaking off or blunting (a point or edge)
pratisaraṇa mfn leaning or resting upon, (ifc. f. *–tā*), n. leaning or resting on (comp.),
pratisarga m. secondary or continued creation out of primitive matter, dissolution, destruction, the portion of a Purāṇa regarding the destruction and renewal of the world
pratisargam ind. in every creation,
pratiśarīram ind. concerning one's own body or person,
pratisārin mfn going round or from one to the other,
pratisārita mfn repelled, removed, dressed (as a wound),
pratiśāsana n. a rival command or authority, 2. giving orders, sending a servant on a message,
pratiśatru m. an adversary, opponent,
pratisavya mfn reversed, inverted,
pratiśayita mfn pressing, importuning, importuned, n. the act of importuning, molestation,
pratisāyam ind. towards evening,
pratiṣedha m. keeping back, warding off, repulsion (of a disease), prohibition, refusal, denial, contradiction, exception, (in gram.) negation, a negative particle,
pratiṣedhya that which is negated,
pratisenā f. an enemy army,
prati√sev A. *–sevate,* to pursue, follow (pleasure), to be kind towards (2nd), serve, honour,
pratiṣevaṇa n. sewing on,
prati-ṣidh (√2.sidh) P. *-ṣedhati,* to drive away, to keep back, prevent, forbid, negate, disallow,
prātisīma m. a neighbour,
pratisiṁhā m. a hostile lion,
pratisīrā f. a curtain, screen, outer tent,
pratiśīta, °śīna, °śīnavat mfn melted, fluid, dropping,
pratiśiṣṭa mfn sent on a message, refused, celebrated, famous,
pratiṣka m. a messenger or spy,
prati√smṛ P.A. *–smarati (te),* to remember, recollect, caus. *–smārayati* to remind,
pratismṛti f. recollection, a kind of magic
pratisnāta mfn bathed, washed,

pratispandana n. throbbing, vibration,
pratispardhā f. emulation, rivalry,
pratispardhin mfn emulous, coping with (6th), a rival, (ifc.) resembling, like,
pratispaśa, -spāśana mfn spying, watching, lying in wait,
pratiśocati P. burns towards or against,
pratiśrama m. toil, trouble,
pratiśrava mfn answering, m.f. promise, assurance,
pratiśravaṇa n. hearkening to, listening, answering, agreeing, promising,
pratiśraya m. refuge, help, assistance, a place of refuge, shelter, asylum, house, dwelling, a receptacle, recipient, an alms-house, a place where food etc. is given away, a place of sacrifice, an assembly,
prati√sṛ P. *–sarati* to go against, rush upon, attack, to return, go home, to go round or from place to place, caus. *-sārayati* to cause to go back, to put back again, restore to its place, to spread over, tip or touch with, put asunder, sever, separate,
pratiśrita n. a place of refuge,
pratisrota , *°tas, °tam,* against the stream, up the stream,
pratiśrotṛ mfn one who promises or assents,
pratisṛṣṭa mfn despatched, despised, celebrated, given,
prati√śru P. *śṛṇoti* to hear, listen, to listen, give ear to, to assure, agree, promise anything, to anyone,
pratiśrut f. an echo, resonance, a promise, assurance,
pratiśruta mfn heard, promised, agreed, promised, accepted, n. a promise, engagement,
pratiśruti f. an answer, promise, assent,
pratistabdha mfn, leaned against, pressed, stopped, checked, obstructed,
pratiṣṭambha m. obstruction, impediment, hindrance, *°bhin* mfn impeding ifc.
pratiṣṭha mfn standing firmly, steadfast, resisting, leading to, ending with (ifc), famous, n. point of support, centre or base of anything,
prati-ṣṭhā (√sthā) P.A. *-tiṣṭhati (te)*, to stand, stay, abide, dwell, to stand still, set (as the sun), cease, to stand firm, be based or rest on, be established, thrive, prosper, to depend or rely on (7th), to withstand, resist (2nd), to spread or extend over (2nd),caus. *-ṣṭhāpayati* to put down, place upon, introduce into (7th), to set up, erect (as an image), to bring or lead into (7th), to establish in, appoint to (7th), to transfer or offer or present to, to fix, found, prop, support, maintain, to hold against or opposite
pratiṣṭhā 671/2 f. standing still, resting, remaining, steadfastness, stability, perseverance in, a standpoint, resting place, foundation, stay, support, a receptacle, homestead, dwelling house, limit, boundary, state of rest, quiet, tranquillity, comfort, ease, pre-eminence, superiority, fame, celebrity
pratiṣṭhāna n. a firm standing-place, ground, foundation, a pedestal, foot, the town, name of an ancient town,
pratisthānam ind. in every place, everywhere,
pratiṣṭhāpya establishing, causing to fix causative gerund *prati √sthā* to be consigned or entrusted to, to be placed or fixed or located,
pratiṣṭhāsu mfn wishing to start, wishing to stay or remain,
pratiṣṭhi f. resistance,
pratiṣṭhikā f. a basis, foundation,
pratiṣṭhita mfn standing, stationed, placed, situated in or on, abiding or contained in, fixed, firm, rooted, founded, resting or dependent on, established, proved, ordained for, applicable to (7th), secure, thriving, well off, transferred to (7th), undertaken,
pratiṣṭithi 671/3 standing firmly, fixed
prātiṣṭhita 706/3 mfn own, not common to others,

pratistrī mfn lying on a woman
pratisupta mfn fallen asleep, sleeping,
pratisūrya m. a mock sun, parhelion, a chameleon, (*am*) ind. opposite to the sun, a comet,
pratisvam ind. one by one, singly,
pratisvara m. a reverberated sound, echo, a focus,
prātisvika mfn own, not common to others, granting to everyone his own due,
pratiśyā, pratiśyāya, m. a cold, catarrh,
pratiśyāyin mfn having a cold,
pratitāḍayati strikes in return, √*ṭad*
pratitālī f. the key of a door,
pratitantram ind. according to each Tantra or opinion,
pratitapati P. throws out or emits heat towards or against, heats, warms, foments, √*tap*
pratīta mfn acknowledged, recognized, known, convinced of anything, trusting in, firmly resolved upon (comp.), satisfied, cheerful, glad, respectful, past, gone, clever, wise
pratitara m. a sailor, oarsman, ferryman
pratitarām ind. (with *bhū*) to retire or shrink more and more,
pratitarkita mfn expected, comprehensible,
pratītārtha mfn having a recognized or acknowledged meaning,
pratitadvid f. recognition of the contrary,
pratīti f. going towards, approaching, being clear or intelligible by itself, clear apprehension or insight into anything, complete understanding or ascertainment, conviction, faith, confidence, belief, trust, credit, fame, respect, delight,
prātītika mfn existing only in the mind, mental, subjective,
pratītya n. confirmation, experiment, comfort, consolation,
prati√*vac* P. *–vakti* to speak back, answer, reply, to refute, to announce, indicate, recommend,
prativāc f. an answer,
prativacas n. an answer, reply, an echo,
prativacana m. a verse or formula serving as an answer, n. a dependent or final clause in a sentence, an answer, an echo, reply,
prativācika n. an answer,
prativācya mfn to be contradicted,
prati√*vad* P. *–vadati* to speak back, answer, reply, to speak to, to repeat,
prativāda m. contradiction, rejection, an answer, reply, rejoinder
prativadati he answers or replies
prativādin mfn contradicting, disobedient, answering, rejoining, m. an opponent, adversary, a defendant, respondent,
pratīvāha m. fee, reward,
prativahana n. leading back, warding off,
prativaira n. revenge,
prativaktṛ answering to (6th), explaining (the law),
prativaktram ind. on every face,
prativākya n. an answer, mfn answerable,
prativākyam ind. in every sentence,
prativanam ind in every wood or forest,
prativāṇi mfn unseemly, unsuitable,
pratīvāpa m. a disease, pestilence,
prativāra m. warding off, resisting,
prativargam ind. group by group,
prativārita mfn kept off, prohibited, n. prohibition,
prativarṇa m. every caste,
prativarṣam ind. every year,
pratīvarta mfn returning into itself,
prativartana n. return, reappearance,
prativartman mfn taking an opposite road
prativārttā f. accout, information,
prati√*vas* A *–vaste* to put on, clothe oneself in, P. *–vasati* to live, dwell, caus. *–vasayati* cause to dwell, to lodge, receive as a guest,
prativāśa mfn to be contradicted/opposed,
prativāsaram ind. every day, daily,
prativāsarika mfn daily
prativasatha m. a settlement, village,
prativāsin mfn neighbouring, a neighbour,
prativāsita mfn dressed or clothed in, inhabited,
prativasati ind. in every house

prativastu n. a counterpart, equivalent, anything contrasted with another
prativāta m. a contrary wind,
(*am*) ind. against the wind,
(e) ind. on the lee side,
prativatsara m. a year, (*am*) ind. every year,
prativedāntam ind. in every upaniṣad
prativedin mfn experiencing, knowing,
prativedita mfn apprised or informed of,
prativelam ind. on every occasion,
prativeṣa mfn neighbouring, a neighbour,
m. a neighbouring house,
-tas ind. from the neighbourhood,
prativeśika m. resident,
prātiveśika m. a neighbour,
prātiveśmika m. a neighbour,
prativeṣya m. a neighbour,
prātiveśya mfn neighbouring, m. an opposite neighbour, any neighbour,
pratīvī mfn receiving gladly, accepting,
m.f. acceptance,
prativi√bhaj to distribute severally, apportion
prativi√budh A. *–budhyate* to be awakened
prati√vī P. *–veti* to receive, accept,
prati√1.vid P. *–vetti,* to perceive, understand, caus. *–vedayati* to make known, report, announce, to offer, present,
prati√3.vid P.A. *–vindati (te),* to find in addition, to be opposite to, to become acquainted with,
prati-vi-√dhā P.A. *–dadhāti, dhatte,* to dispose, arrange, prepare, make ready, to counteract, act against, send out spies, to contradict a conclusion, take precautions,
pratividhāna n. arrangement against, prevention, precaution, care or provision for (comp.), countermeasure,
pratividhi m. a means or remedy against, retaliation,
pratividhitsā desire/intention to counteract
pratividyam ind. in every doctrine,
prativihita mfn counter-acted, guarded against
prativijahati P. quits, abandons √*hā*
prati-vi-√jñā P. *–jānāti* to acknowledge gratefully,
prativīkṣaṇa n. looking upon, returning a look,
prativi√nud P. *–nudati,* to get rid of,
prativiparīta mfn exactly opposite,
prativīra m. an antagonist, well-matched antagonist,
prativi√ram P. *–ramati*, to abstain,
prativīrya n. being a match for in valour,
mfn unequalled, matchless,
prativirati ind. at every pause, at each cessation or disappearance, 2. desisting from, leaving off,
prativiruddha mfn rebellious,
prativiṣaya m. pl. the various objects of sense, (ibc. and *am* ind.) in relation to each single item of sense,
prativiśeṣa m. peculiarity, singularity, a peculiar circumstance,
prativiśeṣaṇa n. detailed specification,
prativiśiṣṭa mfn more distinguished or peculiar, better or worse,
prativiśrabdha mfn full of confidence or trust
prativisṛjati P. sends out, despatches,
prativiśva mfn pl. one and all, √*sṛj*
prativīta mfn covered, *-tama* mfn totally covered, muffled, low (voice)
prati√1.vṛ caus. *–vārayati* to keep back, prohibit, refute, contradict
prati√2.vṛ to choose, elect,
prativrajati P. returns home
prati√vṛj P. *–varjati* to throw against
prati√vṛt A. *–vartate*, to accrue to, caus. *-vartayati* to fling, hurl,
prativṛtta n. an eccentric circle,
prativṛttāntam ind. according to the saying, as they say,
prativṛtti ind. according to the voice modulation
prati√vyadh P. *–vidhyati (te),* to shoot against, hit, wound, pass. *–vidhyate* to be aimed at or hit, to be touched upon or discussed,
prativyāhāra m. an answer, reply,
prativyūḍha mfn drawn out in array against
prati√yā °*ti* P. to come or go to, to go against, to go or come back,

return to or into, to comply with, oblige, please, to equal, be a match for, to be returned or requited,

pratiyacchati P. is equivalent to, worth as much as, grants perpetually,

pratiyāga a sacrifice offered for a result

pratiyajati P. sacrifices in return or with an aim towards anything,

pratiyāta mfn gone towards or against or back or away, turned, returned,

pratiyātana n. requital, retaliation, *(ā)* f. an image, model, counterpart, statue, ifc. appearing in the shape of,

pratiyātabuddhi mfn one whose mind is turned towards (4th),

pratiyātanidra mfn one whose sleep has gone, awakened, awake,

pratiyatate A. guards against, counteracts, caus. *–yātayati* to retaliate, requite,

pratiyatna 669/2 care bestowed upon anything, endeavour, effort, preparation, imparting a new quality or virtue, manufacture, mfn exerting one's self, taking care or trouble, cautious, heedful,

pratiyauti P. ties to, binds, fetters, √2.*yu*

pratiyoddhavya mfn to be attacked in return

pratiyoddhṛ m. an antagonist, adversary, well matched opponent, one who begins a battle,

pratiyodha m. an opponent, adversary,

pratiyodhana n. fighting against,

pratiyodhin m. an antogonist or well matched opponent,

pratiyoga m. resistance, opposition, contradiction, controversy, an antidote, remedy, cooperation, association, being a counterpart

pratiyogam ind. rule by rule,

pratiyogika mfn antithetical, relative, correlative,

pratiyogin mfn as above, m. an adversary, rival, an object dependent on another and not existing without it, a partner, associate, a counterpart,

pratiyogitā f. correlation, dependent existence, mutual cooperation, partnership,

pratiyoni ind. according to source or origin,

pratiyotsyāmi I shall fight against 3/s/fut/*prati* √*yudh*

pratiyuddha mfn fought against, fought, n. fighting against, battle in return,

prati√*yudh* A.P. *–yudhyate, (ti),* to fight against, fight, be a match for, caus. *–yodhayati*

prati√*yuj* P.A. *–yunakti, -yuṅkte,* to fasten on, tie to, A. to pay back (a debt), caus. *-yojayati* to fix on, adjust (the arrow on the bow),

pratiyuta mfn tied to, bound, fettered,

pratiyuvana n. repeated mixture,

pratna mfn former, preceding, ancient, old, customary, traditional,

pratnathā ind. as formerly, as of old, in the usual manner,

pratnavat 1. ind as above, 2. mfn containing the word *pratna*

pratoda m. a goad or long whip,

pratolī f. a broad way, principal road through a town or village,

pratoṣa m. gratification,

pra√*tṝ* P. *–tarati –te,* to go to sea, pass over, cross, to set out, start, A. to rise, thrive, prosper, to raise, elevate, augment, increase, further, promote, extend, prolong, prolong life, caus. *tārayati,* to deceive, trick, mislead,

pratta mfn. given away, offered, presented granted, from *pra* √*dā*

prattavat mfn one who has given/presented

pratti f. giving away, giving, gift,

pratud m. a class of birds, (pecker),

pratuda m. an instrument for piercing,

pratudati P. strikes at, cuts through, pierces, caus. *–todayati* to push on, urge, instigate,

pratūrta mfn quick, fleet,

pratūrti f. rapid or violent motion, haste, speed, mfn hastening, rapid,

pratuṣṭi f. satisfaction, *-da* mfn giving satisfaction,

pratvakṣaś mfn energetic, strong,

praty 663/3 in comp. before vowels for *prati*

prāty 707/1 in comp. before vowels, for *prāti*
pratyabdam ind. every year, yearly,
pratyabhi√dhā to take or draw back, re-absorb, A. to reply, answer,
pratyabhi √jñā to recognize, remember, know, understand, to come to one's self, recover consciousness,
pratyabhijñā f. regaining knowledge or recognition (of the identity of the Supreme and individual soul), (G) recognition, remembrance,
pratyabhinandati greets in return, returns a salutation, bids welcome,
pratyabhipra √sthā A. *-tiṣṭhate* to set out for, depart,
pratyā√bhū P. *–bhavati* to be at hand or at a person's command
pratyabhyāsam ind. at each repetition,
pratyā√brū P. *–bravīti* to reply to, answer,
pratyac mfn backward, south-western, f. southwest,
pratyācāra m. suitable behaviour,
pratyācaṣṭe A. refuses, declines, rejects, answers, refutes,
pratyā√dā A. *–datte*, to receive back, to take back, revoke, to draw forth from (5th), to repeat, return, ,
pratyadana n. eating, food,
pratyādāna n. re-obtaining, recovery, repetition, reiteration,
pratyadhikaraṇam ind. at each paragraph,
pratyadhīyate A. reads through, studies,
pratyā√diś P. *–diśati* to enjoin, direct, advise, to report, relate, summon, to decline, reject,
pratyādeśa m. order, command, an offer, rejection, prevention, warning, obscuring, putting to shame,
pratyādhāna n. a repository, place where things are laid up,
pratyādiśta mfn enjoined, directed, overcome, informed, apprised, warned, cautioned,
pratyādravati P. runs against, rushes upon,
pratyādriyate A. shows respect to,
pratyag in comp. for *pratyañc*
pratyagakṣa n. an inner organ, mfn having inner organs, *-ja* mfn discerned by the internal faculties, visible to the eye of the soul,
pratyagam ind. on every mountain
pratyā√gam P. *–gacchati,* to come back again, return, to come to one's self, recover consciousness, revive,
pratyāgaman n. return,
pratyāgata mfn come back again, returned
pratyāgataprāṇa mfn one who has recovered his breath or life,
pratyāgati f. coming back, return, arrival,
pratyāgamādhvi ind. till (my) return
pratyagni ind. towards the fire, at or near in every fire,
pratyagānanda mfn inwardly rejoicing, appearing as inward delight,
pratyagāśis f. a personal wish, mfn containing a personal wish,
pratyagātma mfn concerning the *ātman*
pratyagātman m. the individual soul, an individual, the inner Self,
pratyagātmatā f. being an individual soul,
pratyagātmatva n. universal permeation of spirit,
pratyagdhāman mfn radiant within, internally illuminated,
pratyagdṛś f. a glance directed inwards, mfn one whose glance is directed inwards,
pratyagekarasa mfn having taste only for the interior, delighting only in one's own soul,
pratyagjyotis n. the inward light,
pratyagra mfn fresh, recent, new, young, repeated, reiterated, pure, (ibc. and *am* ind.) recently,
pratyāgṛṇāti speaks to in return, answers,
pratyaha mfn daily
pratyaham ind. every day, day by day, in the morning,
pratyāhanti P. drives back, keeps away,
pratyāhāra 677/2 m. drawing back, abstraction, withdrawing of created things, re-absorption or dissolution of the world; in gram. the comprehension of a series of letters or roots etc., into one syllable by

combining for brevity the first member with the *anubandha* of the last member, a group of letters so combined, e.g. *ac*, or *hal*

pratyāharaṇa n. bringing back, recovery, withdrawing (esp. senses from external objects), drawing hither and thither,

pratyāharati P. draws in or back, withdraws (senses from worldly objects), replaces, fetches or brings back, continues, √*hṛ*

pratyāhata mfn driven back, repelled, √*han*

prātyahika mfn occurring/happening daily

pratyāhuti ind. at each oblation,

pratyājāyate A. is born again,

pratyak in comp. for *pratyañc*

praty-ā-kalita enumerated, held forth, reproached, interposed,

pratyākaṅkṣate A. is desirous of, longs for, expects,

pratyākāra m. a scabbard,

pratyakcetana one whose thoughts are turned inwards, (*ā*) f. thoughts inward or upon one's self

pratyā√khyā Cl 2 *–khyāti,* to repulse, reject, to deny, refute, to proclaim one by one, counteract by remedies,

pratyākhyāta mfn rejected, disallowed, denied, prohibited, set aside, surpassed, apprised, celebrated, notorious,

pratyākhyāna mfn conquered, overcome (as a passion), n. rejection, refusal, denial, counteracting, combating (of feelings), non-admittance, refutation,

pratyākhyāti P. proclaims one by one, refuses, repudiates, rejects, √*khyā*

pratyākhyātṛ m. a refuser,

pratyākhyāyam ind. enumerating one by one,

pratyakpravaṇa mfn devoted to the individual soul,

pratyākrāmati (te), P.A. steps back, √*kram*

pratyākrośati challenges/reviles in return √*kruś*

pratyākṛṣati P. withdraws √*kṛṣ*

pratyakṣa mfn 674/2 present before the eyes, perceptible, visible, clear, distinct, manifest, direct, immediate, actual, real, keeping in view, discerning, n. direct perception, apprehension by the senses, ind. (also °*kṣa* ibc.) before the eyes, in the sight or presence of, (6th or comp.), clearly, explicitly, directly, personally,(*āt)* ind. actually, really, (*eṇa*) ind. before the eyes, visibly, publicly, (*e*) ind. before one's face, publicly,

pratyakṣabhūta mfn become visible, appeared personally,

pratyakṣacārin mfn walking personally before the eyes of (6th),

pratyakùadakṣina 1. mfn moving to the right, 2. (*am)* ind. to the right, so that the right side is towards an object (a sign of respect), with *kṛ* put (an object) to the right, 3. mfn standing on the right,

pratyakṣadarśana n. seeing with one's own eyes, the power of discerning (the presence of a god), m. an eye-witness,

pratyakṣadarśin mfn seeing anything with one's own eyes, one who has seen with his own eyes, (*a*) n.

pratyakṣadharman mfn keeping in view the merits of men,

pratyakṣadṛś mfn seeing distinctly, one who sees anything clearly as if before the eye,

pratyakṣadṛśya mfn visible, perceptible

pratyakṣadṛṣṭa mfn seen with the eye,

pratyakṣadviṣ mfn not liking that which is clear,

pratyakṣajñāna n. immediate perception,

pratyakṣakaraṇa n. one's own perception,

pratyakṣaṁ brahma 'the direct and immediate Brahman – being proximate and without any intervention, as contrasted with outer organs like the eye etc.' (Gam.)

pratyakṣaparīkṣaṇa n. real observation,

pratyakṣaphala mfn having visible consequences
pratyakṣapramā f. a correct notion obtained through the senses,
pratyakṣara ibc. in each syllable,
pratyakṣatā f. the being before the eyes, being visible, visibility, addressing in the 2nd person, (*ayā*) ind. before the eyes of anyone,
pratyakṣatamāt, °tamām, ind. most perceptibly, or directly or really,
pratyakṣatas ind. before the eyes, visibly
pratyakṣatva n. ocular evidence, explicitness, immediate perception
pratyakṣavat ind. as if it were evident,
pratyakṣasiddha mfn determined by evidence of the senses,
pratyakṣī in comp. for *°kṣa*
prātyakṣika mfn perceptible to the eyes, capable of direct perception,
pratyakṣīkaraṇa n. looking at, viewing, making manifest or apparent,
pratyakṣī√kṛ to make visible or evident, to inspect, look at, see, personally
pratyakṣī√bhū to come before the eye, be visible, appear in person,
pratyakṣīkṛta mfn seen with the eye,
pratyakṣin mfn seeing with one's own eyes, m. an eyewitness,
pratyaktva n. self-awareness, direction towards one's self, backwards direction,
pratyālayam ind. in every house,
pratyamitra mfn opposed as enemy, hostile m. an enemy, an opponent,
pratyaṁśa m. a portion, share,
pratyanantara mfn being in the immediate neighbourhood of, closely connected with, immediately following, standing nearest (as an heir), (*am*) ind. immediately after (5th), next in succession,
pratyānayana n. leading or bringing back, recovery, restoration,
pratyandhakāra mfn spreading shadow,
pratyāneya mfn to be repaired or made good,
pratyānīta mfn led or brought back,
pratyaṅga n. a minor/secondary part of the body, (forehead, nose, chin etc.), a division, section, part, a subdivision (of a science), a weapon, m. a kind of measure,
(ibc. or [*am*] ind.) onevery part of the body, for one's own person, for every part or subdivision,
pratyā√nī P.A. *–nayati (te),* to lead or bring back, restore, to recover, regain, to pour or fill up again,
pratyanīka mfn opposed, injuring, withstanding, resisting, opposite, equal, m. an enemy,m. hostility, enmity, a hostile army,
pratyanīkeṣu in opposing armies 7/pl
pratyanilam ind. against the wind,
pratyañjana n. smearing, anointing,
pratyanta mfn bordering on, adjacent or contiguous to, skirting, m. a border, frontier, bordering country,
pratyantāt ind. in each case to the end,
pratyantika mfn situated at the border,
prātyantika m. a neighbouring chief,
pratyanu√bhū P. *–bhavati* to enjoy singly or severally, 'experiences, appears to experience', (Gam.),
pratyanu√jñā P. *–jānāti* to refuse, reject, spurn,
pratyanumāna n. a contrary deduction, opposite conclusion,
pratyanu√nī P.A. *–nayati, (te),* to speak friendly words, induce to yield, persuade, A. to beg a person's pardon for,
pratyanu√smṛ P.*-smarati,* to remember,
pratyanu√tap pass. *–tapyate,* to feel subsequent remorse, regret, repent,
pratyanu√yāc P. *–yācati* to beseech, implore
pratyapa√kṛ to take vengeance on,
pratyāpanna mfn returned, regained, restored
pratyapapakāra m. offending or injuring in return, retaliation,
pratyāpatti f. √pad, return, turning back (from evil), conversion, restoration, restitution, expiation,
pratyapāya m. perishing again,

pratyāplavana n. springing/leaping back
pratyara a fastener, m. intermediate spoke of a wheel,
pratyārambha m. beginning again, recommencement, prohibition, annulment,
pratyaraṇya ibc. near or in a forest
pratyardhi mfn having equal claims, equal to,
pratyārdra mfn fresh,
pratyari m. an equally powerful enemy,
pratyarṇam ind. at each syllable,
pratyarpaṇa n. giving back, restoring,
pratyarpayati caus. *prati√ṛ* to hand over, give back, (X),
pratyartham ind. in relation to anything, at every object, in every case,
pratyarthin mfn emulating, rivalling, hostile, opposing, opposed to, m. rival, opponent, adversary,
pratyas *prati√as* to be equal to or a match for, to throw to or down, to turn over or round,
pratyāśā f. confidence, trust, hope, expectation,
pratyā√sad P. *sīdati* to be near or close at hand, to wait for, expect,
pratyāśam ind. in all directions,
pratyāsaṁkalita n. the putting together or combining of various evidence, consideration of pros and cons,
pratyāsaṅga m. combination, connection,
pratyāsanna mfn near at hand, close to, imminent, closely connected, feeling repentant, *-tā* n. proximity, neighbourhood,
pratyāsatti f. immediate proximity
pratyāśin mfn hoping, expecting, trusting, relying upon,
pratyāśraya m. a shelter, refuge, dwelling,
pratyaṣṭa mfn fallen to a person's lot/share,
pratyasta mfn thrown down, laid low √2.*as*
pratyasta-gamana n. the setting of the sun
pratyastam ind. with √*gam* to go down, cease,
pratyastra n. missile hurled in return,
pratyāsvara mfn shining back, reflecting,
pratyā√śvas P. *–śvasiti* to breathe again, respire, revive, take heart again,
pratyāśvasta mfn refreshed, revived, recollected,
pratyātanoti, °tanute, P.A. extends in the direction of, shines upon or against, irradiates, bends a bow against,
pratyātāpa m. a sunny place,
pratyātma ibc. or *°mam* ind. for every soul, in every soul
pratyātmaka mfn belonging to one's self, (also *°mika),* original, peculiar,
pratyātmya n. resemblance to one's self, *ena* ind. after one's own image,
pratyavadat (he) repeated verbatim
pratyavamarṣa m. inner contemplation, profound meditation, recollection, consciousness, touch, contact, reflecting upon,
pratyavara mfn lower, more insignificant, less honoured than,
pratyavasthita mfn standing separately or opposite, being in a partic. condition
pratyavāya m. backsliding, reversal, sin, decrease, reverse, contrary course, opposite action, *prati-ava-√i* evil consequences, future sorrow, disappearance of what exists or non-production of what does not exist,
pratyavayava ibc or *°vam* ind. on or at every part of the body, ibc. in every part or particular, in detail,
pratyavekṣaṇa n. looking after, care, attention, f. (*ā*) (Buddhist) one of the 5 kinds of knowledge,
pratyavekṣya mfn to be regarded or paid attention to,
pratyāvartana n. coming back, returning
pratyā√vṛt A. *–vartate* to turn against, return, come back,
pratyāvṛtta mfn turned back (a face), returned, come back, repeated,
pratyaya m. belief, conviction, trust, faith, assurance or certainty of, proof, conception, assumption, notion, idea, ascertainment, definition, analysis, solution, explanation, grond, basis, motive, cause,

an ordeal, want, need, fame, notoriety, a subsequent sound or letter, the name for an affix or suffix to roots (forming verbs, substantives, adjectives and all derivatives),
an oath, usage, custom, religious meditation, a dependent or subject, householder who keeps a sacred fire, fundamental notion or idea (Buddhists and Jainas),
a cooperating cause (Buddhist),

pratyāya m. toll, tribute,

pratyayadhātu the stem of a nominal verb,

pratyāyaka mfn causing to know or understand, convincing, credible,

pratyayakāraṇa mfn one who awakens confidence, trustworthy,

pratyayalopa m. (in gram.) the elision of an affix,

pratyāyati P. comes back, returns to,

pratyāyana mfn convincing, credible, (*ā*) f. convincing, persuasion, consolation, comfort, n. elucidation, explanation,
2. n. setting (of the sun),

pratyayanam ind. every half-year,

pratyayasvara (in gram.) an affix accent

pratyayatva n. the being a cause, causality,
n. consciousness, intelligence, understanding, intellect, buddhi,
m. belief, conviction, trust, faith, assurance or certainty of,
proof, conception, assumption, notion, idea, ascertainment, definition, analysis, solution, explanation, ground, basis, motive, cause, an ordeal, want, need, fame, notoriety, a subsequent sound or letter, the name for an affix or suffix to roots (forming verbs, ubstantives, adjectives and all derivatives),
an oath, usage, custom, religious meditation, a dependent or subject, householder who keeps a sacred fire, fundamental notion or idea (Buddhists and Jainas),
a cooperating cause (Buddhist),

pratyayayātma mfn causing confidence,

pratyayika mfn that of which everybody can convince himself,

prātyayika mfn confidential, relating to confidence, m. a surety for a debt

pratyayin mfn deserving confidence, trustworthy, trusting, believing,

pratyayita mfn proved, trustworthy,

pratyāyita mfn convinced of, trusting, m. a trustworthy person,

pratyayitavya mfn credible,

pratyeka mfn each one, every one, (ibc. or *am* ind.) one by one, one at a time, singly, for every single one,

pratyekabuddha m. a Buddha who lives in seclusion and obtains emancipation for himself alone (as opposed to those who obtain liberation for others also),

pratyekaśas ind. one by one, singly, severally,

pratyenas m. an officer of justice, punisher of criminals, a surety,

pratyeṣ (ā√iṣ) A. *-eṣate* to attach one's self to, enter into(7th),

pratyṛcam ind. at or in each verse,

pratyṛtu ind. in each season,

pratyuccāra m. repetition,

pratyuccāraṇa n. answering,

pratyudadhi ind. at the sea,

pratyudā√hṛ to reply, answer,

pratyudā√vraj to go in a contrary direction

pratyuddhāra m. offering, tendering,

pratyuddhṛta mfn re-obtained, rescued, delivered from (5th), 678/1

pratyud√1.gā to rise before or over, 677/3

pratyud√gam to go out towards, advance to meet, to come forth again, set out for,

pratyudgama m. °*gamana* n. °*gati* f. going forth towards, rising and going out to meet,

pratyudgata mfn gone to meet, met, encountered,

pratyudgīta mfn answered in singing, chanting

pratyudgraha m. *pratyudgrahaṇa* n. setting aside, dismissing,

pratyudgṛhṇāti sets aside, dismisses,

pratyūḍha mfn rejected, refused,

pratyud√i P. *–eti*, to ascend to, to rise and go towards,
pratyūha m. an obstacle, impediment,
pratyūhana n. interruption, discontinuance,
pratyud√īkṣ to look up at, perceive, behold,
pratyudita mfn rejected, repelled,
pratyudyamin mfn maintaining an equipoise, counterbalancing,
pratyudyāna n. the act of going forth against
pratyudyāta mfn met, received,
pratyujjīvati revives, returns to life, caus. *-jīvayati* revivifies, resuscitates,
pratyukta mfn (having been)answered,
pratyukti f. an answer
pratyulūkaka m. a bird resembling an owl
pratyunmiṣati P. rises or shines forth (as the sun), √*miṣ*
pratyupabhoga m. enjoyment,
pratyupadeśa m. instruction/advice in return
pratyupa√dhā to put or place upon, cover,
pratyupāharati P. gives up, desists, √*hṛ*
pratyupa√gam to come near, approach,
pratyupagata mfn come near, approached,
pratyupakāra 678/1 returning a service or favour, gratitude
pratyupa√kṛ A. *–kurute,* to do a service in return, return a favour,
pratyupa√kram to go/march forth against,
pratyupalabdha mfn gained back, recovered,
pratyupamāna n. a counter comparison, the ideal of an ideal,
pratyuparuddha mfn obstructed, choked,
pratyupāsanam ind. for every kind of worship,
pratyupa√sthā P.A. (P.) to insist on A. to stand opposite to, to wait on, caus. *-sthāpayati* to call forth, manifest,
pratyupasthāna n. proximity, imminence,
pratyupasthāpana n. mental realization,
pratyupasthita mfn come near to, approached, arrived, standing or being in (7th), present, assisting at (7th), gone against, standing opposite to, assembled, happened, occurred, imminent, collecting,
pratyupa√yā to go again towards, return,
pratyupeya mfn to be met or dealt with,
pratyupekṣita mfn disregarded, neglected,
pratyupodita mfn addressed offensively,
pratyupta mfn fixed into (7th),
pratyurasam ind. against the breast, upon the breast,
pratyūrdhvam ind. on the upper side of, above,
pratyuṣa m. the daybreak, dawn,
pratyūṣa m. the daybreak, dawn,
pratyuta ind. on the contrary, rather, even,
pratyutkarṣa m. outstanding, surpassing,
pratyutkrama undertaking, the first step or measure in any business, setting out to assail an enemy, declaration of war,
pratyutkrānta mfn about to pass away,
pratyutkrāntajīvita mfn one almost dead,
pratyut√5.pā A. to rise against,
pratyutpanna mfn existing at the present moment, present, prompt, ready, reproduced, regenerated, produced by multiplication, multiplied, n. multiplication or the sum of multiplication,
pratyutpannamati ready-minded, sharp, confident, bold, -
-tva n. presence of mind, m. 'ready-wit' (name of a fish),
pratyut√sad P.*-sīdati* to resort to,
pratyuttara n. a reply to an answer, rejoinder, answer,
pratyuttabdhi f. upholding, supporting,
pratyutthāna n. rising to welcome a visitor, respectful salutation or reception, rising up against,
prauḍha 714/3 mfn raised or lifted up, full-grown, mighty, mature, strong, violent, impetuous (as love), thick, dense (as darkness), full (as the moon), proud, arrogant, audacious, ifc. filled with, full of, f. (*ā*) a married woman aged 30-55 n. a violent or impetuous woman,
pra-uga n. a triangle, the forepart of chariot shafts,
prava mfn fluttering, hovering
pra√vā *P. –vāti,* to blow forth, blow, to smell, yield a scent,

pravā f. blowing forth, blowing,
pra√vac P. *–vakti,* to proclaim, announce, praise, commend, mention, teach, impart, explain, to tell of, betray, caus. *–vācayati* to cause to announce
pravāc mfn eloquent, talkative, boastful,
pravacana m. one who exposes, propounds, n. speaking, talking, teaching, interpretation, announcement, excellent speech or language, eloquence, an expression, term, a system of doctrines, sacred writings, teaching the scriptures, self-recital of the Vedas, study,
pravācana n. a proclamation, promulgation, fame, renown, a designation, name,
pravacanapatu skilled in speaking, eloquent
pravacanīya mfn to be taught, propounded, to be well or eloquently spoken, m. a propounder, teacher, good speaker,
pravācya mfn to be proclaimed aloud, to be spoken to, glorious, praiseworthy,
pra√vad P.A. *–vadati, (te),* to speak out, pronounce, proclaim, declare, utter, say, tell, to raise the voice, to assert, affirm, state, caus. *–vādayati* to cause to sound, play, make music,
pravad in comp. for *pravat*
pravadati 690/3 speaks out, proclaims, declares,
pravāda m. speaking forth, uttering, expressing, mentioning, talk, report, rumour, popular saying or belief, slander, mutual defiance,
pravadana n. a proclamation/announcement,
pravadeta said,
prāvāduka m. an opponent in philosophical discussion, 702/3
pravaga m. = *plavaga* a monkey
pra√vah P. *–vahati,* to carry forwards, drag onwards, to wash away, to lead to, to show, utter, to drive onwards, to rush (as wind), caus. *vāhayati* to cause to go away, send off, dismiss, to set in motion,
pra√vāh A. *–vāhate* to bear down (a woman in labour),
pravaha mfn bearing along, carrying, m. wind, air, a water reservoir, flowing or streaming forth, moving away from,
pravāha m. a stream, river, current, running water, continuous flow, continuity, streaming forth, course of action, activity, a pond, lake, a beautiful horse,
pravahaṇa n. sending away, giving a girl in marriage, a kind of litter,
pravāhin mfn drawing, carrying,bearing along or away, ifc. streaming, abounding in streams, m. a draught animal,
pravāhita n. bearing down, (see *pra√vāh)*
pravahli °likā, °lī f. a riddle, enigma,
pravaka mfn one who goes,
pravāka m. a proclaimer,
pravakṣyāmi I shall speak or talk
pravakṣye I shall speak of, I shall explain, 3/s/fut *pra√vac*
pravaktavya mfn to be announced, explained
pravaktṛ mfn one who tells, imparts, relates, a good speaker, a teacher, announcer
pravāla ifc. f. *ā*, a young shoot, sprout, new leaf or branch, coral, m. an animal, a pupil, mfn having shoots or sprouts, having long or beautiful hair,
pravālaka n. coral,
pravālavat mfn having new leaves or shoots,
pravalha m. a riddle, enigma,
pravalhate A. tests with a question or riddle,
pravalhita mfn enigmatical,
pravaṇa mfn prone,
pravaṇa the side of a hill, slope, declivity, abyss, depth, m. a place where 4 roads meet, a moment, a whirlpool, an access, mfn declining, bent, sloping down, ifc. directed towards, intent upon, full of, decayed, generous, humble,
prāvaṇa mfn among the crags (fire),
pravapaṇa n. shaving off, 2. n. scattering, sowing,
pravara mfn chief, principal, best, eldest (son), better than (5th), greater, eminent, distinguished by,

m.'best of heroes'
a cover, upper garment,
a call, summons, an invocation (Agni), a series of ancestors, a family, race, an ancestor,
pravāra m. a covering, cover, woollen cloth,
pravāraka m.= *pravaraṇa,* woollen cloth
pravarajana m. a person of quality,
pravaraṇa n. the festivities at the end of the rainy season, 2. a call, summons, invocation, any religious observance,
pravāraṇa n. prohibition, 2. n. satisfying, fulfillment of a wish,
pravararūpa mfn having a beautiful form,
pravardhaka mfn augmenting, increasing, enhancing,
prāvarga mfn distinguished, eminent,
pravārita mfn clothed with (3rd), 2. offered, set out for sale,
pravarṣa m. rain √*vṛṣ*
pravarṣaṇa n. beginning to rain, raining,
prāvarṣin mfn raining, showering,
pravarta a round ornament, an ear-ring, engaging in, undertaking, stimulus
pravartaka mf(*ikā)*n acting, proceeding, setting in motion, advancing, promoting, producing, causing, m. a founder, author, originator, a judge, arbiter,
pravartana mfn being in motion, flowing, (*ā*) f. incitement to activity, (in gram.) order, permission, n. advance, forward movement, rolling or flowing forth, walking, roaming, activity, procedure, engaging in, dealing with (3rd, 7th), going on, coming off, occurrence, conduct, behaviour, bringing near, fetching, construction, causing to appear, bringing about, employing, using, informing,
pravartate 693/2 -√*vṛt* to be set in motion or going, sets about, engages in, commences, happens, is intent upon, comes about,
pravartayitṛ m. one who sets in motion, instigator of, a builder, founder,
pravartin mfn issuing, streaming forth, flowing, active, restless, unsteady,
pravartita 693/3 mfn. caused to roll on or forwards, set in motion, set up, established, built, made,
pravartitavya n. (impers.) one should act or proceed,
pravartitṛ m. one who causes or effects, producer, bringer,
pravartya mfn to be (or being) excited to activity,
pravārya mfn to be satisfied,
pravāsa m. dwelling abroad, absence from home, foreign residence,
pravasana n. setting out on a journey, departing, dying, decease,
pravāsana sending away from home, exile,
pravasati sojourns abroad, leaves home, departs, disappears, stops at a place, caus. –*vāsayati* expels, banishes √5.*vas*
pravaste A. puts on clothes, dresses, √4.*vas*
pravat f. the side or slope of a mountain, elevation, height, heavenly height, a sloping path, mfn directed forwards or towards, blazing forth (Agni),
pravaṭa m. wheat,
prāvaṭa m. barley,
pravāta mfn blown forward, agitated by the wind, n. a current or draught of air, windy weather or place,
pravatvat mfn hilly, sloping downwards, affording a swift motion,
pravayas mfn strong, vigorous, in the prime of life, aged, old, ancient,
pravayati P. weaves on, attaches to,
pravedakṛt mfn making known,
pravedana making known, proclaiming,
pravedha m. a bow-shot, measure of length
pravedin mfn knowing well or accurately,
pravedya mfn to be made known,
pravega m. great speed, rapidity,
praveka mfn choicest, most excellent, principal, chief,
prāveṇya n. a fine woollen covering,
praveśa 692/3 entering, entrance, penetration,
praveśaka ifc. entering, entrance,
praveśana 692/3 n entering, entrance or

penetration, sexual intercourse, a principal door or gate, conducting or leading into, introduction
prāveśana n. a workshop,
praveṣṭavya mfn to be entered or penetrated or pervaded, accessible, open to be caused or allowed to enter, n. one should enter or penetrate into,
praveṣṭṛ one who enters or goes into,
praveṭa m. barley,
pravetṛ m. a charioteer,
pra√vī P. *–veti* to go forth, strive after, make for, enter into, attack, fertilize, impregnate, to urge on, animate,
prāvī mfn attentive, heedful, zealous,
pravibhāga m. separation, division, distribution, classification, a part,
pravibhāgaśas ind. separately, singly,
pravibhāgavat mfn having subdivisions, subdivided,
pravi√bhaj P. to separate, apportion, divide,
pravibhajya ind. p. having divided, divided, distributed,
pravibhakta mfn . (having been) divided or distributed, one who has received his share
pravibhāvaka mfn causing to appear, representing,
pravi√cakṣ to declare, mention, name,
pravi√cal to become agitated, confused,
pravi√car to go forwards, advance, to roam about,
pravicāra m. distinction, division, species, kind,
pravicārita mfn examined or investigated accurately,
pravicaya m. investigation, examination,
pravi√ceṣṭ A. to rove about,
pravicetana n. comprehending, understanding,
pravi√cint to think about, reflect upon,
pravicintaka mfn reflecting beforehand, foreseeing,
pravicita mfn tried, proved, tasted,
pravi√2.ci P. *–cinoti* to search through, investigate, examine,
pra√1.vid P. *–vetti* to know, understand, to know or understand right, understand the truth, caus. *–vedayati (te),* to make known, communicate,
pravid f. knowledge, science,
pra√3.vid P.A. *–vindati (te),* to find, find out, invent, to anticipate,
pravi√1.dhā to place apart, divide, A. to meditate, think upon, to place in front, put at the head, pay attention to,
pravidhāna n. a means employed,
praviditsu mfn wishing to perform,
pravidvas mfn knowing, wise,
pravi√gal to stream forth, to cease/disappear
pravigata mfn passed away, disappeared,
pravigraha m. separation of words by breaking up the saṁdhi
pravihāra m. moving onwards,
pravihata mfn beaten back, put to flight,
pravijahāti *√3.hā* to relinquish, give up,
pravijahya mfn to be given up, abandoned,
pravi√jñā P. *–jānāti* to know in detail or accurately,
pravi√jṛmbh A. to open or expand, to appear in full vigour or splendour,
pravikarṣa m. drawing (the bowstring),
pravikaṭa mfn very large, huge
pravikhyāta mfn universally known, renowned, known as, called,
pravi√labh to regain, recover,
pravi√lamb to hang up,
pravilāpana or *–vilāpitatva* n. complete absorption or annihilation
pravi√las p. –lasati to shine forth brightly, to appear in full strength or vigour,
pravilaya m. melting,
pravilayana n. complete dissolution or absorption,
pravi√lī A or pass. *–liyate*, to become dissolved, melt or vanish away, caus. *–lāpayati,* to cause to disappear or dissolve into,
pravilīyate is melted away, dissolves, vanishes, 1/s/pres/indic/pass *pra vi √lī*
pravilokayati looks forward or about, perceives, notices, considers,

pravilola mfn very unsteady,
pravi√mṛś to think upon, ponder, reflect,
pravi√muc to set free, liberate, to give up, relinquish, abandon,
pravīṅa mfn skilful, clever, versed in (7th),
pravinaṣṭa mfn utterly destroyed,
pravīṇatā f. cleverness,
pravīṇī√kṛ to render skilful
prāvīṇya n. cleverness, dexterity, skill, proficiency in (7th or comp.)
pravīra mfn preceding or surpassing heroes, m. a hero, prince, chief among (6th or comp.), a person excellent or distinguished by (comp.),
pravirala mfn well separated, isolated, few,
pravirata mfn one who has desisted from,
pravirūḍha mfn sprouted, grown,
pra√viś P.A. *–viśati (te),* to enter, go into, resort to, to reach, attain, (with partic. words) to ascend the funeral pyre, (with *ātmani* or *cittam*) to take possession of the heart, have intercourse with, to enter upon, undertake, devote one's self to, caus. *–veśayati (te),* to cause or allow to enter, introduce to, usher into, to lead home as a wife, to lay or store up, deposit in, write down, initiate into, instill into, teach, impart, to spend,
pravi√śam caus. *śāmayati* to extinguish, destroy,
praviṣaṇṇa mfn dejected, sad, spiritless,
pravisarpin mfn spreading/diffusing slowly
prāviśat entered
praviśati he enters 1/s/pres/act
praviśata enter!
praviṣaya m. scope, range, reach (of eye etc)
pravi√śiṣ P. *-śinaṣṭi* to magnify, increase augment,
praviśleṣa m. separation, parting,
pravispaṣṭa perfectly visible or evident,
praviṣṭa mfn (having) entered, one who has entered, entered upon, undertaken, occupied with, intent upon, engaged in, initiated into, agreeing with, made use of, come into being,
pravistara m. circumference, compass, extent, also *pravistāra*
praviśuddha mfn perfectly clean,
pravi√śudh caus. *–śodhayati* to clean perfectly
praviśya having entered
pravīta mfn impregnated,
pravitata mfn spread out, expanded, wide, undertaken, begun, arranged,
pravivāda m. altercation, quarrel,
pravivardhita mfn very much increased,
praviveka m. complete solitude
pravivikta mfn separate, solitary, lonely, fine, delicate, sharp, keen,
pravivrajiṣu mfn wishing to take the vow of a monk,
pravlaya m. sinking down, collapse,
pravrāj m. a religious mendicant,
pravrāja m. the bed of a river,
pravrajana n. going abroad,
pravrajita mfn gone astray or abroad, run away (horses), one who has left home to become a wandering mendicant or a monk (Jainas), m. a religious mendicant or a monk, *(ā)* f. a female ascetic or a nun, roaming, wandering about,n. the life of a religious mendicant,
praviyuta mfn completely filled, crammed,
pravrajati P. goes forth, proceeds, sets out for, leaves home as a wandering mendicant, to become a monk (Jain)
pravrājin mfn going forth or after,
prāvrājya n. the life of a religious mendicant, vagrancy
pravṛddha 694/1 fully developed, increased, intense, prosperous, mighty, strong
pravṛddhi f. growth, increase, rising, rise, prosperity, rise in welfare or status,
pra√vṛdh P. *–vardhati* to exalt, magnify, A. *-vardhate,* to grow up, grow, increase, gain in strength, prosper,
pravṛdh f. growth,
pravṛhet one should raise, pull out, separate, 1/s/opt/act *pra√vṛh* cl6
pravṛkta mfn placed in or near the fire,
prāvṛṣ f. the rainy season, the rains, the monsoon,
pravṛṣṭa mfn begun to rain or pour down,

pravṛṣṭe ind. when it rains,

pra√vṛt A. P *–vartate, (ti),* to roll or go onwards (as a carriage), be set in motion or going, to set out, depart, to come forth, issue, arise, originate, be produced, result, occur, take place, begin to, engage in, be intent upon, proceed against, proceed according to, deal with, hold good, prevail, to continue, keep on, to mean, be used in the sense of, caus. *-vartayati* to cause to turn or roll, set in motion, to throw, hurl, to set on foot, divulge, circulate, appoint, install, produce, create, invent, perform, do, make, (with *kathām* to relate a story), to exhibit, show,

pravṛta mfn chosen, selected, adopted (as a son),

pravṛtta 693/3 mfn round, globular, driven up (as a carriage), circulated (as a book), set out from (*-tas*), come forth, resulted, arisen, happened, going to, bound for, engaged in, commenced, begun, proceeding, existing, occupied with, busy, n. with *karman* (action) –causing a continuation of mundane existence,

pravṛttacakra mfn having universal power,

pravṛttatva n. having happened or occurred,

pravṛttavāc mfn of fluent or eloquent speech,

pravṛttavat mfn having set about or commenced to,

pravṛtti participation HH (cf. *nivṛtti* – non- participation)

pravṛtti 694/1 f. active life as opposed to in-active life, moving onwards, progress, manifestation, active life consisting of the wish to act, knowledge of the means, & accomplishment of the object, coming forth, appearance, activity, exertion, efficacy, function, active life (as opposed to *nivṛtti* and to contemplative devotion, and defined as consisting of the wish to act, knowledge of the means and accomplishment of the object), giving or devoting oneself to, course or tendency towards, inclination/predilection for (7th or comp.), application, use, employment, conduct, behaviour, practice, the applicability or validity of a rule, continuance, prevalence, fate, destiny, news, tidings,

pravṛttijña m. 'knowing the news' an emissary, agent, spy,

pravṛttijñāna =*vijñāna*

prāvṛttika mfn corresponding to a former mode of action, ifc. well acquainted with,

pravṛttimārga m. active or worldly life,

pravṛttimat mfn devoted to anything,

pravṛttinivṛttimat mfn connected with activity and inactivity,

pravṛttipratyaya m. a belief in or conception of the things relating to the external world,

pravṛttivijñāna n. cognition of the things belonging to the external world,

pravyādha m. the distance of an arrow-flight

pravyā√hṛ 'to bring forth indistinctly or at intervals', to speak indistinctly or hesitantly,

pravyāhāra m prolongation or continuation of discourse,

pravyāharaṇa n. the uttering of sounds, faculty of speech,

pravyāhṛta mfn speaking, spoken, foretold, predicted,

pravyakta mfn evident, apparent, manifest,

pravyakti f. appearance, manifestation,

pravyasyati P. lays down, places upon √2.*as*

pravyathita 699/2 mfn affrighted, distressed

prāya 708/1 m. going forth, starting, departure from life, probably, ifc. consisting in, mostly, like,

prayā f. onset,

pra√yā *prayāti* to go forth, set out, progress, advance towards or against, to walk, roam, wander, to part, go asunder, be dispersed, pass away, vanish, die, to get into a

partic. state or condition, enter, undergo, incur, to lead into
pra√yāc P.A. *–yācati (te),* to ask for, beg, request,
prayācaka mfn asking, requesting, imploring,
prayācana n. asking, begging, imploring,
prayacchati 687/3 he holds out towards, presents, extends, offers, √*yam*
prayāga m. place of sacrifice, a sacrifice, a horse, confluence of Yamunā and Gaṅgā rivers,
prayāja m. 'pre-sacrifice', preliminary offering, a principal ceremony or sacrifice,
prayaj P.A. *–yajati (te),* to worship, sacrifice to, to offer the *prayāja* sacrifice,
f. an offering, an oblation,
prayajyu mfn worshipful, adorable,
prayakṣa mfn eager, strenuous,
prayāma m. dearth, scarcity, checking, restraining, length (in space or time), extension,
prayāman n. setting out, start,
prayamaṇa n. purification,
prayāṇa n. setting out, starting, advancing, progress, journey, march, invasion, departure, death, onset, beginning,
prayāṇaka n. a journey, march
prayāṇakāle at the time of departure, at the time of death 7/s/m
prāyaṇānta 708/1 m. the end of life, (*am*) ind. unto death,
prayanti they progress, go 1/pl/pres
prayantṛ mfn one who offers or presents, a giver, bringer,
prayāpita mfn driven or sent away, made to go or pass away,
prayāpya mfn to be caused to go, to be sent away,
pra√yas P. *–yasyati,* to begin to bubble, to endeavour, labour, strive after,
prayas 2. n. pleasure, enjoyment, delight, pleasant food or drink,
prāyas 708/2 ind. mostly, probably, commonly, as a general rule, abundantly, largely,
prayāsa m. exertion, effort, pains, trouble, high degree,
prāyaśas ind. for the most part, almost, mostly, most likely,
prayaścitta n. penance, atonement,
prayāsita n. effort, exertion,
prayasta mfn bubbling over, striving, well cooked or prepared,
prāyasya mfn prevalent, dominant,
pra√yat A. *–yatate,* to be active or effective, to strive, endeavour, devote or apply oneself to,
prayata 687/3 mfn dutiful, careful, prudent, pure, controlled, out-stretched, far-extended, placed upon (7th), offered, presented, given, granted, intent on devotion, well prepared (for a sacred rite), ritually pure, self-subdued,
m. a holy or pious person,
-tā f. *–tva* n. purity, holiness,
prayāta mfn set out, gone, advanced, arrived at, gone or passed away, dead,
prayatana n. effort, endeavour,
prayatas ind. with special effort, diligently, carefully,
prayatate he tries
prayati f. offering, gift, intention, will, effort, exertion,
prayāti he/she/it goes forth, sets out, departs or dies *pra* √*yā* 688/1 1/s/pres/indic/act
prayatita n. (impers.) pains have been taken with (7th),
prayatitavya n. pains have to be taken with,
prayatna, 687/3 active efforts, continued exertion, activity, action, act, persevering efforts
commonly, frequently, probably, ibc. and *prayatnāt* ind. great care, caution,
(in phil.) active efforts (3 kinds – engaging in any act, prosecuting it and completing it),
(in gram.) effort in uttering, mode of articulation –distinguished into outer and inner effort,
(*āt, ena*), ind. carefully
prayatnata ind. with special effort, diligently, carefully, zealously,

prayātṛ m. one who goes or can go or fly, seeting out on a journey,
prayatta mfn intent, eager,
prāyatya n. pious disposition or preparation for any rite
prayāyin mfn going forwards, marching,
prāyena ind. mostly, generally, as a rule,
prāyika mfn common, usual, excessive, containing most but not all,
prayoddhṛ mfn one who fights, a combatant
prayoga 688/2 joining together, connection, position, addition (of a word), hurling, casting (of missiles), offering, presenting, undertaking, beginning, commencement, application, employment, a design, plan, device, practice, experiment, (in gram.) an applicable or usual form, utterance, pronunciation, recitation, delivery, sacred text, usury, interest, cause, motive, consequence, result, course of proceeding, a horse, exhibition, representation (of a drama), cause, motive, consequence, result, a horse,
prayogagrahaṇa n. acquirement of practice,
prayogajña mfn skilful in practice,
prayogapradhāna in practice (not theory),
prāyogika mfn applied, used, applicable,
prayogin mfn being employed or used, applicable, usual, having some object in view, m. an actor,
prayogīya mfn regarding the application of medicines etc.
prayogya m. a harnessed or draught animal,
prayojaka mfn causing, effecting, leading to, instigating, instigator, promoter, effective, essential, deputing, anointing, m. an author, composer, lender, employer,
prayojana n. occasion, object, cause, motive, purpose, design, aim, end, (in phil.) a motive for discussing the point in question, *-vat* mfn having or connected with or serving any interest or purpose, interested, serviceable, useful, °*t-tva* having a cause, caused, produced,
prayojanena with a particular intention, at call, on call,
prayojya mfn to be cast or shot (missile), to be used or employed or practised,
prāyojya mfn belonging to necessities,
prayoktṛ m. a hurler, an agent of an action, an employer, actor, reciter, poet, composer, author,
prayoktra m. a harness,
prāyoktra mfn relating to an employer,
prayotṛ m. a remover, expeller,
pra√yuch P. *–yucchati* to be absent, absent in mind, careless, heedless
pra√yudh A.P. *–yudhyate, (ti),* to begin to fight, attack, fight with (2nd),
prāyudh mfn attacking,
prayuddha mfn fighting, one who has fought, n. fight, battle, mfn war, battle, going to war or battle,
pra√yuj A. *–yuṅkte*. P. *–yunakti,* to yoke or join or harness to (7th), to unite with (3rd), to turn the mind to (7th), to prepare for (4th), to set in motion, throw, cast (dice)(4th,7th), to utter, pronounce, speak, recite, to fix, place in or on (7th), to direct, order, urge to, (4th, 7th), to choose for, lead towards, (2nd), to use, employ, practise, perform, display, accomplish, contrive, do, undertake, begin, cause, effect, act, caus. *–yojayati* throw, discharge, (with *manas*) concentrate the mind, urge, direct, undertake, use, employ
prayuj f. a team, impulse, motive, mfn joining, connected with,
prayujyate 688/2 it is used or employed, it is fit or suitable, (pass. *yuj*)
prayukta 688/2 mfn. yoked, harnessed, ordered, directed, used, employed, stirred (by wind), drawn (a sword), undertaken, begun, made, prepared, resulting from (comp.), n. a cause,
prayukti f. impulse, motive, setting in, motion, employment,
prayut mfn stirring, mingling,

prayutsu m. a warrior, a ram, an ascetic, air, wind,

prayuta mfn absent in mind, inattentive, heedless, careless, 2. mfn mingled with (3rd), confused (as a dream), n. a million,

prayuti f. absence,

prayuvana n. stirring, mingling,

√*pṛc* 645/2 Cl 7 P *pṛṇakti* A *pṛṅkte* Cl 2 *pṛkte* Cl 1 P *pṛñcati* Cl 3 P *pipṛgdhi* to mix, mingle, put together with, unite, join, to fill (A oneself), sate, satiate, to give lavishly, grant bountifully, bestow anything richly upon, to increase, augment, DP in *samparka* (Cl 7) bringing contact with, joining, *samparcana* (Cl 2) coming into contact with, *saṁyamana*(Cl 10) joining, uniting,
2. f. food, nourishment, refreshment,

pṛcchati he/she asks

pṛcchāmi I ask

√*pṛḍ* 645/2 Cl 6 P *pṛḍati* to gladden, delight, DP in *sukhana* delighting, pleasing,

prekṣ *pra*√*īkṣ* Cl1 *prekṣate* to look at view, behold, observe, to look on (without interfering), suffer, say nothing,

prekṣā f. seeing, viewing, beholding, looking on (at a performance), a public show or entertainment, circumspection, consideration, reflection, the branch of a tree, ifc. the being understood or meant as,

prekṣāgṛha n. theatre, venue,

prekṣaṇa 712/2 n viewing, looking at or on (at a performance), (ifc *ā*) a view, look, sight, the eye, any public show, (*pra-*√*īkṣ*),

prema 711/2 1. love, affection, 2. in comp. for *preman,* divine love,

preman 711/2 m.n. love affection, kindness, tender regard, love, m. sport, a jest, joke, wind,

preṅkha mfn rocking, pitching, a swing, hammock , f. dancing, m. a partic. pace of a horse, m.n. unsteady boat, skiff,

prepsā 712/3 wish to obtain, desire, longing for, supposition, assumption,

prepsāva desiring

prepsu mfn. wishing to attain, seeking, longing for, supposing, assuming (*-nā*) 3/s/m

preraṇa 712/3 n driving out, setting in motion, urging, inciting, activity, action, the sense of the causal verb,

prerita mfn urged, impelled, dispatched, sent, turned, directed (as the eye), incited to speak, passed, spent (time),

√*preṣ* 712/3 *(pra*√*iṣ)* 1. cl1. A *preṣate* to go, move,
2. *preṣyati* to drive on, urge, impel, direct, to invite, summon, call upon, caus. *preṣayati* to hurl, cast, throw, to turn or direct the eyes, to send forth, dismiss, dispatch, send into exile, banish, to send word, DP in *gati* going,
3. f. pressing, pressure,

preṣaṇa n. the act of sending etc, charge, commission, rendering a service,

preṣita mfn set in motion, urged on, impelled, sent into exile, directed, dispatched on an errand, sent forth,

preṣṭha mfn dearest, most beloved or desired, very fond of, very pleasant, m. a lover, husband, f.(*ā*) a mistress, wife,

preṣya gve. to be sent, m. a servant, menial, slave, n. servitude,behest, command,

preṣyajan m.pl. servants (collectively), household,

preṣyati he sends

preta 711/3 mfn. departed, dead, a dead person, deceased, vampire, goblin, ghost, the spirit of a dead person, an evil being, *pra*√*i*

pretya 712/1 ind. having died, after death, in the next world, hereafter, having desisted, desisting, departing, having departed,

pretyabhāva m. the state after death, future life,

preyas mfn dearer, more agreeable, more desired, m. a lover, a dear friend,

√*prī* 701/1, 709/3 1. Cl 9P A *prīṇāti prīṇīte,*
Cl 4 A *prīyate (ti), priyate (ti),* to please, gladden, delight, gratify, cheer, comfort, soothe, propitiate, to like, love, be kind to, (mostly A. *prīyate*) to be pleased or satisfied with, delight in, enjoy, caus. *prīṇayati, prāpayati, prāyayati* to please, delight, gratify, propitiate, to refresh, comfort,
DP in *prīṇana* (Cl 4) being satisfied, pleased, in *tarpaṇa* (Cl 10) pleasing, or *kānti* (Cl 9) being cheerful or gay,
2. mfn kind, delighted,

prīṇana 711/1 mfn pleasing, gratifying, appeasing, soothing, delighting , n. a means of or the act of pleasing, gratifying, delighting

prīta 711/1 beloved, dear to, delighted, satisfied, joyful, glad, kind (as speech), n. jest, mirth, pleasure,

prītacitta mfn delighted at heart,

prītamanās or *–manas* or *mānasa* mfn whose mind is cheerful, gladdened in mind

prīti 711/1 f pleasurable sensation, pleasure, joy, gratification, gladness personified, satisfaction, friendly disposition, kindness, favour, grace, love, affection, amity, attachment, (with 7th or ifc. or with ind.p.) joy at having done anything,

prītimat mfn satisfied, gratified, having love or affection for, affectionate, kind, having pleasurable sensations, loving, pleased, favourable, glad,

prītipūrvakam ind. kindly, affectionately

prītivacas n. friendly words or talk,

prītyā ind. ina state of joyful excitement, gladly, with joy, in a friendly way, amicably,

priya 710/1 mfn beloved, dear to, devoted to, 2. desired, pleasant, agreeable,
priyaṁ kṛ do a favour,
n. that which is desired, one's wish, to which one is attached, own, agreeably, kindly, in a friendly way, love, kindness, favour, pleasure, loving, willingly, joy derived on seeing a beloved object (U),
m. a friend, lover, husband, son-in-law, kind of deer,
f. (*ā*) a mistress, wife, the female of an animal, news,
(*am*) ind. agreeably, kindly, in a pleasant way,
ifc. fond of, pleasant,

priyā f. the beloved, the wife,

priyacikīrṣā 710/1 f. the desire of doing a kindness to, or serving

priyakṛttama mfn the best accomplisher of what is dear (comparative), doing that which pleases most,

prīyamāṇa mfn being delighted, joyous pres/pass/part

prīyamāṇāya to the delighting one, to the one who is beloved
pres/mid/part 4/s/m

priyaṅgu m.f. a creeping plant,

priyāpriya n. comfort and discomfort,

priyasakhī f. a dear female friend,

priyatara mfn dearer, more pleasing, (comparative)

priyavādin mfn saying pleasant things, a flatterer,

√*pṛj,* √*pṛñj* 645/2 Cl 2 A *pṛkte, pṛṅkte* = *pṛc* to mix, mingle, put together with, to fill, sate, satiate, togive lavishly, grant bountifully, to increase, augment, DP in *varṇa* tingeing, dyeing, colouring,

√*pṛṇ* 645/2 Cl 6 P *pṛṇati,* see √*pṝ,*
to fill (A. oneself), to fill with air, blow into, to sate, cherish, nourish, to refresh, to grant abundantly, to fulfill, to fill with wind, blow a conch, to make complete, cover completely, to spend completely (a period of time),
DP in *prīṇana* delighting,

procyamāna proclaimed, explained, pres/pass/part. *pra* √*vac*

procyate it is said, declared or stated 1/s/pres/indic/pass *pra* √*vac*

prodita mfn spoken out, uttered,

prokta 690/2 mfn. announced, told, said, ppp. *pra* √*vac*

prokta mfn announced, told, said, spoken, meaning,having been spoken of, called, signifying (with 7th),
(*e*) ind. it having been announced,

proktakārin mfn doing what one has been told,

proktavān declaring, having declared, perf/act/part 1/s/m *pra* √*vac*

proktavat mfn one who has said or declared

proṣita mfn one who has set out on a journey, absent from home, abroad, set (the sun), dead,

proṣṭha m. bed or couch, bench, stool, a bull,

proṣṭhe-śaya mfn lying on a couch,

proṣya ind. having set out, abroad, absent, 2. mfn roaming, wandering,

prota 713/2 mfn sewed, strung on, fixed on or in, contained in , set, inlaid, interwoven, m.n. woven cloth, clothes,

√*proth* 713/3 Cl 1 P A *prothati (te*) to be equal to or a match for, be able to withstand, P. to be full, to destroy, subdue, overpower, DP in *paryāpti* being equal to, being a match for,

provāca taught, expounded, said, spoke, answered, described,

√*pṝ* 648/1 Cl 9 P *pṛṇāti,* Cl 6 P *priṇati,* Cl 3 P A *piparti (te*?), to fill (A oneself), to fill with air, blow into, to sate, cherish, nourish, bring up, to refresh, grant abundantly, bestow on, present with, fulfil, satisfy (a wish), to fill –with a noise or wind, blow a conch, draw a bow, make full, complete, cover completely, overspread, bestrew, surround, to load or enrich or present with, to spend completely (a period of time), DP in *pālana* (Cl 3,9) nourishing, *pūraṇa*(Cl 3,9,10)

√*pṛṣ* 647/2 Cl 1 P *parṣati* to sprinkle, to weary, to vex or hurt, to give, Cl 1 A *parṣate* to become wet, DP in *secana* sprinkling,

pṛṣad-ājya n. speckled butter, *ghee* clotted with curds,

pṛṣant mfn speckled,

pṛśni mfn speckled, dapple,

pṛṣṭa 647/3 mfn (having been) asked, inquired, questioned, demanded, wished for, n. a question, inquiry,

pṛṣṭha a ridge, the back or rear of an animal, the upper side, surface, ‘standing forth prominently’ , the heights, top (of a hill or palace),

pṛṣṭha-māṁsa n. back-flesh,

pṛṣṭhatas ind. from behind, with the back, with averted face, m. at the back (with6th),

pṛṣṭvā ind. having asked,

pṛt f. fight, battle,

pṛtanā f. battle, contest, strife, pl. men, mankind, n. an army or a hostile encounter,

√*pṛth* 645/3 Cl 10 P *parthayati* to extend, DP in *prakṣepa* throwing, casting, 2. see *pṛthā*

pṛthā m. the flat or palm of the hand, a partic. measure – tip of the fingers to the knuckles,

pṛthag see *pṛthak*

pṛthagbhāva m. difference, separate state or condition, distinctness, individuality, ‘their nature of being essentially dissimilar to the nature of the Self that is .. pure absolute and consciousness alone’, (Gam.)

pṛthagjana m. blockhead, low man, common people, villain, vulgar man, fool, low person, multitude,

pṛthagvāda who talk of a multiplicity of things, i.e dualistic,

pṛthak ind. widely apart, separately, differently, singly, severally, one by one, without, except, for

one's self,
pṛthak pṛthak one by one, in turn,
pṛthaktvena 645/3 singly, one by one
pṛthivī f. 646/1 the earth or wide world, 'the broad and extended One', land, ground, soil, earth regarded as one of the elements,
pṛthivīkṣit mfn earth-ruling, m. prince,
pṛthivīpāla m. keeper of the earth,
pṛthivīpati m. lord of the earth, king,
pṛthu mfn wide, broad, expansive, extensive, large, great, important, numerous, manifold, prolix, detailed, smart, clever, dextrous,
pṛtsu f. in one place
pṛthagbhāva 646/1separate state or existence, individuality
pṛthagvādin mfn each saying something different
pṛthagvidha 646/1 of diverse kinds, existing in many forms, manifold, various
pṛthak 645/3 ind. widely apart, separately, separately, severally, without,(+5th)
pṛthak pṛthak one by one, in turn,
pṛthaktā f. or –tva n. separateness, severalty, singleness, individuality,
pṛthaktvena 645/3 ind. singly, one by one
pṛthivi m.(f. = *vī*, n.= *tva*) the state or condition of the earth,
pṛthivī 646/1 the earth or wide world, earth regarded as one of the subtle or gross elements having the quality of smell; land, ground, soil,
pṛthivīkṣit mfn earth-ruling, m. (*as*) a king,
pṛthivīpāla m. earth-protector, a king,
pṛthu mfn broad, wide, expansive, m. fire, a measure of length,
pṛthvī 647/1f. the earth, an element,
√pru 711/3 A *pravate* to spring up, caus. *prāvayati* to reach to, DP in *gati* going, jumping,
√pruṣ 1. Cl 5 P A *pruṣṇoti, pruṣṇute* to sprinkle, shower, wet, moisten, Cl 10 P A *pruṣāyati (te)*, Cl 9 P *pruṣṇāti*, to become wet, fill, 3. Cl 1 P to burn DP in *dāha* burning, DP in *snehana* anointing, *secana* becoming wet or moist, or *pūraṇa* pouring out, filling,
√psā 715/3 1. Cl 2 P *psāti* to chew, swallow, eat, consume, to go, DP in *bhakṣaṇa* eating, 2. f. eating, food, hunger,
pu mfn cleaning, purifying,
√pū 640/3 Cl 9 P A *punāti punīte* A, Cl 1 A *pavate* to make clean or clear, or pure or bright, cleanse, purify, purge, clarify, illustrate, illume, metaphysically – to sift, discriminate, discern, to think of or out, invent, compose, (as a hymn), (with *saktum*) to cleanse from chaff, winnow, (with *kratum* or *manīṣām* 'to enlighten the understanding', A. *pavate* to purify oneself, be or become clear or bright, DP in *pavana* cleansing, purifying,
pū mfn cleansing, purifying, drinking, in cpds. purifying,
puccha n. a tail, the hinder part, extreme end (as of a year),
√puḍ 631/3 Cl 6 P *puḍati* to leave, quit, Cl 1 P *poḍati* to grind, pound, DP in *utsarge*, leaving, quitting,
pudgala mfn beautiful, lovely, handsome, m. the body, material object (including atoms) (Jainas), the soul, personal entity, man, the ego or individual, a horse (coloured like rock-crystal)
pūga m. betel-palm, betel nut, an assmbly, country court, a multitude, number, mass, disposition, property, nature,
√pūj 641/1 Cl 10 P A *pūjayati (te)*, Cl 1 P *pūjati* to honour, worship, revere, respect, regard, to honour or present with, to initiate, consecrate, DP in *pūjā* veneration, reverence,
pūjā 641/1 f. honour, worship, respect, reverence, veneration, homage
pūjaka mfn honouring, respecting, worshipping, a worshipper,

pūjana 641/1 n. reverencing, honouring, worship,respect, attention, hospitable reception

pūjanīya gve. to be honoured, revered, worshipped, venerable, honourable,

pūjārī a temple priest,

pūjayitvā ind. having honoured,

pūjita 641/2 mfn. honoured, received or treated respectfully, worshipped, adored,

pūjya mfn worthy of worship, to be worshipped, honoured,gve.
m. an honourable man, father-in-law

√*pul* 638/1 Cl 1.6.10. P *polati, pulati, polayati,* to be great or large or high, to be piled or heaped up, DP in *mahattva* being great, being lofty,

√*pūl* 645/1 Cl 1.10 P *pūlati pūlayati* to collect, gather, DP in *saṅghāta* heaping up, collecting,

pulakā m. bristling hair (pl.) (through pleasure rather than fear),

pulkasa m. one of a despised mixed tribe,

pumāṁ m. man, a male,

puman m. a man, a person, the Absolute Person,

puṁgava m. a bull, chief of, eminent person, hero, kind of drug,

puṁliṅga n. masculine gender, the penis, consciousness, the essence of man, man; power to beget, set in motion; the powerful; generation, mfn having the mark of a man, (in gram.) being masculine,

√*puṁs* 630/3 Cl 10 *puṁsayati* to crush, grind, DP in *abhi-vardhana* crushing, grinding, troubling,
2. m. a man, a male being, (in gram.) a masculine word, a human being, a servant, attendant, the soul, spirit, spirit of man,

√*puṇ* 631/3 Cl 6 P *puṇati* to act piously or virtuously, Cl 10 P *poṇayati* to collect, accumulate, DP in *karman-śubha* being virtuous or holy, acting in a virtuous manner, in *saṅghāta* collecting,

punaḥ see *punar,*

punaḥprāpti f. 'gaining again' regaining,

punaḥsara mfn coming back (as a ghost from the other world), ghostly, running back,

punar (or *punaḥ)* ind. 1. back, home,
with *ā-gam* -go back,
with *vac* -reply,
2. again, anew, further, moreover,
3. but, on the other hand,
punaḥ punaḥ (punaḥ punar) again and again, *kim punas tu* but what besides, how much more?
punar api yet again, once more,
punarukta mfn reiterated, said again,

punarbhava, 633/3 adj. born, new birth, transmigration, m. fingernail,

punargarbhavatī mfn, f. pregnant again,

punarjanma n. rebirth

√*puṇḍ* 631/3 Cl 1 P *puṇḍati* to rub, grind, reduce to powder, DP in *khaṇḍana* crushing, grinding, powdering,

puṇḍarīka a lotus flower, a white lotus, a mark on the fore-head, a white umbrella,

puṅgava bull, hero, best, most eminent,

√*puṇṭ* 631/3 Cl 10 P *puṇṭayati* to speak or to shine, DP in *bhāṣā* speaking, shining,

√*punth* 634/1 Cl 1 P *punthati* to give or suffer pain, DP in *hiṁsā* injuring, hurting, and *saṁkleśana* causing pain,

puṇya 632/1 mfn. auspicious, propitious, good, right, merit, essence of good action, n. (ifc. f.*ā*) the good or right, virtue, purity, good work, meritorious act, moral or religious merit,

puṇyagandha mfn of good or pleasant smell, fragrant,

puṇyamati m. virtuously inclined, (U)

puṇyapāpa n.pl. good and bad deeds,

puṇyāpuṇya virtue and vice, merit & demerit,

puṇyaśloka mfn of good fame, m. epithet of Nala,

puṉs 630/3 a man, a male being, a masculine

word, a human being, = *puṁs*

√*pur* Cl 6 P *purati* to precede, go before, lead, DP in *agra gaman* going in front

pur f. 1. fullness, in abundance, abundantly 2. a rampart, wall, stronghold, fortress, city, castle, town, the body (considered as the stronghold of the city), the intellect,

√*pūr* 636/1 in comp. for √*pur* above before consonant, DP in *āpyāyana* filling, satisfying,

pura n. stronghold, fortified town, city, citadel, the female apartments, a house, abode, residence, receptacle, an upper story, a brothel, the body, the skin, a leaf rolled into the shape of a funnel, mfn a kind of resin, f. (*ī*) a stronghold, fortress,

purā 634/3 ind. long ago, before, formerly, of old, in a previous existence, at first, in the beginning, in the East, in front, formerly, once upon a time, except, beside,

pūra mfn filling, making full, satisfying, m. a large quantity of water, flood, the swelling of a river or the sea, a cake, a breath exercise, the cleansing of a wound, the citron tree,

puraḥsara mfn going before, m. forerunner, pre-cursor, harbinger, attendant, ifc. having ... as forerunner, accompanied by ...

pūraka mfn filling, completing, fulfilling, satisfying, m. flood stream, effusion, (in arithm.) the multiplier, a citron tree, a yogic exercise- closing the right nostril with the forefinger and then drawing in air with the left and then closing the left nostril and drawing in air through the right, *pūraka-kumbhaka-recaka* inhaling, retaining and then exhaling

purāṇa 635 mfn belonging to ancient times, ancient, a class of sacred works, legends, history, science, study, discussions,a measure of silver,

pūraṇa 642/1 filling, completely satisfying, causing, effecting, equipping, m. a dam, bridge, the sea, an embrocation, fulfilling, satisfying, furnishing, equipping, rain, a sort of cake, fully drawing a bow (with *dhanuṣa*), n. the act of filling or filling up, puffing or swelling up,

puras ind. in front, forward, before, at first, in the presence or before the eyes of (2nd, 5th, 6th or comp.), with *kṛ* put in front, before, with *dhā* put in front or in charge esp. of priestly duties,

puraścaraṇa mfn preparatory to, making preparations, n. preparatory or introductory rite, preparation, a repetition of mantra rite,

puraskartum infin. to put in front, appoint, enlist,

puraskārya gve. to be appointed or commissioned,

puras kṛ to place in front or at the head,

puraskṛta mfn placed in front, honoured, esteemed, attacked, accused, led,

purastāt ind. before, forward, in or from the front, in the first place, in or from the East, Eastward, above,

puratas ind. before (in place or time), in front or in presence of (with 6th or in comp.)

purātana 635/1 mfn. belonging to the past, former, old, ancient, m.pl. the ancients, n. an ancient story, legend,

purī f. citadel, fortress, city, castle,

purīṣa n. crumbling earth, loose earth, dirt, excrement,

puriśaya 636/1 mfn reposing in the fortress or fastness, i.e. the body,

purīṣotsarga voiding of waste, faeces,

purītat m. intestines, pericardium or an organ near the heart, a subtle passage in the body,

pūrṇa 642/1 mfn full, filled with, fulfilling, satisfying, complete, perfect, satisfied, contented, n. fullness, plenty, abundance,

pūrṇamāsa m. full-moon and the full-moon sacrifice,
pūrṇayogin m. a full yogi,
pūrṇimā f. the night or day of full moon, an auspicious time,
pūrṇo'ham I am full, perfect, absolute, infinite, Brahman,
purodhas 635/2 'placed at the head' chief priest of a king,
purogama mfn going before, m. leader, ifc. having .... as leader,
purogava m. lead bull, fore-bull, leader,
purohita mfn set before or in charge esp. of priestly service, m. priest, house-priest of a prince, an agent,
pūrta 642/3 mfn filled, full, complete, completed, perfected, covered, concealed, n. fulfilling, fulfillment, granting, rewarding, a reward, merit, a meritorious work, keeping, guarding, an act of pious liberality e.g. feeding a brāhman, or digging a well,
pūrti f. filling, completion, ending, coming to an end, granting, rewarding, reward, satiety, satisfaction,
puru mfn much, many, abundant, (with *simā*) everywhere, (with *siras)* far off, from afar, m. flower pollen, heaven, paradise,
purūci mfn, f. many, abundant, long,
purūravas an ancient king, mfn crying much or loudly,
puruṣa 637/1 m. the soul and original source of the universe, the Supreme Being, person, "the light of the *ātman* illuminating the *antaḥkarana* (mind)." L.M. one who lives in the city i.e. in the *antaḥkarana,* '...There is nothing higher than the *puruṣa*. He is the culmination. He is the highest goal'. HH 'The truth of existence is that the *puruṣa* or *ātman* is the Absolute: within this the universe has its existence.' HH, L. 1. man, 2. servant, 3. see above
puruṣakāra m. deed of a man, human effort (as opposed to *daiva* fate), (in gram.) person *prathamaḥ* first, *madhyamaḥ* second (middle), *uttamaḥ* third
puruṣārtha 'spiritual endeavour' – HH '.. the efforts he will make to realise himself'
puruṣārtha 637/3 spiritual endeavour, any object of human pursuit, any one of the 4 aims or pursuits of existence,
kāma -gratification of desire,
artha - acquirement of wealth,
dharma - discharge of duty or virtue,
mokṣa final emancipation)
m. 7/s in the goal of life
puruṣasiṁha m. man-lion, stout-hearted man,
puruṣavidha 637/2 mfn man-like, having a human form,
puruṣavyāghra m. a man-tiger, a man like a tiger, a brave, courageous man ,
puruṣottama 637/3 highest among men or spirits
purutrā ind. in many places, often,
√*purv* 638/1 Cl 1 P *pūrvati* to fill, Cl 10 *pūrvayati* to dwell, DP in *pūraṇa* filling,
pūrva 643/1 mfn. former, prior, before, East, being before or in front, preceding, previous to, to the east of, eastern, m. an ancestor, forefather, pl. ancients or ancestors, an elder brother, (*am*) ind. before, the day before, formerly +7th,
pūrvabhava 644/1 a former life
pūrvajanman n. former birth, previous state of existence, m. elder brother,
pūrvaka mfn preceding, ealier, former, m. a forefather, ancestor,
pūrvākṣara mfn with the preceding letter,
Pūrva- mīmāṁsā see *mīmāṁsā*
pūrvaniketana dwelling in the past,
pūrvapakṣa prior viewpoint, the objector's or opponent's view in a formal argument, the first objection to an

assertion, anti-thesis, prima facie view,
pūrveṣita 644/3 mfn known from former times, former
pūrvya mfn ancient, former, previous, next, nearest, most excellent, ind. before, formerly, at first, long since, hitherto,
√*puṣ* 1. 638/2 Cl 4 P *puṣyati* to divide, distribute,
2. Cl 1 P *poṣati* to be nourished, to thrive, flourish, prosper, to cause to thrive or prosper, augment, increase, further, promote, fulfil e.g. a wish, develop, unfold, display, gain, obtain, enjoy, possess, caus. *poskayati* to rear, nourish, feed, cause to prosper, A, AA
DP in *puṣṭi* nourishing, fostering, *dhāraṇa* preserving, protecting, ,
3. mfn ifc. nourishing, causing to thrive, showing, displaying,
√*pūṣ* 645/1 = 2. √*puṣ* Cl 1 P *pūṣati* to nourish, increase, DP in *vṛddhi* nourishing increasing,
pūṣā f. the sun, nourisher
pūṣan a Vedic deity, surveyor of the universe, protector of the universe, the sun, growth, increase, the earth,
puṣkala mfn much, abundant, copious, many, excellent, magnificent, numerous, best, powerful, full,
puṣkara n. blue lotus
puṣṇāmi √*puṣ* 638/2 I thrive or flourish
puṣpa 639/2 n. a flower, blossom, *-ika* suffix- pertaining or relating to offerings as of flowers,
puṣpāmoda m. fragrance of flowers,
puṣpadanta m. name of an attendant of *śiva*
puṣpita mfn flowered, bearing flowers, in bloom,
√*puṣpya* 640/2 Nom P °*yati* to bear flowers, flower, blossom, bloom, DP in *vikasana* blossoming,
√*pust* 640/3 Cl 10 P *pustayati* to respect or disrespect, to bind, DP in *ādara* regarding, respecting, noticing, *anādara* disrespecting or condemning,
puṣṭa mfn well fed, fat, having thrived, strong, nourished, cherished, rich in, blessed with, full-sounding, n. growth, increase, gain, wealth, acquisition, property,
pustaka mfn manuscript, book, booklet, m.n. a protuberant ornament, boss,
puṣṭāṅga mfn fat-limbed, well-fed, fat,
puṣṭi 639/1 f. well nourished condition, fatness, growth, increase, prosperity, wealth, comfort, completeness, nourishment,
pustikā f. an oyster, a book,
puṣṭikara mfn causing to thrive or grow,
√*puṭ* 631/2 Cl 6 P *puṭati* to clasp, fold, envelope in, rub together with..,
Cl 1 P *poṭati* to grind, pound, Cl 10 P *puṭayati* to be in contact with, *poṭayati* to speak or shine, to grind or pound, to be small,
DP in *mardana* (Cl 1) crushing, breaking, killing, in *saṁsleśaṇa* (Cl 6) embracing, clasping, intertwining, in *saṁsarga* (Cl 10) composing, putting together, in *bhāṣā* (Cl 10) speaking, shining,
puṭa m.n. fold, cavity, pocket, slit, concavity, a cloth worn to cover the genitals (also *ī*), a horses hoof, an eyelid, m. a cup or basket made of leaves, a casket, enveloping or wrapping for cooking, a cake or pastry filled with stuffing, n. a nutmeg,
pūta 640/3 mfn. cleaned, purified, pure, clear, bright, m. a conch shell, white *kuśa* grass, du. the buttocks,
pūtanā a demoness, a children's disease,
√*puth* 633/2 Cl 4 P *puthyati* to hurt, caus. *pothayati* A P to crush, kill, destroy, to overpower or drown (one sound by another), to speak or to shine, DP in *hiṁsā* hurting, killing, in *bhāṣā* speaking, shining,
pūti 641/1 1.f. purity, purification
2. 641/3 mfn putrid, foul-smelling

m. purulent matter, pus, civet,

pātibhāva m. putrid state, stench,

putra 632/2 m. a son, child. 2. a whelp,

putradāra n. son and wife,

putraka m. 1. little son (as term of endearment), child,

putrī f. daughter, doll or puppet,

putrikā f. daughter, doll,

√*puṭṭ* 631/3 Cl 10 P *puṭṭayati* to be or become small, diminish, DP in *alpībhāva* be or become small, diminish,

puttikā f. white ant, a doll, puppet,

√*pūy* 641/ 3 Cl 1 P *pūyati* A *pūyate* to become foul or putrid, stink, DP in *viśaraṇa* splitting up, in *durgandha* stinking, putrefying,

√*pyai* 652/2 or pyāy Cl 1 A *pyāyate* to swell,be exuberant, overflow, DP in *vṛddhi* training to grow, swelling, increasing,

√*pyāy* 652/2 see *pyai*, DP in *vṛddhi* growing large,

√*ṛ* 223/2 Cl 1.3.5. P *ṛcchati, iryati, ṛnoti, ṛṇvati*, to go, move, rise, tend upwards, go towards, meet with, fall upon or into, reach, obtain, to fall to one's share, occur, befall, to advance towards a foe, attack, invade, hurt, offend, move, excite, erect, raise, cast through, pierce, caus. *arpayati* to transfer, hand over, DP in (cl1) *gati, prāpaṇa*, (Cl 3) in *gati*, (Cl 5) in *hiṁsā*

√*ṝ* not listed, DP in *gati* going

ra mfn acquiring, possessing, giving, effecting, m. fire, heat, love, desire, speed, giving, gold,

√*rā* 871/2 (or *rās*) Cl 2 P A *rāti, (te*), to grant, give, bestow, impart, yield, surrender, DP in *dāna* giving, granting,

rā f. amorous play, ifc. granting, bestowing,

√*rabh* 867/1 (or *rambh)*Cl 1 A *rabhate, (ti), rambhate (ti),* to take hold of, grasp, clasp, embrace, to desire vehemently, to act rashly, DP in *rābhasya* longing for, being eager, embracing,

rabhasa m. violence, impetuosity, energy, rapid, fierce, wild, hurry, haste, speed, passion, mfn impetuous, violent, ifc. eager for, desirous of,

rābhasya 877/1 n. velocity, impetuosity, delight, joy, pleasure

√*rac* 860/3 Cl 10 P *racayati* to produce, fashion, form, make, construct, complete, cause, effect, to compose, write, to place in or on, to adorn, decorate, cause to make or do, cause to move (a horse), DP in *pratipatna* arranging, preparing, making ready,

racana n. preparing, dressing the hair, arrangement, wearing, literary production, composition,

racanā f. creation, order, production, composition, performance, construction (math.),

racita mfn furnished, arranged, prepared, occupied with, engaged in, made of, provided, produced, invented,

√*rad* 866/2 Cl 1 P A *radati (te*) to scratch, scrape, gnaw, bite, rend, dig, break, split, divide, to cut, open (a road or path), lead (a river into a channel), to convey to, bestow on, give, dispense, DP in *vilekhana* splitting, rending, gnawing, digging,

√*radh* 866/3 or *randh* Cl 4 P *radhyati* to become subject to, be subdued or overthrown, succumb, to be completed or matured, to bring into subjection, subdue, to hurt, torment, caus. *randhayati* to make subject, deliver over to, torment, afflict, annihilate, to cook, prepare food, DP in *hiṁsā* injuring or *saṁrāddhi* success, accomplishment,

√*rādh* 876/2 Cl 5.4. P *rādhnoti, rādhyati, rādhati, rādhyate* to succeed (said of things to be accomplished or finished), to succeed (said of persons), be successful, thrive, prosper, be ready for, submit to, be fit for, partake of, attain to, to accomplish, achieve, perform, make ready, prepare, to propitiate, conciliate, gratify, hurt, injure, exterminate, DP in *vṛddhi* (Cl 4) prospering, *saṁsiddhi* completing, finishing,

rādhas n. gracious gift, blessing, success,

√rag 860/2 Cl 1 P *ragati* to doubt, suspect, *āsvādana* tasting, Cl 10 P *rāgayati* DP (Cl 1) in *śaṅkā* doubting, (Cl 10)

rāga 872/1 m. the act of colouring or dyeing, colour, hue, tint, red colour, redness, inflammation, attachment, any feeling or passion, love, affection or sympathy for, vehement desire of, beauty, loveliness, interest in, greed, a musical note, harmony, melody, a partic musical mode or order of sound or formula, seasoning, condiment,

rāga-dveṣa m. likes and dislikes for particulars, love and hatred,

rāgātmaka mfn impassioned, composed of or characterised by passion

rāgavān perf. part. attached

√ragh 860/2 = *√rak*

√rāgh 872/2 Cl 1 A *rāghate* to be able or competent, 2. an able or efficient person, DP in *sāmarthya* sufficing, being able,

rāghava m. descendant of Raghu,

raghu 1.mfn running, darting, swift, m. runner, 2. m. Raghu the runner, name of an ancient king, ancestor of Rāma,

rāgīṇī f. modification of the musical mode called *rāga,*

√rah 871/1 Cl 1 P *rahati* to part, separate, leave, quit, abandon, Cl 10 P to leave, abandon, to cause to give up or abandon, DP in *tyāga* quitting, abandoning,

rahas 871/1 n. loneliness, secrecy, solitude, a secret, mystery, mystical truth, sexual intercourse, swiftness, speed, velocity, ind. secretly,

rahasi n. privacy, solitude, secrecy, loneliness, solitude, a secret, mystery, copulation,

rahasya 871/2mfn. secret, private, concealed,

rahita 871/2 ppp. left, forsaken, deserted, lonely, solitary, separated or free from, devoid of,

rāhu m. 'the seizer' Rahu is supposed to swallow the sun and moon causing eclipses,

rāhukāla inauspicious time,

√rai 888/1 Cl 1 P *rāyati* to bark, bark at, DP in *śabda* sounding,

rai m.f. possessions, wealth, prosperity, barking, sound, noise,

√rāj 872/3 1. Cl 1 P A *rājati (te)* to reign, be king or chief, rule over, direct, govern, be illustrious or resplendent, shine, glitter, to appear as or like, caus. *rājayati (te)* to reign, rule, to illuminate, make radiant, DP in *dīpti* shining, 2. ifc. shining, radiant, m. a king, sovereign, chief, anything the best of its kind,

rāja ifc. for *rājan* m. a king, sovereign, chief or best of its kind,

rājabhavana n. a king's abode, royal palace,

rājadvāra n. king' door, a palace door,

rājadhānī a king's residence, capital,

rājagṛham n. a palace, royal residence,

rajaka m. washerman, also a dyer of clothes,

rājakanyā f. kind of flower, a princess,

rājakārya n. a king's duty or business, state affairs,

rāja-kula n. 1. royal family, (in pl. princes), a royal palace or court,

rājaloka m. an assembly of kings or royalty,

rājan m. 1. king, prince, 2. equiv. to *rājanya,* a *kṣatriya* or man of the military caste, royal,

rājanya mfn royal, princely, m. one of royal race, a noble, oldest designation of a man of the second caste,

rājapuruṣa m. king's man, servant of a

king, a royal official,

rājaputra a prince,

rājarṣi a royal sage or seer,

rajas 863/2 one of the three guṇāḥ "the force of motion within *prakṛti*" HH. including the qualities of activity, urgency, and variability, passion, movement, energy , L. 1. atmosphere, air, region of clouds, vapours and gloom, 2. thick air, mist, gloom, darkness, 3. dust,

rajasa mfn pertaining to *rajas,* passionate, mfn unclean, dusty, dark, living in the dark, f.(ī) ifc. menstrual excretion,

rājasa mfn belonging or relating to the quality *rajas,* endowed with or influenced by the quality of passion, passionate,

rājasika 875/2 mfn belonging or relating to the quality *rajas*, endowed with or influenced by the quality of passion, passionate,

rājasūya n. lotus flower, mountain, kind of rice, a partic. great sacrifice,

rajata 863/1 mfn silvery, made of silver

rājate √*rāj* 872/3 reigns, shines, appears or looks like, illuminates, he she or it shines, 872/3 he reigns, directs, rules, 1/s/pres/indic/mid

rājavat ind. like a king, as towards a king, having a king, having a bad king,

rājayoga 873/3 a constellation under which princes are born, an easy way of meditation, 'the royal way to total unity' HH

rājendra m. best or chief of kings, supreme sovereign,

rājī f. a streak, line, row, black mustard

rajju 861/1 m. f. rope, cord, string, line, a braid of hair, partic. sinews or tendons in the back,

rajjusarpa *rajju* a rope, *sarpa* 1184/1 a snake, a rope -snake, a snake in a rope, a rope seen as a snake

rajjusarpanyāya the analogy of the snake and the rope used to illustrate the appearance of the world in Brahman

rājñī f. queen, princess, ruler, deep-coloured or yellow-red brass,

rajoguṇamaya n. a quality of the universe, having the quality of *rajas*

rajohīna mfn devoid of dust, dustless,

rājya 875/1 mfn kingly, princely, royal, n. kingdom, royalty, kingship, sovereignty, country, realm,

rājyam +*kṛ* reigns

√*rak* 859/3 Cl 10 P *rākayati* to taste, relish, to obtain, get, DP in *āsvādana* tasting,

√*rakh* 860/2 Cl 1 P *rakhati* to go, move, DP in *gati* going

√*rākh* 872/1 Cl 1 P *rākhati* to be dry or to suffice, DP in *śoṣaṇa* drying up, or in *alam* being sufficient,

√*rakṣ* 859/3 Cl 1 P *rakṣati (te*), to guard, watch, take care of, protect, save, preserve, to tend (cattle), to rule (the earth or a country), to keep a secret, to spare, have a regard for other's feelings, observe laws or duties, guard against, ward off, keep away, prevent, frustrate, injure, be wary of, A. to heed, attend to, A. to conceal, hide, caus. *rakṣayati (te*) to guard, watch, save, DP in *pālana* protecting,

rakṣa protect! 859/3 guarding, watching, protecting, a watcher, 860/1 an evil being or demon

rakṣā 860/1 f. protection, the act of protecting or guarding, care, preservation, security, a guard, watch, sentinel,

rakṣaka mfn guarding, watching, protecting, a watcher, keeper, protector, guardian,

rakṣaṇa 859/3 m. protector, f. guarding, protection, n. the act of guarding, watching, protecting, preservation

rakṣas mfn guarding, watching, n. harm, damage, demon, harmer, evil being, injury, anything to be guarded against or warded off, name of nocturnal demons who disturb sacrifices and harm the pious,

rākṣasa m. cruel man-eating ogre

rākṣasī female of above

rakṣati protects, saves

rakṣi mfn ifc. guarding,

rakṣika m. protector,

rakṣita mfn saved

rakṣitṛ m. protector, watcher,

rakta mfn coloured, reddened, n. blood,

√*ram* 867/2 cl1 A *ramate (-ti),* P *ramati or ramṇāti* to stop, stay, make fast, calm, set at rest, to delight, make happy, A. to stand still, rest, abide, like to stay with, be glad or pleased, rejoice at, delight in, be fond of, to play or sport, dally, have sexual intercourse with, DP in *krīḍā* playing, sporting, delighting,

rāma m. 'causing rest',dark, dark-coloured, black, pleasant, beautiful, *Rāmaḥ*

rāmā a beautiful woman, a woman, a dark woman, vermillion

ramaṇīya to be enjoyed, pleasant, agreeable, delightful, charming,

rāmanīyaka mfn lovely, beautiful,pleasing, n. loveliness, beauty, charm,

rāmānuja founder of *Viśiṣṭādvaita* (quailified non-duality) Vedānta School,

ramate 867/2 delights, 1/s/pres/indic/mid rejoices at, stand still, rests,

rāmavat like *Rāmaḥ*

rāmāyaṇa the story of *rāmaḥ* an epic poem,

√*ramb* 868/2 Cl 1 A *rambate* to hang down, 2. to sound DP in *śabda* sounding

√*rambh* 868/2 1. see *rabh*
2. Cl 1 A *rambhate*, to sound, roar, DP in *śabda* sounding, bellowing, lowing,

rambha 867/2 a prop, staff, support, a bamboo, mfn sounding, roaring, lowing,

rambhā f. banana palm, a kind of rice, a cotton string round the loins, a courtesan, sounding, roaring, lowing,

√*raṁh* 859/3 (for *raṅgh*) Cl 1 P A *raṁhati (te),* to hasten, speed, cause to go or flow, to go or flow, caus. *raṁhayati (te),* to hasten, speed, run, cause to run, Cl 10 *raṁhayati* to speak or to shine, DP (Cl 1) in *gati* moving, (Cl 10) in *āpyāyana* increasing,

raṁhas n. impetuosity, eagerness, velocity, speed, quickness,

√*ramph* 868/2 Cl 1 P *ramphati* to go, DP in *gati* going,

ramya gve. to be enjoyed, enjoyable, pleasing, delightful, beautiful, a pleasant abode, f. (*ā*) night,

√*raṇ* 2. 864/2 Cl 1 P *raṇati* to rejoice, be pleased, take pleasure in, to gladden, delight, gratify, caus. *raṇyati te,* to cheer, gladden, be at ease, exhilirate with (3rd), be pleased or satisfied with, delight in (7th),
Cl 1 P to sound, ring, rattle, jingle, caus. *raṇayati* to make resound, DP in *śabda* sounding,
3. Cl 10 P *raṇayati* to go DP in *gati* going,

raṇa 863/3 m. n. delight, gladness, combat, battle as an object of delight, combat, fight, conflict,

raṇakṣetra n. the field of battle,

randhra n. a hole,

√*raṅg* 860/3 Cl 1 P *raṅgati* to move to and fro, rock, DP in *gati* moving,

raṅga m. 1. colour, paint, dye, hue, 2. theatre, amphitheatre, audience, a dancing place, field of battle, diversion, mirth, love,

√*raṅgh* 860/3 Cl 1 A *raṅghate* to hasten, run, caus. or Cl 10 to speak, to shine, DP in *gati* going, (Cl 10) in *bhāṣā* speaking, shining,

rañj 861/2 or *raj*, Cl 1.4. P A *rajati (te), rañjati* or *rajyati (te),* to be dyed or coloured, to redden, grow red, glow, to be affected or excited or moved or glad, be charmed or delighted by, be attracted by or enamoured of, fall in love with, (*rajati °te)* to go, caus. *rajayati, rañjayati (te*), to dye, colour, paint, redden, illuminate, to rejoice, charm, gratify, conciliate, to worship, DP (Cl 1, 4) in *rāga* colouring, dyeing, reddening, feelings, passions, desire,

rañjana 863/3 mfn pleasing, delighting, rejoicing, dyeing, colouring, m. turmeric, saffron, a fragrant perfume, red arsenic, indigo plant, n. colour, giving pleasure, nasalization, act of pleasing, cinnabar, red sandalwood, act of colouring or dyeing, paint, dye, any colouring substance,

√*raṅkh* 860/3 Cl 1 P *raṅkhati* to go, move, DP in *gati* going,

√*raṇv* 864/2 Cl 1 P *raṇvati* to go DP in *gati* going

raṇva mfn pleasant, lovely, agreeable, joyous, delightful,

√*rap* 867/1 Cl 1 P *rapati* to talk, chatter, whisper, DP in *vyaktā-vāc* speaking distinctly,

rapas n. bodily defect, injury, disease,

√*raph* 867/1 Cl 1 P *raphati* to go, to injure, kill DP in *gati* going

√*ras* 1. cl1 to roar, yell, cry, sound, reverberate, to praise, *rasati* DP in *śabda* sounding

√*ras* 2. Cl 10 to taste, relish, feel, perceive, *rasayati,* DP in *āsvādana* 162/1 tasting or *snehana* 1267/3 delighting

√*rās* 879/2 1. Cl 1 A *rāsate* to howl, cry, DP in *śabda* sounding,

rasa 869/2 m. the best or finest or prime part of anything, essence, taste, flavour, a source of joy, water, liquor, drink, juice of sugar-cane, syrup,any mixture, elixir, potion, the sap or juice of plants, juice of fruit, any liquid or fluid, melted butter, milk (with *gavām),* poison (with *viṣasya*), nectar, soup, broth, mercury, semen, a mineral salt, gold, green onion, resin, the tongue, an object of taste, taste or inclination or fondness for, love, affection, desire, charm, pleasure, delight, the prevailing sentiment in human character, disposition of the heart or mind, religious sentiment (5 kinds), a name of the syllable Om, G.254 the essence of things, delight of existence, essence, taste or inclination or fondness for, desire, pleasure, flavour,

rasā f. moisture, humidity, a mythical stream round the earth and atmosphere, the lower world, hell, the earth, ground, soil, the tongue,

rāsabha m. an ass, jackass, donkey,

rasādaya 'the essence of food' (Gam.),

rasāḍhya m. abounding in juice or sap,

raśanā f. cord, strap, rein, girdle, bridle, a ray of light, beam, the tongue, ifc. girt by, dependent on,

rasanā f. sense of taste, tongue as organ of taste, n. tasting, taste, flavour, savour, the tongue as organ of taste, m. phlegm or saliva,

rasāsvāda m. appreciation, sipping of juice or perception of pleasure, enjoying the essence of *savikalpa samādhi* an obstacle on the way to *nirvikalpa samādhi*

rasātala one of seven hells, hell, earth, soil,

rasatanmātra the subtle essence of taste or flavour

rasātmakas mfn having the nature or essence of juice or flavour, consisting of nectar, characterized by sapidity or savour (as water), tasteful, elegant, charming, beautiful,

rasatyāga abstaining from taste or delights,

rasayitā f.the taster,

rāśi m. troop, host, heap, zodiac sign, division of beings, quantity, volume, mass, collection, amount,

rasika mfn tasty, graceful, aesthetic, lustful, sentimental, devoted to, fanciful, m. connoisseur, elephant, one who has a wife liable to strong feelings or emotions,f. (*ā*) chyle, molasses, tongue, emotional wife,

rasikatva n. devotion or addiction to, taste or fondness for, sense of, piling together, accumulation,

raśmi 869/2 m. a string, rope, ray of light, beam, splendour, bridle, rein,

rāṣṭra m.n. kingdom, sovereignty, a people, nation, subjects,

rāṣṭrī f. female sovereign or proprietess,

rāṣṭrīya mfn belonging to the sovereignty, m. an heir apparent or pretender, a king's brother-in-law,

rasya 871/1 mfn. juicy, tasty, savoury, n. blood,

√*raṭ* 863/3 Cl 1 P *raṭati* to howl, shout, roar, yell, cry, to crash (as an axe), ring (as a bell), lament, caus. *raṭayati* to howl, shout etc. DP in *paribhāṣaṇa* speaking much

rata 867/2 mfn pleased, amused, gratified, delighting in, devoted or attached to, fond or enamoured of, intent upon,ifc. having sex with, n. pleasure, enjoyment esp. enjoyment of love, sexual union, the genitals,

√*raṭh* 863/3 Cl 1 P *raṭhati* to speak, DP in *paribhāṣaṇa* speaking

ratha m. wagon, esp. the two-wheeled battle-wagon or chariot, 2. m. pleasure, joy,

rathika m. charioteer, valiant one, a cartwright, mfn going by chariot or carriage, the driver or owner of such

rathin mfn possessing or going in a chariot or carriage, fighting in a war-chariot, m. an owner of a carriage or chariot, charioteer, warrior who fights from a chariot, a *kṣatriya,* driver,

rathopastha m. the well of a chariot, the seat of a chariot,

rathya m. a carriage or chariot horse, n. carriage trappings, a chariot race or match, a carriage or vehicle,

rathyā f. a highway, street, road, fit for a carriage,

rati 867/3 f. comfort, pleasure, the pleasure of love, sexual passion or union, amorous enjoyment, passion, rest, repose, attachment, one of Kama's wives, the pudenda, pleasure-house,

rāti mfn ready to give or bless, generous, gracious, f. grace, gift, oblation,

ratiprīti joy derived from physical love, intense attachment and love (U),

ratna n. a gift, blessing, riches, treasure, (as something bestowed or given), a jewel, precious gem, a magnet, lode-stone, water,

ratnabhūta mfn 'become or being a jewel' jewel-like,

ratna-dhā mfn bestowing blessings, distributing riches or precious things, possessing wealth, procuring wealth,

rātra or rātri m.n.or *rātrī* 876/1 f. (*ī*) night, the darkness or stillness of night ,

ratyā f. sexual passion, sexual desire,(V)

rāvaṇa *Rāvaṇaḥ* -king of the demons

raukma mfn golden, adorned with gold,

√*rauṭ* 891/1 or *rauḍ* Cl 1?. P *rauṭati, rauḍati* to despise, treat with disrespect,

rava m. cry, yell, howl, (wild beasts); song, singing, (birds), hum, humming (bees); clamour, outcry, thunder; any noise or sound e.g. (whizz of an arrow or ring of a bell etc), 868/3

rāva m. cry, yell, howl, any sound or noise, 879/1

ravi 869/1 m. the sun or sun-god, a particular form of the sun, a mountain,

ravi-tulya-rūpaḥ having a brightness like the sun

√*ray* 868/2 Cl 1 A *rayate* to go, DP in *gati* going,

raya m. current, speed, the stream of a river, impetuosity, ardour, zeal, °*eṇa* or °*āt* ind. quickly, immediately, straightway,

rāya a prince or king,

rayi (occurs in a number of other forms), m. or f. property, goods, possessions, treasure, wealth, stuff, materials, 'food' (Gam.), mfn rich,

rāya m. at the beginning or end of a proper name used as a title of honour, = *rājan,* a prince or king, also see *arāya,*
888/1 *rās, rāyam* etc. from √*rai,* goods, wealth, riches
4/s *rāye* for the sake of wealth

rāyaspoṣa m. development i.e. increase of wealth or property or prosperity,

√*ṛc* 225/1 Cl 6 P *ṛcati* to praise, DP in *stuti* praise,

ṛc f. 1. hymn of praise, esp. one spoken rather than sung, a stanza or text referred to,

ṛca 225/2 ifc. well-regulated, metrical verse, sacred verse, ifc. for *ṛc*

√*ṛch* 225/2 Cl 6 P *ṛcchati* to be stiff, to be infatuated or foolish, to go, move, DP in *gati* going, in *indriyapralaya* failing of faculties and *mūrtibhāva* becoming hard or stiff,

ṛcchati 223/2 goes, moves, rises, reaches, obtains, goes towards, meets with, 1/s/pres/act √ *ṛ*

√*ṛdh* 226/1 Cl 6.2.4.5.7.P *ṛdhyati, ṛdhnoti, ṛdhṇadhi,* to grow, increase, prosper, succeed, to cause to increase or prosper, promote, make prosperous, accomplish, pass. *ṛdhyate* to be promoted, increase, proper, succeed, caus. *ardhayati* to satisfy, DP cl 4 and 5 - in *vṛddhi* prospering, growing, increasing,

ṛddha 226/1 mfn. increased, thriving, prosperous, abundant, wealthy, filled with (voices), made to resound, n. stored grain, a demonstrated conclusion, distinct result,

ṛddhi f. welfare, blessedness, increase, prosperity, growth, success, good fortune, abundance, accomplishment, perfection, supernatural power, magic,

re a word of address – O, Ho, often doubled,

√*rebh* cl 1 P. *rebhati,* to crackle (as fire), creak (a carriage), murmur (fluids), to chatter, talk aloud, shout, sing, praise,
DP in *śabda* sounding

recaka mfn emptying, purging, emptying the lungs, emitting the breath, part of a yogic exercise – expelling the breath out of one of the nostrils, m. the act of breathing out, a syringe, saltpetre, a kind of soil or earth, a purge, cathartic,

√*rek* 887/1 Cl 1 A *rekate* to suspect, doubt, DP in *śaṅkā* doubting, suspecting,

rekhā f.a scratch, streak, stripe, line, a continuous line, row, series, outline, drawing, sketch,

reṇu m. dust, pollen, a grain or atom of dust, sand, powder of anything,

√*rep* 887/3 Cl 1 A *repate* to go, to sound, DP in *gati* going,

repha mfn contemptible, vile, low, m. a burring sound (as bees), passion,

√*reṣ* 888/1 Cl 1 A *reṣate* to howl, roar, yell (as wolves), others to neigh or other inarticulate sounds, DP in *avyakta* manifesting and *śabda* sounding,

reṣ mfn any animal that howls or yells, or neighs, howling, neighing,

reṣaṇa n. the howl of a wolf, howling, yelling, roaring, injury, damage, mfn injuring, hurting,

√*reṭ* Cl 1 P A *reṭati (te)* to speak, ask, request, caus. *reṭayati,* DP in *paribhāṣaṇa* speaking,

retas 887/2 n. a flow, stream, current, flow of rain or water, libation, semen, flow of semen, sperm, seed, offspring, desendants, mercury, water, sin (?),

retaso'nte after the discharge of semen,

retaja mfn born from (one's own)seed, one's own or beloved (son),

√*rev* 887/3 (or *reb*), to go, move, leap, jump, DP in *plava-gati* going, jumping,

revā f. a partic.river, the indigo plant,

ṛg-veda the RigVeda each stanza of which is called a *ṛc*

√*rī* 881/2 (or *ri*) Cl 9 P *riṇāti* Cl 4 P *rīyate, riṇīte, riyati,* to release, set free, let go, to sever, detach from, to yield, bestow, A. to be shattered or dissolved, melt, become fluid, drop, flow, caus. *repayati*, DP(Cl 9) in *gati* going, *reṣaṇa* howling, (Cl 4) in *śravaṇa* trickling, dripping, distilling, flowing,

rī f. going, motion,

√*ribh* 880/3 (or *rebh)* Cl 1 P A *rebhati* to crackle like fire, to creak like a car, murmur like fluids, to chatter, talk aloud, to shout, sing, praise, DP in *śabda* sounding

√*ric* 880/2 Cl 7 P A *riṇakti, riṅkte* Cl 1 P *recati,* Cl 4 A *ricyate,*(*ti*) to empty, evacuate, leave, give up, resign, to release, set free, to sell, leave behind, supplant, DP in *virecana* (Cl 7) purging, evacuating, in *viyojana* (Cl 10) separating, or *samparcana* uniting,

ṛddha mfn prosperous, abundant, wealthy, filled with (voices), made to resound n. stored grain, a demonstrated conclusion, distinct result,

ṛddhi f. wealth, supernatural power, good fortune, perfection, success, accomplishment, increase, abundance, magic, m. growth, prosperity,

√*rih* 881/2 Cl 6.2. P *rihati, reḍhi, reḷhi,* A. *rihate*, to lick, kiss, caress, (*rihati* to praise, worship), to ask, implore, DP in *katthana* speaking, boasting, *yuddha* fighting, *nindā* reviling, blaming, *hiṁsā* hurting, killing, *dāna* giving,

√*rikh* 880/1 Cl 1 P *rekhati* to go, move, Cl 6 P. *rikhati* to scratch, scrape, DP in *gati* going,

√*riṅg* 880/1 Cl 1 P Cl 1 P *riṅgati* to move, creep, crawl, advance with difficulty or slowly, DP in *gati* going,

√*riṇv* 880/2 Cl 1 P *riṇvati* to go DP in *gati* going,

√*riph* 880/3 Cl 6 P *riphati* to snarl, to speak or boast, to blame, to fight, to give, to hurt, to kill, DP in *katthana* speaking, boasting, in uttering a rough grating sound, *yuddha* fighting, *nindā* reviling, blaming, *hiṁsā* hurting, injuring, *dāna* giving

ripra n. defilement, impurity, dirt, mfn vile, bad,

ripravāha mfn carrying off or removing impurity or sin,

ripu 880/3 mfn. deceitful, treacherous, m. an enemy, adversary, foe

√*riś* 881/1 Cl 6 P *riśati (te),* to hurt, tear, pluck off, crop, caus. *reśayati* DP in *hiṁsā* hurting, injuring,

√*riṣ* 881/1 Cl 1.4. P *reṣati* or *riṣyati* or *riṣyate* to be hurt or injured, receive harm, suffer wrong, perish, be lost, fail, to injure, hurt, harm, destroy, ruin, caus. *reṣayati,* DP (Cl 1.4) in *hiṁsā* injuring, Cl 4 being angry,

riṣ f. injury or an injurer,

rīti f. manner, style, going, motion, course, a stream, current, a streak, line, row, limit, boundary, general course or way, usage, custom, practice, method, manner, style of speaking or writing, diction, yellow or pale brass, bell metal, rust, oxide coating on metals,

√*ṛj* 225/2 Cl 1 P A *arjati, arjate*, to go, to stand or be firm, to obtain, acquire, be strong or healthy, DP in *gati* moving, *sthāna* standing, *arjana* obtaining, *upārjana* acquiring

ṛjīṣa mfn on-rushing, m. expeller (of

enemies), n. the sediment or residue of soma, the *soma* plant after the juice has been pressed out,

ṛjīṣin mfn on-rushing, receiving the juice or residue of the *soma* pressing,

ṛju 225/2 mfn straight, honest, upright, ind. unswervingly, precisely, in the right manner, correctly,

ṛk a division of the Veda, a hymn,

ṛkṣa m. a bear, species of ape, pl. the Pleiades, mfn bald, bare,

ṛkti f. praise (L) (in *su-v-ṛkti)*

√ṛmph to hurt, kill, reproach, DP in *hiṁsā* injuring, hurting, killing,

√ṛṇ 225/3 Cl 8 P A *ṛnoti or arnoti* to go, move, DP in *gati* going,

ṛṇa mfn (having gone against or transgressed), guilty, going, fleeing, fugitive, n. guilt, debt, duty, anything wanted or missing, anything due, obligation, duty, money owed,

ṛñj 225/3 Cl 1 A *ṛñjate* to fry, Cl 6 P *ṛñjati* A *ṛñjate*, Cl 4 P A, Cl 7A, to make straight or proper, make proper, arrange, fit out, arrange, decorate, ornament, to make favourable, propitiate, gain, obtain, DP Cl 1 in *bharjana* parching,

rocaka mfn brightening, enlightening, pleasing, giving an appetite, agreeable, m. kind of onion, worker in glass or ornaments, sack, hunger, appetite,

rocana mfn shining, light, bright, radiant, n. light, brightness, esp. the bright sky, pl. lights, stars, ifc. the causing a desire for, m. a partic.yellow pigment, the place of the light, ethereal space or spaces,

rocate 881/3 shines, is bright or radiant, is pleasing (with 4th),

rocis n. brightness, light, lustre, grace, loveliness,

rociṣṇu mfn shining bright, fig. blooming, giving an appetite,

√roḍ 889/1 Cl 1 P *roḍati* to be mad, to despise, disrespect, DP in *unmāda* being foolish or mad,

rodana 884/1 n. a tear, tears

rodasī f. du. the two worlds i.e. heaven and earth, name of lightning, the earth,

rodati cries, wails

rodha mfn growing, sprouting, m. growing, ascending, moving upwards, the act of stopping, checking, impeding, suppressing, preventing, besieging, blockading, obstruction of the bowels, attacking, making war upon, a dam, bank, shore, an arrow,

rodhana mfn obstructing, impeding, m. planet Mercury, f. a dam, bank, n. shutting up, confinement, stopping, checking, preventing,

roga 888/3 m. 'breaking up of strength' disease, infirmity, sickness,

rogāpanayana taking away disease, healing

rohaṇa 890/1 a medicine for healing or cicatrizing, n. a means of ascending, the act of mounting or ascending or riding or sitting or standing on, the growing over (healing) of a wound, putting on (a bowstring)

rohati climbs

rohitamatsya m. a kind of fish,

roka m. brightness, light, lustre, n. a hole, vacuity, a boat, ship,

roma m. a hole, cavity, the city Rome, n. water, pl. name of a people; or *roman* 889/3 3. n. body hair

romaharṣaṇa causing the hair to bristle

romāñcā f. goose-bumps,

romānta m. on the hairy side of the hand,

romanthana n. ruminating,

romapulaka m. bristling of the hair,

romāśca m. bristling of the hair,

roṣa 885/1 m. anger, rage, wrath, passion,

roṣaṇa mfn angry, wrathful, passionate, enraged, m. a touchstone, quicksilver,

√ṛph 226/2 Cl 6 P *ṛphati* to hurt, kill, reproach, DP in *hiṁsā* injuring, hurting, killing

√ṛṣ 226/3 Cl 1 P *arṣati* to flow, flow quickly, glide, move with a quick motion, to bring near by flowing, Cl 6 P *ṛṣati* to go, move, stab, kill, push, thrust, DP Cl 6 in *gati* going

ṛṣabha 226/3 m. a bull, a male animal in general, mfn best

ṛṣi m. a seer or sage, a singer of sacred songs, poet, priestly singer, a person renowned for piety and wisdom, in ascending order the ranking of the *ṛṣi(s)* is *rājarṣi, ṛṣi, maharṣi, brahmarṣi,*

ṛṣayas the seers, wise men 1/pl/m

ṛṣiyajña m. sacrifice for the sages, i.e. study of the Veda

ṛṣṭi f. spear, lance, sword,

ṛṣṭimat mfn furnished with spears

ṛṣṭividyut mfn glittering with swords

ṛṣva mfn lofty, elevated, great, sublime,

ṛṣvavīra mfn inhabited by sublime heroes,

ṛta 223/2 mfn. proper, right, fit, brave, honest, true, worshipped, respected, enlightened, able, luminous, suitable n. (*am*), fixed or settled law, order, divine truth, truth in general, righteousness, right,

*ṛtambhara*223/3 mfn. bearing the truth within one self, f. with and without

ṛtambharā f. intellect or knowledge which contains the truth within itself,

ṛtambharaprajñā –intellect or knowledge which contains the truth within itself

ṛtasap mfn following after right, righteous, connected with or performing worship or religious acts,

ṛtasāta mfn filled with truth or righteousness,

ṛtāvan f. *–varī* mfn true to established (natural) order e.g. dawn, , true to sacred law, pious, holy, sacred, keeping within the fixed order or rule,

ṛtāvṛdh mfn rejoicing in right, holy,

ṛte 226/1 ind. excepting, besides, without, unless (with 5th),

ṛtu m. 1. a fixed and settled time esp. time for sacrificing, 2. time of year i.e. season, 3. the menses,

ṛtvij mfn offering at the appointed time, m. a, priest in the ritual, pl. priests,

ṛtvik m. a priest, priest officiating in a sacrifice,

√ru 881/3 1. Cl 2 P *rauti, or ravīti, ruvati, ravoti (te),* to roar, bellow, howl, yelp, cry aloud, make any noise or sound, sing as birds, hum as bees, *rauti* to praise, caus. *rāvayati* cause to roar etc., cause an uproar, DP in *śabda* sounding,
2. m. sound, noise, fear, alarm, war, battle,

√ru 3. Cl 1 A *ravate* to break or dash to pieces, DP in *gati* going, or *reṣaṇa* hurting, killing,
2. m. cutting, dividing,

√ruc, 881/3 Cl 1 A *rocate (ti),* to shine, be bright, or radiant or resplendent, to make bright or resplendent, to be splendid or beautiful or good, to be agreeable to, please, be pleased with, be desirous of, long for, caus. *rocayati (te)* to cause to shine, to enlighten , illuminate, make bright, make pleasant or bright, cause to long for anything, find pleasure in/ like, to purpose, intend, DP in *dīpti* shining, or *abhiprāti* being pleased,

ruci f. light, lustre, splendour, beauty, pleasure, liking, taste, relish, appetite, zest, pleasure in, desirous of, longing for,

rucira mfn bright, beautiful, splendid, radiant, agreeable to, liked by, sweet, dainty, nice,
n. saffron, cloves,

rucirānana mfn fair-faced,

√rud 883/1 Cl 2 P *roditi, rudati (te), rodati (te),* to weep, cry, howl, roar, to bewail, deplore, DP in *aśru-vimocana* weeping, shedding tears,

ruddhvā ind. restraining, having restrained,

√rudh 884/1 1. Cl 1 P *rodhati* to sprout, shoot, grow, DP in *kāma* desiring,

√rudh 884/1 2. Cl 7 P A *ruṇaddhi, runddhe, rundhati (te) rodhati* to

obstruct, check, arrest, stop, restrain, to avert, keep off, repel, to shut, lock up, to besiege, blockade, to cover, conceal, to stop up, fill, to touch, move (the heart), to torment, harass, to lose, be deprived of, rend asunder, DP in *āvaraṇa* covering

rūḍha 885/2 mfn. mounted, risen, ascended

rūḍhi f. rise, ascent, increase, growth, development, birth, production, fame, notoriety, tradition, custom, general prevalence, current usage esp. of speech, the employment of a word in its popular or conventional meaning,

rudhira 884/2 mfn red, blood-red, bloody, m. the red planet – Mars, blood, a kind of precious stone, n. saffron, name of a city,

rudra Rudra, destroyer , leader of the Maruts or storm-gods, *Śiva*

rudrākṣa 'eyed', rosary bead (a tree seed), a rosary, eye of Śiva, sacred to Śiva,

√ruh 885/2 Cl 1 P *rohati (te), ruhati (te),* to ascend, mount, climb, to reach to, attain a desire, to rise, spring up, grow, develop, increase, prosper, thrive, to cicatrize, heal, caus. *rohayati, ropayati,* DP in *bīja-janman* growing, germinating, *prādur-bhāva* becoming visible,

√ruj 882/3 Cl 6 P *rujati (te)* to break, break open, dash to pieces, shatter, destroy, to cause pain, afflict, injure, caus. *rojayati,* DP in *bhaṅga* breaking to pieces, destroying, in *hiṁsā* hurting,

ruj f. pain, disease, sickness, ifc. breaking, crushing, shattering, pain, fracture, disease, fracture, toil, trouble,

rujā 882/3 f. breaking, fracture, pain, sickness, disease, m. sickness, disease induced by passion or love, a ewe,

rujānā f. cleft, rift (of the clouds), a river,

rukma m. ornament of gold, n. gold, iron, a kind of collyrium (eye-wash),

rukmavarṇa the naturally self-effulgent One or the golden-hued (Gam.),

√rūkṣ Cl 10 P *rūkṣayati* to be rough or harsh, to make dry or emaciated, to soil, smear, injure, offend, exasperate, DP in *pāruṣya* being severe,

rūkṣa 885/3 mfn rough, dry, arid, dreary, hard, harsh, unkind, soiled, thin, emaciated, m. hardness, harshness, a kind of grass, n. a good kind of iron, the thick part of curds, a tree,

√ruṁś 881/3 Cl 1.10. *ruṁśati, ruṁśayati* to speak, DP in *bhāṣā* speaking,

ruṇḍa mfn maimed, mutilated, m. a headless body, the offspring of a mule and a mare,

√ruṇṭ 883/1 Cl 1 P *ruṇṭati* to steal, rob, DP in *steya* robbing, stealing,

√ruṇṭh Cl 1 P *ruṇṭhati* to go, to be lame, to be idle, to strike against, to steal, DP in *gati* going, *steya* robbing, stealing,

√rup 884/3 1. Cl 4 P *rupyati* to suffer violent or racking pain, (in the abdomen), to violate, confound, disturb, to break off, DP in *vimohana* troubling

rup f. the earth,

√rūp 885/3 Cl 10 P *rūpayati* to form, figure, represent, exhibit by gesture, act, feign, to view, inspect, contemplate, A °*yate* to show one's self, appear, DP in *rūpa-kriyā* seeing beauty, making beautiful,

rūpa 885/3 n. any outward appearance, or colour, form, shape, or figure, sometimes used after an adj. or part. to emphasize meaning, dreamy or phantom shapes (pl.), loveliness, grace, beauty, splendour, splendid form; nature, character, peculiarity, feature, mark, sign, sympton, likeness, image, reflection, circumstances, sort, kind, mode, manner, way,

(with √*kṛ* or √*bhū*) to assume a form, ifc. having the form or appearance or colour of, formed or composed of, consisting of, like to;
ifc. trace of;
a single specimen or exemplar (and thus a term for the number 1),
a show, play, drama,
(in gram.) any noun or verb form,
(in phil.) the quality of colour,
(Buddhist) material form i.e. the organized body (one of 5 *skandhas*); cattle, a beast, a sound, word, m. a word of unknown meaning,
a people, name of a river,

rūpajitāpsaras mfn surpassing the Apsaras in beauty,

rūpaka mfn having form, figurative, metaphorical, illustrating by figurative language,
m. a coin, rupee, n. form, figure, shape, appearance, image, likeness, feature, sign, sympton, kind, species, a figure of speech, metaphor, simile, comparison,
a drama, play, performance,
a partic. weight,

rūpakabhāṣā a type of utterance. When one has to indicate function and properties of non-physical things, then the poets resort to these styles where similes illustrate with the help of physical forms.

rūpārūpa with form and without form,

rūpaśakti f. the power that creates forms,

rūpasampad f. beauty of form, perfection or excellence of form,

rūpasampanna mfn endowed with beauty, beautiful, modified,

rūpaskandha m. physical element,

rūpatanmātra the subtle element of form and colour, the essence of form,

rūpavant mfn beautiful, handsome, having form or colour, formed, embodied,

rūpavat mfn beautiful, handsome, having form or colour, formed, embodied,

rūpayauvana n. beauty and youth, mfn possessing youth and beauty,

rūpita *rūpita* 886/3 mfn formed, imagined, represented, exhibited, characterisation,

rūpya 886/3 mfn beautiful, well-shaped, n. silver, eye-salve, rupee,

√*ruś* 885/1 Cl 6 P *ruśati* to hurt, injure, annoy, DP in *hiṁsā* hurting,

√*ruṣ* 885/1 Cl 1.4. P *roṣati*, or *ruṣyati (te),* and *ruṣati*, to hurt, injure, kill, to be hurt, take offence, to displease, be disagreeable to,
(cl4) to be vexed or cross, caus. or Cl 10 *roṣayati (te),* to vex, annoy, displease, irritate, exasperate, to be furious or angry,
DP in *hiṁsā* (Cl 1) hurting, *hiṁsā* (cl4) hurting, being angry , *roṣa* (Cl 10) being angry, DP in *bhūṣā* adorning,

√*rūṣ* Cl 1 P *rūṣati* to adorn, decorate, to cover, strew, smear, Cl 10 *rūṣayati* to tremble or burst,

√*ruṭ* 882/3 Cl 1 A *roṭate* to strike against, to shine, Cl 10 P *roṭayati* to be angry, to speak or to shine, DP in *upaghāta* (cl1) striking against, resisting, in *roṣa* (Cl 10) being angry, in *āpyāyana* increasing,

√*ruṭh* 882/3 Cl 1 P *roṭhati* to strike down, fell, Cl 1 A to torment, pain, DP in *upaghāta* striking against, resisting

sa he, this 1111/2 6. the base for the nom. case of the 3rd person pron. *tad,* in the *sāmkhya sa* is used to denote *puruṣa*, that
1111/2 7. ind an inseparable prefix expressing junction, conjunction, possession, similarity, equality; (when compounded to form adjectives and adverbs) with, together with, having, containing, having the same,
4. m. a snake, wind, air, a bird, n. knowledge, meditation, a carriage road, a fence,
5. mfn procuring, bestowing,

sā 1111/2 pron. 1/s/f she or that

sabādh mfn harassed, annoyed, afflicted,

sabādha mfn painful, detrimental to (6th),

sabādhas as *sabādh,* ind. urgently, eagerly,
sabahumānam ind. with great honour or reverence, very respectfully,
śabala mfn dappled, spotted, filled with,
sabala mfn powerful, strong, accompanied by a force or army, together with *Bala*,
sabali mfn endowed with royal revenue,
sabandhu mfn being of the same race or family, related, of kin,
L. having a friend,
śabara mfn brindled, variegated,
sabāṣpa mfn tearful, weeping,
√*śabd* 1052/2 Cl 10 P *śabdayati* to make any noise or sound, cry aloud, to call, invoke, DP in *śabda* sounding, or *āviṣkāra* speaking, calling, revealing,
śabda m. sound, voice, word, space, ether, property of sound, noise, tone, note, speech, language,
the right word, correct expression,
(in gram.) a declinable word or a word-termination (affix),
a name, appellation, title,
a technical term,
verbal communication or testimony, oral tradition, verbal authority or evidence, '..the understanding of a subject that comes without study, from merely hearing of it' (Gam.),
śabdabheda m. difference or distinction of sounds or words, 'difference in word (name) only' (U),
śabdādi m 1053/2 the objects of sense beginning with sound,
śabdapramāṇa n. verbal testimony or proof, oral evidence,
śabdārtha 1053/2 m. sound (or word) and sense, the nature or meaning of sounds, the meaning of a word, sense or meaning of oral tradition (as a source of knowledge),
śabda-brahman 1053/1 n. word-brahman, the Veda considered as a revealed sound or word, and identified with the Supreme,
śabdam kṛ make a noise, raise one's voice,
śabdādhī m. ocean of words,
śabdapramāṇa n. verbal tesimony or proof, oral evidence, scriptural proof,
śabdaśāstra n. word-theory, word-compendium, grammar,
śabdatanmātra n. subtle element of sounds, subtle principle of sounds,
sabhā f. an assembly, congregation, meeting, council, social party, society, good society, a place for public meetings, a court,
a gambling-house, lodging-house,
sabhācāra m. the customs or usages of society, court-manners,
sabhācāturya n. politeness in society,
sabhāga mfn having a share, common, universal, corresponding, answering,
-tā f. participation, companionship,
sabhāgata mfn one who appears before or is present at a court of justice,
sabhāgatā f. participation, friendship, association,
sabhāgya mfn having good fortune, fortunate,
√*sabhāj* 1151/3 Cl 10 P *sabhājayati* to serve, honour, worship, to praise, celebrate, to visit, frequent, to beautify, to show, DP in *prāti* pleasing, *darṣana* showing, or *sevana* serving, associating with,
sabhājana n. service, honour, courtesy, politeness, civility,
sabhakṣa m. a mess-mate,
sabhāpati m. president, chairman,
sabhāratā f. fulness, abundance, prosperity,
sabhārya mfn having his wife with him, i.e. with his wife,
sabhaya mfn fearful, apprehensive,
(*am*) ind. in terror,
sābhra mfn having clouds, cloudy,
sabhya mfn being in an assembly –hall or meeting-room, fit for an assembly or court, suitable to good society, courteous, polite, refined, civilised,
m. an assessor, judge, assistant,
sabīja mfn with seed or germ, containing seed or germ, with attributes,
sabrahmacārin m. fellow-student,

ifc. a fellow, companion,
mfn rivalling, vying with,

sabuddhi 1229/2 mfn wise, clever, intelligent, f. good understanding,

sabva n. digested food,

√*śac* 1048/1 Cl 1 A *śacate* to be strong etc. to speak out, say, tell, speak, DP in *vyaktā-vāc* speaking distinctly

√*sac* 1130/2 Cl 1 A *sacate, sacati, siṣakti*, to be associated or united with, have to do with, be familiar with, associate one's self with, be possessed of, enjoy, to participate in, suffer, endure, to belong to, be attached or devoted to, serve, follow, seek, pursue, favour, assist, to be connected with, to fall to the lot of, to be together, *siṣakti* to go after, follow, accompany, adhere or be attached to, DP in *secana* sprinkling, or *sevana* serving, in *samavāra* being associated with,

sac in comp. for *sat,*

saca mfn attached to, worshipping, a worshipper,

sacā ind. near at hand, along, together, together with, in the presence of, before, in, at, by (with 7th before or after),

sacaitanya mfn having consciousness, conscious,

sacakita mfn trembling, timid, startled,

sacakra mfn having wheels, wheeled,

sacakṣuṣa mfn having eyes, seeing,

sacana mfn ready to befriend or help, kindly disposed, doing kind things,

sacanas mfn being in harmony with,

sacarācara both the animate and inanimate, comprehending both the moving and unmoving, (*cara acara*)

sacāru mfn very beautiful,

sacatha m. companionship, assistance,

sacathya mfn helpful, kind, n. assistance, help,

sācaya mfn joined, united,

saccandrikā f. splendid moonlight,

saccarita n. good conduct, history or account of the good, mfn well-conducted, virtuous,

saccaritra mfn virtuous, n. true or good character,

sacchāya mfn giving shade, shady, having beautiful colours, glittering, ifc. having the same colour as,

saccheda mfn having cuttings or divisions, interrupted,

sacchidra mfn having defects, faulty,

saccid in comp. for *sac-cit*

saccidānanda m.pl. *sat, cid, ānanda* truth, consciousness, bliss, mfn consisting of existence, knowledge, joy, n. (pure) consciousness, knowledge, bliss, = *Brahman*

saccidātman m. the soul which consists of existence and knowledge,

sacchīla n. a good character, mfn of a virtuous disposition, benevolent,

sacchloka mfn having a good reputation,

saccinmaya mfn consisting of existence and knowledge,

saccit n. (pure) existence and knowledge,

sacela mfn having clothes, dressed,

saceṣṭa mfn making effort or exertion, m. the mango tree,

sacetā calm in mind

sacetana mfn having reason or consciousness or feeling, sentient, sensible, animate, rational, (*ā*) f. senses, consciousness,

sacetas 1131/1 mfn. having the same mind, unanimous, M. conscious,

sāceya mfn belonging to, suitable or fit for,

śacī f. 1048/1 the rendering of powerful or mighty help, assistance, aid, kindness, favour, grace, skill, dexterity, name of Indra's wife,

saci ind. together, along with,

sāci mfn following, accompanying, 2. ind. crookedly, awry, sideways,

sacinta 1131/1 mfn absorbed in thought thoughtful

śacīpati m. Lord of might or help (applied to Indra and the Aśvins)

sacit mfn thinking, wise, of same mind,

śacītīrtha n. a place of pilgrimage,

name of a *tīrtha*
sacitka m. thinking,
sacitta mfn of the same mind, endowed with reason,
saciva m. an associate, companion, friend, a king's friend or counsellor,
sācivya n. office of the counsellor or adviser of the king, ministry,
sācya to be assisted or served or honoured,
√*śad* 1. *śāśaduḥ, śāśadmahe, śāśadre, śāśadāna* only, to distinguish oneself, be eminent or superior,
√*śad* 1051/2 2. Cl 1.6 A *śīyate,* to fall, fall off or out, caus. *śādayati* to impel, drive on (cattle), cause to fall off or out, hew or cut off, knock out, to fell, throw down, slay, kill, to disperse, dispel, remove, destroy, DP in *śātana* falling, perishing, decaying,
√*śāḍ* 1063/2 Cl 1 A *śāḍate* to praise, DP in *ślāghā* applauding, praising, boasting,
√*sad* 1138/2 Cl 1 or 6 P *sīdati (te), sadati,* to sit down, sit upon or in or at, to sit down before, besiege, lie in wait for, to sink down, sink into despondency, become faint or wearied or dejected or low-spirited, pine or waste away, perish, caus. *sādayati,* DP (Cl 1) in *viśaraṇa* splitting, bursting, *gati* going, *avasādana* being languid or in distress, Cl 6 in *viśaraṇa* splitting, bursting, *gati* going, *avasādana* being languid or in distress, Cl 10 in *padi* approaching, going to
sad in comp. for *sat*
-sad mfn sitting or dwelling in,
sāḍa mfn having a point or sting (as a stick or scorpion etc.),
sāda m. sitting (on horseback), riding, sinking down, perishing, despair, despondency, purity, clearness, cleanness, going, motion,
sadā 1139/2 ind. always, ever, forever, perpetually, every time, continually
sadābhāsa mfn reflecting the really existent, having the appearance of real existence,
sadābhava mfn perpetual, continual,
sadācāra 1137/2 m. behaviour of the good or wise, 'just action' HH, mfn well-conducted, virtuous,
sadadi ind. generally, usually,
*sadāgama*1137/2 m. a good doctrine, arrival of a good man, 1139/2 m. always moving, wind,
sadguṇa mfn having good quality, virtuous, m. virtue, good quality,
sadāham ind. with a burning sensation,
sadaikarasa mfn having always one object of desire, unchanging essence
sadā jāgrat ever wakeful,
sādaka mfn exhausting, wearying, destroying
sadākārin mfn always active, having a good appearance,
sadakṣa mfn endowed with reason,
sadakṣiṇa mfn having presents, accompanied by gifts,
sadam ind. always, ever, forever, at any time,
sadambha mfn having good water, hypocritical, with hypocrisy
sadaṁśaka mfn having teeth, having nippers
sadana mfn causing to settle down or remain, n. a seat, dwelling, palace, residence, house, home, (ifc. often means –abiding or dwelling in), settling down, coming to rest,
sādana mfn exhausting, wearying, destroying,
n. dwelling, a seat, house, place, home, a vessel, dish, causing to sink, wearying, exhausting, destroying, setting down, arranging (of vessels), sinking in (of wheels), putting together, arranging,
m. a text recited when anything is being set down, exhaustion, decay,
sadānanda m. perpetual bliss, mfn feeling or giving perpetual bliss,
sadanāsad mfn sitting on a seat,
sadani m.f. water,
sādanya mfn belonging to a house,

domestic,
sadara mfn fearful, afraid,
sādara mfn with respect, reverential, considerate, attentive or devoted to ifc., intent upon, *(am)* ind. respectfully, reverentially,
sadāra mfn accompanied by a wife,
sadarpa mfn having pride, arrogant, haughty
sadas n. a seat, residence, abode, place of meeting, assembly, a shed in the sacrificial enclosure, du. heaven and earth,
sadasad for *sadasat* in comp.
sadasadātmaka mfn or *sadasadātmatā* f. having the nature of both entity and nonentity, *-tā* n. original germ
sadasadātmatābhāva m. reality and unreality, truth and falsehood,
sadasadviveka m. discrimination between true and false or good and bad,
sadasat mfn being and not being, real and unreal, true and false, good and bad, n. what is existent and non-existent (also du.), the true and the false, good and evil, existence and non-existence (du.), m.pl. the good and the bad,
sadāśaya mfn of a good or noble mind,
sadāśiva ever auspicious, always happy or prosperous,
sadaśva m. a good horse, mfn drawn by a good horse, possessing a good horse,
sadaśvavat ind. like a good horse,
sadātana mfn continual, perpetual,
sadātman mfn having a good nature, good, virtuous,
ṣāḍava m. a sweetmeat,
sadaya mfn merciful, compassionate, kind, gentle, (*am*) ind. mercifully, kindly,
sadayahṛdaya mfn compassionate hearted, tender-hearted,
ṣaḍāyatana the seats of the six organs, 'six sense gates', the six organs of sense, Buddhist,
sadbhāṣana n. right speech,
sadbhāvanā sadbhāva 1137/2 real being, existence, real state of things, 'pure feelings' HH, the quality of goodness, uprightness, faithfulness
sadbhūta mfn who or what is really good or true,
sādbhuta mfn astonished, surprised,
ṣaḍḍarśana mfn one who is versed in the six systems of philosophy, n. the six systems of philosophy – *nyāya, vaiśeṣika, saṁkhyā, yoga, mīmāṁsā, vedānta,*
sadevaka mfn together with the gods,
saddharma m. the good law, true justice, designation of the Buddhist or Jaina doctrines,
saddhetu m. the existence of cause and effect,
saddhī mfn wise, sage,
sadguṇa 1137/2 m. a good quality, virtue, mfn. having good qualities, virtuous
sadguru a truth guru, true teacher, master,
√*sādh* 1201/1 Cl 1 P A *sādati (te),* Cl 4 *sādhyati*, Cl 5 *sādhnoti, sadhnoti*, to go straight to any goal or aim, attain an object, to be successful, succeed, prosper, to bring straight to an object or end, further, promote, advance, accomplish, complete, finish, to submit or agree to, obey, *sādhyati* to be completed or accomplished, caus. *sādhayati* to straighten, make straight, to guide straight or well, direct or bring to a goal, to master, subdue, overpower, conquer, win, win over, to summon, conjure up (a god or spirit), to enforce payment, recover a debt, collect taxes, heal, cure, set right, to bring to an end or conclusion, complete, make perfect, bring about, accomplish, effect, fulfil, be successful, to make ready, prepare, gain, obtain, find out (by calculation), to grant, bestow, put or place in,
DP in *saṁsiddhi* completing, finishing,
2. ifc. accomplishing, performing,
sadha (= *saha*), with together with, 2. or

sadhā du. heaven and earth,
sādha m. accomplishment, fulfilment,
sādhaka mfn effective, efficient, accomplishing, fulfilling, completing, perfecting, finishing, adapted to any purpose, useful, magical, m. an adept, skilful person, a spiritual aspirant practicing disciplines, (G p.261) one who practises spiritual disciplines, *sādh* – to go straight to the goal,
a spiritual aspirant
sadhamāda m. co-revelry, common feast, drinking together, companionship,
sadhamādam mad revel in bliss with,
sadhana n. common property, mfn wealthy,
sādhana 1201/1 mf(*ī* or *ā*)n. leading straight to a goal, guiding well, furthering, effective, efficient, productive of, self-effort, tool, implement, spiritual practice, f. (*ā*) the act of mastering, overpowering, any means of effecting or accomplishing, propitiation, worship, adoration G.p261 self-effort, spiritual discipline, (from the verb root *sādh* to go straight to the goal, make straight (a path)), (D.P. completing, finishing), the way, generally- the means to release or liberation,
four kinds – discrimination, dispassion/detachment, the sixfold virtues, desire for liberation,
= *sādhanacatuṣṭaya*
sādhanta m. a beggar, mendicant,
sādhāraṇa mfn belonging or applicable to many or all, universal, generic, like, equal, similar to, behaving alike, f. (*ī*) a key,
m. a twig of bamboo,
n. something in common, a league or alliance with, a common rule or one generally applicable, a generic property, (*am*) ind. commonly, generally,
sādhāraṇabhāṣā a type of utterance. 'This is the ordinary, according to fact, language, fully grammatical and simple without any exaggerations.'
sādhāraṇadharma m. common or universal duty, conduct or duty binding on all castes and orders alike,
sādhāraṇakaraṇa common cause,
sādhāraṇatva n. universality,
sadharma m. the same nature or qualities, mfn having the same nature or qualities, subject to the same law, equal, like, virtuous, honest,
sādharmya 1202/2 identity of nature with, likeness or homogeneity with, being of the same religion, equality of duty, office or properties, 'becoming of one law of being and action (with the Divine)'
sādhayitṛ mfn one who brings about, an accomplisher, performer,
śādhi (you) correct! 2/s/impv/act
sādhin mfn accomplishing, performing,
sadhi m. fire, a bull,
sadhis n. the end or goal of any movement, the place where it comes to rest
sādhibhūta mfn (identified) with the Being who is 'the substratum of all material objects',
sādhita mfn brought about, accomplished, perfected, mastered, subdued, proved, demonstrated, made,
sadhri (= *saha*), with, along with, together with,
sadhrīcīna mfn directed to one aim, pursuing the same goal, united, leading to the right goal, correct,
sādhu 1201/2 mfn straight, right, leading straight to a goal, hitting the mark, unerring, straightened, not entangled, well-disposed, kind, willing, obedient, successful, effective, ready, prepared, peaceful, powerful, fit, proper, right, good, virtuous, honourable, righteous, well-born, noble, correct, pure, classical (language),
m. a good or virtuous or honest man, a holy man, saint, sage, seer, a

merchant, usurer, (Jaina) a jina or deified saint,
f. (*vī)* a chaste or virtuous woman, faithful wife, a saintly woman, Jaina nun,
n. the good or right or honest, a good thing or act, ind. straight, aright, regularly, rightly, properly, ind. well done! bravo!

sādhubhāva m. good nature, goodness, kindness

sādhucaraṇa mfn well-conducted, righteous,

sādhudarśin mfn seeing well, well discerning,

sādhudevī f. mother-in-law,
sādhudhī f. a good understanding, mfn having good understanding, wise, well-disposed,

sādhugata mfn respectable, virtuous, resorted to by the good,

sādhuḥ sādhuḥ well done!

sādhujana m. a good person, honest man,

sādhukārin mfn acting well or rightly, skilled, clever,

sādhukarman mfn acting well or rightly, doing kind actions, beneficent,

sādhumat mfn good, f. one of the 10 grades of a *bodhisattva*,

sādhumata mfn well thought of , highly prized

sādhumātrā f. the right measure,

sādhupadavī f. the path or way of the good,

sādhuphala mfn bearing good fruit, having good results or consequences,

sādhusammata mfn approved by the good,

sādhusaṁsarga m. association with the good

sādhuśīla mfn well-disposed, virtuous

sādhutā f. rightness, correctness, honesty, uprightness, goodness, excellence, kindness,

sādhutas ind. from a good man,

sādhutva n. rightness, correctness, goodness, excellence,

sādhuvāda m. exclaiming 'well done!', the name of an honest man, good renown, reputation,

sādhuvāha m. a good/well-trained horse,

sādhuvat mfn right, correct, ind. as if right or correct,

sādhuveṣa mfn well-dressed,

sādhuvṛtta mfn well-rounded, well-conducted, having good manners, m a well-conducted person, virtuous or honest man,

sādhuyā ind. in a straight course, directly towards any mark or aim, plainly, simply, rightly, duly, kindly,

sādhya 1202/1 mfn to be subdued or mastered or won or managed, to be set to rights, to be healed or cured, to be formed (grammatically), to be cultivated or perfected, to be accomplished or brought about, feasible, attainable, taking place, to be prepared or cooked, to be inferred or concluded, to be calculated, to be proved, a class of celestial beings

sādhyābhāva 1202/1 absence of the thing to be proved, impossibility of cure, 5/s because nothing is to be accomplished

sādhyasama 1202/1 m. an assertion identical with the point to be proved,

sādhyasiddha mfn still to be accomplished and already accomplished,

sādhyasiddhi f. accomplishment of what has to be done, the establishing of what has to be proved, the success of an undertaking, accomplishment, fulfilment, proof, conclusion,

sādhyate 1200/3 1. √*sādh* go straight to any goal or aim, attain an object, be successful, prosper, 1/s/pres/mid he is successful

sādi m. a horseman, a charioteer, warrior, wind, a melancholy person,
mfn having a beginning, n. *-tva*

sadīnam ind. lamentably,

sadīpaka mfn together with a lamp,

sadivas ind. on the same day, at once,

ṣadliṅga the six marks of a perfect exposition – unity of thought from beginning to end, reiteration or repetition, novel or uncommon nature of the proof, fruit of the

teaching, convincing expression, illustration or reason,
sadman m. a sitter, assessor, spectator, n. a seat, abode, dwelling, house, mfn dwelling in, inhabiting,
sadoṣa mfn together with the night, wrong, objectionable, with deficiency, faulty,
sadri m. an elephant, a mountain, a ram,
sadṛkṣa mfn like, resembling, similar to,
sadṛś mfn fit, proper, just, right,
sadṛśa 1140/1 like, resembling, similar to, fit, proper, right, worthy,
sadṛśapariṇāma m. 'homogenous change; a change which is not different from the original, like gold into an earring,
sādṛśya n. likeness, resemblance, similarity to, analogy,
sadṛśyata mfn similarity
sadru mfn sitting,
sadruci mfn kindly disposed,
sadrūpatva n. reality,
ṣadūrmi the six waves- grief delusion, hunger, thirst, decay, death,
sadvacas n. a fair speech,
sadvādita mfn well-spoken
sadvārttā f. good news,
sadvelā f. the right moment,
sadvicāra right enquiry, enquiry into Truth,
sadviccheda m. separation from the good,
sadvidya mfn having true knowledge, well-informed, (*ā*) f. true knowledge,
sadvigarhita mfn censured by the good,
ṣaḍvikāra six modifications of the body-existence, birth, growth, change, decay, death,
ṣaḍvikāram ind. in six uncommon ways,
sadvṛtta n. a well-rounded shape, the behaviour of good men, good conduct, mfn well-conducted, containing beautiful metres,
sadvṛtti f. good conduct,
sādya mfn fit for riding, m. a riding horse,
sadyas 1140/1 ind. in the very moment in the present, immediately, on the same day, at once,
sādyanta mfn having beginning and end, complete, entire,
sadyaska mfn belonging to the present day, immediate, present, quick,
sadyastana mfn fresh, instantaneous,
sadyo in comp. for *sadyas*
sadyomukti f. immediate liberation
sadyukti f. good reasoning,
√*sag* 1125/1 Cl 1 *sagati* to cover, DP in *samvaraṇa* covering
sagadgada 1125/1 with stammering
sāgama mfn acquired honestly, legitimate,
sagaṇa mfn having troops or flocks, attended by followers, accompanied by,
sagandha mfn having smell, smelling, fragrant, proud, arrogant,
sagara mfn accompanied by praise, 2. containing poison, poisonous, m. 'provided with moisture', the air, atmosphere, a mythical prince or king of Ayodhyā,
sāgara 1198/2 m. the ocean, sea m. a son of King Sagara,
sāgaraka m.pl. coastal inhabitants,
sāgarānta m. the sea-shore, bounded by the ocean, sea-girt,
sāgarāntargata mfn living in the ocean,
sāgarānukūla mfn situated on the coast,
sāgaravāsin mfn dwelling on the sea-shore
sāgaravat ind. like the ocean,
sāgaraśukti f. a sea-shell,
sagarbha mfn pregnant, f. (*ā*) a pregnant woman,
sāgarodaka n. sea-water,
sāgarodgāra m. the swelling or heaving of the sea, flowing tide, flood,
sagarva mfn having pride, arrogant,proud of
sāgas mfn guilty of a sin or offence,
sagatika mfn connected with a prep. etc.
sagauravam mfn with dignity,
√*sagh* 1125/2 Cl 5 P *saghnoti* to take upon one's self, be able to bear, be a match for, to hurt, injure, kill, DP in *hiṁsā* hurting, killing,
saghan m. a vulture,
saghana mfn thick (hair), clouded, dense,
saghnoti Cl 5 P taking upon oneself, is able to bear, is a match for
saghoṣa mfn pl. shouting together,

saghṛṇa mfn full of pity, compassionate, tender of feeling, delicate, scrupulous
saghṛta mfn mixed with ghee,
sagma m. agreeing, coming to terms,
sāgni mfn together with the fire, maintaining a sacred fire,
sāgnika mfn having Agni with them , together with Agni,
sagotra mfn of the same family or kin, m. a kinsman of the same family,
sāgra mfn with the tip or point, = *sam* + *agra* whole or entire, having a surplus, more than, (*am*) ind. for a longer period, for a whole life,
sagraha mfn filled with crocodiles, taken up by ladles or other vessels, eclipsed (as the moon),
sāgraha mfn persistent
sagṛha mfn with wife and children or with one's house or family,
sagu mfn along with cows,
saguḍa mfn sugared (?)
saguṇa 1125/1 having qualities, qualified, worldly, having good qualities or virtues, virtuous, having particular attributes or properties, furnished with a string or cord,
saguṇin mfn having good qualities, virtuous
saguṇa brahman the *Brahman* with all *guṇa* and manifestations,
sāguṇya n. excellence, superiority,
√*sah* 1193/1 Cl 1 A *sahate (ti), sāhati,* to prevail, be victorious, overcome, vanquish, conquer, defeat, gain, win (battles), to offer violence to, to master, suppress, restrain, to be able to or capable of, to bear up against, resist, to bear, put up with, endure, suffer, tolerate, to be lenient towards, have patience with, to spare anyone, to let pass, approve anything, caus./Cl 10 *sāhayati* to forbear,
DP in (cl1) *marṣaṇa* enduring, forbearing, (Cl 10) in *marṣaṇa* causing to bear or suffer,
2. mfn bearing, enduring, overcoming,
3. 1193/2 Cl 4 P *sahyati* to satisfy, delight, to be pleased, to bear, endure, DP in *caki* satisfying, pleasing,
saha + 3rd together with, with
mfn powerful, mighty, overcoming, vanquishing, bearing, enduring, withstanding, defying, equal to, a match for, causing, effecting, able to, capable of,
2. ind. together with, along with, with, (with 5th) in common, in company, jointly,
also forms adjectives expressing the companion of an action, e.g.
When prefixed to adverbs of time- 'simultaneously, at the same time',
m. a companion, *(ā)* f. a female companion,
sahā f. the earth,
sāha mfn powerful, mighty, resisting, conquering, subduing,
sahabhasman mfn with the ashes,
sahabhū mfn counterpart of, being together, appearing together with, innate, natural,
sahacara mfn going with, accompanying, belonging together, similar, like, m. a companion, friend, follower, a surety, f. (*ī*) a female companion or friend, mistress, wife,
sahacārin mfn going or living together, accompanying, m. comrade, follower, associate, companion,
sāhacarya n. companionship, fellowship,
Sahadeva a *Pāṇḍava* prince (means – accompanied by the gods)
sahadharmacārin mfn sharing the duties of, m. lawful husband,
-*inī* f. lawful wife,
sahādhyayana n. studying together,
sahaja mfn born or produced together or at the same time as, congenital, innate, hereditary, original, natural,
m. natural state or disposition,
a brother of whole blood,
n. emancipation during life,
ibc. by birth, by nature, naturally,

sahajā 1194/1 mfn born or produced together,
sahaja-adhyāsa m. 'the natural error of identifying the *cidābhāsa* (reflection of consciousness) with the ego,' (U),
sahaja-kumbhaka m.n. natural retention of breath,
sahajānanda m. state of bliss become natural,
sahaja-nirvikalpa-samādhi natural non-dual state of Brahmic Consciousness (U),
sahajaniṣṭha natural and normal establishment, establishment in one's own essential nature of *saccidānanda*,
sahajavasthā f. natural and continuous state of consciousness,
sāhajika mfn innate, natural,
sahaka mfn patient, suffering, enduring,
sahakāra 1193/3 m. assistance, acting with, cooperation, n. a mango blossom, mango juice,
sahakārimātra an accessory cause only, a helping factor only as is *māyā* with regard to the world projection of Brahman,
sahakārīn mfn acting together, cooperating, concurrent, m. a concurrent agent, expedient, assistant, e.g. a complement to a text
sāhaṁkāra mfn having egotism, arrogant,
sahana 1193/1 mfn powerful, strong, patient, enduring, n. patient endurance, forbearance,
sahānya m. a mountain,
sahas powerful, mighty, victorious, the winter season, n. strength, power, force, victory, light, water,
sahasā (3rd sahas) suddenly, forcibly, quickly, at once, unexpectedly, fortuitously,
sāhasa mfn precipitate, rash, foolhardy, m.n. punishment, fine, ifc. f. (*ā*) n. boldness, daring, rashness, any reckless act, rape, robbery, felony, aggression, cruelty, adultery, hatred, enmity,
sāhasika mfn bold, daring, rash, cruel, brutal, m. a robber,
sahasra 1195/2 a thousand,
sāhasra mfn consisting of a thousand, thousandfold, relating to a thousand,
sahasradakṣiṇa mfn having a thousand cattle as his gift or reward,
sahasradvār mfn thousand-doored,
sahasrakṛtvas a thousandfold,
sahasrākṣa mfn thousand-eyed, name of Indra, all-perceiving, all-inspecting,
sahasrāmagha mfn having a thousand gifts,
sahasrāṁśu mfn thousand rayed, m. sun,
sahasrāṁśusama mfn sun-like,
sahasraṇītha mfn having a thousand songs, rich in songs,
sahasrāra m.n. the thousand-petalled, the 7th primary *cakra,*mfn thousand –spoked,
sahasraśaḥ 1196/2 ind. by the thousands, innumerably,
sahasraśṛṅga mfn thousand horned,
sahasrin mfn numbering a thousand, thousandfold, etc.
sahasta mfn having hands,
sahastita co-existence,
sahasthiti f. abiding together in
sahasvant mfn mighty,
sahasya mfn powerful,
sahat mfn mighty, strong, lasting, solid,
sahavāhana mfn having their teams along, with their teams, with their vehicles
sahavatsa mfn with the calf,
sahāya m. a companion, follower, adherent, assistant, helper, mfn along with clarified butter,
sāhaya mfn causing or enabling to bear,
sāhāyaka n. assistance, aid, help, auxiliary troops, associates,
sahāyakaraṇa n. the act of rendering assistance, aiding,
sahāyana n. going together, fellowship, company,
sahāyatana mfn along with the fire-place,
sāhāyya n. L. office of attendant, hence – service, aid, help, friendship, fellowship, alliance, used with *Dh°* *kṛ* to mean

giving help – the person being given help is put in the 6th case

sāhāyyam kariṣyati will give help

sahela mfn with levity, full of play or sport, wanton, careless, unconcerned, (*am*) ind. playfully,

sahendra m. a mighty lord,

sahiṣṇutā 1193/2 patient, forbearing

sahita 1. 1193/2 mfn. borne, endured, supported, 2. 1195/1 joined, conjoined, united, all together,

sahitra n. patience, endurance,

sāhitya n. association, connection, society, combination, union with (3rd or comp.) *ena* ind. in combination with, together with', agreement, harmony, rhetoric, poetry,

sāhlāda mfn joyous, cheerful, glad, (*am*) ind. joyfully,

sahottha mfn innate,

sahṛdaya mfn with the heart, hearty, sincere, possessing a heart, good-hearted, full of feeling, sensible, intelligent, m. a learned man,

sāhva mfn having a name, named,

sāhvaya m. gambling with fighting animals

sahya mfn to be borne or endured, able to bear, endurable, agreeable, n. fellowship, assistance, m. convalescence, health,

sāhya n. conquering, overthrowing, aid, assistance, society, fellowship,

saḥ yaḥ anyone that, he who

√*śai* 1089/2 see *śyai, śrai*, to cause to congeal or freeze, DP in *pāka* 2. cooking,

√*sai* 1247/3 Cl 1 P *sāyati* to waste away, decline, DP in *kṣaya* declining,

saiddhāntika mfn connected with or relating to an established truth, m. one who knows an established truth or is versed in a *Siddhānta*

saika mfn added to one, plus one,

saikata mfn sandy, gravelly, n. a sandbank, any bank or shore,

saikṣava mfn sugared, sugary,

śaila mfn stony, rocky, made of stone, stone-like, rigid, m. a mountain, rock, crag,

sailaga m. a waylayer, robber,

saiṁha mfn leonine, lion-like,

saindhava mfn relating to the sea, oceanic, marine, coming from the Indus or Sindh, m. a horse, m.n. a kind of rock-salt, any salt,

saindūra mfn coloured with red lead or vermilion,

sainika mfn relating or belonging to an army, martial, drawn up in martial array, m. soldier, guard, sentinel,

sainya mfn belonging to or coming from an army, m. a soldier, an army, a guard, a body of troops, army,

sairibha m. a buffalo, the sky, atmosphere,

sairika mfn m. a ploughman, plough-ox, the sky, atmosphere,

śaithilya 1089/2 n. looseness, laxity, decrease, flaccidity, smallness, weakness, relaxation, remission, depression (of the mind), unsteadiness, vacancy (of gaze), negligence in, relaxation of rule. inattention, dilatoriness

śaiva mfn relating or belonging or sacred to *śiva* , coming or derived from *śiva* , m. a devotee of *śiva,* concerning *śiva,*

saj = √*sañj, 2.* in comp. for *sat*

sajāgara mfn waking, awake,

sajala watery, wet, humid, containing water

sajambāla mfn muddy, having mud or clay

sajana mfn together with men or people, frequented/inhabited by men, m. a kinsman

sajāni mfn together with a wife,

sajanu mfn born or produced together,

sajātīya mfn of the same caste, kind or species, similar, resembling,

sajātīyabheda difference of one from another of the same species, e.g. the difference between one man and another,

sajāya mfn having a wife, married,

sajīva mfn having life, alive,

√*sajj* 1131/2 to cling, adhere, fasten, fix to, attach to, root *sañj* 1132/3 to be attached, *sajjate* 1132/3 1/s/pres/pass. attached, is attached

sajja mfn fixed, prepared, equipped, ready for, fit for everything (said of hands and feet), dressed in armour, armed, fortified, (*ā*) f. equipment, armour, mail, dress, decoration,

sajjakarman n. the act of making ready or equipping, preparation,

sajjana m. a good or virtuous or wise man mfn well-born, respectable, virtuous,

sajjana mfn hanging round (e.g. round the neck), a flight of steps to water, ferry, equipment, preparation, caparisoning an elephant, a guard, sentry,

sajji√*bhū* to become prepared, make ready,

sajji √*kṛ* he prepares, makes ready, makes strung, strings a bow,

sajjita mfn fastened or attached to, fixed upon, equipped, prepared,

sajjuṣṭa mfn liked by the good,

sajoṣaṇa n. common enjoyment or pleasure,

sajoṣas mfn associated together, united, being or acting in harmony with (3rd), unanimous, kindly disposed, ind. together,

sajṛmbhikam ind. with a yawn, yawning,

sajuṣ mfn an associate, companion, ind. at the same time, besides, moreover,

sajya mfn having its string on, strung,

sajyotis mfn having the same or a common light, ind. according to the light, as long as the sun is in the sky,

√*śak* 1044/1 Cl 5 P *śaknoti* to be strong or powerful, be able to, or capable of, or competent for, to aid, help, assist, to be overcome or subdued, succumb, DP in *śakti* being able, having power, effecting

sāka = *śāka* n. a vegetable, herb, culinary herb,

śākabhakṣa mfn vegetarian,

sakacchapa mfn having tortoises along with them, i.e. along with tortoises,

sakaitava mfn deceitful, fraudulent, a cheat,

śakala m.n. a chip, piece, ½ an eggshell, a potsherd, a spark, n. a half, a half-verse, skin, bark, scales of a fish, the skull,

sakala 1. mfn having a soft or low sound, 2. mfn consisting of parts, divisible, complete, possessing all parts, entire, whole, all, wholesome, sound,

sakāla mfn seasonable, (*am*) ind. seasonable, early in the morning,

sakaladeha m. the whole body

sakalaha mfn having quarrels, quarrelsome,

sakalajana m. every person, everybody,

sakalaloka m. 'all the world', everyone,

sakalārṇamaya mfn containing all sounds,

sakalasiddhi f. the success of all, mfn possessing all perfection,

sakalavedin mfn all-knowing,

sakalavidyāmaya mfn containing all knowledge

sakalayati P. makes full,

sakalika mfn provided with buds,

sakaluṣa mfn troubled, impure,

sākalya n. totality, completeness, (*yena*) ind. entirely, completely,

sākalyaka mfn sick, unwell,

sākam 1197/2 ind. together, jointly, at the same time, along with

sakāma mfn satisfying desires, satisfied, consenting, willing (a girl), acting on purpose or with free will, full of love, a lover, (*am*) ind. with pleasure,

sakāmabhakti devotion with expectation of fruits and with selfish motives, (U)

sakāmabhāva attitude or feeling where there is desire as motive force, (U)

sākāṅkṣa mfn wishing, desirous, longing, requiring a complement, correlative, having significance,

sakara mfn having hands, possessing a trunk, mfn having rays, full of rays, bearing tax, liable to pay tax,

sakāra 3. mfn active, energetic,

sākāra mfn 1197/3 having form, having shape or a definite figure, beautiful,

sākāradhyāna (N) *samādhi* with forms,

sākāra upayoga comprehension, a defined form of experience, a definite imagination (indefinite imagination = *anākāra upayoga*)
sakarmaka mfn having consequences,
sakāśa mfn having appearance or visibility, visible, present, m. presence, nearness, L. m. presence, *tasya sakāśaṁ gam* go to the presence of him, i.e. go to him, *-sakāśe* ifc. in the presence of..., before..., ifc. (or with 6th) in the presence of or before,
sakaṣāya tinged with desire (Gam.), mfn dominated by passion,
sakaṣṭam ind. unhappily, unfortunately,
śakaṭa m. a cart or wagon
sakātara mfn cowardly, timid, (*am*) ind.
sakautuka mfn full of expectation, eager for, expectant of, (*am*) ind.
saketa mfn having the same intention,
saketu mfn having a banner, with a banner,
√*śākh* 1062/3 *śākhati* to embrace, pervade, DP in *vyāpti* pervading, occupying,
śākhā 1062/3 f. a branch, limb of the body, a division, branch of science, sub-division, a branch or school of the Veda (each school adhering to its own traditional text and interpretation, *caraṇa and śākhā* are sometimes used synonymously but *caraṇa* properly applies to the sect or collection of persons united in one school and *śākhā* to the text followed,
sakha m. a friend, companion, attended or ifc. accompanied by ,
sakhāyau (= *sakhāyā*) bear the same names (Gam.)
sakhadga mfn armed with a sword, sword in hand,
sakhe m.voc. my friend!
sakheda mfn having grief, (*am*) ind. sadly,
sakhelam mfn with a gentle motion,
sakhi m. a friend, assistant, companion, brother in law, strong case *sakhā* n. friend,
sakhī f. a female friend or companion, a woman's confidante, a mistress,
sakhīgaṇa m. 'friend-crowd', friends,
sakhījana m. friends
sakhila mfn friendly,
sakhura mfn with the claws or having claws,
sakhya 1130/3 n. friendship, intimacy with, fellowship, community, the attitude of a devotee, expressing the relationship of a friend with God,
sākhya n. association, friendship,
sakman n. association, attendance,
sakmya n. that which belongs to anything, peculiar nature,
śaknomi I am able, I have the power to 3/s/pres/indic/act √*śak*
śaknoti is able
sakopa mfn full of anger, enraged, (*am*) ind. angrily,
śakra 1045/1 strong, powerful, mighty (referring esp. to Indra)
sakratu mfn being of one accord or one mind with,
sakṛcchrutadhara mfn keeping in memory what was heard,
sakṛd in comp. for 1. *sakṛt*
sakṛdāgāmin m. 'returning only once again, being re-born', 2nd of 4 orders (Buddhist)
sakṛdgati f. only a possibility,
sakṛdvidyutteva a flash of lightning,
sakriya mfn having action, active, mutable, movable, migratory, *-tva* n. one who performs his religious acts,
sakṛjjyoti m. everlasting light (Gam.)
sakrodha mfn full of anger, angry, enraged,
sakṛpa mfn compassionate (*am*) ind. accompanied by *kṛpa (grace),*
sakṛt 1.mfn acting at once or simultaneously, ind. at once, suddenly, forthwith, once, formerly, ever, at once, together,

sakṛtpraja m. 'having offspring once a year', a crow, a lion,
sakrudh mfn wrathful, angry,
sakṣ Cl 1 P. *sakṣati* to go,
sakṣa mfn overpowering,
sākṣa mfn having a yoke of oxen, mfn having a rosary, having or with eyes,

plainly, actually, in reality, in person,

sākṣād 1198/1in comp. for *sākṣāt*

sakṣaṇa mfn having leisure for, mfn conquering, victorious,

sakṣaṇi mfn vanquishing, 2. connected or united with (6th, 3rd), a comrade, companion, possessor,

sakṣāra mfn caustic, acrid, pungent,

sākṣāt ind. with the eyes, with one's own eyes, before one's eyes, evidently, clearly, openly, manifestly, in person, in bodily form, personally, visibly, really, actually, in the presence of, immediately, directly,

sakṣata mfn having a crack or flaw eg. jewel

sākṣātkara mfn putting before the eyes, making evident to the senses, direct realisation, experience of Absoluteness

sākṣātkāra m. evident or intuitive perception, realization, experiencing a result of or reward for,

sākṣātkaraṇa n. the act of putting before the eyes, intuitive perception, actual feeling, immediate cause of anything,

sākṣātkartṛ mfn one who sees everything,

sākṣātkṛta mfn clearly placed before the eyes or the mind's eye,

sākṣātkriyā f . intuitive perception, realization,

sakṣatram mfn according to the rule of warriors,

sākṣi m. for *sākṣin,* in comp. for *sākṣin,* the witnessing principle, seer, witness, That which passively observes the actions of the body and the senses,

sākṣī *sa* + *akṣa* having eyes, see *sākṣin* 1198/1 witnessing, an eye-witness

sākṣibhāva m. the state of remaining as the witness alone,

sākṣicaitanya 'the *ātman* or *brahman'* HH, the witness consciousness,

sākṣicetana mfn as above,

sākṣidraṣṭha the witnessing seer, consciousness,

sākṣin 1198/1 mfn seeing with the eyes, witnessing, observing, m. the ever present, self-luminous, conscious, non-acting, witness of all including the mind, (in phil.) the ego or subject (as opposed to the object or that which is external to the mind),

sākṣya mfn visible to, n. testimony, evidence, attestation,

sakta 1132/3 mfn clinging or attached to (7th or comp.), belonging to, committed to, fixed or intent upon, directed towards, addicted or devoted to, fond of, engaged in, occupied with, hindered, impeded, impending, near at hand,

śakta 1044/2 mfn able, competent for, equal to, capable of_, able to be,

śākta mfn relating to power or energy, relating to the *śakti* or divine energy under its female personification, m. a worshipper of that energy, a sect, m. a teacher, preceptor,

saktatā f. *saktatva* n. attachment, addiction (esp. to worldly objects),

sakthi n. thigh, thigh-bone, the pole or shafts of a cart,

śakti 1044/2 f. power, ability, strength, might, effort, energy, capability, faculty, skill, capacity for, power over, the power or force of a *deva* as his wife, the female organ, the power or signification of a word, (in Gram.) the idea conveyed by a case *(kāraka),* the power or force or most effective word of a sacred text or formula, the creative power or imagination (of a poet), help, aid, assistance, gift, a spear, lance, pike, dart, sword,

sakti f. connection, entwinement (of creepers), clinging or adhering to (7th or comp.), attachment, addiction (esp. worldly objects),

śaktibandhana to have virile power

śaktimāna the powerful or that containing all qualities, having the qualities pres/mid or pass/part.

'The śakti belongs to that thing *śaktimāna,* which exists embodying different measures in different things and these measures are ordained by the *śaktimāna* himself.' 'The *śaktimāna* is the Absolute and is seen as sun and sunlight, moon and moonlight, fire and heat. The way the forces work creates the visible world.'
'*śaktimāna* is the conscious being, the Self, and *śakti* emanates from this *śaktimāna.* The *śakti* cannot be separated from the *śaktimāna* under any circumstances'

saktimat mfn attached or devoted to, fond of,

śaktipāta 'descent of grace', spiritual awakening, transmission of spiritual energy,

śaktisaṁcara transmission or transition of energy,

śaktivṛtti the power inherent in a word or sentence, 'manifests the primary apparent meaning of a sentence' (U),

saktu m. coarsely ground parched grains, grits, esp. barley grits,

sakukṣi mfn born from the same womb,

sakula mfn having a family, with one's family, belonging to a noble family, belonging to the same family,

sākula mfn perplexed, bewildered,

śakuna m. a bird, a partic. kind of bird (a vulture, kite, Pondicherry eagle), a kind of Brahman, a sort of hymn or song, n. any auspicious object or lucky omen, mfn indicating good luck, auspicious,

śākuna mfn repentant, regretful, derived from or relating to birds or omens, having the nature of a bird, ominous, portentous, m. a bird-catcher, augury, omen,

śakuni m. a bird,

sakuñjara mfn together with elephants

sakusumāstaraṇa mfn strewn with flowers,

sākūta mfn having significance, significant, having meaning, intentional, (*am*) ind. intentionally, emphatically, accurately, attentively, n. a desired object,

sakūti mfn full of desire, enamoured,

sakutūhala mfn full of curiosity,

sakuṭumba mfn together with one's family

śakya possible, able , capable of being, to be conquered or subdued, liable to be compelled, direct, explicit, literal,

sākyamuni m. Gautama Buddha,

śakyapratikāra mfn capable of being remedied, m. a possible remedy

śakye I am able 1/s/pres/mid

śakyase you are able, you can 2/s/pres/indic/pass. √*śak*

√*śal* 1058/3 Cl 1 A *śalate* to shake or to cover, Cl 1 P *śalati* to go, move, Cl 10 A *śālayate* to praise, DP (Cl 1) in ca*lana* shaking, trembling, *samvaraṇa* covering, *gati* going

śala m. a staff, a hedgehog prickle, a dart, spear,

śāla 1067/1 1. mfn being in a house etc., (*am* ind. at home), a householder, an enclosure, court, wall, fence, a tree, the Sal tree, any tree, a kind of fish,

śālā f. a house, mansion, building, hall, large room, shed, workshop, stable,

śalabha m. grasshopper, locust, moth type

salajja mfn feeling shame or modesty, bashful,

salajjita mfn ashamed, abashed,

salalitam ind, with sport, wantonly,

sālasa mfn languid, tired, lazy, indolent,

salavaṇa mfn with salt, n. tin,

√*śalb* √1059/3 Cl 1 A *śalbhate* to praise, boast, DP in *katthana* praising, boasting,

sālikā f. a flute,

salila mfn flowing, surging, fluctuating, unsteady, internal acquiescence, n. flood, surge, waves, pl. water, rainwater, rain, eye-water, tears, a kind of wind,

salīla mfn playing, sporting (not in

earnest), (*am*) ind. playfully, with ease, coquettishly,

śālin mfn possessing a house or room, ifc. possessing ...., versed in, abounding in, conversant with, distinguished for,

sallakī 1059/2 a plant boswellia thurifera, The sallakī is a medium sized tree with herbal uses for humans and animals. It has similar leaves to those of the bitter neem tree.)

sallakṣya n. a good aim, right aim or object,

sallekhana embracing death voluntarily when one's time is near, (Jaina) such as by gradually abstaining from food and water and meditating on the true nature of the Self, a means to achieve liberation,

salloka m.pl. good people, excellent persons

śālmalī f. the silk-cotton tree,

salobha mfn greedy, avaricious,

sālokya n. residence in the same heaven with, being in the same sphere or world,

śalya m.n. point of spear or arrow, thorn, prickle, m. a porcupine, kind of fish, a fence, boundary,

śalyaka m. hedgehog, porcupine, arrow, dart, spear, a scaly fish,

śalyoddhāra 1059/2 the extraction of thorns or arrows

√śam 1053/3 Cl 4 P *śamyati (te), śanati (te), śamati, (te), śamyati, śimyati,* Cl 9 *śamnāti,* to toil at, fatigue or exert oneself, to prepare, arrange, to become tired, finish, stop, come to an end, rest, be quiet or calm or satisfied or contented, to cease, be allayed or extinguished,
(Cl 9) to put an end to, hurt, injure, caus. *śamayati* to appease, allay, alleviate, pacify, calm, soothe, settle, to put to an and or to death, kill, slay, destroy, extinguish, suppress, leave off, desist, conquer, subdue,
DP in *upaśama* (Cl 4) being tranquil, in *darśana* (Cl 1) seeing, in *ālocana* looking at, inspecting, displaying,

śam n. welfare, happiness, blessing, 2. 1054/2 ind. blissful, auspiciously, fortunately, happily, well,

√sam 1. 1152/1 (or *stam*) Cl 1 P *samati* or *stamati* to be disturbed, (according to some 'to be undisturbed'), Cl 10 P *samayati stamayati,* to be agitated or disturbed, DP (Cl 1) in *a-vaiklavya* being confused, not being confused, (Cl 4) in *pariṇāma* altering, changing,

sam prefix with, together with, along with, altogether, (opp. to *vi*), used as a preposition or prefix to verbs and verbal derivatives expressing conjunction, union, thoroughness, intensity, completeness, sometimes prefixed to nouns like 2. *sama* indicating same, sameness,

śama m. tranquillity, calmness, rest, equanimity, quietude or quietism, absence of passion, abstraction from eternal objects through intense meditation, (śāmaṁ √kṛ to calm oneself, be tranquil), pacification, alleviation, cessation, extinction, absence of sexual excitement, impotence, convalescence, final happiness, emancipation from all illusions of existence, indifference, apathy, the hand, imprecation, malediction, mfn tame, domestic,

sama 1. mfn any, every,

sama 2. same, equal, like, identical with, similar, always the same, constant, unchanged, impartial towards (6th or 7th), even (not odd), a pair, having the right measure, regular, normal, right, equable, neutral, indifferent, equally distant from extremes, ordinary, common, middling, just, upright, good, straight, honest, easy, convenient, full, complete, whole, entire, even, smooth, flat, plain, level, parallel, m. peace, f.(*ā*) a year,

n. (*am*) level ground, a plain, equability, equanimity, equality, imperturbability, likeness, similarity, right measure or proportion, settlement, compensation, good circumstances, ind. in like manner, alike, equally, similarly, just, exactly, precisely, honestly, fairly,
mfn 1153/2 happy, prosperous,

sāma 1. 1204/1 n. likeness, similarity
2.mfn undigested, crude, not sufficiently prepared or matured,
3. in comp. for 2. *sāman, ca*lming, tranquillizing (esp.) kind or gentle words for winning an adversary, conciliation, negotiation,

samā 1152/1 1153/2 f. a year, a plain, equanimity, imperturbability, similarity, right measure or proportion ind. in like manner, alike, equally, together with, exactly, precisely, honestly, a half-year, season, weather, a day,

samā√bhā P. *–bhāti*, to appear like,

samabhāga m. an equal share,

samā√bhāṣ A. *-bhāṣate* to talk with,

samābhāṣaṇa n. talking together, conversation with,

samabhāva m. equability, homogeneousness mfn of like nature or property,

samabhibhāṣaṇa n. conversation with, colloquy with,

samabhi√1.dhā to speak to, address, to direct all one's thoughts to (2nd),

samabhidhā f. ifc. a name, appellation,

samabhi√dhyai P. to reflect deeply on, meditate on, to direct all the thoughts upon, long for (2nd),

samabhihita mfn addressed, spoken to

samabhi√gam P. to go towards together, approach, to go to, have sexual intercourse with,

samabhi√jan A. to spring up together, arise,

samabhi√jñā to recognize fully, entirely acknowledge or perceive,

samabhi√kram to go near to, approach,

samabhi√nand P. to rejoice together with, to greet, salute

samabhinandita mfn rejoiced with, congratulated,

samabhipluta mfn inundated, flooded, washed, overwhelmed, covered,

samabhiṣṭuta mfn extolled, celebrated,

samabhi√tarj P. to threaten/menace greatly,

samabhitas ind. towards, to (2nd),

samabhitiṣṭhati P. to mount upon (elephant),

samabhi√tyaj P. to give up entirely,

samabhityakta mfn wholly given up, renounced, risked,

samabhivyāhāra m. mentioning together, bringing together, association, company

samabhūmi f. even ground,

samabhyā√dā A. *–datte* to comprehend

samabhyā√gam to come near, to meet,

samabhyāgata mfn come near, approached,

samabhyāhāra m. bringing together, association, accompaniment,

samabhyā√nī P. *–nayati*, to lead near or towards, introduce,

samabhyarcita mfn greatly honoured, worshipped, saluted,

samabhy√ārth A. to petition, request

samabhyava√gā P. *–jigati* to go into,

samabhyāśa m. nearness, presence,

samabhyāsa m. practice, exercise, study,

samabhyunnata mfn risen, towering high (as clouds),

samabuddhaya even-minded, dispassionate, indifferent

samabuddhi mfn esteeming all things alike, indifferent,

samacakravāla n. a circle,
samācara mfn practising, observing, 2/s/impv *sam ā √ car* perform! accomplish!

sam ā √car Cl1 *samācarati* to act or behave or conduct oneself towards (7th), to practise, perform thoroughly, do, accomplish, to associate with,

samācāra 1159/1 mfn equal or similar in practice or in virtuous conduct,
m. procedure, practise, conduct, behaviour in(comp.), custom, usage, usual way or method,

observance of duties etc. , news, report, information, tradition, equal manners or customs,

samācaran performing, practising, observing, pres.part.act *ā√car*

samacaturaśra mfn having four angles equal, square, n.m. a regular tetragon, square,

samacaturbhuja mfn having four equal sides, m.n. a square or rhombus,

samacetas see *samacitta*

samacitta mfn even-minded, possessing equanimity, equable, indifferent, thoughts directed to the same subject,

samacittatva n. steadiness of thought, evenness of mind, equanimity towards,

sam√ad P. *–atti,* to eat completely up, devour,

samad f. fight, contest, battle,

samada mfn intoxicated, excited with passion, ruttish,

samā√dā P.A. (P.) to give, bestow, present, to give back, restore, A. to take away fully, take away with one, accept, receive, to apprehend, perceive, comprehend, find out, to take to heart, reflect on, to undertake, begin,

samādāna n. taking fully or entirely, taking upon one's self, contracting, incurring, beginning, undertaking, resolve, determination,

samādara m. great respect, veneration,

samadarśana 1152/2 mfn of similar (or *sama*) appearance, looking on all things or men with equal or indifferent eyes, seeing the same, *samadarśin* mfn regarding all things impartially,

samadarśin mfn looking on impartially, regarding all things impartially,

samadeśa m. even ground,

samādeśa m. direction, advice, instruction,

samā√dhā P.A. *–dadhāti, -dhatte,* to place or put or hold or fix together, to compose, set right, repair, put in order, repair, redress, restore, to add, put on (esp. fuel on the fire), to kindle, stir (fire), to place, set, lay, fix, to direct or fix the eyes or mind upon (with *dṛṣṭim, cittam, cetas, matim, manas*), to resolve or settle in one's mind (with *matim*), make up one's mind (followed by *iti*), to collect the thoughts or concentrate the mind in meditation (with *ātmānam* or *manas*), to be absorbed in meditation or prayer (without 2nd), to impose upon (7th), to entrust or commit to (7th), to establish in (7th), to effect, cause, produce, devote oneself entirely to,

samadhā ind. equally with,

samādhā m. putting together, adjusting, settling, reconciling, clearing up difficulties,completion, accomplishment,

samādhāna n. putting together, laying, adding (esp. fuel to the fire, composing, adjusting, settling, reconciliation, intentness, attention, eagerness, fixing the mind in abstract contemplation (as on the true nature of spirit), religious meditation, profound absorption or contemplation, justification of a statement, proof,

samādhānamātra n. mere contemplation or meditation,

samadharma mfn ifc. of equal nature or character, resembling,

sāmadharmārthanītimat mfn speech that is friendly, just, useful and wise,

samādhātum to keep, to place (infin.)

samādhi 1159/3 putting together, joining with, union, a whole, aggregate, completion, accomplishment, conclusion, setting to rights, adjustment, settlement, justification of a statement, proof, bringing into harmony, agreement, assent, intense contemplation, a unifying concentration, completion, profound or abstract meditation, meditation, intense contemplation of any object or sound (so as to identify the contemplator with that object or sound or the effects of that sound), absorption, union, intense application or fixing the mind on, persevering in difficulties, a state beyond experience and expression, 'wherein the the so-called distinction between the knower and the known is overcome and the consciousness is itself, and shakes not as a flame in a windless place' (U), 'in *samādhi* or absorption there is the transformation of all *vṛtti*s into the *brahmakāra vṛtti* which destroys ignorance, desires and actions, and settles down, extinguishing itself like burnt camphor' (U),

samādhibhāṣā 'a sort of uttering recorded when someone reached a state of *samādhi.* This state, being a state of union and complete peace would produce very nominal use of sound. Thus it is symbolic, and although just few sounds, it would explain much about the subject for which it was intended.'

sam-adhi- √gam 1154/1 to go towards together, come quite near, approach,

samadhigacchati he approaches, comes near, surpasses

samadhika mfn having a surplus with it, superabundant, excessive, exceeding, extraordinary, intense, plentiful,

samādhimat mfn absorbed in meditation, attentive, making a promise/assent

samādhin mfn absorbed in contemplation,

samādhistha mfn absorbed in meditation,

samādhitva n. the state of profound meditation or devotion,

samādhiyoga m. employment of meditation, the efficacy of contemplation

sāmadhvāni m. sound of the *sāman,*

samadhura mfn bearing an equal burden

samadhura mfn bearing an equal burden with, sweet, f. (*ā*) a grape

samadhva mfn being on the same road, travelling in company,

samā√dhyai P. *–dhyāyati* to meditate deeply upon, reflect upon, be lost in thought,

samadhyama mfn moderate,

samadhyayana n. going over or studying together, or, that which is gone over or repeated together,

samādiṣṭa mfn assigned, directed, enjoined (*√diś)*

samadṛś mfn looking indifferently or impartially on, regarding all things impartially,

samadṛṣṭi f. the act of looking on all things equally or impartially, mfn looking on all impartially, even-eyed,

samṛdṛta mfn very respectful,

samaduḥkha mfn feeling pain in common with another, compassionate,

samadvan mfn fighting, warlike,

samadyuti mfn equal in radiance,

samā√gam P. to come together (in a friendly or hostile manner, also sexually), meet, be united with, to come together (heavenly bodies), to come to, come near,

samāgama m. a coming together, meeting, meeting with, association, assembly of, conjunction (planets), approach, arrival,

samāgata 1159/1 mf. come together, assembled, met, joined,

samāgati f. coming together, meeting, union, approach, arrival, similar condition or progress,

samāghāta 1163/3 m. striking together, collision, conflict, war,

sāmagir mfn speaking kind words,

samagra 1153/3 mfn. all, entire, whole, complete, (*am*) ind. wholly, n. all, everything, fully provided with (3rd or comp.), one who has everything or wants nothing, together, in the aggregate

samagraśakti mfn possessing full force,

samagrasampad mfn one who has every happiness

samagravartin mfn entirely resting or

fixed upon,
samagrendu m. the full moon,
sāmagrī f. totality, entirety, completeness, esp. a complete collection of implements or materials,
śama m. tranquillity, calmness, rest, equanimity, quietude or quietism, absence of passion, abstraction from eternal objects through intense meditation, (śāmaṁ √kṛ to calm oneself, be tranquil), pacification, alleviation, cessation, extinction, absence of sexual excitement, impotence, convalescence, final happiness, emancipation from all illusions of existence, indifference, apathy, the hand, imprecation, malediction, mfn tame, domestic,
samaha ind. anyhow, somehow,
samāhāra m. seizing, taking hold of, aggregation, summing up, sum, totality, collection, multitude, (in gram.) conjunction or connecting of words or sentences (as by particle *ca),* compounding of words, a compound, withdrawal (of the senses from the world), contraction, abridgement, a name for diphthongs *ai* and *au,*
samāhartum to destroy, annihilate, *hartum* = infinitive of *hṛ*
samahīdhara mfn mountainous, having mountains,
samāhita 1160/1 put or held together, joined, combined, devoted, one who has collected his thoughts or is absorbed in abstract meditation, quite devoted to or intent upon, devout, steadfast, firm, put in order, set right, adjusted, ended, concluded, granted, admitted, equal to, like, m. a pure or holy man, n. great attention or intentness
samāhitadhī mfn one who has concentrated his thoughts in devotion,
samāhitamanas mfn having the mind absorbed (in anything),
samāhitamanobuddhi mfn having the mind or thoughts collected or composed,
samahyā f. fame, reputation,
samaja m. a multitude of animals, a number of fools, n. a forest,
samāja m. meeting with, falling in with, a meeting, assembly, party, a quantity, plenty, abundance, an elephant,
sāmaja mfn occurring in the *sāmaveda,* an elephant,
samajajyā f. place of meeting, meeting, assembly, fame, celebrity,
samajāti mfn equal in kind,
sāmājika mfn social, relating to an assembly, m. spectator, participator at an assembly,
samā√jñā to know or understand thoroughly, become acquainted with, ascertain, perceive, observe, recognize, caus. *–jñāpayati* to order, command, direct,
samājñā f. name, reputation, fame, cognitions, perceptions,
samājñapta mfn ordered, commanded,
samaka mfn equal, alike,
samakāla m. the same time or moment, ind. simultaneously,
sāmakalam ind. in a conciliatory or firendly tone,
samakālīna simultaneous with (comp.) contemporary, synchronous,
samakakṣa mfn having equal weight, equipoise, equilibrium,
samakara mfn having marine monsters,
samākāraṇa n. calling, summoning,
samākarṣin mfn drawing together, attracting, spreading or extending far, diffusing fragrance,
samākhyā f. name, appellation, explanation, interpretation, report, fame, celebrity,
samākhyāta mfn reckoned up, enumerated,
samakna mfn bent together, moving together or simultaneously,
samā√1.kṛ to bring together, unite, to gather, collect, make ready,
samakriya mfn acting uniformly in or towards (7th),
samākṛta mfn brought/collected together,

samakṣa 1153/2 being within sight or before the eyes, present, visible (*am, āt, e, atas*) ind. visibly, in the sight or presence of, manifestly,
samākṣepa m. hinting at suggestion of,
samakta mfn prepared, made ready, furnished with (3rd), combined or united with (3rd),
samākula mfn crowded together, full of, greatly agitated or troubled,
samala mfn having stains or spots, impure, sinful, n. excrement,
samālabdha mfn taken hold of etc. ifc. come into contact with,
samā√labh A. –labhate, to take hold of, seize, touch, to stroke, handle, obtain, to rub, anoint,
samālagna mfn adhering or united together, closely attached,
samālakṣya mfn visible, perceptible,
samā√lamb to hang on, cling to, to lean on, depend on, trust to, to take hold of, seize, grasp,
samālambana n. the act of clinging to, leaning on, support,
samālambha m. taking hold of, seizing a victim, unguent,
samalaṁkṛta mfn well-adorned,
samālāpa m. talk, conversation with,
samālī f. a collection of flowers, nose-gay
samāloca m. conversation, dialogue,
samālocya ind. having considered,
samāloka m. looking at, viewing/beholding,.
samālya mfn garlanded, crowned,
sam√am A. –amate to ask eagerly, solicit, win over, to fix or settle firmly, to ally or connect oneself with,
samam ind. in like manner, alike, equally, similarly, together with or at the same time with, just, exactly, precisely, honestly, fairly,
samāma m. length,
samamati mfn even-minded, equable,
samamātra mfn of the same size/measure,
samamaya mfn of like origin,
samāmnāta mfn repeated or mentioned together, handed down by tradition or from memory, ifc. mentioned as, n. mentioning together, enumeration,
samāmnāya m. enumeration, sacred texts in general, destruction of the world, mention together, collection or compilation of sacred texts, list, aggregate, traditional collection, handing down by tradition or from memory,totality,
samāmya mfn stretching/extending length
sāman 1205/1 1. n. acquisition, property, wealth, abundance, 2. calming, tranquillizing, kind or gentle words for conciliation or negotiation, 3. a metrical hymn, or song of praise, a partic. kind of sacred text or verse as arranged for chanting, the collection of *sāmans* the *sāmaveda,* any song or tune sacred or profane (also the hum of bees),
samana n. assembly, concourse, festival, intercourse, commerce, pursuit, amorous union, embrace, conflict,
samāna mfn (connected with 1., 2. *sama*), same, identical, uniform, one, alike, similar, equal, homogenous (sound or letter), moderate, common, general, universal, all, whole (number), being (=*sat* after adj.), virtuous, good, (*am*) ind. like, equally with (3rd), m. an equal, friend, digestive function of *prāṇa,* 'the life-breath which controls digestion and assimilation. It keeps an equilibrium in the body', mfn possessing honour or esteem, honoured by (6th), with anger, mfn having the same measure,
samanā ind. in one point, together, at a time, all at once, likewise, uniformly,
samānādhikāra m. the same rule or government or generic character,
samānādhikāraṇa n. grammatical agreement in case with (comp.), same predicament or category, common substratum, having a

common substratum (Vaiśeṣika phil.), the relation of abiding in a common substratum – Brahman, the space in the pot and the space in the cloud have a common substratum where only the limiting adjuncts differ, (U),

samānagati mfn 'going together', agreeing together,

samānagotra mfn being of the same family,

samānagrāma m. the same village,

samānagrāmīya mfn dwelling in the same village,

samānaguṇa mfn having equal virtues,

samānajana m. a person of the same rank,

samānajanman mfn having the same origin, of equal age,

samānajāti mfn of the same kind,

samānakāla mfn simultaneous, (*am*) ind. of equal length/quantity (as a vowel)

samānakalīna mfn simultaneous, contemporaneous,

samānakāraka mfn making all things equal or the same (said of time),

samānākṣara a simple vowel (short or long as opposed to a diphthong or *saṁdhyākṣara*

samānakṣema mfn balancing each other, having the same or an equal basis

samā√nand caus. *–nandayati* to gladden or rejoice,

samanantara mfn immediately contiguous to or following (5th or 6th), (*am*) ind. immediately behind or after,

samānārtha m. equivalence, mfn having the same object or end, having the same meaning as (3rd or comp.),

samānaruci mfn having the same taste,

samānarūpa mfn having the same colour as, having the same appearance as,

samanas mfn being of the same mind, unanimous, endowed with understanding,

samanaska mfn unanimous,

samānasthāna mfn being in the same place, same part of the month, n. interposition,

samānatā 1160/2 f equality with, community of kind or quality

samānatas ind. uniformly, with the same name,

samānatantra mfn having the same chief action, proceeding in one and the same line of action,

samānatejas mfn of equal splendour or glory

samānatra ind. on the same spot,

samānatva n. equality with, (3rd), community of quality,

samānavayas or *–vayaska* mfn the same age

samānayati Nom.P. makes similar or equal, equalises,

samānayoni mfn born of the same womb,

samandhakāra m. great/universal darkness

samaṅga mfn having all limbs, complete, m. a kind of game, name of a people

samaṅgala mfn endowed with happiness, auspicious,

samaṅgin mfn complete in all parts, furnished with all requisites,

sāmañjasya n. fitness, propriety, equity, justice,

samā√nī P.A. *–nayati, (te),* to lead or conduct together, join, unite, collect, assemble, to lead anyone to another, unite one person with another, to lead towards, bring near, to pour together (mingle) liquids, to bring or offer (an oblation), caus. *–nāyayati*

samānitam ind. honourably, respectfully,

samañjana mfn fitting together, n. anointing, particular eye ointment, adjustment,

samañjasa mfn proper, right, fit, correct, n. propriety, fitness, truth, consistency,

samaṅka mfn bearing the same mark/sign, a hook, crotchet,

samanmatha mfn filled with love, enamoured,

samanta 1155/1 mfn. having the ends together, contiguous, neighbouring, ind. on all sides, around, universal, whole, entire, all, f. neighbourhood,

sāmanta mfn being on all sides, bordering,

limiting, m. a neighbour, a vassal, feudatory prince, a leader, champion, n. a neighbourhood,
samantatas ind. on all sides, around, wholly, completely, 'having the ends together' , contiguous, in all respects, neighbouring, adjacent,
samantāt ind. from all sides, on all sides, all around,
samantikam ind. contiguously, near,
samantra mfn acompanied with sacred verses or texts,
samantraka mfn possessing charms/spells,
samantrin mfn together with counsellors,
samanu√bhū to enjoy together, feel, perceive
samanu√cint P. to reflect deeply about, meditate on, remember,
samanu√dhyai P.to reflect upon, think of
samanu√gā to go after together, follow quite closely,
samanu√gai P. –gāyati to repeat in verse or metre
samanu√gam P. *–gacchati*, to go after, follow, pursue,
samanugata mfn gone after or through, followed, pervaded, coherent or connected with,
samanu√grah P.A. *–gṛhṇāti, gṛhṇīte,* to collect or gather together, arrange or put in order,
samanugrāhya mfn to be favoured or treated graciously,
samanu√jñā to fully permit or allow or consent to, to indulge, to pardon, forgive, excuse, to grant leave of absence, dismiss, to take leave of, bid adieu,
samanukīrtana n. praising highly, high praise,
samanu√pad A. to enter into or upon, attain
samanu√paś P.A. to look well after, look at or on, to perceive, observe,
samanuni√śam to perceive, learn,
samanuṣya mfn together with men, visited or frequented by men,
samanu√5.vas P. to abide by, follow, conform to

samanu√1.vid caus. *–vedayati*, to cause to know or remember, remind,
samanvaya m. regular succession or order, connected sequence or consequence, conjunction, mutual or immediate connection, harmony,
samanveṣaṇa n. searching everywhere,
samanvita 1155/2 connected or associated with, fully endowed with, possessing (with 3rd), accompanied by, going along with, corresponding or answering to,
samānyā ind. equally, jointly, together,
sāmanya mfn friendly, favourable, skilful in chanting or singing,
sāmānya mfn equal, alike, similar, joint, common to, whole, entire, universal, common, common-place, vulgar, ordinary, insignificant, (*am*) n. equality, similarity, identity, normal state or condition, universality, totality, general or fundamental notion, common property, *(ā)* f. a common female, prostitute, (*am*) ind. after the same manner as, like,
sāmānyaguṇa general quality, common nature or characteristic (U),
sāmānyavastha undifferentiated condition, unmanifested state, (U),
sāmānyavijñāna (U) pure consciousness, homogenous intelligence, Brahman,

samanyu mfn same minded, unanimous, wrathful, angry, filled with sorrow, name of *śiva*
sam√āp P. *–āpnoti* to acquire or obtain completely, gain, accomplish, fulfil, caus. *–āpayati,* to cause to gain or obtain completely, to bring to an end, finish, to put an end to, put to death, destroy,
samāpa m. sacrificing, offering oblations to the gods,
samā√1.pā P. *–pibati,* to drink in entirely, suck in, absorb,
samāpādana n. the act of bringing about, accomplishing, etc. restoration,
samapa√dhyai to think ill or badly of,

meditate evil or injury against,

samāpadyana n. the being absorbed, absorption into,

samāpana mfn accomplishing, completing, concluding,

samāpanā f. highest degree, perfection, n. the act of causing to complete, completion, conclusion, coming to an end, dissolution, section, chapter, division of a book, profound meditation,

samāpatti f. coming together, meeting, encountering, accident, chance, falling into any state or condition, getting, becoming, completion, yieding, giving way,

samapi√1.dhā to cover completely,

samāpita mfn accomplished, finished concluded, done,

samāplava m. immersion in water, bathing, a bath,

samā√pṝ pass. *–pūryate,* to become completely full, 1161/2

sāmapradhāna mfn perfectly kind/friendly

sāmaprayoga m. the use of kind or friendly words

samāpta mfn completely obtained or attained, concluded, completed, ended, perfect, clever,

samāptāla m. a lord, master,

samāptaśikṣa mfn one who has completed his studies,

samāpti f. complete acquisition (as of knowledge or learning), completion, perfection, reconciling differences,

samāptika mfn one who has completed (esp. a course of Vedic study*),* final, finite

samāptisādhana n. means of completion

samā√pū P. *–punāti*, to purify thoroughly, purge,

samāpūrṇa mfn completely full, whole, entire

samara m. coming together, meeting, concourse, confluence, hostile encounter, conflict, struggle, war,

sāmara mfn with the immortals, accompanied by the gods,

samārambha m. enterprise, undertaking, spirit of enterprise, beginning, commencement,

samaraṇa n. battle, coming together, meeting,

samarcaka mfn worshipping,

samarcita mfn worshipped,adored,honoured

samārabdha mfn taken in hand, undertaken, begun, begun to be built, one who has begun, happened, occurred,

samārādhana n. conciliation, propitiation, gratification, a means of propitiating or winning,

samārambha m. undertaking, enterprise, spirit of enterprise, beginning,

samarana n. coming together, meeting,

sāmarasya (G) homogeneity, even essence, equilibrium, the process of bringing the body into a harmonious resonance with the Divine,

samārata mfn ceased from, desisted,

samārdava mfn having softness, with softness, together with leniency,

samardhaka mfn causing to prosper, granting any advantage,

samardhuka mfn prospering, succeeding, (*ā)* f. a daughter,

samarekha mfn forming an even line,straight

samārgaṇa mfn furnished with arrows,

samargha mfn cheap,

samarhaṇa n. respect, reverence, a respectful gift

samāroha m. mounting, riding upon, agreeing upon,

samāropa m. placing in or upon, stringing a bow, transference to (7th), attribution,

samāropaka mfn making to grow or thrive,

samāropaṇa n. transference, transposition, change of position, stringing a bow,

samāropita mfn caused to mount or ascend, placed in or on, displayed,

samarpaka mfn furnishing, yielding,

samarpaṇa n. the act of placing or throwing upon, delivering or handing over, presenting, making known, communicating,

samarpayati caus. *saṁ√ṛ* sends, gives, hands over,

samarpita mfn fixed, inserted, (like

spokes to the centre of a wheel), delivered to, given to,

sam√arth A.P. *–arthayate, (ti),* to make fit or ready, prepare, to finish, close, to connect with in sense (3rd), construe (grammatically), to judge, think, contemplate, consider, to suppose to be, to notice, perceive, find out, to fix upon, determine, approve, to cheer up, comfort, encourage,

samartha mfn having a similar or suitable aim or object, very forcible or adequate, well answering or corresponding to, suitable or fit for (6th or comp.), very strong or powerful, competent, capable of, having the same sense or meaning, connected in sense, having the same grammatical construction,
m. a word with force or meaning, significant word, the construction or coherence of words in a significant sentence, n. ability, competence, conception, intelligibility,

samarthaka mfn able to, capable of, maintaining, establishing, proving,

samarthana n. f. (*ā),* reflection, deliberation, contemplation, reconciling differences, reconciliation, objecting, objection, (*ā*)f. persuasion, invitation, insisting on the impossible, (*am*) n.establishing, maintaining, corroboration, vindication, justification, energy, force, ability, competence,

samarthanīya mfn to be determined or fixed or established,

samarthatara mfn more or most competent,

samarthatayā (with 6th) sameness of meaning, force or significance (words),

samarthatva n. ability, capability, competence,

samarthayukta mfn adequate to or qualified for (7th),

samārthin mfn seeking/desiring equality, seeking peace with (3rd),

samarthita mfn taken into consideration, considered, judged, regarded, resolved, determined, maintained, established, able, capable,

samarthitavat one who has judged, considered etc.

sāmarthya 1205/3 n. sameness of aim or object, or meaning or signification, belonging or agreeing together, adequacy, accordance, fitness, suitableness, the being entitled to, justification for, ability or capacity for, efficacy, power, strength, force , the force or function or sense of a word,

sāmarthyaṁ kṛ do one's utmost, strength,

samarti f. suffering loss, damage, misfortune

samārūḍha mfn mounted or ridden by (3rd), one who has mounted or ascended, riding upon, one who has agreed upon, grown, increased, grown over, healed,

sam ā √ruh P. *-rohati,* to ascend or rise to or upon, to advance towards or against, to enter upon or attain to, undertake, begin,

samarya Nom.P. (*ti),* to long for battle or war,
mfn attended by many people, frequented (sacrificial ceremony), attended by his followers (Indra), crowd, multitude (festive occasions), an assembly, congregation, community, tumult of battle,

samaryāda mfn bounded, limited, keeping within bounds or on the right course, correct, respectful, neighbouring, (*am)* ind. decisively, exactly, m. contiguity, vicinity,

sam√1.aś P.A. *–aśnoti, -aśnute,* to reach, attain, gain, obtain, to accomplish, to pervade or penetrate thoroughly, P. *–aśnāti* to eat, taste, enjoy, thoroughly enjoys,

sam√1.as P. *–asti,* to be like, equal (2nd), to be united with (*saha),* to be (there) exist,

sam√2.as P. *–asyati* to throw or put together, add, combine, compound, mix, mingle, connect, pass. *–asyate,* to be put together or combined, (in gram.) to be compounded, form a compound

sam√ās A. *–āste* to sit together, sit or assemble round, to sit, be seated, to hold a council, deliberate, to practice, observe, behave like, resemble, to be dejected or low-spirited, to mind, attend to, acknowledge,

samāśa m. a common meal, eating, a meal,

samāsa 1. 1158/2 throwing or putting together, aggregation, connection, union, totality, (*ena* , fully, wholly), succintness, conciseness, (ibc. and –*tas* concisely, briefly, (in grammar) composition of words, a compound word , euphonic combination, reconciliation, 2. 1163/2 m. abiding together, connection

sam ā √sad P. *–sīdati* to be-take oneself to, come near to, approach or advance to, reach, arrive at (2nd), to meet, encounter, attack,

samāsakta mfn suspended, attached to or fixed upon, harnessed with, dependent on, concerning, relating to (7th), intent upon, devoted to,

samāsama mfn du. equal and unequal

samasaṁdhi m. equal alliance, peace on equal terms,

samasaṁsthita mfn being in easy circumstances

samaśana n. eating together, over-eating, eating in general,

samasana n. the act of throwing or putting together, combination, composition, anything gathered or collected, mfn eating collected food,

samāsana n. sitting down, sitting together with (*saha*),

sam ā √sañj Cl1 P. *samāsajati* to fasten or stick together, join or attach to, fix or place on, wrap or suspend on,

samāsena adv. with brevity, briefly, in brief, in summary,

samaśīla mfn having the same customs or character,

sāmāsika mfn comprehensive, concise, succinct, brief, relating/belonging to a compound word, m.n. a compound word,

samāsita mfn formed into a collection, assembled, aggregated,

samaśnute he attains,

samaśnuva mfn reaching, taking hold of,

samāsokta mfn concisely expressed, contained in a compound,

samāsokti f. concise speech,

samasparśa mfn having the same contact, equal in touch,

samaśreṇi f. a straight line,

samaśruti mfn having equal intervals,

samasta 1158/1 mfn combined, united, all whole, inherent in or pervading the whole of anything, the aggregate of all the parts, m. a whole, the aggregate of all parts,

samastha occuring with an even number, being in flourishing circumstances, being level or even, equal, level, uniform, like, similar,

samā√sthā P.A. *-tiṣṭhati* to mount, ascend, to go to, to stop, halt, to undertake (a march), assume (a form), seek (a maintainance), apply (assiduity to), to perform, accomplish, caus. –*sthāpayati,* to cause to stop, cause to be performed or practiced,

samasthala n. even or level ground

samaṣṭi 1158/1 reaching, attaining, conclusion, collective existence, collectiveness, an aggregate, totality, the state of being an aggregate, the universe as a single person or whole,

samaṣṭi-abhimāni a cosmic existence

samāsthita mfn standing or sitting upon, persevering in (7th), one who has entered upon or submitted to (slavery etc.), one who has had recourse to, engaged in, occupied with, intent upon,

samasvara mfn having the same or a similar tone or accent,

samasya mfn to be put together, to be made

whole or complete,
samasyā f. junction, union, the being or remaining together with (comp.),
samatā 1152/2 sameness, impartiality, equanimity, sameness of level, identity with, fairness, impartiality towards, equableness, balanced state of mind, normal condition, mediocrity, benevolence
samātata mfn extended, stretched, strung (as a bow), continuous, uninterrupted
samatikrama m. going entirely over/beyond, deviating from, transgressing, omission,
samatikrānta exceeding, surpassing, fulfilled,
samatīrthaka mfn full to the brim,
samatīta mfn gone or passed by, more than one year old, the departed, the crossed over, the dead
samātmaka mfn possessing equanimity,
samātman mfn possessing equanimity,
samātṛ f. a step-mother,
samatribhuja mfn having three equal sides, m. an equilateral triangle,
samatsara mfn having envy or jealousy, envious, jealous of, indignant,
samatulā f. equal value,
samatulita mfn of equal weight,
samatva n. equality with, equableness, normal condition, similarity, uniform conduct towards, equanimity, indifference,
samatviṣ mfn equally bright or lovely,
samavabodhana n. thorough knowledge, intelligence, perception,
samava√budh to perceive clearly, understand fully, learn, know,
samavacchanna mfn covered all over
samā√vad to speak with certainty, state,
sāmavāda m. a kind word, conciliatory speech,
samavadhāna n. the being brought together, meeting, great attention, preparation,
samavadhīrayati disregards, pays no heed to,
samava√gam P. –gacchati, to perceive or understand thoroughly, become thoroughly acquainted with,
samāvaha mfn bringing about, effecting, causing, producing,
samava√lamb A. *–lambate,* to take hold of, clasp, embrace,
samava√lī A. *–līyate*, to be dissolved
samava√lok P *–lokayati,* to look at or about, to inspect, survey, to behold, perceive,
samavana n. helping, protecting,
samava√nī P.A. *-nayati (te),* to lead together, unite, to pour in together,
samava √āp Class 5 *–āpnoti,* to come to, attain, reach, 1157/3
samava√i Cl 2 *–avaiti* to come together, assemble, approach, to regard, consider,
samāvarjana n. attracting, winning,
samavarṇa mfn of the same colour, being of equal caste, m. community of caste,
samāvarta m. turning back, return to,
samavartin mfn being of a fair or impartial disposition, being equal, acting uniformly, being equidistant,
samavaruddha mfn shut up, enclosed, attained, obtained,
samā√5.vas to dwell or settle in, inhabit, to halt, camp for the night,
samāvāsa m. dwelling place, residence, abode, halting place, encampment,
samavasanna mfn sunk down, depressed,
samavasaraṇa n. meeting, assembling, an assembly, descent (of a *jina* from heaven to earth), or place of descent, aim, goal,
samavaśeṣita mfn left, spared, remaining
samavaskanda m. a bulwark, rampart,
samava√so P. *–syati* , to decide, be in agreement with another (time, place), to reach, attain,
samava√sṛ P. *–sarati* to come down, descend (from heaven to earth),
samavasrava m. flowing off, away or out,
samava√sthā caus. *–sthāpayati* to cause to stand firm or still, stop, to establish
samavasthā f. firm or fixed state or

condition, ifc. a similar state or condition,

samavasthita 1157/3 standing or remaining firm, present equally, arrayed, in full array,

samāvat mfn similar, equally great or much, ind. equally much,

samavatāra m. a sacred bathing place,

samavatta-dhāna mfn containing gathered pieces,

samava√vṛt caus.*–vartayati*, to turn towards,

samavavṛtta mfn turned towards,

samavāya 1157/3 m. coming or meeting together, contact, concourse, congress, assemblage, collection, crowd, aggregate, collision, conjunction of heavenly bodies, (in phil.) perpetual co-inherence, inner or intimate relation, constant and intimate union, inseparable concomitance, expressing relation between a substance and its qualities, between a whole and its parts, (e.g. between cloth and the yarn composing it), course, duration,

samavāyakaraṇa an attendant or concurrent or concomitant cause,

samavāyana n. the act of meeting or coming together etc.

samavāyasambandha m. intimate and constant connection, inseparable relation, connection by inseparable inherence,

samavāyatas ind. in consequence of constant and intimate contact or relation,

samavāyatva n. the state of intimate relation

samavāyin mf n met together, closely connected or united, inherent in (comp.) aggregated, m. a partner, the soul combined with a body, the individual soul,

sāmaveda 1205/2 m. 'veda of chants', name of a principal Veda, it contains a number of verses nearly all of which occur in the Rig-veda and which, modified in various ways, are chanted, mostly, by the *udgātṛ* priests at Soma sacrifices,

samāvedya mfn to be told or communicated fully,

samavekṣita mfn observed, considered, (*ava-√īkṣ)*

samāveśa m. entering together or at once, meeting, penetration, absorption into, simultaneous occurrence, co-existence, (in gram.) applying together, common applicability of a term, agreeing,

samaveta mfn come together, assembled, met, united, all, closely connected with, contained or inherent in,

samavibhakta mfn divided equally, symmetrical,

samā√1.vid caus. *–vedayati*, to cause to know or be known thoroughly, report fully, announce, tell,

samā√viś to enter together or at once, take possession of, occupy, penetrate, fill, sit or settle down on or in, to fall into any state/condition, to apply one's self to, begin, undertake, caus. *–veśayati,* to cause to enter together or thoroughly, introduce, insert, to cause to sit down, to conduct, lead or bring to or into, to place or fix (eyes or mind) on, direct towards, (with *svasmin)* to insert into oneself, A. to deliver over, consign, commit or entrust to,

samāviṣṭa 1162/3 entered together or at once, filled with, imbued with, taught or instructed in,

samā√vṛt A. *–vartate,* to turn back, come back, return, (esp. a Vedic student after completing his studies,) to come near, approach, turn out well, succeed, to come to nought, perish, caus. *–vartayati,* to cause to return, drive away or home, to dismiss (a pupil after his studies), to repeat, recite,

samāvṛta mfn enveloped, covered, surrounded, protected or guarded by (3rd), filled or inhabited by (comp.),

closed to i.e. withdrawn from,
samavṛtta mfn uniformly round,
the prime vertical circle,
samāvṛtta mfn turned back, returned, approached, come from, completed,
samavṛtti f. even state or temper, equable, equanimity, fair, moderate,
samaya P. *–yati*, to level, regulate,
m. a time, coming together, meeting or a place of meeting, intercourse with,
(3rd), coming to a mutual understanding, agreement, treaty, convention, conventional rule or usage, established custom, law, rule, practice, observance, the conventional meaning or scope of a word, appointed or proper time, right moment for doing anything, opportunity, occasion, time, season,
samā√yā Cl 2 *–yāti,* to gather here together, meet, to come near, approach, come from, go to, to elapse, pass away, to fall upon, get into any state or condition,
samayā ind. through, into the middle of or midst of anything, entirely, thoroughly, in the neighbourhood of, near (with 2nd.) 2. in comp. for *samaya*),
samayā√kṛ to pass time, lose time,
√sāmaya 1. 1205/1 Cl 10 P *sāmayati* to conciliate, appease, pacify, tranquillize, DP in *sāntva-prayoga* appeasing, conciliating, soothing, 2. mfn connected with or suffering from disease,
samāya m. a visit, arrival,
samāyata mfn drawn out, lengthened, extended, long, come together or near,
samāyatta mfn resting or dependent on,
sāmayika mfn based on agreement, conventional, customary, of the same opinion, like-minded, seasonable, timely, precise, exact, periodical, temporary,
sāmayikābhāva m. temporary non-existence (as that of a water-jar which has been removed from its place to be again restored to it),
samāyin mfn occurring together or simultaneously,
samayitavya mfn to be levelled, to be adjusted (dispute),
śamayitṛ m. slayer, extinguisher, an alleviator, tranquillizer,
samayocita mfn suitable to the occasion or time or to an emergency,
(*am*) ind. as the occasion demands,
samāyoga m. conjunction, union, contact with, connection, making ready, preparation, fitting an arrow to a bow, aiming, cause, origin,
samāyukta mfn joined, prepared, ready, entrusted, committed, met together, supplied with, intent upon, devoted to,
samāyuta mfn joined or brought together, gathered, collected, made of (comp.), united or connected with, possessed of (comp.)
√śamb 1055/2 Cl 1 P *śambati* to go, Cl 10 P *śambayati* to collect, DP in *sambandhana* (cl10) collecting, heaping together
√samb see *śamb*, DP *sambandhana*
√sāmb 1207/1 see *samb,*
DP in *sambandhana*
sambaddha mfn bound or tied together, joined, connected, connected in sense, coherent, having meaning, shut, closed, connected or covered or filled with, belonging or relating to, combined with i.e. containing, attached to anything i.e. existing, being, found in, ind. jointly, moreover
sambādha m. a throng, crowd, ifc. f. (*ā*) 'crowded with', ' full of', female organ, pressure, affliction, the road to hell, contracted, narrow,
sambahula mfn very much or many, very numerous, plentiful,
śambala n. m. provisions for a journey, envy, jealousy,

sambāḷha mfn firm, strong,
sambandha 1177/3 m. binding or joining together, close connection or union or association, conjunction, inherence, connection with or relation to, (in phil.)- relation or connection is said to be of 3 kinds – *samavāya, saṁyoga, svarūpa,* personal connection by relationship, fellowship, friendship, intimacy with, a relation, relative, kinsman, fellow, friend, ally, a collection, volume, book, prosperity, success, a kind of calamity, fitness, propriety, the application of authority to prove a theological doctrine, mfn able capable, right, proper,
often used in error for *saṁbaddha*
sambandhaka n. connection by birth or marriage, relation, friendship, intimacy, a relation, friend, mfn relating to, concerning, fit, suitable,
sam-bandhi(n) 1177/3 mfn. a relation, kinsman, joined or connected with
sambandhitā f. belonging to (comp.), connection with, relation to, relationship, connection by marriage,
sambandhitva n. relation to or connection with, kinship, relationship,
sambandhu m. a kinsman, relative,
sam√bhā P. *–bhāti,* to shine fully or brightly, be very bright, shine forth, to appear, be visible or conspicuous, seem to be,
sambhajanī f. eating together,
sam bhakta mfn distributed, divided, shared, participating in,
sambhakti 1178/2 f. distribution, allotment, bestowal, possessing, enjoying, favouring, honouring
sambhaktṛ mfn one who distributes, grants, one who shares or participates, one who favours, honours or worships
sambhala a match-maker, a suitor, wooer,
sambhara mfn one who brings together, a supporter, bestower,
sambhāra m. (ifc.f.(*ā*) bringing together, collecting, preparation, equipment, provision, necessaries, materials,
sambharaṇa 1179/2 m. a kind of brick, f. a particular soma vessel, n. putting together, composition, arrangement, preparation, collection, mass, multitude
sambhārin mfn full of (comp.)
sambhāṣa m. discourse, talk, conversation, f. (*ā*) engagement, contract, agreement, watchword, greeting,
sambhava m. (ifc.f.(*ā*) being or coming together, meeting, union, inclusion, intercourse, finding room in, (ifc.= contained in), birth, production, origin, source, being produced from (5th), cause, reason, being brought about, occurrence, appearance, (ifc. = occurring or appearing in), being, existence, capacity, ability, possibility, *ena* according to possibility, as possible
(in phil.) equivalence, (one of the *pramāna*s) e.g. 100 cents/ a dollar, agreement, conformity, compatibility, adequacy, acquaintance, intimacy, loss, destruction, mfn existing, being,
saṁbhavāmi I come into being, I originate myself, 3/s/pres/ind/act *sam √bhū*
sambhavana n. containing,
sambhāvana mfn having a high opinion of (comp.), f. (*ā*), (*am*) n. bringing together, assembling, bringing near, procuring, coming together, meeting with (6th), worship, honour, respect, esteem, regard for, opinion of, imagination, supposition, assumption, fitness, adequacy, competency, ability, fame, celebrity,
sambhāvanā mfn having a high opinion of, f. bringing together, assembling, bringing near, procuring,
sambhavin mfn possible,
sambhāvin mfn faithfully adhering or devoted to, suitable,
sambhaviṣṇu m. a producer, creator,
sambhāvita mfn (having been) honoured, brought together, brought

about, seized, grasped, thought highly of, esteemed, honoured, respected, presented with (3rd), considered, supposed, conjectured, reflected, adequate, fit for, n. conjecture, supposition,

saṁbhāvitasya of the honoured, of the famous, past passive causative part.

sambhāvya gve. to be supposed, supposable, m. to be honoured or respected or well treated, to be honourably mentioned, to be regarded or considered as, to be supposed or expected, possible, probable, suited, fit, adequate, credible, conceivable,

sambheda m. breaking, piercing, becoming loose, falling off, disjunction, division, separation, sowing dissension, a kind, species, union, junction, a mixture, confluence of two rivers,

sambhinna mfn completely broken/divided, interrupted, abandoned,

sambhoga m. (ifc. f. (*ā*) complete enjoyment, pleasure, delight in (comp.), carnal or sensual enjoyment, sexual union with (comp.),

sambhogin mfn enjoying together or enjoying each other mutually, enjoying, using, possessing, m. a sensualist, libertine,

sambhoja m. food,

sambhojaka m. one who serves at a meal, an eater, taster,

sambhojana n. eating together, a common meal, dinner party, food,

sam√bhram Cl 1 *-bhramati,* Cl 4 –*bhrāmyati,* P. to roam or wander all about, go quite astray, to be confused, agitated, be in a flutter,

sambhrama 1179/3 m. whirling round, haste, hurry, flurry, confusion, agitation, activity, eagerness, zeal, awe, deference, respect, error, mistake, delusion, grace, beauty, mfn agitated, excited,

sambhrānta mfn confused, agitated, excited, quickened, brisk, lively (gait),

sam√bhṛ P.A. *–bharati, (te*), to draw together, roll or fold up, A. to close (the jaws), to bring together, gather, collect, unite, compose, arrange, prepare, to pay back, maintain, cherish, to offer, present

sambhṛṣṭa mfn thoroughly fried or roasted, parched, dried, dry, brittle,

sambhṛta mfn brought together, collected, assembled, accumulated, provided, stored, laden, filled, covered, endowed with, carried, borne (in the womb), well maintained or nourished, honoured, respected, produced, caused, made, prepared,

śambhu or *śambhū* mfn being or existing for happiness or welfare, granting or causing happiness, beneficent, benevolent, helpful, kind, Śiva,

sambhu mfn produced from, made of (comp.), m. a parent, progenitor,

sam√bhū P.A. *–bhavati (te),* to be or come together, become, arise, assemble, meet, be joined or united with, to be united sexually with, to be born or produced from, arise, spring up, develop, originate, to happen, occur, be, be found, exist, to be possible, to be or become anything, to accrue to, to prevail, be effective, to be able to or capable of, to enter into, partake of, attain to (2nd), caus. *–bhāvayati,* to cause to meet, assemble etc. to honour, revere, salute, to receive or accept graciously, to imply, suggest a possibility, to regard or consider as, to think it possible that, 1179/1

sambhukta mfn eaten, enjoyed, run through, traversed,

sambhūta 1179/2 mfn being or come together, united or combined with, become, born, produced or arisen, or proceeding from, created, (ibc.) one in whom anything has arisen, become or changed into anything, made or composed of, proceeding from, produced by, originating in, capable, adequate, equal,

saṁbhūtva n. state of union or combination with,

sambhūti f. the fact of being born, birth, origin, production, growth, increase, manifestation of might, great or superhuman power, suitability,

saṁbhūya 1179/2 ind. being together, being united or combined with, as adv. together, in common, in company,

saṁbhūyas 1179/2 Nom P *saṁbhūyasyati* DP in *prabhūtbhāva* being abundant,

sambodha 1178/1 m. perfect knowledge or understanding, *-na* mfn. awaking, arousing, recognizing, perceiving, reminding, the act of causing to know, calling to, the vocative case or its termination

sam√brū to speak well, converse, A. to talk together, agree, to say anything to,

sambuddha mfn wide awake, clever, wise, prudent, well-perceived, perfectly known or understood, completely realised, m. a Buddha or a Jaina deified sage, the enlightened one,

sambuddhi f. perfect knowledge or perception, the vocative case or its termination, calling out to someone (distant), making one's self heard, ,

sam√budh A. *–budhyate*, to wake up, to perceive or understand thoroughly, notice, observe, know, caus. *–bodhayati,* to cause to wake up, rouse, to cause to know, inform, advise, instruct, teach,

saṁcakāsti P. lights up, illuminates,

saṁ√cakṣ A. *-caṣṭe* to look attentively at, observe, notice, consider, survey, examine, reflect upon,

saṁcakṣas m. a priest, sage,

saṁ√cal P. *–calati* to move about or to and fro, oscillate, quiver, to move away, set out, depart from (5th),

saṁcalana 1132/1 moving about, agitation, trembling, shaking

saṁ√car P.A. *–carati (te),* to go or come together, meet, join, to roam, enter, traverse, pervade, to pass over to, to move, live, exist, be, to practise,

saṁcara mfn going about, moving, going together, simultaneous, m. a way, road, path, a difficult passage, defile, bridge over a torrent, evolution, development, the body,

saṁcāra m. walking about, wandering, roaming, driving or riding, any motion, passing over, transition, transference to (comp.), transmission of disease, contagion, course, path, way, track (wild animal), course of life, career, difficult progress, difficulty, distress, leading, guiding, impelling,

saṁcaraṇa mfn fit or suitable for going or walking upon, accessible, practicable, going or coming together, meeting, converging, (*am*) n. going together or through, passage, motion, passing over (from, in, by), with *samudram-* navigation,

saṁcāraṇa n. bringing near, mixing, adding, delivering, insertion, transmission,

saṁcārin mfn going together or about, going hither and thither, roaming, wandering, moving in (7th or comp.), going or passing from one to another, transmitted, infectious, ascending and descending (a note or tone), penetrating into (comp.), coming together, meeting, in contact with, adjacent to, taken with one e.g. umbrella, being in (comp.), engaged in, occupied with (comp.), passing away, transitory, unsteady, inconstant, impelling, difficult, m. incense or the smoke from incense, air, wind, *-tva* n. transitoriness, inconstancy (of feeling),

saṁcaya 1132/1 collection, gathering, accumulation, dense, thick

saṁcayavant mfn possessing an

accumulation of wealth, rich, with *arthais* rich with money, having capital,
saṁceṣṭana moving about restlessly, exerting oneself
saṁcetana to be fully conscious
saṁchinna 1132/3 mfn. cut to pieces, sever
saṁ√1. ci P.A. to heap together, pile up, to arrange, put in order,
saṁ√2.ci to reflect, ponder,
saṁcikīrṣu mfn wishing to do or perform,
saà√cint P. to think about, think over, consider carefully, reflect about, to design, intend, destine,
saṁcintana n. careful consideration or reflection, anxiety,
saṁcintita mfn carefully considered or thought about, deliberated, *-vat* mfn one who has carefully considered or 'he has carefully considered',
saṁcintya ind. intentionally, 2. to be thought over or considered, to be regarded as,
saṁcinvānaka mfn occupied with the accumulation of wealth or treasures,
saṁ√4.cit to observe together, survey, notice, to agree together, be unanimous,
saṁcita mfn piled together, heaped up, collected, accumulated, fitted or provided with, full of (comp.), impeded, obstructed, frequently practised or exhibited,
saṁciti f. a piling, pile, heaping, together, collecting, saving,
saṁcodana 1132/2 urging, exciting, inflaming, arousing
saṁcūrṇana 1132/2 n. the act of grinding to powder, comminution, crushing or breaking to pieces,
saṁ√1.dā to give together, present, grant, bestow, to hold together, to meet,
saṁ√3.dā to cut together, gather by or after cutting, to cut, divide,
saṁ√4.dā to bind together, fasten together,
saṁdadi mfn grasping, comprehending,
saṁdagdha mfn burned up, consumed,
saṁ√dah P.A. – *dahati (te),* to burn together, burn up, consume by fire, destroy utterly,
saṁdāha m. burning up, consuming,
saṁdalita mfn pierced through, pierced,
saṁdāna n. the act of cutting or dividing, 2. m. a bond, halter, fetter,
saṁdānita mfn bound together, tied,
saṁdaṁśa 1143/1 m. a pair of tongs or nippers, thumb and forefinger used together, the nippers of a crab, compression of the lips, a chapter or section of a book, junction, connection, teeth too close together in vowel pronunciation,
saṁdarbha 1143/1 m. stringing or binding together (esp. into a wreath or chaplet), weaving, arranging, collecting, mixing, uniting, a literary or musical composition
saṁdarpa m. pride, arrogance, boasting of (comp.),
saṁdarśa m. sight, appearance, *√dṛś*
saṁdarśana n. the act of looking steadfastly, gazing, viewing, seeing, sight, surveying, inspection, consideration, causing to see, showing, displaying,
saṁ√das to die out or become extinguished,
saṁdaśasyati pardons (a sin), remits,
saṁdaṣṭa mfn bitten, compressed, nipped, a fault in pronunciation, (teeth too close together),
saṁdāya mfn giving, presenting, 2. m. a rein, leash,
saṁdeha 1143/3 m. a conglomeration of material elements (said contemptuously about the body), doubt, uncertainty about, risk, danger,
saṁdehacchedana n. removal of doubt,
saṁdehagandha m. a whiff of doubt,
saṁdehatva n. state of doubt or uncertainty,
saṁdehin mfn doubtful, dubious,
saṁdeśa 1143/2 communication of intelligence, message, information, errand, direction, command, order to, a present, gift, the message words,
saṁ√1.dhṛ P.A. to place, hold, put, draw,

join, fasten, fix, or sew together, unite, combine, connect with, A. to bring together, reconcile, to be reconciled, agree with, to mend, restore, redress, to fix on (arrow etc.), to direct towards, aim at, to be a match for, to comprehend, to use, employ,

saṁdha mfn holding, possessing, joined, united, n. junction, connection,

saṁ√dhā –P.A.*dadhāti, te,* to place or put or hold etc. together, unite, A. to bring together, reconcile, to be reconciled, agree with, to mend, restore, redress,

saṁdhā f. intimate union, compact, agreement, a promise, vow, design, intention, mixture, a boundary, limit, fixed state, condition,

sāṁdha mfn situated at the point of contact,

saṁdhāna mfn joining, uniting, healing, f. mixing, distilling, a metal foundry, (*am)* n. the act of placing or joining together, junction, union, meeting of men, a joint, point of contact, a boundary, a means of union, growing together, healing, fixing on (arrow), aiming at, perceiving, perception, euphonic combination of words, bringing together, alliance, association, friendship, making peace with, compounding, mixing, a link – that by which things are conjoined, a catalytic agent,

saṁdhāraṇa mfn holding together, supporting (life), (*ā)* f. attitude, posture, position, direction (of thoughts), *(am)* n. the act of holding together, supporting, maintaining, bearing, holding in or back, checking, restraining,

saṁdhārtṛ m. one who holds together,

saṁdhayati Nom.P. puts or joins together,

saṁdhi or *sandhi* mfn containing a conjunction or transition from one to the other, m. junction, connection, combination, union with, association, intercourse with, comprehension, totality, the whole essence or scope of, agreement, compact, a putting together, compact, alliance, peace, putting together of sounds in word and sentence, euphonic combination, junction of day and night, i.e. morning or evening twilight, contrivance, management, place or point of connection or contact, juncture, hinge, boundary, critical juncture, crisis, opportune moment,

saṁdhita mfn joined or fastened together, put to or on, fixed (as an arrow), joined or united with, allied, one who has concluded an alliance,

saṁdhiteṣu mfn having an arrow fitted on a bow-string,

saṁdhitsu wishing to make peace or form an alliance with *(saha),*

saṁ√dhṛ P.A. *–dhārayati (te),* to hold together, bear, carry, hold up, support, preserve, observe, maintain, keep in remembrance, to hold back, restrain, to suffer, endure, to hold or fix the mind on, to promise, to hold out, live, exist, to be ready to serve anyone with,

saṁdhṛta mfn firmly held together, closely, connected,

saṁ√dhū P.A. to scatter or distribute liberally, bestow on, A. to seize or carry off,

saṁdhukṣaṇa mfn inflaming, exciting, n. the act of kindling, inflammation,

saṁdhya mfn pertaining to *saṁdhi,* or junction, being on the point of junction, thinking about, reflecting,

saṁdhyā f. time of junction (of day and night) , du. morning and evening twilight, morning twilight (of a *yuga),* prayers recited at dawn, holding together, union, juncture, junction, the period which precedes a *yuga* or 'age of the world', promise, agreement, assent, thinking about, reflection, meditation,

sāṁdhya mfn produced by coalescence (as a syllable), relating to the morning or evening twilight,
saṁ√dhyai P. *–dhyāyati* to reflect or meditate on, think about,
saṁdhyāṁśa m. evening twilight of a *yuga*
saṁdhyāsamaya m. twilight time, evening,
saṁdhyāśaṅka m. the evening conch-shell,
saṁdhyāvandana n. morning and evening prayers and acts of worship,
saṁdhyopāsana worship at the junctions of time – sunrise, sunset, midday,
saṁ√2.dī to shine together, to bestow by shining,
saṁdigdha mfn smeared over, covered with, confused, confounded with, questioned, questionable, doubtful, dubious, uncertain, unsettled, (*am*) n. an ambiguous suggestion or expression,
saṁdīna mfn greatly depressed,
saṁ√dip A. *–dipyate*, to blaze up, flame, burn, glow, caus. *–dīpayati* to set on fire,
saṁdīpana 1143/3 mfn kindling, inflaming, exciting, arousing, n. the act of kindling or inflaming or exciting
saṁdīpta mfn inflamed, flaming, burning,
saṁ√diś –diśati to point out, appoint, assign, to state, tell, direct, command, despatch anyone,
saṁḍiśa m. = *saṁdaṁśa* a pair of tongs or nippers,
saṁdiṣṭa mfn pointed out, assigned, stipulated, promised, n. news, tidings, information,
saṁḍiśṭavat one who has given an order or message to (6th),
saṁḍiśya ind. bidding farewell,
saṁdita mfn cut off, cut, 2. mfn bound or fastened together, detained, caught,
saṁdṛbdha mfn strung together, arranged or bound in a tuft, interwoven, composed, confirmed,
saṁ√dṛś 1144/1 P.A. to see together or at the same time, see well or completely, behold, view, perceive, observe, consider, A. and pass. to be seen at the same time, appear together with, to look like, resemble, be similar or equal, to be observed, become visible, caus. *–darśayati* to cause to be seen, display, show,
saṁdṛś f. sight, appearance, a beholding,
saṁdṛśe 4/s/f as an object of vision
saṁdṛṣṭa mfn completely seen or beheld
saṁdṛṣṭi f. complete sight, full view, aspect,
saṁdṛśyante are seen 1/pl/pres/pass
saṁduṣaṇa mfn corrupting, defiling, depraved, wicked, bad, ill-disposed
saṁduṣyati becomes utterly corrupt, unclean, polluted,
samedha mfn full of strength or vitality,
samedhana n. thriving, prospering, growth,
sameghalekha mfn having streaks of cloud
sameta mfn come together, joined, got into any state or condition, come into collision with, united, possessed of, encountered, in collision with (3rd), come near/to,
sameti √*i* P. to go or come together, meet at (2nd) or with (3rd or 4th), encounter (as friends or enemies), to come together in sexual union, cohabit, to come to, arrive at, approaches, visits, seeks, begins, gets merged,
saṁga m. 'coming together', conflict, war,
saṁ√gam A.P. *–gacchate, (ti),* to go or come together, come into contact or collision, meet, join or unite with, unite sexually with, to harmonize, agree, fit, suit,
saṁgama m.n. (f. ifc.) coming together, meeting, union, intercourse or association with, connection or contact with, sexual union, confluence of two rivers, harmony, adaptation, point of intersection,
saṁgamaka mfn leading to, showing the way,
saṁgamana mfn causing to assemble, gatherer, n. concurrence, meeting with, concur, coming together, partaking of,
saṁgamaṇīya mfn leading to union,

effecting union,
saṁgamita mfn brought together, united,
saṁgara m. agreeing together, agreement, assent, conflict, fight, a bargain,
saṁgata mfn come together, met, encountered, allied with, friendly to, fitted together, proper, suitable, contracted, shrunk up, m. an alliance/peace based on mutual friendship, (*am*) n. coming together, meeting with, intercourse, alliance, association, friendship, the results of good company,
saṁgatha m. meeting place, centre, conflict, (*ā*) f. confluence,
saṁgati f. coming together, meeting with, going or resorting to (7th), association etc., meeting or coming to pass accidentally, chance, accident, adaptation, appropriateness fitness, applicability, connection with, relation to, becoming acquainted, knowledge, questioning for further information,
saṁgāyana n. singing or praising together,
saṁgha m. (*sam* +√*han*) 'close contact or combination', any collection or assemblage, heap, multitude, quantity, crowd, a society, company, community, congregation, church,
saṁgharṣaṇa n. ' rubbing together' friction, rivalry, envy,
saṁghasa m. food, victuals,
saṁghata mfn heaped, piled up,
saṁghāta 1130/1 mfn striking or dashing together, killing, crushing, closing (of a door etc), combat, war, battle, compressing, compactness, hardening, close union, complexity, combination, a company of fellow travellers, caravan, phlegm, a bone, any aggregate of matter, body, (in gram.) a compound as a compact whole as opposed to its single parts, a vowel with its consonant,
(E) p. 102 the body-complex – sense-organs, mind, intellect and ego, organism, organic whole

saṁghāṭa m. carpentry, fitting and joining of timber,
saṁghaṭṭa m. rubbing or clashing together, friction, conflict, junction or union with (3rd), embracing,
saṁgīrṇa mfn agreed, assented to, promised
saṁgīta mfn sung together, sung in chorus or harmony, n. a song sung by many voices, or accompanied, chorus, a concert, any song or music, the art or science of singing with music and dancing,
saṁgīti f. singing together, concert, symphony, the art of singing with music and dancing, conversation,
saṁgopana mfn hiding or concealing well,
saṁ√grah to seize or hold together, take or lay hold of, grab, grasp, encourage, support, favour, protect, to apprehend, conceive, understand, to gather together,
to include, comprehend, contain,
to draw together, make narrower,
to hold in, restrain, close the mouth,
to concentrate the mind, to marry,
caus. *grāhayati* cause to grasp, take hold of, comprehend, understand,
saṁgraha m. holding together, maintenance, 1129/2 bringing together, assembling (of men), a summary, catalogue, list, (in phil.) agglomeration (=*saṁyoga)* sum, amount, totality, *(eṇa* completely, entirely), *(eṇa or āt* shortly, summarily, in few words), making narrower, thinner, the thin part of anything, keeping, guarding, protecting, a guardian, ruler, manager, winning, entertaining, marrying, perception, notion, mention, mentioning, loftiness,
saṁgrāha m. grasping, laying hold of, forcible seizure, the fist or clenching the fist, the handle of a shield,
saṁgrahana mfn grasping, seizing, taking, n. the act of grasping or taking, receiving, obtaining, gathering, accumulating, encasing, inlaying, stopping, restraining, winning

over, propitiation, adultery, intercourse with (comp.),
saṁgrahin m. a collector, procurer,
√*saṁgrām* 1129/3 A. *saṁgrāmayate* to make war, fight, DP in yuddha fighting,
saṁgrāma 1129/3 m. an assembly of people, host, troop, army, battle, war
sāṁgrāmika mfn martial, warlike, relating to war, m. general, commander,
saṁgranthana n. tying together, beginning a quarrel,
saṁgṛhīta mfn grasped, seized, caught, taken, received, gathered, welcomed
saṁguṇa mfn multiplied with (comp.),
saṁguṇayati multiplies,
saṁgupta mfn well-guarded, protected or preserved, well hidden, concealed,
saṁguptārtha m. a secret matter, having a secret meaning,
saṁgupti f. guarding, protection,
saṁ√*han* P. –hanti to strike or put together, join, shut, close (eyes, wings, hands),to beat together, make solid, to put together (frame, fabricate etc.)
saṁhāna mfn narrow,
saṁhanana mfn compact, solid, firm, making compact or solid, striking together, killing, n. the act of striking together, hardening, solidity, robustness, strength, firmness, steadfastness, junction, connection, agreement, harmony, -*vat* mfn strongly built, muscular, robust,
saṁhantṛ mfn one who joins or unites,
saṁhara m. drawing together, contracting,
saṁhāra 1123/2 m. bringing together, collection, accumulation, contraction (organs of speech), drawing in (elephant's trunk), binding together (hair), a compendium, manual, abridgment, comprehensive description, end, conclusion, destruction, (esp. the periodical destruction of the universe at the end of a *kalpa* – 262/3 4,320,000,000 years, a day of *Brahmā*), practice, skill, mfn causing universal destruction,
saṁharaṇa n. drawing together, collecting, gathering, arranging, binding together, taking hold of,
saṁharṣa m. bristling/erection of hair of the body, thrill of delight, jot, pleasure,
saṁhat f. a layer, pile,
saṁhata mfn struck together, closely joined or united with, keeping together, contiguous, coherent, combined, accompanied or attended by, pinned, become solid, compact, strong-limbed, athletic, strong, intensive, -*tā* f. close contact or union, -*tva* n. complexity, close combination, compactness,
saṁhāta m. conciseness,
saṁhatala m. the two hands joined together with open palms brought together
saṁ√*hi* P. –*hinoti* to send forth, bring about, contrive, compose,
saṁhita mfn put together, joined, attached, fixed, settled, composed of (comp.),placed together, uninterrupted (a series of words), abounding in, possessed of, agreeing with, conformable to, relating to, concerning (comp.), √1.*dhā*
saṁhitā f. conjunction, connection, union, (in gram.) the junction or combination of letters according to euphonic rules, (=*saṁdhi*) but sometimes considered rather as the state preparatory to junction, a text treated according to euphonic rules, any methodically arranged collection of texts or verses, the force which holds together and supports the universe,
saṁhiti f. putting together, connection,
saṁ√*5.i* P. –*eti*, to go or come together, meet at or with, encounter, to cohabit, to come to, arrive at, approach, begin,
śamī f. a tree from which the fire-lighting sticks were taken, effort, labour, toil,
samī in comp. for *sama*

sāmi ind. too soon, prematurely, incompletely, imperfectly,
samībhāva m. becoming in a normal state,
samībhūta mfn placed equally, equalized, become indifferent, identified,
samīca m. the sea, ocean,
samīcaka m. copulation,
samīcīna mfn tending in a common direction, going with or in company with or remaining together, connected, united, complete, all, fit, proper, correct, true, right, just,
samid in comp. for *samidh*
samīdā m. fine wheat flour,
samidh 1164/3 mfn. igniting, flaming, burning, f. firewood, fuel,
samidha fuel, wood, m. fire
samiddha mfn. set alight or on fire, lighted, kindled, ignited,
samiddhadarpa mfn inflamed with pride,
samīhana mfn zealous, eager,
samika n. a pike, javelin, dart,
samīka n. hostile encounter, fight,
samīkaraṇa n. equalizing, levelling, assimilation, putting on a level with,
samīkṛta mfn made even, equalized,
sam√īkṣ Cl 1 *-īkṣate,* to look at or inspect thoroughly, investigate closely, view, perceive, to become aware of ascertain, to findout, contrive, invent, to think of, aim at, have in view, bear in mind, to consider well, in quire into, investigate, to look closely at in order to choose, caus. *īkṣayati* to cause to look at or perceive, to let one's self be seen, show one's self, appear,
samīkṣa n. 'complete investigation', name of the *Sāṁkhya* system of philosophy, (*ā*)f. thorough or close inspection, perceiving, beholding, desire or wish to see, a glance, view, opinion in regard to (with *prati*), deep insight, understanding, intellect, investigation, search, the *Mīmāṁsā* philosophy or any work examining or explaining *Vedic* ritual, essential nature or truth or principle, effort,
samīkṣya ind. contemplating, regarding, *sam-√īkṣ* gerund
śamīmaya mfn made of *śamī* wood,
samīpa 1165/1mfn proximate, adjacent, close by, near, (*am*)
n. nearness, proximity, vicinity, presence, immanence, (with 6th or ifc.) to or towards,
-āt from, *-e* near, in the vicinity, close at hand, beside, in the presence of, at the time of, before, at, towards,
samīpadeśa m. neighbouring, close country, neighbourhood,
samīpaga mfn going near, standing beside, accompanying,
samīpagamana n. the act of going near,
samīpaja mfn growing close by, relating to nearness, approaching,
samīpajala mfn being near the water,
samīpakāla m. nearness in time,
samīpanayana n. leading near to, bringing to,
samīpastha mfn (in cpd.) situated in the neighbourhood of, near, approaching, imminent (as death),
samīpatā f. nearness, proximity
samīpatara mfn nearer, neighbouring,
samīpatas from the presence of, near, near at hand, in the presence of, (with 6th) towards, to, very soon, immediately,
samīpatva n. nearness, proximity, contiguity
samīpe near, (see *samīpa*),
sāmīpya mfn neighbouring, a neighbour, n. neighbourhood, nearness, proximity (in space and time), nearness to the deity (one of four states of beatitude),
samira =*samīra* m. breeze, wind, air,
samīraṇa mfn setting in motion, causing activity, stimulating, ifc.f.(ā) breeze, wind, air, breath,
m. wind of the body, a traveller, marjoram,
n. setting in motion, hurling,

throwing,
samiṣ f. a dart, javelin,
śamīśākhā f. branch of the *śamī* tree
samiśra mfn mixing, mingling,
śamīsumanas f. *śamī* tree flower,
śamīsumanomālā a garland of *śamī*-tree flowers
samit f. hostile encounter, battle, war,\ in comp. for *samidh* which see
samita mfn come together, assembled, joined or united with, promised, agreed, finished, completed, mfn measured, meted out, equal to, commensurate, (*am*) ind. continually, always, (*ā*)f. wheat-flour
samiti f. coming together, meeting, assembling, an assembly, council, a flock, herd, association, society, encounter, war, battle, sameness, likeness, rule of life or conduct regarding restraint and moderation in daily life (Jaina),
samitiṁjaya m. victorious in battle or eminent in an assembly,
samitra mfn with a friend,
samīya Nom A. °*yate,* to be treated or accounted as equal by (3rd),
samīya mfn similar, like, of like origin,
saṁja m. 'Universal Creator', (*ā*) f. a she-goat,
saṁjahāti P.gives up, abandons, leave together, √2.*hā*
saṁjalpa m. talking together, conversation, chattering, uproar, mfn spoken together, uttered, n. spoken words, talk,
saṁ√jan 1133/1 A. *saṁjāyate* to be born or produced together with, to be born from (5th), arise or come forth from, come into existence, take place, appear, happen, to bring forth, to become, be,
saṁjanana mfn producing, causing, effecting
saṁjanayan 1/s/m pres. part. *sam √jan* producing, bringing forth
saṁjanita mfn produced, caused, created,
saṁjaya mfn completely victorious, m. conquest, victory,
Saṁjaya a minister in the court of King *Dhṛtarāṣṭra,* the narrator of the B.G.
saṁjāta mfn born, produced, grown, become, (having) arisen,
saṁjāyate is born, is produced, *saṁ√jan* 1/s/pres/indic/pass
saṁ√ji to conquer together or completely
saṁjigati (*saṁ√gā)* P. to come together, to go to, approach,
saṁjit m. a conqueror, winner,
saṁjita mfn entirely conquered or won,
saṁ√jīv P. to live with or together, to live, exist, live by any business or occupation, to revive, be restored to life,
saṁjīva mfn living together, living, making alive, vivifying, m. the act of reviving, revival, a partic. hell,
saṁjīvaka mfn living together, making alive, animating,
saṁjña 1. 1133/2 to agree together, be of the same opinion, be in harmony with, to obey, acknowledge, know well, understand, sentience, the state of consciousness
2. 1133/3 mfn knock-kneed, one who has recovered consciousness, -*tā* f. recovery of consciousness, n. a yellow fragrant wood,
saṁ√jñā 1133/2 P.A *saṁjānāti, saṁjānīte,* A. to agree together, be of the same opinion, be in harmony with, to appoint, assign, attend, direct, order, command, to know well, understand, to watch for, acknowledge, recognize, own, P. to acknowledge, or claim as one's own, to think of, caus. *saṁjñāpayati* to cause to agree, to cause to understand, to command, enjoin, instruct,
saṁjñā 1133/3 f. agreement, mutual understanding, harmony, consciousness, clear knowledge or understanding, any noun having a special meaning, used for technical

terms & definitions which have a specific technical meaning, lit. containing all knowledge (of the named thing)

saṁjñāna 1133/3 mfn producing harmony, n. unanimity, harmony with (3rd or7th), consciousness, right conception, perception, sentience, the state of consciousness, right perception, f. (*ī*) a ceremony for producing unanimity,

saṁjñāpana n. apprising, informing, teaching,

saàjñārtham ind. for the purpose of knowing, for information, for the sake of a sign,

saṁjñāta mfn well-known, understood, intended or destined for (comp.),

saṁjñāti f. agreement, harmony,

saṁjñāyām, f. used as a proper name

saṁjñin mfn having consciousness, conscious of (comp.), having a name, named,

saṁjñita mfn. made known, communicated, known as, called

saṁ√jval P. *–jvalati* to blaze up, flame brightly, caus. *–jvālayati* to cause to flame, illuminate, light,

saṁjvalana n. that which illuminates, fuel,

saṁjvara m. great heat or fever (also applied to the heat of anger or violent agitation),

saṁ√2.kal P. *–kālayati* to drive cattle together for grazing, put to flight, perform funeral honours, 3. to heap together, accumulate, to add, to be of opinion,

saṁkalita mfn heaped together, added, accumulated, intermixed, n. addition,

saṁkalpa 1126/3 m. conception, idea, or notion formed in the heart or mind, will, purpose, resolution, definite intention or determination or decision or wish for, sentiment, conviction, persuasion, (ibc. on purpose, intentionally), declaration of purpose,

saṁkalpaka mfn determining, deciding,

sāṁkalpika mfn based on or produced by the will or imagination,

saṁkaluṣa n. defilement, impurity,

saṁ-kara 1126/2 m. intermixture, confusion, commingling, the offspring of a mixed marriage, mfn soothing,

saṁkāra m. dust, sweepings, the crackling of flame,

śaṁkara another name for *śiva*

saṁkarṣa mfn drawing near, vicinity,

saṁkāśa 1125/3m. having the appearance of, looking like,

saṁkaṣṭa distress, trouble, need,

saṁkasuka mfn splitting, crumbling up,

saṁkaṭa mfn a narrow strait, Slender – name of a gander, narrow passage – a strait, a difficulty 'narrow strait', contracted, closed, narrow,

saṁkathana n. narrating fully, conversation with, narration,

saṁkathita mfn related, narrated,

saṁkaṭin mfn being in danger/difficulties

sāṁkathya n. talk, conversation,

saṁketa m. agreement, compact, stipulation, assignation with (6th), engagement, appointment, allusion, hint, sign, signal, gesture, a short explanation of a grammatical rule, condition, provision,

saṁketagrahaṇa n. making an agreement,

saṁketaka m. an agreement, appointment, rendezvous,

saṁketana n. a place of assignation,

saṁketastha mfn appearing by appointment

√saṁketaya 1127/1 Nom P *saṁketayati* to agree upon, appoint (a time), to be informed, learn, to invite, call, to counsel, advise, DP in *āmantraṇa* inviting

saṁketita mfn agreed upon, fixed, settled,

saṁkhya 1128/1 mfn. counting up, reckoning, n. conflict, battle, war,

sāṁkhya 1199/1 mfn numeral, relating to number (in gram. as expressed by the case terminations), m. one who calculates or discriminates well,

an adherent of this doctrine, a dualistic philosophy of 2 realities – spiritual and *prakṛti*
saṁ√khyā P. to reckon or count up, sum up, enumerate, calculate, to estimate by (3rd), A. to appear along with, be connected with, belong to,
saṁkhyā f. number, numeration, calculation, summing up, reasoning, reflection, reason, intellect, name,
saṁkhyāna 1228/2 becoming seen, appearance, reckoning up, enumeration, calculation, a number, multitude, measurement
saṁkila m. a burning torch, firebrand,
saṁkīrtayati mentions fully, announces,
saṁkīrtita mfn mentioned fully, celebrated, praised,
saṁkīrtyamāna mfn being mentioned or announced,
saṁkleśa m. pain, suffering, affliction,
saṁkleśana 1127/2 causing pain
saṁ√klṛp 1126/2 A. *–kalpate*, to be brought about, come into existence, to be in order or ready, to wish, long for, to determine, fix, settle, to imagine, fancy, take for, consider as,
saṁklṛpta mfn contrived, prepared, made ready, desired, wished, intended,
saṁkoca 1126/1m. contraction, shrinking together, compression, shutting up, closing (of the eyes), crouching down, cowering, humbling one's self, shyness, fear, abridgment, diminution, restriction, limitation, drying up (of a lake), binding, tying, a kind of skate fish, n. saffron,
saṁkocana n. astringent, the act of contracting or closing or having an astringent effect,
saṁ√1.kṛ to put together, compose, arrange,
saṁ√kram 1127/1 P.A. to come together, meet, encounter, to come near, approach, to go or pass over or through, to overstep, transgress, to wander,
saṁkrama m. going or coming together, progress, course, transition, passage or transference to, a bridge or steps down to water, m.n. difficult passage or progress (as over rocks or torrents), a means of effecting a difficult passage,
saṁkrāma 1127/2 m. passing away, m.n. difficult passage or progress,
saṁkramaṇa m. going or coming together, union with, entrance into, entrance, transference to, appearance, commencement (esp. of old age), the sun's passage to another sign of the zodiac, the day the sun crosses the equator northbound, passage into another world, decease, death, a means of crossing, attaining,
saṁkrāmaṇa n. transferring, transporting,
saṁkrāmita mfn transferred, handed over, delivered, communicated,
saṁkrānta mfn gone or come together, met, transferred to a picture, imaged, reflected,
saṁkrānti f. going from one place to another, course or passage or entry into, transference to (7th), transference of an art (from teacher to pupil), transferring to a picture, image, reflection,
saṁ√krīḍ A. *–krīḍate* to sport or play together, play with,
saṁkrīḍa m. sport, play
saṁ√kṛṣ to draw together, contract, tighten,
saṁkṛṣṭa mfn drawn together, contracted (as 2 sounds drawn near to one another)
saṁ√2.kṛt to cut to pieces, pierce,
saṁkṛti mfn putting together, arranging, preparing, making ready, 1126/1
saṁkṛtta mfn cut to pieces, cut through, etc.
saṁkruddha mfn greatly enraged, incensed
saṁkṣālana n. cleansing water, *(ā)* washing
saṁ√kṣap P. *-kṣapati* to emaciate the body by fasting or abstinence, do penance
saṁkṣara m. flowing together,
saṁkṣaya m. complete destruction or consumption, decay, disappearance, the dissolution of all things, *√kṣi*
saṁkṣepa m. throwing together, destruction,

compression, comprehension, conciseness, brief exposition, essence, the whole thrown together, total, aggregate, (*eṇa, °pa-tas* in the aggregate), (ibc. *ṇt, eṇa, am* or *°pa-tas* briefly, concisely, in short),
saṁkṣipta mfn thrown together, abbreviated, condensed, narrow, short, small, taken from or away, *√kṣip*
saṁkṣobha 1128/1 m. agitation, a violent shock or jolt, excitement,
saṁ√kuc 1125/3 (or *kuñc*) to contract, shrink, close (as a flower), to compress, absorb, destry, caus. –*kocayati* to contract, draw in, to narrow, make smaller, lessen, A. to withdraw, internalise, go within,
saṁkucita mfn contracted, shrunk, narrowed shut, crouching, cowering,
saṁkula 1126/1 mfn filled, disordered, crowded together, dense (as smoke), impeded, hindered by (3rd),
n. a crowd, throng, mob, a confused fight, trouble, distress, inconsistent or contradictory speech,
saṁkulita mfn crowded or filled with, abounding in (comp.), confused,
saṁ√labh A. –*labhate,* to take hold of one another, to obtain, receive,
saṁlagna mfn closely attached, adhering, being in contact with, sticking to or in, fallen into (7th or comp.), fighting hand to hand (du), ifc. proceeding from or out of,
saṁlaṅghana n. passing away (time),
saṁlaṅghita mfn passed away, gone by,
saṁ√lap P.-*lapati* to talk together, chat, to be spoken of or to,
saṁlāpa m. (ifc.*ā*) talking together, familiar or friendly conversation,
saṁlapana n. the act of talking or chattering,
saṁlaya m. settling or sitting down, alighting or settling of a bird, sleep, melting away, dissolution,
saṁlekha m. strict abstinence,
saṁlepa m. mud, dirt,
saṁ√lī A. –*līyate,* to cling or adhere to,
saṁlīna mfn clinging or joined together, adhering or clinging to, hidden,
saṁ√lok A. –*lokate,* to look together, look at each other,
saṁlokin mfn being in view of others, observed by others,
saṁlulita mfn agitated, confused, come into contact with,
sam√3.mā to measure out, measure, to make of the same measure, make equal, to compare with (3rd), to mete out, distribute, bestow,
sammā f. equality in size or number, symmetry,
sammada m. exhilaration, joy at, happiness,
sammāda m. great exhilaration, intoxication, frenzy,
sammagna mfn sunk down, immersed in or overwhelmed by (comp.)
sammahas n. common or mutual joy,
sammāna m.n. honour, respect, homage, n. the act of measuring out, equalizing, comparing,
sammānana n. the act of honouring etc.
sammanas mfn unanimous,
sammaniman m. unanimousness, harmony
sammānita mfn honoured, treated with reverence or respect,
sammantavya mfn to be highly valued,
sam√mantr P. –*mantrayati* to consult together, take council with, hold a council, deliberate, advise, greet, address,
sammantrita mfn deliberated, considered,
sammantrya ind. having deliberated, consulted,
sammarda m. pressing or rubbing together, friction, pressure, trampling, impact of waves, meeting, war, battle,
sammārga m. wiping off, cleansing, a wisp of grass for tying faggots together,
sammārjaka mfn sweeping, cleansing, a sweeper, m. a broom,
sammārjana n. act of sweeping or cleansing thoroughly, cleansing, scouring, purifying, brushing, the anointing and washing (of images etc.), a broom, a wisp of grass for wiping plates, food remains wiped off,

sammarṣa m. patience, endurance,
sammarśana n. stroking
sammarśin mfn able to judge, an able deliberator,
sammārṣṭi f. cleansing, purification,
sammata mfn thinking together, being of the same opinion, agreed, assented to, ifc. agreeing with, thought, supposed, considered or regarded as, esteemed, renowned, celebrated, (*am*) n. opinion, impression, consent, approval, concurrence.
sammathita mfn bruised, pounded,
sammati f. sameness of opinion, harmony, agreement, approval, opinion, view, respect, homage, wish, desire, self-knowledge, regard, affection, love, order, command, mfn being of the same opinion, agreeing,
sammātṛ mfn one who measures,
sammatta mfn completely intoxicated, exhilarated, enamoured,
sammegha m. the cloudy season,
sammilāna n. closing (of a flower, eyes etc.) cessation of activity, obscuring,,
sammilita mfn met together, assembled,
sammiśla mfn mixed with, united with,
sammita mfn measured out, measured, meted, measuring so much, measuring just so much, equal, like same (in length, height, number, value), corresponding to, resembling, reaching up to, symmetrical, passing for, consisting of, (*am*) ind. perpetually, incessantly, distance (*e* ifc. at a distance from),
sammocita mfn set free, liberated,
sammoda m. odour, fragrance,
sammoha m. 1181/1 stupefaction, unconsciousness, ignorance, delusion , -*ka* mfn stupefying, infatuating, fascinating, -*nī* f. a kind of fascination or illusion, n. deluding, infatuating,
sammṛṣṭa mfn well swept or scoured, cleansed, strained, filtered,
sammṛta mfn quite dead,
sammud f. joy, delight,
sammūḍha mfn bewildered, unconscious uncertain, confused, foolish, ignorant *sam* √*muh*
sammugdha mfn gone astray, bewildered, not clearly understood, (*am*) ind. furtively,
sammukha facing, confronting, fronting, being face to face or in front of, present, before the eyes, being about to begin or at the beginning of, directed or turned towards, propitious, intent on, adapted to circumstances, fit, suitable, with the mouth or face, (*am*) ind. towards, near to, opposite, in front or in presence of,
sammukhin m. a mirror,
sammūrcha m. thickening, augmenting, increase, expansion, spreading,
sāmna 1205/2 relating to *sāmans* (which see) f. a sort of metre
saṁnaya mfn leading or bringing together, m. a collection, assembly, the rear-guard,
saṁ√*nī* P. –*nayati* to lead or bring or put together, join, connect, unite, mix together, to lead or direct towards, bring, procure, to bring back, restore, to direct the mind towards,
saṁnibaddha mfn firmly bound together, or closely connected with or attached to, dependent on or engrossed by, ifc. planted or covered with,
saṁnibha 1147/1 mfn resembling, like
saṁniboddhavya mfn to be thoroughly perceived or understood, √*budh*
saṁnidāgha m. scorching heat (esp. the sun)
saṁnidha n. juxtaposition, vicinity,
saṁni√*dhā* P.A. –*dadhāti, -dhatte,* to put or place down near together, put down near or into, deposit in, place together, collect, pile up, A. to appoint to, to be present in, be found with, 'absorbs' (Gam.),
saṁnidhāna n. juxtaposition, nearness,

vicinity, presence, (e with 6th or ifc. 'in the presence of'), presence =existence,
a place of deposit, gathering-place,
saṁnidhāne 7/s in the vicinity of,
saṁnidhi m. depositing together or near, juxtaposition, nearness, vicinity, presence, visibility, existence,
L. presence,
sāṁnidhya n. nearness, vicinity, presence,
saṁnihita 1146/3 mfn deposited together or near, contiguous, proximate, present, close, near, at hand, upon, proximate, well-seated,
saṁnikarṣa 1146/2 m. drawing near or together, approximation, close contact, nearness, neighbourhood, proximity, vicinity, connection with, relation to, (in phil.) the connection of an organ of sense with its *viṣaya* or object), a receptacle, repository, mfn near, at hand
saṁnimagna mfn sunk entirely under, immersed, sleeping, asleep, √*majj*
saṁni√mīl P. –*mīlati* to entirely close, completely shut (the eyes),
saṁni√pat Cl 1 –*patati,* to fall or fly down together, alight, descend upon (7th),
saṁnipatita mfn flown or fallen down, descended, met together, assembled,
saṁnir√gam P. –gacchati to go out together, go away, start, depart,
saṁnirmita mfn constructed, composed of (5th)
saṁniruddha mfn kept back, held fast,
saṁni√śam to perceive, hear, learn,
saṁniṣaṇṇa mfn settled down, seated,
saṁnisarga m. good-naturedness,
saṁniścaya m. a settled opinion,
saṁniṣevita mfn served, frequented, inhabited by (3rd),
saṁniśraya m. support,
saṁnisṛṣṭa mfn delivered up or over, entrusted, committed,
saṁniśrita mfn connected with, devoted to,
saṁnisūdita altogether killed, destroyed,
saṁnivāsa m. dwelling or living together, a nest, √5.*vas*
saṁni√1.vid caus. –*vedayati* to cause to know, make known, announce, tell,
saṁniveśa m. arrangement, causing to enter, open place or play-ground in or near a town, putting down together, entering or sitting down together, vicinity, attachment to any pursuit, insertion, construction, position, encampment, seat, fabrication, station, appearance, inclusion,
saṁni√viś A. –*viśate,* to sit or settle down together with, have intercourse or intimate connection with,
saṁniviṣṭa 1147/2 mfn. seated down together with, encamped, assembled, fixed in or on, resting or contained in, being on (a road or path, 7th), dependent on (7th), entered deeply into, absorbed or engrossed in, contiguous, neighbouring, present, at hand, established in the Self,
saṁni√vṛt A. –*vartate*, to turn back, return from (5th), to desist from (5th), caus. –*vartayati*
saṁnivṛtta mfn turned or come back, returned, withdrawn, desisted,
saṁniyacchana n. checking, restraining, guiding (of horses), √*yam*
saṁniyama m. exactness, precision,
saṁniyamya ind. controlling, subduing, having subdued,
gerund *saṁ-ni-√yam* 1147/1
saṁniyoga m. connection with, attachment, application (to any pursuit), appointment, commission, injunction, precept, √*yuj*
saṁniyukta mfn attached to, connected with (comp.), appointed, employed, √*yuj*
saṁ√nṛt P. –*nṛtyati* to dance together,
saṁnyāsa 1148/1 m. giving up the body, complete renunciation, monkhood, profession of ascetism, sudden death, abandonment, resignation, agreement, deposit, laying aside, stake, wager, abstinence from food, complete exhaustion, renunciation of worldly concerns, thrown

down, laid aside, relinquished, renunciation of the world,
saṁnyasta 1148/1 ppp. renounced, abandoned, given up
saṁnyasya relinquishing, renouncing gerund *sam ni √as*
saṁnyāsa 1148/1 m. putting or throwing down, laying aside, resignation, renunciation of the world, giving up the body, sudden death
saṁnyāsin 1148/1 mfn laying aside, giving up, m. one who abandons or resigns worldly affairs, an ascetic, devotee (who has renounced all earthly concerns and devotes himself to meditation and study of the Āraṇyakas or Upaniṣads), a Brāhman in the fourth āśrama or stage of his life, a religious mendicant,
saṁnyasitva n.or *-tā* f. abandonment of worldly concerns, retirement from the world,
samokas mfn living or dwelling together, closely united with (3rd), furnished with, possessed of,
samota mfn woven or strung together,
sampa m. = *patana,* lightning,
sampā P.A. to drink together, f. drinking together,
sampācana n. making ripe, maturing, making tender, softening,
sam√pad A. *–padyate*, to fall or happen well, turn out well, succeed, prosper, to become full or complete (a number), meet or unite with, obtain, to enter into, be absorbed in, be brought forth, be born, to become, turn into,
sampad 1172/1 f. success, accomplishment, completion, fulfilment, concord, agreement, stipulation, bargain, equalization of similar things, attainment, acquisition, possession, enjoyment, advantage, perfection,benefit, blessing, turning into, growing, becoming, being, existence, good fortune, excellence, glory, splendour, beauty, excess, abundance, high degree, fate, destiny, prosperity, riches,
sampada 1172/1 furnished with (ifc.), standing with the feet together (even)
sampādana mfn procuring, bestowing, accomplishing, carrying out, n. the act of procuring/bestowing, bringing about, carrying out, making, effecting, preparing, putting in order,
sampādin mfn coinciding with, fit or suitable for, accomplishing, procuring,
sampādita mfn brought about, accomplished, fulfilled,
saṁpadyate 1171/3 turns out well, becomes full or complete, succeeds, prospers
sampāka cooking or ripening thoroughly, maturing, impudent, lustful, small,
sampakva thoroughly boiled, matured or ripened, ripe for death,
sampālita mfn got over, overcome,
sampanna 1172/1 fallen or turned out well, accomplished or endowed with, perfect, excellent, of perfect or correct flavour, palatable, dainty, possessed of, (ifc.) become, turned into, (*am*) n. dainty food, a delicacy,
sampāraṇa mfn conveying to the further side, leading to a goal, furthering, (*am*) n. accomplishment, fulfilment,
samparāya m. decease, death, calamity, existence from eternity, conflict, adversity, futurity,
samparcana n. combination, a mix, blend, connection or unity with
sampareta mfn liable to die, deceased, dead
samparī (-pari-√5.i) P. *–paryeti* to go round, circumambulate, to embrace, contain, to deliberate, ponder,
sampari√bhū P. *–bhavati*, to despise, slander, caus. *–bhāvayati* to cause to keep together, fix firmly together,
sampari√car P. to attend on, serve,
sampariciṅtita mfn thought out, devised,
samparigraha m. receiving with kindness, property,

sampari√kram to go or walk round, visit in succession,

samparimārgaṇa n. searching about for, search

sampari√mud A. –modate to rejoice or exult far and wide,

sampārin mfn conveying across (as a boat or ship),

samparitoṣita mfn fully satisfied, quite appeased,

samparipālana n. guarding, protecting,

sampariplut a mfn overflowed, overwhelmed (with misfortune),

sampari√rakṣ P. to protect, defend, A. to clasp or embrace together,

samparityakta mfn abandoned, given up

samparivārita mfn surrounded, encompassed

sampari√vṛj caus. *–varjayati* to shun, avoid

sampari√vṛt A. – *vartate*, to turn round, roll round, revolve, roll (as eyes), to exist, turn back, return, turn back or desist from, with *hṛdi* or *manasi* 'to turn over in the mind',

samparka 1173/2 m. mixing together, mixture, conjunction, union, association, touch, contact between or with, bodily contact, sexual intercourse with, addition, sum,

sam√paś to see at the same time, survey, A. to look at each other, (also = to be together), to see, behold, perceive, recognize, look at, inspect, review, to admit into one's presence (to see), to look upon as, regard as, to attend to, consider,

saṁpaśyan seeing, observing pres.part.

sam√pat Cl 1 *–patati,* to fly together,

sampat 1172/1 (in comp. for *sampad),* benefit, blessing, success, prosperity, accomplishment, fulfillment, perfection,

sampāta m. flying or rushing together, collision, concussion, place of contact, point of intersection, flight, swift descent, fall, taking place, happening, remnant, residue,

sampaṭhati P. reads aloud, repeats, recites,

sampatti f. prosperity, welfare, good fortune, success, accomplishment, fulfilment, turning out well, concord, agreement, attainment, enjoyment, possession, acquisition, becoming, turning into, being, existing, existence, good state or condition, excellence, plenty, abundance, affluence,

saṁpatti properties – two types available *sāmānya saṁpatti* worldly properties *daivī saṁpatti* divine properties

sampeṣaṇa 1173/1 n. the act of grinding together, pounding,

samphala mfn rich in fruit or seed, fruitful,

samphāla m. a ram, sheep,

samphulla mfn full-blown, blossomed, fully opened or expanded(as a flower),

sampiba mfn swallowing down,

sampīda m. pressing or squeezing together,

sampīti f. drinking in company,

samplava m. flowing together, flood, deluge

sam√plu Cl1 *-plavate,* to flow together, be heaped together (clouds), to founder, go down (ship), to fluctuate, waver (as the mind), to melt into, merge with, to float over, inundate, submerge,

saṁpluta 1177/2 mfn. flowed or streamed together, met, flooded with water,

sam√1.pṛ P.A. to mix together, bring into contact, caus. *–pārayati,* to bring or convey over to the further side, bring to an end, accomplish,

sam√pī pass. *–pūryate,* to be completely filled, become quite full,

sampra√bhā P. *–bhāti,* to shine forth clearly, be conspicuous, appear,

samprabhagna mfn entirely broken, routed,

samprabhava m. coming forth, rising, appearance,

samprabodhita mfn convinced, persuaded, consulted or deliberated about,

samprabuddha mfn roused up, awakened,

sampra√cakṣ A. *-caṣṭe* to explain, expound, to suppose, assume,

samprada mfn giving, liberal,

sampra√1.dā 1175/1 to give completely up or deliver wholly over, surrender, hand down by tradition, teach, impart, to grant, bestow,

sampradāna the act of giving or handing over completely, presenting, bestowing, (in gram.) the idea expressed by the dative case, the recipient to which the agent causes anything to be given

sampradarśita mfn clearly shown, exhibited, manifested, declared,

sampradatta mfn given over, imparted, transmitted, handed down, given in marriage,

sampradāya m. a bestower, presenter, tradition, established doctrine transmitted from one teacher to another, traditional belief or usage, any sectarian system of religious teaching, sect,

sampradāyin mfn bringing about, causing, effecting, m. 'having a tradition', a holder of any traditional doctrine, a member of a sect,

sampradhāna n. consideration, ascertainment,

sampradhāraṇa n.f. determination, deliberation, deciding on the propriety or impropriety of anything,

sam pra √dhṛ caus. *–dhārayati* to direct towards, deliver over to, (with *buddhim*) to fix the mind or thoughts steadily upon [7th], determine, resolve, settle, decide, to ponder, reflect, consider,

sampradīpta mfn blazing or flaming up, shining very brightly, brilliant,

sampra√diś P. *–diśati* to point out or indicate fully, appoint, designate,

sampradiṣṭa mfn clearly pointed out, indicated, designated, known as, called,

sampradūṣaṇa n. utter deterioration,

sampraduṣṭa mfn wholly corrupted/polluted

sampra√gai P. *–gāyati,* to begin to sing, sing, pronounce by singing,

samprahāra 1177/1 m. mutual striking or wounding, war, battle, fighting with, a strike, blow, going, motion, gait

sampraharṣa m. great joy, thrill of delight,

sampraharṣaṇa mfn exciting sexually,

samprahāsa m. laughing at, loud laughter, mockery, derision,

samprajahāti P. he/she leaves, abandons, *√3.hā*

samprahita mfn thrown, hurled,

sampra√jan to be produced, spring up, arise from, to exist, be existent, to be born again

samprajanya n. full consciousness, introspection, 'mindfulness of purpose',

sampra√jñā to distinguish, discern, recognize, know accurately/perfectly

samprajñāta mfn distinguished, discerned, known accurately,

samprajvalita mfn flaming, blazing, kindled

samprakalpita mfn installed, settled

samprakāśa m. bright appearance,

samprakāśaka mfn manifesting, announcing, directing,

samprakāśaṇa n. manifestation/ discovering

samprakāśita 1173/3 mfn made manifest, displayed,

saṁprakīrtita 1173/3 mfn mentioned, designated, called, declared

samprakḷpta mfn prepared, arranged,

sampra√kram to proceed to do or set about anything, to begin,

samprakṣāla mfn performing the prescribed ablutions, m. a kind of hermit or holy man,

samprakṣālana n. the act of washing entirely away, destruction of the world by inundation, complete ablution, purification by water, bathing,

sampralāpa m. talk, chatter,

sampralīna mfn wholly dissolved or melted away, disappeared, vanished, absorbed,

sampramardana mfn crushing down, destroying,

sampramārga m. purification,

sampramathya ind. violently, by force,

sampramatta mfn very excited (said of an elephant in rut), careless, thoughtless, neglectful, very fond of,
sampramoda m. excessive joy or delight,
sampramoha m. utter bewilderment,
sampra√mokṣ P.A. *-mokṣayati (te)*, to make free, clear away, A. to clear a way for one's self,
sampramoṣa m. carrying off, abstraction,
sampramucya ind. having abandoned, quitted, being quite free from (5th),
sampramūḍha mfn utterly bewildered or confused, perplexed, embarrassed,
sampramugdha mfn completely confused,
sampramukhita mfn placed at the head, foremost, chief, first
sampramukti f. letting loose (cattle),
sampramuṣita mfn distracted, abstracted, carried quite away,
sampraṇāda m. sound, noise,
sampraṇamati P. bows down, bows down before,
sampranaṣṭa mfn vanished, disappeared,
sampraṇetṛ m. a leader, chief (of an army), a ruler, judge,
sampraṇi√dhā P.A. to leave behind in, to put aside, disregard,
sampraṇīta mfn brought together, composed (poetry),
samprānta m. ultimate or absolute end,
sampraṇudita mfn driven or urged on,
sam-prāp (pra-√āp) P. *–prāpnoti* to reach or attain fully to, arrive at, effect, accomplish,
samprapada n. pl. standing on tiptoe,
samprapanna mfn gone together towards, entered, one who has recourse to (2nd), ifc. endowed or filled with,
saṁprāpta 1177/1 mfn well reached or attained, become, one who has reached or attained, arrived at, met with, ifc. extending to, come, become, appeared,
samprāpya ind. having fully attained, obtained, reached realised,
samprarocate A. appears very bright or beautiful, appears good or right,
samprārthita mfn asked for, begged,
samprasāda m. perfect quiet (esp. mental repose during deep sleep), favour, grace, serenity, (in Vedānta) the soul during deep sleep, trust, confidence,
samprasādana mfn calming, sedative
samprasādhana n. accomplishing, arranging, decorating,
samprasahya ind. thoroughly, by all means,
samprasakta mfn devoted to, intent upon, occupied with,
samprasanna mfn soothed, appeased, propitious, favourable, gracious
sampraśānta mfn ceased, disappeared,
samprasāra m. one through whom all goes on well,
samprasāraṇa n. drawing asunder, (in gram.) the mutual interchange of vowels *i,u,ṛ,ḷ* with corresponding semivowels *y,v,r,l,*
samprasava m. admission,
sampraśna m. asking, inquiring about (comp.), inquiry, question,
samprasiddha mfn well-prepared, cooked,
samprasiddhi f. success, good luck,
sampraśraya m. respectful demeanour, modesty, humility,
sampraśrita mfn modest, humble, well-behaved,
sampra√sthā to take up a position together, (before the altar), to set out together,
samprastuta mfn ready to, prepared for,
samprasupta mfn fallen fast asleep, sleeping, closed (as a flower),
samprasūta mfn brought forth, begot, pro-created,
sāmprata mfn seasonable, proper, correct, L. mfn of now, present, (*am*) ind. at present, now,
sampra√tap caus. *–tāpayati* to warm,
sampratapta mfn excessively heated, suffering pain, distressed,
sampra√tark P. to form a clear conclusion, or conjecture, to consider as, think,
samprathita mfn universally known or celebrated,
samprati ind. directly opposite, close in front of (2nd), rightly, in the right way, at the right time, exactly, just,

now, at this moment, at present, immediately or at once (with impf.),

sampratī (-prati-√5. i.) P. *–pratyeti*, to go towards, arrive at, come to a firm conviction, believe firmly in, trust in (6th), caus. *–pratyāyayati* to cause to be meant or understood,

samprati√bhā P. to shine out fully, appear, seem, to appear clearly, be fully understood,

samprati√bhāṣ A *-bhāṣate* to speak in return, answer

sampratibhāṣa m. perception which tends to unite or combine

samprati√budh caus. *–bodhayati* , to rouse or awaken thoroughly,

samprati√grah P.A. to receive hospitably,

sampratigraha m. kind reception, predilection for,

samprati√jñā to promise,

sampratijñāta mfn promised,

sampratīkṣa mfn expecting

sampratīkṣate A. looks out for, waits for, expects, awaits,

samprati√lakṣ pass. *-lakṣyate* to be seen or perceived clearly,

sampratimukta mfn firmly,completely bound

sampratinandita mfn greeted joyfully, attaining to, obtaining, right understanding, presence of mind, agreement, concurrence, acknowledgement, admission, assent, cooperation, bringing about, performing, *-mat* having presence of mind,

sampratipādita mfn delivered over, bestowed, given

sampratipanna mfn gone near, come up to, agreed upon, acknowledged, brought about, performed,

sampratipatti f. going towards, approach, attaining to, obtaining, correct conception, right understanding, presence of mind, agreement, concurrence, acknowledgement, admission, assent, affirmation,

sampratipūjā f. great respect or reverence,

sampratirodhaka m. complete restraint, imprisonment, confinement

sampratisaṁcara m. re-absorption or resolution,

samprati√śru to listen attentively to, assent, promise, caus. *–śravayati* to make to promise, repeat a promise, remind of a promise,

samprati√ṣṭhā 1174/3 P. *-tiṣṭhati,* to stand firmly on, rely on (7th), caus. – *-ṣṭhāpayati* to enclose, confine (as cows), to concentrate in (7th), to make firm, establish, to found, introduce, *√sthā*

sampratiṣṭhā f. perseverance, permanence, continuance (as opposed to beginning or end), high rank or position, final rest,

sampratiṣṭhāna n. a means for supporting the frame or keeping one's self upright,

sampratiṣṭhante proceed towards

sampratiṣṭhanti 1/pl/pres/act they merge, (Gam.),

sampratiṣṭhita mfn standing or resting firmly on, established, fixed, settled, lasting, existing, being,

sampratīta mfn come back again, returned, firmly believing in, fully convinced of, firmly resolved, thoroughly ascertained or admitted, well known, renowned, respectful, compliant,

sampratīti f. complete belief or trust, full knowledge, notoriety, fame, respect for, compliance,

*samprativedhakī (*or *°dhikī)* opening, disclosing,

samprati√1.vid caus. –vedayati, to cause to be fully known, announce, report,

samprativid mfn knowing (only) the present (not what is beyond), having only common-sense,

sampratti 1174/2 ind. directly over-against or opposite, rightly, in the right way, at the right time, exactly, just, at this time, now, immediately, at once, 1175/1 f. giving entirely up, delivering over,

samprattikarman n. the act of delivering over,
sampra√tuṣ P. *-tuṣyati* to be or become quite satisfied, be contented,
sampratyāgata mfn come back, returned,
sampratyavekṣaṇatā f. complete perception or comprehension,
sampratyaya m. assent, agreement, firm conviction, perfect trust or faith or belief, right conception, notion,
sampravadana n. talking together, conversation,
sampravāha m. continuous stream, uniterrupted continuity,
sampravartaka mfn setting in motion, promoting, furthering, producing,
sampravartana n. moving, hurrying about, the act of setting in motion or action, undertaking,
sampravartin mfn putting in order, setting right,
sampra√viś P.A *–viśati (te),* to enter into together or completely,
(with *mānasam* or *dhyānam* to be lost in thought),
sampraviṣṭa mfn entered together or completely, gone into,
sampravṛṣṭa mfn begun to rain, a whole rainfall,
sampra√vṛt A. *–vartate,* to come forth, arise, be produced from, to begin, commence, set about, prepare for, (with *manasi)* to turn or think over in the mind, think deeply about,
saṁpravṛtta 1176/2 mfn. gone forward, proceeded, arisen, existent, present, near at hand, commenced, passed, gone by, setting about anything, engaged in (7th or comp.),
saṁpravṛtti f. coming forth, appearance, occurrence
samprayoga m. joining together, fastening, conjunction, union, connection, contact with, matrimonial or sexual connection with, mutual proportion, connected series or arrangement, correct employment or proper functioning of the senses,
sāmprayogika mfn relating to use or application, name of a work,
sampra√yuj P.A. to yoke or join together, yoke, harness, to employ, make use of, to perform a song, to instigate, incite, induce to;
mfn surrounded or encompassed by,
samprayukta mfn yoked or joined together, yoked, harnessed, joined, united, connected, come into contact, sexually united, engaged in or occupied with, hostile encountering, concentrated, wholly intent on one object, bound to, dependent on, urged, impelled, incited,
samprayuktaka mfn cooperative,
sam√pṛc P.A. to mix together, bring into contact, connect, unite, to fill up, fill or satiate or endow or prsent with, mfn being in or coming into contact,
sampreddha mfn kindled, lighted,
samprekṣaka mfn looking well at, a spectator, beholder,
samprekṣaṇa n. the act of looking well at, beholding, seeing, deliberating about, considering, investigating,
samprekṣita mfn well looked at or seen, beheld, considered, investigated,
samprekṣya looking at, focusing the eyes on, gerund *sam pra √īkṣ* having perceived, seen,
sampriya mfn mutually dear, being on friendly terms with, very dear or beloved, n. contentment, satisfaction, *-tā* f. dearness, the being very dear or dearer than (5th),
samprīṇana n. gladdening, delighting,
samprīṇita mfn made completely happy, thoroughly satisfied, well pleased,
samprīta mfn completely satisfied or pleased, delighted,
samprīti f. complete satisfaction, joy, delight in, attachment, affection, goodwill, friendship with, love for,
sampṛkta mfn mixed together, blended, connected, come into contact with, filled with, inlaid, interspersed,
sampṛṇa mfn filling up, filling,

samprokta mfn spoken to, addressed,
sampṛṣṭa mfn asked, interrogated, inquired about,
sam√pūj to salute deferentially, honour greatly, revere,
sampūjā f. honouring, reverence, esteem,
sampūjaka mfn honouring, revering,
sampūjana n. the act of treating with great respect
sampūjya mfn to be greatly honoured or respected, part. greatly honouring or respecting,
sampūraka mfn filling completely, cramming or stuffing (as the stomach)
sampūrṇa mfn completely filled or full, (also moon), full of, completely endowed or furnished with, complete, whole, entire, abundant, excessive, possessed of plenty, fulfilled, accomplished, n. ether, the ethereal element or atmosphere,
sampūrṇakālīna mfn occurring at the full or right time,
sampūrṇakāma mfn filled with desire,
sampūrṇakumbha m. a full jar,
sampūrṇatā f. complete fullness, perfection, completeness,
sampūrti f. fulfilment, completion,
sampuṭa m. a hemispherical bowl or anything that shape, a jewellery box, a hemisphere, credit, balance,
sampuṭaka m. a wrapper, envelope, casket
sam√ṛ Cl 6 *–ṛcchati, -iyarti, -ṛṇoti, -ṛṇvati,* to come or join together, bring to pass, bring about, bring together, drive together, caus. *samarpayati* sends, gives, hands over,
saṁ√rā to give liberally, bestow, grant,
samrāḍ 1181/3 in comp. for *samrāj* 1181/3 a universal or supreme ruler
saṁ√rādh caus. *-rādhayati* to agree together, agree about or upon, conciliate,
saṁrāddha mfn accomplished, acquired,
saṁrādhaka mfn practising complete concentration of mind, thoroughly concentrated,
saṁrādhana mfn conciliating, satisfying, n. the act of conciliating or pleasing by worship, perfect concentration of mind, thoroughly concentrated,
saṁrādhi 1113/1 accomplishment, success
saṁrāga m. redness, passion, vehemence, attachment to (7th),
saṁ√rāj P. *–rājati* to reign universally, reign over (6th),
samrāj m. a universal or supreme ruler, a sovereign lord, paramount sovereign,
samrājñī f. a queen or female of high rank,
saṁ√rakṣ to protect, guard, watch over, defend, preserve, save from (5th),
saṁrakta mfn coloured, red, inflamed, enamoured, charming, beautiful, angry,
saṁ√ram A. *–ramate* to be delighted, find pleasure in (7th), to have carnal pleasure or sexual intercourse with,
saṁ√rañj A. *–rajyate* to be dyed/coloured, become red, to be affected with any passion, caus. *–rañjayati* to colour, dye, redden, to please, charm gratify,
samṛddha mfn prosperous, prospering, accomplished, succeeded, flourishing, fortunate, full-grown (trees), complete, whole, entire, abundantly endowed with, rich, enriched, plenteous, abundant,
saṁṛddhatejas mfn endowed with splendour or strength,
saṁṛddhavega mfn increasing in speed, excessively swift,
saṁṛddhayaśas mfn rich in fame, renowned
samṛddhi 1171/2 f. great prosperity or success, growth, increase, thriving, welfare, fortune, perfection, excellence, abundance, plenty of, wealth, riches
saṁṛddhin mfn possessing abundance of (comp.), prosperous, happy, blessed,
saṁ√ṛdh P. to succeed well, prosper, flourish, increase or grow greatly, to share in abundantly, be amply furnished with, bestow liberally on,
saṁṛdh f. success, welfare,
saṁrodha m. complete obstruction or

opposition, restraint, hindrance, prevention, limitation, restriction, confinement, siege,
saṁropaṇa mfn causing to grow over or heal, planting, sowing,
samṛta mfn come together, met, come into conflict,
sāmṛta mfn provided with nectar,
samṛti f. collision, shock , 'a coming together' meeting, contact, conflict,
saṁ√ruc A. *–rocate*, to shine together or at the same time or in rivalry, to shine, beam, glitter, caus. *–rocayati* to find pleasure in, like, approve, resolve on
saṁruddha mfn stopped completely, detained, hindered, surrounded by (comp.), held, closed, concealed, withheld, refused,
saṁ√2.rudh P.A. *–ruṇaddhi, -runddhe,* to stop completely, detain, obstruct, block up a road, besiege,
saṁ√rūḍha mfn grown, sprung up, sprouted, grown over, healed, burst forth, appeared, growing fast or taking root firmly, confident, bold,
saṁ√ruh P. *–rohati* to grow together, grow up, increase, to grow over, heal, to break forth, appear,
saṁrujana n. pain, ache,
√śaṁs 1043/3 cl 1 P *śaṁsati* to recite, repeat, to praise, extol, commend, approve, make a vow, relate, say, tell, report, declare, foretell, predict, hurt, injure, be unhappy, caus. cause to repeat or recite, DP in *stuti* praise,
śaṁsa m. recitation, invocation, praise, wishing well or ill to, a blessing or a curse, a promise, vow, a spell, *(ā)* f. praise, flattery, eulogium, wish, desire, speech, utterance, mfn reciting, proclaiming, praising,
sāṁśa mfn having parts or shares,
saṁśabdana 1117/2 n. making a sound, calling out, mentioning, praising,
saṁ√sad P. *–sīdati (te),* to sit down together with (3rd), sit down, sink down, collapse, be discouraged, to meet,
saṁsad f. 'sitting together', an assembly, meeting, a multitude, mfn one who sits together,
saṁsāda m. a meeting, assembly, company,
saṁsadana n. dejectedness, depression,
saṁsādhaka mfn wishing to conquer or win,
saṁsādhana n. performance, fulfilment, accomplishment,
saṁsaha mfn ifc. equal to, a match for,
saṁsahāyaka m. a comrade, companion,
saṁsajjamāna mfn adhering/sticking close together, hesitating, stammering, being prepared or ready,
saṁsakta 1118/3 mfn adhered/stuck together sticking fast, occupied with, intent upon, devoted to, given to mundane pleasures, enamoured, adjoining, contiguous, compact, dense, uninterrupted, dependent,
saṁsaktacitta mfn having their hearts joined, heartily devoted to each other,
saṁsaktajala mfn joining/mingling its waters with (comp).
saṁsaktamanas mfn having the mind attached or fixed,
saṁsaktayuga attached to a yoke, harnessed,
saṁsakti f. close connection or contact with, tying or fastening together, intimacy, intercourse, acquaintance, addiction or devotion to,
saṁ√1.śam P. *-śāṁyati* to become thoroughly calm or pacified, be comforted, to be appeased, make peace with, to be extinguished, to be allayed, cease, to be or become ineffective, to calm, allay, caus. *-śamayati* to tranquillize, calm, pacify, to bring to an end, settle, to extinguish, to bring to rest,
saṁśama m. complete ease, comfort, satisfaction,
saṁsamaka mfn united together,
śaṁsana 1044/1 n. reciting, recitation, prose, report, announcement,
saṁsaṅga m. connection, conjunction,
saṁsaṅgin mfn clinging or adhering to, coming into close contact or

near relation,
saṁ√sañj Pass. *–sajyate, -sajjate* to adhere, stick to, encounter, engage in close combat with, to hesitate, falter (in voice), to flow together, be joined, to arise (as a battle), P. to attach to a yoke, harness,
saṁsanoti P. obtains,
saṁśānta mfn thoroughly pacified or allayed, extinguished, destroyed, dead,
saṁśānti f. extinction,
saṁśapta mfn sworn together, cursed,
saṁśaptaka m. a soldier sworn not to flee or give up fighting, one bound by an oath to kill others,
saṁsāra 1119/2 m. going or wandering through, undergoing transmigration, course, passage, passing through a succession of states, worldly illusion(s), circuit of mundane existence, transmigration, the world, secular life, worldly illusion, repeating births in various bodies, empirical existence,
saṁsārabīja n. the seed/origin of the world
saṁsāracakra n. the wheel of birth and death,
saṁsāragamana n. passing from one state of existence to another, transmigration,
saṁsāraṇa n. setting in motion, also for *saṁsaraṇa* below
saṁśaraṇa n. the commencement of a combat, charge, attack, resorting to, seeking refuge with,
saṁsaraṇa n. going about, walking or wandering through, passing through a succession of states, birth and rebirth of living beings, the world, resorting to, seeking refuge with (6th),
saṁsarga 1119/3 mfn commingling, combining, m. mixture or union together, blending, conjunction, connection, contact, association, society, sexual union
saṁsargābhāva eternal non-existence, the absence of something in something else,
saṁsargadoṣa m. the fault or evil results of association (with bad people),
saṁsargaja mfn produced by union/contact
saṁsargatas ind, through union or contact
saṁsargavat mfn being in contact, connected with,
saṁsargavidyā f. interaction with people, social science
saṁsargī f. purification, purging (in med.)
saṁsargin mfn mixed together, joined, connected, familiar, friendly,
saṁsārin 1119/3 m. a living or sentient being, animal, creature, man, mfn moving far and wide, extensive, comprehensive (intellect), transmigratory, attached to mundane existence, worldly, mundane, mixing with society,
saṁsarjana n. meeting, mixture or combination with (3rd), attracting, winning over, conciliating, discharging, abandoning,
saṁsarpa mfn creeping, gliding,
saṁ√śās P. to direct, instruct, summon, call upon, to arrange, put in order, mfl directing well or instructing,
saṁśāsana n. direction,
saṁśāsita mfn directed, instructed,
śaṁsati 1043/3 *√śaṁs* recites, repeats, praises, extols
saṁśaya 1117/3 m. lying down to sleep, uncertainty, doubt in or of, irresolution, hesitation, danger, a doubtful matter, difficulty, danger, risk, expression of doubt,
saṁśaya bhāvanā feeling of doubt or suspicion, (U)
saṁścat m. a juggler, rogue, n. deceit, trick, illusion,
saṁseka m. sprinkling over, watering,
saṁ√sev A. *–sevate* to be associated with, to frequent, inhabit, to wait upon, attend on, serve, honour, worship,
saṁsevana n. waiting on, serving, doing homage, ifc. using, employing,
saṁ√3.sidh P. *–sidhayati*, to be performed or accomplished thoroughly, succeed,

to attain beatitude or bliss,
saṁ-siddha 1119/2 mfn. fully or thoroughly performed or accomplished, made, done, healed, cured, prepared (food), ready for (4th), firmly resolved, satisfied, contented, clever, skilled in, one who has attained beatitude,
saṁsiddhārtha one who has attained his goal
saṁ-siddhi f. complete accomplishment or fulfilment, perfection, success, perfect state, beatitude, final emancipation, the last consequence or result, fixed or settled opinion, the last or decisive word
sāṁsiddhika mfn effected naturally, belonging to nature, natural, native, innate, self-existent, existing by its own nature or essence, existing absolutely, absolute,
sāṁsiddhikī fully established, effected naturally and existing by its own nature, become natural
sāṁsiddhya n. the state of having attained the highest object, perfection,
saṁsikta mfn well-sprinkled or moistened,
saṁśīlana n. regular practice, habitual performance, frequent intercourse with (6th),
saṁ√śikṣ caus. *-śikṣayati* to teach, try, test,
śaṁsin mfn reciting, uttering, announcing, telling, relating, betraying, predicting, promising,
saṁśiśrīṣu mfn wishing to have recourse to, wishing to rend or tear,
saṁśiṣṭa mfn left remaining,
saṁśita mfn sharpened, ready, made ready, well-prepared, fixed upon, decided, completing, effecting, rigid (as a vow), diligent in accomplishing,
-tapas mfn exposed or subjected to painful austerities/mortifications,
°tātman mfn one who has completely made up his mind, firmly resolved,
-vāc mfn using harsh/ sharp words,
-vrata firmly adhering to a vow or obligation, honest, virtuous
saṁśīta mfn congealed, frozen, cold, cool,
saṁśīti f. doubt, uncertainty,
saṁ√siv P. *–sīvyati,* to sew together,
saṁskāra 1120/2 m. impression on the mind of acts done in a former state of existence, latent impressions, putting together, forming well, making perfect, accomplishment, embellishment, adornment, purification, cleansing, making ready, refining (of metals), polishing (of gems), cleansing the body, rearing plants/animals,
forming the mind, training, education, correction, correct formation or use of a word, correctness, purity, (esp. of pronunciation or expression), making sacred, memory, mental impression or recollection,
a mental creation or conformation of the mind, (such as that of the external world, regarded by it as real though actually non-existent),
a purifying ceremony, cremation ceremony, the faculty of memory, mental impression or recollection, impression on the mind of acts done in a former state of existence,
(Buddhist) a mental conformation or creation of the mind forming the 2nd link in the chain of causation,
a polishing stone,
saṁskaraṇa n. the act of putting together, preparing, cremating (a corpse),
saṁ-s-√1. kṛ P.A. *–skaroti, -skurute,* to put together, form well, join together, compose, A. to accumulate, to prepare, make ready, cook, to form or arrange according to sacred precept, consecrate, hallow, embellish, refine, elaborate, make perfect, (esp.) to form language according to strict rules,
saṁskṛta 1120/3 mfn put together, constructed, perfected, well or completely formed, purified, refined, consecrated, sanctified, initiated, adorned, polished, highly

elaborated, (esp. applied to highly wrought speech, such as the sanskrit language as opposed to the vernaculars),dressed, cooked (food), m. a word formed according to accurate rules, a learned man, a regular derivation, *(am)* n. making ready, preparation or a prepared place, sacrifice, a sacred usage or custom, the Sanskrit language, *-vat* mfn one who has perfected, elaborated or finished,

saṁskṛtātman m. one who has received the purificatory rites, a sage,

saṁskṛti f. making ready, preparation, perfection, consecration, effort,

saṁskṛtrima mfn highly polished,

saṁśleṣa m. (ifc.f. *ā*) junction, union, connection, close contact with, embracing, an embrace,

saṁśleṣaṇa 1118/3 joining, connecting, clinging or sticking to, the act of putting together or joining, a means of binding together, cement, bond

saṁ√śliṣ P.A. *-śliṣyati (te)*, to stick or attach one's self to, to clasp, embrace, bring into close contact or connection with,

saṁśliṣṭa mfn clasped or pressed together, contiguous, coherent, closely connected with, blended together, confused, indeterminate (as an action which is neither good nor bad), endowed with, possessed of, m. a kind of pavilion, a multitude

saṁśliṣṭakarman mfn not distinguishing between good and evil actions,

saṁsmaraṇa 1122/2 the act of remembering, recollecting

saṁsmera mfn smiling at, smiling,

saṁ√smi A. *–smayate* to smile at, to be ashamed, blush,

saṁ√smṛ P. *–smarati* to remember fully, recollect, caus. *–smārayati* to cause to remember, remind of, to cause to be remembered, recall to the mind of (6th),

saṁsmṛta mfn remembered, recollected, called to the mind, prescribed, enjoined, named,

saṁsmṛti f. remembering, remembrance of

saṁsmṛtya remembering, having remembered

saṁśobhita mfn adorned or shining with

saṁśodhana mfn completely purifying, destroying impurity (of the bodily humours), purification or a means of purification, refining, clearing, correction, amendment,

saṁśodhita mfn completely cleansed and purified, corrected, amended,

saṁśoṣa m. complete drying, drying up,

saṁspardhā f. emulation, rivalry, jealousy,

saṁsparśa 1122/1 m. close or mutual contact, touch, conjunction, perception, sense

saṁsparśaja born of contact or touch, produced by contact or sense perception,

sāṁsparśaka n. touch, contact,

saṁsparśana 1122/1 touching, contact, mixture with

saṁspaṣṭa mfn famous, celebrated,

saṁspṛś mfn touching,

saṁspṛṣṭa mfn touched, brought into contact, closely united with (3rd comp.), mixed, combined, attained,

saṁsphuṭa mfn bursting open, blossomed,

saṁ-śrad-√dhā to have complete faith in, believe

saṁśrānta mfn completely wearied, languid,

saṁśrava m. hearing, listening, assent, promise, agreement, mfn audible,

saṁsrava m. flowing together, any remainder, remains, *√sru*

saṁśrāva m. hearing, listening to,

saṁsrāva m. flowing together, the remainder

saṁśrāvaka m. a hearer, disciple,

saṁśravaṇa n. the act of hearing or listening, ifc. hearing about, range of hearing, earshot,

saṁśravas n. perfect glory or renown,

saṁśraya m. (ifc.f.*ā*) conjunction, combination, connection, association, (ifc. joined or connected with, relating to, referring to), *āt* ind.

in consequence of, going or resorting to any person or place for refuge or protection (7th or comp.), relationship or reference to, league, alliance, a refuge, asylum, shelter, resting or dwelling place, residence, home, devotion to, attachment to, (ifc. devoted or attached to), *āt* ind. by means or help of, an aim, object, a piece or portion of something,

saṁśrayaṇa n. ifc. clinging to, attachment,

saṁśrayin mfn having recourse to, seeking protection, m. a subject, servant, ifc. dwelling or resting or being in,

saṁ√śri P.A. *–śrayati (te)*, to join together with, furnish with, attach oneself to, go for refuge or succour to, resort or betake oneself to, cling to for protection, seek the help of (2nd),

saṁ√śī P. *–śīṇati* to join or connect or unite with, cause to partake of (3rd), P. śṛyāti to smash to pieces, crush, to be dissipated or routed, fly in different directions,

saṁ√sṛ P. *–sarati*, to flow together with, to go about, roam or walk through, to walk or pass through (states), undergo transmigration, enter or pass into, to be diffused or spread into, to come forth, caus. *–sārayati* to cause to pass through states, undergo transmigration, to introduce to put off, defer, to use, employ,

saṁśrita mfn joined or united with (3rd or comp.), leaning against, clinging to, clung to, embraced, one who has gone or fled to anyone for refuge, one who has entered the service of (2nd or comp.), one who has taken himself to a place, situated in (7th or comp.), resorted to, sought for refuge or protection, one who is addicted to, indulging in, suitable, fit, proper, m. a servant, adherent, dependant,

-vat mfn one who has joined or united himself with (3rd),

saṁ√sṛj 1119/3 P.A. *–sṛjati (te)*, to join or unite or mix or mingle or endow, to hit with (3rd), to visit or afflict with (3rd), to create, engage in battle, A. to share anything with others, (A. or pass.) to join one's self, be joined or united or mingled, caus. *–sarjayati* to attract, win over, conciliate,

saṁsṛj f. commingling, collision, *saṁsṛjya* ind. joining up, having joined, after projecting (Gam.), having projected,

saṁsṛṣṭa mfn gathered together, collected, associated or connected together, friendly, familiar, accomplished, performed, (*am*) ind. near relationship, friendship, intimacy,

saṁsṛṣṭarūpa mfn mixed in form or kind, adulterated,

saṁsṛṣṭi f. union, combination, association, intercourse, living together in one family, collection, collecting,

saṁsṛṣṭika mfn directly or immediately connected, direct,

saṁsṛṣṭin m. a re-united kinsman, co-partner

saṁsṛti 1119/3 f. passage through successive states of existence or transmigration, course, revolution,

saṁ√1.śru to hear or hear from, attend or listen attentively to, to assent, promise, to be distinctly heard

saṁ√sru P. *–sravati* to flow or run together,

saṁśruta mfn well heard, learnt, read about in (7th), agreed, promised,

saṁstabdha mfn supported, confirmed, firm,

saṁstabhya ind. having supported or strengthened or encouraged, having supported or composed the mind firmly (in affliction), having taken heart or courage, together sustaining, upholding,

saṁ√stambh P. *–stabhnoti, °nāti,* to make firm, to support, sustain, encourage, to make rigid, to restrain, check,

saṁstambha m. obstinacy, pertinacity, firmness in resistance, support, prop, fixing, making firm, stop, stay, paralysis,

saṁstara m. (ifc.f.*ā*) a layer of grass or leaves, a bed, couch, a scattered mass of flowers, a covering, cover, scattering, strewing, spreading, propagation (of laws or customs),

saṁstāra m. a bed, couch, sacrifice, extension, spreading out,

saṁstaraṇa n. a layer of leaves etc. a couch, strewing, covering over,

saṁstava 1121/1 common or simultaneous praise, praise, commendation, familiarity, acquaintance with,

saṁstāva m. praising in chorus,

saṁ√sthā A. P. *-tiṣṭhate, (ti),* to stand together, hold together, to come or stay near (7th), to meet (as enemies), to stand still, remain, abide, stay, to be accomplished, completed (rites), to prosper, succeed, get on well, to come to an end, perish, caus. – *sthāpayati* to cause to stand up or firm, to raise up, restore (dethroned kings), to confirm, encourage, comfort, take heart, to found, establish, fix, settle, set afoot, stop, restrain, accomplish, conclude, kill, put to death,

f. staying or abiding with, shape, form, manifestation, appearance, established order, standard, rule, direction, quality, property, nature, conclusion, termination, completion,

saṁstha 1121/2 mfn standing together, existing, standing or staying or resting or being in or on, contained in, ended, perished, dead,

saṁsthā f. staying or abiding with, shape, form, manifestation, appearance, established order, state, standard, rule, direction, quality, property, nature, conclusion, completion, a complete liturgical course,

-gāra m.n. a meeting house,

-japa m. a closing prayer,

-tva n. being a form or shape,

saṁsthāna mfn standing together, like, resembling, n.f. staying or abiding in, (comp.), standing still or firm (in battle), being, existence, life, strict adherence or obedience to, abode, dwelling place, shape, form, appearance, beauty, splendour, nature, state, condition, an aggregate, whole, totality, conclusion, end, death,

-vat mfn being, existing, having various forms,

sāṁsthānika mfn a fellow countryman, relating to a common living place,

saṁsthāpaka mfn fixing firmly, settling, establishing, forming into a shape/shapes,

saṁsthāpana 1121/3 n. fixing, setting up. establishment

saṁsthita mfn standing, one who has stood or held up (in a fight), placed, resting, abiding, remaining, left standing, lasting, enduring, imminent, future, formed, formed like, being in a partic. state or condition, addicted or given to, intent upon, founded on, relating to, skilled in, concluded, perished, n. conduct, form, shape,

saṁsthiti f. staying together, living in or near, standing or sitting on (7th), duration, continuance in the same state or condition, constancy, perseverance, attaching importance to (7th), existence, possibility of (6th or comp.) form, shape, established order, nature, condition, quality, property, conclusion, end, death,

saṁstir f. contraction,

saṁ√stu to praise together with, to praise all at once, to praise properly or well, laud, celebrate,

saṁstubh f. shout of joy,

saṁstuta mfn praised or hymned together, praised, celebrated, reckoned together, equal to, passing for (3rd or comp.), familiar, intimate,

saṁstutaka mfn affable/condescending/civil

saṁstuti f. praise, eulogy, figurative expression,
saṁstyāna 1121/2 n. the becoming condensed or solid or compact, mfn coagulated, condensed,
saṁ√śubh A. *–śobhate*, to look beautiful, be radiant or splendid, to shine equally with (3rd), caus. *-śobhayati,* to decorate, adorn, beautify,
saṁ√sūc P. *–sūcayati*, to indicate, show, tell, plainly, to imply, betray,
saṁsūcaka mfn indicating plainly, showing, betraying,
saṁśuddha mfn completely purified or cleansed, pure, clean, removed, destroyed, expiated, cleared off, defrayed, paid, searched, tried, examined, acquitted (of a crime),
saṁśuddhi f. perfect purification or purity, cleaning (the body), acquittal, acquittance, correction, rectification,
saṁ√śudh P. *–śudhyati* to become completely pure or purified,
saṁsukhita mfn perfectly delighted/gratified,
saṁśūna mfn much swelled, swollen,
saṁsupta mfn soundly asleep, sleeping,
saṁśuṣka mfn completely dried up/withered
saṁsūte, -sūyate, brings forth, gives birth to, causes, produces √2.*sū*
saṁśyāna mfn contracted, shrunk, collapsed
saṁ√taḍ P. *–tāḍayati* to strike together, hit hard, hit (with an arrow etc.), to beat or play a musical instrument,
saṁtāḍana n. striking/dashing to pieces,
saṁtakṣaṇa n. hurting with words, sarcasm,
saṁ√tam P. *–tāmyati* to be distressed, pine away,
saṁtamas n. great or universal darkness,
saṁtamasa n. as above, great delusion of mind, mfn darkened, clouded,
saṁ√tan P. *–tanoti* to stretch along or over, cover, to unite or join one's self with, to join or connect or keep together, make continuous, to add, to accomplish, to exhibit, display,
saṁtāna 1142/1 m. continued succession, continuance, continuity, an uninterrupted series, continuous flow, coherence, connection, transition, a continuous train of thought, a sinew or ligature (of an animal), m.n. continuous succession, lineage, race, family, offspring, son or daughter,
saṁtānin m. the subject of an uninterrupted train of thought, the upper part of milk, cream,
saṁṭaṇka m. connection,
saṁtani mfn continuing, prolonging, forming an uninterrupted line/series, m.f. sound, harmony, music, a partic. oblation,
saṁ√tap P. *–tapati* to heat thoroughly, scorch, parch, dry up, to feel pain or remorse, to torture, oppress,
saṁtāpa 1142/2 m. becoming very hot, great or burning heat, glow, fire, affliction, distress, torment, agony, remorse, penance, repentance
saṁtapana mfn heating, warming,
sāṁtapana heating, warming, warm relating to the sun,
saṁtāpana mfn burning, paining, afflicting n. the act of burning, paining, afflicting, exciting passion,
saṁtāpavat mfn sorrowful, afflicted with pain
saṁtapta mfn greatly heated or inflamed, burnt up, red-hot, molten, pained, distressed, n. pain, grief, sorrow,
saṁtaptāyas n. heated or red-hot iron,
saṁtāra m. crossing, passing over or through, √*tī*
saṁtaraṇa mfn conveying over or across, bringing out of (a danger), n. the act of crossing over or passing through,
saṁtarati 1142/3 cross or traverse together, brings safely over, rescues, saves
saṁtarjana mfn threatening, abusing,
saṁtarpaka mfn satiating, refreshing, invigorating, n. the act of satiating, refreshing, refreshment, a means of

strengthening, restorative, a partic. luscious dish,
saṁtarutra mfn conveying across, effective, sufficient (as wealth),
saṁtata mfn stretched or extended along, spread over, covered with (3rd), held or linked or woven or sewn or strung together, dense, continuous, perpetual, uninterrupted, stretched, extended
saṁtati f. stretching or extending along, expanse, continuity, uninterruptedness, causal connectedness of things, a continuous line or series, density, intensity (of darkness), uninterrupted succession, lineage, race, progeny, offspring, continued meditation, disposition, feeling,
śaṁtāti f. beneficent, auspicious, benefits,
saṁtejana n. sharpening, exciting,
saṁtoṣa m. (ifc.f.*ā*) satisfaction, contentedness with, content
saṁtrāṇa n. saving, rescuing,
saṁtrasta mfn frightened, alarmed,
saṁtṛṇṇa mfn joined or fastened together, hollowed out, perforated,
saṁtuṣṭa mfn quite satisfied or contented, well pleased or delighted with
saṁtuṣṭi f. complete satisfaction, contentment with (3rd),
saṁtvarā f. great haste, hurry,
saṁtvaritam ind. in a hurry, quickly,
saṁtyāga m. relinquishment, abandonment, renunciation, resignation,
saṁ√tyaj P. *–tyajati* to relinquish altogether, abandon, leave, quit, desert, to avoid, shun, give up,
saṁtyajana n. the act of entirely deserting or abandoning,
saṁtyakta mfn entirely relinquished, or abandoned, left, deprived or destitute of, wanting, lacking,
samubdha mfn confined, closed, covered,
sam√ubj P. to cover over, close up, press together,
samubjita mfn covered over, closed up,
samucca mfn lofty, high,
samuccara m. going or coming forth together, ascending, traversing, flying upwards,
samuccāra m. utterance, pronunciation,
samuccaya m. aggregation, accumulation, multitude, totality, conjunction of words or sentences,
samuccayavāda the doctrine that both *karma* and *jñāna* are necessary for Self-realisation,
samucchitti f. cutting off completely,
samucchraya 1165/3 mfn who or what rises or grows up, m. raising aloft, erection, elevation, height, length, an eminence, hill, mountain, rising, rise, exaltation, high position, increase, growth, high degree, stimulation, accumulation, multitude
samud mfn joyful, glad,
samudā√gam to rise together, to arrive at full knowledge,
samudāgata mfn one who has attained full knowledge, excelling in (comp.),
samudaya m. coming together, union, assemblage, revenue, war, aggregate of the constituent elements or factors of any being or existence, battle, combination, junction, day, income, prosperity, success, aggregate, collection, ind. having spoken together, having concluded or agreed upon,
samudāya m. combination, collection, multitude, mass, totality, a whole,
samudbhāsana n. lighting up, illuminating,
samudbhava m. (ifc. f.*ā*) existence, production, origin, (ifc. either 'arisen or produced from' or 'being the source of'), coming to life again, revival, 1168/2
samud√bhū P. *–bhavati*, to spring up from, arise, be produced, exist, to increase, augment, grow,
samudbhūta mfn sprung up, arisen, born, produced, derived, existing,
samucita mfn well-suited, fit, well-liked, accustomed or used to, right, delighted in, appropriate,

samudbodha m. becoming consciousness,
samud√budh caus. *–bodhayati* to rouse up thoroughly, awaken, animate,
samuddhartṛ mfn deliverer, uplifter, m. an uptearer, extirpator,
samuddhṛtya gerund *sam-ud √dhṛ*, having picked up, gathered, selected
samudeta mfn excelling in (comp.), possessed of all good qualities,
samudghāṭa m. taking away, removal,
samudgīta mfn sung out loud, chanted loudly
samudita mfn gone up, risen, elevated, gathered together, united, well-supplied, wanting nothing, spoken to or with, addressed, accosted, agreed upon, consented, settled, customary,
samudra m. 'gathering together of waters', the sea, ocean, atmospheric ocean, the sky, a large Soma vessel, mfn having a stamp or seal, stamped, sealed, marked,
sāmudra mfn relating to the sea, oceanic, marine, m. a mariner, voyager, sailor, a kind of gnat,
samudrabhava mfn being in the ocean, produced from or in the sea,
samudraga mfn ocean-going, sea-faring, m. a seafarer, seaman,
samudragṛha n. a bath-house, bathroom,
samudraja mfn produced or found in the sea
sāmudraka mfn oceanic, maritime, n. sea-salt, m. a fortune-teller,
samudrakaṭaka a ship,
samudrakallola m. an ocean wave,
samudrakukṣi f. the sea-shore,
samudrāmbhas n. seawater,
samudraphena m. sea-foam, cuttle-fish bone
samudrasāra a pearl, 'quintessence of the sea'
samudrasnāna n. bathing in the sea,
samudraśukti f. a sea-shell,
samudratas ind. from the sea,
samudrataṭa n. the seacoast,
samudratīra n. the sea-shore,
samudratīrīya mfn dwelling on the seashore
samudratva n. the state of the ocean
samudravāsin mfn dwelling near the sea,
samudrayāṇa n. a vessel, ship, mfn flowing to the sea,
samudrayātrā f. a sea-voyage,
samudrayāyin m. a sea-farer,
sāmudrika mfn seafaring, m. a mariner,
samudrikta mfn abundantly furnished with,
samudrīya mfn relating to the sea, marine,
samud√śri Cl 1 *-śrayati,* to raise up,
samudvaha mfn who or what lifts up, moving up an down,
samudvāha m. bearing up, leading away, marriage,
samud√5vas caus. *vāsayati*, to expel, remove
samudvigna mfn greatly agitated/disturbed,
samudvṛtta mfn risen up, swollen,
samudya ind. having spoken together, having concluded or agreed upon,
sam-udyama 1168/2 m. lifting up, raising, setting about, readiness to or for
samudyata 1168/2 part. raised up, lifted up, offered, presented, in raising, arising
samudyāta mfn risen up against, (2nd),
samudyoga m. thorough preparation, making ready, setting about, employment, use, concurrence,
samud√yuj caus.*–yojayati*, to excite, animate
samūha 1170/3 , m. multitude, a collection, assemblage, aggregate, heap, association, community, sum, totality, essence, flock,
samūha sweep together, gather up 2/s/impv *sam √ūh*
samūhana mfn sweeping together, collecting, f. *(ī)* a broom, n. the act of sweeping together,
samūhya ind. having brought together, mfn to be swept together,
samujjhita mfn abandoned, renounced, resigned, free from, rid of, n. that which is left, a remnant, leavings
samujjvala mfn shining, radiant, splendid in or with, *(√jval)*
samukha mfn 'mouthy', talkative, eloquent,
samukta mfn spoken to, addressed, remonstrated or expostulated with,
samūla mfn having roots, together with the

root, grassy, green, root and branch, entire, entirely, based upon, founded,
samūlaka mfn together with the roots,
samulbaṇa mfn strong, big, brawny,
samullāsa m. sporting, dancing, prancing (a horse), excessive brilliance, exhilaration,
samullasati shines forth, gleams, glitters, breaks forth, appears, resounds, sounds, √*las*
samullasita mfn shining forth, gleaming, brilliant, beautiful, sporting,
samundana n. becoming thoroughly wet, moisture, wetness,
samunna mfn well-moistened,
samunnaddha mfn tied or bound up, swollen, pressed up or out, raised up, elevated, exalted, full, excessive, proud, arrogant, unfettered, loosened, produced, born,
samunnamana n. raising, arching (brows)
samunnasa mfn having a prominent nose,
samunnata mfn risen up, lifted up, raised aloft, arched, vaulted, high, sublime, proud, arrogant,
samunnati f. a rising, elevation, i.e. fig. distinction, eminence,
samunnaya m. bringing out, inference, deduction, occurrence, event,
samunnidra mfn wide awake, wide open (eyes),
samupa√dhā to put together, construct, create, produce,
samupa√dhāv Cl 1 *–dhāvati,* run up to together, to run near or towards,
samupa√diś Cl6 -*samupadiśati* to show, assign, point out or indicate fully,
samupa√dru Cl 1 *–dravati,*to run to wards together, run up to, attack,
samupadruta mfn attacked, overrun,
samupa√gam to go or proceed together towards, go or come near to, approach, have recourse to, to go to any state or condition, undergo,
samupā√gam to go up to together, go near to, resort to, approach, meet, undergo, incur, get into any state or condition,
samupagata mfn approached, undergone,
samupāgata mfn gone near to, approached, come, arrived, one who has attained, incurred or undergone,
samupā√ghrā to smell at, kiss,
samupahata mfn stricken, impaired,
samupahava m. invitation with others, a common invitation,
samupahvara m. a hidden place, hiding place,
samupa√i Cl 2 *–eti,* to go to together, assemble,
samupa√jan A. *–jāyate* to arise, spring up, take place, to be born again, caus. -*janayati*, to generate, cause, produce,
samupajanita generated, produced, caused
samupajāta mfn arisen, produced,
samupa√jñā to ascertain fully, find out,
samupā√1.kṛ to satisfy, pay off,
samupa√kram to go up to, approach, to begin, commence to, to step up to,
samupanayana n. the act of leading near to,
samupānayana n. bringing near, procuring,
samupanyasta mfn fully stated,
samupa√śam to become quiet, cease,
samupa√sev to make use of together, to be addicted to, to enjoy,
samupāśrita 1170/1 one who has recourse to, supported by, resting on, resorted to
samupa√ śru to listen to anything, hear, hear or perceive anyone, hear from or be told by anyone,
samupastambha m. propping, supporting,
samupa√sthā to stand near (at anyone's service), to lean on, to go to, approach, to occur, arise, befall,
samupā√sthā to stand near to, to practise, observe,
samupasthā f. standing near, approximation, proximity, happening, befalling,
samupasthita mfn approximated, approached, come to (e.g. a river), sitting or lying on, arisen, appeared, begun, imminent, seasonable, opportune, come upon, fallen to one's share, ready for, undertaken, resolved, attained, acquired,

samupātta mfn gained, acquired, taken, robbed, collected,
samupaveśa m. sitting down together, inviting anyone to sit down or rest, entertaining, a seat,
samupa√viś to sit down together or near, sit or lie down on,
samupa√vṛt to go together towards, proceed together, to behave,
sam-upe *(-upa-√5.i) –upaiti,* to come together, meet, to have sexual intercourse,
samupekṣaka mfn overlooking, disregarding
samupeta mfn come together, arrived, come, furnished or supplied with, abounding in,
samupoḍha mfn brought near, presented, offered, commenced, begun (battle), risen (the moon),
samupoṣaka mfn fasting,
samupoṣita mfn engaged in, devoted to (2nd), one who has fasted,
samūra or *samūru* m. a kind of deer,
samuṣita mfn one who has passed or spent time, dwelled or lived together, stayed with,
samutka mfn desirous of, longing for,
samutkaca mfn beginning to bloom, blooming, expanded,
samut√kram to go upwards, depart from life, to overstep, transgress, violate
samutkrama m. going upwards, rise, ascent, transgressing proper bounds,
samut√pad Cl 4 A *–padyate*, to be brought forth or born of, arise, to spring up together, arise, appear, occur,
samutpanna mfn sprung up together, arisen, produced, occurred, happened, taking place, begotten by (5th), or on (7th),
samut√pat Cl 1 *–patati,* fly up together, spring up, ascend, rise, rush upon, burst forth, arise, appear, fly away,
samutsāha m. energy, force of will,
samutsarga m. an ejecting, discharging, pouring out together (urine) emission (semen),
samutsikta mfn overflowing with, proud of,
samnutsuka mfn very uneasy, longing for (comp.), eager to,
samuttara n. = *uttara* answer, reply,
samuttāra m. passing over safely, deliverance,
samuttha mfn rising up, risen, appearing, sprung or produced from,
samutthā *(ud√sthā)* P.A. *–tiṣṭhati, te,* to rise up together, to rise up (as from death), get up (from sleep), recover (from sickness), rise (in the sky), gather (as clouds), come forth, to awaken, excite, arouse,
samutthita mfn risen up together, risen, raised as dust over a peak, surging (as waves), gathered (clouds), appeared, grown sprung from, ready, ready for, one who withstands all (opponents), cured, healed, swollen,
saṁ√vac P. *–vakti* to proclaim, announce, publish, speak, tell, say to, A. to converse, talk with,
saṁvāc f. speaking together, colloquy
saṁvācya n. the art of conversation, mfn to be conversed with,
saṁ√vad P.A. *–vadati (te),* A. to speak together or at the same time, P.A. to converse with (3rd) or about (7th), P. to sound together or in concord, to agree, accord, consent, fit together (so as to give one sense), to speak, speak to, address, caus. *–vādayati (te),* to cause to converse with (3rd) or about (7th), to invite to speak,
saṁvāda m. speaking together, conversation, assent, concurrence, agreement, information, news, 1114/2
saṁvadana n. the act of speaking together, conversation, a message, consideration, f.*ā* subduing by charms or magic,
saṁvādī mfn corresponding, an error in perception where though the initial perception is a mistake, the end reached is the desired one,
sāṁvādika mfn colloquial, controversial, m. causing discussion, a disputant,

saṁvāha mfn setting in motion, moving, shampooing, a park for recreation, a market-place,
saṁvahana n. guiding, conducting, showing, displaying, bearing, carrying, the moving along or passage (of clouds), rubbing the person, shampooing,
sāṁvaidya n. finding each other, meeting
saṁvalgana n. jumping with joy, exulting,
saṁvalita mfn met, united, joined, mixed with, surrounded by, possessed of,
saṁ√van –vānayati , -vanayati, to cause to like or love, make well disposed,
saṁvanana mfn propitiating, making well disposed to, f. (*ā*) causing mutual fondness, charming, propitiating,
saṁ√vand A. *–vandate,*to salute respectfully
saṁvara mfn keeping back, stopping, m. a dam, mound, bridge, provisions, shutting out the external world, n. restraint, forbearance, 2. choosing, election, choice (of a husband), stoppage of the inflow of karmic matter into a soul (Jaina),
saṁvāra m. ifc. f.*ā*, covering, concealing, compression or contraction of the throat or of the vocal chords (in pronunciation), obtuse articulation, an obstacle, impediment,
saṁvaraṇa mfn covering, containing, shutting, closing, (*am*) n. the act of covering, enclosing, concealing, closing, shutting, concealment, secrecy, a cover, lid, an enclosure, sanctuary, a dam, mound, 1116/1
saṁvardhaka mfn augmenting, increasing,
saṁvardhana n. growing up, complete growth, fostering, a means for causing growth, prospering, thriving, causing to thrive,
saṁvardhita mfn brought to complete growth, brought up, reared, raised, cherished,
saṁvarga mfn rapacious, ravenous, m. gathering for one's self, devouring, consumption, absorption, the resolution of one thing into another,
saṁvargavidyā (in phil.) the science of resolution or absorption
saṁvarmita mfn fully armed,
saṁvarṇana n. narrating, describing, praise,
saṁvarṣaṇa n. raining or showering down,
saṁvarta m. meeting, encountering (enemy), rolling up, destruction, esp. the periodical destruction/dissolution of the world, anything rolled or kneaded, a lump or ball (of cake), a mass of people, a raincloud,
saṁvartaka mfn the end or dissolution of the universe,
saṁvartakalpa m. a particular period of universal destruction,
saṁvartana mfn issuing in, leading to (comp.), a mythical weapon, *(ī)*f. destruction of the world,
saṁvaryati Nom. P. to bring together,
saṁ√ *4. –vaste* A. to be clothed or clad in, *5.vas* to live together, live or associate with, to co-habit with, to meet or assemble together, to stay abide, dwell in (7th), to spend or pass time,
saṁvāsa m. dwelling together, cohabitation, sexual connection, a common abode, settlement, house, an open place for meeting, recreation, association, company, society,
saṁvasana n. a dwelling place, house,
saṁvasatha m. a settlement, village
saṁvasati f. dwelling together,
saṁvat a side, region, tract, 2. a year, in the year,
saṁvatsam ind. for a year,
saṁvatsara m. a full year, a year,
-*am* for a year
-*eṇa* after or in course of a year,
e or *asya* after/within a year
sāṁvatsara mfn yearly, annual, perennial, m. an astrologer, almanac-maker, a lunar month, black rice,
saṁvatsaratama happening after a year, completing a full year,
sāṁvatsarika mfn yearly, annual, relating to a year, produced in a year,
saṁvatsarīṇa mfn yearly, annual

saṁvayati P. weaves together, interweaves,
saṁveda m. perception, consciousness
saṁvedya mfn to be known or understood, intelligible, to be communicated to, 2. m. the junction of 2 rivers,
saṁvedana n. the act of perceiving or feeling, perception, sensation, making known, communication,
saṁvedita 1115/2 mfn made known, informed, instructed, 'becoming enlightened' (Gam),
saṁvega m. violent agitation, excitement, intensity, high degree, desire of emancipation,
saṁveṣṭita mfn surrounded by
saṁvi√bhā P. *–bhāti,* to form ideas about, meditate on, wish for,
saṁvibhāga m. sharing with others, partition, distribution, giving, participation, share,
saṁvibhajana n. the act of sharing with another
saṁvibhakta mfn divided, separated, distributed,
saṁvibhaktṛ mfn one who shares with another (6th),
saṁ√1. vid P.A. cl2. *–vetti, -vitte,* to know together, know thoroughly, know, recognise, to perceive, feel, taste, to come to an understanding, agree with, approve,
saṁ√2.vid A. to find, obtain, acquire, to meet with, be united or joined to,
saṁvid f. consciousness, intellect, knowledge, understanding, (in phil. = *mahat),* perception, feeling, sense of (6th or comp.), a stage of yoga, a mutual understanding, agreement, contract, an appointment, rendezvous, a plan, scheme, conversation, talk about (comp.), news, tidings, prescribed custom, 2. f. acquisition, property,
saṁvida mfn having consciousness, conscious, n. stipulation, agreement,
saṁvidāna mfn joined or united or associated with, agreeing in opinion, harmonious,
saṁviddha mfn ifc. contiguous to, coinciding with,
saṁvidh f. arrangement, plan, preparation,
saṁvidhā f. mode of life,
saṁvi√dhā to dispose, arrange, settle, fix, determine, prescribe, to direct, order, conduct, manage, use, employ
saṁvidhi m. disposition, arrangement, preparation,
saṁvidita mfn known, recognized, understood, searched, explored, agreed upon, admonished, advised,
saṁvidvas mfn one who has known or knows,
sāṁvidya n. mutual understanding,
saṁvigna mfn starting back, recoiling, agitated, disturbed, moving to and fro, ifc. fallen into,
saṁvi√jñā to agree with, recommend, to understand
saṁvijñāna n. agreement, consent, thorough or complete understanding, perception, knowledge,
saṁvi√mṛś to reflect upon, consider,
saṁvi√nī to remove entirely, suppress,
saṁvi√rāj to shine forth, be very illustrious,
saṁ√viś P.A. *viśati (te),* to approach near to, associate or attach oneself to, to enter together, enter into, to merge one's self into, to lie down, rest, sleep with, sit down with, engage in,
saṁ√viṣ to prepare, procure, bestow,
saṁviṣṭa mfn clothed, approached, entered, resting, dressed, reposing, sleeping,
saṁvītaṅga mfn properly clothed, one who has the body covered,
saṁvītarāga mfn one whose passions have disappeared,
saṁvītin mfn girt with the sacred thread,
saṁvi√tark to deliberate about, reflect upon,
saṁvitti f. knowledge, intellect, understanding, perception, feeling, sense of (comp.), mutual agreement, harmony, recognition, recollection,
saṁ√vṛ P.A. *–vṛṇoti, vṛṇute* to cover up, enclose, hide, conceal, to shut, close (a door), to put together or in order, arrange, to ward off, A. to

gather, accumulate, augment, increase,
2. A. *–vṛṇute* to choose, seek for,

saṁvraścam ind. in pieces, piece by piece,

saṁvrāta m.n. a multitude, troop, swarm,

saṁvṛddha mfn full grown, grown up, increased, augmented, thriving, prospering,

saṁvrddhi f. full growth, might, power,

saṁ√vṛdh A. *–vardhate*, to grow to perfection or completion, grow up, increase, to fulfil, satisfy, grant, caus. *–vardhayati,* to cause to grow, bring up, foster, cherish, strengthen, beautify, make prosperous or happy,

saṁ√vṛt A. *–vartate*, to turn or go towards, approach near to, arrive at, to go against, attack, to meet, encounter (foes), to come together, be conglomerated, have sex together, to take shape, come into being, be produced, come to pass, happen, begin, commence, to be, exist, to become, grow, caus. *–vartayati*, to cause to turn or revolve, roll, to turn towards or hither, to clench (the fist), to wrap up, envelop, to crumple up, bring about, accomplish, to fulfil, satisfy (a wish), to think of, find out (remedy),

saṁvṛta mfn covered, shut up, enclosed or enveloped in (7th), surrounded, accompanied or protected by, well provided or filled with, full of (3rd or comp.), concealed, kept, secured, contracted or compressed or closed (throat), articulated with the vocal chords contracted, n. a secret place, *-tva* n. closed condition,

saṁvṛtta 1116/3 mfn arrived, fulfilled, (having) become,

saṁvṛti f. closure, covering, keeping secret, dissimulation, hypocrisy, obstruction, relative truth,

saṁvṛtta mfn approached near to, arrived, happened, occurred, passed, become, grown (with1st),

saṁvṛtti f. common occupation, the right effect, fulfilment (personified), 'an empirical outlook' (Gam.) being, existing, becoming, happening, also for *saṁvṛti,*

saṁvṛtyā ind. 'having an empirical outlook' (Gam.), commonly accepted truth, conventionally real,

saṁvuvūrṣu mfn wishing to cover or conceal,

saṁvyādha m. combat, fight,

saṁvyavahāra m. mutual dealing, dealing with, mercantile business, traffic, addiction to, occupation with,

sāṁvyavahārika mfn current in everyday life, generally intelligible,

saṁya m. a skeleton,

sāmya n. equality, evenness, equilibrium, likeness, sameness, identity with, equality of rank or position,

saṁ√yā P. *–yāti* to go or proceed together, wander, travel, meet, encounter, to come to, attain (state or condition),

śamyā f. a stick, staff, wooden pin, the pin of a yoke,

saṁ√yāc A/ *-yācate* to ask, beg, implore,

samyag in comp for *samyañc* 1181/2 mfn. going along with or together, turned together or in one direction, combined, united, entire, whole, complete,

samyagājīva m. right living,

samyagājñā m. right understanding,

samyagavabhāṣaṇa n. right speech, and *avabhāṣaṇa*

samyagavabodha m. right understanding,

samyagbodha m. right understanding,

samyagdarśana n. right perception or insight, possessing true insight, perfect knowledge,

samyagdarśin, °-dṛś, -dṛṣṭi, right insight or belief, mfn having right belief,

samyagdṛṣṭi f. right insight or belief, mfn having right belief, orthodox,

samyaggata mfn behaving rightly,

samyagguṇa n. right or true virtue,

samyagjñāna n. right knowledge,

samyag-jñāna 1181/3 n. right knowledge

G279 One of the 3 jewels of Jainism, a specialized knowledge of the essence of the Self and not-Self. It is without any defects and beyond all doubt.

samyagvāc f. right speech,

samyagvarṇaprayoga correct pronunciation

samyagvartamāna mfn continuance in right discharge of duty,

samyagvṛtta mfn well-conducted, wholly confiding in,

samyagvṛtti f. regular or complete performance, right discharge of duties,

samyagvyāyāma m. right exertion (Buddhist),

saṁ√yaj P.A. *–yajati (te)*, to worship together, offer sacrifices at the time, to sacrifice, worship, adore, honour, consecrate, dedicate,

saṁyājya mfn to be made or allowed to sacrifice, n. joining or sharing in a sacrifice,

samyak well, perfectly, in comp. for *samyañc,* ind. in the same way, at the same time, in one line, straight, completely, wholly, thoroughly, by all means,

samyakcāritra n. (Jainas) right conduct,

samyakkarmānta m. (buddhist) right action or occupation,

samyakpāṭha m. right pronunciation,

samyakprahāna n. right abandonment, right effort or exertion, (4 kinds for Buddhists) 1. to prevent demerit arising, 2. get rid of it when arisen, 3. produce merit, 4. increase it,

samyakpraṇidhāna n. true or profound meditation,

samyakpravṛtti f. right action or function of the senses,

samyakprayoga m. right use/employment,

samyaksamādhi m. right meditation, (Bud.)

samyaksambodha m. °bodhi f. *°buddhi,* f. complete enlightenment,

samyaksambuddha mfn one who has attained to complete enlightenment, (said of the Buddha),

samyaksaṁkalpa m. right resolve (Buddh.)

samyaksmṛti f. right recollection,

samyakśraddhāna n. right belief,

samyaksthiti f. remaining together,

samyaktā f. rightness, correct manner

samyaktva n. completeness, perfection,

saṁ√yam P.A. *–yacchati,* to hold together, hold in, hold fast, restrain, curb, suppress, control, govern, guide, tie up (hair), bind together (clothing), to put together, to shut up, close a door, press close to, give to,

saṁ-yama 1112/1 m. holding together, restraint, control, esp. control of the senses, self-control, concentration of mind (comprising *dhāraṇā, dhyāna, samādhi,* or the last 3 stages in yoga), effort, exertion, (*āt* with great difficulty) ,

saṁ-yamaka mfn checking, restraining,

saṁ-yamamāgni m. the fire of abstinence,

saṁyamana mfn bringing to rest, n. the act of curbing, checking, restraining, self-control, binding together, tying up, drawing tight, (reins etc) Yama's residence

saṁ-yamavat mfn self-controlled, economical, parsimonious,

saṁ-yamin 1112/1 mfn. one who subdues his passions, self-controlled, tied up (as hair),

saṁ-yamita mfn restrained, checked, bound, clasped in the arms, held, detained, piously disposed, n. subduing the voice,

saṁyamya 1112/1 mfn restraining, holding back, subduing, controlling, to be checked or restrained,

samyaṅ in comp. for *samyañc*

samyañc 1181/2 mfn going along with or together, turned together or in one direction, combined, united, entire, whole, complete, all, lying in one direction, forming one line, correct, accurate, proper, true, right, uniform, same, identical, pleasant, agreeable,

samyaṅmati f. correct opinion,

saṁ√yas cl 4.1. P. *–yasyati, -yasati*

to make effort,
saṁ√yat 1111/3 to unite, meet together, contend, engage in contest or strife,
saṁyat mfn coherent, contiguous, continuous, uninterrupted, f. an agreement, stipulation, a means of joining or uniting, an appointed place, strife, war,
saṁyata 1111/3 mfn. held together, held in, held fast, self-contained, self-controlled, subdued, restrained, m. one who controls himself,
saṁyāta mfn gone together, proceeded together, approached, come,
saṁyatacetas mfn controlled in mind,
saṁyataprāṇa mfn having the breath suppressed or organs restrained,
saṁyatatākṣa mfn having the eyes closed
saṁyatātman mfn controlled in mind,
saṁyatavāc mfn restrained in speech, taciturn, silent,
saṁyatavastra mfn dress or clothes fastened or tied together,
saṁyatavat mfn self-controlled, self-possessed
śāmyate is extinguished, *√śam*
saṁyatendriya mfn having restrained senses, self-controlled,
śāmyati 1053/3 1/s/pres/indic/act. to be quiet, calm, rested, content, satisfied, to cease or be extinguished, is still,
saṁyāti meets with encounters 1/s/pres/indic/act *sam √yā*
saṁyatin mfn controlling, restraining (the senses),
sāṁyātrika m. a voyaging merchant, one who trades by sea, n. any vehicle, the dawn,
sāṁyaugika mfn related, being in relation, connected,
saṁyavana n. mixing, mingling, a square of four houses,
sāmyāvasthā f. state of equipoise, state of equilibrium, harmony of the 3 *guṇāḥ,* the state of the unmanifested being, (U),
saṁyodha m. fight, battle,
saṁyoga 1112/2 m. conjunction, combination, connection, union or absorption with or in, contact (in phil.) direct material contact, (in gram.) , a conjunct consonant, (combination of 2 or more consonants), dependence of one case on another, total amount, sum, agreement of opinion, being engaged in
saṁyogasaṁbandha m. relation by contact, e.g. the stick and the drum (U),
saṁyogin mfn being in contact or connection, closely connected with (3rd or comp.), united (with a loved object, married, one of the consonants in a *saṁyoga,*
saṁyojaka mfn joining together, connecting, bringing together or about,
saṁyojana n. the act of joining or uniting with, all that binds to the world, cause of rebirth, copulation, sexual union,
saṁ√2.yu P.A. to join/unite with one's self, take into one's self, devour,
saṁ√yudh P.A. *–yudhyate* to fight together, fight with, caus. *–yodhayati* to cause to fight together, to fight,
saṁyuga n. union, conjunction, conflict, war
saṁ√yuj P.A. to join or attach together,
saṁyuj mfn joined together, united, connected, related, m. a relation, f. union, connection, (=*saṁyoga),*
saṁyukta mfn joined together, combined, united, conjunct (consonants), connected, related, married to, placed, put, endowed or furnished with, ifc. connected with, relating to, concerning, (*am*) ind. jointly, together, at the same time,
saṁyunaktu may he endow,
saṁyuta mfn joined or bound together, put together, joined with, consisting of, containing, ifc. relating to, in conjunction with,
saṁyuyūṣu mfn wishing to join together or unite with,

saṁyuyutsu mfn wishing to fight,

√*śaṇ* 1048/2 cl 1.10 P *śaṇati, śaṇayati* to give, to go, DP in *dāna* giving, or *gati* going

√*śān* 1064/2 desiderative only, A. *śīśāṁsate* to whet, sharpen, DP in *tejana* sharpening, whetting,

san 1141/1 *sana* old, ancient, (A),(B), being, pres.part √ *as* 1/s/m

√*san* 1140/3 cl 1. P 8. P A *sanati, sanate sanoti* or *sanute* to gain, acquire, possess, enjoy, to gain for another, procure, bestow, give, distribute, to be successful, be granted or fulfilled, DP in *sambhakti* distributing, allotting, bestowing, in *dāna* giving, bestowing,

san in comp. for *sat*

sana m. gain, acquisition, offering, 2. mfn old, ancient, (*am*) ind. of old, formerly, lasting long, 3. the flapping of an elephant's ears,

sanā ind. of old, always, forever,

śanai m. gradually,

śanaiḥ śanaiḥ little by little, gently, slowly

śanais 1051/3 mfn moving slowly ind. quietly, softly, gently

sanaja or *sanajā* mfn born or produced long ago, ancient,

sanaka mfn former, old, ancient,

śanakais ind. quietly, gently, slowly,

sanana n. gaining, acquiring,

sanara mfn together with men and elephants,

sanat also *sanāt* ind. from of old, always, ever,

sanatā ind. from of old, with *na* – never,

sanātana 1141/1 mfn eternal, perpetual, permanent, ancient

sanātana-dharma the eternal law,

sanatkumāra 'always a youth', 'son of *brahmā'*,

sañca m. a collection of leaves for writing, a copy-book,

sañcit (saṁcita) "..that which has been collected (in the *citta)* over a long time." HH, the store of inactivated *saṁskāra* in the causal body, mfn accumulated,

√*śaṇḍ* 1048/3 cl 1 A *śaṇḍate* to hurt or to collect, DP in *rujā* wounding, or *saṅghāta* collecting,

śaṇḍa m. thick sour milk or curds,

sāṇḍa mfn having testicles, (not castrated),

sandhi or *saṁdhi* 1144/3 mfn. containing a conjunction or transition from one to the other, junction, connection, combination, union with, totality, the whole essence, euphonic junction of final and initial letters in grammar, place or point of connection or contact

sandhim etya getting connection

sandhyā see *saṁdhyā*

sāndra mfn thick, dense, oily, intense,

sanemi ind. always, comletely, at all times,

sanīyas mfn being from of old, ancient,

√*śaṅg* 1048/1 ? DP in *gati* going

saṅga 1132/3 m. sticking, clinging to, association with or attachment to, contact, relation, association, addiction or devotion to, propensity for, desire, wish, cupidity, 'the company or environment in which he would find himself and with which he would work' HH76

saṅgama 1128/3 coming together, meeting, union, connection, harmony

saṅgati 1128/2 coming together, meeting with, resorting to, association, society, company, intercourse, agreement or consistency with the rest of a document or argument,

saṅgavarjita mfn free from attachment

saṅgha see *saṁgha*

saṅgharṣa 1130/2 m. rubbing together, friction, mutual attrition, rivalry, envy, jealousy in regard to, going gently, gliding, sexual excitement

saṅghāta 1130/1 m. striking or dashing together, killing, crushing, combat, war, battle, compressing, condensation, compactness, hardening, close union or combination, collection, cluster, any aggregate of matter, intensity, a bone

saṅgin mfn hanging on, sticking in, clinging or adhering to (comp.), coming into contact with, touching, attached or devoted or addicted to, fond of, intent on, connected with, full of affection or desire, worldly, licentious, continuous, uninterrupted

saṅgraha m. gathering, grasp, collecting, collection,

sāṅguṣṭha mfn together with the thumb,

śani m. planet Saturn,

sani m.f. gain, acquisition, gift, reward, mfn gaining, procuring, bestowing, f. a quarter of the sky,

sanīḍa m. proximity,

sanirvāṇa 'co-existent with cessation i.e. liberation,' (Gam.),

sanisrasa mfn falling down or to pieces, frail, fragile,

√sañj 1. 1132/3 cl 1 P *sañjati, sajjati,* to go, move 2. cl 1 P A *sajati (te)* to cling or stick or adhere to, be attached to or engaged in or occupied with, caus. *sañjayati* to cause to stick or cling to, unite or connect with, DP in *saṅga* sticking to, adhering to, clinging to,

saṁjā f. special names, classifications

sañjana n. the act of attaching or fastening, joining, folding (the hands), the act of clinging, adhering, sticking, *(ī)* f. that on which anything is hung,

sañjayati *√sañj* 1132/3 causes attachment 1/s/pres/caus

śaṅk 1047/1 Cl 1 A *śaṅkate* to be anxious or apprehensive, be afraid of, fear, dread, suspect, mistrust, to be in doubt or uncertainty, hesitate, to think probable, assume, believe, regard as *śaṅke* 'I think.. , I suppose..', to ponder over, DP in *śaṅkā* doubting, being uncertain, hesitating, being doubtful, dreading, fearing,

śaṅka 1047/1 m. doubt, fear, hesitation,

saṅkā f. apprehension, care, alarm, fear, distrust, doubt, uncertainty, hesitation, supposition, presumption,

saṅkalpa 1126/3 conception, idea, or notion formed in the heart or mind, will, purpose, resolution, belief (by *Manas)*

saṅkalpamātra mfn mere thought, existing in thought only,

saṅkalparahita mfn without thought, idea or notion,

saṅkalpaśunya mfn devoid of thought

saṅkalpaśūnya n absolute non-existence (buddhist),

saṅkalpavikalpa m. thought and doubt,

śaṅkara or *śaṁkara* 'causing prosperity, auspicious, beneficent', a name for *Śiva,* great philosopher, re-established the vedic tradition, first *śaṅkarācārya*

śaṅkarācārya a fully realized man appointed to the highest position as spiritual leader in the tradition of *advaita vedanta* established by *śaṅkara.* There are 4 such positions in Indiain the north, south east and west,

śaṅkha m.n. a conch shell or horn, the temple area of the forehead,

saṅkhyā see *saṁkhyā*

saṅkoca m. contraction, hesitation, shrinking, together, diminution, humbling one's self, shyness, crouching down,

śaṅku m. a peg, nail, spike, pillar, post, arrow,

sanmāna n. respect or esteem for the good,

sanmārga m. the right path,

ṣaṇmāsa n. a semester, six months,

sanmati mfn well-disposed, noble-minded

sanmātra mfn that of which only existence is predicable, mere existence, mere being, mere beingness,

sanna mfn set down, sitting at i.e. occupied

with, sunk down in (7th), depressed, low in spirits, perished, lost, dead,

sānna mfn together with food, having food,

sannaka mfn low, dwarfish,

sannamaya mfn caused by despair,

sanni f. mental depression, despondency,

sannikarṣa m. vicinity, proximity,

sanniruddha mfn bound,

sannisarga m. good nature, kindness,

sannivāsa mfn staying with the good,

sanniveśa m. entering or sitting down together, entrance into, seat, position, situation, encampment, abode, place, vicinity, an open place or play-ground, assembling together, assembly, crowd,

sanniveśya mfn to be put in (7th), to be put on or drawn (with colours),

sanniviṣṭa 1147/2 mfn. seated down together with, encamped, assembled, fixed in or on, resting or contained in, being on (a road or path, 7th), dependent on (7th), entered deeply into, absorbed or engrossed in, contiguous, neighbouring, present, at hand, established in the Self,

sannyāsa m. giving up the body, complete renunciation, monkhood, profession of ascetism, sudden death, abandonment, resignation, agreement, deposit, laying aside, stake, wager, abstinence from food, complete exhaustion, renunciation of worldly concerns,

sannyāsin 1148/1(*saṁnyāsin)* laying aside, giving up, one who abandons, the fourth stage of life – complete renunciation as a wandering mendicant

sanstyāna see *saṁstyāna* 1121/2 n. the becoming condensed or solid or compact, mfn coagulated, condensed

sant pres.part. √2.*as* true, virtuous, honest, right,

śānta 1064/2 mfn tranquil, calm, free from passions, peaceful, quiet, calmness of mind, undisturbed, 2. appeased, pacified, DP. *śam* in resting, stopping, being quiet

sānta having an end, n. joy,

santaka mfn belonging to (6th),

santam existing, treading the righteous path, being present, existing within oneself, present, situated, (V)

śāntamala mfn having all defilement removed,

śāntamanas mfn composed in mind,

śāntamati m. composed in mind,

śāntamoha n. having delusion dispelled,

santāna m. offspring, family, n. child,

śāntānanda the bliss of tranquillity, the bliss of peace

santaraṇa 1142/3 *saṁtaraṇa* – mfn conveying over or across, bringing out of a danger, n. the act of crossing over or passing through

śāntarūpa mfn calm, tranquil, having a tranquil appearance,

śāntasaṁkalpa he whose mind is freed (from anxiety, distraction etc.)

santati extending, stretching or covering something over, continuity, 'extension of spiritual pursuit ...' f. issue, offspring, progeny, child

santi they (many) are, form of verb *as*

śānti 1064/3 f. peace, tranquillity, quietness of mind, absence of passion, alleviation of evil or pain, indifference to objects of pleasure or pain, propitiatory rites for averting evil or calamity i.e offering water for washing feet, cessation, abatement, extinction, peace, welfare, prosperity, good fortune, happiness, bliss,

śāntikarman n. a ceremony for averting results from something ominous,

śāntirūpa having the nature of peace, having a peaceful appearance,

santoṣa m. contentment,

√*sāntv* 1203/2 (also *śāntv*) Cl 10 P A *sāntvayati (te)*, to console, comfort, soothe, conciliate, address kindly or

gently, DP in *sāma-prayoga*
appeasing, conciliating, soothing,

sāntva n. consolation, conciliation, mild or gentle language or words, mfn mild, gentle, mfn sweet (as sound) , ind. with mild or kind words, in a gentle manner

sāntvana 1203/2 n. the act of appeasing or reconciling, soothing with kind words, consolation or conciliation of

santyaj sam̐ root *tyaj* 1142/3 to relinquish altogether
totally surrender, to be left or abandoned or given up,

sānu n.m. top, surface, ridge, back,

sānurāgā 1203/1 f. feeling or betraying passion, affectionate, enamoured of, passionate

sānuśaya mfn full of repentance, irritable, angry,

sanutar 1141/3 ind. aside, away, off, far off, secretly, clandestinely,

sanutara mfn furtive, clandestine,

sanutya mfn lying in ambush, furtive,

√*śap* 1052/1 3. Cl 1.4. *śapati (te), śapyati (te),* to curse, to swear an oath, swear, to revile, scold, blame, A to adjure, supplicate, conjure anyone, caus. *śāpayati* to adjure, conjure, exorcise (demons), cause to swear by, DP in *ākrośa* cursing,

√*sap* 1148/1 Cl 1 P A *sapati (te),* to follow or seek after, be devoted to, honour, serve, love, caress, do homage, receive homage ? have intercourse, DP in *samavāya* connecting, knowing completely,

sap (in cpds.) following after,

śāpa m. curse

sapa m. penis

sapadi ind. at the same instant, on the spot, at once, immediately, quickly,

śāpādi mfn having the curse first, n. curse and so forth,

sapadma mfn having a lotus,

sapāduka mfn wearing shoes or sandals,

sapakṣa mfn having wings, winged, feathered (as an arrow), having partisans or friends, containing the major term or subject, an adherent, friend, partaker, one in similar circumstances,

sapāla mfn attended by a herdsman, together with a king or kings,

sapaṅkaja mfn provided with a lotus,

sapannaga mfn having serpents,

śāpānta m. end of the curse or period that the curse has effect.

saparibṛm̐haṇa mfn the *Veda* together with its supplements (*Vedānta* etc.)

sapariśeṣa mfn having a remainder, with the rest,

saparivyaya mfn (food prepared) with condiments

saparvatavanadruma mfn with mountains, forests and trees,

√*saparya* 1148/1 Nom P *saparyati* to serve attentively, honour, worship, adore, to offer or dedicate reverentially, DP in *pūjā* worshipping,

saparyā f. worship, homage, adoration,

saparyāṇa provided with a saddle, saddled,

saparyu mfn serving, honouring, devoted, faithful,

śapatha m. a curse, an oath

śāpatha m. a curse, an oath

śapati he curses

sapatna m. a rival, adversary, enemy,

sapatnī f. a woman whose husband has another wife or wives, accompanied with a wife/wives female rival,

sāpatnya n. rivalry among wives of the same husband,

sapaura mfn accompanied by citizens,

saphala mfn together with fruits, fruitful, not emasculated, having good results, productive, successful, fulfilled,

saphalaka mfn furnished with a shield,

sāphalya n. successful, fruitfulness, success

saphena mfn having foam, foamy,

sapīḍa mfn having pain or anguish, painful,

sapiṇḍa mfn having the *piṇḍa* together,

said of persons with a common ancestor up to 6 generations back to whom they offer a *piṇḍa* together, persons related in the 6th generation

sapīti f. drinking together, conviviality, m. a boon companion,

sapitva n. union, communion,

sapota mfn having a ship or boat,

saprabha mfn having the same lustre or appearance, possessing splendour, brilliant,

saprabhāva mfn powerful, mighty,

saprahāsam ind. with laughter,

sapraja mfn together with the children or offspring,

saprajas mfn possessing offspring,

saprajña mfn endowed with understanding,

saprakṛtika along with root or stem or base,

sapramāda mfn heedless, inattentive, off one's guard,

sapramodanam or °dam ind. joyfully,

saprāṇa mfn having breath, living,

saprapañca mfn with all belonging thereto or connected therewith, with manifoldness, a cosmic view or vision, all-comprehensive in its nature,

saprāya mfn like, similar,

sapranāmam ind. with a bow,

sapraṇaya mfn having affection, confident, affectionate, friendly, kind, (*am*) ind.

saprasāda mfn accompanied with favour or kindness, propitious or gracious,

sapraśraya mfn with respectful demeanour, ind. affectionately,

saprathas mfn extensive, wide, effective or sounding or shining far and wide,

sapratibha mfn possessed of quick discernment or presence of mind,

sapratibhaya mfn dangerous, uncertain,

sapratigha mfn having an opposite,

sapratīkṣam ind. expectantly,

sapratīśa mfn respectful,

sapratīvāpa mfn with an admixture,

sapratyāśam ind. hopefully, expectantly,

sapratyaya mfn having trust or confidence, certain, secure, sure,

sapratyayaka mfn together with a suffix,

saprema mfn having love, affectionate,

sapreman mfn rejoicing in,

sapṛṣata mfn accompanied by rain,

sapru mfn attended by lightning,

śapta° cursed

sapta in comp. for *saptan*, seven, also may express an indefinite plurality, e.g. 71, 72

saptaguṇa mfn sevenfold,

saptaka mfn consisting of seven, the 7th, a week,

saptakathāmaya mfn consisting of seven narrations,

saptama seventh

saptamī f. the 7th case or its terminations,

saptan seven,

saptapada mfn making seven steps for the conclusion of the marriage ceremony or ratification of a treaty, consisting of seven *pādas*,

saptarātra n. a period of 7 nights (or days), a week,

saptatantu mfn seven-threaded, consisting of seven parts,

saptatha or *saptama* mfn the 7th

sapti m. a horse, steed, courser,

saptīvat mfn moving with horses,

saptya n. a riding ground for horses, racetrack,

sapuruṣa mfn together with men or followers,

sapūrva mfn along with the preceding (letter or sound), having or possessed by ancestors,

sapuṣpa mfn having or adorned with flowers, flowering,
-*bali* filled with offerings of flowers,

√*sār* see *śar*, DP in *daurbalya* being weak,

śara m. a reed used for arrows, arrow,

sara mfn fluid, liquid, cathartic, laxative, going, moving, m. going, motion, a cord, string, a short vowel, salt, a waterfall, (*ā*) f. moving or wandering about, a cascade, waterfall, n. a lake, pool,

sāra m. course, motion, extension, 2. the core or pith or solid interior of anything, firmness, strength, power, energy, the substance, essence, heart or essential part of anything, best part, quintessence, the real meaning, main point, valid proof (Gam.), a compendium, summary, any ingredient, nectar, worth, value, 4. having spokes,

śarad f. the autumn, poetic for 'years'

śārada mfn autumn, new, shy, diffident, modest, recent, mature, m. cloud, year, autumnal sunshine, n. fruit,

sāragha mfn coming/derived from the bee, m. a bee,

sārathi m. charioteer, assistant, ocean,

saraka mfn going moving, m.n. a drinking vessel, goblet, liquor, rum, drinking liquor, a string of pearls, n. a pearl, jewel, a pond, lake,

sāraka mfn ifc. full of, causing to go or flow, cathartic, n. laxative,

sarala mfn straight (not crooked), right, correct, upright, sincere, candid, easy, honest, artless, simple, outstretched,

saralayati to make straight

saralita mfn made straight, straightened,

sāraloha n. 'essence of iron', steel,

sāralya n. straightness, rectitude, sincerity honesty, easiness,

saramā f. the bitch of Indra or of the gods,

sārameya m. descendant of the bitch, dog, *Saramā,* name of certain dogs,

śaraṇa 1057/1 mfn protecting, guarding, defending, n. place of shelter, refuge, a shed giving shelter from rain, hut

saraṇa mfn going, running, moving, m. a kind of tree, a kind of convolvulus, n. running, quick-motion, a foot-race. running after, iron rust or filings,

śaraṇāgata mfn come for refuge, seeking protection with anyone, m. petitioner, supplicant,

śaraṇāgati f. surrender, surrendering, approach for protection,

sāraṅga mfn dappled, m. antelope,

saraṇi f. a road, path, way, mode, disposition, arrangement of things,

sāraṅi f. a stream, channel, waterpipe,

saraṇyu mfn quick, fleet, nimble, m. wind, a cloud, water, spring,

saras n. a lake, pond, pool, tank, a trough, pail, water, speech (a meaning given to account for *saras-vatī*)

sarasa 1183/3 containing sap, moist, wet, tasty, elegant, bodies of water

sarasa n. a lake, pond, pool,

sārasa coming from a lake or pond, m. a crane or swan, a bird in general, the moon, 2. mfn crying, calling,

sarasara mfn moving hither and thither,

śarāsata n. bow (for arrows),

sarasatā f. juiciness,

sarasi (7th of *saras*), in comp. e.g. *sarasiruha* 'growing in a lake or pond', a lotus,

sarastīra n. shore or bank of a pool or lake,

sarasvant mfn rich in waters, finding pleasure or delight in, elegant, juicy, sentimental,

sārasvata mfn relating or belonging to Sarasva or Sarasvatī (the river or the goddess), eloquent, learned,

sarasvatī f. consort of Brahmā, the power of wisdom, 1182/2 the mother of goddesses, bestower of vitality, renown and wealth, connected with speech, eloquence, learning and wisdom, name of a sacred river, a region abounding in lakes and pools,

sārasya n. abundance of water, relating to ponds or lakes,

saraṭ m. wind, a cloud,

sarat mfn going, flowing, proceeding, m. a thread,

saraṭa m. a lizard, chameleon,

sāratā f. firmness, solidity, worth, value, value, being a chief ingredient, highest degree, strong confidence in,

sāratas ind. according to the nature, essentially, vigorously,

sārathi m. a charioteer, coachman, leader, a helper, assistant, the ocean,

sārathya n. charioteering, being charioteer,

śarāva m.n. flat earthen dish,

śaravya mfn capable of wounding, f (*ā*). an arrowshot, shower of arrows, an arrow, missile, arrow personified, n. a target, aim,
butt or mark for arrows,
sāraya (ti) Nom.P. to be weak ,
sarayu m. air, wind, name of a river passing by Ayodhyā,
√*śarb* 1058/2 Cl 1 P *śarbati* to go or to kill, DP in *gati* going
√*sarb* 1184/3 *sarbati* to go, move, DP in *gati* going,
sārcī mfn flaming, burning,
śardha m. troop, host, breaking wind, flatulence, mfn defiant, bold,
sārdha mfn with a half, increased by a half, having a half over,
sārdham ind. jointly, together, along with,
sārdra mfn wet, moist, damp,
śārdūla m. tiger, ifc. the best of ..., a lion, panther, leopard,
sarga 1183/3 voiding, primary creation, chapter, book, begetting,
a created being, a creature, any troop, host or swarm, a draught of air, gust of wind, a stream, gush, rush, downpour (of any fluid), a dart, shot, L. that which is let loose esp. a herd let loose from the stall,
sargaḍa mfn bolted, barred,
sargaka mfn producing, effecting,
sargakartṛ m. the creator,
sargala mfn obstructed, impeded, prevented
sārgala mfn relating/ belonging to a jackal,
sari f. a cascade, waterfall,
sārī f. a kind of bird, a chessman,
sarid in comp. for *sarit,*
sarila n. water,
sariman m. wind, air,
sarīman the course or passage of the wind, wind, air, proceeding, going,
sarin mfn approaching, coming to aid, in comp. for *sarit*
sārin mfn going, running, hastening, pursuing, following,
sarira n. the heaving sea, flood, tide, the universe,
śarīra 1057/3 n. the body, that which perishes, the bodily frame,
śārīra mfn corporeal, of the body, bodily
śarīraja mfn performed by the body
śarīrāntakara m. destroyer of the bodies, name for Yama the ruler of the dead,
śarīratvāya for embodiment (Gam.), as in 'fit for embodiment',
śarīrin mfn 'having a body' embodied, m. the soul,
sarit f. a river, stream, a thread, string, creek, Ganges, ocean, river,
sarita mfn flowing, fluent (as speech),
√*sarj* 1184/1 Cl 1 P *sarjati* to rattle, creak, 2. Cl 1 P *sarjati* to earn by labour, acquire, gain, DP in *arjana* earning,
sarja m. one who emits or lets go, one who creates or makes,
sarjana n. abandoning, giving up or over, surrendering, ceding, voiding (excrement etc.), the act of creating, creation, the rear of an army,
m. resin
sarju m. a merchant, trader, f. lightning,
sarjū m. a merchant, a necklace, going, following,
sarjūra m. a day,
sārka mfn with the sun, sunny,
śarkara m. brown sugar,
śarkarā 1058/2 1/s ground or candied sugar, sugar, small stones,
√*sal* 1189/3 Cl 1 P *salati* to go, move, DP in *gati* going,
sarma m. going, running, flowing,
śarman 1058/2 n. shelter, refuge, cover, protection, comfort, joy, (common at the end of Brahman names),
śarmavant mfn containing *śarman*
saro in comp. for saras
sāroha mfn having elevation, elevated to, together with a horseman,
sarpa 1184/1 mfn creeping, crawling, stealing along, m. (ifc. f (*ā*) a snake, serpent, serpent-demon, tortuous motion,
sarpadevajanavidyā f. the science of snake-charming and fire-arts, (U)
sarpadhāraka m. a snake-catcher or charmer,

sarpaṇa n. the act of creeping or gliding, stealing away,
sarpat n. a crawling creature, all that crawls
sarpikā f. a little snake,
sarpis n. clarified butter, (warm & fluid or cold and hard) , so not different from *ghṛta* 'ghee'
sarpita n. a snake bite
sarṣapa m. mustard, mustard-seed, used as a weight, any minute weight,
sarṣapakaṇa m. a grain of mustard seed,
sarṣṭika mfn furnished with spears,
sārtha mfn having an object, or business, attained its object, successful (as a request), having property, wealthy, significant, important, useful, m. a caravan of traders or pilgrims, a troop, collection of men,
sārthaja mfn born/reared in a caravan, tame, (as an elephant),
sārthaka mfn having meaning, significant
sārthavat mfn having some meaning or purpose or intention,
sārthika mfn travelling with a caravan, m. a companion on a journey, merchant, trader,
sartṛ m. a courser, (horse),
sārtra n. a house, dwelling,
śaru f. missile, either spear or arrow,
saru mfn minute, thin, fine, m. an arrow, the hilt or handle of a sword,
sarūpa mfn having the same shape or form, uniform, similar, like, beautiful, handsome, of its own kind, of its own form, mfn a consonant,
sārūpya n. similarity of form, mfn seasonable, fit, suitable,
√*śarv* 1058/3 Cl 1 P *śarvati* to hurt, injure, kill, DP in *hiṁsā* hurting, killing,
√*sarv* DP in *hiṁsā* killing, injuring,
śarva m. name of an arrow-slaying god, later a name for *Śiva*
sarva inflected as a pronoun, 1184/3 adj. mfn whole, entire, all, every, (m.s. everyone, pl. all, n.s. everything), sometimes strengthened by *viśva*, of all sorts,, manifold, various, different, with negation- not any, no, none, not everyone, not everything, with another adjective or in comp. altogether, wholly, completely, in all parts, everywhere,
(am) ind. completely,
n. water,
sārva mfn relating to all, fit or good for all, general, universal,
sarvabhāva 1186/2 m. whole being or nature, whole heart or soul, complete satisfaction, all objects, with one's whole soul,
sarvabhāvana mfn all-creating or all-producing,
sarvabhāvānām 6/pl of all entities (Gam.),
sarvabhokta mfn enjoyer of all,
sarvabhūta 1186/2 being everywhere, all beings, m.n. the maker or cause of all things or beings,
sarvabhūtādhivāsa m. dweller in all beings,
sarvabhūtamaya mfn containing in himself all beings, containing or epresenting all beings, m. the supreme pervading spirit,
sarvabhūtahite in the welfare of all beings, mfn serviceable to all beings,
sarvabhūtāntarātmā (or *man*) the self in all beings, the indwelling Self of all, the souls of all beings,
sarvabhūtastha 1186/3 mfn. present in all elements or beings
sarvabhūteṣu in all beings 7/pl/n
sarvābhyantara mfn the innermost of all,
sarvabīja n. the seed of everything,
sarvacārin m. all-pervading,
sarvācārya m. the teacher of all,
sarvada mfn all bestowing,
sarvadā 1189/2 in. always, at all times, ever, (with *na* = never)
sarvadeśika mfn present everywhere, pertaining to all places (U),
sarvadeva m.pl. all the gods,
sarvadevamaya mfn containing in himself all the gods, i.e. representing or being in the name of all the gods,

sarvadevata 1186/1 relating to all the deities
*sarvadevatā*1/pl/m all the gods,
sarvādhāra m. receptacle of everything,
sarvādhika mfn superior to everything,
sarvādi m. the beginning or first of all things, mfn having any kind of commencement whatever,
sarvadravya n.pl. all things,
sarvadṛk the seer of everything, the witness, *turīya,* 'omniscient' (Gam.),
sarvadṛś 1185/3 all seeing, all organs of senses,
sarvaduḥkhanivṛtti removal of all pain (U),
sarvaga mfn all-pervading, omnipresent, m. the universal soul, spirit,
sarvagaṇa m. the whole company, having all kinds of classes, of every kind, n. salty soil,
sarvagandha m. m.pl.all kinds of perfumes mfn containing all odours, m.n. a partic. blended perfume, any perfume, f. a partic. perfume,
sarvagata = *sarvaṁga,* mfn 'going everywhere' all-pervasive like space, omnipresent, universally prevalent,
sarvagatva 1185/1 of universal diffusion, omnipresent, all going, all-pervading, n. universal diffusion, omnipresence,
sarva gati f. the refuge of all,
sarvaguṇa mfn valid through all parts,
sarvaguru mfn long syllables only
sarvahara mfn appropriating everything, inheriting all of a person's property, all destroying,
sarvahāsya mfn derided by all,
sarvahiṁsāvinirmukha against injury of all kinds, (U)
sarvahṛd n. the whole heart or soul,
sarvahṛdṛ ind. with all one's heart,
sarvaiśvarya 1189/1 n. the sovereignty of every one, sovereignty over all
sarvaja mfn wheresoever produced,
sarvajagat f. the whole world, the universe
sarvajana m. every person,
sarvajanīna mfn relating or belonging to everyone, peculiar to everyone,
sarvajanman mfn of all kinds,
sarvajaya m. a complete victory,
sarvajit mfn all-conquering, excellent, all-surpassing, m. death,
sarvajīva m. the soul of all,
sarvajña knower of all, omniscient, knower of all in general
sarvajñāna n. all knowledge,
sarvajñānamaya mfn containing all knowledge,
sarvajñānavid mfn acquainted with all knowledge,
sarvajñanin mfn thinking oneself omniscient,
sarvajñātā f. or *–tva* n. omniscient, 'the state of being all and the knower' (Gam.),
sarvajñātṛ mfn omniscient, *-tva* n. omniscience,
sarvaka mfn all, every, whole, entire, universal *(e)* ind. everywhere,
sarvakāla ibc. at all times, always, *(am)* ind. with *na* never,
sarvakalyāṇa mfn all auspicious qualities,
sarvakāma m.pl. all kinds of desires, mfn wishing everything, fulfilling all wishes,
sarvakāmya mfn loved by all, to be wished for by all,
sarvakara m. maker of all
sarvākāra or *°kāram* ind. in all forms, in every way,
sarvakaraṇa mfn making all, effecting all, causing all,
sarvakāraṇa n. the cause of everything,
sarvakaraṇakaraṇa the cause of all other causes, (U)
sarva kārin mfn making/doing all things, able to do all things, m. the maker of all things
sarvakarman n.pl. all kinds of works or rites or occupations, m. one who performs all acts, mfn containing all acts,
sarvakartā all-doer, doer of everything (U),
sarvakartṛ m. the maker/creator of all,
sarvakartṛtva n. omnipotence,
sarvākṣa mfn casting one's eyes everywhere

sarvakṣaya m. destruction of the universe,
sarva kṣit mfn abiding in all things
sarvaloka m. the entire world,
sarvalokakṛt or *krit* m. maker/creator of the world or worlds,
sarvam all, everything, ind. completely with (*sarveṇa)*,
sarvāmaratva n. absolute immortality,
sarvamaya mfn all-containing, comprehending all,
sarvamedhya mfn universally or perfectly pure,
sarvaṁhara mfn taking/carrying away everything,
sarvamitra m. friend of all,
sarvaṁsaha mfn all-enduring, bearing everything patiently,
sarvanāman words which can be applied to all i.e. pronouns. e.g. me, mine, you, they, which, who
sarvanara m. every man
sarvanaraḥ pron. anyone,
sarvānavadya mfn entirely faultless,
sarvānavadyāṅga mfn having an entirely faultless body,
sarvaṅga mfn all-pervading, omnipresent,
sarvāṅga mfn entire or perfect in limb, complete, n. all the *vedāṅgas,* whole body, all the limbs, ind. in all respects exactly,
sarvāṅgāsāna a shoulder-stand pose in Hathayoga,
sarvānta m. the end of everything,
sarvāntara or *sarvāntarastha* , mfn being in everything,
sarvāntaryāmin m. universal soul, omnipresent,
sarvānubhū mfn all- perceiving,
sarvānubhūti f. universal experience,
sarvapatha m. every direction, every path,
sarvprakāra mfn existing in all forms,
sarvprakāram ind. in every respect, in every manner,
sarvaprathamam ind. before all, first of all,
sarvapratyakṣa mfn being before the eyes of all,
sarvapriya mfn loving all or dear to all,
sarvāpti f. attainment of all,
sarvapuṇya mfn perfectly beautiful,
sarvapūrṇa mfn full of everything,
sarvapūrva mfn the first of all,
sarvapūta mfn completely pure,
śarvara mfn variegated, f. *śarvarī* the night (variegated by stars),
sarvārambha 1188/3 entire energy in the beginning of a work -*eṣu* 7/pl fully dedicated at the beginning of all actions
śarvarī f. the star-spangled night, twilight,
sarvārtha m. pl. (or ibc.) all things or objects, all manner of things, all matters, (*am*) ind. for the sake of the whole, mfn suitable for every purpose,
sarvasāda mfn that wherein everything is absorbed
sarvasādhana mfn accomplishing everything,
sarvasādharāṇa mfn common to all,
sarvasādhu ind. very good! very well!
sarvaśaḥ altogether, wholly, entirely, on all sides, in all respects, adv.
sarvasaha mfn all-enduring, very patient,
sarvasāha mfn all enduring,
sarvaśak mfn all-powerful, omnipotent,
sarvasākṣin m. the witness of all,
sarvaśakti f. power of accomplishing all, omnipotent, entire strength,
sarvaśaktimān omnipotent,
sarvaśaktyā ind. with all one's might,
sarvasamāsa m. complete union, all together,
sarvasamatā f. sameness or identity with all things, equality or impartiality towards everything,
sarvasambhava m. the source of everything,
sarvasampad f. complete agreement,
sarvasampanna mfn provided with everything
sarvasampatti f. success in everything,
sarvasāmya n. equality in all respects,
sarvaśānti f. universal tranquillity or calm
sarvasāra n. the essence or cream of the whole,
sarvaśas ind. wholly, completely, entirely,

thoroughly, collectively, altogether, in general, universally, in every or any way,
sarvaśāstra mfn knowing every science,
sarvāśaya m. refuge of all,
sarvasena mfn leading all the host, the lord of all the host,
sarvasiddhārtha mfn having every object accomplished, every wish gratified,
sarvasiddhi f. accomplishment of every object, universal success, entire proof, complete result,
sarvasūkṣma mfn finest/most subtle of all,
sarvaśūnya mfn completely empty, thinking everything non-existent, -*tā* f. complete void, the theory that everything is non-existent, nihilism,
sarvasva n. (ifc. f. *ā*) all a person's possessions, ifc. entirety, the whole, whole sum of, (*ā*)f. entire property,
sarvasvāmin m. the owner or master of all,
sarvata mfn all-sided,
sarvatā f. wholeness, totality, completeness,
sarvataḥ 1189/1 in comp. for *sarvatas*,
sarvatantra n.pl. all doctrines, m. one who has studied all the Tantras, mfn universally acknowledged, admitted by all schools (as a philsophical principle),
sarvatantramaya mfn containing all doctrines,
sarvatāpana mfn all-inflaming,
sarvatas ind. from all sides, in every direction, everywhere, around, entirely, completely, thoroughly,
sarvatātā ind. all together, entirely,
sarvatāti f. completeness, totality, perfect happiness or prosperity, soundness
sarvatejas n. all splendour,
sarvathā 1189/2 ind, in whatever way, in every way, in every respect, by all means, altogether, entirely, in every way, however
sarvātithi mfn receiving everyone as guest
sarvātmadṛś mfn seeing one's self everywhere,
sarvātmaka the whole soul, (*ena*) ind. 'with all one's soul', mfn all-containing, contained in everything,
sarvātman m. the whole person, (°*nā* ind. 'with all one's soul', the universal soul, the whole being or nature, (°*nā* ind. 'entirely, completely'),
sārvātmya n. the being the Universal Soul,
sarvatobhadra mfn in every direction or on every side good, in every way auspicious,
sarvatra ind. 1189/2 at all times, always, everywhere
sarvatraga mfn everywhere going, all-pervading, omnipresent
sarvatragāmin mfn all-pervading, m. air, wind
sarvatragata mfn extending to everything, universal, perfect,
sarvatrasattva n. omnipresence,
sarvatrāpi mfn reaching everywhere,
sarvatva n. wholeness, totality,completeness
sarvatyāga m. complete renunciation, renunciation of everything,
sarvāvadhi clairvoyance (Jaina),
śarvavarman mfn having *śiva* as protection,
sarvāvasa or °*sin* mfn having one's abode everywhere,
sarvāvat mfn containing everything, entire, complete,
sarvaveda mfn having all knowledge, acqauinted with all the Vedas,
sarvavedas mfn having complete property m. one who gives away all his property to the priests after a sacrifice,
sarvavedasa accompanied by a gift of all one's goods (as a sacrifice)
sarvavid mfn all-knowing, omniscient,
sarvavidya mfn possessing all science, omniscient,
sarvavīra mfn with unharmed heroes or with all heroes, i.e. having lost none,
sarvavit a knower of all things in detail,
sarvavyāpī all-pervasive,
sarvayoni f. the source of all,
sarvavrata n. a universal vow,
sarvavyāpin mfn all-pervading, omnipresent
sarvayoṣit f.pl. all women,

sarvāyu 1188/3 mfn having or bestowing all life, the life of all, full span of life,
sarvāyus n. whole life,
sarve all 1/pl/m
sarveśa m. the Lord of all, the Supreme Being,
sarveṣu 7/pl/n in all
sarveśvara 1188/3 m. the Lord of all, a universal monarch
sarveśvaratva n. almightiness,
sarvopādānatva having the nature of being the material cause of all,
sārya mfn that which may be dropped or omitted (in pronunciation),
√*śaś* 1059/3 Cl 1 P *śaśati* to leap, bound, dance, DP in *pluta-gati* leaping, jumping,
ṣaṣ six
√*śas* 1060/3 Cl 1 P *śasati*, to cut down, kill, slaughter, DP in *hiṁsā* hurting, killing,
√*sas* 1192/1 Cl 2 P *sasti* , *sasāsti,* to sleep, be inactive or idle, caus. *sāsayati*, DP in *svapna* sleeping,
√*śās* 1068/3 Cl 2 P *śāsti, śāste, śāsati (te),* to chastise, correct, censure, punish, to restrain, control, govern, rule, to administer the laws, to direct, bid, order, command, enjoin, decree, to teach, instruct, inform, to confess (a crime), to announce, proclaim, predict, blame, reject, caus. *śāśayati* to recommend, DP in *anuśiṣṭi* (Cl 2) teaching, *icchā* (Cl 1, 2) wishing, desiring
ṣaṣ num. six,
śaśaḥ / śaśakaḥ rabbit, hare,
sasambhrama mfn with excited haste, filled with confusion, agitated,
sasaṁdhya mfn with the morning twilight,
sasaṁdhyāṁśa mfn with the evening twilight,
śāsana 1068/3 mfn punishing, a punisher, n. punishment, correction, chastisement, dominion, rule, order, command, edict, teaching, instruction, discipline a message, self-control,
sasaṅga mfn adhering, attached,
śaśaṅka m. the moon, (having a rabbit as its mark),
saśaṅka mfn fearful, doubtful, timid,
saśaṅkha mfn having a conch-shell,
saśara 1191/3 mfn. furnished with an arrow, together with an arrow,
sāsāra mfn having showers, rainy,
sasarpa mfn with a serpent,
saśarīra 1191/3 with the body, embodied
sāścarya mfn astonished, surprised by, (comp.), wonderful, marvellous,
śaśi m. 'that which contains the rabbit' i.e. the moon
sāsi mfn armed with a sword,
śaśin m. the moon, 'having (the picture of) a rabbit',
saśiṣya mfn with his pupils,
śāsitṛ m. teacher, ruler, governor,
sāśra mfn angular, having angles/corners 2. tearful, weeping, in tears,
sāśru mfn accompanied by tears, tearful, ind. tearfully,
śasta mfn praised, esteemed as good or lucky, commended, happy,
sāṣṭāṅgapāta mfn having or with an *aṣṭāṅgapāta,* (*am*) ind. with profoundest obeisance, i.e with the 8 parts of the body
ṣaṣṭha mfn the sixth, a sixth, the sixth part,
ṣaṣṭi f. sixty,
ṣaṣṭī f. sixth,
śastra n. a sword, weapon, axe, knife, any instrument or tool, iron, steel, n. invocation, praise(applying to any recited verses – as opposed to sung verses), reciting, recitation,
śāstra 1069/1 n. an order, command, precept, rule, teaching, instruction, direction, advice, good counsel, scripture, any instrument of teaching, any sacred book or composition of divine authority, a body of teaching, scripture, science, any compendium of rules, theory, religious treatise, manual, book, what is taught,
śastrabhṛt m. weapon bearing, warrior,

armed man,
śāstrakṛpā the grace of scripture
śastrapāṇi mfn having a sword in the hand,
śastra-saṁpāta mfn clash of weapons
śāstravidhi 1069/2 m. scriptural injunction
śastravṛtti mfn having weapons for subsistence, living by military service,
śāstri knower of the *śāstra (s)*
śāstrin mfn or m.knower of the *śāstra (s),* learned, m. a teacher of sacred books or science, a learned man,
sasmitam ind. with a smile, smilingly
sāsu mfn having life, living,
sāśūka m. a blanket,
sāsusū mfn having arrows,
sāsūya mfn envious, scornful, angry at, L. with impatience,
sāśva mfn with horses,
śaśvant mfn ever repeating or renewing itself,
śaśvat 1060/3 perpetual, endless
śāśvata mfn eternal, constant, perpetual, all, (*am*) for evermore, eternally,
śāśvata 1068/3 mfn. eternal, constant perpetual, all, (*am*) for evermore, incessantly, eternally, about to happen, future,
śāśvatapada n. everlasting abode,
śāśvatatva n. constancy, eternity,
śāśvatī mfn eternal, constant, perpetual, f. earth
śāśvatībhyaḥ for evermore, incessantly, eternally, about to happen, future,
sasya n. corn grain, fruit, a crop of corn, a standing crop, produce of the field, 2. n. a weapon, virtue, merit, mfn a kind of precious stone,
śasya as above
sasyakṣetra n. field of grain,
sasyarakṣaka m. keeper or watcher of the standing crop, f.(*ā*) guarding the fields,
√śaṭ 1048/2 Cl 1 P *śaṭati* to be sick, to divide, to pierce, to be dissolved, to be weary or dejected, to go, Cl 10 A *śāṭayate* DP in *kujā* growing sick, *viśaraṇa* dividing or separating, *gati* going, *avasādana* being weary or dejected,
√saṭ 1134/1 Cl 1 P *saṭati* to be a part of, DP in *avayava* forming a part
sat 1134/2 mf(*satī*)n present part. of √1.*as* being, existing, occurring, happening, being present, real, actual, true, good, right, beautiful, wise, venerable, honest, abiding in (7th), belonging to (6th), living, lasting, enduring, as anyone/thing ought to be, m. a being, pl. beings, creatures, a good or wise man, a sage, good or wise or honest or respectable people, n. that which really is, entity or existence, essence, the true being or really existent, 'the self-existent or Universal Spirit, Brahman', that which is good or real or true, good, advantage, reality, truth, water, (in gram.) present participle endings, *sat* ind. well, right, fitly, "that which exists in truth" HH often used with other participles or an adverb e.g. *tathā sati* 'if it be so' ibc. may = possessed of,
sāt a Taddhita affix which indicates a total change of anything into the thing expressed by that word,
śata n. a hundred, any very large number,
śāta mfn sharpened, whetted, sharp,
saṭā f. an ascetic's matted hair, a braid of hair, the mane of a lion or horse, bristles of a boar, a crest, a multitude, light, lustre,
sāta mfn gained, obtained, granted n. a gift, wealth, riches, m. name of a Yakṣa
śatadhā 1049/2 1. f. Dūrvā grass, 2. ind. in a hundred ways, a hundred-fold, into a hundred parts or pieces,
śataguṇa mfn hundred, hundredfold, hundredfold more valuable, hundred times,
sataḥ in comp. for *satas*

saṭāla m. having a mane, ifc. richly provided with, full of,
saṭālu an unripe fruit,
saṭaṁkāra mfn notorious or famous,
śātana n. the act of sharpening or whetting sharpness, thinness, felling, causing to fall, mfn destroying, felling, hewing, causing to fall,
satas ind. equally, like,
satāsat n.du. the true and the false,
satatam ind. constantly, continuously,
śatātman mfn having a hundred lives,
sātatya 1200/1 n. continuity, constancy, uninterruptedness,
śatāvadhāna m. man with such a memory he can attend to a hundred things at once,
sātatyagamana constant movement, incessant motion
sātatyena continually, permanently,
śatāyuṣaḥ an age or a life of a hundred years 1050/3
sat sat true existence
satandra mfn having lassitude, languid,
satanu mfn having a body, together with the body,
satāpa mfn full of pain or sorrow,
satāra mfn together with the stars,
satarka having argument or reasoning, cautious, considerate,
satarkatā f. watchfulness,
satarṣa mfn having thirst, thirsty,
satas of the real, of the true, of the existent, pres.part √*as* 6/s/n
satata 1138/1 mfn. constant, perpetual, (*am* ind. and in comp.) constantly, ever, always, with *na* never,
satatadhṛti mfn ever resolute,
satatadurgata mfn always miserable,
satatagati m. 'always moving', the wind,
satatajvara m. constant fever,
satataṛāstrin mfn incessantly studying,
satatayukta mfn constantly devoted,
satati mfn coherent, uninterrupted,
satatotthita mfn always intent upon,
satattva mfn knowing the real truth, n. natural property, nature, -*tas* ind. really, in reality,
sātavāhana mfn having Sāta (in the form of a lion) as his beast of burden, riding on Sāta, m. name of a king,
sātayitṛ m. one who cuts in pieces, destroyer,
śatāyuṣa an age or a life of a hundred years 1050/3
ṣat-cakra-nirūpaṇā f. ascertainment or investigation of the six *cakras* (U)
satejas mfn attended with splendour or energy or vital power,
√*śaṭh* 1048/2 1. Cl 10 A *śāṭhayate* to praise, flatter, DP in *ślāghā* praising, boasting,
2. Cl 10 P *śaṭhayati* to speak ill, (according to others 'to speak well', to be true, DP in *sampak* speaking well or elegantly, or *avabhāṣaṇa* speaking ill,
3. Cl 10 P *śāṭhayati* to accomplish, adorn, others – to leave unfinished, unornamented, to go, move, DP in *asaṁskāra* leaving unfinished, unornamented, or *gati* going,
4. Cl 1 P *śaṭhati* to deceive, to hurt, to suffer pain, Cl 10 P *śāṭhayati* to be idle or lazy, DP in *hiṁsā* hurting, *saṁkleśana* causing pain, *kaitava* deceitful,
śaṭha 1048/2 mfn. false, deceitful, m. a cheat, rogue, concealing his powers, a fool, idler, a mediator, umpire, the thorn apple, white mustard-seed, n. saffron,
śaṭhatva roguery, depravity, malice,
satī 1. f. (fem of *sat*) her ladyship, your ladyship, a good and virtuous or faithful wife, (esp. applied in later use to the faithful wife who burns herself with her husband's corpse, a wife, female (of an animal), a female ascetic, a fragrant earth, n. 1134/2 being, existing, being present,
-*tva* n. or –*tā* f. wifely fidelity (esp. as evinced by cremation with a husband's corpse,
sati = *sāti, santi,*

sāti f. gaining, obtaining, acquisition, winning of spoil or property, a gift, oblation, end, destruction, violent pain,

saṭīka mfn accompanied/explained by a commentary, n. water,

satīka n. water

sātīkāśa mfn with or having excessive light,

satīla m. a bamboo, wind,

satīna mfn real, essential, a bamboo, n. water,

sātiśaya mfn superior, eminent, better, best

ṣaṭka mfn consisting of six, n. a whole consisting of six,

satkāma m. pure desire (of a liberated sage), desire for liberation,

satkāṇḍa m. a kite, hawk, falcon,

satkāra 1134/2 m. kind treatment, hospitality, honour, favour, reverence, care, attention, consideration or regard for a thing,

satkaraṇa n. doing the last honours for the dead, cremation, funeral obsequies

satkarman n. a good work, virtuous act, virtue, piety, hospitality, funeral obsequies, expiation, mfn performing good actions,

ṣatkarma cleansing processes in Hathayoga – *neti, dhauti, nauli, basti, kapalabhāti, trataka,*

satkartavya mfn one who is to be honoured,

satkartṛ mfn doing well, acting well, treating kindly or well, a benefactor

sātkarya n. effectiveness, doing anything well,

sātkaryavāda m. the doctrine which holds that the effect is inherent in the cause and that the effect is only a change of the cause (U),

satkīrti f. good reputation, mfn having a good reputation,

satkiṣku m. 48" length,

sat√kṛ P.A. *–karoti, -kurute*, to set right, put in order, arrange, prepare, adorn, to treat well or with respect, honour, be hospitable, pay the last honours to, cremate,

satkṛta mfn done well, adorned with (comp.), honoured, treated with respect or hospitality, adored, n. virtue, respect, honourable reception,

satkṛti f. doing good, virtue, morality, hospitality,

satkriya mfn doing good, *(ā)* f. putting in order, preparation, a good action, charity, virtue,

satkula n. a good or noble family, mfn belonging to a good or noble family

sātma mfn together with one's own person, in comp. for *sātman*

sātman mfn having a soul or spirit, together with the soul, united to the Supreme Spirit,

sātmatā f. absorption into the essence of *Brahmā,* community of essence or nature with (3rd, 6th or comp.)

sātmatva n. having a soul or essence,

sātmī in comp. for *sātma*

sātmībhāva m. becoming a custom or habit, conduciveness, suitableness,

sātmī√bhū P. –bhavati, to become a custom or a habit, become suitable or salutary,

sātmīkṛta mfn one who has made anything part of his nature, become accustomed to,

sātmya mfn agreeable to nature or natural constitution, wholesome, m. suitableness, wholesomeness, habit, habituation, diet,

sāṭopa mfn puffed up, proud, arrogant, rumbling (as clouds), (*am*) ind. haughtily, angrily, with a rumbling sound,

ṣaṭpada mfn having (taken) six steps,

ṣaṭpāda m. a bee, mfn six-footed,

satpatha m. a good or right way, correct or virtuous conduct, orthodox doctrine

satpathīna mfn going on the right way,

satpati m. a mighty lord, leader, champion, a good lord or ruler, lord of heroes, a good husband,

satpātra n. worthy person, worthy recipient,

satphala mfn having good fruit, m.

pomegranate tree, n. pomegranate fruit
satprabhā f. brilliant lustre,
satpuruṣa 1134/3 m. a good or wise man, 'man of truth: usually presumed as subtle form' HH
satpuṣpa mfn in bloom, having good flowers
satputra m. a good or virtuous son,
sato in comp. for *satas*
√*satr* 1138/2 Cl 10 A *satrayate, satrāpayate*, to extend, DP in *santāna kriyā* performing sacrifice,
satrā ind. together, together with, altogether, throughout, always, by all means,
satrāc mfn going together, united, joined, concentrated, whole (as the mind or heart)
satrākara mfn always effective,
satrapa mfn having shame or modesty, modest, bashful,
śatru 1051/1 m. a victorious opponent, an enemy, foe, rival,
śatrughna *Śatrughna,* 'foe-killing',
śatrunandana mfn causing joy to one's enemies,
śatrusaṁkata m. danger from the foe,
satsāra mfn having good sap or essence, m. a painter, a poet,
satsahāya m. a good companion, mfn one who has good or virtuous friends,
satsamāgama m. association with the good,
satsāmānya common substratum, homogenous essence, Being, Brahman, (U)
satsaṁgati = *satsaṅga*
satsaṁgraha mfn understood by the good,
satsaṁkalpa mfn one with good intentions m. true resolve, pure desire,
satsaṁnidhāna n. association or intercourse with the good or wise,
satsampradāya m. good tradition or traditional usage,
satsamprayoga m. right application,
satsaṁsarga m. association with the good, the society of the good,
satsaṁvinmaya mfn consisting of existence and consciousness,
satsaṅga 1134/3 m. intercourse or association with the good, holy company, a meeting of the wise or pious, 'good company' HH, see *saṅga*
√*saṭṭ* 1134/1 Cl 10 P *saṭṭayati* to hurt, to be strong, to dwell, to take or give, DP in *hiṁsā* hurting, injuring,
satta mfn seated,
sattā 1134/3 f. existence, being, goodness, excellence, (in phil.) a partic *jāti* (class)
sāṭṭahāsa mfn with loud laughter,
sattama mfn most excellent, best, most virtuous, very venerable or respectable,
sattāmātra n. mere entity or existence,
sattasāmānya homogenous existence, existence absolute, Brahman, (U),
sattāvat mfn endowed with existence,
satti f. sitting down, sitting, entrance, beginning,
sattṛ mfn sitting down (esp. at a sacrifice)
sattra n. 'session', a great Soma sacrifice, a house, hospital, asylum, an assumed form or disguise, deception, a wood, forest, tank, pond, liberality, munificence, wealth, clothes,
sattragṛha n. place of sacrifice or refuge or asylum,
sattri one who performs sacrifices, a cloud, an elephant,
ṣaṭtriṁśat f. thirty-six,
sattva 1135/2 n. (ifc. f.*ā*) being, existence, entity, reality, true essence, nature, disposition of mind, spiritual essence, life, essence, vital breath, life, consciousness, strength of character, strength, firmness, energy, resolution, courage, self-command, good sense, wisdom, magnanimity, the quality of purity or goodness, regarded as the highest of the three *guṇā* because it renders a person true, honest, wise and a thing pure and clean, material or elementary substance.

the qualities of purity, intelligence and brightness

a substantive, noun, m.n. a living or sentient being, creature, animal, embryo, fetus, rudiment of life,

sāttva mfn relating to the quality *sattva*

sattvaguṇa one of the three *guṇā* m. the quality of purity, or goodness (see above)

sattvaguṇapradhāna mfn sattva-prevailing, sattva-predominating,

sattvaguṇin mfn *sattvaguṇa* predominant,

sattvaka m. the spirit of a departed person,

sattvakartṛ m. the creator of living beings,

sattvaloka m. a world of living beings

sattvapati m. the lord of creatures,

sattvāpatti the fourth step of realisation, natural growth of *sattva* in being, mind and body

sattvaprakāśa m. the manifestation of *sattva*

sattvarāśi m. quintessence of energy,courage

sattvaśālin mfn energetic, courageous,

sattvasaṁāviṣṭa mfn filled or thoroughly pervaded by the quality of goodness,

sattvasampanna mfn endowed with the quality of goodness, good, excellent, equable, even-minded,

sattvasamplava m. universal destruction of beings, loss of vigour,

sattvasaṁrambha m. extraordinary courage, (and) violence or fury of animals,

sattvasaṁśuddhi 1135/2f. purity of nature or disposition, purity of mind or heart

sattvasāra m. essence of strength, extraordinary courage, a very powerful person,

sattvaśīla mfn of a virtuous disposition,

sattvastha mfn being in the nature (of anything), of resolute nature, energetic, clinging to or adherent in the quality of goodness, inherent in animals, animate,

sattvasthāna firm in the quality of goodness,

sattvatā f. purity, goodness, the existence of the *sattvaguṇa*

sattvādhīna mfn depending on courage,

sattvādhika mfn having a noble disposition, spirited, energetic, courageous,

sattvānurūpa mfn according to nature, according to one's innate disposition, according to one's substance or means,

sattvātman mfn having goodness naturally

sattvāvajaya m. self-command, strength of mind or character,

sattvavat mfn endowed with life, living, existent, a living being, endowed with or possessing the true essence, resolute, energetic, courageous,

sattvavihita mfn effected by nature, natural, caused by goodness, virtuous,

sattvaviplava m. loss of consciousness,

sattvavṛtti f. the quality of goodness

sāttvika 1200/1 mfn. spirited, vigorous, energetic, relating to or endowed with the quality *sattva* i.e. 'purity' or 'goodness', pure, true, honest, virtuous, good, internal, caused by internal feeling or sentiment, natural, not artificial, unaffected (style), m. a state of body caused by some natural emotion, an autumn night, n. an offering or oblation without pouring water,

sattvodreka m. excess or predominance of the quality of goodness, superabundance of energy,

sattvodrikta mfn one in whom the quality of goodness predominates,

sattvotsāha m. natural energy, du. courage and energy,

satvan mfn living, breathing, strong, powerful, m. a living being, warrior

satvana m. a warrior,

satvanāyat mfn behaving like a warrior,

satvara mfn speedy, expeditious, quick,

satvaram ind. quickly, immediately, right away, very soon

satvaram ind. quickly

satuhina mfn with frost or ice, wintry,

satvara having or making haste, speedy,

satya 1135/3 mf(*ā*) n. true, real, actual, honest, good, *sat* = existence + termination *ya* = pertaining to, pertaining to true existence = truth

pure, virtuous, good, successful, effectual, valid, the quality of goodness, purity or knowledge, the first of 4 Yugas or ages,
(*am*) n. truth, reality, truthfulness in speech,
satyena truly, certainly, really,
kasmāt satyāt for what reason,
tena satyena for that reason,
satyam tu, kiṁ tu, tathāpi 'it is true.. but yet, however'
yat satyam indeed, certainly,

sātya mfn one whose nature is truth,

satyā 1135/3 f. speaking the truth, sincerity, veracity, truthful, in comp. for *satya*

satyabandha mfn bound by truth, truthful,

satyadarśin mfn truth-seeing, truth-discerning

satyadeva mfn shining through truth,

satyadhāman mfn abiding in truth

satyadhana mfn rich in truth, very truthful,

satyadharma 1136/1 m. the law of truth, eternal truth, mfn one whose ordinances are true,

satyadhṛti mfn sincere in purpose, holding fast to truth, strictly truthful,

satyadṛś mfn truth-seeing, truth-discerning,

satyadūta m. a true messenger,

satyaghna mfn breaking one's word,

satyagir mfn true to one's word,

satyahita mfn really benevolent,

satyajā mfn of a true nature,

satyajit mfn conquering by truth, truly victorious

satyajña mfn knowing what is true,

satyajyotis mfn having real splendour,

satyakāma mfn lover of truth, truth-loving,

satyakarman n. sincerity in action, truthfulness

satyakriyā f. a promise, oath,

satyalaukika n. the true and the worldly, spiritual and worldly matters,

satyam 1135/3 truth, reality, truthfulness in speech, see above, unfailing truthfulness of speech, sincerity, 'the Truth, that which really exists. To perceive that which really exists, to conceive the truth as it ought to exist and speak the truth as it does and has existed in the mind is the aspect of human law, *dharma*. To deviate from the truth is against the law.', 'that which is this subtle essence, all this has got That as the Self',

satyamāna n. a true measure,

satyamanman mfn having true thoughts,

satyamaya mfn consisting of truth, truthful,

satyamedhas mfn having true intelligence,

satyaṁkāra m. a promise, making true/good

satyaṁṛṣāviveka m. discrimination of truth and falsehood,

satyānanda m. true bliss,

satyānandacidātman m. true bliss and true intellect,

satyapa mfn truth-drinking,

satyapara mfn given up to truth, thoroughly honest,

satyaparāmitā f. perfection in truth,

satyāpaya (ti) Nom.P. verifies, speaks the truth, ratifies,

satyapratiṣhṭāna mfn having truth for a foundation, grounded in truth,

satyapūta mfn purified by truth, (as a speech etc),

satyarādhas mfn having real blessings, bestowing real blessings

satyarata mfn devoted to truth, honest,

satyarūpa mfn having a true appearance, probable, credible,

satyasādhana mfn making true,

satyasaṁdha mfn having i.e. keeping true agreement, i.e. faithful, loyal

satyasaṁgara mfn having i.e. keeping true agreement, i.e. true to his word,

satyasaṁhita mfn true to one's agreement,

satyasaṁkalpa mfn true in purpose/resolve, one whose purpose is fulfilled,

satyasaṁrakṣaṇa n. keeping one's word,

satyaśapatha mfn one whose oaths are true or whose curses are fulfilled,

satyaśavas mfn truly vigorous, decidedly impetuous, one whose orders are true or valid,

satyastha mfn holding fast to the truth, keeping one's word,

satyaśīlin mfn addicted to truth,

satyaśravas n. true renown,

satyaśrut mfn listening to the truth,
satyaśuṣma mfn truly valiant,
satyasya as related, i.e. having truth,
satyatā f. reality, truth, love of truth,veracity
satyatama mfn mostly or quite true
satyatapas m. practising true austerity,
satyatas ind. in truth, really, truly
satyātmaka mfn having truth for essence, also = *satyātman* having a true soul,
satyatva n. reality, truth, state of truth,
satyavāc f. true speech, assurance, mfn truth-speaking,
satyavacana n. the speaking of truth, a promise, mfn speaking the truth
satyavacas n. veracity, truth,
satyavāda m. truth-speaking,
satyavādin mfn truth-speaking, truthful,
satyavāhana mfn conveying truth (a dream),
satyavāka m. the speaking of truth,
satyavat mfn truthful, veracious,
satyavikrama mfn having true valour
satyavrata n. a vow of truthfulness, true to one's word, truthful,
satyvṛtta n. true conduct, mfn practising truth, honest or upright,
satyavṛtti mfn devoting one's self to truth,
satyavyavasthā f. ascertainment of truth,
satyayuga n. the first or *kṛta* age the golden age, 1,728,000 years
satyetara n. untruth, falsehood,
Saubhadra son of *Subhadrā*
saubhaga n. happiness, enjoyment, wealth, beauty, welfare, grace, mfn auspicious, from the subhaga tree,
saubhagatva n. condition of happiness,
saubhāgya n. welfare, good luck, success, prosperity, happiness, beauty, charm, grace, affection,
saubhika m. a juggler,
saubhrātra n. good brotherhood, fraternity,
śauca n. cleanliness, cleanness, purity, purification, purity of mind, integrity, honesty, ' the act of purification, bodily, intellectually and emotionally.' '... not to purify body, mind and heart is against the law,'
śaucika m. cleanser, cleaner,
saucika ' one who lives by his needle' m. a tailor
√*śauḍ* 1092/3 = *śauṭ* to be proud or haughty, DP in *varṇa* covering or outer appearance,
saudāminī f. lightning, from *saudāmana* of the rain cloud, cloud-born
saudha mfn plastered, stuccoed, any fine house, n. silver, opal,
saudharmya n. rectitude, probity, honesty,
saudarya mfn brotherly or sisterly, n. brotherhood,
saugatika m. a Buddhist, a mendicant, an atheist, n. atheism, skepticism, buddhistic,
sauhārda n. good-heartedness, affection, friendship for or with,
sauhitya n. satiety, satisfaction, amiableness loveliness, fullness, completion,
sauhṛda mfn relating to or coming from a friend, m. a friend, n. (ifc.f.*ā*) affection, friendship for or with, liking for, fondness of (comp.)
saujanya n. goodness, benevolence,
saujanyavat mfn benevolent, kind, friendly
saukarya n. hoggishness, swinishness, 2. n. easiness of performance, facility, practicability, adroitness, easy preparation of food or medicine,
saukhya n. (ifc.f.*ā*) welfare, comfort, health, happiness, enjoyment,
saukṛtya n. piety, acting well or religiously
saukṣmya n. minuteness, fineness, subtlety,
saukumārya n. (ifc.f.*ā*) tenderness, delicacy, mfn tender, delicate,
saulabhya n. easiness of attainment,
Saumadattis a *Kaurava* warrior 1/s/m son of *Somadatta*
saumanasa mfn coming from or consisting of flowers, floral, flowery, pleasing, m. guardian elephant of the west, cheerfulness, enjoyment, comfort,
saumitra m. friendship,
saumya 1254/1 mfn relating to soma placid, gentle, mild, auspicious, happy, cheerful, cool and moist, northern, m. a *soma* sacrifice,
śaunaka a famous householder
saundarya n. beauty, loveliness, elegance,
saunika m. a butcher, a hunter,
saupa mfn relating to case terminations,
saurabha mfn fragrant, m. coriander,
saurājya n. good sovereignty/government,

saurāṣṭra from Sūrat – a country
saurasya n. tastiness, savouriness,
śaurya 1093/2 n. heroism, valour, prowess, might
saurya mfn relating or belonging to the sun solar, m. a son of the sun, a year,
sauśabda or *–śabdya* m. the right formation of nominal and verbal forms by case and tense terminations,
sauśāmya n. good pacification, reconciliation
sauśīlya n. excellence of disposition, good morals,
sauṣira m. a partic disease of the teeth, n. wind instruments (collectively),
sauṣirya n. hollowness, porosity,
sauśriya n. great fortune or happiness,
sauṣṭhava n. excellence, superior goodness or beauty, extreme skilfulness, cleverness, self-confidence,
√*śauṭ* 1092/3 Cl 1 P to be proud or haughty, see *śauḍ*
sautra mfn made of thread, relating to a *sūtra*, m. a *Brāhman* ,
sautri m. a weaver,
sautrika m. a weaver, a texture, anything woven,
sautya mfn relating to a charioteer, the office of a charioteer,
sauva mfn relating to one's self or property, n. an order, edict, 2. mfn heavenly, celestial,
sauvagrāmika mfn relating to own village,
sauvara mfn relating to or treating of sound or accent,
sauvarṇa mfn made of gold, golden, n. gold, m. a gold ear-ring,
sauvāstava mfn pleasantly situated, having a good site,
sauvastika mfn benedictive, salutatory, m. a family Brāhman or priest,
sauvaśvya n. a horse race,
sauvida m. a guard or attendant on the women's apartments,
sauvratya n. faith, devotion, obedience,
√*śav* 1059/3 Cl 1 P to go, to alter, change, transform, DP in gati going
sava m. pressing out the juice of the Soma plant, pouring it out, the moon, n. the juice or honey of flowers, 2. m. one who sets in motion or impels, an instigator, stimulator, commander, the sun, setting in motion, vivification, instigation, impulse, command, offspring, progeny,
śava m.n. a corpse, dead body, n. water,
śāva m. the young of an animal, mfn relating to a dead body, dead, tawny coloured, n. defilement by corpse contact or death of a relation,
sāva m. a soma libation,
sāvadhāna mfn attentive, heedful, careful, intent upon doing anything, (*am*) ind. attentively, carefully,
sāvadhāraṇa mfn limited, restricted,
sāvadhi mfn bounded, defined, limited,
sāvagraha mfn having an obstacle, restrained, limited, (in gram.) having the mark of separation or elision called *avagraha*, being separated into its component parts or analyzed, withholding (water, a cloud),
sāvahita mfn giving attention, attentive,
sāvajña mfn feeling contempt, despising, disdainful of,
śāvaka m. the young of an animal,
sāvakāśa mfn having an opportunity, applicable, (*am*) ind. leisurely,
sāvalamba mfn supported, leaning for support, having a prop,
savalatā f. the plant yielding Soma-juice,
sāvalepa mfn having pride, proud, haughty,
savana the act of pressing out the juice of the Soma plant, the juice and its libation, a Soma festival, any oblation or sacrificial rite, bathing, religious bathing, instigation, order, command,
savanakarman n. the sacred rite of libation,
sāvaraṇa mfn barred, bolted, locked up, concealed, secret, clandestine,
savarṇa mfn having the same colour or appearance, similar, like, equal to, of the same tribe or class, belonging to

the same class of sounds, homogenous with (comp.),
sāvaroha mfn having shoots or roots sent down from branches,
śavas n. superior might, heroic power, water, a dead body,
savāsa mfn scented, perfumed,
sāvaśeṣa mfn having a remainder, incomplete, unfinished, remaining, left, n. a remainder, residue,
savāsin mfn dwelling together,
sāvaṣṭambha mfn self-reliant, resolute,
savastu 1137/3 n. an excellent work, a good thing, a good plot or story, 'empirical existence' (Gam.),
savayas mfn of like strength or age, m. comrade,
sāvayava mfn having parts, made of parts, with limbs or members,
savicāra mfn that to which consideration is given, with deliberation, reason or enquiry,
savidha mfn of the same sort or kind, proximate, near, n. proximity, *(am)* ind. according to rule or precept,
savidya mfn pursuing the same studies, having learning, versed in science,
savidyut mfn accompanied with lightning,
savidyuta n. a thunderstorm,
savigraha mfn having body or form, embodied, having meaning
savijñāna 1190/3 mfn. endowed with right understanding, with discrimination
savikalpa mfn with attributes, possessing variety or admitting of distinctions, differentiated, admitting of alternative, option or doubt, 1190/3 with doubt and change,
savikāra 1190/3 mfn with its developments or derivatives, undergoing or with modification or transformation, altered in feeling, growing fond of,
savikāśa mfn shining, radiant,
saviklavam ind. piteously, dejectedly,
savikrama mfn vigorous, energetic, with a cry of alarm,
sāvin mfn having good behaviour or propriety, well-behaved, modest, m. kind of *mahāpuruṣa*, f. river,
savinaya mfn having good behaviour,
savinayam ind. politely,
saviśeṣa mfn having specific qualities, peculiar, singular, extraordinary, having discrimination, (*am*) ind. with all particulars, in detail, particularly, especially, associated with attributes,
saviśeṣabrahman Brahman with attributes, *saguṇa brahman,*
saviśeṣatva presence of distinctive attributes
savitāna mfn having a canopy, with a canopy
savitarati Nom.P. resembles the sun,
savitarka mfn accompanied with reason or thought, (*am*) ind. thoughtfully,
savitṛ m. a stimulator, rouser, vivifier, 'the divine influence and vivifying power of the sun', name of a sun-deity, or 'lord of all creatures', the Gāyatṝ is addressed to him, the orb of the sun in its ordinary form,
sāvitra mfn relating to the sun, derived or descended from the sun, an embryo or fetus, the sun, initiation into the twice-born classes by reciting of the *sāvitrī* verse and investing with the sacred thread, a ray of light, solar ray, the ring finger,
sāvitrī f. a verse or prayer addressed to *Savitṛ* or the Sun, also called *Gāyatṝ*, initiation by reciting of the *sāvitrī* verse and investing with the sacred thread, the sacred thread
savitriya mfn relating/belonging to the sun,
saviveka mfn possessed of judgment, discerning
savrata mfn fitting together, harmonious, bound by a rule or law,
savya mfn left, left hand, (*am, ena, ā, e,* ibc. 'on the left'), opposite to left, right, right hand, south, southern (*am* etc.to the south), reverse, contrary, backward, m. the left arm or hand or foot,
savyabhicāra mfn m. (in phil.) an argument

wide of the mark or incompatible with the conclusion drawn from it, an assertion proving too much, as 'fire' to prove 'smoke',

savyabhicaraṇa mfn liable to inaccuracy, possibly inexact or false, not absolutely exact or certain,

savyasācin 1191/3 voc. Oh ambidextrous archer (Arjuna), ambidextrous,

savyatas ind. from or on the left, on the right side,

savyatha mfn with sorrow or trouble, afflicted, sorrowful,

savyāvṛt mfn with a turn to the left, turning to the left,

śaya 1055/3 mfn abiding, resting, sleeping, of cool temperament, m. sleep, sleeping, a bed, couch, a snake, lizard, abuse, the hand,

sāya n. the close of day, evening, (*am*) ind. in the evening, at eventide, m. a missile, arrow, n. unloosing, unyoking, turning in, going to rest

sāyaka mfn intended or fitted to be discharged or hurled, a missile, arrow, a sword, f. (*ikā*) a dagger,

śayālu mfn sleepy, sluggish, slothful, m. a dog, jackal, the boa snake,

śayana mfn lying down, resting, sleeping, n. a bed, the act of lying down, resting, sleeping, copulation,

śayāna mfn lying down, resting, sleeping, m. a lizard, chameleon,

sayana n. binding,

śayanīya n. a bed or couch, satisfactory for lying (on), to be slept or lain on,

sāyāsa mfn beset with difficulties,

sayatna mfn having i.e. taking pains to, i.e. trying to, (with inf.) engaged in

śāyin mfn lying, sleeping, resting, abiding,

śayita mfn sleeping, asleep

śayitā will sleep 1/s/peri.fut., f. state of lying or reposing or abiding in,

śayitvā ind. having lain, having lain down,

sāyojya = *sāyujya,* n. communion with, likeness, absorption, intimate union, identification, similarity,

sayuj mfn united, a comrade, companion,

sayujā ever associated, in close companionship, closely associated, perpetual union,

sayujya mfn closely united with,

sāyujya n. intimate union, communion with, identification, absorption (into the Divine Essence), likeness, similarity

sayujyatā f. intimate union or junction,

śayyā f. bed, couch, mfn sleep, lying down, refuge,

ścandra mfn shining, radiant,

√ścut 1093/3 Cl 1 P (or *ścyut), ścotati,* to ooze, trickle, exude, drop, distil, to shed, pour out, sprinkle, caus. *ścotayati,* DP in *kṣaraṇa* trickling, oozing, flowing,

ścut ifc. dripping, distilling, sprinkling,

se mfn serving,

secaka m. 'sprinkler' a cloud,

secana 1246/1 mfn sprinkling, pouring out, emitting, n. emission, effusion, sprinkling or watering with, a shower bath, casting (of metals), a bucket

sedi f. weariness, exhaustion, decay,

sedhaka mfn driving off, preventing,

√sek 1246/1 Cl 1 A *sekate* to go, move, DP in *gati* going,

śekhara m. crest, crown, diadem, chaplet or wreath of flowers, a peak, summit

sektra n. a vessel for holding or pouring out water,

√śel 1088/3 Cl 1 P *śelati* to go DP in *gati* going

√sel see *śel*

sela a kind of weapon

selaga m. a waylayer, robber,

√śelāya 1088/3 Nom P *√śelāyati* DP in *vilāsa* playing

sena 1246/2 1. having a master or lord, dependent on another, 2. n. the body, 3. in comp. for *senā*

senā army, missile, dart, armament, line of battle,

senānī m. a general, commander, chief,

sendriya 1246/3 possessed of manly

vigour or potency together with the organs of sense, having sense organs

serṣya mfn with jealousy, full of envy, (*am*) ind. jealously, enviously,

śeṣa 1088/3 m.n. remainder, that which remains or is left, leavings, residue, surplus, balance, the rest, that which has to be supplied, *iti śeṣa* 'left to be supplied' a common comment regarding words required to amplify the text, remaining out of or from, end, issue, conclusion, finish, last, last-mentioned, a supplement, appendix, a keepsake, secondary matter, accident, death, destruction, name of a thousand-headed serpent symbolizing eternity, a kind of metre, the remains of offerings, effect, (*ā*) f. pl. the remains of flowers or other offerings afterwards distributed amongst the worshippers and attendants,

śeṣas n. offspring,

śeṣe loc. for the rest, in all other cases,

śeṣin mfn having (little) remainder, (i.e. constituting the 'chief matter ' or 'main point',

seṣu mfn having an arrow,

seśvara mfn having a god, theistical,

śeṣya mfn to be left or ignored or neglected,

śete 1077/1 root *śī* lies down, falls asleep 1/s/pres/indic/mid sleeps

setra n. a bond, ligament, fetter,

seṭu m. a kind of watermelon or cucumber

setu mfn binding, who or what binds or fetters, m. a bond, fetter, a ridge of earth, dike, dam, bridge, separating fields, a landmark, boundary, limit, an explanatory commentary, a fixed rule, the sacred syllable Om,

setum n. a bridge, dam, dike,

setuka a causeway, bridge,

śev 1088/3 Cl 1 A *śevate* to worship, serve, DP in *sevana* serving,

sev 1247/1 Cl 1 A *sevate (ti),* to dwell or stay near or in, to remain or stay at, live in, frequent, haunt, inhabit, resort to, to serve, to attend upon, honour, obey, worship, to cherish, foster (a child), to present with, to enjoy sexually, have intercourse with, to refresh by soft breezes, to devote or apply oneself to, cultivate, study, practise, use, employ, perform, to exist or be found in anything, caus. *sevayati* to attend upon, serve, honour, to tend, cherish (plants), DP in *sevana* serving,

śeva 1088/3 mfn dear, precious, m. the male organ, a serpent, a fish, height, elevation treasure, wealth, n. prosperity, happiness, hail, homage,

seva n. = *sevi* an apple,

sevā 1247/1 f. going or resorting to, service, attendance on, worship, homage, reverence, devotion to

śevadhi m. treasury, wealth, treasure, jewel,

sevaka mfn dwelling in, inhabiting, practising, using, employing, revering, worshipping, m. an attendant, servant, worshipper, 2. one that sews a sewer, a sack,

sevana 1247/1 n. the act of frequenting or visiting or dwelling in or resorting to, waiting upon, attendance, service, honouring, reverence, worship, adoration, sexual enjoyment, intercourse with, devotion or addiction to, fondness for, indulgence in, practice or employment of

sevate he/she serves, honours, obeys

sevi n. the jujube, an apple, in comp. for *sevin,*

sevin frequenting, inhabiting, going or resorting to, attending on, serving, honouring, revering, having intercourse with, addicted to, fond of, enjoying, practising,

sevita 1247/2 mfn. dwelt in, visited, frequented, followed

sevitā f. service, attendance,

sevitṛ mfn one who honours or worships, one who follows or pursues, m. a servant, attendant, *seya* n. obtaining,

√*śi* 1069/3 Cl 3 P *śiśāti* to grant, bestow, to present or satisfy, Cl 5 P A *śinoti, śinute* to sharpen DP in *niśāna* (Cl 5) whetting, sharpening,

√*śī* 1077/1 Cl 2 A *śete* to lie, lie down, recline, rest, repose, to remain unused (*soma*), to lie down to sleep, fall asleep, sleep, caus. *śāyayati* cause to lie down, lay down, put, throw, fix on/in, allow to sleep or rest, DP in *svapna* sleeping,
Cl. 4 A. *śīyate* (connected with √2. *śad*), to fall out or away, disappear, vanish,

śī f. sleep, repose, lying, resting, devotion, tranquillity,

√*si* 1. 1213/1 1212/3 Cl 5.9 P A *sinoti, sinute, sināti* (pres. only), *sinite,* to bind, tie, fetter, caus. *sāyayati,* DP (Cl 5.9.) *bandhana* in binding, fastening,
2. to hurl, cast,
f. service,

√*śībh* 1078/2 Cl 1 A *śībhate* to boast, DP in *katthana* boasting,

√*sibh* or *simbh* 1217/3 see *sṛbh,* to kill, slay, injure, DP in *hiṁsā* injuring, killing,

śibi name of a king,

śibikā f. a palanquin, litter, a weapon,

śibira n. a royal camp or tent, any tent, a protective entrenchment,

√*sic* 1214/10 Cl 6 P *siñcati (te), secate,* to pour out, discharge, emit, shed, infuse or pour into, to emit semen, impregnate, scatter in small drops, sprinkle, to dip, soak, steep, to cast or form anything out of molten metal etc., caus. *secayati (te),* to cause to pour out, to sprinkle, water (plants etc.), DP in *kṣaraṇa* sprinkling, moistening,

sic f. = śic, a net, the border or hem of a dress, the horizon (du.), the wings of an army (du.pl.),

sicaya m. robe, raiment, clothes, cloth, old or ragged clothes,

sīdanti they sit √*2. sad* 1138/2 to sit 1/pl/pres/indic/act

√*sidh* 1. 1215/1 Cl 1 P *sedhati* , to go, move, DP in *gati*, going, warding off, driving,
2. Cl 1 P to drive off, scare away, repel, restrain, hinder, to punish, chastise, to ordain, instruct, to turn out well or auspiciously, caus. *sedhayati,*
DP in *śāstra* ordaining, commanding, instructing, or *māṅgalya* turning out well,
3. Cl 4 P *sidhyati (te*), to be accomplished or fulfilled or effected or settled, be successful, succeed, to hit a mark, to attain one's aim or object, have success, to attain the highest object, become perfect, attain beatitude, to be valid or admissible, hold good, to be proved or demonstrated or established, result from, to be set right, healed or cured, to be well cooked, to conform to a person's will, yield to, to fall to a person's lot, to come into existence, originate, arise, caus. *sedhayati*, or *sāhayati*, to show the knowledge or skill of anyone, (the former with ref. to sacred things, the latter with ref. to secular things), to accomplish, effect, DP in *saṁrādhi* being accomplished or fulfilled,

siddha 1215/1 2. mfn. accomplished, fulfilled, one who has attained his object, endowed with supernatural faculties, sacred, holy, divine, illustrious, a class of demi-gods with supernatural powers esp. flying though the air, healed, cured, driven off scared away, well-known, notorious, celebrated, effective, powerful, miraculous, supernatural, subdued, brought into subjection (by magical powers), subject or obedient to (6th), peculiar, singular, invariable, unalterable,

m. a *siddha* or semi-divine being of great purity and perfection, any inspired sage or prophet or seer, any holy person or great saint, a great adept in magic or one who has attained supernatural powers, a *jina* or *arhat Jaina),* a lawsuit or judicial trial, f.(*ā*) a semi-divine female, n. magic, supernatural power, sea-salt,

siddhānta m. established end, final end or aim or purpose, demonstrated conclusion, right conclusion, settled doctrine, received or admitted truth, any established or received scientific text or treatiseon any subject, a partic. class of Buddhist and Jaina works,

siddhānta śravaṇa scriptural listening, studying the teachings and listening to the wise, (K),

siddhāntin m. one who establishes conclusions logically, one learned in scientific text-books,

siddhārtha mfn one who has accomplished an aim or object, successful, prosperous, leading to the goal, efficient, efficacious, name of the founder of Buddhism, m. white mustard, the Indian fig tree,

siddhārtha-bodha-vākya 'an affirmation of existent facts' (U),

siddhārtha-vākya 'existential statements' i.e. 'they intimate the existent Absolute'(G),

siddhāsana n. a meditation posture (left heel under the body, right heel in front of it, fixing the sight between the eyebrows and mediating on the syllable Om),

siddhi 1216/2 f. accomplishment, performance, fulfilment, complete attainment, fulfilment, perfection, healing of a disease, establishment, substantiation, proof, decision, driving off, putting aside, solution of a problem, cooking, maturing, skill in general, dexterity, art, efficacy, efficiency, understanding, intellect, becoming clear or intelligible, success or perfection personified, personal success, fortune, healing of a disease, readiness, prosperity, supreme felicity, bliss, beatitude, complete sanctification, final emancipation, acquisition of supernatural powers, 'mastery or independence , realization of the Self', HH,

siddhika ifc. = *siddhi* above, supernatural power

siddhīkṛta mfn accomplished, finished,

siddhimant mfn possessing magic power,

siddhisādhana means of obtaining beatitude or perfection or magical power,

sidhma mfn going straight to a goal or object aimed at, white-spotted, leprosy,

sidhra mfn successful, efficacious, perfect, good, m. a kind of tree,

sidhya m. auspicious,

śīghra 1077/3 mfn quick, speedy, rapid

śīghram ind. quickly, rapidly, fast

śīghrataram mfn more quickly, faster, ind. as quickly as possible,

√*śīk* 1077/1 Cl 1 A *śīkate* to rain in fine drops, drizzle, sprinkle, wet, moisten, to go, move, caus. *śīkayati* to besprinkle, Cl 10 to speak or to shine, DP in *secana* (cl1) wetting, sprinkling, Cl 10 in *bhāṣā* speaking, shining, *āpyayana* becoming full, increasing, *āmarṣaṇa* being patient,

śīkara m. spray, drizzle, mist, a fine drop

sikatāḥ f.pl. sand,

sikatila mfn consisting of sand, sandy,

śikhā f. tuft or braid of hair, top, peak,

śikhara mfn peaked, m.n. peak, summit,

śikhari(n) 1070/3 m. a peaked mountain, any mountain, mfn. pointed, peaked

śikhin m. a peacock, a cock, a bull, a horse, having a tuft on top of the head,

√*śikṣ* 1070/1 Cl 1 P A *śikṣati (te),* to wish to be able, P. try to effect, attempt, undertake, A. to learn, acquire knowledge, study, practise, learn from, P. wish to aid, help, befriend, wish to give, A. to offer one's service to, enter the service of, caus. *śikṣayati (te),* cause to learn, inform, instruct, teach, DP in *vidyā-upādāna* learning, teaching

śikṣā (or *śīkṣā*) 1070/1 f. desire of being able to effect anything, learning, study, knowledge, art, skill, teaching, training, pronunciation (one of the *vedāṅgas*), the science which teaches proper articulation, pronunciation and euphony of Vedic texts,modesty, humility, diffidence, chastisement, punishment, √*cakṣ* from √*kāś* to be visible, shine, be brilliant,
'instruction-causing' a teacher, bestowing, imparting,

śikṣāsaṁvara m. the moral life of a monk,

śikṣāvat mfn possessed of knowledge, learned, full of instruction, instructive (as a tale),

śikṣita mfn learnt, studied, practised, taught or instructed in, docile, clever, diffident, modest,

sikṣya m. crystal, glass,

sikta m.n. poured out, sprinkled, wetted,

sikthaka n. beeswax

√*śil* 1073/1 Cl 6 P *śilati* to glean DP in *uñcha* gleaning,

√*śīl* 1079/1 *śīlati* to meditate, contemplate, to serve, worship, act, do, practise, caus./Cl 10 *śīlayati* to do, make, practise repeatedly or exceedingly, be intent upon or engaged in, exercise, cultivate, to wear, put on, visit, frequent, to exceed, excel, DP in *samādhi* (Cl 1), meditation, contemplation, in *upadhāraṇa* (Cl 10) studying or practising repeatedly,

√*sil* see *śil* DP in *uncha* gleaning,

śīla 1079/1 n. habit, custom, usage, natural or acquired way of living or acting, practice, conduct, nature, disposition, tendency, character, a moral precept or moral conduct (Buddhist), form, shape, beauty, m. a large snake,

sīla n., a plough,

śilā f. rock or large stone, crag, red arsenic, camphor, the lower mill-stone, the lower timber of a door, the top of the pillar supporting a house, a vein, tendon,

śilābhāva m. the state or nature of stone,

silha m. incense, olibanum, (*-am, āp)* turn into stone,

śilī f. the beam under a door, a spike, dart, arrow,

śilīmukha m. Block-snout, name of a hare, a fool, a battle, war,

śiloccaya m. crag-pile, craggy hill,

śilpa 1073/3 n. decoration, ornament, artistic work, variegated or diversified appearance, the art of variegating, skill in any art or craft or work of art, ingenuity, contrivance, any act or work, ceremonial act, ceremony, form, shape, mfn variegated,

śilpayoga artistic work? unity through art? artistic yoga,

śilpin m.artist, craftsman, artisan, fashioner of, mfn belonging to or skilled in art,

sīm ind. him, her, it, them, ever,

sima whole, all, every, entire, = *ātman* one's self,

sīmā 1219/1 f. parting of the hair, a boundary, landmark, rule of morality,

sīmaka ifc. a boundary, limit,

sīman m. a hair parting, n. a boundary, border, limit, f. a ridge marking the boundary of a field or village, a bank, shore, the horizon, the utmost limit of anything, furthest extent, summit, acme, the scrotum, a suture of the skull, the nape of the neck,

siṁha m. 'the powerful one', a lion, a hero or eminent person,

sindhi n. rock-salt,

sindhu m.f. a river, stream, esp. the Indus,

m. flood, waters, ocean, sea, the moisture of the lips, water ejected from an elephant's trunk, the country around the Indus (commonly called Sindh), the exudation from the temples of an elephant,

sindhuja mfn ocean-born, river-born, aquatic, born in Sindh, n. rock-salt

sindhuka mfn marine, born or produced in Sindh,

sindhura m. an elephant,

√*śiṅgh* 1071/1 Cl 1 P *śighati* to smell, DP in *āghrāṇa* smelling,

√*śiñj* 1071/2 Cl 2 A *śiṅkte*, Cl 1.10 A *śiñjate, śiñjayate* to utter a shrill sound, tinkle, rattle, jingle, whirr, buzz, hum, twang, bellow, roar, DP in *avyakta-śabda* tinkling, rattling, roaring,

√*śiṅkh* 1071/1 Cl 1 P *śiṅkhati* to go, move, DP in *gati* going,

sīpa m. a vessel (for making libations),

śīpāla m.n. a common water plant or water containing the plant,

sipra m. sweat, perspiration, the moon, f. (*ā*) a woman's zone, a female buffalo,

śira 1072/2 n. the head, skull, a bed, couch,

sīra m.n. a plough, m. an ox for ploughing, draught-ox, the sun,

sirā a stream, water, a nerve, vein, artery, tendon, a bucket, vein-like channel, a baling vessel,

sirājāla a network of vessels or veins,

sīraka m. a plough, a porpoise, the sun,

śiras n. head, skull, the highest part of anything, peak, summit, acme, vanguard of an army, the beginning of a verse, the head, leader, chief, foremost,

sīravāha mfn drawing a plough,

sīravāhaka m. a ploughman,

sirī m.f. a weaver, a shuttle,

śirīṣa m. a tree with a delicate flower n. the blossom,

śiromukha n. head and face,

śirovrata n. a vow of holding fire on the head

śīrṣa n. the head, skull, upper part, tip, top, the fore-part, front, m. a kind of grass,

√*śiṣ* 1076/3 1. Cl 1 P *śeṣati* to hurt, injure, kill, DP in *hiṁsā* (Cl 1) injuring, 2. Cl 7 P *śinaṣṭi* to leave, leave remaining, caus./cl10 *śeṣayati (te),* to cause or allow to remain, leave, spare, DP in *viśeṣaṇa* (cl7) distinguishing or discriminating from others, in *asarva-upayoga* leaving as remainder, sparing,

sīsaka m.n. lead (metal),

śiśira mfn cold, chilly, frigid, m.n. dew, hoarfrost, the cold season,

sisṛkṣu mfn desirous to create, euphony, wishing to let flow, emit,

śiṣṭa 1076/3 mfn 1. left, remaining, residual, remains, n. anything that is left or remains, remnant, rule, 2. taught, directed, ordered, disciplined, cultured, educated, m. a learned or well-educated or wise man, a chief, counsellor,

śiśu m. young, child,

śiśumāra m. a dolphin, alligator,

śiṣya m. to be taught or instructed, a scholar, student, disciple, passion, anger, violence,

√*śiṭ* 1071/2 Cl 1 P *śeṭati* to despise, DP in *anādara* despising, disregarding,

√*siṭ* 1214/1 Cl 1 P *seṭati* to despise DP in *anādara* despising, disregarding,

śīta mfn cold, cool, chilly, frigid, dull, apathetic, sluggish, indolent, n. cold, coldness, cold weather, cold water, m. camphor, liquor,

sitā f. sugar,

sita mfn white, pale, bright, light, pure, m. white (the colour), planet Venus the light half of the month, a handsome woman, liquor, bamboo juice, moonlight, a handsome woman, f. (*ā*) white refined sugar,

n. silver, sandal, a radish,

sītā *Sītā*, a princess, wife of *Rāma*, fabled to have sprung from a furrow, 1218/2 f. a furrow, the track or line of a ploughshare, name of a river,

śītaka mfn cool, sluggish, idle, lazy, healthy, m. feeling of cold, shivering, the cold season, any cold thing, a lazy man, a happy or contented man, a scorpion, a kind of sandal,

śītala mfn cold, cool, cooling, shivering, frosty, cold i.e. free from passion, calm, gentle, not exciting emotion,, not causing painful feelings, *f.(ā)*1078/1/2 - free from passion, cool,

śītāṁśu m. the moon 'having cool rays', cold-rayed, camphor,

śītārta mfn distressed with the cold,

śithila mfn loose, flaccid, unsteady,

śithira mfn loose, flexible, slack,

siti f. binding, fastening, mfn white, black,

śītikā mfn cool, f. coldness,

śītikāvant mfn cool,

√*siv* 1218/1 Cl 4 P *sīvyati (te)*, to sew, sew on, darn, stitch, stitch together, join, unite, caus. *sīvayati* or *sevayati* to sew, stitch, DP in *tantu-santāna* sewing or darning, stitching together,

siva or *sivaka* m. one who sews or stitches, a sewer, stitcher,

Śiva 1074/1 mfn. auspicious, propitious, benign, fortunate, kind, benevolent, friendly, harmonious, conscious, true, m. happiness, welfare, liberation, final emancipation, the Auspicious one, dissolver of creation, destroyer

sivāku m. a *ṛṣi*

śīvan mfn lying, resting, m. a large snake,

sīvana n. sewing, stitching, a seam, suture, *(ī)* f. a needle,

śivapada n. the state of Śiva, blessedness, emancipation,

sivara m. an elephant,

sivasa m. a verse, cloth,

śivira n. a royal camp or tent,

śivo'ham I am Śiva,

sīvya mfn to be sewn,

√*skambh* 1257/1, 1256/3 or *skabh* Cl 5.9.P *skamnoti, skamnāti,* Cl 1 A *skambhate* to prop, support, make firm, fix, establish, caus. *skambhayati* to prop, support, impede, check, DP in *pratibandha* stopping, hindering,

skambha m. a prop, support, pillar, buttress, fulcrum, the Supreme Being,

√*skand* 1256/1 Cl 1 P *skandati (te),* to leap, jump, hop, dart, spring, spurt out, be spilt or effused (semen), A. to emit seminal fluid, to leap upon, cover (said of animals), to drop, fall down, perish, be lost, caus. *skandayati,* to pour out etc., to omit, neglect, thicken, cause to coagulate, DP in *gati* going, *śoṣaṇa* becoming dry,

skanda m. anything which jumps or hops, n. spurting out, emission, effusion

Skanda god of war

skandaka m. one who leaps or springs, a soldier,

skandana n. spurting out, emission, effusion, failing to succeed, miscarrying, purging, clotting of the blood, going, moving,

skandha m. the shoulder, the crown or the trunk of a tree, (buddhism) aggregates – five types of phenomena that serve as objects of clinging and bases for a sense of self, a king, prince, sage, heron, f. (*ā*) a branch, creeper, often used for *skanda*

skandhadeśa m. region of the shoulders, shoulder, part of an elephant where the driver sits,

skandhas n. branches of a tree, tree-top, the shoulder,

√*skhad* 1257/1 Cl 1 A *skhadate* caus. *skhādayati* DP in *skhadana* cutting or tearing to pieces,

*skhadana*1257/1 cutting or tearing to pieces, hurting, killing, discomfiting, firmness

√*skhal* 1257/1 Cl 1 P *skhalati (te)*, to stumble, trip, totter, waver, fluctuate, drop or slip down, stammer, falter (as speech), make mistakes, blunder, err, fail, to gather, collect, to move, to disappear, caus. *skhālayati* to cause to falter, stop, arrest, DP in *sañcalana* stumbling,

skhalana 1257/2 n. stumbling, tottering, faltering, stammering, rubbing, friction, touch, contact, discharge, emission, falling into, being deprived of, mistake,

√*sku* 1257/1 Cl 5.9. P A *skunoti skunute, skunāti skunīte,* and *-skauti,* to tear, pluck, pick, poke, to cover, pass. to be stirred (as fire), caus. *skāvayati,* DP in *āpravaṇa* covering, overspreading,

√*skund* 1257/1 see *skand* Cl 1 A *skundate* to jump, to lift up DP in *āpravaṇa* jumping, raising,

√*ślāgh* 1103/3 Cl 1 A *ślāghate (ti)*, to trust or confide in, to talk confidently, vaunt, boast or be proud of, A. to coax, flatter, wheedle, to praise, commend, eulogize, celebrate, caus. *ślāghayati* to encourage, comfort, console, to praise, celebrate, DP in *katthana* praising, extolling, commending,

ślāghā 1104/1 f. vaunt, boasting, flattery, praise, commendation, pleasure or delight in anything,

ślāghya to be praised, praiseworthy, honourable,

√*ślākh* 1103/3 Cl 1 P *ślākhati* to pervade, penetrate, DP in *vyāpti* pervasion, occupation,

ślakṣṇa mfn slippery, smooth, soft, tender, gentle, small, minute, thin, fine, honest, sincere, (*am*) ind. softly, gently

√*ślaṅg* 1103/3 Cl 1 P *ślaṅgati* to go, move, DP in *gati* going

√*ślaṅk* 1103/3 Cl 1 A *ślaṅkate* to go, move DP in *gati* going,

√*ślath* 1103/3 Cl 1 P *ślathati* to be loose, relaxed or flaccid, DP in *hiṁsā* injuring,

ślatha mfn loose, relaxed, flaccid, weak, languid, unfastened, disshevelled (hair),

śleṣa m. clinging or adhering to, burning, connection, junction, union, embracing, an embrace, a grammatical augment, f. (*ā*) an embrace,

śleṣaṇa 1104/1 n. clinging or adhering to, connection, junction, union, combination, double meaning

śleṣman m. phlegm, mucus, n. a band, cord, string, lime, glue,

√*śliṣ* 1104/1 1. Cl 1 P *śleṣati* to burn DP in *dāha* burning,
2. Cl 4 P *śliṣyati (te)*, to adhere, attach, cling to, to clasp, embrace, unite, join, A. to result, be the consequence of anything, to be joined or connected, to be implied or intimated, DP in *ālaṅgina*(Cl 4) embracing, in *śleṣaṇa* (Cl 10) uniting, joining,

√*ślok* 1104/3 Cl 1 A *ślokate* to compose or be composed, DP in *saṅghāta* heaping together, collecting,

śloka m. (thing heard) i.e. sound, noise, a call or voice (of the gods), fame, renown, glory, praise, a proverb, maxim, a verse esp. the '*anustubh*'
a classic *śloka* form (stanza) in which many stories or scriptures are written,

√*śloṇ* 1104/3 Cl 1 P *śloṇati* to heap, collect, DP in *saṅghāta* heaping together, collecting,

sma or *smā, ṣma, ṣmā* 1271/2 ind. indeed, certainly, ever, always, may be used with present tense or a present participle to give them a past sense, e.g. *praviśanti sma* 'they entered"

smaḥ we (pl) are 3/pl/pres/act √*as*

smara mfn remembering, recollecting, m. (ifc.f.*ā*) memory, remembrance, recollection, loving recollection, love, esp. sexual love, god of love

smāra m. remembrance, recollection of, relating to the god of love,

smāraka mfn recalling, reminding of,

smāram ind. having remembered,

smaran remembering, thinking of, (V),

smaraṇa 1272/1 n. the act of remembering or calling to mind, remembrance, reminiscence, recollection of (gen. or comp.), memory, handing down by memory, tradition, traditional teaching or record or precept, mental recitation (of the name of a deity), f. (*ī*) a rosary of beads,

smarati 1271/3 he remembers, thinks of 1/s/pres/act/indic. √*smṛ*

smārin mfn remembering, reminding,

smārita mfn reminded, called to mind,

smārta mfn relating to memory, recorded in or based on *smṛti,* prescribed or sanctioned by traditional law or usage, an orthodox Brāhmana,

smartavya mfn to be remembered, memorable, living only in the memory (of men),

smārtika mfn based on tradition, traditional,

smartṛ mfn one who remembers, recollects, a teacher, preceptor,

śmaśāna n. the place for burning the corpses and for burying the bones, cemetery, an oblation to deceased ancestors,

śmaśru n. the beard, moustache, beard-hairs

smat ind. together, at the same time, at once, as a prep. with 3rd- together or along with, (often in comp.) having, possessing, provided with,

smaya m. smiling at anything, wonder, surprise, arrogance, conceit, pride

smayamāna smiling,

smayādika mfn beginning with(i.e. based chiefly on) arrogance,

smayin mfn smiling, laughing, *(antaḥsmayin)* laughing inwardly,

smera mfn smiling, friendly, expanded, evident, proud, abounding in, full of, m. a smile, laugh, manifestation,

√*smi* 1271/3 Cl 1 A *smayate (ti*), to smile, blush, become red or radiant, shine, to laugh, to expand, bloom (as a flower), to be proud or arrogant, caus. *smāyayati (te),* cause to smile or laugh, A. to laugh at , mock, despise, DP (cl1) in *īṣat-hasana* smiling, Cl 10 in *anādara* slighting, scorning, despising,

√*śmīl* 1094/2 Cl 1 P *śmīlati* to wink, twinkle, DP in *nimeṣaṇa* closing the eyes, contracting the eyelids,

√*smīl* 1271/3 see *śmīl*

√*smiṭ* 1271/3 Cl 10 P *smeṭayati* to despise, to love, DP in *anādara* slighting, scorning, despising,

smita mfn smiled, smiling, expanded, blossomed, n. a smile, gentle laugh,

smitapūrva mfn previously smiling, with a smile, preceded with a smile,

smitavāc mfn speaking with a smile,

√*smṛ* 1. 1271/3 see *spṛ*
2. 1271/2 Cl 1 P *smarati (te),* to remember, recollect, bear in mind, call to mind, think of, be mindful of, to remember or think of with sorrow or regret, to hand down from memory, by heart, teach, declare, to recite, caus. *smārayati* to cause to remember, be mindful of, regret, to remind anyone of, DP in *ādhyāna* remembering with regret or anxiety, in *cintā* remembering,

smṛta 1272/2mfn. remembered, recollected, referred to, called to mind, thought of, handed down, taught, prescribed, 'held to be' (Gam.), enjoined by *smṛti* or traditional law

smṛti 1272/3 f. remembrance,

reminiscence, thinking of or upon, calling to mind, memory, the whole body of sacred tradition or what is remembered by human teachers (in contra distinction to what is directly heard or revealed to the *ṛṣi*(s), (*śruti*), the whole body of codes of law as handed down through memory or by tradition, and the 16 inspired law-givers, "all that was heard and retained in memory is *smṛti* when recorded" HH , what has been remembered, the teaching of great sages, secondary to *śrūti*, includes Laws of *Manu* etc.

smṛtihetu m. impression on the mind, cause of recollection, association of ideas, recollection,

smṛtiśīla n.du. traditions, usage and moral practices,

√*snā* 1266/3 Cl 2 P *snāti,* Cl 4 P A *snāyati (te),* to bathe, perform a bathing ceremony, to smear oneself with, to wash away, to steep or soak in, to bathe with tears (weep for), caus. *snāpayati*, or *snapayati* to cause to bathe, wash, cleanse, DP in *śauca* cleansing, bathing, 2. mfn bathing, bathed or immersed in,

√*snai* 1268/1 Cl 1 P *snāyati* to clothe, wrap round, envelop, adorn, DP in *veṣṭana* putting on, adorning,

snaigdhya n. unctuousness, oiliness, smoothness, tenderness, fondness

snāna n bathing, washing, religious or ceremonial bathing for purification, washing off, removal by washing, purification, anything used in bathing – water, perfumed powder etc.,

snānaśīla mfn practicing (normal) religious ablutions, fond of bathing,

snapita mfn bathed, washed, sprinkled, wetted, cleansed,

√*snas* 1266/3 see *snus* to eat, to disappear, to take, DP in *nirasana* spitting,

snasā f. a tendon, muscle,

snāta mfn bathed, washed, cleansed or purified from (5th or comp.), immersed or versed in, an initiated householder,

snātaka mfn who has performed the ablution customary at the end of being a religious pupil,

snātra n. a bath, bathing,

snātvā ind. having bathed,

snaya m. bathing, ablution, purification by washing,

snava m. oozing, dripping,

snāva m. any sinew or ligament in a human or animal body, tendon, muscle, nerve, vein, the string of a bow,

snāyin mfn performing religious ablutions

snāyu f.n. any sinew or ligament in a human or animal body, tendon, , muscle, nerve, vein, the string of a bow,

snāyubandha m. sinew-band, bowstring,

sneha 1267/2 mfn. oiliness, fattiness, greasiness, unctuousness, lubricity, viscidity, oil, grease, fat, anything oily, m. smoothness, glossiness, blandness, tenderness, love, attachment to, fondness or affection for, moisture, a fluid of the body

snehaka mfn kind, affectionate, causing affection, conciliating,

snehala mfn full of affection, fond of, tender

snehana 1267/3 mfn anointing, lubricating, feeling, affection, n. unction, lubrication, rubbing or smearing with, being or becoming oily, feeling affection

snehin mfn oily, unctuous, fat, affectionate, friendly, attached to or fond of (comp.), m. a friend, a painter,

snehita mfn anointed, smeared with oil, loved, beloved, kind, affectionate, m. a friend,

snehiti f. slaughter, carnage,

snīḍha mfn bland, attached, tender,

snigdha 1267/2 oily, sticky, viscous, glossy, resplendent , greasy, fat, attached, affectionate, tender, friendly

√snih 1267/1 Cl 4 P A *snihayati (te),* to be adhesive, sticky, glutinous, or viscid or moist, to be fixed upon, to be attached to or fond of, feel affection for, Cl 1 P *snehati,* caus/pass. *snihayate* or Cl 10 P *snehayati* to make unctuous or greasy or moist, to render pliant or subject, subdue, to kill, slay,
DP in *prīti* (Cl 4) feeling or having affection for, (Cl 10) in *snehana* making unctuous, causing to love,
2. f. wetness, moisture, mfn loving, affectionate,

snihiti f. moisture,

snihyati (+7th) falls in love, he loves

√snu 1267/3 Cl 2 P *snauti, snute,* to drip, distil, trickle, emit fluid, yield milk, caus. *snāvayati,* DP in *prasravaṇa* dripping, trickling, distilling,
2. ifc. dripping, trickling, sprinkling,
3. n. the level summit or edge of a mountain, table-land, surface, height,
4. a sinew, tendon, muscle,
5. an affix to roots forming adjectives expressive of an aptitude to do what is implied by the root.

√snuh 1268/1 *snuhayati* to vomit, to be moist, DP in *udgiraṇa* vomiting,
2. mfn vomiting, one who vomits,

√snus 1268/1 Cl 4 P *snusyati* to eat, to disappear, to take, DP in *adana* eating, *ādana* accepting, or *adarśana* disappearing, becoming invisible,

√śo 1091/1 Cl 3 P A *śiśāti , śiśīte,* Cl 4 P *śyati,* to whet, sharpen, (A. one's own weapons or horns), caus. *śāyayati* DP in *tanu-karaṇa* (Cl 4) sharpening, making thin, attenuation,

√so 1. 1248/2 Cl 4 P (usually with prepositions) *syati,* to destroy, kill, finish, caus. *sāyayati,* DP in *anta-karmana* finishing, completing, bringing to an end,

śobha 1092/1 mfn bright, brilliant, handsome, m. lustre,
name of a class of gods,
f. (*ā*) splendour, brilliance, lustre,

śobhana mfn beautiful, brilliant, splendid, excellent, glorious, magnificent, propitious, auspicious, virtuous, moral, correct, right,
ifc, superior to or better than,
m. a burnt offering, a planet, turmeric, a yellow pigment,
f. (*ā*) a beautiful woman,
n. the act of adorning, causing to look beautiful, anything propitious or auspicious, welfare, prosperity, moral good, virtue, brilliance, a lotus, tin,

śobhate 1083/1 beautifies, embellishes, 1/s/pres/indic/mid he adorns,

śobhiṣṭha mfn most swiftly moving onward or most beautiful, most brilliant,

śocanīya, deplorable, lamentable, woeful, pitiable,

śocati 1081/1 root *śuc* to grieve, suffer, 1/s/p/a he or she regrets or grieves

śocis n. flame, beam, heat, light, radiance, colour, splendour, beauty, mfn shining, brilliant,

śociṣ -keśa mfn with locks of flame,

śociṣṭha mfn most brilliant or bright flaming, shining very much,

śocitum infinitive to mourn, to grieve

sodaka mfn having/containing water,

sodara mfn born from the same womb, brother, (*ī*) f. sister

ṣoḍaśa(n) sixteen,

soḍha mfn borne, endured, tolerated, patient, enduring,

śodhana mfn cleaning, purifying, cleansing, refining, purgative,
n. the act of cleaning, purifying, correcting, improving, refining (metals), a means of purification, clearing up, sifting, investigation,

examination, correction, payment, acquittance, justifying, exculpating

soḍhum to endure, bear, tolerate, infin. infin. √*sah* 1192/3

sodvega mfn agitated, disturbed,

sodyama mfn prepared/equipped for battle,

sodyoga mfn energetic, enterprising, violent, dangerous,

so'ham I am he, or I am That,

śoka 1091/1 mfn. burning, hot, *m.* sorrow, grief, anguish, pain, flame, glow, heat,

śokaja mfn grief-born, produced by sorrow,

śokajaṁ vāri grief -born water, tears,

śokamokṣa m. freedom from sorrow

śokātiga mfn having crossed over sorrow, free from mental unhappiness, overcoming sorrow,

sola mfn cold, m. coldness, astringent,

soma m. juice, extract, the juice of the Soma plant, the plant itself, drink of the gods, the moon, nectar,

somapā 1250/1mfn. soma-drinking, m. soma-drinker,

somapeya n. a drinking of soma, (4th) in order to drink the soma,

somavāra Monday, (moonday) *soma* 1249/3 juice, extract from the *soma* plant, one of the most important *Vedic* gods to whom many hymns were dedicated, identified with the moon or the god of the moon, the moon or moon-god.

somya O good looking or amiable one, mfn having to do with soma, i.e. soma-offerer,

√*śoṇ* 1091/2 Cl 1 P *śoṇati* to be or become red, to go, move, approach, DP in *varṇa* becoming red, *gati* going,

śoṇa mfn red, deep red, m. redness, fire,

sonaha m. garlic,

śoṇita n. blood, the sap of trees, resin, saffron, mfn red,

sonmāda mfn mad, insane,

sopādhi mfn restricted, limited, qualified by some condition , ind. conditionally

sopahāsa mfn sneering, sarcastic,

sopalambha 'associated with experience of things' (Gam.),

sopākhya mfn having qualifications, 'one about whom anything can be affirmed,

sopakrama mfn set about, undertaken,

sopāna n. staircase, ladder, steps to,

soparodha mfn obstructed, impeded, favoured, respectful, considerate,

sopasarga mfn meeting with difficulties, obstacles, unbecoming, unpleasant (speech), portentous, possessed by an evil spirit, (in gram.) preceded by a preposition,

sopavāsa mfn one who fasts or fasted,

śoṣa 1092/2 mfn. drying up

śoṣaṇa mfn drying up, draining, parching, removing, destroying, n. drying up, desiccation, suction, making dry, draining, dry ginger

śoṣayati causes to dry up, wither 1/s/pres/indic/caus/act √*śuṣ*

sotu m. extraction of Soma, libation,

sovāla mfn blackish or smoke-coloured, smoky, m. smokiness,

√*spand* 1268/1 Cl 1 A P *spandate (ti),* to quiver, throb, twitch, tremble, throb with life, quicken (as a child in the womb), to kick (as an animal), to make any quick movement, move, be active, to flash into life, come suddenly to life, caus. *spandayati* to cause to quiver or shake, to move, DP in *kiñcit-calana* shaking, trembling,

spanda m. activity, vibration, motion,

spandabhāsa reflection of vibration or movement,

spandana mfn making a sudden movement, kicking (as a cow), m. a kind of tree, n. throbbing, pulsation, twitching, trembling, agitation, throbbing with life, quickening (a child in the womb),

spandavastha state of vibration or motion,

spandita 1268/2 mfn quivering, trembling,

set in motion, produced, n. a pulsation, throb, movement or activity (of the mind), (from caus. √*spand*)

√*spardh* Cl 1 A to emulate, compete, rival, vie or cope with, contend or struggle for, DP in *saṅgharṣa* contending,

spardha mfn emulous, envious,

spardhā 1268/2 mfn emulous, envious f. emulation, rivalry, envy, competition for or with, desire for

spardhita mfn contending or competing together, emulating, envious, jealous contended with challenged, denied,

spārha mfn desirable, enviable, excellent,

spariśa m.touch,

sparśa 1269/1mfn touching, m. touch, sense of touch, contact, collective name of the 25 consonants, (in phil.) the quality of tangibility, any quality perceptible by touching an object –heat, cold, smoothness, etc., feeling, sensation, air, wind,

sparśaka mfn touching, feeling, a toucher,

sparśana mfn touching, handling, affecting, acting upon, m. air, wind, n. the act of touching, touch, contact, sensation, sense of touch, organ of sensation or feeling, sensitive nerve, gift, donation

sparśanaka n. that which touches (the skin),

sparśatanmātra the essence of the sense of touch, subtle sense of touch,

sparśendriya n. the sense of touch,

sparśika mfn tangible, palpable, perceptible,

sparśin mfn ifc. touching, handling, reaching or penetrating to,

sparśitṛ mfn who or what touches, feels or perceives

√*spaś* 1268/2 to see, behold, perceive, espy, caus. *spāśayati (te)*, to make clear, show, to perceive, observe, 2. m. one who looks or beholds, a watcher, spy, messenger, 3. Cl 1 P A *spaśati (te)*, to bind, fetter, stop, hinder, caus. *spāśayati* DP in *bandhana* binding, obstructing, or *sparśana* touching, 4. Cl 10 P *spāśayati* to take or take hold of, to unite, join, embrace, DP in *grahaṇa* taking, or *saṁśleṣaṇa* uniting,

spaṣṭa mfn clearly perceived or discerned, distinct, clear, evident, plain, real, true, correct, intelligible, 2. mfn bound, fettered,

spaṣṭīkṛta ppp. made clear, explained,

√*sphar* 1269/3 Cl 6 P see *sphur*, caus. *sphārayati* to expand, open or diffuse widely, to bend, discharge a bow, DP in *sphuraṇa* throbbing, shaking,

sphara or *spharaka* m. a shield,

sphāra mfn extensive, wide, large, great, abundant, violent, strong, m. a shock, slap, bang, m.n. a bubble or flaw (in gold), much, abundance,

sphaṭa m. a snake's expanded hood, f. alum

sphāṭika m. a drop of water, n. crystal,

sphāti f. breeding, fattening (of cattle), increase, growth, prosperity,

sphaṭika m. crystal, quartz,

sphāṭika mfn made of crystal, crystalline, n. crystal, n. a kind of sandal,

√*sphāy* 1270/1 Cl 1 A *sphāyate* to grow fat, become, bulky, swell, increase, expand, to resound, caus. *sphāvayati* to fatten, swell, strengthen, increase, augment, DP in *vṛddhi* expanding, growing,

spheman m. fatness, abundance,

sphic or *sphij* f. a buttock, hip, (*cau* or *jau* du.) the hips, buttocks,

sphigī f. = *sphic*

sphira mfn fat, much, abundant,

√*sphiṭ* 1270/2 Cl 10 P *spheṭayati* to hurt, injure, kill DP in *snehana* making unctuous, causing to love,

sphīta mfn swollen, enlarged, thriving, prosperous, successful, much abundant, heavy (with rain, a cloud), dense (as smoke),

sphīti f. welfare, prosperity,

√*sphiṭṭ* 1270/2 Cl 10 P *spheṭṭayati* to hurt,

injure, kill, DP in *hiṁsā* hurting, killing,

sphoṭa m. bursting, opening, expansion, disclosure, a swelling, boil, tumour, a little bit or fragment, a roar, (in phil.) sound (conceived as eternal, indivisible, and creative), the eternal and imperceptible element of sounds and words and the real vehicle of the idea which bursts or flashes on the mind when a sound is uttered,
"..a point which expands and in its expansion is its activity. This expansion is very fast, an explosion in consciousness. A *sphoṭa* is a sound, a creative desire, a single particle of consciousness, and it holds the cause, the action and its effects. It also holds the law governing the movement of cause, through action into effect. This is the first step in speech when the forces of *parā* are gathered to a point for action." L.M.

sphoṭana mfn breaking or splitting asunder, crushing, destroying, removing, (in gram.) the separation of certain conjunct consonants by the insertion of an audible vocal sound, m. n.'crusher', (in gram.) 'divider' a kind of vocal sound audible between partic. conjunct consonants,
n. the act of breaking or tearing asunder, winnowing grain, shaking or waving the arms, cracking the fingers,

sphoṭinī f. a cucumber,

√*sphuḍ* 1270/3 Cl 6 P *sphuḍati* to cover, DP in *sañcalana* moving about, agitation

√*sphuṇḍ* 1270/3 Cl 1 A *sphuṇḍate* to open, expand, Cl 10 P *sphuṇḍayati* to jest, DP in *parihāsa* (cl10) jesting, joking, laughing at,

√*sphul* 1271/1 Cl 6 P *sphulati* to tremble, throb, vibrate, to dart forth, to collect, to slay, kill, DP in *sañcalana* trembling, vibrating, collecting,

sphuliṅga m. a spark,

√*sphuṇṭ* 1270/3 Cl 1 P *sphuṇṭati,* to open, expand, Cl 10 P *sphuṇṭayati* to jest, joke, laugh, DP in *viśaraṇa* (cl1) dissolving, opening, expanding, in *parihāsa* (cl10) jesting, joking, laughing at,

√*sphur* 1271/1 Cl 6 P *sphurati (te),* to spurn, to dart, bound, rebound, spring, tremble, throb, quiver, to flash, glitter, gleam, glisten, twinkle, sparkle, to shine, be brilliant or distinguished, to break forth, start into view, be evident or manifest, become displayed or expanded, to hurt, destroy, caus. *sphorayati* to stretch, draw or bend (a bow), to bring forward an argument for consideration, to cause to shine, eulogize, praise excessively, *sphurayati* to fill with, DP in *sphuraṇa* throbbing, trembling, shaking
2. ifc. quivering, trembling

sphuraṇa 1271/1 mfn glittering, sparkling, n. the act of trembling, throbbing, vibration, pulsation, quivering or throbbing of parts of the body (as indicating good or bad luck), springing or breaking forth, expansion, manifestation, flashing, coruscation, twinkling, glittering

spṛhā f. desire, longing, wish, hankering,

√*spurch* 1271/1 see *sphūrch, sphūrj*, DP in *vistṛti* forgetting, spreading, extending,

√*sphūrj* 1271/2 Cl 1 P *sphūrjati* to rumble, roar, thunder, crash, burst forth, be displayed, appear, caus. *sphūrjayati* to crash, crackle, DP in *vajr-nirghoṣa* thundering,

sphūrja m. the crashing sound of thunder, Indra's thunderbolt, sudden outbreak

sphūrti 1271/1 f. breaking forth visibly, manifestation. quivering, throbbing, -*mātra* – 804/2 ifc. measure, quantity, the full or simple measure of anything, nothing but, entirely *sphūrtimātraḥ* (A) pure consciousness

sphūrtimat mfn throbbing, tremulous, agitated, tender-hearted, m. a follower or worshipper of *Śiva*

√*sphuṭ* 1270/2 Cl 6 P, Cl 1 PA *sphuṭati, sphoṭati (te),* to burst or become suddenly rent asunder, burst or split open (with a sound), part asunder, to expand, blossom, bloom, to disperse, run away, to crack (joints of the fingers), to burst into view, appear suddenly, to abate (as a disease), caus. *sphuṭayati* to burst open or into view, to make clear or evident, *sphoṭayati* to burst or rend suddenly, break, split, divide, to put out (eyes), to shake, wag, brandish, to push aside (a bolt), to crackle (as fire), to hurt, destroy, kill, to winnow, DP in *vikasana* (cl6) expanding, opening, blowing, blossoming, in *vikasana* becoming visible, (cl1) , in *bhedana* (cl10) piercing, breaking, in *viśaraṇa* (cl1) bursting open, breaking forth,

sphuṭa mfn open, opened, expanded, blossomed, evident, manifest, clear, distinct, diffused, extensive, wide, extraordinary, strange, full of, filled with, white, m. the expanded hood of a snake, *(am)* ind. distinctly, evidently, certainly,

sphuṭacandratāraka mfn radiant with the moon and stars, (said of night)

sphuṭākṣara mfn having clear words, clearly expressed speech,

sphuṭaphenarāji m. (the sea) bright with lines of foam,

sphuṭapuṇḍarīka n. the expanded (lotus of the) heart,

sphuṭārtha m. clear sense or meaning,

sphuṭatva n. being open, openness, manifestness,

sphuṭavaktṛ mfn speaking distinctly/frankly

sphuṭībhāva m. becoming clear or evident,

sphuṭīkaraṇa n. the act of making clear or evident, manifestation, making true or correct, correction,

sphuṭita mfn burst, budded, laughed at, splay-footed,

sphya m. n. wooden splinter, shaped like a knife and as long as the arm, for use at the sacrifice, a spar or boom, a kind of oar,

√*spṛ* 1268/3 Cl 5 P *spṛṇoti spṛṇute* to release, extricate or deliver from, save, gain, win, caus *spārayati* to attract to oneself, to preserve, save, rescue, to gladden, delight, gratify, bestow, DP in *prīti* gratifying, or *sevana* protecting, or *calana* moving, trembling

spraṣṭā f. the toucher, feeler

spraṣṭavya gve. to be touched,

spṛdh f. rival, opponent, foe, contest, competition, fight, m. a rival, enemy, desirous, mfn emulous, vying with,

√*spṛh* Cl 10 P *spṛhayati (te*), to be eager, desire eagerly, long for, to envy, be jealous of, DP in *īpsā* desiring,

spṛhā 1269/3 f. eager desire, longing

spṛhita mfn desired, wished for,

√*spṛś* 1268/3 Cl 6 P *spṛśati (te*), to touch, feel with the hand, lay the hand on, graze, stroke, to handle, take hold of, to touch or sip water, wash with water, to touch so as to hurt, injure, harm, to perceive or feel by touch, to touch, come into contact, to reach or penetrate to, to come up to, equal, to act upon, affect, to endow or fill with, to fall to the lot of, come upon, visit, afflict, take hold of make one's own, appropriate, attain to, obtain, experience, undergo, to grant, bestow, caus. *sparśayati (te*) to cause to touch, bring into immediate contact with, to convey to, fill or cover with, perceive by touch or feel, to offer, present,
DP in *saṁsparśana* touching,

2. mfn. touching, coming into contact with, reaching to, experiencing, betraying,

-spṛś ifc. mfn touching,coming into contact with,

spṛśa mfn touching, reaching to, m. touch, contact,

spṛśan touching, pres/act/part.

spṛśati he touches

spṛṣṭa mfn touched, felt with the hand, handled, defiled, (in gram.) formed by complete contact of the organs of utterance (all consonants except semivowels and *s, ṣ, ś, h*),

spṛṣṭaka n. a kind of embrace,

spṛṣṭi f. touch, touching, contact,

spṛt mfn ifc. delivering one's self from, removing, avoiding, f. kind of brick

spṛta mfn saved, gained, won,

√*sṛ* 1244/3 Cl 1.3. P *sarati (te),* also *dhārati*, and *sisarti* to run, flow, speed, glide, move, go, exert oneself, to blow (as wind), to run away, escape, run after, pursue, to go towards, to go against, attack, assail, to cross, traverse, A. to begin to flow, (said of the fluid surrounding the fetus), to set in motion, strike (a lute), to remove, push aside (a braid of hair), put in array, arrange, make visible, show, manifest, to nourish, foster, A. *sārayate* to cause oneself to be driven, drive (in a carriage), DP in *gati* going,

√*śī* 1088/2 Cl 9 P *śṛṇāti* to crush, rend, break, (A. with ref. to oneself as in breaking one's arm), to kill (game), to fallout or off, to be worn out, decay, wither, fade,
caus. *śārayati*, DP in *hiṁsā* hurting, killing,

√*sṝ* cl 9 P *sṛṇāti* to hurt, injure, kill,

√*śrā* 1097/2 (or *śrai*) Cl 1 or 4 P *śrāyati* , Cl 2 P *śrāti* to cook, boil, seethe, mature, ripen, caus. *śrapayati* to cause to cook or boil, roast, bake, to make hot, to cause to sweat, DP in *pāka* cooking,

śrad ind. heart, used with *dhā* and 4th of person, e.g. *śrad asmai dhatta* (your) heart to him give ye, i.e. trust in him, have faith in him,

śrad-dadhāna 1095/3mfn. having faith, trustful, full of faith

śrad-dadhat trusting, trustful,

śraddha 1095/3 mfn having faith, believing in, trusting, faithful, having confidence,
n. a ceremony in honour of and for the benefit of dead relatives, (not a funeral ceremony), last rites,

śrad√dhā to have faith or faithfulness, have belief or confidence, believe, be true or trustful, (with *na*) to disbelieve, to credit, think anything true, to believe or have faith in or be true to, to expect anything (2nd) from (5th), to consent, assent to, approve, welcome, to be desirous of (2nd), wish to (inf.),caus. *–dhāpayati* to make faithful, render trustful,inspire confidence,

śraddhā 2. f. faith, trust, confidence, trustfulness, faithfulness, belief in, wish, desire,

śraddhśmaya full of faith, believing,

śraddhāvat mfn assenting, consenting,

śraddhāvirahita mfn devoid of faith, disbelieving,

śraddhayā with faith

śraddhayānvita imbued with faith

śraddhiva mfn credible,

sragvin mfn wearing a wreath, having garlands,

√*śrai* 1102/3 see √*śrā*

śraiṣṭhya n. supremacy, pre-eminence among,

sraj mfn turning, twisting, winding, f. a wreath of flowers, garland, chaplet worn on the head, circle,

sraja (ifc.) a garland

srāk =*drāk* ind. quickly, speedily, immediately,

srakva m. corner of the mouth, mouth, jaws,

√*śram* 1096/1 Cl 4 P *śrāmyati, śramati (te),* to be or become weary or tired, be tired of doing anything, to make effort, exert oneself, labour in vain, caus. *śrāmayati,* to make weary, tire, to overcome, conquer, subdue, to speak to, address, invite, DP in *tapas* perfoming austerities, or *kheda* being afflicted, distressed,

śrama m. weariness, fatigue, exertion, labour, toil, effort, hard work of any kind (as in bodily mortification), religious exercises and austerity, military exercise, drill,

srāma mfn lame, sick, m. lameness, sickness, disease (esp.) animals,

śramaṇa mfn making effort or exertion, toiling, labouring, esp. following a menial or toilsome task, base, vile, bad, naked, one who performs acts of mortification or austerity, an ascetic, monk, devotee, religious mendicant, a Buddhist monk or mendicant, also applied to a Jain mendicant now more commonly called Yati,

√*śrambh* 1096/2 Cl 1 A *śrambhate* to be careless or negligent, to trust, confide, DP in *pramāda* being careless or negligent,

√*srambh* 1274/1 see *śrambh* DP in *viśvāsa* trusting, confiding,

√*sraṁs* 1273/3 or *sras , śraṁś, śraṁs* Cl 1 A *sraṁsate (ti),* to fall, drop, fall down, slip off, get loose from, to fall asunder or to pieces, to hang down, dangle, droop, to be broken, perish, cease, to go, caus. *sraṁsayati* to cause to fall down, loosen, to disturb, remove, destroy, DP in *avasraṁsana* falling, dropping down, slipping off or down,
2. see *śrambh*

√*śraṇ* 1095/3 Cl 1 P *śraṇati* or Cl 10 P *śrāṇayati* to give, grant, present, DP (Cl 1) in *gati* going or *dāna* giving, (cl10) in *dāna* giving

√*śraṅg* 1095/3 Cl 1 P *śraṅgati* to go, move, DP in *gati* going,

√*sraṅk* 1274/1 see *śraṅk*

√*śraṅk* 1095/2 Cl 1 A *śraṅkate* to go, move, creep, DP in *gati* going

śrānta mfn exhausted, wearied,

śrāntāgata mfn wearied and arrived, i.e. arriving wearied,

√*śranth* see *śrath* to be loosened or untied or unbent, become loose or slack, yield, give way, to make slack, disable, disarm, A. to loosen one's own bonds, to remit, pardon, DP (Cl 9) in *vimocana* loosening, liberating, *pratiharṣa* delighting repeatedly, or *saṁdarbha* collecting, Cl 1 in *śauthilya* being weak or loose, Cl 10 in *sandharbha* fastening, tying

sras mfn falling, dropping,

srasta mfn fallen, dropped, slipped off, fallen from (5th), loosened, relaxed, hanging down, pendent, sunk in (as eyes), separated,

sraṣṭāra m. a creator

sraṣṭṛ m. a creator, the Supreme Creator, the creator of the universe, mfn one who emits, discharges, projects, originates,

√*śrath* 1096/1 or *śranth* Cl 9 P *śrathnāti,* also *śrathnīte, śrinthati, śrathati, śrāthayati, śranthati (te),* to be loosened or untied, or unbent, become loose or slack, yield, give way, to make slack, disable, disarm, A. to loosen one's own bonds, caus, *śrathayati,* to loosen, untie, relax, (A. to become loose, yield), to remit, pardon (sin), *śrāthayati* to strive eagerly, endeavour, use exertion, DP (Cl 10) in *mokṣaṇa* untying, loosening, killing, in *prayatna* making effort, in *daurbalya* being weak, impotent, (Cl 1) *hiṁsā* injuring,

śrauta 1103/2 mfn relating to the ear or hearing, to be heard, audible, relating to sacred tradition, enjoined by the *śruti,*

srautika m. a pearl shell,

srautovaha mfn relating to a river,

srava m. flowing, streaming, a flow of (comp.) a waterfall, urine,

śravāka (G) a listener, disciple,

śravaṇa 1096/3 n. the act of hearing, that which is heard, acquiring knowledge by hearing the truth, or by hearing, learning, study. the first stage of reflection. (see *mananam, nididhyāsanam*), m. ear, n. fame,

sravaṇa 1274/2 n. streaming, flowing, flowing off, premature abortion, sweat, perspiration, urine,

srāvaṇa m. a month (=July-August), n. ear, flowing off, urine, flowing, mfn shedding, causing to flow,

sravantī f. flowing (water) stream, river,

śravas n. 1. sounds esp. loud praise, 2. glory, fame,

√*sṛbh* 1245/3 or *sṛmbh* Cl 1 P *sarbhati, sṛmbhati* to kill, slay, injure, DP in *hiṁsā* injuring,

√*śṛdh* 1088/1 Cl 1 P A *śardhati (te*), to fart, mock at, ridicule, defy, to moisten, become moist or wet, caus. *śardhayati* DP in *śabda-kutsā* (Cl 1) farting, *undana* moistening, *prahasana* (Cl 10) insulting, mocking, ridiculing,

√*srek* 1275/1 also *śrek, sek, svek,* Cl 1 A *srekate* to go move, DP in *gati* going,

śreṣṭa mfn classic, best,

śreṣṭatā f. excellence,

śreṣṭha best, most splendid, most excellent, superlative, most auspicious or salutary, chief, distinguished, most excellent, f.(*ā*) excellent woman,

śreyas mfn (comparative) better, preferable, more splendid or beautiful, more excellent or distinguished, most excellent, best, propitious, well disposed to (6th), auspicious, fortunate, conducive to welfare or prosperity, n. the better state, the better fortune or condition, m. good (as opposed to evil), welfare, bliss, fortune, happiness, the bliss of final emancipation, felicity, ind. better, rather, rather than, the higher good, the supreme good, comparative,

śreyāṁsa mfn fairer, more beautiful or excellent, better, n. welfare, prosperity

śreyasa (in cpds.) for *śreyas,* n. welfare, happiness, bliss, (mostly ifc.),

śṛgāla m. fox or jackal, a rogue, cheat, a coward,

√*śri* 1. 1098/1 Cl 1 P A *śrayati (te),* P. to cause to rest or lean on or in, fix on fasten to, direct or turn towards, (esp.) spread or diffuse (light or radiance or beauty) over, A. to lean on, rest on, be supported or fixed on, abide in or on, A.P. to go to, approach, resort or have recourse to, tend towards, A. to go into, enter, fall to the lot ot take possession of, A.P. to attain, undergo, get into any state or condition, to show, betray, to honour, worship, caus. *śrāpayati, śrāyayati,* DP in *sevā* serving, 3. light, lustre, = 3. *śrī*

√*śrī* 1. 1098/2 3. Cl 9 P A *śrīṇati, śrīṇīte* to mix, mingle, cook, to burn, flame, diffuse light, DP in *pāka* cooking,

śrī 2. mfn mixing, mingling, mixed with, f. mixing, cooking,

śrī 3. f. diffusing light or radiance, light, lustre, radiance, splendour, glory, beauty, grace, loveliness, prosperity, welfare, good fortune, success, wealth, treasure, riches, high rank, power, might, majesty, royal dignity, honorific prefix – sacred, holy, respectful title, mfn. diffusing light or radiance, splendid, radiant, beautifying, adorning,

śrībhagavān the Blessed Lord, the Blessed One
√*sridh* cl 1 *sredhati,* P. to fail, err, blunder, f. erring, failing, a misbeliever, foe,
śrīmad bhāgavatam a famous *pūrāṇa* – the life and exploits of *Kṛṣṇa*
śrīmān mister,
śrīmat 1100/2 splendid, glorious, charming, illustrious, eminent, prosperous, of high rank or dignity, wealthy, beautiful, fortunate, lovely auspicious,
√*śriṣ* 1098/2 Cl 1 P *śreṣati* to burn, DP in *dāha* burning,
śrita 1098/2 mfn clinging or attached to , gone to, approached, had recourse to, served, honoured, worshipped, one who has gone or resorted to, having attained or fallen or got into any condition, having assumed a form, subservient, subordinate, auxiliary,
śritakṣama mfn one who has had recourse to patience, composed, tranquil,
śritasattva mfn one who has taken courage or resolution,
śritavat mfn one who has taken refuge with,
√*sriv* 1274/2 or *srīv* Cl 4 P *srīvyati* to fail, turn out badly, to go, to become dry, *srīvayati* to frustrate, thwart, DP in *gati* going or *śoṣaṇa* becoming dry,
śriyā 1100/2 f. prosperity, happiness,
√*sṛj* 1245/2,1 Cl 6 P *sṛjati (te), sarjati,* to let go or fly, discharge, throw, cast, hurl at, to cast or let go (a measuring line), to emit, pour forth, shed, cause to flow (rain, streams), to utter a sound, to turn or direct glances, to let loose, cause (horses) to go quickly, A. to speed, run, hasten, to release, set free, to open (a door), to publish, proclaim, to draw out and twist (a thread), twist, wind, spin, A. *sṛjyate* for oneself, (in older language A. to emit from oneself, create, procreate, produce, beget, to procure, grant, bestow, to use, employ, to get, obtain, acquire, to hang on, fasten to, caus. *sarjayati (te),* to cause to let loose, let go, create, (ifc) letting loose, emitting, discharging, producing, creating, DP in *visarga* quitting, abandoning, leaving,
sṛj ifc. creating, producing, begetting, letting loose, emitting, discharging,
sṛjai let me create! 3/s/impv/mid
sṛjāmi √*sṛj* 1245/1 to let go or fly, emit, pour forth, emit from oneself, create, produce, I create, 3/s/pres/indic/act
sṛjati he sheds
sṛka m. missile or lance, arrow, spear, wind, a lotus flower,
sṛṇi m.f. an elephant goad, m. the moon, an enemy, f. a sickle,
śṛṅga n. the horn of an animal, a tusk, a peak, crag, summit, highest point,
śṛṅgāra m. love, sexual passion or desire, elegant dress, fine garmentts, finery, the ornaments of an elephant, n. gold, red-lead, fragrant powder for dress or person, cloves, undried ginger, black aloe-wood, mfn pretty, handsome, dainty,
sṛṅkā f. necklace
sṛṅkhala m. a chain, a young camel,
śṛṇu listen! 2/s/impv
śṛnvan hearing pres/act/part 1
śṛṇuyāt he should hear/listen 1/s/opt/act √*śru*
śṛṇoti 1100/3 1/s/pres/indic/act hears
śṛṇu listen, hear 2/s/impv.
śṛṇuta listen pl.
śṛṇute hear 1100/3
śṛṇu 1/s/impv/indic/act. hear!
śṛṇvan from *śṛṇoti* pres/act/part. hearing
śromata n. celebrity, renown, glory,
√*śroṇ* 1102/3 Cl 1 P *śroṇati* to collect, accumulate, to go, move, DP in *saṅghāta* collecting,
śrotas n. the ear
srotas n. the current or bed of a river, a river, stream, torrent, water, a nutrient course or current in the

body, a body aperture,

śrotavya to be heard or listened to, audible, worth hearing, n. the moment for hearing, 'it must be heard' fut.part.

śrotṛ m. the hearer

śrotra 1103/1 n. the organ of hearing, ear, the act of hearing or listening to, comprehending the Veda or sacred knowledge,

śrotriya 1103/1 mfn learned in the Veda, conversant with sacred knowledge, docile, modest, well-behaved, m. a Brāhman versed in the Veda, theologian, divine,

śrotriyāḥ 'versed in Vedic studies and observances' (Gam.), (pl.)

śrotṛ 1103/1one who hears, hearing, a hearer

srotyā f. flowing water, a wave, surge, stream, river,

śrotyasi you will hear or listen 2/s/fut/act

śrotavya mfn to be heard or listened to, audible, worth hearing, n. the moment for hearing, impers. 'it must be heard',

śrotavyasya of the to-be-heard, with that which is to be heard, 6/s/m gerundive

√*sṛp* 1245/3 Cl 1 P *sarpati (te),* to creep, crawl, glide, slink, move gently or cautiously, to slip into, caus. *sarpayati,* DP in *gati* going,

sṛpa m. the moon

sṛpra mfn slippery, oily, smooth, supple, lithesome, m. the moon, n. honey,

sṛṣṭa 1245/2 mfn let go, discharged, thrown etc. given up, abandoned, brought forth, produced, created, provided, filled or covered with, engrossed by, intent upon (3rd), firmly resolved upon (4th,7th), ornamented, abundant, much, many, ascertained,

sṛṣṭavat mfn one who has let go or created or made,

sṛṣṭi 1245/2 f. emission, production, procreation, creation, the creation of the world, nature, the absence or existence of properties(?) distribution of gifts, liberality, a kind of brick, procreation, distribution of gifts, letting loose, production, emission, liberality, kind of brick,

sṛṣṭi-bheda difference in creation, i.e. one ego is the result of *sattva* predominance, another of *rajas* etc.

sṛṣṭi-kalpana creative ideation, (U)

sṛṣṭikartṛ mfn creating, a creator,

sṛṣṭimat mfn engaged in the work of creation,

sṛṣṭiunmukha mfn ready or prone to create

sṛṣṭvā having created, having sent forth, having let go

śṛta 1088/1 mfn cooked, boiled, esp. said of water, milk and ghee, n. cooked food, boiled milk,

sṛta 1244/3 mfn. running, going, gone, passed away

sṛti 1245/1 f a road, path, producing,

śru 1100/3 cl5 P *śṛṇoti, śṛṇute* to hear, listen or attend to, study, learn, be attentive, be obedient, obey, to be heard or learnt (from a teacher), to be taught or stated (in a book), caus. *śrāvayati (te) śravayati,* , to cause to be heard or learnt, announce, proclaim, declare, to cause to hear, inform, instruct, communicate, relate, tell, DP in *śravaṇa* hearing,

√*sru* 1274/2 Cl 1 P *sravati (te*), to flow, stream, gush forth, issue from, to flow with, shed, emit, drop, distil, to leak, trickle, to fail, not turn out well, to waste away, perish, disappear, to slip or issue out before the right time (a foetus), to come in, accrue (as interest), caus. *srāvayati,* to cause to flow, shed, spill, to set in motion, stir up, arouse, DP in *gati* going (said of liquids),

srū f. a stream, flow, spring, fountain,

sruc f. a large sacrificial ceremony ladle,

śruta mfn heard, listened to, been heard,

heard of, n. that which is heard from the teacher, that which is learned, learning,

srūta mfn gone, dried, withered,

śrutam n. oral tradition, sacred knowledge, anything heard,

śrutasya of the heard, of that which has been heard, 6/s/m ppp.

śrutavān heard, one who has heard

śrutavant mfn possessing learning, learned,

śruti f.'verbal testimony' HH, what has been heard, revelation, the veda, - word of the Lord, hearing, listening, the ear, organ or power of hearing, that which is heard or perceived with the ear, sacred knowledge orally transmitted from generation to generation, the Veda, as eternally heard by certain holy sages thus differing from *smṛti* (remembered and handed down in writing), learning, scholarship,

śrutimat having ears, having hearing, possessed of knowledge, learned, having the veda as source or authority,

śrutipradhāna superiority of the *śruti* as the basis of scriptural proof,

śrutipramāṇa testimony or proof based on the Veda (U)

śrutvā ind. having heard

śrutya mfn worthy to be heard (of a hymn), goodly, glorious,

srutya mfn relating to a road or path,

sruva m. a small sacrificial ladle,

śrūyatām let it be heard! listen!

stabaka m. a cluster of blossoms, bunch of flowers, a feather of a peacock's tail, a tassel, a quantity, a chapter,

stabakita mfn full of blossoms,

stabdha 1258/1 firmly fixed, supported, immovable, paralysed, stubborn, obstinate, dull, proud, arrogant,

stabdhavastha stunned state of the mind – an obstacle in meditation, (U),

stabdhalocana mfn having immovable i.e. unwinking eyes,

stabdhī kṛ make rigid or stiff (as if dead),

stabha m. a goat or ram,

√*stag* DP in *samvaraṇa* hiding, covering,

stāgha mfn shallow,

staḥ pron. two are, they two are

√*stai* 1260/2 Cl 1 P *stāyati* to put on, adorn, to steal, do anything stealthily, DP in *veṣṭana* putting on, adorning,

stairya n. firmness, hardness, solidity, fixedness, immobility, calmness, tranquillity, continuance, constancy, steadfastness, perseverance, patience,

√*stak* 1257/2 Cl 1 P *stakati* to strike against, DP in *pratīghāta* resisting, repelling, striking against,

√*stam* 1257/3 see 1. *sam*, DP in *avaiklavya* not being confused,

stamba 1257/3 a clump or tuft of grass, any clump, bunch or cluster, a sheaf of corn, a bush, thicket, a post, pillar, the post to which an elephant is tied, a mountain

stambaka m. a clump, bunch, tuft,

√*stambh* 1258/1 or *stabh* Cl 5.9. P *stabhnoti, stabhnāti* or Cl 1 A *stambhate* to fix firmly, support, sustain, prop (esp. the heavens), to support or hold up by contact with, reach up to, to stop, stop up, arrest, make stiff or immovable, paralyse,
A. to rest or lean on, to become stiff or immovable, to become solid,
caus. *stabhāyati* to make firm, support, to stop, arrest, *stambhayati (te)*, to fix, establish, erect, paralyse, make solid, stop, arrest, suppress, check, restrain, DP in *pratibandha* stopping, hindering, paralysing,

stambha 1258/2m. a post, pillar, column, stem, support, propping, strengthening, inflation, pretentiousness, arrogance, fixedness, stiffness, paralysis, becoming hard or solid, stoppage, obstruction, suppression, filling up, stuffing

stambhana stopping the flow of movement,

blocking, paralysing, freezing, stupefaction, promoting contraction

stambhin mfn provided with pillars/columns supporting, puffed up, arrogant, m. the sea,

stambin mfn clumpy, tufty, bushy, shaggy,

√*stan* 1257/2 Cl 1 P *stanati* to resound, reverberate, roar, thunder, to utter inarticulate sounds, caus. *stanayati* it thunders, crackle (as fire), DP in *śabda* (cl1) sounding, in *deva-śabda* thundering, roaring loudly,

stana m. the female breast, nipple,

stanana a hollow cough, rumbling of clouds

stanatha m. roar (of a lion), thunder,

stanathu m. roar (of a lion),

stanita mfn thundering, sounding, n. thunder, loud groaning, the sound of a vibrating bowstring or of hand-clapping,

stara m. a layer, stratum,

staraṇa n. spreading, strewing, scattering, the plastering (of a wall),

stauti 1259/1 he lauds,
1/s/pres/ind/act he praises

stava m. praise, eulogy, song of praise,

stavaka m. praise, eulogy, a praiser,

stavana 1259/1 n. praising, praise

stavaraka m. a fence, railing,

stavi m. m. = *udgātṛ* , a chanter,

stāyu m. thief, robber,

stema m. wetness, moisture,

√*sten* 1260/2 Cl 10 P *stenayati* to steal, rob, with *vācam* to misuse a word, dishonest speech,
DP in *caurya* stealing

stena 1260/2 m. a thief, robber, a kind of perfume, thieving, stealing,

√*step* 1260/2 Cl 1 A *stepate* to flow,
Cl 10 P *stepayati* to send, throw,
DP in *kṣaraṇa* flowing, trickling, distilling, slopping,

steya 1260/2 n. theft, robbery, larceny, anything stolen or liable to be stolen, anything clandestine or private

steyakaraṇa n. the act of stealing or theft

-*stha* suffix, fixed, staying, standing, abiding, being situated in, standing in, dweller

stha 1262/3 mfn. standing, staying, abiding, being situated in, existing or being in or on or among, occupied with, engaged in, devoted to, a place, ground,

stha pron. you (pl.) are
existing, being in on or among

√*sthā* 1262/3, 1262/2 Cl 1 P A *tiṣṭhati* (*te*), to stand, stand firmly, station one's self, stand upon, get upon, take up a position on, to stay, remain, continue in any condition or action, to remain occupied or engaged in, be intent upon, make a practice of, keep on, persevere in any act, to continue to be or exist, endure, to be, exist, be present, be obtainable or at hand, to be with or at the disposal of, belong to, A. plus P. to stand by, abide by, be near to, be on the side of, adhere or submit to, acquiesce in, serve, obey, to stand still, stay quiet, remain stationary, stop, halt, wait, tarry, linger, hesitate, to behave or conduct oneself (with *samam* to behave equally towards anyone), to be directed to or fixed on, to be founded or rest or depend on, to rely on, confide in, to stay at, resort to, to arise from, to desist or cease from, to remain unnoticed, be left alone, caus. *sthāpayati (te),* cause to stand, place, locate, set, lay, fix, station, establish, found, to set up, erect, raise, cause to continue, make durable, strengthen, confirm, to prop up, support, maintain, to affirm, assent, to appoint (to any office), to cause to be, make, appoint or employ as. to fix, settle, determine, resolve, to fix in or on, lead or bring into, direct or turn towards, to introduce or initiate into, instruct in, to make over or deliver up to, to cause to stand still, stop, arrest,

check, restrain, DP in *gati* resorting or going to, *nivṛtti* stopping, being restrained, remain, continue condition,
2. mfn standing, stationary, ifc. standing, being, existing in or on or among,

sthaga mfn cunning, sly, dishonest,
sthāga m. a dead body,
sthagana n. act of covering or hiding,
sthagaṇā f. the earth,
sthagita mfn covered, concealed, closed, shut (as a door), stopped, interrupted
sthaḥ you (two) are
sthairya n. firmness, hardness, solidity, fixedness, stability, immobility, calmness, tranquillity, continuance, permanence, constancy, perseverance, patience, firm attachment to, constant delight in
sthala m. a chapter, section of a book, L. n. dry land, terra firma, a place, spot,
sthāla n. any vessel or receptacle, big tray,
sthalī f. an eminence, table-land, soil, ground, place, spot, n. dry land,
√*sthal* 1261/3 Cl 1 P *sthalati* to stand firm, be firm, DP in *sthāna* standing firm, being firm,
sthāman n. station, seat, place, strength, neighing of a horse,
sthāna 1263/1 n or m. the act of standing, standing firmly, being fixed or stationary, position or posture of the body (in shooting etc.), staying, abiding, being in or on, storing place or storage, firm bearing (of troops), sustaining a charge, state, sphere of activity e.g. the waking state, condition, continued existence, continuance in the same state (i.e. in a kind of neutral state unmarked by gain or loss), continuing as or as long as, a state of perfect tranquillity, station, rank, office, appointment, place of standing or staying, any place, spot, locality, abode, dwelling, house, site, place or room, place for, receptacle of, proper or right place, province, region, domain, sphere, the place or organ of articulation of any sound, any organ of sense, the pitch or key of the voice, note, tone, shape, form, appearance, case, occurrence, cause or object of, a section or division, an open place in a town, plain, square, a holy place, an altar,
sthānabhraṁśa m. abode-ruin, loss of abode, station or rank,
sthānaka n. position, rank, situation, dignity, a place, spot,
sthaṇḍila n. an open unoccupied piece of ground, bare ground, an open field, a boundary, limit, landmark, a heap of clods,
sthānika mfn belonging to a place or site, local, (in gram.) taking the place of anything else, substituted for, m. anyone holding an official post,
sthānin mfn having a place, occupying a position, abiding, permanent, being in the right place, appropriate, (in gram.) that which should be in the place or is to be supplied, m. the original form or primitive element (for which anything is substituted), as opposed to *ādeśa* –the substitute,
sthāṇu mfn standing firmly, stationary, firm, fixed, immovable, m. a stump, trunk, post, pillar (also as a symbol of motionlessness), a kind of spear or dart, a partic. part of a plough, the gnomon of a dial, a partic. perfume,
sthāṇumānuṣya man in the post, a simile used to describe false superimposition due to wrong imagination, (U),
sthāpaka mfn causing to stand, placing, fixing, m. the erector of an image, the directing artist, a kind of stage-director,
sthāpana mfn causing to stand, maintaining,

preserving, fixing, determining, storing, keeping, fixed order or regulation, establishing, establishment, dialectical proof, arranging, regulating or directing, n. causing to stand, placing, fixing, rendering immovable, storage of grain, statement, definition, fixing the thoughts, abstraction, erecting an image etc.

sthāpaya cause to stand, cause to be situated, 2/s/caus/impv/act √*sthā*

sthāpayati (he, she, or it) places

sthāpayitvā ind. causing to stand, having caused to stand, caus. gerund

sthāsnu mfn firm, stationary, immovable, durable, permanent, eternal, patient enduring,

sthāsnutā f. durability, stability, firmness

sthāsu n. bodily strength,

sthātṛ m. a guider, driver (horses etc.), a guide, authority, mfn what stands or stays stationary, immovable,

sthātra n. station, place,

sthaula mfn stout, robust,

sthaulya 1266/2 n. stoutness, bigness, largeness, thickness, grossness, denseness, excessive size or length, doltishness, density of intellect,

sthaura n. firmness, strength, power, sufficient load for a horse or ass,

sthaurin m. a pack-horse, draught-ox,

sthāvara 1264/1 mfn standing still, immovable, L. not endowed with the power of locomotion, n. any stationary or inanimate object, stability, permanence, real estate, a heir-loom, a bowstring, m. a mountain,

sthāvaratā f. condition of being a plant, fixedness, immobility,

sthāvira mfn firm, thick, massy, sturdy, full-grown, old, senile, m. old man, n. old age, commencing at 70 in men and 50 in women, old,

sthāyi 1. f. the action of standing,

sthāyika mfn lasting, enduring, faithful, trustworthy, (*ā*) f. the action of standing,

sthāyin mfn stable, stationary, lasting, enduring, resident, having the form of, faithful, trustworthy,steadfast,

sthāyitā f. *sthāyitva* n. constancy, stability, permanency, steadiness, durability,

stheya mfn to be fixed or settled, placed (as water in a jar),
firmer (comparative of *sthira*),
(*am*) n. 'it is' to be stood still,
it is to be stayed or remained in (7th),
attention is to be fixed on (7th),
m. an arbitrator, umpire, judge,
a domestic priest,

sthin (in cpds.) standing,

sthira 1264/3 mfn. firm, hard, solid, compact fixed, immovable, motion less, still, constant, steadfast, faithful, trustworthy, firmly resolved to, m. the earth,

sthirabuddhi mfn steady-minded, resolute,

sthiramanas mfn firm-minded, steadfast,

sthiramati f. a firm mind, steadfastness, mfn firm-minded, steady,

sthirata steadiness or firmness either of mind (through concentration) or of body (through postures etc.)

sthita 1264/1 mfn standing (firm), staying, resting or abiding in, engaged in, intent upon, devoted or addicted to, performing, protecting, abiding by, conforming to, being in ofice or charge, following, firm, constant, invariable, settled, ascertained, decreed, established, faithful to a promise or agreement, upright, virtuous, being there, existing, present, close at hand, ready, engrossed in, one who has desisted or ceased, standing alone, (*am*) n. standing still, stopping, staying, abiding, remaining, perseverance on the right path,

sthitadhī 1264/2 mfn. steady-minded, firm, unmoved, calm, whose meditation is steady

sthitaprajña 'the man with unshakeable

wisdom', Chapter 2 *bhagavad gītā*, last quarter. 'Essentially, he does everything with utmost attention, great ease and without any claims' HH

sthitasthāpaka elasticity,

sthiti 1264/2 f. standing upright or firmly, not falling, standing, staying, existence, being, remaining, abiding, stay, residence, sojourn, staying, remaining or being in any state or condition, continuance in being, maintenance of life, continued existence, permanence, duration, duration of life, that which continually exists, any situation or state, station, high position, sustenance, maintenance of discipline, establishment of good order, steadfastness in duty, virtuous conduct, rectitude, propriety, constancy, perseverance, devotion or addiction to, intentness on (7th), conviction, custom, usage, settled boundary or bounds, term, limit, standing still, stopping, standing-place, halting, resistance to motion, fixedness, immobility, stability,

√*ṣṭhiv* 1111/1 (or *ṣṭhīv*) Cl 1.4. P *ṣṭhīvati, ṣṭhīvyati* to spit, spit out, spit upon, DP in *nirasana* spitting

√*sthuḍ* 1265/2 = √*thuḍ*, Cl 6 P *sthuḍati* to cover, DP in *saṃvaraṇa* covering, screening,

√*sthūl* 1266/1 Cl 10 A P *sthūlayate, (ti),* to become big or stout or bulky, increase, grow fat, DP in *paribṛṁhaṇa* becoming big or stout,

sthūla mfn large, thick, stout, massive, coarse, gross, rough, dense, dull, stupid, ignorant, tangible, material

sthūla-avidyā f. gross ignorance that envelopes all objects (U)

sthūlabhuk an enjoyer of the gross (material world),

ṣṭhūlabuddhi f. gross intellect,

sthūlaśarīra the gross body, physical body,

sthūlavairāgya dispassion or renunciation of a lower type, (U)

sthūlin m. a camel,

sthūma m. light, the moon,

sthūṇā f. post. pillar, tree trunk or stump, an iron statue, an anvil, a rope, cord,

√*stigh* 1258/3 Cl 5 P *stighnoti stighnute* to step, stride, step up, mount, DP in *āskandana* going towards,

√*stim* 1258/3 or *stīm,* Cl 4 P *stimyati, stīmyati,* to be or become wet or moist, to become fixed or immovable, DP in *ārdrī-bhāva* becoming wet,

√*stīm* 1259/1 see *stim*

stīma mfn sluggish, slow,

stimita mfn wet, moist, fixed, motionless, still, calm, tranquil, soft, gentle, (*am*) ind. pleased, n. moisture, stillness, motionless,

√*stip* 1258/3 Cl 1 A *stepate* to ooze, drip, drop, DP in *kṣaraṇa* flowing, trickling, dropping,

stīrṇa mfn spread, strewn, scattered,

stīrvi m. an officiating priest, a kind of grass, the sky, atmosphere, water, blood, the body, fear,

stiyā f. still or stagnant water,

stobha chanted interjections in a Sāma song, e.g. hum, ho, torpor, paralysis, disrespect,

stoka m. a drop (water etc), a spark, mfn little, small, short, (*am*) ind. a little, slightly, gradually, a *cātaka* bird,

stoma m. praise, a hymn, a chant, a heap, collection, number, n. the head, riches, wealth, grain, corn, an iron-pointed stick or staff, mfn crooked, bent,

stomavardhana mfn delighting in hymns o praise,

√*stomaya* 1259/2 Nom P *stomayati* to praise, laud, hymn, DP in *ślāghā* praising,

stotra 1259/2 n. praise, a hymn of praise, name of the verses or texts which are sung (as opposed to being recited)

stotṛ m. praiser (of a god), worshipper, singer mfn praising, worshipping,

√stṛ 1. 1260/1 Cl 5.9. P A *stṛṇoti stṛṇute* or *stṛnāti striṇīte , starati starate,* to spread, spread out or about, strew, scatter, to spread over, bestrew, cover, Cl 5 P A to lay low, overthrow, slay (an enemy), caus. *stārayati* to spread, cover, DP in (Cl 5) *ācchādana* covering, (Cl 9) in *hiṁsā* injuring, killing,
2. m.pl. the stars (light-strewers),

√stī 1260/1 see *stṛ* , DP in (Cl 5) *ācchādana* covering,

straiṇa mfn female, feminine, relating or belonging to women, subject to or ruled by women, being among women, n. womankind, the female sex. the nature of women,

strī f. a woman, female, wife, the female of any animal, (in gram.) the female gender, a white ant,

strīkāma mfn desirous or fond of women, having desire for female (children), m. desire for women or for a wife,

strīliṅga feminine gender, creative power which brings to birth, the power of the powerful,

strītva n. womanhood, wifehood, (in gram.) feminineness,

√stṛh 1260/2 or *stīh* Cl 6 P *strihati* to injure, do harm, DP in *hiṁsā* injuring,

√stṛkṣ 1260/2 Cl 1P *stṛkṣati* to go DP in *gati* going,

stṛṇas m.pl. stars as the light-strewers or *tāras* the scattered ones.

striyāḥ women 1/pl/f

strīya 1261/2 °*yati* to desire a woman or wife

stṛta mfn bestrewn, covered,

√stu 1259/1 Cl 2 P A *stauti* or *stavīti, stunvanti, stute* or *stuvīte* to praise, laud, eulogize, extol, celebrate in song or hymns, caus. *stāvayati*, to praise, celebrate, *stāvayate*, to cause to praise or celebrate, DP in *stuti* praising,

stubdha mfn chanted, praised, hymned,

√stubh 1. 1259/3 Cl 1 P *stobhati* to utter a joyful sound, hum, make a succession of exclamations, shout, Cl 1 A *stobhate* to pause, stop, cause to stop, paralyze, caus. *stobhayati* to praise in successive exclamations, celebrate,
DP in *stambha* stopping, paralyzing,
2. mfn uttering joyful sounds, praising, stopping, pausing, f. joyful exclamation or cry, praise, m. a praiser,

√stuc 1259/3 Cl 1 A *stocate* to be bright or propitious, DP in *prasāda* being pleased,

stuka a child or young animal, a knot or tuft of hair or wool, thick curl of hair, a hip, thigh,

√stūp 1260/1 Cl 4.10.P *stūpyati* or *stūpayati* to heap up, pile, erect, DP in *samucchrāya* heaping up, erecting,

stūpa m. crest, top (of head), summit, a knot or tuft of hair, a buddhist monument generally of dome-like or pyramid shape, any relic shrine or casket,

stuta mfn praised, hymned, glorified, n. praise, eulogy, 2. dripping, oozing

stuti 1259/1 f. praise, adulation, glorification, commendation,

stuvat mfn praising, m.a praiser,worshipper

stuvati 1259/1 praises, lauds, extols

√styai 1260/3 Cl 1 P *styāyati* to be collected into a heap or mass, to spread about, to sound, Cl 1 A *styāyate* to stiffen, grow dense, increase, DP in *śabda* sounding, *saṅghāta* collecting into a heap,

√su 1219/2 Cl 1 P A *savati (te)* to go, move,
2. Cl 1.2. P *savati, sauti,* to urge, impel, incite, to possess supremacy, DP in *prasava* consenting, conceiving, permitting, or *aiśvarya* possessing power or supremacy,
3. Cl 5 P A *sunoti, sunute,* to press out, extract, (esp. soma juice for libations), to distil, prepare (wines,

spirits), caus. *sāvayati,* or *ṣāvayati,* DP in *abhiṣava* pressing out or extracting juice, distilling,
4. = √2. *sū*

su 5. 1219/3 ind. adj. or adv. good, much, excellent, beautiful, well, greatly, very, rightly, virtuous, beautiful, easy, much, greatly, very, any, willingly, quickly, in later language it is mostly prefixed to substantives, adjectives, adverbs and participles, or rarely to an ind.

√sū 1. 1239/3 Cl 6 P *suvati (te), savati, -sauti,* to set in motion, urge, impel, vivify, create, produce, to hurl upon, to grant, bestow, to appoint or consecrate to, to allow, authorize, DP in *preraṇa* exciting, inciting, impelling,
2. Cl 2 A *sūte,* with *pra-* , *-svati, -sauti,* to beget, procreate, bring forth, bear, produce, yield, DP in *prāṇi-garbha-vimocana* bringing forth, begetting, giving birth to,
3. mfn begetting, procreating, bringing forth, producing, (mostly ifc.), . m. one who begets, a father, a mother, child-bearing, parturition,
4. ind. well, good,

sub in comp. for sup,

subaddha mfn well or fast bound, firmly closed, clenched,

subahu mfn very much, very many, ind. much, very much, greatly,

subāla mfn very childish, m. a good boy

subāndhava m. good friend,

subanta n. a word taking a nominal ending i.e. a nominal, technical expression for an inflected noun ending with a case-termination, 1227/2

subartha m. the meaning of a case-termination, ?

√śubh 1083/1 1. Cl 1 A or 6 P *śobhate, śumbhati, śobhati, śumbhate,* to beautify, embellish, adorn, beautify oneself, A. look beautiful or handsome, shine, be bright or splendid, to prepare, make fit or ready, A. prepare oneself, *śumbhate* to flash or flit, i.e glide rapidly past or along, *śumbhati* to harm, injure, caus. *śobhayati* to cause to shine, beautify, ornament, decorate, A. decorate oneself, to fly rapidly along,
DP in *bhāṣaṇa* (Cl 1) speaking, shining, injuring, in *śobha* (Cl 6) looking beautiful, being splendid, in *dīpti* (Cl 1) shining,
2. f. splendour, beauty, ornament, decoration, flashing or flitting past, gliding along, rapid course or flight,

śubha 1083/2 mfn splendid, suitable, fit, good, blessed, auspicious, beautiful bright, handsome, *śubhe* 'fair one', pleasant, agreeable, suitable, fit, capable, good (in moral sense), righteous, virtuous, honest, pure(as an action), eminent, distinguished, learned, versed in the Vedas, m. water, an assembly of the gods, a ram goat, a cow, an assembly of the gods, n. anything bright or beautiful, n. beauty, charm, good fortune, auspiciousness, happiness, bliss, welfare, prosperity, benefit, service, good or virtuous action,

subhadra mfn very glorious or splendid or auspicious or fortunate,

subhadraka m. a vehicle for carrying the image of a god,

subhaga mfn possessing good fortune, lucky, happy, blessed, liked, beloved, dear (as a wife), delicate, slender, thin, suitable for, (*am*) ind. beautifully, charmingly, greatly, in a high degree, borax, (*ā*) f. good fortune, a beloved or favourite wife, musk, n. good fortune, bitumen,

subhakti f. great devotion to or love for,

śubhamastu farewell,

subhamastu best wishes

śubhānana mfn fair-faced,

subhara mfn well-compacted, solid, dense, abundant, easily carried, well

practised,
subhās mfn shining beautifully,
subhāṣita mfn spoken well or eloquently, eloquent, (am) ind. good or eloquent speech, witty saying, good counsel,
subhāṣin mfn speaking friendly words, spoken mildly or gently,
śubhāśubha mf n agreeable and disagreeable, good and bad, good or bad, agreeable or disagreeable,
śubhāśubhaphala mfn having agreeable or disagreeable fruit, resulting in woe,
śubhavāsanā f. pure desire or tendency, good impression from the past,
śubhecchā f. pure desire, good impulse, the starting point, "Every desire contains a purpose to be fulfilled and a good impulse in this context is Self-realization or Liberation" "willingness to follow *viveka* and willingness to follow *aham*" HH
śubhra radiant, shining, beautiful, splendid, clear, bright-coloured, white, 'free from attributes' (Gam.), m. white (the colour), sandal, heaven,
subhru mfn lovely-browed, f. beautiful eyebrow,
subhrū f. woman with lovely eyebrows, maiden, beautiful brow,
subhū mfn of an excellent nature, good, strong, beautiful etc.
subhūmi f. a good place,
subhūta well made or done (food), (*am*) n. welfare, well-being
subhūti f. welfare, well-being,
subhūyas mfn much more, far more,
subodha m. right intelligence, good information or knowledge, mfn easy to understand, easily taught,
subuddhi f. good understanding, mfn wise, clever, intelligent, of good understanding
subudha mfn vigilant,
√*śuc* 1081/1 1. Cl 1 P *śocati (te), śucyati,* to shine, flame, gleam, glow, burn, suffer violent heat or pain, be sorrowful or afflicted, grieve, mourn at or for, bewail, lament, regret, be absorbed in deep meditation, Cl 4 P A *śucyati (te),* to be bright or pure, to be wet, to decay, stink, caus. *śocayati* to set on fire, burn, cause to suffer pain, to feel pain or sorrow, lament, regret, to purify, DP in *śoka* (Cl 1) grieving, in *pūtī-bhāva* (Cl 4) bathing, performing ablutions, 2. mfn. shining, illumining, f. flame, glow, heat, brightness, lustre, pain, sorrow, grief, or regret, pl. tears,
√*sūc* 1241/1 Cl 10 P *sūcayati* to point out, indicate, show, manifest, reveal, betray (in drama to indicate by gesture, communicate by signs, represent), to trace out, ascertain, espy, DP in *paiśunya* tracing out, spying, ascertaining,
sūca mfn pointing out, indicating, m. a pointed shoot or blade of *kuśa* grass, piercing, gesticulation, spying out, sight, seeing,
sūcaka mfn pointing out, indicating, pointing to, informing, betraying, m. a denouncer, informer, narrator, teacher, demon, imp, villain, dog, jackal, cat, crow, needle, parapet, kind of rice,
sucakṣus mfn name of a mythical river, mfn having good eyes, seeing well, 'the fair-eyed',
sucarita mfn well-performed, well-behaved, one who leads a virtuous life, n. virtuous actions,
sucāru mfn very lovely or beautiful,
sucetana mfn very notable, distinguished,
sucetas mfn having great intelligence, wise well-minded, benevolent,
śuci 1081/1 mfn clear, clean, pure, pure (in a ritual sense), holy, undefiled, honourable (in business), light, bright, beaming, untainted, m. purification, purity, honesty, virtue, fire, ifc. one who has acquitted or discharged a duty,
sūci or *sūcī* a needle or any sharp-pointed

instrument, the sharp point or tip of anything, a rail or balustrade,
sūcika m. one who lives by his needle, a tailor,
sūcikā f. a needle, an elephant's trunk,
sūcīmukha n. the point of a needle, mfn having a needle-sharp beak , pointed or sharp as a needle, narrow, a kind of *kuśa* grass, a gnat or some other stinging insect,
sucintā f. deep thought, due reflection,
sucintana n. the act of thinking well, deliberate consideration,
sūcīprota mfn threaded,
sucira mfn for a long time,very long, (ibc. *am, āya, ena* for a very long time, for a good while, -*āt* after a very long time),
śucismita mfn having a beaming smile, bright-smiling,
sūcisūtra n. a sewing thread,
sūcita mfn pointed out, indicated,
sūcitā f. needlework,
sucitra mfn very distinguished, very manifold, very variegated,
sucitraka mfn very variegated, m. a kingfisher,
sucitta mfn well-minded,
√*śucy* 1081/3 Cl 1 P *śucyati* to distil, poss. to perform ablution, DP in *abhiṣava* expressing juice, distilling,
sūcy in comp. for *sūcī* or *sūci*
sūcyā mfn to be indicated/pointed out,
√*sūd* 1242/2 Cl 1 A *sūdate* to put or keep in order, guide aright, caus. or Cl 10 *sūdayati* to manage, arrange, prepare, effect, contrive, to settle i.e. put an end to, kill, slay, to squeeze, press, destroy, DP in *kṣaraṇa* (Cl 1)effusing, flowing, in *kṣaraṇa* (Cl 10) striking, hurting, killing, pouring out,
sudā mfn giving bountifully, munificent,
sūda m. a well, a hot spring, dried up pool, a sauce or broth, a cook,
sudāman mfn having good gifts, bestowing blessings, m. cloud (as source of rain and from that blessings),the sea,
sūdana 1242/2 killing, destroying
sudarśana mfn having a beautiful appearance, handsome, m. king's name, name of Viṣṇu's discus, 'keen-sighted' a vulture, a fish,
sudāruṇa mfn very hard or severe,
√*śudh* 1082/1 or *śundh* Cl 1 P A *śundhati* (te), to purify (A oneself , become or be pure), to be cleared or cleansed or purified, become pure, to become clear or free from doubts, to be excused or cleared from blame, caus. *śundhayati* to clear, purify, to correct, improve, to remove (impurity), to acquit, exculpate, justify, to put to test, to try, examine, to make clear, explain, to subtract, DP in *śauca* becoming pure or purified,
śuddha mfn 1082/1 cleansed, clean, pure, taintless, (in gram.) a pure simple vowel, complete, entire, unqualified, unmitigated (capital punishment), (in phil.) veritable, unequalled, tried, examined,
śuddhabhakti pure devotion to God (U),
śuddhabhāvanā pure feeling or attitude (U)
śuddhabrahma pure Brahman, free from *māyā, nirguṇa brahman,*
śuddhacaitanya 1082/1 pure intelligence, pure consciousness
śuddhacinmātra pure awareness,
śuddhādvaita pure non-dualism
śuddhakalpanā f. pure imagination (as that of "I am Brahman"), (U)
śuddhamanas pure mind
śuddhamati mfn pure-minded,
śuddhaṁ laukikam pure world view, external objects do not exist but awareness exists, having realized external objects do not exist, still the standpoint is bound to consciousness concerned with external objects, regarded as the state of a practitioner who has not attained,
śuddhānta m. royal harem, private or women's apartments,

śuddhaprema pure love,
śuddharūpin 1082/1 having the nature of purity
śuddhasaṁkalpa pure resolve,
śuddhavicāra pure inquiry into the nature of Brahman,
śuddhi 1082/2 f. cleansing, purification, purity, holiness, freedom from defilement, purificatory rite, setting free, rendering secure, exculpation, acquittal, innocence, (established by trial or ordeal), quittance, discharge (of a debt), verification, correction, truth, clearness, certainty,
suddhyupāsya mfn to be worshipped by the intelligent, (said of the Supreme Being),
sudhā f. welfare, 'good drink' the beverage of the gods, nectar, the nectar of honey or flowers, juice, water, milk, whitewash, plaster, mortar, cement, a brick, lightning, the earth, good place or position, well-being, (good drink)
sudharma m. good law, justice, duty,
sudharman mfn well supporting or maintaining, practising justice, attending well to duty, m. the maintainer of a family, the assembly hall of the gods,
sudhī f. good sense or understanding, intelligence, mfn having a good understanding, wise, clever, sensible, religious, pious, m. a wise or learned man, Pandit, teacher,
sudhīra mfn very considerate or wise, very firm or resolute,
sudhita mfn well-placed or fixed, well ordered or arranged, well prepared or served, fixed upon, meant, intended, well-disposed, kind, benevolent, nectar-like,
sudhiti mfn an axe, hatchet, knife,
suddhyopāsya a form of address indicating respected by the wise
sudeśa m. a fit place,
sudeva m. a good or real god, sporting well, a potent or highly erotic lover,
sudevana n. ardent gambling,
sudhā f. nectar, welfare, ease, comfort
sudharmika mfn very virtuous,
sudhī 1225/3 f. intelligence, good sense or understanding, mfn wise
sudhyupāsya wise, to be honoured or worshipped
sudina mfn clear, bright, (a day, morning), n. a clear, fine, bright or auspicious day, happy time, happiness,
sudinatva n. state of fine weather, an auspicious time, happy days
sudīpta 1224/3 mfn shining bright,
sudīrgha mfn very long (time and space), kind of cucumber,
sudīti f. bright flame, mfn flaming, brilliant,
sudiv mfn shining brightly,
śūdra fourth caste or class, servants, labourers,
sudraṣṭṛ mfn one who sees well, having good insight into (6th),
sudṛś mfn keen-sighted, well-looking, having beautiful eyes,
sudṛśya mfn easily seen, clearly visible,
sudru m. good wood or timber,
suduḥkha n. great pain or sorrow, mfn very painful or troublesome, (*am*) ind. very painfully very uneasily,
sudustyaja mfn very difficult to abandon or risk
sudūra mfn very remote or distant,
sudurācara 1225/1 mfn. very ill-conducted, very badly behaved or wicked, a profligate
sudurbodha difficult to understand,
sudurdarśa m.difficult to see, hard to look at, unpleasant to observe,
sudurjaya mfn mastering utmost difficulties, difficult to overcome or conquer,
sudurlabha hard to find, difficult to obtain
suduṣkara mfn difficult to do or achieve
sudustāra mfn very hard to cross, hard to get over, hard to perform (promise),
suga mfn going well or gracefully, having a graceful gait, easy to traverse, of easy access, easy to obtain, easily

understood, intelligible, n. a good path, faeces,
mfn 2. singing well or beautifully,
sugama mfn easily traversed, easily accessed, easily understood, obvious, easy, practicable,
sugamata mfn the ability to reproduce a passage after reading it once or a few times,
sugambhīra, mfn very deep,
sugandha m. a fragrant smell, fragrance, sulphur, the chick-pea, a trader, f.(*ī*) the small banana, n. small cumin seed, the blue lotus, sandal,
mfn fragrant,
sugandhaka m. having fragrance, the orange
sugandhatā f. fragrance, perfume,
sugandhavat mfn fragrant,
sugandhi mfn sweet-smelling, fragrant, virtuous, pious, m. a perfume, the Supreme Being, a lion, a sort of mango n. sandal,
sugantva mfn easily passed,
sugata mfn going well, one who has fared well, well-bestowed, m. a buddhist, buddhist teacher,
sugataśāsana n. the buddhist doctrine,
sugatāyatana n. a buddhist temple or monastery,
sugati f. a good or happy condition, welfare, happiness, bliss, a secure refuge,
mfn having a good or auspicious position (planet),
sugātra mfn fair-limbed, graceful,
n. a fine or graceful figure,
sugātu m. welfare, prosperity,
sugātuyā f. desire for welfare,
sugava m. a vigorous bull, mfn having fine cows, abounding in cattle,
sughora mfn very fearful or terrible,
sugīta n. good singing
sugo f. an excellent cow,
sugraha mfn easily obtained, easily understood, having a good handle,
sugrahaṇa n. reverential clasping (of a person's feet),
sugṛddha mfn intensely longing for,
sugṛha m. having a good or beautiful house
sugrīva mfn handsome-necked, m. name of a monkey-king, a conch, a goose, a hero,
suguṇa mfn very virtuous or excellent,
sugupta mfn well guarded, well hidden, kept very secret,
sugupti f. good protection, great secrecy,
suguru very heinous (crime),a good teacher
√suh 1239/2 Cl 4 P *suhayati* to satisfy, gladden, to be glad, rejoice, to bear, endure, support, DP in *caki*
satisfying, being pleased,
suhana mfn easily killed,
suhārd mfn having a good or loving heart, kind, benevolent, a friend,
having a good interior (stomach),
suhāsa mfn having a pleasant smile,
suhāsin mfn laughing, radiant or shining with (comp.)
suhasta mfn having beautiful hands, skilful or clever with the hands, trained in arms, disciplined,
suhata mfn thoroughly beaten or slain, justly slain or killed,
suhava mfn easily invoked, listening willingly, n. an auspicious or successful invocation,
suhita mfn very fit or suitable, very beneficial, very satiated, very friendly, affectionate, n. satiety, abundance,
suhṛd 1239/3 m. good-hearted, a friend,
suhṛdbheda m. separation of friends, creating division among friends,
suhṛdvākya n. words of a friend,
suhṛt friend
suhṛttama mfn affectionate, very friendly, close friend,
suhṛtprāpti f. the acquisition of a friend,
sujaghana mfn having beautiful hips, having a beautiful end/conclusion
sujana m. a good, kind, benevolent person,
sujanatā f. goodness, kindness, benevolence
sujaniman mfn having good productions or creations, skilfully fashioning,
sujanman n. noble or auspicious birth,
sujāta mfn well born, produced or made,
sujña mfn. knowing well, conversant

with anything
sujñāna n. easy perception or intelligence, good knowledge, f (*ā*) possessing good knowledge, easy to be understood
sujñeya well-comprehended
śuka m. parrot, 'the bright one', the planet Venus,
suka a parrot,
sūka m. an arrow, air, wind, lotus,
sukalatra n. a good wife,
sukalpa mfn easy to be made, very qualified or skilled,
sukalpita mfn well-equipped or armed,
sukalya mfn perfectly sound,
sukāma mfn having good desires,
sukamala n. a beautiful lotus flower,
sukanda m. an onion, a yam,
sukānta mfn very handsome,
sukaṇṭha mfn sweet-voiced,
sukanyā f. a beautiful girl,
sukanyaka mfn having a beautiful daughter,
sukara mfn easy to be done, easy for (6th), easy to be managed (horse or cow), easily achieving, m. a good-natured horse, (*ā*) f. a tractable cow, (*am*)n. doing good, charity, benevolence,
- *tva* n. easiness, feasibleness,
sūkara m. a pig, swine, boar, a partic. fish, white rice, a potter,
sukarman n. a good work, mfn performing good works, virtuous, active, diligent, m. a good or expert artificer or artist or architect,
sukāśana mfn shining beautifully,
sukāṣṭhaka mfn having good wood or good firewood,
sukathā f. a beautiful story,
śukavat ind. like a parrot,
sukeśa mfn having beautiful hair,
sukeśānta mfn having beautiful locks,
suketa mfn having good intentions, benevolent,
suketu mfn very bright,
√*sukh* 1220/3 Cl 10.4. P *sukhayati, sukhyati,* to make happy, please, delight, gladden, rejoice, comfort, DP in *tatkriyā* giving pleasure,
sukha 1220/3 mfn easy, agreeable, gentle, mild, comfortable, happy, prosperous, virtuous, pious, m. (in phil.) the effort to win future beatitude, piety, virtue, n. ease, easiness, comfort, prosperity, pleasure, happiness, joy, delight in, the sky, heaven, atmosphere, water, ind. easily, comfortably, pleasantly, joyfully,
(N.S.300) sometimes used where *ānanda* would be used in the Upanishads,
sukhabaddha mfn pleasantly formed,
sukhabandhana mfn attached to the pleasures or enjoyments of the world,
sukhabhāga m. a happy lot, good fortune,
sukhabhāgin, or *-bhāj,* happy, fortunate,
sukhabhoga m. the enjoyment of pleasure,
sukhabhojana n. dainty food,
sukhabodha mfn perception of pleasure,
sukhabuddhi f. easy understanding or knowledge,
sukhacara mfn going or moving easily
sukhacāra m. 'easy-going', a good horse,
sukhacitta n. mental ease,
sukhada mfn giving pleasure or delight,
sukhadhana n.pl. comfort and riches,
sukhādi mfn beginning with pleasure,
sukhadṛśya mfn beautiful to look at,
sukhaduḥkha n. du. pleasure and pain, joy and sorrow,
sukhaga mfn going easily,
sukhagama mfn easy to be traversed or travelled over,
sukhagandha mfn fragrant, sweet-smelling,
sukhāgata n. welcome,
sukhagrāhya mfn easy to be grasped, comprehended or understood,
sukhahasta mfn having a soft or gentle hand
sukhakara mfn causing pleasure/ happiness,
sukhākara m. 'making happy, gladdening',
sukhalakṣya mfn easily recognized, easily seen,
sukhalava m. a little pleasure,
sukhāloka mfn pleasant looking, beautiful,
sukham 1220/3 happiness, happily
sukhamada mfn pleasantly intoxicating,

sukhamaya, mfn delightful, consisting of happiness, full of joy and pleasure,
sukhamedhas mfn prospering well,
sukhānta mfn ending in happiness, subversive of happiness,
sukhānubhava m. perception or consciousness of pleasure
sukhāpa mfn easily won or attained,
sukhāpanna mfn one who has attained or gained happiness,
sukhaplava mfn offering a comfortable bath,
sukhaprabodhaka mfn easy to understand,
sukhaprasava mfn bringing forth easily or happily,
sukhapraśna m. welfare inquiry,
sukhaprasupta sleeping placidly,
sukhapravicāra mfn easily accessible,
sukhārha mfn deserving of happiness,
sukharūpa mfn of agreeable appearance
sukhasādhana n. means of obtaining pleasure,
sukhāsakta m. devoted to happiness,
sukhasalila pleasant (i.e. tepid) water,
sukhasambandhi mfn joyful, happy,
sukhasambodhya mfn easy to be explained or taught or to be reasoned with,
sukhasaṁcāra mfn inviting, pleasant to be resorted to,
sukhasaṁjñā f. ease,
sukhasaṁsparśa mfn agreeable to the touch, pleasant to the feelings, gratifying,
sukhasaṁstha or *sukhasaṁsthita* mfn feeling comfortable or happy,
sukhasaṁyāna n. comfortable journey or progress
sukhasaṁyoga m. gain of eternal bliss
sukhāsana n. a comfortable seat,
sukhasaṅga m. attachment to pleasure
sukhasaṅgin mfn attached to pleasure,
sukhaśayana n. placid rest or sleep
sukhaśayita mfn lying or sleeping comfortably on,
sukhasevya mfn easy of access,
sukhāsikā f. well-being, comfort, ease,
sukhāsīna mfn comfortably seated,
sukhaśīta mfn pleasantly cool,
sukhasparṣa mfn an easy life or state of existence,
sukhaśrava mfn sweetly sounding, pleasant to hear,
sukhaśruti f. agreeable to the ear,
sukhāsukha n. pleasure and pain,
sukhasukhena ind. most willingly, with all the heart
sukhasupta mfn sweetly sleeping,
sukhatā f. *–tva* n. ease, comfort, delight, happiness, prosperity,
sukhatas ind. easily, comfortably, happily,
sukhāvagama m. easy perception or comprehension,
sukhavaha mfn easily borne or carried
sukhāvaha mfn bringing or conferring pleasure, delightful,
sukhavartman mfn having easy paths,
sukhavāsa m. a comfortable abode, mfn 'sweet-smelling', a water-melon,
sukhavedana n. consciousness of pleasure,
sukhavihāra m. an easy or comfortable life
sukhī; sukhin, sukhinī happy
sukhin mfn 'having or possessing pleasure', happy, being in comfort
sukhina happy, possessing happiness, 1/pl/m
sukhita ° happy, pleased, comforted,
sukhena ind. happily
sukheṣṭha mfn living in joy,
sukhetara 1222/1 mfn not happy, unfortunate, n.pl in joys and sorrows
sukhi in comp. for *sukhin*
sukhī mfn one who loves pleasure, √*sukh* in giving pleasure, *Aṣṭāvakra* uses *sukhi (ī)* where others might use *ànanda* 139/3 pure happiness, (bliss)
sukhin mf possessing or causing happiness or pleasure, happy, joyful, pleasant, comfortable, easy,
m. a religious ascetic, one who is happy,
sukhita mfn pleased, delighted, comforted,
sukhitā f. ease, comfort, happiness,
sukhocita mfn accustomed to ease/comfort,
sukhodarka mfn causing happiness,
sukhodya mfn easily pronounceable,
sukhopaviṣṭa mfn comfortably seated,

sūkhta n. good works,
sukhya mfn pleasurable,
sukīrti f. good praise, hymn of praise, glorious, well or easily praised,
śukla 1080/2 bright, white, light, pure, spotless, the bright ½ of a lunar month, semen, mucus, saliva,
śuklāmbara mfn having a white garment,
śuklapakṣa the bright lunar ½ month, from new to full moon,
śuklapakṣādi mfn beginning with the bright lunar fortnight,
śukra 1080/1 mfn. bright, resplendent, clear, pure, spotless, white, juice, the essence of anything, semen,
sukratu mfn skilful, wise,
sukṛṣṇa mfn very black,
sukṛt mfn doing good, benevolent, virtuous, pious, fortunate, wise, a skilful worker,
sukṛta 1220/2 n. a good or righteous deed, meritorious act, virtue, doing good, benevolent, fortune, auspiciousness, reward, recompense, well done or made or formed, well-conducted, virtuous, meritorious, (standing for *savkṛta*) – self-creator,
sukṛti f. good or correct conduct, kindness, virtue, righteous, virtuous,
sukṛtin mfn doing good actions, virtuous, generous, prosperous, fortunate, cultivated, wise,
sukṣatra mfn having a good or kind rule, m. kind or gracious ruler,
sukṣetra n. fair field,
sukṣetriya f. desire for fair fields,
sukṣma mfn consisting of good earth,
sūkṣma mfn minute, small, fine, thin, 1240/3 subtle, intangible, intangible matter, the subtle all-pervading Spirit (*am*) ind. nice, exact, precise, subtle, atomic, intangible, m.n. the subtle all-pervading Spirit, an atom, intangible matter, the subtle all-pervading spirit, Supreme Soul, small cardamoms, n. a tooth cavity or socket, woven silk, marrow, Vedānta philosophy, f. (*ā*) sand,
sūkṣma-ati- sūkṣmam subtler than the subtle
sūkṣmabhūta n. subtle element, state of elements, *tanmātra,*
sūkṣmadarśin mfn intelligent, sharp-sighted, of acute discernment, quick, seer of the subtle essence of things, one who has developed the subtle inner eye, a man of wisdom, a sage,
sūkṣmatvāt 1240/3 5/s from subtlety or fineness, because of or through subtlety or fineness
sūkṣma-śarīra the subtle body,
śukta mfn joined, void of men, clean, rough, harsh, united, become acid or sour, stinking, putrid, pure, lonely, m. sourness, n. harsh speech, flesh, sour gruel,
sūkta mfn properly or well recited, speaking well, eloquent, a Vedic hymn, f.(*ā*) a kind of bird, n. good recitation or speech, wise saying, song of praise,
śukti 1080/1 a pearl oyster or oyster shell
sūkti f. a good or friendly speech, wise saying, beautiful verse or stanza
śūktikā f. mother of pearl,
sūtika m. cymbal, kind of cymbal,
śūktikārajata silver seen in mother of pearl, an example of superimposition where one thing is wrongly assumed to be another,
sukula n. a noble family, from a noble family
sukumāra mfn tender, young, delicate,
sukumāraka mfn very tender, m. a tender youth, sugar-cane, rice,
sukumārāṅga mfn with very delicate limbs,
√*śūl* 1086/3 Cl 1 P *śūlati* to hurt, cause pain, DP in *rujā* being ill, or *saṅghāta* making a loud noise, collecting,
śūla m. a sharp, iron stake, pike, spear, spit (for roasting meat), any acute or sharp pain,
śūlā f. a stake, a prostitute,
sulabha 1232/3 mfn easy to be obtained or

effected, feasible, easy, trivial
sulakṣaṇam n. the act of observing or examining carefully, ascertaining, determining, a good or auspicious mark or characteristic,
sulalita mfn very playful or wanton,
sulatāna m. a sultan,
sulavaṇa mfn well salted,
√*śulb* 1084/2 Cl 10 P *śulbayati* to mete out, to create, DP in *māna* measuring, creating,
śūlin 'possessing a spear (trident)'- *Śiva,* one who suffers from sharp internal pain, m. a spearman, lancer, a hare,
√*śulk* 1084/2 Cl 10 P *śulkayati* to pay, give, to gain, acquire, to leave, forsake, to narrate, tell, DP in *atisparśana* gaining, giving, paying, touching,
sulocana mfn fine-eyed, beautiful eyed,
suloha n. a good kind of iron,
sulohaka m.n. 'good metal' brass,
sulohita mfn very red, mfn m. a beautiful red colour
suma m. the moon, the sky, atmosphere, n. a flower
sūma m. the sky, heaven, moon, milk, water,
sumada mfn very drunk or impassioned,
sumadhura mfn very sweet or tender or gentle, m. very soothing speech,
sumadhya mfn good in the middle, slender-waisted,
sumadhyama mfn very mediocre/ middling, slender-waisted, *(ā)* f. a graceful woman
sumahā (for *mahat)* in comp.
sumahākakṣya mfn having very great enclosures, halls or rooms, very high-walled,
sumahant mfn very great or important,
sumahas mfn very glorious or sublime,
sumahat mfn very great, huge, vast, abundant, *(at)* ind. numerous,
sumakha mfn very vigorous or joyous, n. a joyous festival,
sumalina mfn very dirty or polluted,

sumana 1230/3 mfn very charming, beautiful, handsome, m. wheat,
sumanas mfn. good-minded, benevolent, gracious, agreeable, wise, intelligent, calm of mind, m. a god, a good or wise man,
sumānasa mfn good-minded,
sumanaska mfn in good spirits, cheerful,
sumanda mfn very slow or dull,
sumaṅgala f. having or bringing good luck
sumānin mfn very proud or conceited,
sumanman n.pl good wishes, uttering good wishes or prayers, very devout,
sumantra mfn following good advice,
sumantrin mfn having a good minister,
sumantrita mfn well advised, wisely planned
sumantu mfn easily known, well known, m. friendly sentiment or invocation,
sumārdava n. extreme softness,
sumardita mfn much harassed,
sumarmaga mfn deeply penetrating the vital organs (an arrow),
sumarṣaṇa mfn easy to be borne,
sumārtsna mfn very small, minute, fine,
sumat ind. together, along with,
sumati f. good mind or disposition, benevolence, kindness, devotion, a wife of King Sagara, prayer, mfn very wise or intelligent,
sumāvali f. a garland of flowers,
√*śumbh* 1083/1 see *śubh* cl1 P. to kill, harm, injure, DP in *bhāṣaṇa* (Cl 1) speaking, shining, injuring, in *śobhā* (Cl 6) looking beautiful, being splendid,
sumedha mfn very nourishing (pasture -land), loamy,
sumedhas mfn sensible, intelligent, wise, having a good understanding,
sumeka mfn well-fixed or established, firm, constant,
sumeru mfn very exalted, excellent,
sumita mfn well measured out, well fixed,
sumitra mfn having good friends, a good friend,
sumitrā *Sumitrā*
sumitrya mfn having good friends,

sumla mfn very weak or feeble,
sumna mfn benevolent, kind, gracious, favourable, n. benevolence, grace, favour, devotion, prayer, hymn, satisfaction, peace, joy, happiness,
sumnayā ind. devoutly, piously, kindly, graciously,
sumnāyu mfn gracious, favourable, pious,
sumnin mfn gracious, favourable,
sumṛṣṭa mfn well polished, very bright or fine,
sumṛta mfn stone-dead,
sumṛtyu mfn an easy death,
sumukha n. a good or beautiful mouth, a bright face, fair-faced, handsome, bright-faced, cheerful, m. a learned man or teacher,
√*śun* 1082/3 Cl 6 P *śunati* to go, DP in *gati* going,
śuna mfn grown, prosperous, fortunate, n. growth, prosperity, luck, success,
śūna mfn swelled, swollen, increased, grown, n. emptiness, lack, want, absence,
sūna mfn born, produced, budded, empty, vacant, m. a son, n. bringing forth, parturition, a bud, flower, fruit,
sūnā f. a woven wicker basket, a vessel of any kind, a butchery, imminent death,
sūnara mfn glad joyous, merry,
sunāsa mfn having a beautiful nose,
sunāsākṣibhruva mfn having beautiful nose, eyes and brows,
sunaya m. wise conduct or policy,
sundara 1227/1 mfn beautiful, charming, noble, lovely, agreeable,
sundarī f. a beautiful woman, any woman, (also applied to female animals), a kind of tree, turmeric,
√*śundh* 1082/1 see *śudh*, DP in *śuddhi* (Cl 1) being purified or cleansed, in *śauca-karmana* (Cl 10) cleansing
śundhyu mfn pure, unblemished, fair, purified or free from, unmolested by (6th), fire or *agni,*

sūnika m. a butcher, flesh-seller, hunter,
sunirmala perfectly pure, very pure,
sunirvṛta mfn quite at ease, happy in mind,
suniścaya m. firm resolve, perfectly sure,
suniścita mfn firmly resolved, well-ascertained, fixed, settled,
suniścitam ind. definitely, with certainty
sunīta mfn well led or guided, well managed or prepared, n. good or wise conduct, wisdom, prudence,
sunīti mfn guiding well, well conducted, f. good conduct or behaviour, good policy, wisdom, discretion,
sunītha giving or enjoying good guidance, well- conducted, righteous, moral, good,
sūnṛta mfn joyful, glad, friendly, kind, n. pleasant and true speech, sweet discourse, f. (*ā*) gladness, joy, kind and true speech,

śuṇṭh 1081/3 Cl 1 P *śuṇṭhati* to limp, be lame, to dry, become dry, Cl 10 *śuṇṭhayati* to dry, become dry, DP in *pratighāta*(Cl 1) impeded, hindered, in *śoṣaṇa* (Cl 1.10) becoming dry,

sūnṛta mfn joyful, glad, friendly, kind, n. pleasant and true speech, sweet discourse, f. (*ā*) gladness, joy, kind and true speech,
sūnṛtāvan mfn joyous,
sūnu m. an inciter, the sun, 2. m. a son, child, a younger brother, daughter's son,
sunva mfn soma pressing,
śūnya 1085/1 empty, void, a riderless horse, vacant (as a look or stare), without aim or object, void of thinking, (in phil.) vacuity, non-entity, absolute non-existence (esp. with Buddhists), (*am*) solitude,
śūnyacitta 1085/2 mfn vacant-minded, not thinking,
śūnyatā f. loneliness, emptiness, absence of mind, desolateness, ifc. absence or want of, nothingness, non-existence,

non-reality, illusory nature (of worldly phenomena),

śūnyavāda m. the doctrine of non-existence of anything, buddhism, atheism, Buddhist doctrine of non-existence,

śūnyavādin m. atheist, affirmer of a void, Buddhist,

sup a *Pratyāhāra* used as a term for all or for any one of the 21 nominal case terminations,

sūpa m. sauce, soup, broth, a cook, vessel, pot, pan, an arrow,

supad n. having good or beautiful feet, swift-footed,

supada n. a good word,

supadma mfn having beautiful lotuses,

sūpakāra m. soup-maker, cook,

supakṣa mfn beautiful winged, a sort of fragrant mango,

supakṣman mfn having beautiful eyebrows,

supakva mfn well-cooked or matured,

suparṇa n. a beautiful leaf, m. any large bird of prey, any mythical or supernatural bird, a ray, a horse, a cock, the sun, the moon, (*ā*) f. a lotus plant or lotus pool, a name for the mythical bird Garuda, brother in law of King Sagara,

suparṇā = *suparṇau* 'entities who are well-related' (Gam.), f. a lotus plant, a pool abounding with lotuses,

suparvan m. a good period of time, mfn having beautiful joints or knots, highly extolled, m. cane, bamboo, an arrow, smoke, a god, deity, a special lunar day,

supatha 1227/2 m.n. a good road, virtuous course, good conduct, mfn. having a good road

supatnī f. having a good husband,

sūpavañcana mfn easy of approach or access, not repellent, friendly,

sūpāyana mfn easy of access,

suphala mfn yielding much or good fruit,

suprasanna mfn very peaceful, favourably disposed,

supraśānta absolutely tranquil (Gam.)

supratiṣṭhita mfn properly set up,

suprāvī mfn very attentive or mindful, very zealous,

suprīta mfn well pleased,

suprīti f. great joy or delight,

supta 1230/1 mfn fallen asleep, asleep, sleeping, having beautiful braids of hair, paralysed, insensible, closed (as a flower), resting, inactive, dull,

suptajana m. a sleeping person, midnight,

suptaka n. sleep,

suptavat – like those fallen asleep

supti f. sleep, deep sleep, sleepiness, numbness, insensibility, paralysis, carelessness, confidence,

supūjita mfn well or highly honoured, a cup well cleaned,

suputra mfn having good sons,

sup-tiṅ-anta n. an inflected noun or verb as ending with a case termination or verbal termination,

√*śūr* 1086/1 Cl 4 A *śūryate* to hurt, injure, kill, to be or make firm, Cl 10 A to be powerful or valiant, DP in *hiṁsā* (Cl 4) injuring, killing, or *stambhana* being firm,

√*sur* 1234/2 Cl 6 P *surati* to rule, possess supreme or superhuman power, to shine, Cl 10 P *surayati* to find fault, DP in *aiśvarya* ruling and *dīpti* shining,

śūra mfn mighty, bold, m. man of might,

sura 1234/2 m. a god, divinity, deity, a sage, learned man, the sun,

surā f. spirituous liquor, wine, water, a drinking vessel, a snake, name of a goddess,

sūra the sun, a wise or learned man, the *soma* juice from the press,

surabhi mfn sweet-smelling, fragrant, charming, pleasing, lovely, famous, good, virtuous, friendly, a friend, m. fragrance, perfume, the spring season, sulphur, gold, 2. m. an inciter, propellor,

surabhisragdhara mfn wearing fragrant garlands,

surādhas mfn bounteous, well blessed,

having excellent blessings,
suragaṇa a multitude of gods
surahas n. a very lonely place,
surajanī f. night,
surakṣita mfn well-guarded,
surakta mfn well-coloured, deeply dyed, deep red, strongly affected or impassioned, crimson, very lovely or charming,
suraṇa n. joy, delight,
suraṅga m. a good colour or dye, 'bright coloured', the orange tree, crystal, a kind of fragrant grass,
śura m. a hero, a lion,
surasa mfn rich in water, well-flavoured, juicy, sweet, lovely,
surasattama m.pl. the best of the gods,
surata mfn sporting, playful, tender, compassionate, n. great joy or delight, amorous or sexual pleasure,
sūrata mfn well-disposed towards, compassionate, tender, tranquil, calm,
suratha mfn having a good chariot, a good charioteer,
suratna mfn possessing rich jewels or treasure,
surekha mfn forming beautiful lines, *(ā)* f. a beautiful line,
surendra lord of the gods
sureṇu m. a sort of atom,
sūri m. a learned man, sage, L. he who engages priests to perform a sacrifice for his benefit and pays them for it, a sacrifice-master,
sūrin m. a wise or learned man, scholar,
√*surkṣ* 1244/3 or *sūrkṣy* Cl 1 P *surkṣati* or *surkṣyati* to heed, care or trouble about, to disrespect, slight, neglect? DP in *ādara* respecting (*surkṣ),* disrespecting (*surkṣy),*
suroṣa mfn very angry, enraged,
surottama mfn chief of gods,
√*śūrp* 1086/2 Cl 10 P *śūrpayati* to measure, mete out, DP in *māna* measuring, creating,
śūrpa n. a plaited basket for winnowing grain,
śurpanakhā *Śurpanakhā*
suruc f. bright light, mfn shining brightly,
surucira mfn shining brightly, radiant, splendid, beautiful,
suruja mfn very sick, unwell,
surūpa mfn well-formed, handsome, beautiful, wise, learned,
sūrya 1243/1 m. the sun or its deity,
sūryaka mfn resembling the sun,
sūryakāla m. daytime, day,
sūryakānti f. sunlight, sunshine, a partic. flower,
sūryakara 1243/2 m. a sunbeam,
sūryanāḍī another name for the *piṅgalā* psychic tube/nerve
sūryāṇī f. the wif of the god *Sūrya*
sūryapāda m. a sunbeam,
sūryāpāya m. 'sun departure', sunset,
sūryāsta m. sunset,
sūryatejas n. sunshine, mfn having the power or radiance of the sun,
sūryavat mfn sunny, name of a mountain
sūryavid mfn knowing the *sūrya* hymn,
sūryotthāna n. sunrise,
√*śuṣ* 1084/3 Cl 4 P *śuṣyati (te*), to dry, become dry or withered, fade, languish, decay, caus. *śoṣayati* to make dry, dry up, wither, parch, afflict, injure, DP in *śoṣaṇa* being dried, becoming dry or parched, Cl 6 P *śuṣati* to hiss (as a snake), 2. ifc. drying, withering, drying up, parching,
√*śūṣ* 1087/1 Cl 1 P *śūṣati* to bring forth, procreate, DP in *prasava* producing, begetting,
suśabda mfn sounding well, (as a flute)
suśabdatā f. correct grammatical forms, = *sauśabdya*
susādhu mfn quite right or correct,
susādhya mfn easy to keep in order, obedient, amenable,
susaha 1. ind. good company, 2. mfn easy to be borne or suffered,
suśaka mfn easily done, practicable, easy to or to be,

suśāka m. a good herb,
suśākaka n. fresh ginger,
suṣakhi mfn a good friend or having good friends
suśakta mfn well able or capable,
suśakti f. an easy possibility,
susalila mfn having good water,
susama mfn perfectly level or smooth, well proportioned, better than middling,
susamāhita mfn very intent, entirely concentrated upon one thing, well laden (a wagon), well repaired, beautifully adorned,
susāman n. conciliatory words, good negotiation,
susaṁcita mfn well gathered, carefully accumulated,
susaṁdha mfn true to a promise, keeping one's word,
susaṁdhita mfn well reconciled,
susaṁdṛś mfn having a pleasing aspect, agreeable to look at,
suśami or *suśamī* ind. diligently, carefully
susaṁkata mfn firmly closed, hard to explain
susampad f.pl. plenty, abundance,
susaṁrabdha mfn firmly established, very angry,
suśaṁsa mfn saying or wishing good things, blessing,
susaṁśās mfn directing or instructing well,
susaṁskṛta mfn beautifully adorned or decorated, well cooked or prepared, kept in good order, correct *saṁskṛta,* a sacred text or precept,
susaṁsthita mfn well situated, standing firmly, doing well, well brought together, circumscribed,
susaṁtoṣa mfn easily satisfied,
susaṁtuṣṭa mfn well satisfied,
susaṁvigna mfn greatly agitated/perplexed,
susaṁvīta mfn well covered or clothed, well girt, well mailed,
susaṁvṛta mfn well covered, dressed or veiled, wrapped up or concealed in, well hidden, kept very secret, carefully guarding oneself,
susaṁvṛti mfn well concealed,
susaṁvṛtta mfn appearing in good or proper order, well-rounded,
susaṁyatta mfn well prerpared, ready, on one's guard,
susaṁyukta mfn closely joined or united
susaṁyuta mfn well composed or knit together, well joined with,
susaṅga mfn very much liked, adhered to,
susanna mfn completely finished with or done for, frustrated, foiled,
suśānta mfn thoroughly allayed or extinguished, very calm or placid (as water),
suśānti f. perfect calm or tranquillity
suśara mfn easily broken,
susāra m. good essence or sap or substance, competence, mfn having good essence,
suśaraṇa secure refuge or protection,
susaraṇa n. getting on well, easy progress
susārathi m. having a good charioteer,
suśarīra mfn having a beautiful body,
suśarman n. secure refuge or protection, mfn granting secure refuge or protection,
susarva mfn quite complete,
suśāsana n. good government,
suśāsita mfn well governed or regulated, kept under good discipline,
suśasta mfn well-recited,
suśasti f. good recitation, good hymn,
susadṛśa mfn very like or similar,
suśaṭha mfn very deceitful or false,
susattra n. a well managed hospital or hospice,
susattva mfn very resolute or courageous,
susāya n. a good evening,
suśeva mfn very dear or kind or favourable
suśevas mfn very gracious or kind,
suśevya mfn dearly loved,
suśikṣita mfn well instructed, well-informed
suśīla mfn well-disposed, good-tempered, with amiable disposition, well conducted, well made, he whose nature has been purified through

a disciplined life,
suśīma mfn good to lie or sit on,
suśīmakāma mfn deeply in love,
suśīta mfn very cold or cooling,
suśītala mfn very cold or cooling, frigid, freezing, (*am*) n. coldness,
śuṣka mfn dried, dry, withered, 1085/1 to become dry, withered
suślakṣṇa mfn very smooth,
suśleṣa m. close or intimate union, a close embrace, mfn having a close embrace, having a beautiful play on words,
suśliṣṭa mfn closely adhering, well joined or contracted, close, tight, very conclusive or intelligible,
śuṣma m.n. fire, flame, the sun, m. hissing, roaring, whistling, exhalation, breath, fragrant odour (of Soma), strength, vigour, vital sexual energy, impulse, courage, valour, semen, air, wind, a bird, n. strength, mfn hissing, roaring (as water), fragrant, strong, bold,
suśobhita 1237/2 mfn shining brightly,
suśodhita mfn perfectly cleaned,
suśoka mfn shining beautifully,
suśoṇa mfn dark red,
suśrānta 1237/2 mfn very tired, greatly exhausted,
suśrava mfn worth hearing,
suśravas mfn abounding in glory, famous, hearing well or gladly, gracious,
suśravasloka mfn well sounding/speaking, of good renown,
suśravasyā f. willingness to hear,
suśrī mfn very splendid or rich,
śuśruma we have heard, we heard
śuśrūṣā f. obedience, reverence, service, saying, telling, desire to hear,
suśruta mfn very famous, well or correctly heard,
suśruti f. a good or quick ear,
sustha mfn well-situated, faring well, healthy, comfortable, prosperous, happy, safe and sound,
susthacitta mfn easy at heart, feeling happy or comfortable,
susthita mfn well established, firm, unshaken (as a heart), being on the right path, innocent, easy, comfortable, healthy, prosperous, n. a house with a gallery on all sides,
susthiti f. an excellent position, good condition, well-being,
suṣṭhu mfn highly praised or celebrated, aptly, well, fitly, duly, excellently,
suṣū mfn very stimulating, 2. bringing forth easily,
suśuddha mfn perfectly pure or bright,
susukha 1239/1mfn very easy or pleasant
susūkṣma mfn very small or delicate, very subtle or keen (as understanding), very difficult to understand, m.n. an atom,
suṣumṇa or *suṣumna* mfn very gracious or kind, f.*(ā)* one of the passages for breath or spirit lying between the *iḍā* and *piṅgalā* spinal pathways,
suṣumnā G305, the subtle central nerve, the principal nerve

suṣupta 1237/3 fast asleep,
suṣuptasthāna 'whose sphere is that state of deep sleep',
suṣupti f. deep sleep without dreams, in phil. complete unconsciousness,
suṣuptivat ind. as in deep sleep,
suṣūta mfn well-begotten,
sūṣuvāna mfn being consecrated, consecrated,
susvabhāva mfn good-natured,
susvāda having a good taste, sweet,
susvāgata n. a hearty welcome, mfn attended with a hearty welcome,
susvānta mfn having a good or happy mind,
susvāpa m. deep sleep,
susvara mfn harmonious, melodious, loud, having a beautiful voice, m the right tone or accent, a conch,
susvaram ind, very sweetly,
sut mfn ifc. extracting juice, making libations, begetting, generating, m. a praiser, worshipper,

suta 1219 1. mfn impelled, urged, allowed, authorized,
2. mfn pressed out, extracted, m.a Soma libation,
3. mfn begotten, brought forth, a son, child, offspring, (*sutau* du. = 'son and daughter'), a king,

sutā f. ifc. a daughter, a plant,

sūta 1241/2 a charioteer, driver, groom, equerry, master of horse, bard, a carpenter or wheelwright,
1239/3 mfn urged, impelled,
1240/1 mfn born, engendered, m. quicksilver, the sun, a young quadruped, f. (*ā*) a woman who has given birth to a child,

sutala a hell,

sutamām ind. superl. most excellently, best

sutamisrā f. dense darkness,

sutāmra mfn deep red,

sutanu mfn very thin or slender, having a beautiful body,

sutapa m. practising great austerities, a drinker of the *soma* juice,

sutapas mfn very heating or warming, practising severe austerity, m. an ascetic, hermit, the sun,

sutapasvin mfn practising severe austerity or self-mortification,

sutapta mfn very hot, much heated, purified by heat (as gold), greatly harrassed or afflicted, very severe (as an austerity),

sūtaputra son of a charioteer (*Karna*)

sutara mfn easily crossed, easily passed (a night)

sutāra mfn very bright, very loud, having a beautiful pupil (eye), f.(*ā*) one of the nine kinds of acquiescence (*tuṣṭi*), one of the eight kinds of perfection (*siddhi)*

sutāraka mfn having beautiful stars,

sutarām ind. still more, in a higher degree,

sutaṣṭa mfn well-fashioned,

√*śuṭh* 1081/3 Cl 1 P *śoṭhati* to limp or to be obstructed or impeded, Cl 10 P *śoṭhayati* to be dull or slow, DP in *pratighāta* (Cl 1) impediment or hindering, in *ālasya* (Cl 10) idling or lazing

sūti f. birth, production, yielding fruit, parturition delivery, lying in, production of crops, offspring, m. a goose,

sutīkṣṇa very sharp or pungent, acutely painful,

sutin mfn having a son or sons,

√*sūtr* 1241/3 Cl 10 P *sūtrayati, (te), sūtrāpayati,* to string or put together, to contrive, effect, produce, compose, to put in the form of a *sūtra*, teach as a *sūtra* or aphorism, DP in *veṣṭaṇa* tying, binding,

sūtra 1241/3 n. a thread, yarn, string, , that which like a thread runs through or holds together everything, rule, direction, a short sentence or aphoristic rule, any work or manual consisting of strings of such rules... a terse statement

sūtradhāra 1242/1 thread-holder, architect, carpenter, puppet-master

sūtralā f. a spindle, distaff,

sūtraṇa n. the act of stringing together & arranging in aphorisms,

sūtrātman 1242/1 m.the *ātman* or Self like a thread through the universe, 'the immanent deity of the totality of the subtle bodies; the lower Brahman; Hiranyagarbha, (U)'

sūtrita mfn strung, arranged,

sutṛp mfn easily satisfied,

√*suṭṭ* 1223/3 Cl 10 P *suṭṭayati* to slight, disregard, despise, to be small or low or shallow, DP in *anādara* despising, contemning,

sutuṣṭa mfn easily satisfied,

sutyā f. bringing forth a child, parturition

suvāca mfn worth mentioning, sounding beautifully, praiseworthy,

suvacana n. good speech, eloquence, mfn speaking well, eloquent,

suvana m. the sun, fire, the moon,

suvarcasa mfn fiery, splendid, radiant, effulgent, full of life or vigour, *suvargeya* or *–vargya,* mfn leading to heaven, celestial,

suvarṇa mfn of a good or beautiful colour, brilliant in hue, bright, golden, yellow, gold, made of gold, of a good tribe or caste, m. a good colour, a good tribe or caste,

suvarṇaka mfn golden, of a beautiful colour, n. gold, yellow brass,

suvarṇakaṅkana n. gold bracelet,

suveda mfn deeply versed in (sacred) science, 2. easily found/obtained

suvega mfn moving very fast, fleet, rapid

suvela greatly bowed, stooping, humble, quiet,

suvena mfn full of longing or desire,

suveśa or *suveṣa* m. a fine dress/garment,

suvibhakta mfn well separated/distributed, well proportioned, symmetrical,

suvibhāta mfn shining splendidly, very bright, thoroughly clear or distinct,

suvicāraṇā f.good thoughts and reasoning, right enquiry,

suvidatra mfn kindly noticing, i.e. taking kind notice, kindly, very mindful, propitious, n. household, grace, favour, property, wealth,

suvidatriya mfn kindly, favourable, propitious, gracious,

suvidha mfn of a good or kind nature, (*am*) ind. in an easy way, easily,

suvidhāna n. good order or arrangement, mfn well arranged or contrived,

suvidhi m. a good rule or ordinance,

suvidita mfn well-known or understood,

suvidvas mfn very intelligent or wise,

suvidyā f. good knowledge,

suvihita mfn well done or performed,

suvihvala very disturbed or wearied,

suvijñeya 1233/2 mfn. easy to be distinguished, easily comprehensible,

suvilaya mfn easily liquefying, fusible,

suvimala mfn perfectly clear or pure,

suvinaṣṭa mfn quite disappeared/vanished, quite worn out or emaciated,

suvinaya mfn well educated or disciplined,

suvinirmala mfn quite spotless or pure,

suviniścaya m. a very firm resolution,

suviniścita mfn thoroughly convinced,

suvipra mfn very learned (esp. sacred knowledge),

suvīra mfn very manly, heroic, warlike, m. a hero, warrior,

suviraja mfn thoroughly free from passions

suvirūḍha 1233/3 mfn. fully grown up or developed

suvīrya n. manly vigour or deed, heroism

suviśada mfn very clear or intelligible,

suviśāla mfn very large,

suviśārada mfn very experienced/skilful

suvismaya mfn very astonished or surprised

suvismita mfn very surprising or wonderful,

suviśiṣṭa mfn most distinguished/excellent,

suviśodhaka mfn easily improved,

suvispaṣṭa mfn perfectly clear or manifest,

suviśrabdha mfn very beautiful/confident,

suvistara m. great extent, plenty, great diffuseness, mfn very extensive or large, very strong or intense, (*am*) ind. in great detail, at full length, very intensely, vehemently,

suviśuddha mfn perfectly pure,

suviśvasta mfn very confiding, careless,

suvita mfn easily accessed, easy to traverse, prosperous (as a path), faring well, n. a good path, welfare, prosperity, fortune, good luck,

suvivartita mfn well-rounded,

suvivikta very secluded, solitary (a wood), well decided or answered,

suvrata mfn ruling well, strict in observing religious vows, m. a religious student

suvṛddha mfn very old or ancient (as a race)

suvṛkti f. excellent praise or hymn,

suvṛtta mfn well-rounded, beautifully globular or round, well-conducted, virtuous, good,

suvṛtti f. a good way of living, good conduct, life of chastity/continence, the life of a *Brahmacārin*

suvyakta mfn very clear or bright, very plain, distinct or manifest,

suyama mfn easily guided, tractable, easily restrained or kept in order, m. pl. a class of gods,

suyāmuna m. a palace, a kind of cloud,
suyaśas n. glorious fame, mfn very famous
suyata mfn well-restrained or governed,
sūyate it produces, creates, impels, 1/s/pres/indic/mid √*sū*
suyavasa mfn abounding in grass, n. beautiful grass,
suyavasād mfn eating good grass,
suyavasin mfn having good pasture
suyavasodaka mfn abounding in good pasture and water,
suyoga m. a favourable juncture, good opportunity,
suyuddha well fought battle or war,
suyuj mfn well joined or yoked,
suyukta well-joined, harmoniously combined, well-composed, attentive, very auspicious, very fit
suyukti f. a good appliance or contrivance, good argument,
suyuta well accompanied by, well furnished with,
sv for 5. *su* 1219/3 good, excellent, right, virtuous, (due to sandhi),
śva(ḥ) m. or ind. tomorrow,
sva 1275/1 mfn own, one's own, my own, his own, her own, their own etc. referring to all three persons according to context, often ibc. generally declined like the pronoun *sarva* (all) but always like *śiva* when used substantively, sometimes used loosely for my, thy, his, our. Used as a reflexive pronoun (= *ātman*) as appropriate (a reflexive is used when e.g. the person seeing is the same as the person seen, 'I see myself' or 'she sees herself'),
m. one's self, the ego, *ātman,* a kinsman, relative, a man of one's own people or tribe,
(*ā*) f. a woman of one's own caste,
(*am*) n. (ifc.f. *ā*) one's self, the ego e.g. *svaṁ ca Brahma ca* 'the ego and Brahman', one's own goods, property, wealth, riches, (in this sense also said to be m.),
svā f. in comp. for *svar,* a woman of one's own caste
śvaḥ ind. tomorrow,
svabhānu mfn self-luminous,
svābhāsa mfn very illustrious or splendid,
svabhāva 1276/1 m. (ifc. f.*ā*) native place, own condition, or state of being, natural state or constitution, innate or inherent disposition, nature, impulse, spontaneity, sense, natural disposition,
-*vāt* rom natural disposition,
-*vena* by nature, naturally,
-*taḥ* ind. intrinsically,
-*tas* ind. inherently,
-*ta* adv. with 5/s sense, natural disposition
svābhāva m. own non-existence,
svabhāvas mfn being in the Self,
svabhāvaja produced by natural disposition, natural, innate,
svabhāvadveṣa m. natural hatred,
svabhāvajā born of own nature, produced by natural disposition, innate,
svābhāvan 'objects (such as the earth) etc., which are identical with him', (T),
svabhavas mfn being in the Self (said of the breath),
svabhāvataḥ ind. naturally, by oneself, spontaneously, intrinsically,
svābhāvika 1283/3 mfn belonging to or arising from one's own nature, "(knowledge).. that which is provided by the Will of the Absolute to the individual. Natural knowledge is in the design of the individual." HH *a svābhāvika* is created by human beings for their welfare. *A svābhāvika* is also natural but is hidden from the individual and is discovered by intellectual insight. This is learnt and is subject to change.
svābhāvikī belonging to or arising from one's nature, spontaneous, original, natural,
svābhīla mfn very formidable,
√*śvabhr* 1105/2 Cl 10 P *śvabhrayati* to go,

move, to live in misery, to pierce, bore, DP in *gati* going,
svabhū mfn self-existent, f. one's own country, home,
svabhūmi f. one's own land, one's own or proper place,
svabhūta mfn being one's own, belonging to (6th),
√*śvac* (or *śvañc)* 1104/3 Cl 1 A *śvacate, śvañcate* to become open, open, (intrans.)receive with open arms, caus. *śvañcayati* to open (trans.), DP in *gati* going,
svacakṣus n. one's own eye,
svācaraṇa n. good conduct or behaviour,
svacaryā f. one's own nature,
svaccha mfn very transparent or clear, pellucid, crystalline, bright-coloured, clear, distinct (as speech), pure (as the mind or heart), healthy, sound, convalescent, m. rock-crystal, (*am*) n. a pearl, an alloy of silver and gold, pure chalk,
svacchaka mfn very clear/bright (cheeks)
svacchanda 1275/2 m. one's own or free will, one's own choice or fancy, spontaneously, independently, uncontrolled, mfn following one's own will, acting at pleasure, independent, uncontrolled, spontaneous, (*am*) ind.,
svacchandavanajāta mfn spontaneously wood-grown i.e. growing wild in the wood,
svācchandya 1283/2 independence, freedom,
svacetas n. one's own mind, -*sā* 'outof one's own head',
√*svad* 1279/3 Cl 1 A *svadate (ti*), to taste with pleasure, to taste well, be sweet or pleasant to, enjoy, like, delight in, P. to make palatable, season, to make sweet or pleasant, or agreeable, to be pleasant or wholesome, P.A. *svādati (te*), to taste, relish, enjoy, caus. *svadayati (te*), to make savoury or palatable, sweeten, season, prepare, cook, to propitiate, conciliate, *svādayati* to eat, relish, taste, enjoy, DP in *āsvādana* tasting,
√*svād* see *svad* DP in *āsvādana* tasting,
svāda m. taste, flavour, savour, the beauty or charm of a poem,
svādara mfn very considerate, regardful,
svādas n. agreeableness,
svadana n. tasting, licking, eating,
svadhā 1280/1 f. an axe, knife
1278/1 f. self-position, self-power, inherent power, own state or condition or nature, habitual state, custom, rule, law, ease, comfort, pleasure, (*anu svadhām, svadhām anu, svadhayā* etc.) 'according to one's habit or pleasure', spontaneously, willingly, freely, f. self-power, inherent power, self-position, own state or condition or nature, custom, rule, law, ease, comfort, pleasure,
own place, home,
the sacrificial offering due to each god, esp. the food or libation,
the exclamation or benediction used when presenting the offering or libation to the *manes*,
svadharma m. one's own rights, one's own duty or duty of one's own caste, peculiar property, peculiarity,
svadharman mfn abiding in one's own customs,
svadhāvan mfn lawful, constant, faithful, containing homes
svadhāvant mfn keeping to his custom, faithful, constant, (having bliss) i.e. blessed,
svadhāvin mfn containing refreshment, owning the *svadhā*
svadhetika m. armed with an axe,
svādhī mfn well-minded, thoughtful, heedful, devout, pious,
svādhīna mfn independent, free, dependent on one's self, being in one's own power or control,
svadhiṣṭhāna mfn having a good standing place,

svādhiṣṭhāna n. the second of six *cakras* of the body, one's own place,
svadhita mfn firm, solid, = 1. *sudhita*
svadhīta mfn well recited or studied, well read, well instructed,
svadhiti m.f. an axe, knife, saw,
svadhur mfn self-dependent, independent,
svādhyāya m. reciting or repeating the scriptures to one's self, perusal of any sacred texts, study of scriptures and discourses between the aspirant and the wise, '...it removes all doubts, resolves questions and enlightens the way'. HH
svādhyāyati Nom.P. to study, recite, read to,
svādhyāyin mfn repeating/reciting the Veda, m. one who recites or repeats any sacred texts to himself,
svādin mfn tasting, enjoying,
svādiṣṭha mfn sweetest, very sweet/pleasant
svadita mfn well seasoned or prepared, savoury,
svadoṣaja mfn due to one's own fault
svadṛś mfn seeing one's self or the soul,
svādu mfn sweet, savoury, dainty, agreeable, full of tastes, m. sugar, molasses, a grape,
svādukhaṇḍa m. lump sugar,
svāduman m. sweetness,
svāgama m. welcome, salutation,
svagata mfn belonging to one's self, own, passing in one's own mind, spoken to oneself, come of one's self, lawfully earned (money),
svāgata welcome, greeting, well come,
svagata-bheda internal differences, 'difference as between the limbs of one's own body,' (U)
svāgatika mfn bidding welcome to anyone
svagni mfn one who has a good *agni* or fire,
svagocara mfn subject to one's self, m. one's own sphere or range,
svagrāma m. one's own village,
svaguṇa 1275/2 m. one's own merits, mfn having one's own merits, appropriate,
śvaḥ tomorrow
svaḥ we two are,
in comp. for 3. *svar*
svāhā ind. hail! hail to! , may a blessing rest on, an oblation, an exclamation used in making oblations, oblation personified - her body is said to consist of the four Vedas and her limbs of the six Aṅgas,
svāhākaraṇa n. consecration by uttering *svāhā*
svāhāra mfn easy to obtain, m. good food,
svahasta m. one's own hand, own handwriting, autograph,
svahita mfn beneficial to one's self, well disposed to one's self, n. one's own welfare,
svaira mfn going where one likes, doing what one likes, wilful, independent, unrestrained, walking cautiously, voluntary, optional, (*am)* n. wilfulness, unreservedly, confidingly, (*am*) ind. according to one's own will or pleasure, easily, spontaneously, at random, slowly, softly,
svairakam ind. freely, unreservedly, unrestrainedly, straight out, plainly,
svairastha mfn remaining indifferent, unconcerned,
svairavihārin mfn roaming about at pleasure, unimpeded, meeting with no resistance,
svairin mfn going where one likes, free, independent, unrestrained,
śvaitya 1107/3 n. whiteness, white leprosy
√*svaj* or *svañj* 1279/2 Cl 1 A *svajate (ti),* to embrace, clasp, encircle, twist or wind round, caus. *svañjayati*, DP in *pariṣvaṅga* embracing, clasping,
svajana 1275 m. own people, own kindred
svajāta mfn self-begotten, m. a child begotten by one's self,
svajāti mfn f. one's own kind, one's own family or caste,
svajātivṛttipravāha 'the constant flow of the idea of one's own essential state i.e. of the idea of "I am Brahman", (U)
svaka mfn= *sva* , one's own, my own, etc.

m.a relation, kinsman, friend, one's own people, followers, wife, friends,

svakāla m. one's own time, proper time,

svakāle ind. at the right time,

svākāra m. one's own nature, natural disposition, mfn of decent or respectable appearance,

svakaraṇa n. marrying, making a woman one's own,

svakarman n. one's own deeds or duties, one's own business or occupation,

svakarmin mfn selfish,

svakārmin mfn self-pleasing, following one's own wish,

svakāryasaha mfn able to do one's own duty or effect one's own business,

svakṛt mfn doing one's own, performing one's own obligations,

svakṛta mfn done, performed, built etc. by oneself,

svakṣatra mfn master of one's self, free, independent, possessing inner strength

svakta mfn well smeared or anointed,

svakula one's own family or race,

svakuśalamaya mfn relating to own welfare,

svakuṭumba n. one's own household,

√*śval* 1105/3 (or *śvall*) Cl 1 P *śvalati* to go quickly, run, DP in *āśu-gamana* running, going quickly,

svalakṣaṇa mfn having its own specific characteristics, n. peculiar characteristic or property,

svalaṁkṛta mfn well-adorned,

√*śvalk* 1105/3 Cl 10 P *śvalkayati* to tell, narrate, DP in *paribhāṣaṇa* telling, narrating,

svalpa mn little, very small n. a small amount, a little,

svamahimāpratiṣṭhita one who is established in or is dependent on his own greatness or glory, (U)

svamāyā f. own cunning or magical art or skill,

svāmi 1284/1 in comp. for *svāmin*, master, lord, a spiritual preceptor, learned *brāhmin* or *paṇdit*

svāmiguṇa m. ruler-virtue,

svāmihita n. master's welfare, (L)

svāmikārya n. master's business,

svāmikumāra the Lord Kumāra, name of Skanda , god of war,

svāmin m. an owner, proprietor, master, a chief, commander, a husband, lover, (du. husband and wife), a king, prince, spiritual preceptor, learned Brahman or pandit (used as a title at the end of names),

svāmisevā f. the serving one's master, respect or reverence for a master or husband,

svamṛtam 'the beautiful, holy, reality of the Self' (Gam.),

svāmy in comp. for *svāmin*

svāmya n. mastership, lordship, ownership, power over anyone,

svāmyartham 1284/1 ind. for a master's sake

√*svan* 1. 1280/2 Cl 1 P *svanati (te)*, to sound, make any noise, roar, yell, hum, sing, caus. *svanayati* to sound, resound, to adorn, DP in *śabda* sounding, in *avataṁsana* adorning,

śvan m. a dog, hound, cur, f. (*ī*)

svana m. sound, noise, roar (of wind), roaring water, mfn ill-sounding,

svānama mfn easily attracted or captivated,

svānanda m. delight in one's self,

svanagara n. one's own town or native city

svanas n. roar, loud-sounding,

svañc mfn going well, moving swiftly or gracefully, nimble, swift, rapid,

svani m. fire,

√ *svañj* 1279/2 Cl 1 A *svajate (ti),* to embrace, clasp, encircle, twist or wind round, caus. *svañjayati*, DP in *pariṣvaṅga* embracing, clasping,

√*śvaṅk* 1104/3 Cl 1 A *śvaṅkate* to go, move DP in *gati* going,

svanna n. good food,

svanta mfn having a good end, terminating well, auspicious, fortunate,

svānta m. own end, own death, own domain, n. 'seat of the ego', the heart (as seat of the emotions), a cavern,

svāntaja m. 'heart-born' love,

svāntastha mfn being in the heart,
svāntavat mfn having a heart,
svānubhava m. one's own personal experience or observation,
svānubhāva m. enjoyment of or love for property,
svānubhūti f. one's own experience, self-enjoyment, direct experience of one's own Self,
svanuṣṭhita mfn well performed, well observed, duly practised,
svap 1280/2 Cl 2 P *svapiti , svapati (te),* to sleep, fall asleep, to lie down, recline upon, to be dead, caus. *svāpayati,* to cause to sleep, lull to rest, to kill, DP in *śaya* sleeping,
2. mfn having good water, dreaming, sleeping
svapada 1276/1 one's own place or abode, own position or rank, *svapade* 7/s in one's own Self
śvāpada m. a beast of prey,
śvāpaka m. man of an outcaste tribe, a man who cooks dogs,
svapāka mfn skilful, industrious,
svapan sleeping pres/act/part.
svapana mfn sleepy, drowsy, n. the act of sleeping, dreaming, sleep,
svaparāddha mfn very faulty,
svapas mfn doing good work, skilful, artistic, m. a good artificer,
svapasya mfn active, industrious,
svapasyā f. activity, diligence, skill,
svapatya n. good offspring, good work or deeds, mfn having good offspring,
svāpi m. a good friend or comrade,
svapiti he sleeps
svapitṛ mfn asleep, a sleeper, m. one's own father, pl. one's own deceased ancestors,
svapivāta mfn understanding or meaning well, 'whose speech is trustworthy or authoritative',
svapna 1280/3 m. sleep, sleeping, sleepiness, drowsiness, sleeping too much, sloth, indolence, dreaming, a dream, the dream state (also known as *prajñā)*, illusion,

svapnadṛk one who sees a dream (Gam.)
svapnadṛkcittam the consciousness of the dream experiencer, (Gam.)
svapnakalpita imagined in a dream, dream creation,
svapnamānavaka m. the 'dream-manikin', name of a magic for dreams that come true, a kind of charm effecting the realisation of dreams,
svapnamāyāsarūpa 'of the same nature as dream and magic',
svapnas mfn wealthy, rich,
svapnasthāna having the dream state as his sphere of activity, the sire or locality of a dream, a bed-chamber, mfn sleeping, dreaming,
svapnavasthā f. dreamstate, state of dreaming,
svapnavat ind. like a dream, as a dream,
svapnavṛtta mfn occurring in a dream,
svapnayā ind. in dreaming,
svapnya n. a vision in a dream,
svapradhānatā f. one's own natural state, self-dependence,
svaprakāśa mfn clear or evident by itself, self-luminous,
svāpta mfn very abundant, very skilful or trustworthy,
svapū f. a broom,
√*svar* 1. 1281/1 Cl 10 P *svarayati,* to find fault, blame, censure, DP in *ākṣepa* finding fault, blaming, reproving, censuring,
2. Cl 1 P *svarati* caus. *svarayati* to shine, DP see *svṛ*
3. 1281/2 ind. the sun, sunshine, light, lustre, bright space or sky, heaven, the place of the light, the region of the planets and constellations, water,
svara m. (ifc.f.*ā*) sound, noise, voice, tone in recitation (high/low), accent -(3 kinds *udātta*, high pitch, *anudātta* low pitch, *svarita* combination of pitch), a note of the musical scale

a vowel (long, short or extended), air breathed through the nostrils,

svāra m. sound, noise (snorting horse), tone, accent, the *svarita* accent, mfn relating to sound or accent, having the *svarita* accent,

svarabhaṅga m. hoarseness, broken articulation, stammering, choking of the voice (one of the signs of divine emotion),

svarāj mfn self-ruling, m. a self-ruler, self-resplendent or luminous,

svārāj 1282/1 king of heaven *svārājye* 7/s/m in the kingdom or dominion of heaven

svārāma 1277/3 mfn delighting in oneself

svaraṇa mfn loud-sounding, clear-voiced,

svarasa 1276/2 m. one's own pure essence, natural or peculiar flavour, proper taste or sentiment in composition, a partic. astringent juice or decoction, own inclination, feeling for one's own people, instinct of self-preservation? analogy, mfn agreeable or pleasant to one's taste,

svarasādhanā f. regulation of breath, a practice in which the breath is continuously watched and regulated,

svārasya n. naturalness, self-evidence,

svarbhānu m. name of a demon causing the eclipse of the sun,

√*svard* 1282/2 Cl 1 A *svardate* to taste, to please, to be pleasing, DP in *āsvādana* tasting,

svarga 1281/2 mfn. (or *suvarga*) heavenly celestial, going or leading to or being in light or heaven, m. heaven, heavenly bliss.

svargagāmin mfn going to or attaining heaven,

svargakāma 1281/3 mn desirous of heaven

svargaloka m. the heavenly world,

svarganarakau 1281/3 1/du heaven and hell

svargārohaṇa mfn. 151/2 arising, ascending, n. the act of rising,rising to heaven

svargin mfn belonging to or being in heaven, gone to heaven, dead, m. an occupant of heaven, a god, one of the blest

svargya mfn. occupying or dwelling in heaven

svarhaṇa n. great reverence,

svarhat mfn very honourable,

svarita mfn caused to sound, sounded, having an accent, accented, added, admixed, m.n. the *Svarita* accent (a kind of mixed tone, produced by a combination of high and low tone, and therefore named *samāhāra*, the high and low tones being called *udātta* 'raised or acute' and *anudātta* 'low or grave'

svārjita mfn self-acquired,

svarloka the world of heaven, a partic. heaven, 'celestial or bright plane', an occupant of heaven, a god, 'one of the blest',

svarṇa 1282/1 n. gold, a kind of red chalk,

√*śvart* 1105/3 see *śvabhr* DP in *gati* going

svartha mfn pursuing or serving worthy ends,

svārtha m. one's own aim or object, self-interest, personal matter or advantage, mfn directed to one's self, egotistical, adapted to (its) purpose, having one's object, expressing (its) own inherent meaning, having a natural or literal meaning, having similar merits,

svārtham ind. for one's own sake,

svārthin mfn pursuing one's own objects, self-seeking,

svarūpa 1276/2 n. own form or shape, condition, character, true nature, 'the essential nature of Brahman, reality, *saccidānanda*, true nature of being,' (U),

svarūpabhāva m. the use of the true form of a person's name, (a short word) whose essence is of the same efficacy (as that of the full form),

svarūpadhyāna meditation on the reality of one's own real nature,

svarūpaikya 'substance identity' e.g. 'the

mud is the pot' –this is a statement of the oneness of substance between mud and pot, identity of essence, essential oneness,

svarūpalakṣana definition of the essential nature of Brahman, *saccidānanda* – existence, consciousness, bliss,

svarūpānyathabhāva being other than one's own real nature,

svarūpasaṁbandha m. connection with one's own essential nature,

svarūpastha 1262/3 abiding, abiding in your true nature, situated in himself,

svarūpashiti getting oneself firmly established in one's own essential nature,

svarūpapratiṣṭha being established in one's own Self, (U)

svarūpavastha state of being one with Brahman; resting in the absolute reality, or Brahman, (U)

svarūpaviśrānti resting in one's own essential nature,

svarvat m. a good or swift courser, mfn bright, shining, celestial,

svarya mfn sounding, whizzing of a thunderbolt,

√*śvas* 1105/3 Cl 2 P *śvasiti, śvasati (te)*, to blow, hiss, pant, snort, to breathe, respire, draw breath, live, to sigh, groan, to strike, kill, DP in *prāṇana* breathing,

śvas ind. tomorrow, on the next day, a particle implying auspiciousness

svās mfn fair-mouthed, (as Agni), keen-edged, sharp (as an axe),

śvāsa m. breathhard breathing, panting, snorting, inspiration, asthma sighing, hissing,

svāsad mfn sitting happily by,

svaśakti f. own power or strength,

svaśaktyā ind. to the best of one's ability

svasambhava mfn being one's own origin or source,

svasaṁhitā f. connection only with self, being by one self or alone,

svasaṁsiddha mfn perfect in itself (world)

svasaṁsthā f. the abiding in self, absorption in self,

svasaṁvedana n. knowledge derived from one's self,

svasaṁvedya mfn intelligible only to one-self,

svasaṁvid f. the knowledge of one's own or the true essence, mfn knowing only one's self,

śvasan breathing pres/act/part √*śvas* 1105/3

svasara n. a stall, fold, own place, home, nest of birds, day,

svaśarīra 1277/1 own body or person

śvasatha m. a snorting,

√*ṣvaṣk* 1111/2 Cl 1 P A *ṣvaṣkati (te),* to go, move, DP in *gati* going,

svasiddha mfn spontaneously effected, naturally one's own, self-established, self-evident,

svasita mfn very black,

√*svask* 1283/1 see *ṣvaṣk,* DP in *gati* going

svasṛ f. a sister, (also applied to closely connected things of the f. gender),

svasṛt mfn going one's own way,

śvaśrū f. mother-in-law and the other wives,mother in law,

svastaka mfn having a good home,

svastakaraṇa n. reparation,

svastamita n. a beautiful sunset,

śvastana mfn of the morrow, n. the morrow,

svastha 1277/1 mfn abiding in one's self, in one's natural state, (the natural state is that the senses are subordinate to the Self), being oneself, feeling oneself, healthy,

svasthāna n. one's own place, own home

svasthi√*bhū* P. *–bhavati,* to become one's self, return to one's natural condition,

svasthita mfn independent,

svāsthya 1284/3 self-dependence, comfort, contentment, sound state (of body or soul), contentment, satisfaction,

svasti 1283/1 n.f. well-being, luck, success, good fortune, may it be well with thee, hail!, farewell! ind. well, happily, successfully,

svastidā mfn conferring happiness,

svasti iti may it be well

svastika m. a kind of bard, any lucky or auspicious object, (esp.) a kind of mystical cross or mark made on persons and things to denote good luck, the crossing of the arms or hands on the chest, the meeting of 4 roads, a species of garlic, a cock, a libertine,

svasty in comp. for *svasti*

svastya mfn happy, fortunate,

svastyakṣara n. expressing thanks for anything,

svastyayana auspicious progress, success, blessing, benediction, recitation of a mantra for good luck,congratulation, a means of attaining prosperity, mfn bringing or causing good fortune, auspicious,

śvaśura 1105/3 m. father-in-law,

svaśva mfn with very good horses,

svatā f. the state of belonging to one's self, ownership,

svataḥsiddha mfn self-proved, self-demonstrated, self-accomplished, self-evident, self-realised,

svatantra n. self-dependence, independence, self-will, freedom, mfn self-dependent, self-willed, independent, free, uncontrolled, of age, full grown,

svatantrasattabhāva possibility of independent existence,

svatantratva state of (absolute) independence, (U),

svatantrin mfn free, independent, uncontrolled

svatantraya to make subject to one's own will,

svātantrya 1283/3 following one's own will, freedom of the will, independence,

svātantryāt 5/s of one's own free choice, freely, through freedom,

svatas ind. of one's own self, of one's own accord, by nature,

svatastā f. the state of belonging to one's self, ownership, = *-tva*

svatastva being self-proved,

svatavas mfn inherently powerful, valiant,

svatejas n. one's own splendour,

√*śvaṭh* 1104/3 Cl 10 P *śvaṭhayati* = √2. *śāṭh*
2. √*śvaṭh* 1104/3 (or *śvaṇṭh*) Cl 10 P *śvāṭhayati, śvāṇṭhayati,* see 3. *śaṭh* DP in *sampak* speaking elegantly, *avabhāṣaṇa* speaking ill of, *asaṁskāra* not finishing, *gati* going,

svātman 1277/2 m. own self, one-self
svātmani 7/s/m in your own Self

svatra mfn self-preserving, m. a blind man

svatva 1275/2 proprietary right to, self-existence, independence, relationship to one-self

svavaśa mfn having control of one's self independent, free, not at all master of one's self,

śvāvidh m. porcupine,

svavināśa m. self-destruction, suicide,

svavīryatas ind. according to one's power,

svavṛtti f. one's own way of life,

svayam pron. ind. self, one's self, (applicable to all persons, myself, thyself, himself etc.) of or by oneself, spontaneously, voluntarily, of one's own accord, also used emphatically *svayam vṛtavān* I chose it myself

svayamāgata mfn come of one's own accord, intruding,

svayamagurutva n. state of lightness existing in one's self

svayambhāva m. feeling of independence,

svayambhṛta mfn self maintained or nourished,

svayambhu m. self-existent, N.of Brahman,

svayambhū 1278/3 mfn. self-existing, independent, name of *Brahman,* 'm.(*-ḥ*)...is the first-born of his own accord' HH he who exists by himself

svāyambhuva relating to the self-existent i.e. Brahman,

svayaṁjyotis mfn self-shining, self-luminous,

svayammlāna mfn faded/withered naturally

svayammṛta mfn one who has died a natural death, (lit. of his own accord),

svayamprabha mfn self-shining,

svayamprakāśā self-luminous,
svayaṁsiddha self-accomplished, perfect in itself (the world),
svayaṁvara m. self-choice, esp. free choice of a husband, which was allowed to girls of the warrior caste,
svayamvaraṇa n. the free choice of a husband,
svayaṁvedana n. spontaneous consciousness,
svāyasa mfn made of good metal,
svayu mfn left to itself (as cattle), ruling of one's own free will or right (Indra),
svāyu mfn having good people (subjects),
svāyudha mfn well-armed,
svayukti f.pl. own yoke or horse team,
sve in own 7/s/ *sva* , *sve sve* repeated for emphasis,
sveccha ibc. according to one's wish, at will, freely, voluntarily,
svecchā f. one's own wish or will, ibc. at pleasure, according to one's own wish,
svecchayā ind. according to desire, L. according to one's inclination, at will,
sveda m. (ifc. f.*ā*) sweat, perspiration, sweating, warmth, heat, steam, mfn sweating, toiling,
svedaja 1285/1 sweat-produced, engendered by heat and moisture, born of moisture – lice etc.
svedana mfn perspiring, inclined to perspire, causing to perspire, *(ī)* f. an iron pan or plate,
śveta mfn white, bright, m. white (the colour), a white horse, cowry, coin, cloud, planet Venus,
śvetāmbara 'white-robed' one of the two principal Jaina sects and referring to the monks and nuns, the monks of the other (*digambara)* are naked,
śvetaiḥ by or with white
svetara-bheda difference from the rest,
√śvi 1106/2 sometimes written *śvā* cl 1 P *śvayati* to swell, grow, increase, DP in *gati* going, or *vṛddhi* growing,
svī in comp. for 1. *sva*
svid 1. 1284/3 ind. particle of interrogation, inquiry or doubt, 'do you think?, indeed, perhaps, any' 2. cl 1 A cl 4 P *svedate* or *svidayati (te),* to sweat, perspire, *svedate* to be anointed, to be disturbed? caus. *svedayati* to cause to sweat, treat with sudorifics , to foment, soften, 3. mfn sweating, perspiring, DP(cl 1) in *snehana mocana* being greasy, being disturbed, in *avyakta śabda* sounding, cl 4 in *gātra-pakṣaraṇa* sweating, perspiring,
svidita mfn sweated, melted, sweating,
svīkāra m. making one's own, claiming, claim, appropriation, reception, assent, agreement, consent, promise,
svīkāragraha m. robbery, forcible seizure,
svīkaraṇa n. making one's own, accepting, appropriating, acquiring, taking to wife, marrying, assenting, agreeing, promising,
svī√kṛ P.A. *–karoti, kurute,* to make one's own, win, appropriate, claim, to take to oneself, choose, marry, to win power over (hearts etc), A. to admit, assent or agree to, ratify,
svīkśta 1279/1 mfn appropriated, making one's own, claimed, agreed, promised,
√śvind 1107/3 cl 1 A *śvindate* to be white, to be cold, DP in *śvaitya* becoming white,
svinna mfn sweating, perspiring,
√śvit 1106/2 cl 1 A *śvetate* to be bright or white, DP in *varṇa* becoming white, being white,
śvita mfn whiteness, n. whiteness,
svita n. welfare, luck,
svīya mfn relating/belonging to one's self, own, proper, characteristic, m.pl. one's own people or kin, f.(*ā)* one's own wife, a wife solely attached to her husband,
śvobhāvaḥ 1106/1 tomorrow's state of affairs, the affairs or occurrences of tomorrow, ephemeral, whose existence is subject to doubt as to

whether they will exist tomorrow or not,

svojas mfn very strong or powerful,

svopaśa mfn having beautiful locks of hair

svorasa m. a husk, shell, n. the sediment of oily substances ground with a stone,

√*svṛ* 1285/1 cl 1 P *svarati* to utter a sound, sound, resound, to sing, praise, make resound, to shine, caus. *svarayati*, DP in *ṛabda* sounding, *upatāpa* paining or being pained,

sya pron. that

syād in comp. for *syāt*

syada m. driving, rapid motion, speed,

syādasti maybe it is,

syādnāsti maybe it is not,

syādvāda m. assertion of possibility or non-possibility, the sceptical or agnostic doctrine of the Jainas,

√*śyai* 1095/2 cl 1 P *śyāyati* to cause to congeal or freeze, A. *śyāyate* to go, move, to congeal, freeze, be cold, DP in *gati* going

syāla m. a brother-in-law,

√*syam* 1273/2 cl 1 P *syamati* to sound, cry aloud, shout, cry, shriek, to go, cl 10 A *syāmayate (ti),* to consider, reflect, caus. *syamayati,* DP cl 1 in *śabda* sounding, cl 10 in *vitarka* considering, reflecting,

syām I should be, I shall become, 3/s/opt √*as*

syāma we should be, we might be 3/pl/opt/act √*as*

śyāma dark, black, dark blue, a name for *kṛśṇa,*

śyāmala mfn dark coloured, m. black,

syamika m. an ant-hill,

syamīka m. a cloud, time, (*ā*) f. the indigo plant, *(am)* n. water,

√*syand* or *syad*1273/1 Cl 1 A *syandate (ti*), to move or flow on rapidly, flow, stream, run, drive in a carriage, rush, hasten, speed, to discharge liquid, trickle, ooze, drip, sprinkle, to issue from caus. *syandayati* to stream, flow, run, to cause to flow or run, DP in *prasravaṇa* oozing, trickling, distilling, dropping,

syanda m. flowing, running, streaming, trickling, oozing, trickling perspiration, the moon,

syandana 1273/1 mfn. moving on swiftly, running (as a chariot), n. a chariot,

syandanāroha m. a warrior who fights mounted on a chariot,

syandanikā f. a brook, rivulet, a drop of saliva,

syāla 1273/2 brother-in-law 1/s/m

syanda m. flowing, running, streaming, trickling, oozing, trickling perspiration,

syandana mfn moving on swiftly, running (as a chariot), dripping, sprinkling, liquefying, dissolving, a war chariot, chariot, car,

syāt 1273/2 1/s/opt/act verb to be – *as,* expresses possibility, perhaps it is, it may be, perchance, it should be, might it be

śyena m. eagle, falcon, hawk, mfn eagle-like,

syona mfn soft, gentle, pleasant, agreeable, mild, tender, m. a sack, ray of light, (*am*) n. a soft couch, comfortable seat, pleasant situation, delight, happiness,

syota m. a sack

syū f. a string, thread,

syuḥ should be, 1/pl/opt/act √*as*

syūma m.n. a ray of light, water,

syūmaka n. delight, happiness,

syūman n. a band, thong, bridle,

syūna m. a sack, a ray of light, the sun, f. (*ā*) a ray of light, a girdle,

syus they should be, should they be 1/pl/opt/act √*as*

syūta mfn sewn, stitched, woven, sewn on, sewn or woven together, fabricated, pierced, penetrated, m. a sack,

syūti f. sewing, stitching, weaving, a bag, sack, lineage, offspring,

syutna n. happiness, delight,

ta m. a tail, the breast, womb, hip, a warrior, thief, wicked man, a jewel, nectar, n. crossing, virtue,

-tā -ness, a suffix indicating an abstract quality,

√taḍ 432/1 cl 10 *tāḍayati* to beat, strike, knock, strike with arrows, wound, punish, to strike a musical instrument, to speak or to shine, DP in *āghāta* beating, striking, in *bhāṣā* speaking

tad 434/1 that, this, pron 1/s/n
n. this world,
ind. then, in that case, therefore, accordingly, there, in that place, thither, to that spot, \
correlative of *yadā, yatra, yadi,*
ind. thus, in this manner, with regard to that, on that account, for that reason, therefore, consequently, (sometimes corel. of *yatas, yad, yena,* 'because',
ind. now (clause-connecting particle,
ind. so, also, equally, and,
tad tad this and that, various, different, respective,
yad tad whosoever, whichsoever, any, every,
ind. *tadapi* even then, nevertheless, notwithstanding,
tadyathā 'in such a manner as follows', namely,

tadā or *tad*, 434/3 ind. then, at that time, in that case, then (correl. of *yadā* – when…then....),

tadabhivādin mfn signifying that,

tadādi from that time forward

taḍāga n. a lake or pond, a trap,

tadāhāravartman n. the way of that food,

tadājñā f. his (the moon-god's) command,

tadākāra mfn having that appearance, of the same form as That (Brahman),

tadākṛti mfn having the appearance of them,

tādana 441/3 mfn beating, striking, hurting
n. chastising, beating, whipping,

tadānīm then, at that time,

tadānīmtana of that time, in that period,

tadantara 434/1 mfn. nearest to anyone, (*am*) ind. immediately upon that, thereupon, then, immediately adjoining that,

tadaṅga n. his person,

tadānīm 434/3 at that time, then

tadārāma delighting only in the Self,

tadardhika mfn amounting to or lasting half of that, half as much,

tadartham for them, ind. on that account, for that end, therefore,

tadarthīya 434/1 mfn intended for that, undertaken for that end, relating to that, meant for this

tadātmānas those whose selves are fixed on that , BV compound,

tādātmya n. sameness of nature, sameness or identity of nature or character with, of the nature of that,

tādātmyasaṁbandha identical relation, e.g. iron becomes fore (when heated), water becomes white (when mixed with milk),

tadbhāṣā f. that language,

tadbhaya m. fear of it or them,

tadbheda m. differentiation (Gam.),

tadbuddhayas whose minds are absorbed in that BV comp.

tadgṛha n. his house,

taddhita 434/2 m. an affix forming (derivative) nouns from other nouns. *taddhita* is an example of this and means 'good for that or him'

tadīpsita mfn desired by those two,

taḍit ind. lightning,

tāḍita mfn beaten, struck, chastised,

tādītnā ind. then, at that time, (corel. of *yadi*),

tadīya mfn belonging or relating or pertaining to or coming from him, her, it, that, hers, its, theirs, them, such,

tadrasa m. the essence of it, the spirit of,

tādṛś mfn such, suchlike, such a one,

tādṛśa 442/1 mfn in such a manner, such a one, anybody whosoever,

tādṛśāḥ 442/1 such like, such a one 1/pl those like (him)

tādṛśat anybody whosoever,

tadupadeśa m. his advice,
tadvacana n. his words,
tadvana 'derived from t*asya* his and *vanam* adorable, "adorable to all creatures" Brahman to be meditated on as..' *Kena U.* 4.7.6
tadvat ind. in this way, so, likewise, mfn having or containing that,
tadvid mfn knowing that, familiar with that, m. connoisseur, f. the knowledge of that,
tadvidas the knowers of this (or that) pl.
tadvṛddhi f. the interest of them,
ṭagara mfn squint-eyed, m. borax,
tāḥ tāḥ such and such
tāḥ pron. 1/pl/f those,they
taila n. oil,
taijasa 455/1 mfn. originating from or consisting of light (*tejas*) bright, brilliant, the individual being in the dream state,
taikṣṇya n. pungency, severity, sharpness, fierceness, pain,
taila n. sesame oil, oil, olibanum – a fragrant resin,
tailadhārā f. continuous flow of oil, a parallel used to denote the continuous flow of one thought in meditation, as well as the unbroken current of love of the devotee to his beloved God,
tais tais by these and those
taittirīya 'partridge', the name of an upanishad from the Yajur Veda m.pl, the pupils of *Tittīri*
tajjalān tajja – sprung from that, *-lān*, produced, absorbed and breathing in that, 'is born from that Brahman, therefore it is called *tajja*, and it is *talla* because... it gets merged in that very Brahman, becomes wholly identified with that; and it is *tadana* because it continues to live, to function on that very Brahman during its existence.'
tajjña 433/2 (*taj* for *tat* -that*)* knowing That, a knowing man, familiar with, *jña 425/3* intelligent, wise, a wise and learned man,
tajjīvana n. his subsistence, *(tad* +)
√*tak* 431/2 cl 2 *takti* cl 1 *takati* to laugh or to bear, to rush along, DP in *hasana* (cl1) laughing at, deriding, scoffing, bearing, enduring,
takra n. buttermilk mixed with water,
√*takṣ* 431/3 cl1 P A *takṣati (te)* cl 5 *takṣṇoti* to form by cutting, plane, chisel, chop, cut, split, fashion or form out of wood, form in the mind, invent, to make, make able, prepare for, (in math) to reduce by dividing, DP in *tvacana* skinning, in *tanūkaraṇa* n. making thin, attenuation
takṣa m. a wood-cutter, carpenter, mfn cutting through,
√*ṭal* 429/3 cl 1 P *ṭalati* to be disturbed, caus. *ṭālayati* to disturb, frustrate, DP in *vaiklavya* becoming confused or disturbed,
√*tal* 440/2 cl 1.10. *talati, tālayati* to accomplish (a vow), to establish, fix, DP in *pratiṣṭhā* establishing
tala m.n. surface, plane, world, level, base, the part underneath, bottom, a flat roof, the palm of the hand, sole of the foot, the forearm,
tāla m. slapping the hands together, the flapping of an elephants ears, the palmyra tree, a dance, a cymbal,
talātala the name of a hell,
tale at the foot of, ifc. = on
talpa m. couch, bed, seat of a carriage, an upper story, room on the top of a house, a raft, wife, boat,
talpaśīvan mfn lying on a bed(s) or couch(es),
tālu 445/2 the palate, name for palatal sounds,
tālumūla n. the root of the palate,
tallakṣaṇa 435/1 n. his or her or it's or their mark, e.g. 'the target of the soul',
√*tam* 438/1 cl 4 *tāmyati* to gasp for breath

(as one suffocating), choke, be suffocated, faint away, be exhausted, perish, be distressed, or disturbed or perplexed, to stop (as breath), become immovable or stiff, to desire, with *ā* preceding – till exhaustion, caus. *tamayati* to suffocate, deprive of breath, DP in *kāṅkṣā* wishing, desiring,

tam pron. 2/s that, him

tām pron. her (2nd)

tam tam 434/1 this and that

-tama 438/2 2. an affix forming the superlative degree of adjectives and rarely of substantives, added (in older language) to adverbs and (in later language to verbs, intensifying their meaning, ind. in a high degree, much

tamas 438/1 darkness, night, one of the 3 *guṇa(*s) having the qualities of ignorance, illusion, stability, decay, dullness, inertia, regulation, 'it is of the nature of indifference and serves to restrain. It is heavy and deep enveloping.' G. 314

tāmasa mfn dark, pertaining to darkness or to *tamas,*

tāmasāhaṅkāra the lowest or grossest type of egoism characterised by delusion, inertia and deep arrogation, (U)

tāmasika 443/1 mfn. relating to the quality *tamas*

tāmasika tapas exteme austerity of an unecessary, fearful and dire type; self-torture practised by an ignorant person mistaking it for real practice of *tapas,* (ascetism, austerity), (U)

tāmbulam n. betel,

tāmisra m. gloom, a nightwalker, indignation, anger,

ṭaṁkāra m. howl, cry, clang, twang etc. notoriety, surprise,

tamobhūta mfn dark, enveloped in darkness,

tamoguṇa a quality (darkness or ignorance) of nature,

tamomaṇi m. firefly, a kind of jewel,

tamoniṣṭha mfn resting or founded on darkness,

tamonuda mfn darkness-dispelling, m. the sun, the moon,

tāmra of a coppery-red colour, made of copper, n. copper,

√*taṁs* 431/2 cl 1 P *taṁsati* to decorate, A. (*te*) to decorate oneself, to move, pour out (fig.) (a wish), caus.(cl 10) *taṁsayati* to decorate, draw to and fro, to afflict or to be distressed, DP in *alaṅkāra* (cl 10) decorating,

tan 434/3 in comp. for *tad*

√*tan* *cl 1.10. tanati, tānayati* to believe in, to assist or to afflict with pain,
2. cl 4 *tanyati* to resound, roar,
3. Cl 8 P A *tanoti tanute,* to extend, spread, be diffused (as light) over, shine, extend towards, reach to, to stretch (a cord), extend or bend (a bow), spread, spin out, weave, to emboss, to prepare (a way for), to direct (toward), to propagate (oneself, one's family), to protract, put forth, show, manifest, display, accomplish, perform (a ceremony), to sacrifice, to compose (a literary work),
4. m. continuation, uninterrupted succession, propagation, offspring, posterity, ind. in uninterrupted succession, one after another, continually,
DP in *vistāra* (Cl 8) stretching, *śraddhā* (Cl 10) confiding, trusting, placing confidence, *upakaraṇa* helping, assisting, aiding

tān those (many) 2nd m. them

tana n. offspring, posterity,

tāna m. monotonous tone, object of sense, tone, fibre,

tanā one after another, continually,

tanayaḥ/yā mfn propagating a family, belonging to one's family, m. a son, du. son and daughter, n. posterity, family, race, offspring, child, f. daughter,

√*tañc* 432/1 Cl 1 *tañcati* to go, Cl 7

tanakti to contract, DP in *gati* (Cl1)going, in *saṅkocana* (Cl 7) contracting, shrinking

√*taṇḍ* 432/2 = √*taḍ*, Cl 1 A *taṇḍate* to beat, DP in *tāḍana* striking, threshing,

tāṇḍava a violent dance by a male dancer,

tandrā twilight, "neither sleep nor the waking state; always lost somewhere in between" HH
L. f. fatigue, exhaustion, laziness,

tandrālu mfn weary, tired, sleepy,

tandrita mfn wearied,

taṇḍula m. rice, grain, (after threshing and winnowing),

√*taṅg* 432/1 Cl 1 P *taṅgati* to go, to stumble, tremble, DP in *gati* going

tāni pron. 2/pl/n

√*ṭaṅk* 429/2 Cl 10 *ṭaṅkayati* to shut, cover, seal up, DP in *bandhana* binding, fastening,

√*taṅk* 432/1 Cl 1 P to live in distress, DP in *kṛcchra-jīvana* living in distress

ṭaṅka m.n. a spade, hoe, hatchet, stone-cutter's chisel, leg, m. a sword, scabbard,

tanmanas mfn absorbed in mind by that, absorbed therein,

tanmātra 434/3 merely that , only a trifle, a rudimentary or subtle element (5 in number), from which the grosser elements are produced ,

tanmaya 434/3 mfn made up of that, absorbed in or identical with that, consisting of That (where That is the Absolute),

tanmayatā f. being absorbed in or identical with That,

tanniṣṭhās they whose basis is that, they whose foundation is That
BV compound *tan-ni-sthā*

√*tantasya* (intensive of *taṁs*) to afflict or to be distressed, DP in *duḥkha* being miserable

tanti f. cord esp. a long line to which calves are tethered by short ropes,

tantī as *tanti*

tantra n. thread, warp of a web, main point, characteristic feature, model, type, system, framework, division of a work, fundamental doctrine, a class of works teaching magical and mystical methods, a spell, oath or ordeal, an army,
ifc. a row, number, series, troop, a drug, chief remedy, wealth, a house, happiness,
a hindu sect worshipping God as the Divine Mother in a particular form,

√*tantraya* 436/2 Nom. *tantrayati* to follow, as one's rule, to provide for, A to support a family, to regulate, DP in *kuṭumba-dhāraṇa* supporting or maintaining as a family,

tantrī f. lute, the wire or string of a lute, the strings of the heart (fig.), any tubular vessel of the body, sinew, vein,

tāntrika m. follower of the *tantra* doctrine, one completely versed in any science or system, specialist,

tantu 436/1 a thread, cord, string, line

tantunābha m. a spider,

tantusaṁtāna 436/1 weaving of threads,

tanu 435/2 mfn. thin, slender, f. the body, person, self

tanu-avasthā thinned state of mind, (U)

tanūkaraṇa 435/3 1 making thin, attenuation, dilution,
2. body, person, self, formal manifestation,

tanumadhya mfn slender-waisted, n. waist,

tanumānasā f. the third step in realization, experience that impurities and impediments are lessening,

tanumānasī f. thread-like state of mind,

tanumātra M. n. 'a mere that' a mere essence, a potential or subtle element (in the Sāṁkhya system)

tanus n. body

tanutra n. armour, body-guard,

tanutrāṇa n. body-cover,

tanūtyaj mfn abandoning the body, risking life, brave,

tanyatu m. thunder, wind, night,

√tap 436/3 1. Cl 4 A *tapyate* to rule, 2. Cl 1 P A *tapati* give out heat, be hot, shine (as the sun), to make hot or warm, heat, shine upon, to consume or destroy by heat, to suffer pain, to repent of, torment oneself, practise austerity, cause pain to, damage, injure, spoil, Cl 4 A to be heated or burnt, become hot, to be purified by austerities, to suffer or feel pain, undergo austerities, to consume by heat, to cause pain, trouble, distress, to torment oneself, undergo penance, feel violent pain, be in great anxiety, DP in *santāpa* (Cl 1) suffering pain, *aiśvarya* (Cl 4) being powerful, *dāha* (Cl 10) burning, 3. mfn. warming oneself

tapa 436/3mfn. causing pain or trouble, m. heat, warmth, austerity, the sun, the hot season,

tapas n. warmth, heat, pain, suffering, religious austerity, bodily mortification, penance, severe meditation, special observance e.g. sacred learning with Brahmans, 'the concentration of the body, the senses and the mind', endurance of hot and cold etc.

tāpa 442/2 pain (mental or physical), sorrow, affliction, heating,

tapaḥ-prabhāva 437/1 m. supernatural power acquired by austerities, L. efficacy of devotion,

tāpana mfn burning, causing pain, illuminating, distressing, m. sun, hot season, pain, asceticism,

tapanta pres/part burning, consuming, illuminating

tapas disciplined action, (austerities) which purifies and enhances energy, unswerving performance of one's duties, disciplined action that purifies and enhances energy, knowledge, L. mortification, asceticism, devotion, 437/1 n warmth, heat, religious austerity, bodily mortification, penance, severe meditation, special observance,

tāpasa m. an ascetic, the moon,

tapasvant mfn full of devotion, pious, hot, burning, ascetic,

tapasvin 437/2 practising austerities, an ascetic, L. as for *tapasvant*

tapasya 437/2 1. to undergo (perform) austerities, asceticism, 2 produced by heat, devout austerity

tapasyasi 2/s you perform (austerities)

tāpatraya see below

tāpatritayadūṣita impure through 3-fold misery, (the 3-fold misery – from one's body/mind/intellect, from the beings and objects around one, from accidents like floods and earthquakes)

tapodhana mfn 'having austerities as one's wealth' rich in austerities,

tapoja L. mfn asceticism-born, whose element is asceticism,

tapojā mfn born from heat,

tapoloka 'plane of austerity', a heaven,

taponiṣṭha absorbed in austerity,

tapovanam n. hermitage, ascetic's grove,

tapta mfn heated, inflamed, hot, refined (gold etc.), fused, melted, molten, practiced (as austerities) , incensed, undertaken, inflamed with anger,

taptapīṇḍā m. a heated ball,

taptvā ind. having practised (austerities)

-tara 438/3 surpassing (comparative affix intensifying meaning), more notably, particularly,

tara m. crossing, passage,

tāra 443/3 carrying across, a saviour, protector, high, loud, shrill, good, excellent, well-favoured, crossing, saving

tārā f. a star, universal Divine Mother, pupil of the eye,

tāraka m. a helmsman, a raft, n. a star, the pupil of the eye, the eye, the eye, mfn causing or enabling to pass or go over, rescuing, liberating, saving, ifc. f. (*ā*) star,

tārakajñāna the knowledge that leads to liberation,

tarala mfn tremulous, unsteady, vain, m. a wave, necklace, ruby, central stone of a necklace,

taraṁga 438/3 across-goer, a wave, billow, or *taraṅga*

tāraṇa mfn causing or enabling to cross, helping over a difficulty, liberating, crossing, carrying across, crossing over *saṁsāra,*

taraṇi mfn pressing onward, quick, untired, energetic, m. the sun, a ray of light, f (*ī*) a boat,

√*taraṇya* 439/1 Nom *taraṇyati* to go, DP in *gati* going

tarati 454/2 he passes across or over, gets through, attains an end or aim √*tī*

√*tāraya* *tārayati* DP in *karma-samāpti* accomplishing

√*tard* Cl 1 P *tardati* to injure, kill, DP in *hiṁsā* hurting, killing

tarhi ind. then, at that time, at that moment, in that case, correlative of *yadi* if........ then .....

tarī m. f. boat, a barren cow,

taryasi you will pass over or transcend, 2/s/fut/act/ √*tṛ*

tārita mfn rescued, saved, liberated,

√*tarj* 440/1 Cl 1 *tarjati (te)* to threaten, scold, frighten, deride, DP in *bhartsana* abusing, in *tarjaṇa* threatening, menacing

tarjana n. threatening, scolding, fighting, derision, putting to shame,

tarjanī f. 'threatening finger', the fore-finger,

√*tark* 439/3 Cl 10 *tarkayati (te)* to conjecture, guess, suspect, infer, try to discover or ascertain, reason or speculate about, to consider as, to reflect, think of, recollect, have in one's mind, intend (with inf.), to ascertain, to speak or to shine, DP in *bhāṣā* reasoning, arguing, drawing inferences,

tarka m. conjecture, supposition, reasoning, inquiry, speculation, doubt, the number 6, logic, wish, desire, motive, cause,

tarpaṇa 440/1 mfn satiating, refreshing, (esp. of gods and deceased persons) by presenting to them libations of water), n. (*am*) refreshment, food, satisfaction, f.(*ā*) ifc. fuel

tarpaṇīyaḥ to be satisfied

taru m. a tree, mfn quick, speediness,

tarukoṭara m. the hollow of a tree,

taruṇa mfn young, tender, fresh, juvenile, tender (a feeling), m. a youth, -*ka* n. sprout,

tarutale under the tree, (see *tala*)

√*tas* 441/2 Cl 4 *tasyati* to fade away, perish, to throw, DP in *upakṣaya* fading away, becoming exhausted, throwing or tossing away, mfn. throwing

-tas adverbial suffix, through, by

taskara m. robber, thief, ifc. a term of contempt,

tasmai pron. to that, to him

tasmāt 441/2 pron.5/s from that , on that account, therefore

tasmin pron. in that, in him

tasthivas mfn one who has stood, standing, remaining, continuing in, being on or in, one who has stood still or stopped or made a pause, fixed, immovable, stationary, occupied with, persevering, ready to, prepared for,

tasthu mfn stationary, n. 'that which is stationary' i.e. plants,

taṣṭṛ m. carpenter, builder of chariots,

tasya pron. 6/s his, of him

tasya tasya on him, on whoever he is

tasyāḥ pron. 6/s her, of her

tasyai pron. to her

√*taṭ* 432/1 Cl 1 P *taṭati* to rumble, to be raised, caus. *tāṭayati* to strike, DP in *ucchrāya* growing, raising,

tat pron. that, (in a compound indicates

any form of *sarvanāman tad* in any gender, number or case ending,) particle – then, so,

tat api with regard to this also

taṭa m. a slope, declivity, shore, any part of the body with sloping sides,

tata m. father, mfn extended, stretched, spread, diffused, expanded, spreading over, extending to, covered over by(3rd), protracted, bent (a bow), spreading, wide, composed (a tale), m. wind, n. any stringed instrument,

tāta 441/3 m. a father, voc. a term of affection addressed to a junior, dear one, O son

tataḥ adv. from that, resulting from that, due to that, therefore, then, from there,

tataḥ prabhṛti adverbial phrase, from that time on, from then on,

tāṭakā Tāṭakā a demoness,

tatama mfn that one (of many), (superlative), such a one, just that,

tatas 432/2 ind. used for the 5th case thence, after that, from that , from there, from this point, therefore, because of that, *itas tatas* hither and thither, here and there, corel. of *yatas*

tatas tataḥ what next

taṭastha mfn standing on a slope or bank, m. an indifferent person (neither friend nor foe), n. a property distinct from the nature of the body and yet that by which it is known, spiritual essence,

taṭastha-lakṣaṇa an indirect notion of what a thing is; in Vedānta it is the accidental definition of Brahman, as given by the definition that Brahman is the cause of creation, preservation and destruction of the universe, (U)

taṭastha-vṛtti a *vṛtti* of indifference; neutrality wherein there is neither attraction nor repulsion,

tatatama the most pervasive, the fullest, like space

tat tat that (see *yat yat)*

tatas tatas from thence from there

tathā so, just so, 433/3 ind. in that manner, so, thus, likewise, as well (correlative of *yathā* as... *tathā* so) in order that...... thus,
yathā yathā..... tathā tathā
to what degree..... to that degree...
the more................ the more....
yathā tathā in one way or another,

tathagata mfn 'one who has arrived at suchness' being in such a state or condition, of such a quality or nature, 'he who comes and goes in the same way' Gautama Buddha, a Buddhist,

tathākratu mfn so intending,

tathāpi 433/3 even thus, then even, even then, nevertheless, notwithstanding,

tathāsmṛti having that kind of memory,

tathatā f. suchness, thusness, - expresses appreciation of the nature of reality in any given moment (a central concept of Buddhism) (K),

tathāvidha mfn of such sort, in such condition, of such qualities, ind. (*am*) likewise, in this manner,

tathya mfn true, n. *tathyam* truth

tati so many 1/2/pl.

tatkriyā 'doing that', any particular action

tatkṣaṇa m. that moment, (*am*) ind. in that moment, straightaway,

tatkṣaṇe ind. instantly

tatpara 433/1 mfn. following that or thereupon, having that as one's highest object or aim, totally devoted or addicted to, attending closely to, eagerly engaged in, m. 1/50th of an eye's twinkle,
-*tā* f. scope, design, intention, entire devotion or addiction to,
-*tva* n. aiming at, tending to,

tatpārśva his side,

tātparya intention (as in the original intention of an author) (K), mfn intended, meant, deliberate, wilful, n. devoting one's self to,

purpose, aim, purport, meaning, object, intention,
tatprahṛṣṭa mfn pleased with that,
tatpuruṣa 'his man' the name and an example of a class of compounds in which the second term is the main one.
tatsamakṣam in public, in the presence of others, before the eyes, adv.
tatra 433/2 ind. there, in that, over this, about this, in that place, thither, to that place, in that, therein, in that case, on that occasion, under those circumstances, then, therefore, co-rel. of *yad,*
tatrabhavān or *bhavant* refers to a respected person, His Honour,
tatrabhavatī Her Honour,
tatrāntare meanwhile,
tatrastha mfn abiding there, belonging to that place,
tatra tatra there is, here and there, everywhere, to every place,
tatsahacārin mfn accompanying him,
tatsama mfn synonymous with, like that, a modern term for sanskrit loan-words substituted into other similar languages like Bengali (comparable to Greek words like *hubris* used in English),
tatsamīpe ind. near him,
tatsaṁnidhāna n. his presence,
tatsapatnī her co-wife,
tat tad (*tad tad*)this or that, this and that
tattīra n. its bank,
tattva 432/3 n. true or real state, truth, reality, "thatness", truth, in reality, really,
tattvabhāva 433/1 m. true being or nature,
tattvabodha 433/1 1/s/m knowledge or understanding of truth
tattvadarśin mfn seeing the truth, m. one who sees the truth, one who sees the subtle nature of things, a sage,
tattvadṛś mfn perceiving truth,
tattvajña 433/1 1/s/m knowing the truth, knowing the true nature of, knowing thoroughly,
tattvajñāna knowledge of Brahman,
tattvamasi *tat tvam asi* 'thou art that'
tattvaniścaya m. ascertainment of truth, right knowledge,
tattvaniṣṭhatā f. veracity,
tattvanyāsa m. application of true principles, name of a ceremony
tattvaśuddhi f. ascertainment or right knowledge of truth,
tattvatā f. truth, reality,
tattvataḥ 5/s from thatness, from the truth
tattvātita beyond the *tattvas,* beyond the elements,
tattvavat mfn possessing the truth or reality of things,
tattvavid mfn truth-knowing, knowing the true nature of (6th),
tattvāya for the sake of knowlege, for the realisation of truth 4/s
tattvībhūta '(one should) become identified with reality' (Gam.)
tāttvikasattva (N) truth in the absolute sense,
tat u that very thing, that Brahman,
tau pron. 2/du/m they 2, those 2 m.
tava pron. your, of you
tāvacchas ind. so manifoldly,
tāvac-chata mfn having or embracing so many hundreds,
tavaivāham = *tava eva aham*
I am yours alone
tāvaka mfn thy, m. thine,
tāvat mfn so great, so much, so many, extending so far, lasting so long, at once, now, just a little,
(correl. with *yāvant)* as long as ..... so long ....,
also used to emphasize whatever precedes,
ind. meanwhile, in the meantime, very well, all right, indeed, truly, already, really, in that time,
(with *na* or *a*) not yet,
followed by *yāvat*) while,
tāvat-kṛtvas ind. so many times,
taviṣa mfn powerful, strong, energetic,

courageous, m. the ocean, heaven, n. power, strength,

√*tay* 438/3 Cl 1 *tayate* to go towards (2nd),or out of (5th), =√*tāy* to protect, DP in *gati* going, guarding, protecting,

√*tāy* 443/3 Cl 1 *tāyate* to spread, proceed in a continuous stream or line, =√*trai* to protect, DP in *santāna* spreading, extending, or *pālana* protecting,

tayā pron. 3/s. f. by or with her,

tāyin m. a protector, (said of Mahāvīra and of Buddha),

tayoḥ pron. of/in those two

tāyu m. thief,

te pron. they (two) or 6/s your, those many m. pl. or 4/s to thee, to you

√*tej* 454/2 *tejati* to protect, DP in *pālana* protecting,

tejana 454/2 n sharpening, whetting, rendering bright, the shaft of an arrow, a whetstone, tuft, mat

tejas 454/2 n. a sharp edge, point of a flame, ray, glow, glare, splendour, brilliance, light, fire, vital power, spirit, essence, majesty, dignity, authority the element fire with the properties of form and beauty, vigour

tejasvin 454/3 mfn brilliant, splendid, bright, powerful, energetic, violent, inspiring respect, dignified, noble,

tejomaya mfn glorious, full of energy, brilliant, clear, consisting of splendour or light, shining,

tejorāśi 454/3 m. mass of splendour, all splendour,

tena 454/3 pron. 3/s by him, by that, therefore, in that case,

√*tep* 455/1 Cl 1 *tepate* to distil,ooze, drop, to tremble, DP in *kṣaraṇa* sprinkling, or *kampana* trembling

√*tev* 455/1 Cl 1 *tevate* to sport, DP in *devana* playing, sporting,

ṭhakkura m. a deity, object of reverence, man of rank, chief,

theravāda a Pali word –sanskrit = *sthaviravāda* 'the way of the elders' the early system of Buddhists,

thoḍana n. covering,

√*thuḍ* 464/2 Cl 6 *thuḍati* to cover, DP in *samvaraṇa* covering,

√*thurv* 464/2 Cl 1 P *thurvat* hurting, DP in *hiṁsā* hurting

√*tig* 446/1 Cl 5 *tignoti* = √*tik* DP in *gati*

tigma mfn sharp, hot,

√*tij* 446/1 Cl 1 *tejate (ti)* to be or become sharp, to sharpen, caus. *tejayati* to stir up, excite, DP in *niśāna* (Cl 1.10) sharpening,

√*ṭik* 429/3 Cl 1 A to go, DP in *gati* going, moving

√*ṭīk* 430/1 Cl 1 A *ṭīkate* to move (said of a tree), to trip, jump, caus. P *ṭīkayati* to explain, make clear, DP in *gati* going,

√*tik* 446/1 Cl 1 *tekate* to go Cl 5 *teknoti* to assail, wound, challenge, DP in *gati* (Cl 1 and 5) going, attaching or assailing,

ṭīkā f. a commentary esp. on another commentary,

tīkṣṇa 448/3 sharp, hot, pungent, fiery, acid, harsh, rough, rude, vehement, self – abandoning, m. nitre, black pepper, black mustard, marjoram, a resin, an ascetic, n. sharp language, steel, iron, any weapon, sea-salt, nitre, poison, calamine,

tikta mfn bitter, pungent, m. a bitter taste,

√*til* 448/1 Cl 1 *tilati* to go Cl 6.10 *tilati, telayati* to be unctuous, to anoint, DP in *gati* (Cl 1) going, *sneha* (Cl 6.10) becoming unctuous or greasy,

tila m. the sesame plant or its seed,

tilaka m. a mark on the forehead as an ornament or a sectarial division, a freckle, ornament, kind of skinb eruption, kind of horse, n. alliteration, the right lung,

√*till* 448/2 Cl 1 P to go, DP in *gati* going

√*tim* Cl 4 P *timyati* to become quiet, to become wet, DP in *ārdrī-bhāva* becoming wet

√tīm 449/1 Cl 4 *tīmyati* see *√tim* caus. *tīmayati* to wet, DP in *ārdrībhāva* becoming wet

timira mfn dark, gloomy, n. darkness, darkness of the eyes, partial blindness, iron-rust,

tiṅ a *Pratyāhāra* used as a term for all or for any one of the verbal case terminations, a verb ending,

tiṅanta 'having a *tiṅ* ending' a verb

√tip 447/1 Cl 1 P *tepati* to sprinkle, DP in *kṣaraṇa* sprinkling,

ṭippaṇa , *ṭippaṇaka, ṭippaṇī ṭippanī* a gloss (annotation, explanation), comment, subcommentary,

tīra n. a shore, bank, the brim of a vessel, a kind of arrow, m. tin,

tiras 1. prep. through, across, beyond, over, 2. ind. crossways, sideways, aside, so as to pass by, apart from, without, against, apart or secretly from, obliquely, transversely, apart, secretly,
(with *√kṛ)* put aside, treat disrespectfully, scold,
(with√bhū) conceals,

tiraskāra m. a scolding, disdain, placing aside, concealment, a cuirass,

√tirasya Nom *tirasyati* DP in *antardhi* concealing

tiro√bhū causes to disappear,

tirobhāva m. concealment, obscuration, disappearance, veiling,

tirodhāna n. concealment, veiling, obscuration, a covering (sheath etc.)

tirohita mfn removed or withdrawn from sight, hidden

tīrtha 449/1 n. holy waters, a ford, passage, way, place of pilgrimage, a sacred or holy place

tīrthakara 'maker of the ford' one of the 24 Jaina teachers,

tīrthaṅkara as above, called ford makers because they serve as ferrymen across the river of transmigration, G. they are the perfected ones who lead the way to liberation,

tīrthasthāna a sacred bathing place,

tīrtvā having crossed over, crossing over

tiryag see *tiryañc*

tiryak see *tiryañc*

tiryaktva n. the nature of beasts,

tiryaṅ see *tiryañc*

tiryañc see *tiryañc*

tiryañc 1. mfn directed across, horizontal, 2. m.n. beast (going horizontally as opposed to man being upright),

tiṣṭha stay!, stand!

tiṣṭhanta existing, standing, situated pres/act/part *√sthā*

tiṣṭhasi you stand (see *sthā*) 1262/2 to stand, stand firmly, to stay, remain, continue in any action or condition, 2nd pres. act. you stand, remain, etc.

tiṣṭhataḥ 1262/2 stands firmly, remains, to be, abiding, living,

tiṣṭhati 1262/2 he remains, stands, stays

tiṣṭhatu 1/s/pres/impv/act. let remain

tithi m.f. a lunar day,

titikṣā 446/2 f. endurance, forbearance, patience.

titikṣasva you must endeavour to endure 2/s/impv/mid/desid *√tij*

titikṣu mfn enduring patiently, bearing, forbearing, patient,

√tīv 449/2 Cl 1 *tīvati* to be fat, DP in *sthaulya* growing fat,

tīvra mfn severe, violent, intense, fierce, of rigorous austerities,
m. sharpness, pungency,
n. pungency, a shore, tin, steel, iron, black mustard, basil,
(am) ind. severely,

tīvravairāgya intense dispassion,

toḍana 455/3 n. splitting

toka n. creation, progeny,

toraṇa n. arched portal, arch, the neck,

toṣa 456/1 satisfaction, contentment,

toṣaṇa n the act of satisfying, delighting, appeasing, mfn satisfying, gratifying, pleasing, appeasing

toya n. 456/1 water,

tṛ m. star, pl. *tāras*

√tṝ 454/2 Cl 1 P A *tarati*, Cl 5 *tarute,* Cl 3 *titarti,* with prepositions,

Cl 6 PA *tirate,* to pass across or over, cross over (a river), sail across, to float, swim, to get through, attain an end or aim, live through (a definite period), study to the end, to fulfill, accomplish, perform, surpass, overcome, subdue, escape, acquire, gain, A. contend, compete, caus. *tārayati* to carry or lead over or across, to cause to arrive at, to rescue, save, liberate from, DP in *plavana* floating, or *santaraṇa* crossing over

√*trai* 462/1 Cl 1 A *trāyate* to protect, preserve, cherish, defend, rescue from, DP in *pālana* training to protect and cherish

traiguṇya 462/1 the 3 *guṇā*

trailokya the three worlds, the earth, the gods and in between

traivedika mfn relating to the three Vedas,

traividya n. study of or being familiar with the three Vedas,

√*trakh* 457/1 Cl 1 *trakhati* to go, DP in *gati* going

√*traṁs* 457/1 Cl 1.10 *traṁsati, traṁsayati* to speak or to shine, DP in *bhāṣā* shining, speaking,

√*trand* 457/1 Cl 1 to be busy, DP in *ceṣṭā* endeavouring,

√*traṅk* or *traṅkh* or *traṅgh* 457/1 Cl 1 *traṅkhati* to go DP in *gati* going

√*trap* Cl 1 *trapate* to become perplexed, be ashamed, DP in *lajjā* being ashamed,

√*tras* Cl 10 P *trāsayati* to seize, to prevent, Cl 1 *trasati* Cl 4 *trasyati,* to tremble, quiver, be afraid of , DP in *dhāraṇa*, holding, *grahaṇa* taking, *vāraṇa* obstructing
2. Cl 1 *trasati* 4. *trasyati* to tremble, quiver, be afraid of, DP in *advaiga* fearing, trembling

trasa mfn moving, n. the collective body of moving or living beings, m. 'quivering' the heart, n. a wood,

trāsa m. fear, fright, anxiety, a flaw in a jewel,

trāsadasyava m. descendant of *trasadasyu*

trasadasyu m. a generous prince, the favourite of the gods,

trāṭaka n. steady gazing, a process of fixing the gaze on a point,

√*trauk* 462/3 Cl 1 A to go, DP in *gati,* going

traya mfn triple, threefold, consisting of 3

trāyate 462/1 protects, preserves, 1/s/mid

trātṛ m. protector, saviour,

trayī f. the three Vedas collectively,

tredhā in three ways,

tretā yuga the Silver Age 1,296,000 years, man started to want something for himself,

tṛd 453/3 Cl 7 to cleave, pierce, to split open, let out, set free, to destroy, DP in *hiṁsā* hurting, killing, *anādara* disregarding,

√*tṛh* 454/2 Cl 7 to crush, bruise, DP in *hiṁsā* injuring, hurting,

tri 3

tṝ 454/2 cl1 *tarati* to pass across or over, cross over, float, swim, get through, attain an end or aim, fulfil, accomplish

tridaśa 3x10, the thirty, a name in round numbers for the 33 deities,

tridaśeśvara m.pl lords of the gods i.e. the four chief gods – Indra, Agni, Varuna and Yama,

tridhā in three ways, 3 parts, 3 places, triply,

tridhātu mfn having three parts, threefold,

tridiva n. the triple or third i.e. highest heaven

triguṇātmika characterised by the three *guṇas* – *sattva rajas* and *tamas*

trika mfn triple, threefold, forming a triad, happening the third time, m. a place where three roads meet, n. a triad, the loins, hips, the triple,

trikadruka m.pl. the three soma vessels,

trikāla 458/1 n. the three times or tenses past, present, future, mfn relating to them, ind. 3 times, thrice, in the morning, at noon and in the evening,

trikāladarśin m. seer of the past, present and future,
trikālajña mfn knowing past, present and future, omniscient,
trikālajñanin m. one who knows the past, present and future
trikālātīta that which transcends past,present and future (the Self), 'the 3 letters stand for Brahma, Viṣṇu and Śiva and the whole stands for Brahman',
trikarmakṛt one who undertakes 3 types of sacrifice- sacrifice, study of the Vedas and charity, or ceremonies, repeating the Veda, gifts
trilocana mfn three-eyed (Śiva)
trilocanā f. disloyal wife,
triloka the three worlds,
triṁśat f. thirty,
trimūrti the Hindu trinity- *Brahmā, Viṣṇu, Śiva*
trīṇi 3
tripada mfn having (taken) 3 steps,
trividhā threefold, triple, of three kinds,
tripuṭa 459/2 mfn. threefold, triangular, m. a kind of pulse, a kind of measure,
tripuṭī the triad of seer, sight, seen, the knower, the known, the act of knowing
triratna the three jewels – right knowledge, right seeing, right conduct, (Jaina), the Buddha, his doctrine , the Order (Buddhist),
trirātra n. space of 3 nights,
tris ind. thrice, three times,
triśavaṇa mfn pertaining to the three soma pressings, ind, (*am*) at dawn, noon, sunset,
triśula a trident,
tritaya 461/3 a triad, group of three,
triveda (in cpds.) the 3 Vedas, mfn familiar with the 3 Vedas,
triveṇī f. triple braided, place of confluence of the Ganges, Yamuna & subterranean Sarasvati rivers
trividha mfn of three sorts, threefold, triple
trividyā f. the 3 sciences, i.e. Vedas, threefold knowledge,
trivṛt mfn threefold, tripartite, triple, triform, m. a triple cord, an amulet with 3 strings,
trivṛtkaraṇa n. making threefold, intermixture of fire, water and earth, for the formation of bodies,
triyāma f. turmeric, night, mfn the Indigo plant, the river Yamuna, containing 3 watches,
√*tṛkṣ* 453/1 Cl 1 to go DP in *gati* going
√*tṛmp* 454/1 Cl 6 *tṛmpati* see √*tṛp* DP in *tṛpti* satisfying
√*tṛmph* 454/1 cl 6 = √*tṛp, tṛmphati* to satisfy, DP in *tṛpti* satisfying
√*tṛṇ* 453/1 Cl 8 *tṛnoti,tṛṇute*, or or *tarṇute* to eat, DP in *adana* eating grass or grazing,
tṛṇa n. grass, blade of grass, straw,
√*tṛp* cl 4 *tṛpyati* cl 5 *tṛpnoti* cl 6 2/s *tṛmpasi* , to satisfy oneself, become satiated or satisfied, be pleased with, to enjoy, to satisfy, please, cl 1 *tarpati* to kindle, caus. to satiate, satisfy, refresh, gladden, A. to become satiated or satisfied, to kindle, DP in *prīṇana* becoming pleased or satisfied, in *tṛpti* pleasing
√*tṛph* 454/1 cl 6 *tṛphati* to satisfy, to kill, DP in *tṛpti* satisfying
tṛpta 454/1 satisfied with, satiated,
tṛpti mfn giving satisfaction, f. satisfaction, contentment, satiety, disgust, liberation of the *cidābhāsa*
tṛptiyoga satisfaction
√*tṛṣ* 454/1 Cl 4 *tṛṣyati* to be thirsty, thirst, thirst for, DP in *pipāsā* being thirsty
tṛṣ mfn longing for f. thirst, strong desire,
tṛśa 3 stanzas
tṛṣā f. thirst, strong desire,
tṛṣṇā 454/1 thirst, avidity, desire, craving for sense objects,
tṛtīya mfn third
√*trump* see *trup*

√*trumph* see *trup*

√*trup* 462/1 cl 1 *tropate* to hurt, DP in *hiṁsā* hurting, injuring

√*truph* see *trup* DP in *hiṁsā* hurting,

√*truṭ* 462/1 cl 6.4. *truṭati, truṭayati* to be torn or split, tear, break, fall asunder, DP in *chedana* tearing, breaking, cutting, dividing

truṭi m. an atom, a very minute space of time, particle, f. small cardamoms, doubt, cutting, breaking, breaking a promise, mfn broken, divided,

try-adhiṣṭhāna mfn having three manifestations,

tryambaka name of *Śiva*

tryaṇuka combination of three atoms, consisting of three atoms,

√*tsar* 464/2 *tsarati* to go or approach, stealthily, creep on, sneak, DP in *chadnagati* going or approaching gently or stealthily, creeping or crawling, proceeding crookedly or fraudulently,

√*tu* 1. cl 2 *tauti* to have authority, be strong, to go, to injure, caus. to make strong or efficient, DP in *gati* going, *vṛddhi* increasing, *hiṁsā* hurting

tu 2. ind. but, (enclitic), and, or, pray! I beg, do, now, then, and, or, however, though, expletive, indeed, rhythmic filler

ca....na tu	though... still not
na...api tu	not...but
na ca... api tu	not...but
kāmaṁ...tu	though... still
kāmaṁ ca...tu	though... still
kiṁ tu	though... still
paraṁ tu	though...still
kāmaṁ ... na tu	it is true.. but not, ere-than, rather... than
bhuyas...na tu	it is true...but not, ere-than, rather... than
varam...na tu	it is true but not , ere than, rather... than
kiṁ tu	still, nevertheless,
na... paraṁ tu	not... however

√*tubh* 450/3 Cl 1.4. *tobhate, tubhyati* to hurt, kill, Cl 9 , DP in *hiṁsā* hurting, injuring

tubhyam pron. for you 4/s

tuc f. progeny, children,

tuccha mfn empty, vain, small, little, mean, trifling, n. anything trifling, chaff, *-tva* n. emptiness, vanity,

√*tuḍ* 450/1 Cl 1.6. *tuḍati, toḍati* to strike, split, bring near, DP in *toḍana* splitting, breaking,

√*tud* 450/2 Cl 6 P *tudati* to push, strike, goad, bruise, sting, DP in *vyathana* tormenting

tud mfn ifc. pricking, √

√*tūḍ* 452/2 Cl 1 *tūḍati* to split, to slight, disrespect, DP in *toḍana* splitting, pushing, injuring

√*tuh* 452/2 Cl 1 *tohati* to pain, DP in *ardana* distress, pain,

√*tuj* 450/1 Cl 6 to strike, hit, push, to press out, *tuñjati* to give, A. to flow forth, to instigate, incite, pass. to be vexed, Cl 1 *tojati* to hurt, caus. to promote, to move quickly, *tuñjayati* to speak, or to shine, *tuñjayati* or *tojayati* to hurt, be strong, to give or take, to abide, DP in *hiṁsā* (Cl 1) hurting, (Cl 10) in *hiṁsā* hurting, killing, *bala* being strong or powerful, *ādāna* giving or taking, *niketana* living or dwelling

tuj mfn urging, f. (only 3rd *-jā*) shock, impulse, assault

√*tul* 451/2 Cl 10 *tolayati* or *tulayati* to lift up, raise, to determine the weight by lifting up, weigh, compare by weighing and examining, ponder, examine with mistrust, to make equal in weight, equal, compare, counterbalance, outweigh, match, possess in the same degree, resemble, reach, DP in *unmāna* weighing, measuring,

√*tūl* 452/3 Cl 1. 10. *tūlati, tūlayati,* =

niṣkriṣ, also *tūṇ*, DP in *niṣkarṣa* drawing out,

tulā f. balance, scale, weight, equality, equal measure, resemblance, a kind of house roof-beam,

tulanā 451/2 f. rating, equality with, comparison, part. compared

tulasī f. holy basil plant,

tulya 451/3 mfn equal to, of the same kind, similar, L. keeping the balance with, like,

tulyākṛti mfn having like appearance, alike

√*tumb* 450/3 Cl 1 *tumbati* to distress, Cl 10 *tumbayati* to distress or to be invisible, DP in *ardana* (Cl 1) tormenting, (cl10) *adarśana* disappearing, *ardana* distressing,

tumba m. a gourd,

√*tump* 450/3 Cl 1.6 *tumpati, tumphati,* to hurt, DP in *hiṁsā* injuring, hurting,

√*tumph* see *tump*

tumula mfn tumultuous, noisy

√*tuṇ* 450/1 Cl 6 P to curve, DP in *kauṭilya* curving, making crooked, bending,

√*tūṇ* 452/2 Cl 10 *tūṇayati* to contract, *-te* to fill, DP in *pūraṇa* filling, filling up,

√*tuṇḍ* 450/1 Cl 1 A to hurt, DP in *toḍana* breaking, killing

tuṇḍa n. a beak, snout, trunk, the mouth (used contemptuously), an arrowpoint,

tuṅga mfn tall, high, prominent, erect, lofty, m. an elevation, height, mountain, top, peak, a throne, planet Mercury,

tūṇīra m. an arrow quiver,

√*tuñj* see √*tuj*

√*tup* 450/2 Cl 1.6 *topati, tupati, tophati, tuphati,* to hurt, DP in *hiṁsā* hurting, injuring

√*tuph* Cl 1 see √*tup*

√*tur* 450/3 Cl 6 *turati (te)* to hurry, press forwards, Cl 4 to overpower, A to run, to hurt, Cl 3 *tutorti* to run, caus. *turayate* to run, press forwards, 2. mfn running a race, conquering,

√*tūr* 452/3 in comp. for 2. *tur,* DP in *gati* going quickly, *tvaraṇa* making haste, *hiṁsā* hurting, killing mfn. hastening, ind. hastily

tura mfn swift (esp. horses), (*am*) ind. swiftly, mfn strong, mighty,

turaga mfn 'swiftly going' a horse,

turaṁga m. a horse, 'going quickly', the mind, thought,

√*turaṇya* 451/1 Nom *turanyati* to be quick or swift, to accelerate, DP in *tvarā* hurrying,

turīya 451/1 the 4th state of spirit, pure impersonal spirit or Brahman *turīya* the seventh or last step of realisation, "the being itself, the Self alone without a second" HH, the underlying sub-stratum of the waking, dreaming and deep-sleep states, the self beyond the changing modes of existence, "Truth is that which has the capacity to witness all these states." HH

turīyātīta 'beyond the fourth' referring to *turīya*

√*turv* 451/2 Cl 1 P *turvati* to overpower, excel, to cause to overpower, help to victory, save, DP in *hiṁsā* hurting

turya fourth,

tūrya n. a musical instrument

turyā f. superior power,

√*tuṣ* 452/3 Cl 4 *tuṣyati (te)* to become calm, become happy, be satisfied or pleased with anyone or thing, to satisfy, please, appease, gratify DP in *prīti* being pleased or satisfied,

√*tūṣ* 452/3 Cl 1 *tūṣati* = √*tuṣ*

√*tus* 452/2 Cl 1 *tosati* to sound, DP in *śabda* sounding

tuṣāra mfn cold, frigid, m. dew, frost,

tūṣṇīka mfn silent,

tūṣṇīm 453/1 ind. silently, quietly, in silence, quiet!

tūṣṇīm bhava be silent, (silent become)
tūṣṇīṁbhūta-avasthā a state of mind where there is neither attraction nor repulsion; the state of being silent (U)
tuṣṭa 452/1 mfn. satisfied, pleased
tuṣṭi 452/1 m.f. satisfaction, contentment
tuṣṭikara mfn causing satisfaction,
tuṣṭimat mfn satisfied,
tuṣṭuva √*1.stu* 1259/1 perfect active participle, while praising (also *tuṣṭuva* 2/pl/perf/act you praise/ praised
tuṣyati 452/1 Cl 4 is satisfied, calm or pleased, is pleased or content,
√*tuṭ* 450/1 Cl 6 *tuṭati* to quarrel, DP in *kalaha-karman* disputing, quarreling
√*tutthaya* 450/2 Nom P *tutthayati* to cover, DP in *āvaraṇa*
tuvi mfn (in cpds.) mighty, much, many,
tuvibādha mfn distressing many enemies, or besetting them sore,
tuvis n. (in derivatives) might,
tuviṣmant mfn mighty,
tva *or tvat* , *tvad* mfn one, several,
2. base of the 2nd personal pronoun, thy, your,
tva...tva.. one...the other...
√*tvac* 1. Cl 6 *tvacati* to cover, DP in *saṁvaraṇa* covering
tvac 2. 463/3 f. skin (of men, serpents etc.), hide, a leather bag, bark, rind, peel, cinnamon, cinnamon tree, a cover (of a horse), surface (of the earth)
tvaca n. skin, cinnamon, cinnamon tree, bark, (*ā*) f. skin,
tvacana skinning
tvad stem of 2nd person pron. thou/you, = *tvat*
tvadānīm 463/2 ind. sometimes
tvadanya 463/2 mfn. other than thee
tvadīya s. your, thy, thine, yours,
tvadrik ind. towards you
tvādṛk mfn like you, of your kind
tvādṛśa mfn like you, of your kind,
tvadīya thine, your, thy, yours,
tvaj-jāra m. thy lover, (L)
tvak 463/3 in comp for 2. *tvac,* the sense of touch,
√*tvakṣ* 463/2 Cl 1 *tvakṣati* to create, produce, to pare, skin, to cover, DP in *tanūkaraṇa* paring
√*ṭval* 430/1 Cl 1 P = √*ṭal*
-tvam abstract noun suffix –ness, e.g. happiness,
tvam you pron. 1 or 2/s you, thou, that one, applied to *puruṣa* – the Self.
tvām pron. 2/s you
√*tvañc* 463/3 Cl 1 to go, Cl 7 *tvanakti* to contract, DP in *gati* going
√*tvaṅg* 463/3 Cl 1 *tvaṅgati* to wave, tremble, jump, leap, gallop, to flare, DP in *gati* going or *kampana* trembling,
√*tvar* 464/1 *tvarate (ti*) to hurry, make haste, move with speed, DP in *sambhrama* hurrying, making haste,
√*tvār* to convert quickly into the state,
tvara 464/1 ind. hastily,
tvarā f. haste, speed, hastily, quickly
tvaramānā rapidly, in great haste
tvaraṇa mfn produced by hurrying, sweat, n. making haste
tvarita ppp. (having) hastened, hurriedly,
tvaritam ind. quickly, urgent, swiftly,
tvaṣṭṛ m. workman, 2. Twashtar, the artificer of the gods, former of fruit of the womb, giver of growth and long life, father of Saranyū,
tvāṣṭra m. descendant of Twashtar,
tvat from you (s)
tvatkṛte for your sake,
tvatsama like you, same as you
tvāvant mfn like thee, worthy of thee,
tvayā pron. 3/s by you
tvayi 7/s pron. in you
√*tviṣ* 464/2 Cl 1 *tveṣati (te),* to be violently agitated or moved or excited or troubled, P A to excite, instigate, to shine, glitter, DP in *dīpti* shining, glittering, blazing,
tviṣ f. violent agitation, fury, light, brilliance, splendour,

glitter, beauty, authority, colour,
tya pron. that, that well-known,
tyad or *tad* pron. he, she, it, that
tyāga 456/3 m abandoning, renouncing, forsaking, giving up, resigning, gift, donation, distribution, renunciation of egoism, mental tendencies (*vāsanās*) and the world
tyāgī m. abandoner, renouncer
√*tyaj* 456/3 Cl 1 *tyajati (te)* to leave, abandon, quit, to leave a place, go away from, to let go, dismiss, discharge, to give up, surrender, resign, part from, renounce, P A to shun, avoid, get rid of, free oneself from (any passion etc.), to give away, distribute, offer, to set aside, leave unnoticed, disregard, caus. *tyājayati* to cause anyone to quit, to expel, turn out, cause anyone to lose, deprive of, DP in *hāni* abandoning
2. mfn leaving, abandoning, giving up, offering,
tyaja 456/3 *tyaj* leave, avoid, quit, let go, dismiss, impv. set aside
tyaja leave alone!
tyajas n. abandonment, difficulty, danger, alienation, aversion, envy,
m. 'offshoot', descendant,
tyajati leaves, abandons, gives up
tyajet one should abandon or renounce 1/s/opt/act √*tyaj*
tyājya 457/1 ind. to be left, abandoned, given up, sacrificed, excepted,
tyakta 456/3 mfn left, abandoned
tyaktajīvita mfn having life set aside, risking one's life, brave,
tyaktajīvitayodhin mfn bravely fighting, fighting with life at risk,
tyaktena 3/s by or with an abandoned ... by that detachment, through detachment, (*Īṣā up*.)
tyakta jīvitās they whose lives are at risk
tyaktum root *tyaj* 456/3 infinitive form to let go, dismiss, surrender, renounce,
tyaktvā ind. having left, having abandoned, abandoning, sacrificing, relinquishing
u ind. an interjection of compassion or anger, a particle implying assent or command, and, also, further, on the other hand, particle of emphasis, may be used to indicate a conclusion like 'now' in English,
frequently found in interrogative sentences,
a particle implying restriction or antithesis,
√*u* 171/3 cl5 P *unoti* to call, to hail, roar, bellow, DP in *śabda* sounding,
√*ubh* 216/2 Cl 9 P *ubhnāti* to hurt, kill
Cl 6 P *ubhati* to cover over, fill with,
Cl 7 *unabdhi* to bind, compress, confine, contain, include,
DP in *pūraṇa* filling with (Cl 6)
ubha/ubhaya mfn both
ubhaya 216/2 mfn both, of both kinds, in both ways,
ubhayā ind. in both ways, in comp. for *ubhaya*,
ubhayakāma mfn desirous of both,
ubhayataḥ-sasya n. having a crop at both times, i.e. bearing two crops a year,
ubhayathā 217/1 ind. in both ways, in both cases
ubhayatas ind. from or on both sides, to both sides (with 2nd or 6th), in both cases, on both sides of ,
ubhayathā in both ways,
ubhayātmaka mfn of both natures or kinds, belonging to both,
ubhayatra ind. in both places, on both sides, in both cases or times,
ubhayatva intermediacy (Gam.),
ubhayoḥ 6th/du of the two,
√*ubj* 216/2 Cl 6 P *ubjati* to press down, keep under, subdue, make straight, make honest, DP in *ārjava* making straight,
√*uc* 172/3 Cl 4 P *ucyati* to take pleasure in, delight in, be fond of, be accustomed, be suitable, suit, fit, DP

in *samavāya* being suitable, suiting, fitting,
ucca 172/3 mfn. high, lofty, elevated, tall, deep, high-sounding, loud, pronounced with the *udātta* accent, intense, violent, m. height,
uccā ind. above (in heaven), from above, upwards,
uccābudhna mfn being bottom upwards,
uccaghana n, laughter in the mind not expressed in the face,
uccaiḥ in comp. for *uccais*, loudly
uccaiḥkula n. high family, mfn of high family,
uccaiḥśiras mfn carrying one's head high, a man of high rank,
uccaiḥśravasa m. name of a horse, the original horse,
uccaiḥsthāna n. a high place, of high rank or family,
uccaiḥstheya loftiness, firmness of character,
uccair in comp. for *uccais*,
uccairbhāṣaṇa n. speaking aloud,
uccairgotra n. high family or descent,
uccais ind. aloft, high, above, upwards, from above, loud, accentuated, intensely, much, powerfully, loudly, high
uccak *(ud √cak)* P. *–cakati*, to look up steadfastly or dauntlessly, to look up perplexedly,
uccakais ind. very lofty, tall, loud, excessively lofty, tall, with 1.*√kṛ* to make high, set up in a high place,
uccakita mf looking up perplexedly,
uccal *ut√cal* Cl1 *uccalati* to move away, rise,
uccala m. the mind, understanding,
uccalana n. going off or out, moving away
uccaṇḍa mfn very passionate, violent, terrible, mighty, quick, hanging down, expeditious,
uccandra m. the moonless period of the night, the last watch of the night,
uccanīca mfn high and low, variegated,
uccapada n. a high situation, high office,
uccāra mfn rising, m. faeces, discharge, pronunciation, utterance,
uccāraka mfn pronouncing, making audible,
uccaraṇa n. going up or out, articulating,
uccarita mfn gone up or out, risen, uttered, articulated, *(am)* n. dung,
uccaśas ind. upwards,
uccatā or °*tva* n. height, superiority,
uccatāla n. music and dancing at feasts, etc.
uccataru m. any lofty tree, coconut tree,
uccāvaca mfn high and low, great and small, variegated, various, multiform, manifold, irregular,
uccaya m. gathering from the ground, adding to, collection, heap, the knot which fastens the lower garments round the loins,
ucchanna mfn uncovered, undressed,
ucchāstravartin mfn deviating from or transgressing the law-books,
uccheda 173/3 m. cutting off or out, destruction, putting an end to,
ucchedin mfn destroying, cutting off,
ucchesa mfn left remaining, leavings,
ucchidya ind. having cut off or destroyed, having interrupted,
ucchinna mfn cut out or off, destroyed, lost, abject, vile, m. peace obtained by ceding valuable lands,
ucchiṣṭa 173/3 left, rejected, stale, n. that spat out, leavings, fragments,
ucchiṣṭabhoktṛ mfn one who eats leavings,
ucchoṣaṇa 174/1 mfn. making dry, parching
ucchoṣuka mfn drying up, withering,
ucchraya 174/1 rising upwards, elevation, height, growth, increase, intensity, elevation of a tree, mountain, also *ucchrāya*
ucchrāyin mfn high, raised, lofty,
ucchreya mfn high, lofty,
ucchrita mfn raised, lifted up, erected, rising, arising, mounting, high, tall, advancing, arisen, grown powerful or mighty, wanton, luxuriant, excited, grown, huge, enlarged,
ucchritapāṇi mfn with outstretched hand,

ucchṛṅkhala 174/1 mfn unbridled, uncurbed, unrestrained, self-willed, perverse,
uccūḍa m. the flag or pennon of a banner,
ucchvas (ud-√śvas) P.A. *–chvasiti* to breathe hard, snort, take a deep breath, to breathe again, get breath, recover, rest,
ucchvāsa m. breathing out, breath, deep inspiration, expiration, death, froth, yeast, foam, swelling, rising, consolation, encouragement, an air-hole,
ucchvasat mfn breathing, etc. see above, m. a breathing being,
ucita mfn proper, usual, delightful, agreeable, acceptable, convenient,
ucyate 1/s/pres/pass. is called, it is said, it is spoken, he is said to be, he is called, 1/s/pres/indic/pass. 912/1 root *vac* to speak, to be spoken or said, to resound, to be called or accounted,
ud a particle and prefix to verbs, (expressing superiority in place, rank, station, or power), up, upwards, upon, on, over, above, (or implying separation and disjunction), out, out of, from, off, away from, apart, (may also imply) publicity, pride, indisposition, weakness, helplessness, binding, loosing, existence, acquisition, *sometimes repeated in the Veda to fill out the verse,

ud 2. 183/1 or *und* Cl 7 P *unatti* Cl 6 P *undati*
to flow or issue out, spring (as water),
uda n. water, (only ibc., ifc. or in comp.)
udac or 2. *udañc* mfn turned or going upwards, upper, upwards, turned to the north, northern, subsequent, posterior, the northern quarter, north, ind. above, northward,
ud√ac *ud* (prefix expressing superiority–up, upwards, upon, above, over, out, out of, from, off,) +√*ac* to go, move,
udacyate 1/s/pres/pass *acyate* it arises
udācam ind. p. lifting up, raising,
udadhi mfn holding water, m. 'water-receptacle', a cloud, the ocean, sea, river,
udag-ayana n. north-course (of the sun), or the half year from winter to summer solstice,
udagdaśa mfn having the seams upward,
udagra mfn tall, fierce, intense, haughty, advanced (in years), excited, loud,
udāhāra m. an example or illustration, the beginning of a speech,
udāharaṇa n. the act of relating, saying, declaring, declaration, referring a general rule to a special case, an example, illustration, exaggeration
udaharat lifted, lifted up
udāharin mfn relating, saying, calling,
udā√hṛ Cl 1 *–harati,* bring out, express, say,
udāhṛta 185/3 mfn described, explained, called, declared, entitled, ppp.
udāhṛti f. an example, illustration, exaggeration,
udaja mfn produced in or by water, aquatic, watery, m. driving out or forth (cattle), leading out (soldiers to war), n. a lotus,
udaka 183/2 n. water, the ceremony of offering water to a dead person, ablution (ceremonial),
udakta mfn raised or lifted up, drawn up,
uda-kumbha m. water-jar,
udan n. a wave, water,
-*vat* mfn wavy, watery, m.the ocean
ud√an to breathe upwards, to breathe out, breathe,
udāna 184/2 m.breathing upwards, one of the five vital airs of the –body (*prāṇas)*, (that which is in the throat and rises upwards), the navel, an eyelash, a kind of snake, the breath at death,
ud√añc P. *–acati,* to elevate, raise up, lift up, throw up, to ladle out, to cause, effect, to rise, arise,to resound, to come forth, proceed,

udañc mfn directed upward, directed northward, northerly,
udañcana n. a bucket, pail, cover, lid, directing or throwing upwards, rising, ascending,
udañcita mfn raised up, lifted, elevated, tossed up, uttered, caused to resound, worshipped,
udanimat mfn abounding in waves or water,
udanta mfn reaching to the end or border, running or flowing over, good, virtuous, excellent, m. end of the work, rest, harvest time, 'telling to the end' full tidings, intelligence, news, one who gets a livelihood by a trade, by sacrificing for others, (*am*) ind. to the end or border,
udantaka m. news, tidings, intelligence, f. –*ikā* satisfaction, satiety,
udantya mfn living beyond a boundary,
udanya mfn watery, desire of water, thirst -*ja* mfn born or living in water, Nom. P. *udanyati* to irrigate, to be exceedingly thirsty,
udanyu mfn liking or seeking water, pouring out water, irrigating,
udapāna 183/2 a well, water-tank,
udara 184/2 n. the interior or inside of anything, belly, womb etc.
a cavity, hollow, the thick part of anything e.g. the thumb,
udāra mfn high, lofty, exalted, great, best, noble, illustrious, generous, upright, honest, liberal, gentle, munificent, sincere, proper, right, eloquent, unperplexed, exciting, effecting, active, energetic, (as) m. rising fog or vapour, a sort of grain with long stalks,
udārabhāva m. noble character, generosity,
udāracarita mfn of generous behaviour, noble-minded, noble,
udāraka m. honorific name of a man,
udārakīrti mfn highly renowned, illustrious
udāracetas mfn high-minded, magnanimous
udāradarśana mfn of noble appearance,
udāradhī mfn highly intelligent, wise, sagacious,
udāramati mfn noble-minded, highly intelligent, wise
udārasattva mfn of noble character, generous-minded,
udāraśobha mfn of magnificent splendour
udāratā f. or –*tva* nobleness, generousness, liberality, energy, elegance of speech or expression, magnanimity
udārāvastha expanded state (U),
udāravikrama mfn highly brave, heroic,
udāravṛtti generous nature,
udarcis mfn flaming or blazing upwards, brilliant, resplendent, m. fire,
udarila mfn corpulent,
udarka m. arising (as a sound), resounding, the future result of actions, futurity, consequence, future time, a remote consequence, reward, happy future, conclusion, end, repetition, refrain, a tower, look-out place,
ud√as Cl2 *udasyati* to sit idle, to cast or throw up, to raise, erect, to throw out, to throw a weapon,
ud√ās Cl2 *udāste* to sit idle, take no interest in, be unconcerned about, to pass by, omit, to sit on one side or apart, sit separate or away from,
udāsa 1. throwing out, extending, protracting, abortion, 2. m. indifference, apathy, stoicism,
udasana n. throwing up, raising, erecting,
udāsin mfn indifferent, disregarding, m. a stoic, philosopher, ascetic,
udāsīna 185/3 mfn. sitting apart, indifferent, free from affection, inert, inactive, m. a stranger, neutral,
one neither friend nor foe, a stoic, philosopher, ascetic,
udāsīnatā f. indifference, apathy,
udāsīnavat as if sitting apart etc.
udāsitṛ mfn indifferent, disregarding, stoical, void of affection or concern,
udaśru mfn weeping, one whose tears gush forth, shedding tears,
ind. with tears gushing forth,
udasta mfn thrown or cast up, raised,
udātta mfn lifted up, upraised, lofty, elevated, high, arisen, come forth,

highly or acutely accented, high, great, illustrious, generous, gentle, bountiful, giving, a donor, haughty, pompous, dear, beloved,
m. the acute accent, a high or sharp tone, a gift, donation, a kind of musical instrument, a large drum, work, business,
n. pompous or showy speech,

udāttayati Nom P. makes high or illustrious,

udavasāya ind. p. ending, concluding,

udavasita n. a house, dwelling,

udavasya ind p. concluding,

udaya 186/1 m. rising, rising of the sun, dawning, coming up (of a cloud), coming forth, becoming visible, appearance, development, production, creation, conclusion, result, consequence, that which follows, a following word, subsequent sound, rising, reaching one's aim, success, prosperity,

udāya m. emerging, coming forward,

udayana n. rise, rising (of the sun etc.), way out, outlet, outcome, result, conclusion, end, means of redemption,

udayāstamaya m.s. or *yau* du. m. rising and setting, creation and dissolution,

udayavat mfn risen (as the moon),

udayin mfn rising, ascending, prosperous, flourishing, victorious,

udbaddha mfn tied up or upwards, hung, interrupted, compact, firm, hung up, checked, annulled, firm,

udbāhuka mfn having the arms out or extended,

udbala mfn strong, powerful,

ud√bhā P. *–bhāti* to become visible, appear,

ud√bhās P.A. *–bhāsati, (te),* to come forth or appear brightly, shine, to become visible, strike, caus. *bhāsayati, (te),* to illuminate, light up, to make apparent or prominent, cause to come forth, render brilliant or beautiful,

udbhāsa m. radiance, splendour,

udbhāsin mfn shining, radiant, coming forth, appearing, giving or causing splendour,

udbhāsita mfn come forth, appeared, lighted up, illuminated, splendid, ornamented, graced, beautiful,

udbhava 190/2 m.existence, generation, origin, birth, springing from, becoming visible, a sort of salt, association with divine powers (Gam),

udbhāva m. production, generation, rising (of sounds)

udbhāvana n. the act of raising up, elevation, passing over, inattention, neglect, disregard, announcement, communication, making visible, manifestation,

udbhavati arises, is born,

udbhāvin mfn coming forth, becoming visible,

udbhāvita mfn caused to exist, created, produced,

ud√bhid P. *–bhinatti* to break or burst through, break out, to appear above, become visible, rise up, to pirse,

udbhid mfn penetrating, bursting through, coming or bursting forth, overflowing, abounding with, sprouting, germinating, f. (*t*) a sprout or shoot of a plant, a plant, spring, fountain,

udbhida mfn sprouting, germinating, n. a fountain, spring, a kind of salt,

udbhidvidyā f. the science of plants, botany

udbhijja 190/2 mfn. sprouting, germinating, born of earth – trees etc.

udbhinna mfn burst forth, opened, burst, come forth, appeared, brought to light, made to appear,

ud√bhṛ P.A. *–bharati,* (*te*), to take or carry away or out, to take for one's self, choose, select, to raise up, carry above, elevate,

udbhrama m. whirling, excitement, intoxication,

udbhrānta mfn risen, ascended, gone or

jumped up, turned upwards, come forth, disappeared, run away, wandering about, roaming, agitated, bewildered, n. the act of waving a sword, the rising (of the wind), n. excitement, agitation,

udbhrāntaka mfn wandering about, roaming, n. whirling upwards, rising, ascending,

ud√bhū P.Cl 1 *–bhavati*, to rise up, come up to, reach, be equal, to come forth, arise, exist, spring from, shoot forth, increase, grow larger, make apparent, show, explain, to speak of, mention, to consider,
2. mfn 'being up to what is wanted', sufficient, having persistency, persevering,

udbhūta mfn come forth, produced, born, grown, raised, increased, elevated, visible, perceptible, distinct, such as can be comprehended by the senses,

udbhūtarūpa n. visible form or shape, mfn having a visible shape,

udbhūtatva n. the state of being increased,

udbhūti f. coming forth, existence, appearance, elevation, increase,

udbodha m. awaking, coming forth, appearing, reminding, incipient knowledge,

udbodhaka mfn exciting, calling forth, reminding, one who reminds or calls to remembrance,

udbodhana n. awaking, arousing, recalling, reminding,

udbudbuda mfn bubbling out or forth,

udbuddha mfn roused up, awakened, come forth, appearing, budded, reminded, made to think of, recalled,

uddālaka a Vedic teacher and seer, n. a kind of honey,

uddāma unrestrained, unbound, set free, self-willed, unlimited, violent, proud, large, great, (*am*) ind. in an unrestrained manner, without any limits,

uddāna n. binding on, fastening together, taming, subduing, the middle, waist, a fire-place, contents, tax, duty,

uddānta mfn humble, energetic, elevated,

uddarśita mfn made visible, come forth, appearing,

uddeśa m. spot, place, region, an object, the act of pointing to or at, direction, ascertainment, brief statement, illustration, explanation, mentioning a thing by name, prescription, stipulation, bargain, a motion, relative to, aiming at,

uddeśaka mfn illustrative, explanatory, m. an illustration, example, an illustrator, guide, (in math.) a question, problem,

uddeśana n. the act of pointing to or at,

uddeśatas ind. pointedly, distinctly, by way of explanation, for example, pointedly, distinctly, briefly,

uddeśin mfn pointing to or at,

uddhā *ut√hā* Cl3 *ujjīhite* to rise up, start up, depart,

uddhāna n. the act of leaving, abandonment, 2. ejected, vomited, corpulent, n. the act of ejecting, vomiting, a fireplace,

uddharaṇa n. taking up, drawing out, raising, lifting up, taking off (clothes), taking away, removing, putting or placing before, delivering, rescuing, extricating, tearing out,

uddharati lifts,

uddharet one should rise up, lift up, raise up 1/s/opt/act *ud √ dhṛ*

uddharma m. unsound doctrine, heresy,

uddharṣa m. the courage to undertake anything, 2. mfn glad, pleased, happy, m. the flaring up of a fire, great joy, a festival, excessive joy,

uddharṣaṇa mfn animating, encouraging, n. the act of animating encouraging, mfn causing joy, gladdening, n. erection of the hair (through rapture),

uddhasta mfn extending/raising the hands,

uddhata mfn raised (as dust), turned up,

lifted, raised, enhanced, struck (a lute), violent, intense, vain, arrogant, ill-behaved, exceeding, abounding in, full of, stirred up, excited,

uddhati 188/3 f. haughtiness, pride arrogance, a stroke, shaking, elevation,

uddhava m. sacrificial fire, a festival, holiday, joy, pleasure, friend and devotee of *Kṛṣṇa,*

uddhi m. the seat of a carriage,

uddhita *mfn* erected, built up, exposed,

uddhmāna n. a fire-place, stove,

uddhmāya ind. having breathed out, expiring,

uddhura mfn free from a yoke or burden, wild, lively, cheerful, heavy, gross,

uddina n. midday,

uddīpa m. the act of inflaming, lighting, an inflamer, animating,

uddīpaka mfn inflaming, exciting, lighting, rendering more intense,

uddīpana mfn inflaming, exciting, affecting violently (as poison), n. the act of inflaming, illuminating, lighting up, inflaming (a passion), exciting, animating, stimulating, an incentive, stimulus, burning (a body etc), any aggravating thing or circumstance,

uddīpta mfn lighted, set on fire or alight, shining, inflamed, aggravated (as a passion),

uddita mfn bound, tied,

uddiśya 188/1 ind. with regard to, for the sake of, with reference to, having shown or explained, aiming at L. at, towards,

uddiṣṭa mfn mentioned, particularized, described, promised,

uḍḍīyana n. flying up, soaring,

uddyota mfn flashing up, shining, m. becoming bright or visible, light, lustre, revelation, a book chapter,

uddyotaka mfn enlightening, emblazoning,

uddyotakara or *uddyotakarin* mfn causing light, enlightening, illuminating,

uddyotana n. the act of enlightening, illumination,

uddyotita mfn caused to shine, lighted up,

udeti *ud-e* 186/3 *udeti* goes up, rises, 1/s/pres/act/indic it rises

ud√gai P. *–gāyati, -gāti,* to begin to sing, to sing or chant (esp.the Samaveda), to sing out loud, to celebrate in song, sing before anyone, to fill with song,

ud√gam P. *–gacchati,* to come forth, appear suddenly, become visible, to go up rise (as a star), ascend, start up,

udgandhi mfn fragrant,

udgarbha mfn pregnant,

udgata mgn gone up, risen, ascended, come or proceed forth, gone, departed, extended, large, vomited,

udgatāsu mfn one whose life is gone, dead

udgātṛ (tā) m. one of the 4 chief priests, (the chanter of the *Sāmaveda* hymns), a chanter,

udgati f. coming forth, going up, rising

udgha m. excellence, a model, pattern, happiness, the hollow hand, fire, organic air in the body,

udghana m. a carpenter's bench, a plank on which he works,

udghāta m. striking, wounding, a wound, blow, slipping, tripping, raising, elevation, beginning, a thing begun, commencement, breathing through the nostrils (as an exercise), a weapon, a chapter, a club, awakening of the Kundalini śakti,

udghātaka or *udghātya* n. a dialogue in short, abrupt but significant words,

udghātin mfn one who opens or unlocks, commencing, rough, bumpy,

udghus Cl1 *udghoṣati* to cry out,

udgiraṇa 187/1 vomiting, spitting,

udgīta mfn sung, announced, celebrated, n. singing, a song,

udgītha m. chanting of the *Sāmaveda,*

udgīti f. singing, singing loud, chanting,

udgoraṇa n. the act of raising a weapon, threatening,

udgrāha m. taking up, reception, name of a sandhi rule, replying in argument, objection,

udgrāhita mfn taken away, lifted up, delivered, seized, bound, tied,
ūdhan , *ūdhar, ūdhas* n. udder, breast,
udharati lifts, lifts up
ūdhas n. udder,
udhavati he arises, or is born
ud√hṛ or *ud-dhṛ* Cl 1 *–(d)harati,* to take up, lift up,raise, (*dhṛ)* to take out or draw out or bring or tear out or pull out or extricate or eradicate, to draw, ladle up, skim, to take away (fire, or anything from the fire), to rescue,
√*udhras* 193/1 Cl 9 P *udhrasnāti* to gather, glean, Cl 10 P A *udhrāsayati (te),* to gather, glean, to throw or cast upwards, DP in *uñch* gleaning,
udīcīna mfn turned towards the north, northern,
udīcya mfn being or living in the north, the northern region, m.pl. the inhabitants of the north,
udīkṣ Cl1 *udīkṣate* to look at,
udīpa mfn flooded, m. inundation,
udīrita mfn excited increased, proud,
udita mfn. risen, ascended, evolved, high, tall, lofty, conceited, increased, visible
2. said, spoken, proclaimed, declared, authoritative, right, indicated, signified, referred to, ppp of √*vad*
uditi f. ascending/rising (of the sun), setting of the sun, conclusion, end
uditodita mfn conversant with what has been handed down by tradition, learned,
uditvā having said
uditvara mfn risen, surpassing, exceeding, extraordinary,
ud√mad Cl 1 *–madati,* Cl4 *–madyati,* to bubble over with emotion or excitement,
ud√pad Cl 4 *–padyate,* to go forth, arise, come into existence, be produced, caus. *utpādayate,* causes to come into existence, produces,
udra m. a crab, an otter, n. water,
udraṅga or *udraṅka* m. a town,
udṛc f. remainder, conclusion, end,
udṛci ind. lastly, at last, finally,
udreka m. abundance, excess, superiority, predominance,
udrikta mfn prominent, standing out, increased, abundant, abounding,
udriktacetas mfn high-minded, intoxicated
udriktacitta n. a mind abounding in (goodness etc.), mfn having a lofty mind, proud, arrogant,
udrin mfn abounding in water,
ud√sad Cl 1 *-sīdati,* to sink, settle down, decay, go to ruin, caus. *utsādayati* to bring to ruin, destroy,
ud√sah Cl 1 *–sahate,* to hold out, endure, be able, can (with infinitive),
ud√sṛj Cl 6 *–sṛjati,* to let go, release,
ud√sthā Cl 1 *-tiṣṭhati,* to stand up, arise,
uḍu f.n. a star, n. water,
udūḍha mfn borne up, raised, carried, sustained, recovered, acquired, married, coarse, gross, heavy, fat, material, substantial, much,
udūha m. a broom, the highest acute (accent),
udūkhala n. a wooden mortar for rice,
udumbala mfn of widely reaching power, brown or copper-coloured,
uḍupa m.n. a raft or float,
uduṣṭa mfn red-hot, red,
udvaha mfn carrying or leading up, carrying away, propagating, marriage, son, offspring,
udvāhin mfn one who raisesor draws up, one who marries, relating to marriage,
udvahni mfn emitting sparks or fire (as an eye),
udvaṁśa mfn of high descent,
udvana mfn steep, precipitous,
udvāna mfn ejected, vomited, n. the going out, being extinguished the act of ejecting, vomiting, a stove
udvāpana n. the act of putting out (the fire)
udvartman n. a wrong road,
udvasa mfn uninhabited, empty, disappeared, gone, n. solitude,

udvāsa m. banishment, exile, abandonment, setting free, dismissal, carrying out for slaughter, mfn one who has put off clothes (a woman after her period),
udvega 192/1 mfn. going swiftly, a runner, courier, steady, composed, tranquil, ascending, mounting, m. trembling, waving, being offended, admiration, astonishment, absence of passion or emotion, the Areca nut,
udveṣṭ *ud√veṣṭ* caus. *udveṣṭayati* to unwrap open a letter,
udvigna 192/1 terrified, sorrowful, anxious, worried mind, grieving (for an absent lover), melancholy,
udvignamanas mfn having a terrified mind, distressed, depressed, sorrowful,
ud √vij Cl 6 –A.P *vijyate (ti),* to be agitated, or frightened, perturbed, distressed, to gush or spring upward, to shudder, to fear, be afraid of, to shrink from, recede, leave off, to frighten, intimidate,
udvijet one should shudder or tremble, 1/s/opt/act
udvoḍhṛ m. a husband,
udvṛddha mfn grown up, come forth, appearing,
udya mfn to be spoken or pronounced,
udyā *ud√yā* Cl2 *udyāti* to rise up,
ud√yam Cl 1 *–yacchati,* to hold up, raise,
udyama m. the act of raising or lifting up, elevation, undertaking, beginning, the act of striving after, exertion, perseverance, diligence, zeal,
udyamana 191/1 raising, elevation, effort, exertion
udyamya gerund flourishing, brandishing, mfn to be undertaken with exertion, ind. having lifted or taken up, having made exertion,
udyāna n. walking out, the act of walking out, place for walking out –garden or park,
udyānaka n. a garden, park,
udyāna n. small wood, garden , royal garden, purpose, motive,
udyāpana n. the act of bringing to a conclusion, finishing, accomplishment,
udyāpanikā f. return home from a journey,
udyāpita mfn brought to a conclusion, finished,
udyāsa m. exertion, effort,
udyat mfn rising, m. a star,
udyata upraised, uplifted, elevated, high ppp. *ud√yam* eager for, intent on, endeavour, active preparation, trained, exercised, disciplined, active, persevering,
udyāva m. mixing, joining,
udyoga m. the act of undertaking anything, exertion, perseverance, strenuous and continuous endeavour,
udyogin mfn active, energetic,
ud√yuj P.A. *–yunakti, yuṅkte,* to join, be in contact with, to get off or away, go away, to go near, undergo, prepare, to make efforts, be active,
udyuj f. endeavour, striving after,
udyukta mfn undertaking, undergoing, prepared or ready for, labouring for some desired end,
udyuta mfn mixed with, confounded, mad,
ugra mfn terrible, mighty, very strong, high, noble, cruel, fierce, ferocious, savage, hot, sharp, pungent, acrid, turbulent (Gam.),
ugraśāsana mfn having a terrible way of ruling, m. a strict ruler,
√uh 221/1 Cl 1 P *ohati* to give pain, hurt, kill, DP in *ardana* distress, pain
√1.ūh 223/2 Cl 1 P A *ūhati, ūhate*, to push, thrust, move, remove (only when compounded with preps.), to change alter, modify,
2. Cl 1 P A to observe, mark, note, attend to heed, regard, expect, hope for, wait for, listen for, to comprehend, conceive, conjecture, guess, suppose, infer, reason, deliberate upon, DP in *vitarka* reasoning, inferring, deliberating,
ūha 223/1 m. removing, transposition,

change, modification, adding, addition, the act of comprehending, conceiving, consideration, deliberation, examination, supposition, conclusion, inference, 'the knowledge about nature etc. that arises – without instruction- to a seeker of truth as a result of tendencies acquired in past lives' (Gam.),
f. (*ā*) as above,

ūhana n. transposition, change, deliberation, reasoning,

ūhanī f. a broom,

ujjāgara mfn excited, irritated,

ujjayinī f. Oujein, name of a city,

√*ujjha* 174/3 Cl 6 P *ujjhati* to leave, abandon, quit, DP in *utsarga* abandoning,

uj-ji (*uj*-√*ji)* P. *–jayati* to win, conquer, acquire by conquest,

ujjeṣa mfn victorious,

ujjha mfn quitting, abandoning,

ujjhaka m. a cloud, a devotee,

ujjhita mfn left, abandoned, free from,

ujjhiti f. abandoning (the world),

ujjiti f. victory,

ujjīv *(ud-*√*jīv)* P. *–jīvati,* to revive, return to life, caus. *–jīvayati* to restore to life, animate

ujjṛmbhaṇa n. the act of gaping, opening the mouth, coming forth, arising,

ujjval *(ud*√*jval)* P. *–jvalati, -jvaliti,* to blaze up, flame, shine, caus. *–jvalayati* to light up, cause to shine, illuminate,

ujjvala mfn blazing up, luminous, splendid, light, burning, clean, clear, lovely, beautiful, glorious, full-blown, expanded, (*as*) m. love, passion, (*am*) n. gold *(ā)* f. splendour, clearness, brightness,

ujjvalita mfn lighted, shining, flaming, etc.

ukāra 171/3 the letter or sound *u* (partic. of *om),*

√*ukh* 172/2 Cl 1 P *okhati* to go, move, DP in *gati*, going, moving

√*ukṣ* 172/1 Cl 1 P A *ukṣati, ukṣate,* to sprinkle, moisten, wet, sprinkle or scatter in small drops, emit, throw out, scatter, emit seed (as a bull), be strong, DP in *secana* sprinkling,

ukṣ mfn dropping pouring, becoming strong

ukṣita mfn sprinkled, moistened, soaked in, strong, of full growth,

ukta 171/3 mfn. (having been) uttered, said, spoken, ppp. of √*vac*

uktha n. utterance esp. of devotion, praise, hymn of praise, invocation, a subdivision of recited verses in the scriptures,

ukthavardana mfn strengthening, i.e. refreshing or delighting oneself with hymns of praise,

ukti 172/1 f. speech, saying, sentence, a worthy speech or word,

uktvā ind. having said, having spoken,

√*ulaḍ* 218/2 Cl 10 P *ulaṇḍayati* to throw out, eject, DP in *utkṣepaṇa* throwing up, tossing up

ulba 219/1 n. a cover, envelope, membrane covering an embryo, (also *ulva*)

ulbaṇa mfn n. the membrane enveloping the embryo, mfn anything laid over in addition,superfluous, abundant, excessive, much, immense, strong, singular, strange, manifest, evident, ifc. abundantly furnished with, m. a hand position in dancing, f. (*ā*) a particular dish of milk with the juice of melons, bananas etc.

ulkā f. a meteor, torch,

ullaṅgh *ul*√*laṅgh* caus.P. *–laṅghayati* to leap over, pass over or beyond, overstep, transgress, escape, exceed,

ullāsa 219 light, splendour, becoming visible, appearing, happiness, merriness, increase, growth, chapter,section, division of a book,

ullekha m. mentioning, speaking of, description, intuitive description, causing to come forth or appear clearly, description according to different impressions,

ulūka m. owl,

ulūkhala n. a wooden mortar,
umā f. flax, turmeric, splendour, light, fame, reputation, quiet, tranquillity, night, a daughter of Himavat, = Pārvatī, Durgā, wife of Ṣiva and sister of Gaṅgā
√*umbh* see *ubh* Cl 6
ūna mfn lacking, wanting, deficient, short of the right quantity,
√*ūnaya* 221/2 Nom. P *ūnayati,* to leave deficient, not to fulfil, to deduct or lessen, DP in *parihāṇa* lessening, diminishing, leaving unfinished,
√*uñch* 175/1 Cl 1, 6, P *uñchati* to gather, glean, DP in *uñch* gathering bit by bit, gleaning
uñcha 175/1 gleaning, gathering grains
√*und* 193/1 (see 2. *ud*), Cl 7P *unatti, Cl 6P undati* to flow or issue out, spring (as water) to wet, bathe, DP in *kledana* wetting, moistening, bathing,
undana n. wetting, moistening,
uṇḍuka m. a texture, a net, the stomach,
undura = *andura, unduru,* m. a rat, mouse
ūnita 221/2 lessened, reduced, fewer,
√*uṅkh* 172/3 Cl 6 P *uṅkhati* to go, move, DP in gati going, moving
unmada mfn mad, furious, extravagant, drunk, m. insanity, intoxication,
unmāda 194/1 m. mad, insane, extravagant, m. insanity, madness, hysteria,
unmadana mfn inflamed with love, intoxication,
unmadita mfn excited, wrought up into an ecstatic state, mad,
unmajjana n. act of emerging, emergence,
unmāna 194/3 n. measure, weight, value, price, worth, a partic. measure,
unmanas mfn excited or disturbed in mind
unmanī-avasthā f. mindless state of a yogin,
unmanībhāva m. absence of mind, mindlessness,
unmarda m. rubbing off, rubbing,
unmārga m. by-way, evil way, wrong way,
unmārgagāmin mfn going in evil ways,
unmārjita mfn polished, clean,
unmāttha m. snare, trap, murderer, act of shaking, killing, slaughter,
unmatta mfn disordered in intellect, distracted, frantic, mad,
unmattadarśana mfn having a frantic look,
unmedā f. corpulence, fatness,
un√*mīl* P. *–milati* to open the eyes, to open (as an eye), to become visible, come forth, appear, caus. *–mīlayati,*
unmīla m. becoming visible, appearance,
unmīlati 194/2 opens the eyes 1/s/pres/indic/act opens the eyes
unmīlita mfn opened (as an eye or flower), caused to come forth, made visible,
unmiṣ *(ud*√*miṣ)* P. *-miṣati* to open the eyes, draw up the eyelids, to open (as buds or eyes), to come forth, originate, to shine forth, become brilliant,
unmiṣa m. the act of opening the eyes,
unmiṣan opening the eyes, pres/act/part *ud miṣan*
unmiṣati opens the eyes, winks, blinks
unmiṣita mfn opened (as an eye), expanded (as a flower), open (as the face), smiling, (*am*) n. the opening of the eyes,
unmita mfn ifc. measuring, having the measure of,
unmiti f. measure of altitude, measure, value, price,
unmocana n. the act of unfastening, unbinding, giving up or away,
unmṛṣṭa mfn stroked, rubbed or wiped off, effaced, blotted out,
unmudita mfn exulting, rejoicing,
unmudra mfn unsealed, opened (a flower), unbound, unrestrained, wild through joy,
unmugdha mfn confused, silly, stupid,
unmukha mfn raising the face, looking up or at, expecting, near to, ready, erect, waiting for,
unmukta mfn taken off, laid aside, thrown out, uttered, free from, deprived of, wanting,
unmukti f. deliverance,
unmuṣita mfn stolen,

unna mfn wetted, wet, moistened, moist, kind, humane
unnāda m. crying out, clamour,
unnaddha mfn tied or bound up, swollen, increased, unbound, excessive, impudent, conceited,
unnāha m. excess, abundance, impudence, haughtiness, sour gruel,
unnahana freed from fetters, unbound,
unnasa mfn having a prominent nose,
unnata mfn high, tall, prominent, lofty, eminent, sublime, great, noble, having a large hump, bent or turned upwards, elevated, lifted up,
m. a boa, n. elevation, ascension, elevated part, means of measuring the day,
unnati f. rising, ascending, swelling, elevation, height, advancement, prosperity,
unnaya m. the act of leading up, raising elevating, conclusion, inference, *(ud√nī)*
unneya mfn to be inferred or ascertained by analogy,
un-nī *ud-√nī* P.A. *–nayati, (te),* to lead up or out, lead upwards or up to, to bring or fetch out of, free from, help, rescue, redeem, to raise, set up, erect, to put up, lay up, press or squeeze out, to lead away (a calf from its mother),
unnī mfn bringing or leading upwards,
unnidra mfn sleepless, awake, expanded (as a flower), budded, shining,
unnidraka n. sleeplessness,
uñśiṣṭa see *ucchiṣṭa*
upa ind. a preposition or prefix to verbs and nouns expressing towards, near to, (opp. to *apa* away), by the side of, with, together with, under, down, e.g. *upa√gam* to go near, undergo, *upagamana* approaching,

As a prefix to nouns *upa* expresses, direction towards, nearness, contiguity in space, time, number, degree, resemblance and relationship but with the idea of subordination and inferiority (e.g. *upa-purāṇam – a* secondary or subordinate Purāṇa. *upa-kaniṣṭhikā* the finger next to the little finger),

sometimes forming compound adverbs e.g. *upa-mūlam* at the root,

prefixed to names may indicate a younger brother e.g. *upendra* 'the younger brother of Indra', (in Buddhist lit. a son),

as a separable adverb it may (rarely) express – there-to, further, moreover,
as a separable preposition – near to, towards, in the direction of, under, below,

with 2nd - near to, at, on, upon, at the time of, up to, in, above,

with 7th – with, together with, at the same time with, according to,
upa may also imply disease, extinction, ornament, command, reproof and more,
upabaddha mfn tied up, fastened,
upabandha m. union, connection, tie bond, rope, quotation, use (of a word etc.), a particular manner of sitting, an affix,
upa barha m. a pillow,
upabhoga m. enjoyment, gratification
upabhogin mfn enjoying, making use of,
upabhojin mfn eating, enjoying,
upabhoktā the enjoyer, consumer,
upabhrita mfn brought near, procured for
upabhṛt f. wooden cup (sacrificial use),
upa√bhū P. to come near to, approach, to help, assist,
upa√bhuj Cl7 *upabhuṅkte* to enjoy, eat, eat up, consume, spend, partake of, experience,
upabhukta mfn enjoyed, eaten, consumed
upabhukti f. enjoyment, use,

upa√bhūṣ P. *-bhūṣati,* to approach (in order to revere), to regard, be careful, pay attention to, observe, obey,

upabṛṁhana n. 'the act of making strong' invigoration, strengthening,

upa-brū A. *–brūte*, to speak to, address, to invoke for, entreat, ask for, persuade,

upacakṣus n. a superhuman or divine eye, spectacles,

upacara mfn accessory, supplementary,

upacāra m. approach, service, attendance, proceeding, procedure, established use (of a word), usage, custom or manner of speech, a figurative or metaphorical expression, act of civility, obliging or polite behaviour, reverence, a figurative or metaphorical expression, offerings to a deity, present, offering, bribe, solicitation, request,

upacaraṇa n. approach,

upacārika mfn ifc. serving for, belonging to,

upacaya 197/3 accumulation, quantity, heap, elevation, excess, increase, growth

upacāyin mfn honouring, revering, mfn ifc. causing to increase or succeed

upacchanda m. a requisite,

upacchandana n. persuasion, conciliation by coaxing, enticing,

upacchandita mfn persuaded, coaxed, enticed,

upacīrṇa mfn attended upon, assisted,

upācīrṇa mfn deceived,

upacita mfn heaped up, increased, thriving, increasing, prospering, succeeding, big, fat, thick, covered over, well furnished, plastered, smeared,

upacitra mfn variegated, coloured,

upa√1.dā P. *–dadāti*, to give in addition, add, to give, grant, offer, to take upon one's self,

upadā mfn giving a present, f. a present, offering, a bribe,

upadagdha mfn burnt, set on fire,

upadāna n. a present, offering,

upādāna 213/2 n. the act of taking for oneself, perceiving, learning, acquiring, accepting, including, cause, motive, material cause,

upadarśana n. the act of exhibiting, representing, a commentary,

upadarśita mfn caused to appear, shown, perceived, explained,

upadātṛ mfn one who gives, grants or confers,

upādāya ind.p. having received or acquired, receiving, acquiring, taking with, together with, including, by help of, by means of,

upadeha 199/2 a cover, liniment, ointment, a secondary growth of the body

upadekśyati he will point out, instruct or teach, 1/pl/fut/act *upa √ diś*

upadeśa 199/1 specification, teaching, instruction, advice, prescription, initiation, reference, communication of the initiatory mantra or formula, original enunciation – the original form in which a root, base, affix, augment or any word or part of a word is enunciated in grammatical treatises,

upadeśaka mfn giving instruction, instructive, teacher, instructor,

upadeśana n. the act of advising, instruction, information, doctrine,

upadeśin mfn advising, teaching, informing, m. a teacher, adviser, L. mfn giving (good) instruction, a word or affix used in an *upadeśa*

upadeṣṭāram upadeṣṭā 199/1 one who teaches, a guru or spiritual guide, *tara* – surpassing, comparative 2/s surpassing guru

upadeṣṭavya gve. to be taught,

upadeva m. an inferior or secondary deity,

upādeya 213/2 to be taken or received, not to be refused, acceptable

upa√dhā P.A. *–dadhāti, -dhatte*, to place or lay upon, place near to, put on or into, to place, lay, put, to yoke (horses), to give or make over, hand over (knowledge), teach, to impose, commit, consign, to place under one's self, lie down upon, to communicate, cause to share in, to use, employ, to place in addition, add, connect, to cause to rest upon or depend upon,

upā√dhā P.A. to place upon, put on, to seize, lay hold of, take up, to keep, hold back, to seduce (a woman),

upadhā *2.* f. imposition, forgery, fraud, deceit, trial or test of honesty, (in gram.) a penultimate letter, condition, reservation,

upadhāna mfn placing upon, (*am*) n. the act of placing or resting upon, a pillow, cushion, cover, lid, peculiarity, singularity, affection, kindness, religious observance, poison, footstool, fetching, procuring,

upadhāraṇa 200/1 the act of considering, consideration, reflection

upadhāraya understand, comprehend, consider, reflect
2/s/pres/indic/caus/act *upa √dhṛ*

upadharma m. a minor or subordinate duty, a by-law, a false faith, heresy,

upadhārya mfn to be comprehended, ind. having taken or held up etc.

upa√dhāv Cl 1 *–dhāvati,* to run up to, run near, approach hastily,

upādhāya ind.p. taking up or with, together with,

upadhi m. the act of putting to, adding, addition, a part of a wheel, fraud, circumvention, condition, peculiarity, attribute, support,

upādhi 213/2 1. m. a substitute, superimposition, substitution, anything which may be taken for or has the mere name or appearanceof another thing, appearance, phantom, disguise, (said to be applied to forms or properties considered as disguises of the spirit), anything defining more closely, a peculiarity, an attribute, title, limitation, qualification, disguise, limitation, deception, deceit, G.328 adventitious condition, limiting condition, limitation, that which is put in the place of another thing, a substitute, substitution, an attribute, 2. m. point of view, aim, reflection on duty, virtuous reflection, a man who is careful to support his family,

upādhi-dharma characteristic of the limiting adjunct, (U)

upādhika mfn exceeding, supernumerary,

upadhṛti f. a ray of light,

upadhvasta mfn speckled, spotted,

upadhyāta mfn remembered, thought of,

upādhyāya m. a teacher, preceptor (who subsists by teaching part of the Veda, grammar etc. and is distinguished from the *ācārya),*

upadigdha mfn smeared, covered,

upa√diś Cl 6 *–diśati,* to point out, teach, instruct, explain,

upadiś mfn pointing out to, showing,

upadiṣṭa mfn specified, particularized, taught, instructed, mentioned, prescribed, initiated, (*am*) n. counsel, advice,

upadraṣṭā the Witness, he who while staying nearby does not Himself become involved 1/s/m 199/2

upadraṣṭṛ m. a looker on, spectator, a witness, supervisor,

upadrava m. that which attacks or occurs suddenly, any grievous accident, misfortune, calamity, mischief, national distress (famine, plague etc.), national commotion, rebellion,

upadravin mfn attacking suddenly, falling on, m. a tyrant, oppressor, rebel,

upa√dṛś to catch sight of, perceive, to look at or regard (with indifference), 2. f. aspect, look, appearance,

upadrāva n. a side door,

upa√1. gā P. *–gāti,* to go near to, arrive at, to come into, arrive at, undergo, to go, walk,

upaga mfn approaching, going towards, being or staying in or on, following, belonging to, fit for, conducive to, approached, furnished with,

upagā f. accompaniment of a song,

upagacchati 196/2 goes near, comes

toward, attains, approaches
upa√gai P. *–gāyati,* to sing to anyone, to join in singing, accompany a song, to sing before, sing, praise in song, celebrate, 'fill with song', to sing near,
upagata mfn gone to, met, approached, (esp. for protection or refuge), attained, obtained, arrived, happened, undergone, experienced, allowed,
upa√gam to go near to, come towards, approach, arrive at, reach, attain, to come upon, attack, to press hard upon, to occur, happen, to undertake, begin, to enter any state or relation, undergo, obtain, participate in make choice of, to admit, agree to, allow, confess,
upā√gam Cl 1 *–gacchati,* to come up to, approach, step near, come towards
upagama m. approach, coming to, approximation, entering (state or condition), obtaining, acquiring, approaching respectfully, veneration, coming near to, perceiving, acquaintance, society, sexual intercourse, undergoing, suffering, feeling, agreement,
upagamana n. the act of going towards, approaching, attaining, the act of coming near, perceiving, undertaking, addicting oneself to,
upagati f. approach, going near,
upagāyana n. singing,
upageya mfn to be approached, to be observed or kept, to be sung or celebrated, n. song,
upaghāta 197/1 a stroke, hurt, violation, injury, damage, offence, wrong, weakness, sickness , oblation,
upaghna m. contiguous support, resting-place, shelter, refuge,
upagiram ind. near or at a mountain,
upāgra n. a secondary member, the part next to the end or top,
upagraha m. seizure, confinement, a prisoner, addition (of a sound), alteration, change, propitiation, conciliation, a kind of sandhi or peace, winning over,
upagraha m. seizure, confinement, a prisoner, handful of *kuśa* grass, alteration, change, addition, propitiation, conciliation, – the *pada* or grammatical voice of a verb, , there are 3 voices- active (*kartari prayoga),* middle (*ātmanepada),* and passive (*karmaṇi prayoga)*
upagrāha m. a complimentary gift, present to a superior,
upagrantha m. 'minor work' a class of writings,
upagṛhīta mfn held from below, supported, subdued, mastered,
upagupta mfn hidden, concealed,
upa √han 211/3 Cl 2 P.*-hanti,*A. *-jighanti* to beat, hit at, strike, touch, hurt,
upahanana reduction, destruction, deficiency, error, ?
upahanyām I should destroy or smite 3/s/opt/act above
upahāra m. offering, oblation (to a deity), a gift or present to a superior, food distributed to guests,
upahāraka m.f. an offering, oblation, gift,
upaharaṇa n. offering, taking, serving out food, seizing, act of bringing near, presentation,
upahārin mfn offering, presenting, sacrificing,
upahartṛ mfn one who offers or presents, one who serves out (food), a host,
upahārya mf to be offered as an oblation, n. an offering, oblation,
upahāsa m. ridicule
upahāsaka mfn ridiculing others, jocose, m. a jester, n. drollery, fun,
upahāsāspada n.a laughing stock,
upahāsapātra n. a laughing stock,
upahāsin mfn ifc. deriding, ridiculing,
upahasita mfn laughed at, derided, laughter accompanied by shaking the head,
upahasta m. the act of taking with the hand, receiving,

upahasvan mfn laughing at, deriding,
upahata 211/3 mfn hurt, damaged, injured, overpowered, covered, affected, transported (with passion), seduced, misled, distressed, weakened, discouraged, killed, scattered over, covered, *upa-√han*
upahava m. calling to, inviting, invitation
upahita mfn put on or upon, placed, deposited, put into, joining, connected with, mixed, (in gram.) immediately preceded by, resting or depending upon, having as a condition, used, employed for, brought near, handed over, given, misled, deceived, the conditioned, 2. mfn good in a secondary degree, somewhat good, n. a secondary good,
upāhita mfn put or placed on, deposited, caused, effected, agreed, m. outbreak of fire, fire,
upahitacaitanya intelligence associated with upādhis; individual soul,
upa√hṛ Cl1 *upaharati* offer, offer up, sacrifice, place before, gather, apply (medicine), to destroy,
upahṛta 212/2 mfn brought near, offered, taken, collected, presented, immolated, sacrificed (as a victim), served out (as food),
upāhṛta mfn brought, offered, given,
upahūta mfn called near, invited, summoned, invoked,
upahūti f. calling (to fight), challenging,
upahvara m. a circuitous course with rough ground , slope, etc. a car, carriage,
upaiti approaches, attains, 1/s/pres/indic/act *upa √i*
upaja mfn additional, accessory, produced or coming from,
upajalpin, mfn talking to a person, giving advice,
upajalpita n. talk,
upa√jan A. *–jāyate,* to be produced or originate in addition, to be added or put to, to follow (as a consequence), to be born, originate, come forth, appear, become visible, happen, to come into being, be roused,
upajana m. addition, increase, addition of a letter(s), syllable(s) or word(s),
upajanam ind. near the people,
upajanana n. generation, procreation,
upajāpa secret communication, act of rousing to rebellion, 'overtures',
upajarasam ind. towards or near old age,
upajāta mfn added, additional, produced,
upajāyate it is born, it is produced, 1/s/pres indic/pass *upa√jan*
upāje ind. so as to help or support,
upājinam ind. on a skin,
upa√jīv P. Cl 1 *–jīvati,* to live or exist upon (food), subsist, support one's self on, be supported by, make use of (2nd), derive profit from, be dependent on, serve, caus. *–jīvayati* to use, make the most of,
upajīvaka mfn living upon, subsisting by, depending on, subject to, a dependant, a servant, f.n. subsistence, livelihood,
upajīvana n. livelihood, subsistence, dependance, submissiveness, economical dependence,
upa√jñā A. *–jānīte,* to ascertain, invent, find out, hit upon,
upajñā f. knowledge found out or invented by one's self (not handed down by tradition), invention, mfn ifc. invented or first taught by, unknown before,
upajñāta mfn invented, found out, ascertained by one's self, unknown before,
upajoṣa m. desire, pleasure, liking, silently, quietly,
upajvalita mfn lighted up,
upāka mfn brought near to each other, joined, approximate,
upakalpa m. a belonging,
upakalpana n. the act of preparing,
upakalpita mfn assigned, prepared, procured, fetched, arranged,
upakalpya ind. having prepared/procured,
upakaniṣṭhikā mfn f. next to the little i.e. the third finger,

upakāntam ind. near a friend, lover or loved one,
upakāra m. 195/2 help, assistance, benefit, service, favour,
upakāraka mfn doing a service or favour, assisting, helping, benefiting, suitable, requisite, subsidiary, subservient, accessory,
upakaraṇa 195/2 the act of doing anything for another, doing service for another, helping, instrument, machine, engine, apparatus, implement, anything added, contribution, means of subsistence, anything supporting life, any object of art or science, anything fabricated,
upākaraṇa n. the act of bringing near, fetching, setting about, preparation, beginning, commencement,
upakārapara mfn intent on doing benefits or good, beneficent,
upakāri f. a royal tent, a palace, a caravanserai,
upakārin mfn helping, assisting, a benefactor, subsidiary, subservient
upākarman n. preparation, commencement (esp. reading the Veda),
upakartṛ mfn one who does a favour, one who benefits, a helper,
upakāśa m. aurora, dawn, ifc. aspect, appearance,
upāke f. du. joined (night and morning), ind. in the next neighbourhood, in the presence of, before,
upākecakṣas mfn standing present before the eyes, to be seen from near at hand,
upākhya mfn discernible, observable by the eye
upākhyā 212/3 A. to give an account about anything, relate, f. a secondary name, surname,
upākhyāna n. a subordinate tale or story, episode, anecdote, repetition of an event,
upakiraṇa n. the act of scattering or throwing over, burying, covering up (with earth),
upakleśa m. a lesser *kleśa* or cause of misery (as conceit, pride etc.)
upaklinna mfn wet, moist, rotten, putrid,
upa√klṛp *-kalpate* to be fit for, ready at hand, become, to serve as, lead to (with 4th), caus. *–kalpayati* to prepare, make ready, equip, assign,
upaklṛpta mfn ready, prepared,
upa√1.kṛ P.A. *–karoti, -kurute,* to bring or put near to, to furnish with, provide, to assist, help, favour, benefit cause to succeed or prosper, to foster, take care of, to serve, do homage to, to undertake, begin,
upā√1.kṛ P.A. to drive or bring near or towards, fetch, to commit to, deliver, give, grant, make preparations (ceremonial), undertake, begin,
upa√kram P. *–krāmati, -kramati,* A. *–kramate,* to step up to, go toward, go near, approach, come to, to rush upon, attack, to approach with any object, have recourse to, set about, begin, to treat or attend upon as a physician,
upā√kram to fall upon, attack,
upakrama m. beginning, the act of coming or going near, approach, setting about, undertaking, commencement, beginning, enterprise, planning, original conception, plan, a means, expedient, stratagem, exploit, remedy, treatment, attendance on a patient, practice or application of medicine, the rim of a wheel, heroism, courage, effort, endeavour,
upakramaṇa mfn approaching, complying with, granting, n. attendance (on a patient), treatment,
upakrama-upasaṁhāra-ekavākyatā consistency of thought from beginning to end; the first of the 6 signs of a perfect exposition,
upakramya mfn to be treated (as a patient), ind. having approached undertaken or commenced,
upa√krī Cl 9 *–krīṇāti,* to buy,

upakrīya ind. having bought,
upakriyā f. the act of bringing near to, favour, assistance, benefit, help, means, expedient, remedy,
upakroṣa m. reproach, censure,
upakṛta mfn helped, assisted, benefited, done kindly or beneficently,
upākṛta mfn brought/driven near, fetched,
upakṛti f. assistance, help, favour,
upākṛti f. setting about, beginning,
upākṛtin mfn one who prepares or begins
upakṣaya 196/2 decrease, decline, decay, waste
upakṣepa m. threat, allusion, throwing at, threatening, mention, hint, poetical or figurative style
upakṣepaka mfn alluding, suggesting,
upakṣepaṇa throwing at or down, allusion, hint, suggestion,
upakṣīṇa mfn exhausted, consumed, absorbed, lost in, vanished,
upa√kṣip Cl6 *upakṣipati* to throw at, hurl against, to beat, strike, insult, accuse, to speak of, describe, hint at, to commence, set about a work,
upakṣit mfn dwelling near, clinging to, adhering,
upākta mfn anointed, greased,
upakūla mfn being or growing near the bank,
upakūpa m. a small well, *(e)* ind. near a well,
upakurvāṇa one who will become a householder after religious study,
upakurvāṇa-brahmacārin m. a student who takes the vow of continence for a limited period only,
upala m. a rock, stone, jewel, a cloud, upper mill-stone,
upalā f. upper mill-stone,
upalabdha mfn obtained, received, conceived, perceived, heard, understood, learnt, known, guessed
upālabdha mfn reproached, reviled,
upalabdhavya mfn 205/3 to be perceived, known or realized,
upalabdhi f. obtainment, gain, observation, perceiving, perception, becoming aware, understanding, mind, knowledge, perceptibility, appearance,
upalabdhṛ mfn one who perceives,
upa√labh 205/3 A *–labhate,* to seize, get possession of, acquire, receive, obtain, find, to understand, learn, know, ascertain, caus. P. *lambhayati,* to cause to obtain or take possession, to cause to hear or learn or know, to cause to be known or distinguished,
upā√labh Cl1 *upālabhate* to reproach, rebuke, blame,
upalabhya mfn obtainable, perceivable, to be understood, ind.p. having obtained, having perceived,
upalabhyate is known, perceived, is perceptible or attainable *upa √labh* 205/3 1/s/pres/pass
upalālana f. caressing, fondling,
upalakṣa m. distinction, distinguishing,
upalakṣaka mfn observing closely or with attention, implying, designating by implication,
upalakṣaṇa n. the act of observing, designation, implying something that has not been expressed, using a term metaphorically or elliptically in a generic sense,
upa√lakṣaya Nom. P. (*ti),* to mark, notice,
upalakṣita mfn beheld, perceived, looked at, observed, distinguished, implied, (having been) noticed, expressed by implication or elliptically,
upalambha m. obtainment, perceiving, ascertaining, recognition,
upālambha m. abuse, taunt, reproach, abuse
upalambhaka mfn perceiving, causing to perceive, reminding,
upalambhana n. apprehension, perceiving, the capacity of perceiving, intelligence,
upalambhya mfn worthy to be acquired,
upalepana 206/1 the act of be-smearing (with cow dung), anointing, plastering, an ointment

upaliṅga n. a portent, natural phenomenon considered as boding ill,
upalipsu mfn wishing to learn or hear,
upalipta mfn besmeared, anointed (with cow-dung),
upalipyate is defiled or smeared
upama mfn highest, uppermost, best, most excellent, first, resembling, similar, eminent, nearest, equal, like
-upama similar to
upamā 203/3 ind. in the closest proximity or neighbourhood, to measure one thing by another, f. comparison, resemblance, equality, similarity a resemblance (as picture, image etc.),
upa √1.mad P. *–madati* to cheer up encourage,
upamāda m. enjoyment, amusement,
upamādravya n. any object used for comparison,
upamajjana n. bathing, a bath,
upamām ind. in the highest degree,
upamāna n. comparison, resemblance, analogy, simile, recognition of likeness,the object with which anything is compared,
mfn similar, like,
upamānatva n. similarity,
upamantraṇa n. the art of persuading,
upamantrita mfn called near or hither, summoned, invited, persuaded,
upāmantrita mfn addressed, called upon summoned,
upamanyu mfn striving after, zealous, knowing, understanding,
upamarda m. friction, rubbing down, pressure, injury, violation,
upamardin mfn ifc. destroying, annulling,
upamarṣita mfn borne patiently, tolerated, granted, not begrudged,
upamārtha m. purpose of an image, (*ena*) figuratively, comparative sense,
upamaśravas mfn having highest glory,
upamāt f. a prop, support,
upamathita mfn stirred, churned, mixed,
upamāti f. comparison, similarity,
upamātṛ mfn one who compares, an image-maker
upamekhalam ind. on the slopes or sides of a mountain,
upameya mfn comparable with,
n. that which is compared,
the subject of comparison,
upameyopamā f. the resemblance of any object to that compared with it, reciprocal comparison (as of a moon to a beautiful face),
upamita mfn compared, comparable with, illustrated by comparison,
stuck or fastened on, put into,
upamiti f. comparison, resemblance, likeness, similarity, analogy, knowledge of things derived from analogy or resemblance,
upamitra n. a minor friend,
not an intimate friend,
upamṛta mfn died, dead,
upāṁśu mfn in a low voice, in a whisper,
m. a prayer uttered in a low voice,
ind. secretly, in secret,
upāṁśu-japa japa done with a humming sound; semi-verbal repetition of a mantra
upa√muc A. *–muñcate*, to put on e.g. shoes,
upamukham ind. on the mouth,
upamūlam ind. on or at the root,
upanadam ind. near or on the river,
upanaddha mfn covered with, inlaid,
upanagara n. a suburb, (*am*) ind. near the city,
upānah f. sandal, shoe,
upanāha m. a bundle, a plaster, poultice,
upānahin mfn having shoes, shoed,
upanāman n. a surname, nickname,
upanamra mfn coming to, being present,
upanata mfn bent towards or inwards, subdued, subjected, surrendered, dependent on, brought near to, approached, near (in form or space), fallen to one's share, produced, existing, being,
upanati f. inclination, affection,
upanaya m. the bringing near, procuring, attaining, obtaining,
upanayana 201/2 n. the act of leading to or

near, bringing, employment, application, introduction (to any science), leading or drawing towards oneself, initiation, investiture,

upanāyana n. initiation,

upāṅga n. a minor limb or member of the body, minor sciences or texts, a subdivision, a sectarial mark on the forehead, m. the act of smearing, anointing,

upa√nī Cl 1 *–niyati,* to bring to (some-one), to lead or drive near, bring near, bring, to bring information, communicate, to lead or bring near to one's self, take possession of, to lead, guide, to lead or draw towards one's self, to initiate with the sacred thread,

upanetṛ mfn one who brings near, (*tā)* m. the spiritual preceptor,

upanibaddha mfn adhering to, written, composed, arranged, spoken of,

upanibandha m. obligation, oath,

upanibandhana mfn manifesting, explaining, n. description,

upanibha mfn ifc. similar, equal,

upanidhāna n the act of putting down nearby, a deposit,

upanimantraṇa n. invitation, inauguration,

upanipāta m. acceding, accession, taking place, occurring,

upanirgama m. a main or royal road,

upaniṣad 201/1 a class of philosophical writings (100+) regarded as the source of the Vedantic and some other philosophies, 'setting at rest ignorance by revealing the knowledge of the supreme spirit',

upaniśamya ind.p. having perceived, perceiving,

upanīta mfn led near, brought near, led to a man, married, presented, initiated, m. a boy initiated with the sacred thread,

upaniveśa m. a suburb,

upaniveśin mfn adherent, belonging to,

upaniviṣṭa mfn besieging, occupying, occupied, inhabited,

upanṛtya n. a place for dancing,

upānta mfn near to the end, last but one, n. proximity to the end or edge or margin, border, edge, the last place but one, immediate or close proximity, nearness, (*e*) ind. in the proximity of, near to, (*am,āt*), ind. (ifc.) near to, towards, the last letter but one, the corner of the eye,

upāntika n. vicinity, proximity, (*am)* ind. near to, towards, (*āt)* ind. from the neighbourhood, mfn near, neighbouring,

upāntima mfn the last but one,

upanunna mfn driven near, wafted,

upanyāsa m. putting down, placing near, bringing forward, speaking of, statement, suggestion, hint, quotation, reference, proof, reason, a deposit, pledge, pawn,

upanyāsya mfn to be adduced or stated,

upāpa m. the act of obtaining, acquirement,

upa√pad Cl 4 *–padyate,(ti),* to be fit for (with 7th), to gpo towards or against, attack, come to, arrive at, enter, to approach or come to a teacher, (as pupil), to approach for succour or protection, to approach or join with in speech, to reach, obtain, partake of, to enter into any state, to take place, come forth, be produced, appear, occur, happen, to be present, exist, to be possible,

upapad f. happening, occurring, taking place,

upapada n. a word standing near or accompanying another to which\ it is subordinate,

upapāda m. happening, accomplishing,

upapādaka mfn causing to occur or happen,

upapādita mfn effected, accomplished, performed, done, proved, cured,

upapāduka mfn having shoes, shod, self-produced, m. a superhuman being, a god, demon,

upapādya mfn to be effected or done,

to be shown or proved, being produced, coming into existence,
upapadyate goes towards or against, arrives at, enters, comes, is fit for, occurs, happens, is according to the rules, suitable to1/s/pres/indic/mid/pass *upa √pad*
upapanna mfn one who has approached a teacher (as a pupil), one who has approached for protection, one who has obtained or reached, obtained, reached, gained, happened, produced, existing, being near at hand,
upaparīkṣaṇa n. inquiring into, investigation, examination,
upapāta m. accident, occurrence,
upapātaka n. minor offence, secondary crime,
upapatha m. appendix, (*am*) ind. on the road,
upapati m. a paramour, gallant,
upapatti happening, occurring, taking place, proving right, resulting, 201/3
upaplava m. any public calamity, misfortune, disturbance,
upapluta mfn overflowed, invaded, afflicted, distressed, pained,
upāpnoti he attains or masters,
upapraiṣa m. invitation, summons,
upaprāṇa m. a secondary vital air of the body,
upaprāpta mfn approached, come near,
upapṛc mfn clinging close to (with 6th),
upaprekṣaṇa n. the act of overlooking, disregarding, looking at without interest,
upāpti f. reaching, obtainment,
upapura n. near the city,
upapurāṇa n. a secondary or minor *purāṇa*
upapurī f. the environs of a city,
upara mfn situated below, under, posterior, later, nearer, approximate, a cloud, region,
upāra m. offence, sin, transgression,
uparacita mfn constructed, formed, made,
uparāga m. the act of dying or colouring, colour, darkening, influence, an eclipse, affecting, misbehaviour, ill-conduct, reproach, abuse,
uparāja m. a viceroy,
uparajya ind. p. having dyed/coloured, darkening, obscuring,
uparakṣaṇa n. a guard, outpost,
uparakta mfn dyed, coloured, coloured red, heated, inflamed, distressed,
upa√ram P.A. *–ramati (te),* to cease from motion, stop, be inactive or quiet, to pause, stop (speaking or doing anything), to leave off, desist, give up, renounce (5th), to await, wait for, to cause to cease or stop, to render quiet, cease, die, caus. *–ramayati* to cause to cease or stop, to render quiet,
uparam stop!
uparama m. cessation, stopping, expiration, leaving off, desisting, giving up, death,
uparāma m. ceasing, stopping, desisting, renunciation, detachment,
upārama m. the act of ceasing,
upārāma m. rest, repose,
uparāmam ind. near Rāma
uparamaṇa n. abstaining from worldly actions or desires, ceasing, discontinuance,
upārāmata calmness of mind, cessation of action,
uparamati stops
uparamet he should cease, he should be quiet, 1/s/opt/act *upa √ram*
upāraṇa n. offence, sin,
uparasa a secondary mineral or feeling or passion or flavour,
uparata 204/3 mfn. ceased, stopped, quiet, indifferent, ceasing to exist, from *upa√ram*
upārata mfn resting, lying upon, fixed upon, ceasing, returning, giving up, free from,
uparatāti ind. in the proximity, a circumference,
uparati f. cessation, stopping, death, desisting from worldly action,

absolute quietness, tranquillity, renunciation, quietism, 'control of the mind in all its 5 modifications (*vṛttis)*... total absence of practical concern with the world of duality is the consequence or result' (U)

uparāva m a near sound,

upārdha n. the first half, the half,

upari ind. (as a separable adverb) upon, on, upwards, on top, above, towards the upper side of, besides, in addition to, further, afterwards, higher and higher, repeatedly, continuously,
(as a separable prep. with 2nd, 6th, 7th), over, above, upon, at the head of, on the upper side of, beyond, in connection with, with reference to, with regard to, towards, after, (may stand first in a compound),

uparicara mfn moving or walking above or in the air,

upariga mfn moving or soaring above,

uparija mfn growing upwards or out,

uparikuṭī f. an upper room,

upariṣṭāt ind. (adverbial) above, from above, on the upper part, behind, further on, later, below, afterwards, (prepositional) over, upon, down upon (with 2nd and 6th), behind (with 6th), with reference to, about (with 6th),

uparisthita mfn staying above,

uparitala n. the upper surface,

uparitana mfn upper,

uparitas ind. over, above,

upārjana 214/1 the act of procuring, acquiring, gaining

upārjita mfn procured, acquired, gained,

uparodha m. beseiging, blockading, trouble, disturbance, damage, disunion, quarrel, regard, respect,

uparodhana n, beseiging, obstructing,

upārohati ascends, goes up to, mounts, arrives at, reaches,

uparotsīḥ 2/s/aorist *upa√2. rudh* you lock in, shut up, besiege, obstruct, hinder, press, trouble, importune,

upa√rudh Cl7 *–ruṇaddhi* to beseige, molest, hinder, invade, obstruct, annoy, cover, conceal,

uparuddha mfn locked in, shut up, besieged, hindered, obstructed, m. a captive,

uparūḍha mfn healed over, altered, changed

upārūdha mfn mounted, ascended, one who has arrived, approached,

upāruh f. a shoot, sprout,

upās 3. *upa* + *√ās* to sit near, serve, honour, revere, be devoted to, worship, to wait upon, approach respectfully, serve, honour, revere, respect, acknowledge, do homage to, worship, be devoted or attached to, to pay attention to, be intent upon or engaged in, perform, converse, to sit near, be in waiting for, expect, wait for, to sit, occupy a place, abide in, reside, to be present at, partake of, to approach, go towards, draw near, arrive at obtain, to enter into any state, undertake, to remain or continue in any action or situation, see *upāsana*

upāsā f. homage, adoration, worship,

upa√sad P. *–sīdati,* to sit upon (2nd), to sit near to, approach (respectfully), revere, worship, to approach (a teacher in order to become his pupil), request, crave for, to approach in a hostile manner, to possess,

upasad mfn approaching (respectfully), worshipping, serving,
m. a particular fire,
f. attendance, worship, service, siege, assault,

upasada mfn one who goes near,

upasadana n. the act of approaching (respectfully), respectful salutation, setting about, undertaking, approaching or going to a science or art teacher, performing a ceremony or sacrifice, neighbourhood,

upasādana n. the act of placing or putting

upon, approaching respectfully, reverence, respect,
upasādita mfn caused to come near, led near, conveyed to,
upasadvan mfn receiving reverence or worship,
upasadya mfn to be respectfully approached, to be revered or worshipped,
upaśāka m. a helper, companion,
upāsaka mfn serving, a servant, worshipping, a worshipper, follower, intent on, engaged or occupied with, a Buddhist lay worshipper (as distinguished from the *Bhikṣu*), a *śūdra*
upaśākhā f. a small branch,
upaśālam ind. near a house,
upaśalya m. a small spear/lance tipped with iron, n. the ground near a village, the environs, the ground at the base or edge of a mountain,
upa√śam P.A. *–śāmyati (te),* to become calm or quiet, to cease, become extinct, caus. *–śamayati* and *śāmayati* to make quiet, calm, extinguish, to tranquillize, appease, pacify, mitigate,
upaśama 207/3 the becoming quiet, stopping, cessation, calmness, patience, tranquillity of mind, (N) annihilation, = *nirvāṇa*
upaśāmaka mfn calming, quieting, affording repose, making patient,
upaśamana mfn calming, appeasing, n. becoming extinct, ceasing, calming, appeasing, mitigation, an anodyne,
upasaṁbaddha mfn tied on,
upasaṁbhṛta mfn brought together, prepared
upasaṁ√dhā P.A. to put to, add, annex, increase, put together, join, connect, join together with, to place befor oneself, aim at, take into consideration,
upasaṁ√gam A. *–gacchate*, to approach together, join in approaching, to unite, join, to go or come near, to enter into any state or condition,
upasaṁgamana n. the act of coming together, sexual union,
upasaṁgamya having approached, gerund
upasaṁgata mfn come together, assembled, united, joined,
upasaṁgraha m. the act of clasping round (the feet), embracing, embrace, respectful salutation, polite address,
upasaṁgrahaṇa n. the clasping and taking to oneself (the feet of another, as a sign of great respect),
upasamhāra 208/3 m the act of withdrawing, taking away, drawing towards oneself, conclusion, end, suppression, subduing, summarizing, summing up, death, destruction
upasaṁhita mfn connected or furnished with, having, attached to, devoted,
upasaṁhṛta mfn drawn near, brought into contact, withheld, drawn back, stopped, suppressed, absorbed, destroyed, dead, comprehended, excluded,
upasaṁhṛti f. comprehension, conclusion,
upasaṁ√jan A. tp present one's self, appear,
upasaṁ√klṛp caus. P. *–kalpayati* to put upon, set, cause to settle,
upasaṁ√kram to step or go to the other side
upasaṁkramana n. going over towards,
upasaṁkrānta turned to, changed into (as a word employed in another meaning),
upasaṁkṣepa m. a concise abridgment or summary,
upasaṁ√pad A. *–padyate,* to come to, arrive at, reach, obtain,
upasaṁpadā f. entering an order of monks,
upasaṁpanna, mfn arrived at, reached, one who has reached,
upasaṁpatti, f. approaching/reaching or entering into any condition
upasaṁ√prach P. to question about,
upasaṁsthita mfn one who has stopped,
upasaṁvāda m. agreement,

upasaṁyama m. wedging in,
upasaṁyamana n. fixing one thing to another, a means of fastening together,
upasaṁyata mfn wedged in,
upasaṁyoga m. a secondary or subordinate connection or modification,
upāsana 2. 215/1 *am, ā*, n. f. the act of sitting or being near at hand, serving, service, homage, adoration, worship (consisting of 5 parts , viz. *abhigamana* or approach, *upādāna* or preparation of offering, *ijyā* or oblation, *svādhyāya* or recitation, and *yoga* or devotion). Grimes p.330 It is of 3 kinds (1) *aṅgāvabodhopāsana* – something is worshipped or meditated on as a limb of a rite e.g. a piece of grass is thought of as a deity, (2) *pratīkopāsana* – an idol or picture is worshipped as God, (3) *ahaṁgrahopāsana* – the worshipper equates himself with a deity, 'in the realm of devotion and service' HH '*upāsanā* means being close or united through physical, mental and emotional means.'
upāsanamūrti the form of God chosen for worship,
upāsāniśita sharpened by devotion, i.e. 'purified by constant meditation',
upāsanīya mfn to be attended on, worthy to be engaged in,
upa√śaṅk A. to suspect, suppose, think,
upasanna mfn put or placed upon, being on, come near, approached (for protection or instruction or worship), bestowed upon, given
upaśānta 207/3 mfn calmed, appeased, ceased, calm, tranquil, intermitted, (conditioning) extinct,
upaśāntātman mfn one whose mind is pacified, placid,
upaśānti f. cessation, intermission, remission, tranquillity, Calmness,
upasāntvana n. the act of appeasing, soothing, kind words,
upaśaradam ind. at or near autumn,
upasarga 210/2 m. obstacle, addition, misfortune, trouble, a natural phenomenon portending evil, change caused by disease, indication or symptom of death,
(in gram.) a *nipāta* or particle joined to a verb or noun denoting action... These are used like prefixes and are said to 'change the direction' or sense of the word to which they are prefixed.
upasargin mfn adding, one who adds,
upasarjana n. pouring upon, infusion, inauspicious phenomena,
anything or any person subordinate to another, a substitute, representation, (in gram.) subordinate, secondary, - 'any word which by composition or derivation loses its original independence while it also determines the sense of another word',
upasarjita mfn sent off or out,
upasarpa m. approaching, approach, sexual approach,
upaśāstra n. a minor science or treatise,
upasat in comp. for 2. *upasad*,
f. attendance, service, worship, siege, assault, name of a festival,
upāsate they worship or honour 1/pl/pres/indic/mid *upa √ās*
upasatti f. connection with, union, service, worship, gift, donation,
upasattṛ m. one who has seated himself near or at (esp. at the domestic fire), the inhabitant of a house, anyone domiciled,
upaśaya mfn lying near at hand or close by, lying ready for use,
upasecana mfn pouring upon, sprinkling, a pouring ladle,
upa√sev A. *–sevate,* to frequent, visit, stay at (a place), to stay with a person, attend on, serve, do homage, honour, worship, to practice, pursue, cultivate, study, make use of, be addicted to,
upasevā 210/3 f. homage, worship, use, courting, addiction to, employment, enjoyment, serving,

upasevaka mfn ifc. doing homage, courting (e.g. the wife of another),
upasevin mfn ifc. serving, doing homage, worshipping, addicted/devoted to,
upasevate 210/3 frequents, abides or stays at, visits, serves, does homage, honours, worships
upaśikṣā f. desire of learning, learning, acquisition,
upaśikṣita mfn learnt, studied, trained,
upāsita mfn. served, honoured, worshipped, one who serves or offers worship,
upāsīta he should worship 1/s/opt, *upa√ās*
upāsitavya to be meditated on
upaskāra 195/3 m. anything additional, a supplement, decoration, any utensil, any article of household use, appurtenance, apparatus, an ingredient, condiment, spice,
upaślāghā f. boasting, brag, swagger,
upaśleṣa m. close contact, contiguity,
upa√śliṣ *-śliṣyati* to come near to or into close contact with, cling to, caus. *śleṣayati* to bring near or into close contact,
upaśliṣṭa mfn brought near or into close contact, contiguous, adjoining,
upasmāram ind.p. having remembered,
upa√smi A. to smile upon,
upa√smṛ P. to remember,
upasmarati he/she remembers intimately
upāśnute 214/3 to reach, attain, meet with, enjoy, 1/s/pres/indic/mid enjoys
upasparśa m. touching, contact, bathing, washing, sipping water (ceremonial)
upasparśana n. the act of touching, ablution, bath, sipping water,
upa√spṛś P. to touch above, reach up to, touch
upaspṛś mfn touching,
upaśobhā f. ornament,
upaśobhana n. the act of ornamenting,
upaśobhin mfn of beautiful appearance, brilliant,
upaśoṣita mfn made dry, dried, dry,
upa√sṛ Cl1 *upasarati* to go up to, approach,
upa√śram P. *–śrāmyati,* to rest, repose ,
upa√śri P. *–śrayati,* to lean (anything) against, A. *–śrayate*, to lean against, support, prop,
upaśrita mfn placed near, brought to the attention of, leaning towards/upon,
upāśrita 214/3 mfn. having recourse to, taking refuge with, relying upon clinging to, adhering to, beset with, lying or resting upon, leaning against,
upāśritya resorting to, following, depending on, taking refuge in
upaśrotṛtā m. a listener, hearer,
upa√śru P. *–śṛṇoti,* to listen to, give ear to, hear,
upaśruta mfn listened to, heard, promised, agreed,
upaśruti f. giving ear to, listening attentively, range of hearing, hearing, rumour, report,
upaśrutya ind. p. having listened to, listening to, hearing,
upastabdha mfn supported, stayed,
upastava m. praise,
upastambha m. stay, support, strengthening, encouragement, incitement, excitement, base, basis, ground,
upastambhaka mfn promoting, encouraging, supporting, instrumental cause,
upastara m. anything laid under, substratum
upastaraṇa n. the act of spreading over, a under-mattress, pillow, a substratum, pouring out to form a substratum,
upāste he worships, pays attention to, meditates on,
upastha mfn standing upon or beside, being near at hand, near, 211/1 'the part which is under', a seat or stool, lap, 'sex' (Gam.), the generative organs
upa√sthā P.A. *-tiṣṭhati (te),* to stand or place one's self near, be present, stand beside, come together or meet with, become friendly with, conciliate, to stand near in order to serve, attend, serve,
upā√sthā A. *-tiṣṭhate,* to betake one's self to, approach, set about, devote one's self to,

upasthāna n. placing one's self near, going near, coming into the presence of, worshipping, waiting on, attendance, standing near, presence, proximity, a place of abiding, abode, assembly, a sanctuary, abode of a god,
upasthāpaka mfn causing to remember, causing to turn one's attention,
upasthāpana n. placing near, having ready for, (*ā*) f. the act of ordaining a monk, causing to remember, calling to mind,
upasthāpya mfn to be produced or effected,
upasthātṛ mfn one who is near at hand, an attendant, servant, waiter, nurse, one who makes his appearance,
upasthāvan mfn standing near or at hand,
upasthāya ind.p. having approached, standing by the side of, attending on,
upasthāyaka m. a servant,
upasthāyika m. a servant, keeper, nurse,
upasthita mfn come near, approached, arisen, arrived, present, near at hand, ready for, near, impending, fallen to one's share, received, gained, obtained, happened, caused, felt, known, clean, cleansed,
upāsthita mfn one who has mounted, standing or being in a carriage, one who has devoted himself to,
upasthiti f. standing near, approach, presence, proximity, accomplishing, completeness, obtaining, getting, remaining, memory,
upastir f. anything spread over, a cover,
upāstra n. a secondary or minor weapon,
upaṣṭut mfn praised, invoked,
upastuta mfn invoked, praised,
upastuti f. celebration, invocation, praise,
upastutya mfn to be praised,
upaśvasa m. breeze, draught of air,
upāsya 215/1 1. 1. mfn to be revered or honoured or worshipped
2 ind. having served or worshipped,
upatalpya m a kind of wooden seat or stool,
upatāpa 198/3 heat, warmth, heating, pain, trouble, sickness disease, hurt
upatāpaka mfn causing pain, paining,
upatapta mfn heated, hot,
upataptṛ mfn heating, burning, m. interior heat, disease,
upatīram ind. on the shore,
upātta mfn received, accepted, gained, obtained, seized, gathered, felt, perceived, regarded, used, employed, allowed in argument, granted,
upāttaśastra mfn one who has taken up arms, armed,
upāttavidya mfn one who has acquired knowledge, learned,
upatya mfn lying under, (L)
upatyakā f. land at the foot of a hill or mountain, lowland, a vale, valley, foothill,
upātyaya m. transgressing, neglect or disobedience of customs.
upa√vac to address, praise, to animate by the voice, rouse, impel,
upa√vad P. *–vadati,* to speak ill of, decry, abuse, curse, to speak to, address, A. *–vadate,* to talk over, conciliate, to flatter, cajole, court secretly,
upavāda m. censure, blame,
upavāha m. driving, riding,
upāvaharaṇa n. taking or bringing down,
upavaiṇava n. the three periods of the day, (morning, midday and evening),
upavāka m. addressing, praising,
upavaktṛ m. one who rouses, animates,
upavalha m. impetuosity, superiority,
upavana n. a small forest or wood, grove, garden, a plantation,
upavanam ind. near or in a wood,
upavañcana n. a faltering approach, tottering towards, crouching or lying close to,
upa√varṇ P. *–varṇayati* to tell fully, describe minutely or particularly, communicate, relate,
upavarṇana n. description, minute description, delineation,
upavarṇita mfn described minutely,
upāvarohaṇa n. the act of causing fire to

come from two sticks by friction,
upavartana n. the act of bringing near, a place for exercise, a country,
upavāsa m. a fast, fasting, abstinence in general, kindling a sacred fire, a fire altar,
upavasana n. a fast, fasting, the state of abiding or being near,
upāvasāyin mfn attaching one's self to, submissive, compliant,
upāvasita mfn settled or living near by,
upavasta n. a fast, fasting,
upavasatha m. a fast-day,
upavāta mfn dried up, dry, blown upon,
upaveda m. 'secondary knowledge', a class of writings subordinate or appended to the four vedas,
upavedana n. ascertainment, learning,
upavedanīya mfn to be learnt or found out,
upaveśa m. sitting, resting, the act of sitting down, the act of applying one's self to or being engaged in,
upaveśana 207/1 n the act of sitting down, a seat, being devoted to or engaged in. directing one's mind to, evacuation or motion of the bowels,
upaveśi m. name of a man,
upaveśin mfn ifc. devoting or applying one's self to, one who has an evacuation or motion of the bowels,
upa√vī P. to hasten near, come near, obtain, attain,
upāvī mfn cherishing, pleasing,
upavicāra m. environs, neighbourhood,
upavid f. ascertainment, learning,
upa√1.vidh P. to honour, worship,
upavidyā f. inferior knowledge,
upa √vīkṣ A. *-vīkṣate*, to look at or towards, to regard as fit or proper,
upa√viś P. *–viśati* to go or come near, approach, to sit down, take a seat (men), lie down (animals), to enter, to stop, to settle one's self, to sit near to, to set (the sun), to apply or devote one's self to, cultivate,
upā√viś P. to enter, enter into any state,
upa√viṣ P. 207/1 *-viveṣṭi* to be active for, to obtain or gain by activity, to perform service, be effective or useful for,
upaviśa sit down!
upaviṣa n. a narcotic, any deleterious drug, (opium, datura etc.)
upāviśat sat down 1/s/imperf/act *upa ā √viś*
upaviśati sits down
upaviśrambhayya ind. p. having inspired with confidence,
upaviṣṭa mfn seated, sitting, come to, arrived, ifc. having obtained,
upaviṣṭhā A. *-tiṣṭathe,* to be or stand here and there,
upaviśya having sat down, sitting down,
upavīta mfn invested with the sacred thread, n. being invested with the sacred thread, the sacred thread or cord,
upavīya ind.p. having put on the sacred thread
upavrajya ind.p. having gone towards, coming near, approaching, going behind, following,
upavṛtta mfn come near, approached, come back, recovered,
upavṛtti f. motion towards (one's place),
upavyāghra m. the small hunting leopard,
upavyākhyāna n. explanation, interpretation, clear exposition,
upavyuṣam ind. about dawn,
upāya 215/2 m. that by which one achieves one's aim, a means or expedient, way, stratagem, artifice, method , coming near, approach, arrival,
upa √yā 204/2 to come near, go near, or towards, approach (a woman for sex), to arrive at, reach, obtain, to get into any state or condition, to occur, befall, to give one's self up to,
upayācana n. approaching with entreaty or prayer,
upa√yam -yacchati, -te, to seize, lay hold of, touch, marry, to take for one's self, to take as one's wife,
upayama m. appropriation, taking possession of, marrying, marriage,

kindling a fire, a support, stay,

upayamana mfn serving as support (as grass), a ladle, n. a support, stay, marrying, sleeping with a woman,

upayāna n. coming near, arrival,

upāyana n. approach, going to a teacher, becoming a pupil, engaging in religious observance, undertaking, an offer, present, gift,

upayāta mfn approached, visited, one who has obtained, n. arrival,

upāyāta mfn approached, arrival,

upayoga m. employment, use, application, to be employed (√*gam,* √*vraj*), enjoyment, consuming, an agreement, fitness, acquisition (of knowledge), good conduct, observing established practices, calculation,

upayogin mfn serving for use or application, useful, convenient, appropriate, favourable, propitious, ifc. using, employing, touching, in contact with,

upa√*yuj* A. –*yuṅkte,* (P. rarely), to harness to, take for oneself, appropriate, to follow, attach one's self to, be devoted, to undertake, to use, employ, have the use of, enjoy,

upayukta mfn enjoyed, eaten, consumed, employed, used, suitable, fit, proper,

upe upa√*i* Cl2 *upaiti* to go or come or step near, arrive at, reach, enter into any state, fall into, undergo, suffer,

upekṣ A.P.(*upa -īkṣate*) to look at or on, to perceive, notice, to wait on patiently, expect, to overlook, disregard, neglect, abandon, to connive at, grant a respite to, allow, to regard,

upekṣa 215/3 part. overlooking, disregarding, indifferent,

upekṣā f. indifference, overlooking, disregard, negligence, contempt, endurance, patience, dissent, deceit (in war),

upeta 215/3 mfn. one who has come near or approached, arrived at, abiding in, endowed with, come to, fallen to the share of, a pupil who has approached a teacher, initiated,

upetya mfn to be set about or commenced, having approached, approaching

upeya mfn to be set about or undertaken, a thing undertaken, to be approached sexually, to be striven after or aimed at, that which is aimed at, aim,

upoḍha mfn brought near, effected, appeared, near (in time and space),

upoṣaṇa n. a fast, fasting,

upoṣita mfn one who has fasted, fasting, n. a fast, fasting,

upota mfn put into, wrapped, enveloped,

uraga 217/2 m. a serpent, snake,

uraṇa m. a ram, sheep, young ram,

uraṇayuga n.. a pair of rams,

uras n. breast, chest (of the body),

√*urasya* 217/3 Nom P to be strong-chested, be strong, DP in *bala* being strong mfn pectoral, belonging to or coming from the chest, produced from oneself (as a child), m. the female breast,

√*urd* 218/2 see *ūrd*

ūrdhva 222/1 mfn rising or tending upwards, raised, elevated, erect, upright, high, (*am*) n. after, height, elevation, anything placed higher, after the death of, in a high tone, aloud, in the sequel in the later part, to go upwards or to heaven (die), (*am*) ind. upwards, towards the upper part, aloft, above, in the upper regions, higher, where the gods reside (Jaina),

ūrdhvadṛṣṭi mfn having an upward gaze,

ūrdhvapavitra mfn pure above, 'whose cause is purifying',

ūrdhvam āyan going up

ūrdhvamūlaḥ that which has it's roots above (and branches down)'the tree of the world from the unmanifested to the immovables (Gam.)', peepul tree

ūrdhvaretoyogin the yogin in whom the seminal energy flows upwards, (U)

urī 1. a particle implying assent, admission or promise,

√*ūrj* 221/3 P (caus.) connected with √*vṛj*, *ūrjayati* to strengthen, invigorate, refresh, A *ūrjayate* to be strong or powerful, be happy, to live, DP in *bala* strengthening, or *prāṇava* living, breathing,

ūrj f. sap, strength, nourishment, vigour,

ūrjana 221/3 strong, powerful, eminent, invigorating, strengthening

ūrjānī f. strength personified,

ūrjas n. vigour, strength, power,

ūrjita 221/3 n. strength, power, valour, (*am*) ind. excellently,

ūrmi m. f. wave, (lit. roller), billow, an evil,

ūrṇa 221/3 m. a spider, having wool in the navel,

ūrṇā f. wool, a wollen thread, thread, cobweb,

ūrṇābhi m. a spider,

ūrṇamradas mfn having the softness of wool, soft as wool,

ūrṇāstukā f. braid or plait of wool, skein, a tuft of wool,

√*ūrṇu* 221/3 Cl 2 P A *ūrṇuti* or *ūrṇauti, ūrṇute*, to cover, invest, hide, surround, A to cover oneself, DP in *ācchādana* covering,

uru 217/3 mf(*vī*)n wide, broad, spacious, extended, great, large, n. wide space, space, room, ind. widely, far, far off,

ūru 221/2 m. thigh, shank, mfn wide,

urukrama mfn far-stepping, making wide strides, m. wide stride,

urukṣiti f. spacious dwelling or habitation,

urūṇasa mfn having broad snouts

urvaśī f. name of an Apsara,

uruvyacas mfn having wide embrace, wide extending,

√*urv* 218/2 see *ūrv*

urvī f. the earth,

urviya or *urvyā* ind. far, far off, to a distance,

√*uṣ* 220/1 Cl 1 P *oṣati* , Cl 9 P , to burn, burn down (active), to punish, chastise, DP in *dāha* burning,

√*ūṣ* 223/1 Cl 1 P *ūṣati* to be sick or ill, DP in *rujā* being ill

usanā a seer 1/s/m

uśanas 219/3 name of the planet Venus

uśanā ind. with desire or haste, zealously

uṣas f. morning red, dawn, (personified) Dawn,

uṣasya 220/1 N P *uṣasyati* to grow light, dawn, DP in *prabhātabhāva* becoming dawn, mfn sacred to the dawn,

uśīra mn the fragrant root of a plant, f. a species of grass,

uśita part. √*vas* lived, past, one who has stayed, one who has halted, spent, one who has been absent, retired or resorted to, lived,

uśitvā having dwelt, dwelling, having stayed, remained, gerund √ 3. *vas*

uṣman m. heat, ardour, steam,

ūṣmapa 223/1 steam-eater, m. fire,

uṣṇa n. heat, mfn hot,

uṣṇīṣa m. turban,

usra mfn bright, of or pertaining to the dawn, daybreak, a cow, m. a ray of light,

usrā f. dawn,

uṣṭra m. a camel, buffalo,a cart, f. *(ī)*

uṣyate is lived 1/s/pres/pass *vas*

ut ind. a particle of doubt or deliberation as a prefix –see *ud*

uṭa m. leaves, grass, (used for huts etc.)

uta 175/2 2. sewn, woven

2. ind. and, also, even, often used for emphasis, especially at the end of a line after *iti* or a verb, also used as an interrogative, as a particle of wishing, or (preceded by *kim)* 'on the contrary','how much more', 'how much less', or when preceded by *prati* 'on the contrary', 'rather',

uṭaja m. a hut of grass, a house,

√*uṭh* 175/1 Cl 1 P *oṭhati* or *ūṭhati* to strike or knock down, DP in *upaghāta* striking,

ūti f. furtherance, help, blessing, refreshment, food, enjoyment, play, dalliance,

utka mfn longing for, wishing for, regretting, sad, sorrowful, absent, thinking of something else,

utkaca mfn hairless, full-blown,

utkala m. a porter, a bird-catcher, present day Orissa,

utkalikā f. longing for, regretting, dalliance, a bud, a wave,

utkalita mfn unbound, loosened, opened, blossoming, brilliant, bright, coming forth, becoming visible, regretting, longing for, prosperous, increasing,

utkaṇṭha mfn ready, eager, having the neck uplifted (on the point of doing anything), having the throat open (as in crying), m. longing for, a kind of sexual union, regretting or missing any thing or person,

utkara m. anything dug out or scattered upwards, rubbish, a heap,

utkarṣa mfn superior, eminent, m. pulling upwards, drawing, pulling, elevation, increase, rising to something better, prosperity,

utkarṣaṇa n. the act of drawing upwards, taking off, pulling off (a dress),

utkarṣin mfn superior, better,

utkartana cutting up, cutting to pieces,

utkartṛtva n. being a helper, the state of being conducive to,

utkāśa n. going out, coming forth,

utkaṭa mfn exceeding the usual measure, immense, gigantic, richly endowed with, drunk, furious, excessive, much, superior, proud, haughty, uneven, difficult,
m. fluid from the temples of an elephant, intoxication, pride,

utkhāta mfn dug up, excavated, eradicated, pulled up by the roots, n. a hole, cavity, a deepening, uneven ground, undermining, hollowing out, destroying, eradicating,

utkhāthin mfn rugged, destructive, uneven, having cavities or holes,

utkīrtita mfn proclaimed, promulgated, praised, celebrated,

utkleda m. becoming moist or wet,

utkleśa 177/1 m. excitement, disquietude, disorder or corruption, sickness, nausea,

utkoca m. winding off, unbinding, bribery, corruption,

utkocaka mfn receiving a bribe, corrupt,

utkocin mfn corruptible, to be bribed,

utkoṭi mfn ending in a point or edge,

ut-kṛ (*ud-√kṛ*) P. *–karoti* to do away with, eradicate, A. *–kurute* to inform against, to promote, help,

ut-kram (*ud-√kram*) P.A. to step up, go up, ascend, to step out, go out or away, to pass away, die, to pass over, omit, not to notice, to neglect, transgress,

utkrama m. going up or out, inverted order, progressive increase, going astray, acting improperly, deviation,

utkrāma m. going from or out, going above, surpassing, deviating from propriety, transgression, opposition, contrariety,

utkramaṇa n. going up or out, soaring aloft, flight, stepping out, surpassing, departing from life, dying, death,

utkrāmanta pres/part departing, stepping away, leaving the body,

utkramya ind. having ascended, ascending, stepping up, having neglected,

utkrānta mfn having gone forth or out, gone over or beyond, passed, surpassed, trespassing, exceeding,

utkrānti f. stepping up to, going out, passing away, dying, departure of the soul from the body,

utkṛṣṭa 176/3 mfn drawn up or out, attracted, extracted, taking a high position, excellent, eminent, superior, best, much, most, excessive,

utkṛṣṭā f. or *–tva* n. excellence, superiority,

eminence,
utkṣepaṇa n. the act of throwing upwards, tossing, sending, sending away, vomiting, a kind of basket or bowl for cleaning corn, a fan,
utkula mfn fallen from or disgracing one's family, an outcast from the family,
utkūla going uphill, passing beyond the bank (overflowing), ind. (*am*) uphill,
utkūlita mfn brought to the bank or shore, thrown up on a bank, stranded,
utkumuda mfn having lotus flowers on the surface,
utkūṭa m. an umbrella or parasol,
utkuṭaka mfn sitting on the hams, squatting,
utkutuka mfn ifc. amusing one's self by,
ut-pad (*ut√pad*) A. *–padyate*, to arise, rise, originate, come forth, become visible, appear, to be ready, to take place, begin, caus. *utpādayati* cause to arise, cause,
utpāda m. coming forth, birth, production, origination, mfn having the legs stretched out, standing on the legs,
utpādana n. procreation, mfn bringing forth, producing, productive,
utpādasya ind. having originated, origination
utpādita mfn produced, effected, generated, begotten,
utpādyamāna mfn being produced or generated,
utpala n. the blossom of the blue lotus, any water-lily, any flower, 2. fleshless, emaciated,
utpanna mfn risen, gone up, arisen, born, produced, come forth, ready, mentioned, quoted,
utpannabuddhi mfn one in whom wisdom is produced, wise,
utpāra mfn endless, boundless, *utpala* n. the blossom of the blue lotus, any water-lily, any flower, 2. mfn fleshless, emaciated,
utpāraṇa n. transporting over,
ut-paś *(ud-paś)* P. *–paśyati* to see overhead, to foresee, expect, to behold, perceive,
utpaśya mfn looking up or upwards,
ut√pat Cl1 *utpatati* to fly up,
utpata m. 'flying upwards', a bird,
utpāṭa m. pulling up by the roots,
utpāta m. flying up, jumping up, a spring, jump, rising, arising, a sudden event, unexpected appearance, a calamitous portent, any public calamity or phenomenon, (earthquake etc.),
mfn causing misfortune or calamity, flying upwards,
utpatāka mfn with raised flags or banners
utpatha m. wrong road, bad way, error, evil, mfn one who has left the right path, lost, stray,
utpāṭita mfn pulled out by the roots, torn out, eradicated, driven away, banished, de-throned,
utpatita mfn springing up, risen, ascended,
utpattavya mfn to be produced or born,
utpatti f. arising, birth, production, origin, resurrection, profit, productiveness, producing as an effect or result, giving rise to, occurrence, being mentioned or quoted (as a Vedic passage),
utpattināśa m. beginning and destruction,
utpāva m. purifying ghee,
utpavana n. cleaning, cleansing, straining liquids, any cleaning tool,
utpavitṛ mfn purifying, a purifier,
utphulla mfn wide open (as eyes), swollen, sleeping supinely, looking at with insolence, insolent, impudent, a kind of coitus,
urpīḍita mfn squeezed,
utpiñja m. sedition, revolt,
utpiñjala mfn let loose, unfolded, unrolled
utpiñjalaka mfn tumultuous, disordered (as a battle),
utpiñjara mfn uncaged, set free, out of order, very confused, let loose, unfolded, expanded,
utpṛ *(ud√1.pṛ)* caus. *–pārayati,* to transport over, conduct out of (the ocean), to save,
utpī to fill up,

utprabha mfn flashing forth or diffusing light, shining, m. a bright fire,
utprāsana n. derision, jocular expression
utprasava m. abortion,
utprekṣā f. overlooking or disregarding, carelessness, indifference, observing, comparison, simile, illustration, metaphor, a parable,
utprekṣaka mfn observing, considering,
utprekṣaṇa n. looking into, observing, foreseeing, anticipating, comparing, an ironical comparison,
utprekṣita mfn compared (as in a simile)
utpraveṣṭṛ mfn one who enters or penetrates,
ut-pū (ud√pū) P.A. *–punāti. –punīte*, to cleanse, purify, to extract (anything that has been purified),
utpulaka mfn having the hairs of the body raised (through joy or rapture),
utpūta mfn cleaned, cleansed,
utsa m. a spring, fountain (metaphorically applied to the clouds),
utsāda m. ceasing, vanishing, ruin, one who disturbs or destroys,
utsādaka mfn destroying, overturning,
utsādana n. putting away or aside, suspending, interrupting, omitting, destroying, overturning, rubbing, anointing, healing a sore, a means of healing a sore, going up, ascending, raising, elevating, ploughing a field twice or thoroughly,
utsadhi m. a well, the receptacle of a spring,
utsādyante they are withdrawn, disappear, a 1/pl/pres/indic/pass/caus *ud √sād*
utsāha m. cheerfulness, enthusiasm, 182/1 power, strength, strength of will, resolution, effort, energy, perseverance, strenuous and continuous exertion, fortitude, joy, happiness, a thread,
utsāhaka mfn active, persevering,
utsāhayoga m. bestowing energy, exercising one's strength,
utsaṅga m. the lap, hip, a horizontal area,
utsanna mfn obliterated, disappeared, in ruins, fallen into disuse, raised, elevated,
utsaraṇa n. going or creeping upwards,
utsarga 182/3 m. pouring out, pouring forth, emission, excretion, laying aside, (in gram.) any general rule or precept, abandoning, resigning, rejecting,
utsargin mfn leaving out or off, abandoning, quitting,
utsarpin mfn soaring upwards, mounting upwards, appearing, coming forth,
utsatti f. vanishing, fading, absence,
utsava m. festivity, enterprise, beginning, a festival, jubilee, joy, gladness, blossoming,
utsecana n. the act of foaming or spouting upwards, boiling over,
utsedha m. height, elevation, altitude, thickness, bigness, excelling, sublimity, the body,
utseka m. foaming upwards, showering, overflow, increase, enlargement, superabundance, haughtiness, pride
utsīdeyus they would sink down or perish 1/pl/opt/act/ *ud √sad*
utsikta mfn overflowing, superabundant, elevated, raised, haughty, proud, wanton, rude, crack-brained, disturbed in mind,
utsita mfn fettered, entangled,
ut √sṛj 182/2 let loose, set free, open, lay aside, abandon, send forth, to discontinue, suspend, cease,
utsṛjāmi I set free, let loose, send forth
utsṛṣṭa mfn let loose, set free, released,
utsuka mfn eager, restless, uneasy, anxious, zealously active, eager for, fond of, attached to, regretting, missing, *(am)* n. sorrow, longing for, desire, eagerness,
utsukatā f. or*–tva* n. restlessness, uneasiness, disquiet, sorrow, regret,
utsūra the evening, sunset,
utsūtra mfn unstrung, out of rule, deviating from or disregarding rules, (policy and grammar), anything not contained in a rule, loose, detached,

utsya mfn coming from a well or fountain,
utsyūta mfn sewn up, sewn to,
utta 183/1 mfn moistened, wet
uttadhi (*udadhi)* mfn holding water, m. 'water-receptacle', a cloud, river, sea, the ocean,
uttāla mfn great, strong, high, loud,
uttama mfn (superlative) best, uppermost, highest, chief, most elevated, principal, excellent, the highest tone, (*am*) ind. most, in the highest degree, In Sanskrit grammar the *uttama puruṣaḥ* or best person is the 3rd person i.e. I or we e.g.
uttamādhamamadhyama mfn highest and lowest and midmost,
uttamagandhāḍhya mfn rich in excellent odours or scents,
uttamakoṭī-adhikārī m. qualified person of the highest order,
uttamāṅga 178/1 n. the head (highest limb)
uttamapuruṣa highest person –God, the Absolute,
uttamarahasya n. highest secret, deepest mystery,
Uttamaujas a warrior 'of highest power'
uttamavid mfn having supreme knowledge,
uttāna mfn stretched out, spread out, Buddhist – clear, distinct,
uttānita mfn wide open (as the mouth),
ut-tap *(ud√tap)*P. *–tapati,* to make warm or hot, to heat thoroughly, A. *–tapate,* to shine forth, give out heat, to warm one's self or a part of the body,
uttāpa m. great heat, glow, ardour, effort, excessive energy, affliction, excitement,
uttapta mfn burnt, heated, red-hot, glowing, pained, pressed hard, bathed, washed, anxious, excited, n. dried flesh, great heat,
uttāpita mfn heated, made hot, pained, excited, roused,
uttara 1. 178/1 mfn. upper, higher, superior, northern, left, later, following, subsequent, future, (*am*) n. answer, reply, upper surface or cover, the following member, the last part of a compound, superiority, competency, result 2. mfn crossing over, to be crossed
uttarā ind. north, northerly, northward,
uttaradāyaka mfn giving answer, contradicting, impertinent,
uttarāhi ind. northerly, from the north
uttāraka a deliverer, Śiva
uttaraloman mfn hairy side up,
uttaramārga 178/3 m. the way leading to the North, the Path of the Sun,
uttaraṁga a high wave, rough with high waves, washed over by waves, flooded,
uttāraṇa mfn transporting over, bringing over, rescuing, (*am*) n. the act of landing, rescuing, delivering,
uttarapaścima mfn north-westerly,
uttarāpatha n. the northerly way, the north country,
uttarapurastāt ind. north-east of (with 6th),
uttaratas ind. northward, to the north of (with 6th), at the top, above, from the north, to the left,
uttarāyana n. the northern phase of the sun, the northern summer solstice,
uttareṇa ind. northerly, north of, on the left side of,
uttarjana n. violent, threatening,
uttarottara mfn higher and higher, more and more, (*am*) ind. one on the other, more and more, higher and higher, n. answer to an answer, a rejoinder, conversation, excess, succession, gradation, descending,
uttata mfn stretching oneself upwards, rising upwards,
uttejaka mfn instigating, stimulating,
uttejana n,f. incitement, instigation, encouragement, stimulation, exciting, animating, sending, despatching, urging, driving, whetting, sharpening, polishing, an inspiring or exciting speech, n. an incentive, inducement, stimulant,
uttejita mfn incited, animated, excited etc.

n. an incentive, inducement, moderate velocity in a horses pace,

uttha 179/3 mfn (generally ifc.) standing up, rising, coming forth, originating, derived from, m. arising, coming forth,

utthāna n. the act of standing up or rising, rising of the moon etc. resurrection, rising from the ground, rising up to depart, leaving off, coming forth, appearing, tumult, sedition, effort, exertion, manly exertion, manhood, an army, joy, pleasure, a book, a courtyard, a term, limit, the care of subjects or dependents, reflection,

utthānīya mfn belonging to the completion, forming the conclusion,

utthāpaka n. causing to get up, who or what raises etc. exciting, animating,

utthāpana n. causing to rise or get up, causing to leave, causing to come forth, bringing forth, exciting, instigating, bringing about, causing to cease, finishing,

utthātṛ m. one who rises, resolving,

utthāya ind. having risen (from a seat), having risen (in rank etc.), standing up,

utthita mfn . √*sthā* risen, rising

utthitā f. state of activity or readiness to serve,

uttīrṇa mfn landed, crossed, traversed, rescued, liberated, escaped, released from obligation, thrown off, one who has completed his studies, experienced, clever,

uttiṣṭha stand up 2/s/impv/act *ud*√*sthā* you may stand up,

uttiṣṭhate 179/3 comes forth, arises, results, 1/s/pres/indic/mid arises

uttiṣṭhati he/she stands, stands up

uttolana n. lifting up, raising, elevating by means of a counter-poise or balance),

uttolita mfn raised, lifted up,

ut-tī *(ud√tṛ)* P. *–tarati, -tirati,* to pass out of (esp. water), to disembark, to come out of, to escape from (misfortune, affliction), to come down, descend, to pass over, to cross (river with 2nd), to vanquish, to give up, leave, to elevate, strengthen, increase, caus. *–tārayati* to cause to come out, to deliver, rescue, to make anyone alight, to take down, take off, to cause to pass over, to convey or transport across, land, disembark,

uttrāsa m. fear, terror,

uttripada n. an upright tripod,

uttuda mfn one who stirs up,

uttyāga m. throwing up, abandonment, secession from worldly attachments,

uttyakta mfn thrown upwards, left, abandoned, free from worldly passion,

uvāca he said, he spoke, 1/s/perf/ act √*vac* speak

√*ūy* 221/2 Cl 1 A *ūyate* to weave, sew, DP in *tantusantāna* weaving, sewing

va 910/1 2. m. air, wind, the arm, the ocean, water, addressing, reverence, conciliation, auspiciousness, a dwelling, a tiger, cloth, n. a weaver, mfn strong, powerful,
2. ind. = *iva*, like, as,

vā or, as well as, also,
f. going, hurting, an arrow, weaving,

vā... vā either... or

√*vā* 934/2 cl.2 P *vāti* to blow (as the wind), to procure or bestow anything (acc.) by blowing, to blow towards or upon, to emit an odour, be diffused (as perfume), to smell, to hurt, injure, caus. *vāpayati,* DP in *gati* going, or *gandhana* 344/3 blowing

vā yadi vā whether... or if...
yadi vā... vā whether.... or...
vā... vā ... either… or…
na... na vā... neither… nor…

√*vabhr* 920/2 Cl 1 P *vabhrati* to go, go astray, DP in *gati* going,

√*vac* 912/1 Cl 2 P *vakti*, Cl 3 P *vivakti* to speak, say, tell, utter, announce, declare, mention, proclaim, recite, describe, to reproach, revile, to resound, to be called or accounted, be regarded as, caus. *vācayati (te)*, cause to say or speak or recite or pronounce, to read out loud, to say, tell, declare, DP in *paribhāṣaṇa* speaking

vāc 936/1 f. speech, voice, talk, language, sound, a word, saying, phrase, sentence, speech personified,

vaca mfn. speaking, talking, m. a parrot, the sun, n. the act of speaking, speech,

vācā 937/2 f. 1. speech, a word, the goddess of speech, a holy word, sacred text, an oath,

vācaka mfn speaking, saying, telling anything (6th), speaking of, treating of, declaring (6th or ifc.),expressing, signifying, berbal, expressed by words, m.a speaker, reciter, a significant sound or word, a messenger,

vācāla mfn talkative, chattering said aslso of birds), boastful, full of noise and bustle, ifc. filled with the song or noise of,

vācālatā f. talkativeness, loquacity,

vācālatva n. as above

vācaṁyama mfn restraining or holding one's voice, silent,
m. sage who practises silence,

vācaṁyamatva n. silence,

vacana 912/3 mfn. speaking, a speaker, indicating,eloquent,
ifc. mentioning, indicating, expressing, meaning, (*-tā* f. *–tva* n.)
n. the act of speaking, utterance, command, statement, word, speech, pronunciation,
used to express number in grammar e.g. *ekavacana* speaking of one, lit. the act of speaking,
rumour, dry ginger,

vacārambhaṇa 'ornament of speech', existing in speech alone; not real, as in a gold ornament – gold is the reality and the ornamentation is only an expression of this,

vacas 912/3 n. speech, voice, word, singing, song (of birds), advice, (in gram.) number,

vācāṭa mfn talkative, boastful,

vācāvirudha mfn unsuitable for words, not describable with words,

vācika mfn verbal, consisting of words, news, tidings, intelligence,

vācya gve. to be spoken, to be spoken to, to be directed to, to be told about, to be spoken against, blamable, that which is denoted by speech (U)

*vācyartha*937/3 m. directly expressed meaning, literal meaning,

√*vad* 916/1 Cl 1 P A *vadati (te)* also *vādati,* to speak, sat, utter, tell, report, speak to, talk with, address, to praise, recommend, adjudge, adjudicate, to indicate, designate, proclaim, announce, foretell, bespeak, allege, affirm, declare to be, call, to raise the voice, sing, utter a cry, A. to say, tell, speak to, to mention, state, communicate, name, to confer or dispute about, to contend, quarrel, lay claim to, be an authority, be eminent in, to triumph, exult, caus. *vādayati (te)*, DP in *vyaktāvāc* speaking distinctly, in *sandeśa-vacana* causing to speak or sound

√*vāḍ* 939/1 see √*bāḍ* DP in *āplāvya* diving, emerging, bathing,

vada speak! say! 2/s/impv. you speak,

vāda 939/3 mfn. speaking of or about, causing to sound, playing,
m. speech, discussion, discourse, proposition, argument, doctrine, demonstrated conclusion, result , a saying, a word,

-vāda m. the 'doctrine of ...'

vādaka mfn making a speech, speaking, a speaker, m. a musician,

vadan mfn saying

vadana m 916/2 n. the act of speaking, the mouth, face, countenance,

vadati he says, speaks

vādayati plays (an instrument)

vadeta he should expound, 1/s/opt/mid/ √*vad* cl1

√*vadh* 916/3 *vadhati* to strike, slay, kill, DP in *bandhana* binding, *saṁyamana* restraining,

vadha m. killing, slaughter, murderer, weapon of death esp. Indra's thunderbolt,

vadhar n. weapon of death, Indra's bolt,

vadhasna 3rdpl. only, Indra's bolts, (weapons of death),

vadhati slays, strikes,

vādayuddha n. speech-fight, i.e. controversy, war od words,

vādayuddhapradhāna mfn devoted to controversy, m. eminent controversialist,

vadhri mfn whose testicles have been crushed, emasculated, impotent,

vādhrīṇasa m. rhinoceros,

vadhū f. bride, woman, young wife,

vadhūvastra n. bride's garment,

vadhya gve. to be struck, i.e. punished, to be harmed or slain, going to be killed, should be killed,

vādi in comp. for *vādin* 940/1 mfn saying, speaking, a speaker, learned, wise,

vādin 940/1mfn. saying, talking about, proclaiming, m. teacher of any doctrine, speaker, disputant, accuser, plaintiff, prosecutor,

vaditavya gve. to be spoken, n. instrumental music

vāditra 940/1 n. a musical instrument, music, musical performance,

vadya gve. to be spoken of, worthy of (favourable) notice, praiseworthy,

vādya n. a musical instrument, instrumental music,

vādyamāna part. being played (music, instrument),

vādyavidyā f. the art of playing a musical instrument,

vāg-doṣa m. speaking badly or ill, abusive or ungrammatical speech,

vāg-doṣāt by or as a bad consequence of his voice, i.e. because he was fool enough to let his voice be heard,

vāghat m. the pledging one, i.e. institutor of a sacrifice, not he priest but the *yajamāna*

vāgmin 937/1 eloquent, speaking well, loquacious, talkative, below, m. a parrot, planet Jupiter,

vāgvistara prolixity, diffuseness (in speech)

√*vah* 933/2 Cl 1 P A *vahati (te)* to carry, transport, convey, to lead, conduct, to bear along (water, said of rivers, to draw (a car), guide (horses etc.), to lead towards, bring, procure, bestow, to cause, effect, offer (a sacrifice), to spread, diffuse (scent), to shed (tears), to carry away, carry off, rob, to lead home, take to wife, to bear, suffer, endure, to forbear, forgive, pardon, to undergo (ordeals), to drive, ride, go by or in, be borne or carried along, run, swim, to pass away, elapse, caus. *vāhayati*, DP in *prāpaṇa* carrying, conveying,
ifc. carrying, drawing, bearing,

vāha 949/1 mfn bearing, drawing, m. the act of a draught animal, any vehicle, conveyance, car, a bearer, porter,

vahāmi 933/2 √*vah* I lead, carry, bear

vāhana mfn carrying off, drawing, bearing, conveying, bringing, n. endeavouring, exertion, driving, riding, beast of burden, beast for riding, team, vehicle, the carrying,

vāhanā f. an army,

vahati he carries

vahatu m. wedding procession, wedding, means of furthering, an ox, a traveller,

vāhin mfn carrying, bearing, drawing, effecting, wearing, conveying along, bringing, causing to flow, undergoing,

vāhinī f. army, host, body of forces, a river, a channel,

vahni 933/3 m. any animal that bears or draws along, horse, team, charioteer, rider, bearer of oblations, fire in general or the god of fire, the digestive fire,

vahya n. portable bed, litter, mfn fit to bear or to be borne or to draw or to be drawn, (*ā*) f. the wife of a *muṇi*

vahye-śaya mfn lying on litters,

√*vai* 1019/3 1. Cl 1 P *vāyati* to become languid or weary, or exhausted, to be deprived of, also A. to blow, DP in *śoṣaṇa* drying, being, languid or weary,

vai 1019/3 a particle of emphasis – certainly, truly, indeed, common in poetry as an expletive,

vaicitrya n. variety, diversity, sorrow,

vaicitya 1021/1 mental confusion, absence of mind, a swoon

vaidagdhya n. cleverness, proficiency, skill, dexterity, acumen,

vaidarbha mfn belonging to Vidarbha, m. the Vidarbhan, king of Vidarbha, Vidarbhī – the princess of Vidarbha, i.e. Damayantī,

vaideha m. belonging to the country of Videha, king of Videha,

vaidehī a name for *Sītā*

vaidharmya n. unlawfulness, injustice, difference of duty or obligation, difference, diversity in kind or nature,

vaidhibhakti formalistic devotion, practice of devotion through rituals,

vaidhika mfn ritual, in accordance with rule, ceremonial, instructive,

vaidika mfn Vedic, prescribed by or conformable to the Vedas,

vaidya mfn having to do with science, versed in science, learned, relating or belonging to the Vedas, conformable to the Vedas, m. a physician, a learned man, a follower of the Vedas or one well versed in them, skilled in the art of healing,

vaijayantī f. necklace of Viṣṇu, banner, flag, ensign, a plant,

vaikalya 1020/1 n. imperfection, defect, weakness, defectiveness, frailty, incompetency, insufficiency, despondency, confusion,

vaikārika mfn based on or subject to modification, modifying or modified, m. a class of deities, the time necessary for formation of a fetus (with *kāla)*, n. emotion, flurry, the *sattvika* or godly aspect of *ahaṁkāra,*

vaikhānasa relating to or belonging to *vaikhānasa*s or religious recluses,

vaikharī 4th stage in the manifestation of sound or speech, "when the sounds are manifest in the physical form, through the use of tongue and mouth, and are expelled to vibrate in the open space, then it is *vaikharī"*

vaiklavya 1020/3 n. frailty, feebleness, mental weakness

vaikṛta mfn disfigured, undergoing change, derivative, not natural, subject to modification, deformed, mofified, secondary, n. mental change, unnatural phenomenon, alteration, hostility, aversion,

vaikṛtya 1020/2 mfn changed (in form or mind), n. change, alteration, deterioration, degeneration, ugliness, portent, hostility, woeful state,

vaikuṇṭha name of Viṣṇu's heaven

vaimanasya n. dejection, depression, melancholy, sickness,

vaimānika mfn riding in a sky-traversing car called, *vimāna*

vaiṇava mfn of reed, esp. of bamboo,

Vainateya 1023/2 m. the son of Vinatā, name of Garuda the bird transport of *Viṣṇu*

vaira n.m. enmity, hostility, mfn hostile,

vairāgya 1025/2 n. freedom from all worldly desires, indifferent to worldly objects, and to life, renunciation, aversion, distaste for, life (A), detachment, 'power of detachment' HH
change or loss of colour, growing pale, disgust, aversion, distaste for

or loathing of,
vairasya 1025/2 tastelessness, disgust, insipidity, bad taste,
vairi 1025/1 m. an enemy,
vaiśākha m. a month, (April-May), a churning stick,
vaiṣamya n. unevenness of ground, inequality, oddness, diversity, disproportion, difficulty, trouble, distress, calamity, injustice, unkindness, harshness, wrongness, an error, solitariness,
vaiṣamyāvasthā f. a state in which the equilibrium of the three gunas is disturbed,
vaiśāradya n. experience, skill in (7th), expertness, wisdom, clearness of intellect, infallibility, 'perfection' (Gam.), 'peace of mind' (N),
vaiṣayika 1027/2 belonging or relating to an object of sense, sensual, carnal, mundane, having a partic. sphere or object or aim,relating to, concerning, m. a sensualist, one addicted to the pleasures of sense or absorbed in worldly objects,
vaiśeṣika mfn special, peculiar, specific, characteristic, distinguished, excellent, pre-eminent, excellence , distinction, n. the name of a particular philosophy (a division of the Nyāya school), peculiarity, distinction, m. a follower of that doctrine,
vaiṣṇava mfn relating to Viṣṇu, worshipping Viṣṇu,
vaiṣṇavī personified *śakti* (energy, power) of Viṣṇu,
vaiśvānara 1027/1 mfn. relating or belonging to all men, omnipresent, known or worshipped everywhere, universal, general, common, -- consisting of all men, the sun, sunlight, name of the supreme Spirit or intellect when located in a supposed collective aggregate of gross bodies, the digestive fire of all men, name of Agni or fire, ' the universal consciousness in forming this physical realm is known by the name *Vaiśvānara* or *Virāṭ* (the totality of the material universe)(U)
vaiśya m. the third class or caste, merchants, producers, farmers,
vaitālika mfn out of time, m. bard, minstrel, magician, watchman, servant of a *vetāla* (ghost, spirit),
vaitaraṇī f. a river that flows between earth and hell, a cow that transports a dead person across that river,
vaitathya 1021/2 falseness, unreality, from *vi-tatha*
vaitatya n. great extension from *vi-tata,*
vaitṛṣṇya 1022/1 n. freedom from desire, indifference to, quenching of thirst,
vaivāhika mfn nuptial, n. nuptial festivities, wedding, marriage, alliance by marriage, preparations for a wedding,
vaivasvata mfn coming from or belonging to the sun, relating or belonging to Yama m. Vaivasvata (son of the sun – Death) O Death, *Vaivasvata* 1026/1 a *Manu* the son of *Vivasvat* , the Sun,
vaiyākaraṇa mfn relating to grammar, grammatical, m. a grammarian,
√*vaj* 913/1 Cl 1 P *vajati* to go, caus. or Cl 10 *vājayati* to prepare the way, to trim or feather an arrow, to be hard or strong, DP in *gati* going,
vāja m. swiftness, courage esp. of the horse, race, struggle, prize of race or contest, booty, reward (in general), treasure, good, a swift or spirited horse, war-horse, the feathers on an arrow, a wing, sound, n. ghee, an oblation of rice, rice or food in general,
vājin m. a horse, warrior, man, steed of a war-chariot, a bridle , bird, an arrow, mfn swift, spirited, impetuous, heroic, warlike, strong, manly, procreative, potent, winged, feathered (as an arrow),

vajra 913/1, m.n. Indra's thunderbolt, a mythical weapon, diamond, rock-like firmness,

vajrabāhu mfn having the thunderbolt on his arm (Indra), lightning-armed,

vajranirghoṣa a thunderbolt, thunderclap

vajrayāna 'thunderbolt vehicle or diamond vehicle' a form of Tantric Buddhism principally in Tibet,

vajrin mfn having the thunderbolt, m. thunderer,

vāk statement, in comp for *vāc* 936/1 speech, voice talk, language, primordial rd, logos,

√*vakh* 911/3 Cl 1 P *vakhati* to go, move, DP in *gati* going,

vākovākya dialectic, dialogue, the science of logic,

vākpati m. the ruler of the organs of speech, planet Jupiter, a master of speech, an eloquent man

vakra mfn crooked, 2. fig. disingenuous, ambiguous,

√*vakṣ* 911/3 Cl 1 P *vakṣati* to grow, increase, be strong or powerful, to be angry, caus. *vakṣayati* to make grow, cause to be strong, DP in *roṣa* being angry, or *saṁghāta* accumulating,

vāksamudāya m. collection of words,

vakṣaṇā f.pl. belly, bellies (of cloud-mountains),

vakṣas n. the breast, bosom, chest,

vāksiddhi perfection in speech, in which whatever is spoken turns out to be true; the result of the observation of truthfulness, (U)

vākskhalana

vāk speech, voice, talk

skhalana 1257/2 stumbling, tripping, unsteady, stammering faltering (speech)

stammering or faltering speech

vaktā he/she will speak 1/s/peri fut, speaking, fluent speaker, an instructor, orator,

vaktavya gve. to be said or spoken,

vakti 912/1 root *vac* 1/s/pres/indic/act speaks

vaktṛ m. speaker,

vaktra n. mouth, face

vaktrasamyoga kissing

vaktum infin. of *vac* 912/1 to say , speak, utter

vākya a sentence lit. that which is spoken 936/2 n. word, speech, saying, assertion, statement, command, a statement, a sentence, a rule, an argument, mode of expression

vākyaprabhanda 936/2 connected flow of words, connected composition or narrative

vākyārtha m. the meaning or contents of a sentence,

vākyārthabodha (G) verbal judgment, knowledge gained by sentence meaning,

vākyasiddha 'whatever one would say would duly come to pass'

√*val* 927/3 Cl 1 A P *valate (ti),* to turn, turn round, turn to, to be drawn or attached towards, be attached to, to move to and fro, to go, approach, hasten, to return, turn back or home, depart or go away again, to break forth, appear, to increase, to cover or enclose, or to be covered, DP in *samvaraṇa* covering, enclosing, or *sañcalana* going,

vala m. name of a demon

vāla m. bristle, hair of any animal's tail, any tail or hair,

valavṛtra Vala and Vritra

valavṛtra-han m. slayer of Vala and Vritra i.e. Indra, mfn slaying V° and V°,

valavṛtra-niṣūdana m. destroyer of Vala and Vritra,

valaya m.n. bracelet,

√*valbh* 928/2 Cl 1 A to take food, eat, DP in *bhojana* eating,

√*valg* 928/2 Cl 1 P *valgati (te*), to spring, bound, leap, dance, to sound, A. to take food, DP in *gati* going

valgu mfn handsome, beautiful, attractive,

√*valguya* 928/2 Nom P *valguyati* to treat kindly, to exult, DP in *pūjā* praising or honouring, *mādhurya* being handsome, mild or gentle,

√*valh* 929/1 Cl 1 A *valhate* to be excellent, to speak, to kill, to hurt, to give or to cover, Cl 10 P *valhayati* to speak or to shine, DP (Cl 1) in *paribhāṣā* speaking, *hiṁsā* hurting, killing, *chādana* covering, (Cl 10) in *bhāṣā* speaking, shining,

valī f. a fold, wrinkle, a wave,

vālī brother of *sugrīva*

√*valk* 928/1 Cl 10 P *valkayati* to speak, DP in *paribhāṣaṇa* speaking around, telling, narrating,

valkala m. tree-bark,

valkya m. bark of a tree,

√*vall* 928/2 Cl 1 P *vallate* to be covered or to go DP in *samvaraṇa* covering, or *sañcalana* going, moving,

vallabha m. beloved, a favourite, friend,

vallarī or *vallī* a creeper, creeping plant,

valmīka m. ant-hill, mole-hill,

vālmīki a great sage who wrote the *Rāmāyaṇa*

vāluka mfn containing or resembling sand, powder, made of salt, m. a kind of poison, *(ī)* f. a sandbank, camphor,

vālukā f. sand, gravel, powder,

√*vam* 920/2 Cl 1 P *vamati* to vomit, spit out, eject, emit, send forth, give out, reject, DP in *udigaraṇa* vomiting,

vām you, enclitic 2nd pers. pron. dual 2nd,4th, 6th

vāma mfn lovely, pleasant, n. a lovely thing, a joy, left, on the left side, m. the female breast, the god of love, a she-ass, a female camel or jackal, a young female elephant, n. a lovely thing, any dear or desirable good (gold, horses,etc.), wealth, fortune, mfn relating to a mare, left (not right),reverse, adverse, contrary, opposite, unfavourable, crooked, oblique, refactory, coy (in love), acting in the opposite way or differently, hard, cruel, vile, wicked, base, low, m.n. the left side,

vāmana mfn dwarfish, short in stature, a dwarf, small, minute, short (also of days), bent, inclined,

vami f.nausea, vomiting, m. fire, a rogue, cheat,

vaṁśa 910/1 m. lineage, race, family, a dynasty, offspring , L. cane ,stock or stem of bamboo, the upper timbers or beams of a house, the rafters or roof-laths,

vaṁśaḥviśuddha mfn made of unblemished bamboo, 2. of pure lineage,

vamana 920/2 n. the act of vomiting, emitting, emission, offering oblations to fire, pain, paining, m. hemp,

√*vaṁh* 910/3 see *baṁh,* DP in *vṛddhi* increasing,

vamra m. ant, f. (*ī*),

vaṁśa 910/1 m. lineage, race, family, a dynasty, offspring, L. cane ,stock or stem of bamboo,

vaṁśa m. a flute

vaṁśakara mfn making a family or dynasty, m. an ancestor, a son,

vaṁśī f. a flute, pipe, artery, vein,

vāṅ 937/1 in comp. for *vāc*

√*vaṇ* 917/2 Cl 1 P *vaṇati (te*), to sound, DP in *śabda* sounding,

√*van* 917/2 Cl 1 P *vanati (te),* Cl 8 P A *vanoti, vanute,* to like, love, wish, desire, to gain, acquire, procure, to conquer, win, become master of, possess, to prepare for, aim at, attack, to hurt, injure, to sound, to serve, honour, worship, DP (Cl 1) in *śabda* sounding, *sambhakti* possessing, *hiṁsā* hurting, *gati* going, (cl8) *yācana* begging, asking, requesting,

vana 917/2 n. forest, wood, grove, plenty, a single tree, abundance, timber, adorable,

vāṇa 939/2 m. sounding, a sound, an arrow, the sound of a partic. drum, music esp. flutes, harps etc.

vanamālā f. a kind of metre, a garland of forest flowers, a garland worn by Kṛṣṇa, mfn wearing a garland of forest flowers,
vananā f. desire,
vanaprastha m.n. forest-plateau, wooded table-land,
vānaprastha a forest dweller, the third stage of life for a *brāhman,* having passed through the stages of student and householder he abandons his house and family for an ascetic life in the woods, hermit, anchorite,
vānara n. monkey, ape,
vanaspati m. tree, 'lord of the wood', a forest-tree,
a stem, trunk, beam, timber, post,
'lord of plants' the soma plant,
anything made of wood,
an ascetic, du. a pestle and mortar,
vanaukas m. forest-dweller, anchorite,
a forest animal, a wild-boar, ape,
vanavāsa m. living in a wood,
wandering habits,
-tas owing to (his) forest- life,
vanavāstin mfn forest-dwelling, m. forest-dweller,
√*vañc* 914/2 Cl 1 P *vañcati* to move to and fro, go crookedly, totter, stagger, to go, go to, arrive at, go slyly or secretly, sneak along, to pass over, wander over, go astray, caus. *vañcayati (te)* to move or go away from, avoid, shun, escape, cause to go astray, deceive, cheat, defraud of, DP in *gati* going, in *pralambhana* (Cl 10) deceiving, cheating,
√*vāñch* 938/3 Cl 1 P *vāñchati* to desire, wish, ask for, strive after, pursue, to state, assert, assume, DP in *icchā* desiring,
vāñchā f. desire, wish, longing for,
vañcaka mfn cunning, deceitful, a deceiver, fraudulent, crafty, m. a jackal, a tame or house mongoose, a low or vile man,
vañcana mf cheating,
vāñcati he/she desires
938/3 1/s/pres/act/indic. of *vāñch*
938/3 desire, he desires
vañcavitavya gve. to be deceived, n. a to-be-practised deceit,
√*vaṇḍ* Cl 1 A *vaṇḍate* to partition, share, divide, to surround, cover, Cl 10 P *vaṇḍayati* to partition, share, DP in *vibhājana* sharing out, dividing,
√*vand* 919/1 Cl 1 A *vandate (ti),* to praise, celebrate, laud, extol, show honour, do homage, salute respectfully or deferentially, venerate, worship, adore, to offer anything respectfully, DP in *abhivādana* saluting or *stuti* adoring, *vanda* mfn. praising, extolling
vanda mfn. praising, extolling
vandana (m) n 919/2 the act of praising, praise, reverence, worship, adoration, offering gratitude, thanking,
vandanam thank-you,
vandhya n. barren,
vandhyaputra the barren woman's son, a symbol of non-existence,
vanditṛ m. praiser,
vandya 919/2 mfn to be praised, saluted, praiseworthy
vanecara mfn forest-dweller,
√*vaṅg* 912/1 Cl 1 P *vaṅgati* to go, to go lamely, limp, DP in *gati* going,
vaṅga m. Bengal, m.n. cotton, n. tin or lead
√*vaṅgh* 912/1 Cl 1 A *vaṅghati* to go, set out, to begin, to move swiftly, to blame or censure, DP in *gati* going
vāṇī f. sound, voice, music, speech, language, diction, 'following true perception with exact expression'
vaṇij m. a merchant,
vaṇijya trade, traffic, commerce
vāṇija 939/2 a merchant, trader, trade, traffic, commerce,
vaṇik-putra m. merchant's son,
vanitā f. a loved wife, mistress, any woman
√*vaṅk* 911/3 see 2. *vak*, DP in *kauṭilya* going or moving crookedly, in *gati* going
√*vāṅkṣ* Cl 1 P *vāṅkṣati* to wish, desire, long

for, DP in *kāṅkṣā* desiring, wishing for,

√*vaṅkh* 911/3 *vaṅkhati* to go, move, DP in *gati* going

vāñ-manasa 937/2 speech and mind,

vāṅmātra n. mere words, only speech,

vāṅmaya mfn consisting of voice or utterance, whose essence is speech, relating to speech, n. speech, language, eloquence, rhetoric, manner of speech,

√*vaṇṭ* 915/2 Cl 1.10. P *vaṇṭati* or *vaṇṭayati,* to partition, apportion, share, divide, DP in *vibhājana* dividing, *prakāśana* making clear,

√*vaṇṭh* Cl 1 A *vaṇṭhate* to go or move alone, go unaccompanied, DP in *eka-caryā* going alone,

√*vap* 2. 919/3 Cl 1 P A *vapati (te*), to shear, shave, cut off, strew, sow, scatter, throw, cast, beget, throw or heap up, caus. *vāpayati* sow, plant put in the ground, DP in *bīja-santāna* sowing seed, begetting, producing,

vapā f. a caul, an anthill, a cavity, hollow,,hole, a prominent navel,

vāpi whether, f. a pond,

vāpī f. oblong pond, lake, well,

vāpījala n. lake-water,

vapra m.n. a rampart, earthwork, mound, slope of a hill, table-land, the gate of a fortified city, a sown field, any field, dust,

vapus 920/1 mfn. having form or a beautiful form, handsome, L. admirable, n. a wonder, wonderful appearance, a wonder to see,

vapusāt ind. into the form of a body,

vār n. water, urine, the ocean, stagnant water, a pond, m. a protector, defender,

vara L. 1.m. choice, wish, a thing to be chosen as gift or reward, gift, boon, reward,
ind. *varam vṛ* wish a wish, make a condition, *varam dā* give a choice, grant a wish, *prati varam* or *varam ā* according to one's wish,
2. mfn most excellent or fair, best, ind. *varam...na ca* the best thing is.. and not ....
921/1 m. 'enclosing', circumference, space, stopping, checking
2. 922/1 select, choicest, best,
3. choosing, m. chooser,
(ifc. TP.) best of such and such, the best such and such, suitor,
n. (*am*) width, breadth, expanse, room, space,

vāra 943/3 1. the hair of any animal's tail (esp. that of a horse), 2. keeping back, restraining, anything enclosed or circumscribed in space or time – appointed times, times e.g. 3 times, a moment, occasion, opportunity, a day of the week

varada mfn boon-granting, gift-giving, m. a benefactor, fire for burnt offerings of a propitiatory nature,

varadā f. a young woman, girl, maiden, the yam root,

vāraḥ a turn

varāha m. a boar, cloud, bull, ram,

varāka mfn vile, pitiable, wretched,

vāraka m. kind of vessel, resister, sort of horse or any horse, opposer, seat of pain, obstacle,

varam ind. it is better that, it is better than, rather than, it would be best if, rather, preferably, better,

vāraṁ vāram ind. time and again, sometimes,

varaṇa 921/1 m. a rampart, mound, causeway, bridge, a camel
L. n . a choosing

vāraṇa 944/1 mfn warding off, restraining, all-resisting, invincible, relating to prevention, dangerous, forbidden m. an elephant, elephant-hook, armour, mail. the act of restraining or keeping back or warding off,

vārāṇasī f. now called Benares

varāṅganā f. most excellent woman,

a beautiful woman,
varāroha mfn having fair hips or buttocks, m. an excellent rider, a rider on an elephant, a rider in general, mounting, riding,
varas n. width, room, expanse, space,
vara-varṇa m. most fair complexion, best-coloured, gold,
varavarṇin mfn having a fair complexion, *-inī* f. a fair-faced woman,
√*varc* 924/1 Cl 1 A *varcate* to shine, be bright, DP in *dīpti* shining
varcas n. vitality, vigour, the illuminating power in fire and the sun, splendour, form, figure, shape, fig. glory, colour, excrement, feces,
vardhana mfn 1. increasing, growing, thriving, m. increaser, delighting in, bestower of prosperity, increase, groeth, prodperity, success, enlarging, magnifying, strengthening, promoting, a means of strengthening, restorative, comfort, educating, rearing, 2. n. the act of cutting or cutting off, often ifc. causing to increase, strengthening, granting prosperity, mostly ifc. animating, gladdening, exhilirating,
vardhate he/she/it grows
vardhiṣyate will grow
vareṇya mfn desirable, best among, to be wished for, excellent, n. saffron, supreme bliss,
varenya gve. to be desired, longed for, excellent, mfn most excellent, best,
vareṇyakratu mfn having excellent understanding, wise, intelligent,
varga m. group, division, class,
√*varh* 927/3 see *barh* DP in *paribhāṣā* speaking, *hiṁsā* hurting, *chādana* covering,
vāri 943/1 1/s water, rain, fluidity, f. a place for tying or catching an elephant, a rope for tying an elephant, a captive, prisoner, a water-pot, pitcher, jar,
vāridhi m.the sea, the ocean, the fourth,
variṣṭha 921/2 1. mfn. (superlative) widest, broadest, largest, most extensive, 923/1 mfn. the most excellent or eminent among, best, most preferable among, better than, most excellent, valuable, precious , chief (in a bad sense) – worst, most wicked,
vāristha mfn situated in the water, i.e. of the sun's disk – reflected in the water,
varivas n. breadth, fig. freedom from constraint, ease, gladness, bliss, wealth, treasure,
varīyāṁs mfn very broad, extended wide,
varja mfn. (ifc) free from, devoid of, ifc.ind. except, excluding,
varjaka mfn. (ifc.) shunning, avoiding,
varjana 924/1 n. leaving, avoiding, excluding, neglect, omission, exception, hurting,
varjita 924/1 mfn. excluded, abandoned, avoided, deprived of, wanting, without
varman n. envelope, coat of armour, protection, at end of *kṣatriya* names,
√*varṇ* 924/2 Cl 10 P *varṇayati* to paint, colour, dye, to depict, picture, write, describe, relate, tell, explain, to regard, consider, to spread, extend, to praise, extol, proclaim qualities, DP in *varṇa* colouring, *kriyā* exerting, *vistāra* extending, *guṇavacana* praising, explaining, in *preraṇa* sending, *varṇana* describing,
varṇa 924/2 m. ifc f. *(ā)* a covering, cloak, mantle, exterior or outer appearance, form, figure, shape, colour, colour of the face (esp.), good colour or complexion, lustre, beauty, tint, dye, pigment (for painting or writing), colour (= race), species, kind, sort, character, nature, quality, class of men, tribe, order, caste – *brāhmaṇa* – priests, teachers, *kṣatriya*- warriors, kings, statesmen, *vaiśya* – merchants, producers, farmers, *śūdra* – servants, labourers

(the more modern word for caste being *jāti*), a letter, sound, vowel, syllable, word, alphabet, a musical sound or note, praise, renown, glory, the figure 'one', n. saffron,

varṇaka mfn painting, picturing, representing, m. a strolling player or singer, fragrant ointment, mfn colour for painting, adorning etc., m. sandal, f. woven cloth, a mask, dress of an actor, a pencil or brush for painting or writing, kind, description, fine gold, n. a chapter, a circle, orb, the red colouring marking the bride and groom, ifc. a letter or syllable,

varṇanā f. description, the act of painting, colouring etc. delineation, description, explanation, writing, embellishment, decoration, praise, commendation,

varṇāśrama n. caste and order, class and stage of life,

varṇātmaka mfn having articulate sound,

varṇātmakaśabda lettered sound with meaning as opposed to auditory sound,

varṇavyavasthā 924/3 the caste-system, institution of caste,

varṇayati colours, paints, describes,

varṇyamāna part. being described.

varpas n. assumed appearance, image, form, any form or shape, figure, image, aspect, artifice, device, design,

varṣa 926/3mfn raining, m. raining, rain, a cloud, rainy- season, a year, a shower, a division of the earth,

varṣā f. the rains, rainy season, rain-water,

varṣakarman n. the act of raining,

varṣaṣaṭka n. period of six years, (L)

vārṣika mfn annual, belonging to the rainy season, growing in the rainy season or fit for or suited to it, having water only during the rains (as a river), sufficient or lasting for a year,

varṣman m. height, top, crown of the head, n. height, top, surface, greatness, extent, measure, body, a handsome form or auspicious appearance, holding rain,

vārṣṇeya voc. 'O clansman of *vṛṣṇi' (Kṛṣṇa)*

varta m. subsistence, livelihood, the urethra,

vartamāna 925/2 mfn. turning, moving, unfolding, existing, living, abiding, present, (*ā*) f. the terminations of the present tense, n. presence, the present time, (in gram.) the present tense,

vartamānakāla m. present time, present tense,

vartamānākṣepa 925/2 m. denying or not agreeing with any present event or circumstances

vartamānatā 925/2 f. or *tva* n. the being present, the condition of present time, the dwelling or abiding in (with loc.)

vartana 925/2 n. or f. the act of rolling, or rolling on or moving forward or about, staying on, mfn. abiding, staying, setting in motion, L. n. means of subsistence, occupation, earnings, wages, commerce, conduct, behaviour,

vartate 1009/1 turns, revolves, proceeds, is, lives, exists 1/s/pres/indic/mid he lives

varte (or *vartate*) I turn, move on, live, continue 3/s/pres/indic/mid √*vṛt*

varteyam I should continue 3/s/opt/act √*vṛt* 1009/1

varti or *ī* f. a bandage round something, a lamp wick, a lamp,

vartikā f. a lamp wick, a stalk, a paint brush, colour, paint,

vartin mfn resting, abiding, behaving properly towards, engaged in, practising, behaving, acting, ifc. behaving properly towards, turning, moving, going, m. the meaning of an affix,

vartma in comp. for *vartman*

vartman 925/3 n. the track or rut of a wheel,

path, road, way, course, an edge, border, rim,an eyelid, basis, foundation,

vartmanā ifc. by way of, through,

vartṛ m. restrainer, stayer, mfn one who keeps back or wards off, expeller,

vartra mfn warding off, holding back, n. a water-stop, dam, weir,

vārttā f. news,

vārttika mfn skilled in a profession or business, relating to news, delivering intelligence, explanatory (gloss), relating to a gloss, m. a business-man, trader, an emissary, envoy, conjurer, physician, the egg-plant, f. business, trade, n. an explanatory or supplemental rule, critical gloss or annotation, -the exposition of the meaning, a marriage feast,

vārttikā f. business, trade

vārttikakāra m. a commentator (composer - of *vārttika(s),*

vartula mfn round, circular, globular, a ball,

Varuṇa the supporter, the supreme god of the Veda, the personification of truth, one of the *ādityas*, presiding over the element water,

varuṇabija the syllable *vaṁ*

varūtha n. cover, protection, defence, shelter, secure abode, a house or dwelling, armour, a coat of mail, a shield, a multitude, host, swarm, quantity, m. the Indian Cuckoo, time,

varūthya mfn protecting, safe, secure,

√*vaś* 929/1 Cl 2 P *vaṣṭi* , Cl 1 *vasati,* Cl 3 *vivaṣṭi,* to will, command, to desire, wish, long for, be fond of, like, to aver, maintain, affirm, declare for, caus. *vāśayati* to cause to desire, get in one's power, DP in *kānti* wishing for

√*vāś* 947/1 Cl 4 A *vāśyate, (ti*), to roar, howl, bellow, bleat, low, sing (like a bird), sound, resound, DP in *śabda* sounding

√*vaṣ* 930/1 Cl 1 P *vaṣati* to hurt, strike, kill, DP in *hiṁsā* hurting, killing,

√*vas* 932/1 3. Cl 10 P *vāsayati* to love, to cut off, to accept, take, to offer, to kill, DP in *sneha* loving, *cheda* cutting, dividing, or *apaharaṇa* taking

√*vas* 1. 930/1 Cl 6 P. connected with √1. *uṣ, ucchati,* to shine, grow bright,

√*vas* 4. 932/1 Cl 2 A *vaste*, to put on, invest, wear, (clothes etc.), assume (a form), enter into, caus. *vāsayati, (te),* to cause or allow to put on or wear, clothe, (A. oneself), DP in *ācchādana* wearing, putting on, ifc. clothed in , wearing,

√*vas* 5. Cl 1 P *vasati (te*) to dwell, live, stop (at a place), to remain, abide with or in, to remain or keep on or continue in any condition, Cl 10 P *vasayati* to dwell, caus. *vāsayati (te),* pass. to cause to halt or stay overnight, lodge, receuve hospitably or as a guest, t0 cause to have sexual intercourse with (7th), to let anything stand overnight, cause to wait, keep in suspense, delay, retard, to cause to exist, preserve, to cause to be inhabited, populate a country, to put in, place upon, DP (Cl 1) in *nivāsa* living, dwelling, (cl10) in *nivāsa* dwelling

√*vas* 8. 933/1 Cl 4 P *vasyati* to be or make firm, DP in *stambha* fixing,

√*vās* 947/2 Cl 10 P *vāsayati* to perfume, make fragrant, scent, fumigate, incense, steep, DP in *upasevā* scent perfume, incense, fumigating, making fragrant,

vas enclitic pron. you,

vaśa 929/2 1 m. will, wish, desire, power, control, dominion, 'passion for the company of women' –Gam.
to fall into a person's power (with 2nd case and verbs of 'going' and some others,) by force of, on account of, by means of, birth, origin, a brothel, mfn willing,

submissive, obedient, subject to or dependent on,

vāsa 947/2 n. cloth, clothes, garment m. abiding, dwelling, abode, habitation, perfuming, perfume, to take up one's abode, place or seat of (6th), a day's journey, state, situation, condition, staying overnight,

vaśā f. cow, female elephant, a ewe, a barren woman, any woman or wife, a daughter,

vāsabhūmi f. dwelling-place, homestead,

vaśakara mfn subjugating, winning,

vaśakāraka mfn leading to subjection,

vasana 932 n. clothes, dress, garments, dwelling, abiding, residing in, investment, siege, a leaf of the cinnamon tree, an ornament worn around the loins by women,

vāsanā 947/3 f. thinking of, longing for, desire , the impression of anything remaining unconsciously in the mind, the present consciousness of past perceptions, latent tendencies, idea, imagination, liking, respectful regard, trust, confidence,
(in math.) proof or demonstration

vāsanākṣya annihilation of subtle desires,

vāsanārahita devoid of subtle desires,

vāsanātyāga renunciation of subtle desires,

vaśanī mfn bringing into one's power, performing the will of another, subject, vessel of, m. controller,

vasanta m. spring,

vāsara mfn (Vedic)of the dawn, (Classic) time of dawn, day in general, m. time, turn, succession,

vāsas n. garment, clothing, the feathers of an arrow, cotton, a pall, a screen, a cobweb, lodging for the night,

vasati he lives, dwells,

vasati f. a dwelling, home, residence, mfn dwelling, abiding, fixing one's residence,

vāsava m. a name of Indra as chief of the Vāsus, Indra's energy, the east,

vāsaveśman n. chamber for spending the night, sleeping room,

vaśī 929/31. in *urvaśī* 'widely extending' 2. in comp. for 1. *vaśa* having mastery, a ruler, controller, a sage with subdued passions

vaśīkara mfn making anyone subject to one's will, bringing into subjection, subjugating, control,

vaśī-kṛ make submissive, enthral, ensnare,

vaśin mfn having will or power, having authority, a ruler, lord ('over' 6th), compliant, obedient, master of one's self, having the mastery of one's passions, void, empty, m. a ruler, a sage with subdued passions,

vāsin mfn dwelling, dweller, staying, abiding, dwelling, living, inhabiting, having or wearing clothes, fragrant, ifc. clothed or dressed in, living in or among in a partic. manner or condition,

vasiṣṭha mfn most excellent, best, m. a famous sage who wrote the Supreme Yoga , 'the most wealthy', n. flesh,

vaśitā f. subjugation, dominion, the power of subduing all to one's will, subduing by magical means, fascinating, bewitching,

vāsita 947/2/3 mfn.infused, steeped, perfumed, scented,affected with, influenced by, spiced, seasoned (as sauces), caused to dwell or live in, peopled, populous (as a country), n. the art of rendering populous, knowledge (esp. derived from memory = *vāsanā*),

vaśitva n. freedom of will, being one's own master, power or dominion over(7th), power of subduing to one's own will, mastery of one's self, self-command, fascinating, bewitching,

√vaṣk 933/1 Cl 1 A *vaṣkate* to go, DP in *darṣaṇa* seeing, (Cl 10) in *gati* going,

vāśra mfn lowing of cattle, m. a day, a mother, n. a place where four roads meet, dung,

vāstava 948/3 substantial, real, genuine, true, fixed, determined, demonstrated, n. an appointment,

vāstavya mfn belonging to an abode, an inhabitant, left on any spot (as a worthless remainder),

vāstoṣ-pati m. lord of the dwelling, 'house-protector', the name of a deity who presides over the foundation of a house or homestead,

vastṛ mfn shining, illumining, clothing, covering, putting on (clothes), m. illuminer, mfn lighting up,

vastra n. clothing, garment, cloth, a cinnamon tree leaf,

vastrānta m. the hem/ border of a garment,

vastraveṣṭita mfn covered with clothes, well clad,

vastu 932/3 f. becoming light, dawning, morning, n. the seat or place of anything, any really existing or abiding substance or essence, thing, object, article, (in phil.) the "real", the real as opposed to that which does not really exist, the right thing a valuable or worthy object, goods, wealth, property, the thing in question, matter, affair, circumstance, subject, subject-matter, contents, theme, plot, a kind of musical composition, natural disposition, essential property, the pith or substance of anything,

vāstu m.n. dwelling, the site or foundation of a house, site, ground, building, house, an apartment, chamber, a kind of grain,

vastutā f. ifc. the state of being the object of,

vastutas ind. in fact, really, actually, indeed, essentially, owing to the nature of things,

vastvābhāsa 'appears to be an object' (N)

vastvabhāva m. absence of reality, unsubstantial essence, loss or destruction of property,

vasu 930/3 mfn excellent, good, beneficent, sweet, dry, n. goods, wealth, m. 1. good (of gods), name of the gods (as the 'good or bright ones'), 2. m.pl. the good ones the Vasus, a class of gods closely associated with Indra,

Vāsudevānanda

Vasudeva was the father of *Kṛṣṇa* so another name for *Kṛṣṇa* is *Vāsudeva* which indicates the relationship by the addition of a measure of the letter *a*. Therefore *vāsudevānanda* can mean the bliss of *Kṛṣṇa* which could be another way of saying the bliss of the Absolute. Other meanings may also be derived.

vasu-dhā mfn yielding good, liberal, f. the earth, the land, a country, soil

vasu-dhādhipa m. king, prince 'lord of the earth',

Vāsuki king of serpents,

vasuṁdhara mfn or (*ā*) f. holding goods or treasures (the earth), a country,

vasusampatti f. accession or acquisition of wealth,

vasusampūrṇa mfn treasure-filled, filled with wealth,

vasuśravas mfn having good fame, famous for weath,

vasūya f. desire for good, longing, Nom. P °*yati* to desire weath,

vaśya 929/3 mfn. to be subjected, subdued, obedient to another's will, dutiful, humble, at the disposal of, m. a slave, a dependent, f.n. the (magical) power of or the act of subjecting to one's will, m. cloves, M. mfn being under one's control, submissive, obedient,

vaśyatā f. obedience, humility, being under the control of or fit for being under the control of,

√*vaṭ* 914/3 Cl 1 P *vaṭati* to surround, encompass, Cl 10 P to tie, string, connect, divide, partition, to speak, DP in *veṣṭana* surrounding, *grantha*

stringing, *paribhāṣaṇa* speaking, *vibhājana* distributing,
2. ind. an exclamation used in sacrificial ceremonies,

√vāt 939/3 Cl 10 P *vātayati* to fan, to serve, make happy, to go, DP in *gati* going, *sukha* making happy, *sevana* serving,

-vat a suffix – like, as

vaṭa m. a kind of fig tree, the Banyan tree, a kind of bird, cowry shell, a chess pawn, sulphur,

vāṭa mfn made from the Banyan tree or its wood, m. an enclosure, garden, park, plantation, a district, road, house-site, the groin,

vāta 934/2 mfn blown, the wind, solicited, wished for, desired, injured, hurt, dried up,
m. wind, air, god of the wind, body-wind,flatulence, gout, rheumatism,

vātaikabhaṣa mfn having wind alone as food, i.e. fasting,

vataṁsa m. a ring-shaped ornament, a garland, crest,

vātasvanas mfn having the roar of the wind, i.e. blustering, tumultuous,

vātāyana mfn moving in the air or wind,
m.'fleet as the wind' a horse,
n. 'wind passage' a window, air-hole, loop-hole,
a balcony, roof-terrace,

√vaṭh 915/1 Cl 1 P *vaṭhati* to be big or fat, DP in *sthaulya* being strong or powerful or fat,

vaṭhara mfn stupid, dull, a fool,
m. a physician, a water-pot,

vatsa m. young, young of a cow, calf, yearling, a son, boy, a year,

vatsala mfn tender, kind, child-loving,
m. the tender sentiment in a poem, a fire fed with grass (quickly burning away',

vātsalya n. affection or tenderness (esp. toward offspring), fondness or love for (6th,7th or comp.)

vatsara a year, the year personified, the 5th year in a cycle of 5 or 6,

vāva 947/1 ind. a particle laying stress on the word preceding it, esp. in relative clauses, just, indeed, even,

vavri m. place of hiding or refuge, body

√vāvṛt 947/1 Cl 4 A *vāvṛtyate* to choose, select, DP in *varaṇa* choosing, selecting,

√vay 920/2 Cl 1 A *vayate* to go, DP in *gati,* going,

vayā f. strengthening, vigour, strength, a branch, twig,

vayam we pron. 1/pl

vayas n. a bird, any winged animal, bird (collective),
2. food, meal, (enjoyment),
3. strength –of body and of mind, energy, health, the time of strength – youth, marriageable age, any age or period of life, years (of life), any age, aged, old, degree, kind,

vāyasa m. a bird esp. crow, turpentine, a house facing north-east,
mfn relating or peculiar to crows, consisting of birds,
n. a multitude of crows,

vayasya m. friend, a contemporary, associate, companion,
mfn being of an age or of the same age, contemporary

vayogata mfn. advanced in years, old,
n. advanced age,

vayogate ind. 'when youth is passed'

vayohāni 921/1 loss of youth or vigour, growing old

vāyos of the wind 6/s/m

vāyu 942/2 m. air, wind, the element air, has the property – touch,
the god of the wind, breathing, breath, a vital force or energy,

vayuna 920/3 mfn. moving, active, alive, agitated (the sea), restless, clear (as an eye), a path, way, means, expedient, rule, order, custom, according to rule (3rd), distinctness, clearness, knowledge, wisdom, brightness, a mark, aim,
f. (*ā*) a mark, aim, knowledge, wisdom,

vayunā-vid mfn learned in rules, well-versed in ordinances,
vāyuputra son of the wind - *hanuman*
√*ve* 1013/2 Cl 1 P A *vayati (te)* to weave, interweave, braid, plait, string or join together, make, compose, to make into a cover, or web, overspread as with a web, DP in *tantu-santāna* weaving,
vāyutattva the principle of air,
veda 1015/1 1. m. knowledge, true or sacred knowledge or lore, knowledge of ritual, name of 4 celebrated works - *ṛgveda, yajurveda, sāmaveda* and *atharvaveda.* The concluding portions of each (*vedanta* – end of the *vedas*) are the *upaniṣad*s, feeling, perception,
property, goods, a broom,
veda he knows 1/s/perf/act √*vid*
veda meditates on
veda tuft of strong grass tied to form a broom,
vedabāhya mfn being outside of the Veda, differing from or conflicting with the Veda,not founded on i.e. contrary to the *veda,*
m. an unbeliever, skeptic,
vedādhyayana n. vedic study, scripture reading, the repetition or recitation of the Veda, 1016/2
vedana mfn announcing, proclaiming,
n. perception, knowledge, making known, proclaiming,
feeling, sensation, the act of finding or falling in with, the act of marrying, property, goods,
f. (*ā*) pain, torture, agony,
vedanaśakti power of cognition or sensation,
vedanaskandha bodily sensations, the aggregate of feeling/sensation, (Buddhist),
vedāṅga support (limb) of the Veda in six sciences – pronunciation, metre and singing of verses (poetry), grammar, meaning of words, astronomy and planetary influence, sacrifices and ritual
vedānta 1017 m. end of the *veda* – see above. One of the great branches of Indian Philosophy, (called *Vedānta* either as teaching the ultimate scope of the *veda* or simply as explained in the *upaniṣads* – its chief doctrine is that of *advaita* i.e. that nothing exists in reality but the One Self or Soul of the Universe called *Brahman* or *Paramātman* and that the *jīvātman* or individual human soul and indeed all the phenomena of nature are really identical with the *paramātman.....*
m.pl. the Upanishads or works on the *vedānta* philosophy
vedāntaniścaya (N) 'the fixed theories of the Vedānta',
vedanindaka m. one who scoffs at the Veda, infidel, unbeliever, Buddhist etc.
vedāntin 1017/2 follower of the *vedānta* philosophy
vedapāraga 1015/3 m. 'one who has gone to the further end of the Veda', a Brāhman skilled in the Veda,
vedapuṇya n. merit from Veda study
vedas n. knowledge, property, wealth, science,
vedatraya n. the 3 Vedas,
vedavid 1016/1 mfn. knowing the Veda, conversant with it
vedayajña m. sacrifice for the divine, a Vedic sacrifice,
veditavyaḥ is to be known, fut.pass.part. √*vid* cl.2
veddhavya mfn to be penetrated (by the mind), to be pierced or hit (a mark)
vedhas mfn worshipper of the gods, worshipping, pious, devoted, (generalised) faithful, true, (used of Indra),
m. a worshipper of the gods, creator (Brahmā and others), an arranger, disposer, creator,
vedi m. a wise man, teacher, Pandit,

f. knowledge, science, a seal ring, sacrificial bed, serving as a kind of altar, a covered verandah or balcony in a courtyard, a stand, basis, pedestal, bench, in comp. for *vedin,*

vedī f. altar,

vedikā f. raised seat, stage, balcony, pavillion, sacrificial ground, altar, m. seat, bench,

vedin mfn knowing,

vedi-purīṣa n. loose earth of the *vedi,*

veditum to know (infin. √*vid)*

vedya n. the to-be-known, an object of knowledge, recognized or understood, to be acquired, notorious, celebrated, that which is learnt, 1/s/n gerundive √*vid*

vedyatva n. knowableness, intelligibility,

vega 1013/3 m. rush, dash, speed, haste, agitation, shock, jerk, impetus, momentum, vehemence, the flight of an arrow, outbreak, outburst of passion, expulsion of feces, semen,

vegena ind. quickly,

√*veh* 1019/3 Cl 1 A *vehate* to strive, make effort, Cl 1 P *vehati* = *vehāya*, DP in *prayatna* endeavouring,

√*vel* 1. 1018/2 Cl 1 P *velati* to move shake, DP in *calana* moving, playing
2. Cl 10 P *velayati to* count or declare the time, DP in *kāla-upadeśa* counting the time,

velā f. end-point, limit, esp. limit of time, point of time, hour, sea-shore, the last hour, hour of death, easy or painless death, tide, flow (opp. to ebb), stream, current, the gums, speech,

√*velāya* Nom. from *velā* DP in *vilāsa* playing,

√*vell* 1018/3 Cl 1 P *vellati*, to shake about, tremble, sway, be tossed or agitated, caus. *vellayati* cause to shake, to knead dough, DP in *calana* trembling, playing, sporting,

√*veṇ* 1014/1 to go, move, know, think, discern, to play on an instrument, to hold or take, DP in *gati* going, *jñāna* knowing, *cintā* reflecting, *niśāmana* perceiving, *vāditra* playing an instrument, *grahaṇa* taking,

√*ven* 1018/2 Cl 1 P *venati* to care or long for, be anxious, yearn for, to tend outwards (said of the vital air), to be homesick, envious or jealous, DP in *gati* going, *jñāna* knowing, *cintā* reflecting, *niśāmana* perceiving, *vāditra* playing an instrument, *grahaṇa* taking,

veṇi f. weaving, braiding, a braid of hair, braided stream (*veṇī*), cascade

veṇu m. reed esp. bamboo reed, a flute,

vepamāna part. trembling,

vepas 1018, trembling, quivering

vepathu 1018/2 m. quivering, trembling

veśa m. settler, neighbour, dwelling, small, farmer, tenant, neighbour, house, dwelling, brothel, trade, business,

veṣa m. work, management, activity, dress, apparel, artificial exterior, assumed appearance, often for *veśa,* mfn working, active, busy,

veśman n. dwelling, house, chamber, an astrological house,

√*veṣṭ* 1019/2 cl 1 A *veṣṭate* to wind or twist round, to adhere or cling to, to cast the skin (of a snake), to dress, caus. *veṣṭayati (te),* to wrap up, envelop, enclose, surround, cover, invest, beset, to tie on, wrap round (a turban), cause to shrink up, DP in *veṣṭana* surrounding,

veṣṭana the act of surrounding or encompassing, or enclosing or encircling, surrounded, beset, anything that surrounds or wraps, headband, girdle, enclosure, wall,

vetāla m. vampire, goblin, ghost,

vetana n. wages, hire, salary, livelihood,

vetasa m. rod, stick, reed, cane, rattan or similar cane,

vettha you know 2/s/perf/act √*vid*

vetti root *vid* 1. to know, 1/s/pres/act he, she knows

vettṛ m. a knower, experiencer, witness,

√*vevī* 1019/1 cl 2 A *vevīte* to go, pervade, conceive, desire, throw, to eat, DP in *gati* going, *vyāpti* pervading, *prajana* bringing forth, *kānti,* being beautiful, *asana* throwing, *khādana* eating,

vi 1. m. a bird,
2. ind. an artificial word = *anna*
3. ind. in two parts, apart, asunder, in different directions, to and fro, about, away, away from, off, without,

may denote 'through' or 'between' as a preposition with 2nd case.

as a prefix to verbs, nouns and other parts of speech derived from verbs to express – division, distinction, distribution, arrangement, order, opposition or deliberation,

may express- outwards, in different directions, in all directions.

sometimes gives a meaning opposite to the idea contained in the simple root, or intensifies that idea,

in some cases does not seem to modify the meaning of the simple word at all,

may be used in forming compounds not immediately referable to verbs, in which cases it may express difference in terms of change or variety,

also used to form proper names out of other proper names,

√*vī* 1. 1004/1 cl 2 P *veti* to go, approach (as a friend {accept, enjoy}or enemy {attack, assail, punish}), to set in motion, arouse, excite, impel, to further, promote, lead, or bring or help anyone to, to get, procure, caus. *vāyayati* or *vāpayati* to cause to go or approach, to impregnate, DP in *gati* going, *vyāpti* pervading, *prajana* bringing forth, procreating, *kānti* being beautiful, *asana* throwing, *khādana* eating,
2. mfn. going to, eager for, desirous or fond of, set in motion, m. the act of going,
3. *(vi* √5. *i)* P. *vy-eti* to go apart or in different directions, diverge, be diffused or scattered, or distributed or divided or extended, to be lost, perish, disappear, A. *vīyate* to pass through, traverse,

vibaddha mfn bound or fastened, obstructed, constipated,

vi√*bādh* A. *–bādhate,* to press or drive asunder in different directions, drive or scare away, oppress, harass, injure,

vibādhā 977/1 f. pressure, pain, anguish

vibādhana expelling, removing,

vibala mfn having no strength, weak,

vi√*bandh* P.A. *–badhnāti, -badhnīte,* to bind or fasten on different sides, stretch out, extend, to seize or hold by,

vibandha m. encircling, encompassing, a circular bandage, obstruction, constipation,

vibandhu having no relations,

vi√*bhā* P. *–bhāti* to shine or gleam forth, come to light, become visible, appear, to shine upon, illumine, to kindle, to shine brightly, glitter, be resplendent or beautiful, strike or catch the eye, to strike the ear, be heard (as sound), to seem or appear as, look like, shines variously, 'shines surpassingly' (Gam.)
2. mfn shining, bright, f. light, lustre, splendour, beauty,

vibhāga 977/2 m. distribution, division, apportionment, partition of patrimony, law of inheritance, a share, portion, separation, distinction, difference, a part of anything,

vi√bhaj P.A. *–bhajati (te),* to divide, distribute, apportion,to separate, part, cut, to divide (aritmetically), to open (a box or chest),to worship, A. to share together or with each other,

vibhājana 977/3 n. division, distinction, the act of causing to share or distribute, participation

vibhakta 977/2 mfn. divided, distributed among, parted, one who has received his share, one who has caused partition, isolated, secluded, divided into regular parts, harmonious, symmetrical, decorated, n. seclusion, solitude,

vibhakti f. separation, partition, division, distinction, modification, (in gram.) inflection of nouns, declension, an affix of declension, case.

vibhaṅgi f. mere appearance or semblance,

vi√bhāṣ A. *-bhāṣate* to speak variously, speak against, abuse, revile, to admit an alternative, be optional,

vi√bhās A. *–bhāsate* to shine brightly or pleasantly, be bright, caus. –*bhāsayati* to cause to shine, illuminate, brighten,

vibhās f. brightness, splendour,

vibhāṣā 1. 951/3 a class of *prākṛt* languages
2. 978/1 f. an alternative, option, one of two ways,

vibhāṣita 978/1 mfn. admitting an alternative (esp. in gram. = optional)

vibhāskara mfn having no sun, without the sun,

vibhāt mfn shining, splendid

vibhavati reveals itself, see *vi√bhū*

vibhāta mfn shone forth, grown light (as in dawning), become visible, appeared, n. dawn, daybreak, morning,

vibhava 978/2 mfn powerful, rich, m. being everywhere, omnipresence, development, evolution, power, might, greatness, exalted position, dignity, majesty, dominion, wealth, money, luxury, magnanimity, lofty-mindedness, emancipation from existence, destruction of the world (Buddhist),

vibhāva 1. 977/3 brilliant, light
2. 978/3 m. any condition which excites or develops a particular state of mind or body, any cause of emotion e.g. persons and circumstances, *-tva* a friend or acquaintance,

vibhāvaka mfn causing to appear, procuring or intending to procure,

vibhāvan f. *–varī* mfn shining far and wide, brilliant, bright,

vibhāvana mfn causing to appear, developing, manifesting, n. examination, manifesting on, causing to appear or become visible, creation, development, showing, clear perception, judgment, reflection on, act of producing a particular emotion by a work of art, clear ascertainment,

vibhāvanā f. (in rhet.) description of effects the causes of which are to be conjectured, ‘description by negatives’,

vibhavin 978/3 mfn rich, wealthy,

vibhāvin 978/3 mfn inherent cause, mighty, powerful, arousing a particular emotion,
ifc. causing to appear,

vibhaya n. freedom from danger, mfn not exposed to danger,

vibheda m. breaking asunder, splitting, piercing, division, separation, knitting, interruption, disturbance, dissension, variety,

vibhedaka mfn distinguishing anything, splitting, cleaving,

vi√bhī P. *–bibheti,* to be afraid of, fear, caus. *-bhīṣayati (te),* to frighten, terrify, intimidate

vibhī mfn fearless,

vi√bhid P.A. *–bhinatti, -bhintte,* to split or break in two, divide, separate, to pierce, sting, loosen, untie, to

scatter, disperse, to alter, to change (the mind),
vibhīdaka m.n. a large tree, the nuts were used for dice, a die, dice,
vibhinna mfn split or broken in two, altered, changed, alienated, become faithless, separated, disunited,
vibhīṣaṇa brother of *rāvaṇa*
vibhīṣikā 978/1 f. frightening, terrifying, the act of terrifying, fear, an object of fear, frightened
vibhīta mfn afraid, intimidated,
vibhraṣṭa 979/2 mfn. sunk, fallen, disappeared, useless, vain, gone, lost, strayed from, deprived of
vi√bhṛ P.A. *–bharati (te),* to spread out, A. to distribute, diffuse, to bear, endure,
vi√bhrāj A. *–bhrājate*, to shine forth, be bright or radiant,
vibhrāj mfn shining, splendid, luminous
vi√bhram P. *–bhramati –bhrāmyati,* to wander, roam or fly about, roll, hover, whirl, to fall into disorder or confusion, be bewildered, to drive away, to move the tail about,
vibhrama m. moving to and fro, rolling or whirling about, restlessness, unsteadiness, violence, excess, agitation, error, feminine coquetry, amorous getures or action of any kind (esp. play of the eyes, illusion, illusive apearance or mere semblance of anything, caprice, whim,
vi√bhraṁś A. *-bhraṁśate* to fall off, fail, be unsuccessful, be unfortunate, to be separated from, desert,
vibhraṣṭa mfn fallen, sunk, disappeared, gone, lost, useless, vain,
vibhrāṣṭi f. radiance, flame, blaze,
vibhreṣa m. commission of an offence, transgression,
vibhṛta mfn spread out, distributed, upheld, supported, maintained,
vibhru a prince, king
vi√bhū P. *–bhavati* to arise, be developed or manifested, expand, appear, to suffice, be adequate or equal to or a match for, to pervade, fill, to be able to or capable of, to exist (in *avibhavat* not existing), caus.°*bhāvayati* to cause to arise or appear, develop, manifest, reveal, to pretend, feign, to divide, separate, to perceive distinctly, find out, discover, know, recognise as, to regard or consider as, to suppose, fancy, imagine, to think, reflect, to make clear, establish,
vibhu or *vibhū* 978/3, being everywhere, far-extending, all-pervading, omnipresent, eternal, abundant, plentiful, a Lord, ruler, sovereign, king - *vibho* voc. sing - Oh, all pervading One
vibhudravya omnipresent substance,
vibhugna mfn bent, bowed, crooked
vibhūta mfn arisen, produced, great, mighty,
vibhūti 978/3 mfn. penetrating, pervading, plentiful, powerful, f. expansion, development, multiplication, manifestation of might, superhuman powers, 'manifestation; divine glory and manifestation of divine power; pervasion; the special forms in which the Lord exhibits Himself (U)'
vibhūtimat mfn powerful, splendid,

vibhūṣ P. *-bhūṣati* to be brilliant, to adorn, decorate,
vibhūṣaṇa mfn adorning, n. f. (*ā*) decoration, ornament, splendour, beauty,
vibhūti 978/3 mfn. penetrating, pervading, mighty, manifestation of superhuman power
vibhūtimat mfn powerful, splendid, smeared with ashes, superhuman,
vibhvan mfn far-reaching, penetrating, pervading; skilful, m. an artificer
vibodha 1. 951/3 m. inattention, absence of mind,
2. 977/1 m. awaking, perception, intelligence,

vi√brū P.A. *–bravīti –brūte,* to speak out, express one's self, state, declare, explain, propound, teach, to interpret, decide (a law), to make a false statement,

vibubūṣā f. the wish or intention to manifest one's self

vibuddha 1. 951/3 without consciousness, 2. 977/1 mfn awakened, wide awake, clever, experienced,

vibuddhi 1. mfn without consciousness 2. mfn unreasonable,

vi√budh A. *–budhyate,* to awake, be awake or awakened, to become conscious or aware of, perceive, learn, know, caus. *vibodhayati* to awaken, to restore to consciousness,

vibudha 1. destitute of learned men, 2. mfn very wise or learned, m. a wise or learned man, teacher, a god

vibudhānucara m. attendant of a god,

vibudheśvara m. a lord of the gods,

√vic 958/1 cl 7 P A *vinakti, vinkte*, to sift, separate (winnow), to separate from deprive of, to discriminate, discern, judge, DP in *pṛthag-bhāva* separating, discriminating,

vicacakṣire 1/pl/perf *vi-√cakṣ* they explained

vicakra mfn wheelless, having no discus,

vi√cakṣ A. *vicaṣte* to appear, shine, to see distinctly, view, look at, perceive, regard, to make manifest, show, to proclaim, announce, tell, caus. *vicakṣayati* to cause to see distinctly, make clear, proclaim, tell,

vicakṣaṇa 958/2 mfn. conspicuous, visible, bright, radiant, clear-sighted, wise, 'adept, omniscient' (Gam.),

vicakṣus mfn eyeless, blind,

vi√cal 958/3 P. *vicalati* to move about, shake, waver, to move away, depart or swerve or deviate or desist from, to fall off or down, to go astray,

vicālayet he should cause to waver 1/s/caus/act/opt *vi√cal*

vicalita mfn gone away, departed, deviated from, troubled,

vicālyate he is shaken or moved 1/s/pres/indic/caus/pass

vicandra mfn moonless (as a night)

vi√car P. *vicarati* to move in different directions, spread, extend, be diffused, to ramble about or through, traverse, pervade, make an attack or assault, to wander from the right path, to run out, come to an end, to act, proceed, practise, perform, make, do, caus. *vicārayati* to cause to roam about, to cause to go astray, to move hither and thither (in the mind), ponder, reflect, examine, investigate, ascertain,

vicara mfn wandered or swerved from,

vicāra 958/2 m. consideration, reflection, discrimination, mode of acting or proceeding, investigation, inquiry, examination, self-inquiry, hesitation, deliberation, discrimination between the real and the unreal, enquiry into the Self,

vicaraṇa mfn footless, n. wandering, motion,

vicāraṇa n. also f. (*ā*) consideration, reflection, discussion, doubt, hesitation, changing a place,

vicāraśakti power of inquiry,

vicārita 958/3 mfn deliberated, considered, examined, discussed, judged, n. anything under discussion, dubious, doubtful, uncertain, ascertained, settled,

vicaya m. search, investigation, examination, gathering or putting together, arrangement,

vicchad caus. (√1. *chad*) *vicchādayati* to uncover, unclothe, 2. caus. *vichandayati* to render or return homage,

vicchanda consisting of various metres

vicchāya mfn without shadow, lacking colour or lustre or distinction, pale, m. a jewel, gem,

viccheda m. separation, cutting asunder, cleaving, piercing, breaking, division, interruption, cessation, end, removal, destruction, distinction, difference, division of a book, section, chapter, space, interval, ifc. injury to,

vi-cchid (*√chid)* P. *vichinatti vichintte,* to cut or tear or cleave, cut off, divide, separate, to interrupt,

vicchinna mfn cut or torn or split or cleft, interrupted, disconnected, incoherent, ended, ceased, no longer existing, crooked, anointed

vicchinnāvasthā hidden state of *vāsanās* (latent tendencies)

vi√ceṣṭ 959/2 P.A. *viceṣṭati (te*), to move the limbs about, writhe, struggle, exert oneself, be active or busy, act or proceed against, deal with, caus. *viceṣṭayati* to set in motion, rouse to action,

viceṣṭa mfn motionless,

viceṣṭā f. motion, acting, proceeding, conduct, behaviour, effort,

vicetana 1. mfn senseless, unconscious, absent-minded, inanimate, dead, foolish, stupid, 2.mfn. visible, clearly seen, discerning, wise,

vicetas 1. mfn unintelligible, absent-minded, confounded, perplexed, 2. mfn. visible, clearly seen, discerning, wise

√vich 959/3 cl 10 P *vicchayati* to speak or to shine, to go, caus. *vicchāyayati* to press, bring into straits, DP in *bhāṣā* (cl 10) speaking, in *gati* (cl 6) going,

vi√ci 1. P.A. *vicinoti, vicinute*, to segregate, select, pick out, cull, to divide, part hair, to take away, remove, disperse, to clear, 2. to discern, distinguish, to make anything discernible or clear, cause to appear, illumine, to search through, investigate, examine, to look for, long for, strive after,

vīci 1004/3 f. going or leading aside or astray, aberration, deceit, seduction, m. a wave, ripple

vicikitsā 959/1 f. doubt, uncertainty, question, inquiry *vi √4. cit*

vi√cint P.A.1 *–cintayati, te,* to perceive, discern, observe, reflect upon, ponder, consider, find out, devise, fancy, imagine,

vi √4. cit P.A. *vicetati (te),* to perceive, discern, understand, A. to be or become visible, appear, caus. *vicitayati* to perceive, distinguish, Desid. *vicikitsati* to wish to distinguish, to reflect, consider, doubt, be uncertain, hesitate,

vicitra mfn very variegated, 2. differently coloured, varied, 3. (full of variety and surprises) entertaining, beautiful,

vicitta 950/2 mfn unconscious, not knowing what to do, helpless, f. (*ā*) helplessness, unconsciousness,

vicitti f. perturbation,

vi√cumb P. to kiss, kiss eagerly, *vicumbati*

√viḍ 1. cl 1 P. *veḍati* to call, cry out, 2. f. a bit, fragment, in comp. for 3. *viṣ*

√vid 1. cl.2 P *vetti, vedati (te), vidati (te), vindati (te),* to know, understand, learn, perceive, be conscious of, *viddhi yathā* know that, *vidyāt* one should know, to know or regard or consider as, take for, declare to be, to mind, notice, observe, remember, to experience, feel, to wish to know, inquire about, caus. *vedayate (ti)* to make known, announce, report, tell, to teach, explain, DP (cl 2) in *jñāna* knowing, (cl 10) in *cetanā* feeling, experience, *ākhyāna* telling, declaring, *nivāsa* dwelling

vid 2. 963/3 mfn. knowing, understanding, a knower (mostly ifc.), planet Mercury, f. knowledge, understanding

√vid 3. cl 6 P A *vindati (te), vitte, vide,* to find, discover, meet or fall in with, obtain, get, acquire, partake of, possess, to get or procure for, to seek out, look for, attend to, to feel, experience, to consider as take for, to come upon, befall, seize, visit, to contrive, accomplish, perform, effect, produce, to take to wife, find (a husband), to be found, exist, be , caus. *vedayati* to cause to find etc. DP (cl 4) in *sattā* being, existing, (cl 6) in *lābha* getting, obtaining,

vid 4. ifc. finding, acquiring, procuring

√vid 5. 965/2 cl 7 A *vintte* to consider as, take for, DP in *vicāraṇa* considering, regarding,

-vid ifc. knowing, learned in,

vida mfn. ifc. knowing, knowledge, discovery, m. knowledge, discovery,

vi√dā 1. P. *vidadāti* to give out, distribute, grant,
3. *vidāti,* or *vidyati* to cut up, cut to pieces, to untie, release, destroy,

vidagdha 1. mfn undigested, 2. mfn burnt up, consumed, digested, decomposed, spoiled, turned sour, clever, shrewd, knowing, m. a clever man, a scholar,

vidagdha śākalya a clever man, scholar,

vi√dah P. *vidahati to* burn up, scorch, consume or destroy by fire, to cauterize a wound, to decompose, corrupt, to burn, be inflamed, to suffer from internal heat, to be consumed by grief, waste, pine, to be puffed up, boast,

vidāhin 965/3 mfn burning, scorching, hot, pungent, acrid,

vidalati breaks or bursts asunder,

vi√ḍamb A. *viḍambate* to imitate, vie with, P. *viḍambayati* to imitate, copy, emulate, equal, be a match for anyone or anything, to mock, deride, to impose upon, take in, cheat,

viḍamba mfn imitating, representing, m. mockery, derision, distressing, annoyance, degradation, desecration,

viḍambita mfn imitated, copied, disguised, transformed, distorted, vexed, mortified, low, poor, abject, disappointed, frustrated, deceived, n. an object of ridicule or contempt, despicable object,

vidanta toothless, deprived of tusks,

vidāra 966/1 m. tearing or rending asunder, cutting, splitting, war, battle, an inundation, overflow,

vidāraṇa 966/2 mfn tearing or rending asunder, breaking, splitting, n. the act of tearing asunder, hewing down, opening wide (the mouth)

vidarbha m. 'without *darbha* grass" the name of a country now the 'Hyderabad assigned Districts', probably arid and dry this was the country of Damayantī who became the wife of Nala,
m. pl. the inhabitants of Vidarbha,

vidarbhanagarī city/capital of Vidarbha

vidarbhapati m. lord or king of Vidarbha,

vidarbharājan m. king of Vidarbha,

vidarśanā f. right knowledge

vidārya ind. having cleft or torn asunder

vi√dāś P. *vidāśati* to reject, deny,

vidaśati 1/s/pres bites to pieces,

vidāsin mfn becoming exhausted, drying up

vidasta mfn wasted away, exhausted,

vidasyati or *vidasati* wastes away, become exhausted, comes to an end,

vidatha 963/3 n. knowledge, wisdom, (esp. knowledge given to others, i.e. instruction, direction, order, a meeting, assembly, congregation, a host, army, body of warriors, war, fight, a sage, scholar,

vidatra mfn (in cpds.) noticing,

vidatta mfn distributed, given out,

viḍāyate flys out,

vidayate 1/s/pres. divides, severs, destroys,

viddhi 963/2 from root *vid* to know, understand, perceive, learn, be

conscious of – 2/s/impv/act. know!
viddhi yathā know that,
ātmānam viddhi know thyself,
f. perforating, piercing,

viddhi sutrāṇi state the rules of grammar in Pāṇini's grammar

videha mfn bodiless, incorporeal, deceased, dead, *Videhā* – the capital city of *Videha* (*Mithilā)*

videhakaivalya liberation from the body and limited self-existence while still in the body, liberation after leaving the body,

videhamukti liberation at the time of death,

videśa mfn foreign, m. another country, foreign country,
abroad, °*ga* going abroad,

videva godless, hostile to gods (as demons), performed without gods (a sacrifice),

√vidh 967/2 cl6 P *vidhati* to worship, honour a god, ,dedicate, to present reverentially, offer, to be gracious or kind, befriend (said of Indra), DP in *vidhāna* according to rule or precept, *vidhema* we offer

vidh ifc. boring through, wounding, piercing, penetrating,

vidha m. piercing, perforating, measure, form, kind, food for an elephant,

vi√dhā 967/2 P.A. *–dadhāti, -dhatte*, to distribute, apportion, grant, bestow, (with *kāmam* to fulfil a wish), to furnish, supply, procure, (with *ātmanaḥ* 'for one's self'), to spread, diffuse, to put in order, arrange, dispose, prepare, make ready, to divide, parcel out, to ordain, enjoin, direct, fix, settle, to form, create, build, establish, found, to perform, effect, produce, cause, make, do, pass. *–dhīyate* to be distributed, to be allotted or intended for, caus. – *dhāpayati* to cause to put, cause to be laid, cause to put in order, fix or arrange,

vidhā f. division, part, portion, kind, sort,

vidhāna mfn disposing, arranging, regulating, acting, performing, possessing, n. order, measure, disposition, arrangement, regulation, rule, precept, method, manner, , setting up, creating, performance, fate, destiny, making, doing, accomplishing, (in gram. affixing, prefixing, taking as an affix), an elephant's food,
-tas ind. according to rule or precept

vi√dham P. or *vi√dhmā* P. *vidhamati (te*), to blow away, scatter, disperse, n. the act of blowing away,

vidhamana mfn blowing out, extinguishing, blowing away, destroying,

vidhana mfn devoid of wealth, poor,

vidhāna 967/3 mfn disposing, arranging, regulating, acting, performing, possessing, prescription, precept, disposing, n. order, measure, regulation, rule

vidharaṇa 968/3 mfn checking, restraining, *(ī)* f. maintaining, supporting,

vidhārayitavya mfn to be (or being supported or maintained),

vidharma wrong, unjust, unlawful, m. wrong, injustice, *-tas* ind. wrongly, unlawfully,

vidharman mfn acting wrongly or unlawfully, m. a maintainer, arranger, disposer, n. that which encircles or surrounds, receptacle, boundaries, circumference, disposition, arrangement, order, rule,

vidharmin mfn transgressing the law (as speech), of a different kind,

vidhartṛ m. a distributor, arranger, supporter, *√dhṛ*

vidhātavya gve. to be shown, to be fixed or settled, to be got or procured, to be performed, to be striven after or cared for, n. (with *yathā*) 'care must be taken that', to be used or employed or appointed,

vidhātṛ mfn distributing, arranging, m. creator, maker, author, a granter, giver, disposer, fate or destiny personified,

vi√dhāv 1. P. *vidhāvati* to run or flow off, trickle through, flow away, disappear, be scattered or dispersed, 2. to wash off,

vidhavā f. widow, a country without a king,

vidhāvana n. running hither and thither

vi-dheya 968/2 mfn to be bestowed or procured, to be enjoined, governed or controlled, docile, compliant, subject or obedient to work. to be drawn (a line), to be kindled (fire), to be exhibited or displayed or betrayed,

vidhi 967/2 1. m. a worshipper, one who does homage

vidhi 2. 968/1 m. a rule, formula, law, rules of behaviour, a grammatical rule or precept, use, employment, application, a prescribed rite or action, method, way of acting, mode of life, conduct, behaviour, a means, any act or action, performance, work, business, creation, fate, destiny, the creator,

vidhi L. m.1. a disposition, ordering, ordinance, prescription, rule, method, 2. (method i.e.) way, procedure, 3. destiny, fate,

vi√dhī 1. to be uncertain, hesitate,

vidhipūrvaka in accordance with scriptural injunctions (U),

vidhidṛṣṭa 968/1 mfn. prescribed by rule

vidhihīna 968/1 mfn destitute of rule, unauthorised, opposed to what is enjoined, contrary to injunction

vidhivākya 'divine rules', G343 injunctive sentences containing the essence and purport of the Veda (according to Mīmāṃṣā)

vidhivat ind. according to rule, duly,

vidhīyate it is granted, it is given 1/s/pres/indic/pass *vi√dhā*

vi√dhṛ P.A. *vidharati* to hold, bear, carry, keep apart, divide, distribute, arrange, manage, to keep off, withhold from, seize, hold fast, check, restrain, support, maintain, (with *manas)* to keep the mind fixed upon, to preserve, take care of,

vi√dhṛṣ caus. *vidharṣayati* to violate, spoil, injure, annoy, trouble,

vidhṛta mfn kept apart, divided, separated, kept off, avoided, stopped, checked, restrained, held, borne,

vidhu mfn lonely, solitary, m. the moon, miserable, helpless, palpitation, throbbing (of the heart),

vi√dhū P.A. *vidhūnoti, °nute*, to shake about, agitate, to kindle (fire), to shake off, A. to shake off from oneself, relinquish, abandon,

vidhūma smokeless, not smoking (fire),

vidhūmra quite grey

vi√dhūp P. *vidhūpāyati* to emit vapour, smoke,

vidhura mfn alone, bereft, suffering, lack, miserable, wanting, disagreeable, m. a widower, n. trouble, adversity,

vidhura-darśana n. sight of adversity

vidhūya having shaken off or driven away, *√dhū*

vidhūnana mfn causing to move to and fro, n. shaking, agitation, waving, undulation, repugnance, revulsion,

vi√dhvaṁs or *dhvas* A. *vidhvaṁsate (ti),* to fall to pieces, crumble into dust or powder, be scattered or dispersed or destroyed, caus. *vidhvaṁsayati* to cause to fall to pieces or crumble, crush, destroy, annihilate,

vidhvaṁsa m. ruin, destruction, hurt, injury, cessation (of a disease), violation (of a woman), insult, offence,

vi√dīp 965/3 A. *vi-adīpanta* to shine forth, shine very brightly, caus. *vidīpayati* to shine upon, illuminate

vidīpta mfn shining, bright

vidita 963/3 mfn. known, understood, perceived, learnt, knowing, promised, agreed, represented, apprised, informed, m. knower, a learned man, sage,

n. information, representation,

viditvā knowing, having known,

vi√div 2. 965/3 P.A. *vidivyati (te),* to lose at play, to play

vidman n. knowledge, intelligence, wisdom,

vidmanāpas mfn working carefully or skilfully,

vidmas we know, 1/pl/perf/act √*vid*

vi √dṝ P *vidṛṇāti* to tear asunder, cleave, split open, to be torn with grief,

vidrava m. running away, flight, panic, melting, liquefaction, censure, reproach, intellect, understanding,

vidrāva m. flight, retreat, liquefaction,

vidraṣṭṛ mfn seeing clearly or distinctly,

vidṛ 950/3 1.mfn. eyeless, blind

vi√dṛś 2. 966/1 A. pass. *vidṛśyate* to be clearly visible, become apparent, appear, caus. *vidarśayati* to cause to see, show, to teach,

vidṛti f. cleft, split open, the cleft one, a suture in the skull,

vi√dru p. *vidravati* to run apart, or in different directions, disperse, run away, escape, to become divided, burst, caus. *–drāvayati* to cause to disperse, put to flight,

vidruma 1 treeless, 2. m. a young sprout or shoot, coral,

vi√du 2. P. *vidunoti* to consume or destroy by burning, A. *vidunute* , *vidūyate*, to be agitated or distressed, or afflicted,

vidu mfn intelligent, wise,
m. the hollow between the frontal globes of an elephant,

vi√duh P. *vidogdhi* to milk out, drain, exploit,

vidūna mfn distressed, afflicted,

vidura mfn knowing, wise, intelligent, skilled in (comp.), an intriguer,
m. a learned or clever man,

vidūra mfn very remote or distant, far removed from, not attainable by (6th), not caring for (ifc.),

vi√duṣ P. *viduṣyati* to be defiled, commit a fault or sin, transgress, caus. *vidūṣayati* to defile, corrupt, disgrace, to deride, ridicule,

vidus(ḥ) 3/pl/perf 1. √*vid* 963/2 they knew or with present meaning, they know,

vidus mfn wise, attentive, heedful,

viduṣā f. very learned man, understanding, possibly – an apparently learned man,

vidūṣaka mfn witty, facetious, defiling,
m. a jester, clown,

viduṣkṛta mfn free from sins or faults or transgressions,

vidvajjana m. a wise man, 'knowing-man'

vidvān 'one who knows', the wise, the wise one, the illumined soul, √*vid*1
tvaṣṭā vidvān a cunning workman,

vidvas mfn one who knows, knowing, understanding, learned, intelligent, wise, mindful of, familiar with, skilled in (2nd, 7th, comp.), m. a wise man, sage, seer,

vidvatsannyāsa renunciation after the attainment of the knowledge of Brahman,

vidveṣa m. hatred, dislike, contempt, aversion to, proud indifference,

vi√dviṣ P. A. *vidveṣti, vidviṣte*, to dislike, hate, be hostile to (2nd), A. to hate each other, dislike one another, caus. *vidveṣayati* make hostile towards one another, *vidviṣāvahai* 3/du/mid/impv. may we two dislike

vidviṣ 2. mfn hating, hostile, an enemy to (mostly ifc.)

vidyā 963/3 f. scholarship, science, learning, philosophy, knowledge, 'The knowledge or *vidyā* belongs to the *ātman* and out of *vidyā* comes the world. having taken a form, it must perish and go back to *vidyā* again' HH
vidyā 'is implied as *adhyātmavidyā*, the knowledge of the Self,'

vidyādhara (ī) f. mfn keeping or possessed of knowledge or the magic art, m. a Vidyādhara, one of a class of genii who are attendants on Ṣiva and

reputed to be magicians, f. fairy, sylph,
vidyādhāra m. great scholar, receptacle of knowledge,
vidyāmada m. knowledge-intoxication, i.e. infatuated pride in one's learning,
vidya-santati continuity of spiritual knowledge through practise, the spreading of liberating truth, connection and succession, knowledge-continuance,
vidyāt may it be known, let it be known, it should be known, 1/s/opt/act √*vid*
vidyate 1/s/pres/indic/pass 2. √*vid* 963/2 it is known, understood, perceived, learned, is conscious of, has an understanding of, he is
vidyeta it should be understood, perceived, etc. 1/s/opt/pass √*vid* cl2
vidyāvayo-vṛddha mfn grown old in knowledge and years, distinguished for learning and age,
vidyopādana
vidyā 963/3 f. knowledge, science, learning, scholarship, philosophy,
upādana 213/2 n. the act of taking for oneself, appropriating to one's self, perceiving, noticing, learning, acquiring (knowledge), saying, speaking, abstraction, cause, motive, material cause,
vidyotayitavya mfn to be illustrated or illuminated, 'the object revealed' (Gam.),
vidyullatā f. a lightning flash, forked lightning, 'lightning-creeper',
vi√dyut 966/3 A. P. *vidyotate* to flash forth, lighten, shine forth (as the rising sun), to hurl away by a stroke of lightning, to illuminate, caus. °*dyotayati* to illuminate, irradiate, enlighten, make brilliant,
vidyut mfn. flashing, shining, glittering, f. lightning, a flashing thunderbolt, the dawn, L. also mfn lightening,
vidyutā lightning flashes,
vi√gā to go or pass away, disappear,
vigāḍha mfn plunged into, entered, begun, set in, set in place, flowing copiously, deep, excessive,
vigāman n. a step, pace, stride,
vigada mfn free from disease, healthy, well, m. confused shouting,
vi√gāh A. *vigāhate (ti),* to plunge or dive into, bathe in, enter, penetrate, pervade, to pierce, agitate, be engrossed or intent upon, ponder, to follow, practise, to reach, obtain, approach,
vi√gal 957/1 P. *vigalati* to flow or ooze away, drain off, dry up, melt or pass away, disappear, vanish
vigalita mfn drained off, dried up, melted away, dissolved, slackened, untied, dishevelled, passed away, disappeared, vanished,
vi√gam P. vigacchati to go asunder, sever, separate, to go away, depart, disappear, die,
vi√gaṇ P. *vigaṇayati* to reckon, compute, calculate, to deliberate, consider,
vi√garh A. *vigarhate (ti),* to blame, abuse, revile, reproach, despise,
vi√garj P. *vigarjati* to roar out, cry out
vigarjā the roaring/thundering of the ocean
vigata 949/3 the flight of birds
956/3 disappeared, ceased, gone, free from, devoid of
vigatasaṁkalpa mfn aimless, purposeless, 'whose purpose has gone away'
vigataspṛha mfn gone away desire, whose desire has gone away,
vi√ghaṭ A. *vighaṭate* to go or fly apart, become separate, disperse, to be broken,
vighāta m. a stroke, breaking off , warding off, driving back, ruin,
vighaṭana mfn warding off, averting, n. breaking up, separation, dispersion, destruction,
vi√ghaṭṭ A. *vighaṭṭate* to smash or break to pieces, P. *vighaṭṭayati* to strike or force asunder, open a door, sever,
vighna n. an obstacle, impediment,

hindrance, interuption, any difficulty or trouble, m. a breaker, destroyer,
vighnadhvaṁsa m. the removal of obstacles,
vighneśa a god who removes obstacles, (same as Ganeśa), name of those who have attained a particular degree of emancipation,
vi√ghrā P. *vijighrāti* to smell or scent out, find out by smelling, to smell, sniff, smell at,
viglāpana n. weariness, fatigue,
viglāpayati 1/s he wearies, is distressed, afflicted,
vigna ppp. darted (from fear), moved suddenly,
vi√grah P.A. *vigṛhṇāti , °ṇīte,* to stretch out or apart, spread out, to distribute, divide, to hold apart, separate, isolate, (in gram.), to analyse, to wage war, to quarrel, to seize, lay hold of,
vigraha 957/2 mfn freed from the seizer (*rāhu* the moon), m. keeping apart or asunder, the body, embodied, shape, form, expansion, analysis, individual form or shape, discord, war with, element, independence, strife, resolution of a compound word into its component parts, division, enmity, individual form or figure, separation,
vigrāha m. partic. kind of recitation,
vigrahaṇa n. diffusion, distribution, taking hold of, seizure,
vigṛhīta mfn stretched out or apart, changed,
vigulpha mfn abundant, plentiful,
viguṇa 950/2 mfn deficient, imperfect, wicked, bad, unsuccessful, ineffective,
viha the sky, air,
vi√hā A. *–jihīte* to go apart, become expanded, open, fly open, gape, yawn, caus. *–hāpayati*
2. *vihā* ind. heaven,
3. *–jahāti* to leave behind, quit, abandon, to be deprived of, lose, to get rid of or free from, to desist, stop, pause,
vihaga sky-goer, a bird, an arrow, the sun, moon, etc.
vi√han P. *–hanti* to strike apart, disperse, break, to unbind, loosen, to ward off, to keep back, withhold, to hinder, interrupt, annihilate, caus. *–ghātayati (te),* to beat, defeat, A. to afflict, distress, annoy, disturb,
vihaṅga mfn sky-going, flying, m. a bird
vihara 1003/2 m. taking away, removing, separation, shifting, changing, separation, disunion, absence
vihāra 1003/3 m. distribution, transposition, arrangement or disposition, too great lengthening or drawling in pronunciation, sport, play, pastime, enjoyment, pleasure, walking for pleasure or amusement, a place of recreation, a monastery or temple (Buddhist), the shoulder, a partic. bird,
viharaṇa n. the act of taking away or removing or changing or transposing, opening, expanding, stepping out, going about for pleasure or exercise, strolling,
vihārin mfn wandering about for pleasure, going as far as, extending to, dependent on (comp.), enjoying one's self with, delighting in, fond of (comp.), charming, beautiful,
viharṣa 1. m. excessive joy or gladness, 2. mfn joyless, sad,
vi√hary P. *–haryati* to scorn, repudiate,
vi√has P. *–hasati* to laugh loudly, burst out laughing, to laugh at,
vihāsa m. laughing, laughter, mfn opened
vihasatikā or *vihasana* gentle laughter, smiling,
vihasta mfn having the hands away, handless, awkward, perplexed, not handy, inexperienced, clumsy, adroit, skilled, experienced, wise, learned,
m. a eunuch,
ifc. completely absorbed in,

vīhasta for *vihasta*
vihastita mfn confused, embarrassed,
vihasya laughing at, smiling, disregarding the etiquette,
vihata mfn torn up, furrowed, warded off, repelled, rejected,
vihati f. a stroke, blow, striking, killing,
vihāya 1003/2 ind. notwithstanding, leaving behind, setting aside, at a distance from, forsaking, giving up,
vihāyas 953/2 vigorous, active, mighty, mn the open space, air, sky, atmosphere, m. a bird,
vihāyasā 1003/1 3/s/n 'through the sky' , m. a bird
vi√hel Caus. A. *–helayate* to vex, annoy
vi√hiṁs P. *-hiṁsati* to injure severely, hurt
vihiṁsita mfn injured, hurt, damaged,
vihiṁsra, see *vihita*
vihīna 1003/2 mfn entirely abandoned or left, absent, free from, low, vulgar, destitute or deprived of or free from (3rd, 5th, or comp.), f. ifc. absence or want of,
vihita 1 953/2 1. improper, unfit, not good, 2. 1003/2 distributed, apportioned, bestowed, ordered, determined, ordained, put in order, arranged, fixed, prescribed, decreed, enjoined, (having been) ordained,
vi√hṛ P. *–harati (te),* to put asunder, keep apart, separate, open, to distribute and transpose verses, to disperse (clouds), to shift, let pass from hand to hand, to divide or construct (mathematically, geometrically), to cut off , sever, extract from, carry away, remove, move on, walk, wander through or about (esp. for pleasure),
vihṛdaya n. want of courage,
vihṛta mfn set or put asunder, distributed, disposed, transposed, varied, hesitation, reluctance, bashful silence,
vihṛti f. expansion, increase, growth, sport, pleasure, taking away,
vi√hru P. *–hruṇāti* to cause to deviate, turn aside, frustrate, spoil,
vihruta mfn crooked, dislocated, injured,
vi√hurch P. *–hūrchati* to waddle, (a fat person's gait), to stagger, totter, stumble,
vihutmat mfn presenting no offerings,
vi√hval P. *–hvalati* to shake, be agitated or unsteady
vihvala mfn agitated, perturbed, distressed,
vi√hve A. *–hvayate* to call in different places, call, invoke, contend for anything,
vi√hvṛ to stagger, stumble, fall,
vihvarita mfn staggered, fallen,
√vij 1. 959/3 cl 6 A *vijate, vijati, vejate,* cl 1 P *vinakti*, cl 3 P A *vevekti, vevikte* to move with a quick darting motion, heave (waves), speed, start back, recoil, flee from , caus. *vejayati* to speed, accelerate, DP in (cl 6,7) *bhaya* being afraid, or *Calana* shaking, trembling, in (cl 3) *pṛthag-bhāva* separating, dividing,
√vīj Cl1 P.A. to fan, coll by blowing or fanning, to sprinkle with water, caus. or Cl10 *vījayati* to fan, blow, kindle (fire),
vijala mfn waterless, dry, sauce etc., mixed with rice-water or gruel, n. drought,
vijalpa m. an unjust reproach, speech, talk
vijāman mfn related, corresponding,
vijāmi mfn related,
vi√jan A. *vijāyate* to be born or produced, originate, arise, to be transformed, turn into, become, to bear young, generate, bring forth, produce,
vijana mfn free from people, solitary, deserted, lonely,
vijanana n. the act of generating, bringing forth, birth, delivery,
vijānat 961/1 mfn knowing, understanding m. a wise man, sage
vijānāti 961/1 he distinguishes, discerns, knows,
vijanita 959/3 mfn born, begotten

vijānītas they two know, understand, 1/du/pres/indic/mid

vijāni mfn strange, foreign, having no wife,

vijānīyām I should understand or comprehend, I shall know 3/s/opt/act *vi √jñā*

vijānīmaḥ we are aware, we understand, we know, 3/pl/pres/act *vi√jñā*

vijanman n. separate birth, birth in general, m. illegitimate child, the son of an out-caste or degraded *vaiśya*

vijara mfn not growing old, m. a stalk

vijātīyabheda difference of one from another of different species,

vijaya 960/1 m. contest for victory, victory, conquest, name of a rabbit, mfn leading to victory, proclaiming victory, victorious, triumphant,

vijayin mfn. victorious, triumphant, m. a conqueror, subduer,

vijenya mfn lonely, solitary,

vi√ji A. *vijayate (ti),* to conquer, win or acquire by conquest, to vanquish, defeat, subdue, overpower, master, control, to be victorious or superior,

vijighatsa mfn not becoming hungry, not subject to hunger,

vijigīṣā 960/3 mfn desirous of victory, *(ā)*f. wishing to overcome or surpass, ambitious, mfn desirous to overcome or surpass

vijigīta mfn celebrated, famous,

vijihma mfn crooked, bent, dishonest,

vijihva mfn tongueless

vijijñāsitavya to be desired to be known,

vijita mfn conquered, subdued, to be apprehended or feared, m.n. a conquered country, m. any country or district, conquest, victory,

vijiti f. conquest, contest for victory,

vijitendriya mfn having the organs of sense subdued,

vi√jīv P. *vijīvati* to revive, return to life,

vijīvita mfn lifeless, dead,

vijjala slimy, smeary, sauce etc., a kind of arrow,

vijña 961/1 mfn. knowing, intelligent, wise,discerning, m. a wise man, a sage

vi√jñā 961/1 P.A *vijānāti, vijānīte* to distinguish, discern, observe, ascertain, know, understand, have right knowledge, become wise or learned, explain, declare, caus. *vijñapayati* or *vijñāpayati (te),* to make known, declare or tell that, to apprise, teach, instruct,

vijñāna 961/2 the act of distinguishing or discerning, understanding, comprehending, intelligence, knowledge, faculty of right judgement, consciousness, pure knowledge, nothing but intelligence, has been used in the sense of 'right apprehension' in *Advaita* text, has been used with the sense of 'proper analysis of the *jñānam'* q.v. also see *prajñānam ,* knowledge of the arts etc. secular knowledge, knowledge of the Self,

vijñānamaya mfn consisting of knowledge or intelligence, all knowledge, full of intelligence,

vijñānamayakośa the sheath of intellect,

vijñānārtham for the sake of understanding

vijñānaspanditam 'the vibration of consciousness' (Gam.),

vijñānata knowing, wise pres.part.

vijñānātmā 'the entity that is by nature a knower' (Gam.), cognitional Self,

vijñānavāda 961/2 the doctrine (of the Yogācāras) that only intelligence has reality, (not the objects exterior to us),

vijñāpanā f. request, tender,

vijñapta ppp. (having been) informed,

vijñāpta informed, made known, reported,

vijñapti = *vijñāpti* 961/1 f. information, report, address (to a superior), request, entreaty of (6th), imparting, giving, (N) the Absolute Self, the essence of Ātman,

vijñaptimātra N) the Absolute Self, the essence of Ātman, synonym of *vijñāna,*

vijñāta discerned, well known, understood,

vijñātṛ m. the knower,

vijñāya mfn recognizable,

vijñeya mfn to be known, perceived or learned, to be realised, understood, or heard, (-*tva* n.) to be recognized or considered or regarded as

vijoṣas mfn deserted, alone,

vi√jṛmbh A. *vijṛmbhate* to open the mouth, yawn, gape, to open, expand, become expanded or developed or exhibited, spread out, blossom, to extend, become erect, to arise, appear, awake, to begin to feel well or at ease,

vijṛmbhita 960/3 mfn become expanded, appearance, manifestation,

vijugupsate 957/2 shrinks away from, wishes to conceal from, dislikes, hates, √*gup*

vijvara 950/3 free from distress or anxiety, cheerful

vikaca 1. mfn hairless, bald,
2.mfn opened, blown, shining, resplendent, brilliant, expanded,

vikacayati to open, expand (a blossom),

vikala 953/3 mfn crippled, impaired, exhausted, weakened

vikāla m. twilight, evening, afternoon, (am) ind. in the evening, late,

vikalaṅka mfn spotless, bright

vikalmaṣa mfn spotless, sinless, guiltless

vikalpa 955/2 m. alternative, option, different, doubt, conflicting ideas, 'the oscillating condition of the mind as to the true nature of the thing known' (U),

vikalpanā 955/2f. false notion or assumption, fancy, imagination

vikalpita 955/2 mfn from *vikalpa* diversity, imagination, arranged, false notion, imagined,

vikāma free from desire

vi√kamp 953/3 Cl 1 –*kampate,* tremble greatly, quiver,

vi√kāṅkṣ P.A *vivikāṅkṣati (te)* 954/1 to have anything in view, aim at, tarry, linger, hesitate,

vikāṅkṣa °*kṣin* mfn free from desire,

vikara mfn deprived of hands (as a punishment), m. disease, sickness

vikāra 954/2 m. change of form or nature, alteration or deviation from any natural state, modification, transformation, coming into being, changing, and passing away, change, emotion, agitation, passion, , change of sentiment, hostility, defection, change of bodily or mental condition (esp. for the worse), a product, 7Vikāras - *buddhi, ahaṁkāra* and the 5 *tanmātra*s
an apparition, spectre,
contortion of the face, grimace

vikarāla mfn very formidable or dreadful,

vikarālin mfn hot, m. heat

vikāraṇa mfn causeless

vikaraṇa mfn deprived of organs of sense, m. producing a change (in gram.), the term for the affix or conjugational characteristic placed between the root and terminations, n. change, modification,
a disturbing influence

vikarman n. prohibited or unlawful act, fraud, mfn acting wrongly or unlawfully, not acting, free from action,

Vikarṇa m. a Kaurava warrior, 'without ears', deaf, a kind of arrow,

vikarṣaṇa mfn destroying, removing, taking away, n. searching, investigation,

vikarṣaṇaśakti power of repulsion,

vikartana mfn cutting asunder, dividing,

vi√kas cl 1 P *vikasati* to burst, become split or divided, to open, expand, blossom, to shine, be bright, beam (with joy etc.),

vi√kāś cl 1 A *vikāśate* to appear, become

visible, shine forth, illuminate, make clear, publish,

vikāśa 1. m. absence of manifestation or display, loneliness, privacy,
2. m. brightness, radiance, manifestation, appearance,

vikasa 954/1 m. the moon,

vikāsa m. expanding, budding, blowing (of flowers), opening (of the mouth or eyes), opening (of the heart), cheerfulness, serenity, expansion, devlopment, growth,

vikasana 954/1 developing, expanding, opening, blowing, blossoming

vikāsana mfn causing to blow or expand, n. developing,

vikāsin mfn blossoming, blooming, opened, open (as the eyes or nose), expanding, developing, extensive, great, rich or abounding in (ifc.),dissolving, relaxing, paralysing,

vikasvara mfn opened (as eyes), expanded, clear (as sound), candid,

vikaṭa mfn having an unusual size or aspect, horrible, dreadful, unusually handsome, obscure, obsolete, having no mat,

vikathā useless or irrelevant talk,

vi√katth A. *katthate* to boast, vaunt, brag, to praise, extol, commend, to mock or blame, caus. *vikatthayati* to humiliate, humble,

vikautuka mfn showing no interest or curiosity, indifferent,

vi√khan P. *vikhanati* to dig up

vi√khid P. *vikhidati* to tear asunder

vi√khyā P. *vikhyāti* to look about, look at, view, see, behold, to shine, shine upon, lighten, illuminate, caus. *vikhyāpayati* to show, make visible, to make known, announce,

vikiṣku a carpenter's measure – 42 inches,

vi√klav A. *viklavate* to become agitated or confused,

viklava mfn overcome with fear or agitation, confused, bewildered, distressed, timid, shy, unsteady,
n. agitation, bewilderment,

vi√kḷp 955/1 A *kalpate* to change or alternate, change with (3rd), to be undecided or questionable or optionable, to be doubtful or irresolute, waver, hesitate, caus. °*kalpayati* to prepare, arrange, contrive, form, fashion, choose one of 2 alternatives, to call in question, prescribe variously, to state a dilemma, to suppose, conjecture,

vi √1. *kṛ* P.A *vikaroti, vikurute,* to make different, transform, change the shape (or the mind), cause to alter or change, pervert, spoil, to develop, produce, to embellish, decorate, distribute, divide, destroy, represent, A. to move to and fro, be restless, to act in various ways, diversify,

vi√kṝ 955/1 Cl 6 *vikirati* to scatter, throw or toss about, disperse, dishevel, pour out, utter, heave sighs, cleave, split, to scatter over, cover, fill with (3rd),

vi√kram 955/2 P.A *vikrāmati,-kramate,* to step beyond or aside, move away, depart from, to move apart or asunder, become divided, to go or stride through, traverse, to move on, walk, go, advance, to bestride, show valour or prowess, attack, caus. *vikramayati* to cause to step over or through,

vikrama m. a step, stride, pace, going, proceeding, walking, valour, courage, heroism, power, strength, force, intensity, high degree, stability, duration, a foot,

vikramya ind. having attacked, by force,

vikrānta mn striding forth, courageous

vikrānta mfn stepped beyond, courageous, bold, strong, mighty, m. a warrior, a lion, n. a step, stride, bold advance, courage,

vikrānti f. stepping or striding through, striding everywhere i.e. all-pervading power, heroism, prowess, courage, strength, might

vikraya m. sale, selling, vending,

vikretṛ m. seller,
vi√krī 956/1 A *krīṇīte* to buy and sell, barter, trade, to sell
vi√krīḍ P. °*krīḍati* to play, jest, sport with,
vikrīḍa m. a playground, plaything, toy, f. play, sport,
vikrīḍita played, played with, made a plaything of, n. play, sport
vikriyā f. change, alteration, variation, changed condition, change for the worse, deterioration, disfigurement, ailment, indisposition, affection, agitation, hostile feeling, rebellion, alienation, injury, harm, failure, misadventure, extinction (of a lamp), a strange phenomenon, any product or preparation, contraction or knitting (of the brows), bristling (of the hair),
vikrodha free from anger,
vi√kṛṣ P *vikarṣati, vikṛṣati,* to draw apart or asunder, tear to pieces, to bend a bow, draw a bowstring, to widen, extend, to draw along, to lead (an army), to pull out, withdraw, keep back, to deprive, *vikṛṣati* to plough, draw a furrow,
vi√kṛt 955/1 P. *vikṛntati, kartati* to cut into or through, divide by cutting, tear asunder,
vikṛta mfn transformed, altered, changed, deformed, disfigured, unnatural, strange, incomplete, sick, diseased, m. capital punishment with mutilation, sick, diseased, n. change, alteration, disgust, aversion, misshaped offspring, abortion, untimely silence caused by embarrassment, °*tva* the state of being changed, transformation, ready or prone to create,
vikṛti 954/3 f. change, modification, agitation, emotion, changed condition of body or mind, alienation, hostility, defection, an apparition, phantom, any production, anything made of (ifc.), derivative products of *prakṛti – mahat, buddhi,* mind, the senses, the *tanmātras* in gram. a derivative,
vi√kruś P. °*krośati* to cry out, exclaim, revile
vīkṣ *vi√īkṣ* Cl 1 *vīkṣate* A P 1004/2 to look upon, regard, see, see in the heart, ponder, to consider, observe, discern, ascertain, understand, to think fit or proper, to look over, peruse, study,
vikṣaṇam ind. momentarily, for a moment,
vikṣepa m. inattention, distraction, mental agitation due to *rajas,* projection, the projecting power of *māyā* (having 5 forms – the principles of sound, touch, sight, taste, and smell; confusion, "due to non-stop use of the subtle body" (Jaiswal), inattention, scattering, shaking,
vikṣepaśakti the power of *māyā* that projects the universe and causes movement and superimposition, (U)
vi√kṣip P.A. *vikṣipati (te),* to throw asunder or away or about, cast hither and thither, scatter, disperse, to remove, destroy, extend, stretch out, to bend (a bow), to handle, manage, to separate,
vikṣipta 956/2 mfn agitated, scattered, dispersed, bewildered, distraught, frustrated, sent, dispatched, refuted, falsified, projected, n. being dispersed in different places,
vikṣobha m. shaking, agitation, motion, distraction, alarm,
vi√kṣubh A *vikṣobhate* to be shaken about, agitated, to confuse, disturb, caus. *kṣobhayati* to agitate, disturb,
vi√kṣudh to be hungry, *vikṣudhyati*
vikṣudra 950/1 mfn comparatively smaller, each smaller than another,
vīkṣya mfn seeing, astonishing, wonderful, m. a dancer, actor, horse,, n. wonder, surprise, wonderful object,
vi√kūj cl 1 P. *kujati* to chirp, sing, hum, warble,

vi√kūṇ to contract, wrinkle (the face),
vikuṇṭha mfn sharp, keen, penetrating, irresistible, f. (*ā*) inward glance, mental concentration,
vi√kup caus. *–kopayati,* to disturb
√vil 984/2 cl 6 P *vilati* to cover, conceal, clothe, cl 10 P *velayati* to throw, cast, send, DP (cl 6) in *varaṇa* covering, concealing, (cl 10) in *kṣepa* throwing,
vi√labh A. *–labhate* to part asunder, separate, to take away, remove (dung from a stable), to procure, bestow, grant, deliver up, caus. –*lambhayati* to cause to receive, or fall to the share
vi√lag P. *–lagati,*to hang to, cling to
vilagita mfn attached to etc.
vilagna 984/3mfn fastened or attached to, connected with, pendulous, flaccid (breasts), caged (as a bird), gone by, passed away, thin, slender, m. or n. the waist, middle, n. the rising of constellations, a horoscope,
vi√lajj A. *–lajjate* to become ashamed or abashed, blush,
vilajja shameless
vilajjamāna pres.part. being ashamed,
vilajjita ashamed, abashed
vi√lakṣ P.A. *-lakṣayati (te),* to distinguish, discern, observe, perceive, notice, to lose sight of one's aim, become bewildered or embarrassed,
vilakṣa having no fixed aim, missing its mark, unusual, embarrassed, ashamed, having no characteristic mark or property,
having uncharacteristic properties,
vilakṣaṇa mfn having different marks, varying in character, different, differing from, various, manifold, not admitting of exact definition,
n. any state or condition which is which is without distinctive mark or for which no cause can be assigned, vain or causeless state, the act of distinguishing, perceiving, seeing,
vilakṣita 1. undistinguished, unmarked, undiscriminated, distinguished, marked by ($3^{\text{rd or comp.}}$), perceived, observed, noticed, confused, vexed, annoyed,
vi√lamb A. *–lambate* to hang down, hang on, be attached to, to sink, set, decline, linger, delay, tarry, caus. –*lambayati* cause to linger, cause to waste time, lose time, procrastinate,
vilamba mfn hanging down, pendulous, m. hanging or falling down, slowness, tardiness, procrastination, delay,
vilambhāt with delay
vi√laṅgh P.A. *–laṅghati (te*), to leap, jump, rise up to, caus. *–laṅghayati* to leap or jump over, cross, traverse, overstep (bounds), to transgress, neglect, violate, to rise up to, ascend to, to rise beyond, overcome, subdue,
vilaṅghana n. leaping over, crossing, offence, injury, pl. fasting,
vilaṅghanīya to be passed over or transgressed,
vi√lap P. *–lapati* to wail, lament, to chatter, caus. *–lāpayati* to cause to mourn, cause to speak much,
vilāpa m. lamentation,
vilāpana mfn causing moaning or lamentation, dissolving, destroying, removing, melting, n. death, the act of causing moaning or lamentation, wail, lamentation, destruction, a means of destruction, melting or a means of melting, a partic. milk product,
vilapati he laments
vi√las P. *–lasati* to gleam, flash, glitter, to shine forth, appear, rise, to sound forth, echo, to play, dally, be amused or delighted, to vibrate, caus. –*lāsayati* to cause to dance
vilāsa 985/1 m. shining forth, appearance, manifestation, joy,
sport, play, pastime, coquetry, liveliness, joviality, wantoness, lust, grace, charm, beauty,

vilasana n. gleaming, flashing of lightning, play, sport
vilasati 985/1 gleams, flashes, shines forth, sports, plays,
vilaya 985/3 m. disappearance, dissolution, liquefaction, death, destruction, decomposition, n. corrosion, melting, corroding,
vilayana mfn dissolving, liquefying, n. dissolution, liquefaction, melting, corroding, attenuating,
vilekha m. scratching, wounding
vilekhā f. a scratch, furrow, mark
vilekhana 985/2 mfn scratching, lacerating, n. the act of making an incision, mark or furrow, scratching, lacerating, the course of a river, dividing, splitting,
vilepa m. ointment, unguent, anointing, plastering, f. (*ī*) rice-gruel
vilepana n. ointment, anointing, personal perfume, mythical weapon, smearing,
vi√lī A. *–līyate,* to cling or cleave or adhere to, to hide or conceal one's self, disappear, to be dissolved, melt, caus. *lāpayati* to cause to disappear, destroy, to cause to be dissolved or absorbed in, to make liquid, dissolve, melt,
vi√lih P.A. *–leḍhi, -līḍhe,* to lick, lick up,
vi√likh P. *–likhati* to scratch, scrape, tear up, lacerate, to rub against, to touch, to wound (the heart), to vex, offend, to scratch in or on, make a furrow or mark, write, delineate, paint,
vilikhina n. the act of scratching, scraping
vilīna mfn clinging, sticking, attached to, fixed on, immersed in, alighted or perched on, sticking, hidden, disappeared, perished, absorbed in, dissolved in, melted, united or blended with, infused into the mind, imagined,
viliṅga n. absence of marks, mfn of a different gender,
vi√lip P.A. *–limpati (te)*, to smear or spread over, anoint,
vilipta mfn (having been)smeared all over, anointed,
vi√liś A. *–liśate* to become out of joint, be disarranged or disordered, break off, become torn,
viliṣṭa mfn broken off, out of due order,
vilobha m. attraction, delusion, seduction,
vilocana mfn causing to see, seeing, distorting the eyes, name of an antelope, n. the eye, sight,
viloḍa m. rolling, wallowing,
viloḍana 985/3 n. stirring up, churning, splashing (in water), agitating
vilohita deep red, m. a kind of onion, name of a hell,
vi√lok to look at or upon, regard, examine, test, study, caus. *–lokayati* to look at, consider, observe, regard, examine, try, inspect, to be able to see, possess the faculty of seeing, to have regard to, to look over or beyond (2nd), pass. *–lokyate* to be seen, be visible,
viloka n. absence of man, mfn apart from the world, solitary, °*stha* mfn living apart from the world,
2. m. a glance, view
vilokana n. the act of looking or seeing,
vilokya 986/1 to be or being looked at, visible,
vilola mfn moving to and fro or from side to side, rolling, waving, tremulous, unsteadier than (with 5th),
vilolupa mfn free from all desires,
viloma mfn against the grain, turned the wrong way, inverted, opposed, m. reverse order, opposite course, reverse, a snake, a dog, n. a water-wheel or machine for raising water from a well, (*am)* ind. backwards,
vilopa m. carrying off, taking away, interruption, disturbance, injury, ruin, loss,
vi√lū 986/1 to cut off, sever,
vi√lubh *-lobhayati* to lead astray, perplex, confuse, allure, entice, tempt, to divert, amuse, delight,

vi√luḍ *-loḍayati* to stir about, stir up, mingle, to upset, confuse,
vi√luṇṭh P. *–luṇṭhati* to carry off, plunder, steal, ravage,
viluṇṭhana n. the act of plundering, robbing, hanging down, dangling,
vi√lup P. *–lumpati* to tear or break to pieces, wound, lacerate, tear away, rob, destroy, confound, ruin,
A. to fall to pieces, be ruined, disappear, caus. *–lopayati,* to tear or carry away, withhold, suppress, extinguish, destroy,
vilupta mfn torn or broken off, carried away, destroyed, ruined, lost,
vi√2.luṭh P. *-luṭhati* to roll, move to and fro, quiver, flicker,
viluṭhita mfn agitated, excited, n. rolling, wallowing,
vi√mā 3. P.A. *–māti, mimīte*, to measure, mete out, pass over, traverse, to enumerate, to ordain, fix, set right, arrange, make ready, prepare,
vi√mad P. *–mādyati, -madati,* to be joyful or merry, to become perplexed or discomposed, to confound, embarrass, disturb,
vimada mfn grown sober, free from pride or arrogance, joyless
vimadhya n. the midst, middle,
vimadhyama middling, indifferent,
vimahas mfn merry, joyous,
vimahat mfn very great, immense,
vimahī mfn exhilarating, inspiring,
vi√majj P. *–majjati* to plunge or dive into, enter into, caus. *–majjayati* to submerge, lead into, cause to plunge
vimala 979/3 stainless, spotless, pure, clean, bright, pure, clear, transparent, white, m. a lunar year, n. silver gilt,
ind. at daybreak,
vimalaya Nom P. °*yati* to make clear or pure,
vi√maṁh A. *-maṁhate* to distribute, bestow

vi√man A. to distinguish, caus. *–mānayati* to dishonour, slight, treat with disrespect,
vimana mfn dejected, downcast,
vimāna mfn devoid of honour, disgraced, measuring out, traversing, traversing the sky,
m. disrespect, dishonour,
m.n. a car or chariot of the gods, a horse, ship, boat, n. measure, extension, the science of (right) measure or proportion (partic. the state of the body with regard to remedies etc),
vimanas mfn having a keen or penetrating mind or understanding, sagacious, dejected, downcast, out of one's mind or senses, perplexed, heart-broken, destitute of mind, foolish, silly, changed in mind or feeling, averse, hostile,
vimanāya Nom. A. °*yate* to be out of one's mind, disconsolate or downcast,
vimanthara mfn rather slow or dull,
vimānuṣa mfn without or except men
vimanyu m longing, desire,
mfn free from anger or fury,
vimanyuka mfn not angry, allaying anger or wrath
vimarda m. destruction, disturbance (of sleep), crushing, bruising, rubbing, friction, trampling, hostile encounter, conflict, touch, contact, refusal, rejection, total eclipse, weariness, tediousness,
vimardana mfn pressing, squeezing,
m, fragrance, perfume,
n. the act of rubbing or grinding, hostile encounter, fight, battle, devastation, destruction, an eclipse,
vimārga m. a wrong road, evil course,
mfn being on a wrong road,
vimārga 2. m. wiping off, a broom, brush
vimārgaṇa n. the act of seeking for,
vimārjana n. cleansing, purifying, wiping off
vi-marśa 981/*1* m. consideration, deliberation, critical test, examination, reasoning, discussion, knowledge, intelligence,

vi-marṣa as above, m. irritation, impatience, displeasure,
vimātra mfn unequal in measure,
vimata mfn disagreed, at variance, hostile, slighted, offended, m. an enemy,
vi√math (or *manth*) P.A. *–mathati (te), mathnāti °nīte*, to tear off, snatch away, break in pieces, rend asunder, bruise, to confuse, perplex,
vimātha m. the act of crushing or destroying utterly,
vimati of different opinion, stupid, silly, f. difference of opinion, dissent, dislike, aversion, doubt, uncertainty, error,
vimātṛ f. a stepmother,
vimātra mfn unequal in measure,
vimatsara mfn free from greed, malice or envy,
vimatta mfn discomposed, perplexed, being in rut, ruttish, intoxicated,
vimauna mfn breaking silence,
vimaya m. exchange, barter,
vimāya mfn devoid of magic, free from illusion,
vimauna breaking silence,
vimegha cloudless,
vi√1.mi P.A. *–minoti, -minute,* to fix, build, erect,
vi√miśr P. *–miśrayati* to mix or mingle together,
vimiśra mfn mixed, mingled, miscellaneous,
vimita mfn fixed, built, n. a square shed or large building resting on four posts,
vi√mlai P.A. *–mlāyati (te)*, to wither away, languish, become weak or weary, caus. *–mlāpayati* to cause to wither or languish,
vimlāna mfn unfaded, faded or withered away, bereft of lustre or beauty, fresh, pure,
vimocana mfn unyoking, loosening, n. deliverance, liberation, giving up, abandoning, stopping for rest, relief,
vimogha mfn quite fruitless, idle, vain,
vimoha m. confusion of the mind, perplexity, a kind of hell,
vimohana n. confusion, perplexity, the art of confusing, bewildering
vimohayati causes to confuse, confuses, deludes, 1/s/pres/indic/act *vi√muh*
vi√mokṣ P. *-mokṣayati* to set free, let loose, liberate,
vimokṣa m. release, deliverance, liberation of the soul, final emancipation, giving up, abandoning, letting flow, shedding of tears, gift, bestowal (of wealth), discharge (of arrows),
vimokṣana 981/2 mfn liberating from (ifc.), n. untying, loosening, liberating, deliverance from, taking off, casting away, giving up the ghost, discharging (arrows),
vimokṣyase you shall be liberated 2/s/fut/pass *vi√muc*
vimoktavya mfn to be let loose or liberated,
vi√mrad only impv *–mradā,* to make soft or tender, soften
vi√mṛd P. *–mṛdnāti –mardati,* to crush or press to pieces, grind down, destroy, to rub together,
vi√mṛj P.A. *-mārṣṭi –mṛṣṭe,* to rub off or out, purify, cleanse, rub dry, anoint, wipe off, rub, stroke, caress,
vi- √mṛś 981/1 *-mṛśati* to touch (with the hands) stroke, feel, (mentally), be sensible or aware of, perceive, consider, reflect on, deliberate about, investigate, examine, DP in *āmarśan* rubbing, stroking, touching, handling
vi√mṛṣ P.A. *–mṛṣyati (te)*, or *marṣati (te),* to be distressed, bear hardly,
vimṛśa 981/1 reflection, consideration,
vimṛśata mfn reflecting,
vimṛśya 981/1 mfn to be tried or examined, ind. having deliberated or considered, reflecting on
vi√mṛt P. *–mrityati* to fall to pieces, crumble away, decay,
vimṛtyu mfn immortal, not liable to death,
viṁśati twenty
vi√muc P.A. *–muñcati (te),* to unloose, unharness, unyoke, set free, liberate, to leave, abandon, quit, give up, shun, to lose (consciousness), to pardon,

forgive, emit, discharge, 2. f. unyoking, stopping, putting up,

vimucya ind. relinquishing, abandoning, having relinquished or discarded, being delivered from, having become free from, after clearing, after releasing him,

vimūḍha mfn not foolish, m. a kind of divine being, ifc. perplexed as to, uncertain about, stupid, foolish,

vimudra mfn unsealed, opened, blown, abundant,

vimugdha mfn confused, bewildered, infatuated,

vi√muh P.A. *–muhyati (te),* to be confused, become bewildered, faint away,.

vimuhyati 980/3 1/s/pres/ind/act is confused/bewildered

vimukha mfn having the face averted, turning away from (6th), disappointed, downcast, averse or opposed to, indifferent to (ifc.), adverse, hostile, wanting or lacking (ifc.),

vimukhaya Nom P. °yati to render averse, mfn averse, hostile,

vimukhin having the face averted, hostile,

vimukta 980/2 mfn unloosed, unharnessed, set free, liberated (esp, from mundane existence), freed or delivered or escaped from, given up, abandoned, launched (as a ship), emitted or discharged by, flowing from (comp.), shed or bestowed on, a snake which has recently cast its skin, dispassionate,

vimūla mfn uprooted,

vimuñcati 980/2 he shuns, avoids, keeps off, relinquishes, frees oneself, rejects,

vimuñcata discarded, abandoned, relinquished, rejected,

vimūrchana n. modulation, melody,

vimūrchita mfn thickened, coagulated, become solid, full of or mixed with (ifc.), resounding with, n. 'becoming stiff, fainting, a swoon,

vinā ind. without (after 3rd), except, short or exclusive of, exceptionally (ifc.),

vīṇā f. the Indian lute, lightning,

vi√nad P. *vinadati* to sound forth, roar, thunder, caus. *vinādayati* to cause to sound or resound, fill with noise or cries, to sound aloud,

vinada m. sound, noise

vinaddha mfn untied, set free,

vinadya sounding forth, vibrating, resounding,

vinagna mfn quite naked

vi√nam P.A. *vinamati (te),* to bend down, bow down, stoop, caus. *vināmayati, vinamayati* to bend down, incline, bend (a bow), (in gram.) to change a letter to *mūrdha*,

vinamra mfn bent down, stooping

vi√nand P.A. *vinandati* to rejoice, be glad or joyful,

vinaṅkṣyasi you will be lost, you will perish 2/s/fut/act *vi* √2. *naś*

vi√naś 1. P. *vinaśati* to reach, attain, 2. P. *vinaśati* or *vinaśyati* to be utterly lost, perish, disappear, vanish, to come to nothing, be frustrated or foiled, to be deprived of, to destroy,

vināśa 969/3 m. destruction, utter loss, decay, death, perdition, removal,

vināśana n. destruction, causing to disappear, removal,

vināśin mfn perishing, perishable, undergoing transformation, destroying (mostly ifc.),

vinaṣṭa mfn utterly lost or ruined, corrupted, spoilt, perished, destroyed, disappeared, n. dead carcase, carrion,

vināśvara 969/2 m. liable to be lost or destroyed, f. perishable,

vinaśyatsu 7/pl among the perishable

vinaśyati 969/2 is lost or destroyed

vinata mfn bent, curved, bent down, bowed, inclined, sunk down, depressed, deepened, stooping, m. a kind of ant,

vinātha mfn having no master, unprotected, deserted,

vinaya humility or sense of propriety, manners, educationmental culture and refinement (U),
971/3 mfn leading away or apart, separating, cast, thrown, secret, separating,
m. taking away, leading, guidance, training, education, the rules of discipline for monks (Buddhist), formation of manners, discipline, decency, modesty, mildness, manners, good breeding, good conduct, decency, modesty, a man of subdued senses, an office, business, a merchant, trader,
vinayabhāj mfn possesing propriety or modesty,
vinayagrahin mfn conforming to rules of discipline, compliant, tractable, m. an elephant which obeys orders,
vinayakarman n. instruction,
vinayapiṭaka m. 'basket of discipline' the collection of treatises on discipline (Buddhist),
vinayapradhāna mfn having humility pre-eminent,
vinayapramāthin mfn violating propriety, behaving ill or improperly,
vinayatā f. good behaviour, modesty,
vinayayogin mfn possessing humility,
vinda mfn finding, getting, gaining, m. a partic hour of the day,
vindu mfn as above, m. a drop,
vindati knows, understands, perceives, learns, experiences, feels, considers as, takes for, √ 3. *vid*
vindhya m. name of the range of hills across the Indian peninsula and north of the Deccan, a hunter,
vindhyāṭavī f. the *vindhya* forest,
vinetra mfn eyeless, blind, red-eyed, m.a teacher, preceptor,
vinetṛ m. a leader, guide, instructor, king, teacher, a tamer, trainer, prince,
vi√nī P A *–nayati (te),* to lead or take away, remove, avert, to throw off, drive away, dispel, expel (a disease), part the hair, stretch, extend, train, tame, guide (horses), to educate, direct, instruct, to induce, lead or cause to, to chastise, to spend, pass time, perform, accomplish,
A. to elicit, draw from,
to pay off or restore a debt,
vinibandha m. being attached or attachment to anything,
vinidhā P.A. *vinidadhāti, vinidhatte,* to put or place or lay down in different places, distribute, to put off, lay down or aside, to put by, store up, to fix upon (mind, eyes), (with *hṛdi*) to fix in the heart, bear in mind
vini√dhṛ P. *vinidhārayati* to fix (the eyes) upon,
vinidra mfn sleepless, awake, opened (as eyes), occurring in the waking condition, passed sleeplessly,
vinigamanā f. decision between alternatives
vinighna mfn multiplied (√*han*),
vinighnat mfn striking down
vini√guh P. *vinigūhati* to cover over, conceal, hide,
vinigūhita mfn covered, concealed, hidden,
vinigūhitṛ m. one who conceals, keeper of a secret,
vini√han P. *vinihanti* to strike down, slay, slaughter,
vinihata mfn struck down, dispelled (darkness), disregarded (command), afflicted (the mind), m. a great or unavoidable calamity, a portent, comet, meteor,
vinihita mfn put or laid down, placed or fixed upon, directed towards, appointed to (7th), separated,
vini√hnu P. *–hnauti* to deny, disown,
vinihnuta mfn denied, disowned, hidden, concealed,
viniketa mfn having no fixed abode,
vini√kṛ 969/3 *vinikaroti, °kurute*, to act badly towards, ill-treat, offend
vini√kī to cast off, abandon,
vini√kṣ P. *-nikṣati,* to pierce, penetrate,
vinikṣip P.A. *vinikṣipati (te),* to throw or

put down, insert, fasten, (with *manas*) to fix the mind upon, entrust with, charge with, appoint to,

vinīla dark blue, blue

vinimagna mfn bathed or immersed in, dived under,

vinimaya m. exchange, barter, reciprocity, a pledge, deposit, security,

vinimeṣa winking or twinkling of the eyes, a wink, sign,

vinimitta mfn having no real cause, not caused by anything,

vi√nind or *nid* P. *vinindati* to reproach, revile, abuse,

vinindana mfn. mocking, reproach, reviling, abusing, surpassing,

vini√pat vinipatati to fall down, fall in or into, to flow down, fall upon, attack,

vini√pīḍ vinipīḍayati to torment, annoy

vinirbandha m. persistence or perseverance in,

vinirdagdha mfn completely burned up or consumed, utterly destroyed,

vinir√dah P. *–dahati* to burn completely, consume by fire, destroy,

vinir√diś P. *–diśati* to assign, point out, indicate, state, declare, to determine, resolve, fix upon,

vinir√gam P. *vinirgacchati* to go out or away, depart or escape from,

vinirgata 970/3 liberated or freed from, gone out, come forth 2/s

vinirhata mfn completely destroyed,

vinir√hṛ P.A. *-harati (te),* to take out, extract, remove, destroy,

vinirjaya m. complete victory,

vinir√ji P. *°jayati* to conquer completely, win, overpower, subdue,

vinirjita mfn entirely conquered, subdued, won,

vinir√jñā to distinguish, discern, find out,

vinir√likh P. *–likhati,* to make incisions in, scarify, scratch or scrape off,

vinirmala mfn extremely pure,

vinirmāṇa meting out, measuring, building, forming, creating,

vinirmita mfn formed, created, built, laid out (as a garden), fixed, appointed, destined to be, kept, celebrated, observed (as a feast),

vinirmokṣa m. emancipation, liberation, exclusion, exemption, release from

vinir√muc P. *–muñcati* to abandon, relinquish (the body, i.e. die), pass. *–mucyate* to be liberated, or set free,

vinirmukta 971/1 liberated, escaped, free

vinirṇaya complete settlement or decision,

vinirṇī to decide or determine clearly

vinirṇīta mfn determined clearly, ascertained, certain,

vinirodha mfn. uninfluenced, inactive

vinirodhin mfn checking, obstructing,

vinirvṛtta 971/1 proceeded, come forth, completed, finished, issued from,

vinir√yā P. *–yāti* to go forth, go out, issue, set out,

viniryāṇa n. act of setting out, going forth,

viniryat mfn going forth, issuing,

viniścala mfn immovable, firm, steady

viniś√car P. –carati to go forth in all directions

viniścaya 971/2 m. deciding, settling ascertainment

viniścaya m. deciding, settling, ascertainment, settled opinion, decision, firm resolve regarding,

viniścayin mfn settling finally, deciding,

viniścatya ind. having considered or deliberated,

viniś√2. *ci* to debate about, deliberate, consider,

viniścita mfn ascertained, determined, settled, firmly resolved upon, (*am*) ind. most certainly, decidedly,

viniṣ√pat P *–patati* to fall out of, fly forth from, rush forth, issue, to fly or run away,

viniṣ√piṣ Cl 7 *-pinaṣṭi* to crush to bits,

viniṣpiṣṭa mfn crushed to bits, ground down, crushed into powder,

vinismṛta mfn recorded, mentioned,

vinis√sṛ Cl 3 *–sisirti,* go forth hither and thither,

vinīta mfn led or taken away, removed, tamed, trained, educated, well-behaved, humble, modest, versed in, accomplished, one who has subdued his passions, lovely, handsome, plain, neat,

vinīti f. (good breeding esp.) modesty,

vinivartana n. turning back, return, coming to an end, cessation,

vinivartate 971/2 turns back, returns, turns away, ceases from, renounces

vinivarteta would discontinue, would cease, 1/s/opt/mid 1.√*vṛt*

vinivartya having witnessed, turn away, desist from, extinguish,

vini√1. *vid* caus. *vinivedayati* to make known, announce, inform, report,

vinivedana n. the act of announcing, announcement,

vini√*viś* *viniveśayati* to cause to enter into, set down or place in, to fix (the eyes or mind) upon, to erect (a statue), found (a city),

vini√*vṛt* A. *–vartate* to turn back, return, turn away, desist or cease from, to cease, end, disappear, to be extinguished(as fire), to be omitted, caus. *–vartayati*

vinivṛtya ind. having turned away or desisted

vini√*yam* *P. viniyacchati* to restrain, check, control, regulate, to draw in, withdraw, to keep off,

viniyama m. limitation, restriction, restraint,

viniyamya restraining, subduing, gerund mfn to be restricted or limited,

viniyata 970/2 mfn. restrained, checked, regulated, limited

viniyoga m. apportionment, distribution, task, employment, use, application, relation, correlation,

vini√*yuj* A. *viniyuṅkte,* P. *viniyunakti* to unyoke, detach, separate, assign, commit, charge or entrust with, destine for (7th), apply, use, employ,

viṇmūtra n. faeces and urine,

vinoda m. driving away, removal, diversion, sport, pleasure, amusement, eagerness, vehemence, a kind of embrace,

vi√*nṛt* P. *–nṛtyati* to begin to dance,

vi√*3. nu* A. *–navate* to go or spread in different directions,

vi√*nud* P.A. *–nudati (te),* to drive away, scare away, dispel, remove, to strike chords, play an instrument, caus. *nodayati* to spend time, amuse, entertain, to amuse one's self with, delight in(3rd), caus. *vinodayati* to drive asunder or away, dispel, to spend time, to divert, amuse, entertain, amuse one's self with, f. a stroke, blow, thrust,

vinyāsa 972/3 m. putting or placing down, arrangement, disposition, putting together, composing, displaying, a deposit, movement, position of limbs, attitude, connecting (words), composition (literary works), exhibition, display, the utterance of words of despair, assemblage, collection, a site or receptacle for depositing,

vi-ny√*2.as* P. *–asyati, -asati,* to put or place down in different places, spread out, distribute, arrange, to deposit, place or lay on, turn or direct toward, apply to, to mark or designate by (3rd), to entrust or make over to (7th),

vinyaya m. position, situation,

√*vip* or *vep* cl 1 A. *vepate (ti*), to tremble, shake, quiver,
2. mfn inwardly stirred or excited, inspired, f. 'easily moved or bent', flexible, a switch, rod, arrow-shaft, a finger,

vipa m. a learned man, f. speech,

vi√*pac* *-pacati,* to cook thoroughly, dissolve by cooking or boiling, pass. *–pacyate* to be cooked or baked or roasted, to be digested, to be completely matured, ripened or developed, to bear fruit, develop consequences, caus. *–pācayati* to cook thoroughly, dissolve by cooking, melt, liquefy,

vi√*pad* A. *vipadyate* to fall or burst asunder, to come between, intervene, prevent, hinder, fail, miscarry, perish, die, *vipad* f. misfortune, trouble, calamity, failure, going wrongly, ruin, death

vipāka mfn ripe, mature, m. cooking, dressing, maturing (esp. of the fruit of actions), effect, result, digestion, bad digestion, any change of form or state, calamity, distress, withering, fading, sweat or flavour, ibc. subsequently, afterwards (comp.),

vipakṣa mfn deprived of wings, an opponent, adversary, enemy, female rival, in logic – a counter statement, in gram. an exception, a disputant,

vipakva mfn well cooked, well done, matured, ripe, fully developed, perfect,

vipāla unguarded, having no attendant,

vipalāśa leafless,

vi√paṇ P. *vipaṇati* to sell, A. *vipaṇate* to bet, wager

vipaṇa m. selling, sale, wager, shop, market-place, the organ of speech or the energy of activity,

vipaṇin m. shopkeeper, trader, merchant,

vipanna mfn gone wrong, failed, afflicted, distressed, ruined, destroyed, m. a snake,

vipāpa 951/2 mfn sinless, faultless,

vipāpman mfn free from suffering,

viparīta 974/1 mfn. turned round, reversed, inverted, being the reverse of anything, opposite, contrary to, perverse, wrong, inauspicious, false, untrue,

viparīta bhāvanā error, opposite stream of thought, habitual wrong thinking, thinking opposed to the teaching,

viparītatā f. counterpart, contrariety, inversion,

viparyāsa 974/2 m. overturning, upsetting (of a car), transposition, transportation, expiration, lapse(of time), reverse, contrariety, opposition, opposite of, change for the worse, deterioration, perverseness, error, mistake, delusion, imagining what is unreal or false to be real or true, false perception or non-perception,

viparyasta 974/2 mfn overthrow, opposite of, contrary, turned over, reversed, opposite, inverted, standing round, erroneously conceived to be real, (in gram.) interchanged,

viparyastatā f. perverseness,

viparyaya mfn reversed, inverted, perverse, contrary to, m. turning round, revolution, running off, coming to an end, transposition, change, alteration, inverted order or succession, opposite of, exchange, barter, change for the worse, reverse of fortune, perverseness, overthrow, loss, change of opinion, change of purpose or conduct, hostility, misapprehension, error, mistaking anything for the reverse of what it is, shunning, avoiding, patic. forms of intermittent fever, 'erroneous knowledge born of defects in the perceptive organs or confusion in the mind…' (U),

viparākrama mfn without courage or energy,

viparicchinna mfn cut off on all sides, utterly destroyed,

vipari√dhā A. –dhatte to exchange, alter

vipari√gā P. *viparijigati* to go over, be upset (a cart),

vipariharaṇa n. transposition, exchange,

vipari√hṛ P.A. *–harati (te),* to transpose, exchange

vi-pari-√kram P.A. –krāmati to step or walk around, circumambulate,

viparikrāmam ind. having walked round, going all about,

viparikrānta mfn one who has shown valour (in battle), courageous, powerful

vipari√muc pass. *–mucyate* to be freed or released from,

vipariṇam –ṇamyate pass. to undergo change or alteration, caus. *vipariṇamayati* alters, changes into,

vipariṇāma m. change, exchange, transformation, ripening, maturing,

vipari√pat P. *–patati* to fly round or back,
viparīta mfn turned round, reversed, inverted, being the reverse of anything, acting in a contrary manner, opposite, contrary to, various, different, perverse, wrong, contrary to rule, adverse, error, inauspicious, false, untrue
viparītaka mfn reversed, inverted, inverted coitus,
vipari√vṛt A. *–vartate,* to turn round, revolve, move about, roam, wander, turn round or back, return, to be transformed, change, alter, to visit or afflict continually, caus. *viparivartayati,*
viparivartate it revolves, exists 1/s/pres/indic/mid *vi pari √vṛt*
viparivatsara m. a year
viparus, mfn without knots or joints,
viparva without joints, or vulnerable points,
viparyak ind. invertedly,
viparyāṇa mfn unsaddled,
vipary√as A *–asyate* to turn over, turn round, overturn, reverse, invert, to change, interchange, exchange, caus. *viparyāsayati*
viparyāsa 974/2 m. overturning, overthrow, upsetting (of a car), transposition, transportation, expiration, lapse (of time), inversion, change, interchange, reverse, contrariety, opposition, deterioration, perverseness, error, mistake, delusion, imagining what is false or unreal to be real or true, in Buddhism there are 4 kinds of *viparyāsa* (false notions) – i.e. suppositions of being permanent (*nitya*), happy (*sukha*), ego , and pure (*śuddha*) ,
viparyasta mfn turned over, reversed, opposite, contrary, erroneously conceived to be real,
viparyaya mfn reversed, inverted, contrary to, perverse, m. turning round, revolution, running off, , coming to an end, alteration, transposition, change, inverted order or succession, opposite of, *buddhi-viparyaya* the opposite opinion, *svapna- viparyaya* state of being awake, change for the worse, reverse of fortune, calamity, misfortune, perverseness, overthrow, ruin, loss, destruction (esp. of the world), change of purpose or conduct, enmity, hostility, misapprehension, misconception, error, mistake, mistaking anything to be the reverse or opposite of what it is, shunning, avoiding, exchange, barter,
vipaścit 972/3 mfn. inspired, wise, learned, the intelligent Self, -intelligent because its nature of consciousness is never lost, versed in,
vi√pat P. *–patati* to fl or dash or rush through, to fly apart, fall off, be divided or separated, caus. *vipatayati* to fly in various directions, cause to fly asunder or off, strike down, kill, in comp. for *vi-pad,*
vipat 973/3 causing misfortune, calamitous, *vipatsu* 7/s in adversity
vi√paṭh P. *-paṭhati* to read through, peruse,
vipatha m.n. a different path, wrong road, evil course, a kind of chariot (fit for untrodden paths),
vipatti f. going wrongly, adversity, misfortune, failure, disaster,
vipavana mfn windless,
vipavya mfn to be thoroughly cleansed or purified,
vipayas mfn waterless,
viphala mfn bearing no fruit, useless, ineffectual, futile, idle,
vipīḍam ind. without harm or injury,
vipina n. forest, stirring or waving, quantity, multitude, grove, thicket,
vipinaukas m. monkey, ape,
viplava mfn having no ship or boat, confused (as words),

m. confusion, trouble, disaster, evil, calamity, misery, affray, revolt, violation of a woman, loss, profanation, rust on a mirror, damage, shipwreck, evil omen, terrifying an enemy by shouts and gestures, divulging,

viplavin mfn fugitive, transitory,

vi√plu A. *–plavate* to float asunder, drift about, be dispersed or scattered, to fall into disorder or confusion, go astray, perish, caus. *viplāvayati* to cause to swim or float about, to spread abroad, make known, to bring to ruin,

vipluta drifted apart, scattered, dispersed, gone astray, lost, perished, dimmed (eyes), excited, troubled, broken, violated (as chastity or a vow etc.), vicious, immoral, committing adultery with (*saha*), wrongly treated (with *karmaṇā*), depraved, wicked, contrary, adverse, inundated, immersed, n. springing or bursting asunder,

vipra mfn stirred or excited (inwardly), inspired, wise, gifted with superior insight, m. a sage singer, seer, poet, a priest, a Brahman, the moon the month *bhādrapada,*

vi√prā to fill completely

viprabodhita mfn mentioned, discussed,

viprabuddha mfn awakened, awake,

vipracchanna mfn hidden, concealed, secret,

vi√prach P. *–pṛcchati (te),* to ask various questions, make various enquiries,

vipra√cint to meditate on, think about

vipradharṣa m. harassing, annoyance,

vipra√dhāv P. *–dhāvati* to run in different directions,

vipra√dru P. *–dravati* to run away, flee, disperse,

vipra√duh P. *–dogdhi* to milk out, drain, exploit, to take,

vipraduṣta mfn very corrupt or corrupted, very sensual or dissolute, very bad,

vipra√gam –gacchati to go apart or asunder, be dispersed or scattered

vipragīta mfn that about which opinions differ, not agreed upon,

vipra√hā P. *–jahāti* to give up, abandon,

viprahāṇa n. disappearance, cessation,

viprahata mfn (√*han*) struck down, beaten, defeated (as an army),

vi-pra-√kṛ P. *–karoti* to treat with disrespect, hurt, offend,

viprakāra m. treating with disrespect, hurt, injury, wickedness,

viprakarṣa m. dragging away, carrying off, remoteness, distance, difference, contrast, the separation of 2 consonants by inserting a vowel,

viprakāśa mfn resembling, similar to,

vipra√kṛṣ P. *viprakarṣati* to drag or draw apart, lead away or home,

viprakṛt mfn hurting, offending,

vipra√labh A. *–labhate* to insult, violate, mock at, cheat, deceive, to regain, recover,

vipralabdha mfn insulted, violated etc., *(am)* ind. deceitfully, falsely,

vipralambha m. deception, deceit, disappointment, disjunction, quarrel, disagreement, separation of lovers, disunion, disjunction,

vipra√lap P. *–lapati* to discourse or speak about variously, be at variance, disagree, A. to complain, lament,

vipralāpa 1. mfn free from mere chatter, (as truth), 2. m. discussion, explanation, prattle, breaking of a promise, deception,

vipralāpin mfn prattling, a prattler,

vipralapita mfn discussed, debated about,

vipralapta n. discussion, debate

vipralaya m. extinction, annihilation, absorption in (7th),

vipraloka a bird-catcher,

vipra√2. ṇaś P. *–ṇaśyati* to be lost, perish, disappear, to have no effect or result, bear no fruit,

vipramādin mfn heeding nothing, heedless,

vipramanas mfn dejected, low-spirited,

vipramāthin mfn destroying everything, destructive,

vipramatta mfn not neglected,

vipra√muc P. *muñcati* to loosen, take off, to liberate, set free, pass. *–mucyate* to be liberated or released from,
vipra√muh caus. *–mohayati* to throw into confusion, render confused,
vipraṇī to turn the mind to, to let elapse or pass away (time),
viprapāta m. a particular way of flying, a precipice, abyss,
viprasāraṇa stretching out (limbs),
vipraśna m. interrogation of fate,
vipraśnika m. a fortune-teller,
vipra√sṛ P. *–sarati* to spread, be expanded, or extended,
viprasṛta mfn spread, extended, diffused,
vipra√sthā A. *-tiṣṭathe (ti),* to spread in different directions, go apart, be diffused, to set out, depart,
viprasthita mfn set out on a journey, departed
vipratāraka m. an impostor, deceiver,
vipratārita mfn imposed upon, deceived,
vi√prath P.A. –prathati (te), P. to spread, A. to spread out, extend, be wide, caus. *–prathayati* spread out or abroad, celebrate, to unfold, exhibit, display,
viprati√bhā P. *–bhāti*, to appear as, seem to be,
vipratikāra m. counter-action, opposition,
viprati√1.kṛ P. *–karoti* to counteract, oppose,
vipratikṛta mfn counteracted, opposed, requited,
vipratikūla obstinate, refractory,
vipratīpa reversed, inverted,
viprati √pad 975/2 to go in different or opposite directions, turn here and there, to roam, wander (said of the senses) to differ or diverge in opinion, be perplexed, be mistaken, have a false opinion about, to reply falsely or erroneously,
vipratipadya mfn to be opposed or contested, to be variously acquired,
vipratipadyate is contradicted, 1/s/pres/pass.
vipratipanna mfn. averse, gone in different directions, having a false opinion, wrong, uncertain, perplexed,
viprattipatti f. divergence, difference or opposition, contrariety, contradiction, incompatibility of two conceptions, opposition of one rule to another, erroneous perception, suspicion about (7th), aversion, hostile feeling or treatment, error, mistake, false reply or objection, mutual connection or relation,
vipratisāra 975/2 n. repentance, evil, wickedness, anger, wrath,
vipratiṣiddha mfn prohibited, forbidden, contradicted, opposed, (*am*) ind. of opposed meaning,
vipratyanīka mfn hostile,
vipratyaya m. distrust,
vipra√vad P.A. *–vadati (te*), to speak variously, be at variance, disagree,
vipravāda m. disagreement,
vipra√5. vas 976/3 P. *–vasati*, to set out on a journey, go or dwell abroad, caus.-*vāsayati* to expel from, banish,
vipravāsana n. expulsion, banishment,
vipravasita mfn withdrawn, departed,
vipra√vraj P.*–vrajati* to go away in different directions, to depart from,
viprayāṇa n. going away, flight,
viprayāta mfn gone apart, fled in all directions,
viprayoga 975/3m disjunction, dissociation, separation from, absence, want, quarrel, disagreement, the being fit or deserving,
viprayogin mfn separated from a beloved object,
vipra√yuj P. *–yunakti* to separate from, deprive of, 975/3
viprayukta mfn separated or removed or absent from, destitute of, free from, without, ‘ specifically applied to a single object alone’ (Gam.),
vi√pṛc P. *vipṛṇakti* to isolate, separate, scatter, dispel, fill, satiate,
vi-pre (*pra* + 5. i) P. *vipraiti* to go forth in different directions, disperse, depart
vipreks A. *-prekṣate* to look here and there,

viprekṣaṇa n. looking round

viprekṣita n. a look, a glance,

viprekṣitṛ mfn one who looks round

vipreman n. estrangement,

vipṛkvat mfn unmixed, pure,

vipriya mfn disaffected, disagreeable, unpleasant to, estranged, n. anything unpleasant or hateful, offence, transgression,

viproṣita mfn. dwelling abroad, set out or gone away to,

vi√pru A. *–pravate* to sprinkle about, scatter

vipruta mfn borne away, cast or carried away, vagrant,

vipsā f. repetition, succession,

vi√pū P. *–punāti* to cleanse thoroughly, purify effectually,

vipula mfn large, extensive, wide, thick, long, abundant, numerous, important, m. a respectable man, f. (*ā*) the earth, *-tva* largeness, greatness, extent, width,

vipulaka very extensive,

vipulamati mfn endowed with great understanding,

vipuṁsaka unmanly, not quite manly

vipura n. the intellect, 2. having no fixed abode or home,

vipuruṣa mfn void of men, empty,

vipuṣpa mfn flowerless,

vipuṣṭa mfn illfed, underfed,

vipuṣṭi f. perfect welfare or prosperity,

vipūya mfn cleansing, purifying,

√*vīr* 1005/2 2. cl 10 A *vīrayate* to be powerful or valiant, display heroism, P *vīrayati* to overpower, subdue, DP in *vikrānti* acting the hero, being powerful,

vīra mfn brave courageous, heroic, m. a man, a brave or eminent man, hero, chief, a hero, a husband, a male child, son, the male of an animal, warrior, actor, fire (esp. sacred fire,

vi√rac P. *–racayati* to construct, contrive, form, fashion, make, arrange, to build, erect, invent, produce, compose, write, to put on, don, wear,

viracana n. f(*ā*). arrangement, disposition, embellishment,

vi√rad P. *–radati*, to rend, sever, to open to, to bestow,

virāddha mfn opposed, thwarted, offended, reviled, abused,

vi√rādh P. *–rādhyati* to hurt, injure, to lose, be deprived of, caus. *rādhayati*, to become disunited, be at variance, disagree,

virāga 952/1 passionless, without feeling, aversion, dislike, indifferent (to everything), m. change or loss of colour, excitement, irritation, aversion, dislike or indifference to,

vi√rah P. *–rahayati* to abandon, desert, relinquish, leave,

viraha m. abandonment, desertion, parting, separation, absence from, lack, want, agony due to separation from the Lord,

virahita mfn deserted, abandoned, lonely, solitary, separated or free from,

vi √rāj 982/3P. A *virājati (te)*, to reign, rule, govern, master, excel, be illustrious or eminent, shine forth, shine out, glitter, caus. *virājayati* cause to shine forth, give radiance or lustre, brighten, illuminate,

virāj 982/3 2. mfn. ruling far and wide, the first progeny of Brahmā, sovereign, excellent, splendid, a ruler, chief, f. excellence, pre-eminence, high rank, dignity, majesty, 1. m. the king of birds,

viraja free from dust, clean, pure, free from passion, free from taint, free from all taints of *rajas*, free from menstrual excretion,

virāja mfn shining, brilliant,

virajas mfn dustless, pure,

virājati 982/3 reigns, rules, is illustrious, shines forth, shines out, appears as

virājita mfn adorned, 'caused to shine far and wide', eminent, illustrious, brilliant, splendid, glorious,

vi√rakṣ P. *-rakṣati* to watch over, guard, protect,

virakta 981/3mfn discoloured, changed in disposition, estranged, disaffected, averse, indifferent to, having no interest in, unattached,

virakti 982/1 f. change of disposition or feeling, alienation of mind, freedom of passion, indifference to (6th or 7th with *upari* or 2nd with *prati*), indiffernce to worldly objects,

viraktimat mfn indifferent to (7th), connected with freedom from worldly attachment,

virala 982/2 mfn rare, scarcely found, scanty, few, separated by intervals (whether of space or time), loose, thin sparse, wide apart, n. sour curds,

vi√ram P. A. *–ramati,* to stop, pause, cease, come to an end, to give up abandon, abstain or desist from, caus. –*rāmayati* to cause to stop or rest, bring to an end, finish,

virama 982/2 m. cessation, end

virāma m. stop! cessation, termination, end, grammatical stop at end of line or verse, desistence, abstention, exhaustion, languor,

virāmaka mfn ifc. ending in,

viramati stops,

vi√2.raṇ *-raṇayati* to cause to sound, make to resound, play upon (an instrument),

vi√rañj P.A. *–rajyati (te),* to be changed in colour, discoloured, lose one's natural colour, to become changed in disposition or affection, become indifferent to, take no interest in, caus. *–rañjayati* to discolour, stain,

vi√rapś A. *–rapśate*, to be full to overflowing, abound in (6th), have too much of (3rd),

virapśa mfn copious, abundant, m. superabundance,

vi√1.ras P. *–rasati* to cry out, yell, shriek,

virasa mfn without essence, juiceless, sapless, unseasoned, flavourless, tasteless, insipid, unpleasant, disagreeable, painful, ifc. having no taste for, m. pain, *(am)* ind. unpleasantly,

vīrasena mfn having a hero-army, m. a king (father of Nala),

vīrasenā f. her-army, army of heroes,

vīrasena-suta m. son of *vīrasena*

vīrasū mfn bringing forth heroes (sons), the mother of a male child,

virāṭ 983/1 in comp for 2. *virāj* see *virāj* '..the macrocosm, universe in full manifestation' HH.
-'the cosmic person embodied in the gross universe', 'who exists as fire, air and the sun'

viraṭa m. the shoulder

virata 982/2 stopped, ceased, ended, one who has given up or resigned or ceased or desisted from,

virāṭpuruṣa deity presiding over the universe, the cosmic or universal aspect of the deity, (U)

virātra m. or n. the end of night,

virathya m. delighting in byroads

virathyā a bad road or a byroad

virati 982/2 f. cessation, stop, pause, end, one who has given up, resignation, abstention, desistence from, detachment

virava m. roaring, thundering, noise,

virāva m. sound, noise, buzzing,

vīravat mfn having or rich in men or heroic sons, manly, heroic, n. wealth consisting in men or sons,

vīrayate see *vīr*

virecana 983/2 mfn opening, n. purging or any purging substance, a means for making the head clear,

vireka m. purging, making the head clear, a purgative, cathartic,

virepas mfn faultless, blameless,

virepha m. absence of an *r,* a river,

viribdha m. a note, tone, sound,
vi√ric pass. *–ricyate* to reach or extend beyond, to be emptied or purged, caus. *–recayati* to empty, drain, purge, emit,
virikta mfn evacuated, emptied, purged,
virocana mfn shining upon, brightening, illuminating, m. the sun, the god of the sun, the moon, fire, *Viṣṇu,* n. light, lustre,
virodha m. opposition, hostility, quarrel, contradiction, inconsistency, calamity, misfortune, incompatibility, hindrance, prevention, blockade, siege, adversity, perversity, an apparent contradiction or incongruity (in rhetoric), conflict with (ifc.),
virodhin mfn hindering, disturbing, opposing, obstructing, besieging, blockading, dispelling, removing, adverse, hostile, opposed, contradictory, rivalling with, contradictory, contentious, quarrelsome,
viroga m. absence of illness, mfn healthy
viroha m. growing out, shooting forth, source, origin, 'place of growth',
viroka m. shining, gleaming, effulgence, a ray of light, a hole, cavity, chasm,
viropaṇa mfn causing to grow, planting, n. the act of planting, the act of healing,
viropita mfn caused to grow, planted, caused to grow over, healed,
viroṣa mfn free from anger, very angry,
vi√1.ru P. *–ruvati –ravati –rauti* to roar aloud, cry, buzz, hum, yell, sing, to break to pieces, crush, destroy,
vi√ruc A. *–rocate* to shine forth, be bright or radiant or conspicuous, or visible, to appear as or like, to outshine, excel, to please, delight, to cause to shine, illuminate, caus. *–rocayati* to cause to shine, brighten, illuminate, to find pleasure in, delight in,
vi√rud P. *–roditi* to weep or cry aloud,
vi√rudh 1. to shoot forth,
2. P.A. *–ruṇaddhi –runddhe* P. to hinder, obstruct, invest, besiege, A. to encounter opposition from, to be at variance with, pass. *virudhyate,* caus. *–rodhayati,* to oppose, fight against or contend,
viruddha mfn opposed, hindered, restrained, surrounded, blockaded, forbidden, odious, (*am*) ind. perversely, incongruously, n. opposition, hostility, repugnance
virūḍha mfn shot out, sprouted, budded, grown, come forth, formed, produced, born, arisen, ascended, mounted, ridden, *-bodha* one whose intelligence has increased or matured,
virudita mfn wailing, grief,
vi√ruh P. *–rohati* to grow out, shoot forth, sprout, bud, caus. *–rohayati* to cause to grow, pass. *–ropyate* to be planted, to be caused to grow over, heal,
vi√ruj P. *–rujati* to break to pieces, crush,
viruj 1. f. violent pain, a great disease
2. mfn free from pain, healthy,
virukmat mfn shining, brilliant, bright, m. a brilliant ornament, bright armour, a bright weapon,
virūkṣa mfn rough, harsh (as speech),
virūpa mfn many-coloured, variegated, multi-form, manifold, various, altered, changed, deformed, less by one, m. jaundice, n. deformity, difference of form, the act of disfiguring, variety of nature or character,
virūpākṣa m. the elephant holding up the Eastern corner of the earth, mfn having deformed eyes, having various occupations,
viruta mfn roared, cried, etc. invoked, made to resound, filled with the cries of, n. shrieking, howling etc. any sound or noise,

vīrya 1006/3 n. (ifc.) manliness, valour, strength, power, energy, splendour, lustre, dignity, consequence,
f. (*ā*) vigour, energy, virility, heroic deed,
mfn. strong, powerful, 'power of potentiality' HH

vīryavān mfn valorous, full of heroism, the most powerful, the omnipotent,

viś 989/1 1. cl 6 P *viśati* to enter, enter in, to pervade, settle down on, go into, to re-enter, return, come back, to be absorbed into, ascend the funeral pyre, to appear (on the stage), to go home or to rest, to sit down upon, to resort or betake one self to, to flow into and join with (rivers and armies), fall to the share of, to occur to (as a thought), to fall or get into any state or condition, to enter upon or undertake, to begin, to mind (any business), to attend to, caus. *veśayati (te)* cause to enter into etc., DP in *praveśana* entering,
2. f. a settlement, homestead, house, dwelling, a community, tribe, race, also 'subjects, people, troops', (pl) property, wealth, entrance,
mf a man in general, person,

√*viṣ* 1. 995/2 cl 3 P *viveṣṭi*, cl 1 P *veṣati* to be active, act, work, do, perform, to be quick, run, speed, flow (as water), work as a servant, serve, overcome, subdue, rule, caus. *veṣayati* to clothe, DP in *secana* pouring out, emitting, effusion, DP (cl 3) in *vyāpti* spreading through, extending, pervading
2. mfn consuming,
3. f. faeces, excretion, dirt,

√*viṣ* 4. 996/2 cl 9 P *viṣṇāti* to separate, disjoin, DP in *viprayoga* disjoining,

√*vis* 1000/2 see *bis*, DP in *preraṇa* inciting, driving or urging on, instigating,

poison, venom, anything active

viṣa 995/2 mfn poisonous, m. a servant, attendant, n. anything active, poison, venom, water,

viṣā f. a kind of aconite (a plant), faeces, the *ati* tree, ind. = *buddhi*

viśabda 952/3 (ibc.) words of various kinds

viśabdana 989/3 = *pratijñāna* (666/1 admission, assertion, assent, agreement, promise)

viśabdita mfn mentioned, indicated,

visabhāga mfn having no share,

viṣad √*sad* P. -*ṣīdati* to be exhausted or dejected, despond, despair, to sink down, be immersed in,

viśada 989/3 mfn bright, brilliant, shining, splendid, beautiful, white, spotless, pure, calm, easy, cheerful, clear, intelligible, tender, ifc. skilled in, fit for,

viṣāda 996/3 m.depression, despondency, despair, aversion, disgust,

viṣādī m.despondent, depressed, morose,

visadṛśa mfn dissimilar, different, not corresponding, unequal,

visadṛśapariṇāma a change different from the original, like that of milk to curd; one relation of the Gunas changes into another different from it and so on (U),

vi-ṣah *(√sah)* A. -*ṣahate*, to conquer, subdue, overpower, be a match for, to be able to or capable of, to bear, withstand, resist, to endure, suffer, put up with,

viṣahya mfn bearable, tolerable, conquerable, resistible,
with *kartum* – possible, practicable, ascertainable, determinable,

viṣajjat devoted to worldly objects,

viṣajjita mfn clinging or sticking or adhering to,

viśakala mfn fallen into pieces,divided,

viśākha mfn branched, forked, branchless, m. a beggar, a spindle, f. (ī) a forked stick, n. a fork, -*ja* the orange tree

viśākhila m. name of a merchant,

viṣakta mfn hung to or upon, hung or suspended to, firmly fixed or fastened or adhering to, turned or directed towards, spread over, produced, implanted, stopped,
viṣakumbha m. jar of poison,
viśāla great, broad, huge, vast, illustrious, eminent, ifc. abundant in, full of,
viṣama 996/3 uneven, rough, irregular, difficult, dangerous, bad, wicked
visāmagrī f. the absence of means, (in phil.) the absence of causes calculated to produce an effect,
visamāpti f. non-completion,
visambhoga m. separation,
visaṁcārin mfn moving hither and thither
visaṁdhi jointless, without (gram.) *saṁdhi*
visaṁgata unconnected, inconsistent, not in harmony,
visaṁhata disjoined, loosened,
visaṁjña mfn unconscious, bereft of sense, lifeless,
visaṁjñita mfn deprived of consciousness,
visaṁkula not confused, self-possessed,
visaṁmūḍha utterly bewildered,
visaṁśaya mfn free from doubt, certain,
visaṁsthita mfn not finished, unachieved,
visaṁsthula mfn unsteady, infirm,
visaṁ√vad P. *–vadati* to break one's word or promise, to fail in an agreement, contradict, raise objections,
visaṁvāda m. false assertion, breaking one's word, disappointing, contradiction,
visaṁyoga m. liberation from worldly fetters, disjunction, separation,
visaṁyukta mfn disjoined, detached or separated from, omitting, neglecting,
viśana n. entering, entrance into,
viṣāṇa n. a horn, a tusk, crab-claws, a peak, top, point, summit, the chief or best of a class or kind,
viṣāṇin mfn horned, tusked, m. an elephant,
viṣañj *√sañj* P. *-ṣajati* to hang on, hang to, attach, *-ṣajjate* to be attached or devoted to,
viśaṅka mfn fearless, not afraid of
viśaṅkā 952/2 mfn fearless, not afraid of, causing no fear, free from danger, safe, ind. fearlessly,
f. absence of fear,
2. suspicion, doubt in, apprehension, fear of, hesitation
viśaṅkāṭa extensive, large, big, strong, vehement, ghastly, hideous,
viṣaṇṇa mfn dejected, sad, downcast,
viśāpa mfn freed from a curse,
viśapta n. forswearing, abjuring, taking an oath against,
visara m. going forth or in various directions, spreading, a multitude, quantity, plenty, abundance, bitterness, mfn bitter,
visāra m. spreading, extension, diffusion,
viśārada mfn experienced, proficient, learned, wise, holy, of a clear or serene mind, beautifully autumnal, lacking the gift of speech, bold, impudent,
visarjana n. cessation, end, relaxation (of the voice), the letting go, evacuation, abandoning, deserting, discharge, emission, sending forth, dismissal, driving out (cows to pasture), setting a bull at liberty, giving, bestowing, hurting, casting, shooting, creating, product, creation, answering a question, 'removal; the final item in upāsanā or worship by which the worshipper devotedly prays to the divine presence invoked in the idol, to return to its original abode,' (U)
viśaraṇa 1. mfn without protection,
2. dissolution, killing, slaughter
visaraṇa 1000/3 n. the act of going forth, becoming loose or slackened or released,
visārathi mfn being without a charioteer
visarga 1001/1 m. sending forth, letting go, liberation, emission, discharge, a release of breath, shown as :, giving, granting, producing, creating

viṣāsahi mfn victorious,
vi√śās P. *–śāsti* to give different directions (concerning),
viśasta mfn praised, celebrated, cut up, dissected, rude, ill-mannered,
viśastra mfn weaponless
viśati 989/1 retires, resorts to, enters,
viśaya 991/1 m. the middle, centre, doubt, uncertainty,
viṣaya m. object of the senses – sounds, textures, colours, tastes, smells 997/1 sphere (of influence or activity), dominion, kingdom, territory, region, district, country, abode, scope, compass, horizon, range, reach (of eyes, ears, mind), period or duration (of life), peculiar field or province of action, peculiar element, concern, ifc. (f. *ā*) concerned with, belonging to, an object of the senses, sphere of influence or activity, matter, subject or topic, anything perceptible by the senses, pl. objects of the senses, the subject of a comparison, a thesis,
viṣayabhoga sensual enjoyment,
viṣayacaitanya consciousness as objects, the object known; the consciousness determined by the object cognised, (U)
viṣayaka having anything for an object or subject, relating to, concerning,
viṣayaśakti attachment to sensual objects,
viṣayasaṁsāra objective or sensual world,
viṣayavṛtti thought of sensual objects,
viṣayavṛttipravāha the continuous thought-current of worldly objects; the flow of objective thinking,
viṣayin mfn relating or attached to worldly ob jects, sensual, carnal, m. a sensualist, materialist, a prince, king, a subject of (6th), (in phil.) the subject, the ego, the god of love, n. an organ of sense,
viścakrada m. a dog-keeper(regarded as a low man), a dog,
viśeṣa 990/2 m. distinction, difference, characteristic difference, peculiarity, a kind, species, individual, distinction, excellence,
a sectarian mark, any forehead mark, name of the primary elements, the earth as an element, the mundane egg, ifc. a particular or special…
(in gram.) a word which defines or limits the meaning of another word,
(in phil.) particularity, individuality, essential diference or individual essence,
(in med.) a favourable turn or sickness crisis,
(in rhetoric), statement of difference or distinction, individualization, variation,
(in geom.) the hypotenuse,
viśeṣaguṇa special quality,
viśeṣajñāna special knowledge, detailed knowledge
viśeṣaṇa 991/1 mfn distinguishing, discriminative, specifying, qualifying, distinctive (as a property), n. the act of distinguishing, distinction, discrimination, particularization, (in gram.) a word which - particularizes or defines, attribute, adjective, species, kind,
viśeṣeṇa (3rd) ind. especially
'brings out a quality of a *nāman* (an adjective) "the act of expanding the remainder"'
-pada epithet,
viśeṣatas ind. especially, particularly, above all, individually, singly, according to the difference of.., in proportion to (comp.)
viśeṣāvasthā f. differentiated condition,
viśeṣavijñāna special knowledge, knowledge of the Self,
viśeṣin mfn distinct, individual, ifc. vying with, rivalling,
viśeṣita mfn distinguished, defined, characterized, preferred, superior to, better than, surpassed, exceeded, attributed,

viśeṣya mfn to be (or being) distinguished or qualified or particularized, n. (in gram.) the word to be distinguished from another word, a substantive, noun, the object or subject of a predicate,

vi-ṣic *(√sic)* P. *-ṣiñcati* to shed, spill

vi-ṣīdati 996/2 is exhausted or dejected

vi√1. sidh P. *–sedhati* to resort to,

viṣīdan pres.part.despairing, despondent, while lamenting, *vi√sad*

viśikha bald, pointless, blunt, flameless, unfeathered (an arrow), m. a spear, javelin, reed,

vi√śikṣ to impart, share out,

viśīla mfn ill-behaved, ill-mannered, badly conducted,

viśiras mfn headless, topless,

vi√śiṣ P. *-śinaṣṭi* to distinguish, make distinct or different, particularize, specify, define, to distinguish (from others), to augment, enhance, caus. *-śeṣayati* to distinguish, define, specify, to prefer, to enhance the worth or value of, to surpass, excel,

viśiṣṭa mfn 'left apart', separated, distinct, distinguished, particular, peculiar, complex, qualified, excellent, that which is qualified, characterized by (3rd or comp.), chief or best among (6th), better or worse than (5th or comp.),

viśiṣṭādvaita qualified non-dualism, a prominent branch of philosophy of which a prominent exponent was Rāmānuja, a doctrine that the spirits of men have a qualified identity with the one Spirit,

viśiṣṭādvaitavāda the *viśiṣṭādvaita* doctrine

viśiṣṭatā f. condition of being distinguished, distinction, superiority, difference, speciality, peculiarity,

viśiṣya mfn without pupils,

viśita sharpened, sharp,

viṣita mfn let loose, released, relieved (the sun immediately before setting),

vi-ṣiv *(√siv)* P. *-ṣivyati* to sew or sew on in different places,

√viṣk cl 10 P *viṣkayati* to see, perceive, DP in *darśana* seeing, *hiṁsā* injuring,

vi-ṣkambh (√skambh) P. *–skabhnoti* or *–skabhnāti* to fix, support, prop, to hurl, cast, to come forth, escape,

vi-ṣkambha m. a prop, support, the bolt or bar of a door, the supporting beam or pillar of a house, a post, the diameter of a circle, a mountain range, an obstacle or impediment,

viślatha mfn relaxed, loose,

viśloka mfn without fame,

vi√śliṣ P.A. *-śliṣyati (te),* to be loosened or dissolved or relaxed, to be divided or separated, to fall wide of a mark, miss the aim, to divide, caus. *-śleṣayati* to cause to be disunited, separate from, deprive of

viśleṣa m. loosening, dissolution, disjunction, separation (esp. lovers), a chasm, subtraction,

viśleṣaṇa mfn dissolving, n. separation, dissolution,

viśliṣta mfn loosened, disunited, separated,

vismāpana 1002/2 m. a juggler, conjurer, illusion, deceit, the god of love, n. an act or means of surprising, a miraculous sign or phenomenon

vismaraṇa 1002/2 the act of forgetting, oblivion,

vismarati forgets

vismārita mfn caused to forget, caused to be forgotten, lost to memory,

vismaya 1. 953/1 mfn free from pride or arrogance, 2. 1002/2 m. wonder, surprise, amazement, bewilderment, pride, arrogance,

vismayana n. astonishment, wonder,

vismayānvita mfn filled with astonishment,

vi√smi A. *–smayate* to wonder, be surprised or astonished at,

vismita mfn amazed, astonished, proud, arrogant, wondered at,

vi√smṛ 1002/2 P. *–smarati*, to forget, be unmindful of, caus. *–smārayati* to cause to forget,

vismṛta mfn one who has forgotten anything, forgetful of all, forgotten by (3rd),
vismṛtāḥ 1002/2 pl. forgotten all
vismṛti f. forgetfulness, loss of memory, oblivion,
viṣṇu sustainer of the universe, preserver, universal *citta,*
viṣṇugranthi the knot of ignorance at the *maṇipūra* (navel) *cakra,*
viṣṇumāyā illusion wielded by the Supreme Lord so that the unreal seems real (U)
viṣṇu purāṇa famous book
viṣṇuśarman m. name of a sage,
viṣṇuśarmanāman mfn named *viṣṇuśarman*
viṣṇuvrata a vow to propritiate *viṣṇu*
viṣo (√*so*) P. -*ṣyati* to let loose, release, set free, flow, shed, cause to flow, to unharness, unbridle, to open, relax, mollify,
visoḍha mfn endured,
vīśodhana mfn cleansing, purging, washing away, n. cleansing, purification (in a ritual sense), subtraction,
viśoka m. cessation of sorrow, n. free from sorrow, removing sorrow, exemption from grief, at ease,
viśoṣa dryness, drought,
viśoṣaṇa mfn drying, dessicative, healing (a wound), n. dessication

vi√spardh A. –*spardhate* to emulate, vie with
vispardhā f. emulation, rivalry, absence of emulation or rivalry,
vispaṣṭa mfn very clear or apparent, manifest, evident, plain, intelligible, -*tā* f. great clearness or perspicuity,
vispaṣṭārtha mfn having clear or intelligible meaning,
viśpati m. master of the house or of the people(also applied to *agni* and *indra*), du. master and mistress of the house, the chief of a settlement or tribe, pl. kings or head-merchants,
vi√sphar caus. –*spharayati* to open wide (eyes), to draw, discharge (a bow),
visphāra m. opening wide, discharging a bow, the twang of a bowstring,
visphāraṇa n. spreading (wings),
vi√sphāy A. –*sphāyate* to swell,
visphīta mfn abundant, plentiful,
vi√sphul -*sphulati,* -*ṣphulati,* to wave or flicker to and fro, move hither and thither,
visphuliṅga m. a spark of fire, a sort of poison, f. a spark,
vi√sphur P. –*sphurati* -*ṣphurati,* to dart asunder, to writhe, tremble, flash, glitter, to break forth, appear,
visphura opening the eyes wide,
visphuraṇa n. quivering of lightning
vi√sphūrj P. –*sphūrjati* to resound, thunder, roar, caus. –*sphūrjayati* to cause to resound or twang (a bow),
visphūrja m. roaring, thundering, breaking forth like thunder,
vi√sphuṭ P. -*sphuṭati* -*sphoṭati,* to burst open, be split, cleft, rent asunder
visphuṭa mfn burst open, gaping,
viṣpanda m. throbbing, beating,
viṣpardhas mfn emulating, vying, envious,
viṣpita n. peril, difficulty,
vi√sṛ Cl 3P. –*sarati,* –*sisarti,* to go in various directions, to run or flow through, extend, A. to open or unfold one's self, to be separated, part from (3rd), caus. –*sārayati* causes to go in different directions, directs,
viśrabdha mfn confiding, confident, fearless, tranquil, calm, trusting in, relying on(*prati*), (*am*) ind. quietly, confidingly, without fear or reserve, confidently, without hesitation,
viśrabdhatva n. trustworthiness,
vi√śram P. –*śramyati,*-*śramati (te),* to rest, repose, recreate one's self, to rest from labour, cease, stop, to rest or depend on, to trust or confide in, rely on, to feel at ease or comfortable, caus. – *śrāmayati*

to cause to rest, cease, stop,
viśrama m. rest, repose, quiet,
viśrāma 992/1 m. rest, repose, calm, tranquillity, deep breathing (after exertion),cessation, abatement, a pause, a house,
vi√śrambh or *–srambh,* A. *–śrambhate* to confide, be confident, trust in or rely on, to inspire with confidence, encourage,
viśrambha m. relaxation of the organs of utterance, cessation, trust, confidence in, absence of restraint, familiarity, intimacy, a playful or amorous quarrel,
viśrambhakathā f. a confidential or intimate conversation,
viśrambhālāpa m talk with confidence familiar conversation,
vi√sraṁs A. *-sraṁsate* to fall apart, break down, collapse, become loose,
visraṁsa m. falling apart, dropping down, relaxation, weakness,
vi√śraṇ caus. *–śrāṇayati* to give away, distribute, present,
viśraṇana n. gift, donation
viśrāṇana 991/3 n. gift, donation
viśrānta 991/3 rested or ceased from, stopped, reposed, abated, ceased, coming to rest or to an end, feeling at ease in or with (7th), destitute of (in comp.),
viśrānti f. rest, repose, abatement, cessation, coming to an end,
visras f. dropping down, debility, decay
visrasā f. decrepitude, infirmity, senility,
viraśmi mfn rayless
visrasya mfn to be loosened or untied
visrava m. a flow, stream, efflux,
visrāva m. flowing forth, issuing,
viśrāva m. noise, sound, great fame or celebrity, flowing forth, dropping,
viśrāvaṇa n. causing to hear, narrating, causing to flow forth, bleeding,
viśravas n. great fame, mfn famous,
viśraya m. having recourse to, dependence on, asylum,
vi√sṛ P. *–sarati, -sisarti* to run or flow through, to spread out in various directions, A. to open or unfold one's self, to be separated, part from, to disperse, to come forth, issue from, caus. *–sārayati* to send forth, extend,
vi√śri P.A. *–śrayati (te),* to set or put asunder, separate, throw open, open, A. be opened or separated, or spread or diffused, to have recourse to, rely on,
m. death,
vi√sṛj P. *–sṛjati (te),* to send or pour forth, let go or flow, discharge, emit, turn the eye upon, to shed (tears), to utter (sounds or words), to set free, release, send away, dismiss, despatch, pass over, overlook, abandon, to produce or create, to answer questions,
visṛjāmi I send forth, I create 3/s/pres/indic/act *vi √sṛj*
visṛjan excreting, discharging, pres/act/part *vi√sṛj* 1001/1
visṛjya 1001/2 mfn. to be sent out or let go, to be produced or effected, effect ,
viśṛṅkhala mfn unfettered, unbounded, dissolute, sounding or tinkling excessively, abounding excessively in (ifc.),
vi√sṛp P. *–sarpati* to glide, move along or about, sneak, steal, to be spread or diffused over, to spread, diffuse, divulge,
visṛṣṭa mfn sent or poured forth, let go, discharged, spat out, turned, directed, deprived or destitute of, spread, diffused, opened, produced, created, founded, having been released, bestowed on (ifc.), mfn streaming or yielding milk,
vi√śru P. *–śṛṇoti* to hear distinctly, A. *-śṛṇute* to be heard or be heard of far and wide, become known or famous, caus. *–śrāvayati* to cause to be heard everywhere, narrate,

communicate, to make famous, to cause to resound,

vi√sru P. *–sravati* to flow forth or away, issue from, to discharge or emit any fluid, melt, dissolve, come to nothing, caus. *srāvayati* to cause to flow forth or away, to wash away, to let blood (with 6th or 2nd),

visruh f. a plant, shoot,

viśruta mfn flowed forth, flowed away, 2. mfn heard of far and wide, heard, noted, notorious, famous, known as, passing for, named, pleased, happy,

viśruti f. oozing, flowing, celebrity, fame, notoriety,

vi√stabh see *viṣṭambh* below,

viṣṭabha m. fixed or firmly planted, the world

viṣṭabhya supporting, having stopped, gerund *vi√stabh*

*vi-ṣṭambh(√stambh)*P. to hold or keep apart, prop, fix, fasten, support, to strengthen, encourage, to settle, ascertain, to stop, check, restrain,

vi-ṣṭap f. top, summit, surface, highest, part, height (esp. of heaven),

viṣṭara expansion, 999/1 anything spread out, rushes or grass for sitting on, a tree, mn any seat or couch, chair, stool, mfn extensive, wide,

vistara 1001/3 mfn extensive, long, m. spreading,expansion, a multitude, pl. great wealth or riches, detail, particulars, full or detailed description, amplification, an extensive treatise, affectionate solicitation, a layer, bed, couch, a partic. *śakti,*

vistāra 1001/3 m. spreading, expansion, extent, width, becoming large or great (said of the heart), a diameter, specification, detailed description, branch of a tree with new shoots, a shrub,

vistaraśa ind. in detail (adv.)

vistarata adv. in detail,

vistaratā f. spreading, extension,

vi-ṣṭhā 2. *(√sthā)* A. *-tiṣṭathe* to stand or go apart, be spread or diffused, or scattered over or through, to be removed or separated from, to stand, be stationary, stand still, remain firm, abide, dwell, stop, to keep ground, not to budge, to be present or near, to be engaged in (7th), 3. f. place, position, station, form, kind, feces, excrement,

viṣṭhala n. a remote place, a place at a distance,

visthāna mfn belonging to another place or organ (as a sound),

viṣṭhita 999/1 mfn. standing apart, scattered, standing, fixed, standing or being on or in, being present or near, situated,

vistīrṇa mfn broad, extensive, expanded, numerous, long, copious, large,

vistṛti 1001/3 f. extent, width, breadth, spreading, expansion, a circle diameter,

viṣṭu (*√stu*) P. *-ṣṭauti* or *-ṣṭaviti* to praise very much, extol with praises,

viṣṭuta mfn praised highly, extolled,

viṣu ind. on both sides, in both directions, in various directions, similarly, equally, 2. to press or squeeze out (Soma plant),

viṣū (√2. *sū*) to bring forth (a child) impf only *vyasūyata*

vi√śubh A. *–śobhate*, to shine brightly, be beautiful,

visūcana n. making known,

viśuddha 991/2 mn. completely cleansed or purified, clean, clear, pure, free from vice, virtuous, honest, (ifc.) one who has gone through or thoroughly completed, cleared i.e. exhausted, empty (as a treasury), n. a *cakra* in the region of the throat,

viśuddhabodha m fully realized man

viśuddhasattva m. of a pure character, one who has become pure in mind, *viśuddhi* f. complete purification, purity, holiness, virtue, rectification, removal of error or doubt, retribution, retaliation, perfect, knowledge,

visuhṛd mfn friendless

visukha mfn joyless,

visukṛt mfn doing no good work,

viṣuṇa mfn different, various, manifold, changing (as the moon), averse from, ind. aside, apart, m. the equinox,

viśūnya mfn perfectly empty,

viṣupta mfn fallen asleep, sleeping,

visūraṇa n. sorrow, distress,

visūrya mfn deprived of the sun

vi√1.śuṣ cl 4 P.A. *-śuṣyati (te),* to become very dry, dry up, wither away,

viśuṣka mfn dried up, withered, parched, thirsty,

visuta mfn childless

vi√sūtr P. *–sūtrayati* to drive away, remove, to throw into confusion,

viṣuvat 1. mfn having or taking part on both sides, i.e. keeping or being in the middle, 2. m. middle day (of a long sacrifice), 3. middle day (between the solstices), the vernal or autumnal equinox, top, summit, vertex,

viṣuvat-saṁkrānti f. the equinox, passage of the sun from one zodiacal sign to the next, the time of equinox,

viśva 992/2 mfn all, every, everyone, whole, entire, universal, all pervading, omnipresent, n. the whole world, the universe, dry ginger, myrhh, m. (in phil.) the intellectual faculty, Grimes 351, the individual form of the Self having egoism in a gross body while awake, the form of the Self in its waking state according to *Advaita Vedanta* 'a name of the *jīva* in the waking state (U),

viṣvā f. the earth, dry ginger, a partic. weight,

viśvabheṣaja mfn all-healing, containing all remedies, m. a universal remedy, n. dry ginger,

viśvacakṣas mfn all-seeing,

viśvācī f. universal,

viśvād mfn all-consuming,

visvāda mfn tasteless,

viśvadarśata mfn to be seen by all, all-conspicuous, to be honoured by all,

viśvadeva m. all divine, pl. the all-gods,

viśvādhipa m. lord of the universe,

viśvāhā ind. = *viśvahā* at all times, always, for evermore,

viṣvak for *viṣvañc* in comp.

viśvakarmā 'whose work is the universe',

viśvakṛt mfn creator of all things, m. architect and artificer of the gods, maming, creating all,

viśvam 992/2 n. whole, the All, entire, universal, the world, the universe,

viśvāmitra *Viśvāmitra* –'friend of all' a sage,

viṣvañc 998/2 going in both or all directions, all-pervading, ubiquitous, general, going asunder or apart, separated or different from, following in inverted order, n. the equinox, in two, in all directions, all around, everywhere,

viṣvañj (√svañj) A. *-ṣvaṇati* to embrace

visvapna, visvanaj, visvara m. discord, mfn having no sound, dissonant, discordant, *(am)* ind. pronoun ced with a wrong accent,

viśvarūpa mfn many coloured, variegated, wearing all forms, manifold, various, the form of all, n. various forms, 'cosmic form; having all forms, (U)'

visvara soundless, dissonant, discordant,

vi√śvas P. *–śvasiti* to draw breath freely, be free from fear or apprehension, be trustful or confident, trust or confide in, rely or depend on, caus. *viśvāsayati* to cause to trust, inspire with confidence, console, comfort, encourage,

viśvāsa 995/1 m. confidence, trust, faith or belief, reliance, a confidential communication, secret,

viśvāsabhūmi f. proper vessel for confidence, one who may be trusted,

viśvāsakaraṇa n. reason for confidence,

viśvasākṣin 994/1 mfn all-seeing

viśvasana n. trusting, confiding,

viśvaścandra mfn all-sparkling,

viśvasṛj mfn all-creating, m. creator of the universe, m.pl. all-creators (10),

viśvasta mfn full of confidence, fearless, bold, unsuspecting, trusted, faithful,

viśvāsya ind. having inspired confidence, to be trusted or confided in, trustworthy, to be inspired with confidence, liable to be consoled or encouraged or comforted,

viśvataijasaprajñā jīva in the waking, dreaming and deep sleep states respectively, in the individual aspect, (U)

viśvatas mfn from or on all sides,universally,

viśvātman m. Soul of the Universe, Universal Spirit, sun,

viśvatomukha mfn having a face on all sides, whose face is turned everywhere,

viśvāyu mfn general, n. all people,

viśvāyus mfn belonging to or appearing to all life or living creatures, n. all-life, all living creatures, universal life, universal health,

viśve m.pl. all-gods, ind. in the world,

viśvedeva a class of divine beings,

viśya mfn forming or belonging to a community, m. a man of the people or of the 3rd caste,

viṣyand (*vi-√syand*) A. -*ṣyandate* to flow in streams or abundantly, to dissolve, melt, to cause to flow,

viṣyaṇṇa mfn overflowed, overflowing,

viṭ 1. in comp for 2. *viś*, 3. *viṣ*

-vit knower

√viṭ cl 1 P *veṭati* to sound, DP in *śabda* sounding,

viṭa m. a bon-vivant, boon-companion, rogue, knave,

vīta 1004/1 mfn gone, approached, desired, liked, loved pleasant, straight, smooth, trained, quiet, gone away, departed, disappeared, worn out, useless, f. a line, row, n. a wish, desire, the guiding of an elephant with a goad, a useless horse or elephant,

vīta-darpa mfn pride departed, humbled,

vi√taḍ P. *vitāḍayati* to strike back, strike against, wound

vi√takṣ P. *vitakṣati* to cut off, cleave, split

vitala n. one of seven hells, depth of hell,

vitāla mfn (in music) breaking time, m. wrong time or measure, f. an instrument for beating time,

vitamanyu mfn free from anger, free from sorrow,

vitamas mfn free from darkness, light

vitamaskatā f. exempt from the quality of ignorance,

vi√tan P.A. *vitanoti, vitanute,* to spread out or through or over, cover, pervade, to spread, stretch, extend (a net, snare, cord),

vitāna mfn dejected, sad, empty, dull, stupid, wicked, abandoned, 2. mn great extent or quantity, plenty, abundance, extension, n. leisure, opportunity,

vitaṇḍā f. fallacious controversy, perverse or frivolous argument, criticism, a ladle, spoon,

viṭaṅka m. n. the loftiest point, pinnacle, top, an aviary, m. a big cucumber, mfn trim, nice, pretty, handsome,

vitantu m. a good horse, f. a widow

vitanu mfn extremely thin, bodiless, having no essence or reality, m. the god of love

vitanvānā an increaser, (Gam.),

vi√tap P.A. *vitapati (te)*, to give out heat, to force asunder, tear, penetrate, to burn, to warm oneself, caus. *tāpayati* to heat, warm,

viṭapa 961/3 mn a young branch of a tree

or creeper, twig, sprout, shoot, a bush, shrub, cluster, thicket, tuft, expansion, spreading, m. a keeper of catamites,

viṭapaka a tree, a rogue, voluptuary,

vitāra mfn starless, without a nucleus (as a comet)

vītarāga 1004/2 mfn dispassionate, calm, (*vita-* gone away *raga-* passion), desireless, tranquil, unattached, colourless, bleached, 'free from such drawbacks as attachment,' (Gam.) m. a sage with subdued passions,

vi√tark P. *vitarkayati* to reflect, think, believe, suppose, conjecture, consider as or take for,

vitarka m. conjecture, supposition, guess, fancy, imagination, opinion, doubt, uncertainty, purpose, intention, a teacher, instructor in divine knowledge, a dubious or controversial matter, reasoning, deliberation, intention, a teacher, a partic. class of *yogī*

vitaram ind. farther, farther off, more distant, more

vītaśoka 1004/2 mfn free from the disturbance of sorrow, m. the *aśoka* tree,

vitasti f. a span (about 220mm/12 fingers)

vitata 962/2 mfn. spread out, extended, diffused, drawn (as a bow-string), bent (as a bow), n. any stringed instrument,

vitatha mfn untrue, false, incorrect, unreal, free from,

vitathābhiniveśa m. inclination towards that which is false,

vitathatā f. untruth, falsehood,

vitathavat mfn prone to falsehood,

vitati f. extent, length,

vītatṛṣṇa 1004/2 mfn free from all passions or desires

√vith 963/2 cl 1 A *vethate* to ask, beg, DP in *yācana* begging,

vīthikā f. tie or fastening, row, street, road, line, sort of drama, picture gallery,m. sort of drama, picture-gallery, terrace in front of a house,

vitilaka mfn having no mark on the forehead

vi√tī P. *vitarati, vitirati,* to pass across or through, traverse, pervade, to bring away, carry off, remove, to cross, frustrate, disappoint, to extend, prolong, to give away, grant, bestow, yield, caus. *vitārayati* to comb out, to carry out, accomplish,

vi√tṝ P. *–tarati,-tirati,* to pass across or through, traverse, pervade, to bring away, carry off, remove, to cross, frustrate, disappoint, to extend, prolong, to give away (also in marriage), grant, bestow,

vi√tras P. *vitrasati, vitrasyati,* to tremble, be frightened,

vitrāsa m. fear, terror, alarm,

vitṛṇa mfn grassless,

vi√tṛp P. *vitṛpyati* to be satisfied, become satiated with,

vitṛpta mfn satisfied, satiated,

vi√tṛṣ P. *vitṛṣyati* to be thirsty,

vitṛṣ mfn free from thirst,

vitṛṣṇa mfn free from desire,

vitṛṣṇā thirst for, ardent desire,

vitṛṣṇatva 950/3 n. freedom from desire

vitta 963/2 mfn known, understood, celebrated, notorious, famous for, found, gained, obtained, n. anything found, a find, m. wealth, fame

vittārtha m. one who knows the matter, an expert,

vittasamutsarga pouring forth of riches, creation of wealth

Vitteśas another name for *Kubera*

vitti 963/3 f. consciousness, understanding, intelligence, finding, acquisition, gain, a find, the being found, existence, (ifc.) a term of praise,

vi√tud P.A. *vitudati (te),* to pierce, tear, strike, play (an instrument), caus. *vitudāyati* to prick, sting,

vituṣṭa mfn displeased, dissatisfied,

vi√vā P. *–vāti* to blow on all sides, or in every direction, blow through, blow,
vi√vac P. *–vakti* to declare, announce, explain, solve (a question), to decide, to discuss, to impugn, A. to speak variously or differently, dispute with one another about (7th),
vivāc mfn crying aloud, screaming, f. opposing shout, contest, battle,
vivācas mfn speaking in various ways,
vi√vad P.A. *–vadati (te),* to contradict, oppose, be at variance, contest, litigate, fight
vivāda m. a dispute, quarrel
vivadanta m. talking contrari-wise (Gam.),
vivadha m. a shoulder yoke or carrying burdens, a store of grain or hay, provisions, a road, highway, a ewer, pitcher, the income of a king from his subjects,
vivadita mfn disputing, quarrelling, disputed, litigated,
vi√vah P. *–vahati* to bear or carry off, remove, lead away the bride from her father's house, to marry,
vivāha m. fetching home of the bride, wedding, marriage, a partic. wind
vivāhacatuṣṭaya n. the marrying of 4 wives,
vivāhāgni m. wedding-fire,
vivāham + *kṛ* he gets married
vivāka m. one who decides causes or pronounces judgment,
vivakṣita mfn favourite, to be urged, expressly meant, essential, literal, chief, intended, n. any desired object or aim, what is wished or intended to be spoken,
vivakṣitā f. meaning, purpose, wish,
vi√val P. *–valati,* to turn away, or aside,
vi√valg P. *–valgati* to leap, jump, spring,
vivāna n. plaiting, twisting,
vivara m.n. a fissure, hole (of creatures that live in the ground), chasm, slit, cleft, hollow, intermediate space, difference, breach, fault, flaw, weak point, injury, opening,
vivāra m. dilation, expansion, open or expanded state of the organs of speech (throat), one of the particular 'efforts' of articulate speech for certain letters,
vivaraṇa mfn the act of uncovering, spreading out, laying bare or open, explanation, exposition, interpretation, gloss, commentary, translation, a sentence,
vivarcas mfn without splendour,
vivardhana 989/1 mfn augmenting, increasing, furthering, promoting, n. the act of cutting off, cutting, dividing, growth, increase, prosperity,
vivarjaka mfn shunning, avoiding,
vivarjita mfn avoided, left, abandoned by, destitute or deprived of, free or exempt from (3rd or comp.), that from which anything is excluded (ifc.), excepting, excluding, that from which anything is subtracted, diminished by, distributed, given,
vivarman mfn without armour
vivarṇa pale, colourless, low, vile, m. a man of low caste or outcaste,
vivarṇa-vadana mfn pale-faced,
vivarta 988/3 m. 'the revolving one' name of the sky, turning round, revolving, rolling onwards, changing from one state to another, alteration, an appearance e.g. a snake seen as a rope, transformation, illusion,
vivarta upādāna a kind of material cause in which the effect is apparent without undergoing any changein itself e.g. a snake seen as a rope,
vivartasṛṣṭi creation where the original reality remains what it is and yet apparentlybrings about the effect, according to *Advaita* school of thought (U),
vivartate 988/3 change from one state to another, turn, revolve, turn round, 1/s/pres/indic/mid rolling onwards
vivartavāda a method of asserting the Vedanta doctrine (maintaining the

development of the universe from brahma as the sole real entity). (N) the temporary-manifestation or *māyā* theory,

vivartman n. a wrong road,

vivartopādāna a material cause which does not undergo the slightest substantial change in the production of the effect. e.g. Brahman as cause of the universe,

vivaruṇa keeping off *Varuṇa* i.e. death

vi√2.vas P. *vyucchati* to shine forth, shine, dawn, caus. *–vāsayati,*

vi√4.vas A. *–vaste* to change clothes, to put on, don

vi√5.vas P. *–vasati* to change an abode, depart from, enter an apprenticeship, become a pupil, abide, dwell, live, to pass, spend (time), caus. *–vāsayati,* to cause to dwell apart, banish, expel, send forth, dismiss,

vivaśa mfn deprived or destitute of will, powerless, helpless, unwilling, involuntary, spontaneous, unrestrained, independent, subject, apprehensive of death, desirous of death, m. a town, suburb,

vivāsa mfn without clothes, naked, m. unclothed, naked, leaving home, banishment, shining forth, dawning, ind. at dawn, *vi* 2. *√vac* leaving home, banishment, separation from

vivasana mfn unclothed, naked, m. a naked mendicant,

vivasvabhis ind. so that it lights up, n. perhaps, flash, spark,

vivasvan mfn lighting up, n. flash, spark,

vivasvant mfn lighting up, the sun, name of a god,

vivasvat 987/1 mfn. shining forth, diffusing light, name of the sun (the brilliant one), the *soma* priest, ,

vivat mfn containing the word *vi*

vivavri mfn unveiled, bare,

vivayana n. plaited work,

vivecaka mfn discriminating, distinguishing, judicious, wise,

vi√ve P.A. *–vayati (te),* to interweave

vivejita mfn terrified, frightened,

viveka 987/3 m. true knowledge, right judgement, the power of separating the invisible Spirit from the visible world, truth from untruth, reality from illusion, "The result of *viveka* is such that in appreciation of the separation of the two, there is no binding force for the limited knowledge. In *viveka* the limit is broken and the vision goes beyond the limit. It transcends." HH 'discrimination between the conscious and inanimate' HH 'Only through true understanding, *(viveka)* can one experience *aham* and segregate *ahaṅkāra*' HH "*Viveka* is the reasoning system to acquire the truth about the Self." HH

vivekin 988/1 mfn discriminating or distinguishing, separated, kept asunder, examining, investigating, discriminative, judicious, prudent, discreet, wise, a discriminating man

vi√ven P. *–venati* to be hostile or indisposed,

vi√vic P. *–vinakti* to sift (esp. grain), divide, separate from, to cause to lose, to distinguish, discern, discriminate, decide, examine, ponder, investigate, to show, manifest, declare, caus. *–vecayati* to separate, distinguish, investigate,

vi√1.vid to discern, know, (only pf. *–veda)*

vividha mfn of various sorts, manifold, diverse, n. variety of action or gesture, *(am)* ind. variously,

vivigna mfn very agitated or alarmed,

vivikta 987/3 mfn separated, discriminated, isolated, alone, solitary, kept apart, free from, pure, clean, neat, trim, clear, distinct, discriminative, judicious, profound, n. separation, solitude, a lonely place, clearness, purity,

vivikti f. separation, division, discrimination, discernment, *vi√viś* P. *–viśati* to enter, penetrate,

vivīta m. an enclosed ground, paddock, the owner of same,

vivitti f. gain, acquisition,

vivoḍhṛ m. a husband

vi√1.vṛ P.A. *–vṛnoti –vṛṇute* to uncover, spread out, display, show, reveal, open, to unsheathe (a sword), to part, comb (hair), to explain, describe,comment upon, to cover, cover up, stop up,

vivrata mfn reluctant, refractory, performing various actions,

vi√vṛdh A. *–vardhate* to grow, increase, swell, become large or powerful, thrive, prosper, be lengthened, be lucky or fortunate, to spring up arise, caus. *–vardhayati* cause to grow, increase, prosper, to gratify, exhilarate, gladden,

vivṛddha 989/1 grown, increased, grown up, enhanced, fully developed, n. (*am*) grown powerful, increased,

vivṛddhi f. growth, increase in size, increase, enlargement, furthering, promotion, prosperity, lengthening (of a vowel),

vi√vṛj caus. *–varjayati* to exclude, avoid, shun, abandon, to distribute, give

vivṛkta mfn abandoned, left,

vi√vṛṣ caus. *-varṣati* to rain, rain upon, besprinkle or cover with,

vi√vṛt A. *–vartate,* to turn round, revolve, roll, struggle, move about, turn back, depart, go astray, expand, develop, caus. *–vartayati* to turn round, turn, roll, etc. to cause to turn away, remove, withdraw, to keep asunder, leave behind, cast o (a garment, to accomplish, execute,

vivṛta mfn uncovered, unconcealed, exposed, naked, bare, unclosed, open, also applied to the organs of speech when articulating partic. sounds, extensive, wide, explained, divulged, public, maniest, evident, known, presented or offered (as an opportunity), n. the bare ground, (*am*) ind. openly, publicly,

vivṛtta mfn turned or twisted round, whirling round, flying in different directions (a thunderbolt), opened, uncovered, shown, displayed,

vivṛtti f. going asunder, opening, expansion, development, turning round, revolution, rolling, whirling, tumbling, development, (in gram.) the opening of two vowels upon each other without blending, hiatus,

vi√vyadh P. *–vidhyati* to pierce through, transfix,

vivyādhin mfn piercing, transfixing

vi√yā P. *–yāti* to go or pass through, traverse, cross, drive through (with a car), cut through (with wheels), destroy, to depart, turn away

viyac in comp. for *viyat*

viyaccāra mfn flying through the air,

viyad in comp for *viyat*

viyadgata mfn moving or flying in the air,

vi√yam P. *–yacchati* to spread out, extend, to stretch out the legs, step out (as a running horse), to hold apart or asunder, caus. *–yāmayati*

viyāma m. a measure of length (the two extended arms), forbearance, restraint, rest, stop, cessation, pain, distress,

viyan in comp for *viyat*

viyat A. *–yatate,* to dispose in various rows, caus. *–yātayati* to place in rows, arrange, to do penance, to torment, pain, punish,

viyat mfn going apart or asunder, being dissolved, passing away, vanishing, n. the sky, heaven, air, atmosphere, ether (as an element),

viyata mn stretched out, extended, kept apart,

viyāta mfn gone apart or from the right path, shameless, impudent,

viyodha mfn deprived of combatants,

viyoga 981/3 m. disjunction, separation (esp. of lovers), loss or absence or want of, giving up, getting rid of, abstention from (comp.), subtraction,

viyogin mfn separated or absent from, liable to separation, m. the ruddy goose,

viyoginī f. a woman separated from her husband or lover,

viyojana 981/3 n. detaching or liberating from, separation from,

viyoni f. the womb of animals, mfn contrary to one's own nature, of low origin, an animal,

viyotṛ mfn one who divides or separates,

vi√yu P. *–yuyoti, -yauti,* to separate, part, to be separated from or deprived of, to separate, divide, detach or exclude from, deprive of, keep off, avert, scatter, to open,

viyugala mfn not fitting together

vi√yuj P.A. *–yunakti –yuṅkte*, to disjoin, detach, divide, separate from or deprive of, A. to forsake, abandon, to relax, abate, yield, caus. *–yojayati (te),*

viyukta 981/3 mfn detached, separated, disunited, ailing, deficient,

viyuta mfn separated from, deprived of, diminished, that from which something has been subtracted,

viyuti f. the difference between two quantities,

√vlī 1043/3 cl 9 P *vlīnāti* or *vlināti* to press down, crush, cause to fall, caus. *vlepayati* DP in *varaṇa* going, choosing, supporting,

vlīna mn crushed, sunk down, collapsed, gone, held, supported,

voḍhṛ mfn wafting, carrying, bearing, drawing, bringing, m. bridegroom, husband, porter, carrier, ox, bull, draught horse, charioteer,

√vṛ 1. cl 5.9.1. P A *vṛṇoti vṛṇute, vṛṇāti vṛṇīte, varati varate,* (mostly cl 5 and with prepositions *apa* or *vi*, to cover, screen, veil, hide, surround, obstruct, to close (a door), to ward off, check, keep back, prevent, hinder, restrain, caus. *vārayati (te*), to cover, conceal, hide, keep back, hold captive, exclude, prohibit, forbid, DP in *āvaraṇa* covering,

√vṛ 2. 1007/3 cl 5,9 P A *vṛnoti, vṛṇute, vṛṇāti vṛṇīte* to choose, select, choose for one's self, choose as, to choose in marriage, woo, to ask for, request that, to prefer to, like better than, to like, love, grant a boon, caus.*varayati (te),* to choose, choose for one's self, choose as, DP in *varaṇa* (cl 5), selecting, choosing, in *sambhakti* (cl 9) dividing,

√vṝ 1013/2 see √2. *vṛ* DP in *varaṇa* choosing, selecting,

√vraj 1041/3 cl 1 P *vrajati (te)* to go, walk, proceed, travel, wander, move, retire, withdraw, pass away (as time), to undergo, go to any state or condition, obtain, attain to, become, cl 10 P *vrājayati* to send, drive, to prepare, decorate, DP in *gati* (cl 1) going, in *mārga-saṁskāra* (cl 10) trimming, preparing, in *gati* going,

vraja m. a way, road, n. wandering, roaming, ifc. m.f (*ā*) a fold, stall, cow-pen, cattle-shed, station of herdsmen, a herd, flock, swarm, troop, host, multitude,

vrāja m. going, movement, motion,

vrajeta he might go, he should travel, he should proceed 1/s/opt/mid *vraj*

vrajita mfn gone, proceeded, walked, n. going, roaming,

vrajitvā ind. having gone, having walked,

√vraṇ 1042/1 1. cl 1 P *vraṇati* to sound, DP in *śabda* sounding,
2. cl 1 P *vraṇati* to wound, cl 10 P *vraṇayati,* DP in *gātra –vicūrṇana* (cl10) wounding

vraṇa m. a wound, sore, ulcer, tumour, cancer, boil etc. a flaw, blemish,

vraṇita mfn wounded, sore, ulcerated,

√vraśc 1043/1 cl 6 P *vṛścati* to cut down or off or asunder, cleave, hew, fell (a tree), caus. *vraścayati,* DP in *chedana* cutting,

vrata 1042/2 n. will, command, law, vow ordinance, rule, obedience, service, mode or manner of life, conduct, manner, usage, custom, fulfilling religious vows, rules and observances faithfully,

vrāta 1043/1 m. a multitude, flock, assembly, group, the company or attendants at a wedding feast, the descendant of an outcast Brahman, n. manual labour, day labour,

vratya mfn engaged in a religious observance, obedient, faithful, fit for a religious observance,

vrātya m. tramp, low or vile person, outcaste, man of the vagrant or mendicant class,

vṛddha mfn old, grown larger, aged, grown up, full grown, advanced in years, eminent in, important, distinguished by (3rd or comp.) experienced, wise, learned, cut off, destroyed, exalted, joyful, glad, (in gram.) vowel increased by *vṛddhi* n. what is cut off, m. an old man (ifc. eldest among), a religious mendicant,

vṛddhi 1010/2 cutting off, abscission, (in law) forfeiture, deduction, 1011/1 growth, increase, rise, success, gain , augmentation, advancement, extension, welfare, prosperity, success, fortune, happiness, elevation of ground, old, prolongation of life, gain, profit, usury, interest, the second modification or increase of vowels (in certain conditions), a strengthened vowel, an elder male or female descendant,

√*vṛdh* 1010/2 cl 1 A *vardhate (ti*), to increase, augment, strengthen, cause to prosper or thrive, to elevate, exalt, gladden, cheer, to grow, grow up, increase, be filled or extended, become longer or stronger, thrive, prosper, succeed, to rise, ascend (as the scale of ordeals), to be exalted or elevated, feel animated or inspired, become joyful, caus. *vardhayati, (te*), cause to increase or grow etc., to rear, cherish, foster, bring up, to elevate, cause to prosper, to speak or shine, DP in *vṛddhi* (cl 1) growing, increasing, in *bhāṣā* (cl 10) speaking, shining,

vṛdh being pleased, rejoicing,

√*vṛh* 1013/2 see √1.2.*bṛh* DP in *udyamana* growing, increasing, expanding,

vṛhat (or *bṛhat* in earlier language) lofty, high, tall, extended or bright, name of a man, name of a *marut,* name of various *sāmans*, (a metrical hymn or song of praise) composed in *bṛhatī* form, name of *Brahman,*

√*vrī* 1043/2 cl 9 P , 4 A *vrīṇāti, vriṇāti, vriyate*, to choose or to cover, caus. *vrāyayati, vrepayati,* DP in *varaṇa* (cl 9), selecting, *vṛṇoti (*cl 4) choosing, selecting,

√*vrīḍ* 1043/2 cl 1 A *vrīḍate* cl 4 P *vrīḍyati* to be ashamed, feel shame, be bashful, or modest, cl 4 P to throw, hurl, cl 10 P *vrīḍayati, vīḍayati,* to make firm, DP in *codana* throwing, casting, or *lajjā* being ashamed, feeling shame, (cl4)

vrīḍā f. shame, modesty, bashfulness

vrīhi m. rice pl. grains of rice, a field of rice, rice ripening in the rainy season, any grain,

vrīhī m. rice,

√*vṛj* 1008/3 cl 1.7.P *varjati, vṛṇakti,* cl 2 A *vṛkte* to bend, turn, twist off, pull up, pluck, gather, wring (a neck), to avert, remove, A. to keep anything from, divert, withhold, exclude, A. choose for one's self, select, appropriate, caus. *varjayati,* to remove, avoid, shun, relinquish, abandon, give up, renounce, to spare, let live, to exclude, omit, DP in *varjana* avoiding, shunning, *vṛjana* n. enclosure, esp. enclosed settlement, dwelling place, dwellers, crookedness, wickedness, deceit, wile, intrigue, strength, the sky, atmosphere,

vṛjina 1009/1 bent, crooked, false, wicked, m. curled hair, hair, n. sin, vice, wickedness, distress, misery, affliction,

vṛka m. wolf

vṛkka m. du. the kidneys,

vṛkṣa m. tree

vṛkṣatraya n. three trees,

vṛkṣatraya-tale under three trees,

vṛkṣopari on the tree,

√*vṛk* 1008/1 cl 1 A *varkate* to take, seize, DP in *ādāna* taking, seizing,

vṛka m. wolf, dog, jackal, crow, owl, thief, a plough, thunderbolt, the moon, sun,

√*vṛkṣ* 1008/2 cl 1 A *vṛkṣate* to select, accept, to cover, keep off, DP in *varaṇa* accepting, selecting, covering,

vṛkṣa *vṛṣaka* m. tree

√*vṛṇ* 1009/1 cl 8 P A *vṛṇoti, vṛṇute*, to consume, eat, cl 6 P *vṛṇati* to please, gratify, exhilarate, DP in *prīṇana* delighting,

vṛnda mfn many, much, all, n. a multitude, a bunch, cluster (flowers or berries etc.), a chorus, m. a throat tumour,

vṛṇe I ask for, I seek for 3/s/mid/pres/ mid cl9

vṛṅkte excludes 1/s/pres/mid *vṛj*

vṛnoti he chooses, adopts,

vṛṇīṣva you ask for 2/s/impv √*vṛ* cl9

√*vṛś* 1011/3 cl 4 P *vṛśati* to choose, select, DP in *varaṇa* choosing, selecting,

√*vṛṣ* 1011/3 cl 1 P *varṣati,(te), vṛṣate,* A. *varṣate vṛṣate* to rain, rain down, shower, pour forth, effuse, shed, A. to bestow or distribute abundantly, caus. *varṣayati*, to cause to rain, to fall down as rain (flowers), to rain upon (arrows etc.), A. to have manly power, generative vigour, DP in *secana* (cl1) sprinkling, in *śakti-bandhana* (cl 10), being powerful or eminent, having the power of pro-creation,

vṛṣa ifc. for *vṛṣan* , or = *vṛṣan*

vṛṣabha same as *vṛṣan,* bull as type of greatness and might etc., of Indra – most mighty one,

vṛṣadhvaja m. having virtue for a mark, having a rat for a sign, virtuous man, Śiva,

vṛṣala m. manikin, little man, (as a term of contempt) a low person, *śūdra* ,

vṛṣan mfn all that was distinguished for its strength and virility, m. man as opposed to a castrated person, the male of any animal - stallion, bull, bear, etc. of gods – manly, mighty, great, of Indra and others, a strong or potent man, the most excellent or pre-eminent of anything, best of its kind, justice or virtue as a bull, semen, water, a mouse or rat, an enemy, a partic. form of a temple, suitable ground for a house foundation, n. a woman's apartment, a peacocks plumage or tail,

vṛṣṇi 1013/2 mfn manly, strong, powerful, angry, passionate, heretical, heterodox, m. a ram, a bull, a ray of light, air, wind, family or tribe (of *Kṛṣṇa*)

vṛṣṭi f. rain, (ifc. often a shower of flowers), a form of internal acquiescence (Sāṁkhya),

vṛṣṭibhū m. 'rain-born', a frog,

vṛṣṭijīvana mfn 'living by rain', land nourished by rain

vṛṣṭikāma n.f. desiring rain,

vṛṣṭikāla m. the rainy season,

vṛṣṭikara mfn producing rain, sprinkling,

vṛṣṭimat mfn rainy, raining,

vṛṣṭipāta m. a shower of rain,

√*vṛt* 1009/1 cl 1 A *vartate (ti), vavartti,*

vartti, to turn, turn round, revolve, roll, to move or go on, get along, advance, proceed, take place, occur, be performed, to be, live, exist, be found, remain, stay, abide, dwell, to live on, subsist by, to pass away (time), to depend on, be engaged in, be intent on, attend to, to act, conduct oneself, to act or deal with, follow a course of conduct, show, display, employ, use, to be alive or present, to continue, to hold good, continue in force, to become, to associate with, caus. *vartayati,* to cause to turn or revolve, whirl, wave, make anything round, cause to proceed or take place, or be or exist, do, perform, accomplish, display, spend, pass, lead a life, live, to set forth, relate, recount, to begin to instruct, to speak or to shine, DP in *varttana* (cl1) being, existing, abiding, remaining, staying, in *bhāṣā* (cl 10) speaking, shining,

vṛt 1009/1 lives or exists

vṛt in cpds.) turning, ifc. surrounding, enclosing, obstructing, a troop of followers or soldiers, army, host,

vṛta mfn chosen, selected, preferred, loved, liked, asked in marriage, covered, enclosed, surrounded, stopped, checked, held back,filled or endowed or provided or affected with, n. a treasure, wealth,

vṛthā 1007/3 at will, at pleasure , i.e. not for the sake of the gods, in vain, wrongly, falsely, incorrectly, unduly, ind. aimless

vṛthāpaśughna mfn slaying cattle for pleasure, m. one who slays cattle for pleasure, i.e. not for sacrifice,

vṛtra 1.n. that which wards off or holds in check, i.e. the enemy, 2.m. coverer, encloser, name of a demon of drought and darkness, darkness, a thunder-cloud, a wheel, mountain, a stone, n. wealth, sound, noise,

vṛtraputra having *vṛtra* as son, (*ā*) f. the mother of *vṛtra*

vṛtratara comparative of *vṛtra,* the arch-withholder,

vṛtta mfn turned, set in motion (as a wheel), round, rounded, circular, occurred, happened, ifc. continued, lasted for a certain time, completed, finished, absolved, past, elapsed, gone, quite exhausted, deceased, dead, studied, mastered, existing, effective, unimpaired, become..., acted or behaved towards, fixed, firm, chosen, m. a tortoise, a kind of grass, a round temple, n. a circle, the epicycle, occurrence, transformation or change into (ifc.), appearance, formed or derived from (ifc.), procedure, practice, action, mode of life, conduct, behaviour (esp. virtuous conduct, good behaviour), an event, adventure, means of life, subsistence,

vṛttānta mfn alone, solitary, m. n. 'end or result of a course of action', news, report, occurrence, incident, course, manner, way, method way something is done), tidings, rumour, report, account, tale, story, history, a chapter or section of a book, a topic, subject, sort, kind, nature, property, leisure, opportunity, a whole, totality, adventures, story,

vṛttaujas mfn one who has effective power or energy,

vṛtti the fluctuations of reflected consciousness, the waves of mental activities (*citta vṛtti*) of thought and perception, thought-wave, mental modification, mental whirlpool, 1010/1 f. rolling, rolling down of tears, mode of life or conduct, course of action, behaviour, moral conduct, common practice, mode of being, kind or respectful behaviour or treatment, nature, kind, character, disposition, state, condition, being, existing, accurring or appearing in (7th or comp.), devotion to, occupation with, working, activity, function, the use of a word in a particular way, (in gram. – a complex formation which requires explanation or separation into its parts e.g. some compounds), a commentary , comment, gloss, explanation, style of composition, alliteration,

vṛttijñāna secular science, knowledge obtained through the mind, experience of the world,

vṛttilaya dissolution of the mental modification,

vṛtti-nibandhana n. means of support,

vṛttisahita mfn associated with thought,

vṛtti-vyāpti 'the mind enveloping the object and taking the shape of the object, 'whenever an object is perceived, there is a corresponding *vṛtti* in the mind,'

√*vruḍ* 1043/3 cl 6 P *vruḍati* to cover, to heap, to sink, DP in *saṃvaraṇa* covering,

vyabhicāra m. going apart or astray, deviating, being separated or isolated, trespass, transgression, crime, vice, sin (esp. infidelity of a wife), violation, disturbance, (in phil.) wandering from an argument, erroneous reasoning, (in gram.) deviation from or exception to a rule, irregularity, anomaly,

vyabhicārin mfn going astray, doing what is improper, unchaste, changeable, transgressing, wanton, faithless towards, irregular,

vyabhicāriṇibhakti wavering, unsteady devotion,

vyabhra mfn cloudless

√*vyac* 1029/1 cl 6 P *vicati*, cl 3 *vivyakti* to encompass, embrace, comprehend, contain, *vicati* to cheat, trick, deceive, caus. *vyācayati,*
2. P A *vyacati* (*te*), to bend apart, make wide, extend,
DP in *vyājīkaraṇa* deceiving,

vy-ā-√*cakṣ* 1036/3 cl2. to explain, comment upon, recite, rehearse,

vyācacakṣire they explained, they spoke clearly, 1/pl/perf.

vyacas n. compass, extent, expanse, wise space, free scope, room,

vyadadhāt has allotted or distributed in the proper way, made into, offered, performed, awards,

vyadārayat it caused to burst, it tore, it rent, 1/s/caus/imperf/act *vi* √*dṛ*

√*vyadh* 1031/1 cl 4 P *vidhyati (te)* to pierce, transfix, hit, strike, wound, to pelt with, to inflict, attach to, affect with, to shake, wave, cling to,(with *sirām*) to open a vein or bleed, caus. *vyādhayati, vedhayati,* to pierce, open a vein, DP in *tāḍana* piercing,

vyādha m. a hunter, 'one who pierces', a low man, wicked person,

vyādhi m. disease, ailment, sickness, disease personified (as a child of death), any tormenting person or thing, ifc. a plague of a woman i.e. a troublesome woman,

vyādhita mfn diseased, sick,

vyāghāta m. striking against, a defeat, commotion, agitation, an obstacle, impediment, hindrance, (a figure of speech in which different or opposite effects are seen to arise from the same cause, (in phil.) contradiction or inconsistency of statement,

vyāghra 1036/2 m. a tiger, a pre-eminently strong or noble person,

vyāghraśarman n. tiger-skin,

vyāghratā f. tigerhood, condition of being a tiger,

vyagra m. tiger, mf(*ā*)n inattentive, distracted, agitated, (*am*) ind. in an agitated manner, engrossed by,
-*tā* f. intense occupation, eagerness, intentness (ifc.), perplexity,
-*tva* n. distraction, confusion, (ifc.) intentness on

vyāharaṇa n. the act of uttering, speaking, pronouncing, utterance, speech,

vy-ā-√hṛ P.A *°harati (te),* to utter or pronounce a sound, say to, converse with, name, call by name, answer questions, to begin to talk (said of a child), to confess, avow to, to utter inarticulate sounds,

vyāhṛti 1039/3 f. utterance, speech, declaration, the mystical utterance of the names of the seven worlds (*bhūr, bhuvaḥ, svar, mahar, janar, tapar, satya)* the first three of which, called 'the great *Vyāhṛti*s are pronounced after *om* by every Brāhman in commencing his daily prayers and personified as the daughters of *Savitṛ* and *Pṛśni*

vyāja 1036/3 m. deceit, deception, fraud, imitation, disguise, an artifice, device, contrivance, means, wickedness,

vyajana n. a palm-leaf used as a fan, a fan,

vyājīkaraṇa n. fraud, deception

vyākaraṇa 1035/3 separation, distinction, discrimination, explanation, detailed description, grammatical analysis, grammar, grammatical correctness, polished or accurate language, the science of grammar, putting asunder,

vy-ā-√khyā 1036/1 P. *–khyāti* , to explain in detail, tell in full, discuss, to relate, communicate, to name, call, *√cakṣc* derived from *√kāś*

vyākhyāna explanation and commentary,

vyākhyāsyāmaḥ we shall explain, 'we shall speak clearly (*vi)* and fully (*ā*)', (Gam.)

vyākhyāta mfn explained, fully detailed, related, told, fully dealt with,

vyākhyātṛ m. explainer, commentator, expounder,

vy-ā-√kṛ 1035/3 P.A *°karoti, °kurute*, to undo, sever, divide, separate from (3rd), to expound, explain, declare, '*vyākaroti vācam* –utters speech' to prophesy anything (2nd) about anyone (2nd), to predict (esp.future births) (Buddhist),

vyākriyate is differentiated,

vyakta mfn. adorned, embellished, beautiful, caused to appear, manifested, apparent, visible, distinct, intelligible, perceptible by the senses, specified, distinguished, specific, individual, hot, wise, learned, m. heat, a learned man, an initiated monk,
(*am*) ind. apparently, evidently, certainly,

vyaktāyām vāci
' in the sense of becoming visible (and) of speech', apparent in Vedic instruction, ? apparent in the words?

vyakti f. visible appearance or manifestation, becoming evident or known or public, specific appearance, distinctness, individuality, an individual, (in gram.) gender, the proper form of any word, case, inflection,

vyaktitva n. personality, identity, individuality, distinctness,

vyaktīkaraṇa n. the act of making manifest or clear or distinct,

vyākula mfn intently engaged in or occupied with (comp.), confused, puzzled, full of, quivering (as lightning),

vyākulatva 1035/3 n. agitation, bewilderment, alarm,

vyalkaśā mfn having various branches, f. a certain plant,

vyāma m. a stretch-out, the distance covered by the stretched out arms,

vyāma-mātra mfn having a *vyāma* as measure,

vy-ā-miśra mfn. mixed together, blended, manifold, of various kinds

vyāmoha 1038/2 loss of consciousness, delusion, embarrassment,

vyaṁsa mfn having the shoulders apart, i.e. broad-shouldered, –name of a demon slain by Indra,

vyaṁsaka m. a cheat, rogue, juggler,
vyāna 1031/2 m. one of the 5 vital airs or *prāṇas,* that which circulates or is diffused through the body, diffused breath, the *prāṇa* which governs the circulation of blood in the body,
vyañjana mfn clear, manifest, indicating, manifesting, n. dry curry, curry, n. figurative expression, irony, suggestion, sign, mark, (in Gram.) consonant, f. (*ā*) allusion, suggestion, implied indication,
vyanunādayan causing to resonate, thunder, howl, *vi-anu-√nad*
vyā√pad Cl 4 *–padyate,* falls away, perishes f. misfortune, calamity, disorder, failure, ruin, death,
vyāpāda m. destruction, ruin, death, evil intent or design, malice,
vyāpādaya kill!
vyāpādayati he kills
vyāpādayiñyati will kill
vyāpādayitavya to be destroyed or killed,
vyapadeśa m. designation, information, statement, a name, representation, title, a family, race, summons (of an army), appeal to (6th),talk, speech, a partic. form of speech, fame, renown, making a false show of, an unauthorized referring to, using the name of an authority,
vyāpādita mfn destroyed, killed,
vyāpādya gerund, having killed
vyāpaka 1037/2 mfn pervading, diffusive, comprehensive, widely spreading or extending, spreading everywhere, (as an attribute always found (like smoke) where some other (like fire) is found, invariably pervading or inherent or concomitant,
vyāpakātmā all-pervading Self,
vyāpāra 1038/1 m. occupation, employment, exertion, activity, business, affair, workplace, profession, performance, engaging, exertion,
vyāpāra-śata n. exertion-hundred, a hundred attempts,
vyapāśraya 1028/3 1. mfn. devoid of reliance or support, self-centred, self-dependent *vi- apa- ā √śri* 1032/1 2. 2. going away, secession, place of refuge, shelter, support, ifc. being in or on,
vyapāśritya taking refuge in, having recourse to, gerund
vyāpatti f. falling into misfortune, suffering injury, loss, ruin, death,
vyapeta mfn passed away, ceased, opposed to, separated, gone away, vanished,
vyāpi in comp. for *vyāpin*
vyāpin mfn reaching through, pervading, covering, diffusive, comprehensive, spreading everywhere, ifc. extending or reaching or continuing to or filling up or containing, one who pervades,
vyā√pṝ
vyāpṛta mfn . busied with or engaged in, occupied, employed, m. minister, official,
vyāpta 1037/2 pervaded , (as the universe by spirit), spread through, pervaded, filled with, permeated,
vyāpti 1037/3 f. invariable concomitance, ubiquity, universal rule without an exception, acquisition, attainment, accomplishment, pervasion, universal pervasion, inherence, inherent and inseparable presence of any one thing in another, e.g. oil in sesame seed, omnipresence, universality,
vyāpya 1037/3 permeable, penetrable, the site or locality of universal pervasion, proof, reason, cause, gerund.. pervading, having pervaded,
vyāpyatā f. permeableness,
vyartha mfn useless, unavailing, unprofitable, futile,
-tā falseness, uselessness, absence of meaning, nonsense, inoffensiveness,
-tva n. contradictoriness, absence of meaning,

vyāsa the sage who composed the *Mahābhārata* and compiled the *Veda*

vyasana n. separation, individuality, attachment, throwing one's self away (upon a thing), inability, passionate devotion or addiction to a thing, an overpowering passion, vice, difficulty, evil result, bad habit, favourite pursuit or occupation, ill-luck, wind, assiduity, individuality, crime,

vyaśema *vy√1.aś* 1034/3 P.A. to reach, attain, obtain, 3/pl/opt/act may we attain,

vyaṣṭi 1034/3 f. attainment, success, singleness, individuality, a separated aggregate, (such as a man) viewed as a part of a whole, individual acting as a separate unit

√*vyath* 1031/1 cl 1 A P *vyathate* *(ti)*, to tremble, waver, go astray, come to naught, fail, lose, fall on the ground, to be dried up, to cease, become ineffective (as poison), to be agitated or disturbed in mind, be restless or unhappy, be afraid of, caus. *vyathayati* to disquiet, frighten, agitate, pain, afflict, cause to tremble, cause to swerve from,DP in *bhaya* being afraid, or *sañcalana* trembling,

vyathā f. feeling of painful unrest, agitation, perturbation, loss, damage, ill-luck, (with *hṛdi or hṛdaye*) palpitation of the heart,

vyathana mfn greatly disturbing or perplexing, tottering, alteration, feeling pain, tormenting, piercing,

vyathate he is agitated, churned up,

vyathayanti they cause to tremble 1/pl/caus/act √*vyath*

vyatikara mfn acting reciprocally, reciprocal, m. reciprocity, reciprocal action or relation, a mixing or blending together, confusing, confusion, disaster, contact, contiguity, incident, opportunity, reverse, misfortune, calamity, accident, destruction, end, a resemblance (confusing or striking), (ifc.) performing, joined with, spreading through or over, pervading,

vyatireka 1030/2 distinction, difference, separation, exclusion, negation, logical discontinuance, (opp. to *anvaya* q.v.), contrasting of things compared in some respect to each other, the presence as separate (and conjoint (*anvaya*), (V), 'The way of discrimination, starting with earth is called *vyatireka.* It starts with any idea of limit and leads to the unlimited' 'Thus the Self is distinguished from the body, thoughts, etc.'

vyatirekin mfn excepting, distinguishing, reverse, different, negative, m. an exclusive mark (logic), negative property (logic),

vyati√tī cl 1 *–tarati* to cross over completely, overcome,

vyatitariṣyati 1030/1 will pass completely across or overcome, 1/s/fut/act

vyatītāni passed away, gone away, ppp *vi ati* √*i* 1/pl/n

vyātta mfn . 'taken apart', wide open (esp. the mouth), n. the opened mouth, open jaws,

vyavahāra m. worldly life, doing, action, performing, practice, conduct, procedure, way of acting, way of acting with others, intercourse, usage, custom, ordinary life, common practice, mercantile transaction, trade with dealing in (comp.), a contract, legal procedure, contest at law with (*saha),* litigation, lawsuit, practices of law and kingly government, mathematical process, administration of justice, punishment (fig.), competency to manage one's own affairs, majority (in law), propriety, adherence to law or custom, with regard to, speaking about, designation, compulsory work, a sword, a sort of tree,

vyavahārapekṣa with a view to the world of appearance or relativity,

vyāvahāra-satya (N) practical truth, the truth which has *māyā* as its limiting adjunct, e.g. the sky, accepted as true in daily life but false from the standpoint of the highest truth,

vyāvahārika mfn relating to common life or practice or action, practical, empirical, actual, ordinary life, sociable, affable, relative viewpoint, (in phil.) practical existence, the empirical nature, (opposed to *paramāthika* real and *pratibhāsika* illusory), m. the experiencer of the waking state,
m. a counsellor, minister, official, name of a Buddhist school,

vyāvahārikasatta empirical reality,

vyāvahārya 1039/1 m. mfn able, capable, not worn-out,

vyavahita mfn placed apart or asunder, separated, not contiguous, concealed, covered, hostile, opposed, remote, distant, passed over, surpassed, excelled, put to shame,

vyava√hṛ P.A. *–harati, te,* to transpose, exchange, to have intercourse with (3rd or 7th), to meet (as foes), fight with, to be active or busy, work, to carry on commerce, trade, deal in (7th3rd or 6th), to bet at, play for (6th), to manage, employ, make use of, be intent on, care for, cherish,

vyāvartaka mfn separating, removing, excluding, excepting, distinguishing, distinctive, turning away from, encircling, encompassing,

vyavasāya m. settled concentration and perseverance, determination, resolve, purpose, intention to, strenuous effort or exertion, resolution (personified), trade, business, an act, action, performance, first impression or perception, state, condition, artifice, stratagem, boasting,

vyavasāyātmika one with resolution and determination,

vi-ava √so P. *–syati* to settle down or dwell separately, to differ(in opinion), contest, quarrel, to separate, divide, to determine, resolve, decide, be willing to, to ponder, reflect, consider, to settle, ascertain, caus. –*sāyayati* to cause to resolve, encourage to undertake, embolden, to incite or instigate to,

vyavasāyin mfn determined, resolute, persevering, untiring,
m. practitioner,

vyavasita mfn determined, resolved, ended, undertaken, known, persevering, decided, done, finished, one who has resolved upon or is determined or willing to, cheated, deceived, energetic, making effort or exertion,

vyavasthā 1033/3 A. -*tiṣṭhate,* to go apart, separate from, to differ respectively, to halt, stop, stay, to prepare or make ready for, to be settled, be logically true or tenable, to appear as (1st), caus. *–sthāpayati,* to put down, place, to fix on direct towards (7th), to charge with, appoint to (*artham*), to stop, hold up, prevent from falling, to restore, re-establish, prove to be (logically), to give a name, to perform,
f. respective difference, abiding in one place, statute, law, rule, steadiness, fixity, constancy, establishment, state, condition,

vyavasthita 1034/1 mfn placed in order, drawn up (in battle), standing on the side of, standing here and there, contained in (7th), used in the meaning of (7th), signifying (as a word), based or dependent on (7th), one who has waited or stayed, persevering in, sticking or adhering to (7th or comp.), arrayed, arranged, stationed, settled, established, fixed, exactly determined, persevering in, placed in order, settled, constant, unchanging, existing, present, turning out or appearing as,

vyavasthiti f. being placed apart or separate, separation, distinction, difference, staying, abiding, perseverance in (3rd or 7th), constancy, steadfastness, fixity, fixed rule or statute, decision, determination,

vyā√vṛt A. *–vartate* (rarely P.) to become saparated or singled out from (3rd), to become separated or distinct, be distinguished as or in some partic. form,to turn or wind in different directions, divide (as a road), to be dispersed (as an army), to be opened, to turn away from, part with, get rid of, to diverge from, be inconsistent with (5th), to go away,

vyāvṛtta mfn turned away from, freed from, split asunder, opened, ifc. different from, averted, distorted, turned back, returned from (5th), ifc. incompatible or inconsistent with, thoroughly liberated or emancipated, ceased, disappeared, gone, 'chosen' or 'fenced' = *vṛta* excepted, excluded, praised,

vyāvṛtti f. turning away, turning the back, rolling the eyes, deliverance from, getting rid of, being deprived of, separation, exclusion, removal, rejection, discrimination, distinction, difference, cessation, distinctness (of sound or voice), difference, cessation, a kind of sacrifice, praise

√vyay 1032/2 cl 1 P A *vyayati (te)*, to expend, spend, waste, cl 10 P *vyayayati* to go, move , throw, DP in *vitra-samutsarga* (cl1) dissipating, expending wealth, in *gati* (cl 10) going,

vyaya mfn passing away, changeable, decayable, going asunder or to pieces,
m. spending, loss, expense, outlay, (as opposed to *–āya* income), wealth, money,
(in gram.) inflection, declension,

vyāyāma 1038/2 m. dragging different ways, contest, strife, struggle, exertion, manly effort, athletic exercise, right exercise or training (Buddh.), a measure of length, fathom, dancing, a difficult passage,

√vye 1041/2 cl 1 P A *vyayati, (te)*, to cover, clothe, wrap, envelop, caus. *vyāyayati,* DP in *samvaraṇa* covering,

vyoma 1041/2 in comp. for 2. *vyoman* - heaven, sky, atmosphere, air, ether (as an element), space thoroughly occupied or penetrated by, pervaded, wind or air (of the body), water, talc, mica, a temple sacred to the sun, preservation, welfare,

vyomaga mfn moving through the air, flying, m. a being that moves in the air, a divine being,

vyoman mfn one who cannot be saved, m. heaven, sky, atmosphere, air, space, ether (as an element), wind (bodily),water, talc, mica, a temple sacred to the sun, preservation, welfare,

vyuda mfn waterless, dry,

vyudasya ind. having rejected or abandoned, laying aside, given up or giving up completely,

vyūḍha 1. mfn led home, married, divided, distributed, arranged, transposed, altered, expanded, developed, wide, broad, large, compact, firm, solid,

vy √ 1 ūh P. *–ūhati,* to push apart, place asunder, remove, to arrange, place in order, draw up in battle array, to shift, transpose, alter, to separate, resolve vowels (sandhi), A. *–ohate,* to forebode, perceive,

vyūha *(you)* remove, place apart, 2/s/impv

vyūha m. placing apart, distribution, orderly arrangement of the parts of a whole, shifting, transposition, displacement, separation, resolution (of vowels,

syllables etc.), detailed explanation or description, a section, division, chapter, emanation, manifestation, battle array, an army, host, squadron, form, structure, manufacture, an aggregate, flock, multitude, the body, breathing, reasoning, logic,
a name for three forms in which *nārāyaṇa* appears for the creation, support and dissolution of the world,

√vyuṣ 1040/3 1. cl 4 P *vyuṣati* to burn, to divide, distribute, cl 10 P *vyoṣayati* to reject, discharge, emit, DP in *dāha* burning (cl 4), in *vibhāga* (cl 4) dividing,
f. dawn, daybreak,

vyutthāna n. rising up, awakening (a partic. stage in *yoga*), yielding, giving way in, swerving from the right course, neglect of duties, opposition, independent action, a kind of dancing or gesticulation,

vyutpanna mfn arisen, originated, derived (esp, in grammar), to be explained etymologically, learned, accomplished, experienced, versed in,

vyutpatti f. learning, production, origin, derivation, etymology, development, perfection, growth (esp. knowledge), proficiency (esp. in literature and science), comprehensive learning or scholarship, difference of tone or sound,

vyutsarga m. renunciation, resignation, (G) indifference to objects,

ya pron. who, which, what,
ya ya whoever, whichever, whatever, whosoever,
ya ka ca, ya ka cid, ya ka cana, anyone soever no matter who,
ya if anybody
ya and .... he..
m. a goer or mover,
wind, joining, restraining, fame, barley, light abandoning,
f. going, a car, restraining, religious meditation, attaining, the vulva,

√yā 849/1 cl 2 P *yāti* to go, proceed, move, walk, set out, march, advance, travel, journey, go away, withdraw, retire, to flee, escape, go or come to, enter, approach, arrive at reach, to go to for any request, implore, solicit, to go to for any purpose (inf.), to extend to (2nd), to last for (2nd), to pass away or elapse (time), to vanish or disappear (wealth), to come to pass, prosper, succeed, to proceed, behave, act, to undertake, undergo, caus. *yāpayati,* to cause to depart, cause to go or march, dismiss,
to direct the gaze towards,
to drive away/remove/cure a disease
to cause to pass or elapse (time), pass or spend (time), to live, to cause to subsist, support, maintain, to induce,
DP in *prāpaṇa* going,
m. a goer, mover, wind, joining, restraining, fame, barley, light abandoning,
f. going, a car, restraining, religious meditation, attaining, the vulva,

√yabh 845/2 cl 1 P A *yabhati (te*), to have sexual intercourse, DP in *maithuna* having sexual intercourse with,

√yāc 850/2 cl 1 P A *yācati (te*), (usually A. in sense of asking for oneself), to ask, beg, solicit, entreat, require, implore, caus. *yācayati,* DP in *yācñā* begging, asking, soliciting,

yācaka m. beggar, petitioner

yācana 850/2 asking, entreaty, begging, soliciting, f.(*ī*) a female beggar,

yaccittam *yat* pronoun – who or which, *citta* 395/3 the heart or mind, whose mind

yacitṛ m. proposer, wooer, applicant, petitioner, suitor,

yācñā 850/2 f. begging, asking for, asking alms, mendicancy, any petition or request, prayer, entreaty

yad who, which, what, whichever, whatever, that, also used to introduce direct assertions,
yad....tad....., since...... therefore.....
yad...tasmāt... inasmuch as... therefore
tad...yad... then... when..
yad... tatas... when...then...
m. = *puruṣa,*
yadā 844/1 ind. when, at what time, whenever,
yadā.... tadā when..... then....
yadā aiva as soon as
yādas 851/2 n. a large aquatic animal, a sea monster, water, semen, a river,
yadbhaviṣya mfn what will be, who says
yad bhaviṣyati (tad)bhaviṣyati 'what will be, will be,' m. fatalist, name of a fish,
yadi ind. if, or else, or rather, or
yadi api (*yadyapi*) even if, though,
yadi...tarhi.. if...then...
yadṛccha 844/3 mfn spontaneous, accidental, f.*(ā)* self-will, spontaneity, accident, chance, (ibc or *ayā* ind. spontaneity, unexpectedly, accident, chance, 3/s by accident, accidentally, that which is presented or happens by chance, visible, apparent,what is seen,
yadṛcchayā (ibc. or ind.) by luck, by chance, by good fortune, by accident,
yadi 844/3 ind. if, in case that , even though
yady api even if, although,
yadi ... tarhi if..... then...
yadṛcchayā by luck, by chance, by good fortune, by accident,
yādṛcchika mfn dependent on circumstances i.e. dependent on what comes to him by chance, m. a son who offers himself for adoption,
yādṛś 851/2 mfn which like, as like, of whatever kind or nature
yādṛśa anyone whatever, anybody whatsoever, of which kind, such as, just as,
yadvā f. = *buddhi,* perception, mind, intelligence,
yad vā whether, if, if either
yad vā..... yadi vā if... or if... whether..... or.....
yadvat 844/3 in which way, as, correlative of *tadvat* as/so,
yadyad whatever
yadyāpi although
yadyapi.... tathāpi although... nevertheless ......
yāga m. sacrifice, offering, oblation, ceremony for the above, presentation, grant,
yaḥ 838/1 pron. he who, who or which 1/s/m
yaḥ.... saḥ... (he who..... he....)
yaḥ kaścit whoever,
√*yaj* 838/3 cl 1 P A *yajati (te),* to worship, adore, honour, to consecrate, hallow, honour, to offer, present, grant, yield, bestow, to be sacrificed or worshipped, caus. *yājayati* to assist anyone at a sacrifice, cause anyone to sacrifice, DP in *deva-pūjā* worshipping with sacrifice, *saṅgati-karaṇa* consecrating or *dāna* bestowing,
yajamāna 839/1 mfn sacrificing, worshipping, m. the person paying for the sacrifice, the patron, the master of the sacrifice,
yajanta m. a sacrificer, worshipper,
yajante they sacrifice, they worship, 1/pl/pres/indic/mid √*yaj*
yajatra 839/1 worthy of worship or sacrifice, deserving adoration,
yajīyas mfn (compar.) sacrificing excellently, worshipping more or most
yajña 839/2 m. sacrifice, worship, devotion, act of worship, devotion, prayer, praise, a worshipper, sacrificer, fire, sacrifice personified,
yajñabhāvita mfn honoured with sacrifice (as the gods),
yajñacchāga m. sacrifice-goat,
yajñakratu m. sacrifice ceremony, rite

yajñapātra n. a sacrificial vessel,
yajñārtham ind. for a sacrifice,
yajñarūpa n. the form or attribute of a sacrifice, the constituents of the sacrifice, the accomplishers of the sacrifice,
yajñāśiṣṭa 840/1 n. the remnants of a sacrifice after the gods and priests have consumed their share
yajñavalkya a great Vedic seer,
yajñiya mfn worthy of worship or sacrifice, reverend, holy, divine, active or skilful in sacrifice, pious, m. offeror, M. sacrificial 'belonging to or connected with the sacrifice',
yajñopavīta mfn the sacred thread, sacred cord worn over the left shoulder,
yajūṁṣi the Yajur Veda, verses whose letters, feet and lines are not fixed, taking the form of sentences,
yajur-veda m. the Veda of sacrificial texts,
yajus a division of the *Veda,* n. sacred reverence, sacrifice, , worship, sacrificial text, rites,
yajuṣmant mfn accompanied by sacrificial texts,
yajuṣmatī name applied to certain bricks in building the sacred fire-place,
yajvan mfn worshipping, sacrificial, sacred, m. worshipper, sacrificer,
√*yakṣ* 838/2 cl 1 P A *yakṣati, (te*), to be quick, speed on, to explain, cl 10 A *yakṣayate* to worship, honour, DP in *pūjā* worshipping
yakṣa a ghost or spirit,(usually benevolent), attendant to Kubera, a class of semi-divine beings regarded as of a benevolent and inoffensive disposition,
yakṣin mfn having life, living, really existing,
yakṣma m. sickness, disease in general, pulmonary disease, consumption, ,
√*yam* 845/2 cl 1 P *yacchati (te), yamati (te)*, to sustain, hold up, support, A. oneself, to raise, wield (a weapon etc.), to raise, extend or hold over (as a screen), A. to extend oneself before, to raise (the other scale), weigh more, stretch out, expand, spread, display, show, hold in, hold back, restrain, govern, subdue, control, to give oneself up to, be faithful to, obey, to utter a sound, to fix or establish, caus. *yāmayati (te)* to restrain, hold in, control, keep or put in order, DP (cl 1) in *upasama* checking, curbing, (cl 10) in *pariveṣaṇa* surrounding, enclosing,
yama 846/1 m. a rein, curb, bridle, a driver , charioteer, the act of checking or curbing, suppression, restraint, self control, forbearance, any great moral rule or duty, self-restraint (in yoga), any rule nor observance, the Lord of death, controller and ender of all, a twin, one of a pair or couple, a symbolical name for the number 'two', the planet Saturn, a crow, a bad horse (limbs too large or small), mfn paired, twin-born , forming a pair,
yāma mfn of or coming from Yama, m. course, going, progress, a road, way, path, a carriage, chariot, course (of a feast), cessation, end, f. watch of the night, a class of gods,
yama & niyama = behaviour codes of conduct, *yama* =a traditional code of restraints-non-violence, truthfulness, non-stealing, continence faithfulness when married), patience, steadfastness, compassion, honesty, neither eating too much or too little, purity in body, mind and speech, 'control of body and senses and observance of moral injunctions' (Gam.)
yamaja mfn twin-born, m. twins,
yamarājan mfn having Yama as their king, m. subject of Yama
yāmika m. watchman,
yāminā f. night,
yam yam whatever
yamunā f. a river,
yān whom, 2/pl/m

yāna mfn leading, conducting (to or in),
m. way, path, teaching
n. wagon, vehicle (fig. Buddhist)),

yānti they go, 1/pl/pres/act √*yā*

√*yantr* 845/2 cl 10 P *yantrayati* or 1 P *yantrati* to restrain, curb, bind, to bind up, bandage, DP in *saṅkocana* restraining, checking

yantra n. a prop, support, barrier, a means or implement for holding, a fetter, band, tie, a surgical instrument esp. a blunt one e,g, tweezers, any instrument or apparatus, engine, machine, restraint, force, -*eṇa* ind. forcibly, violently,
an amulet, mystical diagram,

yantraṇa n. or f. (*ā*) restriction, limitation, pain, constraint, force, compulsion,
n. guarding, protection,

yarhi ind. when, at which time, whenever, while, whereas, sometimes, since, as, because,

√*yas* 849/1 cl 4 P *yāsyati, yasati* to froth up, foam, to heat or exert oneself, to strive after, caus. *yāsayati* DP in *prayatna* striving, endeavouring,

yaśas 848/2 n. beautiful appearance, beauty, splendour, worth, honour, glory, fame, mfn honoured, splendid,

yaśasvin mfn 'possessing glory', glorious, celebrated, famous, splendid,

yasmāt ......tasmāt ....,
because, ... therefore.......

yaśodā mother of Kṛṣṇa

yaṣṭi f. staff, stick, pole, pillar, support, rod, mace, club, cudgel,
stalk, stem, branch, twig,
anything thin or slender (ifc.), the blade of a sword, a thread, string (esp. of pearls), a partic. kind of pearl necklace, liquorice, sugar-cane, any creeping plant,

yasya who, whose

yas yas whoever

yāsyasi you shall go, you shall come, 2/s/fut/act √*yā*

yat pron. who, which

yat yat whatever.... *tat tat* that

√*yat* 840/3 cl 1 A P *yatate (ti),* P. to place in order, marshal, join, connect, P or A. to keep pace, be in line, rival or vie with, A. to join, associate with, march or fly together or in a line, to conform or comply with, to meet or encounter in battle, to seek to join oneself with, make for, tend towards, endeavour to reach, strive after, be eager or anxious for, DP (cl 10) in *nikāra* piling up, collecting, or *upaskāra* endeavouring, (cl 1) in *prayatna* striving
mfn going, moving,

yāt mfn going, moving,
ind. so long as, inasmuch as,
so far as,

yata 845/2 mfn restrained, controlled, subdued, held in, held forth, kept down or limited, ppp. √*yam,* n. restraint, the spurring or guiding of an elephant by the rider's feet,

yāta ppp. (having) gone, proceeded, marched, gone away, fled, escaped, passed by, elapsed, entered upon, pursued (as a path), gone to, come or fallen into, situated (as a heavenly body), become, turned out, known, understood, n. motion, progress, gait, course, the place where a person has gone, the past time, the guiding or driving of an elephant with a goad,

yatacetas 845/2 mfn. restrained or subdued in mind

yataḥ..... tataḥ..... since.... therefore.....

yatāhāra m. temperate in food, abstemious,

yatamānasa mfn controlled, restrained

yātanā f. requital, esp. punishment, pains of hell, torment, anguish,

yatārtha mfn real, accurate, exact, genuine,
ind. really, truly,

yatārthasvarūpa essential nature,

yatas ind. from what time or place or reason, where, because, for,
yatas.....tena, since ... therefore....

yatas....atas, yatas....tad,
yatatas of the striving, of the one who strives, pres.act.part. √*yat* 6/s/m
yatati he strives, stretches
yatātman 845/3 mfn self-restrained,
yatātmavān m. controlled in mind, self-controlled
yatayas ascetics, performers of austerities, 1/pl/m
yatayāmam spoiled, stale
yat yat whatever
yatas yatas whensoever, wheresoever
yatendriya mfn having the organs of sense restrained, of subdued passions, chaste, pure,
yat yat...... sat sat whatever.... that
yathā 841/2 ind. as, like , according as, correlative *tathā* 433/3 ind. so *yathā..., tathā...,* as .... , so....,
yathābhāgam according to each share, each in his respective place
yathābhimata mfn as desired, that one likes
yathābhimatadeśa m. desired place, place that one likes,
yathāgata mfn as gone, as previously gone, as one came (into the world), without sense, stupid, ind. by the way one came,
yathākāla m. the proper time, suitable moment, *(am)* ind. according to time, in due time, at the right or usual time,
yathākalpam ind. according to or in conformity with the ritual,
yathākāma mfn as you please, according to desire, agreeably, in an easy-going way, slowly,
yathākarma according to actions,
yathākartavya mfn proper to be done, the proper course of action,
yathākārin acting in such or whatever way,
yathākārya = *yathākartavya*
yathākramam ind. according to order, in regular series, in succession,
yathākṛta mfn. made or done according to rule, agreed, *(am)* ind. according to usual practice,
yathāmānam ind. according to a particular measure or dimension,
yathāmanasam ind. to the heart's content,
yathāṅgam ind. limb after limb or limb on limb
yathānyāyam ind. according to rule, rightly, fittingly,
yathāprāpta 842/2 as met with, the first met with, the first that is met with or occurs.
yathāprāptavartī
yathāprāpta 842/2 as met with, the first met with, the first that is met with or occurs. *vartī* 925/3 see *vartin* resting, abiding, behaving properly towards one who rests in life's situations as they arise
yathārtha 843/1 accordant with reality, conformable to truth, true, right (*am*) ind. suitably, according to one's dignity, - *ta* ind. truly
yathārūpa of whatever form, of a corresponding form or appearance, extremely beautiful, exceedingly great,
yathāśakti ind. according to power or ability, to the utmost of one's power,
yathāśāstram ind. according to precept or rule, according to the codes of law,
yathāsatyam ind. in accordance with truth,
yathāśraddham ind. according to inclination, according to faith, in all faith or fidelity, confidently,
yathāsthiti 843/3 accordant with usage, certainly, assuredly, ind. according to usage, as on previous occasions,
yathāsukham ind. according to ease or pleasure, at ease, at will or pleasure, comfortably, agreeably,
yathā tathā in whatever manner, as..... so
yathātatham ind. as it really is, accurately, as is becoming or proper, fitly, duly,
yāthātathya 851/1 real state or condition, truth, *-ta* as it should be, consistent with endeavour and result

yathāvastham ind. according to state or condition, whenever the same circumstances occur,
yathāvastu ind. according to the state of the matter, precisely, accurately,
yathāvat ind. duly, properly, rightly, as, like,
yathāvidhi ind. according to prescription or rule or merit of,
yathāvidyam 843/1 ind. according to knowledge,
yathāvṛtta mfn as happened, as occurred, as ensued, as behaving one's self, n. a previous occurrence or event, the circumstances or details of an event, ibc. or (*am*) ind. as anything happened, circumstantially,
yathāyatanam ind. each in his own place or abode,
yathāyogyam ind. as is fit, according to propriety,
yathepsita mfn as desired, (*am*) ind. according to one's wish,
yatheṣṭam according to wish
yathokta mfn as said or told previously just as .... said, (*am*) ind. as said or told previously,
yati, yatin 841/1 mfn. an ascetic, a devotee, one who has restrained his passions and abandoned the world
yati as many as, as often, how many or often,
yati 845/3 f. restraint, control, guidance, stopping, ceasing, a pause in music, a widow,
yāti 849/1 √*yā* to go to, proceed, 1/s/pres/indic/act he goes, attains, undergoes
yatna 841/1 m. activity of will, volition, effort, performance, work, effort, exertion, energy, care
yatna ind. in or to which place or where, wherein, in which
yatnavat 841/1 possessing energy, making effort, aspiring after, striving
yātṛ m. avenger, pursuer, mfn going, travelling, marching, being on a journey, going for, seeking, going to or in or riding on ifc., f. a husband's brother's wife,
yatra where, if, when, since, in which case, in order that,
yatra yatra wherever...*tatra tatra*....there...
yātrā 849/3 f. going, setting off, journey, procession, support of life, maintenance, going on a pilgrimage, a feast, festival, livelihood, way, means, expedient, passing away time, practice, usage, custom,
yatra tatra in whatever, in whatever place, anywhere, to any place whatever, at any rate, indiscriminately,
yatra tatra .... *tatra tatra* wherever there is .... there is
yatra yatra ind. wherever
yatra.... *tatra* where..... there..
yatta 841/1 1. mfn endeavoured, striven, engaged in intent upon, prepared for, ready to, on one's guard, watchful, cautious, attended to, guided (as a chariot),
yat satyam (what is true) in truth, (X)
yat yat whatever, (+ *tat tat*) that...
yaugika mfn useful, applicable, remedial, connected with or suiting the derivation, having an etymological meaning, relating to or derived from the *yoga*
√*yauṭ* 859/1 cl 1 P *yauṭati* to join or fasten together, DP in *bandhana* joining together,
yauvana n. youth, period between childhood and maturity,
yauvana-daśā f. time of youth,
yauvarājyam immediate heir to the throne,
yava m. orig. any grain or corn yielding flour, later, barley-corn, barley,
yāvad as many, as much, until, as often, as frequent, as far, as long, as old
yāvajjīvam 852/2 ind. life-long, lasting for life, as long as life
yava-madhyama mfn having a barley-corn middle, i.e. big in the middle and small at the ends,

yavana m. a greek, a swift horse, wheat, a carrot, pl. the greeks, n. salt (from saline soil), mfn keeping away, averting, quick, swift,

yāvān *(yāvat, yāvad)* as much, so much , having which measure, how great, how much, until,

yavapūrṇa mfn filled with barley,

yavau barley

yāvat as many, as much, until, as often, as frequent, as far, as long, as old (with 2nd) during, up to, till, while,
yāvat tāvat as much as,
(with 1/s/pres/) meanwhile, just,
na yāvat...tāvat... scarcely... when.. no sooner... than...
na param...yāvat... =
not only... but even..
sūryodavat yāvat until sunrise,

yāvat ..... tāvat as long as .... for so long

yāvatī fem. of above

yāvayad-dveṣas mfn driving away foes,

yaviṣṭha mfn youngest, esp. of a fire just born or just set on the altar,
m. a younger brother,

yaviṣṭhya mfn =*yaviṣṭha,* always at the end of a *pada,*

yavīyas mfn younger, lesser, worse,
m. younger brother,
f. (*ī*) younger sister,

yayā pron. 3/s/f by which, with which

yayāti a patriarch of the old time, son of Nahusha

ye pron. 1/pl/m who

yena for which reason

yena ... saha together with whom, by which

yena 3/s pron. by or with whom
ind. in which manner, on what account, why

yeṣām pron. of whom, among whom, according to whom, 6/pl/m

ye ye all things

yeṣṭha mfn 'best going' swiftest,

yeṣu pron. in which

yoddhṛ m. fighter, warrior,

yoddhukāma mfn anxious to fight, hungry for battle,

yodha m. a fighter, warrior, battle, war,

yodhamukhya m.a chief warrior, leader,

yodhavyam to be fought, √*yudh* gerundive,

yodhin mfn ifc. fighting, m. a warrior, conqueror,

yoga 856/2 m. union, abstract meditation or union with the Supreme Being, a yoke, team, vehicle, the act of yoking, joining, attaching, use, application, a means, method, work, fixing (an arrow on a bow-string), putting on (armour), a remedy, cure, a means, expedient, device, way, manner, method, a charm, incantation, a trick, stratagem, fraud, deceit, business, acquisition, gain, profit, wealth, property, occasion, any junction, union, combination, contact with, mixing of various materials, mixture, fitting together, fitness, propriety, opportunity, connection, use, application or concentration of thoughts, abstract contemplation, a follower of the yoga system,
union of soul with matter (*sāṁkhya*)
union of the individual soul with the universal soul (*pāśupata*), devotion, piously seeking God (*pāñcarātra*)
contact or mixing with the outer world (*jaina*)
meditation (esp. self-concentration), abstract meditation and mental abstraction practised as a system ... to teach the means by which the human spirit may attain complete union with the Supreme Spirit

yogabala 857/1 n. the force of devotion, the power of magic,

yogabhraṣṭa mfn fallen from yoga, lost from practice of yoga,

yogābhyāsa m. practice of yoga

yogācāra m. 'one whose practice is yoga', a Buddhist Mahāyāna School,

yogadarśana yoga philosophy,

yogadhāranā 857/1 f. continuance or perseverance in meditation or concentration

yogadṛṣṭi yoga-vision,
yogaja mfn produced by or arising from *yoga* or meditation,
yogakṣema 856/3 m. acquisition and preservation of property, protecting or holding on to what has been acquired
yogamāyā (the power of) divine illusion (U)
yogāṅga n. a part of the *yoga,* means of attaining it,
yoganidrā f. 'meditation-sleep' a state of half-meditation half sleep (which admits of the full exercise of the mental powers), light sleep. the sleep of *Brahmā,*
yogarūḍha mfn having a special as well as etymological and general meaning - e.g. *paṅkaja* means 'growing in mud' and 'a lotus flower',
yogastha mfn abiding in discipline, absorbed in yoga,
yogavasiṣṭha a work on Vedānta
yogavittama having best knowledge of yoga
yogayukta 857/1 mfn. immersed in deep meditation, absorbed in yoga, steadfast, disciplined, yoked steadfast in yoga
yogeṣvara Lord of Yoga, Kṛṣṇa,
yogī 857/3 usually called *yogin,* a contemplative saint, devotee, or ascetic a *yogin,* f. *yoginī,*
yogigamya attainable only by a *yogin*
yogya mfn of use, suited for use, fit, fitting, fit for the yoke, useful, perceptible, m. a draught animal, a calculator of expedients,
yogyatā f. suitableness, fitness, propriety, ability, *yojaka* 858/1 m. a yoker, harnesser, a user, employer, an arranger, preparer, contriver,
yojana n. joining, yoking, harnessing, that which is yoked or harnessed, a team, vehicle, course, path, (also applied to words addressed to the gods), (sometimes m. f. *ā* ifc.), a distance (traversed in one harnessing), instigation, stimulation, mental concentration, abstraction, directing the thoughts to one point, the Supreme Spirit, a finger, f. (*ā*) use, application, arrangement, erecting, constructing, junction, union, combination, application of the sense of a passage, grammatical construction,
yojayati he/she harnesses, yokes
yoktavya to be joined or yoked or united (as the mind) to be prepared or practised, gerundive √*yuj*
yoni 858/2 m.f. womb, place of birth, source, origin, spring, place of rest, receptacle, seat, abode, home, family, race, caste, the form of existence, or station, fixed by birth, seed, grain, a mine, copper, water, part of a fire-pit,
yonitas ind. from birth, by blood, out of a place of rest or stable,
yoṣit f. young woman, maiden,
yotsyamānān those who are about to give battle, √*yudh* 854/3 fut/mid/act/part. 2/pl/m
yotsye I will fight, I shall fight 3/s/fut/mid √*yudh*
√*yu* 852/3 1. cl 3 P *yuyoti* to separate, keep or drive away, ward off, exclude or protect from, to keep aloof, to be or remain separated from, caus. *yavayati* or *yāvayati,* DP in *jugupsā* dislike, abhorrence,

2. cl 2 P *yauti,* A *yute,* cl 6 *yuvati* (*te*), cl 9 *yunāti yunīte,* to unite, attach, harness, yoke, bind, fasten, to draw toward oneself, take hold or gain possession of, hold fast, to push on towards, to confer or bestow upon, *yauti* to worship, honour, DP (cl 2) in *miśraṇa* joining, mixing, or *amiśraṇa* loosening, in *bandhana* (cl 9) binding, fastening, mfn going, moving,
√*yuch* 853/1 cl 1 P *yucchati* to go away,

depart, keep aloof, vanish, DP in *pramāda* error, mistake, carelessness about,

√yudh 854/3 cl 4 A P *yudhyate (ti)* cl 1 P *yodhati,* to fight, wage war, oppose or overcome in battle, fight with or against, to go, to move, fluctuate (as waves), caus. *yodhayati* to cause to fight, lead to war, engage in battle, be a match for, to defend, DP in *samprahāra* fighting, struggling,

yudh m. a fighter, warrior, hero, f. fight, war, combat, struggle,

yuddha 854/3 mfn fought, encountered, conquered, n. battle, fight, war, opposition ,
(*am*) with *kṛ* makes battle)

yuddha-varṇa m. a sort of battle, a battle, so to speak,

yuddha-viśārada m. skilled in battle, battle-skilled

Yudhāmanyus 1/s/m name of a warrior 'fighting with spirit'

Yudhiṣṭhira son of *Kuntī* and *Dharma*, eldest of the *Pāṇḍava* princes, to whom Brihadaśva tells the story of Nala

yudhya fight! join battle! 2/s/impv/act

yudhyasva fight! join in the battle! 2/s/impv/mid

yuga 854/1 n. a yoke, team, an age of the world of which there are four – *satya* or *kṛta, tretā, dvāpara* and the present *kaliyuga* (432,000years).
a yoke , team, couple, pair,
(with *mānuṣa)* a human generation,

yugapad 854/1 ind. 'pair-foot', together, at the same time, simultaneously, (being in the same yoke),

yugapat ind. together

yugapat-prāpti f. simultaneously reaching or arriving at,

yuge yuge from age to age, in age after age

yugma mfn paired, even, n. pair, couple, twins, junction, confluence,

√yuj 853/2 cl 7 P A *yunakti, yuṅkte, yuñjati (te), yojati (te),* pass. *yujyate* to yoke or join or harness or fasten, to make ready, prepare, arrange, fit out, set to work, use, employ, apply, to offer, perform (prayers or sacrifice), to put on (arrows on a bowstring), fix in, insert, to appoint to, charge or entrust with, command, enjoin, to turn or direct or fix or concentrate (the mind, thoughts, etc.) upon, to concentrate the mind in order to obtain union with the Universal Spirit, be absorbed in meditation, to recollect, recall, to join, unite, connect, add, bring together, to confer or bestow anything upon, to become possessed of, to join oneself to, to accrue to, to be fit or proper or suitable or right, caus. *yojayati* DP in *yoga* (cl 7) joining, uniting, (cl 4) in *samādhi* concentration of the mind, in cessation of the modification of the thinking principle,

yuj mfn yoked together, paired, even, m. yoke-fellow, comrade, a sage who devotes his time to abstract contemplation,

yujya mfn united, combined, connected, related, allied, homogenous, similar, equal in rank or power, suitable, proper, capable, n. union, alliance, relationship,

yujyasva join, engage, yoke!, yoke thyself!, join thyself, 2/s/impv/mid *yuj*

yujyate it is used, 1/s/pres/indic/pass

yukta mfn proper, right, yoked or joined or fastened, or attached or harnessed to, set to work, made use of, engaged in, intent upon, ready to, prepared for (4th), absorbed in abstract meditation, concentrated, attentive, skilful, clever, experienced in, joined, united, connected with, disciplined, applied, auspicious, favourable, prosperous, thriving, (in gram.) primitive (as opposed to derivative),
added to, increased by (ifc.), connected with, concerning (ifc.),

subject to, dependent on (ifc.), (*am*) ind. fitly, suitably, justly, properly, rightly,
m. fit, proper, n. a team, yoke, junction, connection, fitness, suitableness, propriety,
yuktacetasa those whose thought is steadfast, whose mind is steady,
yuktatamas most devoted, most steadfast, superlative of *yuktas*
yuktātmān of steadfast self 853/3 mfn. concentrated in mind, ever merged in deep contemplation (Gam.), ifc. wholly intent upon,
yukte joined, in yoke
yukti 853/3 f. union, junction, combination, practice, usage, suitableness, fitness, propriety, meditation on the Supreme Being, contemplation, union with the universal spirit, reasoning, argument, proof, deduction from circumstances, reason, skill, cleverness, a yoking, harnessing, yoke, team,
in gram. connection of words, a sentence, connection of letters, mixture or alloying of metals, sum, total,
yuktyā 853/3 (see *yukti*) 3/s by means of reasoning, by logical argument,
yūna n. a band, cord, string,
yūnas a weak form of *yuvan,* see *yuvan,*
yunakti √*yuj* yokes, joins, makes ready, uses, concentrates the mind on, engages,
√*yuṅg* 853/1 cl 1 P *yuṅgati* to desert, relinquish, abandon, DP in *varjana* leaving,
yuñjaka mfn applying, performing, practising,
yuñjan practising, performing yoga, disciplining, concentrating
yuñjāna mfn uniting, joining, arranging, performing, appointing to, entrusting with, suitable, proper, successful, prosperous, m. a driver, coachman, a yogin,
yuñjat he should practice/concentrate 1/s/opt/act √*yuj*
yuñjīta he should concentrate the mind on, come into union with, discipline himself, 1/s/opt/mid √*yuj*
√*yup* cl 4 P *yupyati,* to debar, obstruct, disturb, trouble, confuse, efface, remove, destroy, DP in *vimohana* troubling, effacing, making level or smooth,
yūpa m. post, pillar, sacrificial post,
√*yūṣ* cl 1 P *yūṣati* to hurt, kill, DP in *hiṁsā* hurting, killing,
yuṣmābhiḥ by you pl. pron.
yuṣmabhyam pron. for you pl.
yuṣmad you
yuṣmadīya pl. your,
yuṣmākam of you pl.
yuṣmān you pl. 2nd
yuṣmāsu in you pl.
yuṣmat pron. from you pl.
√*yut* 854/3 cl 1 A *yotate* to shine, DP in *bhāsana* shining,
mfn keeping off,
yuta mfn concerning, made or consisting of, accompanied by, connected with, separate, occupied in, added, fastened,attached, united, combined, possessed of,
yūtha m.n. herd, flock, troop, etc.
f. a kind of jasmine,
yūtha-nātha m. protector or leader of the herd,
yūtha-pa m. keeper or protector of the herd, esp. the elephant that leads the herd,
yūtha-pati m. lord of the herd, esp. the elephant that leads the herd,
yuvābhyām pron. by/for/from you two
yuvām pron. you two 1st or 2nd
yuvan mfn young, young man, youth,
yuvayoḥ pron. of/in you two
yuvan 855/2 mfn young, youthful, adult, (applied to men and animals), strong, good, healthy, m. a youth, young man, young animal,
yuvarāja m. a crown-prince, heir-apparent,
yuvatiḥ f. young woman,
yūyam you pl. 1st

yuyodhi destroy! remove!
yuyutsu 855/2 mfn. wishing to fight, desire for war, combativeness,

yuyutsavaḥ desiring to fight or do battle, √*yudh* 1/pl/m desiderative adj.

Verb/Upasarga List

Frequently used roots are given with basic meanings and prefixed meanings.

root class, Parasmai, Ātmane, meaning

ah to say, call, speak,
pra+ declare to be
akṣ 5 P to reach,
aṁs 10 PA to divide
an 2P to breathe,
pra+ to be alive, breathe,
aṅgīkṛ 8 PA to accept,promise, admit,
añj 1 PA to bend, to worship,
pari+ to twist,
7 P to anoint,
vi+ to reveal, show,
āp 5 P to obtain, reach, gain,
abhi+ reach to a thing, attain,
desid. strive to win,
caus. carry out fully,
ava+ to secure, come upon,
fall in with, incur,
pari+ to be competent,
pra+ to get, reach, arrive
sam + to complete,
vi+ to pervade,
arc 1 PA to worship
arh 1 P to deserve,
arj 1 P to gain, to earn,
upa+ to earn
arth 10 PA to request,
abhi+ to beg,
pra+ to ask, so wish,
prati+ to challenge,
arthayati(te) to seek for an object,
abhi+ ask, entreat,
pra+ desire, sue for,
aś 5 A to pervade, reach, enjoy,
aś 9 P to eat,
pra+ to taste, eat, partake of,
as 2 P to be,
as 4 P to throw,
apa+ to cast away,
abhi+ to practice, direct one's
attention to, study,
ni+ to put down, throw down,
deposit, commit,
parini+ throw down over,
stretch over,
nis+ throw out, root out,
sanni+ to give up,
vi+ cast or throw away,
vipari+ to upset,
vyati+ throw over, cross,
ās 2 A to sit, to be,
adhi+ to occupy, take one's place in,
put on (e.g.shoes),
ud+ to be indifferent,
upa + to serve, worship, sit by,
sit waiting for,
asūyati Nom. envies,
aṭ 1 P to wander,
ātmasāt + kṛ to appropriate,
av 1 P to deserve,
pra+ show favour,
be attentive or heedful,
bādh 1 A to thwart,
adhi+ to harass,
anu+ to vex,
apa+ to drive away,
ava+ to restrain,
pari+ to ward off,
pra+ to repel,
vi+ to distress,
bandh 2 PA to bind,
ā+ to hold fast,
anu+ to combine,
ni+ to check, bind, fasten,
write down,
nis+ to importune,
pari+ to surround,
pra+ bind on, form a series,
sam+ bind together, connect,
ud+ to suspend,
bhā 2 P to shine,
ā+ to look like, illumine, shine upon
ava+ to appear,
nis+ shine forth from (5th),
pra+ shine forth, begin to be light,
prati+ to illumine,
ud+ to shine forth,
bhaj 1 PA to share, adore,
ā+ give a person, deal out to,
pravi+ divide,
saṁvi+ divide a thing with

a person, present a person (3rd) with a thing (2nd),
vi+ to divide,

bhaṇ 1 P to speak,

bhañj 7 P to break,
ava+ to destroy,
nis+ to defeat,
sam+ to shatter,
vi+ to dispel,

bharts 1 P to threaten,
abhi+ to mock
ava+ to abuse,
nis+ to deride,

bhāṣ 1A to say,
ā+ to converse,
abhi+ to address,
ava+ to revile,
pari + to explain
pra+to declare
prati+ to reply, speak back,

bhās 1 A to shine,
ā+ to appear,
ava+ to shine,
prati+ make a show, appear well,

bhī 3 P to fear,

bhid 7 P to split,
antar+ to plot,
pra+ split forth or open,
prati+ to betray,
ud+ to pierce,
vi+ to destroy, split asunder,

bhṛ 1 PA, 3 P, to hold,
ā+ bear to, bring to,
apa+ carry off, take away,
ava+ bear down, ward off,
ni+ to fix,
pra+ bring forward, offer,
sam+ to prepare,
upa+ to procure, bring to,

bhrāj 1 A to shine,

bhram 1 P, 4 P to roam, wander around,
pari+ to turn round,
sam+ to fall into error, be confused,
vi+ to be perplexed, shine,

bhraṁś 4 PA to fall,
pari+ to escape,
pra+ to disappear,
vi+ to fail,

bhrasj 6 P to fry

bhū 1 P to become,
abhi+ to overcome, oppress,
abhisam+ enter into, become by a process of change,
anu+ to experience, attain,
parā+ to vanquish
pari+ to surpass, surround,
pra+ to be produced, to rule,
sam+ to be possible,
sam+caus. to honour,
ud+ to arise,

bhuj 6 P to curve,

bhuj 7PA to enjoy, eat,
anu+ reap the fruit (of good or evil deeds),
sam+ to enjoy,
upa+ to enjoy,

budh 4 A to awake,
anu+ to think of,
ava+ to perceive,
pra+ to awake,
prati+ to observe, awake,
ud+ to awake,
sam+ to recognise,
ud+ to awake,
vi+ to learn,

brū 2 PA to say,
anu+ to repeat,
apa+ try to console a person,
ava+ to console,
nis+ to explain,
pra+ to proclaim,
prati+ to answer, speak back to,
upa+ to invoke,

cakṣ 2 A to appear, look upon, speak,
ā+ to look on
sam+ look upon, consider,
vi+ appear far and wide, shine,

cal 1 P to go,
vi+ to shake,

cam 1 P to sip,
ā+ to rinse the mouth,

car 1 P to move,
ā+ to practise, approach, set about,
abhi+ to offend, trepass against,
anu+ to follow,

apa+ go off, be absent,
parā+ move away from,
pra+ to set forth,
samā+ proceed, do, perpetrate,
ud+ go up, rise (of the sun),
caus. cause to go out, evacuate,
udā+ rise up out of,
upa+ to serve, come to (esp. in order to serve), attend, wait upon politely, proceed with, undertake,
vi+ move in different directions, wander about, caus. cause to go hither and thither in thought, ponder,

chad 10 P to cover,
ā+ to cover, conceal,
pari+ envelope, cover over,
pra+ cover, dress oneself with,

chid 7 PA to cut,
ā+ to rob,
apa+ to sever,
pari+ to divide,
ud+ to destroy, cut out,
vi+ to separate, cut asunder,

ci 5 PA to collect,
ā+ to heap up,
ava+ to gather,
nis+ to ascertain,
pari+ to recognise, find out,
sam+ gather together, collect,
ud+ to arrange, heap up, collect,
vi+ to select,
vinis+ ponder, consider,

cint 10 P to think,
anu+ to remember,
pari+ to reflect,
sam+ to ponder, think to oneself,
vi+ to discern, reflect,

cirāyati Nom. he delays

citrayati Nom. decorates,

cṛt 6 P to tie, hurt, shine,
pra+ caus. drive on, inspire,

cud 10 P to urge,
abhi+ to impel,
pra+ to command, drive on, further, inspire,
sam+ to stimulate,

cumb 1 P to kiss,

cur 10 PA to steal,

curṇ 1 A to waver, fail,

cyut 1 P to drip, fall,

dā 2 P to cut,
ava+ to cut off,
samava+ cut in pieces and collect

dā 3 PA to give,
ā+ to receive, take, grasp,
anu+ to yield, grant, admit,
pari+ to entrust, deliver over,
pra+ give, grant, impart,
prati+ to give back,
upā+ A. to acquire, appropriate,
vi+ to distribute,

dah 1 P to burn,

dal 1 P to burst,

dam 4 P to be tamed,

ḍamb 10 P to push, throw,
vi+ to deceive,

daṁś 1 P to bite,

daṇḍ 10 P to punish,

daridrā 2 P to become poor,

day 1 A to have pity,

dhā 3 PA to lay, hold, maintain,
ā+ to deposit, set in or on, put on (wood on the fire), take on, take or take away,
abhi+ to address, put on, designate, name, address, speak to,
adhi+ A. to wear,
antar+ to conceal, put in the interior,
(a)pi+ to close, cover,
ava+ to heed, put down in, esp. down into water,
ni+ to entrust, lay down, set down (sacred fire),
pari+ to put on, put around,
pra+ set forward,
prati+ to adjust,
pratini+ to substitute,
sam+ to dispose,
samā+ to concentrate, put upon,
samni+ lay down together,
upa+ put on (brick/stone on altar),
upasamā+ set together (wood onto a burning fire), put (fuel) on,
vi+ to prescribe, distribute, spread abroad, arrange, determine,
vyā + pass. be separated, be sick,

ḍhauk 1 A to approach,
dhāv 1 P to run,
abhi+ to rush at,
anu+ to pursue, run after,
ava+ to drip down,
pra+ to run away, flow, run,
samupa+ run on to,
upa+ run to,
dhe 1 P to suck,
dhīrayati encourages,
dhmā 1 P to blow,
ā+ to inflate, blow up,
nis+ to blow out,
dhṛ 1 P to hold,
dhṛ 10 P to hold, owe,
ava+ to determine,
nis+ to pick out,
upa+ to support,
dhṛṣ 1 P to be bold,
ā+ venture against,
prati+ hold out against, withstand,
dhū 9 PA to shake,
ava+ to shake off, shake down,
dhvaṁs 1 PA to perish,
dhvan 1 P to sound,
dhyai 1 P to meditate,
abhi+ to desire,
anu+ to reflect,
ḍī 1 A, 4 A to fly,
ud+ to fly up,
dih 2 P to smear,
dīp 4 A to blaze,
ud+ to flame up,
diś 6 PA to show,
ā+ to prescribe, point out to,
anu+ to refer to,
apa+ to feign, to show,
nis+ to specify,
pra+ point out to, designate,
sam+ to assign,
samā+ point out to, direct,
ud+ to point out,
upa+ to instruct,
vyapa+ make a false show of,
div 10 to suffer, lament,4 PA to play,
du 1 to go, 5 P to burn, suffer,
dṛ 6 A to heed,
ā+ to respect,
dṝ 9 P to tear,
ā+ to split,
ava+ to burst,
vi+ to tear,
dṛp 4 P to become crazy,
dṛṣ 1 PA to see,
anu+ to behold,
pra+ to foresee,
prati+ appear before one's eyes,
sam+ to perceive, behold,
upa+ to observe,
vi+ pass. be seen far and wide,
dru 1 P to melt, run, 5 P to hurt,
ā+ run to, make an attack, charge,
abhi+ to assail,
anu+ to pursue,
apa+ to flee,
ati+ run past or by, escape,
pra+ to rush upon,
samupa+ run to rush at,
upa+ to hasten, run to,
vi+ to flee, burst,
druh 4 P to hurt,
abhi+ to do harm,
duh 2 PA to milk,
duḥkhayati P afflicts,
duḥkhāyate A feels pain,
dyut 1 A to gleam,
abhi+ to shine,
ud+ to shine forth,
vi+ to flash,
gad 1 P to speak,
ni+ to declare,
gāh 1 A to plunge,
ava+ to dive,
upa+ to penetrate,
gai 1 P to sing,
ava+ to censure,
gal 1 P to drip, fall, perish,
galbh 1 A to be bold,
gam 1 P to go,
ā+ to come to, go to, return,
abhi+ to approach,
abhyā+ come unto, visit,
adhi to acquire, go to attain,
antar+ go within, enter,
anu+ to follow, go after,
api+ go unto, join,

ava+ to know, come down,
nis+ to go out, proceed from,
prati+ to return, come back,
sam+ A. to meet,
samā+ to meet, assemble,
samupā+ to go to together,
ud+ to rise, go out, proceed from,
upa+ to approach, go unto,
upā+ approach,
vi+ to pass away, go asunder,

gaṇ 10 PA to count,
ava+ to disregard
pari+ to consider,

garh 1 A to censure,

garj 1 P 10 PA to roar,

ghaṭ 1 A to strive, to happen,
sam+ to be united,
vi+ to break down,

ghrā 1 P to smell,

ghṛṣ 1 P to rub,
sam+ to vie with,
ud+ to scratch,

ghuṣ 1 P to proclaim,

ghūrṇ 1 A,6 P to whirl,

gṝ 6 P to swallow,
ud+ to vomit,

grah 9 PA to seize,
ā+ to persist in
anu+ to favour,
ava+ to resist,
ni+ to check,
pari+ to clasp,
prati+ to accept, take hold of
sam+ to collect, hold together,
vi+ separate, make a division, quarrel, fight,

granth 9 P to fasten,

gras 1 A to swallow,
sam+ to destroy,

guh 1 PA to hide,

guṇ 10 PA to multiply,

gup to shun, abhor,

hā 3 A to go

hā 3 P to leave,
pari+ to forsake,
vi+ to cast off,

han 2 P to kill,
ā+ to beat, strike upon,
abhi+ to smite,
apa+ to drive away,
ava+ strike down, bring to nought,
ni+ to fall upon, strike down, slay,
pra+ to strike,
pari+ strike around, encompass,
prati+ to check, strike back at, strike against so as to transfix,
sam+ to join, strike together,
ud+ force up,

has 1 P to laugh
ava+ to deride,
pari+ to ridicule,
pra+ laugh out, laugh,
vi+ laugh out,

hi 5 PA to send,
pra+ to despatch,

hiṁs 7 P to injure,

hlād 10 PA to refresh,
ā+ to gladden,
pra+ to gladden, refresh

hṛ 1 P to take,
ā+ to obtain, eat, fetch, receive,
abhi+ to offer,
anupra+ throw in the fire or on a fuel pile,
apa+ to take away,
ava+ move down,
pari+ to avoid, carry around,
pra+ to strike, attack,
pratyā+ get back again,
pravyā+ utter, speak,
sam+ to check, bring or draw together, contract, withdraw,
samā+ to collect,
ud+ to lift, rescue, take out,
udā+ say, tell,
*upa+*to offer,
upasam+ bring or draw together to one's self,
vi+ to enjoy oneself, take apart, divide, pass one's time, esp. pleasantly, enjoy one's self, wander about,
vyā+ to utter, bring out,
vyava+ to behave, move hither and thither, go to work, proceed,

hreṣ 1 PA to neigh

hrī	3 P to be ashamed,		*prati*+ to wait for,
hṛṣ	1 P, 4 P, to rejoice,		*sam*+ look upon, behold, perceive,
hrus	1 PA to decrease,		*upa*+ to neglect, overlook,
hu	3 PA to sacrifice,		*vi*+ to look, look on,
hve	1 P to call,	*indh*	7 A to kindle,
	ā+ to summon,	*īr*	2 A to move, arise,
	ā+ A. to summon,		*pra*+ caus. drive or steer a vessel onward ,
i	1 A to go,		*sam*+ caus. bring together i.e. into shape or form , create,
	ā+ to come near, hither,		*samud*+ to utter,
	with *punar* go back,		*ud*+ rise up, caus. rouse, send out, announce,
	abhi+ go unto, become embodied in	*īrṣ*	1 P to envy (with 4th)
	abhipra+ to intend,	*iṣ*	6 P to wish,
	abhyā+ to approach, go near,		*abhi*+ seek for
	adhi+ to study, learn,		*anu*+ 4 P to search, seek after
	antar+ go within, retire, withdraw,		*prati*+ to accept
	anu+ accompany, go after,	*īś*	2 A to rule, to be able,
	anuparā go forth (along a path),	*jāgṛ*	2 P to awaken,
	apa+ to depart, go off, slink away,	*jakṣ*	2 P to eat,
	ati+ *to* go beyond, transcend, leave behind, escape,	*jalp*	1 P to murmur,
	ava+ approach,		*pari*+ to prattle,
	ni+ go into or in, (e.g. *nyāya*)		*sam*+ to converse,
	parā+ go away, depart,	*jan*	4 A to be born,
	pari+ to circumambulate, walk round (the fire),		ā+ breeding (as with horses), lineage,
	pra+ go forward or onward, come out, be prominent,		*abhi*+ pass. be born unto, be destined for from birth,
	prati+ go against, go back, withstand,		*pra*+ be born, caus. procreate,
	sam+ come together, assemble,		*sam*+ to arise, happen, be produced,
	samanu accompany, go after,		*upa*+ to be born, arise,
	samava+ to assemble,	*jap*	1 P to mutter,
	samupa+ to obtain, come hither,		*upa*+ to whisper,
	ud+ to arise,	*jhaṇajhaṇāyati*	Nom. he,she,it rattles
	upa+ to approach,	*ji*	1 P to conquer,
	upā+ go unto,		*ava*+ to deprive of,
	vi+ go asunder, separate, disperse,		*nis*+ to overcome,
	viparā go away separately,		*parā*+ A. to defeat,
īh	1 A to strive,		*ud*+ to conquer, pass. be conquered,
īkṣ	1 A to see,		*vi*+ A. to vanquish, subdue,
	anu+ to seek,	*jīv*	1 P to live,
	apa+ to expect, to need,		*anu*+ to live upon,
	ava+ to look after, look after one's self, i.e. look behind or around,		*ati*+ to survive,
			ud+ to live again,
			upa+ to maintain oneself,
	nis+ look after, contemplate,	*jñā*	9 PA to know,
	pari+ to examine, investigate,		*ā*+ to attend to, notice,

	abhi+ to recognise, know,	*kḷp*	1 A to be fit for,
	anu+ to permit,		*pari+* to decide,
	ava+ to despise,		*vi+* to doubt,
	pari+ carefully observe, find out,	*kliś*	4 A to suffer
	pra+ to know, know what to do,		9 P to torment,
	prati+ to promise, allow,	*kṛ*	8 PA to make, do, perform,
	pratyabhi+ recognize,		*ā+* bring hither, prepare, fashion,
	sam+ A. to agree,		*adhi+* to refer to, put in office,
	samanu+ to wholly acquiesce in,		*alam+* to adorn,
	vi+ to ascertain, understand, know,		*anu+* to imitate,
jṝ	4 P to grow old,		*apa+* to harm, injure,
jṛmbh	1 A to yawn,		*āvis+* to reveal,
	ud+ to expand,		*namas+* to salute,
juṣ	6 PA to relish,		*pari+* to surround, make ready, adorn,
	abhi+ to frequent,		*pariṣkṛ+* to polish,
	anu+ to visit,		pra+ carry forward, accomplish, set before, make the subject of discussion or treatment, (buddhism) put a plan before oneself,
jval	1 P to blaze,		*prati+* to remedy, to counteract,
kal	10 P to drive (cattle),		*sam+* put together, prepare, consecrate, abide by rites,
	anusam+ to lead along after		*saṁskṛ+* to refine
kamp	1 A to tremble,		*tiras+* to abuse,
	anu+ to feel pity,		*upa+* to help, do someone a service, bring something to someone,
kaṇ	1 P to sound		*upas+* to decorate,
kāṅkṣ	1 P to wish,		vi+ to change,
	ā+ to long for,		*vipra+* to tease,
	abhi+ to desire,		*vyā+* to explain, separate, analyse,
karṇ	10 PA to pierce, bore,	*kṛ*	3 P mention with praise
	ā+ to hear,	*kṛ*	3 P pour out, scatter abundantly (e.g. hailstones)
kāś	1 A to shine,		*ā +* scatter abundantly, cover over, fill,
	ā+ to look on,		*ava+* strew (loose earth) throw in,
	ava+ be visible, lie open,		*samā+* bestre, cover,
	pra+ shine out, become clear,		*vyati+* be scattered in various directions,
	pra+ to shine,	*kṝ*	6 P to scatter,
	vi+ to bloom,		*ā+* to spread,
kās	1 A to cough,		*sam+* to mix,
kath	10 P to tell,		*ud+* to carve,
khād	1 P to eat,		*upa+* to buy,
khan	1 PA to dig		*vi+* to strew, to sell, sell for (w 3rd)
	ā+ dig, burrow,	*kram*	1 PA 4 P to go,
	ni+ to bury		
	ud+ to uproot,		
khid	4 A to suffer,		
khyā	2 P to tell,		
	ā+ to declare, show, narrate, name		
	parisam+ reckon up completely,		
	pratyā+ to deny, turn away, repulse,		
	sam+ to count, tell together, sum up,		
	vyā+ show to discriminately,		
klam	1,4 P to be tired,		

ā+ to attack, step near to, come upon, overpower
abhi+ to approach,
abhyud+ caus. cause to step out,
ati+ to cross, o step beyond, excel, overcome
nis+ to leave, go out,
parā+ step forth, advance boldly (show one's strength or courage),
pari+ go around, circumambulate,
pra+ step forward, set out, start from
sam+ come together, approach, enter
samati+ excel,
ud+ go out, depart (vital spirit), caus. cause to disembark,
upa+ A. to begin, approach,
vi+ move away or on, proceed,

krand 1 P to cry
ā+ to cry out,

krī 9 PA to buy,
pari+ A. to hire,
vi+ A. to sell,

krīò 1 P to play,

kṛṣ 1 P to pull,
ā+ to attract, draw on, draw from (a source),
ni+ to lessen,
pra+ draw forward, place in front,
ud+ to enhance, elevate,

kṛt 6 P to cut,
ud+ cut out/off/up, butcher,

kruś 1 P to cry,
ā+ to carry out,
anu+ to pity,
vi+ to call aloud,

kṣal 10 PA to wash,
pra+ to cleanse,

kṣam 1 A 4 P to suffer, forgive,

kṣaṇ 8 P A to hurt,

kṣi 1 P to decay,
5, 9 P to destroy,
apa+ be afflicted, suffer loss (pass.)

kṣip 6 PA to throw,
ā+ to allude, throw at,
adhi+ to offend,
ni+ to entrust, throw down,
sam+ to abridge, dash together in a heap, destroy,
vini+ lay down separately/orderly

kṣu 2 P to sneeze,

kṣubh 4, 9P to shake,

kṣud 7 PA to crush

kṣudh 4 P to be hungry,

kūj 1 P to hum, warble,

kup 4 P to be angry, (with 4th)
pra+ be angry, boil with rage,

kus = *kuś* 4 P to embrace,

kuts 10 A to abuse,

lā 2 P to take,

labh 1 A to obtain, find,
pra+ to deceive,
upa+ to perceive,
upā+ to blame,
vi+ to hand over
vipra+ to mock at,

lag 1 P to adhere,
ava+ to linger
vi+ to cling to,

lakṣ 10 P to mark,
ā+ to observe,
upa+ to consider,
vi+ to perceive,

lal 1 P to frolic, play

lamb 1 A to hang down,
ā+ to grasp,
ava+ to cling to,
pari+ to linger,
vi+ to delay,

laṅgh 1 PA to cross, leap,
ati+ to transgress,
ud+ to cross,
vi+ to leap,

lap 1 P to chatter,
ā+ to address,
apa+ to deny,
pra+ to prattle,
sam+ talk with,
vi+ to lament,

laṣ 1 P to desire,
abhi+ to long for,
ud+ glance, play, be overjoyed,
vi+ glance play, be overjoyed or wanton,

las 1 P to shine,

lī 4 A, 9 P, to adhere,
abhi+ to clasp,

ava+ to lurk,
ni+ to cling,
pra+ to disappear,
vi+ to perish,
lih 2 PA to lick,
likh 6 P to scratch,
ā+ to sketch,
abhi+ to write,
ava+ to erase,
pari+ to copy,
pra+ to draw,
ud+ to polish,
lip 6 PA to anoint,
anu+ smear over, cover with,
vi+ besmear,
loc 1 A to see, behold,
ā +to appear or be seen, bring to sight or mind,
paryā+ reflect, deliberate,
samā+ reflect,
lok 10 P to behold,
ā+ to consider,
ava+ to look at or upon,
vi+ look at, inspect, behold,
lū 5 P 9 PA to cut,
lubh 4 P to covet,
pra+ to allure,
upa+ caus. to entice,
vi+ caus. to seduce,
luṇṭh 10 P to plunder,
lup 6 P to break,
ava+ to snatch,
pra+ to rob,
vi+ to lacerate
vyā+ to dispel,
luṭ 4 P, 5 P, to wallow,
mā 2 P, 3A, to measure,
anu+ to infer, re-create in imagination, conceive,
nis+ to fashion, make out of,
pari+ to estimate, measure around, limit,
pra + measure,
prati+ to imitate,
upa+ to compare, measure with,
vi+ measure out,
vinis+ lay-out (garden),
mad 4 PA to rejoice,
pra+ to neglect,
ud+ to be mad,
man 1 A, 4A, to think,
abhi+ to desire, put one's mind upon
anu+ to agree, approve,
apa+ to despise,
ava+ to despise, look down upon,
sam+ to esteem,
manth strong form of *math* 9 PA to churn,
nis+ to thrash,
ud+ to stir up,
vi+ A. to tear,
mantr 10 PA to consult,
ā+ to take leave,
abhi+ to address,
ni+ to invite,
sam+ to consult,
samni+ invite together
marg 10 PA to seek,
mi or *mī* 9PA to lessen, bring low, bring to nought,
pra+ bring to nought, pass. come to nought, perish,
miṣ 6 P to wink,
ni+ to close the eyes, fall asleep, wink,
ud+ to bloom,
miśrayati Nom P mixes
mlai 1 P to fade,
mṛ 6 A to die,
mṛd 9 P to crush,
abhi+ to trample
ava+ to rub,
pari+ to pound,
pra+ to devastate,
vi+ to lay waste,
mṛj 2 PA to cleanse,
apa+ to wipe away (also fig. guilt),
pra+ to stroke, wipe off, polish,
sam+ to rub
vi+ to smear,
mṛś 6 P to touch,
abhi+ touch
vi+ to consider,
muc 6 PA to release,
ā+ to put on,
abhi+ to discharge,
ati+ to avoid,

ava+ A. to take off,
nis+ to loosen,
pari+ to abandon,
ud+ to free,
vi+ to loosen, e.g. a bond (with 2nd), loosen from (with 5th), untie, free, pass. be freed or separated from or be deprived of (with 3rd or 5th),

mud 1 A to rejoice,
ā+ to be fragrant,
anu+ to approve,
pra+ to rejoice,

muh 4 P to lose sense,
ati+ to be at a loss,
pari+ to be confused,
vi+ to faint,

murch 1 P to faint,
sam+ to coagulate,

nam 1 P to bow,
ā+ bow down to,
ava+ to stoop, bow down,
pari+ to change into,
samud+ rise,
ud+ to rise, raise, arise,
upa+ to occur,

namaskṛ to pay homage,

nard 1 P to roar,

naś 4 P to perish,
vi+ to be lost,

nī 1 PA to lead,
ā+ to fetch, bring to, mix,
abhi+ to act (as actor), bring to,
anu+ to request, try to win or conciliate by friendly words,
apa+ to carry away,
nis+ to decide,
pari+ lead around a cow, or a bride in the wedding ceremony,
parinī+ to marry,
pra+ bring forward (one's feelings or sacrificial components),
sam+ to unite,
vi+ to dispel, lead, guide, train,
ud+ to raise, bring up, rescue,
upa+ to offer, take unto oneself, (teacher who receives a youth and confers spiritual re-birth),

nij 3 PA to cleanse
ava+ to purify,

nind 1 P to blame,

nu 2 P to shout,

nud 6 PA to impel,
apa+ to drive away,
nirṇud to remove
praṇud to dispel,

pā 1P to drink,
ā+ to absorb,

pā to protect,

pad 4 A to fall,
ā+ to gain, happen, get into trouble,
anu+ to agree,
ati+ to postpone,
pra+ to seek refuge,
prati+ to receive, step to, enter upon get into a condition,
sam+ to succeed, turn out well,
ud+ to arise, go out of, come into existence, be produced,
upa+ to occur, happen,
vi+ to fail, fall apart,
vyā+ fall away, perish, caus. destroy, kill,

pāl 10 P to protect,
pari+ to expect,
prati+ to observe,

pat 1 P to fall,
abhi+ to rush at
ati+ to neglect,
ni+ to fall down, fly down,
anu+ to fly after, pursue,
parā+ to fly off,
praṇi+ to prostrate oneself
samni+ fall together, come together
samud+ to fly up together,
ud+ to fly up

pīḍ 10 P to afflict, press,
ā+ press out,

piṣ 7 P to grind,

plu 1 A to float or leap,
ā+ bathe,
ava+ to submerge,
samā+ bathe,
ud+ spring up
upa+ hover unto,
vi+ to drift,

pṝ 3 P,9 P to fill,
ati+ bring across,
pari+ to fulfill,
pra+ to complete,
sam+ to fulfill, becomes full,
prā to fill,
ā+ to fill
prach 6 P to ask,
ā+ to take leave,
pari+ to enquire, ask,
sam+ to converse, consult with,
vi+ find out by asking,
prakaṭayati Nom P to manifest,
prath 1A to spread out
vi+ to spread out wide,
psā 2 P to chew, eat
pū 9 PA to purify
niṣpū to winnow,
pūj 10 P to worship,
adhi+ to honour,
pari+ to venerate,
puṣ 4 P,9 P to nourish,
pyai 1 A to swell,
ṛ 1 P to go, 5 P to injure,
ā+ get into trouble,
nis+ dissolve connection with,
sam+ meet, go along with,
caus. deliver to, consign,
ud+ to rise, raise,
upa+ go against, transgress,
rā 2 P to give,
rabh 1 A to grasp,
ā+ to begin, take hold upon, touch
anvā+ take hold of from behind,
prā+ to undertake,
pari+ to embrace,
sam+ to become excited, take hold of each other (for dance, battle,..),
samā+ undertake,
samanvā+ hold onto each other (said of several),
rac 10 P to fashion,
ā+ to prepare, caus. make happy, satisfy,
upa+ to construct,
vi+ to compose,
rādh 5 to prosper,
ā+ caus. to propitiate,
apa+ to offend,
rah 1 P to separate, abandon
vi+ separate from, abandon, leave,
rakṣ 1 P to protect,
abhi+ to observe,
pari+ to guard,
pra+ to save,
sam+ to preserve,
ram 1 A stop, stay, make fast rest, abide, find pleasure in,
ā + P stop,
abhi+ A. stop, find pleasure,
upa+ stop, *uparata* ceased,
vi+ P. stop, pause,
rañj or *raj* 4 PA to be glad,
abhi+ to be devoted,
anu+ to love, take the tinge of,
apa A. to lose colour,
sam+ A. to redden,
vi+ to lose interest, lose colour, be indifferent towards,
raṭ 1 P to cry,
ṛdh 6,2,4,5,7, P to grow, increase, prosper, succeed,
sam+ to be fulfilled,
ric 7 PA to empty,
ati+ pass. to surpass,
ud + pass. to excell,
ruc 1 A to please, to shine,
abhi+ to please,
ati+ to shine,
pra+ to shine forth,
prati+ appear good to, please,
rud 2 P to cry,
pra+ to wail,
vi+ to weep,
rudh 7 PA to obstruct,
ā+ to besiege,
anu+ 4 A to obey,
ava+ to confine,
ni+ to check,
prati+ to resist,
upa+ to molest,
vi+ 4 A to contend,
ruh 1 P to ascend,
ā+ to ascend, seat oneself upon, climb (tree), ascend (hilltop, life, place), embark upon (boat, ship),

fig. get into danger,
ā+caus. to ascribe,
adhi+ to mount,
ava+ to descend,
pra+ to grow
sam+ to grow,
vi+ to shoot up,

ruj 6 P to break,
ā+ to tear,
pra+ to shatter,

rūp 10 P to represent, form,
ni+ to observe,
pra+ to explain,
vi+ to disfigure,

sā = *so*

sad 1 P to sit,
ā+ to find, sit upon,
lie in wait for, get to, reach,
ava+ to collapse,
ni+ sit down, take one's seat,
set, install as,
niṣad + to sink,
pra+ to be pleased,
be favourable or gracious,
sam+ to lose heart, to sit together,
ud+ to perish
vi+ sink, be dejected, come to grief,
viṣad + to be dejected,

śam 4 P to be calm,
pra+ to be quiet, come to rest, stop,
upa+ to cease, be quiet, stop,

śaṁs 1 P to praise
ā+ A. to hope, wish, bless,
abhi+ to accuse,
pra+ to extol, praise,

sañj 1 P to adhere,
ā+ to fasten,
ava+ to entrust to,
pra+ to result, follow,

śaṅk 1 A to fear,
ā+ to be apprehensive
abhi+ to distrust,

śap 1 PA to curse,

śās 2 P to rule
ā+ A. to hope,
anu+ to instruct,
pra+ to rule,

ścut 1 P to trickle,

sev 1 A to serve,
ni+ to frequent,
samā+ to practice
upa+ to reverence,

śī 2 A to lie (down),
ā+ lie in,
adhi+ to dwell, dwell in,
anu+ to repent,
lie down after another,
ati+ to surpass,
prati+ to importune
sam+ to hesitate, be in doubt,
upa+ lie by,

sic 6 PA to sprinkle,
ā+ pour into,
abhi+ pour upon, sprinkle,
anoint, consecrate,
ava+ pour upon,
ni+ pour down or in (semen)
ud+ to be arrogant,

sidh 1 P to drive away,
apa+ to ward off,
niṣidh to forbid
pratiṣidh to forbid

sidh 4 P to succeed,
sam+ to be accomplished

śiṣ 7 P to remain,
ud+ leave remaining,
vi+ to distinguish, hence
distinguished, eminent,

skhal 1 P to stumble,
pari+ to stagger,
vi+ to falter,

śliṣ 4 PA to cling to,
ā+ to embrace,
sam+ to clasp,
vi+ to be loosened,

smi 1 A to smile,
pra+ to laugh,
anu+ caus. to remind,
vi+ to forget
vi+ to be astonished,

smṛ 1 P to remember,

snā 2 P to bathe,

snih 4 P to love,

spand 1 A to throb,

spardh 1 A to compete

sphāy 1 A to swell

sphur 6 P to quiver,
sphuṭ 1 P to burst,
spṛdh 1 A to emulate, compete,
spṛh 10 P to long for,
spṛś 6 P to touch,
upa+ to caress, touch,
so = *sā* 4 P to finish,
adhyava+ to resolve, decide upon, undertake,
ava+ to conclude, unbind, unharness, turn in, go to rest, go home,
udava+ set out,
vyava+ to decide, determine,
sṛ 1 P to move,
ā+ run to, run
abhi+ to assail,
anu+ to follow, go after,
apa+ to depart, remove, take out,
ava+ go down,
nis+ to emerge, go out, caus. drive out,
pra+ to gush, go forth,
*pra+*caus. to stretch,
sam+ flow together, wander
upa+ go to, approach,
śṝ 9 P to crush,
sṛj 6 PA to emit, hurl, utter,
ati+ to grant,
pra+ to renounce,
ud+ to discharge,
vi+ to dismiss,
sṛp 1 PA to creep,
ud+ creep out or up,
upa+ approach gently,
vi+ move apart, disperse, move about,
śram 4 P to grow weary,
pari+ to be exhausted,
vi+ to rest, stop,
sraṁs 1 A to fall,
vi+ to collapse,
śrambh 1 or *srambh* A to be negligent, usually with *vi,*
vi+ to trust in, confide,
śri 1 PA to lean, rest on,
ā+ to seek refuge, lean upon, seek support,
adhi+ to resort to,
pari+ A. lay about, enclose,
pra+ lean forward,
upa+ A. lean against,
śru 5 P to hear,
ā+ to listen,
prati+ answer, say yes to, make a promise to, not turn a deaf ear to – answer,
sam+ hear, accede to the request of,
vi+ be heard of far and wide, be famous,
sru to shed, emit,
prati+ to promise,
stambh or *stabh* 9 P to prop, support,
ava+ to fix,
sam+ to benumb,
ud+ prop up,
vi+ to check, prop apart,
sthā 1 PA to stand,
ā+ take one's place at, resort to
abhi+ set the foot upon, vanquish, withstand,
adhi+ to dwell, stand upon,
anu+ to perform, take one's place by, support, devote oneself to a thing, carry out a plan, accomplish
anūpa+ A. approach one after another,
anuvi+ spread oneself over, pervade,
ava+ to stand still, stand off, abide, remain,
ni+ to be versed in, stand in, rest on,
pari+ stand round about, encompass, restrain,
pra+ A. to set out, go off, caus. send away, dismiss,
prati+ stand, be established, get a foothold,
pratyud+ rise up to meet (in respect)
sam+ A. remain with, come to a standstill, get through, finish,
samud+ rise up, spring up,
samupa+ approach one after another
ud+ stand up, rise up, spring up,
upa+ to wait upon,
utthā to rise,

vi+ A. spread itself,
vyava+ to remain,
ṣṭhīv 1 P to spit,
stṛ 5 PA to strew,
ā+ to cover, spread out,
anu+ cover over,
ava+ to scatter,
upa+ spread upon,
vi+ to spread,
stu 2 P to praise,
su 5 PA to press,
sū 2 A to beget, set in motion,
śubh 1 A to look beautiful,
śuc 1 PA to grieve, shine, burn,
ā+ bring hither by flame,
abhi+ burn,
anu+ to regret,
apa+ drive away by flame,
sūd 1 A to put in order, guide aright
10 P to kill,
niṣud to destroy
śudh 4 P to purify, become pure,
sukhayati Nom P delights,
sukhāyate Nom A feels happy,
svād 1 A to taste,
ā+ to relish,
svan 1 P to resound,
svañj 1 A to clasp,
pari+ to embrace,
svap 2 P to sleep,
śvas 2 P to breathe, get one's breath,
become quiet, caus. quiet, comfort
ā+ to revive,
abhipra+ blow forth upon,
ni+, nis+ to sigh, breathe out,
pra+ blow forth,
ud+ to expand,
vi+ to confide in, have confidence,
be unsuspecting,
svid 1 P to sweat,
svīkṛ 8 A to agree,
syand 1 A to flow,
taḍ 10 P to beat,
pari+ to strike,
vi+ to wound,
tan 8 PA to stretch, extend, spread over,
ā+ to pervade,
adhi+ to string (a bow)
ava+ to descend,
pari+ to clasp, surround, envelope,
vi+ to spread, stretch out, cover,
tap 1 P to heat, suffer, practice
austerities
tap 4A to be heated, to suffer,
do penance, be purified,
tarj 1 P, 10 P, to threaten,
abhi+ to revile,
vi+ to threaten,
tark 10 PA to surmise,
tṝ 6 PA to cross,
abhyud+ come out of the water to,
cross the water to,
at+ to overcome,
ava+ to descend esp. divine beings
as men,
nis+ to overcome,
pra+ take to the water, start on,
ud+ to escape, come up out of the
water,
vi+ to bestow, cross through,
traverse,
trā 4 A to rescue, (form of *tṛ* ?)
trap 1 A to be ashamed,
tras 1 P to tremble,
apa+ to flee,
pari+ to be afraid,
sam+ to dread,
tṛh 7 P to crush,
tṛṣ 4 P to be thirsty,
tud 6 P to strike,
tul 10 P to weigh,
tuṣ 4 P to be pleased,
pari+ to be satisfied,
sam+ to rejoice in,
tvar 1 A to hasten,
tyaj 1 P to abandon,
pari+ to forsake, leave to one's fate
sam+ to give up,
ud or *und* 7 P to flow or issue out, wet,
sam+ flow together, wet,
ūh 1 PA to push, attend to, expect,
guess, suppose,
apa+ to remove,
api+ to grasp, understand,
prati+ to impede,
vi+ to arrange troops,

ujjh 6 P to leave,
ukṣ 1 PA to sprinkle, wet, emit,
pra+ sprinkle before one for consecration,
uñch 1,6 P to gather, glean,
pra+ to wash away, wipe out,
uṣ 1 P to burn,
vā 2 P to blow,
ā+ blow here,
nis+ to go out (flame etc.), be extinguished,
parā+ blow away,
pra+ blow or move forward,
vi+ blow asunder, scatter to the winds,
vac 2 P to say, speak,
abhyanu+ say with regard to, say after the teacher, learn, study,
anu+ to recite, repeat (prayers), say,
nis+ to explain, speak out clearly,
pra+ to announce, tell forth,
prati+ to reply, answer,
sam+ say together,
vi+ to explain,
vad 1 P to speak, say,
ā+ speak to,
abhi+ to address, speak to, salute,
apa+ to abuse,
pari+ to blame,
pra+ speak forth, say, declare to be,
pratyabhi+ caus. A.salute in return,
sam+ A. to converse, consider,
vi+ A. to quarrel,
vah 1 PA to bear, to carry, to flow,
ā+ to cause, bring hither or to,
apa+ to carry away,
ati+ to pass (time),
nis+ to carry out,
pari+ lead about,
pra+ to blow, carry onward,
sam+ carry, carry together,
ud+ to marry, bear or bring up, lead a bride from her father's house,
vi+ to marry, lead away (the bride from her parent's house),
vam 1 P to vomit,
van 8 PA to desire,
vañc 10 PA to cheat, go crookedly,
vāñch 1 PA to desire,
vand 1 A to salute, honour, praise,
vap 1 P to sow, strew,
ā+ throw upon, strew,
abhi+ bestrew,
apa+ cast away, fig. destroy,
ni+ throw down,
nis+ throw out, deal out (oblation),
vas 2 A to put on,
vas 1 P to dwell, live,
ā+ to abide, take up one's abode in, occupy, enter upon,
adhi+ to occupy,
ni+ to dwell (men and beasts),
pra+ to live abroad,
prati+ have one's dwelling,
ud+ caus. remove from its place,
upa+ to stay, to fast, stay with, wait,
vi+ to depart,
vāsayati Nom P perfumes,
ve 1 P to weave, interweave,
vep 1 A to tremble,
veṣṭ 1 A to wind round
pari+ caus. to surround,
ud+ caus. to loosen,
vic 7 P to sift,
vi+ to discern,
vid 2 P to know,
anu+ know thoroughly, from end to end
*ni+*caus. to inform, cause to know, announce, communicate,
vid 6 P to find,
anu+ to find,
vij 3 PA to separate,
vij 6 A, to shake,
ud+ to shudder,
vīj 1 P to fan
viś 6 PA to enter,
ā+ to overpower, enter, go into,
abhini+ A. to resort to, settle down to, be inclined towards,
ni+ A. to retire, go in, go home,
pra+ to enter, get into,
sam+ enter together, i.e. make their appearance together,
sampra+ go in,
upa+ to sit down, settle down upon

vṛ 5 PA to cover,
ā+ to cover,
abhi+ cover,
anu+ to conform, cover over,
apa+ to depart, uncover, open,
ati+ to surpass,
ni+ to return, keep down, suppress, ward off,
nis+ to arise, uncovered
nirvṛta – pleased, contented, free from care (not covered over),
pari+ to turn round, surround,
pra+ to set out, cover,
sam+ to be, to occur,
samā+ cover,
sampra+ A. cover completely,
upa+ to approach,
vi+ uncover, open, make open or clear, illumine

vṛ 5,9, PA to choose, prefer,
ā+ to choose, desire,

vraj 1 P to go,
ā+ come hither, go to,
pari+ to wander, wander around,
pratyā march or go back

vṛdh 1 A to increase,
pra+ grow on, grow up,
sam+ grow, caus. cause to grow, bring up, nourish, feed,
*vi+*grow, increase,

vṛṣ 1 P to rain,

vṛt 1 A to turn, turn round, revolve,
ā+ P. turn hither, A. turn, roll back
abhyaryā+ turn around to,
anu+ roll after, follow, continue,
ni+ turn back, flee, turn away, turn from, abstain,
nis+ roll out, develop, come into being, evolve itself, create from (with 5th),
pari+ turn around, move in a circle,
pra+ turn or move forward, set out, begin, set about, engage in, caus. set in motion,
pratini+ turn back from (5th),
sam+ unite, take shape, form itself, come into being,
samā+ turn back to meet, go home (esp. a pupil who has finished his studies),
ud+ turn out, fly asunder,burst open,
upā+ turn to here,
vi+ turn away, part with, caus. whirl about,

vyadh 4 P to pierce,
apa+ to cast aside,
nis+ to slay,

vyath 1 A to suffer,

yā 2 P to go,
ā+ to come,
ati+ to overcome,
anu+ to follow,
nis+ to go out,
pra+ to set out, go forth,
samā+ assemble, come together,
ud+ go forth, go out,
upa+ to approach, go or attain to,

yāc 1 A to beg,
abhi+ to implore,
anu+ to beseech,
sam+ to solicit,

yaj 1 PA to worship,
ā+ get a thing as a result of sacrifice,

yam 1 P to curb, sustain, support,
ni+ to check, restrain,
pra+ to bestow,
pratipra+ offer in turn, pass (food) (with 6th),
sam+ to curb, hold or reach out, hold together,
samud+ raise, set about,
ud+ to strive, undertake, raise (the arms or weapons),
upa+ hold onto, take hold of, A. take to wife, marry,
vi+ hold asunder, stretch out,

yat 1 A to strive
pra+ to endeavour,

yuj 7 PA to join, prepare, employ
abhi+ to accuse,
anu+ to instruct,
ni+ to appoint, fasten to,
pra+ apply, use,
sam+ to unite, join together,
ud+ to get ready,
upa+ to use, enjoy,

Abbreviations

A	Atmanepada (middle voice)
(A) to (W)	references to bibliography sources
acc	accusative case
act	active voice
adj	adjective
adv.	adverb
aor	aorist
caus	causative
comp.	compound
compar.	comparative
corel.	correlative
denom	denominative
desid.	desiderative
du	dual number
e.g.	for example
esp.	especially
f.	feminine
fig.	figuratively,
fut.	future
gram.	grammar
gve	gerundive - future passive participle – indicating an action to be carried out
fut	future
ibc	at the beginning of a compound
i.e.	that is
ifc	at the end of a compound
impers.	impersonal
impf	imperfect tense
impv	imperative tense
ind	indeclinable
indef	indefinite
inf	infinitive
intens	intensive
Gam.	Svāmī Gambhīrānanda – Upaniṣad translator for Advaita Ashrama
HH	His Holiness *Śṛī Śāntānanda Saraswati*
lit.	literally
LM	Leon McLaren
loc.	locative case
m.	masculine
mfn	masculine, feminine or neuter = adjective
mid	middle voice
n.	neuter gender
Nom.	Nominative verb
opt	optative tense
P	Parasmaipada (Active voice)
p.	page
part.	participle
partic	particular
pass	passive voice
perf	perfect tense
phil	philosophy
pl	plural
ppp	past passive participle
prep	preposition
pres	present tense
pron	pronoun
s	singular
Ved	Vedic
voc	vocative case – used to address somebody (oh Rāma)
1st	1st case – nominative (the subject)
2nd	2nd case – accusative (the object)
3rd	3rd case – instrumental (by or with)
4th	4th case – dative (to or for something)
5th	5th case- ablative (from or through)
6th	6th case – genitive (of something)
7th	7th case – locative (in or on something)

Bibliography and Reference List

A Sanskrit-English Dictionary – Sir Monier Monier-Williams, Motilal Banarsidass, Delhi, 1993 (all page references unless otherwise noted)
(A) Aṣṭāvakra Saṃhitā – Swami Nityaswarupananda, Advaita Ashrama, Mayavati 1981
(Apte) The Student's Sanskrit English Dictionary – VS Apte, Motilal Banarsidass, Delhi 1997
(B) Sanskrit Manual – Roderick S. Bucknell –Motilal Banarsidass, Delhi 1996
(C) Ashtavakra Gita translated by Hari Prasad Shastri –Shanti Sadan London 1961
(D)The Heart of Awareness a translation of the Ashtavakra Gita by Thomas Byrom – Shambhala Dragons 1990
(E)Aṣṭāvakra Gītā – Commentary by Swami Chinmayananda – Central Chinmaya Mission Trust – Revised Edition May 1997 – Mumbai
(F) Teach yourself Sanskrit –Michael Coulson, Teach Yourself Books, Hodder, England 2001
(G) A Concise Dictionary of Indian Philosophy – John Grimes, SUNY, NY, 1996
(Gam.) Eight Upanishads – Advaita Ashrama –Gambhīrānanda
(H) A practical aid for the study of Sanskrit Dhātus – The School of Economic Science, London
(HH)Quotations from his Holiness Śrī Śāntānanda Saraswatī Śankarācārya
(I) Dhātu Pātha – Hill and Harrison – Duckworth 1991
(J) The roots, verb-forms and primary derivatives of the Sanskrit language –WD Whitney reprint 1994 Motilal Banarsidass Delhi
(K) Wikipedia
(L) A Sanskrit Reader – C. R. Lanman - Motilal Banarsidass, Delhi. orig 1884, reprint 2007
(LM) Quotations from Mr. Leon McLaren in various publications
(M). The Sanskrit Language -Walter Harding Maurer –Routledge Curzon 1995
(N) A History of Early Vedanta Philosophy, Pts 1 and 2, Prof. Hajime Nakamura, Motilal Banarsidass Delhi, 1983, 2004
(O) A Sanskrit Manual (for High Schools) Parts 1 and 2, R.Antoine S.J. Xavier Pubn. Calcutta,
(P) Pāṇini
(Q) Materials for a Dictionary of the Prajñāpāramitā Literature, Edward Conze, Suzuki Research Foundation 1973
(R) A Sanskrit-English Dictionary AA Macdonell, 1924 MLBD
A Sanskrit Grammar for Students A.A. Macdonell reprint 1997 Motilal Banarsidass, Delhi
(S) Śaṅkara
(T) Svetasvatara Upanishad Trans. Swami Tyagisananda, Sri Ramakrishna Math Chennai 2006,
(U) The Philosophy of the Panchadasi Swami Krishnananda, The Divine Life Society, Rishikesh
(V) Bhaktivedanta Vedabase
(W) Encyclopaedia of the Hindu World, Gaṅga Rām Garg, Concept Publishing, New Delhi, 1992
(X) Teach Yourself Sanskrit, Michael Coulson, Hodder and Stoughton Educational, London 2004
Devavāṇīpraveśikā – An introduction to the Sanskrit Language – RP Goldman & SJS Goldman 1980 et al, University of Clifornia, Berkeley
Introduction to Sanskrit, parts 1 and 2 - Thomas Egenes 1989, 1985 Motilal Banarsidass, Delhi
Pāṇini –His Description of Sanskrit Jag Deva Singh
Sanskrit Grammar for Beginners – – Max Müller –Hippocrene Books, New York 2004 (M)
Sanskrit Grammar – William Dwight Whitney – Bodhi Leaves Corp. Delhi reprint 1990 (W)
School of Economic Science London Sanskrit Faculty numerous texts
The Bhagavad Gita Winthrop Sergeant SUNY 1994
Bhagavad Gita translated by Swami Gambhirananda, Advaita Ashrama May 2000
Eight Upaniṣads translated by Swami Gambhirananda, Advaita Ashrama 1958

www.ingramcontent.com/pod-product-compliance
Lightning Source LLC
Chambersburg PA
CBHW080631230426
43663CB00016B/2834